Companions of Honour

Peter Galloway

The heights by great men reached and kept
Were not attained by sudden flight,
But they, while their companions slept,
Were toiling upward in the night.

Henry Wadsworth Longfellow

Chancery Publications

Published by Chancery Publications
Copyright © Peter Galloway 2002

The moral right of Peter Galloway to be identified as the author of this work has been asserted in accordance with the Copyright, Designs and Patent Act of 1988

A catalogue record for this book is available from the British Library

ISBN 0-9543381-0-3

All rights reserved. No part of this publication may be reproduced, stored in a retrieval system, or transmitted, in any form, or by any means, electronic, mechanical, photocopying, recording or otherwise, without the prior permission of the author.

Printed in Great Britain by Stephen Austin and Sons Ltd
Printers at Hertford since 1768

I'm not at all sure what a Companion of Honour actually is . . . so now I have to find out just what it is about.
                        Paul Scofield

BUCKINGHAM PALACE

In 1917 my grandfather, King George V, instituted the Order of the Companions of Honour as a way to honour those who had rendered conspicuous service of national importance during the years of the 1914-18 war.

Over the eighty-five years of its existence, membership of the Order has been conferred to recognise those who have reached the highest levels of attainment in the arts, the sciences and in government. Many of its members have gained an international reputation through their work.

I am pleased to see that this book includes not only an account of the history of the Order and its badge, but also a biographical gallery of the distinguished men and women who have been honoured with membership. The sum total of their lives constitutes an impressive array of eminent achievement in the life of this nation and in the Commonwealth.

CONTENTS

Message from Her Majesty The Queen

Acknowledgements

1	In the beginning: *a new Order comes to life*	1
2	The dogs of war: *a miscellany of war services*	11
3	In God's name: *bishops, priests and pastors*	39
4	All the pride of power: *statesmen and politicians*	67
5	Bright is the ring of words: *writers, novelists, poets*	165
6	Famed in all great arts: *artists, architects, sculptors, curators, potters*	205
7	Music of the spheres: *composers, conductors, singers, musicologists, impresarios*	231
8	Portals of discovery: *scientists and physicians*	258
9	To the well-trod stage: *actors, choreographers, producers*	289
10	Interpreters of life and living: *philosophers, historians, archaeologists, economists*	310
11	Campaigning spirits: *social and humanitarian pioneers*	335
12	Sharp quillets: *lawyers*	357
13	National voices: *journalists and broadcasters*	369
14	Forth to his work: *industrialists and trades unionists*	387
15	A grant of honours: *the 1943 enlargement and the Commonwealth quotas*	405
16	Over the bright blue sea: *overseas appointments*	424
17	Emblem of honour: *the ribbon and badge of the Order*	489
18	Gallery of conspicuous service: *a retrospect of eighty-five years*	505

Appendix 1 *Members of the Order*   516

Appendix 2 *Officer of the Order*   545

Bibliography   546

References   551

Index   564

ACKNOWLEDGEMENTS

I am grateful to Her Majesty the Queen for giving me permission to write this the first history of the Order of the Companions of Honour. Papers from the Royal Archives at Windsor Castle are quoted in the text by gracious permission of Her Majesty.

Lieutenant Colonel Robert Cartwright, Secretary of the Central Chancery of the Orders of Knighthood at St James's Palace, and ex officio Secretary and Registrar of the Order of the Companions of Honour, kindly allowed access to the Central Chancery files relating to the Order, and allowed the insignia of the Order to be photographed. Rachel Wells LVO and the staff of the Central Chancery were as always unfailingly friendly and helpful.

My thanks also go to the Ceremonial Officer, Cabinet Office, for allowing access to the records of the Ceremonial Secretariat and also providing space for research and writing. My warm thanks go to Ruth Gardner LVO OBE of the Cabinet Office Ceremonial Secretariat, who was willing to spend her time reading and re-reading successive drafts of the chapters of this book, thereby precluding including factual and typographical errors, and for providing the encouragement needed to see this book through to publication.

I would also express my thanks to the many unnamed staff of the British Library, the University of London Library and the Foreign and Commonwealth Office Library who gave valuable assistance in identifying and obtaining relevant publications. My thanks also go to Richard Roscoe, Honours Secretary at 10 Downing Street.

I make no claim to be an expert in many of the categories included in this book. For example, the world and work of the scientists in chapter 8 was approached with a considerable degree of nervousness, and I had no hesitation in relying on the greater knowledge of others. So my thanks also go to the following: Sir Robert Balchin and Robert Harrison of the House of Lords Record Office for their help with chapter 4; Professor Alan Downie, Professor of English Literature at Goldsmiths College, University of London, for his help with explaining the origin of the motto of the Order and for his comments on chapter 5; The late Reverend Alfred Pryse Hawkins, for translating from Welsh into English sections of the biography of Elfed Lewis, who appears in chapter 5; Mrs Marlene Burston for her comments on chapter 6; Philip Dukes for his comments on Chapter 7; Professor Alan Bevan, Emeritus Professor of Genetics, Queen Mary and Westfield College, University of London, and Dr Terence Kealey, vice-chancellor of the University of Buckingham, for their comments on chapter 8; Peter Morris of the Society of London Theatres for his comments on chapters 5 and 9; Dr Donald Adamson, formerly of Goldsmiths College, University of London, friend and biographer of the late Dr A. L. Rowse, for his comments on the details of Rowse's life in chapter 10; Professor Ben Pimlott FBA, warden of Goldsmiths College, for his comments on chapter 10; The Right Honourable the Lord Slynn of Hadley, for his comments on chapter 12; Christopher McCreery of Queen's University, Kingston, Canada for his help with the Canadian recipients of the Order included in chapter 16; Brigadier General Harry Bendorf USAF (retd), for his help in locating a surviving prototype badge of the Order.

Most of the present Companions of Honour willingly and generously provided photographs of themselves for inclusion in the present volume. Desirable as it would have been to include illustrations of all the departed as well as the living members of the Order, the cost in reproduction fees would have been prohibitively expensive. Andrew Smart of A. C. Cooper and Son expertly photographed the insignia of the Order.

The attempt to create and assemble succinct biographies of more than three hundred diverse individuals inside the covers of one book has been a mountainous task, and I take full responsibility for the selection that had to be made. No inference on relative merit should be drawn from the varying lengths of each entry. Length depended to a great extent on available material. There was, for example, no difficulty in assembling a life of Sir Winston Churchill. But not all the Companions of Honour have reached the level of his renown, and several did not merit obituaries in *The Times* or entries in the *Dictionary of national biography*. What has been included and what has been omitted is entirely arbitrary, and designed to do no more than provide a portrait of each of the Companions of Honour. No doubt some will criticise what has been said or left unsaid, but the line had to be drawn somewhere.

The gathering of the Companions into subject groups is purely a literary convenience; to divide the book into chapters. The Order has no 'categories' of membership which have to be 'represented' in its ranks. Each Companion of Honour stands alone on the basis of his or her national renown.

Peter Galloway

CHAPTER ONE

In the beginning

A NEW ORDER COMES TO LIFE

'Well! What are you?' said the Pigeon. 'I can see you're trying to invent something.'
'I – I'm a little girl,' said Alice, rather doubtfully, as she remembered the number of
changes she had gone through that day.
'Advice from a caterpillar', *Alice's adventures in wonderland*, Lewis Carroll

In his book *The queen's orders of chivalry*, published in 1964, Sir Ivan De la Bere described the Order of the Companions of Honour as being 'something in the nature of a junior class of the Order of Merit'.[1] Though there is a very slight element of truth in that statement, it was not the best way to summarise the essence of an Order that occupies a very high level in the honours system. The word 'junior' suggested a slightly dismissive tone towards the honour. This image has hung like a shadow over the Order for most of its existence, and arguably impeded recognition of its high rank.

The foundation of the CH on 4 June 1917 is an inseparable adjunct to the foundation of the Order of the British Empire on the same day, and the two honours themselves originate in the first of the two international conflicts of the twentieth century – 'the Great War', later and for depressingly similar reasons re-titled 'the First World War'. The war began after the assassination of the Archduke Franz Ferdinand of Austria, and his wife Sophie, Duchess of Hohenberg, in Sarajevo on 28 June 1914. The archduke, and the Austro-Hungarian Empire over which his family ruled, are now distant memories, but the year of his death has come to be seen as an historic milestone in European history. The assassinations in Sarajevo provided the excuse for the launch of a cataclysmic war, after which Europe was never to be the same again.

The war was the first for a century to be fought on a European dimension, and because of the development of increasingly sophisticated weaponry, the loss of human life was on a scale never before seen. Every section of society in the United Kingdom played a role during the four long years of war. The nation was mobilised, and because the rarefied and restricted United Kingdom honours system was unequal to the task of recognition of such service, it quickly became apparent that a new and widely distributed honour was needed to recognise service by and for the nation. The question of creating a new honour was the subject of informal discussion by December 1915, and the debate culminated in the establishment of the Order of the British Empire and the Order of the Companions of Honour in June 1917.

The former effectively gave birth to the latter, because the long and wearisome debates on the issue concluded that one Order was not enough. The Order of the British Empire emerged as a traditional five-class confraternity of knights and dames grand cross (GBE), knights and dames commander (KBE and DBE), commanders (CBE), officers (OBE) and members (MBE), with an accompanying medal (BEM). Following the pattern of other British Orders, admission to the first and second classes brought the conferment of knighthood with the title of 'Sir' for men, and introduced the innovative title of 'Dame' for women. But this traditional pattern of title and honour was unacceptable to certain sections of British society in the early twentieth century. Socialism, trade unions and the Labour Party were rising forces in the land, and there appeared men and women whose pre-eminent commitment to the war effort was beyond question, but who, for ideological or other reasons, would not accept an honour that conferred a title. Because their contribution to the war effort was at such a high level, there was a need for a correspondingly high honour to recognise their work, an honour that would not inflict upon them, in the words of Thomas Jefferson 'the opprobrium of a title'. The result was the Order of the Companions of Honour.

Throughout the debates on the creation of the Order of the British Empire during the second half of 1916 and the first half of 1917, there ran a continuous concern about the most appropriate way to include at a high level within the new Order, those who would not accept a knighthood. The progress of the debate is chronicled in *The Order of the British Empire* by the present author and published in 1996, and no more than a summary is needed in the present work. The earliest proposals recommended that none of the classes of the new Order should carry the honour of knighthood, which would therefore make the Order 'acceptable to many to whom this title is not an object of ambition'.[2] Although the Order of Merit, itself conferring no title on its members, had been founded in 1902, the proposal for the new Order was innovatory in that it would be more widely conferred than the Order of Merit. 'The general feeling seems to be that it is a distinctly good idea. There are a large number of people who dislike knighthoods, not only the Labour members, but such men as Arthur Balfour [first lord of the admiralty and a former prime minister], Walter Long [president of the local government board], etc., and while they would like to have some Order, it would hardly do to relegate them to the lower classes [of the Order of the British Empire].'[3] The words were those of Sir Frederick Ponsonby, keeper of the privy purse to King George V, and one of the principal figures in the honours debate of 1915–17. The difficulty of the proposal was that all those appointed to the first class, and who would still remain 'Mr' would be given precedence over all the knights commander of the other Orders. Sir John Brown, whether KCB, KCSI, KCMG, KCIE or KCVO, would be outranked by Mr Smith GBE, and even more seriously, Mrs Smith would outrank Lady Brown! 'What is the fundamental objection? If the Order is to rank in its proper place with Orders and not be considered an inferior affair, the first and second classes would confer the honour of knighthood . . . Surely the dignity of the Order about to be created by the King should be considered and not the ambitions of the recipients.'[4] The dignity of the new Order was a valid consideration. If there were no knighthood, and precedence was strictly adhered to, the unknighted members of first class (GBE) would be pushed far down the table of precedence and rank after knights bachelor, in turn pushing the fifth class (MBE) even further down. Would this not jeopardise the public reputation of the new Order?

A multi-class Order with no knighthood, while a superficially attractive proposition, was something of a novelty and could not easily be integrated into early twentieth century British society where rank and precedence were still subjects of sometimes worrying importance. Even the radical Sir Frederick Ponsonby was brought to understand that such things simply could not be done without seriously upsetting a well-established and well-accepted system. 'Hideous problems of precedence which seemed to me quite inane were brought forward. I quite realised, however, that although the points seemed to me ridiculous they might possibly assume gigantic proportions in a small town. I therefore asked him to communicate his objections to our scheme to the Central Chancery . . . so that they might be properly considered by people competent to express an opinion on such matters. Personally I was quite incompetent to venture even to consider such conundrums.'[5]

In October 1916, consideration of an Order with no knighthood was replaced by consideration of an Order with optional knighthood. King George V discussed the problem with David Lloyd George, his new prime minister, on 3 October 1916, and the two men agreed on a curious compromise, which only caused further debate and delay. They decided that the first and second classes should, in common with the other Orders, carry the honour of knighthood, but only for those who wanted it. For those who did not, on ideological or other grounds, the option to accept the class but decline the knighthood was to be available. Although the decision now seems odd, and further debate brought the realisation that it was unworkable, it was neither a foolish nor a frivolous proposal. The king and the prime minister both wanted the new Order to begin its working life with the widest possible spectrum of support. It was a compromise, but it was unworkable because it similarly foundered on the entrenched rock of precedence that in 1916 was accorded a level of significance that no longer seems important in a more egalitarian age. Could Sir John Smith GBE and Mr John Smith GBE really be of equal status in the table of precedence? No, they could not, and by December 1916, 'optional knighthood' for the new Order had been rejected; attractive in theory, it was impossible in practice. 'Any attempt to place Members of the Order of the British Empire, without Knighthood, in the same precedence as that accorded to those of other Orders would cause an outcry, not only from Knights Commanders of other Orders, but from the whole community of Knights Bachelors. Further it would cause endless confusion in assigning precedence at Functions, and give rise to bickering and annoyance . . . I believe that an Order of Chivalry without Knighthood, yet conferring precedence, would be proved, before the new Order was a week in existence, to be unworkable and unpopular, while it would become the object of derisive criticism'.[6]

The earliest evidence of a solution to the problem came on 5 March 1917 when Ponsonby was summoned to a meeting of the war cabinet. There he heard Arthur Henderson, chairman of the parliamentary Labour Party, argue that the only way forward was to have a one-class decoration, while Andrew Bonar Law, chancellor of the exchequer, argued that the new decoration should have no knighthood. The only possible solution was to combine these two arguments into a small new one-class Order without an accompanying knighthood, leaving the Order of the British Empire with a traditional format. This decision was finally agreed at a meeting on 26 March 1917, attended by Prince Louis of Battenberg, Ponsonby, Earl Curzon, lord president of the council, Sir George Cave, home secretary, Sir Douglas Dawson, state chamberlain, Henry Farnham Burke, Garter King of Arms, and three permanent secretaries: Sir George Fiddes of the colonial office, Sir Thomas Heath of the treasury and Sir Edward Troup of the home office. The meeting decided to abandon all idea of optional knighthood. The Order of the British

Empire should be a five class Order, either with or without knights. If it was to have knights, then another single class decoration, to be called the War Service Order or the National Service Order, should be created. It would carry no precedence, but the postnominal initials WSO or NSO could be used.

Curzon submitted this recommendation to the war cabinet in a memorandum dated 1 April 1917. He gave a frank exposition of the problems faced by the group. The cabinet, he said, was faced with the task of establishing an honour that would be suitable for presentation to a number of entirely different classes, and would satisfy those classes. Quite apart from foreigners, there would be persons 'who attach a good deal of importance to social precedence and to titular prefixes to their names'. There would also be persons of distinction 'to whom it would be absurd to offer the style and title of Knight' [he did not supply a list of names, nor suggest any general group from which they might be drawn]. There would also be those 'who would not refuse a decoration but would, for reasons entirely honourable to themselves, abjure a title'. To satisfy the claims of all these conflicting parties was an almost impossible task, and the only way ahead was to submit two alternative schemes to the war cabinet, 'for both of which there is something to be said, but neither of which is free from objection. Objections, indeed, are inseparable from any solution that can be proposed'. The first scheme envisaged a five class Order to be styled the 'Order of the British Empire', without knights and with precedence that recognised that fact. The second scheme called for the said five class 'Order of the British Empire', to include provision for knighthood, and a one class 'War Service Order', or 'National Service Order' if continued in peacetime, that bestowed neither title nor precedence. 'It would indeed be the equivalent for civilians to the DSO for soldiers, would be open to both sexes, would raise no pretence of title or precedence, and would largely depend for its distribution upon the list of first appointments and upon a none too profuse distribution afterwards.' Curzon's final note summed up the essence of the problem. 'The two schemes are submitted with no sort of exhilaration to the War Cabinet. Were it not for the insatiable appetite of the British-speaking community all the world over for titles and precedence, the first would be unhesitatingly recommended'.[7] Ponsonby reported that the king was 'much amused' by these remarks.[8]

The war cabinet met on 6 April 1917 and decided in favour of the second scheme. The Order of the British Empire should be a five-class order, with knighthood for the first two classes, and for those who did not wish to be knights, there would be a one-class National Service Order. The precedence of the Order of the British Empire was clear; as the newest of the multi-class Orders, it could be placed next to and after the Royal Victorian Order. The precedence of the National Service Order took a little while longer to settle. In depicting it as a civilian DSO, Curzon was clearly proposing that its status should be low, roughly equivalent to the fourth class of the Order of the British Empire. Curzon's view lasted only a few weeks. By the end of April 1917, it had been agreed that the NSO would be equivalent in rank to the first two classes of the Order of the British Empire, for those who had no desire to receive the title and rank of a knight.

On 25 April 1917, the secretary of state for the colonies sent a circular telegram to the governor-generals of Canada, Australia and South Africa and the governors of New Zealand and Newfoundland announcing the impending establishment of the two honours and inviting the submission of names. In the case of the National Service Honour: 'It is intended to meet the case of those who would otherwise be recommended for the 1st two classes [of the Order of the British Empire] but who object to receive Knighthood. It will carry no precedence but will be of high value being strictly guarded by merit of service. For the present, qualification for both orders should be valuable war work.'[9]

Ponsonby himself circulated the news to government departments in the United Kingdom, and the very vagueness of the new honour inevitably brought forth requests for elucidation. 'Would you be so good as to let me know generally on what basis the National Service Order is to be constituted', wrote the permanent secretary at the board of education.[10] To which Ponsonby could only reply that he was hardly in a position to say more than he had already said. 'The War Cabinet have merely informed me that these two Orders are to be instituted, but have left the details to be decided by a committee . . . My own idea is that the National Service Order will be restricted to those to whom the honour of knighthood is distasteful: it will, therefore, be kept as a sort of "Order of Merit".'[11] This is the first reference to the Order of the Companions of Honour being viewed as a 'brother' to the Order of Merit, the eminent honour instituted by King Edward VII in 1902. It was a view that gained momentum with the passing of years, but in 1917 there was really no discussion of the relationship between the two Orders, the Order of the Companions of Honour still being principally viewed as an honour for those engaged in the war effort who decried titles. In view of the imminent public announcement of the two new Orders, criteria for the new honours had to be established, and on 1 May 1917 Curzon alerted Ponsonby to the fact that the two honours could not be announced in the press until a clearer distinction between the two had been decided.[12]

The proposed new honour was not well received in some quarters. The National Service Order, with its decidedly functional and proletarian-sounding title, was to be created solely for the purpose of pandering to ideological whim. Admittedly there were people whose principles would preclude them from accepting a title, but did their numbers really justify the creation of a new Order with such a narrow purpose? On 15 May 1917, Prince Louis of Battenberg, Ponsonby, Dawson, and Farnham Burke met at the lord chamberlain's office and concluded that the new Order should be opposed on grounds that it undermined a still rigidly divided class system. 'The necessity for the creation of this Order was merely the outcome of the attitude of a small minority of the King's subjects, including one or two persons of distinction but mainly composed of labour members and trades-unionists . . . Such being the case, it was decided to suggest that there was no necessity for the creation of the National Service Order at all. The few persons of distinction whom it was proposed to place in the First Class of the O.B.E. but who declined the Honour of Knighthood, could be included in the Order of Merit, after a slight alteration to the Statutes. The labour members and trades-unionists who declined the Honour of Knighthood could be placed in the Third Class of the Order of the British Empire.'[13] From the point of sense and practicality, it would avoid the creation of yet another new honour, the announcement of which might detract from the launch of the Order of the British Empire. But the memorandum of the meeting was marked by a hint of a snobbish disdain for those influenced by an ideology that itself disdained the use of titles, and a view, typical of its time, that the upper and lower classes really could not be given the same honours. 'Persons of distinction' who declined a title could go to the Order of Merit. For 'Labour members and trades unionists', a CBE would be quite sufficient. The memorandum of the meeting dismissed the National Service Order as 'merely the outcome of the attitude of a small minority of the King's subjects'. But that conclusion was reached by four very ceremonially-minded individuals for whom the maintenance of tradition was paramount, and whose attitudes could not or would not accept and embrace the need for a new development in the world of honours; one that would meet the sincerely-held beliefs of an increasingly numerous and powerful British socialist movement.

A distant member of the royal family and three courtiers might easily agree on a course of action in an office in St James's Palace, but their plan was effectively demolished when King George V refused to allow the Order of Merit to be touched, and their only success was to change the name of the nascent Order. The war cabinet opposed 'War Service Order' with its temporary connotations, but even the agreed working title of 'National Service Order' did not long survive. The future of the two emerging Orders was discussed at a meeting at Buckingham Palace on 1 May 1917, to which Ponsonby summoned a group of permanent secretaries and other representatives of several government departments. Their task was to produce standards and criteria for the Order of the British Empire and the National Service Order. The verbatim record of their conversations illustrates the emergence of the new honour, its status and its title.

The high rank of the National Service Order was now clear. It was confirmed that it should equate to the first two classes of the Order of the British Empire, and Ponsonby's vision of the NSO being comparable to the Order of Merit was echoed by Theo Russell, the representative of the foreign office. 'I do not think it probable that we should have any candidates for the NSO. Our recommendations would have to be divided up into classes, and with perhaps the exception of the Secretary of State himself, I do not think we should have any candidate for the NSO. I should like to see that made into an Order corresponding with, though perhaps not quite so high as, the Order of Merit, and only given to very few.' Ponsonby supported Russell's position. 'I am quite sure of it, and we do not want another ISO [Imperial Service Order]; it would become a war ISO and would not be wanted.'[14] The Imperial Service Order was primarily for civil servants, both at home and abroad, and effectively a fourth class of the Orders of the Bath and St Michael and St George.

The name of the Order was raised by the delegates to the meeting. As a companion to the Order of the British Empire, itself now acquiring the status of a permanent honour, the alternative title of 'War Service Order' was swiftly disposed of, but even the somewhat anaemic title of 'National Service Order' aroused understandable criticism. 'I take it the WSO disappears in favour of the NSO', said Sir George Fiddes of the colonial office. 'I do not know whether we could think of a better word', replied Ponsonby. 'The unfortunate thing about a National Service Order is that the public will get the idea that it has something to do with Mr Neville Chamberlain's scheme.'[15] The point was well made, but the Order would soon have eclipsed the 'scheme'. Chamberlain, whose reputation was to be almost irretrievably tarnished by the events of 1938–9, was called to London by Lloyd George from a successful career in the municipal and business world of Birmingham, and given the title of director general of national service. Powerful orator and enthusiast that he was, Lloyd George's schemes were occasionally based on little more than impulse and passion. More than one of them foundered on the lack of a basic strategic plan, and the national service department was one victim among several. In December 1916 the prime minister was making eloquent speeches calling for volunteers to undertake unspecified tasks, and summoned Chamberlain to head this new department to coordinate a redistribution of labour on strictly voluntary lines. The task was virtually impossible on several grounds. Lloyd George did not realise that departments which already controlled most of the labour supply would be unwilling to surrender their powers, and the powers and responsibilities of Chamberlain himself were undefined. He lacked both resources and assistance and he had no seat in the house of commons from which to defend his work. Lloyd George came to view him as too rigid and stubborn, lost patience, and effectively forced his resignation after only seven months. It therefore seems a reasonable hypothesis that had there not been a national service department, there could well have been a National Service Order.

After the meeting on 1 May, Ponsonby wrote to the prime minister's principal private secretary, recommending a new name. 'Some exception was taken to the title "National Service Order" as being too much associated in the public mind with Mr Neville Chamberlain's scheme, and the words "Patriotic Service Order" were suggested as an alternative.'[16] [This title does not appear in the verbatim minutes of the meeting.] Ponsonby also consulted Prince Louis of Battenberg who agreed that the title did have 'a definite and restricted meaning', and proposed 'Meritorious Service Order' instead.[17] But these ephemeral titles – 'War Service Order', 'National Service Order', 'Patriotic Service Order' and 'Meritorious Service Order' are scarcely worth mentioning and were soon consigned to the dustbins of history. Few people, beyond a select group of high-ranking officials, were ever aware that they had been suggested or considered. As blandly unimaginative as they were functionally descriptive, none of them had a serious future.

The name of the Order was finally resolved in an exchange of letters between Ponsonby and Curzon in the period 23–26 May 1917. On 23 May Ponsonby wrote to Curzon, reciting and rehearsing the objections to the provisional title, and suggesting a version of the name that was eventually to be adopted. 'The first gazette of the Order of the British Empire will come out on the King's birthday in spite of innumerable difficulties and conundrums, but the National Service Order is not going well. In the first place, the name "National Service Order" does not seem to appeal generally to the officials of this country. They seem to think that the words "National Service" have become so associated with Mr Neville Chamberlain's schemes, that the public will imagine that this decoration is reserved as a reward for those who have helped Mr Neville Chamberlain. A suggestion has been put forward that the new decoration should be called "The Companion of Honour" with the initials CH after the man's name. When framing the statutes of the new Order it was found that they were precisely similar to those of the Order of Merit, and the question was raised whether it would be possible to enlarge the Order of Merit to suit modern requirements, but the King firmly refused to allow the Order of Merit to be touched, and so it will be necessary after all to have another decoration, but it is a nice point whether it should only be reserved for the War; the duplication of our decorations is always a mistake, if it can be avoided.'[18]

Reading through correspondence for the early months of 1917, leads the reader to sympathise with Ponsonby in his efforts to create a sensible scheme that would appeal to the divergent backgrounds and views of politicians serving in the same cabinet. On 9 February 1917 Ponsonby was summoned to a meeting of the cabinet at Downing Street, to find himself confronted by Curzon, who only knew about grand crosses, Arthur Henderson, leader of the Labour Party, 'who had not the foggiest idea of what we were talking about the whole time, as Orders and Decorations had never come his way', and Lloyd George, the prime minister, who explained that he had had no time to read any of the papers on the subject. 'I could see,' wrote Ponsonby, 'that with the exception of Curzon, I was not being understood at all.'[19]

Curzon was very much the viceregal grandee. A former viceroy of India, he had once admitted to Ponsonby that although he had some idea of decorations from his days in India, he had only been referred to in cases of grand crosses, and knew very little about the conferment of the lower classes.[20] He was an earl, a Knight of the Garter, and a Knight Grand Commander of the Orders of the Star of India and the Indian Empire. The OBE, the MBE and the NSO were a little outside and well below his level of experience and interest. 'I see no objection to the second Order standing over for the present', he wrote to Ponsonby. 'Even if it never materialises I don't suppose many of us would shed a tear. It might not be at all a bad idea to connect it with the idea of "Honour" on the lines of the Legion d'Honneur. CH might even stand for "Corps of Honour".'[21] Although Ponsonby did not divulge the identity of the person who had suggested the title 'Companion of Honour', he was prepared to accept it. 'It is a fine title,' he said, 'but, of course, it lacks originality, as it is a slavish copy of the "Legion of Honour".'[22] It was a surprising comment for Ponsonby to make; beyond the word 'honour' there was not remotest connection between the new restricted one class British Order and the vast five class French Legion of Honour. With the restriction of numbers to fifty, it rapidly became clear that Curzon's memorandum of 1 April 1917 in which he imagined the new National Service Order to be the civilian equivalent of the military Distinguished Service Order was inaccurate. The Companions of Honour were daily advancing in status, and the DSO, given to junior officers below the rank of colonel, was hardly its equal. 'I think, therefore, it would be best to use the OM as an example when describing the CH.'[23]

The Order of the Companions of Honour had emerged from the nest of the Order of the British Empire, principally because those to whom it would be given disliked titles. But although this was privately debated and accepted in Whitehall, it could not very well be stated in a press release without introducing an unwise note of ideology into the inauguration of these latest two additions to the honours system. 'The Central Chancery of Orders very much object to my suggestion that anything should be said with regard to the CH being given to those already in possession of British Orders, or, to those to whom the Honour of Knighthood is distasteful. They argue that the first is detrimental to the CH, and the second implies that a British subject has the right to refuse an honour offered by the King', wrote Ponsonby to Curzon. But the two Orders could not be publicly inaugurated without any comment. 'People will wonder why two decorations have been instituted, and not one. Whether it would be possible to construct some nebulous paragraph hinting at the raison d'être of the second Order without putting it into such bald terms is a matter for you to decide.'[24] Curzon obliged with a few nebulous words: 'The Order will carry with it no title or precedence but will be conferred upon a limited number of persons for whom this special distinction seems to be the most appropriate form of recognition, constituting as it will, an honour dissociated either from the acceptance of title or the classification of merit.'[25]

The statutes
The original statutes of the Order were drafted by Farnham Burke, Norroy King of Arms, in January 1918.[26] Retrospectively dated 4 June 1917, they were not published in the *London Gazette* until 26 February 1918, after the design of the insignia had been finally approved. Slight changes were made in June 1919, because the interested eyes of the foreign office and the colonial office were being directed towards the Order.

The possibility of further anomalies such as the appointment of a United States citizen as a substantive member, was excluded by the 1919 revisions, which instituted the category of 'honorary member'. The original wording of statute 2 read: *It is ordained that the said Order shall consist of the Sovereign and one class of Members, as in our said Letters Patent is provided.* The statute was altered in 1919 to read: *It is ordained that the said Order shall consist of the Sovereign and Members, Ordinary and Honorary.* Other consequential changes continued throughout the statutes, by the insertion of additional wording, indicated in the following by underlining. Statute 4: *It is ordained that not more than fifty <u>Ordinary</u> Members shall be admitted to this Order.* Statute 5: *It is ordained that the persons to be admitted as <u>Ordinary</u> Members of this Order shall be such persons, male or female being subjects of Our Crown, <u>and such Native Princes and Chiefs of India and such subjects of Native States of India,</u> as may have rendered conspicuous services of National importance, <u>and that persons to be admitted as Honorary Members shall be such Foreign Princes and Persons upon whom We may think fit to confer the honour of being received into this Order</u>.*

The provision for honorary members was made at the request of the foreign office, and the unusually specific mention of India and its princes and chiefs was included at the request of the colonial office. In the latter case, the provision for India proved to be virtually redundant from the beginning. Only two Indian nationals have received the CH, and the first – Valingaman Sankarana-Rayana Srinivasa Sastri – not until 1930. But the Indian provision of 1919 could be said to mark the beginning of a significant and occasionally problematical component of membership until the end of the 1980s – the Commonwealth.

The first references originate in a request by Lloyd George to the Earl of Crawford and Balcarres, lord privy seal, to examine the question of honorary membership and the possibility of using the Order in the colonies. Crawford spoke to Sir Douglas Dawson in April 1918, who wrote back informing him that there was 'no provision' for the appointment of honorary members to the Order, and that Indian princes counted as British subjects.[27] Crawford pressed on. 'The Foreign Office is anxious to recommend for 5 honorary. The India Office likewise wants to recommend for 5, of which at least 2 should be honorary, as the Amir of Afghanistan for instance isn't eligible for the British appointments.'[28] In reply, Dawson proposed an informal allocation of 37 for the United Kingdom, 3 for India, and the remaining 10 for the colonies. 'With regard to honorary appointments, should the King approve such appointments being made to the Order, they would, as is the case with all the Orders, be unlimited in number, and I do not think it would be advisable to allot any specific number of honorary appointments to the India Office and Foreign Office, but to leave each case for submission to the King to be judged on its merits.'[29] Crawford accepted Dawson's allocation and informed Lloyd George accordingly, pointing out the absence of any provision in the Statutes, and noting that Smuts should count as one of the colonial allocation.[30]

Nothing further was done – the 1914–18 war was reaching a climax – until January 1919 when the India office took the matter further. The secretary of state for India was considering the question of appointing a 'ruling chief' or the 'subject of a native state', but Dawson's statement that the Indian princes were British subjects was challenged. 'The ruling chiefs are not British subjects, but . . . they should be regarded as eligible for ordinary appointments, and that statutory provision should be made for the purpose.'[31] In May 1919, the India office made a firm proposal that the statutes of the Order should be amended to make formal provision.[32] Dawson approached Crawford again to say that as a provision for India was now to be made in the statutes, did he still wish to argue, on behalf of the foreign office, for a provision for honorary members? Yes indeed was the reply. 'A limited number of honorary companionships should be reserved for award on Foreign Office nomination in most exceptional cases to really distinguished foreigners. Up to the present no case of the kind has arisen, but we certainly think it desirable that provision for honorary appointments should be made, even though, as is contemplated, such appointments would be very few and far between.'[33] Instructions were duly sent to Farnham Burke to revise the statutes, and he had completed the task by 26 June 1919.[33] The revised statutes were promulgated on 15 October 1919. The provision for honorary members remained dormant for many years, the first appointment being that of René Massigli in 1954.

The statutes of an Order are its governing regulations and each new member is issued with a current set at the time of his or her appointment. In pale reflection of their medieval origins, Orders of chivalry are theoretically societies or confraternities, into membership of which people are admitted (in contrast to 'medals' which are merely 'awarded'), and such societies are governed by a code of rules. In most organisations it would be usual first to establish the rules and then to admit the members. But the speed with which the Order of the British Empire and the Order of the Companions of Honour were created, in the light of the perceived need for these new honours, reversed this usual process, and the statutes trailed behind the first appointments. Twenty-one members had been appointed to the new Order before its rules were formally agreed and promulgated in February 1918. The anomaly bothered no one. The new honours were needed and the paperwork could follow at its own pace. What was needed in the summer of 1917 was a list of names of potential recipients. On one level it would be an honour for them; an expression of thanks for their good works. On another level, it was a form of canonisation. This select group of Companions of Honour were to be lifted high as exemplars of what was right and good in the prosecution of the war that was still far from won. Their work and commitment should inspire others to follow. But where and how were they to be found?

CHAPTER TWO

The dogs of war

A MISCELLANY OF WAR SERVICES

'Get to your places!' shouted the Queen in a voice of thunder, and people began running about in all directions, tumbling up against each other: however, they got settled down in a minute or two, and the game began.
'The Queen's croquet-ground', *Alice's adventures in wonderland*, Lewis Carroll

The letters patent creating the Order of the Companions of Honour were passed on 4 June 1917, as were those creating the Order of the British Empire, and the date is recorded in the statutes as the foundation day of the Order, but a delay of eleven weeks occurred before the public were aware that there was a new Order. The first appointments did not appear in the *London Gazette* until 24 August 1917, the delay being partly due to consideration of the first recipients. Names of possible recipients of the Order of the British Empire were already being circulated, but at the request of the prime minister, a meeting was convened at the privy council office on 7 June 'to reconsider the lists of recommendations and to see whether we could not give the *Gazette* a more democratic aspect.'[1] Those present, apart from Sir Frederick Ponsonby and Lord Curzon, included Christopher Addison, parliamentary under secretary at the ministry of munitions, George Nicoll Barnes, Labour member of parliament and a member of the war cabinet, Sir Edward Troup of the home office, E. H. Phipps, general secretary (executive) of the ministry of munitions, and J. T. Davies, private secretary to the prime minister. The same meeting also turned its attention to the Order of the Companions of Honour, on which Curzon in particular focused his attention, much to Ponsonby's annoyance. Ponsonby, who was more concerned with the Order of the British Empire, described him as 'much exercised with the other decoration', and it was at this meeting that the names of the first Companions of Honour began to appear. 'A list of suitable people for this Order was slowly brought out by everybody round the table suggesting a name . . . I am glad to say that I was able to keep in all the big names I wanted [for the Order of the British Empire], although I should have preferred to retain some which Lord Curzon took away for the CH.'[2]

Ponsonby's letter implies that most if not all of the earliest recipients of the CH were effectively decided at the meeting on 7 June, but this cannot be verified since his letter is not accompanied by the provisional list. There was in any case a delay in the public announcement of the Order, at least in part due to Ponsonby's difficulty in obtaining the prime minister's agreement, and the need to secure his approval of the first seventeen names. 'A week ago I asked the private secretaries at 10 Downing Street to get the Prime Minister's approval of this second Order, but in spite of several telephone messages I have not been able to get the matter through. It seems very dangerous for me to communicate any details respecting these Orders to the press until the Prime Minister has officially put forward for the King's approval a submission instituting this second Order.'[3]

Rather surprisingly for one who knew much about honours, Ponsonby thought that the Order would get off to a good start if the members of the war cabinet would award themselves the CH. Arthur Henderson, leader of the parliamentary Labour Party was an obvious candidate, but if he was the only CH from the war cabinet, 'it may give a wrong impression.'[4] Curzon promised to do no more than talk to the prime minister, and he suggested Arthur Balfour, the foreign secretary, in recognition of his work in persuading the United States to enter the war on the side of the allies. A blanket conferment on the war cabinet was not a serious starter and Balfour had already received the Order of Merit in June 1916.

The names of the first seventeen appointments to the Order were announced on 24 August 1917, but backdated to 4 June 1917, a technical if not farcical device to tie them to the date on which the letters patent were signed by the King, and therefore the date on which the Order officially came into being.

The new Order was inevitably overshadowed by its junior partner, and any public reaction to the Order of the Companions of Honour was obliterated by reactions to the Order of the British Empire as Lord Stamfordham reported to the governor-general of Australia. 'As to the new Orders, the Order of the British Empire and the Companions of Honour, His Majesty fully appreciates the reason for delay in forwarding names by your government: indeed the difficulty here at home in making a selection has been very great, and the first list has caused anything but public satisfaction!'[5] Another three appointments were gazetted on 22 January 1918, and a further appointment on 25 February 1918. These first twenty-one members were gazetted under the heading 'To be Companions of the Order'. In every subsequent gazette, from 3 June 1918 to the present day, recipients have been gazetted 'To be Members of the Order'. There is no known reason for the change, except that the style 'member' follows the practice of the Order of Merit. But in common parlance a recipient is often referred to as 'a Companion of Honour' rather than the correct but more cumbersome style: 'a member of the Order of the Companions of Honour'. The seventeen original members were joined by ten more at various dates from January 1918 to January 1920, and together these twenty-seven members comprise the war service section of the Order. Their contributions to the war effort were solid, consistent and reliable, but mostly, it has to be said, quite unspectacular. In some cases, their reputations survive among those who still practice in the relevant specialist subject area, but beyond that their names and their war efforts have been generally forgotten.

When Curzon submitted his memorandum to the war cabinet on 1 April 1917, he referred to a category of persons of distinction 'to whom it would be absurd to offer the style and title of Knight', and those 'who would not refuse a decoration but would, for reasons entirely honourable to themselves, abjure a title'. A trawl of the first twenty-seven members yields a fairly obvious list of those who might, in the class conscious world of 1917, fall into the first category: these were the seven Labour members of parliament and general secretaries of trades unions – those members of the Independent Labour Party who gave the most obviously patriotic and unstinting support to the war effort and to the coalition government, if need be at the expense of their positions within their own party. At that time the Labour members of parliament were little more than parliamentary spokesmen for the trades unions and generally supported the Liberal government in return for political favours. Many, if not all of them, might be additionally included in the second category of abjuring a title for reasons 'entirely honourable to themselves'. Others who could fall into both categories would include Jan Smuts, the South African politician, and Kenneth Quinan, the American explosives expert. Of the remaining eighteen, three were women, and eleven were already in possession of a title of some kind.

If there was a public statement about the nature and direction of the new Order, it was there for all to see and note in the two names that followed Smuts. In second and third place respectively, stood the general secretary of a trade union, and a marchioness. Harry Gosling, president of the transport workers' federation, and the Marchioness of Lansdowne, president of the officers' families fund. The trade unionist preceding the marchioness summed up the decidedly classless structure, inclusive nature and meritocratic purposes of the new Order.

The source of the war service recommendations cannot be determined with precision, though there is no reason to doubt that they 'emerged' from the meeting on 7 June 1917 and afterwards, that Lord Curzon played a principle role in forming the first list, and that a certain amount of 'horse-trading' occurred before the list was finalised and names were swapped between the two new Orders. Curzon reminded Ponsonby not to overlook any names from the departments; if they were being excluded from one Order they should go into the other Order. 'When putting Gosling and Hill into the first tentative group of CH . . . we [must] not forget to put the other nominees of the Admiralty, viz Wardle, Gilmour, O'Grady, Havelock Wilson into some class of the British Empire?'[6] Wardle, acting chairman of the Labour Party, was included in the first CH list. Havelock Wilson, of the sailors and firemen's union, was made a CBE and received the CH in 1922. J. Hill was from the boilermakers' association; J. Gilmour from the miners' association; and J. O'Grady from the general federation of labour unions.

The names would have been submitted to Lloyd George and approved by him, though it is doubtful if he was interested in more than a handful of them. In his *War memoirs*, published in six volumes in 1933–36, surprisingly few of the war service Companions of Honour receive more than a passing mention, and most of them are not mentioned at all. He warmly applauded the work of Jan Smuts, found Lord Chetwynd and his work fascinating, May Tennant was 'useful', Lord Burnham 'broad-minded', Walter Layton 'eminent', Thomas Royden 'able' and George Barnes 'level-headed and respectable.' Alexander Faringdon, Alfred Keogh and George Wardle were only noted in passing. There is no mention at all of Harry Gosling, William Davies, Alexander Wilkie, Kenneth Quinan, Maud Lansdowne, Elizabeth Haldane, William Ripper, Violet Carruthers, Frank Swettenham, Henry Babington Smith, Gerald Strutt, John Furley, James Seddon, James Parker, Hebert Perrott, Samuel Provis and Philip Kerr. The names of four 'labour' men, two from outside the house of commons and two from inside – Harry Gosling, William Davies, George Wardle and Alexander Wilkie (all appointed in 1917) were almost certainly supplied by George Barnes, a member of the inner 'war cabinet', himself to be made a Companion of Honour in 1920. 'I understand,' wrote Ponsonby, 'that Mr Barnes is putting forward a list of Labour Members, and these of course will be added to the first list since the Prime Minister approved of the general principle.'[7] Barnes' list duly arrived and Ponsonby forwarded it to Curzon, prefacing it with the acid remark: 'it seems to be a complete and accurate list of all his friends, with their addresses.'[8]

Although their names are mostly forgotten, and question marks might be made against their suitability for the Order in succeeding ages, the 1917–20 war service Companions of Honour include a broadly-based cross-section of people who, politically or practically, together helped on the home front to maintain the morale of the nation during the war.

Lieutenant General Jan Smuts 4 *June 1917*

The Companion of Honour named at the head of the first list was an implicit statement about the importance of the empire, and of the distance travelled by one who had once despised it.

Jan Christian Smuts was born in 1870 and educated at Victoria College, Stellenbosch and Christ's College, Cambridge where he took a double first in the law tripos. He was called to the bar and practised at Cape Town. He was appointed state attorney of the South African Republic (the Transvaal) in 1898. He fought against the British during the South African War (1899–1902), and was given supreme command of the Boer forces in 1901.

After the establishment of the Union of South Africa in 1910 his sentiments became progressively more pro-British, and he held a succession of portfolios: interior and mines (1910–12), defence (1910–20), and finance (1912–13).

In 1915 he led South African forces in the conquest of German South West Africa, and in the following year he was given command of all the imperial forces in east Africa with the rank of lieutenant general in the British army. In January 1917 he was sent to London to represent the South African government at the imperial conference and in the imperial war cabinet. Lloyd George invited him to join the cabinet in an unpaid capacity with the title of minister without portfolio, while remaining a member of the South African parliament and cabinet, and so Smuts became the empire spokesman in London at a time when empire troops were playing a significant role in the allied forces. This unprecedented status accorded to a man who had been one of the principal enemies of the empire that he now sought to defend, did much to boost morale and give added impetus to the war effort. Smuts was generally highly regarded by his contemporaries in Britain, and in September 1917, the King's private secretary praised him as 'one of our most intelligent, far-seeing public men'.[9] 'His creation as a Companion of Honour ... caused Smuts some embarrassment. Boer principles opposed the acceptance of distinctions of that sort, but for Smuts they were quickly submerged in his satisfaction that his many services to Britain had been formally recognised.'[10]

Smuts continued his political career on his return to South Africa and was twice prime minister of the union (1919–24 and 1939–48). During the course of the royal visit to South Africa in 1947 he received the Order of Merit from King George VI. His party was defeated in the 1948 general election and he died in 1950.

Smuts was gazetted a CH in 1917 as 'Lieutenant-General The Right Honourable Jan Christiaan (sic) Smuts' No citation or description of appointment appeared next to his name.

Harry Gosling 4 *June 1917*

Henry (usually known as Harry) Gosling, was the first of a group of four members of the Order appointed in 1917, who could be grouped under the heading of 'labour', and who helped to recruit to the army in the days before conscription.

He was born in 1861 into a relatively prosperous household in Lambeth. His father was a journeyman lighterman on the River Thames and his mother was a teacher. He had a weak heart and although he followed his father's profession and enjoyed working on the river, a collapse in 1887 caused him to spend three years in and out of St Thomas' Hospital. He tried to return to the work in 1890 but another collapse in 1891 caused him to leave work on the river forever. The 1889 dock strike created a new enthusiasm for trade unionism among those whose work centred on the river, and Gosling was an enthusiastic supporter, joining the amalgamated society of watermen and lightermen in 1890, becoming its full time general secretary in 1893, which post he held until 1921. In 1911 he became additionally president of the National Transport Workers' Federation, an amalgamation of sixteen unions. In 1908 he was appointed to the board of the port of London authority and served on it until his death. His attitude to the war was one of total support and he was appointed by the government to the port and transport executive committee, a body set up in 1915 to deal with congestion in the ports. In 1915 he became chairman of the parliamentary committee of the Trades Union Congress. He was elected to parliament at a by election in 1923 and became minister of transport in the first labour government in 1924. He published a volume of reminiscences, *Up and down stream*, in 1927.

He was gazetted a CH in 1917 as 'President of the Transport Workers' Federation', and died in 1930.

William Davies 4 June 1917
William John Davies was general secretary of the brassworkers' trade union and helped with recruitment in the days before conscription.

He was born in Birmingham in 1848, the son of a brassfounder. Unlike Gosling, Davies' family was poor and he had no early education beyond two and a half years at a dame school. He entered the brass trade in 1861 as a chandelier maker and assembler and worked for various employers. He became a foreman and developed an interest in politics. In 1869 he represented the Barr Street Reform Association at the second Trades Union Congress. In 1871 the brassworkers of Birmingham began to agitate for a fifteen percent rise in wages and, as a result, in April 1872, a trade union called the Amalgamated Society of Brassworkers was founded and Davies was unanimously chosen as first general secretary. With one break (1883–9) when he was a factory inspector, he continued in that office until he retired in 1921. By July 1872 the society had branches in nearly a dozen towns and 6000 members. His attitude to female labour was typical of many of his generation; in 1874 he organised a strike in protest against the employment of women instead of skilled brass workmen. He remained all his life Liberal-Labour in his politics, insistent upon the independence of labour but within a Liberal political framework. He was a mid-Victorian radical who had no great liking for doctrinaire socialism. His name was submitted for appointment as a justice of the peace in 1892 but rejected apparently because of his prolonged warfare with the stipendiary magistrate, T. M. Colmore, against whose judgements, Davies repeatedly and often successfully appealed. Davies was finally appointed a justice of the peace in 1906, Colmore having retired in 1905.

Between 1880 and 1900 he declined several invitations to become a candidate for parliament but in 1892 he agreed to stand as a Gladstonian Liberal for the Bordesley division of Birmingham. He was an active supporter of the government during the war, assisted in recruiting and was a member of several advisory committees set up in connection with the ministries of national service and munitions. After the war he continued to serve on a number of government committees. For all his limited education he was remembered as a fluent and cogent writer and frequently contributed to the press. He wrote to the local daily newspapers on any matter on which he thought labour or trade union views should be represented or had been misrepresented, and he wrote articles for labour and trade union journals. He wrote a two-volume history of the TUC and two books on token coinage of which he had an extensive collection. He also designed a number of tokens and medals and enjoyed playing chess, becoming vice-president of the Birmingham chess club. He retired, unwillingly, as general secretary of the brassworkers in 1921, and soon afterwards decided that he and his daughter Mabel would go to live in France, where he died at Rueilville near Paris in 1934.

He was gazetted a CH in 1917, his name accompanied only by the description 'Brass Workers and Metal Mechanics'.

George Wardle 4 June 1917

George James Wardle was a railwayman and Labour member of parliament, and helped with recruitment in the days before conscription.

He was born in Derbyshire in 1865, the second of eight children of a collier (later railway horsekeeper). He followed his father in working on the railways, and between the ages of fifteen and thirty he was employed as a clerk on the Midland Railway at Keighley. Although having a limited education, he was widely read and was influenced in his younger days by the writings of George Dawson, Charles Kingsley and George Macdonald, and by Carlyle and Ruskin, when he began to take an interest in social and labour questions. At Keighley he became one of the first railway clerks to join the local branch of the Amalgamated Society of Railway Servants. At the conference of trade union and socialist bodies held in London on 27 February 1900 he seconded Keir Hardie's fateful amendment in favour of the establishment of a distinct Labour group in parliament. In 1906 he was elected Labour member of parliament for Stockport. Given his background, it was not surprising that on railway issues he adopted an advanced position for his time, being an early advocate of nationalisation. On all other issues he belonged to the moderate wing of the Labour Party, which caused a growing opposition to him in his own constituency. He was an ardent patriot at the outbreak of war, emphasising that the war was one for freedom, honour, justice and truth, but insisted that the working class must not be alone in being called upon to make sacrifices. He campaigned vigorously for army recruitment, and a visit to France in 1915 only increased his ardour. Although he voted against the Military Service Bill in January 1916, which introduced conscription, and then abstained on the second reading, his general attitude to the war was not affected and he was made a CH for his services to recruitment. From 1913 he served on the executive of the Labour Party, and from 1916 he was its acting chairman. When the war ended a special conference of the Labour Party (14 November 1918) resolved to end all co-operation with the war cabinet, and advised all the party's members who held office in the government to resign. Wardle, who had been made parliamentary under secretary to the board of trade in 1917, refused to comply, in company with G. N. Barnes, G. H. Roberts and James Parker. In January 1920 the Hornsey branch of the National Union of Railwaymen, to which he belonged, demanded his expulsion from the union for his refusal to leave the coalition government, but the national executive refused to comply on the grounds that he had 'ceased to exercise any influence either for or against the interest of the members.'[11] He deplored the wave of strikes that affected Britain after the war, and he denounced the railway strike as revealing the effects of the poison of 'Bolshevism in the industrial system'.[12] The strain of the war years and the struggles of the post war years took their toll on his health, and in March 1920 he resigned both his office and his seat in parliament. In 1922 he retired to Hove where he took an active part in social affairs and charities, but played no further part in national politics. The break with the national union of railwaymen was so complete, that his death in 1947 went unnoticed in the *Railway Review*, the paper he had formerly edited for twenty-one years.

Wardle was gazetted a CH in 1917 with the description 'National Union of Railwaymen'.

Alexander Wilkie 4 June 1917

Alexander Wilkie was general secretary of the shipwrights' union, a Labour member of parliament and a supporter of the policy of conscription during the 1914–18 war.

He was born in 1850 at Leven on the coast of Fife. At the age of thirteen he went to work as an apprentice in a shipbuilding yard at Alloa. After a spell travelling the high seas as a ship's carpenter, he found employment in Greenock and later in Glasgow where he joined the Glasgow Shipwrights' Society, and was elected secretary of the society in 1872. A vigorous advocate of a closer unity among the shipwrights' unions, he became general secretary of the Associated Shipwrights of Scotland in 1877, and was a leading personality in the move to consolidate the nation's shipwrights into a single national union – the Associated Shipwrights' Society – and became its first general secretary in 1882. He was elected Labour member of parliament for Dundee at the general election in 1906, and held the constituency until 1922 when he did not seek re-election. During the war he was an enthusiastic supporter of the British Worker's National League, and in 1916 he voted in favour of conscription. He deplored the 1926 general strike and urged his members to remain at work. 'His experience, as he often said, was that more concessions were gained from employers by conciliation and arbitration than were ever secured by force. Throughout his long career he was a strong advocate of these methods. He used also to say that the extremists did not want production; they wanted revolution. He urged at all times that masters and men should unite in trying to further the prosperity of the country as a whole.'[13] He continued as general secretary of the shipwrights' union after 1922, despite declining health, until shortly before his death in 1928 at the age of seventy-eight.

He was gazetted a CH in 1917 with the description 'Ship Constructors and Shipwrights' Association'.

Kenneth Quinan 4 June 1917

Given the significance of the munitions industry in the war, three names on the first list were cited for their contribution to munitions work: Kenneth Quinan,

Viscount Chetwynd and William Ripper. Kenneth Bingham Quinan was a chemical engineer, explosives technologist, farmer and sportsman.

He was born in 1878 in East Orange, New Jersey but little is known of his early life. After a period on a sailing ship, he worked as assistant chemist at the Hercules Powder Company's explosives factory at Pinole, California, of which his uncle Colonel William Russel Quinan was the manager. The latter went to South Africa at the request of Cecil Rhodes in 1899 to build an explosives factory for De Beers Consolidated Mines at Somerset West and was joined by his nephew in 1901. By 1905 Quinan had become works manager of the plant. W. R. Quinan's health was beginning to fail, and more responsibility fell on the shoulders of his nephew, who was appointed general manager of the renamed Cape Explosives Works in 1909. In December 1914 he went to England at the request of the British government and was attached to the ministry of munitions as head of the factories branch of the department of explosive supplies. He designed and supervised the construction of a TNT plant at Oldsbury and three large munitions factories at Queen's Ferry, Sandycroft and Gretna Green, which were operating in 1916. His department not only brought into production a large number of chemical and poison gas factories, but aimed at giving chemists and engineers a thorough training which would qualify them to play their part in the postwar build up and development of chemical industries.

Quinan's appointment as a CH was an unusual one in that despite being an American citizen, he was made a substantive rather than an honorary CH for one simple reason: there was no choice. The hastily drafted statutes of June 1917 made no provision for honorary members. Quinan either had to be made a substantive CH or not be made a CH at all. In 1918 he was offered a knighthood, which he declined. With the ending of the war he received an honorarium of £10,000 from the British government and was thanked in the house of commons by Lloyd George for his unique contribution to the war effort. After the war he returned to South Africa and became a naturalised South African in 1939. He died in 1948

Quinan was gazetted a CH in 1917 with the description 'Explosives Supply Department, Ministry of Munitions.'

Because of the long delay in the appearance of the insignia of the Order, Quinan was never formally invested. The other CHs were summoned to Buckingham Palace for an investiture on 17 December 1918. Quinan replied that he was leaving for South Africa before that date, and after several efforts to get him to an investiture, the central chancery sent his badge to the colonial office in June 1921, asking for it to be sent to the South African government for a formal presentation to be made locally.[14]

Viscount Chetwynd 4 June 1917
Godfrey John Boyle Chetwynd, eighth Viscount Chetwynd, was the inheritor of a viscountcy and an Irish barony, created in 1717. Both titles were created in the peerage of Ireland, but none of the holders had any connection with that country.

He was born in 1863, the second son of the seventh viscount and succeeded his father in the peerages in 1911. His war services were other than what might have been expected of an hereditary peer. Chetwynd was managing director of the national shell filling factory at Chilwell, Nottinghamshire (1915–19), and his claim to the honour was the rapidity with which his workers produced the shells that devastated the landscapes of Belgium and northern France. 'He had as far as I remember,' wrote Lloyd George, 'no practical experience in dealing with explosives, but he had a tremendous store of resource and ingenuity. I was, however, warned that he was very sensitive to any attempt to control him by a bridle of red tape. We told him he was wanted to build and run a factory that would fill a thousand tons a week of high explosive shells. He stipulated for and got a free hand, without control by the departmental managers of the Ministry [of munitions], and a contract valid until after the cessation of hostilities. Thus equipped, he went straight ahead in glorious independence. He found a site at Chilwell, near Nottingham, and designed and built his own factory there. While it was being erected, he went over to France in October 1915, as one of a deputation I sent to study the French methods of shell-filling . . . His initiative in this matter was of incalculable benefit for the country, and made possible an immense increase in both the speed and the volume of shell-filling. The Chilwell factory was an amazing place, where powerful explosives were milled and mixed like so much flour. Lord Chetwynd designed his own plant and processes, aiming always at speed, simplicity, and the fullest use of machinery on mass production lines . . . Chilwell was the largest of our national filling factories and was our principal source of supply for the heavier natures of filled shells.'[15]

Chetwynd was completely dedicated to the task and had the temperament of a maverick. In January 1916 a Zeppelin flew over Nottinghamshire by night, in an attempt to locate and bomb the factory. A rumour spread that Chetwynd had caught three German agents trying to signal the Zeppelin with lights and had them shot without trial. Chetwynd turned the rumour to advantage. He set a policeman on guard outside an empty room one day, and during the following night he employed a labourer to dig three graves on a hillside. He filled them with stones and placed a black post at the head of each. 'That turned the rumour into unquestioned history, and discouraged would-be spies from prying round the place.'[16]

Little else is known of his life, except that he was a justice of the peace for the west riding of Yorkshire. In 1927 he claimed, before the royal commission on awards to inventors, an award for improvements to the manufacture of amatol and in the filling of high explosive shells; the claim was unsuccessful. He died at San Angelo, Texas, in 1936.

Chetwynd was gazetted a CH in 1917 as 'Managing Director Chilwell National Shell Filling Factory.'

William Ripper 4 June 1917
William Ripper was professor of engineering and dean of the faculty of applied science at Sheffield University.

He was born at Plymouth in 1853. He served an apprenticeship as a marine engineer at Plymouth and at Stockton-on-Tees. He won a queen's scholarship and was trained at the Exeter training college for teachers. For a period he was science master at the Central Secondary School at Sheffield. He did research on superheated steam, continuous indicators and machine tool testing, among other areas. He was president of the Sheffield Society of Engineers and Metallurgists, founder of the Sheffield trades technical societies, a member of the board of education departmental committee on science museums (1910), and a justice of the peace.

He was the author of two works which became standard textbooks. The first edition of *Steam engine theory and practice* was published in 1899. It was one of the pioneers of this branch of technical literature, and ran through seven editions, the last being published in 1914. In 1928 William J. Goudie was asked by the publishers to act as editor of an eighth edition. Owing to his advanced age and indifferent health, Ripper had felt unable to undertake the task. 'Within recent years great advances, some of them almost revolutionary, have taken place in the theory and practice of steam engineering, and in consequence the writer found that a large part of the text was out of touch with modern conditions. He decided therefore to rewrite and considerably enlarge the text. The result of this task is a new text, containing about thirty percent of the original illustrations.'[17] Despite such extensive revision, it was still entitled *Ripper's steam engine theory and practice*. Ripper's *Heat engines* was first published in 1909, and was continually reprinted until 1938. A second edition was published in 1939 and a third edition, revised by A. J. T. Kersey, appeared in 1950. Like its companion volume, it was entitled *Ripper's heat engines*. He published a third book entitled *Machine drawing and design*. He retired to Brighton and died there in 1937.

He was gazetted a CH in 1917 as 'Vice-Chairman of the Sheffield Munitions Committee.'

The Marchioness of Lansdowne 4 June 1917
As the Order of the British Empire was open to women from the beginning, so was the Order of the Companions of Honour, and four women were named among the first seventeen members of the Order, for a high level of voluntary service: the Marchioness of Lansdowne, Elizabeth Haldane, Margaret Tennant and Violet Markham.

Maud Lansdowne was born in 1850 and her family and connections were impeccably aristocratic. She was the daughter of the first Duke of Abercorn, married to the Marquess of Lansdowne, a former viceroy of India, governor-general of Canada, secretary of state for war and foreign secretary, and was herself a lady of the bedchamber to Queen Alexandra. She was the antithesis of the world of labour and munitions and the epitome of that now vanishing breed, the aristocratic lady with a great deal of time and a great number of important 'connections', both of which enabled her to give full and effective rein to the benevolent spirit for voluntary work that she undoubtedly possessed in abundance. The CH was for her work as president of the officers families' fund, and she became one of the few to bridge the gulf between the CH and the GBE, receiving the latter honour in 1920. She had already merged the two in 1917, in her letter of thanks to the King for making her a 'Companion of Honour of the British Empire'. The King's private secretary reported that her description of the honour, 'has taken the King's breath away.'[18] She died in 1932.

Lady Lansdowne was gazetted a CH in 1917 as 'Member of the Council of the British Red Cross Society, President of the Officers' Families Fund.'

It was as well that she received the CH in August 1917. Her husband's long and distinguished service was finished by the famous 'Lansdowne letter' to the *Daily Telegraph* in November 1917, in which he outlined possible peace terms to end the war. Repudiated by the government and by his own party, he became an isolated figure for the remainder of the war.

Elizabeth Haldane 4 June 1917

Elizabeth Sanderson Haldane had a long tradition of social work, including the provision of pensions for the elderly, improving housing conditions of the poor, child welfare, nursing and adult education.

She was born in 1862, a scion of the distinguished Scottish Haldane family. Among her brothers were Richard Haldane (1856–1928), secretary of state for war (1905–1912), who reorganised the army and established the territorial army in 1908, and John Scott Haldane (1860–1936), an occupational health physician, who later followed his sister in being appointed a CH. They were the only known example of a brother and sister being Companions of Honour. Elizabeth benefited from the highly cultivated atmosphere in which she was raised at home. 'She shared her brother's tutors and entered into their discussions on philosophy, science and politics, which undoubtedly helped to develop her unusual mental attainments. About the age of fifteen she attended a private school in Edinburgh where her pre-eminence in literature, mathematics and languages rapidly became apparent.'[19]

Although the *London Gazette* recorded her appointment as a CH for being vice-chairman of the advisory council of the territorial force nursing association, her life encompassed a range of voluntary social service, primarily a fundamental interest in the welfare of humanity. She was prominently associated with the formation of the Scottish women's benefit society in 1890, the members of which were later admitted to the ancient order of foresters, the pioneers of old age pensions for women in Scotland. She worked for some time in London with Octavia Hill in her efforts to improve the housing conditions of the poor, and in 1884 she helped to establish a similar organisation in Edinburgh. In the pioneer days of the Westminster health society (founded in 1903) she proved a tower of strength on the national council for maternity and child welfare. In the years before the 1914–18 war, when her brother Richard was secretary of state for war, she played a large part in encouraging the extension of nursing services especially in connection with the territorial association. During the war she was mentioned in despatches and received the Reine Elisabeth medal for work on behalf of Belgian soldiers and the housing of Belgian refugees. She was the first woman to receive an LLD degree from the University of St Andrews (in 1911), the first to become a member of the Scottish savings committee (1916), and the first woman justice of the peace in Scotland (1920). She was a member of Queen Alexandra's imperial military nursing service board, the general nursing council (1928), the board of management of the Edinburgh royal infirmary, the Scottish universities committee (1909), the royal commission on the civil service (1912) and the advisory committee under the Insurance Act of 1912.

When the women's suffrage movement was at its height, she was opposed to its militant methods, but she worked steadily for enlightened freedom for women in education and the professions. In politics she remained a staunch liberal all her life, and her publications included a translation of Hegel's history of philosophy (1892), *The wisdom and religion of a German philosopher* (1897), *Life of James Ferrier* (1899), *Life of Descartes* (1905), *Descartes' philosophical works* (1912), *George Eliot and her times* (1927), *British nurse in peace and war* (1928), *Mrs Gaskell and her friends* (1930), *The Scotland of our fathers* (1933), and *Scots gardens in old times* (1934). 'The outstanding features of her character were love of humanity, courage, and ability, coupled with a clarity of vision, and force which enabled her to overcome any obstacles which she encountered in her way. Her life throughout was marked by an absence of self-consideration, and an abundant flow of little kindnesses which did much to lighten for many the daily path of life . . . She was of medium height, rather thick set, not exactly good looking, but with a high forehead and an expression of extreme intelligence and benevolence. Her practical hands betokened capability in what they undertook.'[20] She died in 1937.

Elizabeth Haldane was gazetted a CH in 1917 as 'Vice-Chairman, Advisory Council of the Territorial Force Nursing Association.'

May Tennant 4 June 1917

The reputation of Margaret Edith (known as May) Tennant was formed on the basis of her pioneering social work.

She was born May Abraham in Dublin in 1869. She moved to London at the age of eighteen and became secretary to Lady Dilke (wife of Sir Charles Dilke), the promoter of women's trade unions. She lived with the left-wing Dilkes at their house at 76 Sloane Street, a hub of enlightened representatives from the world of politics, literature and art which stimulated her mind. She became great friends with Lady Dilke's niece, Gertrude Tuckwell (herself later to become a CH), and for a while the two women shared a house in Chelsea, encouraging and firing each other with infectious enthusiasm.

She learned a great deal from Lady Dilke about the working conditions of women, including the perils of white lead, phosphorus and other hazardous industrial processes. She became treasurer of the women's trade union league and was prominent in the struggle for state inspection of laundries. In 1893 she was appointed by Herbert Asquith, then home secretary, as the first woman factory inspector in the country, and was vigilant in matters such as illegal overtime, bad sanitation and dangerous trades. In 1895 she was appointed a member of the departmental committee on dangerous trades, under the chairmanship of the Liberal member of parliament John Tennant, whom she married in 1896, and who was briefly secretary of state for Scotland in 1916. She made the decision – not an easy one – to relinquish her career. It was a decision that dismayed her colleagues. 'It is only by degrees that we can realise the extent of our loss,' wrote her successor in the annual report of the factories department, 'as we miss her knowledge and insight in the work for which we could not fail, while she was with us, to feel her rare gifts.'[21] After marriage she tried for a while to retain her position as superintending inspector of factories, but it proved impossible, and the birth of her eldest son ended her career.

She was not entirely lost to the causes that meant so much to her, and there followed a succession of public appointments: chairman of the industrial law society, and the maternal health committee; member of the royal commission on divorce, member (and treasurer) of the central committee on women's employment. During the 1914–18 war she was chief adviser on women's welfare in the ministry of munitions, and in 1917, director of the women's section of the ill-fated national service department. When that ephemeral department was closed down Tennant served on the health of munitions' workers committee, and acted as an adviser in the department. Despite the failure of the national service department, Lloyd George later declared that it began a good deal of useful work 'in particular, the organisation of women's service by the Women's Branch under Mrs Tennant, which gave us the WAAC's and the Land Girls.'[22]

Although she continued to be passionate in her commitment to improving the conditions of working men and women, the death of her eldest son, Henry, in May 1917, was a shock. 'Her mind still reacted almost automatically to the old stimulus of the worker's needs. But those of us who knew and loved her realized how mortal was the blow she had received. She was made a Companion of Honour . . . but no honour could reach out to comfort the place of desolation into which her spirit had been swept.'[23] She died in 1946.

May Tennant was gazetted a CH in 1917 as 'formerly Director of the Women's Section, National Service Department.'

Violet Carruthers 4 June 1917
Violet Carruthers was May Tennant's deputy in the women's section of the national service department, and had long been interested in social problems and in practical schemes for brightening the lives of workers.

She was born in 1872, the youngest daughter of a wealthy colliery owner and grew up in a house in which mining problems were discussed, but rarely the living conditions of the miners. She developed a concern for the slum conditions in which they lived and in 1902 started a settlement in Chesterfield, which aroused opposition, incredulity and sometimes ridicule.

She received a legacy that made her financially independent and in her house at 8 Gower Street, London, she created an informal meeting place for people interested in politics, the arts and public service. Her idealism and social passion was infectious and she gathered around herself a wide collection of those who shared her concerns. One of those who became an occasional attender was the Canadian politician William Mackenzie King. 'She was a healthy influence on the idealistic young politician and later, on the solemn self-absorbed prime minister, and tried, as she once wrote, "to direct his mind from the turbid oratory in which all colonial premiers seem to indulge".'[24] Another Canadian, Vincent Massey, who was high commissioner in London before and during the 1939–45 war, and governor general in the 1950s, became a great friend. 'We called her "the lioness" because she never hesitated to roar when she disapproved of something or some person concerned with the affairs of the moment – and how often she was right! She had the tough common sense and forthrightness that came from her North Country background, and great ability as a writer [as Violet Markham] and public servant.'[25]

For many years she was a chairman of the central committee on women's training and employment. She was appointed a member of the industrial court in 1919 and became a member of the lord chancellor's advisory committee on women justices. She married Lieutenant Colonel James Carruthers MVO DSO in 1915. They had no children and he died in 1936. Strongly influenced by Bishop Hensley Henson of Durham, her Christian faith sustained her when coping with blindness in her last years. At time of her death in 1959, she was the last survivor of the founding members of the Order of the Companions of Honour.

Violet Carruthers was gazetted a CH in 1917 as 'formerly Assistant Director, Women's Section, National Service Department.'

Viscount Burnham 4 June 1917
Propaganda was a prominent part of the war effort, and the press played a significant role in encouraging and bolstering popular support for the war. Lord Burnham was primarily a newspaper proprietor, although his range of public ser-

vice was much wider. Lloyd George praised him as 'broad-minded, liberal and a man of business.'[26]

Harry Lawson Webster Levy-Lawson was born in 1862, educated at Eton and Balliol College, Oxford, and called to the bar in 1891. He succeeded his father as the second Baron Burnham in 1916. In 1903 he inherited from his father the managing proprietorship of the *Daily Telegraph*, which became the principal interest and the pride of his life. As long as he held it, he declined to accept ministerial office on the ground that the independence of his newspaper might be compromised, and during the twenty-four years of his control he became a leading figure in the London newspaper world and its chief spokesman throughout the empire, holding for long periods the presidency of the newspaper press fund, the chairmanship of the newspaper proprietors' association and the presidency of the institute of journalists and the empire press union. He was president of the imperial press conferences held in Ottawa and Melbourne in 1920 and 1925. He relinquished control of the newspaper in 1928, with deep regret, after his appointment to the Indian statutory commission (1927–30).

Although the *London Gazette* cited his presidency of the empire press union, Burnham made other contributions to the war effort. The firm foundation of Anglo-Belgian friendship owed much to the advocacy of the *Daily Telegraph*, and he did all that he could to advance the cause of the territorial army. For many years he held a commission in the Royal Buckinghamshire Hussars and commanded the regiment from 1902–1913. On the outbreak of war in 1914 he rejoined and took a leading part in training the second reserve regiment.

Burnham's public service was wide ranging. He moved in and out of the house of commons until succeeding his father in 1916. He was member of parliament for West St Pancras (1885–92), East Gloucestershire (1893–95), and Tower Hamlets, Mile End Division (1905–06). He also served on London County Council, representing West St Pancras (1889–92) and Whitechapel (1897–1904), and was mayor of Stepney (1907–1909). He served as a member of the royal commission on civil establishments (1889–94), the speaker's conference on electoral reform (1916), during which he moved the resolution which led to the enfranchisement of women (1918), and the joint conference on the reform of the house of lords (1918), and acquired a reputation as the ideal chairman for public assemblies of every kind. He was president of the international labour conference at Geneva (1921–22 and 1926), president of the press experts' conference (1927 and 1929), president of the public health conference (Bordeaux 1924, Ghent 1927), chairman of the standing joint committees of education authorities and teachers, president of the imperial press conferences (Ottawa 1920, Melbourne 1925). 'Apart from his wide experience of public affairs he was fitted for the duties of chairmanship by his fair-mindedness, moderation and genial temper. Governments in need of a workable report on a matter of difficulty turned naturally to Burnham.'[27] He remained active to the end and died of heart failure in his sleep in 1933.

Burnham was created a viscount in 1919 and appointed a GCMG in 1927. He was gazetted a CH in 1917 as 'President, Empire Press Union,' but perhaps he never did quite grasp the place of the honour, like Maud Lansdowne before him. He listed the honour in his *Who's Who* entry as 'Companion of Honour of the British Empire'.

Sir Frank Swettenham 4 June 1917
Frank Swettenham was joint director of the official press bureau (1915–19), but had previously enjoyed a distinguished career in the colonial service, spent mostly in the Malay states.

He was born in Derbyshire in 1850. He began his career as a colonial administrator in Singapore in 1871. He was deputy commissioner with the Perak expedition (1875–76), British resident at Selangor (1882–89), Perak (1889–95), resident general of the Federated Malay States (1896–1901), and governor and commander in chief of the Straits Settlements (1901–04). He retired in 1904 and refused the offer to become governor of Kenya. He chaired a royal commission to enquire into the affairs of Mauritius (1909), and was given the ceremonial appointment of king of arms of the Order of St Michael and St George (1925–38). His publications included *Malay-English vocabulary* (1880), *Malay sketches* (1895), *Unaddressed letters* (1898), *The real Malay* (1899), *British Malaya* (1906), *Also and perhaps* (1912), *Arabella in Africa* (1925), and *Footprints in Malaya* (1942).

At the outbreak of the 1914–18 war he became assistant director of the press bureau, and in the following year joint director. The principal sadness of his life was his first wife who developed mental instability at an early date, and whom he divorced in 1938 after sixty years of marriage. He died in 1946.

Swettenham was made a GCMG in 1909 and gazetted a CH in 1917 as 'Joint Director, Official Press Bureau.'

Sir Henry Babington Smith 4 June 1917
Henry Babington Smith was a civil servant and a financier of conspicuous ability, the emphasis being on the latter during the 1914–18 war.

He was born in 1863 and educated at Eton and Trinity College, Cambridge, from where he graduated with a first class in the classical tripos. A career in the civil service beckoned and after a period as an examiner in the education department, he became private secretary to the chancellor of the exchequer (1891–92), clerk in the treasury (1892–94) and private secretary (1894–99) to the earl of Elgin, viceroy of India. He represented the treasury in Natal, was British representative on the council of administration of the Ottoman public debt (1901) He was secretary of the post office (1903–09) when his financial acumen attracted the attention of Sir Ernest Cassels and he left the civil service to become, through Cassels' influence, administrateur directeur-général of the national bank of Turkey (1909). During the war he served on most of the more important financial committees and in 1915 was chairman of the royal commission on the civil service. After the war he was assistant commissioner for Great Britain to the United States (1918–19), chairman of the committee on Indian currency (1919), chairman of the railways amalgamation tribunal (1921–23), deputy governor of the British trade corporation, and a director of the bank of England. He died in 1923.

Smith was made a CSI in 1897, a CB in 1905, a KCB in 1908, and GBE in 1920. He was gazetted a CH in 1917 without any accompanying citation or description of appointment.

The Honourable Gerald Strutt 4 June 1917
During the war, food production was as important as the production of munitions, and Edward Gerald Strutt was a renowned and competent agriculturalist who effectively framed government agricultural policy during the war.

He was born in 1854, fifth son of the second Lord Rayleigh, and was educated at Winchester and Trinity College, Cambridge. In 1877 he went into partnership with Charles Parker, to form Strutt and Parker, land agents and surveyors, to manage the Lincolnshire and Essex estates of Guy's Hospital. As the land agent, he also transformed the Rayleigh estates in Essex after a disastrous fall in wheat prices in 1878.

He was an alderman on Essex County Council and chairman of the Essex County Small Holdings. An authority on commercial agriculture with extensive farming interests (eventually 25,000 acres of farmland), he introduced a scheme of agricultural co-partnership with the workers on his farms. During the war he served on Lord Milner's food production committee (1915), and on Lord Selborne's committee on post war agricultural policy (1916). 'He was consulted on most matters of real difficulty and it was largely in reliance on his advice that compulsion was applied to secure the ploughing up of additional grasslands. He judged that most British farmers would loyally accept such a policy, if prices were guaranteed.'[28] He was proved right. He died in 1930.

Strutt was gazetted a CH in 1917 as 'Agricultural Adviser to the Board of Agriculture and Fisheries.' His entry in *Who's Who* inserted the word 'unpaid' after Agricultural Adviser.

Lord Faringdon 4 June 1917

Alexander Henderson, first Lord Faringdon, was a financier, politician, country squire and justice of the peace.

He was born in London in 1850 and educated privately. He trained as an accountant with Deloitte and Co., where he attracted the attention of Thomas Greenwood, senior partner in a stock exchange company who took him into his business. Greenwood's knowledge of railway finance (he had been associated with the Great Western Railway) and Henderson's capacity for figures made a powerful combination. Henderson took over the running of the old Manchester, Sheffield and Lincolnshire Railway, later the Great Central, of which he became chairman, and greatly improved its financial position. During the war he launched the British Trade Corporation of which he became the chairman and was also vice chairman of the shipping control committee. He was Liberal Unionist member of parliament for West Stafford (1898–1906) and for St George's Hanover Square (1913–16). His obituary in the *The Times* in 1934 summed him up. 'In his long career he was associated with great undertakings, especially railways, and he showed a remarkable gift for reorganizing and restoring to prosperity concerns which had fallen into difficulties.'[29]

Henderson was created a baronet in 1902 and a baron in 1916 with the title of Lord Faringdon. He was gazetted a CH in 1917 as 'Vice-Chairman of the Shipping Control Committee.'

Sir John Furley 1 January 1918

Sir John Furley was a leading figure in organising the work of the St John Ambulance Association (of which he was the first director of stores) and the British Red Cross Society.

He was born at Ashford, Kent in 1836 and educated at Harrow. As far back as 1864 he had visited the Danish army during the Schleswig-Holstein campaign and saw the plight of the wounded, and from that beginning there developed a lifelong interest in caring for the victims of war. In 1868 he joined Sir Edmund Lechmere and other members of the Order of St John in a provisional committee for the establishment of a national Red Cross society, and during the Franco-Prussian war (1870–71) he was commissioner of the British Aid Society; for his services he received the Prussian war medal. Furley never seemed to be far from the field of action in war or natural disaster. He was director of *ambulances volantes* of the French army during the war of the commune (1871); delegate of the British seed fund committee for French peasant farmers (Lord Vernon's Fund) (1871); director of ambulances in Spain during the Carlist war (1874); special commissioner of the Mansion House fund for the relief of sufferers from inundations in the Garonne valley (1875); special commissioner of the British national aid society to inspect and report on ambulance arrangements and to afford necessary assistance to the wounded in Montenegro during the Russo-Turkish war (1876). He was one of the original founders of the St John Ambulance Association in 1877, and deputy chairman and director of the ambulance department of the Order of St John. He also held high office in the Red Cross and attended a series of international conferences from 1868 to 1908, usually as honorary secretary or vice-president.

He was chief commissioner of the British Red Cross central committee during the South African war (1898–1902), for which he was twice mentioned in dispatches, and received the South African war medal with two clasps. He was appointed delegate of the foreign office for the revision of the Geneva convention in 1906, and honorary president of the first international life-saving congress at Frankfort on Main in 1908.

In 1889 he was described as 'one of the most distinguished wearers of the Red Cross. The stretcher of which he is the inventor is used by ambulance corps in all parts of the world. It has greatly facilitated their labours and rendered Sir John Furley's name familiar wherever ambulance work is going on.'[30] The stretcher (named 'the Furley') was awarded a silver medal at the Brussels international exhibition in 1877. Furley was also credited with an ambulance hamper, horse-ambulance carriages, and an electric light device for searching the battlefield, each of which was either invented or modified by him, and he was acknowledged as one of the greatest pioneers of the ambulance movement. In spite of his advanced age, he was active during the 1914–18 war. 'The original 25 huts, the nucleus of the great base hospital at Netley, were designed under his personal supervision, and these served as the model for later additions. He also devoted all his skill and experience to the designing of hospital trains at the front, and their efficiency was in no small degree due to him.'[31] He published a number of volumes of reminiscences, including the two-volume *Struggles and experiences of a neutral volunteer* (1871), *In Spain amongst the Carlists* (1876) and *In peace and war* (1905). He also translated from French, Moynier and Appia's *La guerre et la charité* (1870) and Moynier's *La Croix Rouge, son passé et son avenir* (1883). The advertisement for *Struggles and experiences of a neutral volunteer* sums up the essence of John Furley. 'It is true that Mr Furley won no victories, bombarded no cities, but he has saved many lives, alleviated much suffering, and displayed an amount of foresight and administrative talent of which even a Von Moltke might have been proud.'[32]

Furley was knighted in 1899 and appointed a CB in 1902. He was gazetted a CH in 1918 without any accompanying citation or description of appointment. Aged eighty-one at the time of receiving the CH, he died less than two years later in 1919.

James Seddon 1 January 1918

James Seddon was a doubtful addition to the ranks of the Companions of Honour, but was an enthusiastic supporter of the war and a strong supporter of the coalition government.

He was born in 1868, the eldest son of a Lancashire nail maker. After education at national and board schools, his early working life consisted of sixteen years as a grocer's assistant, followed by ten years as a commercial traveller. In 1898 he became a member of the executive committee of the amalgamated union of shop assistants, and was president of that union in 1902. He was president of the Trades Union Congress in 1915. He was elected Labour member of parliament for the Newton division of Lancashire in 1906 but was defeated at the general election in December 1910.

He used all his influence to encourage pro-war attitudes. In 1916 he was one of the signatories of the British workers' national league manifesto, which called for an all-out effort to achieve victory. In 1918 he left the Labour Party and joined the National Democratic Party, formed to support the coalition government. He was elected member of parliament for the Hanley division of Stoke-on-Trent in December 1918 as a National Democratic Party candidate, but lost the seat in 1922, when he fought it as an independent. The last years of his life were spent in political obscurity until his death in 1939 from a heart attack while taking a bath.

Seddon was gazetted a CH in 1918 without any accompanying citation or description of appointment.

James Parker 1 January 1918

James Parker was one of the few Labour members of parliament who supported the war and in 1918 broke with the party rather than Lloyd George's coalition government

He was born in born 1863 in Lincolnshire, the son of a farm labourer. During his teenage years he worked successively as a greengrocer's assistant, doctor's groom, milkman and barman, until the age of nineteen when he moved to Halifax where he worked first as a labourer with the corporation and later as a packer and warehouseman. In 1897 he was elected to the town council and served until 1906. In 1906 he was elected Labour member of parliament for Halifax. He was secretary of the Labour Party in the house of commons (1909–12) and its vice-chairman (1912–13), and was possibly the least able of the Labour members. He was described as a 'plodding' party secretary in Halifax and dismissed by Beatrice Webb as a 'feeble creature' for his lack of enthusiasm for the 1912 'war against poverty' campaign.

With the outbreak of war, Parker was among the minority within the Independent Labour Party who took a pro-war line. He became a member of a government committee to stimulate recruiting and was rewarded with the minor government post of junior lord of the treasury in January 1917. He often spoke at meetings of the war savings certificate scheme, which he claimed to have originated. He was Labour chief whip in the house of commons (1916–18) and held his treasury post until 1922, and acted as a whip of the coalition government (1918–22). At the general election of December 1918 he was returned for Cannock as a Coalition Labour candidate, but chose to leave the Labour Party rather than give up his government office. In November 1922 he contested the same seat as an Independent with National Liberal support but was defeated by the Labour candidate and retired from politics. 'His last few years in Parliament were lucrative, as he showed a readiness to pick up investment tips dropped to him by the wealthy.'[33] He spent the last twenty-six years of his life in obscurity in Halifax, dying in 1948 at the age of eighty-four.

Parker was gazetted a CH in 1918 without any accompanying citation or description of appointment.

Lieutenant General Sir Alfred Keogh 25 February 1918

Sir Alfred Keogh had created an efficient army medical service and retired from the army in 1910. Such was his reputation that he was recalled to the post in 1914 and headed the service again until the end of the war.

He was born in 1857 at Roscommon in Ireland. He qualified in medicine at the age of twenty-one and entered the army in 1880 after serving as a house physician at Brompton hospital and as an assistant at the Westminster ophthalmic hospital. He was first deputy director general of army medical services (1902–05) and director general (1905–10). He established the Royal Army Medical College at Millbank in 1907 and founded an army school of hygiene. The many station hospitals distributed over the country were replaced by central hospitals, equipped and staffed on a scale impossible in small establishments. When R. B. Haldane organised the territorial army, Keogh was responsible for the creation of a medical service for the new armies. With the co-operation of the civil profession, the teaching hospitals were brought into the scheme, and the staff trained in military duties. During his first tenure of office, he succeeded in bridging the gulf between the civil and military branches of his profession, and raised the standard of medical practice in the army. He left the army on his appointment as rector of Imperial College (1910–22), but on the outbreak of war in 1914, he returned to the war office at the request of Lord Kitchener, on the condition that he was granted exceptional powers. Keogh's reforms were far-reaching in their effect, and the great army medical machine that he had built up worked smoothly and developed under his supervision. He died in 1936.

Keogh was gazetted a CH in 1918 without any accompanying citation or description of appointment.

Colonel Sir Herbert Perrott 3 June 1918

With John Furley, Herbert Perrott was a pioneer of the work of the St John Ambulance Association, and the development of St John into the great national institution that it became was to a large extent due to him.

He was born at Charlton, Kent in 1849, and inherited from his father in 1886 a baronetcy created in 1717. He was educated at Ipswich grammar school, and after service in the army he began a long career with the St John Ambulance. He was chief secretary of the St John Ambulance Association from its foundation in 1877 until he retired in 1915. He was also assistant secretary (1875–88), secretary (1894–1910) and secretary-general (1910–15) of the Order of St John. In 1915 he was appointed to the titular office of Bailiff of Egle.

In October 1914 he was appointed vice chairman of the joint war committee of the Order of St John and the British Red Cross Society, an office he held throughout the war, to the detriment of his health. 'He had never spared himself and had never taken a real holiday, and the increasing strain of the war led to a breakdown in health'.[34] He died in 1922 from the effects of influenza and bronchial pneumonia.

Perrott was gazetted a CH in 1918 without any accompanying citation or description of appointment.

Sir Samuel Provis 3 June 1918

Sir Samuel Provis was a long-serving civil servant whose 'war service' was the unspectacular but important national organisation of war pensions committees throughout the country. Long steeped in the administration of local government he was an obvious candidate to be entrusted with the task.

He was born at Warminster in 1845 and educated at Queens' College, Cambridge. He was called to the bar in 1866 and began a long acquaintanceship with local government when he was appointed junior legal assistant to the local government board in 1872. Promotion to assistant secretary of the board followed in 1882 and then his ultimate appointment as permanent secretary (1889–1910). During his career, Provis witnessed and assisted in a complete revolution in the system of English local government, which through the Local Government Acts of 1888 and 1894, established county councils and parish and district councils, transferred local affairs from the control of justices to that of popularly-elected bodies. From 1914 he was also chairman of the weekly board and convalescent home committee of Chelsea Hospital for Women. After his retirement he did further work in connection with the administration of pensions and was a member of the commission of inquiry into the working of the local pensions committees. As adviser to the ministry of pensions, he organised local and joint war pensions committees throughout the United Kingdom. His obituary that appeared in *The Times* said much about the nature of the man. 'An excellent type of old-fashioned civil servant who brought to his duties the highest character, untiring industry, and good sense which made for a soundness of judgement that was seldom impugned . . . Of an extremely retiring and modest disposition, Provis was hardly known outside official circles, and his type has now passed out with the calmer atmosphere that prevailed in administration before the war. But at the Union Club and elsewhere many will hear with sorrow that the kindly and courteous old gentleman will not be seen again.'[35]

Provis was gazetted a CH in 1918 without any accompanying citation or description of appointment. He died in 1926.

Sir Frederick Treves – the first refusal

Also published on 3 June 1918, and sandwiched between Perrott and Provis, was the name of Sir Frederick Treves GCVO, CB. He was gazetted without any accompanying citation or description or appointment, but his time as a CH was short-lived. On 25 June 1918, the London Gazette published a notice announcing that the name of Treves should be omitted from the list published on 3 June, 'at his own request.' Sir Frederick Treves (1853–1923) was serjeant surgeon to the King and surgeon in ordinary to the Queen, and Sir Frederick Ponsonby described him as 'a man with a keen sense of humour but a certain contempt for the human race.'[36] The prevailing opinion of his contemporaries was that Treves was 'aggressive, ambitious, sarcastic, dismissive, and somewhat vain,'[37] and even his biographer described him as 'terse and opinionated.'[38] But against these criticisms can be set the great kindness and compas-

transport advisory committee and a member of the shipping control committee, and Lloyd George described him as 'one of the three ablest shipowners in the world.'[47]

He was born in 1871 and educated at Winchester and Magdalen College, Oxford. From his ancestry he had a lifelong interest in the sea and ships. His grandfather began shipbuilding on the Mersey in 1820. His father was the founder of the Indra line of steamers and was created a baronet in 1905. He began work in his father's firm in 1895. He was also a director of the Cunard Steam-Ship Company from 1905 and of Cunard White Star from its inception in 1934, and remained on the boards of both companies until his death. He was deputy chairman of Cunard (1909–22) and then chairman (1922–30). He was Conservative member of parliament for Bootle (1918–22), but resigned on his appointment as chairman of Cunard.

In 1913 he shared in the preparation of a confidential plan for the transport of troops and munitions across the channel, a plan brought into operation at the outbreak of the war. As well as his work on the admiralty transport advisory committee and the shipping control committee, he was also a member of the royal commission on wheat supplies. When the USA joined the war in 1917 he visited that country to take part in arranging the transport of troops and war materials to Europe.

Royden had succeeded his father in the baronetcy on his death in 1917. He was lengthily gazetted a CH in 1919 as 'Vice-Chairman of the Cunard Company. Devoted himself entirely to public service since the beginning of the war. Member of the Shipping Control Committee. Has twice acted as Chief Representative of the Ministry of Shipping in America.' He was created a baron in 1944 as Lord Royden. His marriage was childless and the barony became extinct on his death in 1950.

George Barnes 1 January 1920
George Nicoll Barnes was one of a group of Labour members of parliament who enthusiastically supported the war, and also the coalition government of Lloyd George after the Labour Party withdrew from it in 1918. In his memoirs, Lloyd George praised him as 'one of the most level-headed and respected trade union leaders in the world.'[48]

He was born in 1859, the second of the five sons of a journeyman machine maker, who was managing a jute mill in Dundee at the time of his son's birth. George Barnes himself began work in a jute mill at the age of eleven. He went to evening classes to study mostly technical drawing and machine construction. He worked for a period in the London docks and, like many others at the time, he was affected by the 1889 dock strike and the new stirrings of trade unionism. He joined the amalgamated society of engineers, and was general secretary of the union from 1896 until 1908, and was his union's delegate at the founding of the Labour Party in 1900. In 1906 he was elected Labour member of parliament for the Blackfriars and Hutchestown (later Gorbals) division of Glasgow, which he held with increasing majorities until his retirement from politics in 1922.

He was a firm supporter of the war, taking the view that Britain had to defend her international obligations. In the early months he was active in recruiting campaigns throughout the country, taking a particular interest in the pensions and allowances paid to families of recruits. From May to September 1914 he was on a mission to Canada to persuade Canadian mechanics to migrate to England to replace engineers who had joined the army. The death of his youngest son at the battle of Loos in 1915 only served to reinforce his conviction that the war was just and had to be won. In 1916 he became chairman of the savings committee, in December that year he was appointed minister for pensions, and in 1917 a member of the war cabinet. When the Labour Party decided to withdraw from the coalition government in 1918 he resigned from the party rather than surrender his ministerial office, believing that Labour would be denied the chance to influence the peace conferences. He was asked to attend the Versailles conference and signed the treaty of Versailles as the government's labour representative. In 1919 he led the British delegation to the first international labour conference in Washington, which led to the establishment of a permanent office in Geneva. He resigned from the government in 1920, feeling that his work was finished. His continued participation in government made him widely unpopular in the Labour movement and he did not contest his seat at the 1922 election, his chief regret being that the international labour office would no longer have a spokesman in the house of commons. He was the author of a number of publications including, *The history of the amalgamated society of engineers* (1901), *An eastern tour* (1921), *From workshop to war cabinet* (1923), *Industrial conflict: the way out* (1924), and *The history of the international labour organization* (1926). Barnes died at his home in London in 1940.

He was gazetted a CH in 1920 without any accompanying citation or description of appointment.

Philip Kerr (Marquess of Lothian) 1 January 1920
Philip Henry Kerr was a journalist and, to a lesser extent, a politician. His influence on public affairs far outweighed his comparatively few public offices.

Kerr was born in 1882, scion of a Scottish aristocratic family. He was educated at the Oratory School, Birmingham and New College, Oxford. His career began in the colonial service in southern Africa: he was assistant secretary of the intercolonial council of Transvaal and Orange River Colony and of the railway committee of Central South African Railways (1905–08), and secretary of the Transvaal indigency commission (1907–08). A period of journalism followed with his editorship of *The State* (1908–09), a new journal dedicated to the promotion of union of the South African colonies and the formation of a South African identity. In 1910 he became the first editor of *Round Table*, a quarterly magazine which functioned as the organ of the 'Milnerites', the young men who had worked with Lord Milner to reconstitute South Africa as part of the British Empire after the South African War (1899–1902). The journal was strongly orientated towards the organic union of the empire. While writing on imperial and American affairs, he also used its columns to give periodic warnings of the danger that Germany posed to the British empire.

His career took a very public turn in December 1916 when he was called away from his editorial desk to become private secretary to Lloyd George. More than anyone else, he was responsible for the drafting of the document with regard to Germany which formed a preface to the treaty of Versailles, and was strongly criticised by Lloyd George's opponents for what was perceived to be his unwise influence over the prime minister in the matter of the Russian civil war. He left politics in 1921 to join the board of United Newspapers, owners of the *Daily*

Chronicle. He was secretary of the Rhodes Trust (1925–39). He inherited the marquessate of Lothian (and ten other peerages) on the death of his cousin in March 1930. In 1931 he joined the coalition government of Ramsay Macdonald as chancellor of the duchy of Lancaster (August-November 1931) and parliamentary under-secretary of state at the India Office (1931–32). With a number of other Liberal Party members he resigned in September 1932 on free trade issues. He had never liked being in government and resigned with relief. During the 1930s he was at first inclined towards appeasement of Germany, but became less conciliatory after the Austrian *Anschluss* in 1938 and was strongly opposed to the Munich settlement.

In 1939 he accepted the appointment of ambassador to the USA at the suggestion of Lord Halifax. He liked the United States and the American people and it was a pleasant ending to his career and his life; he died in Washington in 1940. In his *Truth about the peace treaties* published in 1938, Lloyd George praised his former private secretary and acknowledged the 'priceless help' that Kerr had given him, and Kerr remains the only private secretary of a prime minister to have been appointed to such a high honour for his services.

Kerr was gazetted a CH in 1920 as 'Member of the Prime Minister's Secretariat.' He was made a KT in 1940, a month before his death. He never married and the peerages were inherited by a cousin.

And who next?
Sir Frederick Ponsonby was unenthusiastic about the list of the first twenty-seven Companions of Honour, most of whom were not immediately recognisable figures, and about the ability of the prime minister's office to make any sense of the Order, and his view was shared by others. In 1918 he asked Sir Douglas Dawson for suggestions, and Dawson duly obliged with a list of names. Although he appears to have given little serious consideration to the task, he produced a list of eleven names which in his opinion, would enhance the social status of the new Order and mark a distinct move away from the 'common touch' of the first list: Princess Arthur of Connaught, Princess Patricia of Connaught, Princess Alice, Countess of Athlone, the Dowager Countess of Dudley, the archbishops of Canterbury and York, Lord Finlay (lord chancellor), Viscount Northcliffe, Sir George Buchanan (former ambassador at Petrograd), Vice Admiral Sir William Pakenham and Lieutenant General Sir Jacob Van Deventer, commanding forces, East Africa. Pakenham and Van Deventer were hardly serious contenders for another honour. Pakenham had been made a KCB in May 1916 and a KCVO in June 1917. Van Deventer had been made a KCB as recently as December 1917. But Dawson had tried: 'Herewith a list of suggested names, which you asked me to let you have. I have included one naval [and] one military with dates of last honours conferred. Pakenham because I understand him to be second to Beatty as regards naval operations and Van Deventer because his Colonial War record was longer and more strenuous than others. Lord Northcliffe for his wonderful propaganda work, silently done, Lady Dudley for her Red Cross equally silent. If we can get all this list to accept, in spite of the unknown names already appointed, we shall introduce a leaven of a new standard which should be adhered to in future. But, will they accept, under the circumstances?!!!'[49] Not one of Dawson's suggestions was admitted to the new Order.

A correspondence in 1919–20 between Sir Arthur Stanley, chairman of the British Red Cross Society, and Sir Frederick Ponsonby, demonstrated some of the problems that surrounded the gathering of names for the new Order. Stanley wanted to recommend the Duchess of Beaufort for the CH, for her work with the Red Cross.[50] Ponsonby's answer was terse and forthright. 'The CH is entirely run by the P. M.'s Private Secretary and a nice mess he has made of it. Will you write to him about it?'[51] Stanley's reply showed a prevailing feeling of frustration. 'My heart sinks within me when I am told to apply to the P. M.'s secretaries for anything, as I know it means many letters and even more months of waiting and generally nothing done in the end. But I get back to London on Saturday . . . and I will make a determined onslaught on Downing Street.'[52]

Whether or not Stanley made an 'onslaught' on Downing Street in August 1919, nothing happened, and he returned to Ponsonby in April 1920, this time adding the name of Sir William Bennett to that of the Duchess of Beaufort.[53] This time Ponsonby elaborated on his powerlessness and added some background. 'The Companionship of Honour is most jealously guarded at 10 Downing Street and they seem there to resent my interference. I suggested last year to George Curzon that we should try and make that Decoration a success. He cordially agreed and said he would consider a list of suitable people, but on referring to Downing Street he was told that the list was entirely in the hands of the Prime Minister and that while the King could, of course, nominate anyone he pleased, the ordinary procedure must be kept at Downing Street. I have therefore decided to let this Decoration slide and it has developed into a vague honour, which no one quite understands.'[54]

Ponsonby did his best but in December 1920 wrote to Stanley saying why he thought the nomination of the Duchess of Beaufort was being thwarted. 'I am told that owing to the duke having expressed a wish years ago to hand over Lloyd George to his pack of hounds, her name has invariably been taken off every list.'[55] The last letter on the subject was from Ponsonby to J. T. Davies, Lloyd George's private secretary in the same month. 'The Duchess of Beaufort is very strongly recommended by the Red Cross and I spoke to the King on the subject. His Majesty does not know whether the Prime Minister intends to put forward any names for this Order [for the New Year List 1921], but in any case the King considers that the Duchess should receive recognition for the excellent work she did during the war. Perhaps you will let me know what it is proposed to do with this Order.'[56] It was to no avail; the 'pack of hounds' story was either true or it was a piece of unsubstantiated folklore, but the duchess and Sir William Bennett were passed over.

The Red Cross was nothing if not persistent and after the fall of Lloyd George in 1922, they tried again, in the spring of 1923, to secure the CH for the Duchess of Beaufort, Sir William Bennett and on this occasion they added the name of Sir Richard Temple. Ponsonby reported to the prime minister's office that once again he had been approached by 'the Red Cross people'. 'I have replied that all recommendations for this Honour must be sent to you at Downing Street, but that I would pass on these names. It seems to me that the Duchess of Beaufort and Sir William Bennett would help the Order very much, as at one time there was the danger of the Order not being appreciated because it was given to people unknown to the public. Sir Richard Temple, however, is hardly known to anybody, except as the son of his father, and if you have too many names, possibly you might omit this one.'[57] Even the departure of Lloyd George had not persuaded Downing Street that there was any merit in selecting the Red Cross names.

Temple stood no chance, but once again Beaufort and Bennett were passed over. The Duchess of Beaufort, who lived on until 1945, received no state recognition for her war services, and had to be content with being a dame grand cross of the Order of St John. As for Sir William Bennett – he too received nothing, and had to rest with the KCVO he had been given in 1901.

The appointment of Philip Kerr in 1920 had set a precedent and possibly whetted appetites. As Lloyd George's private secretary had been made a CH, there was surely no reason why other private secretaries should not be included. In 1924 Ramsay MacDonald, the country's first Labour prime minister submitted his resignation honours list to King George V, recommending the names of Sir Ronald Waterhouse and Sir Patrick Gower for the CH. Ronald Waterhouse (1878–1942) and Patrick Gower (1887–1964) were private secretaries to successive prime ministers in the years 1922–28 and Macdonald simply wanted to thank the two men for their service to him during his difficult and brief minority government. The King thought it his duty not only to restrain Macdonald's generosity but also to preserve the reputation of the new Order. 'The King desires me to express his regret,' wrote Lord Stamfordham, 'at being unable to bestow the Order of the Companion of Honour upon Sir Ronald Waterhouse and Sir Patrick Gower. His Majesty wishes me to point out that the former was made a KCB only last year, for his services as Private Secretary to Mr Bonar Law: while Gower was made a KBE this year, for his services to Mr Baldwin, a CB in 1922, and a CVO last year. The King cannot recognise what seems to be now regarded as a rule, that the Private Secretaries to out-going Prime Ministers are to receive decorations.'[58]

Macdonald enlisted the aid of his successor, Stanley Baldwin in trying to get the two men honoured. While agreeing with the principle that no prime minister on relinquishing office should as a matter of course submit the names of his staff ex officio for the grant of any honour or reward, 'I recognise that the nature of these appointments differs very materially in these days both in its duties and responsibilities from that of any other personal Staff, and it appears to me natural therefore that a retiring Prime Minister might wish to emphasise this fact not in respect of the actual appointment held, but rather on account of the personal assistance which in his judgement had been rendered to him. In these circumstances I feel sure that His Majesty would wish to be guided in the submission of his final Resignation List by the same considerations which had previously influenced him during his tenure of office, and to judge accordingly as to the merits of his personal staff.'[59]

The King held his ground, pointing out that complications could arise if members of secretarial staff continued to serve successive prime ministers – as happened in the case of Waterhouse and Gower – but he was also concerned to protect the still young honour. 'The King hopes . . . that the Companion of Honour will be reserved for bestowal upon persons who do not wish to receive Knighthood, as this was one of the chief reasons for the creation of the Order.[60] The point was well made and Baldwin retreated. 'I fully agree as to the usage of this Order and will deal with it accordingly when considering submissions to the King.'[61] The firm line taken by King George V prevented the needless appointment of further private secretaries to the Order and helped a little to ensure that the CH remained a high honour, but where was it to go? The lives of the twenty-seven men and women who inaugurated the Order of the Companions of Honour were linked by their common contribution to the 1914–18 war effort, and few of them would now be reckoned to have risen to the later and higher standards of a CH, although echoes can be found in the twenty or so appointments made during the 1939–45 war. It is difficult to believe that an explosives expert, a newspaper proprietor, a shipowner, a munitions expert, or the prime minister's private secretary would now be seen as natural CH recipients. On paper, the honour matched one of its early provisional names – the War Service Order. But the madness of the long and debilitating 1914–18 war was finished and it remained to be seen how the Order would develop in peacetime, and what new categories of Companions of Honour would emerge in the decades ahead.

CHAPTER THREE

In God's name

BISHOPS, PRIESTS, PASTORS

'Alice tried a little to fancy to herself what such an extraordinary way of living would be like, but it puzzled her too much.'
'A mad tea-party', *Alice's adventures in wonderland*, Lewis Carroll

The first of the postwar appointments to the Order, categorically not for war service, was an unusual choice and pointed to the establishment of a precedent that continued throughout the 1920s and 1930s and dwindled away in the second half of the twentieth century. The 1921 new year honours list named two new Companions of Honour, the first of whom was John Clifford, a Baptist pastor. Only on the rarest of occasions were clergy given honours before the beginning of the twentieth century, and usually in the 'colonial' Order of St Michael and St George. From 1902 a few were appointed to the Royal Victorian Order on the initiatives of King Edward VII and King George V, usually for services rendered to the royal family. But from 1917 the new 'open' Orders – of the British Empire and the Companions of Honour – provided a way of honouring clergy for more general services, though at first not without opposition from King George V.

Any reaction by the King to the recommendation of Clifford appears not to have survived, but Clifford's appointment to the Order had opened the gate to admission of further clergy, and in May 1921, the King endeavoured to have it shut. Randall Davidson, archbishop of Canterbury, in the approach to the birthday honours list 1921, launched the first salvo. Among the earliest names considered for the list was that of Sir William Robertson Nicoll, a minister of the Free Church of Scotland, and editor of a number of journals. J. T. Davies, the prime minister's private secretary suggested that outstanding churchmen (i.e. members of the Church of England) should also be considered, and proposed to Lord Stamfordham, the King's private secretary that the views of the archbishop of Canterbury should be sought.[1] Stamfordham advised that the prime minister should himself contact the archbishop, but in the meantime he noted that 'the King does not wish a churchman yet'.[2] The archbishop had views of his own which ran counter to those of the King and went further still. 'Is there any reason why a man nominated to be a Companion of Honour should not be a clergyman? I have looked at the list . . . and though there are no clergy as such [the archbishop appears to have been unaware of the appointment of Clifford, or more probably discounted it] it does not seem that there is anything unsuitable, and as a matter of fact Robertson Nicoll is a Dissenting Minister as well as a politician and the editor of a weekly newspaper. What should you think of Professor Headlam of Oxford? He is an eminent theologian, an eminent thinker, and a leading university man.'[3] Davidson was not about to see the Church of England left out of the running, but to the prospect of a clergyman, the King was decidedly opposed, though no reason is on record. 'The King is against conferring decorations other than VO [the Royal Victorian Order] on clergymen. I told the PM so who did not agree and thought it hard on the clergy!!'[4] It was the King's misfortune that the said prime minister was David Lloyd George, the most difficult and devious of any of his prime ministers, and certainly the most determined and the most stubborn, and there was no love lost between the two men. When the prime minister submitted the name of the mayor of Colchester for a CBE in 1922, the King wrote to the left of the name 'No' and to the right of the name 'For giving oysters to L.G.'[5] But when Lloyd George was determined that something would be done, opposition – even that of the King – was swept aside, and a combination of the prime minister and the archbishop of Canterbury was not something that the King could easily resist. 'The Prime Minister told Lord Stamfordham that he wished to make a Companion of Honour of an English Churchman, a layman, as he was giving that honour to Robertson Nicoll, who was a Nonconformist. Lord Stamfordham advised him to consult the Archbishop of Canterbury, and himself repeated the conversation he had with the Prime Minister. The King afterwards agreed to the CH being conferred upon a clergman *(sic)*.'[6] The clergyman concerned was Arthur Headlam.

Although the way was now permanently open, the King occasionally intervened to stop a flood of appointments. In 1922 the names of the bishop of Worcester, John Shakespeare (secretary of the Baptist Union of Great Britain and Ireland since 1898) and John Jowett (minister of Westminster Chapel) were under consideration. When the list of suggested honours was submitted to the King, he wrote against the names of the clergy, 'only one',[7] and only Jowett was appointed.

John Clifford was the first of twenty-seven clergy appointed to the Order of the Companions of Honour in the twentieth century. Ten were Anglicans (nine from the Church of England and one from the Church of Ireland), one was Roman Catholic, five were Baptists, two were Presbyterians, five were Congregationalists, one from the United Reformed Church (a 1972 fusion of Presbyterians and Congregationalists in England), one Methodist, one Jewish and one Salvation Army officer.

The word 'clergy' is a convenient rather than accurate description of these twenty-seven Companions of Honour. Judaism has the teaching office of 'rabbi', the Salvation Army is staffed by 'officers', and the 'ministers' and 'pastors' of the nonconformist churches would probably resist being defined as 'clerks in holy orders' in the traditional sense, but there seems to be no other all-embracing heading. The grouping of these individuals under the title is arguably further flawed, since none of them was honoured purely for undertaking their traditional pastoral duties. Each of these 'clergy' had a 'value added' aspect that secured them a reputation often beyond their own communion. But without fragmenting this book into smaller chapters, it seemed appropriate, with two exceptions, to assemble their diverse contributions to national life under the broad genre of primary vocation. In many cases it was the wellspring of their activity, or it contributed to their activity, or it provided a backdrop or a field in which their sometimes esoteric cultural interests could flourish.

The appointment of John Clifford in 1921 was itself a notable development, in that it marked the fact that the Order could be used to honour distinguished ministers of the nonconformist churches. For centuries the historic free churches had suffered from the public image of being 'nonconformists' or 'dissenters'. Usually though not always for doctrinal reasons, they had refused to conform to the

Church of England, the church 'by law established', and were consequently labelled 'nonconformists' or 'dissenters' and viewed by the 'establishment' as being on the margins of the spiritual life of the nation. Until they were swept along by the juggernaut of the Gothic revival style in the nineteenth century, nonconformist chapels or meeting houses were architecturally humble and undistinguished structures, usually found on the edge of villages or in the poor back streets of industrial towns. There, the simple preaching of their ministers or pastors, themselves usually from humble backgrounds, found fertile and untilled soil in the shape of a working class that was mostly alienated from the confident self-importance of the middle and upper class Church of England. The arrival of a Welsh nonconformist prime minister in Downing Street in 1916, and the creation of the Orders of the British Empire and the Companions of Honour in 1917, began the process of recognising nonconformity for the valuable contribution it had made to the life of the nation. David Lloyd George was so proud of his origins that at times he seemed almost a professional Welsh nonconformist.

Other factors were at work, not least the *Appeal to all Christian people* that emerged from the Lambeth Conference of 1920. The work of Archbishop Cosmo Gordon Lang of York, 'it expressed, and on the whole generously expressed, the new wind blowing across Christendom.'[8] The *Appeal* was a visionary if impractical call for a non-specific unity among Christian denominations, and it inaugurated a series of discussions between the Church of England and the English nonconformist churches throughout the 1920s, encouraging nonconformists to break free from their narrow sectarianism and embrace the ecumenical spirit that pervaded the interwar years. In 1920 the University of Oxford at last allowed non-Anglicans to receive its higher theological degrees, and there seemed to be a new spirit of trust and cooperation between the established church and the denominational descendants of those who, long ago, had refused to 'conform' to its liturgies and doctrines. The admission of nonconformist ministers to the new high-ranking Order of the Companions of Honour was at last a recognition of their place in British public life.

Some of the clergy were conscientious and zealous contributors to the flurry of ecumenical activity, national and international, that emerged after the 1914–18 war, including John Jones (1927), John Scott Lidgett (1933), John White (1935), Melbourn Aubrey (1937) and Ernest Payne (1968). Some, for example Arthur Headlam (1921), Herbert James (1926), Hugh Martin (1955), John Baillie (1957) and Walter Matthews (1962), held high academic appointments. Some were motivated by a strong social conscience to lead personal crusades that led to the bettering of the lot of their fellow human beings. Into this category fall the work of Wilson Carlile (1926) and the Church Army, Dick Sheppard (1927) and his social work at St Martin-in-the-Fields, Bramwell Booth (1929) and the Salvation Army, 'Tubby' Clayton and the Toc H movement (1933). Some were eminent theologians, including C. H. Dodd (1961) and Nathaniel Micklem (1974).

Other CHs are not easily assigned to categories; the fiery political and social populist radicalism of John Clifford is in sharp contrast to the almost patrician political tact of Archbishop John Gregg (1957) and Bishop Henry Williams (1945). Chief Rabbi Joseph Hertz (1943) was in a category of his own, but coming at the height of the 1939–45 war, his CH was certainly a well-timed symbol of honour for the head of a Jewish community, whose brethren on the European mainland were suffering under a particularly vicious form of anti-Semitism. The powerful oratory of John Jowett (1922), both in New York and Westminster, was almost certainly recognised because he was known to be dying. The work and qualities that led to John Carlile (1929) being made a CH are less apparent, although he was twice president and once acting secretary of the Baptist Union at difficult periods for that organisation, and he was editor of the *Baptist Times* at the time of his appointment. Maude Royden (1930), part of the movement for the rights of women, abandoned the Church of England for the Congregational Church to become a pioneer woman preacher.

Two clergy – Edmund Fellowes (1944) and Elfed Lewis (1948) – were recognised for their services to music and to literature and are included chapters 7 and 5 respectively. Chad Varah (1999) was honoured for his work in founding the Samaritans and is included in chapter 11.

Beginning in 1921, appointments of clergy to the Order were made fairly regularly until 1974, an average of one every two years. But the graph revealed a steady downward drift after the 1939–45 war, reflecting the numerical decline of the churches in the second half of the twentieth century. With historic nonconformity in steep decline, the appointment of the theologian Nathaniel Micklem in 1974 was the last of a line of distinguished Free Church ministers to appear in the ranks of the Companions of Honour. The appointment of Archbishop Derek Worlock (1995), a long overdue recognition of the significant place of the Roman Catholic church in the life of the nation, was essentially for his community services in Liverpool.

With the Christian churches generally now on the margins of national life, the once relatively numerous class of eminent clergy who appeared in the ranks of the Companions of Honour has effectively ceased to exist.

John Clifford (Baptist) *1 January 1921*

John Clifford was very much of the self-taught working class background that was a feature of the earliest Companions of Honour. He was a fiery Baptist preacher of (for his time) liberal principles.

Born at Sawley in Derbyshire in 1836, the elder son of a factory worker, his mother came from an old-established Baptist family and three of his uncles were preachers. After an elementary education, he went to work in a lace factory at the age of eleven. By the age of thirteen he was able to read, and the writings of the American essayist and poet, Ralph Waldo Emerson, strongly influenced his life. He was 'converted' in 1850 and baptised on 16 June 1851. He trained for the Baptist ministry at the Midland Baptist College at Leicester in 1855, and in 1858 he was chosen to be pastor at Praed Street Baptist Church in Paddington, London. He stipulated that he should be free to continue his studies, and between 1861 and 1866 graduated from the University of London with degrees in arts, science and law. The church flourished under his pastorate and, having outgrown the chapel, built a new church in Westbourne Park where he remained until 1915.

Given his thirst for knowledge and a voracious reading schedule, Clifford was a man of broad sympathies in his time – too broad in the opinion of some of his fellow Baptists. He was an ardent evangelical, to whom a personal experience of redemption in Christ was of the essence of the Christian life, but his religious beliefs were not purely internal. He was raised in a working class household and could remember 1848 and the last and greatest of the Chartist marches. The social and political implications of religious faith concerned him as deeply as did any internal sense of redemption. He was no advocate of class warfare, but given the poverty of his childhood he was sensitive to the glaring and prevalent inequalities of the class-ridden age in which he lived, and there was something of the agitator about him. Social concerns led him to join the Fabian Society and to support the dock strike of 1889, and in 1894 he founded the Christian Socialist League. Some labourers were once rash enough to ask him what he knew about hard work. Clifford rose in wrath and told them of his youth in a factory in the days before the factory acts and how he was sometimes made to work sixteen or twenty hours a day.[9] His social conscience was paralleled by a liberal theology that sometimes troubled his fellow Baptists. He was proud of the fact that his own denomination had no formal creed, and he claimed the freedom to interpret the will of Christ in the light of growing knowledge and experience, rather than simply accept the precise wording of the biblical texts as the unchanging standard. He kept abreast of scientific advances and regarded Charles Darwin as a fellow worker in the kingdom of truth, accepting Darwin's evolutionary theory at a time when it aroused heated controversy. He welcomed the new spirit of informed criticism of the biblical texts that emerged in the second half of the nineteenth century, typified by *Essays and reviews* (1860) and *Lux mundi* (1889). In 1887, his fellow Baptist preacher Charles Haddon Spurgeon, withdrew from the Baptist Union of Great Britain and Ireland partly on the ground of its tolerance of biblical criticism. Clifford, then vice-president of the union, defended its position. He respected Spurgeon, but liberty of conscience was of such paramount importance to him that he firmly and successfully resisted Spurgeon's demand that the union should adopt a definite creed. In later years, he opposed any thought of Christian reunion, on the ground of a belief that it would lead to the sacrifice of truth and freedom, but his liberal views did not prevent him from being president of the Baptist World Alliance (1905–11).

His libertarian principles extended to the world of education. He welcomed the 1870 Education Act, which created a system of national education because the church schools could not cover the entire country, but he held that no religious test should be imposed on the teachers in these new board schools. In 1902 a new Education Bill effectively sought control of denominational schools by placing them on the rates and making them eligible for maintenance grants on the same scale as the board schools. Clifford was a strong opponent, arguing that these church schools, almost entirely Anglican and Roman Catholic, should not receive state funding, and he mounted a campaign of protest. When the act was passed, he championed a passive resistance movement whose members refused to pay part of their rates in protest. Clifford's vehement opposition at least in part, revived both nonconformity and the Liberal Party, and led to the defeat of the Conservative government at the 1906 general election.

Nonconformity in general and Clifford in particular, found their natural home in the Liberal Party, but Clifford like many others eventually lost patience with Lloyd George's policies, especially conscription, which ran counter to the free church tradition, and he backed the Labour Party at the 1918 general election. He was eighty-two years old, but still commanded great respect and was the most uninhibited leader of nonconformity. There is no doubt that he deserved the CH that he received on new year's day 1921, but whether that was the only consideration that motivated Lloyd George to give the honour to the old man is another matter. No specific citation or description of appointment appeared in the *London Gazette*. Clifford died less than two years later, in 1923.

Arthur Cayley Headlam (Anglican) 4 June 1921
Arthur Headlam was one of the most influential prelates of the Church of England in the inter-war years.

He was born in 1862, the eldest son of a parish priest in County Durham. A first class degree in greats at Oxford and a fellowship of All Souls pointed to an academic career, and after seven years as rector of Welwyn, Hertfordshire (1896–1903), he was appointed principal of King's College, London. 'There he found scope for his energy, powers of organisation and for a determination which did not easily brook opposition.'[10] His strengths were needed. On his arrival in 1903 the college was bankrupt; on his departure in 1913 it was solvent and secure. King's College was a composite educational establishment consisting of a motley collection of teaching departments at various levels, including even a school. In the light of the establishment of the University of London, hitherto only an examining body, as a teaching institution in 1900, Headlam was faced with the task of rationalising the college and formally incorporating it into the university. The school, the hospital and the ladies department were hived off to form separate institutions, while the remainder of the college was divided into two parts. The larger, consisting of the secular departments, in which religious tests for the staff were abolished, was incorporated into the university. The smaller, Kings College Theological Department, kept its independence with its own council as a denominational body of teachers and students. Headlam's scheme was described as a remarkable piece of statesmanship, but it was not achieved without considerable heartache as the college parted company with historic parts of its teaching life. The standard of the theological department was raised, and among its students was Walter Robert Matthews, himself later to become a CH.

Headlam resigned in 1913 on the ground that he wanted to spend more time in reading and writing. He was a prolific writer and the author of a series of works on biblical and theological subjects, as well as being editor of the *Church Quarterly Review* 1901–21. In 1918 he became regius professor of divinity at Oxford, and his Bampton Lectures of 1920 on *The doctrine of the church and Christian reunion*, was the most notable achievement during his professorship. Headlam, who had long been interested in the prospect of Christian reunion at home and abroad, chose the subject with a view to the 1920 Lambeth Conference and the move towards ecumenism. His utterly central churchmanship (he disliked evangelicals, anglo-catholics and modernists in equal measure) and his strong adherence to the historic episcopate was balanced by an equally strong conviction of the validity of the ministries and sacraments of the nonconformist churches, and he argued that a recognition of that validity would be a great step towards reunion.

He was consecrated bishop of Gloucester in 1923 and was chairman of the Church of England council on foreign relations (1933–45), and brought to his diocese the same edge of steel that had marked his ministry at King's. 'In his work as a bishop, as in many other areas of his life, he could appear brusque and insensitive, even hard and unsympathetic. He knew his own mind and expressed himself with uncompromising clearness; a characteristic reserve and unsentimentality combined with a quick temper and a disregard for criticism often made him seem difficult and unapproachable. Certainly he could be bluntly impervious to the effect of his words. But he welcomed and respected forthrightness in others; differences of opinion did not damage old friendships, and there was a strong sense of justice and kindness in his dealings with those in trouble. In his theological and biblical studies, he was an enlightened conservative, keeping in touch with new knowledge and new theories, but strongly critical of views which seemed to strain the evidence or to move far from the positions which his own studies had tested and his own mind had established.'[11] Troubled by deafness for many years, he retired in 1945 to live at Whorlton Hall, his ancestral home in County Durham, where had been born and where he died in 1947. His wife had died in 1924 after twenty-four years of marriage; they had no children.

He was appointed a CH in 1921 for his services as 'Regius Professor of Divinity, Oxford University, and Canon of Christchurch, Oxford, since 1918.'

John Henry Jowett (Congregationalist) 19 October 1922
John Jowett was a powerfully vigorous nonconformist preacher who made his name at a time when the oratorical skills of a preacher were paramount in the world of nonconformity.

He was born into a working class family at Halifax in 1863. Educated at Hipperholme Grammar School, he won a scholarship to the University of Edinburgh, followed by a time at Oxford. At Edinburgh he acquired the enthusiasm for preaching which distinguished his work throughout his life as a Congregational minister. His books and his life are now forgotten, but his appointment as a CH is evidence of the national esteem in which he was once held. His first appointment was at St James' Congregational Church, Newcastle on Tyne (1889–95), but fifteen years (1895–1910) of sermons at Carrs Lane Chapel, Birmingham saw his reputation and popularity soar to international heights and in 1911 he finally accepted a repeated invitation to become minister of the great Fifth Avenue Presbyterian Church in New York, where he had preached on a visit in 1909. He remained there until 1918 when, 'notwithstanding considerable indignation in America,'[12] he returned to England in reply to an invitation to become minister of Westminster Chapel in London. In about 1920 his health began to fail, and though he continued to preach both in England and abroad, he was compelled to resign from the chapel a few months before his death in December 1923. Among the honours he acquired was a DD degree from Edinburgh in 1910 and another from New York University in 1911, the chairmanship of the Congregational Union, and the presidency of the Free Church Federal Council in 1910. He published a number of homiletic and devotional books, with titles such as *From strength to strength* (1898), *Meditations for quiet moments* (1899), *Apostolic optimism* (1901), *Brooks by the travellers' way* (1902), *The epistles of St Peter* (1905), *The high calling. Meditations on St Paul's letter to the Philippians* (1909), *Thirsting for the springs*, *The passion for souls*, *Silver lining*, *The transfigured church*, *The preacher: his life and work*, *Things that matter most*, *Daily meditations*, *The redeemed family of God* (1919), *The eagle life* (1921), *The friend on the road* (1921), *God – our contemporary* (1922), *Life in the heights. Studies in the epistles* (1924), and *The daily altar* (1925). All of them were 'characterised by the same literary grace and charm, which were a feature of his sermons.'[13]

He was made a CH in 1922, but no citation or description of appointment appeared against his name in the *London Gazette*.

Wilson Carlile (Anglican) 1 January 1926
Wilson Carlile is remembered principally as the founder of the Church Army, an Anglican society of lay evangelists, sometimes thought of as the Church of England's answer to the Salvation Army.

Born in Brixton in 1847, the eldest of the twelve children of a city merchant, he was educated at a private school. In 1862, he entered the business of his maternal grandfather, a silk merchant. He travelled widely in France during the Franco-Prussian War (1870–71), taking advantage of the unsettled state of the silk market, and learned to speak fluent German and Italian. Inheriting his grandfather's business when he came of age, he suffered the cathartic experience of being financially ruined in an economic collapse, and like others before and since, turned his interest to religion of which previously he had been only a conventional practitioner. His parents, previously Congregationalists, had recently joined the Church of England, and Carlile took an interest in his new communion. He was confirmed and, in partnership with his father, used his spare time for mission work in the parish of Holy Trinity, Richmond, where his family had settled. He was a competent musician and acted as deputy to the piano-playing Ira Sankey during the great Moody and Sankey mission (1872–75). In 1878 he abandoned a business career forever to be trained for holy orders at St John's College, Highbury. Ordained deacon in 1880 and priest in 1881, he served his title at St Mary Abbots in Kensington.

Carlile was concerned by the evident failure of the Church of England to build any meaningful bridge with the English working classes and by the absence of the working classes from any positions of responsibility within the church, and he was additionally convinced that the gospel could be preached equally well by lay people; it was a radical and not altogether welcome view at the time. Like John Wesley and William Booth before him, he began to hold open air meetings on the pavements of Kensington High Street, which eventually caused so much obstruction to traffic that he was asked to give them up. In 1882 he resigned his curacy and founded the Church Army. Like the Salvation Army, founded four years earlier, the Church Army met with hostility and violence in its early days in the slums of Westminster, and Carlile himself was injured on two or three occasions. Opposition also came from within the Church where his unconventional methods were greeted with suspicion. At a church congress in Carlisle in 1884, he was howled off the platform when he urged that laymen should be allowed to lead prayers in churches. He travelled continuously around the country persuading less than enthusiastic clergy to allow the Church Army to work in their parishes and by 1885 the army had forty-five evangelists and 4,000–5,000 active members. A Church Army Training College was established, first at Oxford and after 1885 in London, in which working men, without cost to themselves, were trained to be full time evangelists. Groups of fifteen or twenty men at a time lived in a house above a shop in Edgware Road, studied the bible and the prayer book and practised preaching in Hyde Park and in the slums. Like the officers of the Salvation Army, they had to abstain from alcohol and nicotine. Carlile's work was recognised in 1897 when, under an Order of Convocation, male students who had successfully completed their training, were admitted by the bishop of London 'to the office of evangelist in the church of God' with the title of 'captain'. Women, known as 'sister' were admitted in 1921. Unlike the Salvation Army, the Church Army remained firmly within the fold of the Church of England and its officers were based in parishes, but in common with the Salvation Army, the Church Army placed a strong emphasis on social work. In 1889 Carlile established Church Army homes for ex-prisoners, tramps and destitute, and two or three times each week during the winter, he would spend the night on the Thames embankment. Sometimes 2000 homeless men and women would gather for Church Army food and shelter. He was criticised on the ground that the work was merely palliative, but the fact remains that his work alleviated a great amount of misery and did much to rouse social conscience.

In 1891 he became rector of St Mary at Hill, an empty city of London church that he filled to overflowing until he retired in 1926. At the rectory adjoining the church, he established a 'City Samaritan Office', which constituted in his own words, 'a free club conducted by evangelists of the Church Army, to aid destitute but deserving clerks, warehousemen, and hopeless starving outcasts.'[14] He preached on the test match and on night clubs, and instituted a 'Doll Sunday' and a 'Bun Sunday', when gifts of these items were made, and during his incumbency, St Mary at Hill became the fullest and liveliest church in the city. That his movement thrived was due at least in part to Carlile's personality, which was marked by personal humility, an absence of fanaticism, and a sense of humour. He died in 1942 in his ninety-sixth year.

He was made a CH in 1926, allegedly at the behest of King George V, for his services as 'Prebendary of St Paul's Cathedral 1906. Founder and Honorary Chief Secretary Church Army since 1882.'

Herbert Armitage James (Anglican) 5 June 1926

For more than half a century Armitage James held an almost unbroken succession of educational appointments, culminating in the presidency of St John's College, Oxford.

He was born in 1844, son of the rector of Panteg, Monmouthshire. He was educated at Abergavenny Grammar School and Jesus College, Oxford, followed by a scholarship to Lincoln College, and gained a first class degree in moderations and literae humaniores. In 1869 he was elected a fellow of St John's College and two years later became president of the Union. He was an assistant master at Marlborough College (1872–75), during which time he was ordained and took a BD degree in 1874. After Marlborough, he was headmaster of Rossall School (1875–86), but the strain affected his health and he resigned after eleven years. For what seems to have been almost a period of convalescence, he then spent three years in the relatively tranquil post of dean of St Asaph Cathedral, resigning his fellowship at St John's on his acceptance of the deanery. In 1889, his health recovered, he became headmaster of Cheltenham College. During his time there, he was offered the headship of Clifton College, but so popular had he become that he was exhorted to stay, and so he did. He left in 1895 to become headmaster of Rugby, where he remained for fourteen years. On his appointment at Rugby, he was given an honorary fellowship at St John's College, and in 1909 he returned to Oxford as president of the college where he remained until the end of his life. He was too old to make any distinctive mark in the university, 'But he became something of a leader of the Church and the Conservative Party . . . exercising a healthy and valuable influence, and, however much anyone might differ from him in opinion, winning all hearts by his geniality, his good sense, and his readiness to help all with whom he was brought into contact. No one probably ever retained a firmer hold over a greater variety of pupils . . . He was, in truth, a discriminating judge of boys and men, often predicting subsequent distinction in what seemed unlikely characters, and in not a few cases smoothing their path to success by his own quiet generosity.'[15]

James was not a prominent figure on the national stage, but many of his former pupils were, and his CH in 1926, at the age of eighty-one, was almost certainly the result of their abiding affection for their old teacher whom many now regarded as the doyen of the educational world. At a dinner held in his honour on 15 October 1926, and attended by more than two hundred of them, the chairman was Viscount Cave, the lord chancellor, and James' health was proposed by Sir Austen Chamberlain, the foreign secretary. Cave was almost certainly responsible for instigating the CH for James, via the president of the board of education; he had been an undergraduate at St John's College, and the college had given him an honorary fellowship in 1915.

For one who occupied such prominent teaching posts, it may seem surprising that James' publications consisted only of an edition of Cicero and a book of sermons preached at Rossall, but that was only a reflection of the fact that his entire adult life was devoted to teaching rather than writing, and to great effect. He was regarded as one of the ablest preachers and speakers of his day, 'businesslike, effective, and, when roused, either by the cause or the occasion, to display his Celtic fire, rising to heights of real eloquence.'[16] He never married, and died in 1931 at the age of eighty-seven.

He was made a CH in 1926 for his services as 'President of St John's College, Cambridge.'

Hugh Richard Lawrie Sheppard (Anglican) 1 January 1927

'Dick' Sheppard, as he became known, was vicar of the central London church of St Martin-in-the-Fields in the 1920s and achieved fame as the most prominent religious broadcaster of his day.

He was born in 1880, the younger son of Edgar Sheppard, sub dean of the Chapels Royal. He was educated at Marlborough, Trinity Hall, Cambridge and Cuddesdon Theological College, Oxford. With such an influential background, and in the days when such things mattered, Sheppard might have been destined for great things, and he was certainly given a number of senior appointments in the church, the longest and most prominent of which was that of vicar of St Martin's-in-the-Fields, London (1914–27). But if his contemporaries expected high preferment to come his way, they were to be disappointed. Part of Sheppard's problem was that he suffered throughout his life from chronic asthma, and it led to his resignation from St Martin's. His work at the church in Trafalgar Square was unparalleled and unprecedented, and he brought it everlasting fame through the development of religious broadcasting and the use of its position as a church that was open day and night.

In 1917, with William Temple, he inaugurated the Life and Liberty Movement that led in 1919 to the establishment of the Church Assembly and the beginnings of a democratic government of the church. In 1929 Archbishop Cosmo Gordon Lang of Canterbury, to whom Sheppard had been a close friend and almost a son, was delighted when the latter was appointed dean of Canterbury Cathedral. But he worried that Sheppard's health would break down again, and his fear proved correct. Recurrent asthma forced Sheppard to spend most of his time at

Broadstairs and to resign the deanery in 1931. 'Yet in spite of all this, even in the two short years he had greatly improved the cathedral and city by his so lovable personality. Crowds came to hear his simple vivid messages of the love of God. He endeared himself to everyone in the cathedral, from the chapter to the vergers and the workmen. He passed like a meteor of light and love.'[17] In his last years, he became a convinced pacifist and founded the peace movement in 1935. In 1934 he was appointed canon and precentor of St Paul's Cathedral and died in office in 1937, a few months after the students of Glasgow University had elected him rector of the university, in preference to J. B. S. Haldane and Winston Churchill. Sheppard wrote a number of books, including: *The human parson* (1924), *Two days before* (1924), *The impatience of a parson* (1930); *My hopes and fears for the church* (1930), *If I were dictator* (1934), *We say 'no'* (1935), *The root of the matter* (1937), *Sheppard's pie* (1937), *More Sheppard's pie* (1938) and *Some of my religion*. When he heard of Sheppard's death, Archbishop Lang wrote: 'We shall never see his like again. How I wish that somehow the course of his life had been different and that the dear man had never written those very tiresome and unhelpful books, but simply allowed his unique personality to radiate its influence of love and goodwill.'[18]

The CH was conferred on him in 1927 for his services as 'Chaplain to The King and lately Vicar of St Martin's-in-the-Fields.' He died in 1937.

John Daniel Jones (Congregationalist) 3 June 1927
John Jones was minister of a Congregational church in Bournemouth for nearly forty years, and by the power of his oratory he gave it an international reputation.

He was born in Denbighshire in 1865, the third son of a schoolmaster and composer. His father died in 1870 and his mother married again, to a Congregational minister at Chorley. Jones graduated from the University of Manchester in classics, then trained for the Congregational ministry at Lancashire College, of which later in his life he was invited to become principal. – an invitation that after much thought he declined. His first appointment was at Newland Church, Lincoln, but in 1898 moved to Richmond Hill Church, Bournemouth where he remained until his retirement nearly forty years later. Like his contemporary John Henry Jowett, Jones was a vigorous nonconformist preacher in an age when the worth of a pastor was estimated by the effectiveness of his preaching and little else. Under his leadership, Richmond Hill Church became a widely known and popular conventicle with an international reputation. It was filled each Sunday, not only by the regular congregation, but by visitors to Bournemouth who came to listen to him. He was described as 'pre-eminently an expository preacher, with a gift of telling application to the problems and needs of contemporary life.'

He retired in 1937 and was made a freeman of Bournemouth in the following year. He was twice chairman of the Congregational Union (1909–10 and 1925–26). Further appointments included honorary secretary of the Congregational Union (1919), moderator of the Free Church Federal Council (1921–23), moderator of the International Congregational Council (1930), and chairman of the National Free Church Council (1938–39). He played a leading part in the discussions on church unity that followed the Lambeth *Appeal* in 1920, although he thought it unlikely that any specific act of reunion would result. But he welcomed the increased understanding that arose from these conversations and preached from time to time in Anglican churches. Through his preaching and through the many books of sermons and addresses that he published, he left a marked impression on the whole religious life of his age. 'But his renown as one of the outstanding Free Church leaders rested not so much upon the high offices which he filled or the honours which came to him as upon the simplicity and strength of his faith and the devotedness of his service of his church.'[19] He died in 1942.

He was made a CH in 1927 for his services as 'Chairman of the Congregational Union of England and Wales, 1909–10 and 1925–26.'

John Charles Carlile (Baptist) 1 March 1929
John Carlile was a prominent Baptist pastor who gave more than thirty-five years of service in a range of public services, including national and county committees dealing with secondary and elementary education.

He was born in London in 1862, the only child of Scottish parents, and educated at Royal Schools of Science, London and trained for the Baptist ministry at Spurgeon's College. His first pastorate was at Abbey Street, Dockhead (1884–93), on the south bank of the Thames, where he spent what he himself described as 'the most romantic period of my life.' Dockhead was followed by Trinity Baptist Church, Marylebone (1893–98), and from there he moved to Rendezvous Street, Folkestone in Kent where he remained for forty years until his retirement in 1938.

With a church in docklands, Carlile showed an early interest in social questions, and at the time of the dock strike of 1889, he worked with the archbishop of Westminster, Cardinal Henry Manning, in organising the dock strike mediation committee. During the 1914–18 war he visited France on five occasions, organising lectures for officers and men, though on what subject and with what effect is unknown. He was one of the original members of the united army and navy board and advisory council to the war office, and at Folkestone he was an officiating chaplain to the royal air force. He was appointed a CBE in 1920 for his war services and decorated by King Albert I of the Belgians. Journalism had always interested him, and he took on the editorship of the *The Baptist Times* in 1925, holding it until his death in 1941. His publications – none of great substance – included *The royal life* (1900), *Alexander Maclaren DD* (1901), *Talks to little folks* (1903), *A history of the English Baptists* (1905), *Short talks to boys and girls* (1912), *Christian union in social service* (1913), *Vision and vocation* (1919), *A colony of heaven* (1923), *The necessity of the advent* (1926), *The greatest adventure* (1926), *Sermons without words* (1931), *The challenging Christ* (1932), *An interpretative history of C. H. Spurgeon* (1933), *Portraits of Jesus* (1933), and an autobiography entitled *My life's little day* (1935). He served for many years on the general committee of the Baptist Missionary Society, and on the council of the Baptist Union, being twice elected president (1921–22 and 1922–23). Following the breakdown in health of the previous occupant, he served as acting secretary of the Union (1924–25). He was twice married, but his only child – a son – died tragically, soon after arriving home at the end of the war. Carlile died in 1941.

He was made a CH in 1929 as 'Editor of the "Baptist Times". For public and social services.'

William Bramwell Booth (Salvation Army) 30 April 1929
Bramwell Booth was the eldest son of William Booth, founder of the Salvation Army, and succeeded his father as the second general of the army.

Born in 1856 he saw the army grow from an obscure Christian mission in Whitechapel in 1865 into an international organisation with numerous and varied social activities. Despite being affected throughout his life by deafness, the result of sickness following injuries received while at school, he became an enthusiastic and lifelong supporter of the aims and ideals of his father. In 1870 he began to help in the management of his father's mission and in the cheap food kitchens established in its early days. The hereditary principle was strong in the family, and the younger Booth was chief of staff of the army from 1880 until the death of his father in 1912, when he succeeded him as general. In 1885 he was associated with William Thomas Stead in a campaign for the suppression of criminal vice, which resulted in the Criminal Law Amendment Act of 1885, raising the age of consent to sixteen. Owing to a technical breach of the law in their method of collecting evidence, Booth and Stead were arrested and tried at the Central Criminal Court, though Booth was discharged. It was through his guidance that the right to hold open air meetings – a matter which had brought the army into conflict with many local authorities – was firmly established, and certain local by laws were declared *ultra vires* by the High Court. Booth did much to develop foreign missions and he visited most of the larger cities in Europe, where he conducted public meetings and officers' councils. During his time in office, the army made rapid progress and he continued to visit European capitals after the war and to be received by their leading statesmen. He also travelled on behalf of the army to India, Ceylon, Korea, Japan, the Dutch Indies, Australia, New Zealand, Canada and the USA.

The younger Booth was quite different from his father in his style of delivery. The elder Booth was an old-fashioned platform orator, appealing to the emotions of those who heard him. His son, who was described as something of a mystic, relied on calm and reasoned argument. But there was no disputing the key role he played in consolidating and extending the work of the Salvation Army. It was only unfortunate that he stayed in office past the time when he should have gone, and the time arrived when the army could cope with him no longer. He held the position of general until 1929 when he was effectively deposed. A meeting of the high council of the army was convened in January that year to consider his fitness, and resolved to ask him to retire, although allowing him to retain his title and honours. He declined and the high council then adjudicated by 55 votes to 8 that he was unfit to hold the office. Booth's supporters went to the High Court and an interim injunction restraining the council from electing a new general was granted on 18 January. A substantive injunction was granted on 30 January, to be in force until Booth had been heard by the high council. He was represented by counsel, but on 13 February, by 52 votes to 5, the high council reaffirmed his deposition. It was a sad end to his life's work, but there was no doubt that he had stayed too long.

In what was obviously a compensatory gesture, Booth was made a CH on 30 April, six weeks before his death. He could have had the honour three years earlier. He was offered the CH in 1926 at the same time as Wilson Carlile – and declined. As the end drew closer, voices were raised in support of an honour for the dying man. 'Such an honour . . . could by none be taken as a taking of sides in any little misunderstanding that may have lately taken place, and which obviously is at rest now.'[20] 'It would I know give intense joy to him, it might be the rallying point of his few grains of strength which he is not now allowed to use even in speaking beyond a word to his nurse.'[21] When the question of Booth's 1926 refusal was raised, he was informally sounded to avoid a repetition. 'I am now in a position to say that were you now to recommend His Majesty to confer upon him some signal mark, it would be welcome and accepted from his heart. Is the OM too full?'[22] It was the CH rather than the OM, and the citation simply read 'late General of the Salvation Army'. Booth died on 16 June 1929, before he could be invested, and the badge was presented to his widow at her home on 1 July.

Maude Royden (Congregationalist) 1 January 1930

Maude Royden was a supporter of the movement for women's rights and a pioneer woman preacher.

She was born in 1876, the daughter of Sir Thomas Royden Bt, a former mayor of Liverpool. She was educated at Cheltenham Ladies' College and at Lady Margaret Hall, Oxford. After graduation she worked for three years at the Victoria Women's Settlement, Liverpool, then went to help G. W. Hudson Shaw, vicar of the country parish of South Luffenham, before being appointed a lecturer in English literature in the Oxford University Extension Delegacy. She was a strong supporter of the rights of women and in 1908 she joined the National Union of Suffrage Societies. She was a natural and persuasive public speaker and her gifts and abilities ensured that she was made a member of the executive committee and editor of *Common Cause* in the same year. She held both positions until her resignation from the executive in 1914. A pacifist by nature during the 1914–18 war and again in the 1930s, she joined the Fellowship of Reconciliation when it was founded in December 1914, and as its clerical membership was overwhelmingly Congregationalist, it was not long before she found a spiritual home in that denomination.

She was a devout Anglican and could have been a very able preacher from the pulpits of its churches. But the very idea of the ordination of women was alien to the Church of England in her day and remained so until the last decade of the twentieth century. But Maude Royden was well ahead of the Church of England and not one to be put off in her desire to preach by official church policy. She was a member of the council of William Temple's 'Life and Liberty' movement, but when the council went into retreat at Cuddesdon Theological College in October 1917, she was forbidden to sleep on the premises by the college principal. Temple acquiesced and Royden resigned. In the same year she distressed her fellow Anglicans by accepting a pastoral ministry at the City Temple – then the most important Congregational church in London – where, to the horror of some, she preached and baptised. Her reputation as a preacher soon began to spread and in 1919, G. W. Hudson Shaw, now rector of St Botolph's Church, Bishopsgate, London, invited her to preach for the three hours service on Good Friday. She was prohibited from doing so by the bishop of London, but the bishop's injunction was circumvented when the service was held in an adjoining room. Two years later she preached in the church without the bishop's approval, but without his inhibition.

She resigned as an assistant preacher at the City Temple to begin holding 'Fellowship Services' in Kensington Town Hall with Percy Dearmer, the Anglican liturgist. In 1921 Eccleston Square Congregational Church was acquired for the Fellowship Guild and reopened under the name of the Guildhouse, Eccleston Square.

Her reputation rising, she travelled widely in the USA in 1923 and a few years later in Australia, New Zealand, India and China. She made a deep impression on those who heard her, though her appearance in the cathedral pulpits at Adelaide and Wellington caused controversy. She was one of the founders of the Peace Army in 1932, and in 1936 she resigned from the Guildhouse to devote herself to the promotion of world peace.

She was made a CH in 1930 for being 'Eminent in the religious life of the nation', and died at her home in Hampstead in 1956. Canon Sir Percy Maryon-Wilson paid tribute to her remarkable character: 'The debt of gratitude which this century owes her is incalculable. By her outstanding intellectual ability, combined with invincible Christian faith and personal devotion, and remarkable gifts of human sympathy – to say nothing of her charm and sense of humour – she is numbered among those whom the wisdom of God "entering into holy souls" has made "friends of God and prophets".'[23]

In October 1944 she married her old friend G. Hudson Shaw, who was then over eighty years old and had retired from the living of St Botolph's. The marriage lasted only until his death in the following December. She and Shaw had loved each other for many years, in a ménage à trois shared by Shaw's first wife – though with no violation of the marriage bed. The story was movingly told by Royden in her book *A threefold cord*, published three years after his death.

Philip Thomas Byard Clayton (Anglican) 2 January 1933
'Tubby' Clayton ranks with Dick Sheppard and Woodbine Willie as one of the legendary Anglican priests who acquired fame and reputation in the years during and after the 1914–18 war. Clayton himself is remembered chiefly as the founder of the Toc H movement, itself a product of the fighting conditions of that war.

He was born in Australia in 1885, the third son of a sugar plantation manager. His family returned to England in 1886. A stay at Exeter College, Oxford produced an inauspicious third class degree in moderations in 1907, followed by a much more promising first class degree in theology in 1909. Ordained in 1910, he served his title at the parish of St Mary, Portsea, during the time of Cyril Garbett (later archbishop of York) as incumbent. Like many others of his profession, Clayton volunteered as an army chaplain at the outbreak of war, and his service might have been unremarkable but for the intervention of Neville Talbot, senior chaplain of the 6th division. Talbot had seen the effects of stress on British troops at the front, and conceived the idea of establishing a rest house for the troops on their way to and from Ypres. He aroused Clayton's interest, and together the two men transformed an empty mansion at Poperinghe. The house was in the nature of a non-residential club and had a canteen, recreation and writing room, library, chaplain's room and chapel. The house was named Talbot House in memory of Talbot's brother, who had been killed in action a few months previously, but the troops rapidly abbreviated it to TH or 'Toc H' in morse code. Clayton himself used it as a base for visiting men in the front line. 'Tirelessly energetic, his magnetic personality became known and loved by thousands behind and in the front line.'[24] He was awarded the Military Cross in 1917.

After the war, he assisted F. R. Barry for four years as chaplain and tutor of a theological college in a derelict prison at Knutsford. The scheme was an attempt to relieve the acute national shortage of ordinands in the Church of England. Some 675 men went to Knutsford and 435 were eventually ordained, and its less 'class-conscious' style of training was a significant change from most other colleges at the time. Clayton established a Talbot House in London in 1920 and began the Toc H movement which had forty branches by 1922, the year in which it became an association incorporated by royal charter. The reputation of the movement was such that in 1923 Archbishop Randall Davidson gave the London church of All Hallows by the Tower to Clayton as the spiritual centre of Toc H, and Clayton remained the vicar until 1963. A lamp, which became the movement's symbol, was lit by the Prince of Wales in the Albert Hall in 1923 and still remains in the church today. The movement was based on the principles of fellowship, service, fairmindedness and the kingdom of God. It struck a chord in the 1920s and eventually numbered a thousand branches in Britain, hundreds overseas, and a women's association.

A strenuous tour of southern Africa in 1934 brought on a nervous breakdown, and Clayton recuperated by spending a year in India with his brother Sir Hugh Clayton, a commissioner with the Indian Civil Service. For a few months in 1935 he was chaplain to HMS Codrington and then HMS Beagle, stationed at Malta, and early in 1936 he returned to All Hallows. He spent the early years of the 1939–45 war in Orkney with the royal navy, establishing Toc H clubs around Scapa Flow. In 1940 All Hallows Church was gutted by a bomb and Clayton was given the chaplaincy of a tanker fleet which took him to various parts of America. In 1943 he sailed to Gibraltar and then went on tour to Karachi, Ibadan, Basra, Baghdad and Haifa, returning to Gibraltar late in 1944.

At the end of the war discussions began on rebuilding All Hallows Church. Clayton was active in raising funds, undertaking a tour of Canada and the USA, which resulted in the Americans sending the Winant Volunteers to help rebuild the church, which was rededicated in 1957. 'A man of enormous sympathy and courage, never sparing himself, convinced that his work was God-ordained, Clayton was unaware of time or his own appearance. He was frequently late for appointments, causing much distress to his ADCs and to those who awaited his arrival. He was an imaginative and original speaker with a retentive memory and a sense of humour that made him excellent company. His voice had a deep growling resonance and his eyes were mischievous. His way with people of all ages and circumstances was renowned, but he was rarely at ease with women. Despite his thousands of admirers and disciples he was a deeply lonely man with very few close friends. His constant companion was his dog.'[25]

He was made a CH in 1933. The citation read: 'Vicar of All Hallows, Barking-by-the-Tower. Founder of Talbot House.' In 1969 it was suggested that he be appointed to the Order of Merit, long after his principal days of activity were over, but the CH was the natural honour for him, and he enjoyed it for nearly forty years, dying in 1972 at the age of eighty-seven.

John Scott Lidgett (Methodist) 2 January 1933

For more than half a century, Scott Lidgett was regarded as the personification of British Methodism, and called by some 'the greatest Methodist since Wesley'.[26] When president of the Wesleyan Methodist Church in 1908, he could claim to have been personally acquainted with fifty of the ninety-one presidents who had occupied Wesley's chair, and lived to see another forty-four holders of the office.

He was born in Lewisham in 1854 into a Methodist family. His father was a successful city businessman and his mother helped to found what became known as 'Women's Work' of the Methodist Missionary Society. Her father was twice president of the Methodist conference, first principal of Westminster Training College and a powerful influence on his grandson's early days. Scott Lidgett graduated from the University of London in logic and philosophy and in 1876 was accepted for the ministry of the Wesleyan Methodist Church. His first fifteen years were spent in places as diverse as Tunstall, Southport, Cardiff, Wolverhampton and Cambridge, and it was at Cambridge that he was influenced in a way that was to affect the rest of his life. There he became acutely aware of the gulf between rich and poor, and the effects of poverty, bad housing and unemployment in different parts of the country. Stimulated by W. F. Moulton, headmaster of the Leys school and one of the foremost scholars of New Testament Greek in his day, Scott Lidgett decided to establish in Bermondsey, one of the most neglected districts of London, 'a colony, evangelical, but with the broadest possible educational and social aims.'[27] It would be a meeting place for all classes of society, to provide facilities for the study of literature, science and art, to encourage participation in local administration and philanthropy, and to be inspired throughout by nonsectarian motives. In 1891 the Bermondsey Settlement was founded with Lidgett as warden and a group of permanent residents who mainly worked in London during the day. It was part residential community, part club and part adult educational institute and ranked with places such as Toynbee Hall and Oxford House. Scott Lidgett loved his settlement and stayed at Bermondsey for fifty years, until his retirement in 1949 at the age of ninety-five.

His passion for education also found expression elsewhere in London. In 1897 he was elected a member of the London School Board and represented the free churches in the controversy sparked by the Education Bill of 1902. He welcomed the impetus it gave to higher education but was a strong critic of its provisions that seemed to deny justice to nonconformists, although he declined to support the passive resistance movement. He was an alderman on London County Council (1905–10 and 1922–28) and represented Rotherhithe (1910–22). In 1918 he was elected leader of the progressive group on the council, and although they were then losing ground he succeeded in keeping the dwindling group together for ten years. His paramount interest on the council was Christian education and he was a member of the council's education committee (1905–28), serving as deputy chairman (1917–19). In 1922 he was elected a member of the senate of the University of London, becoming vice-chancellor (1930–2). He continued to represent the arts graduates until he retired in 1946 at the age of ninety-two.

He took a leading role in his own church, being editor for many years of the *Methodist Times*. He was also the principal architect of the union of the Wesleyan, Primitive and United Methodist Churches and was elected the first president of the united church in 1932. He was a member of the joint committee set up by the Free Church Federal Council in 1920 in response to the appeal of the 1920 Lambeth Conference, and a leading member of the committee of bishops and Free Church leaders which met at Lambeth in 1922–25, and again, when it resumed, in 1930–8. He was a trusted friend of Archbishop Randall Davidson of Canterbury and pressed for the creation of a Council of Churches of Great Britain and welcomed the establishment of the British Council of Churches when it was founded in 1942. He was described as 'an austere and exacting man with few intimate friends. Of his sanctity, which was inseparable from devotion to human need, there was no doubt.'[28] By 1950, at the age of ninety-six, he had virtually completed the painful process of official retirement from his various offices. He died at Epsom in 1953, in his one hundredth year.

'President of the Methodist Church. Honorary Secretary of the National Council of Evangelical Free Churches of England and Wales since 1914. Vice-Chancellor of London University 1930–31 and 1931–32. Warden of the Bermondsey Settlement since 1891,' was the lengthy citation that announced his appointment as a CH in 1933.

John White (Presbyterian) 3 June 1935

As John Scott Lidgett played a fundamental role in the reunion of the three principal Methodist denominations in 1932, so his contemporary, John White, performed a similar role in Scotland in 1929, and White was honoured with the CH for his distinguished services to religious life in Scotland.

During the eighteenth and nineteenth centuries, the Church of Scotland suffered numerous schisms, with various groups seceding from the established church for what now seem to be the slightest of reasons. Moves towards reunion produced the United Free Church in 1900 (a merger of the Free Church and the United Presbyterian Church) and then in 1929, the union of the United Free Church and the Church of Scotland. John White was the spirit behind the 1929 reunion and a major architect of the united church. Born in Glasgow in 1867, the son of a grain merchant and flour miller, he graduated from the university of Glasgow in 1891 and was ordained in 1893. During his ministry he held most of the key convenorships in the committees of the church and was first president of the Scottish Churches Council, and a chaplain to King George V, King Edward VIII and King George VI. Moderator of the Church of Scotland in 1925 and first moderator of the united church in 1929, he was one of the most revered and influential Scottish churchmen of the twentieth century. For forty years (1911–51) he was minister of the Barony Church in Castle Street, Glasgow, an appointment that was only terminated by his death at the age of eighty-four in 1951. Although the church has been converted into the ceremonial hall of Strathclyde University, it still houses the John White Memorial Chapel, and a stained glass representation of White, together with the badges of the institutions and buildings with which he was associated, can still be seen.

He was made a CH in 1935 for his services as 'Minister of the Barony of Glasgow, First Moderator of the General Assembly of the United Church of Scotland, 1929.'

Melbourn Evans Aubrey (Baptist) 11 May 1937

Melbourn Evans Aubrey was unusual in being a Baptist minister strongly committed to ecumenism in an age when the Baptist Union, a denomination never very enthusiastic on the subject, was sharply divided.

Born in 1885, Aubrey came from a Baptist family, his father being pastor of Zion Baptist Church at Pentre. He was trained at Mansfield College, Oxford and ordained in 1911 to serve at Victoria Road Church in Leicester. After only eighteen months, he was appointed pastor of St Andrew's Street Church, Cambridge in 1913 where his gifts as a preacher and speaker drew large congregations. In 1925 he was chosen to be general secretary of the Baptist Union of Great Britain and Ireland in succession to J. H. Shakespeare who had left because of ill-health, and the interim appointment of John Carlile. At a time when the Church of England was actively pursuing discussions with the historic nonconformist churches, Aubrey found himself in a church that was sharply divided on the subject. But to the end of his life, he retained an undimmed enthusiasm for the ecumenical movement.

He was moderator of the Federal Council of the Evangelical Free Churches of England (1936–38), chairman of the United Committee of Churches for Christian Reconstruction in Europe (1943–50), and was one of the first British churchmen to visit Germany at the end of the war in 1945. In 1947 he was appointed a member of the royal commission on the press. From 1948–50 he was a vice-president of the British Council of Churches. He helped to draft the constitution of the World Council of Churches and served on the central committee of the World Council (1948–54). For all his wider involvements, he retained a constant concern for the spiritual welfare of Baptist churches and successfully held together the diverse elements in the Baptist denominations at a time of decline. Widely respected, and on the eve of retirement in 1951 as general secretary, he was elected president of the Baptist Union for 1950–51. His publications were few, principally *A manual for Free Church ministers* (1926), *The work of a minister* (1929), *Three Baptist heroes* (1935), and *The Free Churches in our national life* (1936)

He was made a CH in the Coronation Honours List in 1937 for his services as 'Moderator of the Federal Council of the Evangelical Free Churches. General Secretary of the Baptist Union of Great Britain and Ireland.' He died in 1957.

Joseph Herman Hertz (Jewish) 1 January 1943

Amid the British Christian luminaries appointed to the Order of the Companions of Honour, the name of Joseph Herman Hertz, chief rabbi of the United Hebrew Congregations of the British Empire, at first seems to sit somewhat awkwardly.

Hertz was born in Slovakia in 1872 and, with his family, emigrated to the USA in 1884. He was educated at New York City College and at Columbia University (obtaining a PhD in 1894), and became the earliest graduate rabbi of the newly founded Jewish Theological Seminary of America (1894). After four years as rabbi at Syracuse, New York, he went to South Africa in 1898 as rabbi of the Witwatersrand Old Hebrew Congregation of Johannesburg, where he aroused the dislike of Paul Kruger, president of the Transvaal republic. At the outbreak of the South African War in 1899, Hertz's sympathies were decidedly pro-British, and that, combined with his condemnation of religious discrimination against Jews and Catholics, caused his expulsion by Kruger shortly after the outbreak of the South African War. He served as a member of the high commissioner's consultative committee in 1900 and returned to his congregation in 1901. In 1906–08 he was professor of philosophy at Transvaal University College.

In 1911 he went back to the USA as rabbi of the Orach Chayim congregation in New York, but in 1913, partly through the efforts of Lord Milner, whom he had known in South Africa, Hertz was elected chief rabbi of the United Hebrew Congregations of the British Empire in succession to Hermann Adler who had died in 1911. The contrast between the two men was great. Although born in Hanover, Adler was brought to England as a child and educated at University College, London, and was thoroughly English. Adopting clerical garb and assuming the style of 'Very Reverend', Adler was on friendly terms with leading church and public figures, including King Edward VII, and was instrumental in raising the chief rabbinate to the position of distinction, dignity and national prominence that it still enjoys today.

Hertz was a fiery and fearless individual. He 'threw himself into his duties with an almost explosive energy which almost scandalized the conservative elements of his flock. In contrast to his gentle, highly anglicized predecessor, he adopted the standpoint of the Eastern European immigrants who in the past generation had become a majority in the Anglo-Jewish community; denounced the Russian persecutions of the Jews . . . adopted a militant attitude towards the newly founded Liberal Jewish movement, and carried on a perpetual polemic with its advocates in his sermons and publications. His very strong Zionist sympathies proved decisive when he was consulted by the government in 1917 before the publication of the "Balfour Declaration", the policy of which was opposed by some of the most distinguished Jews.'[29]

In 1920–21 he carried out the first pastoral tour of Jewish communities of the British Empire. In his last years his attention was absorbed by the rise of anti-Semitism in Germany and the almost virtual destruction of Jewish faith and culture by the Nazis. He repeatedly attempted to raise public awareness of the danger that faced his people in continental Europe, and to demonstrate the necessity of providing a Jewish homeland in Palestine. 'Bursting with energy; stocky; with a square-cut black beard, ultimately grizzled, and a somewhat rasping voice; full of himself, but at the same time overflowing with native kindliness; somewhat bellicose – it was once said of him that he never failed to seek a peaceful solution when all other possibilities had failed; constantly swayed by an overwhelming compassion for his suffering co-religionists; which would impel him to display on occasion a lion-like courage, Hertz was certainly the most remarkable character who has filled the English rabbinate since its inception.'[30]

The CH for this passionate Jewish firebrand came in his thirtieth year as chief rabbi, and at the height of the Jewish holocaust when such a sign of affirmation would have been particularly comforting for that community. The citation read 'Chief Rabbi of the United Hebrew Congregations of the British Empire.' He died in 1946.

Edmund Horace Fellowes (Anglican) 1 January 1944 (see Chapter 7)

Henry Herbert Williams (Anglican) 14 June 1945
Henry Williams was one of the more distinguished academic Anglican bishops of the first half of the twentieth century, but who is now completely forgotten.

He was born in 1872, son of the vicar of Poppleton. He was educated at St Peter's School, York and Queen's College, Oxford from where he graduated in classical moderations and literae humaniores. He was elected a fellow of Hertford College, Oxford in 1898 and was ordained deacon in 1900 and priest in 1901. His career included periods as a tutor at Hertford College (1909–14), rector of Gatcombe (1914–17), and additionally principal of St Edmund Hall, Oxford (1913–20).

In 1920 he was consecrated bishop of Carlisle where he stayed for the remainder of his ministry. Perhaps it was a misfortune that he was bishop of that northern borders diocese and living in the fastness of Rose Castle, because his conscientious devotion to his diocese prevented his intellectual gifts from being fully used in the service of the church. He contributed a series of articles to the *Encyclopedia Britannica*, in an age when that publication was revered as the ultimate repository of a general knowledge on any subject. 'His article on "will" in particular was considered one of the ablest statements ever penned of the issues in the controversy between libertarianism and determinism. The case against the latter, based on the facts of moral consciousness, can rarely have been stated more cogently or more fairly. He repeated the substance of the arguments in one of the best official sermons ever preached before the British Association for the Advancement of Science.'[31] He published only one volume, *Scientific necessity and the miraculous* (1911), a collection of articles that had appeared in the *Manchester Guardian*.

Outside the dioceses of Oxford and Carlisle he was best known to the general public for his chairmanship of the archbishop's commission on the ministry of women, which was set up as a consequence of the report of the committee on ministry of the church to the 1930 Lambeth Conference. Williams had one trait in his character which would have gladdened the hearts of many later generations, a distrust of new organisations, 'maintaining that "the Church of England already possesses the machinery necessary for its life and needs if it had the will to use it," and he himself never spared pains to make existing organisations work.'[32] He retired as bishop of Carlisle in 1946 and died in 1961.

He was made a CH in 1945, the citation only recording that he was 'Bishop of Carlisle'.

Howell Elvet Lewis (Congregationalist) 10 June 1948 (see Chapter 5)

Hugh Martin (Baptist) 1 January 1955
Hugh Martin was the first managing director and editor of SCM Press, one of the principal religious publishing companies.

He was born in Glasgow in 1890, the son of a Baptist minister. In 1910, at the age of twenty, he attended the world missionary conference at Edinburgh as a student observer; an experience which became a permanent inspiration to him. Educated at Glasgow University and then trained at the Baptist Theological College of Scotland he could have had a career in the regular Baptist ministry, but he had become fascinated with the possibility of work among students, and in 1914 he was appointed assistant secretary of the rapidly developing Student Christian Movement and given responsibility for publications. His work with SCM introduced him to the World's Student Christian Federation and he developed friendships with many students who were to become church leaders in North and South America. He was honorary treasurer of the world federation (1928–35). A competent chairman and committee member, he chaired the preparatory committee (1920–24) for the 1924 conference on politics, economics and citizenship, Archbishop William Temple chairing the conference itself. The conference at Birmingham, attended by 1,400 delegates, was one of Temple's enthusiasms. As with all such conferences, the immediate results were negligible, but the longer-term effects were significant. 'Its importance lay within a longer process of adult education whereby the leadership, clerical and lay, of the Church was being weaned from high Tory attitudes to an acceptance of the Christian case for massive social reform and the development of the welfare state.'[33]

The aftermath of the conference did create a new attitude to social affairs and politics in the life of the churches, and Martin saw a fertile ground for publications. In 1929 he persuaded SCM to establish its publishing department as a separate company known as SCM Press, of which he became the first managing director and editor. He built up a varied list of significant theological and sociological titles. and it is due primarily to Martin that SCM Press achieved the high reputation that it enjoyed for some decades afterwards.

In 1937 he established the Religious Book Club which attracted a membership of 18,000. Each member received six books a year of a standard length at two shillings a copy. All the books were specially commissioned and dealt with contemporary public and theological issues, especially during the Munich period and beyond. Martin himself edited or wrote several of the books. On the outbreak of war, he became director of the religious division of the ministry of information (1939–43) because of his wide knowledge and experience of religions both at home and abroad, especially in enemy nations. Unlike the behaviour of some clergy during the 1914–18 war, who shamelessly led recruiting drives, Martin was careful to elucidate the spiritual issues at stake in the war, and to avoid propaganda that appeared to support war aims which were unChristian. He returned to SCM Press in 1943 as managing director and in the same year became free church leader of the newly-formed British Council of Churches, which was initially housed in the offices of SCM Press in Bloomsbury Street. After the war he served on the Council of Christian Reconstruction in Europe. He saw SCM Press as an instrument of debate and concern for unity and was happy to have authors of all Christian traditions on his list. After retirement from SCM Press in 1950, he was vice-president of the British Council of Churches (1950–52), moderator of the Free Church Federal Council (1952–53), and finally chairman of the executive committee of the British Council of Churches (1956–62).

Baptist though he was, Martin was primarily a Christian educator of ecumenical sympathies. The citation for his CH in 1955 honoured him 'For services to the National Free Church Federal Council and to the British Council of Churches.'

John Baillie (Presbyterian) 1 *January 1957*

John Baillie was a distinguished Scottish academic who taught theology at the University of Edinburgh for more than twenty years.

He was born in Gairloch, Ross-shire in 1886, the son of a Free Church minister. He was educated at Inverness Royal Academy, where he was a gold medallist in classics, and then at Edinburgh University, where he was awarded a first class honours degree in mental philosophy in 1908, and at the universities of Marburg and Jena. That seemed to mark him out for an academic career, and after the 1914–18 war he remained in the world of academe until his retirement in 1956, occupying a succession of increasingly distinguished theological teaching posts. He trained for the ministry of the Church of Scotland at New College, Edinburgh, and was assistant minister at Broughton Place Church (1912–14). During the 1914–18 war he served with the YMCA in France, and was assistant director of education on lines of communication (1917–19).

After the war he went to the USA where he was Richards professor of Christian theology at Auburn Theological Seminary, New York (1919–27), professor of systematic theology, Emmanuel College, University of Toronto (1927–30), and Roosevelt professor of systematic theology at Union Seminary, New York (1930–4). In 1934 he returned to his native Scotland as professor of divinity at Edinburgh University (1934–56), and was additionally principal of New College and dean of the faculty of divinity (1950–56). He was moderator of the general assembly of the Church of Scotland (1943–44), a chaplain in Scotland to King

George VI and then to Queen Elizabeth II (1947–56) and then an extra chaplain (1956–60). He was also co-president of the World Council of Churches (1954–60). He published a number of theological works, including *The roots of religion in the human soul* (1926), a devotional classic, *A diary of private prayer* (1936) and *Our knowledge of God* (1939), and was chairman of the influential church committee that produced the report *God's will for church and nation* (1946), in favour of the welfare state and state intervention in the economy. He was a key contributor to mid-century religious, social and intellectual life in Scotland.

The CH came just after his retirement, in the New Year List 1957 for his services as 'Lately Professor of Divinity, Principal of New College and Dean of the Faculty of Divinity, University of Edinburgh.' He died in 1960.

John Allen Fitzgerald Gregg (Anglican) 13 June 1957
John Gregg was archbishop of Dublin and then archbishop of Armagh for a total of thirty-seven years. He was a tactful and sensitive head of the Church of Ireland at a time when most of Ireland was disengaging itself from the United Kingdom.

Although born in Gloucestershire in 1873, his father being then rector of St Nicholas' Church, Deptford, London, he came from stock that was both impeccably Irish and also impeccably episcopal, both his grandfather and his uncle occupying the see of Cork, Cloyne and Ross. His grandfather, Robert Gregg, was the prime mover in giving the city of Cork the fabulous French Gothic style cathedral of St Fin Barre.

John Gregg was educated at Bedford School, Christ's College, Cambridge where he was awarded a first class classical tripos degree, and Trinity College, Dublin. He served as a curate in Ballymena (1896–99), then at Cork Cathedral (1899–1906), and then as incumbent at Blackrock (1906–11). He was appointed Archbishop King's professor of divinity at Trinity College, Dublin (1911–15), and chaplain to the lord lieutenant of Ireland in 1912. He was elected bishop of Ossory, Ferns and Leighlin in 1915, archbishop of Dublin in 1920 and finally archbishop of Armagh and primate of All Ireland in 1939. His occupancy of the see of Dublin coincided at a time of substantial political change; firstly with the independence of the Irish Free State in 1922 and secondly with the introduction of the republican constitution in 1937. Gregg was statesmanlike and diplomatic, and sufficiently respected by that fiery embodiment of Irish nationalism, Eamonn de Valera, to be consulted by him on the drafting of the 1937 constitution. In 1949, when southern Ireland left the Commonwealth, Gregg unhesitatingly told the Church of Ireland, that 'in our prayers, above all, there must be reality.' and so new state prayers were included in the *Book of common prayer* to satisfy the consciences of those who lived in the republican south of Ireland. Gregg's primacy included the 1939–45 war, during which his son died in a Japanese prisoner of war camp, and Gregg found himself presiding over a church that spanned two political jurisdictions, one of them neutral. His few publications, which appeared between 1897 and 1913 were mostly commentaries, but his addresses had considerable theological content, and he was also respected for his business acumen and legal competence.

He was appointed a CH at the age of eighty-three, two years before his retirement in 1959. The citation simply read 'Archbishop of Armagh and Primate of All Ireland'. The archbishop of Canterbury described Gregg as a towering figure in the Anglican communion and probably the greatest leader and scholar the Irish church had had since the days of Archbishop Ussher in the seventeenth century. He died in 1961.

Charles Harold Dodd (Congregationalist) 10 June 1961

C. H. Dodd was one of the foremost biblical scholars of the twentieth century, and his principal contribution was to oversee the *New English Bible* translation of the New Testament.

The eldest of four sons of a headmaster, he was born at Wrexham in Wales in 1884 and learnt Welsh as a boy on his own initiative. It was to stand him in good stead when he became one of the very few New Testament scholars who could be called on to examine Welsh theses for higher theological degrees. Educated at Wrexham and University College, Oxford, he was awarded a first class honours degree in honours moderations and literae humaniores, and for a short period taught classics at the University of Leeds. After beginning research at Magdalen College, Oxford, he transferred to Mansfield College in 1910 to study theology. He was ordained in 1912, and spent three years at Brook Street Congregational Church, Warwick. In 1915 he returned to Mansfield as Yates lecturer in New Testament Greek and Exegesis. 'This appointment launched him on a life of scholarship so free of major crises that his bibliography is virtually his biography.'[34] The first of his twenty books, *The meaning of Paul for today*, was published in 1920 and displayed a consuming interest in the background of early Christianity and a meticulous handling of language which characterised all his work. In 1935 he produced *The parables of the kingdom*, expounding the view that in the work of Jesus, defined in his parables, the kingdom of God had been inaugurated. This revolutionary affirmation came to be known as 'realised eschatology' and won wide acceptance. In 1930 he moved to Manchester to succeed A. S. Peake as Rylands professor of biblical criticism and exegesis.

In 1935 he succeeded F. C. Burkitt as the Norris-Hulse professor of divinity in Cambridge and became the first non-Anglican since the sixteenth-century reformation to hold a chair of divinity at either of the ancient universities, and held that chair until he retired in 1949. 'Dodd was always too enthusiastic a teacher and churchman to accept a view (especially prevalent in Cambridge) that popular lectures and broadcast talks were beneath the dignity of a scholar and, since he nearly always wrote his lectures and published everything he wrote, a large number of small books (rarely equalled for their clarity) extended his influence far beyond the universities.'[35] He was at his greatest as a Johannine scholar, and the two great works of his retirement, *The interpretation of the fourth gospel* (1953) and *Historical tradition in the fourth gospel* (1963), 'opened a new era in the discussion of the mystical and historical, Jewish and Hellenistic elements in St John.'[36]

In retirement his formidable learning led to the most sustained enterprise of his whole career, and the project for which he was honoured by appointment as a CH. In 1950 he was appointed general director of the project for a new translation of the bible, which led to the appearance of the *New English Bible*. The translation was designed as a translation of the bible into contemporary English, to be made from original languages and drawing on the best scholarship and literary judgement. The panels of translators worked under Dodd's chairmanship (1950–65) when he was joined as co-chairman by Sir Godfrey Driver. Because of its academic flavour, the NEB was never widely popular, and a more conservative revision, the *Revised English Bible*, appeared in 1989. Some considered the project a misguided dissipation of his time and energy, but he clearly enjoyed the task immensely. 'To observe him at work with the translation panels over a period of twenty years was to know beyond a doubt that it engaged all his gifts and fulfilled all his deepest aspirations.'[37]

The publication of the New Testament in 1961 earned him the CH, the citation reading 'Director of the recent translation of the New Testament.' He died in 1973.

Walter Robert Matthews (Anglican) 1 January 1962
Walter Robert Matthews was for thirty-three years dean of St Paul's Cathedral, a record unlikely to be matched in the future.

Born in 1881, he was the eldest of four children of a banker, and after school he spent five years as a bank clerk. The sense of a vocation took him to King's College, London to train for the priesthood of the Church of England. Ordained in 1907, he was lecturer in philosophy at King's (1908–18) and additionally lecturer in dogmatic theology (1909–18). He was also vicar of Christ Church, Crouch End (1916–18). From 1918 to 1932 he was dean of the college and professor of the philosophy of religion. He was a chaplain to King George V (1928–31), but had to relinquish the office on his appointment as dean of Exeter. He stayed at Exeter only three years before his appointment as dean of St Paul's in 1934. During his time in London he aroused controversy because of his opposition to unilateral disarmament, perhaps born of the death of one of his sons in action in 1940. But his main interest was in philosophical theology and he produced a stream of books, articles, reviews and published sermons over a period of more than fifty years. Reckoned by some to be the equal of William Temple and John Baillie, his approach was always objective. He rarely referred to his own religious experiences, even in his autobiography, *Memories and meanings*, published in 1969. 'Among his personal qualities those that especially impressed people who knew him well were his modesty and his combination of firmness with gentleness. He also possessed a distinctive sense of humour.'[38]

For his work in hosting and organising the service of thanksgiving to celebrate the Silver Jubilee of King George V in 1935, Matthews was appointed a KCVO. Appointment as a CH for his services as 'Dean of St Paul's Cathedral' in the New Year list 1962 came three months after his eightieth birthday. He died in 1973.

Ernest Alexander Payne (Baptist) 1 January 1968
Ernest Payne was general secretary of the Baptist Union of Great Britain and Ireland (1951–67) and the leading ecumenical figure in England after 1954.

Born in 1902, he was educated Hackney Downs Secondary School, King's College, London, Regents Park, St Catherine's and Mansfield Colleges at Oxford, and the University of Marburg. Four years at Bugbrooke Baptist Church (1928–32) was followed by eight years on the headquarters staff of the Baptist Missionary Society (1932–40), and then eleven years as senior tutor at Regents Park College (1940–51) before his appointment as general secretary. Payne was a prominent figure in the Baptist Union, but he gave a great deal of his time to ecumenism. He was vice-chairman of the central committee of the World Council of Churches (1954–68) and joint president (1968–75); moderator of the Free Church Federal Council (1958–59); vice-president of the British Council of

Churches (1960–62) and chairman of the executive committee (1962–71); and vice-president of the Baptist World Alliance (1965–70). 'A historian of sound judgement and quiet manner, he fulfilled these duties with admirable discretion despite some disquiet on the part of his Baptist constituency – perhaps more abroad than at home – at so ecumenical a commitment.'[39]

A CH for this committed ecumenist came in 1968, 'General Secretary, Baptist Union of Great Britain and Ireland. For services to the British and World Councils of Churches.' The archbishop of Canterbury praised Payne's outstanding services to the British Council of Churches, and described him as being among the foremost figures of ecumenical influence in the country. He died in 1980.

Nathaniel Micklem (Congregationalist/United Reformed Church) 15 June 1974
Nathaniel Micklem was a biblical scholar, dogmatic theologian, liturgist, poet and politician.

He was born in 1888, the eldest of the four sons of a chancery QC and Liberal member of parliament. Educated at Rugby and New College, Oxford, he went to Mansfield College to study theology and 'During his years in Oxford he showed as an outstanding president of the union in 1912, the clarity and wit which were always to characterise his speech.'[40] When the union was reestablished in 1919, Micklem was asked to accept the unique honour of holding the presidential office for a second time. After toying with the thought of following his father into the house of commons, he became a congregational minister in 1914. From 1918–21 he was chaplain of Mansfield College, where he developed a lifelong friendship with C. H. Dodd. From 1921–27 he was professor of Old Testament literature and theology at Selly Oak Colleges, Birmingham, then professor of New Testament literature and criticism at Queen's Theological College at Kingston, Ontario (1927–31). He returned to Oxford to become professor of dogmatic theology and principal of Mansfield College (from 1932), combining the roles until his retirement in 1953. He emerged as one of the foremost free church leaders of his day but he was ill at ease in his ministry and unpopular with many of his fellow Congregationalists. The origins can be dated to 1931 when Micklem was asked to speak at the assembly celebrating the centenary of the Congregational Union. Micklem's depth of intelligence and breadth of intellectual sympathy could not be contained within the narrow confines of sectarian Congregationalism and he called on his church to play its full part both in the ecumenical movement generally and in seeking union with the Presbyterian Church of England. The fundamentally 'independent' nature of Congregationalism did not take kindly to this, and for some years, he was regarded with suspicion by his fellow Congregationalists. Then there was the question of his background. 'Socially, Micklem, like many others, had moved too far up the scale. His father was a prosperous Liberal MP, and he had been educated at Rugby and New College. One would have expected him to become an Anglican in such circumstances, but he disagreed with the idea of the Establishment and remained a Free churchman. Nevertheless, socially and intellectually he was only too clearly an Anglican . . . Theologically he had moved in a very Catholic direction; he gave lectures on St Thomas Aquinas, encouraged students to attend courses by the Dominicans at Blackfriars, and threw himself into the liturgical movement.'[41] But his stature could not be ignored and his worth was eventually recognised when he was elected chairman of the Congregational Union for the year 1944–45. He continued to work for the union of Congregationalists and Presbyterians in England and lived to see that union result in the creation of the United Reformed Church in 1972. True to his origins, he remained an active member of the Liberal Party, and was president of the party in 1957–58. He used his presidential address to remind his audience of the moral foundation of the liberal movement. 'His candour, perspicacity, esprit and warmth drew the friendship of scholars, but no less of people who would have followed only a little of the intricacy and subtlety of "Nat's" mind.'[42]

A CH in 1974 'For services to Theology', came at the age of eighty-six, and within three years of his death. He was put forward for a CH by the incoming prime minister, Harold Wilson, although no one was quite sure why Wilson had decided to use the only vacant CH at the time to recognise Micklem. He died 1977.

Derek Worlock (Roman Catholic) 30 December 1995
Derek Worlock was the ecumenically-minded Roman Catholic archbishop of Liverpool from 1976 until shortly before his death in 1996.

He was born in London in 1920 to parents who were converts to the Roman Catholic Church. His father was the Conservative agent for the Winchester constituency and his mother was a prominent supporter of the suffragette movement. Worlock was ordained priest in 1944 and was clearly marked for preferment when in the following year he was appointed private secretary to the archbishop of Westminster, a post he held until 1964, serving Archbishops Griffin, Godfrey and Healey in succession. He was not a charismatic figure, but his thoroughgoing knowledge of the administration and successive archbishops ensured promotion. He spent less than two years as a parish priest in the east end of London, clearly only a preparation for episcopacy, but he was effective and took his responsibilities seriously, developing a ministry to the homeless and establishing a pastoral service to the Irish immigrants who arrived in London homeless and penniless.

He was consecrated bishop of Portsmouth in 1965 and translated to be archbishop of Liverpool in 1976, though many thought he would have been a natural candidate to succeed Cardinal Heenan as archbishop of Westminster. As private secretary to three of Heenan's predecessors he had unfortunately acquired the unfair reputation as a hatchet man who had to carry out tough decisions on behalf of his superiors. 'More than anything else that counted against him and he felt a sense of bitterness at what seemed to him to be a diocesan plot to keep him out . . . He was prone to depression, even a touch of paranoia [but] he was certainly more popular and liked by his flock and by those around than he seemed willing to allow.'[43]

At Liverpool he struck up a remarkable and famous friendship with the Anglican bishop of the city, the charismatic David Sheppard, and together they demonstrated the ecumenical character of their faith, not least by the attendance of Pope John Paul II at a crowded service in the Anglican cathedral on his visit to England in 1982. Worlock and Sheppard did much to heal decades of suspicion and bitterness between the two Christian denominations in Liverpool. Worlock presented a bible to the dean of the Anglican cathedral, at its dedication in the presence of the Queen, a gesture that would have been unthinkable in former times. He attended the Second Vatican Council (1962–65), and pressed his liberalising views on such issues as the marriage of divorced persons. Consequently he was little liked by more conservative elements in his communion. The national pastoral congress, which met in Liverpool in May 1980, prepared and chaired by Worlock, was the point at which the teaching and spirit of the Vatican Council were formally adopted by the Roman Catholic Church in England. It was the product of Worlock's kindness, tolerance and drive towards ecumenical cooperation, and it was not his fault that the conference of bishops stalled its application for many years afterwards.

Worlock identified himself with the poor and the disadvantaged of his industrial archdiocese, and initiated the Michaelmas group, which attempted to assess and correct some of the long term problems which faced the city. At the time of the Toxteth riots in 1981, sometimes accompanied by Sheppard and sometimes alone, he made it his business to intercede with the police and the black community.

Appointment as a CH 'lately Roman Catholic Archbishop of Liverpool. For services to the Roman Catholic Church and to the community in Liverpool' came in 1995, sadly only a few weeks before his death from lung cancer.

Edward Chad Varah (Anglican) 31 December 1999 (see Chapter 11)

CHAPTER FOUR

All the pride of power

STATESMEN AND POLITICIANS

'I don't think they play at all fairly,' Alice began in rather a complaining tone, 'and they all quarrel so dreadfully one can't hear oneself speak – and they don't seem to have any rules in particular; at least, if there are, nobody attends to them.'
'The Queen's croquet ground', *Alice's adventures in wonderland*, Lewis Carroll

'Politicians are not popular as a species,' wrote Selwyn Lloyd in his autobiography, 'they have rude things said about them all the time.'[1] Those who enter the field of politics rapidly find that they have to develop tough outer shells because of the abuse to which they are regularly subjected. When others have been exonerated, absolved or excused, politicians remain the ultimate scapegoats because, in the public opinion, they are ultimately and always responsible and answerable by virtue of their election to national power, and the hunting season is open all year. Successive prime ministers have made much use of the CH to recognise service given by their colleagues; service that has sometimes led to a severe battering by press and public.

The 'politician' Companions of Honour easily outnumber any one of the other non-political categories, and while it is not true to say that they have saturated the Order, significantly large numbers have been admitted from time to time, usually on the personal recommendation of the prime minister of the day. There is nothing to be gained in arguing that 'too many' politicians have been made CH; but there is an argument for examining appointments – occasionally made in batches – to understand the political expediencies that lay behind them.

In the political field the CH is generally though not always associated with service in senior ministerial office. The list of politicians suggests that the CH has been used by prime ministers of both parties mainly in recognition of distinguished political services by ministers at or towards the end of their careers, although very rarely a serving minister – such as Michael Stewart (1968) or William Whitelaw (1974) – has been appointed. On several occasions the CH has been quite obviously used as a consolation prize for a minister dropped from the cabinet for whatever reason. There is a strong case for saying that this is an abuse of the Order. The CH was and is a very high honour, a companion to the Order of Merit in style and status, and not to be used as a sop to console discarded ministers. This practice was very apparent in 1962 when Harold Macmillan used the CH to sweeten the bitter pill of dismissal for Jack Maclay, Harold Watkinson and Selwyn Lloyd in the 'night of the long knives'.

In the world of politics, the CH has taken on the appearance of a long and faithful service medal to be given to those who have decided voluntarily to leave the cabinet but remain in the house of commons. There is an argument for saying that this is not in keeping with the original purposes of providing a high honour for those who would decline to take a title, because the number of politicians who have received both the CH and a peerage is numerous. The conferral of the Order on retiring cabinet ministers before the inevitable promotion to the house of lords, as an hors d'oeuvres to a peerage, departed from the fundamental purpose for its creation. The only rider to that statement is that the reforms to the house of lords, at the end of the twentieth century, have made it less likely for cabinet ministers generally to find themselves promoted to 'the other place'.

The difficult question to answer is whether the CH should be used to recognise political service. The principal qualification enshrined in the statutes, 'conspicuous service of national importance', has remained unaltered since 1917. Some might claim that the standard required for the politician Companions of Honour has been lower than the exacting standards in the non-political categories, and that politicians are generally appointed at a younger age; there is truth in that claim. Others might say that the work of politicians in government and parliament is a more measurable form of service to the nation than some of the other categories, and that the politicians are the truer lineal descendants of the 1914–18 war service members. The truth of the matter is that standards have varied in this category as in every other category, and that for reasons of political expediency, the choice of candidates has sometimes been less discriminating than it should have been.

Although rather more from the Conservative benches have been appointed CH than those from other parties, this is only a result of the Conservative Party being in power for more years in the twentieth century. A better subdivision is an analysis of the 'political' use of the Order made by successive prime ministers.

The political figures who received the CH between 1917 and 1939 were few in number and individual in nature; pattern and precedent were still well into the future. The line begins with Winston Churchill (1922), renowned for his leadership of the coalition government during the 1939–45 war, although he received the CH in Lloyd George's resignation honours list while still a backbench Liberal MP. John Davidson (1923) was an eminence grise who received the honour for securing the Conservative Party leadership for Stanley Baldwin. Thomas Jones (1929) was a state servant rather than a politician. A long-serving deputy secretary to the cabinet, he was well-liked by successive prime ministers of different political hues. Hugh Pollock (1936) had been minister of finance in Northern Ireland for more than fifteen years and was over eighty years old and close to the end of his life when he was made a CH. The redoubtable Nancy Astor (1937), first woman to take her seat in the house of commons, was made a CH more for being Nancy Astor than for anything else.

The frequency of political appointments began during the 1939–45 war when Winston Churchill habitually used the CH to recognise the war services of ministers in the coalition government: A. V. Alexander (1941) at the admiralty; Lord Woolton (1942) for his work as minister of food; Frederick Leathers (1943) for war transport; Henry Snell (1943), Viscount Swinton (1943), resident minister in West Africa; Robert Hudson (1944), minister of agriculture and fisheries; the Earl of Selborne (1945), minister of economic warfare; Clement Attlee (1945), deputy prime minister and leader of the Labour Party; Arthur Greenwood (1945), deputy leader of the Labour Party; General 'Pug' Ismay (1945), the wartime coordinator of the chiefs of staff; Leo Amery (1945), secretary of state for India and Burma; and Ernest Brown (1945), minister of health. The exception to the general rule was John Miller Andrews (1943), probably the least successful prime minister of Northern Ireland, who was made a CH after his own political party had forced his resignation.

Clement Attlee (1945–51) made four distinctively 'Labour' appointments during his tenure: Margaret Bondfield (1948), the first Labour woman cabinet minister; William Whiteley (1948), the chief whip; Sir Stafford Cripps (1951), chancellor of the exchequer; and Herbert Morrison (1951), in compensation for having thwarted Morrison's chances of succeeding to the leadership of the party.

Winston Churchill (1951–55) added Walter Elliot (1952), a cabinet minister in the late 1930s but still a popular figure in Scottish life; Chuter Ede (1953), Labour home secretary in Attlee's government but a widely respected figure in the commons; Thomas Johnston (1953), Labour Scottish secretary during the 1939–45 war; R. A. Butler (1954), who was good enough to become prime minister but never did. Harry Crookshank (1955) held a series of second rank ministerial offices and would have been a better speaker of the commons than cabinet minister.

Anthony Eden (1955–57) appointed only one CH: Lord Robert Cecil (1956) was over ninety years old but a revered internationalist.

Harold Macmillan (1957–63) began the practice of using the CH as a thank you present to those moved into the departure lounge. James Stuart (1957), secretary of state for Scotland, was tired of front line politics and left the cabinet as soon as Macmillan replaced Eden; Alan Lennox-Boyd (1960), had disagreed with Macmillan over colonial policy. Jack Maclay (1962), Scottish secretary, Harold Watkinson (1962), defence secretary, and Selwyn Lloyd (1962), chancellor of the exchequer, were sacrificed in the 'night of the long knives'. Patrick Buchan-Hepburn (1962) could have been appointed for his work as a charming and successful chief whip; instead he was honoured for undertaking the impossible task of governor general of the doomed federation of the West Indies.

Alec Douglas-Home (1963–64) held office for barely a year and his sole CH appointment was Henry Brooke (1964), who had been home secretary for two years.

Harold Wilson (1964–70) made a succession of recommendations that seemed to be a 'mopping-up' exercise of old cabinet ministers from Clement Attlee's government: Lewis Silkin (1965), Manny Shinwell (1965), Edith Summerskill (1966) and Jim Griffiths (1966). Megan Lloyd George (1966) was in mould of Nancy Astor. She was made a CH more for playing the passionate maverick character of Megan Lloyd George; she was also seriously ill. Following Macmillan's precedent, Douglas Houghton (1967) and Patrick Gordon-Walker (1968) were honoured after being dropped from the cabinet. Michael Stewart (1969) was the first secretary of state for foreign and commonwealth affairs. He was not the best, but he was conscientious and had to cope with extreme opinions about American involvement in Vietnam.

Edward Heath (1970–74) recommended Duncan Sandys (1973), a member of Harold Macmillan's cabinet; Irene Ward (1973), a worthy successor of Nancy Astor and Megan Lloyd George in her spirited feminist independence; and William Whitelaw (1974) for his attempts to bring peace to Northern Ireland.

Harold Wilson (1974–76) made only two political recommendations during his final brief term as prime minister. Bert Bowden (1975) was honoured for his work as chairman of the Independent Television Authority, although he had previously been an effective chief whip. Ted Short (1976), deputy leader of the party, received the CH in Wilson's resignation honours list, perhaps a signal that his ministerial career was not destined to continue under Wilson's successor.

Jim Callaghan (1976–79) similarly added only two names to the political CHs. Cledwyn Hughes (1976) had not been in government since 1970, but he had immersed himself in service to his native Wales. Denis Healey (1979) was Callaghan's deputy and chancellor of the exchequer. His time at the treasury was one of the most difficult in the twentieth century.

Given that she was prime minister for more than ten years, Margaret Thatcher (1979–90) made few political recommendations for the CH. She was generally uninterested in the honours system and only interested in those high honours that would not cause a by-election. She remembered Peter Thorneycroft (1979), a minister in the administration of Harold Macmillan, for his stand on curbing public expenditure. Christopher Soames (1980) was honoured for his role in the transition of Rhodesia into Zimbabwe. Edward Boyle (1981), another minister in the governments of Harold Macmillan and Alec Douglas-Home, had found a new career as a university vice-chancellor. Peter Carrington (1983) resigned as foreign secretary, taking responsibility for failing to predict the Argentine invasion of the Falklands Islands. Margaret Thatcher took the view that the resignation was unnecessary and that an otherwise unblemished ministerial career should not go unrecognised. David Eccles (1984), whose ministerial career extended from Winston Churchill to Edward Heath, was honoured for his services to the arts. Keith Joseph (1986) and Norman Tebbit (1987), both highly regarded by Margaret Thatcher, were honoured with the CH on leaving the government.

John Major (1990–97) similarly honoured departing cabinet ministers: Ken Baker (1992), home secretary; Peter Brooke (1992), Northern Ireland secretary; Tom King (1992), defence secretary and Douglas Hurd (1995), foreign secretary. Geoffrey Howe (1996), former deputy prime minister, received the CH four years after leaving government and parliament, and six years after bringing down Margaret Thatcher. David Owen (1994), the former Labour foreign secretary was given the CH for his endeavour, futile though it proved to be, to bring peace to the former Yugoslavia.

Tony Blair (1997-) has made only three political recommendations for the CH – all Conservative – Michael Heseltine (1997), the former deputy prime minister; Christopher Patten (1997), the last governor of Hong Kong; and lastly John Major (1998), only the third former prime minister (after Winston Churchill and Clement Attlee) to be honoured with the CH.

Refusal of the CH by politicians is almost unknown, although it is thought that *Malcolm MacDonald* (1901–1981) did so. Son of the Labour prime minister Ramsay MacDonald, he served as cabinet minister in the 1930s and then after the war served abroad in dismantling various parts of the British empire. It is known that he refused the GCMG (knight grand cross of the Order of St Michael and St George) on two occasions, once from Winston Churchill and once from Clement Attlee. On the first occasion he declared that the prime minister's confidence was reward enough, and 'I should be sorry to cease being a plain Mister.'[2] On the second occasion he was more explicit. 'I was averse to honours, and especially to those which conferred titles. They seemed to me to make false distinctions between a few human beings and millions of equally worthy others – to establish something like a caste system in our society.'[3] It was also said that he had refused a peerage.[4] Having refused such high honours as a GCMG and a peerage and signalled his dislike of titles, he would certainly have been offered a CH. It is thought that he declined that honour on at least two occasions before accepting the OM in 1969.

The following list includes principally those identified as 'politicians' in the public mind. Two notable backbenchers in the house of commons – Ian Fraser (1953) and Jack Ashley (1975) – made outstanding reputations in the world of the blind and the deaf are included in chapter 11.

Sir Winston Churchill 19 October 1922
A fearless and unorthodox politician who more often followed the dictates of his conscience than the dogma of his party, Winston Churchill, was the most renowned British politician of the twentieth century and principally remembered as the prime minister who led the nation through the dark years of the 1939–45 war.

He was born at Blenheim Palace, Woodstock in 1874, the son of Lord Randolph Churchill. He was educated at Harrow and Sandhurst and commissioned in the Fourth Hussars in 1895. He saw action on the north-west frontier of India and in the Sudan where he took part in battle of Omdurman in 1898. In the same year he went to Bangalore and published the first of his many historical books, *The story of the Malakand Field Force*, and his sole novel, *Savrola. A tale of revolution in Laurania*. He left the army in 1899 to become a war correspondent for the *Morning Post*. While reporting from South Africa he was taken prisoner by the Boers but made headline news when he escaped. On returning to England he wrote a book about his experiences, *London to Ladysmith* (1900).

Although Churchill's political career began in 1900, the earlier phase was overshadowed by his inspired leadership of the nation during the 1939–45 war. Thereafter, estimates of his life and work tended to be devotional and reverential. Of more interest were the assessments made before the war – which showed traits of character that reached their apotheosis between 1940 and 1945. Beatrice Webb met Churchill in July 1903 and formed a mostly unfavourable impression, though she discerned early signs of greatness: 'restless, almost intolerably so, without capacity for sustained and unexcited labour, egotistical, bumptious, shallow-minded and reactionary, but with a certain personal magnetism, great pluck and some originality, not of intellect but character.'[5] J. R. Clynes, later leader of the Labour Party, met Churchill in 1901 and formed an altogether different impression, though as he wrote down his memories in 1937, it was filtered by later history. 'I found him a man of extraordinarily independent mind, and great courage. He absolutely refused to yield to our persuasions, and said bluntly that he would rather lose votes than abandon his convictions . . . Churchill was, and has always remained, a soldier in mufti. He possesses inborn militaristic qualities, and is intensely proud of his descent from Marlborough. He cannot visualize Britain without an Empire, or the Empire without wars of acquisition and defence. A hundred years ago he might profoundly have affected the shaping of our country's history. Now, the impulses of peace and internationalism, and the education and equality of the working classes, leave him unmoved.'[6] Philip Snowden, the Labour politician, painted a picture of Churchill in his autobiography published in 1934. 'However much one may differ from Mr Churchill, one is compelled to like him for his finer qualities. There is an attractiveness in everything he does. His high spirits are irrepressible. Mr Churchill was as happy facing a Budget deficit as in distributing a surplus. He is an adventurer, a soldier of fortune. An escapade has an irresistible fascination for him.'[7]

In the 1900 general election Churchill was elected Conservative member of parliament for Oldham, having unsuccessfully contested the seat in the previous year. In 1904, critical of Joseph Chamberlain's tariff reform policy, he crossed the floor of the house of commons and continued to represent Oldham for the Liberal Party. 'So it continued all through his life – the habit of following his own judgement, his own intuition, and his own impulses.'[8]

In the 1906 election he won the seat of North-West Manchester for the Liberals and immediately became a member of the new government as under-secretary of state for the colonies. When Asquith replaced Campbell-Bannerman as prime minister in 1908, Churchill was promoted to the cabinet as president of the board of trade, having refused the local government board on the ground that he did not wish 'to be shut up in a soup kitchen with Mrs Sidney Webb.'[9] In 1910 Asquith made him home secretary. He introduced several reforms to the prison system, including the provision of lecturers and concerts for prisoners and the setting up of aftercare associations to help convicts after they had served their sentence. But he was criticised for using troops to maintain order during a Welsh miners' strike. In 1911 he exchanged ministries with Reginald McKenna, first lord of the admiralty, with a mandate to prepare the navy for war. He was one of the first people to grasp the potential of airplanes in war and he established an air department at the admiralty. His enthusiasm for the air extended to him taking flying lessons.

At the outbreak of the 1914–18 war, he joined the war council, but he was blamed for the failure at the Dardanelles in 1915 and on the formation of a coalition government in the same year the Conservative Party insisted that the renegade be moved to the relatively minor office of chancellor of the duchy of Lancaster. Resentful of being marginalised and unable to influence the government's war policy, he resigned after six months, rejoined the army and commanded a battalion of the Royal Scots Fusiliers. When Lloyd George replaced Asquith as prime minister in 1916, he brought Churchill back into the government as minister of munitions and for the final year of the war, he was in charge of the production of tanks, aircraft, guns and shells.

After the war he was secretary of state for war and air (1919–21), for air and the colonies (1921) and for the colonies (1921–22). He was defeated in the 1922 general election, rejoined the Conservative Party and was elected to represent Epping in the 1924 election. The new prime minister, Stanley Baldwin, made Churchill chancellor of the exchequer. In 1925 he returned Britain to the gold standard, thereby, according to general wisdom, inaugurating the economic disasters of the late 1920s and 1930s. In 1926 he took a strong line against the general strike. He edited the government's newspaper the *British Gazette* during the dispute where he argued that 'either the country will break the General Strike, or the General Strike will break the country.' From the defeat of the government at the 1929 election, Churchill was out of power, though not out of parliament, for the next ten years. He was not invited to join the national government in 1931 and spent the next few years concentrating on his writing, including his multi-volume *History of the English speaking peoples*, published in the 1950s.

A staunch critic and opponent of appeasement, Churchill was appointed as first lord of the admiralty at the outbreak of the 1939–45 war. When Neville Chamberlain resigned in May 1940, Churchill succeeded him as prime minister.

He formed an all-party coalition government to unite public opinion behind the war effort. Enough has been written about his inspirational leadership of the country during that war and it need not to be repeated here. His unusual daily timetable – he would go to bed and sleep soundly each afternoon and then begin work again, regularly convening meetings of the cabinet at 11pm – seemed to underpin and enhance rather than reduce the effectiveness of his leadership.

After the defeat of Germany, the Labour Party withdrew from the coalition government and insisted on a general election. The swing against the Conservative Party – which had begun before the war – led to a resounding Labour victory in the 1945 election. Churchill's behaviour during the campaign did him no credit. 'He indulged in accusations, imputations and even personal abuse against his wartime colleagues [including his successor Clement Attlee] which shocked his hearers – even his friends – and embittered his opponents.'[10]

He spent the next six years as leader of the opposition, irrationally and furiously denouncing the decision to grant independence to India, Burma and Ceylon, and when visiting the USA in March 1946 he made the famous 'iron curtain' speech at Fulton, Missouri in condemnation of the effective Soviet occupation of the eastern European states. He began work on a six volume history, *The second world war* (1948–54), for which he was awarded the Nobel prize for literature in 1953.

In August 1946 he suffered the first of several strokes but it was never publicly revealed and he remained leader of the Conservative Party, leading it to victory in the 1951 election. This second administration (1951–55) was little more than a postscript. He became prime minister for the second time a month before his seventy-seventh birthday. His health continued to deteriorate and shortly after the coronation in June 1953 he suffered a severe stroke and was barely able to function as prime minister. His son-in-law, Christopher Soames, became his guardian and decided which ministers should be allowed to see Churchill and for how long. He returned to office in October 1953 but he was noticeably weaker than before. By 1955 he was past eighty and incapable of leading the Conservative Party into another election. He reluctantly resigned as prime minister in April that year (he had become too attached to the reins of power and tried to defer resignation), though he remained a member of the house of commons until 1964. He died in 1965.

Churchill was made a CH in the 1922 dissolution list; there was no citation, but he had been a loyal supporter of Lloyd George. He was appointed to the Order of Merit in 1946 and to the Order of the Garter in 1953 (having refused it in December 1944). He was offered a dukedom nervously by Queen Elizabeth II on his retirement in 1955, but only after it had been informally ascertained that he would decline. A policy had been agreed whereby dukedoms would in future only be conferred on members of the royal family. There was no doubting Churchill's exceptional service to the nation – but was it enough to justify a departure from policy? After Churchill returned from his audience with the Queen he reported the outcome to his private secretary. 'Do you know, the most remarkable thing – she offered to make me a Duke . . . I very nearly accepted, I was so moved by her beauty and charm and the kindness with which she made this offer, that for a moment I thought of accepting. But finally I remembered that I must die as I have always been – Winston Churchill. And so I asked to forgive my not accepting it. And do you know, it's an odd thing, but she seemed almost relieved.'[11]

Viscount Davidson 25 May 1923

John Davidson was the eminence grise to prime ministers Andrew Bonar Law and Stanley Baldwin, and played a significant role in securing Baldwin's appointment as prime minister in 1923.

He was born at Aberdeen in 1889, the only son of Sir James Davidson, a physician. He was educated at Westminster and Pembroke College, Cambridge, and called to the bar at Middle Temple in 1913. In 1910 he had become private secretary to the marquess of Crewe, then secretary of state for the colonies. He was well thought of and remained in office under the next two colonial secretaries, Lord Harcourt (1910–15) and Andrew Bonar Law (1915–16). A friendship developed between Davidson and Bonar Law that lasted until the latter's death in 1923. Bonar Law was leader of the Conservative Party (1911–21 and 1922–23) enabling Davidson to become a power behind the scenes. He stayed with Bonar Law when the latter became chancellor of the exchequer and a member of the war cabinet (1916–19) and lord privy seal and leader of the house of commons (1919–21). In 1920 Davidson was returned to the commons at a by-election at Hemel Hempstead and became Bonar Law's parliamentary private secretary (he was defeated in December 1923 but regained the seat in October 1924). 'He had made a niche for himself as a discreet, high-powered and very well-informed private secretary, who was an ideal aide-de-camp to people in high places. His exquisite manners, combined with great tact and discernment and a gift for modestly effacing himself while playing an important part in state business, made him greatly liked.'[9]

In March 1921 Bonar Law resigned his offices and retired from politics through ill-health, and Davidson temporarily became private secretary to Stanley Baldwin, president of the board of trade. He kept in touch with Bonar Law who was convalescing in the south of France, and when Lloyd George's coalition government collapsed in October 1922, Bonar Law returned to be leader of the Conservative Party and prime minister. His time in office was short-lived because his illness was terminal and, seriously ill, he resigned in May 1923.

Davidson's position gave him power to influence the succession. King George V desired to know the views of the outgoing prime minister on who should be invited to form a new government. Colonel Sir Ronald Waterhouse, who had succeeded Davidson as his private secretary, conveyed Bonar Law's letter of resignation to the king. The letter was accompanied by an unsigned memorandum, which strongly pressed the case for the appointment of Stanley Baldwin. Waterhouse informed the king that the memorandum practically expressed the wishes of Bonar Law. What he did not say was that it been written by Davidson. Later it was disputed whether it was a true representation of Bonar Law's feelings and whether Davidson had intended it to be used in the way it was used. What is certain is that the king consulted others and the result of his consultations was the appointment of Baldwin rather than Lord Curzon

Davidson became as attached to the Baldwin family as he had been to Bonar Law, and Baldwin treated him as a confidential adviser. His services were recognised by his appointment to the cabinet as chancellor of the duchy of Lancaster (1923–24), but he was never destined to be a successful minister. He was moved in January 1924 to be parliamentary and financial secretary to the admiralty (1924–26), and then chairman of the Conservative and Unionist Organisation (1926–30). He was better as a mover behind the scenes and not temperamentally suited to the very public role of party chairman. The Conservatives were defeated at the 1929 election and Davidson resigned in May 1930.

He actively worked for the creation of the national government in 1931 and returned to his first office as chancellor of the duchy of Lancaster (1931–37). Baldwin sent him to India in 1932 as chairman of the Indian states advisory committee, to prepare the way for an all-India federation. When Neville Chamberlain succeeded Baldwin in May 1937 Davidson was dropped from the government. In the early part of the 1939–45 war he was for a short time controller of production at the ministry of information, and in 1942 he was sent on an official tour of South America, but Churchill did not entrust him with any other role.

In the years following the 1939–45 war he busied himself with pressing for a rather grandiose building development at the Queen's Chapel of the Savoy (the chapel of the Victorian Order) in London. The plans envisaged the erection of a 'Knight's Hall', domestic offices and a cloister. The proposed development, which would have overshadowed the chapel and enclosed the graveyard did not meet with universal approval and was never implemented. He died in 1970.

Davidson was made a CB in 1919, a CH in 1923 (there was no citation or description of appointment) and a GCVO in 1935. He was created a viscount in 1937 on leaving the government. With the exception of the GCVO from King George V, his other honours were due to the regard felt for him by Andrew Bonar Law and Stanley Baldwin, the two politicians who were his closest friends. To the general public, he was unknown.

Thomas Jones 3 June 1929

Thomas Jones (he became known as T. J.) was deputy secretary to the cabinet (1916–30) and a significant influence in Welsh cultural affairs

He was born at Rhymney, Monmouthshire in 1870 where his father was the manager of the shop and farm of the Rhymney Iron Company. He left school at fourteen to work as a timekeeper with the company but saved as much of his wages as he could with the intention of being able to continue his studies at a future date. He had envisaged a career in the civil service, but it was not then practicable and in 1890 he was encouraged to become a candidate for the ministry of the Methodist Church. A vocation never materialised, but with the money he had saved, and with help from his father, he went to University College, Aberystwyth, the University of Glasgow and the London School of Economics. His latent intellectual abilities flowered and in 1905 he was given a lectureship in economics at Glasgow. He was also a special investigator for the Poor Law Commission (1906–09). He was briefly professor of economics at Queen's University, Belfast (1909–10), then secretary of the Welsh national campaign against tuberculosis (1910–12) and secretary to the national health insurance commissioners for Wales (1912–16). In 1916 he was appointed deputy secretary to the cabinet and remained there until he left the civil service in 1930.

As a civil servant Jones never enjoyed (and never wanted) the spotlight that fell on politicians. He was a sensitive self-effacing individual who was content to work quietly on the Whitehall backstage in the best civil service tradition of anonymity and his name was not familiar to the general public. He had strong and independent convictions but his profession taught him to analyse a problem impartially, present the best solution or give the best advice to a minister, and then loyally accept and implement whatever decision the minister then chose to make (even if it was not in accord with the advice tendered). Consequently he was able to work on terms of friendship with four very different prime ministers: David Lloyd George, Andrew Bonar Law, Stanley Baldwin and Ramsay MacDonald. He had a wide range of contacts outside the civil service and 'he had the gift of making people talk freely to him, as if to a friend, and it was this faculty for gaining the confidence of all sorts of men that enabled him to play so well an unobtrusive part in the negotiations about the labour disputes that characterised the inter-war years.'[13]

He left the civil service in 1930 to become the first secretary of the Pilgrim Trust. Many of the trustees, including Stanley Baldwin and John Buchan were already his friends. He resigned in 1945, was immediately appointed a trustee, and served two years as chairman of the trust (1952–54). He was a member of the Unemployment Assistance Board (1934–40), charged with dealing with the problems of those who had been unemployed for so long that they had almost reached the stage of being unemployable. His south Wales background gave him a deep concern for the underprivileged (although he had no time for indolence) and the trust in particular allowed him an active interest in various aspects of social service including housing, education and unemployment. He was a strong supporter of adult education and one of the group instrumental in founding Coleg Harlech (of which he was president). He was equally at home with the privileged and enjoyed being a guest at weekend gatherings in country houses. But he was quite unaffected by it, and totally indifferent to social advancement.

Unsurprisingly Wales and its culture had a special place in his affections. He was fluent in Welsh and loved Welsh literature. He was a member of the court of the University of Wales, a governor of the National Library of Wales and of the National Museum of Wales, and chairman of the Royal Commission on Ancient Monuments in Wales and Monmouthshire (1944–48). He was also chairman of the Gregynog Press, founded by Gwendoline Davies (who herself received the CH in 1937), and of which he wrote a history in 1954. He also wrote *Rhymney memories* (1939), a nostalgic volume of autobiography, a biography of Lloyd George (1951) and *A diary with letters* (1954) an account of politics behind the scenes between 1931 and 1950. Of his cabinet years he was totally discreet and revealed nothing.

By his marriage he had a son and a daughter. His son was killed in a car accident, but he lived to see his daughter Eirene (1909–99) elected Labour member of parliament for East Flint in 1950. She served as a junior minister in the 1964–70 Labour government and was created a life peer as Baroness White. He died in 1955

Jones was made a CH in 1929 for his services as 'Deputy Secretary to the Cabinet'. The honour, a highly unusual one for a civil servant, was a tribute to the regard in which a diverse range of political opinion held him.

Hugh Pollock 23 June 1936
Hugh Pollock was the first minister of finance and deputy prime minister of Northern Ireland after the partition of Ireland in 1921.

He was born at Bangor, County Down, in 1852, the son of a master mariner. He was educated at Bangor Endowed School and then went into the world of commerce. He was managing director of Shaw, Pollock and Co., a firm of flour importers, a director of the Belfast Ropeworks, a member of the Belfast Harbour Commissioners for thirty-six years (and chairman, 1918–21), and president of the

Belfast Chamber of Commerce. During the 1914–18 war he was a member of the Belfast Committee, which encouraged subscriptions to the war loan, and was largely responsible for Belfast's contribution reaching the total of over £12 million. In 1917 he was nominated to represent the chamber of commerce as a member of the abortive Irish convention, a last attempt to reconcile the divergent views between the north and the south of Ireland, and was remembered as one of the few members of the convention to approach the question of home rule dispassionately. 'Swayed by no political prejudices, he saw it as an economic problem and, having examined the data of Anglo-Irish finance, he concluded that the preservation of fiscal unity with Great Britain was essential.'[14]

With the partition of Ireland in 1921, Pollock was elected member for South Belfast in the new Northern Ireland parliament and then, from 1929 for the new constituency of Windsor, which included part of his former constituency. Typical of the first generation of Northern Ireland ministers in being drawn from the upper layers of commercial society, he was appointed minister of finance and deputy prime minister in June 1921. Few finance ministers could probably equal Pollock's record of presenting fourteen budgets, every one of which showed a surplus. Among his achievements were the continuance of the Loans Guarantee Act – which assisted shipping companies and enabled them to place orders in Belfast shipyards – and the efforts he made in negotiating the Reinsurance Agreement with Britain, which made it clear that unemployment insurance was a United Kingdom not a Northern Ireland liability. His argument was that equal taxation entitled the people of Northern Ireland to the same social benefits as those of Great Britain, and that only after these were provided should the statutory contribution towards imperial expenditure be assessed. He remained minister of finance and deputy prime minister until his death in 1937 at the age of eighty-four.

He was made a CH in 1936 for his services as 'Minister of Finance, Northern Ireland.'

Viscountess Astor 11 May 1937
An American-born feminist and politician, Nancy Astor was the first woman member of parliament to take her seat in the house of commons.

She was born Nancy Witcher Langhorne in 1879 in Danville and raised in Richmond, Virginia, U.S.A. Her family had lost most of their money in the American civil war (1861–65), but recovered its fortune by the 1890s. She married her first husband, Robert Gould Shaw, in 1897, but the marriage did not last and she divorced him in 1903 (he died in 1930). On a visit to England in 1906, she met and married Waldorf Astor, a member of America's first millionaire family. (His father had come to England in 1890 and was a naturalised British subject in 1899.) He was elected to parliament in 1910 and Nancy became involved in her husband's work. In 1919 he succeeded his father as the second Viscount Astor and was obliged to resign his seat in the house of commons. At the ensuing by-election, Nancy stood as the Conservative Party candidate and was elected by a substantial majority to succeed her husband as member for the Sutton division of Plymouth. She was the first woman to take her seat in the house of commons. (Countess Constance Markievicz preceded her, at the general election in December 1918, but following the policy of her fellow Sinn Fein members, she refused to take her seat at Westminster.) Her main focus in parliament was on issues affecting women and children, and she introduced a bill prohibiting the sale of alcohol to persons under the age of eighteen. She was a tough and forceful personality, but as the first woman in the house of commons, she had to be. 'She made a great many speeches on her feet and still more interjectory remarks from her seat; she could answer the Labour members in banter or in anger and be equally effective in either mood. She was adored by her constituents but disliked by the classic parliamentarians, who considered her repartees undignified.'[15] She never held office in government and frankly acknowledged the reason: 'Nobody wants me as a cabinet minister and they are perfectly right. I am an agitator, not an administrator.'

Many witticisms are attributed to her. On the rights of women: 'We are not asking for superiority for we have always had that; all we ask is equality.' On her own achievements: 'The penalty of success is to be bored by the people who used to snub you.' On her marriage: 'I married beneath me. All women do.' On the wealthy: 'The only thing I like about rich people is their money.' On men: 'In passing, also, I would like to say that the first time Adam had a chance, he laid the blame on a woman.' On the consumption of alcohol: 'One reason I don't drink is because I wish to know when I'm having a good time.' Her relationship with Winston Churchill was based on mutual antipathy and their verbal fights were legendary. Meeting an intoxicated Churchill in a corridor in the palace of Westminster one day she said: 'Mr Churchill, you are drunk.' The latter replied: 'Madam, I am drunk. You are ugly. In the morning, I shall be sober.' In about 1912, the two met each other at Blenheim Palace, and she shouted: 'If I were your wife I would put poison in your coffee.' With equal heat and sincerity he replied: 'And if I was your husband I would drink it.'[16]

Her husband persuaded her to retire from the house of commons at the 1945 general election. She was sixty-six and her performance in the house had deteriorated over the years, and in the Labour landslide she would probably have been defeated. The Labour candidate won her constituency with a majority of more than 5,000. She resented not being in the commons and blamed her husband, and relations between the two were strained until his death in 1952. 'Her finest qualities were courage, generosity and zest; her principle defects, insensitivity, prejudice and a streak of cruelty. She was a curious mixture of religious maniac and clown, oscillating between the extremes of earnestness and levity.'[17]

She died in 1964, at the age of eighty-four. Seeing her children around her during her last illness, she said: 'Am I dying or is this my birthday.'

She was made a CH in the Coronation Honours List in 1937 for services as 'Member of Parliament for the Sutton Division since 1919.'

Earl Alexander of Hillsborough 12 June 1941

Albert Victor Alexander was the longest serving first lord of the admiralty in the twentieth century, but his political service was unremarkable, and he was over-decorated with a number of high honours.

He was born at Weston-super-Mare in 1885, the son of a blacksmith. He went to Barton Hill elementary school in Bristol but left at the age of thirteen to work as a junior clerk in the offices of Bristol education committee. Five years later he transferred to Somerset education committee, where he stayed until the outbreak of the 1914–18 war, rising to the rank of chief clerk.

In 1914 he joined the Artists' Rifles and was demobilised in 1919 with the rank of captain. He returned to his old profession as education officer to the south-western district. In 1920 he was appointed secretary to the Co-operative Congress, which coordinated the co-operative organisations as did the TUC for the trades unions. In 1922 he was elected to the house of commons as member for the Hillsborough division of Sheffield and became parliamentary secretary to the board of trade in the first Labour government (1924). When Labour returned to power in 1929 he was appointed first lord of the admiralty and took part in the London naval conference. The conference was much criticised in subsequent years for its restrictive effects on the size of the royal navy. Despite the concerns of others, he remained proud of his contribution to the Naval Treaty 1930 which, as a socialist, he regarded as a substantial step towards international agreement.

He lost his seat in the 1931 election but regained it in 1935 and held it until he moved to the house of lords in 1950. He was opposition spokesman on naval matters at the outbreak of the 1939–45 war, gave Churchill his full support, and was in turn kept fully briefed on all naval matters. When Churchill succeeded Chamberlain in 1940, Alexander was made first lord of the admiralty in the coalition government and held the office throughout the war. There was not a great deal for him to do as Churchill kept full control in his own hands. Alexander was given no access to secret materials and no entry to the most secret war room.

He was replaced by Brendan Bracken in the postwar caretaker Conservative government (1945), but resumed the office (1945–46) in the following Labour government. In 1946 the three service departments were reorganised and a ministry of defence was created and Alexander became its first minister (1947–50). He was not a great success and vacillated badly over the length of national service, on which he seemed to be incapable of being decisive. 'Although a hard and unobtrusive worker and a conscientious administrator, he was not at home in the world of grand strategy.'[18] Field Marshal Montgomery (chief of the imperial general staff 1946–48) later revealed that he, with the service chiefs of the navy and the air force, had asked the prime minister to remove Alexander on the ground that they had no confidence in him.

In time-honoured fashion, he was 'kicked upstairs' in the New Year Honours List 1950 with a viscountcy, and when Labour was returned to power a few weeks later with a majority of only six, he was replaced by Emanuel Shinwell. With such a slender majority, it was essential that the defence secretary should be in the house of commons. He was given the titular office of chancellor of the duchy of Lancaster, continuing as defence spokesman for the government in the house of lords. In 1955, though now seventy years old, he was unanimously elected to succeed Lord Jowitt as leader of the Labour peers in the lords. 'He proved a hardworking, devoted, but somewhat pedestrian leader. Conscientious in attendance, assiduous in challenging the government, weighty in manner, what he lacked was the light touch.'[19]

Outside the world of politics he was a Baptist lay preacher with extreme protestant opinions. In a 1964 debate on whether the clergy of the Church of England should be allowed to wear vestments (a substantial minority had done so for more than a century), Alexander appeared pedantic, discourteous and foolish when he attempted to oppose the measure and challenged Archbishop Michael Ramsey of Canterbury to declare publicly that he was a 'protestant'. He was no match for the theological mind of the archbishop and when the vote came, the measure was passed and Alexander was one of only a tiny number of opponents.

He was made a CH in 1941 for his services as 'First Lord of the Admiralty.' He was created a viscount in 1950 as Viscount Alexander of Hillsborough, and, rather pointlessly, an earl and a baron in 1963 as Earl Alexander of Hillsborough and Baron Weston-super-Mare. The last of his high honours – Knight of the Garter – was conferred in 1964. As Alexander had only one daughter by his marriage, all three peerages became extinct at his death in January 1965.

Earl of Woolton 11 June 1942

Frederick James Marquis, first Earl of Woolton, had the career of a chameleon, moving through a series of very different phases and brilliantly adapting to each. He began his working life as a social worker in the back streets of Liverpool, and moved on to be a businessmen, a non-party minister in the 1939–45 war, and finally a very successful chairman of the Conservative Party.

He was born in Manchester in 1883 and educated at Manchester Grammar School and the University of Manchester. After graduation he was awarded a research fellowship in economics. In 1908 he became warden of the David Lewis men's clubs and the university settlement in Liverpool. He was rejected for military service in the 1914–18 war on health grounds, but he worked at the war office in connection with the allied commission and raw materials sections. He became secretary to the leather control board and controller of civilian boots. His became so proficient at the task that he spent two years after the war in reorganising the Boot Manufacturers' Federation. Then he was asked to join the staff of Lewis's, the first gentile to be part of the management of a hitherto wholly Jewish owned company, and became joint managing director in 1928 and chairman in 1936.

A gift for administration led to a series of government appointments including membership of the overseas trade development council (1930–33), the advisory council of the board of trade (1930–34), the advisory council of the post office (1933) and the Cadman committee on civil aviation (1937) During his business days in the north-west he was also chairman of the Liverpool medical research council, a member of the council of the University of Liverpool and chancellor of the University of Manchester (1944–64).

In 1939 the government decided to double the size of the territorial army and he was appointed honorary adviser to the secretary of state for war, for the purpose of clothing the army. In September the same year he was appointed director-general of equipment and stores, ministry of supply. In April 1940 Neville Chamberlain invited him to join the government as minister of food. Woolton was primarily an industrialist with no taste for politics and accepted only with reluctance. But his job description hardly required political skills. His task was to supply the country with food while simultaneously rationing that supply, and the sign above his door recalled a fundamental trait in his character that recalled his days as a social worker in Liverpool: 'we not only cope, we care.'

In 1943 Churchill persuaded him to become minister of reconstruction with full authority to deal with all aspects of postwar reconstruction policy. It was a coordinating role and he had no separate department of his own, but the force of his personality and the strength of his integrity brought respect and cooperation from his colleagues. He was known for never making a promise that he could not fulfill. He gave priority to the provision of decent housing for those serving in the armed forces and in 1944 he announced proposals for the creation of a ministry of social insurance, the provision of family allowances and a comprehensive social insurance bill.

Hitherto apolitical, Woolton decided to join the Conservative Party in 1945. He was briefly lord president of the council in the 1945 caretaker government, and after the election defeat, Churchill made him party chairman in 1946. He was to hold office for nearly ten years, during which time he rebuilt the party and became renowned as one of its most successful chairman ever. 'Avuncular in manner, perceptive in judgement, and thorough in action, he was repeatedly underestimated by his critics at large. He had a broader mind and a stronger will than might have been recognised from that bland smile and hearty chuckle. Above all he had those immense assets, the ability to profit from his mistakes and to work within his limits.'[20]

When the Conservative Party returned to government he was again lord president of the council (1951–52), with the task of supervising and coordinating the policies of the ministries of food and agriculture, and then chancellor of the duchy of Lancaster (1952–55) with the additional rank of minister of materials and responsibility for winding up that ministry. After the resounding Conservative victory in the May 1955 election he resigned as chairman in June and from the government in December. He died in 1964.

He was knighted in 1935, created a baron in 1939 as Baron Woolton, a viscount in 1953 as Viscount Woolton, and an earl and a viscount in 1956 as Earl of Woolton and Viscount Walberton. He was made CH in 1942 for his wartime services as minister of food, but no citation appeared in the *London Gazette*.

Viscount Leathers 1 January 1943

Frederick Leathers was more a businessmen than a politician, but was called upon by Churchill to be minister of war transport during the 1939–45 war as a result of his lifetime experience of coal and shipping.

He was born in Stowmarket in 1883. His father died when he was young and at the age of fifteen he began a career in commerce. He became managing director of William Cory and Sons in 1916, and eventually became chairman or director of a large number of companies involved in mining, shipping and cement. It was the shipping aspect of his interests that was to bring him into the orbit of government. Like a number of businessmen with shipping interests, including Lord Faringdon, Lord Royden and Sir John Ellerman, Leathers had worked with the ministry of shipping in the 1914–18 war.

By the outbreak of the 1939–45 war, he had become a shipping expert of international repute and in May 1940 he joined the ministry of shipping as an adviser on fuel problems and the shipping of coal and fuel. In 1941 he was created a baron and appointed minister of the new department of war transport, an amalgamation of the departments of shipping and transport. It was one of those backroom ministries that undertook essential but unglamorous and unspectacular work. 'It fell to Leathers to face the immense problems not only of the external but also of the internal communications of the country at a period when its existence as well as its war effort depended on them. From the first he saw transport as a continuous process from the interior to the coast and to its overseas destinations. Indeed the unification of the national system of transport which did so much to overcome the difficulties he encountered was primarily due to him . . . The transport of the United States forces to Europe and north Africa, and the success of the Normandy invasion, depended greatly on Leathers' knowledge of shipping and his remarkable gifts of organisation and improvisation. He was, in fact, the one man responsible for all the nation's communications by land and sea.'²¹

The war years were Leathers' 'finest hour'. When the Conservative Party returned to government in 1951, Churchill recalled Leathers to office as secretary of state for the co-ordination of transport, fuel and power. It was one of a number of 'overlord' appointments devised by Churchill. But it was a nearly impossible task to co-ordinate transport and the production of fuel and power and the appointment was abolished in September 1953. Leathers returned to his business interests and died in 1965.

He was created a baron in 1941, made a CH in 1943 for his services as 'Minister of War Transport', and created a viscount in 1954.

John Miller Andrews 21 May 1943

Holding the office for only three years (1940–43) between the lengthy tenures of Viscount Craigavon (1921–40) and Viscount Brookeborough (1943–63), John Miller Andrews ranks as the least known and the least effective prime minister of Northern Ireland.

He was born in County Down in 1871 and educated at the Royal Academical Institution in Belfast. He left school to serve an apprenticeship in his father's flax spinning firm at Comber, County Down and later became managing director of the company. He was chairman and later president of the Ulster Labour Unionist Association and a member of the executive committee of the Ulster Unionist Council. When the parliament and government of Northern Ireland was formed in 1921 he was returned as member for County Down. He held the seat until 1929 and then represented Mid-Down until his retirement in 1953. His commercial experience made him well qualified for the two cabinet posts that he occupied in the province: minister of labour (1921–37) and minister of finance (1937–40). On the death of Hugh Pollock CH in 1937, Andrews' appointment to succeed him as minister of finance was warmly welcomed, and his talent in this area was recognised by his obituarist in *The Times*. 'His honesty of purpose and his skill in handling the problems of his department were recognised even by those who politically were strongly opposed to him.'²²

In politics he was a hardline and unapologetic unionist. In 1933 he claimed to have investigated the thirty-one porters employed at the newly-opened Northern Ireland parliament building at Stormont and found that there were thirty Protestants and one Catholic, the last being 'there temporarily' he added ominously.²³ On the death of Lord Craigavon in November 1940, Andrews was deputy prime minister and the generally accepted choice to succeed him. But he was nearly seventy and only one year younger than his predecessor. '[He] had neither the health nor the vision to provide the leadership now desperately required.'²⁴ The 1939–45 war had begun and Belfast was the most unprotected city in the United Kingdom. The anti-aircraft strength was less than half the approved strength and the city did not possess a single searchlight; no other town in Northern Ireland had any defence at all. When the bombing of Belfast began in April 1941, the people of Northern Ireland quickly realised how vulnerable they were, and within four weeks, a quarter of the population of Belfast had fled to the countryside. Andrews had no idea of how to cope in a war situation. He could not put Northern Ireland into a European situation. He was a doggedly conservative unionist with very clear priorities. Under Andrews, the Northern Ireland cabinet spent much of its time arranging camouflage for the parliament building at Stormont and debating at length how to protect the bronze statue of Sir Edward Carson in its grounds from bomb damage.[25]

Andrews was impervious to criticism and seemed incapable of action in the crisis. He was obsessed by the infiltration of 'Free Staters' and instituted an investigation to discover how many Roman Catholics were in the higher ranks of the civil service. Despite having a number of weak and ineffectual ministers in his government, he steadfastly and repeatedly refused to reshuffle his cabinet and bring in new blood. Labour disputes began to increase and an extensive series of strikes took place in the autumn of 1942. In early 1943 the IRA made successful gaol breaks in Londonderry and Belfast, and wartime output was paralysed by a series of unofficial strikes. Andrews still refused to reorganise his government and a rebellion among junior ministers and backbenchers gained ground. On 28 April 1943, having rejected compromise proposals from members of his own party, he was forced to resign and replaced by Sir Basil Brooke. Although Churchill was shocked by the ineffectiveness of the Northern Ireland government, his letter to Andrews, on the latter's resignation, was a typically fulsome concentration on broader principles. 'But for the loyalty of Northern Ireland and its devotion to what has now become the cause of thirty governments or nations we should have been confronted with slavery and death and the light which now shines so brightly throughout the world would have been quenched . . . During your premiership the bonds of affection between Great Britain and the people of Northern Ireland have been tempered by fire and are now, I believe, unbreakable.'[26]

Andrews remained a member of the Northern Ireland parliament until 1953, but devoted more of his time to the family flax business and to the Orange movement. He was grand master of the Orange Institution of All Ireland (1948–54) and grand master of the Imperial Grand Council of the World (1949–54). He died in 1956.

He was made a CH three weeks after his resignation from the premiership of Northern Ireland. Some thought was given to creating him a peer, but he had been prime minister for a comparatively short period and concerns were voiced that perhaps it was too high an honour and might create a precedent that would lead to an automatic peerage for all future prime ministers of the province. No citation or description of appointment appeared against his name, but it was difficult to know what to say about him. In the light of his inability to do anything more than display a regrettable intransigence in the face of a series of external and domestic crises, it is questionable whether Andrews should have received any honour at all.

Lord Snell 2 June 1943

Henry Snell was a socialist, secularist and rationalist who began his life as an illegitimate farm boy and ended it as captain of the Honourable Corps of the Gentlemen-at-Arms and a peer of the realm.

He was born in 1865 at Sutton-on-Trent, Nottinghamshire, the son of Mary Snell, formerly Clarke. His mother never revealed the identity of his father. He was raised by his mother and his stepfather and at the age of eight he began work as a cattle-minder and bird-scarer. His formal education was scanty and consisted of casual and seasonal attendance at the village school. At the age of twelve he was sent to the hiring-fair at Newark and employed by a farmer as a servant. From there he was employed in a succession of public houses, mostly in Nottingham, where these experiences gave him a lifelong dislike of alcohol and tobacco. He also worked as a groom, a ferryman and a potman, but there were long periods of unemployment.

His enquiring mind led him gradually to read and think for himself (and attend evening classes at University College, Nottingham) and led him to secularism (he described himself as passionately anti-clerical in outlook and temper), briefly into membership of the free-thinking Unitarian Church, and eventually to socialism and rationalism. Having been a clerk at the Nottingham Blind Institution, he went to London in 1890 as assistant to the secretary of the Woolwich Charity Organisation Society. In 1895 he became secretary to the London School of Economics and Political Science. He joined the Social Democratic Federation and then the Independent Labour Party and became committed to the Ethical and Fabian movements. In 1900 he was an organiser and lecturer in the Union of Ethical Societies, and secretary of the Secular Education League (1907–31).

He stood unsuccessfully as Labour candidate at Huddersfield in the general elections of 1910, and again in 1918. He was Labour member for East Woolwich on London County Council (1919–1925) and in 1922 he was elected to parliament as Labour member for East Woolwich. He was a founder member of the Labour Commonwealth group and gave much of his time to the imperial interests, visiting South Africa, India, Palestine and British Guiana. He was a member of the Imperial Economic Committee (1930), vice-president of the Royal Empire Society, joint treasurer of the Empire Parliamentary Association, vice-chairman of the British Council, and vice-chairman of the Royal Institute of International Affairs (1940–43).

He had only one brief taste of ministerial office – as parliamentary under secretary for India from March to August 1931. There was no place for him in the national government, but he was given a barony, and although he preferred the more stimulating atmosphere of the house of commons, he soon took to the work of the lords 'acquitting himself with dignity and aplomb, earning much praise for his well-argued and well-expressed speeches.'[27] In 1934 the Labour Party won a majority of seats on London County Council and Snell was recalled to be its chairman, serving until 1938. With the formation of the coalition government in 1940, Snell was made captain of the Honourable Corps of Gentlemen at Arms and deputy leader of the house of lords, serving in both offices until his death in 1944.

He wrote two volumes of autobiography: *Daily life in parliament* (1930) and *Men, movements and myself* (1936) and various pamphlets on cooperation, immigration and secular education. He was austerely devoted to his work, and under 'recreations' in his entry in *Who's Who* he entered the word 'none'. 'Snell spent a laborious and penurious life in devoted service to the rationalist and Socialist causes. He had no hobby but reading, and much of that was in subjects connected with his work. His sensitive conscience and keen sense of duty drove him so hard that from time to time his constitution rebelled and he was forced to rest. Although at times he could be witty and good company, he did not make friends easily, and his unremitting preoccupation with ethics and sociology, unrelieved by any winning weaknesses, often made him seem bleak to more human mortals.'[28] Although he was never embarrassed about his early life as a poor farm boy, he must have been sensitive about his illegitimacy and never named his mother in *Who's Who*.

He was appointed a CBE in 1930, created a baron in 1931 and made a CH in

1943 for his services as 'Captain of the Honourable Corps of the Gentlemen at Arms. Deputy Leader of the House of Lords'. He never married and the barony became extinct on his death in 1944.

Earl of Swinton 9 August 1943
Philip Cunliffe-Lister, first Earl of Swinton was a Conservative politician who was given his first cabinet post at the age of thirty-eight and retired from his last when he was past seventy.

He was born Philip Lloyd-Greame in 1884, the youngest son of a Yorkshire squire. He and his wife assumed the surname of Cunliffe-Lister under the terms of the will of his wife's aunt, Lady Cunliffe-Lister. He was educated at Winchester and University College, Oxford. He was called to the bar in 1908 and practiced until the 1914–18 war. He was commissioned in the King's Royal Rifle Corps and was awarded the Military Cross. In 1918 he was elected Conservative member of parliament for Hendon and held the constituency until he was created a peer in 1935. He was parliamentary secretary to the board of trade (1921–22), secretary of the department of overseas trade (1922), and president of the board of trade (1922–24, 1924–29 and in 1931). In 1923 he presided over the imperial economic conference, the first of its kind, which brought agreement on an extension of the system of reciprocal tariff preferences. In his second term of office he helped the struggling British film industry by, among other things, establishing a compulsory quota in cinemas for British films. He was president of the board for three months in 1931 before being moved to be secretary of state for the colonies (1931–35). 'During his four years in office he brought in businessmen as advisers, advanced young men to posts of authority, started an immediate economic survey of the colonies, established a system of entry to the colonial service by selection and required all new entrants to the colonial office to be prepared to serve overseas as well as at home. He also insisted that there should be more business done by direct contacts and less writing of voluminous minutes.'[29]

He was secretary of state for air (1935–38) and achieved a massive expansion of the air force, with manpower increasing from 29,000 to 90,000 and the expansion of the aircraft industry. Among his many decisions was to order the Spitfire and Hurricane fighters straight off the drawing board. He also recruited Winston Churchill as a member of the committee on air defence research in 1935, at a time when Churchill was still in the political wilderness. It proved valuable to both men. Swinton moved to the house of lords in 1935 when he was created a viscount, but in the quieter pastures of the upper chamber, he was not able to reply to those who criticised his pace of rearmament. After a stormy debate in May 1938 Chamberlain decided that his air minister had to be in the commons and Swinton had to go. It was a pity because Swinton was an excellent cabinet minister and but for the misfortune of being a peer, he would have continued and gone to even greater offices. 'His appearance and manner were deceptive and the unwary were apt at first sight to regard him as something akin to the Frenchman's conventional image of a dilettante English "milord". Anybody who fell into this error was quickly disabused on closer acquaintance. He was a man of tough fibre who did not suffer fools gladly. He detested stuffiness and red tape and his vigorous personality blew strong gusts of fresh air through many government departments and offices.'[30]

Swinton's recruitment of Churchill in 1935 was a gesture that was not forgotten after the latter became prime minister. In 1940 Swinton was made chairman of the United Kingdom Commercial Corporation, the agency that was the executive arm of the ministry of economic warfare. Its task was to purchase supplies and materials from neutral countries before they were purchased by enemy nations for the purposes of war production. Also in 1940 Churchill invited Swinton to become chairman of the security executive with responsibility for the security of British ships and supplies.

In 1942 he was appointed to the unprecedented post of cabinet minister resident in West Africa, charged with ensuring the effective cooperation in the prosecution of the war of all the services, civil and military, throughout the British colonies in West Africa; in effect the mobilisation of West Africa's war effort. In October 1944 Churchill recalled him to be the first minister of civil aviation, but there was hardly any time for him to make a mark on his new ministry before the Conservative government was defeated at the election in July 1945. His last two ministerial offices were chancellor of the duchy of Lancaster and minister of materials (1951–52) and secretary of state for commonwealth relations (1952–55). He died in 1972.

He was created a viscount in 1935 as Viscount Swinton, and an earl and a baron in 1955 as Earl of Swinton and Baron Masham. He was appointed a KBE in 1920, a GBE in 1929 and CH in 1943 as 'Minister Resident in West Africa.'

Viscount Hudson 1 January 1944
Robert Hudson was a Conservative politician who as minister of agriculture and fisheries during the 1939–45 war, effectively framed the government's agricultural policy and in many ways was the counterpart of Edward Strutt CH who had done much the same in the 1914–18 war.

He was born in 1886, the eldest son of a wealthy soap manufacturer. He was educated at Eton and Magdalen College, Oxford. He joined the diplomatic service in 1911 and was posted to the embassies in St Petersburg, Washington, Athens and Paris, retiring as a first secretary in 1923. He left the service to enter politics, unsuccessfully contesting Whitehaven in 1923 and winning it in 1924. He was defeated in 1929 but elected for Southport in 1931, and retained the seat until he was created a peer in 1952. His early ministerial offices were parliamentary secretary, ministry of labour (1931–35), minister of pensions (1935–36), parliamentary secretary, ministry of health (1936–37) and parliamentary secretary, ministry of overseas trade (1937–40). In the last of those posts he was among a group of junior ministers who voiced their concern to Neville Chamberlain in December 1938 about the defence programme. Early in 1939 he submitted his resignation to Chamberlain which the latter refused to accept. International developments were beginning to gather pace and Hudson did not press his desire to go.

In April 1940 he was made minister of agriculture and fisheries in the coalition government and continued in office until the defeat of the Conservative caretaker government in 1945. He made spectacular progress in the office, though he had the advantage of a succession of good harvests and there were factors on his side in wartime that would not have been present in time of peace. Food was needed and there was less restraint on departmental expenditure. He had the active support of the agricultural community as part of the civilian war effort. Mechanisation, increased knowledge and the work of the women's land army all helped to ensure that by 1942 the country was two-thirds self-supporting in its food needs. But Hudson had great personal qualities, including a personal interest in farming that made him the successful leader of the wartime agricultural revolution. 'Able, masterful and energetic, he made up for a somewhat brusque manner by the force of his intelligence . . . He spoke plainly and was respected for it. He worked strenuously and others emulated him. Although the support he received, and was always ready to acknowledge, was great in quality and extent, there remained a measure of personal accomplishment for which he richly deserved the gratitude of his fellow countrymen.'[31]

Hudson had farms in Wiltshire and after the war he was able to spend more time with his pedigree herd of British Friesians and was president of the British Friesian Cattle Society. He was also president of the Imperial Institute in South Kensington (later Imperial College) (1953–57) and the United Kingdom's representative on the United Nation's Trusteeship Council. He died in 1957.

He was made a CH in 1944 for his successful revolution of agricultural policy and the citation simply recorded him as 'Minister of Agriculture and Fisheries'. He was created a viscount in 1952.

Earl of Selborne 1 January 1945
Roundell Cecil Palmer, third Earl of Selborne, was a close friend of Winston Churchill, and was minister of economic warfare (1942–45) in the wartime coalition government.

He was born in 1887, scion of a family distinguished for attainment of high office. His father had been first lord of the admiralty and governor-general of South Africa. His father's father had been lord chancellor and his mother's father had been prime minister. With such a pedigree, politics was in his blood. He was educated at Winchester and University College, Oxford and in 1910 he stood for parliament in the Lancashire seat of Newton-le-Willows. He was defeated in the January election that year, but won the seat in the December election and held it until 1918. In 1914 he was commissioned in the Hampshire Regiment and served in the 1914–18 war. In the 1918 election he won the Aldershot division of Hampshire and held the seat until moving to the house of lords in 1941. He showed sufficient promise to be offered minor ministerial rank in two Conservative governments: parliamentary secretary to the board of trade (1922–24) and assistant postmaster-general (1924–29). Although he remained a member of parliament, he held no further ministerial office until the 1939–45 war. In the intervening years he occupied himself as a member of the house of laity of the church assembly of the Church of England, and with managing his estate on the borders of Hampshire and Surrey. In 1934 he became chairman of the Cement Makers' Federation and in 1939 director of cement in the ministry of works and buildings. To be relieved of constituency work he resigned his seat in 1941 and was called to the house of lords as Baron Selborne, one of his father's junior titles.

He became third Earl of Selborne on the death of his father in 1942. In the same year Churchill made him minister of economic warfare in the coalition government. Selborne and Churchill had become close friends during the fight over the Government of India Bill in 1935, admiring each other's gifts and sharing a common political standpoint. Selborne's greatest weakness was his inability to be pragmatic in changing times and he never attained high political office because he appeared a relic of a passing age. 'His uncompromising principles and independence of mind often made him seem like the embodiment of an uneasy conscience in a party busy abandoning so many tenets of its former faith.'[32]

The function of the economic warfare department was primarily to deny the enemy any materials that could nourish their war effort. That meant using the regular intelligence channels of the forces and other government agencies, and the seemingly innocent commercial title of the ministry concealed the fact that it supervised the sabotage work of the Special Operations Executive.

Selborne resigned at the conclusion of the war in Europe on the ground that the waging of economic war against Japan could be better handled by the United States. He returned to the Cement Makers' Federation, remaining chairman until 1951 when he became chairman of the National Provincial Bank (1951–54). He was also a director of the Boots Pure Drug Company from 1936, resigning as deputy chairman in 1963, and chairman of the house of laity of the church assembly (1955–59). He died in 1971.

He was made a CH in 1945 for his services as 'Minister of Economic Warfare since 1942.'

Earl Attlee 8 June 1945

Clement Attlee was a sincere, quiet and self-effacing politician who was prime minister from 1945 to 1951, and the first Labour prime minister to head a government with an independent majority.

He was born in Putney in 1883, the fourth son of a solicitor. He was educated at Haileybury and University College, Oxford, graduating with a second class degree in modern history. He was called to the bar at Inner Temple in 1906. In his early adult life Attlee's politics were essentially Conservative, but with his brother, Tom, he developed an interest in social problems while doing voluntary work in the east end of London. He was converted to socialism by reading the works of John Ruskin and William Morris, and with his brother he joined the Fabian Society in 1907 and became a member of the London School Board. Soon afterwards they also joined the Independent Labour Party. He had a variety of experiences designed to give him insight into working class conditions, beginning with a visit to a boy's club in Stepney in 1905. He lived in east London for fourteen years (for a time in a workman's dwelling in Poplar), where took the post of secretary of Toynbee Hall, was manager of Haileybury House, Stepney and worked for a while in the docks. 'I soon began to learn many things which had hitherto been unrevealed. I found there was a different social code. Thrift, so dear to the middle classes, was not esteemed so highly as generosity. The Christian virtue of charity was practised, not merely preached . . . I found abundant instances of kindness and much quiet heroism in these mean streets. These people were not poor through their lack of fine qualities. The slums were not filled with the dregs of society. Not only did I have countless lessons in practical economics but there was kindled in me a warmth and affection for these people that has remained with me all my life . . . From this it was only a step to examining the whole basis of our social and economic system, I soon began to realise the curse of casual labour. I got to know what slum landlordism and sweating meant. I understood why the Poor Law was so hated. I learned also why there were rebels.'[33]

By 1911 he was lecturing at Ruskin College on trade unionism and trade union law and had abandoned any thought of practising as a barrister. In 1912, largely through the influence of Sidney Webb, he was appointed a lecturer in social science and administration at the London School of Economics, not on the basis of his academic qualifications but because he was considered to have a practical knowledge of social conditions. At the outbreak of the 1914–18 war he was commissioned in the sixth battalion of the South Lancashire Regiment and served in Gallipoli and Mesopotamia, where he was badly wounded at El Hanna. After convalescence in England, he was sent to France in 1918 and served on the western front for the last few months of the war.

He returned to teaching at the London School of Economics and became involved in local politics. In 1919 he was elected mayor of the metropolitan borough of Stepney. He was chosen to head an association of London mayors and led a deputation on foot to Downing Street to convince the prime minister of the gravity of unemployment. In the 1922 general election he was elected Labour member of parliament for Limehouse and held it until its identity was lost in the redrawing of constituency boundaries in 1948. At the 1950 general election he was elected member for West Walthamstow and held the seat until he left parliament in 1955.

Ramsay MacDonald recruited Attlee as his parliamentary secretary (1922–24) and in the short-lived 1924 Labour government he was appointed under secretary of state for war. In 1927–29 he was a member of the statutory commission on India and was principally occupied with a study of the political problems of India. The experience did much to form his later attitudes towards Indian aspirations and his decision as prime minister in the late 1940s that independence could not be refused or delayed. After the Labour victory in the 1929 general election, MacDonald appointed him chancellor of the duchy of Lancaster (1930–31) in succession to Sir Oswald Moseley, and then postmaster-general (1931). Like many of his Labour colleagues, he refused to serve in the national government formed by MacDonald in 1931 and went into opposition. He was one of the few Labour members to retain his seat in the 1931 general election and became deputy leader of the party under George Lansbury. When Lansbury resigned shortly before the 1935 general election, Attlee won the leadership on the second ballot.

The later 1930s were a difficult time for him because he headed a party which included a substantial pacifist element, and which he could not afford to ignore, and his own position remained equivocal until increasing Nazi aggression brought him face to face with the growing threat from the totalitarian powers. During the Spanish civil war he supported the British volunteers fighting against Franco and even visited the International Brigade on the front line in December 1937. He had himself been a zealous pacifist in the years after 1918, but by the late 1930s he was pragmatic enough to accept that this option was no longer viable. Even then he had to face demonstrators in his own constituency chanting 'we want peace: Attlee wants war.'[34]

The military disasters of the spring and summer of 1940 brought Attlee and his Labour colleagues into the coalition government headed by Winston Churchill. He was virtually deputy prime minister although this post did not formally become his until 1942. He never rivalled Churchill for supremacy in the war cabinet and the two men worked together harmoniously to win the war. He first served as lord privy seal (1940–42). The 1942 Japanese advance through Malaya and Singapore caused anxiety in Australia and New Zealand. The methods of reassurance included Attlee taking on the additional post of secretary of state for dominion affairs for sixteen months (1942–43). He then served as lord president of the council (1943–45), with responsibility for the coordination of home policy.

After the conclusion of the war in Europe, Churchill proposed that the coalition should remain in office until the conclusion of the war with Japan. Attlee was inclined to agree but he could not take his party executive with him, and so the Labour Party left the coalition. Churchill formed a caretaker Conservative administration from May to July 1945. The Labour Party swept to power with a substantial majority of 146 over all other parties and launched a massive legislative programme of reform. The Bank of England, the coalmines, civil aviation, cable and wireless services, gas, electricity, railways, road transport and steel were nationalised, and the national health service was created. The government repudiated imperialism by granting independence to India and Pakistan (1947) and to Burma and Ceylon (1948), ending the Palestine mandate (1949) and withdrawing from Egypt. But he also managed to persuade India, intent on republican status, to remain within the commonwealth in spite of that impending change, and devising the 'head of the commonwealth' title for the United Kingdom sovereign as a way of retaining the preeminence of the British crown in the newly developing organisation.

The postwar years were economically severe, not least in 1947 and Attlee, who had no personal charisma, had to face attacks from within his party and even from among his own cabinet colleagues. The problems seemed to have eased when he decided to call a general election in February 1950. With the establishment of the welfare state, exemplified by the health service, family allowances and social insurance, Attlee had reason to hope for a reasonably comfortable majority. In fact the Labour Party was returned to power with a majority of only ten seats, and there began an eighteen months Labour government that remained perilously close to defeat. The great strain on Attlee was made greater by the resignations and deaths of two of his most talented and trusted colleagues – Stafford Cripps and Ernest Bevin – and he never established as close a relationship with their successors Hugh Gaitskell and Herbert Morrison. Bevin in particular had been a very effective and important foreign secretary and a loyal supporter of Attlee against Morrison. A mounting economic crisis brought bitter and personal divisions between cabinet ministers and led to Attlee spending time in hospital to be treated for duodenal ulcers. The Iranian government's decision to nationalise the assets of the Anglo-Iranian oil company only added to the government's embarrassment and difficulties, although Attlee remained convinced that local nationalism must be allowed to take its course.

The Labour Party was defeated in the 1951 general election, and Attlee never again held office. He was tired and weary (he was by now sixty-eight) and the factionalisation of the Labour Party was almost more than he was able to cope with. 'Bitter and prolonged disputes broke out, all turning in reality on a struggle for the succession to the leadership of the party. Attlee assumed almost the attitude of a detached observer to the intrigues and manoeuvres that rent the party and brought it low in public esteem.'[35] He led the party into the 1955 election but with an air of tiredness and with little confidence in victory. The Conservative Party increased its majority to sixty and shortly afterwards he suffered a slight stroke. Although he made a complete recovery he resigned the party leadership in December 1955 with a quietness and minimum of fuss. 'He was a guide rather than an imaginative leader, a pilot in charted waters rather than a pioneer . . . He inspired respect more than devotion. He was a man who stood aloof and whose intimate friendship was rarely given. A steadiness of judgement, a matter-of-fact honesty of approach, and a quite uncommon degree of common sense mark him out as one of the least colourful and most effective British prime ministers.'[36] Few people, even his closest colleagues ever really understood him. It was said that a conversation with Attlee was like throwing biscuits to a dog – 'all you could get out of him was yup, yup, yup.'[37]

Winston Churchill was noted for his Attlee jokes, although he busily denied that he had ever said most of them. Among the many was his remark that an attack by Attlee was 'like being savaged by a pet lamb.' A version of the phrase was used in 1978 by Denis Healey and became enshrined in folklore.

Attlee was made a CH in the dissolution honours list of June 1945, the citation reading, 'Lord President of the Council, 1943–1945. Member of Parliament for the Limehouse division of Stepney since 1922.' Churchill personally added his name to the Labour Party list. He was appointed to the Order of Merit in 1951, and created an earl and a viscount in 1955 on his resignation as Labour leader, taking the titles Earl Attlee and Viscount Prestwood. He was appointed a Knight of the Garter in 1956. He himself wrote the brief rhyme that summed up his rise.

> *Few thought he was even a starter*
> *There were many who thought themselves smarter*
> *But he ended PM, CH and OM,*
> *An earl and Knight of the Garter.*

He published a dry and unrevealing volume of memoirs in 1954 entitled *As it happened*. In old age he attended debates in the house of lords and he seemed to enjoy himself more in retirement than he had in office. He died in his sleep at Westminster Hospital in 1967.

Arthur Greenwood 8 June 1945

Arthur Greenwood was a Labour politician who was undistinguished in his brief ministerial offices but regarded with great affection by both sides of the house of commons.

He was born at Hunslet, Leeds in 1880. His father owned a painting and decorating company and the family was comfortably middle class. He was educated at a local dame school, a Church of England school, Leeds Higher Grade School and then won a scholarship to what is now the University of Leeds. After graduation he was a schoolteacher for a short period and then became head of the economics and law department at Huddersfield Technical College and then lecturer in economics at the University of Leeds. At the same time he developed an active interest in the burgeoning activity of the Workers' Educational Association, becoming chairman of the Yorkshire district and a vice-president of the national organisation.

In 1914 he went to London as general secretary of the council for the study of international relations. He quickly moved into the world of politics as one of Lloyd George's secretariat and was appointed assistant secretary to the reconstruction committee (1917) and then assistant secretary to the ministry of reconstruction (1917–19). In 1918 he unsuccessfully fought Southport for the Labour Party, and in 1920 he was made secretary of the Labour Party's research department. In 1922 he was elected member of parliament for Nelson and Colne. He was parliamentary secretary to the ministry of health in the first Labour government (1924) and minister of health in the second (1929–31). His principal work in the latter appointment was the passing of the Widows, Orphans and Old Age Pensions

Contributory Pensions Act (1929) that increased grants to widows and lowered the age of eligibility.

He opposed the formation of the national government in 1931 and was defeated in the general election that year, but he was never bitter about his Labour colleagues who stayed with prime minister Ramsay MacDonald to form a government with the Conservative Party. 'I have parted company with men who were in the Labour movement as a child', he said. 'Nothing will ever tempt me to say a word against the men who built up that movement.'[38] He returned to the commons at a 1932 by-election as member for Wakefield. His majority was only 344 but he continued to hold the seat with substantially increased majorities until his death. He was elected deputy leader of the Labour Party in 1935 and became an outspoken critic of appeasement. Such was his reputation that he earned himself a personal attack from Adolf Hitler in 1938. In the summer of 1939 the party leader Clement Attlee was ill and Greenwood acted as leader of the opposition during the crucial debate in the commons on 2 September 1939. He spoke for only eight minutes but it was a triumph of measured determination and marked by a lack of rhetoric, a refusal to be contemptuous of the government, and a refusal to villify prime minister Neville Chamberlain. With Herbert Morrison and Hugh Dalton, Greenwood was nominated for the leadership of the Labour Party in November 1939, but the three men later stood aside allowing Attlee to be unanimously reelected.

A few days later his doctors ordered him to rest and thereafter ill-health constantly interrupted his work. On the formation of the coalition government in 1940 he was made minister without portfolio and leader of the parliamentary Labour Party. In January 1941 he was given charge of the government's reconstruction plans and invited Lord Beveridge to make the inquiry that resulted in the Beveridge Report. He was dropped from the government in 1942. After the Labour victory in 1945 he was made lord privy seal and given responsibility for coordinating the work of all government departments concerned with national insurance. He was additionally paymaster-general (1946–47). In April 1947 he was moved to be minister without portfolio and left the government five months later at the request of the prime minister to make way for 'some younger members of the party.'[39] It appeared that Greenwood had become reluctant to conduct his morning's business from anywhere except the 'snuggery' of the Charing Cross Hotel.

A more ruthless and less scrupulous politician would have held on to ministerial office, but it was not in Greenwood's nature. He was a modest and humane man, free of personal ambition and any tendency to be histrionic, loyal to his colleagues and to the end principally concerned with working class education. Although his ministerial record was limited and undistinguished, his total integrity was never in doubt and he was regarded with warmth and affection across party boundaries. Before his death, in 1954, he had the pleasure of seeing his son Anthony (1911–82) elected to parliament in 1946.

He was made a CH in 1945. The citation perhaps pointedly made no mention of his ministerial offices, merely describing him as 'Member of Parliament for Nelson and Colne, 1922–1931, and for Wakefield since 1932'.

General Lord Ismay 17 August 1945
Although reaching the army rank of general, the military career of Hastings Lionel

'Pug' Ismay was quite unexceptional. He was less a soldier and more a liaison officer between the government and the armed forces during the 1939–45 war, and later a cabinet minister and the first secretary-general of NATO (1952–57).

He was born in 1887, the younger son of Sir Stanley Ismay, a barrister who rose to become chief judge of the Mysore Chief Court, India. He was educated at Charterhouse and the Royal Military College, Sandhurst. He joined the 21st Cavalry in 1907 and returned to India where he began a distinguished military career serving initially on the north west frontier from 1908. He was promoted captain in 1914 and saw active service in Somaliland (1914–20). He was mentioned in despatches and appointed to the DSO but never reached the main theatre of war. 'He thus faced a heavy handicap in his profession, and he overcame it by becoming a bureaucrat.'[40]

He returned to India again after the war and served on the staff of the commander-in-chief of the Indian army. He was promoted brevet-major (1918), brevet-lieutenant-colonel (1928) and colonel (1932), but from the mid-1920s, his military career took a decided turn away from the front line towards the civil service and the politics of Whitehall. In 1925 he returned to London from India and was successively: assistant secretary to the committee of imperial defence (1926–30), military secretary to the viceroy of India (1931–33), general staff officer at the war office (1933–36) and deputy secretary (1936–38) and secretary (1938) to the committee of imperial defence. In 1936 he was faced with the choice of the committee or command of a brigade and he chose the former. 'It was like saying goodbye to the dreams of my youth,' he said later, 'but reason quickly banished sentiment and I never regretted my decision.'[41] It was an accurate self-assessment of where his own abilities lay.

At the outbreak of the 1939–45 war, Ismay was made deputy secretary (military) to the war cabinet, becoming the chief of staff to Winston Churchill and later to Clement Attlee when the latter became prime minister and minister of defence in 1945. Churchill made him a member of the chiefs of staff committee and Ismay was later thought of as a fourth chief of staff. He became one of Churchill's ablest and most loyal lieutenants and almost worshipped him as a hero. 'My whole heart went out to him in his superhuman task, and I made a silent vow that, whatever he asked of me, I would do my utmost to give.'[42] Despite his primarily civilian role, his army promotion was rapid: major-general (1939), lieutenant-general (1942) and general (1944). He participated in a number of the important international conferences, including Moscow, Tehran and Yalta, and retired in 1946. In 1946–47 he was chief of staff to Lord Mountbatten in the negotiations for India's independence, and remained in India until the autumn of 1947. In 1948 was made chairman of the council responsible for organising the 1951 Festival of Britain.

When Churchill returned to power in October 1951. Ismay was called out of retirement and made secretary of state for commonwealth relations, but held the office only until March 1952 when he was chosen to be the first secretary general of NATO. He was simultaneously vice-chairman of the North Atlantic Council. The chairmanship of the council itself continued to be held by the foreign minister of one of the member countries rotating annually, until 1956 when the secretary general of NATO became the chairman of the North Atlantic Council at whatever level of government representation it chose to meet. He was an ideal candidate for the post, not because he was a general but because he was a gifted politician who knew how to handle people. He had 'an almost uncanny skill for smoothing over difficulties and averting friction. His power resided in friendliness, unlimited patience, and a quick sense of humour, combined with a high degree of intelligence and a wide knowledge of the processes of government.'[43] He retired as secretary general in 1957 and died in 1965.

He was made a CB in 1931, a KCB in 1940, a CH in Churchill's resignation honours list in 1945 for his services as 'Chief of Staff to the Minister of Defence since 1940'. His biographer, Sir Ronald Wingate, thought the CH a curious honour to give to Ismay when the three chiefs of staff were given peerages in the same list, and when the CH was not given to soldiers. Wingate trumpeted his belief that Ismay was really a fourth chief of staff and should have received similar recognition. In fact the CH was an entirely appropriate honour for a man who had not functioned as a soldier for many years and was being honoured for his work as a civilian liaison officer and trusted confidant of Churchill. But it was not to be Ismay's final honour. Wingate claimed that Attlee felt that Ismay's services had been inadequately recognised,[44] and he was made a GCB in June 1946. After leaving government service he was created a baron in 1947. The supporters to his armorial bearings recorded his distant military career: a private of the Somaliland Camel Corps and a sowar of the Indian Cavalry. He was made a privy councillor in 1951 on entering the cabinet, and his final honour was to be made a KG in 1957 on retirement from NATO. He and his wife had no sons and the barony became extinct on his death.

Leopold Amery 17 August 1945
Leo Amery was a Conservative politician and a dedicated though liberal imperialist who found his niche as secretary of state for the colonies in the 1920s and then as secretary of state for India and Burma during the 1939–45 war. He had a quick and intellectual mind and sometimes found it difficult to restrain himself from interfering in matters that were none of his concern. He is chiefly remembered for bringing down the government of Neville Chamberlain in 1940.

He was born at Gorakpur, India in 1873 where his father was working for the Indian forest department. He claimed that his mother was Hungarian and fled Hungary after the uprising of 1848. He did not divulge the fact that she was also Jewish, and he did his utmost to conceal this for the rest of his life. In his autobiography he referred to her Jewish born Hungarian stepfather, Dr Johann Moritz Leitner, and to her brother Gottlieb only by the initials of their forenames. He never disclosed his mother's name at birth, nor the identity of her real father. Amery himself always recorded his name as Leopold Maurice Stennett Amery; in fact it was Leopold Moritz Stennett Amery.

He was educated at Harrow and Balliol College, Oxford. His time at Oxford was distinguished by first class honours in classical moderations (1894) and literae humaniores (1896), and election as a fellow of All Souls in 1897. After leaving Oxford he pursued the study of modern languages and foreign politics, travelling through Turkey and the Balkans. There he attracted the attention of *The Times* and was offered first a temporary appointment in Berlin and then in London as a member of the editorial staff until 1909.

He was called to the bar by Inner Temple in 1902 but never practised. In 1906 he unsuccessfully contested East Wolverhampton as a Unionist and Tariff Reformer. He stood again in 1908 and in January 1910, on the second occasion losing by only three votes. In December 1910 he stood against George Lansbury at Bow and Bromley but was again defeated. In May 1911 he was returned unopposed for South Birmingham (later the Sparkbrook division), which he represented until his defeat in 1945. He served in the 1914–18 war in Flanders and the Balkans before returning to the commons in 1916. On the formation of the war cabinet, Amery became assistant secretary. He produced the final draft of the 1917 Balfour declaration that committed the United Kingdom to establishing a Jewish national homeland in Palestine. Despite his desire to conceal his own Jewish origins, Amery used his influence on behalf of Jewish causes whenever he could. In 1919–21 he was parliamentary under secretary to Lord Milner at the colonial office. In 1921 he moved to be parliamentary and financial secretary to the admiralty, and on the fall of the coalition government in 1922, first lord of the admiralty (1922–23).

With the return of a Conservative government in 1924, he was made secretary of state for the colonies, a position to which he was well suited as a lifelong imperialist devoted to the development and solidarity of the empire. The development of imperial trade appeared as a theme in many of his speeches and in 1925 he was given the additional title of secretary of state for dominions affairs on the creation of a separate department. In that capacity Amery became the first Conservative minister to visit the Irish Free State, and from July 1927 to February 1928 he made a six months tour of the now independent dominions. He had travelled 55,000 miles and delivered 300 speeches, some of which were published in his book *The empire in the new era* (1928).

The defeat of the Conservative government in 1929 excluded him from the cabinet for more than eleven years. 'He half minded and half did not. Whenever a reshuffle became imminent he began to quiver with anticipation, but then some mixture of integrity and over-excitement made him constantly blot his copybook with some unfortunately timed piece of over-criticism.'[45] From the backbenches he continued to expound his views in writing: *Empire and prosperity* (1930) presented his arguments against free trade and in favour of imperial preference; *A vision of empire* (1935) was his personal confession of faith; *The German colonial claim* (1939) and *Days of fresh air* (1940) were travelogues. The theme was continued by *In the rain and the sun* (1946), an account of his walking and mountaineering experiences.

In the early months of the 1939–45 war, Amery made his celebrated and devastating speech against Chamberlain in the house of commons, when he cruelly quoted Cromwell's contemptuous dismissal of the Long Parliament: 'You have sat here too long for any good you have been doing. Depart, I say, and let us have done with you. In the name of God, go!'

In the coalition government of Winston Churchill, his imperial experiences were put to use as secretary of state for India and Burma (1940–45). His loyalty to the concept of empire caused certain misgivings among Indian nationalists, but Amery was not a diehard colonialist. His tour of the dominions had given him firsthand experience of their successful development as independent nations within the empire and he envisaged complete autonomy for India, outlined in his book *India and freedom* (1942). 'He might have secured more active support from his colleagues in the coalition cabinet had not his restless energy and amazing industry made him prone to write letters and memoranda to them on any matters, whether directly affecting his own office or not.'[46] It was also said that he might have been prime minister had he been half a head taller (he was 5 feet 4 inches) and his speeches half an hour shorter.

'He was a man not so much of government as of ideas and public concern. He would be ill at ease in any party today and he was altogether rather admirable.'[47]

He lost his seat in the 1945 general election and although he harboured hopes of returning to the commons, he was over seventy and the possibility was remote. He continued to write, commenting shrewdly on the issues of his day: *The Washington loan agreements* (1946), *The Elizabethan spirit* (1948), *A balanced economy* (1954), and three volumes of memoirs entitled *My political life* (1953–55). The last years of his life were overshadowed by an appalling personal tragedy: his elder son, John Amery (1912–45), was hanged for treason at Wandsworth prison on 19 December 1945 as a wartime Nazi. Leo Amery died in 1955.

He was made a CH in the coalition resignation list in 1945 for his services as 'Secretary of State for India and for Burma, 1940–1945. Member of Parliament for the Sparkbrook (formerly South) Division of Birmingham, 1911–1945.'

Alfred Ernest Brown 17 August 1945
Ernest Brown was a competent and hardworking minister with a stentorian voice who served in the national and coalition governments of the 1930s and 40s. He was heavily criticised from time to time, but it was due more to the inherently difficult ministries that he was given than to any ineptitude on his own part.

He was born at Torquay in 1881 and educated there. His father was a Baptist preacher, and from him he learned the art of public speaking. 'Gifted with a tremendous and far reaching platform voice and an unusual aptness and power of persuasion, he soon found himself employing them on behalf of the Liberal cause and in due course became one of the most effective of the Liberal platform speakers, especially in the open air.'[48]

His early life was spent in the service of the Baptist Union. In the 1914–18 war he was commissioned in the Somerset Light Infantry, mentioned in dispatches, and awarded the Military Cross. After the war he unsuccessfully stood for election to parliament, in Salisbury in 1918 and 1922, and in Mitcham in February 1923. He won Rugby in November 1923 but was defeated in 1924. In 1927 he won Leith and continued to represent it as a Liberal National until he was defeated in 1945. He held a series of increasingly important ministerial offices: parliamentary secretary to the ministry of health (1931–32), secretary of the mines department (1932–35), minister of labour (1935–40) and additionally minister of national service (1939–40). He was responsible for the Agricultural Unemployment Insurance Act 1936, which extended the principle of insurance to all workers in agriculture, horticulture and forestry. In 1937 the Trades Union Congress passed a unanimous resolution of thanks to him for the part he had played in organising the workers in the distributive trades.

With the formation of the coalition government Brown was briefly secretary of state for Scotland (1940–41) and then minister of health (1941–43). In the latter department he faced criticisms over the accommodation of workers and other housing difficulties and in June 1943 he faced a vote in the commons that was in effect an attack on his competence, though no one doubted his sincerity and conscientiousness. In November 1943 he was moved to the office of chancellor of the duchy of Lancaster and remained there until the end of the coalition government in 1945. He was minister of aircraft production in the Conservative caretaker government of May to July 1945. Defeat in the 1945 general election ended his political career. He died in 1962.

He was made a CH in the coalition resignation list. The citation was the usual record of his ministerial career: 'Minister of Labour 1935–1940, and Minister of National Service 1939–1940; Secretary of State for Scotland 1940–1941; Minister of Health 1941–1943; Chancellor the Duchy of Lancaster 1943–1945; Minister of Aircraft Production, May-July 1945. Member of Parliament for Leith 1927–1945.'

Margaret Bondfield 1 January 1948
Minister of Labour in Ramsay MacDonald's national government 1929–31, Margaret Bondfield was the first British woman cabinet minister.

She was born in Chard, Somerset in 1873, the daughter of textile worker, who was well known in the area for his radical beliefs. At the age of fourteen she left home to serve an apprenticeship in a draper's shop in Brighton in poor conditions. She had to 'live in', sleeping in a dormitory. Her personal belongings were stored in a box under the bed and entering the dormitory during daytime incurred a fine.

She struck up a friendship with a customer – Louisa Martindale – a strong advocate of women's rights, and an importance influence on her political development. When Martindale died in 1914, Margaret Bondfield wrote to her daughters saying how much she owed to their mother. 'Your mother is one of the great immortals who cannot die as long as memory lasts. She was a vivid influence in my life, the first woman of broad culture I had met, she seemed to recognise me and make me recognise myself as a person of independent thought and action . . . My first talk with your mother was the great event of that period of my life . . . She put me in the way of knowledge that has been of help to many score of my shop mates. She lent me books on social questions, which prepared me to take my proper place in the Labour movement.'[49]

In 1894 she went to live with her brother Frank in London and found work in a shop. After a short period she was elected to the Shop Assistants Union District Council and began contributing articles to the union journal *The Shop Assistant*. In 1898 she created a storm when she described the ideal married couple as one in which both went out to work and shared the household tasks between them. In 1896 Clementina Black of the Women's Industrial Council asked her to investigate the pay and conditions of shop workers. Her report was published in 1898 and in the same year she was appointed assistant secretary of the Shop Assistants' Union.

As a result of her work for the Women's Industrial Council, she became known as the country's leading expert on shop workers and gave evidence to the select committee on shops (1902) and the select committee on the truck system (1907). She resigned from the Shop Assistants' Union in 1908 and became secretary of the Women's Labour League. She was also active in the Women's Co-operative Guild that was campaigning for minimum wage legislation, an improvement in child welfare and action to lower the infant mortality rate. She was a member of the TUC general council 1918–24 and 1926–29, and chairman in 1923.

In 1910 the Liberal government asked her to serve as a member of its advisory committee on the Health Insurance Bill. Her efforts were rewarded when she persuaded the government to include maternity benefits and she also influenced their decision to make the benefit the property of the mother.

She was chairman of the Adult Suffrage Society, but unlike some members of the National Union of Women's Suffrage Societies and the Women's Social and Political Union, she was totally opposed to the idea that initially only certain categories of women should be given the vote. She believed that a limited franchise would disadvantage the working class and feared that it might act as a barrier against the granting of adult suffrage. Consequently she was unpopular with middle class suffragettes who saw limited suffrage as an important step in the struggle to win the vote. She also disagreed with the pro-war position that the WSPU took during the 1914–18 war over the recruitment of men to fight in the army. She vigorously opposed the war and conscription and instead supported a negotiated peace with Germany.

In 1923 she was elected Labour member of parliament for Northampton. When Ramsay MacDonald became prime minister in 1924 he appointed Bondfield as parliamentary secretary to the minister of labour. She was defeated in the 1924 general election, but re-elected, for Wallsend, in 1926. When MacDonald became prime minister for a second time in 1929 he appointed Bondfield as his new minister of labour, and she became the first woman cabinet minister. In the financial crisis of 1931, she upset many members of the Labour Party when she supported the government policy of depriving some married women of their unemployment benefit and she lost her seat in the general election later that year. Like other Labour Party members who chose to support MacDonald's national government, she was never forgiven by the party and never returned to the house of commons.

She remained interested in social issues and was chairman of the Women's Group on Public Welfare (1939–45), vice-president of the National Council of Social Service and served as a justice of the peace. She died in 1953.

She was made a CH in 1948 'for public services.'

William Whiteley 10 June 1948
William Whiteley was chief whip in the 1945–51 Labour government. Like many chief whips before and after him, of any political party, he was one of the least known members of parliament, and one of the most powerful.

He was born in 1882 in Elland, County Durham where his father was a colliery check-weighman. He was educated at Brandon Colliery School near his home. He was raised in an atmosphere of trade union activities and the Labour Party, although he was a late entrant to politics. He taught accountancy and short hand in night schools before his first and unsuccessful attempt, in 1918, to enter parliament. He was elected for the Blaydon division of Durham in 1922 and held the seat until 1931. Recognised for his strong will, he was made a Labour whip in 1927, and continued in that post in the Labour government (1929–31). 'He was in appearance and demeanour the least likely man imaginable to have come into public life from the pits – tall, good-looking, always immaculately dressed, genial, but a man of iron will when necessary – he might have passed for a bishop in mufti.'[50]

After losing his seat in 1931 life was financially difficult and he never had full time employment. But he won Blaydon again in 1935 and retained the seat until his retirement in 1955. He resumed his work as a whip in May 1940 when he was appointed comptroller of the household. In March 1942 he became joint parliamentary secretary to the treasury and chief Labour whip. He became chief government whip with the Labour Party victory in 1945. The government had a large majority that presented no difficulties in the division lobbies. But he did from time to time have to deal with impending revolts on the backbenches, awkward members who were not inclined always to follow the party line, and incipient rebellions against the authority of the prime minister.

Between the elections of February 1950 and October 1951 the situation changed dramatically. The Labour Party governed with a slender majority in the house of commons. Defeat was a very real possibility and in August 1950 one Labour member left the party to sit as an independent. Numerous crises could have brought down the government, but it was due to the efforts of Whiteley and his team that the government lasted as long as it did with such a small majority. He continued as Labour chief whip on the opposition benches (1951–55) but was forced to resign through ill-health in June 1955 (much to his bitter resentment) and died a few months later.

Whiteley was made a CH in 1948. The citation read: 'Parliamentary Secretary to the Treasury since 1945. Joint Parliamentary Secretary to the Treasury, 1942–1945. Member of Parliament for the Blaydon Division of Durham, 1922–1931 and since 1935.' The honour was conferred on the personal initiative of Clement Attlee. It was a tribute from a prime minister who recognised how much he owed to his chief whip. But cautious voices were raised: 'In addition you mentioned to me that the Chief Whip might be considered for a CH. This would be the first time I think that a serving Chief Whip had received such an honour and you may wish to consider whether it would be desirable to start the practice now.'[51]

The Honourable Sir Stafford Cripps 1 January 1951
Lawyer, statesman and diplomat, and probably the most distinguished cabinet minister in the government of Clement Attlee (1945–51), Stafford Cripps was an upper class radical who approached politics not with the desire for self-advancement, but with incisive common sense and almost as a messianic visionary intent on salvation.

He was born in 1889, the youngest son of the first Lord Parmoor, a Conservative member of parliament who was a staunch advocate of peace in the 1914–18 war. He was educated at Winchester and University College, London (where he studied chemistry), and called to the bar at Middle Temple in 1913. Being unfit for service in the 1914–18 war he worked in a government factory as an assistant superintendent in 1915 but suffered a breakdown in health between 1917 and 1919. After the war he returned to the bar and specialised in patent and corporation work. He was made King's Counsel in 1927.

He joined the Labour Party in 1929 and was solicitor general (1930–31), receiving the customary knighthood on his appointment. He resigned on the formation of the national government in 1931 but was elected member of parliament for Bristol East in the general election that year. He became a leading spokesman of the left wing of the Labour Party, championing a united front by the parties of the left, and helped to found the Socialist League in 1932. A 1933 assessment by the *British Weekly* summed up his charisma. 'This tall, buoyant scientist with the dark, piercing eyes, has about him the candour of a boy. That is the secret of his present stand. Comparatively new to political leadership, his interest is to discover with a scientist's logic and lack of sentimentality, the exact implications of the present position and, having discovered them, to take the people . . . into his confidence . . . He has given a lead which has rallied the whole of the younger generation of socialists to his side.'[52] In 1936 he advocated a united front with the communists, which widened in 1938 as an anti-fascist popular front, and led to his expulsion from the Labour Party in 1939. He felt the bruising of that experience until the end of his life. Denis Healey described Cripps as 'a political ninny of the most superior quality,' and remembered some of Cripps' more naive comments from the pre-war years. 'He told the people of Stockport that he did not believe that "war would be a bad thing for the British working class; it would be a disaster for the profit-makers and the capitalists, but not necessarily for the working class".'[53]

In the early months of the 1939–45 war, Winston Churchill who appointed him ambassador to the Soviet Union in May 1940 put his communist ties to good use. On his return in January 1942 Churchill brought him into the war cabinet as lord privy seal and leader of the house of commons. In the same year he was sent to India with a self-government plan. The meetings, known as the Cripps mission, took place in Delhi between 22 March and 12 April 1942. The talks failed and increased the breach between British government and the Indian Congress Party. In November 1942 he was made minister of aircraft production and held the office for the remainder of the war.

In 1945 he was readmitted to the Labour Party and appointed president of the board of trade (in the new Labour government of Clement Attlee), initiating the postwar export drive. He returned to India to negotiate independence in 1946, and the failure of this further mission (because of the antagonism between Hindus and Muslims) is often seen as the point at which the partition of India became inevitable. In September 1947 he was appointed to the newly created office of minister of economic affairs and in November the same year became additionally chancellor of the exchequer in succession to Hugh Dalton who had been forced to resign in the wake of a financial scandal. The country was in the throes of a severe economic crisis, which Cripps sought to counter with a policy of austerity. By continuing rationing and imposing strict economic controls, he was able to slow inflation while maintaining full employment and without cutting back the government's welfare programmes. However, despite a vigorous export drive, the country's balance of payments situation remained serious, and in 1949 he was reluctantly forced to devalue the pound by 30%.

The onset of cancer compelled him to resign from the government and from parliament in October 1950 and he went to Switzerland for treatment in November. There was some improvement in the following year and he returned to his home in the Cotswolds in October 1951; it was only a brief respite. He returned to Switzerland early in 1952 for further treatment and died at Zurich in April. Cripps was a devout member of the Church of England and his faith sustained him during his last declining months. A testament that he had written in the summer of 1950 was found two years after his death. 'I want no memorial except this. I would like some really capable person to try to translate my actions and my hopes and what I have tried to do for the world. Not because I want my name to live on but because I want my effort to live on and to inspire others to work for the eventual salvation of mankind which we all look for.'[54]

He was made a CH in 1951 for his services as 'Lately Chancellor of the Exchequer'. Because of his illness and long absences abroad, he was never invested with the badge, which was posted to his widow in April 1952.

Lord Morrison of Lambeth 30 November 1951
Herbert Morrison organised the Labour Party in London and was the most prominent Labour politician in London local government in the 1920s and 1930s. A

career in national government in the 1940s was less successful and bore too much evidence of his frustration at being denied the leadership of the Labour Party.

He was born in Brixton in 1888, the son of a policeman. He was educated at a board school but left at the age of fourteen to become an errand boy. After periods as a shop assistant and a telephone operator, he earned a living as a journalist and worked as circulation manager for the first official Labour paper, the *Daily Citizen* (1912–15). He had joined the Brixton branch of the Independent Labour Party in 1906. In 1910 he became honorary secretary of the south London federation of ILP branches, and his work led to the decision of the London Trades Council to call a conference and form the London Labour Party, and Morrison became its secretary (1915–47) and London became his power base. He had no interest in doctrinaire politics or ideology. As a child from the inner city, he had a lifelong preoccupation with such urban concerns as housing, transport, health and education, and the remedying of social grievances. 'He was, in fact, a rather unusual type of Labour leader. He had not come up through the trade union movement, nor was he one of the middle-class intellectuals who formed the other major group in the senior ranks. A working class boy who was largely self-educated, he had risen by virtue of his organisational skills, tactical and argumentative skills, and he had no sign of an inferiority complex. Indeed his bearing was a mixture of Cockney brashness and the self-confidence which arises from knowledge, competence and a solidly-based political position.'[55]

He began attending meetings of Lambeth Metropolitan Council and in 1912 he unsuccessfully contested the Vauxhall division on behalf of the London Labour Party. As he had lost the sight of one eye in an accident shortly after his birth, he was not a combatant in the 1914–18 war but he kept his organisation going and in 1919 it won 15 out of 124 seats in the elections for London County Council. The London Labour Party won a majority or became the largest party in sixteen of London metropolitan boroughs. Morrison became mayor of Hackney (1920–21), an alderman on Hackney borough council (1921–25) and a member of the LCC (1922–45, leader of the council 1934–40). He was first elected to parliament in 1923 and served as member for South Hackney (1923–24, 1929–31 and 1935–45), East Lewisham (1945–51) and South Lewisham (1951–59).

He was a strong supporter of Ramsay MacDonald and was rewarded with appointment as minister of transport in the second Labour government (1929–31). He was responsible for the London Passenger Transport Act 1931 which created the London Passenger Transport Board. But for his defeat at the 1931 election he might have become leader of the Labour Party on the retirement of George Lansbury in 1935, but he had been out of the commons for four years, and Clement Attlee was preferred (by 88 votes to Morrison's 48).

On the formation of the coalition government in 1940, Morrison was made first minister of supply (1940) and then home secretary and minister of home security (1940–45). The latter post arose from his close knowledge of London and its citizens, because his chief task was to reassure Londoners that all possible measures were being taken to protect them against air raids. He rose to the task, visiting all areas involved in civil defence, creating a national fire service and instituting a fire guard with regular fire-watching duties. 'Morrison typified the irrepressible London civilian who made a joke out of nights at the office or the factory, who rallied round after the raids and would not let any German actions depress him.'[56]

The period after the Labour victory in 1945 was a less fruitful period. Morrison repeatedly and unsuccessfully renewed his ambitions for the highest office. Attlee made him lord president of the council, leader of the house of commons and deputy prime minister (1945–51). As soon as the election victory was secure there was evidence of a move to push Attlee to one side and replace him with a more vigorous candidate. Morrison supported the move but denied that he himself had any interest – although he was the preferred candidate of Harold Laski and Edith Summerskill. In 1947 there were further moves, led by Stafford Cripps, to persuade Attlee to stand aside. According to Hugh Dalton, Morrison initially supported the plan on the understanding that he himself would replace Attlee, and withdrew his support when he discovered that Ernest Bevin was the favoured candidate. In March 1951 Morrison replaced Bevin as foreign secretary. He suggested that he got the office on the ground of his seniority; Attlee later said that Morrison had demanded it. Whatever the truth, it was a bad move. Friendly critics observed that Morrison knew Londoners perfectly and other English fairly well. The Scots and the Welsh were strangers to him, and foreigners were incomprehensible. His period also coincided with the Iranian government's nationalisation of British-owned oil wells. Morrison favoured direct military action. Attlee had to restrain him, saying that the age for that kind of action was well past. Morrison had an exceptionally deep knowledge and understanding of domestic politics, but he was a poor foreign secretary who never mastered his brief.

In 1956, he tried one last time for the leadership of the Labour Party, but it was then too late. Attlee had held on to the leadership (deliberately) until Morrison was sixty-eight, and then declared that his successor should be someone who had been born in the twentieth century rather than the nineteenth. Morrison came third with 40 votes (behind 70 votes for Aneurin Bevan and 157 votes for Hugh Gaitskell). Time had run out for Morrison and ignoring requests to the contrary, he resigned as deputy leader. He retired from the commons in 1959 and died in 1965.

He was made a CH in the 1951 resignation honours list, the citation reading 'Secretary of State for Foreign Affairs, March–October, 1951. Lord President of the Council, 1945–1951. Member of Parliament for South Lewisham since 1950, for East Lewisham, 1945–1950, and for South Hackney, 1935–1945, 1929–1931 and 1923–1924.' He was created a life peer in 1959, taking the title Lord Morrison of Lambeth.

Walter Elliot 5 June 1952

Walter Elliot was a Scottish medically trained Conservative politician who held a number of cabinet offices in the 1930s.

He was born in 1888 and educated at Glasgow Academy and the University of Glasgow. He graduated with degrees in science (1910) and medicine (1913). He served in France in the 1914–18 war, finishing with the rank of colonel, and was awarded the MC.

In 1918 he was elected Unionist member of parliament for Lanark. With a degree in medicine, it was not surprising that he should have been appointed parliamentary under secretary of health for Scotland in 1923. He lost his seat in the general election that year but was returned as member of parliament for the Kelvingrove division of Glasgow in 1924 and resumed his government office, holding it (with a slight change of title) until 1929. With the formation of the national government in 1931 he was financial secretary to the treasury (1931–32), minister of agriculture (1932–36), secretary of state for Scotland (1936–38) and then minister of health (1938–40). He was dropped from the government when Churchill formed his administration in 1940, but took on the role of public relations officer at the war office (1941–42). He was defeated at Kelvingrove by 88 votes in the 1945 general election, but he returned to the commons the next year as member for the Scottish universities. When the university constituencies were abolished in 1950, he was returned for Kelvingrove with a majority of 1,224, holding it until his death in 1958. The last of his public appointments was as lord high commissioner to the general assembly of the Church of Scotland in 1956 and 1957. A popular figure in Scottish life, Elliot was elected rector of the University of Aberdeen (1933–36) and of the University of Glasgow (1947–50).

His domestic life was marked by an early tragedy. He married his first wife in 1919. While on their honeymoon on the island of Skye, they were on a mountain walk when a mist descended. Helen Elliot fell down a mountainside and was killed. Walter Elliot also fell and was seriously injured. He married again in 1934, and after his death in 1958 his widow was created Baroness Elliot of Harwood as one of the first four life peeresses. She died in 1993.

Elliot was an exuberant figure in the house of commons and in government, and was respected for his sincerity and for his intellectual ability to grasp a problem and deal with the tasks before him. The principal criticism of him was the way in which he cascaded his thoughts on to his hearers. 'Elliot's wealth of ideas and the eagerness with which he poured them out as he turned rapidly from point to point, detracted from the full power of his argument. It was written of him in his early days in the house that he had none of the airs and graces of debate, that he "attacks instead of wooing his subject", and that "his speech has the jerky, breathless movement of thought".'[57]

He was made a CH in 1952. The citation read: 'Member of Parliament for Lanark, 1918–1923; for Kelvingrove Division, 1924–45; for Scottish Universities, 1946–1950; and for Kelvingrove Division since 1950. Minister of Health, 1938–1940; Secretary of State for Scotland, 1936–1938; Minister of Agriculture and Fisheries, 1932–1936; Financial Secretary to the Treasury, 1931–1932. For political and public services.'

Lord Chuter-Ede 1 June 1953

James Chuter Ede was a former teacher who became home secretary in the post-war Labour government of Clement Attlee. His patience, judgement and common sense made him a highly respected figure in the house of commons.

He was born at Epsom in 1882 and educated at the Epsom National Schools, Dorking High School, Battersea Pupil Teachers' Centre and Christ's College, Cambridge. He was a schoolteacher in Surrey elementary schools until 1914. In the 1914–18 war he served in the East Surreys and the Royal Engineers as a non-commissioned officer. He had a parallel career as a member of Epsom Urban District Council (1908–27 and 1933–37) and Surrey County Council (1914–49, vice-chairman 1930–33, chairman 1933–37). He was charter mayor of Epsom and Ewell in 1937.

Beginning his political life as a Liberal, he moved to the Labour Party and first entered national politics as member of parliament for Mitcham (March–November

1923). He was elected for South Shields in 1929, defeated in 1931, reelected in 1935, and held the seat until his retirement in 1964. In the wartime coalition government his experience was put to use as parliamentary secretary to the ministry of education (1940–45) and he carried responsibility for preparing the 1944 Education Act and guiding it through the committee stage in the commons. With the Labour victory in 1945 he was made home secretary and held the office until the government was defeated in 1951. His time at the home office was marked by a period of turbulent disagreement between the two chambers of parliament over the Criminal Justice Bill in 1947–48 and the fate of the death penalty. Ede promised a free vote on the issue but strongly recommended that hanging be retained. The commons decided on a five-year suspension and Ede then announced that he would recommend commutation of all death sentences in anticipation of the law being permanently changed. For that he was much criticised by the judiciary. The lords reversed the commons vote and Ede then announced that each case would be considered on its merits. The lords then rejected a compromise clause prescribing hanging for certain categories of murder, and Ede advised the commons not to persist with the compromise. Important penal reform was at stake and therefore it was pointless to provoke an unnecessary fight with the upper chamber. His own views eventually moved towards abolition and he was able to vote for it in the lords a few weeks before his death in 1965. He was briefly leader of the house of commons for seven months in 1951. There his patience, tact and good humour secured the passage of legislation at a time when the government had no more than a single-figure majority. The Labour defeat that year relegated him to the opposition benches and he never held office again. He retired from the shadow cabinet in 1955 and from the house of commons in 1964 and died in 1965.

'His wit and wisdom were a constant refreshment to the house and a salutary corrective to vagaries and vacuity. He brought to it the finest qualities of the best type of schoolmaster – patience, good humour, tolerance and an acute instinct for detecting humbug and woolly-mindedness. His sympathy for the weaknesses of humankind and his understanding of the criminal mind, derived from long experience on the bench, were invaluable assets to him as home secretary . . . Ede was no puritan. He wanted his fellow citizens to enjoy life as fully as he did. Horse racing was one of his passions. Nothing would keep him from the Derby. He thought betting was folly but he saw no sin in it and he had a soft spot for the street bookmaker. Although he was a total abstainer he saw no reason to deny reasonable indulgence to others. His was indeed a remarkably balanced and well rounded personality of a quality which can ill be spared from public life.'[58]

He was made a CH in the Coronation Honours List 1953. The usual record appeared in the *London Gazette*: 'Labour Member of Parliament for Mitcham, 1923, and for South Shields, 1929–1931 and since 1935. Secretary of State for the Home Department, 1945–51; Leader of the House of Commons, March-October, 1951. For political and public services.' He was created a life peer on leaving the commons in 1964.

Thomas Johnston 1 June 1953
Tom Johnston was secretary of state for Scotland during the 1939–45 war.

He was born at Kirkintolloch, Dunbartonshire in 1882, and educated at Lairdsland Public School, Lenzie Academy and the University of Glasgow where he was a contemporary of Walter Elliot CH.

After a number of commercial experiences, he developed a taste for journalism and founded the weekly socialist journal *Forward* in 1906 and edited it for twenty-seven years (1919–46). It became the most prominent socialist publication in Scotland and its influence probably secured the election of a number of Labour members from Clydeside in the 1922 general election. Johnston was prominent in Clydeside local politics, having been a member of Kirkintilloch town council and was elected member for West Stirling and Clackmannan. He was defeated in 1924 but won Dundee at a by-election in the same year. He was again elected for West Stirlingshire in 1929 and was appointed parliamentary under secretary for Scotland (1929–31) and lord privy seal (1931) before losing his seat in the 1931 election. He was re-elected for his old constituency in 1935. In 1939 he was appointed regional commissioner for civil defence in Scotland and in 1941 he joined the coalition government as secretary of state for Scotland. From his socialist Clydeside background he became a vigorous, forthright and practical spokesman for his native country. But that was as far as his career went. Although he could perhaps have become leader of the Labour Party he never aspired to be prime minister and was perhaps too focused on Scotland to concern himself with the wider national picture. He devoted much of his energy to editing *Forward*. He was modest by nature and his comments were never marked by personal ambition. Throughout his time as Scottish secretary he declined to take his cabinet minister's salary of £5,000 pa. He acquired a reputation in the commons for 'informed, dour and sardonic criticism . . . Johnston's skill in using facts and figures, which lent an engaging touch of Scots didacticism to his combative debating style, was joined to a genuine moral passion. Of sincerely Puritan temperament (he was a teetotaller by principle), he was a formidable Socialist propagandist.'[59]

He did not stand again in the 1945 general election, but took on a number of public appointments including chairman of the North of Scotland Hydro-Electric Board (until 1959), the Scottish National Forestry Commissioners (until 1948), the Broadcasting Council for Scotland, and the Scottish Tourist Board, and was chancellor of the University of Aberdeen (1951–65). He also served as the BBC national governor for Scotland. At the end of his life, Johnston had come to be seen as the elder statesman of Scotland. He died in 1965.

He refused the peerage that was offered in 1945, but accepted a CH in 1953 'for public services in Scotland.'

Lord Butler of Saffron Walden 8 January 1954
'Rab' Butler, as he was known from childhood, was a Conservative politician who held the highest cabinet offices and could have become prime minister but never did.

He was born at Attock Serai in the Punjab, India, in 1902, the eldest son of Sir Montague Butler, a civil servant who later became governor of the Isle of Man. He was educated at the Wick Preparatory School at Hove, Marlborough and Pembroke College, Cambridge, from where he graduated in the modern and medieval languages tripos (1923) and in history (1925). Born into a privileged family, Butler married into a wealthy one in 1926, his wife being the daughter of the industrialist Samuel Courtauld, who gave his son-in-law a lifelong tax-free annual income of £5,000. He did not even have to compete for a parliamentary seat; the Courtauld family secured Saffron Walden in Essex while the Butlers were honeymooning.

He won the seat at the 1929 general election and held it until his retirement in 1965. He was destined for high office, but in a sharp exchange in *The Times*, he crossed swords with Harold Macmillan, advising him to seek 'a pastime more suited to his talents' than politics, and in 1963, Macmillan did his utmost to prevent Butler from succeeding him as prime minister.

Butler's career in government began in the national government when he was made parliamentary private secretary to Sir Samuel Hoare (1931–32) and parliamentary under secretary at the India Office (1932–37). Neville Chamberlain made him parliamentary under secretary at the ministry of labour (1937–38) and then at the foreign office (1938–41) where he was a supporter of appeasement. Churchill viewed him with suspicion but kept him in post, the foreign office being a backwater department in the 1939–45 war. In 1941 Churchill moved him to be president of the board of education and even further from the war. But it was here that he had his greatest achievement. The 1944 Education Act gave every child a right to free secondary education, and provision was made for the expansion of nursery and further education and for the raising of the school leaving age. He was briefly minister of labour in the postwar caretaker government (1945).

In 1941 he was made chairman of the Conservative Party's postwar problems central committee and after the war chairman of the Conservative research department and the industrial policy committee. He exerted a major influence in reshaping Conservative policy and 'even more than Macmillan, was chiefly responsible for the civilised conservatism of the postwar party.'[60] His 1947 *Industrial Charter* called for full employment, social security and the acceptance of the welfare state, and condemned mass unemployment as a thing of the past. Some of the more right wing elements of the party branded Butler as an incipient socialist, but his policies were an important factor in securing successive Conservative victories in the 1950s.

When the Conservative Party returned to office at the 1951 general election, he was made chancellor of the exchequer, tackling a financial crisis by a mixture of import controls and monetary policy and encouraging expansion and enterprise, and producing two successful and popular budgets He was twice head of the government – in September 1952 when both Churchill and Eden were away, and in the summer of 1953 when both were ill (Butler chaired sixteen cabinet meetings in a row). Everything seemed to go well until December 1954 when the death of his wife came as a shattering blow. Growing inflation, balance of payment difficulties and a run on the pound compounded his problems. Eden asked Butler to leave the Treasury after the May 1955 election. Butler refused and was removed in December of the same year, being replaced by Harold Macmillan. Butler accepted the offices of lord privy seal and leader of the house of commons but they were no compensation. He could have seized the initiative at the time of the Suez crisis and nailed his colours firmly to the mast. But he displayed a lack of tactical skill at a time of international crisis and when the party was divided, and for a seasoned politician, he was surprisingly indiscreet to back bench groups. He was left as acting head of the government when Eden departed for rest in the West Indies, but he was too unpopular to succeed when Eden finally resigned in January 1957. When Macmillan was appointed prime minister, Butler asked for but was refused the foreign office and accepted the home office in addition to his post as leader of the house. He was a liberal in favour of penal reform, at a time when most of his party stood firmly at the other end of the spectrum. But he was reckoned as an outstanding home secretary, reforming the laws on gambling, public houses, prostitution and charities. In October 1961 he was replaced as leader of the house (to allow Iain Macleod a way out of the colonial office) but remained home secretary. In March 1962 Macmillan persuaded him to take charge of a new central Africa department, which he kept after losing the home office in the night of the long knives in July 1962. He was given the additional and quite meaningless title of 'first secretary of state' and the intimation that he would be deputy prime minister. His principal achievement was the orderly dissolution of the Federation of Central Africa in July 1963 without conceding full independence to Southern Rhodesia.

When Macmillan resigned in October 1963 he managed to keep a degree of control over the choice of his successor, and was determined that it would not be Butler. A group of cabinet ministers encouraged Butler to fight the choice of Lord Home (the result of informal consultation, and before the days of ballots and votes). Despite support, Butler's heart was not in a fight. He accepted Alec Douglas-Home as prime minister and in return was rewarded with the foreign office that Macmillan had denied him in 1957. But his political days were almost finished. The Conservative defeat was followed by the offer of an earldom (which he refused) and the mastership of Trinity College, Cambridge (which he accepted). He then accepted a life peerage in 1965, taking the title of Lord Butler of Saffron Walden, and sat on the cross benches.

He was also rector of the University of Glasgow (1956–59), high steward of the University of Cambridge (1958–66), chancellor of the University of Sheffield (1960–78), chancellor of the University of Essex (1962–82) and high steward of the city of Cambridge (1963–82). He retired from Trinity College in 1977 and died in 1982.

Butler was certainly capable of becoming prime minister and would have been a competent occupant of the office, but lacking charisma and determination he never reached his potential. 'But behind it there was a Rolls Royce mind and a sharp sardonic wit which he enjoyed exerting at the expense of his colleagues. He ... had a strong vein of innocence, rare in sophisticated politicians. He was also abnormally good-natured and inspired great affection.'[61]

He was made a CH in 1954 (there was no citation) and a KG in 1971.

Viscount Crookshank 1 January 1955
Harry Crookshank was a Conservative politician who held a number of second rank ministerial posts, but who was more at home in the house of commons than in the government. He had a extensive knowledge, and a reverence, for parliamentary traditions and usage, and perhaps might have made a better speaker of the chamber than cabinet minister.

He was born in Cairo in 1893, the son of a surgeon. He was educated at Eton and Magdalen College, Cambridge. In the 1914–18 war he was commissioned in the Hampshire Regiment and after 1915 on the special reserve of the Grenadier Guards. He served in France and Salonika and was twice wounded. Demobilised in 1919 he spent the next five years in the diplomatic service, being posted to Constantinople and Washington. He resigned in 1924 when he was elected as Conservative member of parliament for Gainsborough and retained the seat until 1955.

Over more than thirty years he became well versed in the procedures of the commons and acquired a reputation for ability and soundness among his fellow members. He was not a great success as a minister and was not well known in the country. The ministerial posts that he did hold were not of the first rank and mostly undemanding. He served as parliamentary under secretary to the home office (1934–35), secretary for mines (1935–39), financial secretary to the treasury (1939–43), where his task was largely to remind the public that there was a financial cost side to the war and they should save as much as they could), and finally postmaster-general (1943–45). When the Conservative Party returned to government in 1951, Crookshank was made minister of health (1951–52) and additionally leader of the house of commons (1951–56). The additional responsibility of the health ministry was deemed too great a burden and he resigned in 1952 and was made lord privy seal (1952–56), continuing as leader of the house. He retained office when Anthony Eden became prime minister in April 1955, but Eden reshuffled his government in December that year and Crookshank was one of the casualties. In his memoirs Eden shed crocodile tears. 'I had to lose the services of Mr Crookshank, which I much regretted, for his Parliamentary experience and independence of mind, and for his loyalty.'[62]

Crookshank had many gifts but sometimes he lacked the ability to compromise tactfully to facilitate the passage of government business. 'He often seemed to invite trouble by sticking with undue rigidity to the pattern he had set, and his manner of doing so irritated and angered the opposition . . . He was never flurried, never lost his poise, seldom raised his voice. Indeed he could often infuriate his opponents with the dry, laconic, mocking manner which he brought to issues on which their feelings were passionately engaged.'[63]

He was made a CH in 1955 for his services as 'Lord Privy Seal since 1952 and Leader of the House of Commons since 1951. Minister of Health 1951–1952; Postmaster-General 1943–45; Financial Secretary to the Treasury 1939–43. Member of Parliament for Gainsborough since 1924.' The honour was a parting gesture of thanks from his old friend Winston Churchill, then on the verge of retirement as prime minister. Crookshank was created a viscount in 1956 after leaving the government. He never married and the viscountcy became extinct on his death in 1961.

Viscount Cecil of Chelwood 2 January 1956

Edgar Algernon Robert Cecil, known as Lord Robert Cecil, was a lawyer, parliamentarian, cabinet minister, and a passionate internationalist. He was one of the principal architects of the League of Nations, and always faithfully defended it against its detractors.

He was born in 1864, the third son of the third Marquess of Salisbury, who had been foreign secretary under Benjamin Disraeli, and three times prime minister (1885, 1886–92, and 1895–1902), and served as private secretary to his father (1886–88). He was educated at Eton and at University College, Oxford, and was called to the bar in 1887, at the age of twenty-three. His legal career (which lasted until 1906) included most of the forms of common law, some work in chancery, and a steadily increasing parliamentary practice. He also collaborated in writing *Principles of commercial law*.

In 1906 he turned to politics and was elected Conservative member of parliament for East Marylebone. He was defeated in the two general elections in 1910 and then won as an Independent Conservative in 1911 as member for the Hitchin division of Hertfordshire, remaining in the commons until 1923 when he was made a viscount. Settled in that county, he resumed his legal work as chairman of the Hertfordshire quarter sessions (1911–20).

With the formation of the coalition government in 1915, he became under-secretary for foreign affairs for a year, served as minister of blockade (1916–18), being responsible for devising procedures to bring economic and commercial pressure against the enemy, and early in 1918 became assistant secretary of state for foreign affairs.

The 1914–18 war deeply affected him as it did so many of his contemporaries and from 1916 he became absorbed by the pursuit of peace. Appalled by the war's destruction of life, property, and human values, he became convinced that civilization could survive only if it could invent an international system that would insure peace. In September 1916, he circulated a memorandum making proposals for the avoidance of war, which he claimed was the first document from which sprang British official advocacy of the League of Nations. In 1919 he collaborated with President Woodrow Wilson of the USA in drafting the covenant of the League.

From the inception of the League of Nations to its demise in 1946 Cecil's public life was almost totally devoted to the League. At the Paris peace conference in 1919, he was the British representative in charge of negotiations for a League of Nations. In 1920–22, he represented South Africa in the League assembly. In 1923 he made a five-week tour of the United States, explaining the League to American audiences. In 1923–24, with the title of lord privy seal, and from 1924–27, with that of chancellor of the duchy of Lancaster, he was the government minister responsible, under the jurisdiction of the foreign secretary, for British activities in League affairs.

Not all of his colleagues shared his enthusiasm for the effectiveness of the international body, and in 1927 he resigned from the government disagreeing with the government's policy on disarmament. Thereafter, although an official delegate to the League as late as 1932, he worked independently to mobilise public opinion in support of the League. He was president of the British League of Nations Union (1923–45), and joint founder and president of the international peace campaign, known in France as rassemblement universel pour la paix. Among his publications were *The way of peace* (1928), a collection of lectures on the League; *A great experiment* (1941), a personalised account of his relationship to the League of Nations; *A real peace* (1941), *An emergency policy* (1948); and *All the way* (1949), a complete autobiography. In the spring of 1946 he participated in the final meetings of the League at Geneva, ending his speech with the sentence: 'The League is dead; long live the United Nations!' In his last years, he was an occasional attender at the house of lords and supported international efforts for peace through his honorary life presidency of the United Nations Association.

Cecil's devotion to internationalism was matched by his devotion to his Christian faith and he became an adherent of the anglo-catholic tradition within the Church of England, and denounced the government's decision to disestablish the Anglican church in Wales. 'Lord Robert . . . with a permanent stoop . . . gave one the impression when he was denouncing the Bill of a benevolent hawk, if there be such a bird, anxious to swoop upon the Liberal Party to remove it from its evil environment of radicalism and nonconformity and secure it body and soul for the Church.'[64]

Cecil received wide public recognition for his work. He was elected chancellor of Birmingham University (1918–44) and rector of Aberdeen University (1924–27), was given the peace award of the Woodrow Wilson Foundation in 1924 and the Nobel peace prize in 1937. He was created a viscount in 1923 with the title Cecil of Chelwood and made a CH in 1956 'for public services'. He married Lady Eleanor Lambton in 1889 but they had no children and the viscountcy became extinct at his death in 1958.

Viscount Stuart of Findhorn 14 January 1957

Bearing a distinctly Jacobite name, James Stuart was a descendant of King James V of Scotland. Stuart was a handsome, witty, persuasive, charming, and self-confident philanderer who abandoned a brief career in royal service for one in politics, and served as a whip and as secretary of state for Scotland in the governments of Winston Churchill and Anthony Eden.

He was born in 1897, third son of the seventeenth Earl of Moray, and educated at Eton. He left school at the outbreak of the 1914–18 war to join the Scots Guards and was twice awarded the Military Cross. In 1918 he was introduced to the duke of York (the future King George VI) and spent eighteen months as his equerry (1920–21). He later claimed in his memoirs to have introduced the duke to his future bride at a dance in the Ritz Hotel in 1921. He may well have done so, but the duke and duchess had met on previous occasions. Stuart was a smooth-talking, extremely good-looking lady-killer with a reputation for being a heart-breaker,[65] and it was rumoured that he had proposed to Lady Elizabeth Bowes-Lyon and that the two might have married. Others claimed that he was certainly in love with her. 'Perhaps she was just a little with him. He was awfully attractive. Everybody was in love with James Stuart.'[66] He was not the most competent of equerries. 'He brought a cheerful insouciance to his duties. Once when the duke wanted to watch cricket, his equerry took him to a deserted Lord's; the match was being held at the Oval. He had similar difficulty in finding Lambeth Palace, where the duke was late in arriving for the archbishop of Canterbury's dinner party.'[67] In 1922 he resigned as the duke's equerry and travelled to seek his fortune in the oilfields of Oklahoma. One account has it that it was because of the low rate of pay (£450, from which he had to pay a valet). Another account held that his love for Elizabeth Bowes-Lyon was awkward and embarrassing, given that his employer was himself ardently in love with same woman, and that a temporary exile was the best solution. He left for the USA in January 1922 and spent three months in the office of the American Petroleum Company in New York and ten months in the Oklahoma oilfields.

The exile was not long. The following year he was back in Britain and in April 1923 he was married to Lady Rachel Cavendish, daughter of the Duke of Devonshire. In the general election of December 1923 he fulfilled an ambition to enter politics and was elected to the house of commons as Conservative member for Moray and Nairn (1923–59). It says much about his character that for thirteen years he was a government whip: firstly in the national government (1935–40) and then in the coalition government (1940–41). Then he became Conservative chief whip in the coalition government (1941–45) and in the brief pre-election Conservative government (1945), and then chief opposition whip (1945–48). He became one of Churchill's most trusted colleagues and friends.

Despite his debonair and slightly decadent lifestyle, he was an effective whip, as a colleague recalled. 'James was a deeply attractive chap. He was laid-back to the point of insolence and yet he had a cutting edge. As Churchill's chief whip, if a young MP stepped out of line he would snap and they would never forget it. His air was deceptive. He had bite.'[68] 'His laconic, rather languid manner in the House concealed an immense capacity for hard work. He took great pains to perfect himself in a subject. Before a debate he would spend half the night in preparation; but he saw no point in burdening the House with gratuitous information. He never wasted words in public or in private. His training as a whip had bred in him a firm conviction that a politician who talked too much was likely to get himself into trouble. He distrusted oratory and made no claim to any gift for it . . . Indeed he sometimes gave the impression that he found the making of speeches a boring occupation. He once yawned in the middle of one of his own.'[69]

Despite his marriage Stuart's nature remained, and his career as a whip ended in 1948 when he was cited as co-respondent in a divorce case. It could have been a permanent conclusion to his political career, but Churchill thought highly of him, and when the Conservative Party formed a government in 1951, Stuart was made secretary of state for Scotland (1951–57). He had been a great success as chief whip for his party and that office was more to him than the Scottish office, which became a burden. He left the cabinet when Harold Macmillan became prime minister in January 1957, at his own request, but remained in the house of commons until the 1959 general election.

He was a member of the royal commission on the working of the Tribunals of Inquiry (Evidence) Act 1921 from 1966 until his death in 1971, and published an autobiography, *Within the fringe*, in 1967. His memories of his days as an equerry were not tinged with nostalgia, and he remembered the job as a cross between an ADC and a glorified bell-hop, and displayed coolness in references to his former employer. 'He was not an easy man to know or to handle, and I cannot pretend that I ever became a close friend.'[70]

He remained on cordial terms with the royal family for the rest of his life. Accidentally peppered with shot by his neighbour on the grouse moor, he once arrived at Balmoral with his face covered with sticking plaster. In reply to the Queen's anxious enquiry, he told her how he had first driven to the local hospital for an injection of penicillin, then to the nearest hotel for a "small refreshment", (a double whisky). 'James,' said the Queen, 'you should surely not have had that after the penicillin?' 'You know, Ma'am, that's exactly what the barmaid said.'[71] In 1971 he telephoned Queen Elizabeth the Queen Mother, as she had now become, and asked to see her. She invited him to lunch, and he died two days later.

He was made a CH in 1957 as compensation for leaving the cabinet, and was created a viscount in 1959 on leaving the house of commons.

Viscount Boyd of Merton 1 January 1960

Alan Lennox-Boyd was a right wing maverick in the 1930s, yet he had a wide circle of friends from a diversity of race, colour and social origin, deplored racial prejudice, had no ambition to be anything other than secretary of state for the colonies, and became the second longest serving and most influential occupant of that office in the twentieth century.

Alan Boyd (he assumed the additional surname of Lennox in 1925) was born at Boscombe, Bournemouth in 1904, the son of a barrister. He was educated at a preparatory school in Bournemouth and then at Sherborne and Christ Church,

Oxford, graduating in modern history. He unsuccessfully stood for parliament as a Conservative for the Gower division of Glamorgan in 1929. He was elected for mid-Bedfordshire in 1931 and held the seat until he retired from politics in 1960. In 1938 he married a member of the Guinness brewing family that brought him a substantial fortune and made him financially independent

In the 1930s he was an ally of R. A. Butler and a supporter of appeasement. He served as parliamentary secretary at the ministry of labour (1938–39), the ministry of home security (1939) and the ministry of food (1939–40). He left the government in May 1940 to serve as a lieutenant commander in the RNVR. Churchill recalled him to the government as a parliamentary secretary in the ministry of aircraft production (1943–45). During the years of opposition Lennox-Boyd, who had always shown a strong interest in overseas affairs, travelled widely in the colonies, and often spoke from the opposition front bench on imperial issues.

When the Conservative Party returned to government in 1951 he was made minister of state at the colonial office (1951–52), where he firmly resisted European settler influences in Kenya and Tanganyika, and then minister of transport and civil aviation (1952–54). He had no desire for the ministry and accepted it only on the understanding that he would be given the colonial office when it became vacant – which it did in 1954. It was as secretary of state for the colonies (1954–59) that he attained the job that he wanted above all others, and became the longest serving colonial secretary since Joseph Chamberlain (1895–1903). His capacity for work was phenomenal. 'He would start work early, between five and six in the morning, arriving in the office having already mastered his briefs. Thereafter he would seldom read or write in the office but spend the day listening to advice or giving it. He was persuasive in council and in the house of commons on colonial affairs, not so much by his oratory as by his knowledge of facts and his grasp of the arguments involved.'[72]

He was pragmatic enough to recognise that there was no halting the progress towards decolonisation; that it was inevitable and even desirable. In his own party he took a middle ground between those who wanted to go slower and those who wanted a faster process. In his view there should be no hastiness in granting independence. It had to be accompanied by economic underpinning, and he devised a series of federations for south-east Asia, south Arabia, central Africa and the west Indies. The arguments were logical, but the concepts included an element of dreaming that took no account of local political realities and rivalries, and with the exception of Malaysia, itself prone to internal strife, the others soon collapsed. The rapid decolonisation of the French empire in Africa in 1958 and Macmillan's interest in pursuing links with the European Economic Community meant that Lennox-Boyd's more gradual and more careful steps towards independence were not in accord with Macmillan's more rapid timetable, nor if truth be told with many of the colonies themselves. He offered to resign, but was persuaded with difficulty to remain until after the 1959 general election. The election concluded, he made it clear that he was disinclined to have anything further to do with parliament and, to the irritation of the party whips, he was abroad for much of his remaining time as a member of the commons. He left the house of commons and the world of politics in July 1960.

The remaining twenty-three years of his life were spent in a variety of commercial and public appointments, including being a trustee of the British Museum (1962–78) and of the Natural History Museum (1963–76), and the presidency of the Royal Commonwealth Society (1965–83). After leaving the commons in 1960 he and his wife left London to live in a fortified seventeenth century manor house in Cornwall where the garden was patrolled by a collection of fierce white peacocks. They travelled widely, visiting east Africa, India and the Galapagos Islands.

His life ended suddenly and sadly in 1983 when he was hit by a car driven by a young uninsured student as he was crossing Fulham Palace Road in London. Shortly after his death, his son received a telephone call from Lee Kuan Yew, prime minister of Singapore, who said: 'I just wanted you to know that without your father, my country would not exist.'[73]

He was made a CH in 1960 and created a viscount later in the same year, taking the title Viscount Boyd of Merton (from Merton-in-Penninghame in Scotland).

Lord Hailes 2 June 1962
Patrick Buchan-Hepburn was principally remembered as a charming, urbane and intuitive chief whip of the Conservative Party (1951–55). His four years as governor-general of the doomed federation of the West Indies (1958–62), for which he received the CH, was only a coda to a long and successful career in parliament.

He was born in 1901, the third son of a baronet and educated at Harrow and Trinity College, Cambridge. His family was wealthy and he was able to travel for much of his youth. He spent a few months as an honorary attaché at the British embassy in Constantinople (1926–27) but he did not otherwise need to work for his living. On his return to England he was appointed private secretary to Winston Churchill, a position that was to be crucial to the development of his career. Politics beckoned and he unsuccessfully contested Wolverhampton in 1929. He briefly tried local government, as member for North Kensington on London county council (1930–31), before being elected for the Toxteth East division of Liverpool. He was not an orator and never cabinet minister material. His talents were best used behind the scenes. He had, 'an almost preternatural flair for estimating people, managing their foibles and penetrating their motives.'[74] A period as parliamentary private secretary to Oliver Stanley took him on a tour of the home office, the ministry of labour, the ministry of transport, the board of education and the board of trade, and although contemporary observers interpreted this as Stanley being destined for the highest office, it benefited his parliamentary secretary, who became a whip in 1939 and remained in the whip's office until 1955 apart from a short period of service with the Royal Artillery (1940–43) in the 1939–45 war. He was recalled from active service by Churchill to become a junior Conservative whip. He was promoted to deputy chief whip in 1945 and chief whip in 1948, and was the first not to come from a military background 'although his displeasure normally proved no less deadly than his predecessors.'[75] He spent a year in the cabinet as minister of works (December 1955 to January 1957) but asked to retire from politics when Harold Macmillan succeeded Anthony Eden as prime minister.

Within a few months he was called out of retirement to become first (and only) governor-general of the recently created federation of the West Indies in May 1957. A colonial office convinced that the West Indian islands could not exist as individual administrative units conceived the federation; they had to be federated to ensure 'viability'. Buchan-Hepburn's appointment as governor-general was conceived on the basis of the personal qualities of charm and strength that he had displayed as chief whip. It was greeted with opposition on the ground that West

Indian politicians had not been consulted and that a man with local experience would have been a better choice. In fact the selection and identity of the governor-general was really irrelevant. A product of the colonial office in London, the federation took no account of the incompatibility of interest between its member states and no one person could have held it together. The hope was that the federation would evolve into a fully independent state, and the colonial office announced a projected independence date –31 May 1962 – in May 1961. In September 1961 Jamaica voted in a referendum to secede and in February 1962 the British government announced that legislation would be brought in to dismantle the federation. Buchan-Hepburn returned to London in May that year. His last appointment – a reflection of his love of historic monuments – was to be chairman of the Historic Buildings Council for England and Wales (1963–73). He died in 1974.

He was appointed a GBE in 1957 for his services as chief whip, and was created a life peer on his appointment as governor-general of the West Indies also in 1957, taking the title Lord Hailes. He was made a CH in 1962 on the dissolution of the federation. His citation read: 'Parliamentary Secretary to H. M. Treasury, 1951–1955; Minister of Works, 1955–1957. Governor-General and Commander-in-Chief of the West Indies, since 1957.' He and his wife had no children and the barony became extinct on his death.

Viscount Muirshiel 20 July 1962
With Harold Watkinson and Selwyn Lloyd, Jack Maclay (later Viscount Muirshiel) was one of the three cabinet ministers to receive the CH as compensation in July 1962 after being sacked by Harold Macmillan in the infamous 'night of the long knives'. A patient, courteous, modest, conscientious and fair-minded man, Maclay was too self-critical and too sensitive to criticism to be a successful politician and was probably far happier after his departure from the tempests of politics and parliament.

He was born in 1905, the younger son of the first Baron Maclay, who was minister of shipping and a member of the cabinet in the 1914–18 war. He was educated at Winchester and Trinity College, Cambridge and joined the family shipping business until the outbreak of the 1939–45 war when he joined the Royal Artillery. In 1940 he was seconded for duties at the ministry of war transport, and travelled to Washington to assist Sir Arthur Salter (later Lord Salter) whom he succeeded as head of the British Merchant Shipping Mission. Also in 1940 he was returned unopposed to parliament as National Liberal member for Montrose Burghs. In 1945 he was appointed parliamentary under secretary at the ministry of production in the brief postwar Conservative caretaker government. During the years of opposition he was chairman of the British committee of the International Chamber of Commerce (1947–51).

Among other reforms, the Labour government's Representation of the People Act proposed the abolition of his constituency. Maclay tried but failed to stop the incorporation of Montrose Burghs into the new constituency of South Angus. He decided not to stand in South Angus and was returned for West Renfrewshire in 1951.

In the new Conservative government Maclay became minister of transport and civil aviation, but a number of crises led to his early resignation in May 1952 on the grounds of health. A crisis over increased fares in the London area and the need to devise policies for the denationalisation of road transport, proved too great a pressure and he needed two months in recuperation in Scotland after his resignation. Although it was not to his credit that he had effectively cracked under pressure, he was well regarded by Anthony Eden, who brought him back into the government as minister of state for the colonies in October 1956. In January 1957 he was brought into the cabinet as secretary of state for Scotland by Eden's successor Harold Macmillan, and there he remained until 1962. He was an effective and conscientious Scottish secretary whose methods were marked by patience and persuasion, and a number of new works, including the construction of the Forth and Tay road bridges, the inauguration of the first nuclear power station, the Glasgow redevelopment plan, the modernisation of the fishing fleet, rating reform, hospital building and the liberalisation of the licensing laws, were to his credit. But there were lingering problems, notably the level of unemployment in Scotland which was well above the national average. 'He got more blame for his failures than praise for his achievements. He ran into stormy trouble over his refusal in May 1961 to be stampeded into hasty action by a strike of teachers, but he inaugurated a useful review of conditions in the profession. In the same year his housing bill came under heavy Opposition attack. But he endured one of the most uncomfortable half-hours of his political career one afternoon in July 1962 when he had to face the fury of Scottish Labour members over a decision, not of his making, to close more than a score of Scottish coal mines in the ensuing four years.'[76]

A few days later he was removed from office in the 'night of the long knives'. It was later revealed that he had given notice to the prime minister some months before that he was beginning to sink under the burden of the office. It was a sad way to go and those in his private office felt that he had been badly treated. 'Imagine our dismay, even fury, when his name appeared among that sorry list of ministers who were dismissed ... This was grossly unfair to Jack and also misleading. Not only was his work exemplary, but he had been expressly asked to stay on previously. His resignation could have been postponed for a few weeks and the reasons for it clearly and explicitly given, but he never complained.'[77]

After leaving the commons, he was well occupied in business and public affairs. He was chairman of the Joint Exchequer Board for Northern Ireland (1965–73) and held several directorships of leading companies. He was lord lieutenant of Renfrewshire (1967–80) and, concerned about Scotland's environment and man-made heritage, he was an assiduous and effective chairman of the Scottish Civic Trust (1967–89).

He was made a CMG in 1944 for his wartime services in Washington, and a CH seven days after being removed by Macmillan in 1962. There was no citation or description of appointment in the *London Gazette*. He was created a viscount in the Birthday Honours List 1964, taking the title Viscount Muirshiel. For his long and varied service to Scotland, he was created a KT in 1973. Retirement from politics led to longevity and Maclay died in 1992 at the age of eighty-six.

Viscount Watkinson 20 July 1962
By the time of his death, Harold Watkinson was remembered as a competent businessman and virtually forgotten as a politician. He was sacked in the 'night of the long knives' due mostly to his disagreement with Macmillan over issues of defence policy.

He was born in Walton-on-Thames in 1910, the son of Methodist parents. He was educated at Queen's College, Taunton, and at King's College, London, which he left without taking a degree in order to enter the family business of light engineering. He spent the 1939–45 war in the royal naval volunteer reserve, rising to the rank of lieutenant commander and becoming an expert in anti-aircraft gunnery. He had developed an interest in politics through conversations with the son (a Liberal member of parliament) of the family's local Methodist minister, and after the war he decided on a career in the Conservative Party. He had become chairman of the Conservative constituency association in Dorking before being elected to parliament as member for Woking in 1950. It was the beginning of a political career that was over and done with in only fourteen years. Eighteen months after his election to parliament, he tasted his first experience of government as parliamentary under-secretary at the ministry of labour, being appointed because of his experience of the publishing and machine tool industries. In January 1957 Harold Macmillan brought him into the cabinet as minister of transport and civil aviation, and in October 1959 he became minister of defence.

His departure from the government in the 'night of the long knives' was more the result of a conflict with Macmillan than with inadequate performance as a minister. 'Watkinson always favoured a businessman's approach. He deplored the proneness of governments to adopt short-term expedients and consistently sought to strengthen the managerial process within Whitehall. He could appear brusque or even peppery certainly his dogged debating style was seldom redeemed by any elegance or finesse. But he took his place on the centre-left of the party and it was characteristic that his main difference with Macmillan should have arisen from their contrasting strategic views.'[78] Watkinson believed that the United Kingdom could no longer afford to deploy its forces worldwide, nor could it make a meaningful contribution to the western nuclear deterrent. Macmillan took the opposite view in both cases, partly because of his desire to maintain Britain's prestige in the world and partly to please the United States. The conflict almost certainly played a role in Macmillan's decision to dispense with Watkinson's services in July 1962. Macmillan told Watkinson that he wanted to reduce the average age of the cabinet, yet Watkinson's successor, Peter Thorneycroft, was a year older.[79]

Watkinson was shocked and hurt by his dismissal and remained bitter. In his memoirs he recalled the embarrassment of the next few days. On the afternoon he was due to attend a garden party with his wife and elder daughter, the latter of whom he had arranged in advance to present to the Queen. 'I had to do it,' he writes ruefully, 'in the knowledge that I was no longer a Minister of the Crown. If the Queen knew, she very kindly did not let it become obvious'.[80] The next evening he was scheduled to preside at a performance of the royal tournament as minister of defence. While still in office he had invited the American ambassador to be his guest. He was allowed to occupy the royal box but not to take the salutes that were part of the display, the role being delegated to an army officer.

The termination of his ministerial career left a void that needed to be filled. He left the house of commons in 1964 election. But he was still only fifty-four years old, and too young and active to play the role of an elder statesman in the house of lords. Instead he turned his mind and talents to the world of industry. He served for six years as a member of the British Exports Council and was chairman of the Committee for Exports to the United States (1964–67). His principal work was done as group managing director (1963–68) and then as chairman (1969–74) of

Cadbury Schweppes, one of the country's largest and most successful companies. In 1976 he was elected president of the Confederation of British Industry, though ill-health forced him to leave the office four months early. He remained as a main board member of the Midland Bank until 1983.

Watkinson declined Macmillan's initial offer of a baronetcy but accepted the CH as a consolation for leaving the cabinet. He left the commons at the 1964 election and was created a viscount. By his marriage he had two daughters and the viscountcy became extinct at his death in 1995.

Lord Selwyn-Lloyd 20 July 1962
Selwyn Lloyd was a Conservative politician who held the high offices of foreign secretary and chancellor of the exchequer, was sacked in the 1962 'night of the long knives', and several years later returned to become a respected speaker of the house of commons.

He was born in Liverpool in 1904 and educated at Fettes College and Magdalen College, Cambridge. He was called to the bar at Gray's Inn in 1930. During the 1939–45 war he served on the general staff of the Second Army and proved himself to be a first rate soldier. He had joined the territorial army just before the war and by the end of 1939 he had passed through staff college and was a brigade major. 'He never commanded troops, but he was a staff officer of the highest quality who ended the war as one of the select band of "civilian" brigadiers. He loved the army because it filled his life, kept his endemic loneliness at bay, provided him with official accommodation, demanded the loyal and efficient discharge of higher orders, and rewarded him with the prestige of rapid promotion. Much of his remarkable political career he spent in trying to get the same benefits out of political life, and succeeding for a high proportion of the time.'[81]

Determined to enter the house of commons from the age of sixteen, he was elected in 1945 as member for the Wirral division of Cheshire and retained the seat until 1976. He continued to practice as a barrister and was made a KC in 1947 and was recorder of Wigan (1948–51). After the Conservative victory in 1951 he served as minister of state at the foreign office (1951–54), minister of supply (1954–55) and minister of defence (1955). But his political career took off with his long period as secretary of state for foreign affairs (1955–60) It was almost immediately dominated by the intervention in Suez, an episode planned and pushed through by Anthony Eden. Lloyd was prepared to negotiate with the Egyptians, and could hardly be held responsible for the imperialist bellicosity of a prime minister over whom he had no control. Those who worked for him at the time remembered his 'erratic style, disorder with papers and bantering sense of humour [but] he was a kind man and scrupulously fair. He welcomed advice even when it was unsolicited, but always took full responsibility for his decisions.'[82]

Though his tenure as chancellor of the exchequer (1960–62) was relatively short, his time was seen with hindsight as the most reforming period since the work of Stafford Cripps a decade earlier. He established the national economic development council which made long-term planning respectable for the private sector, attempted to restrain public expenditure by way of long-term planning, raised the starting level of surtax, introduced economic regulators, giving the chancellor power to vary tax between budgets, reformed the archaic budget accounts, and developed a new and positive policy towards the nationalised industries. His dismissal by Macmillan in the 'night of the long knives' in July 1962 was a completely unexpected and shattering blow but he accepted it with philosophical calm and remained tight-lipped about this perceived injustice. Later he was to say that 12 July 1962 was the day 'on which my house of cards collapsed.'[83]

He forged a friendship with Macmillan's successor, Alec Douglas-Home, who made him lord privy seal and leader of the house (1963–64). 'In this post, which seemed to require most of the qualities he did not possess – delicacy of touch, wit and detachment – he was a considerable success. It lasted only a year . . . but was the indispensable foundation of his 1970s Indian summer of five years as speaker.'[84] He was elected speaker of the house of commons in 1971 to a chorus of criticism. By custom the ancient office was held by backbenchers, not by former cabinet ministers, and fifty-five members (some of them with memories of Suez) voted against him. In the event he proved to be an excellent speaker. His fairness, firmness, humour, tolerance and impartiality won him cross-party acclaim by the time of his retirement in 1976.

Harold Macmillan called him 'a little country notary'[85] and Roy Jenkins described him as a second rate lawyer and a middle rank politician but 'an unusually nice although sad man.'[86] There was sadness in his life – the dissolution of his marriage in 1957 and his hurtful dismissal in 1962, but he had the endearing qualities, rare among politicians, of a simple personal life and a spiritually-based humility. He was a conscientious godparent (another rarity among a group usually wilfully blind to their responsibilities) and customarily sent out his *Letter to a young relative* at the time of a confirmation: 'If you can force yourself to acquire as a habit, as something coming naturally to you, the feeling of pleasure at the successes of others, even though you are yourself in direct competition with them, you will gain much in happiness. Friendship is giving, not getting. You must disburse if you are to receive, love if you are to be loved, push out if you are to draw in. Life is not a single engagement, it is a campaign. One can lose a number of engagements and yet win the campaign.'[87]

He was appointed a military OBE in 1944 and military CBE in 1945. After the night of the long knives, Macmillan offered him a peerage, expecting that he slip smoothly into a business career in the city. To Macmillan's surprise and discomfiture, Lloyd said that he had no intention of giving up his constituents in the Wirral and that he would stay in the house of commons and support the financial policies he had established. Then came the CH. On the following day, Lloyd was telephoned and told that Macmillan 'in his distress' had forgotten to offer him the CH – and would he like it? In response to a request for time to think about it, Lloyd was told that he had half an hour. Lloyd speculated later as to whether the prime minister had genuinely forgotten and concluded that as the other sacked ministers had been given a sprinkling of honours to sweeten their dismissal, it would look odd if he was not given something, especially as his refusal of a peerage could not be made public. So he believed that his name was added to the list of honours at the last minute. He accepted the honour with reluctance, rightly associating it with figures distinguished in the worlds of music, literature and the sciences, and believing that it should not be handed out to superannuated and redundant politicians.[88] When he retired as speaker in 1976 he was given the traditional peerage. He followed the contemporary trend of hyphenating his first and surnames to produce the title Lord Selwyn-Lloyd. His retirement was short; he died of an inoperable brain tumour eighteen months later in 1978.

Lord Brooke of Cumnor 1 December 1964
Henry Brooke was a conscientious but uncharismatic Conservative politician who had a difficult tenure as home secretary (1962–64).

He was born at Oxford in 1903, the son of an author and illustrator of children's books. He was educated at Marlborough (where he was a contemporary of R. A. Butler) and Balliol College, Oxford where he read classics, mathematics and literae humaniores. On graduating in 1926 Balliol offered him a fellowship in philosophy, which he declined, and went instead to work at a Quaker settlement for the unemployed in the Rhondda valley (1926–27). After work as a journalist on the *Economist*, he became a member of the Conservative research department (1930–38).

He entered politics as a member of Hampstead Borough Council (1936–57) and was elected to parliament in 1938 as Conservative member for Lewisham West and retained the seat until he became one of the victims of the Labour landslide in 1945. In the same year he was elected to London County Council (1945–55) and pursued business interests, becoming the last deputy chairman of the Southern Railway (1946–48) before the nationalisation of the railways. He was returned to the house of commons in 1950 as member for Hampstead and held the seat until 1966.

In 1954 he was appointed financial secretary to the treasury, while his old school friend, R. A. Butler, was chancellor of the exchequer. As minister of housing and local government (1957–61) he succeeded in eliminating the famously unhealthy London smog and implementing the unpopular Rent Act devised by his predecessor. The act removed restrictions from privately owned housing, but simultaneously removed security of tenure from many tenants of small means and created a good deal of bitterness (it was repealed in 1965). He was appointed to the new post of chief secretary to the treasury (1961–62), effectively a deputy chancellor of the exchequer. He was responsible for public expenditure, the civil service, the universities and the arts, and found that his unenviable task 'was to play the role of Scrooge towards popular proposals for public expenditure.'[89] To provide him with a salary, he was given the ancient but sinecure office of paymaster-general. His last ministerial appointment was home secretary (1962–64). No one doubted his integrity, but it was an office that required flexibility and lightness of touch. He made a number of decisions on immigration and deportation issues that infuriated libertarians. 'He seemed to display a certain insensitivity in these cases – an impression enhanced by his somewhat pedantic way of speech.'[90] Although he retained his seat at the 1964 election, with a reduced majority, he was defeated in 1966.

He was given a life peerage in 1966 and spoke frequently in the house of lords until the onset of Parkinson's Disease made it impossible. His wife had been created a life peeress in 1964 as Baroness Brooke of Ystradfellte and they became the first couple in parliamentary history to sit together on the front bench of either chamber. He died in 1984.

He was appointed a CH in 1964, a few weeks after the defeat of the Conservative Party in the general election. The citation read: 'Conservative Member of Parliament for West Lewisham 1938–1945, and for Hampstead since 1950. Financial Secretary to HM Treasury, 1954–1957; Minister of Housing and Local Government, and Minister for Welsh Affairs, 1957–1961; Chief Secretary to H. M. Treasury and Paymaster-General, 1961–1962; Home Secretary 1962–1964. For political and public services.'

Lord Silkin 1 January 1965

After a long apprenticeship on the housing committee of London County Council, Lewis Silkin was the Labour cabinet minister charged with rebuilding the nation's urban housing after the 1939–45 war and was responsible for the creation of the 'new towns' in the 1940s.

He was born in London in 1889, the eldest of the seven children of Baltic immigrant parents. He was educated at a junior school in Stoke Newington and the Central Foundation School, City Road, London. He won a scholarship to read mathematics at Worcester College, Oxford, but his parents were too poor to allow him to take it up. He managed a year's study at the University of London. After working as a clerk in the docks he joined a firm of solicitors, qualified, and set himself up in practice. He was a lifelong supporter of the Labour movement and first stood for parliament, unsuccessfully, at Central Wandsworth in 1922, but was elected to London County Council in 1925. In 1934 he was elected chairman of the LCC's housing and public health committee and took on the leadership of the council's housing drive. In 1935 a visit to continental housing convinced him that flats rather than houses were the only solution to densely populated areas. In the same year he was appointed a member of the central housing advisory committee and in 1936 he was elected member of parliament for Peckham. As chairman of the LCC's town planning committee (1940–45) he became even more convinced of the advantages of flats over houses.

He held no office in the wartime coalition government but with the formation of a Labour government in 1945 and the question of rebuilding many urban areas, he was a natural choice to be minister of town and country planning. With his experience of slum housing in London before the war, the bombing of London had presented him with the opportunity for a new start. Although temporary housing had to be constructed as quickly as possible, the concept of 'new towns' emerged. 'Housing districts should be separated from industrial districts, and the countryside should enjoy many of the amenities of the towns, and the towns the advantages of open spaces and easy access to green belts and the country itself . . . Sites were chosen which were likely to attract industry, and usually with an already existing town as a nucleus. In the case of towns like Stevenage and Hemel Hempstead he had to meet much opposition from the citizens whose lives were about to be unsettled.'[91] Among the significant pieces of legislation that he piloted through parliament were: the New Towns Act (1946), the Town and Country Planning Act (1947) and the Countryside Act (1949).

Silkin was shy and not a good public speaker, and diligent rather than brilliant. Town and country planning was the only ministerial office that he held (1945–50) but his effect on the townscape and landscape of south-east England has been indelible.

He was created a peer as Lord Silkin in 1950 and served as deputy leader of the Labour Party in the house of lords. He was made a CH in 1965. The citation read: 'Labour Member of Parliament for the Peckham Division of Camberwell, 1936–1950. Minister of Town and Country Planning, 1945–1950. Deputy Leader of the Opposition in the House of Lords, 1958–1964. For political and public services.' Without decrying the importance of his work in the house of lords, the CH might have been better linked to his planning work. He died in 1972.

Lord Shinwell 12 June 1965
From a background in London's east end Jewish rag trade Emanuel 'Manny' Shinwell lived to become the abrasive yet lovable and outspoken elder statesman of the Labour Party. A man of fiery temperament and sharp wit, he was a vividly individual personality and his political life was punctuated by some colourful incidents. But they never diminished the great affection in which he was held to the end of his long life

He was born in Spitalfields, east London, in 1884, the son of Samuel Shinwell, a clothing manufacturer. He left school at the age of eleven to be apprenticed in the tailoring trade. He soon went to Scotland and became interested in Clydeside politics. In 1906 he was elected to the Glasgow Trades Council, of which he was twice president, and in 1911 he helped to organise the seamen in the Clyde ports into a trade union. On 'Red Friday' (31 January 1919), a strike led to a clash with the Glasgow police and Shinwell spent several months in jail. He spent seven years as a councillor on Glasgow city council and was elected to parliament in 1922 as member for Linlithgow. He was parliamentary under secretary in the ministry of mines for a few months in 1924 during the first brief Labour government but lost his seat in the general election that year. He was returned again for Linlithgow in 1928 and was financial secretary to the war office in 1929–30, and then returned to his post at the ministry of mines until he lost his seat in the 1931 election.

He was bitterly opposed to the national government, formed in 1931, and delivered a stinging attack on Ramsay MacDonald at Seaham Harbour during the 1935 election. He was returned for the seat and held it until 1950. He then represented Easington until he retired from the commons in 1970.

Shinwell was as pugnacious in behaviour as he was in appearance and in 1938, provoked by a remark from Commander Robert Bower, a Conservative member and former naval boxing champion, he crossed the floor of the house and struck him in the face. Shinwell then turned on his heels and stalked out of the chamber, muttering angrily to himself.

He was given no office in the coalition government during the 1939–45 war and instead became a mostly constructive critic of government policies. It was commonly believed that Shinwell stayed out of the government because he had refused a junior post. He would like to have been minister of fuel and power, and he was given the ministry when Labour won the 1945 election. His first effort was the implementation of a long-standing Labour commitment – nationalisation of the mines – but it coincided with an economic crisis and proved his downfall. The date of nationalisation was set for 1 January 1947. Because of the crisis Shinwell warned that there might be shortages but denied that there would be any dislocation of industry or closing of factories. It was an unwise pledge. On 10 February he was forced to announce in the house of commons that much of the nation's industry would have to close because of coal shortages. He was fiercely criticised for making the original statement and for the perfunctory way in which he had made the closure announcement. It was a scarring experience and thereafter he became wary of nationalisation, arguing that nationalised industries should be demonstrably successful before any further nationalisation took place.

He remained in office, but not for long. Although prime minister Clement Attlee expressed confidence in him (a standard but meaningless procedure for criticised ministers) Shinwell was moved to the war office in October of the same year and ceased to be a member of the cabinet. He was bitter at being transferred from such a prize ministry, and failed to see that he had only himself to blame for having failed to plan for an impending crisis. It could have been difficult for a radical working class activist with a prison record to deal with the patrician ranks of senior army officers, but he adjusted to the problems of his new ministry and got on well with his army colleagues.

He returned to the cabinet in March 1950 as minister of defence and had to face the war in Korea, mounting tension in Berlin, terrorism in Malaya, and Russian nuclear tests. He did his utmost to modernise the armed forces and was a strong supporter of NATO. In office he had supported the concept of a British nuclear deterrent, but in opposition he became a strong opponent of nuclear weapons.

His influence in the Labour Party began to wane after the 1951 election and he never held office again. He had been unseated from party's national executive in 1941 and failed to gain re-election in 1952 and 1953. He left the shadow cabinet in 1955 and moved to the backbenches where he remained until he left the house of commons in 1970. When Labour came back to power in 1964 he was eighty years old and, despite a youthful vigour, he was too old for ministerial office. He was elected (and twice re-elected) chairman of the parliamentary Labour Party in 1964 and proved to be loyal and able if authoritarian. In later years he developed a passionate dislike of the European Economic Community as it was then, and in 1967 he bitterly opposed the government's decision to apply for membership of the EEC and at a party meeting he lost his temper and a furious row ensued with the foreign secretary and the leader of the house. Discontent grew and he eventually resigned in 1967.

Although his vigour was undimmed, he did not stand at the 1970 election (he was then eighty-five). He was made a life peer in 1970, and was an active, alert and outspoken member of the house of lords until well into his nineties. For one who had himself once been a militant rebel his resignation of the Labour whip in 1982 was a surprise. He had chaired the influential all-party house of lords defence study group for several years and resigned in protest against left-wing militancy. He remained a member of the Labour Party, but sat thereafter on the crossbenches. He was only the second centenarian member of the house of lords, and in 1984 the house gave him a reception to mark his one-hundredth birthday. He was three times married and three times widowed, and having reached the milestone of his first century, he began to fail and died seven months after his one hundred and first birthday.

He published a number of volumes of reminiscences: *Conflict without malice* (1955), *The Labour story* (1963), *I've lived through it all* (1973), *Lead with the left* (1981) and *My first ninety-six years* (1981).

He was made a CH in 1965 with an unnecessarily long citation: 'Member of Parliament for Linlithgow 1922–1924 and 1928–1931; for the Seaham Division of Durham 1935–50 and for Easington since 1950. Minister of Fuel and Power 1945–1947; Secretary of State for War 1947–1950; Minister of Defence 1950–1951. Chairman of the Parliamentary Labour Party since November 1964. For political and public services.'

Baroness Summerskill 1 January 1966
Edith Summerskill was a feminist physician and politician whose contributions to the house of commons centred on health issues and the rights of women.

She was born at Doughty Street, London in 1901, the daughter of a physician of radical views who strongly supported the right of women to vote. She was educated at Eltham Hill Grammar School, King's College and later Charing Cross Hospital where she herself qualified as a doctor in 1924. She practised medicine in Wood Green, London, and in 1928 was invited to become a co-opted member of the maternity and child welfare committee. She became a member of the Labour Party and the Socialist Medical Association and in 1934 she was elected to Middlesex County Council, winning the Green Lanes division of Tottenham from the Conservative Party and holding it until 1941. She stood unsuccessfully for parliament at a by-election in Putney in 1934, and again at Bury in the 1935 general election. In 1938 she won West Fulham from the Conservatives in a by-election. With constituency boundary changes in 1955 she went to the north to represent Warrington until she left the house of commons in 1961.

She was a radical combative feminist whose main concerns – clean food, abortion, medicine, boxing (which she fiercely opposed) and the rights of married women – sprang from her family background and her medical training. In the postwar Labour government she was appointed parliamentary secretary to the ministry of food (1945–50) and minister of national insurance and industrial injuries (1950–51). She campaigned against tuberculosis and for the pasteurisation of milk in 1949, which she afterwards referred to as her 'finest hour'. Her publications included *Babies without tears* (1941), *The ignoble art* (1956), *Letters to my daughter* (1957), and *A woman's world* (1967). She died in 1980.

She was created a life peer in 1961 and a CH in 1966. The citation read: 'Member of Parliament for West Fulham, 1938–1955, and for Warrington, 1955–1961. Parliamentary Secretary, Ministry of Food, 1945–1950; Minister of National Insurance, 1950–1951; Chairman of the Labour Party, 1954–1955. For political and public services.'

James Griffiths 19 May 1966
Jim Griffiths was a garrulous and warm-hearted Labour politician who came from a background in the mines of south Wales to become the first secretary of state for Wales in 1964.

He was born at Ammanford, south Wales, in 1890, the youngest of the ten children of a local blacksmith, and only spoke Welsh until he was five years old. He was educated at Bettws council school and went from there to work at the local anthracite colliery at the age of thirteen. Four years later he joined the local branch of the Independent Labour Party. In 1919 he was awarded a scholarship to the Labour College in London and studied there for two years. In 1921 he returned to his work as a miner in Wales but spent four evenings a week teaching classes in economics and industrial history. In 1922 he took on his first full-time political post, as agent of the Llanelly Labour Party and in 1925 he became miners' agent in the Anthracite Mines Association. He became active in the South Wales Miners' Federation at a time of growing industrial unrest and became known as a skilful and patient negotiator. In 1934 he became president of the federation and was elected to the executive of the Miners' Federation of Great Britain.

He was elected to parliament at a by-election in Llanelly in 1936 (retaining it until his retirement in 1970) and in 1939 he was elected to the Labour Party national executive. His early working experiences had given him a lasting sense of indignation at the sight of deplorable working conditions and hatred of social injustice (though he was never embittered), and in the commons he denounced the means test, attacked mine owners and advocated social insurance. With the Labour victory in 1945 he was made minister of national insurance and charged with implementing the Beveridge report by providing a nationwide system of insurance against sickness, unemployment and old age. At the 1950 general election he retained his seat with a majority of 31,626, the highest in Wales and the fourth highest in the country. Surprisingly he was moved by Attlee to be secretary of state for the colonies, but he gave the job his utmost, travelling widely throughout the empire and devoting time to increasing native participation in colonial government. He would later boast that twelve new constitutions were effected while he was colonial secretary. 'His simple duty, as he conceived it, was to apply on a worldwide scale the liberalising benefits of the welfare state. If, in the eyes of his critics, he strayed into errors of judgement in colonial policy, his mistakes were those of a man whose heart ruled his head.'[92]

The Labour defeat in 1951 brought thirteen years on the opposition benches. But Griffiths was widely respected for his evident sincerity and he was elected deputy leader of the parliamentary Labour Party in 1955 (defeating Aneurin Bevan) and held the post until he retired in 1959. When Labour returned to power in October 1964, Griffiths was seventy-four years old, but he was respected by all sections of the party and Harold Wilson gave him the post that was the culmination of his political career and one which gave him the greatest pleasure. Wilson established a new department, headed by a minister with a seat in the cabinet: secretary of state for Wales. It was a fitting and crowning end to a man who had begun his working life in the grim conditions of a south Wales colliery more than sixty years earlier. Griffiths was a radical Welsh nonconformist revivalist orator whose political formation owed much to the influences of his early working life and his homeland. 'Cynics might sneer when Jim Griffiths, hand on heart in that familiar gesture, poured out a flood of Celtic emotion. In his highest flights of Welsh fervour he could be prolix, repetitive and often obscure, but real sincerity shone through the welter of words. He beguiled by lack of guile. Much more than by what he said – and he said a great deal – Jim Griffiths commanded respect and affection by what he was, a man who enriched and sweetened political life by rare qualities of heart and mind.'[93] Because of his age, he was never going to be long in the cabinet. He retired from the government in April 1966 and from the house of commons in 1970. He died in 1975.

He was made a CH in 1966 as 'Member of Parliament for Llanelly Division of Carmarthenshire since 1936. Minister of National Insurance, 1945–1950; Secretary of State for the Colonies, 1950–1951; Secretary of State for Wales, 1964–1966. For political and public services.'

Lady Megan Lloyd George 19 May 1966
Megan Lloyd George was very much the daughter of her father. She was like him in temperament, inheriting his passionate radicalism (which never mellowed or diminished with age and ill-health) and maintaining in parliament – first as a Liberal and then as a Labour member, a spirited independence. In 1949 all the women members of the house of commons presented her with a book to commemorate her twenty years as a member. In it she was described as 'a true daughter of the Welsh Wizard: she bewitches friend and foe alike.'[94]

She was born at Criccieth in 1902, the younger daughter of her famous father, and for the first four years of her life she could only speak Welsh. From the age of eight until she was twenty-two she lived with her father in Downing Street, firstly at number eleven (when her father was chancellor of the exchequer) and then at number ten (when he was prime minister), and she accompanied him to the peace conference at Versailles in 1919, where she often acted as his hostess. In 1924–25 she spent a year in India as the guest of the viceroy, Lord Reading but on her return developed an interest in politics and was elected Liberal member of parliament for Anglesey in 1929, the first successful woman candidate in Wales. Major Gwilym Lloyd George, her younger brother, was also a member of parliament 'and with three members of the Lloyd George family in the House together harmony was often strained in the parliamentary Liberal Party.'[95] After their father's death in 1945 Gwilym and Megan drifted apart politically – she to the left and he to the right – but they remained personally close.

In 1949 she was appointed deputy leader of the party but condemned its gradual drift to the right as contrary to the old radical Liberal tradition in which she had been reared, and often found herself at variance with her colleagues. She held on to her seat until 1951 when Cledwyn Hughes defeated her in a three-cornered fight. It was a blow as she had represented the constituency for twenty-two years and increased her majority at the 1950 election. But she was increasingly out of step with the Liberal Party and announced in 1952 that she would not contest Anglesey again as a Liberal.

While she was out of the commons she became president of a campaign to press for the establishment of a Welsh parliament, and in 1955 she joined the Labour Party which more closely matched her radical tradition. She campaigned for the party in the 1955 election and in 1957 she won the seat of Carmarthen (previously held by the Liberals) at a by-election. One of her opponents was another woman, Jennie Davies of Plaid Cymru. Labour returned to power in 1964 but there was never any question of ministerial office. She was sixty-two and her reputation as an uncontrollable maverick was sufficient for any government to be terrified of giving her a post. 'She was primarily a Welsh radical, of a very independent turn of mind, and she did not always march very precisely in step or seem completely at home with her Labour colleagues . . . She undoubtedly liked best the freedom of the back benches to campaign independently for the causes she had most at heart – against privilege, the House of Lords, rural slums, Tourism, the under-payment of agricultural workers, and generally, as champion of the underdog . . . She had her roots in rural North Wales and always proudly belonged to her native countryside and people, among whom she mostly lived. She was sometimes the despair of party managers but she remained true to her life-long political instincts and was a charming embodiment of Wales and Westminster.'[96] She died in harness in 1966.

Plans to make her a CH in 1966 were made when she was known to be dying, but she died five days before the honour was publicly announced. She never married and the badge was sent to her next of kin Lady Owen Carey Evans. Lady Megan's citation read: 'Member of Parliament for Anglesey, 1929–1951. Member of Parliament for Carmarthen, since 1957. For political and public services.'

Lord Houghton of Sowerby 5 January 1967
Douglas Houghton was one of the last survivors of the battle of Passchendaele, a trade unionist, a broadcaster, a Labour member of parliament and government

minister, who infamously took a significant role in wrecking the Labour government's plan for trade union reform in the summer of 1969.

He was born at Long Eaton, Derbyshire in 1898, and educated at a county secondary school. He worked briefly in London as a post office clerk before joining the Civil Service Rifles at the outbreak of the 1914–18 war. At the age of nineteen he fought at the third battle of Ypres (Passchendaele) where the allies suffered 300,000 casualties. Memories of the injustices perpetrated during that war remained with him to the end of his life and in 1993 he tried to obtain pardons for the 300 soldiers who had been shot for cowardice or desertion.

After demobilisation he joined the inland revenue and became a prominent figure in the Association of Officers of Taxes, being appointed general secretary in 1922, and through his organisational skills, built the union into the Inland Revenue Staff Federation. In 1936 he noticed a young clerk named James Callaghan and got him elected assistant general secretary. Although Houghton had left the house of commons and was in any case too old for ministerial office when Callaghan became prime minister in 1976, they remained firm friends.

The IRSF was a comparatively small white-collar trade union and never had the serious political influence of the larger unions, but Houghton became a national figure during the 1939–45 war by way of the media. The government and the BBC chose Houghton to explain, through broadcasting, the way the tax system worked, to the large number of people who were having to pay income tax for the first time. The programme was a success and developed beyond the world of finance. 'He found himself answering queries about the worries and secret fears of ordinary people and his programme was renamed *Can I help you?* Houghton, authoritative, reasonable and helpful, became a national institution.'[97]

The fame that came to Houghton through the media made him an ideal candidate for a parliamentary by-election in the Yorkshire constituency of Sowerby. In 1949 the former member, John Belcher, resigned after implication in a financial scandal, and the government were concerned that seat would be lost to the Conservatives (from whom Labour had won it in the 1945 election). 'The Labour Party wanted somebody who would be a picture of responsibility and probity. Houghton, a Labour alderman on London County Council with his outstanding broadcasting reputation, fitted the bill. He repaid his party's confidence by retaining the seat and holding it comfortably for the rest of his Commons career.'[98]

Houghton's parliamentary style was at first disappointingly clumsy, but he quickly improved and Hugh Gaitskell promoted him to the front bench as an opposition Treasury spokesman. In 1963 he succeeded Harold Wilson as chairman of the important public accounts committee and with Labour's victory in the 1964 election, he joined the cabinet as chancellor of the duchy of Lancaster, with practical responsibility for coordinating social security services and revitalising the welfare state. He retained the brief in a reshuffle in April 1966, exchanging his archaic but exact title for the more vague one of minister without portfolio. Without a department of his own, he had no power to implement his plans and his hopes for a radical reorganisation of the social security and pensions system never materialised. He was dropped from the government in January 1967 ostensibly on the grounds of age – he was sixty-eight.

Wilson thought that Houghton would settle into a comfortable and uncontroversial retirement. Houghton thought otherwise. The chairmanship of the

Parliamentary Labour Party became vacant; Houghton was elected and almost immediately became embroiled in the government's ill-fated plans to reform trade unions, including the introduction of the law into trade union disputes by outlawing unofficial strikes. Opposition to the plan was led by Houghton and by James Callaghan, the home secretary. Houghton was later bitterly accused by Harold Wilson and the responsible cabinet minister, Barbara Castle, of sabotaging the policy. In *The Crossman diaries* Wilson talked of 'treacherous deals' between Houghton and the TUC general council, and Castle described Callaghan and Houghton as 'playing in double harness like a comic and his feed-man.'[99]

He remained a tough and effective chairman of the parliamentary party until 1974, but he voted with the Conservative Party on the principle of entry into the European Economic Community in 1971. Mutterings of discontent surfaced in his constituency and he decided not to stand in the February 1974 general election. Created a life peer he was a regular contributor to the work of the house of lords. He chaired the inquiry into teachers' pay and the committee which recommended financial help for political parties from public funds. With memories of his first career he spoke on the tax system, and also on birth control, sexual law reform and animal rights. He survived to become the oldest living parliamentarian at the time of his death in 1996 – at the age of 97 and after a public life of more than 70 years.

He was made a CH in 1967 on his retirement as minister without portfolio; no citation or description of appointment accompanied his name. On 9 January 1992 he asked a curious parliamentary question about the Order, wanting to know 'whether facilities exist for them to meet in companionship and to confer on matters of public concern'.

Lord Gordon-Walker 8 June 1968

Patrick Gordon Walker was one of the unluckiest politicians of his generation. He could have been an eminent foreign secretary, but the loss of his parliamentary seat in 1964 ended his chances.

He was born at Worthing in 1907, the elder son of a Scottish judge of the supreme court of Lahore in the Indian civil service. After his early years spent in the Punjab, he was educated at Wellington and at Christ Church, Oxford where he took a degree in history. Graduation was followed by a thesis on the national debt, and election in 1931 as a Student and history tutor at Christ Church. A year spent at German universities left him fluent in German and with a passionate hatred of totalitarianism in all its forms. His father was a Fabian and he inherited from him a strong sense of social justice and of responsibility for the welfare of the population of the empire, and became a convinced democratic socialist.

He unsuccessfully contested the city of Oxford at the 1931 general election, but withdrew from the 1938 by-election. During the 1939–45 war his knowledge of German was put to use when he broadcast for the BBC. He accompanied the invasion force in 1944 and was among the first British broadcasters to take possession of Radio Luxemburg which became the allies' main radio station on the European mainland. He returned to Britain to be director of the German service at the BBC and in October 1945 he was elected to parliament at a by-election in the Birmingham constituency of Smethwick. In 1946 he became parliamentary private secretary to Herbert Morrison and in 1947 parliamentary under secretary at the Commonwealth Relations Office. It was a time made difficult by Burma's decision to leave the Commonwealth and by India's determination to move to republican status which could have led to the same outcome. He was sent to India as Clement Attlee's personal representative and by his delicate negotiating won the trust of Nehru and agreed a formula that would allow a republican India to remain with the Commonwealth. After the 1950 election he joined the cabinet as secretary of state for commonwealth relations, but found himself embroiled in difficulties surrounding the government's refusal to recognise Seretse Khama as head of the dominant Bamamgwato tribe in Bechuanaland, and black African hostility towards plans for the creation of a central African federation.

While Labour was in opposition from 1951 to 1964 he was the party's principal spokesman on international affairs and travelled widely in the Commonwealth. He was on the social democratic 'right wing' of the Labour Party and a trusted lieutenant of both Hugh Gaitskell and Harold Wilson. In 1951 he published a work of political philosophy entitled *Restatement of liberty*, in which he outlined his belief in 'the third way' – more than forty years before that phrase became politically fashionable.

In 1963 Wilson appointed him shadow foreign secretary, and in the 1964 general election he could have expected to hold the substantive office. Every general election throws up a fluke result in which a party wins the election but some of its MPs lose their seats; Gordon Walker was one such case in 1964. He was defeated in Smethwick by 1,774 votes, the only member of the shadow cabinet to be so humiliated. The circumstances of his defeat were thought to arise from his opposition to the Immigration Act of the previous Conservative government. Birmingham was afflicted by extreme racism at the time and Gordon Walker fell victim.

For a brief few months (October 1964 to January 1965) he was actually secretary of state for foreign and commonwealth relations, though he was a member of neither house of parliament. The unusual appointment was made on the understanding that a seat would be found for him. In January 1965 Reginald Sorensen, Labour member for the London constituency of Leyton was persuaded to accept a peerage and resign to make way for Gordon Walker. But the voters of Leyton were not so easily persuaded to take on someone who had been defeated in another constituency and whereas it had been thought to be a safe enough seat (7,926 majority at the 1964 election) he lost the by-election by 205 votes. When the result was declared, he resigned as foreign secretary.

To his credit he refused to look for a safer seat, and stood for Leyton again at the 1966 election, winning it by more than 8,000 votes. He joined the cabinet as minister without portfolio (January to August 1967) and secretary of state for education and science (August 1967 to April 1968), but the interregnum had finished his chances of resuming the office of foreign secretary. It was all the more galling because his successor, Michael Stewart, had little experience of foreign affairs. He left the government at a reshuffle in the spring of 1968 and never returned. He went to the house of lords in 1974 and was a member of the European parliament (1975–76). His fellow cabinet minister and obituarist delivered an assessment of a man with whom fate had dealt unkindly. 'Gordon Walker may well be considered the unluckiest and most ill-starred of his generation of political leaders. He would undoubtedly have made a wise and courageous foreign secretary. In the sense that parliamentary politics are as important a test of character as of ability he will be remembered as having personal qualities rare in public life. In the face of heart-breaking disappointment that might well have crippled his spirit, he remained totally without self-pity or bitterness. He had a quiet depth of conviction and a magnanimity of spirit that set an example of dignity in the face of adversity.'[100]

He was made a CH in 1968 for his services as 'Member of Parliament for Smethwick 1945–1964; and for Leyton since 1966. Parliamentary Under Secretary of State, Commonwealth Relations Office 1947–1950; Secretary of State for Commonwealth Relations 1950–1951. Secretary of State for Foreign Affairs October 1964 – January 1965. Minister without Portfolio 1967. Secretary of State for Education and Science 1967–1968.' He was created a life peer in 1974, adding a hyphen to his names to become Lord Gordon-Walker. He died in 1980.

Lord Stewart of Fulham 1 January 1969
Michael Stewart was a teacher turned politician who held three important ministries in Harold Wilson's first government (1964–70), but never quite seemed to reach the potential of his offices.

He was born in 1906 and educated at Christ's Hospital and St John's College, Oxford. On graduation he began a career as a schoolmaster, firstly at Merchant Taylors' School (1930–31) and then at the Coopers' Company's School (1931–42). He was also a tutor with the Workers' Educational Association (1931–42). In 1931 and 1935 he unsuccessfully contested West Lewisham as a Labour candidate. He joined the Army Intelligence Corps in 1942 and was transferred to the Educational Corps in 1943. He won East Fulham in a by-election in 1945 and held it (it was twice renamed) until 1979. He was a government whip (1946–47) and then parliamentary under secretary of state at the war ministry (1947–51) and at the ministry of supply (1951).

After thirteen years on the opposition benches, Labour was returned to power in October 1964. 'Harold Wilson admired and came to rely upon Stewart's qualities. He . . . saw in Stewart a man broadly of the right wing of the Party who was not tainted as a 'Gaitskellite'. This, together with his high ability and wide range of knowledge, made Stewart one of Harold Wilson's most trusty and hardest worked lieutenants.'[101] Stewart remained in the cabinet throughout the 1964–70 Labour government, but in a variety of appointments beginning with secretary of state for education (1964–65). It was an obvious appointment for a former teacher, but his tenure was brief. In January 1965 he was moved to the appointment of foreign secretary on the resignation of Patrick Gordon Walker. Stewart had no experience of foreign affairs and he was not an obvious candidate in the eyes of many. But it was a relatively short occupancy, and in August 1966 he exchanged jobs with George Brown, this time to the newly created post of first secretary of state and secretary of state for economic affairs, with responsibility for introducing the government's prices and incomes policy.

The grand title of 'first secretary of state' placed Stewart immediately below the prime minister in rank but it was otherwise meaningless. More significantly it carried more than a suggestion that the occupant was heir apparent to the prime minister, and its high domestic profile caused speculation in the press that Stewart would be the most likely successor to Wilson. Stewart himself harboured hopes that he might become prime minister, and he remained disappointed that he had not launched a vigorous campaign to succeed Hugh Gaitskell as leader in 1960.

In March 1968 George Brown resigned over the conduct of government business and Wilson returned Stewart to the foreign office where he stayed for the remainder of the Labour government's term. In October 1968 the foreign and commonwealth relations offices were merged and he became secretary of state for foreign and commonwealth affairs. It was a difficult time. He had to face the civil war in Nigeria and the increasing American involvement in Vietnam. The latter campaign aroused heated emotion and Stewart came under attack from extremes of opinion. One side argued that the United Kingdom should give a concrete expression of their support by committing British troops to south-east Asia. The other side demanded an unequivocal condemnation of American involvement in Vietnam. Invited to speak at an Oxford union debate, Stewart had to abandon the attempt in the face of shouts of 'Murderer Stewart' and 'Stewart, we want you dead.' Denis Healey, his contemporary in the Wilson cabinet, remembered that he was perhaps the wrong man for the job 'He had total moral and intellectual integrity, but perhaps lacked the drive and imagination the job needed at that time.'[102]

As a former teacher he was used to dealing with passionate and intemperate youth by patience, reason and logic, but feelings about the war ran very high, and calm, measured and rational debate was rarely possible. He could be impatient of ill-founded criticism of his policies and delighted in exposing faults in the arguments of his opponents. But he was never theatrical and consequently never sufficiently charismatic to arouse the recognition and approval of the public. 'He was always well-briefed and showed himself a master of fact and argument in the many difficult debates in which he figured as a minister in the house of commons. But he never used a resonant or telling phrase or struck an attitude calculated to fire or move the public.'[103]

After defeat of the Labour government in 1970, Stewart stood as a candidate in the elections for the shadow cabinet and suffered a crushing defeat. His political career was at an end. 'Stewart was cheated of his highest ambitions. But neither ambitions nor disappointment could mar or warp him. Not even his bitterest enemies doubted his personal and political probity and honour nor his unswerving service to the Labour Party.'[104] When the Labour Party returned to power in 1974, Stewart was by then aged sixty-seven and remained on the back benches. He retired from the commons in 1979, accepted a life peerage, and died in 1990.

He was made a CH in 1969, nine months after the beginning of his second term as foreign secretary. The entry in the *London Gazette*, no more than a recital of his political offices, occupied eighteen lines and was the longest entry for any CH: 'Member of Parliament for East Fulham, 1945–1955; and for Fulham since 1955. A Lord Commissioner of HM Treasury, 1945–1946; Comptroller of HM Household; Vice-Chamberlain of HM Household, 1947; Parliamentary Under-Secretary of State, War Office, and Financial Secretary, 1947–1951; Parliamentary Secretary, Ministry of Supply, 1951; Secretary of State for Education and Science, 1964–65; Secretary of State for Foreign Affairs, 1965–1966; First Secretary and Secretary of State for Economic Affairs 1966–1967; First Secretary of State, 1967–1968; Secretary of State for Foreign Affairs, 1968; Secretary of State for Foreign and Commonwealth Affairs since 1968.'

Lord Duncan-Sandys *1 January 1973*
A son-in-law of Winston Churchill, Duncan Sandys was a cabinet minister in every Conservative government from 1951 to 1964. He was charming, dynamic, courageous as much as he was stern, ruthless, unscrupulous and contemptuous, and not for nothing was described as a political commando who undertook a series

of ministries requiring a strong and determined hand on the tiller at a time of unpopular change.

He was born in 1908, the only son of Captain George Sandys, member of parliament for Wells (1910–18). He was educated at Eton and at Magdalen College, Oxford. He was called to the bar at the Inner Temple but never practised as a barrister. He decided in 1930 to join the diplomatic service and served in Berlin as a member of the embassy staff. In 1933 he returned to London and represented the foreign office in negotiations for commercial treaties with the northern European countries, and was a member of the British delegation to the abortive world economic conference. He resigned from the diplomatic service at the end of 1933 to enter politics and in 1935 was returned as Conservative member for the Norwood division of Lambeth. He attracted attention by a complaint to the Speaker in 1938 that he had been summoned, in his capacity as a territorial officer, to appear before a military court of inquiry to answer for the source of certain allegedly secret information contained in a question which he proposed to put to the secretary of state for war. A report by the committee of privileges cleared the reputations of all concerned but left the impression on many 'that Sandys had courted martyrdom by announcing his intention to ask publicly a question he had never intended to put down.'[105]

At the outbreak of the 1939–45 war he joined the army and served with the Norwegian expeditionary force. He was promoted to the rank of lieutenant-colonel in 1941, but injury in a car crash released him from the army on disability grounds and allowed him to resume his political career. He had married Winston Churchill's daughter in 1935 and it was Churchill, by now prime minister, who made him financial secretary to the ministry of supply (1941–43), parliamentary secretary (responsible for armaments production), ministry of supply (1943–44) and minister of works (1944–45). More important than the titular ministerial appointments was his chairmanship of the war cabinet committee (1943–45) charged with defending the country against the V1 and V2 missiles. Sandys was largely responsible for devising the successful policy of anticipating attack by the sustained bombardment of the German research station at Peenemunde and the rocket bases in the Pas de Calais and elsewhere.

With many other Conservative MPs, Sandys lost his seat in the 1945 election, and instead founded the European Movement in 1947 (he was chairman of the international executive until 1950), which was to become the most important political theme of the rest of his life. He returned to the commons in 1950 for the south London constituency of Streatham and held it until 1974. With the return of a Conservative government in 1951, he was made minister of supply (1951–54) and was charged with the task of denationalising the iron and steel industry in the face of bitter Labour opposition. As minister of housing and local government (1954–57) he oversaw the more controversial abolition of rent restriction, the government arguing that it would eventually create an adequate supply of property for rent. As minister of defence (1957–59) it fell to him to implement Macmillan's radical reform of the nation's defence. It was predicated on the beliefs that the nation's safety depended on the nuclear deterrent, that there was no effective defence against a nuclear attack, and that the principle thrust of defence policy should be the avoidance of a major war. The country would be best served by a small, efficient, well-paid and highly mobile army, and that would mean a reduction in conventional armaments and abolition of conscription.

His stay at the defence ministry was followed by a short nine-month tenure as minister of civil aviation (1959–60), charged with helping the aircraft industry face the reduction in the demand for military aircraft involved in the new defence policy.

His last ministerial appointment was his longest. In July 1960 he became secretary of state for commonwealth relations, and additionally secretary of state for the colonies in 1962, holding both offices until the Conservative defeat in October 1964. It was a transitional age for Britain, its colonies and the emerging independent Commonwealth states. Sandys was not a sentimental imperialist and was convinced that the dismantling of the empire was inevitable. He had failures as well as successes. Many thought that he could – had he behaved with greater diplomatic patience between Sir Edgar Whitehead and Joshua Nkomo – have secured a multiracial parliament for Southern Rhodesia. In 1963 he drove unprotected through the streets of Accra at the side of President Kwame Nkrumah, who had recently been the target of an attempted assassination, as proof that there would be no danger to the Queen in her forthcoming state visit to Ghana. 'In the eyes of a succession of Conservative prime ministers, Sandys' role seems to have been that of a kind of political commando, specially equipped for tasks of extreme peril. His dominant characteristics were toughness, fortitude and almost incredible industry. The impression produced by his early political career turned out to be surprisingly inaccurate. The ebullient young man, who threw himself wholeheartedly into Churchill's campaign against the Chamberlain leadership, was considered by many to be something of a lightweight. It was a very different figure who emerged as a leading member of the wartime coalition. From then onwards, Sandys' critics might be disposed to accuse him of ruthlessness and even of lack of subtlety, but none could deny his iron nerves . . . Nevertheless, he lacked the flexibility necessary to win wide favour in the House of Commons, and also to some extent the common touch indispensable to a popular leader. He never became a serious contender for the leadership of the Conservative Party.'[106]

The defeat of the Conservative Party in the 1964 election spelled the end of his political career. In the years of opposition he worked for his favourite causes, including the Civic Trust, Europe, conservation and the environment, and he indulged his hobby of abstract painting. He was not given ministerial office in the government of Edward Heath (1970–74). At the age of sixty-two, he was too old. Instead he began a new career in 1972 as a chairman of Lonrho, the conglomerate built up by 'Tiny' Rowland. In 1973 a public boardroom split over Rowland's style of management led to a court case in which it was revealed that Sandys had been paid £130,000 to give up a consultancy to become chairman, and his salary as chairman had been paid in part into overseas tax havens. Edward Heath famously described the affair as 'the unpleasant and unacceptable face of capitalism,' and a department of trade report criticised Sandys for being 'less than frank with boardroom colleagues'. But he remained loyal to the company until his retirement in 1984.

In 1935, he married Winston Churchill's daughter Diana. She was long affected by ill-health and they divorced in 1960. She committed suicide three year later. His second wife was Marie-Claire Schmitt, daughter of Adrien Schmitt and former wife of Viscount Hudson CH. He died in 1987.

He was created a life peer in 1974, adopting the then fashionable trend of hyphenating his first and surnames to produce the composite title of 'Lord Duncan-Sandys'. He was made a CH in the New Year Honours List 1973 'for political and public services', a few months before the Lonrho 'affair.'

Baroness Ward of North Tyneside 2 June 1973

Irene Ward was a rumbustious and indomitable backbench Conservative member of parliament. She was the counterpart of the equally formidable Bessie Braddock on the Labour backbenches, and was the longest-serving woman member of the house of commons.

She was born at Newcastle in 1895, the daughter of an architect. After leaving school she became a secretary, working for an industrialist. In her spare time she was honorary secretary of the Northumberland Conservative Association. After unsuccessfully contesting Morpeth in 1924 and 1929, she won Wallsend in 1931, defeating Margaret Bondfield, the first Labour woman cabinet minister. She was defeated, with many other Conservatives, in the Labour landslide of 1945, but returned to the house of commons in 1950 as member for Tynemouth. She also served as a justice of the peace for Newcastle from 1949.

Irene Ward was a joyfully independent spirit, too much so ever to be considered for government office, and she never expected it. She embarrassed successive prime ministers with her awkward questions and on one occasion she occupied the traditional seat of the prime minister on the front bench and refused to move, stating that she was carrying out a peaceful picket in aid of pensioners' rights. She remained loyal to the constituency which returned her to parliament from 1950 to 1974 and saw her primary duty as being to defend the interests of the shipyard workers and industries of Tyneside. She became notorious for badgering ministers on local issues. When she once barracked a Labour cabinet minister during his speech, he finally snapped and accused her of behaving like a fishwife. She swiftly retorted that she represented a fishing constituency and was proud of it. In 1968 she was suspended for five days by the speaker of the commons (Horace King) for protesting on the floor of house in a debate over the Finance Bill, arguing with the speaker and getting in the way of the tellers at the end of a division. King later remembered how much it had upset him to suspend a member that he regarded as an old friend.

Her concern for Tyneside was matched by her concern for nurses, although she had never been one herself, and she regularly challenged governments on the low pay of nurses. She acted as their spokesperson in the commons and served on committees of the Royal College of Nursing and the Royal College of Midwives. She was publicly thanked for her commitment to nursing when she was made an honorary vice-president of the Royal College of Nursing. In 1955 she wrote a history of the First Aid Nursing Yeomanry entitled *FANY Invicta*.

Irene Ward was known for her colourful flowered hats and during one division in the commons, she lent her hat to three male members in succession to allow them to make points of order – the house rules requiring members to be 'seated and covered' when making points of order during a division. 'She got a great deal of fun out of politics – and gave a lot. Her entry into the Chamber was a bustling zestful progress as she disposed herself and her enormous handbag on her seat, rubbing her hands and peering eagerly about her.'[107]

She retired from the house of commons in 1974 and was created a life peer, taking the title of Baroness Ward of North Tyneside. She was never seduced by the superficial sophisticated charm of the capital city and she lived in Newcastle until her death in 1980.

She was made a CBE in 1929, a DBE in 1955 and a CH in 1973 'for political and public services.'

Viscount Whitelaw 1 January 1974

Willie Whitelaw was a delightfully old-fashioned Conservative politician whose warmth, compassion, flexibility, pragmatism and honourable nature won him widespread respect. 'Large, ebullient, amiably noisy and sometimes marvellously confused in his use of the English language (he once warned against the dangers of prejudging "the past"), he made friends and disarmed enemies with remarkable ease. His highly idiosyncratic comments on life and politics, known as "Willieisms", were widely savoured – none more so than his celebrated complaint in 1974 that the Labour Party was "going around the country stirring up apathy".'[108]

He was born in 1918 into a Scottish family with substantial property in the Glasgow district and in the Scottish lowlands. His great-grandfather and grandfather were both members of parliament, and a great-uncle married Disraeli's niece. He was educated at Winchester and Trinity College, Cambridge, where he took a third in law and a second in history. On leaving Cambridge, he joined the army and served as a regular officer in the Scots Guards (1939–47). Throughout the war he was in a Scots Guards tank battalion, reaching the rank of major in 1942. He was awarded the MC in the Normandy campaign and was twice mentioned in despatches. After leaving the army he managed the family estates in Lanarkshire, but with such an ancestry, the call to politics soon came. He fought East Dumbartonshire unsuccessfully in the general elections of 1950 and 1951. In 1954 he was adopted for Penrith and the Border, was elected in 1955 and retained the seat until the aftermath of the 1983 general election.

In 1956–58 he was parliamentary private secretary to his relative, Peter Thorneycroft, when he was president of the board of trade and then chancellor of the exchequer. He was appointed an assistant government whip in 1959 and then parliamentary under-secretary at the ministry of labour (1962–64). After the Conservative defeat in 1964 he was given the thankless task of chief whip and found it sometimes impossible to avoid damaging splits on key votes. After the Conservatives were returned to power in the 1970 election, he became lord president of the council and leader of the house of commons.

With the suspension of the Northern Ireland parliament in March 1972 and the imposition of direct rule, he became first secretary of state for Northern Ireland, faced with the near impossible task of breaking the fifty-year-old mould of Ulster politics. For such a genial man intent on compromise and consensus rather than confrontation, the sharp divisions and hereditary hatreds of the province came as a shock and left a lasting impression on his mind. He left the Northern Ireland office at the end of 1973, but those twenty-two months overshadowed everything else in his long political career. 'When he came to write his memoirs after his retirement in 1988, his publishers had the utmost difficulty in persuading him to give serious attention to his other political work. His most vivid and powerful memories were all of Ulster.'[109]

At the time he was acclaimed for bringing together leading political representatives from both communities in a power-sharing executive responsible to a new elected assembly, but his work had collapsed within six months. It was always going to be difficult to eradicate generations of deep hostility on both sides, and the institutions that he had created were innately frail in the face of unrelenting attacks from a widespread and extremist unionism which was determined not see the end of its historic rule of the province. It was typical of his candour that in later years he admitted that he had made mistakes. His genuine and good-natured desire to achieve consensus, which he rightly saw as the only route to a lasting peace, led him to introduce 'special category status' for senior IRA terrorists, exempting them from ordinary prison rules, and to engage in fruitless talks with leaders of the IRA in London in July 1972.

He returned to London in December 1973 to be secretary of state for employment where it was hoped that his conciliatory work in Northern Ireland could be used to end a bitter dispute with the miners. He proposed an improved pay offer, conditional on a firm pledge by the TUC that other unions would not base their pay claims on it, but it was rejected by prime minister Edward Heath in favour of an immediate general election in February 1974, to which Whitelaw was totally opposed.

He stood for the leadership of the Conservative Party in the second ballot in February 1975 and came second to Margaret Thatcher. His relations with her were always warm and she revived the post of deputy leader for him, giving him responsibility for shaping Conservative policy on law and order and other Home Office issues. With the formation of a Conservative government in 1979 he was appointed home secretary. 'His overriding concern as Home Secretary was to create conditions in which those responsible for law and order could operate more effectively. Where the previous Labour Government had cut, Whitelaw spent. He increased police pay substantially, making it possible to recruit an extra 10,000 officers by 1983. He began the largest programme of prison building and improvement this century. He also increased the range of penalties available to the courts so that they could punish serious criminals more severely, but also provide non-custodial sentences more easily for less serious offenders and young people.'[110] He was proud of his other achievements including: the creation of an independent complaints commission, preparing the way for the introduction of Channel 4, and the British Nationality Act 1981 which clarified and redefined the status of British citizens. His otherwise successful term of office was overshadowed by the unfavourable publicity that accompanied the riots and racial disturbances of 1981.

After the 1983 election, Whitelaw reluctantly agreed to become leader of the house of lords, but only agreed to go with an hereditary viscountcy. He retained the unofficial title of deputy prime minister until 1991 and Margaret Thatcher came to rely on his loyalty and trust his judgement. 'He certainly felt no reluctance about warning Mrs Thatcher privately against what he felt, sometimes with excessive nervousness, to be the faults of her policies.'[111] His good-nature and charm had to be used to the full in the upper chamber since, despite its inbuilt and overwhelming Conservative majority, it had inflicted a series of defeats on government legislation. Whitelaw accustomed the cabinet to the inevitability of defeat in the house of lords, but he succeeded in securing general agreement, on amendments to legislation which left the central principles of the government's policies intact. He retired from politics in 1991 and returned to his Scottish estates.

He was made a CH in 1974 'for political and public services' in recognition of his strenuous efforts in Northern Ireland, and a KT in 1990. He was created a viscount in 1983. His happy marriage produced four daughters but no sons and the viscountcy became extinct on his death in 1999.

Lord Aylestone 14 June 1975

Bert Bowden was a largely unknown Labour Party politician who, previously a military policeman, served as an effective whip, then as a less distinguished cabinet minister, and finally as a well regarded chairman of the Independent Television Authority.

He was born in Cardiff on 20 January 1905, the eldest of the eleven children of a baker. He had a secondary school education, then worked as a shop assistant and went to evening classes. He joined the Independent Labour Party but left it the moment it broke with the Labour Party over the latter's passive attitude to the Spanish Civil War.

In 1933 he moved from south Wales, after the failure of a tobacconist's shop which he had opened, and worked as a radio salesman in Leicester. He delved into local politics and became president of the Leicester City Labour Party and a member of the city council. At the outbreak of the 1939–4 war he spent three years as a regimental policeman before being commissioned into the RAF as an administrative officer. He won the previously Conservative constituency of Leicester South in the 1945 election. When it disappeared in the 1948 boundary redistribution, he moved to Leicester South-West until his retirement from the commons in 1967.

Bowden was a solid and dependable member and began his government career as parliamentary private secretary to the postmaster-general (1947–49). As a former military policeman, he was a natural candidate for the whips' office, which he joined in 1949. With Labour in opposition he was made deputy chief whip in 1951, and in 1955 succeeded William Whiteley as chief whip. Within a few months it fell to Bowden to meet with Attlee and tell him that he thought the time had come for him to make his mind up about his future. Two weeks later Attlee showed that he had taken the hint and told Bowden that he had decided to go.

Bowden was an admirer and supporter of Hugh Gaitskell and wanted him to win the leadership contest. When Gaitskell won on the first ballot Bowden spent the next seven years as Gaitskell's loyal supporter. In 1960 he made it clear that if Gaitskell were voted out of the leadership, he would resign, and he was later to say that the worst moment of his political life was when he heard of the death of Gaitskell in January 1963. Again it fell to him to organise the election, and again he knew whom he wanted to succeed – Harold Wilson. His behaviour was somewhat devious in that he instructed his fellow whips that they must not attempt to influence the outcome of the contest, but then broke the rule by confiding in Wilson (who made good use of the knowledge) that he preferred him to George Brown and Jim Callaghan. Though his relationship with Wilson was never as close as it had been with Gaitskell, it was sufficient for Wilson to repose trust in his chief whip.

Bowden was ever the disciplinarian in the party and his colleagues nicknamed him 'the Sergeant Major'. Even as a government minister (1964–67) he was incapable of changing habits. As leader of the house of commons (1964–66) he was a rigorous and unimaginative traditionalist who strongly opposed the televising of parliament and ignored demands for procedural reform put forward by the younger members. He was moved to be secretary of state for commonwealth relations (1966–67) to make way for Richard Crossman, but was no great success in this office. He spent most of his year in office trying to bring an end to the unilateral declaration of independence by the government in Southern Rhodesia, but although he tried hard (visiting Salisbury on three occasions) he made no headway.

In 1967 he left the government (and the house of commons) to become chairman of the Independent Television Authority. A claim, never substantiated, had it that he was put in as a successor to the disciplinarian Charles Hill who had left to 'deal' with the BBC. But it was known that Bowden, a man of few words, who had never felt easy with life on the front bench, wanted to leave the government. There was also evidence that Bowden himself was offered the choice of the BBC or the ITA. He fell naturally into the habit of a whip and 'managed' to secure the retirement of Sir Robert Fraser, the long-serving director-general. But his time as chairman was remembered with affection as a surprisingly tranquil one.

He retired into private life in 1975, but had to endure being cited by his next-door neighbour in an unsavoury divorce case in 1976. In 1981 he became leader of the peers of the new Social Democratic Party, having left the Labour Party when the SDP was formed that same year. He was in office only for a year, making way for Lord Diamond in 1982. He subsequently became a deputy speaker in the house of lords, publicly revealing that he was joining the Liberal Democrats on retirement from the deputy speakers' roster in 1992. He died in 1994.

He was appointed a CBE in 1953, created a peer in 1967 taking the title of Lord Aylestone (there was already a Lord Bowden) and made a CH in 1975 for his services as 'lately Chairman, Independent Broadcasting Authority.'

Lord Glenamara 27 May 1976
Ted Short was a Newcastle-based teacher and local politician who entered parliament in 1951 and became a trusted lieutenant of Harold Wilson during his two administrations (1964–70 and 1974–76) and served as deputy leader of the Labour Party for four years.

He was born in 1912 and educated at Bede College, Durham and at the University of London where he read law. He served in the 1939–45 war with a commission in the Durham Light Infantry. He became a teacher after the war and was headmaster of Princess Louise County Secondary School, Blyth, Northumberland (1947–51). He followed a parallel career in local politics, beginning as president of the North Newcastle Labour Party (1946). He was elected to Newcastle city council and was leader of the Labour group (1948–51). In 1951 he was elected member of parliament for Newcastle upon Tyne Central, and held the seat until his retirement in 1976. He served as an opposition whip (1955–62), deputy chief whip (1962–64) and chief whip (1964–66). He entered the cabinet in 1966 and served as postmaster general (1966–68) and secretary of state for education and science (1968–70). In opposition he served as spokesman on education (1970–72) and house of commons affairs (1972–74). When Labour returned to power in 1974 he was appointed lord president of the council and leader of the house of commons (1974–76). He was elected deputy leader of the Labour Party in December 1972, winning by the narrow margin of 145 votes to 116 cast for Michael Foot. He left the government in April 1976 when Harold Wilson resigned as prime minister, and retired from the house of commons and from the deputy leadership of the party in October of the same year on his appointment as chairman of the then state-owned Cable and Wireless Co.

He remained devoted to his homeland in the north-east and served as chancellor of the University of Northumbria at Newcastle (Newcastle Polytechnic until 1992) (from 1984); president of Finchale Abbey Training College for the Disabled (Durham) (1985-); and North East People to People (1989-). He was also a member of the council of the World Wildlife Fund (1983–92). He was the author of two publications reflecting his early army interests: *The story of the Durham Light Infantry* (1944) and *The infantry instructor* (1946). Two publications emerged from his government work as education spokesman: *Education in a changing world* (1971) and *Birth to five* (1974). He produced two volumes of autobiography: *I knew my place* (1983) and *Whip to Wilson* (1989).

Ted Short was a man of integrity who was widely admired on both sides of the house of commons. He was made a CH in 1976, one of the non-controversial names in Harold Wilson's controversial resignation honours list. The citation read: 'Lately Lord President of the Council. Member of Parliament for Newcastle upon Tyne, Central.' He was created a life peer in 1977, taking the title of Lord Glenamara.

Lord Cledwyn of Penrhos 31 December 1976

Cledwyn Hughes was an effective and skilled Labour cabinet minister who was largely unknown to the public because his ministerial career encompassed three departments of which the public knew little: the Commonwealth, Wales and agriculture.

He was born in Anglesey in 1916, the son of a Presbyterian minister, and educated at Anglesey Grammar School and University College, Aberystwyth, graduating with a degree in law. He qualified as a solicitor in 1940, served with the RAFVR (1940–45), and then began a career in local politics. He was a member of Anglesey County Council (1946–52), having already contested Anglesey in the 1945 general election. The constituency was traditionally Liberal, and was held by Lady Megan Lloyd George, daughter of the great Welsh prime minister. Hughes unsuccessfully contested the seat again in 1950 and succeeded in 1951 at the third attempt, with a very slender majority of 595 votes. After a period as a backbencher, his experience as a local politician (he had also been town clerk of Holyhead) made him an ideal opposition spokesman on housing and local government (1959–64).

When Labour won the 1964 election, Harold Wilson made Hughes a minister of state at the commonwealth relations office and in 1965 he became involved in the crisis over the illegal declaration of independence by the government of Southern Rhodesia. In 1966 he entered the cabinet as secretary of state for Wales, in succession to James Griffiths. His last cabinet appointment was as minister of agriculture, fisheries and food (1968–70), and he continued as the opposition spokesman on agriculture (1970–74).

The Labour defeat in 1970 ended his ministerial career. He was given no office in the Labour governments of Harold Wilson and James Callaghan (1974–79). It was thought that he might have been too pro-Europe at a time when the party was moving against membership of the EEC. He pursued an alternate career as a moderate within a divided and fractious party that enjoyed a wafer-thin majority in the commons. In July 1974 he was one of a group of fifty Labour backbenchers who resolved at a secret meeting to fight against domination of the party by left-wing militants. He challenged Ian Mikardo, recently elected chairman of the parliamentary Labour Party and won the post, by 163 votes to 131.

He found himself in the position of attempting to hold the Labour Party together. In 1978 Callaghan asked him to undertake a mission as 'envoy to southern Africa'.

He decided not to stand for parliament at the 1979 election and was given a life peerage. In 1982 he repeated in the house of lords, his 1974 challenge in the commons. Some colleagues suggested that he should replace Lord Peart as leader of the Labour Party in the house of lords. Peart, to whom Hughes had been deputy for a year, declined to stand down. In the ensuing vote Hughes won by 60 votes to 37. He achieved more prominence than his predecessors because of the recently introduced televised coverage, and because of the chamber's confident rejection of several pieces of legislation by the government of Margaret Thatcher. He retired as leader of the Labour peers in 1992, but remained active in the lords almost until the end of his life.

Hughes was a devoted child of his nation, and his Welsh sympathies deeply affected his views. He was a strong supporter of the proposals for devolution in Wales and attended the opening session of the new Welsh assembly in 1999. He was fluent in Welsh and used to claim that if he met ten people on the way to his office in Holyhead, nine of them would address him in Welsh. He was entrusted with the task of instructing the Prince of Wales in Welsh affairs prior to his investiture in 1969. He also pressed for a Welsh-language television channel. After leaving the commons he took up a number of public appointments in Wales including president of the University College of Wales at Aberystwyth (1976–85), pro-chancellor of the University of Wales (1985–94) and president of the University College of Wales at Bangor (1995–2001). A puritanical Welsh nonconformist background made him one of 24 Labour peers to vote in 1998 against the government bill to reduce the age of homosexual consent from 18 to 16. The lords overwhelmingly rejected the bill on that occasion. In 2000 he was one of 15 Labour peers to vote in defiance of the government whip to retain Section 28. He died in 2001.

He was made a CH in 1976 'for public service in Wales', and created a life peer in 1979 as Lord Cledwyn of Penrhos.

Lord Healey 12 June 1979
Denis Healey was a Labour chancellor of the exchequer of considerable intellect, whose misfortune it was to have to cope in the 1970s with the worst monetary crisis to face the country since the 1939–45 war.

He was born in Kent in 1917, the son of an engineering teacher and grandson of an Irish Fenian. In 1922 the family moved to the west riding of Yorkshire when his father was appointed principal of Keighley Technical School. He won a scholarship to Bradford Grammar School and another to Balliol College, Oxford, graduating with a first in moderations (1938) and a first in literae humaniores (1940). He joined the army in 1940 and served in the Royal Engineers in north Africa and Italy.

While at Oxford Healey was a member of the Communist Party and although he subsequently joined the Labour Party he began on its 'far left'. He contested Pudsey and Otley in 1945, and although he was defeated, the Conservative majority was reduced from 10,000 to fewer than 2,000. Afterwards he worked for six years at the Labour party's headquarters at Transport House. Watching the iron curtain fall across eastern Europe cured him of his extreme left-wing views and he published several anti-Soviet pamphlets. In February 1952 he was returned for South-East Leeds at a by-election. The seat became Leeds East in 1955 and he retained it until his retirement from the commons in 1992. In 1959 Hugh Gaitskell brought him into the shadow cabinet and, whether the Labour Party was in or out of power, he remained a front bench spokesman until 1987.

Throughout the Labour administration of 1964–70 Healey was secretary of state for defence. Despite making substantial cutbacks to British forces in the far east, Healey did much to calm the fears of the armed forces about what a Labour government might do to Britain's defence capacity. In 1972 Harold Wilson made him shadow chancellor of the exchequer and he held the substantive office (1974–79) when Labour returned to power. When Harold Wilson resigned as prime minister in April 1976, Healey stood in the leadership election, but came bottom of the poll in the first and second ballots.

It was a difficult time and events overtook him. In the aftermath of the Arab-Israeli war oil prices had risen dramatically, there were high wage demands, inflation was at nearly 20% and sterling was being battered in the currency markets. In 1975 he had to face the ignominy of being forced to go to the International Monetary Fund for a loan. He secured special drawing rights of £1000 million and a stand-by credit of £700 million. The financial crisis continued and in 1976 the IMF demanded public spending cuts of £3 billion. The experience was doubly humiliating – for a Labour chancellor and for a British chancellor. By 1978 the monetary crisis was over and the economy had returned to something approaching normal, but Healey's reputation had taken a hammering. That he survived was due to the unswerving support that he received from prime ministers Harold Wilson and James Callaghan, to his status as an intellectual heavyweight, to his down-to-earth style (he always retained a recognisable though cultured Yorkshire accent) and to his reputation for toughness. Nicknamed 'the old bruiser', he was not a person to engage in battle without a well-stocked intellectual armoury, and when roused his demeanour and temperament could be terrifyingly fierce and he could turn on his opponents with the force of a juggernaut. His most famous comment was in a debate on his budget proposals on 14 June 1978. On being attacked by Sir Geoffrey Howe, the Conservative shadow chancellor, Healey replied: 'That part of his speech was rather like being savaged by a dead sheep.' The phrase passed into folklore, although Healey later revealed that he had adapted it from a similar comment used by Churchill about Attlee.

The opposition years were in some ways as difficult as the years in government. When Jim Callaghan resigned in 1980, Healey again stood for the party leadership, this time against Michael Foot. He was defeated in the second ballot by only ten votes. He was elected unopposed as deputy leader in 1980 and served as foreign affairs spokesman (1980–87). But he was on the right wing of the party at a time when it was lurching to the left. In October 1981 he faced a challenge from Tony Benn and won by a margin of only 852 votes in a ballot of 100,000 (from 1981 election was by the party conference and no longer by MPs alone). The Social Democratic Party was founded in the same year and succeeded in recruiting 25 sitting Labour members. Tony Benn was to claim that he was the true deputy leader of the party, 'as Denis Healey's entire majority has now defected to the SDP.' He resigned as deputy leader of the party after the 1983 election. He retired as deputy leader and as a front bench spokesman in 1987 and from the house of commons in 1992. He published a volume of autobiography *The time of my life* in 1989.

He was made a CH in 1979 in James Callaghan's resignation honours list. The citation read: 'Member of Parliament for the East Division of Leeds. Lately Chancellor of the Exchequer.' He was created a life peer in 1992.

Lord Thorneycroft 31 December 1979
Peter Thorneycroft was a Conservative cabinet minister long remembered for resigning as chancellor of the exchequer with a flourish in January 1958. He was a jolly and kindly man, full of life, and in character resembled his fellow Conservative, William Whitelaw, but the office had been the high point in a career which never recovered from the dramatic gesture.

He was born in 1909, the son of Major Mervyn Thorneycroft, DSO, of Dunston Hall, Staffordshire. He was educated at Eton and the Royal Military Academy, Woolwich, and commissioned in the Royal Artillery. He soon resigned his commission and was called to the bar by the Inner Temple in 1935, after which he practised in Birmingham. In 1938 he abandoned the law in favour of politics and won Stafford at a by-election in 1938. During the 1939–45 war he served again in the Royal Artillery. He returned to commons towards the end of the war, playing an active role in the Tory reform committee which, with the assistance of the Labour Party, succeeded in inflicting on the coalition government its one defeat in the years 1940–45 over equal pay for men and women teachers. The victory was short-lived. Two days later the Conservative rebels were forced to humiliate themselves by voting for a government confidence motion. Churchill did not hold a grudge against Thorneycroft and the latter was given the post of parliamentary secretary to the ministry of war transport in the brief Conservative 'caretaker' government of May 1945. In the July 1945 election he was narrowly defeated in Stafford but the death of the Conservative member for Monmouth after polling day allowed him to return to the commons in October 1945 and he was to represent Monmouth for the next 21 years. His instinct for following his conscience led to a further rebellion when he defied the party whip and voted against the American loan agreement in the commons debate of December 1945.

Defiance of the whip excluded him for consideration for the shadow cabinet, but he was an influential backbencher until the Conservative Party was returned to office in 1951, when he was made president of the board of trade. The apotheosis of his career came in January 1957 when he was made chancellor of the exchequer by Harold Macmillan, whose campaign manager he had been in the struggle to succeed Anthony Eden. His main claim to fame as chancellor was to be known as 'Mr Seven Per Cent' a reference to his raising the bank rate to a higher level than it had been since 1921. His control of the nation's economy lasted barely a year. He resigned abruptly in January 1958 on the issue of cuts in defence spending. The treasury team had asked the cabinet for cuts of £150 million and had been offered £100 million. 'The rest of the Cabinet was said to be astonished that the figure could not be negotiated, not least because the supposedly "stern, unbending" Chancellor had been in politics quite long enough to understand the importance of give-and-take in Cabinet decision-making.'[112] But Thorneycroft would not compromise and his resignation was accompanied by those of Enoch Powell (financial secretary to the treasury) and Nigel Birch (economic secretary). Powell and Birch were said to be the architects of resistance and to have swept the chancellor along with them. Macmillan was about to leave London for a Commonwealth tour and at the airport he famously dismissed the three resignations as 'a little local difficulty'. Thorneycroft was only forty-eight and with the chancellorship to his credit, he could have laid claim to the leadership of the party; but from then on he was on the downhill slope.

His isolation on the backbenches lasted until July 1960 when Macmillan, remembering old times, magnanimously brought him back into the cabinet as minister of aviation with responsibility for persuading the cabinet to support the Concorde project. In July 1962 'the night of the long knives', resulted in his promotion to be minister and then secretary of state for defence and he kept the post until the government was defeated in October 1964. However his standing in the Conservative Party had diminished and he was never considered to be a serious contender for the leadership in 1965.

He was defeated at Monmouth in the 1966 general election and was created a life peer in 1967. He regularly appeared in the house of lords mainly to speak in economic debates, 'where he could be counted upon to restate his faith in free enterprise and his hatred of corporatism.'[113] Like almost every other former cabinet minister, he quickly entered the world of business and accepted a number of company directorships. From 1972 to 1975 he was the chairman (unpaid) of the British Overseas Trade Board.

He could have disappeared permanently into commercial obscurity but for the fact that one who had not even been a member of parliament at the time remembered his 1958 stand on principle many years later. Margaret Thatcher was elected to the commons in 1959 and was elected leader of the Conservative Party in 1975. She was a passionate believer in the necessity of curbing public expenditure. Thorneycroft, who was already sixty-six and not in the best of health, was called out of retirement to become chairman of the Conservative Party. Instead of the customary two years he remained in post for six years (longer than any post-war chairman except Lord Woolton, who lasted nearly ten). He upset central office by some of the changes he made, but his considerable contribution to the Conservative victory in 1979 was undeniable. Superficially he was a dated relic of another age. 'His manner, especially in the rotund, florid tone of his speeches, was that of a bygone era: he was one of the last debaters in both Houses of Parliament to deploy the fashionable 1930s' cockney twang at the end of his sentences. This did not necessarily endear him to all the party's professionals. It was hard for them to appreciate that a man who sounded like a throwback to the age of the Duke of Windsor could be in touch with modern developments.'[114] But he would not have kept the post for six years without being attuned to contemporary needs. 'During his reign in Smith Square he developed the party's trade union and community affairs activities. He greatly improved Conservative fundraising, the treasure chest having been seriously depleted by the two lost elections of 1974. His advice was heard with respect in the shadow Cabinet. His speaking to any party audience had both vigour and panache even if its echoes tended to smack of the Edwardian music-hall stage.'[115]

By 1981 his days were numbered. Apart from any other factor he was seventy-two that year and well past normal retirement age. The Conservative government was at the usual mid-term low point ebb. As party chairman he had a duty to report constituency anxieties to the government but with rising unemployment and an economy failing to respond to monetarism, 'the view seems to have been taken that he was doing so with rather too much relish.'[116] He resigned in September 1981 and died in 1994.

He had been created a life peer in 1967, and was made a CH in 1979 'for political and public service'.

Lord Soames 14 June 1980
Christopher Soames was a Conservative politician and diplomat whose career was launched by his advantageous status as a son-in-law of Winston Churchill. But his innate talents were proved in a succession of distinguished public appointments culminating in the difficult and sensitive role as the last British governor of Southern Rhodesia.

He was born in 1920 and educated at Eton and Sandhurst. During the 1939–45 war he served in the Coldstream Guards in the Middle East, Italy and France until his fighting career was ended when a mine explosion shattered his right leg. He later served as liaison officer with Charles de Gaulle's Free French movement in North Africa, Italy and Normandy. At the end of the war he was appointed assistant military attaché in Paris (1946–47). In 1947 his life changed decisively in more ways than the merely domestic when he married Mary Churchill, daughter of Winston Churchill. Politics beckoned and in 1950, he won Bedford from Labour. After the Conservatives won the 1951 general election, he became parliamentary private secretary to his father-in-law (1952–55). Theoretically the lowest rank in government, Soames' position soon became influential and pivotal. In 1953 Churchill suffered a severe stroke and was barely able to function as prime minister. Soames slipped into the role of deciding which ministers would be allowed to see the prime minister and for how long. 'He played the part with discretion, earning the respect of leading Tory politicians who might well have resented his premature importance ... In this vital role of guardian at the gate he made few mistakes.'[117]

His ministerial career began after Churchill's retirement. In 1955 Anthony Eden made him under-secretary for air. In 1957 Harold Macmillan appointed him parliamentary and financial secretary to the admiralty. In the following year he was made secretary of state for war. In 1960 he was made minister of agriculture. In this post he displayed a talent for negotiation in the negotiations for British entry into the European Economic Community. It was not his fault that de Gaulle vetoed Britain's application in January 1963.

With the Conservative Party in opposition, Soames was spokesman on defence (1964–65) and foreign affairs (1965–66). He lost his seat at the 1966 election and tried unsuccessfully to seek another seat. In 1968, George Brown, then foreign secretary, appointed him ambassador in Paris. Although a seasoned European, Soames was able to do little with de Gaulle still in office. There was little chance that Britain's fresh application to join the EEC would succeed, and the situation was not helped when the British government revealed the contents of a discussion between Soames and de Gaulle to other EEC countries and to the USA. The French government denied the British version of what had transpired and relations were distinctly cool for some while afterwards. Relations quickly improved after de Gaulle's resignation in 1969. After the Conservative victory in 1970 Edward Heath asked Soames to stay on in Paris. 'His convivial personality and his special position as Churchill's son-in-law had won him greater popularity than any British ambassador had enjoyed since Duff Cooper; and Foreign Office ministers at the time also readily acknowledged that without Soames's personal contribution Great Britain would probably not have entered the Community.'[118]

When Britain joined the EEC in 1973 he became a vice-president of the commission (1973–77) with responsibility for the community's foreign affairs. He helped the Labour government to strengthen its case that continued British membership was a matter of vital national importance; and in the approach to the 1975 referendum on continued membership he addressed large pro-common market rallies organised by the Conservative Party. As his term on the commission drew to an end he harboured hopes of returning to the house of commons, but prolonged ill-health ended his chances. In 1978 he accepted a life peerage, and after the Conservative victory in 1979 he became leader of the house of lords and the minister responsible for the civil service department. Seven months later Margaret Thatcher sent him to Southern Rhodesia, as the last British governor (1979–80), to implement the Lancaster House conference agreement on independence for the country. 'Apart from supervising the end of a murderous civil war and trying to ensure that the electoral rules were not flouted, Soames had to reassure a sullen white community, repair the broken morale of the local administration, and attempt to soothe the bitter factional and tribal divisions in the African community.'[119] He was successful, given his extremely limited powers, but it was a job that required only the implementation of already agreed policy and left him no room for personal initiative.

After independence he briefly returned to his cabinet post, but his patrician style was perhaps better suited to diplomatic negotiation than to the rough and tumble world of domestic politics. As minister responsible for the civil service, he was held responsible for a series of strikes that disrupted the public service for several months. Inclined to yield further to trade union demands than was the prime minister, he was sacked from the cabinet in September 1981. It came as a shock to realise that his former achievements were no protection, and his letter of resignation was written in a tone of resentful disbelief. He died in 1987.

He was made CBE in Churchill's resignation honours list in 1955, a GCMG after the successful conclusion of the EEC negotiations in 1972, and GCVO after the visit of Queen Elizabeth II to Paris in 1972. He was made a CH in 1980 'for public service, particularly in connection with Rhodesia.'

Lord Boyle of Handsworth   13 June 1981
Edward Boyle was a Conservative politician who developed an interest in the world of education during his years in the house of commons, and left it to become vice-chancellor of a university.

He was born at Queen's Gate, London in 1923, elder son of a baronet and grandson of a Conservative member of parliament, and was educated at Eton. Towards the end of the 1939–45 war he served for a short period in the foreign office and then went to Christ Church, Oxford to read history. He left the university in 1949 with a third class degree, a surprisingly poor result. It must be an encouragement to many undergraduates that with such a degree, Boyle should have finished his life as the vice-chancellor of a university. But despite the grade, he had many gifts. 'He was considered to be exceptionally mature, a charming and persuasive, though not rhetorical, speaker, and one who was likely to make his mark in the outside world . . . His intellectual characteristics, however, comprised a wide breadth of interest, a remarkable store of information, and phenomenal memory for everything which he encountered, but his was not a mind full of innovative ideas or of penetrating analysis. His strength lay in his deep-seated and moderate convictions which guided him all through his life.'[120]

In 1948 he unsuccessfully contested a by-election in the Perry Bar division of Birmingham, and lost again in the same constituency in the 1950 general election. Later in the same year he contested the Handsworth division of Birmingham and won at the age of twenty-seven. He remained a member of the house of commons until 1970. His ministerial career began as parliamentary secretary to the ministry of supply (1954–55) and economic secretary to the treasury (1955–56). He resigned from the government when Eden announced that British forces would be used to regain control of the Suez Canal. After the fall of Eden, Boyle was brought back into the government as parliamentary secretary to the ministry of education (1957–59), financial secretary to the treasury (1959–62), minister of education (1962–64), and minister of state with responsibility for higher education (1964). His last post was an ostensible demotion because Quintin Hogg was brought in above him as secretary of state for the new department of education and science. But Boyle had long been urging the creation of such a department and he retained a seat in the cabinet.

After the Conservative defeat in 1964, Boyle became opposition spokesman on home affairs but disliked the job because his own liberal views brought him into conflict with the right wing of his party. In 1965 he became opposition spokesman on education and retained that portfolio, despite requests from Edward Heath to move, until he retired from the commons in 1970. Education had become his overwhelming interest (he was pro-chancellor of the University of Sussex 1965–70) and in 1970 he was appointed vice-chancellor of the University of Leeds. It was a difficult time because of increasing radicalism in student communities opposed to the unfolding horrors of the Vietnam war. But a reasonable stability was maintained at Leeds because of Boyle's diplomatic skills, sharpened and polished by twenty years in the house of commons, and by his genuine concern for the welfare of his students. Although he was elected chairman of the committee of vice-chancellors and principals (1977–79) he was at his happiest when among his own students in his own university. After a lingering illness he died at the vice-chancellor's lodge at Leeds in 1981.

He was made a life peer in 1970 and a CH in 1981 three months before his death 'for public service.'

Lord Carrington 11 June 1983

Peter Alexander Rupert Carrington, sixth Baron Carrington, was the holder of a barony created in 1796 and was probably the last hereditary peer to hold a high cabinet office by virtue of his membership of the house of lords.

He was born in 1919, son of the fifth baron by his wife, the daughter of the second Viscount Colville. His family traced its line back to a seventeenth century Nottingham draper. The family home was at Wycombe Abbey, now a girls' boarding school. He was educated at Eton and the Royal Military College, Sandhurst. During the 1939–45 war he was commissioned in the Grenadier Guards, served in north-west Europe and was awarded the Military Cross in 1945. The death of his father in 1946 brought succession to the peerage and the right to a seat in the house of lords. He began to attend the lords regularly and came to the attention of Winston Churchill who appointed him parliamentary under secretary at the ministry of agriculture (1951–54) and then at the ministry of defence (1954–56). In November 1956 he was appointed United Kingdom high commissioner in Australia. In October 1959 he returned to the United Kingdom and to the government where he was appointed first lord of the admiralty (1959–63), and then minister without portfolio and leader of the house of lords (1963–64). During the 1964–70 Labour government he was leader of the Conservative peers in the lords. With the return of a Conservative government he was appointed secretary of state for defence (1970–74) and secretary of state for energy (January to February 1974), and also chairman of the Conservative Party (1972–74). In Margaret Thatcher's government he fulfilled a schoolboy ambition to become secretary of state for foreign and commonwealth affairs (1979–82), and he was chairman of the Lancaster House conference, which led to the end of the illegal independence of Rhodesia and the creation of the independent republic of Zimbabwe in 1981. He enjoyed a good relationship with Margaret Thatcher. When the two were entertaining a VIP from overseas, he scribbled a note and slipped it in front of her. It read: 'The poor chap's come 600 miles, do let him say something,'

Carrington remarked that in the world of foreign affairs the only certainty is that the unexpected always happens. It happened on 2 April 1982 when Argentina invaded the British dependent territory of the Falkland Islands. Because of a failure of intelligence, the United Kingdom was completely unprepared. As a direct result Carrington resigned as foreign secretary three days later in the face of a public outcry. He took the view that it was the right thing to do. The country was now going to have to fight a very difficult war far away, and there were recriminations about who was responsible. Although Margaret Thatcher thought it unnecessary Carrington decided to take the blame and resign as a way of ending recrimination. 'The anger of the British people and Parliament at the Argentine invasion of the Falklands was a righteous anger, and it was my duty and fate to assuage it; the rest was done by brave sailors, soldiers and airmen, too many of whom laid down not office but their lives.'[121]

He was briefly chairman of the General Electric Company (1983–84) but relinquished the office on his appointment as secretary-general of NATO (1984–88). He was effectively the last secretary-general of the organisation while the Soviet Union was the potential enemy. The collapse of communism across eastern Europe and the Soviet Union in 1989 changed the direction of the organisation.

In 1991–92 he chaired the European Community's peace conference on Yugoslavia. Far from the sometimes racial violence in that disintegrating state, the conference was always going to be faced with an uphill struggle. But its work was undermined when the EC decided to recognise Croatia and Slovenia, and then asked Bosnia whether it wanted independence. Carrington had warned that it would lead to civil war. After eighteen months in post he decided there was nothing more he could do and resigned. His successors, Cyrus Vance and David Owen, found themselves in an equally impossible situation.

He held a number of other business and public appointments including chairman of the board of trustees of the Victoria and Albert Museum (1983–88), resigning to become chairman of Christies International (1988–93); president of Voluntary Service Overseas (1993-), chancellor of the University of Reading (1992-); and chancellor of the Order of St Michael and St George (1984–94).

Carrington was one of a caste that has now disappeared because of 'time, circumstance and parliamentary enactment': an hereditary aristocrat who fought in the 1939–45 war, entered politics largely 'because it was fun', never had to fight an election and held high cabinet rank. A cultured and honourable old Etonian guardsman, he was the last echo of a time when it was both natural and normal for hereditary peers to be liberally sprinkled through government ranks. He was undeniably one the best representatives of his class.

He was made a KCMG in 1958 while high commissioner in Australia. Initially reluctant, he was appointed a CH in 1983 for his services as 'Secretary of State for Defence 1970–74. Secretary of State for Foreign and Commonwealth Affairs 1979–82.' It was a token of Margaret Thatcher's regard for her colleague whose cabinet career seemed to have ended unnecessarily in her view. His highest honour was to be made a KG in 1985, but it was not his last. He was promoted to GCMG in 1988 at the conclusion of his time at NATO.

Viscount Eccles 16 June 1984
David Eccles was a prominent minister in the Conservative governments of Winston Churchill, Anthony Eden, Harold Macmillan and Edward Heath. He was a wealthy, handsome, elegant, fastidious and cultured individual whose confidence was interpreted as arrogance by his critics.

He was born in 1904 in Harley Street, London where his father was a distinguished surgeon. The medical theme continued with his future wife, Sybil Dawson, daughter of Lord Dawson of Penn, physician to King George V. She was born a few months later in Wimpole Street. He was educated at Winchester and at New College, Oxford. University was followed by work in the city where he made a great deal of money. During the 1939–45 war he was enlisted by the ministry of economic warfare and sent to Spain. His official title was economic adviser to the British ambassadors in Madrid and Lisbon, but his real role was to use trade agreements and all other possible means to persuade Spain and Portugal to remain neutral. He described himself as 'the apostle of bribery' and admitted handing out vast sums of money to generals, politicians, diplomats, and anybody credited with having influence. He was successful and the two Iberian countries remained outside the conflict.

He returned to Britain in 1942 and in the following year he was elected for the constituency of Chippenham, which had become vacant by the death of Peter Cazalet in an air-crash. He had never contemplated a political career but enjoyed the commons and spoke as often as possible. In the years of opposition (1945–51), he was a frontbench economics spokesman. With the Conservative victory in 1951, Eccles was made minister of works. It was not a significant cabinet post, but the death of King George VI in February 1952 raised the profile of the office and required him to play a prominent role in preparations for the coronation of Queen Elizabeth II. In an off-the-cuff remark he described the new queen as a perfect leading lady. It was an affectionate and innocuous remark by later standards, but in 1952 some regarded it as disgracefully over-familiar, and Randolph Churchill, who resented Eccles's rise in the party, blew up the consequential fuss.

There were no lasting consequences however, and after the coronation he was promoted to be minister of education. He called for more scientists and technologists and led a big expansion in technical training. In 1957 he became president of the board of trade and in 1959 Harold Macmillan returned him to the ministry of education. He was less successful and a fight with the teachers when a Burnham pay award was not met in full proved his undoing. On 13 July 1962 he was summoned to see Macmillan and entered the meeting hoping to be appointed chancellor of the exchequer. Instead, he left as one of the seven victims of Macmillan's infamous night of the long knives. He was offered another post, but refused and accepted a barony instead. He regretted that he had not held out for a viscountcy (he was given it by Alec Douglas-Home in 1964), but enjoyed returning to his earlier life of making money. He had begun by selling rare books while he was still at Oxford. He was a collector of paintings, sculpture and rare books and a member of the leading British bibliophile circle, the Roxburghe Club. When his turn came to produce a volume, he was determined to produce its most imposing and impressive publication ever. He approached the map librarian of the British Library, Helen Wallis, and the result, printed by Oxford University Press, was a folio facsimile of the Rotz Atlas, a manuscript world atlas produced for King Henry VIII, which includes the shadowy presence of the as-yet-undiscovered continent of Australia. In his old age he donated his collection of twentieth century English and American private press books to Winchester College. His addiction to culture was demonstrated by the way in which he furnished his government offices. Other ministers borrowed state-owned works of art for their offices; Eccles installed his own.

With the Conservative victory at the 1970 general election, Edward Heath made Eccles paymaster-general with responsibility for the arts. His term of office was dominated by the museum charges he was forced to introduce as his contribution to the new government's first economic crisis and his refusal to make exceptional grants to prevent art treasures being sold to the USA did not help. After eight years out of the commons, he was not really at ease in the government and he left it with relief in a 1973 reshuffle. He had served as a trustee of the British Museum (1963–70, chairman 1968–70) and then as first chairman of the British Library (1973–78). He died in 1999 at the age of ninety-four, the last survivor of the night of the long knives.

He was made a KCVO in 1953 for his services to the coronation festivities and a CH in 1984 'for political and public services, especially to the arts.'

Lord Joseph 21 May 1986
Keith Joseph was a wealthy, cultivated and intellectually gifted Conservative politician with a civilised taste for literature and the arts. He was generally regarded as the chief intellectual influence on much of the domestic and economic policy of Margaret Thatcher in the years 1975–86. He was a passionate libertarian whose faith in liberty was founded on the religious conviction that man's moral nature could only be expressed in a society in which he was free to make important personal choices.

He was born in 1918 into a prosperous Jewish family. He was the only child of Sir Samuel George Joseph, who became lord mayor of London during the 1939–45 war and received the then customary baronetcy (which his son inherited in 1944) at the end of his term of office. He was educated at Harrow and at Magdalen College, Oxford, graduating in jurisprudence in 1939. On the outbreak of the 1939–45 war he joined the Royal Artillery, was wounded in the Italian campaign, mentioned in despatches and reached the rank of captain. After the war he was called to the bar, and in 1947 won a prize fellowship to All Souls College. He was not an academic by instinct and he failed to finish research on the concept of tolerance. While at All Souls, he devoted more time to his family business, and became chairman of the company for a while.

He followed his father into public life in the city of London as a councillor and alderman, although he resigned before proceeding to the mayoralty. He took a great interest in charitable works within the Jewish community, especially in education and housing. Later he founded and controlled the Mulberry Trust, a non-profit making housing association.

When he entered the house of commons at a by-election in 1956, he was one of only two Jewish Conservative MPs. He was elected for Leeds North East, a constituency which he was to represent for the rest of his commons career. He entered Harold Macmillan's cabinet in 1962 as minister of housing and local government. In opposition (1964–70) he was a frontbench spokesman on social services and trade, including technology and power. In Edward Heath's government he served as secretary of state for health and social security (1970–74). He never disguised his own failings and after 1974 he often repented of his activities at both ministries. At health and social security 'he had encouraged ever-accelerating public expenditure, as well as equipping the national health service with a bureaucratic structure of mind-boggling complexity; while at housing he was accused of building concrete jungles, and in the aftermath of Rachmanism of having done too much to protect tenants against landlords. He especially regretted the tower blocks he had built as part of the architectural and social legacy of the early 1960s. Congratulating one newly appointed Housing Minister in the 1980s he said: "Well done. You'll find lots of problems in your new job. I caused many of them".'[122]

After Edward Heath's second defeat in October 1974 his clumsy public utterances ruled out any leadership ambitions that he may have had. In particular, he suggested in a public speech at Birmingham that the poor were naturally both promiscuous and improvident. Denis Healey recalled Joseph at the time: '[Joseph] was too bizarre a character to win the leadership of the British Conservative Party . . . A Fellow of All Souls, he could easily hold his own in academic circles; but politically he was a mixture of Hamlet, Rasputin, and Tommy Cooper.'[123] Instead Joseph supported the election of Margaret Thatcher who was thereafter devoted to him. She appointed him secretary of state for industry in 1979. It was not a particularly happy period for him. He began to dismember the large government subsidies but could not avoid large payments to British Leyland and British Steel. In 1981 he asked to be moved to the department for education where he remained until 1986. 'He probably found his natural intellectual niche as Secretary of State for Education, although some thought his apparent slowness in promoting change was due to his way of conducting departmental business. He did this by endlessly (and courteously) arbitrating between the views of ministers and officials as though he were conducting a seminar. He wanted to cut public expenditure which prevented him from seeking greater funds for his department, 'and just as he was beginning not only to gain the confidence but even to charm a hitherto surly and suspicious teaching profession, he lost it through an inflexible determination not to breach the government's pay aims that year.'[124] It was a deeply unhappy time for Joseph, as well as for education, and he asked to be relieved of his post in the spring of 1986 on the ground that he would not be standing at the next election. 'Tense and intense, and much moved by his religious certainties as a Jew, his personality, despite public parody, was not that of someone given to extreme views. He was kind, diffident in the extreme, courteous and an agonisingly scrupulous man.'[125]

Despite his great intellectual capacity, he was curiously inept at politics and had lapses of judgement which an astute politician would have avoided. However, there was an attractive air of innocence and naiveté about him. 'On one occasion he was to be seen totally flummoxed standing in front of the closed booking office at Westminster Underground station. The intimation from a fellow passenger that it was possible as it was in those days to pay at the other end was received with professions of undying gratitude. Equally guileless was his approach to the mass media. He once found himself involved in a television interview that had not gone well. When the lights went down, he asked the interviewer "Not your fault of course, entirely mine" if he could do it again. "But I thought you realised, Sir Keith," said his interrogator "that this was a live interview." "Yes, yes, I know that," came the slightly impatient reply, "that's why I want to do it again." Not merely the interviewer but the whole camera crew hardly knew where to look. Their bewilderment might have been marginally tempered had they realised that for many years he stood out against even having a television set in his home.'[126]

A slightly pained expression resulted from an intensely nervous disposition related to a chronic, persistent and often painful set of physical ailments. Ill-health combined with a considerable touch of moral austerity could make him seem remote in public though he was friendly and warm in private. He died in 1994.

He was made a CH in 1986 on leaving the cabinet; no citation accompanied the announcement in the *London Gazette*. He was created a life peer in 1987.

Lord Tebbit 31 July 1987

Norman Tebbit, always firmly on the right wing of the Conservative Party, acquired a reputation for being Margaret Thatcher's trusted confidant and hard man in her first and second administrations.

He was born in the working class north London suburb of Ponders End in 1931, the son of the assistant manager of a jeweller's and pawnbroker's shop. His father lost his job soon after the birth of his son and set out on his bike each day to look for work. Many decades later his son was to make that bike famous. After a brief period of evacuation in Wales his parents brought him back to London where he remained for the rest of the 1939–45 war. He was educated at Edmonton County Grammar School. The bike theme continued in his teenage years when he saved enough money to build a bicycle for himself.[127] On leaving school he had set his heart on journalism and spent two years working on the *Financial Times* (1947–49), before doing national service in the royal air force (1949–51) where he qualified as a pilot. It was an unusual form of national service (most national servicemen served in the army), but the cold war had begun and the air force was facing a potential shortage of serving and active reservist aircrew. Tebbit loved flying and memories of his national service days feature prominently in his autobiography. For two years (1951–53) he worked, with no great enthusiasm, for a company that sold advertising space in overseas newspapers, and in his spare time flew with the royal air force volunteer reserve. By the spring of 1953 he was 'head over heels in love with flying again'[128] and decided to join the British Overseas Airways Corporation as a civil pilot. He narrowly avoided death in an air crash in July 1954 and thereafter 'I have regarded each day of my life, however hard or disagreeable, as a bonus.'[129]

He had joined the Conservative Party in 1946, founding a branch of the Young Conservatives in Enfield and by 1966 he had begun seriously to consider standing for parliament. He was elected for Epping (1970–74) and for Chingford (1974–92), taking a pay cut from £5,000 that he earned at BOAC to £3,250 as an MP. His political views were too far to the right for him to be comfortable with the more centrist policies of Edward Heath, but with the advent of Margaret Thatcher (who found in him a close ally) his career prospered. He was made parliamentary under secretary, department of trade (1979–81), minister of state, department of industry (1981) and secretary of state for employment (1981–83). In that role he became famous (or infamous depending on point of view) for his instruction to the unemployed to follow the example of his father – to get on their bikes and look for work. Few observers of his apparently tough and unsympathetic public manner could have guessed that a hard exterior concealed a kind and sensitive man.

A major turning point of his life occurred in 1983 when, at the party conference, in Brighton a bomb planted by the IRA devastated the Grand Hotel where he, his wife and the Conservative Party hierarchs were staying. Tebbit himself suffered painful injuries and his wife, Margaret, was left paralysed from the neck down.

His last ministerial appointments were secretary of state for trade and industry (1983–85) and chairman of the Conservative Party (1985–87), the latter post held in conjunction with the ancient cabinet rank office of chancellor of the duchy of Lancaster (1985–87). As chairman of the party he was a crucial figure in securing Margaret Thatcher's third electoral victory in 1987. Because of his wife's injuries and the need to rebuild their new and different life, Tebbit decided against further ministerial office after the 1987 election and retired from the house of commons in 1992.

He was made a CH in 1987 on leaving ministerial office for his services as 'Member of Parliament for Epping 1970–74; Chingford since 1974. Chancellor of the Duchy of Lancaster 1985–87. Secretary of State for Trade and Industry 1983–85. Secretary of State for Employment 1981–83. Minister of State for Industry 1981. Parliamentary Under-Secretary of State, Department of Trade 1979–81.' He was created a life peer in 1992.

Lord Baker of Dorking 13 April 1992

Ken Baker served as a cabinet minister in the governments of Margaret Thatcher and John Major, culminating in his appointment as home secretary. But he had a parallel career as an acknowledged expert on the history of caricature and published a number of volumes on the subject.

He was born in 1934 and educated at St Paul's School before undertaking the then obligatory two years of national service (1953–55). He went to Magdalen College, Oxford (1955–58).

He was elected to Twickenham Borough Council (1960–62) and unsuccessfully contested Poplar (1964) and Acton (1966) for the Conservative Party. He won Acton from Labour at a by election in March 1968 but lost it by only 660 votes at the 1970 general election. He was not long out of the commons, winning St Marylebone in October 1970 at the by election caused by the elevation of Quintin Hogg to the house of lords. He held the constituency until its disappearance in the 1983 boundary reorganisations and represented Mole Valley from 1983 until he retired from the house of commons in 1997.

He was a strong supporter of Edward Heath who appointed him a parliamentary secretary at the civil service department (1972–74). He was parliamentary private secretary to Heath in opposition (1974–75), and after Heath's defeat by Margaret Thatcher in 1975 he returned to the backbenches where he stayed for six years. Thatcher brought him back into the government as minister for information technology at the department of trade and industry (1981–84), minister for local government at the department of the environment (1984–85) and into the cabinet as secretary of state for the environment (1985–86) and secretary of state for education and science (1986–89). He was responsible for the 1988 Education Act which began the process of delegating power from local education authorities to schools, and school governors found, sometimes to their dismay, that they would now actively have to 'govern' their schools instead of hitherto doing little more than being ceremonial adornments on prize days.

Baker was made chairman of the Conservative Party (1989–90) with the cabinet office of chancellor of the duchy of Lancaster. He was home secretary (1990–92) but left the government after the 1992 election. He was known as an ebullient supporter of Margaret Thatcher and was perhaps too associated with the Thatcher regime. Additionally there was no other cabinet rank to which he could have aspired after the home office. The foreign office had the incumbent Douglas Hurd, and he had no desire to be chancellor of the exchequer.

He is a cultured man, who lists 'collecting books' among his hobbies and has several examples of incunabulae in his collection. He is also a noted authority on the history and traditions of British caricature, building up an exceptional collection in the field. His publications included: *I have no gun but I can spit* (1980), *London lines* (1982), *The Faber book of English history in verse* (1988), *Unauthorized versions: poems and their parodies* (1990), *The Faber book of Conservatism* (1993), *The prime ministers: an irreverent history in cartoons* (1995), *The Faber book of war poetry* (1996) and *The kings and queens: an irreverent cartoon history of the British monarchy* (1996), which coincided with his series on BBC television on the cartoon history of British monarchs, and *A children's English history in verse* (2000). An autobiography *The turbulent years: my life in politics*, was published in 1993.

He was made CH in 1992 on leaving the government. No citation appeared against his name in the *London Gazette*. He was created a life peer in 1997 taking the title of Lord Baker of Dorking (from the largest town in his former constituency of Mole Valley) on retiring from the house of commons.

Lord Brooke of Sutton Mandeville 13 April 1992
Peter Brooke held a number of cabinet offices in the governments of Margaret Thatcher and John Major, of which the most difficult was that of Northern Ireland secretary.

He was born in 1934, the son of Henry Brooke, Conservative home secretary in 1962–64. He was educated at Marlborough and Balliol College, Oxford, and studied for an MBA at Harvard Business School. After returning from Harvard he began a career in business, working for Spencer Stuart & Associates, a firm of management consultants (1961–79), and being chairman of the company (1974–79). He was briefly a member of Camden Borough Council (1968–69) before his work took him to live in New York and Brussels (1969–73).

He contested Bedwellty for the Conservative Party in the October 1974, but there was never a chance of winning it. It was a Welsh constituency with a rock solid Labour majority, and Brooke's opponent was the future Labour leader Neil Kinnock who won the seat with a majority of more than 21,000. In October 1977 he won the safe seat of the Cities of London and Westminster at a by election and held it until retiring from the commons in 1997. He was brought into the Conservative government in 1979 as a whip (1979–83), parliamentary under secretary of state at the department of education and science (1983–85), minister of state at the treasury (1985–87), chairman of the Conservative Party (1987–89) with the cabinet office of paymaster-general. After three years in the challenging and arduous office of secretary of state for Northern Ireland (1989–92) he left the government after the 1992 general election. He stood in the election for speaker of the house of commons in April 1992 but was defeated by Betty Boothroyd. He might have remained on the backbenches, but a personal scandal forced the resignation of David Mellor as secretary of state for the national heritage in September 1992, and John Major brought Brooke back into the government as his replacement, to avoid a reshuffle so soon after the general election. Brooke held the office until leaving the government – again – in July 1994.

Peter Brooke had the advantage of being an hereditary Conservative. Both his parents were Conservative life peers – Lord Brooke of Cumnor and Baroness Brooke of Ystrafellte – but his ministerial career was achieved on merit. Although he never held any of the principal cabinet offices he was personally well liked in the house of commons. He became chairman of the council of the University of London in 2002.

He was made CH in 1992 after leaving the government for the first time. No citation appeared against his name in the *London Gazette*. Henry Brooke and Peter Brooke, with John Christie and George Christie, are the only examples of fathers and sons being made Companions of Honour. Peter Brooke was created a life peer in 1997 on leaving the house of commons, taking the title Lord Brooke of Sutton Mandeville.

Lord King of Bridgwater 13 April 1992
Tom King held a number of cabinet offices in the governments of Margaret Thatcher and John Major, including an unprecedented four year period as Northern Ireland secretary.

He was born in 1933 and educated at Rugby and Emmanuel College, Cambridge. During his two years of national service (1951–53) he joined first the Somerset Light Infantry (commissioned in 1952) and then the King's African Rifles, serving in Kenya and Tanganyika. Leaving Cambridge in 1956 he began a career in business, joining E. S. & A. Robinson of Bristol and staying with the company in various positions until 1969.

In 1970 he was elected member of parliament for Bridgwater and served as a parliamentary private secretary to the minister of posts and telecommunications (1970–72) and to the minister of industrial development (1972–74). During the opposition years he was front bench spokesman on industry (1975–76) and energy (1976–79). Margaret Thatcher made him minister of local government and environmental services at the department of the environment (1979–83), and brought him into the cabinet in January 1983 as secretary of state for the environment (January to June 1983), for transport (June to October 1983), for employment (1983–85), for Northern Ireland (1985–89) and for defence (1989–92). During his tenure of the Northern Ireland office the historic Anglo-Irish agreement – promising a new dimension in relations between Ireland and the United Kingdom – was signed on 15 November 1985. King had only taken office two months previously and much of the credit for the agreement went to his predecessor. His settling-in period was difficult and complaints were made about his 'negative' performance in the last round of negotiations. But his stature rose as he proved himself under fire in a demanding job, as Geoffrey Howe recalled: 'Tom had not exactly endeared himself to any of us in his first few weeks, but that may have been scarcely his fault – and his courage and firmness later, when he was inevitably exposed to all the assaults and pressures that went with his job, were to win him widespread respect.'[130]

He left the government after the 1992 general election and retired from the house of commons at the 2001 election.

He was made CH in 1992 on leaving the government. No citation appeared against his name in the *London Gazette*. He was created a life peer in 2001, taking the title Lord King of Bridgwater.

Lord Owen 11 June 1994
David Owen was a right-wing Labour foreign secretary who left the party when it moved rapidly to the left, and later attempted to mediate without success in the violent civil war that unfolded in Yugoslavia in the 1990s.

He was born at Plympton, South Devon in 1938, the son of a medical practitioner. He was educated at Mount House School, Bradfield College, Sidney Sussex College, Cambridge and St Thomas' Hospital. Initially he had thought of studying law and going to Oxford, but at the age of sixteen he decided to follow his father and study medicine. He qualified in 1962 and held various house appointments at St Thomas' Hospital (1962–64), was neurological and psychiatric registrar (1964–66) and a research fellow in the medical unit (1966–68).

His political career began in 1964 when he unsuccessfully contested Torrington for the Labour Party. He was elected for Plymouth Sutton (1966–74) and for Plymouth Devonport (1974–92). His first appointment was as parliamentary private secretary to the minister of defence (1967) and his first government appointment was as parliamentary under secretary of state at the ministry of defence (for the royal navy) (1968–70). As a junior member of the Harold Wilson government he witnessed Wilson's failure to weld together a team of talented but disparate individuals who spent part of their time manoeuvring against each other.

He was opposition defence spokesman (1970–72) but resigned over his party's attitude towards the European Economic Community. When Wilson returned to power in 1974 he brought Owen back into government as parliamentary under secretary of state at the department of health and social security, and rapidly promoted him to be minister of state in the same department later that year, and then minister of state at the foreign and commonwealth office (1976–77). When Anthony Crosland died suddenly in February 1977, Owen was ideally placed to succeed him as foreign secretary (1977–79). He was thirty-nine years old and the youngest foreign secretary in living memory. His appointment was not welcome to some of his colleagues, including Denis Healey: 'It was probably a premature promotion . . . He began to mask his insecurity with an arrogance which was found offensive by many of those who worked for him.'[131]

It was to be a brief experience of power. The Labour government was defeated in the general election of May 1979 and at the age of only forty-one, Owen left government office, never – because of his own change of political direction – to hold it again.

After its electoral defeat, the Labour Party lurched to the left and Owen, with others, found himself out of sympathy with a party that had abandoned the centre ground. In 1981 he left the Labour Party and, with Roy Jenkins, Shirley Williams and Bill Rodgers, founded the new Social Democratic Party as a centrist answer to the very left-leaning Labour. He served as deputy leader (1982–83) and leader (1983–87) of the SDP. The Social Democratic Party never prospered. It was formed almost entirely of centrist-leaning politicians within the Labour Party, and it never seemed to break out of a public perception of it as a protest against that party, and take root in the nation's political consciousness as a significant political entity. As a separate party it participated in two general elections, winning 3.5 million votes and 6 seats in 1983, and 3.1 million votes and 5 seats in 1987. After the 1987 results, recognition that the party had failed to make a breakthrough, and the emergence of a new and more central leadership in the Labour Party, brought calls for a merger between the Social Democratic and Liberal parties. Owen would have none of it and resigned as leader of the Social Democrats. The union of the two parties went through and he was re-elected leader (1988–92) of a small rump of Social Democrats who refused to join the united party. It was no more than a small splinter group that quickly withered away. Owen announced his intention not to seek re-election to parliament in the 1992 election, and the party's remaining two members of parliament were defeated.

He held only one further notable public appointment – European Union co-chairman of the international conference on the former Yugoslavia (1992–95), succeeding Lord Carrington. Although Owen did his best to secure a negotiated peace, it was impossible for a group of diplomats to bring order out of the civil war that was sweeping through the disintegrating state. While Owen and his colleagues drew thoughtful boundaries on neat maps, the military situation in Yugoslavia was changing hourly and the work of the conference appeared to make little practical difference.

Good-looking and charming with a suave appearance and a slightly supercilious manner, Owen was disliked by many of his contemporaries, including his staff at the Foreign Office. Roy Jenkins, the first leader of the Social Democratic Party, likened Owen to a Javanese upas tree, poisoning all other life nearby.[132] Denis Healey delivered a more direct verdict. 'The good fairies gave the young doctor almost everything: thick dark hair, good looks, matinée idol features, a lightening intelligence – unfortunately the bad fairies also made him a shit.'[133] Owen himself admitted his 'infuriating habit of retrospective analysis and carping criticism.'[134]

He was created a life peer in 1992 and a CH in 1994 as 'EU Co-Chairman of the International Conference on the former Yugoslavia.'

Lord Hurd of Westwell 30 December 1995

Douglas Hurd was a former professional diplomat who turned Conservative politician and served for ten years as a minister in the foreign office.

He was born at Rainscombe Farm, near the Wiltshire town of Oare in 1930, the son and grandson of members of parliament. His grandfather, Sir Percy Hurd (1864–1950) was member for Somerset and Frome (1918–23) and Devizes

(1924–45), and his father, Anthony Hurd (1901–1966), was member for the Newbury division of Berkshire (1945–64), and became a life peer on leaving the commons.

Douglas Hurd was educated at Twyford Preparatory School, Eton and Trinity College, Cambridge. After graduation he joined the diplomatic service (1952–66), serving in Beijing (1954–56), the United Nations (1956–60), and Rome (1963–66). After leaving the diplomatic service, he joined the Conservative Party's research department and served as private secretary to Edward Heath (1968–74). He followed his father and grandfather into parliament in 1974 as member for Mid Oxfordshire (1974–83) and Witney (1983–97). He was sufficiently ambitious to seek a place on the front bench and he began relentless attacks on prime minister Harold Wilson for his failure to construct a national government to deal with a worsening economic climate. His strongest attack on Wilson was made in June 1976, after the publication of the latter's resignation honours list. He described the honoured individuals as 'a bizarre collection' and condemned the list as an abuse of the honours system. His views of the famous 'lavender list' were widely supported. Hurd always strongly believed that the honours system should 'reflect the unsung feats of those performing public service for the good of the community and the nation.'[135]

Hurd's former career made him a natural opposition spokesman on foreign affairs (1976–79), and when the Conservatives returned to power under Margaret Thatcher, he was a natural choice to be minister of state at the foreign office (1979–83), and was in office at the time of the Argentine invasion of the Falkland islands. He alone of the ministerial team in that department decided not to resign. The department had been criticised for failing to predict the invasion and its ministers were held responsible for that failure and the prime minister's antipathy towards the foreign office was legendary. Hurd had no responsibility for the Falkland islands and became a figure of continuity in the department while the new ministers mastered their briefs.

He moved to be minister of state at the home office (1983–84). There he was less successful because he had no experience and little interest in the world and detail of domestic politics. From there he was moved to his first cabinet appointment as Northern Ireland secretary (1984–85). The Northern Ireland office was a bush of thorns and not one that was actively sought by aspiring cabinet ministers, but Hurd, who occupied it for slightly less than twelve months, was remembered as one of the architects of the Anglo-Irish agreement which set the province on the long slow journey to peace. Diplomats were trained to deal swiftly and effectively with crises, and as home secretary (1985–89) Hurd proved capable of dealing with a department notoriously prone to crises. The diplomatic theme ran strongly through his ministerial career in the way that he eschewed ideology and favoured compromise. Consequently, his relationship with Margaret Thatcher was not entirely easy, but she made him foreign secretary (1989–95). It was a rare achievement for a former professional diplomat and he loved the job. He was also well liked in the foreign office who recognised him as one of their own and one who would look after their interests. It was therefore all the more difficult for him, after the 1993 review of the honours system, to have to explain to the diplomatic service that there would be fewer honours for them in the future.

Hurd presented the classic appearance of an upright, tolerant and civil English gentleman, and when he spoke it was always with a slightly reserved, grave and solemn air. He disdained tactic and political intrigue, and although he was widely respected for his calm authority, he was not popular and charismatic enough to acquire a backbench following. When Margaret Thatcher resigned in 1990 he stood in the second ballot, but attracted only 56 votes, compared with 185 for John Major and 131 for Michael Heseltine. He resigned from the cabinet in June 1995 on the day following John Major's decision to submit himself for reelection as leader of the Conservative Party. He had already signalled in the spring of 1994 that he wanted to go in the summer of 1995 and Major's decision gave him the excuse he needed. He had no wish to become tangled up in the leadership election and so he went. He retired from the commons in 1997.

He was appointed a CBE in 1974 and a CH in 1995. The citation read: 'Member of Parliament for Witney and Secretary of State for Foreign and Commonwealth Affairs 1989–95. For political services.' He was created a life peer in 1997. As his father had been ennobled as Lord Hurd, his son took the title of Lord Hurd of Westwell, from the Cotswold village to which he had retired.

Lord Howe of Aberavon 15 June 1996

Geoffrey Howe was a Conservative lawyer who served as a cabinet minister for all but the last three weeks of Margaret Thatcher's government (1979–90). It was his devastating resignation speech on 13 November 1990 that finally brought about her resignation.

He was born in Port Talbot, South Wales in 1926. He was educated at Winchester College, served in the Royal Signals (1945–48), read law at Trinity Hall, Cambridge and was called to the bar at Middle Temple in 1952. He was appointed a Queen's Counsel in 1965 and was deputy chairman of the Glamorgan quarter sessions (1966–70), and elected a bencher of Middle Temple in 1969.

He contested Aberavon for the Conservative Party at the 1955 and 1959 general elections. He was elected member for Bebington in 1964 but was defeated in 1966. It was a traumatic moment; he had inherited a Conservative majority of 10,000 in 1963 only to see it change to a Labour majority of 2,337 in 1966 as the area had begun to change. He returned to practise at the bar for the next four years and took a series of important briefs, including representing local officials at the tribunal of enquiry following the Aberfan disaster.

Howe had set his sights on ministerial office, and Bebington had become too marginal for him to try again. After a number of rejections, he was finally selected for the safe seat of Reigate and won it in 1970, holding it until he retired from the commons in 1992. The boundaries of the constituency were redrawn and it was renamed Surrey, East in 1974. When Edward Heath formed a government in 1970, Howe was appointed solicitor-general (1970–72), and minister for trade and consumer affairs, department of trade and industry (1972–74). When Margaret Thatcher challenged Edward Heath in February 1975 for the leadership of the Conservative Party, Howe entered the race in the second ballot but he won only 19 votes (compared with 140 for Thatcher and 79 for William Whitelaw) Howe was not a natural political plotter and he had no network of supporters to campaign on his behalf. Thatcher appointed him economics spokesmen instead of Keith Joseph and he began a long duel with the Labour chancellor, Denis Healey, during which the latter famously described part of one speech by Howe as 'like being savaged by a dead sheep.' Howe later responded by including in his coat of arms a wolf dressed in a sheepskin. The two men never developed a friendship,

Howe regarding Healey as a rogue lacking integrity of purpose and Healey regarding Howe as a dullard and bore.[136] Howe did have a donnish style of delivery that completely concealed any passion he might have felt and his speeches in the commons fell well short of being described as rousing. 'If you listened to Sir Geoffrey Howe for oratory you would hang yourself,' wrote one journalist.[137]

With the return of a Conservative government he became chancellor of the exchequer (1979–83), secretary of state for foreign and commonwealth affairs (1983–89), and finally deputy prime minister and leader of the house of commons (1989–90). As chancellor Howe helped to launch the free market programme, commencing with the abolition of exchange controls, and he succeeded in reducing inflation from 22% to 4% on the basis of strict monetary discipline. As foreign secretary he was responsible for the preparation and passage through parliament of the principal legislation providing for the United Kingdom's membership of the European Community, for the 1986 enlargement of the community and for the European Community's 1992 programme. He served as chairman of the International Monetary Fund interim committee (1982–83) and attended the world economic summits every year from 1979 to 1989.

He served nearly six years as foreign secretary and, on 24 January 1989, recorded with pride that he had surpassed the record set by Sir Edward Grey who left office in 1916.[138] Howe was an internationalist with a degree of sensitivity towards Europe and its affairs not possessed by his prime minister. Perceived as too pro-European, and unwilling to continue in office unless the government was committed to joining the European exchange rate mechanism, Howe was eventually removed as foreign secretary in 1989 and made leader of the house of commons. It was an obvious demotion and was made only slightly less bitter for Howe when (at his own request) he was given the additional and mostly meaningless title of deputy prime minister. Relations with Margaret Thatcher continued to deteriorate and Howe eventually resigned on 1 November 1990 over Thatcher's hostile attitude towards the European Community generally and in particular to joining the exchange rate mechanism of the European monetary system.

He delivered his famous resignation speech on 13 November 1990 to a packed house of commons and, intentionally or not, precipitated a leadership challenge and brought down a prime minister who had once seemed invincible. Howe's resignation speech was a calmly-delivered vitriolic statement of why the parting of the ways had come, and it was all the more effective because of the control with which it was delivered. He began statistically by remarking that he had shared with the prime minister some 700 meetings of cabinet or shadow cabinet during the previous eighteen years, and some 400 hours alongside each other, at more than 30 international summit meetings. Then he reached the crux of his speech, quoting several of Margaret Thatcher's famed anti-European phrases. 'The European enterprise is not and should not be seen like that – as some kind of zero sum game. Sir Winston Churchill put it much more positively 40 years ago, when he said: "It is also possible and not less agreeable to regard" this sacrifice or merger of national sovereignty "as the gradual assumption by all the nations concerned of that larger sovereignty which can alone protect their diverse and distinctive customs and characteristics and their national traditions." I have to say that I find Winston Churchill's perception a good deal more convincing, and more encouraging for the interests of our nation, than the nightmare image sometimes conjured up by my right hon. Friend, who seems sometimes to look out upon a continent that is positively teeming with ill-intentioned people, scheming, in her words, to "extinguish democracy", to "dissolve our national identities" and to lead us "through the backdoor into a federal Europe." . . . What kind of vision is that for our business people, who trade there each day, for our financiers, who seek to make London the money capital of Europe or for all the young people of today? . . . The tragedy is – and it is for me personally, for my party, for our whole people and for my right hon. Friend herself, a very real tragedy – that the Prime Minister's perceived attitude towards Europe is running increasingly serious risks for the future of our nation. It risks minimising our influence and maximising our chances of being once again shut out. We have paid heavily in the past for late starts and squandered opportunities in Europe. We dare not let that happen again. If we detach ourselves completely, as a party or a nation, from the middle ground of Europe, the effects will be incalculable and very hard ever to correct.' Arguments there would certainly be with Europe. 'But it is crucially important that we should conduct those arguments upon the basis of a clear understanding of the true relationship between this country, the Community and our Community partners. And it is here, I fear, that my right hon. Friend the Prime Minister increasingly risks leading herself and others astray in matters of substance as well as of style.'[139]

The day after the speech, Michael Heseltine challenged Margaret Thatcher to a leadership election. In the first ballot on 20 November she won by 204 votes to 152, four votes short of the required majority for an outright victory. Inclined to fight on, she was forced to resign by her own cabinet on 21 November, when hardly any of her ministers offered strong support. She announced her resignation on 22 November. Howe was bitterly attacked by Thatcher's supporters for his part in her downfall and the following few weeks were difficult. 'I have never seen or heard,' he wrote, 'views more vehemently expressed. Bitter charges of treachery, cards bearing the simple word "Judas", even bags with thirty pieces of cupronickel, arrived by almost every post.'[140]

The new prime minister was John Major, Margaret Thatcher's favoured candidate, and there was no place for Howe in the new administration. It was unlikely in any case. Thatcher still commanded a strong following in the party, both in the commons and in the country, and there could be no question of a return to office for the man who had brought her down.

Howe retired from the house of commons in 1992 and began a new career of appointments in a large number of companies, charities and educational foundations.

He was knighted in 1970 (a then traditional honour for the solicitor general), created a life peer in 1992 as Lord Howe of Aberavon, and made a CH in 1996 (the dust clouds of 1990 having settled) 'for political service.'

Lord Heseltine 2 August 1997
Michael Heseltine is a strikingly tall, long-haired, blond, charismatic and colourful Conservative millionaire who unashamedly harboured an ambition to be prime minister,

He was born at Swansea in 1933, the son of an army colonel. He was educated at Shrewsbury School and at Pembroke College, Oxford, where he read philosophy, politics and economics. A commission in the Welsh Guards followed national service. He unsuccessfully contested Gower in 1959 and Coventry North in 1964, but was elected member for Tavistock (1966–74) and for Henley (1974–2001). Before entering the commons he was a successful businessman with interests centred on publishing, and this continued on a lower key basis as a parallel to his ministerial career, but were renewed after the Conservative defeat in 1997. He was director of Bow Publications (1961–65), chairman of Haymarket Press (1966–70), and a director of the Haymarket Publishing Group (1997-). Haymarket specialises in the production of smart, laminated corporate magazines. From 1970 to 1997, Heseltine was virtually a sleeping partner, but after 1997 he returned full-time as chairman and expanded the company. It was an unusual destiny for someone who was mildly dyslexic as a child and never liked reading.

In parliament he was vice-chairman of the Conservative parliamentary transport committee (1968) and opposition spokesman on transport issues (1969). When the Heath government came to power in 1970, Heseltine became parliamentary under secretary at the department of transport (June to October 1970), parliamentary under secretary at the department of the environment (1970–72), and minister of aerospace and shipping at the department of trade and industry (1972–74). In the opposition years he was spokesman on industry (1974–76) and the environment (1976–79). With the advent of the Thatcher government he was secretary of state for the environment (1979–83) and for defence (1983–86).

Heseltine seemed set for further promotion until the 'Westland affair' when he abruptly left a cabinet meeting and resigned from the government on 9 January 1986. Few people can remember, or care about, the details of the European versus American helicopter row. It centred on the fate of Westland, a failing helicopter manufacturer that supplied the ministry of defence, and whether the company should be saved by a European rather than an American buyer. Pro- and anti-Europe factions had emerged in the cabinet with Margaret Thatcher in the latter group and Heseltine in the former. He resigned because he refused to accept Thatcher's insistence that all ministers should refer statements on the Westland issue to the Cabinet Office for clearance. The two politicians intensely disliked each other from that day onwards. Although it was a turning point for the worse in his career, he declared that he had never regretted the decision to leave the cabinet. He regarded the affair as a scandal and could not keep quiet.

In his memoirs he criticised the prime minister's total absence of any notion of team building. 'The "one of us" mentality turned the cabinet into a kind of solar system, in which ministerial planets revolved in fluctuating elliptic orbits, whose shape depended largely upon her solar attention. Seldom, if ever, did ministerial constellations come together for long enough for them to make any significant impact upon the Prime Minister's inter-galactic control.'

Heseltine remained on the backbenches of the commons until the crisis that brought down Margaret Thatcher in November 1990, and in which he played a major role. He had long intended to bid for the party leadership, but not until the time was ripe. As the result of Howe's speech, the time had suddenly arrived and there could be no delay. On the day after the famous resignation speech of Sir Geoffrey Howe, Heseltine challenged Thatcher to a leadership election. In the first ballot on 20 November she won by 204 votes to Heseltine's 152, four votes short of the required majority for an outright victory. Inclined to fight on, she was forced to resign when hardly any of her ministers offered strong support and she had clearly lost the confidence of her colleagues. She announced her resignation on 22 November. In the second ballot on 27 November, John Major, Thatcher's favoured candidate, polled 185 votes to 131 for Heseltine and 56 for Douglas Hurd. Thatcher and Heseltine had defeated each other. He had brought her down, but he failed in his dream of becoming prime minister. It later transpired that one of her last acts in cabinet was to secure from her colleagues a commitment to stop Heseltine at all costs.[141] He had the qualities – courage, conviction, and leadership skills – that would have made him a good prime minister, but her supporters took their own revenge and never forgave him.

His ministerial career was not over. John Major soon proved that he was his own man when he brought Heseltine back into the government as secretary of state for the environment (1990–92), president of the board of trade (an ancient title that Edward Heath had abolished in October 1970, but which Heseltine rather liked and asked to be revived) (1992–95), and finally as first secretary of state and deputy prime minister (1995–97). The Conservative defeat in the 1997 general election ended his political career. He remained a member of parliament until the 2001 general election when he retired, but he was later to say that psychologically he left the house of commons in 1997. He had enjoyed an extraordinarily privileged career and it was difficult for him to go back to being in opposition.

When asked what he would most like to be remembered for he included 'Liverpool' on the list. He virtually became the 'minister for Merseyside' and spent a good deal of time in the city, devising policies to renew its economic and social life after the devastating riots of the 1980s.

Heseltine's tactical challenge to Thatcher's leadership was not the only cause of failure to achieve the highest office. He had a reputation as a loner, for being cold and distant, having few friends, and being difficult to get to know, and although he was ambitious, he was not good at nurturing relationships with the influential. A famous story records Heseltine as an undergraduate at Oxford pondering his future and mapping out his career on the back of an envelope: 'Fifties: millionaire. Sixties: MP. Seventies: minister. Eighties: Cabinet. Nineties: Downing Street.' He achieved everything except the last.

He was made a CH in 1997 in John Major's resignation honours list. The citation was a traditional one for politicians: 'Member of Parliament for Henley. Secretary of State for the Environment, 1979–83 and 1990–92, for Defence, 1983–86; President of the Board of Trade, 1992–95; First Secretary of State and Deputy Prime Minister.' He was created a life peer on retiring from the house of commons in 2001.

Christopher Patten 31 December 1997
Intellectual, popular and with a strong moral sense born of his Catholic faith, Christopher Patten is remembered principally as the Conservative Party chairman who was architect of the 1992 Conservative victory, but who lost his own seat in the same election, and then later as the last governor of Hong Kong.

He was born in 1944 and educated at St Benedict's School, Ealing and at Balliol College, Oxford where he read history. After graduation he won a travelling scholarship to the USA where he was given a job as a researcher with the team running John Lindsay's 1965 campaign to become mayor of New York. Returning to London he decided against a career in the BBC and joined the Conservative party's research department (1966–70) and then the cabinet office (1970–72). He became private secretary to the party chairman Lord Carrington (1972–74) and then returned to the research department. With a great many other people he fell foul of Margaret Thatcher who regarded him as hostile to her radical vision and ostracised him thereafter. The feeling was reciprocated. On the left wing of the Conservative Party he was more Christian Democrat than Conservative. If he had not stood out against the policies of Margaret Thatcher for so long, he might have entered the cabinet earlier than he did.

He was elected member of parliament for Bath in 1979 and became a parliamentary private secretary (1979–81). He joined the government in 1983 and served as parliamentary under secretary of state at the Northern Ireland office (1983–85), minister of state at the department of education and science (1985–86), and minister of overseas development at the foreign and commonwealth office (1986–89), responsible for the United Kingdom's aid programme to developing nations. He entered the cabinet as secretary of state for the environment (1989–90), charged with introducing the hated community charge (which became known as the 'poll tax'). Although he personally viewed it as a serious mistake he forced it through the house of commons, obedient to the principal of collective responsibility. As chairman of the Conservative Party (1990–92), with a seat in the cabinet as chancellor of the duchy of Lancaster, he led the party organisation to win the 1992 election, only to be defeated in the hour of his victory by losing his own seat at Bath. It was a marginal constituency and the Liberal Democrats won it with a majority of 4,351.

Out of parliament at the age of only forty-eight, he still had a long future ahead of him. He could have had a peerage, but declined it on the grounds that it would prevent him from holding any senior cabinet offices. He could have waited for a by-election, engineered or otherwise, although that was a risky return route that could not guarantee success. He came to the conclusion that his career in domestic politics was finished. 'I still wanted to work in public service and was drawn to the prospect of spending some time abroad, which would save me from becoming one of the wallflowers of Westminster, pining for the next dance.'[142] On the day following the election, John Major offered him the post of governor of Hong Kong and Patten accepted the challenge with alacrity, becoming the last governor of the last substantial colony of the British empire.

Patten's appointment was viewed with surprise in that he was neither a diplomat nor a Sinologist. He succeeded David Wilson, a competent high-flying diplomat who was rumoured to be bitterly disappointed at his removal, and resentful that the government failed to quash publicly rumours that he had been sacked to make way for a figure of greater resolution and substance.[143] Many felt that a more cautious and delicate hand than that of a politician was needed in the closing years of British rule, before the colony was returned to China in 1997. In fact Patten proved to be a popular and successful governor. He had harboured political hopes that he would one day be foreign secretary, and his capacity for charm and wit were essential qualities for life as a diplomat, but he was a politician who could sense a national mood and he was popular with the people of Hong Kong. The Chinese government disliked him for his introduction of democratic government to the colony, but he was never interested in 'appeasing' the future rulers of the colony, only in doing the best for its people. He did not get everything right, but he was well-liked. 'He was a good Governor,' said a Chinese taxi driver, 'even when he was wrong.'[144]

He left Hong Kong in 1997 and spent a time on 'sabbatical' at his house in France. In 1999 he accepted appointment as one of the two British members of the European commission.

On his appointment as governor of Hong Kong he declined to wear the traditional ceremonial diplomatic uniform and also refused the traditional knighthood that went with the appointment. 'I've got my house colours as a privy councillor, which, for a politician, is the most important honour you can have . . . I think the time for an additional honour, if there does come a time, should be when I've actually done something for Hong Kong, not just because I've taken the job.'[145] Having 'done something' for Hong Kong, he was made a CH in the New Year Honours List 1998. The citation read: 'Former Governor and Commander-in-Chief, Hong Kong. For public service.'

John Major 31 December 1998
John Major was the Conservative politician who unexpectedly succeeded Margaret Thatcher as prime minister. His unexpectedly swift rise to the highest office in 1990 made him, at the age of forty-seven, at that time the youngest British prime minister of the twentieth century.

He was born in 1943, the son of Thomas Ball, a theatrical artist (who used the stage name of Tom Major) who later ran his own garden ornaments business. He was educated at Cheam Common Primary School and Rutlish Grammar School, Wimbledon. He lived with his family in a two-room apartment in Brixton, south London. He left school at sixteen and worked at first for a firm of insurance brokers and then in various manual jobs. He was denied a job as a bus conductor because his knowledge of mathematics was poor and at the age of nineteen he was unemployed for eight months. In 1965 he began a career in banking, qualifying as an Associate of the Institute of Bankers, and worked for the District Bank (later Standard Chartered Bank) in various posts in the UK and overseas (1965–79), including a period in Nigeria (1966–67), becoming assistant to the chairman.

He first visited the house of commons in 1956 and joined Brixton Young Conservatives in 1959. He became founder chairman of Lambeth Young Conservatives (1965–67), a member of Lambeth Borough Council (1968–71) – winning the previously solid Labour ward of Ferndale – and chairman of its housing committee (1970–71). He unsuccessfully contested St Pancras North at the two general elections in 1974, and in 1979 he was elected Conservative member of parliament for Huntingdonshire (Huntingdon from 1983).

His career in government began as a parliamentary private secretary to ministers of state at the home office (1981–83). Margaret Thatcher noticed him during a working dinner in 1983 when he challenged her on policy issues. She was impressed with those who opposed her as long as they stood their ground and their ground was sure, and so Major started a rapid rise. He was moved to the whips' office (1983–85), to be parliamentary under secretary of state for social security (1985–86), and then minister of state for social security (1986–87). In 1987 he was appointed to the cabinet as chief secretary to the treasury (1987–89). This was said to be at the request of Nigel Lawson, who was the chancellor of the exchequer at the time. Two years later he became secretary of state for foreign and commonwealth affairs (1989), an astonishing promotion from the most junior office in the cabinet to one of the most senior. At the time the appointment was seen as a surprise, and was taken as a snub by Geoffrey Howe the previous foreign secretary. His tenure lasted only three months until he became the chancellor of the exchequer after the resignation of Nigel Lawson. By this time Margaret Thatcher's popularity in the parliamentary party was rapidly waning after damaging statements by former cabinet ministers, the poll tax debacle and divisions within the party over attitudes to the European Community. After presenting one budget, Major became prime minister in November 1990 after Margaret Thatcher's resignation, she having made it clear that he was her preferred successor. In the second ballot on 27 November John Major won 185 votes to 131 for Michael Heseltine and 56 for Douglas Hurd. Two votes short of technical victory, his rivals immediately acknowledged Major as the new leader.

His election as leader of the Conservative Party extinguished the lead in the opinion polls enjoyed by the Labour Party and to the surprise of many observers Major led his party to victory (albeit with a substantially reduced majority in the 1992 general election. In June 1995, to counter damaging party splits, he resigned as Conservative Party leader (though not as prime minister) to fight a leadership contest. He won a substantial victory over his sole opponent, John Redwood, and stayed as party leader and prime minister, with the understanding that there would be no further leadership contests until the general election.

Hampered by a divided party and a small majority which later became a minority, the Conservatives were defeated by a Labour landslide in the 1997 general election. The end did not come as a complete surprise. By 1997 the country was tired of eighteen years of rule by a Conservative Party that seemed to be increasingly mired in personal scandals, and his bland style and lack of charisma succumbed to a resurgent Labour Party. Economically the country was in good shape, with falling unemployment and rising productivity, but it was not enough. He was forced to live in Margaret Thatcher's shadow and his managerial, collegiate and negotiating style contrasted strongly with her authoritarian personality cult. 'Overall public opinion seems likely to remember him as caring but weak; honest, but not really in charge and, likeable but, ultimately, unable to unite either the Conservative Party or the nation.'[146] That said, it was to John Major's credit that he did his utmost to hold the party together by consensus.

As soon as the scale of the defeat was clear, he swiftly resigned the leadership of the Conservative Party (almost it seemed with relief), remarking that when the play was over it was time to leave the stage, and embarked on writing his memoirs which were published in 1999. He remained a backbench member of parliament until the 2001 general election when he did not stand again, simultaneously making it clear that he would not necessarily accept a place in the house of lords.

The CH that he received in 1998 was recommended by his successor and was perhaps the honour that he most desired, having given it freely and generously to many of his former colleagues. The citation, far shorter that it would have been in former times, read: 'Member of Parliament for Huntingdon. Prime Minister and First Lord of the Treasury 1990–97. For services to Peace in Northern Ireland.' It was a recognition of the strides that he had made to bring peace to that province. He was the third British prime minister (after Winston Churchill and Clement Attlee) to be made a Companion of Honour.

CHAPTER FIVE

Bright is the ring of words

WRITERS, NOVELISTS, POETS

'Tell us a story!' said the March Hare. 'Yes, please do!' pleaded Alice.
'And be quick about it added the Hatter, 'or you'll be asleep again.'
'A mad tea-party', *Alice's adventures in wonderland,* Lewis Carroll

The 'literary' Companions of Honour represent a diversity of styles. Their collected works form a fair representation of English literature throughout the twentieth century, but their interests, their specialities, their styles of writing and public assessment of their writings, has led in some cases to total eclipse, and in the case of others, to fame for the foreseeable future. If public opinion can be ephemeral and fickle, then the same judgment can be applied to public taste, and the reputations of the literary Companions of Honour will always be subject to the vagaries of trend and fashion.

A book collector with a two-volume edition of the collected short stories of Somerset Maugham decided to sell them, and was told by a secondhand bookshop dealer that Maugham was 'not flavour of the month, or the year, or the decade.' Yet Maugham's reputation as the principal British exponent of the art of writing short stories was great enough for him to be made a Companion of Honour in 1954. Each of the literary Companions has been a highly regarded and popular 'flavour of the month and the year and the decade' in their own lifetime, but changing tastes have either erased that popularity or come to a different assessment of the once honoured literary skills. Unlike other disciplines, the value or significance of achievement or merit in the arts is often assessed more by the extent of popular acclaim than by empirical verification or measurement against objective standards. The ability to spell and punctuate and construct grammatical English might once have been deemed a basic prerequisite for any writer, but even that now seems less important than a general ability to enthral the reader.

The nautical ballads of Henry Newbolt (1922) evoking the glories of a maritime nation back to the glowing days of Sir Francis Drake must have been thrilling to a victorious Great Britain that was proud of its empire and its imperial navy. But in a post-imperial, multicultural, egalitarian age of defence cuts, the work of Newbolt speaks of an almost foreign world. The novels of the Manx novelist, Hall Caine (1922), enjoyed phenomenal popularity until the 1939–45 war, but his books have long been out of print and forgotten. Thanks in part to the work of Alfred Hitchcock, John Buchan (1932) continues to be remembered for his adventure stories, especially *The thirty-nine steps,* but few people would know that he was once a member of parliament, lord high commissioner to the general assembly of the Church of Scotland and governor-general of Canada. The name of Laurence Binyon (1932) is now virtually unknown, although in November of each year many will still recite the most famous words of one of his poems: 'They shall grow not old as we that are left grow old.' Elfed Lewis (1948) was a Welsh

Congregationalist minister whose poems won him a crown and a chair at the National Eisteddfod. Vita Sackville-West (1948) is probably now better remembered for the beauty of the garden that she created at Sissinghurst Castle than for her gardening and other books. The charming children's books of Walter de la Mare (1948) ensured him a wide audience in his day, but his standing has declined since his death. The reputation of E. M. Forster (1953) has widened in recent years with the film and television productions of *Maurice*, *Howard's end*, *A room with a view* and *A passage to India*. The films of *The third man* and *Our man in Havana* have similarly widened the popular appeal of Graham Greene (1966). The pendulum may swing back in favour of the short stories of Somerset Maugham (1954), although at present his standing is low. Whether the witty and self-indulgent writings of Osbert Sitwell (1958) and Sacheverell Sitwell (1983) will survive the passage of time is questionable. A. P. Herbert (1970) was a leading wit in London society, a crusader against injustice and an independent member of parliament, and BBC Television filmed his *Misleading cases* in the 1960s, but his writings have faded from the public mind. The stature of Philip Larkin (1985), never a prolific writer, and comparatively unknown during his lifetime, has increased since his death in 1985. The chronicles of Anthony Powell (1987), the short stories of V. S. Pritchett (1992), the poems of C. H. Sisson (1993), the novels of Doris Lessing (1999), and the plays of Harold Pinter (2002) are too recent to assess whether their reputations will last.

The contributions of the other 'literary' Companions of Honour were more editorial or critical than creative. Thomas Page (1934), John Dover Wilson (1936), David Cecil (1949), Arthur Waley (1956), Ivor Richards (1964), Maurice Bowra (1971) and Frank Leavis (1977) hold a different place in the literary category because of the primarily academic thrust of their work. Page played a pivotal role in editing the writings of Greek antiquity. Wilson made not always well-received critical assessments of the plays of Shakespeare. Cecil, one of many distinguished scions of the Gascoyne-Cecil family, was an academic of broad cultural interests, who was equally at home in the fields of literature, history and art. Among sinologists, Waley remains a renowned figure for his work in translating Chinese and Japanese poetry. Richards wrote a few volumes of poetry and drama late in his life, but he is principally remembered as the father of practical literary criticism, and for his campaigns for 'Basic'. In his editorial work on Greek poetry, Maurice Bowra was a successor to Thomas Page, and their joint interest in the writings of antiquity gave them a shared interest with the translation work of C. H. Sisson. Leavis was a controversial figure whose work led to a major reassessment of English literature in the twentieth century.

This chapter collects writers, novelists, poets, essayists, editors and critics together for the reason that many of the literary Companions produced work in more than one category, and a chapter on each would have led to repetition and an increase in detail. Some were more successful at writing novels than they were at poetry, some were better poets than novelists, and some were better at writing short stories than full-length novels. Some proved their expertise in travelogues and artistic studies, and some, especially in the case of Laurence Binyon, wrote learned and pioneering academic studies as well as poetry. Some of them published extensively on a wide range of subjects and some, like Philip Larkin, produced very little. But quality and public opinion were the criteria, especially when set against public taste.

Not every writer has welcomed the offer of appointment to the Order, and a number of distinguished literary figures are known to have declined the CH for a variety of reasons. Writers are usually highly individual people, whose individuality can result in eccentricity as much as creativity. It is often commonly assumed that because an individual does not have an honour, they have been 'overlooked' or 'forgotten'. In the case of particularly prominent individuals the names and brief biographies of the 'refusals' are included to show that they were considered and an offer was made, but for diverse personal reasons they chose to decline the CH.

Virginia Woolf (1882–1941). Novelist, essayist and critic, and one of the leaders in the literary movement called modernism. This elite group also included Gertrude Stein, James Joyce, Ezra Pound and T. S. Eliot. Her most famous novel *To the lighthouse*, examines the life of an upper middle class British family, portraying the fragility of human relationships and the changing social values at the turn of the century. Her feminist ideas are expressed in essays such as *A room of one's own*. She kept an extensive diary, wrote numerous literary reviews and hundreds of letters to friends and acquaintances in her lifetime. She was the most prominent member of the early twentieth century Bloomsbury Group. The group sought to criticise the institutions of society, political, legal and moral, by the yardstick of their tendency to promote or impair the greatest happiness of the greatest number of people. They were criticised as a group of precious and well-to-do intellectuals who talked and wrote a great deal, but in fact 'did' very little. Anything but happy herself, Virginia Woolf was prone to bouts of depression and instability and lived through six major breakdowns before drowning herself, fearing another breakdown, in the River Ouse in 1941. She refused the CH in 1935 (and an honorary degree from the University of Manchester), regarding such tributes almost as trivialities.[1]

Edward Garnett (1868–1937) was a writer, critic and editor who published several volumes, including novels, plays, and critical works, but is chiefly remembered as publisher's reader for several successive firms, the last of which was Jonathan Cape. His own work never achieved great distinction, but as a reader and critic he fostered, encouraged and guided the careers of many writers, including Joseph Conrad, John Galsworthy, F. M. Ford, W. H. Hudson and D. H. Lawrence. He was the author of a number of plays, but is better known as editor of the letters of Conrad and Galsworthy. His wife Constance Garnett (1862–1946) was famous for her translations from the Russian, including the novels of Dostoyevsky and Tolstoy. He indignantly refused a CH in 1935 in the rather quaint belief that it would compromise his independence. 'A few months ago I refused the Birthday Honour that has, I see, been conferred on Dr Dover Wilson – because for me a writer loses part of his independence, when he is honoured by the Government which expects conformity with the ruling powers, such as the Censorship – at least no opposition.'[2]

Hilaire Belloc (1870–1953) was an essayist, poet, novelist, historian, biographer and critic. He was the son of a French father and an English mother, and was born in St Cloud near Paris. The family moved to England when Hilaire was two years old. After being educated at the Oratory School, Birmingham he served in the French army. He returned to England in 1892 and became a student at Balliol College, Oxford. He graduated with a first class honours degree but was disappointed not to be offered a fellowship and was convinced that he had been rejected because of his Roman Catholic faith. He went on a lecture tour of the United States and also had two books of verse published: *A bad child's book of beasts* (1896) and *Verses and sonnets* (1896). He returned to England and in 1902 became a naturalized British subject. A member of the Fabian Society, he became friends with George Bernard Shaw and H. G. Wells who helped him obtain work with newspapers such as the *Daily News* and *The Speaker*. Eventually he became literary editor of the *Morning Post*. In 1906 he purchased a house and land near Horsham and he developed a love for Sussex and over the next thirty years wrote numerous articles and several books on the subject. He was elected to the house of commons at the 1906 general election as Liberal member for South Salford, but was defeated at the December 1910 general election. He returned to journalism and over the next couple of years wrote for the *Pall Mall Gazette*, *Glasgow Herald*, *The Academy* and the *New York World*. He became editor of the political weekly, *The Eye-Witness*, and attacked political corruption in his book *The party system* (1911). Politically, he moved to the right and in *The servile state* (1912) he attacked welfare programmes such as social insurance and minimum wage levels. He was also a successful novelist and historian and his books included *Mr Clutterbuck's election* (1908), *A change in the cabinet* (1909), *Pongo and the bull* (1910), *The French revolution* (1911) and *The history of England* (1915). He was a strong supporter of Britain's involvement in the 1914–18 war and was recruited by the war propaganda bureau, by writing *The two maps of Europe* (1915). Belloc had always been hostile to Germany but he portrayed the war as a clash between pagan barbarism and Christian civilization. His estimates of German casualties were often highly inflated and he constantly made inaccurate estimates about when the war would be over. His son, Louis Belloc, who joined the royal flying corps, was killed while bombing a German transport column in 1918. After the war Belloc wrote a book propounding his Roman Catholic faith, *Europe and faith* (1920). He also published a series of historical biographies: *Oliver Cromwell* (1927), *James II* (1928), *Richelieu* (1930), *Wolsey* (1930), *Cranmer* (1931), *Napoleon* (1932) and *Charles II* (1940). He suffered a slight stroke in January 1942 and refused the CH in the same year.[3]

Robert Graves (1895–1985) was a poet, historical novelist and critic. He was born in Wimbledon and grew up in a protected middle-class environment with an unchallenged belief in 'God, King and Country'. His beliefs were shattered by his experiences as a twenty-year old officer in the Royal Welch Fusiliers during the 1914–18 war. He translated his observations of the brutality and stupidity of war, and his own personal disillusionment, into an early volume of autobiography entitled *Good-bye to all that* (1929). Graves was well known for his historical novels, including *I, Claudius* (1934) and *Claudius the god* (1934), though he wrote them in a hurry to secure much needed funds. His later books included *The Greek myths* and *The Hebrew myths*, and he became increasingly fascinated with the earliest history of Christianity. He produced a novel entitled *King Jesus* (1946) and *The new Nazarene gospel restored*, which he quixotically hoped would revitalise the Christian churches. He always thought of himself primarily as a poet and was professor of poetry at Oxford (1961–66), and was awarded the Queen's Gold Medal for Poetry in 1968. He refused a CBE in 1957, and it was rumoured a CH in 1984, on the ground that he believed an honour to be incompatible with his vocation as a poet. He was, he said, primarily a poet and poetry was a private activity that should not be recognised by the award of an honorific appropriate to public servants. He professed himself content with the three campaign medals awarded to him for his service in the 1914–18 war. For many years until the end of his life he lived on the Mediterranean island of Mallorca.

Leonard Woolf (1880–1969) was best known for being the husband of his wife Virginia Woolf. He was born in London in 1880 into a middle class Jewish family. He was educated at St. Paul's School and Trinity College, Cambridge and then worked for the Ceylon Civil Service. On his return to England in 1912 he married Virginia. He never seemed bothered by her affairs with women (including Vita Sackville-West) and was a supportive husband. His first novel *The village and the jungle* was published in 1913, followed by the *Wise virgins* in 1914. An opponent of Britain's involvement in the 1914–18 war, Woolf was spared declaring himself a conscientious objector by being rejected by the military as unfit for duty. Woolf joined the Fabian Society in 1916 and the following year founded the Hogarth Press. Over the next few years Leonard and Virginia Woolf became the centre of what became known as the Bloomsbury Group. Leonard Woolf was literary editor of *The Nation* (1923–30) and wrote several books including *Socialism and co-operation* (1921), *After the deluge* (1931) and *Principia politica* (1953). He also published several volumes of autobiography: *Sowing* (1960), *Growing* (1961), *Beginning again* (1964), *Downhill all the way* (1966) and *The journey not the arrival matters* (1969). His refusal of the CH in 1966 was due to an antipathy to honours, as he said in his letter of refusal. 'I have always been (heretically) against the giving and accepting of honours and have often in the past said so. Much as I appreciate your kindness, I cannot therefore accept it, but I hope that you will not think the worse of me. Years ago Ramsay MacDonald offered the same honour to Virginia, and sharing my views, she asked to be forgiven for not accepting it, and I drafted her reply in much the same words as I am now using for my own.'[4]

J. B. Priestley (1894–1984) was a versatile journalist, novelist, playwright, and essayist from Yorkshire. He wrote over one hundred and twenty novels, plays, and essays, all usually light and optimistic in tone. He was born in Bradford, Yorkshire, the son of schoolmaster. He was educated at Bradford Grammar School, leaving it at the age of sixteen to work as a junior clerk (1910–14). In Bradford he began to write poetry for his own pleasure and contribute articles to local and London papers. During the 1914–18 war he served with the Duke of Wellington's and Devon regiments, and survived the front lines in Flanders. After the war he went to Cambridge where he studied literature, history and political science and graduated in 1921. From 1922 he worked as a journalist in London, starting his career as an essayist and critic at various newspapers and periodicals, including the *New Statesman*. His first collection of essays *Brief diversions* appeared in 1922. He achieved popularity with his novel *The good companions* (1929), a tale about the adventures of a troupe of travelling players. *Angel pavement* (1930) depicted the people of London and what happens to them when an adventure comes to them in the person of the mysterious Mr Goldspie. As a playwright (he wrote some fifty in all) he began in the 1930s with *Dangerous corner* (1932) *Laburnum grove* (1933), and *Time and conways* (1937). He also founded his own production company, English Plays, Ltd., and in 1938–39 he was director of the Mask Theatre in London. Among his other books were *English journey* (1934), a seminal work in arousing social conscience in the 1930s, *Literature and western man* (1960), a survey of Western literature over the past 500 years, and his memoirs, *Margin released* (1962). His novel *The magicians* (1954) showed the influence of the Swiss analytical psychologist Carl Jung. The last of his novels was *Found, lost, found* (1976), an old-fashioned fairy tale and love story in a modern setting. After the outbreak of the 1939–45 war he gained fame as 'the voice of the common people'. He was a patriotic radio broadcaster, second only to Churchill. At the early stage of the cold war, he became a supporter of the Campaign for Nuclear Disarmament. In *Britain and the nuclear bombs* (1957) he argued for the moral superiority that unilateral nuclear disarmament would bring. He is known to have refused a knighthood and a life peerage and the CH went the same way in 1969.[5] He was a known critic of honours and objected in particular to the appointment of politicians as Companions of Honour. In his book *The Edwardians* (1970) he gave a hint of his heart's desire, by praising King Edward VII for instituting the Order of Merit in 1902. To that Order he was appointed in 1976.

It could be argued that the lives of Virginia Woolf, Edward Garnett, Hilaire Belloc, Robert Graves, Leonard Woolf and J. B. Priestley should not be mentioned in this chapter or anywhere in this book because they were never made Companions of Honour and do not qualify for inclusion. A better argument asserts that as they were offered the honour, their work and reputation was judged to be of CH standard and therefore it should be publicly noted that they were not overlooked. It seemed appropriate to include this group in this chapter rather than relegate them to an appendix, and they merit at least a footnote because they were not prepared to accept even this classless egalitarian honour.

Disposal of the literary CH 'could have beens', leads to a record of the substantive literary Companions of Honour.

Sir Henry Newbolt 2 January 1922
First of the 'literary' Companions of Honour, Henry Newbolt was long remembered as the author of rousing patriotic nautical ballads, of which *Drake's drum* was the best known, and many regarded him as the nautical counterpart of his contemporary, Rudyard Kipling.

Newbolt was born in 1862, eldest of the three sons of the vicar of St Mary's Church, Bilston. He was educated at Clifton College and in 1881 went by scholarship to Corpus Christi College, Oxford where he graduated with a first in classical moderations in 1882 and a second in literae humaniores in 1885. He contemplated a legal career, was called to the bar at Lincoln's Inn in 1887 and practised as a barrister for twelve years. But a developing interest in literature gradually supplanted the world of the inns of court, and his first book, *Taken from the enemy*, a tale of the Napoleonic wars, was published in 1892, and a second, *Mordred: a tragedy*, appeared in 1895. Six poems, including *Drake's drum*, were published in Longman's magazine in 1896. *Drake's drum* appeared again in a collection entitled *Admirals all and other verses*, published in 1897. According to Newbolt himself, his friend Robert Bridges, later poet laureate, read it and said: 'It isn't given to a man to write anything better than that. I wish I had ever written anything half so good'.[6] *The island race* followed in 1898, and two later collections: *Songs of the sea* (1904) and *Songs of the fleet* (1910) were set to music by Sir Charles Villiers Stanford. Newbolt was generally best known for his sea poems.

The origin of his affinity with the sea probably derived from his maternal grandfather, a naval officer, but his spirited sea poems were only one aspect of his literary career. 'Many books followed from 1898 to 1932, various in theme and kind, but consistent in the fastidious care and thought expended upon their making; indeed, owing in part perhaps to his training in the law, but much more to native impulse, inclination and character.'[7] In 1923, at the request of the committee of imperial defence, he undertook to complete the last two volumes of the five-volume official history of the naval operations of the 1914–18 war, of which the first three had been written by Sir James Corbett. He served on many councils, committees and commissions, such as the Royal Literary Fund, the Central Council for the Care of Churches and the Royal Society of Literature, and he was a trustee of the National Portrait Gallery (1928–37). 'His faith in Christianity and the influence of tradition, social, historical and literary, was paramount in his mind and work. He was haunted too by the seductive problem of Time, not that of the clock but of the self within, and by a "sense of the past" allied to the idea of the Supreme Consciousness . . . He was not a born story-teller; but his romances have a serene and imaginative grace now rare in English fiction . . . Throughout his life he was faithful to his ideal of England and Englishness. In spite of so many literary pursuits that called him away from it, poetry was his inmost and lifelong devotion.'[8] His *Vitaï Lampada*, inspired by his experiences at Clifton, with its refrain "Play up, play up! and play the game!" was at one time known by almost every schoolboy in England.[9]

During the 1914–18 war he was controller of telecommunications, for which he was knighted in 1915, and the conferment of a CH in 1922 described him blandly as 'Barrister and Author'. He died in 1938.

Sir Hall Caine 19 October 1922
Hall Caine was a novelist who sprang to fame in the last fifteen years of the nineteenth century and set many of his books against the backdrop of the Isle of Man.

He was born at Runcorn, Cheshire in 1853, the eldest son of a ship's smith from the Isle of Man. Although his father had migrated to Liverpool, much of Caine's childhood was spent living with relations on the Isle of Man, and that island featured prominently in his life and writings. He left an elementary school in Liverpool at the age of fourteen to become the pupil of a local architect, though his entry in *Who's Who* stated that he 'never practised'. He contributed articles on architectural criticism to *The Builder* and *Building News* which brought him to the notice of John Ruskin. In 1878 he delivered a lecture on Dante Gabriel Rossetti's poetry that was published in 1879 and led to a friendship between the two men. In 1881 he decided to devote himself entirely to writing and he was invited by Rossetti to live with him at his house, becoming the poet's constant friend and companion until Rossetti's death in 1882. He published *Recollections of Rossetti* in 1892 and a new and enlarged edition on the occasion of the poet's centenary in 1928.

Like other writers, he tried a career in journalism and worked for six years on the *Liverpool Mercury*. His first novel, *Shadow of a crime*, appeared in 1885 as a serial in that paper and he then abandoned journalism and Liverpool to settle in his beloved Isle of Man in 1895. The publication of *The deemster* (1887), a story set on the island, marked the beginning of his extraordinary popularity. Other novels followed, including *The bondman* (1890), *The scapegoat* (1891), *The Manxman* (1894), *The eternal city* (1901), *The prodigal son* (1904), *The woman thou gavest me* (1913) and *The master of man* (1921). He also wrote a *Life of Christ* (1938) and an early autobiography *My story* (1908). The islanders resented his vision of Manx life, riddled with steamy sexuality, illegitimacy and superstition, but it had a very wide public appeal. He claimed that the central motive of his books was 'the idea of justice, divine justice, the idea that righteousness always works itself out, that out of hatred and malice comes love.'[10] There was a religious streak to his nature and the plots of some of his novels were derived from biblical stories. *The deemster* was based on the parable of the prodigal son, *The bondman* on Jacob and Esau, and *The scapegoat* on Eli and Samuel. He also wrote plays. The lord chamberlain stopped one about Mohammed after pressure from Indian Moslems.

Although he was principally a novelist, he undertook other work. In 1892–3 he visited Poland and the frontier towns of Russia at the request of the Russia-Jewish committee to investigate the facts of the Jewish persecutions, and he wrote a series of articles for *The Times* describing his experiences. In 1895 he was sent on behalf of the Incorporated Society of Authors and the colonial office to Canada where he conducted successful negotiations with the dominion government on the subject of Canadian copyright.

After their coronation in 1902, King Edward VII and Queen Alexandra travelled on a cruise up the west coast of England and Scotland. They made a short visit to the Isle of Man where they were Caine's guests. Caine described the encounter: 'The Queen . . . talked continuously, hardly ever waiting for a reply . . . She was all nerves and emotions.'[11] Queen Alexandra described Caine as 'a curious-looking man, the same as his books.'[12] (Caine had a high balding forehead and cultivated an alleged resemblance to Shakespeare by growing a pointed beard.) Nonetheless, despite that unpromising beginning, a friendship seems to have developed between the author and the royal party. Either Caine or his son seem to have suggested that a gift book associated with Queen Alexandra and produced for Christmas might be sold in aid of the queen's charities. The result was *The queen's Christmas carol*, published in 1905. A book of photographs, *Queen Alexandra's gift book*, appeared in 1908 and was published by the *Daily Telegraph*, where Caine was a part-time journalist.

From 1903–08 he was a member of the house of keys of the Manx parliament. During the 1914–18 war he devoted his energies to allied propaganda in the USA writing streams of articles which were published in a syndicate of American newspapers, principally the *New York Times*, urging the USA to join the war on the side of the allies. He also edited *King Albert's book* (1914), a tribute to the Belgian king and people, for which he was made an Officer of the Belgian Order of Leopold.

Caine's novels were astonishingly popular and his books were translated into many languages, several being adapted for the stage. 'Over a million copies were sold of *The eternal city* (1901), and *The Christian* (1897) was hardly less popular, but the success of books such as these should not obscure the genuine merit of some of his Manx novels, notably *The Manxman* (1894). He had a real knowledge of the Manx people, their history and customs, and in the Isle of Man he found a setting, hitherto unknown to novelists, which exactly suited his romantic and picturesque stories.'[13] Others were more critical of his ranting sentiment, and his pretensions to prophetic wisdom were increasingly mocked. In 1941 the *Cambridge history of English literature* did not rate his 'numerous novelistic melodramas' as worthy of any discussion.

He was appointed a KBE in 1918 for his war services, and his CH in 1922 was conferred 'For services to Literature.' He died in 1931.

Lord Tweedsmuir 1 January 1932
Forever remembered as the author of *The thirty-nine steps*, and other fast-moving adventure stories, John Buchan's career extended to the world of journalism and politics.

He was born at Perth in 1875, his father a minister of the Free Church of Scotland and his mother, the daughter of a farmer from Peeblesshire. After attending a grammar school and lectures at Glasgow University, Buchan was awarded a scholarship to Brasenose College, Oxford in 1895. Thereafter his life was spent in England, South Africa and Canada, but his childhood and formative years in Scotland left a deep impression on him. As he said, quoting Wordsworth, Scotland 'haunted him like a passion'.[14] He remained a devout Christian throughout his life, saying his prayers and reading the bible, and he knew *The pilgrim's progress* almost by heart.

At Oxford in 1897 he won the Stanhope historical essay prize on the subject of 'Sir Walter Raleigh' and in 1898 the Newdigate prize for English verse with the 'Pilgrim Fathers' as its theme. He was president of the Union in 1899 and was awarded a first class degree in literae humaniores in the same year. He already had two books to his credit, *Sir Quixote of the Moors* (1895), *Scholar gipsies* (1896), and he was commissioned to write the history of Brasenose for the Robinson series of college histories. It was published in 1898 while he was still an undergraduate, but was severely criticised by antiquarian reviewers who were unaccustomed to so unconventional a style of historical writing.

After graduation he was called to the bar at Middle Temple in 1901 but earned his living by journalism. His legal career was cut short when he was summoned to South Africa by Lord Milner to be one of his assistant private secretaries. He was only two years in Africa 1901–03, but it was a significant step in his career. Daily association with Milner and his modest tasks in resettlement of the country, 'where his warm human desire to make friends with the Boers and bury the hatchet gave him a horizon and a sense of size, and his imperialism, cleansed of vulgar jingoism, became elevated above the patronising "trust" conception into an association of free peoples in loyalty to a common throne.'[15]

At the conclusion of his South African sojourn, he was disappointed in his desire to go to Egypt and work with Lord Cromer, and returned to London to practice as a barrister. His work was never distinguished enough to ensure a future at the bar, and he was never committed enough to make a success of it. He produced one legal book, *Law relating to the taxation of foreign income* in 1905. A last echo of this phase of his life occurred in 1935 when Middle Temple made their distinguished alumnus a bencher. In 1907 a publisher whom he had known from Oxford, invited Buchan to join him as a literary adviser. Five novels had appeared between 1895 and 1902, and two partly autobiographical books on Africa in 1903 and 1906. *Prester John* (1910) was the first of the long series of adventure stories which made his reputation. He attempted a work of history *The marquis of Montrose* (1913), but it contained so many elementary blunders and showed so much bias in favour of the character of Montrose that he was severely criticised. Other historical biographies included Sir Walter Scott (1932), Oliver Cromwell (1934) and Augustus (1937).

A serious carriage accident in 1914 left him confined to bed for more than a year and the task of having to learn to walk again. During this time, he began work on *A history of the great war* which was published in twenty-four volumes in

1921–22, but the publication of *The thirty-nine steps* (1915) made his reputation with its mixture of espionage and excitement, and introduced Richard Hannay to the world. *Greenmantle* (1916) and *Mr Standfast* (1919) completed the trilogy. Other adventure stories included *Huntingtower* (1922), *The three hostages* (1924), *John MacNab* (1925), *Witch wood* (1927), *The courts of the morning* (1929), *The island of sheep* (1936) and *Sick heart river* (1941). Apart from *The thirty-nine steps*, memorably filmed by Alfred Hitchcock in 1935 with Robert Donat in the lead role of Richard Hannay, and a silent version of *Huntingtower* in 1927, Buchan's books have been oddly neglected by the film industry.

After recovery, Buchan worked as a journalist on *The Times*, then at the foreign office under Lord Grey and Lord Robert Cecil, and in the early months of 1917 was appointed by Winston Churchill as head of the department of information, where he laid the foundation of the success of British propaganda. Then he acted as director of intelligence under Lord Beaverbrook, and was one of the principal officials of the ministry of information.

Throughout the 1920s, a succession of novels appeared, but politics beckoned and in 1927 he was elected member of parliament for the Scottish Universities. Always a practising Presbyterian, he was made an elder of St Columba's Church in Oxford, and then in 1933 and 1934 he was appointed lord high commissioner to the general assembly of the Church of Scotland. He was president of the Scottish History Society (1929–32). In 1935 this literary son of Scotland achieved his highest office when his fellow-Scot, Prime Minister Ramsay MacDonald, recommended to King George V that Buchan be made governor-general of Canada. It was an unusual and inspired choice. The fame of his novels had preceded him and he received a warm welcome in the dominion, not least because he was fluent in French and took a special interest in the French-Canadian culture of Quebec. He also possessed qualities essential to the holder of any viceregal post – discretion, tact and charm. He became a close friend of President Roosevelt and with Lord Lothian, the British ambassador in Washington, who had served with him under Lord Milner in South Africa. Buchan was a success as governor-general. 'He retained royal protocol in Ottawa, but combined it with an easy democratic approach in his travels. His speeches were opportunities to talk about matters of general concern, and he spoke with a brevity and a cogency that sharply contrasted with the interminable woolliness of the Mackenzie King school of oratory.'[16]

He was considered for a KCMG in 1922,[17] but his honours began with the CH in 1932 'For public, educational and literary services', and continued with a GCMG in 1935 on his appointment as governor-general, and a GCVO in 1939 on the occasion of the visit of the king and queen to Canada. He was made a privy councillor in 1937, elected chancellor of Edinburgh University in 1937 and an honorary fellow of Brasenose College in 1934.

Since the accident of 1914 his health had never been strong, and the strain and anxiety of the royal visit led to his premature death in 1940 at the age of sixty-five.

Laurence Binyon 3 June 1932
In his day, he was a poet, art historian and critic, but the name of Laurence Binyon is no longer widely known, beyond his authorship of a poem, a few lines of which have enshrined the memory of war. 'They shall grow not old as we that are left grow old. Age shall not weary them nor the years condemn. At the going down of the sun and in the morning, we will remember them.'

Laurence Binyon was born in Lancaster in 1869, the second son of the vicar of Burton-in-Lonsdale. He was educated at St Paul's School and Trinity College, Oxford where he won the Newdigate Prize for English poetry. He entered the department of printed books at the British Library in 1893 but was transferred to the department of prints and drawings in 1895, becoming assistant keeper in 1909. As a boy he had hesitated between poetry and art as a means of expression, and as an undergraduate he contributed to a slim volume of poems in 1890 and continued to publish small volumes of lyrics and dramas until 1931. His first volume of verse, *Lyric poems*, was published in 1894, and his best work appears in *Odes* (1901). Had he not been a diligent and thorough expert in his professional life, he might have written and published more. 'He issued at intervals a considerable number of annotated catalogues, of lectures and essays, in many of which the affinity of poetry with the visual arts was felt or actually indicated.'[18] His first official work was the production in four volumes (1898–1907) of the *Catalogue of drawings by British artists and artists of foreign origin working in Great Britain preserved in the department of prints and drawings in the British Museum*. He became an expert on eastern art, and 'did more than anyone to spread the appreciation of the art not only of China and Japan, but of India and Persia,'[19] and his *Painting in the far east* (1908) was the first book on the subject in any European language. He was also an expert on western art, including the work of Blake and Botticelli. Verse and art overlapped in his mind, and verse was as much a part of his nature as the study and interpretation of visual art. His love of the English earth and legends pervades much of his poetry and appears in such prose as *Landscape in English art and poetry* (1931) and *English watercolours* (1933). He also wrote plays – *Paris and Oenone*, *Attila*, *Arthur* – which had successful runs, and translated Dante's *Divine comedy* into terza rima (1933–43), but composition was limited by the zealous discharge of his professional duties, as he himself remarked. 'Having a seven-hours official day to put in, I rarely have time to write on a first stimulus: I am obliged to keep things in my mind for months, and so they tend to grow and expand of themselves . . . I long in my heart to get away from the museum and write a magnum opus, cherished for twenty years or more, though not a line of it has been written.'[20] His poetry, lyrical in the style of Wordsworth and Matthew Arnold, was never widely popular. 'His style was too refined, his thought too swift and subtle for the generality of even the reading public,'[21] but his elegy of affecting melancholy, *For the fallen*, published in *The Times* on 21 September 1914, met with universal acclaim. It was set to music by Sir Edward Elgar and it has been said or sung at countless memorial services and is inscribed on countless memorial stones, including the one at the British Museum. His *Collected poems* was published in 1931.

His CH in 1932 cited his twin careers as 'Poet. Deputy Keeper, Sub-Department of Oriental Prints and Drawings, British Museum.' He died in 1943.

Thomas Ethelbert Page 1 January 1934
Classical scholar, teacher, editor and political critic, Thomas Page was born in 1850. He was reticent about his origins and private life, excluding details of his parentage in his entry in *Who's Who*, and including his wife only by way of her initials, 'D.C.E.'. He was educated at Lincoln Grammar School, Shrewsbury School and St John's College, Cambridge, where he was an outstanding classics scholar. He was Porson prizeman in 1870, Brown medallist (for Latin ode) 1870–72, won

the chancellor's medal for English poem in 1872, was Porson university scholar in 1871 and Davies university scholar in 1872, and won the chancellor's classics medal in 1873. Despite these achievements, which clearly pointed to talent, he left Oxford with a second class degree in classics, and for the next thirty-seven years, he was a sixth form master at Charterhouse. There he produced the standard sixth form editions of the *Odes* of Horace and the *Aeneid*. In 1911 he unsuccessfully stood for parliament as an independent for Cambridge University. He was a regular contributor to *The Times Educational Supplement*, a member of Surrey County Council and its education committee, and served for the thirty years on the town council of Godalming.

In 1912 he was invited to be editor in chief of the Loeb classical library, holding that position for the last twenty-five years of his life, 'editing the various editions with laborious care and fine critical judgement, and handling the translators, both English and American, with tact and considerateness. His magnificent presence, tall stature, and noble head with fine eyes and close-cropped beard attracted the notice of strangers. Those who conversed with him found a courteous listener and a weighty and witty talker, who touched no subject that he did not illuminate.'[22] On his eightieth birthday in 1930 he received a Latin address of congratulation from 500 men eminent in politics, scholarship, art and literature.

At the age of eighty-one, St John's College, Cambridge made him an honorary fellow. The CH, conferred on him in 1934 as 'Editor-in-Chief of the Loeb Classical Library. For services to scholarship and letters', came two and half years before his death in 1936.

John Dover Wilson 1 January 1936
John Dover Wilson was a distinguished textual critic and educationalist who became absorbed by his attempts to recover the original texts of Shakespeare's works.

Born in Cambridge in 1881, the son of a lithographer, he was educated at Lancing College and Gonville and Caius College, Cambridge, where he was a history scholar, graduating in 1903. He was an assistant master at Whitgift Grammar School (1904–05), taught English at the University of Helsingfors, Finland (1906–09), was lecturer in English language and literature at Goldsmiths College, London (1909–12), and then on the staff of the schools inspectorate (1912–24). In 1919 he served on a committee on the teaching of English under the chairmanship of Sir Henry Newbolt. He was professor of education at King's College, London (1924–35), and regius professor of rhetoric and English literature at Edinburgh (1935–45). He retired from Edinburgh to concentrate on his work as chief editor of the New Cambridge edition of William Shakespeare's plays (1921–66). He was a trustee of Shakespeare's birthplace (1931–69) and also of the National Library of Scotland (1946–69), serving a term as vice-chairman (1954–57).

Wilson's special interest was the speaking and writing of English and even before he left Cambridge he had begun to focus on Shakespeare's works. His first book was published in 1911 under the title *Life in Shakespeare's England: a book of Elizabethan prose*. His analysis of the development of the texts of Shakespeare's works was intensely detailed, and he used the insights of psychology and history in his interpretations. His contributions to Shakespearean scholarship were certainly controversial and his critical judgments were variously labelled extreme, faulty, or inspired, but his theories made fascinating reading. He held that it was only after the problems of the text had been solved that the dialogue could be properly interpreted and understood, and he established this doctrine most effectively in his book *What happens in Hamlet* (1935). He reviewed the intricate plot and arrived at the ingenious and plausible theory that a missing stage direction lay underneath the mountain of critical doubt and confusion on the subject. 'If only [he] maintained, it can be assumed, as it should be assumed, that Hamlet overheard the plot hatched between Polonius and Claudius – why, then, a great deal which is now obscure or contradictory becomes intelligible and illuminated, and with that transformation the plot of Hamlet can be shown to be completely watertight.'[23] Another radical theory was posited in *The fortunes of Falstaff* (1943) where he presented a picture of Falstaff as a force of evil ultimately rejected by the king. His other works include: *Shakespeare's hand in the play of Sir Thomas More* (1923); *Shakespeare's happy comedies* (1962); and *Shakespeare's sonnets* (1963). *The essential Shakespeare: a biographical adventure* (1932) captured public imagination more than any other Shakespearean scholar and confirmed his reputation. 'He was a popular lecturer in the best sense, whether to a learned or an unlearned audience. He had the manner of one who had just discovered the secret of Shakespeare for the first time and was anxious to share it with his listeners.'[24]

The CH was conferred on him in 1936 'For services to Literature'. He died in 1969.

Vita Sackville-West 1 January 1948
Born in 1892, the only child of Lionel Sackville-West, later third Baron Sackville, Vita Sackville-West was a poet, novelist, columnist and gardener, who enjoyed a very privileged life from birth until her marriage. She lived at Knole, one of the largest houses in England, a Tudor palace built around seven courtyards in a 1000 acre park, 'and her romantic love of her aristocratic home, combined with her disappointment that as a female she could not inherit it, did much to form both her personal character and her professional career.'[25]

Devoted to her father, she was critical of her eccentric half-Spanish mother. Educated at Knole by governesses until she was thirteen, her childhood was inevitably lonely. The result of her isolated and privileged lifestyle was at least in part responsible for her voracious appetite in reading and writing. By the age of eighteen, she had written numerous poems, eight novels (one in French) and five plays, all on historical themes. A childhood spent against the backdrop of Knole at the beginning of the twentieth century, led to a deep love of country pursuits and the fertile farmland of Kent. In her teens she enjoyed travel, visiting France and Italy on numerous occasions, learning to speak both languages fluently, and toured Russia, Poland and Austria with her mother.

She developed as a writer, successful in the fields of poetry, the novel and biography. Her first published works were a collection of poems, *Poems of east and west* (1917) and a novel, *Heritage* (1919). *Knole and the Sackvilles*, a history of her home and ancestors, was published in 1922, and in 1930 she published *The Edwardians*, a novel based on Knole, the Sackvilles and Edwardian society at its peak. 'It was an instant best seller, and though perhaps over-intense, it will hold its place as a period piece, a record of the sumptuous standard of living in a great house where the servants were numbered in hundreds, before the war of 1914–18.'[26] Her love of her home county emerges in *Orchard and vineyard* (1921) and in a long poem, *The land* (1927).

In 1913 she married the diplomat Harold Nicolson, and there began half a century of a happy and enduring if unusual marriage. Nicolson was already third secretary at the British embassy in Constantinople, where they lived for a short time after their marriage. Her personal life between 1914 and 1930 was emotional and sometimes stormy. In 1918–21 she had a passionate love affair with Violet Trefusis with whom she went off on several occasions. But she returned eventually to her husband who was both understanding and forgiving. In 1925 Nicolson was posted to Persia, but Vita stayed in England. She hated diplomatic life and preferred her writing and her garden. But they wrote to each other every day, a habit they continued to the end of their lives, and she twice went to Persia to visit him, and recorded the events in *Passenger to Teheran* (1926). 'Although their marriage was unconventional in every way, because both were basically homosexual, it had become extremely happy . . . each needed the other to advise, amuse, sustain and understand.'[27] Her most significant relationship during this period was with Virginia Woolf with whom she remained close friends, and Woolf's suicide in 1941 was deeply distressing to Vita who had been the model for Woolf's *Orlando*. Nicolson summed up his emotional wife. 'She is a dark river moving deeply in shadows. She really does not care for the domestic affections. She would wish life to be conducted on a series of *grandes passions*. Or she thinks she would. In practice, had I been a passionate man, I should have suffered tortures of jealousy on her behalf, have made endless scenes, and we should now have separated, I living in Montevideo as H. M. Minister and she breeding Samoyeds in the Gobi desert.'[28]

In 1929, Nicolson retired from the diplomatic service, and in 1930 they purchased Sissinghurst Castle, a decayed Elizabethan mansion in Kent. They spent a considerable amount of time and effort restoring and transforming the house and gardens, both of which passed to the National Trust after Nicolson's death in 1968. Vita continued to write prolifically, chiefly historical biography, and wrote a gardening column for the *Observer* (1948–61). Her horticultural interests were reflected in a series of books with increasingly insistent titles. *The garden* (1946), *In your garden* (1951), *In your garden again* (1953), *More for your garden* (1955) and *Even more for your garden* (1958). The poet Stephen Spender described her thus: 'Working always in her garden, caring for her friends, her flowers and her poetry, modest and never interesting herself in literary disputes, her friendship had the freedom of silence and watchfulness about it.'[29]

The CH was conferred on her in 1948 'For services to Literature'. At a cocktail party at Buckingham Palace early in December 1947, she was introduced to Clement Attlee, the prime minister. Two days later she received a letter from Attlee's office offering her the CH. She showed the letter to her husband, who was surprised at her lack of excitement, based apparently on her belief that her writing days were over. It transpired that the King's private secretary, Sir Alan Lascelles, had suggested the honour and that Attlee himself was a passionate admirer of *The land*. Her husband made it clear that the CH was to be announced as to 'V. Sackville-West' and not to Mrs Harold Nicolson, but despite his request, correct form took precedence, and Vita was gazetted as 'Victoria Mary, The Honourable Mrs Harold Nicolson (Miss V. Sackville-West). For services to Literature.'[30] She didn't quite know what to do with the badge. 'I would like to know', she wrote to the Central Chancery of the Orders of Knighthood, 'on what occasions one is entitled to wear the Decoration, on which shoulder one pins it; and whether I have correctly been informed that there is no ribbon or miniature, i.e. that one wears only the large locket with which the King presented me. It seems so enormous compared with other medals.'[31]

Vita Sackville-West was diagnosed with inoperable cancer in 1961 and died in June 1962.

The Reverend Howell Elvet Lewis 10 June 1948

Howell Elvet Lewis, known by his Gorsedd name 'Elfed', was a minister of the Welsh Congregational Church, and a poet and hymn writer of considerable fame in his native land.

He was born in 1860 at Cynwyl Elfed, Carmarthenshire, and educated at the Presbyterian College in Carmarthen. His ministry was spent at churches at Buckley, Hull, Llanelli, Harecourt (Canonbury) and finally at the Welsh Congregational Church at King's Cross where he spent thirty-six years (1904–40), his sermons attracting large numbers of the then numerous Welsh expatriate community in London. He was also chairman of the Union of Welsh Independents in 1925, president of the National Free Church Council (1926–27), and chairman of the Congregational Union of England and Wales (1933–34). In its heyday the Welsh Congregational Church in King's Cross Road, with those at Charing Cross and Westminster, was one of the three largest Welsh churches in London. His ministry there was brought to a reluctant conclusion in the dark days of 1940. With the outbreak of war, Elfed's friends made attempts to persuade him to retire. He refused to go until the increasing severity of the blitz caused him to leave on 14 April 1940 – his eightieth birthday – and retire to Penarth, Glamorgan.

Although Elfed was a powerful and prominent preacher in his day, his fame rests more on his interest and proficiency in the Welsh language and its culture, which won him the crown at the national eisteddfod in 1888 and 1891, and the chair in 1894. From 1923–27 he was archdruid of Wales. Lewis was an important figure in the history of modern Welsh poetry, and his lasting contribution was his collected poems *Caniadau [Songs]*, published in two volumes in 1895 and 1901. Some of the more socialist and patriotic elements of his verse brought him fame, and his romantic lyrics about the beauty of nature were more popular, particularly the poems *Gwyn ap Nudd, Pan Ddaw'r [When it comes]* and *Y Ddau Frawd [The two brothers]*. None of his later poetry reached the standard of his earlier work. In the art of hymn writing, he produced verses that were lyrical, devotional meditations, and published *Sweet Singers of Wales* c.1890, a study of Welsh hymns and their authors. He also wrote authoritatively on the history of the Welsh sermon, particularly in his volumes *Planu Coed [Planting trees]* (1894) and *Lampau'r Hwyr [Lamps of the evening]* (1945), both books proving that his principal interest was more moral and devotional than theological.

By the late 1940s, Elfed was blind and in his late eighties, but he had become something of a legendary figure in Wales and his contribution to Welsh culture was recognised with three high honours in 1948. In January, he was presented with a national testimonial, containing contributions from all of Wales, in the Temple of Peace in Cardiff. His response was according to the spirit of his faith. 'And this I would say without being argued against, that none of us shall expect honour for his gifts that he has received as a birthright from the author of life. In his faithfulness to nurture and use his gifts to the best purpose is the true worth of every man. After all it is not the prize that is the chief treasure, but the enjoyment of service.'[32]

In June 1948 he was appointed a CH, 'For services to Welsh religious and social life and letters', and he was always fond of reciting the story of his investiture by King George VI. He spent nearly half an hour with the king, who spoke to him of their earlier meetings, especially at the Eisteddfods. As Elfed was leaving, he turned to the king and showed him the stick that he carried, saying that it had come 'every step from Nazareth'. The king placed his hand on the stick, and Elfed responded by 'asking a blessing of the man of Nazareth on him'.[33] Finally, in December 1948, he was honoured for the third and last time by the University of Wales. He had been given an honorary MA in 1906 and an honorary DD in 1933, and now he was given an honorary LLD. The vice-chancellor, Professor Emrys Evans, paid tribute to Lewis' eminence. 'From now on there are no honours left to give him unless we create new ones. We love him for the sweet verses and gentle hymns that we've had consistently from him. A true successor to the enchanting Gwyn ap Nudd, hymnwriter of the dawn and the designer of our evening prayer. Archdruid, archpreacher and archpoet, we cannot today but offer him the only convenient degree that we have and to express to him our good feelings and admiration. May he long voyage on the evening of life.'[34]

The evening of his life lasted five more years. Elfed died in 1953 at the age of ninety-three. A memorial of this great son of Wales, *Cofiant Elfed 1860–1953*, was written by Emlyn Jenkins and published in 1957 – in Welsh. Although Jenkins concluded his work with a piece of hyperbole, describing Elfed as 'the idol of Wales and the beloved of the nation,'[35] it was an indication of the extent of affection for the old man. Nearly half a century after his death, some of his beautiful hymns are still sung in the churches and chapels of Wales.

Walter de la Mare 10 June 1948
Walter de la Mare was a popular novelist and poet in the first half of the twentieth century, whose high honours came only in the last few years of his life.

He was born in 1873 at Charlton in Kent, the sixth child of an official in the Bank of England. His French-sounding surname derived from his Hugenot ancestry. He was educated at St Paul's Cathedral Choristers' School where he edited the school magazine. Then he joined the Anglo-American Oil Company in 1890, working for them until 1908 when he left to become a full-time writer. His literary career began with *Songs of childhood* (1902), published under the pseudonym of Walter Ramal ('Ramal' was an adaptation of his surname spelt backwards), followed by the vast opus of poems, stories, novels, books for children, and anthologies. 'His first prose book, *Henry Brocken* (1904), is a romance using famous figures from the literatures of Europe. It sets the perspective line of all his subsequent work. The background of his view of life was to remain fixed in the world of books. If incongruity threatened, then life had to be refashioned by fantasy to fit that background, whether it was life of children or adults.'[36] A children's story, *The three mulla mulgars* (1910) and a novel of the occult, *The return* (1910) demonstrated the breadth of his skills. Volumes of poetry included *The listeners* (1912), *Peacock pie* (1913) and *The veil* (1923), and books of short stories included *On the edge* (1930). In 1953 he published a new volume of lyrics *O lovely England*.

De la Mare delighted children and adults alike with his words, but there was a less comfortable and darker side to him. 'Within his own universe de la Mare was a highly complicated organism, compounded of subtly articulated nervous tensions which made his contacts with the outside world oblique, tentative sometimes even bizarre... It was as though he were endowed with several sets of eyes, which he was able to set out in strategic positions to get a many intelligenced-view of any given situation, mood, fear, or passion, person or place... His was a mind, a personality, which loved dangerous living. He would not be content to bask by the fireside of accepted values. The certainties of life must always be opened, disrupted by him in his almost irresponsible inquisitiveness. In the most ordinary and innocuous of things and events he saw a force which was always a threat... He drew again and again towards this brink of the abyss which most people ignored or denied, and there he stood, fascinated, wondering what might be the result if a mortal defied this pervasive latency.'[37] Because of this, de la Mare's poems do always not make comforting reading. 'The best poems are shot through with a disturbing sense of mystery and unease in which dream can shift into nightmare.'[38]

He was made a CH in 1948, the citation simply stating that he was a 'Poet'. He was given the Order of Merit in the Coronation Honours List in 1953. He died in 1956 and was buried in Westminster Abbey.

Lord David Cecil 1 January 1949
David Cecil was an historian of nineteenth century English literature who spent thirty years teaching it at the University of Oxford.

He was born in 1902, son of the fourth marquess of Salisbury. Officially his surname was Gascoyne-Cecil, but he was always known as Lord David Cecil. 'A delicate child, he was much at home and benefited in this from the company of his brilliant aunts and uncles, notorious for their eccentricities, wit and zeal.'[39] He was educated at Eton and Christ Church, Oxford where he took a first class degree in modern history. Elected to a fellowship at Wadham in 1924 to teach modern history, he was simultaneously working on his first book, a life of the poet William Cowper, entitled *The stricken deer*. It was published in 1929 and won the Hawthornden prize in 1930. The success led him to resign his fellowship and take up writing in London. Marriage in 1932 led to a move to the country, and then, missing academic life, he accepted a fellowship in English at New College, Oxford in 1939, and it was here as tutor and from 1948 as Goldsmiths' professor of English literature that he exercised his widest influence and produced much of his best work. 'He had a genius for teaching, communicating enjoyment, and drawing out the best from others. A brilliant conversationalist, his wit consisted in verbal sharpness and accuracy, together with a peculiarly sympathetic humour that was always adapted to the company and the occasion. He was a celebrated lecturer, but his influence was most felt in tutorials, classes, or small, intimate groups. He and his wife, naturally hospitable, were eager to mix their friends and share them with young unknowns. Without condescension or pretension they spread over a wide circle of acquaintances and pupils the best-known cultural, political, and artistic influences of the mid-twentieth century.'[40] He retired from Oxford in 1969 but continued to write and entertain until death.

After his biography of Cowper, he produced biographies of Lord Melbourne (1939 and 1954), Jane Austen (1935 and 1978), Sir Walter Scott (1933) and Charles Lamb (1983). *Early Victorian novelists* (1934) included a subtle analysis and discussion of the structure of *Wuthering Heights*. *Hardy the novelist* (1943) was a classic exposition of one of his favourite authors. The breadth of his knowledge was indicated by his other works: *Poets and story tellers* (1949), *The fine art of reading* (1957), *Visionary and dreamer: two poetic painters – Samuel Palmer and Edward*

Burne-Jones (1969), *The Cecils of Hatfield House* (1973), *Library looking-glass* (1975), *Some Dorset country houses* (1986). 'Born into one of the first families in the land, gifted with intellectual sympathies of a high order, professionally successful, idyllically happy in his family life, he might well have grown complacent and a figure of envy. But complacency was not in his nature or his background; he was self-critical and self-aware. As for enemies, he had few if any. He was greatly loved because of the unusual sweetness of his temper and his genuine humility. Naturally high-spirited and with some vanity, he felt most strongly an inherited impulse of service and purpose.'[41]

He was a trustee of the National Portrait Gallery (1937–51), president of the Poetry Society (1947–48) and president of the Jane Austen Society (1966–83).

The CH was conferred in 1949 for his services as 'Writer. Goldsmiths Professor of English Literature, University of Oxford', at the unusually early age of forty-six. He died in 1986.

Edward Morgan Forster 1 January 1953

E. M. Forster was a novelist and critic and author of a number of classic works including *Howard's End*, *Maurice* and *A passage to India*.

He was born in London in 1879, the only son of an architect. When he was an infant, his father died, and he was raised 'by his mother and by a gaggle of maiden aunts in an atmosphere suffused with doting care.'[42] His childhood home at Rooksnest in Stevenage was evoked in his novel *Howards End*, but his mother moved in 1893 to enable him to go to Tonbridge School as a day boy. He disliked the experience and described the products of public school as having 'well-developed bodies, fairly-developed minds and undeveloped hearts.' A bequest of £8,000 from a great-aunt, enabled him to go to King's College, Cambridge as a classical exhibitioner and be financially independent enough to exist as a writer. The great-aunt had died when Forster was only eight, but he never forgot her, and repaid the debt by writing a biography of her, published as *Marianne Thornton 1797–1887. A domestic biography* (1956). At Cambridge he revelled in the 'Bloomsbury Circle' of G. E. Moore, G. M. Trevelyan and Lowes Dickenson, with the last-named of whom he founded the *Independent Review* in 1903, and a series of mentors encouraged him to write, taught him to be sceptical of worldly values, and to value truth rather than victory in discussion. The essence of his undergraduate life is recorded in the first two chapters of his novel *The longest journey* published in 1907, which also included his indictment of public schools.

Graduation in 1901 was followed by a period of travel in Italy and Greece, countries that meant much to him and symbolised a style of life which contrasted with the puritanism of northern Europe. His Italian travels provided material for *Where angels fear to tread* (1905), his first novel. His third novel, *A room with a view* (1908) was also set in Italy and *Howards end*, followed in 1910. His famous novel on homosexuality, *Maurice*, was completed in 1914, but it was unpublishable at that repressive time, and only appeared in print in 1971, after his death. Forster was not embarrassed by his sexual orientation but he was never as outré as Oscar Wilde. He longed for a loving and stable relationship; it came in the 1930s and endured until his death.

He travelled in India and in 1921 was appointed private secretary to the Maharaja of Dewas State Senior, a curious experience which he described in *The hill of Devi* (1953). This second stay in the subcontinent produced his acknowledged masterpiece, *A passage to India* (1924) in which he examined the clash of English values and Indian susceptibilities. Collections of short stories include *The celestial omnibus* (1914) and *The eternal moment* (1928), and collections of essays, *Abinger harvest* and *Two cheers for democracy*, appeared in 1946 and 1951 respectively. In 1915 T. E. Lawrence assessed Forster's world as 'a comedy, neatly layered and staged in a garden whose trim privet hedges were delicate with gossamer conventions. About its lawns he rolled thunderstorms in teacups, most lightly, beautifully.'[43]

In the 1930s he became more concerned with political and social questions. The liberty of the individual was the cause closest to his heart and he was twice president of the national council for civil liberties. Despite a distaste for politics he felt obliged to join the international pen club and protest against the developments of nazism in 1930s.

He had been a fellow of King's College (1927–33) and in 1946, after the death of his mother, he was invited to make his home there, occupying a set of rooms which had once been used by his old tutor Nathaniel Wedd. Life at King's enabled him to make friends with successive generations of undergraduates. In the 1930s he was a close friend of T. E. Lawrence and Siegfried Sassoon, and he knew Thomas Hardy, D. H. Lawrence and W. H. Auden particularly well. In 1951 he collaborated with Eric Crozier on the libretto of Benjamin Britten's opera *Billy Budd*. 'Second only to D. H. Lawrence, Forster was the most important British novelist of his generation. His works were translated into twenty-one languages, and his work began to be intensively studied, especially in America where Lionel Trimming's perceptive study in 1944 established his place in the canon. He was particularly venerated in India for his sympathy with the movement for independence and with both Hindu and Muslim culture . . . Forster spoke for liberal humanism. No one spoke with greater simplicity or originality in defence of such well-worn concepts as liberty, democracy and tolerance . . . He distrusted size, pomp, the Establishment, empires, politics, the upper classes, planners, institutions. He put his trust in individuals, small groups and insignificant people, the life of the heart and mind, personal relations.'[44]

It is thought that he declined a knighthood, but he accepted the CH in 1953 as a 'Writer' and the OM on his ninetieth birthday in 1969. He died in 1970.

William Somerset Maugham 10 June 1954

In his day Somerset Maugham was renowned as a master of the art of writing short stories.

He was born in Paris in 1874, the youngest son of the solicitor and legal adviser to the British embassy. His mother died when he was eight and his father when he was ten. Maugham then left Paris and went to the guardianship of his uncle, Henry Maugham, vicar of Whitstable in Kent. Thereafter his childhood was unhappy. He was educated at King's School, Canterbury, but as his first language was French, he was virtually a foreigner in his own country. He spent a time at Heidelberg University, but did not take a degree. His escape was travel which was to become a lifelong habit. At sixteen, on the suspicion of tuberculosis, he was sent for a time to Hyères on the French Riviera. He read de Maupassant and became familiar with French authors. His uncle wanted him to study for ordination, but he had £150 from his father's estate and in 1892 he enrolled as a medical student at St Thomas's Hospital. He qualified in 1897 but soon abandoned medicine for literature. His first novel, *Liza of Lambeth*, a vivid portrayal of the low life of the district where he served as an obstetric clerk, was published in 1897 and became a success as Maugham himself recalled. 'Edmund Gosse admired and praised it. After that I published other books and became a popular dramatist . . . I used to meet Gosse once or twice a year and continued to do so for twenty years, but I never met him without his saying to me in his unctuous way: "Oh, my dear Maugham, I liked your Liza of Lambeth so much. How wise you are never to have written anything else".'[45]

In 1903 his first play, *A man of honour* was performed by the Stage Society, but not until 1907 at the age of thirty-three, did he become famous with the performance of *Lady Frederick* at the Court Theatre. Its success was so sweeping that within a short time Maugham had four plays running simultaneously in the west end. 'By the mid twenties he was an acknowledged master of light, sometimes mordant comedy. He attempted serious themes with courage and assurance, but the public wanted to be amused.'[46] In 1933 he ceased writing plays altogether, but as early as 1911 he had retired temporarily from the theatre to work on his long novel *Of human bondage*. It was published in 1915 to acclaim in New York though less so in war-torn London, and remains Maugham's most impressive literary work. It was followed by *The moon and sixpence* (1919), based on his travels in the South Pacific, *The painted veil* (1925) and the astringent and satirical *Cakes and ale* (1930), but he made his reputation in the fertile territory of the short story and was widely regarded as its supreme English exponent. Several of his short stories were filmed under the titles *Quartet* (1949), *Trio* (1950) and *Encore* (1951).

In 1915 he was recruited for intelligence work in Geneva and Petrograd, his aptitude for languages made him an ideal candidate, and his 1928 novel *Ashenden* (filmed in 1938 by Alfred Hitchcock, with the title *Secret agent*, and starring John Gielgud), was based on these experiences. In 1917 he developed tuberculosis and spent the next two years in a Scottish sanatorium. A marriage in 1916 proved to be unhappy and was dissolved in 1927, though they had one daughter. In the meantime he had taken up a friendship with a young American, Gerald Haxton, who became the companion of his middle years, and because Haxton was viewed as an undesirable alien by the British, the two men established a home in the south of France in 1928. They left France in 1940, Maugham being on the Nazis' wanted list, and went to America where, although now wealthy, he lived quite modestly. Some regarded his decision to go to the United States as a defeatist attitude, and although he did useful propaganda work during the war, there was a suggestion that it suited him to be out of the United Kingdom for the duration.

In 1944 he published his last substantial novel, *The razor's edge* in which he paid tribute to the ascetic mysticism he had encountered in India. After the liberation he returned to France. Haxton had died in America in 1944 and his place was taken by Alan Searle. For the remaining twenty years of his life, he continued to write short stories and historical novels. 'He was tortured by his stammer, and by the conviction that he was unloved. He was drawn to religion though he affected a sturdy agnosticism. He was very widely read, though he claimed to be uneducated. His tongue was sharp and he could make enemies easily, yet he was capable of great courtesy, and his uncensorious scepticism brought comfort as well as diversion both to millions of readers and to private acquaintances . . . However, he could be kind as well as caustic. He was a thoughtful correspondent and a generous private critic of unsolicited manuscripts.'[47]

At the age of eighty he was made a CH for his services as 'Author and dramatist', and on his eightieth birthday the Garrick Club gave a dinner in his honour, an honour previously enjoyed only by Dickens, Thackeray and Trollope. In his autobiography, *The summing up*, Maugham was candid about his talents: 'I discovered my limitations and it seemed to me that the only sensible thing was to aim at what excellence I could within them. I knew that I had no lyrical quality. I had a small vocabulary and no efforts that I could make to enlarge it much availed me. I had a little gift of metaphors; the original and striking simile seldom occurred to me. Poetic flights and the great imaginative sweep were beyond my powers . . . I knew that I should never write as well as I could wish, but I thought with pains I could arrive at writing as well as my natural defects allowed.'[48]

His old age was soured by public wrangles with his daughter and, in the regrettable memoir *Looking back* 1962, with the ghost of his wife who had died in 1955. He died in hospital at Nice in 1965 and left a substantial legacy, including his books, to King's School, Canterbury, where his ashes were interred next to the library he had endowed.

Arthur Waley 2 January 1956

Arthur Waley was a scholar and poet who introduced Chinese and Japanese literature to the west. He was born in 1889, the son of David Schloss, an economist and Fabian socialist. At the outbreak of the war in 1914, the family found it prudent to replace their surname with 'Waley', the maiden name of David Schloss' wife.

Arthur Waley, as he became, was educated at Rugby and King's College, Cambridge. In 1913 he started work at the British Museum in the newly formed sub-department of oriental prints and drawings under its first head Laurence Binyon. His task was to make a rational index of the Chinese and Japanese painters represented in the museum's collection. It was a formidable task; Waley had no formal education in the subject, but he immediately started to teach himself Chinese and Japanese. By 1916 he was printing his first fifty-two translations of Chinese poems. By 1918 he had completed enough translations of poems to have a volume entitled *A hundred and seventy Chinese poems* accepted by Constable for publication. In 1919 Sir Stanley Unwin became his publisher and remained his constant friend and admirer.

He remained at the museum for sixteen years, retiring in 1929 on the grounds of health – he had been told to spend winters abroad. His official publications consisted of the index of Chinese artists (1922), at that time the first in the west, and a catalogue of the paintings recovered from Tun Huang by Sir Aurel Stein (1931). *An introduction to the study of Chinese painting* (1923) was a by-product of his unpublished notes on the national collection and its relation to the great tradition of Chinese painting. In 1925 he began publication of his best known translation – of the *Genji Monogatari* by Murasaki Shikibu, the late tenth century Japanese classical novelist, the sixth volume of which did not appear until 1933. 'He aimed at an interpretation of the sensibility and wit of the closed Heian court, described in the idiomatic English of his day.' He continued to produce translations of Chinese poetry for the rest of his life, trying to evoke the mood and intention of the original text. 'He enjoyed meeting the sympathetic and their conversation but never spoke himself unless he had something to day; he expected the same restraint in others . . . As a scholar Waley aimed always to express Chinese and Japanese thought at their most profound levels, with the highest standard of accuracy of meaning, in a way that would not be possible again because of the growth of professional specialization . . . Although he never travelled to the Far East and did not seek to confront the contemporary societies of China or Japan, he was scathingly critical of the attitude of the West to their great cultures in the world in which he grew up: hence his scorn for the older generation of sinologists and his hatred of imperialism, as shown in his *The opium war through Chinese eyes* (1958).'[49]

He was an honorary fellow of King's College, Cambridge. He was made a CBE in 1952 and a CH in 1956 'for services to the study of Chinese literature', and died of cancer of the spine in 1966. From 1918 his companion, and wife in all but name, was Beryl de Zoete, who, like Waley himself, hovered on the fringes of the Bloomsbury Group. But from 1929, for more than thirty years he maintained an on-off relationship with a New Zealand girl, Alison Robinson, as well as with Beryl. 'Waley, a mixture of scholar and bard, recluse and social celebrity, nursed her [Beryl] devotedly until her death in 1962. Being a secretive wimp, Waley was unable to resolve the triangle until then.'[50] He married Alison a month before his own death in 1966, and thereafter she became 'the priestess who tended the flame of his memory, making their house in Highgate a shrine of pilgrimage for Chinese and Japanese scholars,'[51] until her own death in 2001 at the age of 100.

Sir Osbert Sitwell 12 June 1958

Osbert Sitwell, 'the witty controversialist and polemicist of a famous and eccentric family,'[52] made his name as a man of letters and a champion of new movements in the arts in the first quarter of the twentieth century.

He was born in London in 1892, the elder son of Sir George Sitwell. As the eldest son of a wealthy baronet, he was born into a life of privilege, spent partly at Renishaw Hall, near Chesterfield, the family's ancestral summer home, and the medieval castle of Montegufoni near Florence, acquired by his father in 1909. Educated at Eton and then sent to a military crammer, he deliberately failed his entrance examination to Sandhurst, but his father's persistence brought him a commission first in the Sherwood Rangers in 1911 and then in the Grenadier Guards Special Reserve in 1912. The 1914–18 war gave him a lifelong hatred of war, and the best of his verse is strongly pacifistic. Many of his satirical poems were collected in *Argonaut and juggernaut* (1919) and *Out of the flame* (1923), but poetry was the least important part of his work.

He left the army in 1919 and moved into his London home, 2 Carlyle Square Chelsea, 'from which address he directed his unceasing war against everything that smacked to him of the philistine or pompously conventional, in a series of caustic and highly individual pronouncements and polemics.'[53] One of his chief gifts was satire, and satire marks the three novels that he wrote between the wars: *Before the bombardment* (1926), *The man who lost himself* (1929), and *Miracle on Sinai* (1933). 'With their passages of bravura description and frequent touches of lively invention, they are highly individual works, although it is difficult not to think that Sitwell lacked some essential gift that goes to make the true novelist. The same limitation may perhaps be found in his short stories. Surprisingly diverse in mood and theme, many of them were delightful and remained fresh to read, although the raconteur rather than the imaginative creator was a little too frequently uppermost.'[54]

A more significant contribution to literature was the series of travelogues that he published, which reflected his travels in the aristocratic style: *Discursions on travel, art and life* (1925), *Winters of content* (1932), *Brighton* (1935) and, perhaps his best, *Escape with me* (1939), describing a journey to China.

His first poem was published in *The Times* in 1916 and he continued to write satirical poetry to end of his life. But his finest achievement was his five-volume autobiography, *Left hand right hand* (1944), *The scarlet tree* (1946), *Great morning* (1947), *Laughter in the next room* (1948) and *Noble essences* (1950). A postscript volume, *Tales my father taught me*, appeared in 1962. 'An exploration of the author's family history and the experiences and encounters of his own life, constructed according to a poetic logic of association rather than chronological sequence, this unique and highly wrought, but always fascinatingly readable, work is remarkable for its combination of shrewd social observation, portraits that are often wittily critical and affectionate at the same time, interspersed with romantic reverie and rhapsodic descriptions of places he had loved.'[55]

'His formally courteous and aristocratic manners concealed a warmth and generosity of heart which manifested themselves without reservation towards young writers, musicians and artists, whose gifts he had with immediate discernment judged to be outstanding. He could be malicious towards those he thought less outstanding and he enjoyed conducting vendettas against hostile critics and writers who had lost his favour.'[56]

In his last years, he was seriously incapacitated by Parkinson's disease and came to rely heavily on his new assistant and secretary, Frank Magro, who cared for him until he died in 1969. This caused distress to Sitwell's previous companion of some thirty years David Horner, who at one time had expected to be left Montegufoni.

Sitwell was appointed a CBE in the New Year List 1956, and although he accepted it, there were those who felt he should have been offered something more. Harold Macmillan, the prime minister, was rebuked by Peter Simple in the *Daily Telegraph*, who asked what were we to think of a prime minister who offered a Sitwell a CBE, and what were we to think of a Sitwell who accepted it.[57] The rebuke was noted and Sitwell was made a CH only two and half years later, in the Birthday Honours List 1958, for his services as 'Writer and Poet'. It was a questionable move and a more decent interval might have been allowed to elapse. For all that the CBE might have been 'not quite the right award', the short gap between the two honours left no one in any doubt that the CH was a substitute honour.

Ivor Richards 1 January 1964

Ivor Richards had a lifelong love of language and poetry, part philosophical and part mystical, which led to a working life dedicated to literary criticism and a late flowering as a poet and dramatist. With F. R. Leavis, his work transformed the study of English literature in the twentieth century.

He was born in Sandbach, Cheshire in 1893, the son of an engineer. He was educated at Clifton College and Magdalen College, Cambridge where he read moral sciences. Tuberculosis contracted as an undergraduate delayed his graduation until 1915. The disease recurred in 1916 and he spent a long period of convalescence in north Wales until his return to Cambridge in 1917. Early interests in medicine, psychoanalysis and mountaineering were put to one side when he was invited to teach for the new English Cambridge tripos in 1919. From that decision there sprang a lifetime of literary research and a reputation as the father of practical literary criticism. His first book, The *foundations of aesthetics*, written jointly with C. K. Ogden and James Wood, was published in 1922, but his first significant work, *The meaning of meaning* appeared in 1923, again written in collaboration with Ogden.

Richards taught two courses at Cambridge, one on the theory of criticism and one on the modern novel, and his lectures on criticism led to *Principles of literary criticism* (1925), his first sole-authored work. It laid down a method of literary criticism, according to which the words in a work of imaginative literature are examined, not in the light of psychoanalysis of the author, but for their psychological impact on the reader.'[58] The book inaugurated the modern critical movement, and his theories were further developed in *Practical criticism* (1929)

The language of poetry fascinated him and he used it as a teaching tool. 'He distributed an unfamiliar poem; the students commented in writing; and he subsequently used their remarks to categorise common faults of reading. This may have been the origin of his lifelong passion for cleansing the channels of communication, and removing impediments to the understanding of language at all levels from the highest to the lowest.'[59] In *Science and poetry* (1926), he envisaged poetry and reading fulfilling at a time of national crisis, the role formerly played by religion. He was to say that ambiguity was 'the indispensable means of our most important utterances.'[60] He continued his studies in the language of poetry in *Coleridge on imagination* (1934) and *The philosophy of rhetoric* (1936).

He visited China in 1927 and taught at the Tsing Hua University in Peking (1929–31). In 1932 he published *Mencius on the mind*, which studied the difficulties of translating Chinese into English. He returned to Cambridge (1931–36) and then to China (1936–38) where he taught at the Orthological Institute in Peking. *Interpretation in teaching* (1937) developed methods for the teaching of prose. After a brief sojourn in Cambridge (1938–39) he was persuaded go to Harvard, where he taught until his retirement in 1963. There a crusading element appeared. He was appalled by the misunderstandings of language that he found among university students and launched a campaign to provide the world with a simple precise international language called Basic English. The concept had been invented in the 1920s by C. K. Ogden as a fundamental selection of 850 English words, designed to assist in the teaching of English and as an auxiliary language. The word 'Basic' was an acronym of British, American, Scientific, International, Commercial. Richards took up the cause with enthusiasm and was still campaigning for it at the end of his life. Such a language was necessary, he said, to save the planet. He supported his arguments in a succession of publications: *How to a read a page* (1943) was a study of a hundred words. He translated Plato's *Republic* into Basic English (1942). *Basic English and its uses* appeared in 1943. It was an entirely artificial language and never gained widespread popularity.

Not until the age of sixty-five did he turn his pen to writing poetry. *Goodbye earth and other poems* appeared in 1958, *The screens* in 1960 and *Internal colloquies* in 1972. He also wrote a number of plays, including *A leak in the universe* (1956), *Tomorrow morning, Faustus!* (1962) and *Why so, Socrates?* (1964).

In 1973 Richards returned to live in Cambridge, though he stayed at Harvard for a few months each year. In 1979 he accepted an invitation to revisit China where he taught in universities and continued to campaign for Basic. He fell ill on the tour. The Chinese government flew him home and he died at Cambridge in September that year.

He was made a CH in 1964, after his retirement from Harvard, 'For services to Literary Criticism.'

Henry Graham Greene 1 January 1966
Graham Greene was a novelist, short-story writer, essayist and biographer whose works included *Brighton rock*, *Our man in Havana* and *The third man*.

He was born in 1904 and educated at Berkhampstead School where his father was headmaster – a factor that made his schooldays rather difficult – and at Balliol College, Oxford. Two volumes of autobiography, *A sort of life* (1971) and *Ways of escape* (1980) recount his experiences. He joined the staff of the *The Times* in 1926 and worked for the newspaper until 1930, when he left to make his career as a writer. He began his career as a novelist with *Babbling April* (1925), published while he was still an undergraduate at Balliol. His next three novels *The man within* (1925), *The name of the action* (1930) and *Rumour at nightfall* (1931) made little impression, and he subsequently disowned them, and *Stamboul train* (1932) was his first great success. 'Like many of his subsequent novels it is sombrely romantic, fusing comedy and tragedy in a peculiar no-man's land that critics christened "Greeneland".'[61] He was a prolific writer of novels, stories, plays and biographies as well as film criticism, and his unguarded words were partly responsible for the demise of *Night and day* when that magazine was successfully sued after he had accused Twentieth Century Fox of 'procuring' Shirley Temple for immoral purposes.

He joined the Roman Catholic Church in 1926 and Catholicism strongly influenced his writing thereafter. 'His novels were much concerned with shabby souls in the process of disintegration veering towards damnation, but not beyond reach of salvation. The combination of religion with crime or degeneracy is found nauseating by a minority of readers but inspiring by others. As a storyteller Greene is in the tradition of John Buchan whose influence he acknowledged, as also that of the French novelist, Mauricac, whose religious outlook he shared.'[62] *Brighton Rock* (1938), filmed in 1947 by John Boulting, was a thriller which asserted that human justice was inadequate and irrelevant to the real struggle against evil. His frequent use of the word 'seedy' popularised it, much to his later regret. He was not always orthodox in his writings and some of his more unorthodox novels led him into controversy with the authorities of his adopted communion. The image of the whisky priest in *The power and the glory* (1940) was an uncomfortable and embarrassing image. Other novels included *The heart of the matter* (1948), *The third man* (1950), *The end of the affair* (1951), *The quiet American* (1955), *Our man in Havana* (1958), *A burnt-out case* (1961), *The comedians* (1965), *Travels with my aunt* (1969), *The honorary consul* (1973), *The human factor* (1978), *Doctor Fischer of Geneva* (1980), *Monsignor Quixote* (1982) and *The captain and the enemy* (1988). Some of his books were filmed, perhaps most famously *The third man* in 1949 and *Our man in Havana* in 1959. The uncomfortable if not dangerous settings of his novels – Argentina, the Congo, Mexico, Vietnam – reflected his own fascinations and his disregard for personal safety. He published travel books: *Journey without maps* (1936), *The lawless roads* (1939), and *In search of a character: two African journals* (1961). *Collected essays* appeared in 1969 and *Collected stories* in 1972. His plays include *The living room* (1953), *The potting shed* (1957) and *The complaisant lover* (1959). *A world of my own – a dream diary*, appeared in 1992. The range and power of his writing was considerable and he was often cited as the greatest novelist of his time.

He married in 1927 but was later separated from his wife, although they never divorced. He settled in a modest flat in Antibes in 1966 where he stayed for the rest of his life. The CH in 1966 for his services as 'Writer' was followed by an OM in 1986, a high double honour that he shared with his fellow writers, Walter de la Mare and E. M. Forster. He died in 1991.

Sir Alan Herbert 1 January 1970

Alan Herbert was a sharp, amusing and witty writer of novels, articles and plays. He became famous for brushing away the cobwebs of the law by making fun of it.

He was born in 1890, the son of an Irishman who served as a civil servant in the India Office. His mother was the daughter of a lord justice of appeal and died when Herbert was eight. Herbert was educated at Winchester where he was awarded the King's medal for English speech and the King's medal for English verse. While at school he published the first of his many later volumes of light verse, a genre which became one of the several main strands of his versatile writing career. He went to New College, Oxford in 1910, at the same time becoming a free-lance contributor for *Punch*, and came down in 1914 with a first class degree in jurisprudence.

He served in the royal navy during the 1914–18 war, but was wounded and invalided home in 1917. During convalescence he wrote *The secret battle* on the theme of cowardice, but it attracted little attention when published in 1919, at a time of general war weariness. With the approach of the 1939–45 war it was reissued as a classic of its kind and had the reverberating after-effect of bringing about an improvement in court martial procedure. He was called to the bar in 1918 but never practised. After two years in chambers he joined the staff of *Punch* in 1924. His long-running series of articles for that periodical, entitled *Misleading cases* and published in book form in 1927, pungently satirised the law and its anomalies and brought him celebrity in legal circles throughout the English-speaking world. It was 'a sustained and compulsive argument for the sovereignty of common sense.'[63]

Until his forties, Herbert's reputation was mainly metropolitan, resting on his *Punch* connection, his *Riverside nights* (1926) revue at the Lyric Theatre, Hammersmith, his sequence of libretti for operettas that followed it there: *La vie parisienne* (1929), *Tantivy towers* (1931) and *Derby day* (1932). He frequently appeared in the correspondence columns of *The Times*, where his letters were often the talk of the west end clubs. He wrote a novel about the canal people, *The water gipsies* (1932). A further novel, *Holy deadlock* (1934) exposed the problems of the English divorce laws and was later credited with helping to create a more favourable attitude to reform. In 1935 he was elected independent MP for Oxford University, and within a year his Matrimonial Causes Act 1936, improving divorce conditions, had received the royal assent.

In 1939 he joined the river emergency service which operated on the Thames as part of London's defences. When the service was merged with the royal naval auxiliary patrol, he was given the rank of petty officer RN and the right to fly the white ensign on his converted canal boat, *Water Gipsy*. His entry in *Who's Who* noted that he received two good conduct badges, and after the war he was a trustee of the National Maritime Museum 1947–53. In June 1940 he did battle in the house of commons with the chancellor of the exchequer, who was proposing to subject books to purchase tax. 'His speech was a philippic of outraged sensibility. The chancellor exempted books from tax three weeks later.'[64] Herbert received a knighthood in Churchill's resignation honours list in 1945. The abolition of the university franchise in 1950 ended his parliamentary career, but his memoir, *Independent member* (1950), affirmed his belief in the value of independence in the house of commons.

After the war, Herbert deployed his talent to amuse in a number of spectacular musical plays for the west end stage, of which the conspicuous success was *Bless the bride* (1950). The bright lights did not distract him from the serious business of campaigning: for a passenger traffic service on the Thames, against the entertainments tax, for a public lending right for authors, against a spelling reform bill, for a betting tax, against bureaucratic and business jargon, and for a Thames barrage.

Herbert was first thought of for a CH in 1967. His knighthood had been conferred twenty-two years earlier, and the sum total of his life indicated that a rather more considerable honour was overdue. The honour was conferred in 1970 'For services to Literature' when he was seventy-nine, a little less than two years before his death.

Sir Maurice Bowra 1 January 1971
Maurice Bowra was a distinguished scholar of classical languages and literature.

He was born in China in 1898, the youngest son of an official in the Chinese customs service, he was educated at Cheltenham College. At the age of nineteen he joined the Royal Field Artillery and served in France in 1917–18. After the war he went to New College, Oxford where firsts in classics and literae humaniores pointed towards an academic career. He was appointed a fellow and tutor at Wadham College in 1922, and at that college he remained until retirement nearly half a century later. In 1938 he was elected warden of the college and held the post until 1970. He was professor of poetry (1946–51) and vice-chancellor of the university (1951–56).

He wrote or edited books in many areas of literature, and was highly regarded as a contributor to classical scholarship, European literature and English literature, but he was particularly known for his studies of ancient Greek poetry and culture. He made his reputation as a classical scholar for his interpretation of Pindar's poetry, but he always believed that those who did not know Greek and Latin should be given a glimpse of classical literature, and he edited the *Oxford book of Greek verse*, and his popular work *The Greek experience* sold nearly one hundred thousand copies on both sides of the Atlantic. His book *Heritage of symbolism*, published in 1943, was the first attempt by an English author to explain the revolutions which took place in European poetry at the turn of the nineteenth and twentieth centuries. He also wrote books on the epic, which few if anyone could have attempted because he wrote of poetry in French, German, Portuguese, Italian, and Old Norse, all of which he knew, and of many eastern European and Asian languages, of which he learnt sufficient to enable him to make comparisons. With these considerable linguistic skills, it was said that no one excelled him as a master of comparative literature and that nobody had a wider knowledge of the literature of all languages and ages.

His publications included translations of *Pindar's Pythian Odes* (1928 and 1969), *The Oxford book of Greek verse* (1930), *Tradition and design in the Illiad* (1930), *Ancient Greek literature, Pindari Carmina* (1935), *Greek lyric poetry* (1936), *Oxford book of Greek verse in translation* (1937), *Early Greek elegists* (1938), *The heritage of symbolism* (1943), *A book of Russian verse* (1943), *Sophoclean tragedy*

(1944), *From Virgil to Milton* (1945), *The creative experiment* (1949), *The romantic imagination* (1950), *Heroic poetry* (1952), *Problems in Greek poetry* (1954), *Inspiration and poetry* (1955), *The Greek experience* (1957), *Primitive song* (1962), *In general and particular* (1964), *Pindar* (1964), *Landmarks in Greek literature* (1966), *Poetry and politics 1900–1960* (1966), *Memories 1898–1939* (1966), *On Greek margins* (1970), and *Periclean Athens* (1971).

Bowra had an impressive and vivid personality, and was fondly remembered as a guide, philosopher and friend, particularly to the young. He was an indefatigable entertainer of undergraduates, and made a point of helping young dons through the university and in the country as a whole by drawing on his vast range of knowledge. In the eyes of those who knew and respected him, he was the model of a don; devoted to his pupils, dedicated to learning and willing to sacrifice his leisure time for the good of the society to which he belonged.

He was elected a fellow of the British Academy in 1938 and was its president 1958–62. He was knighted in 1951 and received the CH in 1971 'For services to Literature', six months before his death.

Frank Raymond Leavis 31 December 1977
Despite his explosive irascibility, F. R. Leavis was one of the most influential literary critics of the twentieth century.

He was born in Cambridge in 1895, the son of a local businessman. Although his family was of Hugenot origin, his father was a Victorian radical and a promoter of the Rationalist Press Association who took the side of the Boers during the South African War. He was educated at Perse School, and read history and English at Emmanuel College, Cambridge. After service in the 1914–18 war (he was said to have translated German poetry in the trenches), he returned to Cambridge to become a lecturer in English at Emmanuel College (1925), and later a fellow (1936–62) and honorary fellow (1962–64) of Downing College, Cambridge.

From the beginning, Leavis was a formidable controversialist and his academic career suffered as a result. He was over forty when he was made a part-time lecturer, well into his fifties before attaining a lectureship, and was only made a reader in his early sixties. His departure from Downing College in the early 1960s was the result of academic politics. The negative adjectives used against him were many: foolish, rude, silly, petty, and petulant, and his use of language could be spiteful and cruel. 'There's something wrong with T. S. Eliot down there (pointing towards his waist) – or even lower,' he once said. 'Occasionally he would risk a full bayonet charge at the main critical enemy – the mandarins, the Neoplatonists, anyone whose seriousness about the fertilising relation between literature and life seemed more dilettante than his. When all the imaginary smoke and gunfire died away he was left standing – a bald, touchingly slender man, worn down by his own putdowns, his invariably and defiantly open-shirted neck mottled with sunburn like a gipsy's hand. He was the Max Miller of the lecture circuit, a one-line virtuoso . . . He encouraged his pupils to apply this yardstick not only to literature but to newspapers, television, advertisement hoardings, letters and common speech. He was ruthless in using it. He revered most of Shakespeare but, in tutorials, dismissed much of *Othello* and *Antony and Cleopatra* as an attempt to soup up emotion about the doings of great babies . . . Perhaps the most telling counter-assault on him was by C. S. Lewis, who said that the use of subliminal code words like 'maturity' and 'relevance' smuggled in an entire value system that was never made explicit for scrutiny. Others accused him of being a crypto-Marxist. Leavis never replied, which was a pity, but then his weapons during his long career of humiliations in the Cambridge English faculty also included silence, internal exile and cunning. His most murderous and underestimated weapon was ridicule, which he deployed in lectures with the virtuosity of a music-hall star and with an insensitivity verging on paranoia . . . He also alienated generations of pupils from the journalism of critics of integrity like Cyril Connolly and Philip Toynbee because he resented – with only some justification – the way they dominated the review pages. But any primary school teacher who as a matter of course now pays sensitive attention to the speech and writing of children and of people outside school has Frank Leavis to thank for it, among others.'[65]

He despised 'mass culture' and excoriated it in his writings on education and society. Throughout his work, much of it shared with his wife Queenie Dorothy Leavis (1906–91), he stressed the moral value of literary study and deplored the decline in English literature. He passionately lamented the perceived decline of an educated literary public, a result, in his view, of debased educational standards at home, school and university. At one end of the spectrum, he condemned railway bookstalls for their racks of what he called 'pornography', and at the other he vehemently denounced the *Times Literary Supplement*, Radio 3 and the Arts Council for 'killing English literature'. He was editor and cofounder of the influential quarterly *Scrutiny* from 1932 until its demise in 1953. It included contributions from some of finest literary, philosophic, scientific and musical minds of the time, and Leavis abruptly closed it down when the flow of aspiring unpaid contributors began to slow down and commercial reward began to loom. Its content was as forthright as Leavis himself and Virginia Woolf was said to be furious at the reviews of her novels.

His publications included *Mass civilization and minority culture* (1930), *D. H. Lawrence* (1930), *New bearings in English poetry* (1932), *For continuity* (1933), *Culture and environment* (1933), *Revaluation: tradition and development in English poetry* (1933), *Education and the university* (1943), *The great tradition: George Eliot, James and Conrad* (1948), *The common pursuit* (1952), *D. H. Lawrence. Novelist* (1955), *Two cultures. The significance of C. P. Snow* (1962), *Retrospect of Scrutiny* (1963), *Anna Karenina and other essays* (1967), *A selection from Scrutiny* (1968), *Lectures in America* (1969), *English literature in our time and the university* (1969), *Dickens the novelist* (1970), *Nor shall my sword: discourses on pluralism, compassion and social hope* (1972), *Letters in criticism* (1974), *The living principle: English as a discipline of thought* (1975), and *Thought, words and creativity* (1976).

For all his spite, he was the most creative, serious and influential literary critic since his Victorian model, Matthew Arnold. He wanted the Oxford professorship of poetry in 1956 because Arnold once held it. To his grief W. H. Auden beat him in the election. After his departure from Downing College, he had a few enjoyable years as a visiting professor at the University of York.

At least in part because of the passions that he aroused, both for and against him, the question of an honour was delayed almost until the end. The unguarded frankness of his tongue and his invincible belief in the rightness of his own beliefs, both redolent of the denunciatory vocation of the Old Testament prophet, caused many to regard him as insufferable, and perhaps prevented earlier recognition. Some thought that his style of teaching English was unacceptable, that his 'popular' works were not distinguished, that his work had deteriorated over the years and that it too often showed an element of personal bitterness. Others felt that, for all his faults, he was a great figure in English literature, that he had given the art of literary criticism a tremendous impetus, that he was well known and that he had made a significant difference to the study of English both nationally and internationally, despite the fact that, in the opinion of one he was 'as mad as a hatter.' The sole honour that he eventually received was the CH, conferred in 1977 'for services to the study of English Literature'. At last he had received the recognition that he probably felt he deserved. But it was too late to mean very much; he died four months later.

Sir Sacheverell Sitwell 31 December 1983

Sacheverell Sitwell was the dilettante author of a series of works on the history of art and architecture, travelogues, and biographies of composers.

Born in 1897, youngest of the three famous children of Sir George Sitwell, Sacheverell Sitwell was educated at Eton and then gazetted an ensign in the Grenadier Guards. He was spared the trenches of the 1914–18 war because of a weak heart. His duties at Aldershot were compensated for by an obsession with poetry. He began writing poetry with the encouragement and for the amusement of his sister Edith. His first volume of poetry *The people's palace* was published in 1918 and had a moderate reception. 'John Lehmann considered his poetic inspiration the fruit of great works of art rather than life's experiences. Yet it was deeply tinged by the blood bath in which "my schoolfriends were killed with hardly an exception." For the rest of his life he was haunted by a macabre pessimism made all the more tormenting by a total lack of religious faith.'[66]

Demobilised in 1918 he went to Balliol College, Oxford, but it offered little to the ex-Guards officer whose acquaintances were artists, writers, musicians and actors, and he left in 1919 to set up home with his brother Osbert. 'Already a leader of the avant-garde, Sacheverell organised an exhibition of modern French paintings in London and helped to introduce Modigliani, Utrillo and Dufy to the British public. He discovered the composer William Walton and promoted the author Ronald Firbank.'[67]

In 1920 he made an expedition to Fiume to see its leader Gabriele d'Annunzio, whom he admired as the greatest poet of the age. In the autumn he accompanied his brother Osbert to Naples and Caserta, and the next year to the southern extremities of Italy, then exceedingly remote and beyond the tourist horizon. These visits fired enthusiasm for baroque and rococo architecture, the track of which he pursued to Spain, Portugal, Bavaria and Latin America. The outcome was *Southern baroque art* (1924). A masterpiece in the delineation of the style, the book caused a sensation and was followed by *German baroque art* (1927). 'He made it his life's work to see every beautiful place and thing in the world. He became the modern equivalent of an eighteenth century English gentleman making the grand tour, seeking enlightenment by picking over the remains of other civilizations, staggering home with any marble, bust or artefact not screwed down to embellish country house or museum.'[68]

Unlike his older brother and sister, he was modest and shy and was always overshadowed by them. 'His manner to old and young was exquisite, and towards children of the poor deeply compassionate. His memory, like his imagination, was prodigious. As a raconteur he was spellbinding, his humour impish and bubbling. Before exhausting one subject he was launched upon another.'[69]

He wrote eighty books on a diverse range of subjects. *The Gothic north* (1929), which appeared in three volumes, gave as much rein for fantasy as *Southern baroque art*. He wrote a series of lively but idiosyncratic and subjective travelogues, *Roumanian journey* (1938), *Mauretania* (1939), *The Netherlands* (1948), *Spain* (1950), *Portugal and Madeira* (1954), *Denmark* (1956) and *Malta* (1958). Love of music was reflected in his biographies of Mozart (1932) and Liszt (1936). Of more serious consideration are his travel books of the mind and spirit, of which *Sacred and profane love* (1940) an aesthetic journey during the stresses of war was the first, and *For the want of the golden city* (1973) was the last. 'They are written in a genre he invented himself – a mixture of fantasy and realism . . . The world he presents in these pages is not a comforting one, where macabre horrors are emphasized only by their juxtaposition with some celebration of beauty.'[70]

He was included in Michael Robert's *Faber book of modern verse*, published in 1936, but it proved to be a premature assessment. 'Interest in his rather eccentric but frequently diffuse and inconsequential poetry diminished.'[71] He published nineteen collections of verse between 1918 and 1972 and a further forty-three were printed privately between 1972 and 1978. It was capable and interesting work, but never captured popular imagination and is now hardly read. His reminiscences attracted some attention, but Sacheverell Sitwell was the least gifted of the three famous siblings.

It was his fate forever to be compared, unfairly, with Osbert and Edith. Some thought his poetry fresh and powerful, and his travelogues scholarly, imaginative and well written, but there was no widespread support for this view and he was seen as a figure from the past who had written many books which few now read. It was said that he felt unfairly discriminated against as compared with his brother and sister. His output had been no less prolific and some thought that there was a greater element of learning in his work than there was in either of theirs. The postwar literary establishment had viewed Osbert and Edith as emblems of upper class literary dilettantism, and the less flamboyant and unconventional Sacheverell suffered as a result and received less public acclaim. His proponents argued that his poetry was hardly less distinguished than that of his sister, and the distinction of his prose writing was no less great than that of his brother, and his scholarship was a good deal better than either of them.

He gave up writing on the death of his wife in 1980, after fifty-six years of marriage. By 1982 he was eighty-five and frail, his memory was beginning to fail and the time was not far off when it would be too late to recognise him. In December 1981 he was awarded the rare Benson Silver Medal by the Royal Society of Literature (only twenty-seven having been awarded since 1916) and many saw it as an overdue recognition of his talents. The CH was conferred on him in 1983. The citation was unusually unimaginative, describing him simply as an 'Author'. 'I am an absolute mine of useless information,' he once said. 'I have a huge repertoire of knowledge which interests nobody except myself.'[72] He died in 1988.

Philip Larkin 15 June 1985
Philip Larkin was a reclusive and self-effacing poet, librarian and jazz critic who spent the last thirty years of his life living in Hull in suburban anonymity.

He was born in 1922 and raised in Coventry where his father served as city treasurer. He was educated at King Henry VIII School and St John's College, Oxford, where he obtained a first in English language and literature, and where he formed a lasting friendship with Kingsley Amis. Oxford in his time is evoked in his early novel, *Jill* (1946). Poor eyesight prevented him from undertaking military service.

After graduation he became a librarian, a profession in which he stayed until the end of his life, working at Wellington Library in Shropshire (1943–46), and then in the university libraries of Leicester (1946–50), Belfast (1950–55) and Hull (1955–85). An echo of his early days in Wellington can be seen in his only other novel, *A girl in winter* (1947), which tells the story of a day in the life of a refugee librarian employed in a drab English provincial town. He began work on a third novel, but it was never published, and thereafter he confined himself to poetry. He published only four slim volumes in his lifetime: *XX poems* (1950), *The less deceived* (1955), *The Whitsun weddings* (1964) and *High windows* (1974). He also edited the *Oxford book of twentieth century English verse* in 1973. His work is not uplifting. 'His imagination conceives of a postwar, postimperial England of drab suburbia and Welfare-State-sponsored lives in which traditional pieties, either of religion of self-fulfilment, can only be approached with scepticism or, at best, regret.'[73]

He was awarded the Queen's Gold Medal for poetry in 1967, and after the death of Sir John Betjeman, he was offered the poet laureateship in the autumn of 1984, but declined it. Throughout his life he was regarded as a minor poet with a narrow range of subject matter, but his stature has grown since his death and *Collected poems*, published posthumously in 1988 was a bestseller. He published little after 1974, feeling that poetry 'had given him up', and became particularly deaf, which prevented him from enjoying his favourite jazz. He remained an atheist till the end and his work repeatedly denied the possibility of life after death. He never married and liked to portray himself as a hermit-like bachelor, although he maintained a strong and lasting friendship with Monica Jones, a lecturer at the university of Leicester who shared his passion for privacy and equally disliked the age in which they both lived. After a bout of ill-health, she went to live with him in Hull for the last two years of Larkin's life. 'Her rigour had helped Larkin to escape his earlier recourse to blarney when he couldn't work out quite what he felt, and spurred him to keep revising until he achieved the plain but exacting emotional statement.'[74] *The less deceived* was dedicated to her.

As a reviewer he wrote perceptively about jazz and poetry often taking the side of the pleasure seeking audience against the drabness and difficulty of modernism. He reviewed jazz records for the *Daily Telegraph* (1961–71), and his jazz articles were collected and published in *All what jazz?* (1970). Superficially he presented the appearance of a depressive, xenophobic, reactionary old fogey who would rather be anywhere than in the modern world, and he was said to resemble Badger in Kenneth Graham's novel, *The wind in the willows*, but his talent for poetry was indisputable. 'Though detractors continue to speak of his gloom, philistinism, insularity, and anti-modernism, the authority and grandiloquence of his long poems, and the grace, sharpness, or humour of his shorter ones now seem indisputable, as does his clear-eyed engagement with love, marriage, freedom, destiny, ageing, death, and other far from marginal subjects.'[75]

Larkin was appointed a CBE in 1975 and a CH in June 1985 'For services to Poetry'. Larkin was already seriously ill and was never invested with his CH badge. Although he was invited to be invested at a private audience, he was in hospital in June and the Queen was away in Scotland and then in the Caribbean from early August until the end of October.[76] By that date he was too ill to make the journey to London for a private investiture. He died in December 1985, and the badge was posted to Monica Jones in February 1986. Faithful to his death bed request, though in contradiction to the terms of his will, she maintained his desire for privacy by destroying the thirty or so volumes of his diary after his death, depriving the literary world of much that might have been fascinating and giving the lie to the statement that he wrote nothing worth preserving in the last ten years of his life. She accompanied Larkin to Buckingham Palace to receive his CBE, and survived him by fifteen years, dying in 2001.

Anthony Powell 31 December 1987
His life may have been unobtrusive but his life's work – the twelve novels published between 1951 and 1975 under the collective title *A dance to the music of time* – was formidable. Powell was the friend and contemporary of Evelyn Waugh, George Orwell, Henry Green, Cyril Connolly, Malcolm Muggeridge and Graham Greene. He overlapped at school or university with Harold Acton, Brian Howard and Robert Byron. But in a generation dominated by conspicuously high aesthetic profiles, 'Powell turned no heads and cut no dash in his own or other people's memoirs.'[77]

He was born in 1905, the son of a serving officer in the Welch Regiment, and educated at Eton and Balliol College, Oxford. 'An abnormally isolated, reflective, peripatetic childhood and, by his own account, often melancholy childhood left him with a number of useful gifts . . . the habit of solitude coupled with a love of company, gossip and parties . . . an appreciative eye for detail, balanced by the outsider's alertness to overall pattern; an ingrained sense of life as fluid, shifting, unstable, together with a corresponding urge to put down roots, discern principles of order and continuity, establish some sort of perspective, plus a bottomless absorption and – perhaps most precious of all – an almost total lack of preconception as to how they might be expected, or ought to behave.'[78] He drifted into his first job in publishing in 1926, working for Duckworth. The publishing house vetoed his attempts to publish Christopher Isherwood, Nathaniel West and Antonia White. In the 1930s he had five satirical novels published: *Afternoon men* (1931), a satire of the Bohemian world of Chelsea and Bloomsbury 'which maps a characteristically seedy section of pleasure-loving, party-going London,'[79] *Venusberg* (1932), *From a view to a death* (1934), *Agents and patients* (1936) and *What's become of Waring* (1939), which earned him the reputation of being a satirist or comic lightweight. In 1935 he left Duckworth to seek his fortune in films, turning out scripts for Warner Bros. at Ealing. After the 1939–45 war he worked as a journalist with the *Times Literary Supplement* and *Punch* and as a book reviewer for the *Daily Telegraph*. He joined the Welch Regiment in 1940, serving briefly in Northern Ireland and then in the Intelligence Corps. In the years after the war he turned his attention to the inauguration of a long-term serious project. Taking its title from Nicolas Poussin's painting in the Wallace Collection, *A dance to the music of time*, it covered fifty years of British upper middle-class life and attitudes. *A question of upbringing* (1951) would be the first instalment of a sequence roughly following the contours of its author's life, seen through the eyes of a narrator, Nicholas Jenkins, who is clearly in some sense a self-projection. The generations grow up in the shadow of the 1914–18 war to find their lives dislocated by the 1935–45 war. There are haunting scenes of the war itself in Normandy, the post-war socialist world, and the frivolous dissident world of the 1960s. Admirers eagerly awaited succeeding volumes which appeared every two years or so, and the series closed with *Hearing secret harmonies* in 1975. The work was described as:

'This higgledy-piggledy, jampacked, panoramic view of England. The narrative is part humorous, part melancholy, and at times so funny that readers have tended if anything to underrate its sombre, even tragic sweep and range . . . Few writers have explored the ravages of madness, despair, destruction, desolation, and death more comprehensively than Powell.'[80] Others were more critical of Powell's literary talents, one describing the *Dance* as little more than an upmarket soap opera, and criticised the evident vein of snobbery that ran through all his writings. After the completion of the *Dance*, Powell published his memoirs in four volumes (1976–82) under the general title *To keep the ball rolling*, two novels, *O, how the wheel becomes it!* (1983) and *The fisher king* (1986), and two volumes of criticism, *Miscellaneous verdicts* (1990) and *Under review* (1992).

He was appointed a CBE in 1956 and is later thought to have refused a knighthood. For his services as an 'Author', he was made a CH in 1987. In his memoirs he noted the receipt of the 'sounding' letter on 13 November 1987. 'Post arrived. OHMS envelope first thought Income Tax, then saw 'Prime Minister' in corner. Letter, topped and tailed by Mrs T. herself, asking would I be agreeable to being recommended to HM the Queen for the CH. Replied I should like that very much.'[81] The personal investiture, which took place on 21 January 1988, was recorded by Powell in minute detail, including the instructions. 'We walk in, pause, bow from the neck . . . You walk forward towards the Queen at the far end of the room, stop, bow again. The Queen will shake hands. She will then give you the decoration, possibly hang it on you, indicate the chair in which you are to sit, sit down herself, have a short talk. She will indicate to you when the audience is at an end and get up. You will get up, bow, shake hands, turn your back on the Queen, walk to the doors, turn round, bow again, smile . . . After I had bowed for the second time, shaken hands, she handed me the CH, the case open, saying: "It's a nice light decoration to wear round the neck".' Light in weight it may be, but Powell himself was not overly impressed with the design. 'The CH is an Order established in 1917 by George V,' he wrote, 'its design enormously characteristic of that period. It might be called the last gasp of the Art Nouveau Movement.'[82]

Powell lived at Frome, Somerset with Lady Violet Pakenham, to whom he was married for sixty-six years, until his death in 2000 at the age of ninety-four. She died in 2002.

Sir Victor Pritchett *31 December 1992*

V. S. Pritchett was a man of letters with a prolific output that included short stories, novels, biographies, travelogues and reviews.

He was born in Ipswich in 1900 and raised in London. His first name derived from his parents' respect for Queen Victoria, but he never liked it, partly because as a child he had known a vicious baby-biting dog called Victor. For most of his life he hid behind his initials, and was always known as VSP to family and friends. 'His mother, Beatrice, he described as "a rootless London pagan, a fog-worshipper, brought up on the London streets". His father was a Micawberish figure, perennially insolvent but strutting through life in a natty suit, eternally optimistic that his latest business venture would come good. Together they drifted from suburb to suburb, from one red-brick villa to the next, the only continuity in the young Victor's life a moveable clutter of potted palms and mottoed ornaments. On the morning of each move, he recalled, a cab would draw up at the door, while his mother wept and his father tried to jolly her along, singing old music-hall songs: "Oh dry those tears, oh calm those fears, life will be brighter tomorrow".[83]

He was educated at Alleyn's School, Dulwich and Dulwich College where his first attempt at writing was provoked by a desire to record the sight of a zeppelin crash. His parents decided that he should leave school at fifteen to work in the leather trade, and for two years he was employed as a clerk in a tannery in Bermondsey. At the age of nineteen he went to Paris where he worked as a commercial traveller, selling shellac, glue and ostrich feathers from shop to shop.

In 1923 he applied for a job as a foreign correspondent for the *Christian Science Monitor* (his father had been a Christian Scientist). He was sent to Ireland during the civil war, and then to Madrid. His first travel book was called *Marching Spain* (1928). In succession to Somerset Maugham, Pritchett is best remembered for his short stories, the first of which appeared in *Cornhill* and the *New Statesman*, in the 1920s. His first collection of short stories was called *The Spanish virgin and other stories* (1930). 'They are distinguished by their wide social range, shrewd observation of the quirks of human nature, and humane irony.'[84] His first novel *Clare drummer* (1929) was followed by several others including *Shirley Santz* (1932), *Nothing like leather* (1935), *Dead man leading* (1937) and *Mr Beluncle* (1951). His novels were never as good as his short stories, and Pritchett was always ready to admit that they took second place. His other works include *The living novel* (1946), scholarly biographies of Flaubert, Balzac (1973) and Turgenev (1977) and two volumes of autobiography, *The cab at the door: early years* (1968), the title referring to his household's frequent removals, which he claimed gave him a lifelong love of travel, and *Midnight oil* (1971), which ends with the 1939–45 war. Both volumes are 'redolent of the bowler-hatted, Edwardian era of gaslight, smogs and Wesleyan chapels, breweries, tan-yards, port and stout.'[85] He also edited the *Oxford book of short stories* (1981). Some believed that his concentration on the art of the short story rather than the novel excluded him from consideration for the Nobel prize for literature and the Booker prize,

In 1928 he began working as a book reviewer for the *New Statesman*, initially as a way to supplement his income. In fact he reviewed for the next fifty years. In the 1950s he was briefly literary editor and in 1951 he joined the board of directors. Office management and the world of business were never to his liking and he made few contributions to meetings. He was a writer and his book reviews were his main strength and described as a mixture of 'generous connoisseurship and inspired psychology'. 'With a modesty characteristic of his refined civility, he did not, as a reviewer, consider himself interesting beyond his reaction to the author he was writing about. He never pompously brandished the personal pronoun, or succumbed to what he called "the technological habits" of academic criticism. He vigorously refused to view literature as some sort of esoteric game, played for the benefit of the literary establishment.'[86]

During the 1939–45 war he was employed by the government to write pamphlets, surveying factories, shipyards and mines and travelled round Britain making a study of the railway networks.

From the 1950s he discovered an appreciative audience for his works on the other side of the Atlantic. In 1953 he was Christian Gauss lecturer at Princeton University and in 1962 Beckman professor at Berkeley. He spent periods as writer-in-residence at Smith College, Massachusetts, and Vanderbilt University in Tennessee, and was visiting professor at Brandeis and Columbia universities.

'American students warmed to the tweedy Englishman with his pipe and thick-framed spectacles. He, on his side, was attracted by their refreshing directness and lively vernacular, though he did admit to finding American earnestness sometimes exhausting.'[87]

He was viewed as a brilliant exponent of the English language and one of the most clear-sighted and respected literary figures of his day. He was appointed a CBE in 1968, and knighted in 1975. His CH in 1992 was for his services as a 'Writer'. At the conclusion of the musical accompaniment to his investiture in the ballroom at Buckingham Palace in 1993, he was heard to mutter, 'bloody awful band'. He died in 1997 in his ninety-seventh year.

Charles Hubert Sisson 12 June 1993

Although not widely known, C. H. Sisson has a high reputation in literary circles as a distinguished classical scholar and poet.

He was born in Bristol in 1914, and read English at Bristol University before pursuing his studies at the universities of Berlin and Freiburg (1934–5) and at the Sorbonne (1935–6). Apart from active service in India (1942–5) – where his first novel *An Asiatic romance* (1953), a musing satire – is set, he worked from 1936 in the civil service, rising to be an under secretary in the ministry of labour before his retirement in 1971. His dissatisfaction with the civil service is registered in *The spirit of British administration* (1959), the result of a Simon research fellowship.

Sisson was proud of the fact that he had been brought up among working class people, 'an experience which gave him a life-long distaste for the sentimental socialism of Auden, Spender and Day-Lewis: "I could not help noticing," he said, "that it was not from a world I inhabited -which actually contained working people – that these three Saint Georges came riding to the relief of the poor. They came, it seemed, from what they represented as the closed middle class of majors, vicars, lawyers, doctors, advertisers, maiden aunts . . . whom they made a special point of denouncing . . . When they spoke of the workers it was as if they were speaking of people in some far-off fairyland, or alternatively of a remote race of South Sea Islanders, or of a favourite breed of beetles.'[88] His novel, *Christopher Gomm* (1965), reckoned by some to be his masterpiece, is a depressing account of working-class life.

Although he had published *Poems* (1959), *London zoo* (1961), *Numbers* (1965) and *Metamorphoses* (1968), he achieved a wider recognition only with *In the Trojan ditch: Collected poems and selected translations* (1974). 'The unfashionable nature of his opinions and the frequently sour manner of their expression, caused his existence as an essayist to go for many years unnoticed'[89] and he only became well-known as a poet with *Collected poems 1943–1983* (1984).

An Anglican, Sisson has a passing resemblance to T. S. Eliot, but his Anglicanism is less high church and he refused to attend church after the general abandonment of the seventeenth-century *Book of common prayer* and the introduction of more contemporary liturgies. His austere poems about age, decline and death do not resemble the tranquil visions of Eliot, and the dark depressiveness of Thomas Hardy is a stronger influence, and his extreme bitterness about contemporary life is most evident in *The spectre*, a satirical account of a modern intellectual going through familiar stages of pseudo-development. 'His poetry had not yet entered the mainstream, owing to its persistently exasperated tone and its apparently anti-liberal stance. But it is powerfully representative of what is left of the Christian tradition in English poetry.'[90]

He is also a distinguished classical scholar and has published translations, including Heine (1953), Catullus (1966), Horace's *Ars poetica* (1975), Lucretius' *De rerum natura* (1976), *La fontaine* (1979), Dante's *Divine comedy* (1979), *The song of Roland* (1983), Du Bellay's *The regrets* (1984), and Virgil's *Aeneid* (1986). His critical works, *English poetry 1900–1950. An assessment* (1971) and *The avoidance of literature: collected essays* (1978) are 'characterised by a desire to debunk received opinion and a forceful independence of mind.'[91]

The CH was conferred on him in 1993 as a 'Writer and Poet. For services to Literature'. Eminent poet and scholar though he is, Sisson is not widely established with the general public, but deeply appreciated amongst his followers, who include many of the leading critics and editors in the country. He is a complex and meditative writer who has undoubtedly kept alight a kind of carefully constructed intellectually informed poetry which has been far from fashionable in recent times.

He has never been a great contributor to public affairs, but that reflects his shyness and belief in the essential privacy which should be accorded writers; in that view he is not dissimilar to Robert Graves. His contribution to literature is in a narrow field, his writing is inaccessible to most, and he has a limited appeal. But his Englishness, his Anglicanism, his acerbic sense of history and contempt for the merely fashionable, have made him a distinctive figure, and as he approached his eightieth birthday, it was appropriate that he should be recognised for the unmodish distinction that he brought to English poetry.

Doris Lessing 31 December 1999
Doris Lessing is a novelist and short story writer whose work has concentrated on social, political and feminist issues.

She was born in Persia in 1919 of British parents, who moved to Salisbury (now Harare) in Southern Rhodesia (now Zimbabwe) when she was five. She left school at fifteen and worked as a housemaid, shorthand typist and telephone operator. She continued her own education while living on the family farm by reading European and American literature and starting to write novels. She lived in Salisbury itself from 1937 to 1949 where she became involved in politics and helped to start a non-racialist left-wing party. She married twice in Rhodesia and left for England in 1949 with the manuscript of her first novel, *The grass is singing*. Published in 1950 it is the story of a complex relationship between a white farmer's wife and her black servant and its violent conclusion. Her experiences of life in working-class London are described in *In pursuit of the English* (1960). She was briefly a member of the Communist Party but left it at the time of the Hungarian uprising in 1956, in which year the Southern Rhodesian government declared her a 'prohibited immigrant'. Several of her novels, *Martha Quest* (1952), *A proper marriage* (1954), *A ripple from the storm* (1958), *Landlocked* (1965) and *The four-gated city* (1969) were to an extent autobiographical, exploring contemporary social and psychological problems through the life of the heroine Martha. *The golden notebook* (1962) and *Briefing for a descent into hell* (1971) are studies of mental breakdown and a return to normality, which question the definitions of 'sanity' and 'insanity'. Collections of short stories include *A man and two women* (1963), *African stories* (1964) and *The story of a non-marrying man* (1972). Politics and social issues dominated her writing throughout the 1950s and 1960s.

Subsequently, her novels, such as *The fifth child*, became more conventional in form. She moved into the world of science fiction with a quintet of novels entitled *Canopus in Argos: archives* (1972), of which *The making of the representative of planet 8* (1982) formed the basis of a libretto (1988). Her principal concerns are politics, communism, the changing destiny of women, with a fear of technological disaster, and an interest in Sufi thought. *The golden notebook* has been credited with changing the consciousness of many young women. 'Her commitment to exploring political and social undercurrents in contemporary society has never wavered and can be seen to potent effect in *The good terrorist* (1985) and *The fifth child* (1988).'[92]

The CH was conferred on her in 1999 'For services to Literature'. Honours would undoubtedly have come her way in previous years but for her understandable if slightly old-fashioned dislike of the title of the Order of the British Empire.

Harold Pinter 15 June 2002

Actor, playwright and director, Harold Pinter was one of the two or three most important British playwrights of the second half of the twentieth century.

He was born in Hackney, London in 1930, the only child of a Portuguese Jewish tailor, and educated at Hackney Downs Grammar School. During the war he spent a year as an evacuee in Cornwall and later talked of a childhood that was lonely and dislocated. He refused to do national service, on the grounds of conscientious objection, and defended himself at two trials and two tribunals. It was, he said, beyond 'human understanding and my moral conception' that anyone would want to join an organisation whose 'main purpose is mass murder.'[93]

He went to the Royal Academy of Dramatic Art, but left after two terms, and then stayed three terms at the Central School of Speech and Drama. He began work as an actor in 1949, touring with provincial repertory companies and acting under the name of David Baron. Living in shabby digs he began to concentrate on writing. 'The world of old lino floors, bare light bulbs, fly papers and washing up mouldering in the bed-sit sink suffuses his early plays. Later they moved up-market with him.'[94]

In 1957 he wrote three important plays: the one-act *The room* and *The dumb waiter* and the full-length *The birthday party*. Although the last was roughly treated by the critics (*The Times* spoke of its 'off-beat note of madness, a sort of delirium') it established his method in dialogue and to a large extent the air of despair, menace, obscure violence and repressed anger that has dominated his work. The critic Martin Esslin, who coined the term 'theatre of the absurd', saw in Pinter's work an absurdist strain, especially in the nihilism – the belief in nothing – that sometimes appears in his work. His sometimes degenerate characters usually reveal no spiritual awareness and no longing for spiritual values. The first of his plays to catch the public attention was *The caretaker* (1960) in which two brothers invited a revolting tramp to share their attic. His '*The homecoming* (1965) had a brutal shocking quality with its account of tensions and sexual revelations in the house of a retired London butcher. Throughout the 1970s he directed many plays by other playwrights and acted on films and on stage. In the 1980s he produced *The hothouse* and wrote the screenplays for *The French lieutenant's woman* (1981) and *Betrayal* (1983), both of which received an Academy Award nomination for Best Film, and adapted Kazuko Ishiguro's *Remains of the day*, and Franz Kafka's *The trial* (1993) for screen. He has occasionally appeared on screen, usually in threatening roles.

Pinter is probably best known as a playwright and he was associate director of the National Theatre (1973–83). His plays include *The room* (1957), *The birthday party* (1957), *The dumb waiter* (1957), *The hothouse* (1958), *A slight ache* (1958), *A night out* (1959), *The caretaker* (1959), *Night school* (1960), *The dwarfs* (1960), *The collection* (1961), *The lover* (1962), *Tea party* (1964), *The homecoming* (1964), *The basement* (1966), *Landscape* (1967), *Silence* (1968), *Night* (1969), *Old times* (1970), *No man's land* (1974), *Betrayal* (1978), *Family voices* (1980), *A kind of Alaska* (1982), *Victoria station* (1982), *One for the road* (1984), *Mountain language* (1988), *The new world order* (1991), *Party time* (1991), *Moonlight* (1993) and *Ashes to ashes* (1996). His screenplays include *The caretaker* and *The servant* (1962), the latter adapted from Robin Maugham's downbeat melodrama in which a rich and ineffectual young man is gradually degraded and overruled by his sinister manservant, *The pumpkin eater* (1963), *The Quiller memorandum* (1966), *Accident* (1967), *The birthday party* and *The homecoming* (1968), *The go-between* (1969), *Langrishe, go down* (1970), *A la recherche du temps perdu* (1972), *The last tycoon* (1974), *The French lieutenant's woman* (1981), *Betrayal* (1981), *Victory* (1982), *Turtle diary* (1985), *The handmaid's tale* (1987), *The heat of the day* (1988), *Reunion* (1989), *The trial* (1989), and *Comfort of strangers* (1990). Apart from his plays, his publications include *PEN anthology of poems* (1967), *Poems and prose 1949–1977* (1978), *Collected poems and prose* (1986), *100 Poems by 100 poets* (1986), *The dwarfs* (1990), *99 poems in translation* (1994) and *Various voices: prose, poetry and politics 1948–1998* (1998).

His work has been widely produced internationally, and is part of the GCSE and A-level syllabus. Because of their immediacy, plays are the least enduring of literary works, and there is no guarantee that Pinter's will survive long in the canon, but even if they became dated and unperformable, his work is significant. For the time being his plays are constantly being revived, unlike many of his contemporaries from the 1960s, and they remain continuously popular with actors. 'He stamped a new perception on his generation. After Pinter we listen differently. We overhear with new glee the snatched absurdities of conversations in the bar, from a crossed line on the telephone or from the next door restaurant table. He has taught us to become attuned to the cadences, the non-sequiturs, the significant silences, the hidden jockeying for power underneath everyday phrases. He has turned the apparently banal into the surprisingly significant.'[95]

The 1973 American-backed coup in Chile, that deposed President Salvador Allende and brought Augusto Pinochet to power, was a catharsis that honed and sharpened his socialist politics. Thereafter he espoused an often emotional and unbalanced anti-Americanism. At one point the American ambassador to London published a withering criticism of Pinter. 'He would not be Vaclav Havel even if Britain were Czechoslovakia. He brings to mind Goethe's comment that when ideas fail, words come in very handy.'[96] Throughout the 1980s and 1990s he was active on behalf of writers in countries that emerged from eastern Europe's economic and political shifts. He championed the works of Vaclav Havel, and when the Czech writer was sentenced to four years in prison, Pinter put on a benefit night to provide money for his destitute family. In the 1980s his politics grew ever more extreme. He detested the Conservative government of Margaret Thatcher, and in 1988 he and his wife founded a philosophical circle of anti-Thatcher writers to meet regularly in their London house. In 2001–02 he was a leading campaigner against the intervention in Afghanistan, fearing the madness of a new world war. In December 2001 he was diagnosed with cancer of the oesophagus and underwent a course of radiotherapy early in 2002.

He was made a CBE in 1966, but refused a knighthood in 1996, his left wing politics apparently unable to reconcile acceptance of an honour on the prime minister's list when a Conservative government was in power. An article in *The Times* of 21 November 2000 recorded Pinter's refusal of a knighthood and then complained that David Hare and Tom Stoppard had both been knighted and a Labour government was now in power but Pinter was still waiting for a further honour. The waiting was nearly over. He was made a CH in 2002 as 'Playwright. For services to Literature.'

CHAPTER SIX

Famed in all great arts

ARTISTS, ARCHITECTS, SCULPTORS, CURATORS, POTTERS

'It seems very pretty,' she said when she had finished it, 'but it's rather hard to understand!' (You see she didn't like to confess, even to herself, that she couldn't make it out at all.)
'Looking-glass house', *Through the looking-glass*, Lewis Carroll

A visitor to an art gallery looked at a particular exhibit and said to his companion, 'what is it meant to be?' Back came the crushing reply: 'you shouldn't ask that question; it's art'. The work of an artist, like the work of a composer, can arouse strong feelings, either positive or negative, on first encounter. As a musical composition needs to be heard more than once for a critical assessment of its worth, so a piece of art often needs to be seen more than once by the observer, before he or she can appreciate and interpret the often highly individual skills of the artist. A single look can lead to an elementary dismissal of a piece of modern art as 'rubbish', whereas a longer and more thoughtful reflection can lead to a more positive assessment and insight into the mind and purpose of the artist. That art was so late in joining the ranks of the Companions of Honour is almost certainly due to a long prevailing conservatism that decried contemporary art, so far removed from the photographic portraits and landscapes of the past (occasionally dismissed by radical opinion as merely ornamentation) as the product of talentless painters. In the world of art more than any other profession, artistic reputation is often fashionable and therefore ephemeral. The conferment of so high an honour as the CH on an artist needs as firm an assurance as possible that their work is not only nationally well known, but will not quickly fade into oblivion when the fashion has passed.

Seventeen individuals are grouped into this broadly 'artistic' category: eight artists, two sculptors, two architects, one potter, and four individuals loosely assembled under the heading of 'curators'. With one atypical exception, all of them have been appointed since 1955.

Artists have only been appointed to the Order since 1972, and the eight 'artist' Companions have been John Piper (1972), whose diverse talents extended from lithographs to stained glass; David Jones (1974), an artist and poet who lived almost his entire life in England but never lost his love for his Welsh roots; Victor Pasmore (1980), who abandoned figurative painting for abstract art; Lucien Freud (1983), a painter of anonymous portraits; Carel Weight (1994), in his own words a painter of emotions; David Hockney (1997), an exponent of Pop Art; Bridget Riley (1998), one of the foremost exponents of Optical Art; and Richard Hamilton (1999), another painter in the tradition of Pop Art.

Only two sculptors have received the CH: Henry Moore (1955) and Elizabeth Frink (1992). The massive and solid forms of Moore's work are unmistakable and his international reputation was considerable, even though opponents dismissed his work as a cult of ugliness. Frink was his successor as Britain's foremost sculptor, and her relatively early death from cancer was a loss.

Only two architects, Philip Powell (1984) and Denys Lasdun (1995), have received the CH. Powell's major works are the University of East Anglia and the Queen Elizabeth II Conference Centre in Westminster. Lasdun's lasting memorial is the cubist Royal National Theatre on London's south bank.

At the time of writing, only one potter, the unique Bernard Leach (1973), has been made a CH. Learning his skills in Japan before the 1914–18 war, Leach lived to become the most famous potter in the west.

The 'curator' group were more diverse in their interests. Viscount Dillon (1921) was curator of the Tower of London armouries, but his CH was conferred for twenty-seven years work as chairman of the trustees of the National Portrait Gallery. John Summerson (1984) was trained as an architect, but abandoned architectural practice to become curator of a museum of artefacts and write books on architectural history. Kenneth Clark (1959) and Hugh Casson (1984) were two of a kind. Clark was an art historian and Casson an effectively non-practising architect. Both served as curators – Clark of the National Gallery and Casson of the Royal Academy – but both were essentially media figures who competently popularised the history of art and architecture.

Three artists are known to have refused the CH. The first, for reasons and in tones that were entirely unworthy, was that of the artist *Ben Nicholson* (1894–1982), who refused both a knighthood and the CH. He was offered the CH in 1965 at the same time as his former wife, the sculptress Barbara Hepworth, was offered the DBE. 'Whereas Barbara accepted the honour with aplomb . . . Ben was playing for higher stakes, and politely declined his CH. As a Swiss resident, he said, he already had those letters on the back of his car.'[1] If he was indeed 'playing for higher stakes', he won the game in 1968 when he was appointed to the Order of Merit.

The second refusal demonstrated complete indifference to honours. *Francis Bacon* (1909–92) was famous for his paintings of people distorted by anger and violence. But he was important enough to represent the United Kingdom (with Ben Nicholson and Lucien Freud) at the 1954 Venice Biennale. He refused a CBE in 1960 and a CH in 1977. 'I always decline these honours', he said, 'I never want them. I have no opinion on the honours system. It might be fine for other people, but I want to stress I don't want anything for myself.'[2]

The third refusal, couched in tones of gracious humility, was that of *L. S. Lowry* (1887–1976), a significant twentieth century British artist famous for his paintings of matchstick figures set in northern industrial townscapes. But Lowry is known to have refused every honour he was offered: an OBE (1955), a CBE (1960), a knighthood (1967) and the CH twice. When he was offered the CH by Edward Heath in 1971, he replied: 'I have at all times tried to paint to the best of my ability and I would only hope that any remembrance people may have of me when I am gone may be based on my work, rather than any decoration I may have collected on my journey.'[3] When Harold Wilson repeated the offer in 1975, Lowry was equally firm: 'I only ask that I may be allowed to live the remainder of my life in peace free from publicity which would naturally accompany such an honour.'[4]

Dillon's CH in 1921 was a one-off and did not establish a trend; more than thirty years elapsed before the appointment of Henry Moore in 1955. Although Dillon was highly regarded in his day, he published nothing of note, and his lengthy tenure at the National Portrait Gallery would not today of itself warrant the conferment of a CH. The age of the fixed term contract will ensure that his record is unlikely to be equalled. It was the appointment of Henry Moore in 1955 that inaugurated the entrance of the world of art to the ranks of the CHs, but although Kenneth Clark followed him in 1959, it did not at first seem to presage a new dawn; another thirteen years passed before the appointment of John Piper in 1972. Since that date thirteen 'artistic' Companions have been gathered into membership, an average of one every two years, although the frequency increased towards the end of the twentieth century.

The work of the artist Companions spans a range of styles: from the relatively traditional work of Piper, Jones and Freud, to the hurrying figures of Weight, to the abstract work of Pasmore, to the Pop Art of Hockney and Hamilton and the geometrically-based Optical Art of Riley. New conceptions of art will doubtless emerge in the years ahead, and as examples will be given honoured places in the caverns of the Tate Modern, so their imaginative compositors will be welcomed into the ranks of the Companions of Honour.

Viscount Dillon 4 June 1921
Harold Arthur Dillon-Lee, seventeenth Viscount Dillon, was an expert on the history of arms and armour, and the first curator of the Tower of London armouries.

He was born in 1844, into an Anglo-Irish family of landowners since the twelfth century. He was educated at Eltham in Kent and spent twelve years in the Rifle Brigade (1862–74) and seventeen years in the Oxfordshire Militia (1874–91). An interest in antiquities from an early age led to appointments as president of the Royal Archaeological Institute (1892–98), president of the Society of Antiquaries (1897–1904), chairman of the trustees of the National Portrait Gallery (1894–1928), a trustee of the British Museum (1905–12), and of the Wallace Collection (1918–31). His knowledge was wide-ranging, but his primary interest was the history of arms and armour, medieval costume and kindred subjects, and he became the first curator of the Tower of London Armouries (1892–1913).

Dillon was never a collector himself, considering that the keeper of a national armoury should not have a private collection, but his knowledge of the subject was extensive, and based on meticulous research of the pieces in his care. 'He took all the important armours in the Tower to pieces in order to learn their construction and made minute studies of the locks, crossbows and firearms. His knowledge of medieval and later periods was encyclopaedic . . . He had two maxims, one that "Duty is doing more than you are paid for", the other being, "Never say you do not know, but find out and then reply".' 'In any case where finance was involved Dillon was very exact, and he would never give an official signature until he had checked the accounts before him. His knowledge of his own library was such that he could tell the shelf, the colour of the binding and the page of the work that was asked for. He would never put forward theories unsupported by evidence, and when at a trial which involved the authenticity of a suit of armour the opposing counsel questioned his opinion, he replied: "My opinions *are* facts". A true aristocrat, he was equally at home in a royal palace and in a third class carriage of the Great Western Railway by which he travelled from Charlbury to London and back several times a week for many years'.[5] His first wife died in 1895 after twenty five years of marriage; their only child, a son, died in 1923. After thirty-one years as a widower, Dillon married secondly in 1926 and died in 1932.

His entry in *Who's Who* recorded that he 'owned about 3,000 acres in England'. He made a number of contributions to archaeological and antiquarian journals, but published no major works. He was given the honorary degree of doctor of civil law from Oxford and was a fellow of the British Academy. The CH in 1921 was accompanied by the citation that he had been 'Chairman of Trustees, National Portrait Gallery, since 1894'.

Henry Moore 9 June 1955

The large abstract sculptures of Henry Moore made him the best-known British sculptor of the twentieth century.

He was born in Yorkshire in 1898, the seventh child of a coalminer. Educated at Castleford Secondary School, he returned there as a student teacher in 1915, his family intending that he should adopt teaching as a career, to gain practical experience before going to a teacher-training college. He served in the Civil Service Rifles during the 1914–18 war and returned to the school at Castleford in 1919. It was expected that he would become an art teacher, and in 1920 he began formal training at Leeds School of Art. His outstanding talents became apparent and he finished the two-year course in one year. During his second year he studied sculpting and won a scholarship to the Royal College of Art where he studied sculpting (1921–24). He spent time studying the sculpture collections in the British Museum and the Victoria and Albert Museum, and became fascinated by Greek, Egyptian, and Assyrian worlds and by art from pre-European Mexico, Africa and Oceania. 'He was attracted by their intensity, unconventional beauty, powerful sense of mass and form, and feeling for the particular character of the materials – the weight and immovability of stone or the organic quality of wood.'[6]

A six-months travel scholarship to Italy in 1925 was followed by a part-time teaching position in the sculpture school of the Royal College of Art, which gave him time to sculpt and prepare for his first exhibition in January 1928. It was a success and brought his first public commission – an invitation to carve part of the facade for the new London Underground headquarters near St James's Park. During the 1930s he taught part-time at the Chelsea School of Art, working at his studio in Hampstead, and making larger works at his cottage in Kent. His reclining figures of 1929–30 show breasts and upraised knees projecting upwards like hills, and the association of the human figure with the landscape has been a recurrent theme of his work.

In 1940 bombing damaged his Hampstead studio and he moved to Hertfordshire where he remained for the rest of his life. In the 1930s abstract art and surrealism began to make an impression on his work and he began to carve holes through his figures, creating interior spaces like caves in rocks. 'It was the natural world, and the human presence in it, that lay at the heart of all Moore's work, in whatever medium. He did not seek to express beauty, rather an image of power and vitality.'[7] It was not always appreciated, and in 1931 the *Morning Post* condemned his work: 'The cult of ugliness triumphs at the hands of Mr Moore.'

In 1940–42 he worked as an official war artist in the scheme supervised by Kenneth Clarke, an admirer of Moore's work. Until the 1939–45 war, Moore was principally an artist of the avant-garde with a cult following, but in response to Clarke's commission, he produced drawings of sleeping figures in the London Underground, which became one of the most powerful images of the 1939–45 war. In 1943 he produced a *Madonna and Child* for St Matthew's Church,

Northampton. It aroused feelings of anger and dismay at the time, but it remains a work of simple beauty. These two commissions made his international reputation and he was promoted abroad by the British Council. 'By the time he was sixty Moore was generally regarded as Britain's greatest artist and the world's greatest living sculptor. More than 200 museums worldwide own examples of his work, with particularly strong holdings in the Art Gallery of Ontario, Toronto, and the Tate Gallery, London. In over fifty cities his sculpture stands in prominent public places, notably outside the National Gallery of Art in Washington, the Lincoln Centre in New York, the Houses of Parliament in London, and in Dallas, Chicago, Amsterdam, Zurich, Berlin, Singapore and Hong Kong. By the time of his death he had had more exhibitions than any other artist, with the exception only of Pablo Piccasso.'[8] Centres of cultural, political and financial power were not the only places to find Moore's sculptures, the classical and ample figure of the *Draped seated woman* (1962), can be found on an east London housing estate, where she is known locally as 'Old Flo'.

The march of artistic progress inevitably led to a time of opposition from younger artists, who viewed Moore's work as outdated and out of touch with contemporary ideas. In 1967 when there were proposals for a Moore gallery at the Tate, forty-one artists (including his former assistant, Anthony Caro) signed a letter to *The Times*, protesting against the allocation of state funds. To think of Moore's work as old-fashioned in the 1960s was an irony considering that in the 1970s his works were being daubed with the words 'hideous' and 'grotesque'. This opposition did nothing to damage his international reputation, which had made him a very wealthy man; by the mid-1970s he was paying more than £1 million in tax each year. But his fame and his riches seemed never to affect his nature. 'He kept a light Yorkshire accent all his life, and expressed himself in simple straightforward terms, avoiding any philosophising. Interpretations of his work he left to others; he was the maker, driven by some creative force that he could not and perhaps did not wish to understand. At times he seemed almost surprised by his own reputation, expressing a boyish delight at visits from prime ministers and presidents.'[9]

He was a trustee of the Tate Gallery (1941–48 and 1949–56), the National Gallery (1955–63 and 1964–74), a member of the Arts Council (1963–67) and of its art panels for many years from 1942. He was appointed a member of the National Theatre board in 1957 and the Royal Fine Art Commission (1947–71). Those who knew Moore remembered him as a delightful man to deal with, a firm character without any affectations, but quick in decision and as warm and reliable a friend as one could hope for.'[10] The charitable trust to which he assigned his income, allowed him a modest income, sufficient to maintain his economical way of life.

In keeping with his principles of simplicity and modesty, he declined a knighthood in 1952 (he didn't relish the idea of his assistants greeting him with the words 'Good morning Sir Henry'). 'I didn't want to be rude, but titles change one's name and one's opinion of oneself. The initials aren't so bad. No-one comprehends them.'[11] So he accepted the CH in 1955 for his services as a 'Sculptor' and the OM in 1963. He died in 1986 at the age of eighty-eight.

Lord Clark 1 January 1959
Kenneth Clark was a patron and interpreter of the arts who became popular through the medium of television.

He was born in 1903, the only child of a wealthy Scottish industrialist, sportsman, gambler and alcoholic. The wealth derived from a textile firm, and enabled Clark to maintain a level of financial independence throughout his life. He was educated at Winchester and Trinity College, Oxford where he took a second class degree in modern history in 1925. 'A first had been expected, but his interests had already turned exclusively to the study of art. An inborn sensitivity of response (sometimes described in almost mystical terms) to works of art, together with an insatiable appetite for them, allied to an acute, fastidious and articulate intelligence, had developed from childhood on. He was a workmanlike draughtsman himself, and read wide and voraciously.'[12] In 1925–27 he spent two years at the house of Bernhard Berenson in the hills above Florence, assisting him in the revision of his work on Florentine drawings, and working on his first full-length book, *The Gothic revival*, published in 1928.

In 1929 Clark was offered the task of cataloguing the collection of Leonardo da Vinci drawings in the royal collection at Windsor Castle, and, his reputation now established, he accepted the post of keeper of the department of fine art at the Ashmolean Museum in Cambridge in 1931. In 1933, aged only thirty-one, he was appointed director of the National Gallery in London, where he remained until 1945, and was additionally surveyor of the king's pictures (1934–44). During his directorship the gallery acquired a number of masterpieces, established a scientific department and embarked on a programme of picture cleaning. He was less successful as an administrator and alienated the senior staff of the gallery. In 1937, against the advice of professional staff, he acquired four small minor Venetian School paintings and declared them to be Giorgiones. 'The virulent subsequent controversy became a public scandal and contributed to a lingering mistrust of his integrity, especially amongst some fellow art historians, that was perhaps never quite dispelled. On the other hand he fought off the reappointment of Lord Duveen as a trustee, believing that a dealer's interests were irreconcilable with those of a trustee and that although Duveen's natural charm and indeed generosity were compelling, they were about matched by his natural duplicity.'[13]

In 1946, following the return of the National Gallery's collection after war time evacuation, he resigned to become a full-time writer. His 1935 catalogue of the Windsor Leonardo collection remains a respected addition to the literature of that field. In 1939 he produced *Leonardo da Vinci . . . His development as an artist*, which was acclaimed as the best general introduction in English, and a new edition was published in 1967. His other books, which often accompanied his lectures, included *Piero della Francesca* (1951), *Moments of vision* (1954), *The nude* (1955), *Looking* (1960), *Ruskin today* (1964), *Rembrandt and the Italian renaissance* (1966), *A failure of nerve* (1967), *Civilisation* (1969), *Looking at pictures* (1972), *Westminster Abbey* (1972), *The artist grows old* (1972), *The romantic rebellion* (1973), *Henry Moore drawings* (1974), *The drawings by Sandro Botticelli for Dante's divine comedy* (1976), *Animals and other men* (1977), *An introduction to Rembrandt* (1978), *The best of Aubrey Beardsley* (1979), *Feminine beauty* (1980). He published two volumes of autobiography: *Another part of the wood* (1974) and *The other half* (1977)

Clark was Slade professor of fine art at Oxford (1946–50 and 1961–62), and professor of the history of art at the Royal Academy (1977–83). He was also chairman of the Arts Council (1953–60) in which he emerged as a frustrated figurehead, but a three-year stint as chairman of the Independent Television

Authority (1954–57) was more rewarding, and although he was not reappointed in 1957, he became celebrated as a writer and performer for television, most notably for his series entitled *Civilisation*. '[It] was avowedly a very personal, selective interpretation and illustration of the title's grandiose theme. Though in it he ranged widely, with great erudition, in time and space, his conceptions generally were conditioned by Mediterranean values . . . Though he recognised the achievement of Mondrian, and even of Jackson Pollock, he did not respond generally to abstract art, and his primary concern was to arouse response in individual human beings to individual works of art, essentially by accounting for his own response. If he was in a sense old-fashioned . . . he made art accessible to a whole generation as no other English-speaking writer was able to do.'[14]

Clark was made an honorary fellow of his alma mater Trinity College, Oxford, in 1968. He was also chancellor of the University of York (1969–79). He was appointed a KCB in 1938 at the very early age of thirty-seven. The CH was conferred in 1959 for his services as 'Chairman, Arts Council of Great Britain'. He was created a life peer in 1969, and received the OM in 1976. A few days before his death in 1983 he was received into the Roman Catholic Church.

John Piper 3 June 1972
John Piper was an artist who worked in a wide variety of fields: painter in oil, watercolour and gouache, a poet, potter, draughtsman, lithographer, decorator, photographer, book illustrator and designer for the theatre. His work prominently featured the art, architecture and topography of England.

He was born in 1903 at Epsom, Surrey, the son of solicitor. He was educated at Epsom College. In his teenage years he made topographical notebooks of the architecture of southeast England, illustrated with drawings and photographs and it was said that he had visited every church in Surrey by the age of twelve.[15] From 1921 he worked as an articled clerk in his father's office. When the latter died in 1926, Piper seized the opportunity to abandon law and went to study at Kingston and Richmond Schools of Art and then at the Royal College of Art (1928–29). He had written and illustrated a book of poems, *The wind in the trees*, in 1924, and from 1928 he was a regular contributor to the *Nation and Athenaeum* and to the *New Statesman* as a critic of painting and a reviewer of concerts, plays and books. In 1927 he exhibited wood engravings at the Arlington Gallery and held his first one-man exhibition at the London Gallery in 1938. During the 1930s he contributed art and theatre criticism to *The Listener* and the *New Statesman* and exhibited with the London Group. In 1937 he made his first stage designs for Stephen Spender's *Trial of a judge*.

A visit to Paris in 1933 caused a fascination with abstraction which lasted for a while in the mid-1930s. In 1934 he was elected a member of the 7 & 5 Society which was dedicated to 'non-representational' art. By 1937 he rejected abstraction and returned to representational painting, including misty landscapes. He was influenced from 1936 by a meeting with the poet John Betjeman. 'They travelled the country together preparing the Shell Guides to the counties of England, combining their disciplines to develop an appreciation of the visual heritage of Britain which the war served to intensify and deepen and make more immediate, more vital and more national. It began to transcend the conventional labels of "romantic nostalgia" and "neo-romanticism". "Visionary topography" might be a better description of Piper's work of this period.'[16] He shared Betjeman's love of architecture and architectural detail that others dismissed as too ordinary.

He was an official war artist (1940–42) and came to public attention with his paintings of bombed buildings during the war, notably the studies of Coventry and the palace of Westminster. The theme of destruction continued throughout his life as he used his art to record the threatened buildings of England. In 1941–42 he was commissioned by Queen Elizabeth, at the suggestion of Sir Kenneth Clark, to make a series of twenty-six watercolours of Windsor Castle. Part of the impulse for the commission was the fear in 1941 that Windsor Castle itself could be bombed at any time. He won a reputation in the 1940s as a brilliant exponent of the romantic, picturesque, topographical tradition, though his work was not to the liking of some critics, who dismissed him as a 'romantic' or 'poetic' representative of 'Anglo-Saxon twilight'. To those who thought him too insular, Piper replied that Constable went no further than the Lake District.

In his painting and printmaking he concentrated on landscape, particularly the wild mountainous country of Wales, and the buildings of England, France and Italy. He also illustrated several books of poetry by Betjeman and others. He was a distinguished photographer, and designed tapestries, posters and pottery. Throughout his long working life he had a deep and continuing involvement with graphics and printmaking, from early work with small woodblocks during the 1920s, through pre-war aquatints, like those of Brighton and Stowe, and the many series of autolithographs which he made at different printing works.

From 1945 he illustrated the five volumes of Sir Osbert Sitwell's autobiography. In 1946 he designed the scenery and costumes for the premiere of Britten's *Rape of Lucretia* at Glyndebourne, to be followed by *Albert Herring* in 1947. For the Festival of Britain in 1951 he designed the mural for the exterior of the Homes and Gardens pavilion and, with Osbert Lancaster, he was responsible for the decoration of the Main Vista. Also in 1951 he designed four major theatrical productions, for the English Opera Group, Sadler's Wells Ballet, Glyndebourne, and Britten's *Billy Budd* at Covent Garden, and two exhibitions in Philadelphia and London. In 1953 he designed sets and costumes for Britten's *Gloriana* and designed the settings for many of Britten's operas, including *Death in Venice* (1973).

From the mid–1950s he designed stained glass windows, chiefly for churches and became the country's foremost designer of stained glass. In 1957 he was commissioned to design the stained glass wall of the baptistery at Coventry Cathedral, in collaboration with Patrick Reyntiens. Coventry was followed by Eton College Chapel (1958), Nuffield College Chapel, Oxford (1961) St Margaret's, Westminster (1967), Liverpool Cathedral (1967), the chapel of Robinson College, Cambridge (1979) and the Benjamin Britten memorial window at Aldeburgh.

There seemed to be no end to his versatility. In 1964–65 he worked on the tapestry for a screen behind the high altar at Chichester Cathedral. In 1972 he had his first exhibition of ceramics, and in 1979 he designed the firework display at the opening of the extension to the Tate Gallery.

He had many exhibitions, culminating in the retrospective at the Tate Gallery, and he served as a trustee of the Tate (1946–53, 1954–61 and 1968–75). There he was praised for his 'enthusiasm, his openmindedness, his good sense, his natural modesty and his excellent taste'.[17] He was a member of the Arts Council Panel (1952–57), the Royal Fine Art Commission (from 1959), and the Oxford Diocesan Advisory Committee (from 1950). 'A born collaborator, who leaves a huge wake of friends from his multitude of enterprises (for he treated all around as equals), Piper's most elusive achievement is that he was one of a group of mid-twentieth century men Niklaus Pevsner, J. M. Richards, John Betjeman, Osbert Lancaster, Gordon Cullen among them who have taught us to look at Britain's visual heritage and see it, not in vain nostalgia, but with enjoyment and for what it is. He is an artist whose stature is to be measured by the sum total of moments of individual human awareness, exhilaration and vision. These he brought to those who look at pictures, to theatre audiences, to readers of books and to church congregations alike.'[18] His reputation as an interpreter of the landscape of Britain, and his contribution to British twentieth century design give him an assured place as one of the great artists of his age.

He received the CH in 1972 for his services as a 'Painter'. Other honours might have been expected to come to him in earlier years, not least a CBE and a knighthood, the latter at least at the time of the completion of Coventry Cathedral, but he was a private individual who never sought honours and was not a self-publicist. His supporters pointed to his complete integrity, his unselfish public service, his wide contribution to the raising of English prestige and his reputation as an enchanting man who was kind and encouraging to the young and talented. He died at his home in Henley-on-Thames in 1992.

Bernard Leach 2 June 1973

Bernard Leach studied the art of pottery in Japan and became the most influential potter of his age in the west.

He was born in Hong Kong in 1887, the only child of a barrister and his wife who died in childbirth. The first three years of his life were spent in Japan with his grandparents. When his father remarried in 1890 he was returned to Hong Kong. He moved to Singapore in 1894 when his father was appointed British colonial judge there, and was taken to England in 1897 to spend six years at the Beaumont Jesuit College near Windsor. In 1903 he went to the Slade School of Art to study drawing. The death of his father in 1904 deprived him of a source of income, and Leach temporarily reconciled himself to work in the Hong Kong and Shanghai Bank. A new opportunity for resuming his art studies led in 1908 to the London School of Art where he studied the art of etching. With the aim of introducing this unknown art in Japan, he moved there in 1909 living first in Nagasaki and then in Tokyo. In 1910 he experimented with a kiln for the first time, and in 1911 he decided to become a potter. He remained in Japan, with visits to Peking and Korea, until 1920, falling profoundly under the influence of living masters of the Japanese 'tea ware' tradition. His first book, *A review 1909–1914*, contained poems, prose pieces and illustrations of etchings, drawings and pots. 'This was the start of a long series of books in which Leach propounded his personal philosophy, his aesthetic, moral and religious concepts . . . He became interested in the Baha'i faith (1932), and in 1940 he declared himself to be a believer in Baha'u'llah, the Persian prophet's creed.'[19] His books included *A potter's outlook* (1928), *A potter's book* (1940), his best-known book, *A potter's portfolio* (1951), *A potter in Japan* (1960), *A potter's work* (1967), *The unknown craftsman* (1972), *Drawings, verse and belief* (1973), *Hamada* (1976), *The potter's challenge* (1976), and *Beyond east and west* (1978).

On his return to England in 1920 he established a pottery at St Ives, building the first oriental climbing kiln in Europe, and more than one hundred pupils learned the art of pottery under Leach's instruction. 'At the height of its activity the pottery produced some 22,000 pieces of domestic ware; Raku soft ware was dominant in the beginning and later stone ware, some porcelain, and salt glaze ware were produced.'[20] He worked predominantly in earth glaze colours, black to red, and implanted in western ceramics the oriental idea that glaze decoration and body should be felt as one. He stressed the calligraphic use of the brush in decoration and his pots became works of art in their own right, although they were always usable and sold as such. 'Two fundamental ideas dominated his working life: hand production by studio potters against a background of industrialism, and the bridging of the cultural gap between east and west (Tao and Zen – European humanism and depth psychology) in an attempt to create a wholeness of human spiritual achievement. He stood for the honest and personal involvement of the potter with his philosophical and religious overtones; this was a social service to the community, his was not to be dominated by purely economic (mass production) and rationalistic considerations.'[21] He absorbed the ideas and methods of traditional Japanese pottery, revived aspects of English medieval pottery, and during more than fifty years of activity amalgamated the two.

In 1974 Leach suffered the loss of sight in his right eye through the effects of glaucoma. The deterioration in the sight of his left eye brought his unique career to an end. He was appointed a CBE in 1962 and a CH in 1973, his last pot-making year, 'For services to the Art of Pottery.' He died at Hayle in 1979.

David Jones 15 June 1974
David Jones was a painter, poet and essayist who was influenced by his Welsh ancestry and by the misty world of Arthurian legend.

He was born in 1895 at Brockley, then in Kent, the youngest son of a printer from Flintshire and half-Italian mother. He claimed a happy childhood and began drawing animals at the age of six. He was educated at Camberwell School of Art (1910–14). He enlisted in the Welch Fusiliers in 1915 and was demobilised in December 1918. He worked at Westminster School of Art (1919–21), and in the latter year was received into the Roman Catholic Church, to the grief of his Welsh nonconformist father, and joined Eric Gill's craft community, first at Ditchling in Sussex and then at Capel-y-ffin in the Black Mountains of Wales, where he apprenticed himself to the carpenter. He was engaged to Gill's daughter in 1924 but, he having little money or prospects, she broke off the engagement in 1927 to marry someone else. In 1928 Ben Nicholson had him elected to the 7 and 5 Society where he exhibited with Henry Moore, Barbara Hepworth, John Piper, and others.

His work was interrupted by eye problems from 1930 and by severe nervous breakdowns in 1934 and 1947. His writings began with *In parenthesis* (1938), on which he worked for nine years, and which drew on his experiences in the 1914–18 war, won the Hawthornden prize, was praised by T. S. Eliot as 'a work of genius' and published by Faber. *The anathemata* (1952), originated with a journey to Jerusalem, prescribed as therapy after his breakdown in 1934. W. H. Auden described it as 'very probably the greatest long poem in English this century.' *The anathemata* is a meditation on the origins of man and of Britain projected through the events of the mass. He published a series of a fragments of another large religious work, *The sleeping lord* (1974), but never finished it. A posthumous selection, *The Roman quarry*, was published in 1981. His essays were collected in *Epoch and artist* (1959) and *The dying Gaul* (1978).

Despite the undoubted quality of his literary works, he was probably best known as a painter, and the CH was conferred on him for that field of his talents. He worked mainly in pencil and watercolour, his subjects including landscape, portraits, still-life, animals and imaginative themes (Arthurian legend was one of his main inspirations). 'The delicacy and freshness of his colours, and the purity and power of his forms as a painter, let alone the strength and grace of his engraving work and his occasional wooden sculpture, would be enough to win him a high place among the artists of his generation and in a tradition that goes back to William Blake, whose nature and genius with many differences Jones recalls.'[22]

After 1947 he lived in a set of rooms in Harrow, then in a small hotel in the town. 'Jones had boyish gaiety and a charmingly wide smile. His conversation was full of humour and inventive parody, his sympathy and range of interest were extraordinarily wide . . . Under stress he would drop his shopping, lose his papers, or find himself smoking two cigarettes, one in each hand. His notes became long writings, and his letters, annotated in several colours, tumbled effortlessly from sheet to sheet, and subject to subject like the dialogues of Plato.'[23]

He was never prominent in public life and held no public appointments, but he was sufficiently highly-regarded to be appointed a CBE in 1955. Further honours might have come his way sooner had he undertaken the round of trusteeships of art institutions and memberships of committees; but it was not in his nature to concern himself with such things. By the end of 1970 he was resident in the Calvary Nursing Home at Harrow, where he was cared for by the sisters of the Little Company of Mary, a Roman Catholic community. There, he devoted himself mainly to calligraphic inscriptions in the Welsh language and lived in a fug of cigarette smoke. He lived in an untidy jumble and was interviewed in 1972 where he was seen sitting in a chair 'wedged between a slagheap of unanswerable correspondence on the table at the foot of his bed, and a chest of drawers on which a continuing detritus of books, devotional, historical and poetical [was] suffered to find its own level . . . He has about 40 biros and a claspknife with the manuscript on his working trolley. His hands are never still: cupped to contain and isolate an idea when talking, impatiently fending off some scholar's well-meant but wholly irrelevant gloss, taking the knife to chivvy wood like intractable verbiage, following a ballpoint in a touring line over paper . . . "Life is too bloody long for comfort," he says, "and too bloody short to get everything done".'[24]

Some thought that the Welsh office should have recommended this distinguished son of Wales for an honour (despite the fact that he had not been born in Wales and had only lived there briefly in the 1920s). It was claimed that there was 'acute disappointment' in Wales at the lack of any further honour for Jones.

He received the CH four months before his death in 1974, for his work as an 'Artist'. He was unable to attend an investiture and the badge was posted to him at the nursing home.

Victor Pasmore 31 December 1980
Victor Pasmore was an artist who caused a shock in the art world in 1947 by publicly abandoning the beautifully poetic and lyrical style that had been the hallmark of his work, and turning to abstraction.

He was born at Chelsham in Surrey in 1908. He was educated at Harrow School (1922–26), having to leave on the death of his father. His mother moved to London from rural Surrey and from 1927 to 1937 he worked as a clerk in the public health department of London County Council, and attended evening classes at the Central School of Arts and Crafts until 1931. He painted in his spare time, experimenting with fauvism, cubism and abstraction. He was a member of the London Artists' Association (1932–34) and the London Group (1934–52). His work at this time was still figurative, but the work of his fellow exhibitors led him to experiment with abstractionism. He reverted to naturalistic painting and in 1937 he combined with William Coldstream and Claude Rogers to open a studio in Fitzroy Street, moving later in the same year to Euston Road, in an attempt to revive impressionism. The 'Euston Road School' closed in 1939 after the outbreak of war, which led to a general diaspora of the London art groups.

He registered as a conscientious objector, married in 1940, and lived briefly in Ebury Street before moving to Chiswick in 1942. 'Characteristic of his work at this time and in the early 1940s are some splendid female nudes and lyrically sensitive Thames-side landscapes that have been likened to those of Whistler.'[25] During the late 1930s and 1940s he produced some of the most beautiful British figurative painting of the period, among them the misty and poetic scene depicted in *The quiet river. The Thames at Chiswick* (1943–44). As late as 1963 he was still being described as 'Whistler's true heir and the most ravishing painter we have.'[26] 'He made pictures in the tradition of Bonnard and Sickert which were masterly. His skill was great: his sensibility never grew mechanical. Collectors would have been content to acquire flower paintings, nudes and still lifes of his of a realistic kind for many years.'[27]

His postwar life was affected by the revelation of Picasso's wartime paintings at the Victoria and Albert Museum in 1946. In 1947 he created a sensation by concluding that there was no future to figurative painting, and went 'abstract'. It caused howls of dismay and a minor crisis in domestic art history. The shock waves lasted for several years and in the 1950s critics complained that he had declined as an artist and that abstraction was a vehicle unsuited to his otherwise excellent talents. He had abandoned his extraordinary gifts for the poetic interpretation of nature in favour of abstract art that few people could understand. Some said bluntly that he was no longer any good.

After the war he moved to St German's Place, Blackheath, which remained his base for the rest of his life. In 1950–51 he visited Ben Nicholson and Barbara Hepworth, exhibiting with them at the Penwith Society, St Ives, which held the first postwar exhibitions of abstract art. He developed a personal style of geometrical abstraction and began to make three-dimensional constructions, although a carpenter usually did the carpentry for him. 'He started with spirals, moved through triangles, lines, blots then constructions and more recently poured or dribbled paint. With all points of departure the principle remained the same. "It's just starting with a different element and building it up organically. The objective factor is deciding not on image but on the process and material I am going to deal with".'[28]

He was an influential teacher, being a visiting teacher at the London County Council Camberwell School of Arts (1945–49) and the Central School of Arts and Crafts (1949–53). He was master of painting in the department of fine arts at King's College, Newcastle upon Tyne (1954–61) (then part of Durham University, now Newcastle University).

In 1955 he was asked to take charge of a team of architects to design the southwest area of Peterlee – a typically idealistic product of the post-war Labour years – planned as a new modern town for Durham miners, and he remained consulting director of urban design for the area until 1977. His principal work there became known as the Pasmore Pavilion. The pavilion is unique among British public sculptures. A massive, functionless reinforced concrete structure, it has been described as not so much a sculpture as an integration of painting and architecture. It was intended as an emotional and social centre; not surprisingly it became a graffiti-ridden haunt of local youth. At one point it was suggested that it should be blown up, but Pasmore visited the place and perversely announced his complete approval of the graffiti. 'The children had done what I couldn't: they had humanised the place and made it a social centre.'[29] In 1999 the structure acquired the honour of inclusion in the second edition of the book on British follies by Gwyn Headley and Wim Meulenkamp. 'This graffiti-stained bridge . . . has been listed by English Heritage. But is has so persistently been targeted by local saddies that it has become a deeply-scarred, deeply unpleasant environment, fit only for demolition . . . The Pasmore Pavilion was designed to be "an architecture and sculpture of purely abstract form through which to walk, on which to linger, and on which to play." The structure has now become a shabby dump . . . With the wind howling through it and the rain lashing the concrete it is not difficult to see this as one of the more depressing sites of "modern" British architecture.'[30] Pasmore also made a number of mural paintings and reliefs commissioned for public buildings, the first being a mural in 1950 for a canteen in the drivers' and conductors' bus garage at Kingston in Surrey.

Retrospective exhibitions of his work were held at the Venice Biennale (1960), the Musee des Arts Decoratifs, Paris (1961), the Louisana Museum, Copenhagen (1962), the Tate Gallery (1965), the Sao Paolo Biennale (1965), and the Marlborough New London Gallery (1966, 1969 and 1972). Kenneth Clarke described him as one of the two or three most talented painters of this century. 'At the heart of his work there has always been that marvellous reflection of our indigenous light. He captures it not only with the brush, but even in his constructions in wood and plastic. Everything that comes from his hand somehow contains that particular light as marble contains its own inner light.'[31]

Pasmore was a trustee of the Tate Gallery (1963–66). In 1966 he bought the house on Malta that became his principal home. From that date some critics pointed to a decline in the standards of his work. 'Since then his work has seemed increasingly out of touch, and even anachronistic. Many of these new faults were always there, but checked by a dogged mental engagement that have now gone; which is a pity. But Pasmore remains what he is, an artist particularly of the 1940s and 1950s, and his work of that time remains significant and will stand.'[32]

Despite the ripples caused by his conversion to abstraction he was appointed a CBE in 1959 and a CH in 1980 for his services as an 'Artist'. He died in 1998, less than a year before his ninetieth birthday.

Lucian Freud 11 June 1983
Lucien Freud is a portrait artist whose desire for privacy has been reflected in the anonymity of many of his works.

He was born in Berlin in 1922 the son of Ernst Freud, an architect and the youngest son of Sigmund Freud, the founder of psychoanalysis. He came to England with his family in 1933 and has lived in London since that time. His childhood was comfortably bourgeois and he was educated at the Franzoisches Gymnasium. He was reluctant to talk about his childhood years or to divulge any information about them and was for long estranged from his brothers Stephen and Clement. On his arrival in England he was sent to Dartington Hall School in Devonshire and then to Bryanston School in Dorset. By that time a career as an artist seemed to be beckoning and he went to the Central School of Arts and Crafts in London in 1938–39. He became a naturalised British subject in 1939 and in the same year transferred to the East Anglian School of Painting and Drawing in Dedham, Essex, run by the painter Cedric Morris. Even though Freud's habit of smoking at night started a fire that destroyed the school, Morris recognised Freud's talent and kept him on in his own home as a special student.

After leaving Dedham, Freud led an independent bohemian life in London with a studio of his own in Maida Vale. He spent a year with the merchant navy (1941–42) being invalided out, and then returned briefly to the East Anglian School before going for a year of drawing lessons at Goldsmiths College in 1942. A period of travel and painting in Paris and Greece marked the immediate postwar years (1946–48). On his return, his marriage marked a four-year period in which his wife's face dominated his paintings, and since that time his paintings have always been of those close to him, women he has loved, friends and fellow artists, a process of recording faces that were meaningful to him.

He won an Arts Council prize at the Festival of Britain Exhibition in 1951. He taught at the Slade School of Fine Art (1948–58), and in 1964–65 he was a visiting teacher at Norwich School of Art. In 1972 he embarked on a series of paintings of his mother after she had recovered from the bout of depression caused by the death of Freud's father in 1970. It was said of him that not since Rembrandt had any artist so movingly revealed his feelings towards his mother.

Two daughters were born of his first marriage which ended in divorce. A second marriage also ended in divorce after only three years, but he was not an easy person to live with. 'Freud's well-known eccentricities include reckless gambling, refusing to have a telephone in his studio, in which he spends long hours at work, occasionally throughout the night. If he feels so moved he will call friends from a pay phone, but invitations to visit him . . . are rare.'[33]

A tendency to secretiveness and a shunning of publicity finds an echo in the vague titles of his portraits: e.g. *Girl with roses* (1951), *A woman painter* (1954), *Woman smiling* (1958–59), *Sleeping head* (1962), *The big man* (1976–77), *Boy with a rat* (1977–78), *Boy and his friend* (1978–80), *Two Irishmen in W11*, (1984–85), *Night portrait* (1985–86), *Girl with closed eyes* (1986–87). Further identification, in the opinion of Freud himself, would only detract from the knowledge to be derived from the painting itself. 'Just as few of his subjects are named on the labels of his paintings, the backgrounds against which they were portrayed are similarly nonspecific and reduced to a minimum, though they often include large and rather sinister-looking houseplants.'[34] His *Baby on a green sofa* (1961) was later acquired by the Duke and Duchess of Devonshire. When the duchess asked Freud the identity of the subject he replied: 'I don't know, it's just a baby'. Four decades later Freud mentioned in passing that it was his daughter Bella.[35]

Freud's portraits are not at all in the tradition of the romantic and heroic portraits of de Lazslo. His painting of the faults and flaws of individual human bodies is perceptive to the point of being merciless. 'The frankness with which he explores bodies at their most unflattering can be alarmingly stark: at times Freud's pictures dwell on physical disintegration with the sternness of a preacher warning us to beware of our own imminent decay. But he discovers dignity in these sprawling limbs as well. Indeed by confronting their awkward nakedness he implies that we ought to accept human vulnerability, not shy away from it.'[36]

Freud said that people interested him more than anything else and most of his works are portraits, but he has painted some scenes, latterly of drab neighbourhoods. It has been said of him that he talks a great deal while he paints and needs numerous sittings. He was in the process of painting the philosopher Sir Isaiah Berlin when the latter died. The painting was never finished because they both talked too much. Another candidate, approached directly by Freud, was Lord Goodman. 'Whether he was seized by an impulse or had been contemplating it for some time he announced to me that he would very much like to draw me . . . He started work in the early 1980s and thereafter continued for several years, making in all no fewer than four drawings of me, and at the end one etching.'[37]

Private and reclusive though he is, Freud is probably no more eccentric and difficult than many other creative artists. 'Freud is, in fact, an anomalous figure, a socially sought-after solitary with a seemingly facile mind to whom the pursuit of his vocation is a sombre ordeal daily renewed, a seemingly material temperament, who . . . is without the acquisitive urge, and whose successive studios would be rejected as unfit to live in by the student of today.'[38]

Exhibitions of his work have been held at the Lefevre Gallery, the London Gallery, the Venice Biennale (1954), and the Marlborough Fine Art Gallery. A retrospective of his work was held in the Tate Britain in 2002 to commemorate his eightieth birthday. Most of his works are in the hands of individuals, but examples can be found in public galleries in London, Liverpool, Manchester, Paris, Perth (Australia), Fredericton (Canada), and New York.

He was made a CH in 1983 for his services as a 'Painter' and an OM in 1993.

Sir Philip Powell 16 June 1984
Philip Powell has the distinction of being the first architect to be appointed a Companion of Honour.

He was born in 1921 and educated at Epsom College and the Architectural Association's School of Architecture. He started his architectural career in 1948, by winning, with J. H. Moya, the architectural competition for the large Churchill Gardens Flats development for Westminster City Council. This scheme put the stamp of quality on their work from the outset and it was a tribute to them that the development remains an elegant addition to this part of the Thames embankment. They also won the competition for the Skylon at the Festival of Britain in 1951. Subsequently they carried out schemes that ranged from private housing to major public buildings, including schools, hospitals, and extensions to Oxford and Cambridge colleges. Among their commissions are the Chichester Theatre, the Cripp's Building for St John's College, Cambridge, Wolfson College, Cambridge, the Museum of London, Winslade Manor, the National Westminster Bank in Shaftesbury Avenue and the Queen Elizabeth II Conference Centre in Westminster.

The design of Wolfson College, Cambridge was not altogether well received. 'It looks like just another of the sprawling rectangular complexes of concrete and plate glass which have been allowed to rise beside the River Cherwell since the war,' was one comment. 'One of the first postgraduates finds its design "the ideal compromise between friendliness and privacy." One of the first photographers to see a print says disparagingly – that it reminds him of the new Covent Garden.'[39] Another prominent commission was the distinctive Queen Elizabeth II Conference

Centre, that stands across Victoria Street from Westminster Abbey. Although surrounded by buildings of such clearly identifiable styles as the Flemish Gothic Middlesex Town Hall, the neo-Baroque Central Hall, and the partially medieval Westminster Abbey, the Conference Centre is a striking and eye-catching addition to this part of Westminster.

The work of leading architects by its nature attracts considerable comment, and usually some criticism, not least from other members of the profession, but Philip Powell is a rare example of an architect who is universally admired by his fellow practitioners. It is not just a compliment but confirmation of the general quality and integrity of his work.

He was appointed an OBE in 1957, knighted in 1975 and appointed a CH in 1984 'For services to Architecture'. His CH was the first to be granted to an architect and was particularly timely, being conferred in the European Year of Architecture.

Sir Hugh Casson 31 December 1984

Hugh Casson could have been successful in a number of professions, including architecture, theatre, literature, journalism and teaching. He was a qualified architect, but he was at his best as a journalist and teacher.

He was born in 1910, the son of Randall Casson of the Indian Civil Service. He was educated at Eastbourne College and St John's College, Cambridge. He studied architecture at Cambridge and at University College, London, was Craven Scholar at the British School at Athens in 1933 and became an Associate of the Royal Institute of British Architects in 1934. From 1937 until the war he practised architecture in partnership with Christopher Nicholson. He served from 1940 to 1944 as a camouflage officer with the Air Ministry and from 1944 to 1946 as a technical officer with the ministry of town and country planning. In 1948 he set up in private practice with Neville Conder, and in the following years the firm of Casson, Conder & Partners was responsible for a quantity of well-thought-out buildings including work for Birmingham and Belfast universities, civic buildings at Swindon, a banking headquarters at Manchester and the Ismaili Centre in Cromwell Road, London, opposite the Victoria and Albert Museum.

For nearly thirty years (1948–76) he was the senior partner in the architectural practice. But despite his early training, he was not an outstandingly good architect and is remembered more as a general expert in the arts and the holder of a series of distinguished public appointments. He was director of architecture for the Festival of Britain (1948–51), a member of the Royal Fine Art Commission (1960–83), a trustee of the Natural History Museum (1976–86), a trustee of the National Portrait Gallery (1976–84), a member of the board of the British Council (1977–81), president of the Royal Academy (1976–84), professor of environmental design (1953–75) and provost (1980–86) of the Royal College of Art (although he never did very much teaching), and a member of the Royal Mint Advisory Committee (from 1952 until his death).

Although he was an important procurer of clients for his architectural practice, his heart was never in the work and he once admitted that modern architecture was not much fun to draw. 'His buildings often lacked conviction. His group of arts buildings, for example, in Sidgwick Avenue for Cambridge University, designed in 1956, were sensitively laid out in the informal manner of the South Bank, but there were so many changes of motif, variations of fenestration and ingenious details of all kinds that the effect was weak and somewhat fussy.'[40] He was more in his element in designing the light and ephemeral architecture of exhibitions and stage sets, the former beginning with his work at the Festival of Britain. Casson was never really suited to the routine work of the architectural profession with its regular battles with planning committees and visits to muddy building sites. Visits to the architectural glories of Venice and designing stage sets for Glyndebourne were more to his taste. He was a talented interior designer; it suited his appreciation of changing fashions and his subtle sense of style and atmosphere. He designed interiors for passenger liners, for restaurants and offices, for numerous private clients and for the Queen at Windsor Castle. He was a favourite with the royal family and was responsible, in consultation with the Queen and the Duke of Edinburgh, for the interior design of the Royal Yacht Britannia.

Casson also practised as a journalist and wrote after the war on architecture for *The Observer* and gossip columns for the architectural magazines. He was devoted to the theatre, to which he had family links (the late Lewis Casson was his uncle), and designed sets for Covent Garden and Glyndebourne. After his retirement from practice and from the Academy presidency, Casson took to painting in watercolour more regularly, also tutoring the Prince of Wales.

He was sometimes dismissed as a lightweight but, like Kenneth Clarke, he was at his best as a communicator and populariser of what he knew, the evidence lying in the titles of some of his publications: *New sights of London* (1937), *Bombed churches* (1946), *Homes by the million* (1947), *Houses – permanence and prefabrication* (1947), *Victorian architecture* (1948), *Inscape: the design of interiors* (1968), (with Joyce Grenfell) *Nanny says* (1972), *Diary* (1981), *Hugh Casson's London* (1983), *Hugh Casson's Oxford* (1988), *Japan observed* (1991), *Hugh Casson's Cambridge* (1992), *The Tower of London: an artist's portrait* (1993).

He was a warm-hearted and public-spirited man whose diplomatic skills were brought to bear in a number of situations, not least his presidency of the Royal Academy, and who was prepared to accept ideas that he might not have liked himself. During his time at that venerable and august institution he persuaded academicians and staff to join him in a crusade to transform a dusty, antiquated and reactionary institution. He founded the Friends' organisation in 1977 and set up a development office in order to raise funds to modernise an historic building in need of upgrading. 'Casson had great personal charm and an instinct for seeing the best in everyone. However, his tolerant acceptance of many points of view sometimes gave the impression that he was on all sides at once. This became a difficulty in his professional life, when as a consultant he several times found himself in an awkward position. He puzzled his admirers by remaining architectural adviser to Bath City Council while much of the city's Georgian heritage was being destroyed, and as adviser to Brighton while that city was permitting developments damaging to its Regency character. At the same time Casson was an assiduous supporter of conservation organisations such as the Georgian Group and the Victorian Society. It is not that he was insincere; but he liked to please, and toughness was not in his nature. He was simply too nice a man.'[41]

He was made an honorary fellow of University College, London. He was knighted in 1952 for his work in the Festival of Britain, made a KCVO in 1978, and a CH in 1985 'For services to Architecture and the Arts.' He died in 1999.

Sir John Summerson 31 December 1986
John Summerson, curator of Sir John Soane's Museum in London for nearly forty years, was at the time of his death the doyen of English architectural historians.

He was born in 1904 and educated at Harrow and at the Bartlett School of Architecture, University College, London. He worked for short periods in various architect's offices from 1926, but soon gave up a prospective career as an architect in favour of teaching and writing. He was an instructor at the school of architecture in the Edinburgh College of Art (1929–30), and assistant editor of *The architect and building news* (1934–41). His first book, *John Nash. Architect to George IV*, was published in 1935, and became the standard work on the subject. He was deputy director of the National Buildings Record (1941–45), during which time he walked the streets of London taking photographs of endangered buildings. He was then appointed curator of Sir John Soane's Museum in 1945 and held that post until his retirement in 1984. He was also a member of the council of the Architectural Association (1940–45); lecturer in the history of art at the Architectural Association (1949–62), at Birkbeck College (1950–67); Slade professor of fine art at Oxford (1958–59) and at Cambridge (1966–67); Ferens professor of fine art at Hull (1960–61 and 1970–71); and held lectureships at several American universities. He held numerous public appointments: he was a member of the Royal Fine Art Commission (1947–54), the Royal Commission on Historical Monuments (England) (1953–74), the Historic Buildings Council (1953–78), the arts panel of the Arts Council (1953–56), the Historical Manuscripts Commission (1959–84), the listed buildings committee of the ministry of housing (1944–66, chairman 1960–62), and a trustee of the National Portrait Gallery (1966–73). He was also chairman of the National Council for Diplomas in Art and Design (1961–70), but modern art education never really interested him, and there was criticism in his time that the council's recommendations did not meet contemporary needs. He was forced to confront modern art on a more domestic front as the brother in law of the sculptor Dame Barbara Hepworth.

His natural reserve produced 'a somewhat aloof and seemingly haughty style', but he was an effective broadcaster. 'Both as a writer and a speaker he was remarkable for his polished elegance and fluency, peppered by a dry wit.'[42] His publications were numerous and included: *Architecture here and now* (1934), *Georgian London* (1946), *Ben Nicholson* (1948), *Heavenly mansions* (1949), *Sir John Soane* (1952), *Architecture in Britain 1530–1830* (1953), *A new description of Sir John Soane's museum* (1953), *Sir Christopher Wren* (1953), *Inigo Jones* (1966), *The classical language of architecture* (1964), *The London building world of the eighteen-sixties* (1974), *The life and work of John Nash, architect* (1981), *The unromantic castle* (1990), and two volumes to *The history of the king's works* (1976 and 1982).

His preference for the past extended to his working conditions at Sir John Soane's Museum where for thirty-nine years his management style was quaint to say the least. He worked on an antique typewriter and usually answered the museum's only telephone himself. But he could be impish. 'Summerson's reserved and sometimes severe manner concealed a dry sharp humour. His opinions were positive, but when expressed in public were sometimes deliberately provocative. He was fond, for example, of testing out the climate of a meeting by making some outrageous statement and then sitting back, completely impassive, while others argued round it. Later, quite unabashed, he would speak out from the opposite point of view, leaving the meeting deflated and confused. The most extreme example of this contrariness was when he was asked to Dublin to support the fight for a long run of Georgian houses in Fitzwilliam Street that the Electricity Board was seeking to demolish. Summerson's crushing judgement "one damned house after another" set back the preservation of Georgian Dublin, a far more complete Georgian city, for years.'[43]

He was elected a fellow of the British Academy in 1944. He was made a CBE in 1952, knighted in 1958 and appointed a CH in 1986 'For services to the history of Architecture.' He died in 1992.

Dame Elizabeth Frink 13 June 1992

Elizabeth Frink was an outstanding sculptor who shunned the development of a personality cult and was never as widely known as she could have been. Her work had three themes: the nature of man; the 'horseness' of horses; and the divine in human form.

She was born at Thurlow, Suffolk in 1930, the daughter of an army officer of Dutch, German and Hugenot descent. She was educated at the Convent of the Holy Family, Exmouth. She trained at Guildford School of Art (1947–49) and Chelsea School of Art (1949–53), and then taught at Chelsea (1953–61) and St Martin's School of Art (1954–62). In 1964 she became a visiting instructor at the Royal College of Art.

Her father was a polo player, who at one point was attached to an Indian regiment as riding instructor. In Trieste in 1946 he had charge of the hundreds of horses liberated throughout Europe at the end of the war. Frink grew up with horses and she learned to ride at the age of four. She grew up during the 1939–45 war and lived near an airfield in Suffolk where aircraft crashes were a common sight. By 1949 two themes were already evident: naked men on powerful horses, and predatory, menacing birds crows, hawks and eagles. She said that her birds were 'vehicles for strong feelings of panic, tension, aggression and predatoriness.'[44]

She came to prominence in the 1950s when her prize entry for the 'Unknown Political Prisoner' international competition in 1952 brought her to the attention of other sculptors. The Tate Gallery had already bought in 1953 her *Bird* (1952), which was exhibited at the Beaux Arts Gallery in London. Her first one-person show was at St George's Gallery in 1955. The birds led on to figures of 'birdmen' commissioned by London County Council in 1958 and Sedgehill School, Lewisham, in 1961. Her reputation grew stronger for her work in the humanist school, in which the human and mostly male figure remained her central motif. Heads of all sizes, torsoes and full size figures all convey the strengths and vulnerabilities of man (she rarely sculpted female figures). 'During the 1960s her figures – typically bronze horses and riders or male nudes – became smoother, but she retained a feeling of the bizarre in her over-life-size heads.'[45] In 1967–73 she lived in France. From that period, came her 'goggle heads.' 'The power of these images lies in their ambivalence: bull-necked, hair cropped, thin-lipped, eyes shaded, hiding moral weakness under a show of physical strength.'[46] Her work included numerous commissions beginning with the concrete *Wild boar* (1957) for Harlow New Town, and a typical piece is *Horse and Rider* (in London's Piccadilly, at the corner of Dover Street), commissioned by Trafalgar House Investments. *Blind beggar and his dog*, in Roman Road, London E3 was listed by English Heritage in 1996. She was influenced by her Christian upbringing and undertook a number of religious commissions including the *Eagle Lectern* (1962) for Coventry Cathedral, *Risen Christ* at Solihull, *Crucifixion* in Belfast, *Walking Madonna* (1981) for Salisbury Cathedral and her bronze *Christ* unveiled at Liverpool Cathedral in the month of her death.

Frink was a trustee of the British Museum (1975–89), and of the Royal Fine Art Commission (1976–81). In the 1980s there was a move to elect her as the first woman president of the Royal Academy. But she declined involvement on the ground that it would take too much time from her work as a sculptor.

She was an honorary fellow of St Hilda's College, Oxford and Newnham College, Cambridge. She was appointed a CBE in 1969, a DBE in 1982, and a CH in 1992 for her services as a 'Sculptor'. She died of cancer less than a year later.

Carel Weight 31 December 1994

Carel Weight was a visionary artist with a talent for depicting the everyday life of the urban areas in which he spent his childhood. His relish for the ordinary and the commonplace details of street furniture and facade, led a critic to describe him as something of a 'John Betjeman of painting'.

He was born in Paddington, London in 1908 into a family of partly German and partly Swedish descent. His mother worked as a chiropodist and manicurist mainly to the acting profession. His father was an unwilling bank cashier. From the age of a few months up to 18, their son was 'put out' during weekdays with a poor family in a derelict area of Chelsea, and later Fulham. He was educated at the local Board school for poor children and then at Sloane Secondary School. '[His] playgrounds as a lonely child were the shabby streets and alleys and the public parks of south-west London, in particular Bishop's Park in Fulham and Battersea Park. These provided the setting for many of his subsequent paintings, against which he pieced his disturbing human psychodramas – acted out by a cast of remembered characters of run-down London and fantasy figures called up by the imagination of a lonely child. "A fairly lonely childhood is, I think, rather a good thing for an artist," he once said.'[47]

He originally trained to be a singer (he had a fine baritone voice), but changed to painting and studied at Hammersmith School of Art (1928–30). From there he won a scholarship to the Royal College of Art, but could not afford to take it up. Instead he studied two days a week at the School of Art at Goldsmiths College (1930–33). At Goldsmiths he met his life partner Helen Roder whom he married in 1990 when he was eighty-two.

His work was first exhibited in 1931 at the Royal Academy (he was elected a fellow in 1965), and led to a part-time teaching post at Beckenham College of Art (1932–42). He had his first solo show at Cooling Galleries in 1933. During the 1939–45 war he served (from 1942) in the Royal Engineers and the Royal Army Education Corps. He was an official war artist (1945–46) and worked in Austria, Greece and Italy.

In 1946 he joined the Royal College of Art as a teacher of painting. He was made a fellow of the college in 1956 and was professor of painting (1957–73), when he became professor emeritus. He was the senior fellow of the college from 1984 until his death. He presided over the remarkable flowering of individual talent that took place there over those years – particularly in the Pop Art generation of David Hockney and his contemporaries. He was regarded with affection by many of his students who achieved prominence long before he did. 'Several of his students won international fame almost on graduation, while he and his fellow teachers were dismissed as hopeless reactionaries in thrall to a moribund tradition. He was always open to new ideas, but his belief in the necessity of sound technique, and his insistence that art should be essentially a humanist activity, left him out of sympathy with many of the developments of the 1960s and 1970s.'[48]

After a retrospective exhibition at the Royal Academy in 1982, his work became more fashionable, and another retrospective was held at the Newport Museum and Art Gallery in 1993. 'His adoption of a style of slightly awkward naive realism, sometimes loosely brushed and veering towards the surreal and expressionist. . . He moved into that vital (but often neglected) artistic realm of psychological, emotional and spiritual realism, where by exaggeration and distortion of physical form, "ordinary" people in an "ordinary" scene are shown pulled, twisted, and swept away by the revealed force of the movement of their minds, the violence of their emotions and the ghosts of their shared past disturbing the calm of their spirit . . . His eye for the colours of the urban scene – particularly the London sooty air and acid soil before the Clean Air Act of 1963 – was vividly precise.'[49]

He was regarded as one of the most important British artists of his generation and had a unique reputation for representing the anxieties and personal disturbances caused by the twentieth century. In 1979 he said, 'I aim to create in my painting a world superficially close to the visual one but a world of greater tension and drama . . . My art is concerned with such things as anger, love, fear, hate and loneliness, emphasized by the ordinary landscape in which the dramatic scene is set.'[50]

He once declaimed, 'I don't like the art world very much, I don't like the dealers and I don't like the critics.'[51] He held exhibitions at private galleries only when he couldn't get out of it. He painted about fifty pictures a year, but was never ruthless in marketing them. He preferred them to go to those who would appreciate them rather than selling them for the highest possible price.

He was made an honorary fellow of Goldsmiths College, elected an associate of the Royal Academy in 1955, and a full academician in 1965. He was appointed a CBE in 1961, and a CH in 1994 as 'Professor Emeritus, Royal College of Art. For services to Art.' He died in 1997.

Sir Denys Lasdun 17 June 1995
Denys Lasdun was considered one of the most influential and highly-regarded architects of his generation, with an international reputation.

He was born in 1914, and educated at Rugby and the Architectural Association's School of Architecture. His career began in 1935 soon after modernism was introduced to Britain from continental Europe, and his primary inspirations were Le Corbusier and cubist painting, but there was a classical echo in his work reinforced by his study of the English Baroque, especially the work of Nicholas Hawksmoor. His first work was the house at 32 Newton Road, Paddington, London, designed in 1937 and commissioned by an artist. His principal works include schools in London, including Hallfield Primary School in Paddington, his pioneering 'cluster' blocks of flats at Bethnal Green in east London, the London offices of the New South Wales government, the Royal College of Physicians building, Fitzwilliam College and the extension to Christ's College, Cambridge, the University of East Anglia (1962–68), buildings for Liverpool, Leicester and London universities, and the first phase of the European

Investment Bank, Luxembourg (1974–80), commissioned by the EEC. At East Anglia he 'arranged living and teaching accommodation in the form of concentrated masses which merged in the distant view into one highly impressive, fascinatingly modulated sequence of ziggurats.'[52]

Lasdun's most well known work is the cubist mass of the Royal National Theatre (1963–76) on London's south bank. Arnold Goodman related the story of the choice of Lasdun to design this landmark. 'A committee of three met with a number of architects picked at random and interviewed them. Their innermost souls told them, possibly rightly, that the best applicant was Mr Denys Lasdun and so this immensely talented peacock of the slide-rule was installed in office to produce designs which will be the subject of controversy for a generation. His concept was vast, massive and expensive. For every inch of auditorium and every millimetre of stage, he had feet, if not acres, of foyers, vestibules and other aesthetic irrelevancies that delighted our hearts and tortured the representatives of the Greater London Council on the South Bank Theatre Board.'[53]

In 1962–63 he was Hoffman Wood visiting professor in architecture at the University of Leeds. He was a member of the international committee invited to Jerusalem in 1970 to advise on the planning of that city, and designed the new Hurva Synagogue for the Old City. In 1971 he acted as an assessor in the competition for the Belgrade opera house. He served as a trustee of the British Museum (1975–85), the Victoria and Albert Museum advisory committee (1978–83) and the arts panel of the Arts Council (1980–84). But he never played any significant role in architectural politics or the work of the professional institutions, perhaps due in part to his often uncompromising temperament. 'When he had arrived at what he was convinced was the right solution to a problem, he adhered to it with a firmness and an unwillingness to compromise which sometimes seemed to amount to obstinacy . . . This self-belief led him to defend some of his buildings against threats to alter them, or even to demolish them – threats which distressed him profoundly. His department store in the Strand was demolished . . . but his fight to save the Bethnal Green flats eventually succeeded . . . Although in the 1990s he stopped the destruction of one of the first-floor balconies at the National, essential to the order of the entire building, he failed in his attempt to preserve his treasured porte-cochere, vital to his vision of the entrance. His lifelong insistence on the rightness of his own judgement was a contrast to his quiet, reasonable personality and his unassertive manner. He was often unforthcoming with strangers, but always affectionate with friends.'[54]

He was made a military MBE in 1945, the result of service with the Royal Engineers in the 1939–45 war, a CBE in 1965, knighted in 1976, and appointed a CH in 1995 'For services to Architecture.' He died in 2001.

David Hockney 14 June 1997
David Hockney has been one of the most widely discussed and documented artists of his generation. He achieved international success by his mid-twenties, based not only on the flair, wit and versatility of his work, but also on his colourful personality. This has made him a recognisable figure, even to those who have no interest in art, and he was the subject of a 1974 film, *The bigger splash*, named after one of his paintings, which featured a Californian swimming pool.

He was born at Bradford in 1937. Between 1953 and 1957 he studied at the Bradford School of Art. A conscientious objector, he spent his national service working in a hospital until 1959. From 1959 to 1962 he studied at the Royal College of Art, London where he met the founders of Pop Art, including Richard Hamilton, and his early work was associated with that movement which flourished from the late 1950s to the early 1970s in the United Kingdom and the USA, and was based on the imagery of consumerism and popular culture.

From 1960 he began showing in the Young Contemporaries exhibitions at the RBA Galleries. By 1961 he had done his first *Tea paintings* and *Love paintings*, painted compositions consisting of consumer goods images and psychograms. More than any others, these pictures showed his proximity to Pop Art. In 1961 he was represented at the Paris Biennale and awarded the Guinness Award for Etching. He also visited New York for the first time. He taught at Maidstone College of Art in 1962. In 1963 he travelled to Egypt and Los Angeles, where he met Henry Geldzahler and Dennis Hopper. He did his first paintings of showers at this time. From 1963 to 1964 he taught at the University of Iowa. In 1964 he settled in Los Angeles, painted his first swimming-pool pictures and made his first polaroids. About that time he began to paint more directly and to show increasing interest in rendering what the eye saw. 'His painting have since tended to become more straightforward, with a regard for light, space and volume, and are usually executed either from drawings or from his own photographs . . . including a number of portraits of his friends. He has worked much in California, which has provided the themes of many of his pictures. His paintings, drawings and prints have a strongly individual flavour and often provide an irreverent and amusing commentary on contemporary life.'[55] His paintings included one of Sir John Gielgud at the age of seventy. Gielgud's published reaction was probably genuine. 'I thought that if I really looked like that, I must kill myself tomorrow.'[56]

From 1965 to 1967 he held teaching posts at the University of Colorado and the University of California, Berkeley. He had a retrospective exhibition in London in 1970, also shown at Hanover and Rotterdam. Between 1973 and 1975 he lived in Paris. An exhibition of his works was shown at the Musée des Arts Décoratifs in 1974. He created his first opera design for Igor Stravinsky's *The rake's progress*, performed at Glyndebourne in 1975. In 1978 he designed the décor for Mozart's *The magic flute*, also produced at Glyndebourne, and in 1980 he developed a programme for the Metropolitan Opera with works by Satie, Poulenc, Ravel and Stravinsky. From 1976 he began to experiment extensively with photography, producing photographic collages and prints created on photocopiers. In 1981 he travelled in China, following which *China diary* (written with Stephen Spender) was published. He designed covers for *Vogue* in 1984 and 1985, the set for Wagner's *Tristan and Isolde* at the Los Angeles Music Centre in 1986–87, and carpet patterns for a company in 1988. His book *David Hockney by David Hockney* (1976) became one of the most popular art books of the time.

In 1999–2000 he drew portraits of twelve warders working at the National Gallery, rather than the trustees of the gallery because he knew they would be on duty in the very rooms where his drawings would be displayed, offering the visitor an unparalleled opportunity for comparing the portrait with the actual person. 'He also liked the fact that they tended to be shy people whom others normally do not notice, since their job is to sit in a corner and observe visitors without drawing attention to themselves. By nature patient people, they were likely to make good models, able to sit still for long periods, even though most of them had never been drawn before.' The sitters were chosen from the greatest variety of male and female, different ages, races and physical types.

It is difficult to imagine the title 'Sir' as a prefix to David Hockney's name, and the CH that he accepted in 1997, 'For services to Art', was the first state honour accorded him.

Bridget Riley 31 December 1998
Bridget Riley is an abstract painter who is recognised as a pioneer of the school of 'Optical Art' painting that developed in the 1960s.

She was born in 1931 and educated at Cheltenham Ladies College. She was trained at Goldsmiths College (1949–52) and the Royal College of Art (1952–55). She has a distinguished role in the British art scene as a painter, writer and organiser of exhibitions. She has been an artist of international reputation since the early 1960s with one-man exhibitions in London, New York, Los Angeles, Hanover, Turin, Berne, Basle, Zurich, Dusseldorf, Prague, Rome, Stockholm, Sydney and Tokyo. She was given retrospective exhibitions at the Hayward Gallery in 1972 and 1992, and she became widely recognised as the outstanding abstract painter of her generation. In 1965 she represented Britain at the Paris Biennale where she was awarded the Chief International Prize, and the Venice Biennale in 1968 where she won the International Painting Prize.

For those who met her, Bridget Riley had all the determination and discipline of an old-fashioned hospital matron (with an impish but kindly sense of humour), a trait observed by Arnold Goodman. 'There is no doubt that she is an artist of great talent, but more than that she is a person of great determination and character. I met her first when she refused to join the Arts Council, and in fact had a view that she should have nothing to do with the Establishment. In later years this has altered: she has become a trustee of the National Gallery [1981–88, during the period of considerable controversy about the nature and quality of the extension] and is regarded as the natural leader of the artistic proletariat. I recollect when I was at the Arts Council, how intensely she worked to organise accommodation for a great number of artists at St Katherine's Dock, where she exercised an iron discipline with those who took the accommodation, requiring them to keep it clean and tidy and, although a slight and attractive figure, instilling in them such a terror that not a single one of them would dare to deviate from the rules.'[57]

She has specialised in the art form known as 'Optical Art'. The term was coined in the 1960s to describe the work of a growing group of abstract painters who specialised in a mathematically-oriented form of usually abstract art, which uses repetition of simple forms and colours to create vibrating effects, moiré patterns, an exaggerated sense of depth, foreground-background confusion, and other visual effects. All painting is based on tricks of visual perception: using rules of perspective to give the illusion of three-dimensional space, mixing colours to give the impression of light and shadow. With Optical Art, the rules that the eye applies to make sense of a visual image are themselves the 'subject' of the artwork. By her careful juxtaposition of colours, her paintings often create effects of vibration and dazzle and a less sophisticated assessment was delivered by the *Daily Telegraph*, which described her as 'famous for creating migraine-inducing hallucinatory images.'[58] But she also designed a decorative scheme for the interior of the Royal Liverpool Hospital (1983) using soothing bands of blue, pink, white and yellow which was reported to have caused a drop in graffiti.[59] Examples of her work can be found in the Tate Gallery and the Victoria and Albert Museum in London, Hull, and Ulster, in Buffalo, New York and Pasadena, and in Amsterdam, Berne, Canberra and Tokyo.

She is an honorary fellow of Goldsmiths College. She was made a CBE in 1972 and a CH in 1998 as 'Artist. For services to Art'.

Richard Hamilton 31 December 1999
Richard Hamilton is a painter and printmaker and regarded as the founder of British 'Pop Art'.

He was born in London in 1922 and left school at fourteen. In 1936 he worked in the publicity department of an electrical company and attended evening classes in painting. He studied at Westminster Technical College and St. Martin's School of Art. In 1937 he worked in the publicity department of the Reimann Studios. From 1938 to 1940 he studied painting at the Royal Academy Schools. During the war he worked as an engineering draughtsman. He was readmitted to the Royal Academy Schools in 1946 but was expelled in the same year as a result of apparently unsatisfactory work. He studied painting at the Slade School of Art (1948–51). His etchings from this period were exhibited at his first one-man exhibition at Gimpel Fils, 1950. The first exhibition he designed himself was *Growth and form* at the Institute of Contemporary Art, London, 1951. In 1952 he became a teacher of silver work, typography and industrial design at the Central School of Arts and Crafts. One of his colleagues there was Eduardo Paolozzi, with whom Hamilton was a founder member of the 'Independent Group' at the ICA. This was a group of artists and intellectuals who met to discuss cultural change in the age of technology. In 1953 he became a lecturer in the fine art department at King's College, Newcastle upon Tyne. In this post he worked with Victor Pasmore and taught a course in basic design which was also attended by art students, and he became a figure of extraordinary influence on two generations of British artists. As a maker of exhibitions he was responsible for some of the most important exhibitions of the postwar years, notably *Growth and form* and *Man, machine and motion*, both at the ICA and *This is tomorrow* at the Whitechapel Art Gallery.

In 1955 he exhibited his own paintings at the Hanover Gallery in London. His paintings at this time were influenced by cubism. During the early part of his career he worked in a variety of styles, including paintings with a small number of points related to one another by criss-crossed lines, and organized several didactic exhibitions. In 1956 he made the collage *Just what is it makes today's homes so different, so appealing?* as a design for the poster and catalogue of the exhibition *This is tomorrow* (a satire on suburbia and consumerism) at the Whitechapel Gallery, which he had helped to organize with other members of the Independent Group. It was his first and the probably the first true Pop work to be made anywhere and reflects his interest in mass commercial culture, advertisements and pin-ups. In spite of this interest in ephemeral, glamorous and gimmicky non-fine art imagery, his work has remained intellectual and highly complex. It often combines painted areas with photographic images drawn from a wide range of sources, so as to draw attention to a process of ambiguity, or to allude to the characteristics of some earlier style such as cubism.

From 1957 to 1961 he taught interior design at the Royal College of Art, and painting at King's College, Newcastle upon Tyne (1953–66) (the University of

Newcastle from 1963). In 1960 he was awarded the William and Norma Copley Foundation Prize for Painting. He also published a typographical version of Marcel Duchamp's *Green Box*. In 1965 he began his reconstruction of Marcel Duchamp's *Le Grand Verre*. He organised the Duchamp retrospective at the Tate Gallery in 1966. His works on the theme of the Guggenheim Museum were also shown at the Robert Fraser Gallery. In 1969 he helped to make a film of his work for the Arts Council. In 1970 he showed his *Cosmetic Studies*. He was given his first comprehensive retrospective exhibition in 1979 at the Tate Gallery, also shown at the Kunsthalle, Berne. In 1974 he had retrospectives at the Guggenheim Museum, New York, the Städtische Galerie, Munich, and the Kunsthalle, Tübingen. In 1982 his writings, notes and documents were published under the title *Collected words 1952–82*. A second retrospective exhibition took place at the Tate in 1992 (a recognition only matched by Francis Bacon). He was British representative at the Venice Biennale in 1993.

The CH was conferred on him in the New Year List 2000 'For services to Art.'

CHAPTER SEVEN

Music of the spheres

COMPOSERS, CONDUCTORS, SINGERS, MUSICOLOGISTS,
IMPRESARIOS

Of all the strange things that Alice saw in her journey through the looking-glass, this was the one that she always remembered most clearly . . . All this she took in like a picture, as, with one hand shading her eyes, she leant against a tree . . . listening in a half-dream, to the melancholy music.

'It's my own invention', *Through the looking-glass*, Lewis Carroll

The musical category includes the diverse work of a group of individuals for whom music has been a lifelong profession or love. The art of music is as creative as the art of writing, though less dependent on the vagaries of public taste rising and falling from one generation to another. Whereas some of the 'literary' Companions have been forgotten and their writings lie unread, the names and reputations of the 'composer' Companions mostly continue to endure, even if some of their works do not. Although many composers have been completely forgotten, their compositions unpublished and no longer performed, others have remained prominent because of the abiding popularity of a few of their works, and a few are remembered because of the brilliance of most if not all their compositions. The works of a composer survive partly by the extent to which they continue to be performed and partly by the extent to which recordings of such performances are continually released in one or more of several formats in the changing world of technology. The interpretative techniques of the conductor and the vocal skills of the singer are similarly enshrined in their performances, and similarly dependent on whether recordings of their particular interpretations continue to be re-issued.

Music entered the ranks of the CH with the appointment of Frederick Delius (1929), and then only after the repeated attempts of Sir Thomas Beecham to secure an honour for the composer whose profile he had done so much to raise. Delius remained the sole 'musical' member of the Order for its first twenty-seven years, and his dreamlike and misty music, so evocative of the beauty of the natural world that enchanted him, continues to be performed and recorded. It was an auspicious beginning.

Nearly a quarter of a century passed before the appointment of the next composer, Benjamin Britten (1953) at the youthful age of forty. Britten had made his reputation with his opera *Peter Grimes* in 1945. His less successful opera *Gloriana* (about the life of Queen Elizabeth I) was composed to commemorate the coronation of Queen Elizabeth II, and his CH was conferred in the coronation honours list. His standing continued to rise; he was appointed an OM in 1965, following Edward Elgar and Ralph Vaughan Williams as the third composer to enter the ranks of that Order, and received a life peerage in 1976. More than twenty-five years after his death his reputation remains high in musical circles and his *Young person's guide to the orchestra* continues to teach successive generations of children.

Able and competent rather than outstanding, Arthur Bliss (1971) was not in the first rank of British composers. He acquired a reputation for composing music to accompany films and ballets, and for producing fanfares to commission. His ability to compose to order and his competency in administration and committee work made him a natural candidate to be master of the queen's music.

Although Herbert Howells (1972) composed on a wider basis, he is principally remembered as an archetypal 'church' composer, and his anthems for church and cathedral choirs, notably *A spotless rose*, have given him an enduring reputation in those circles.

Contemporary and equal of Benjamin Britten, Michael Tippett (1979) was, like Britten, a conscientious objector during the 1939–45 war, and suffered a brief period of imprisonment in 1943 which may have delayed his first honour – a CBE – until he was fifty-four. His oratorio – *A child of our time* – was the product of those war years and is probably his most well known composition. In 1984 he followed Britten into the ranks of the Order of Merit.

The demanding music of Harrison Birtwistle (2000) is far removed from the tranquil dreaming melodies of Frederick Delius, and the passage of time will judge which of his compositions will endure. To a contemporary generation the originality of his style is beyond question.

The first conductor was Henry Wood (1944), whose reputation as a populariser of music is forever associated with the annual BBC Promenade Concerts at the Royal Albert Hall in London. Thomas Beecham (1957) is remembered for his indefatigable promotion of the music of Frederick Delius, and also for a devastating and razor-sharp wit. Adrian Boult (1969) was a personal friend of Elgar, Vaughan Williams and Holst, and championed the work of British composers throughout his long life. The name of John Barbirolli (1969) is linked with the reconstruction and resurgence of the Hallé Orchestra, and will be as long as that orchestra survives. Arnold Goodman had no hesitation in exalting the three 'Bs' as he called them. '[They] were in their different ways the outstanding British conductors of my day – Beecham, Barbirolli and (perhaps a controversial choice) Adrian Boult – and they stand out from all the others.'[1] Colin Davis (2001) was renowned as an interpreter of the works of Berlioz, conductor of the London Symphony Orchestra and music director at the Royal Opera House, London. Bernard Haitink (2002) was Davis' successor at the Opera House after successful terms with the London Philharmonic Orchestra and the Glyndebourne Festival. He succeeded in maintaining the music at a high standard despite recurring financial crises.

An outstanding mezzo-soprano, Janet Baker's appointment (1993) was in part due to her many non-musical commitments.

Three 'musical' individuals in this chapter were providers of the stage rather than performers on it; music lovers rather than musicians. The work of John Christie (1954) revolved solely around Glyndebourne, the extraordinary operatic dream that he brought to fruition in his own back garden. George Christie (2001) essentially continued the work begun by his father and rebuilt the opera house at Glyndebourne. Patted on the head by Brahms at the age of eleven for his performance on the piano, Robert Mayer (1973) spent his adult life as a stockbroker and made his money dealing in non-ferrous metals on both sides of the Atlantic. So much money did he make that he was able to retire at the age of fifty and devote the rest of his long life (he lived to be one hundred and five) to introducing children and young people to the delights of music, that had played such an important part in his own childhood.

Edmund Fellowes (1944) was a musicologist who made pioneering studies of English renaissance music.

The 'musical' Companions of Honour amount to a small percentage of the total membership of the Order, but the number of outstanding British composers and conductors is also small, and those appointed to the Order have been highly esteemed by their musical contemporaries.

Frederick Delius 1 March 1929
Frederick Delius was a composer of misty and dreamy works that captured the beauties of nature.

He was born in Bradford in 1862, the second son of a wool merchant of German ancestry. Both his parents were born in Germany, but his father had become a British national in 1850. He was educated at Bradford Grammar School and at the International College at Isleworth, before the young Delius, who wished to make music his career, was ordered into the family business. Typical of the time, Delius' father did not consider music a proper livelihood, but he encouraged its performance in the home as a social pastime. The young Delius learned to play the piano and violin, but after college, he worked in his father's wool business for over three years as a travelling representative, visiting Sweden, Germany and France. His interest in music continued to be a passion, to the neglect of his business duties. Heated arguments followed until a compromise was agreed; the frustrated Julius Delius allowed his son to move to Florida to manage his orange plantation at Solano Grove, south of Jacksonville. 'There the solitude of the grove, the resplendent tropical scenery, and the strange music of the negroes combined to set the youth's imagination ablaze.'[2] A romantic streak in his nature absorbed the unique natural beauty along the St John's River, as well as the rich harmonic vocal improvisations of the local black slaves. He acquired a piano and met Thomas F. Ward, an organist from Brooklyn who was convalescing in the state and who spent six months improving his piano playing. He later wrote: 'In Florida, through sitting and gazing at Nature, I gradually learnt the way in which I should eventually find myself . . . [and] hearing singing in such romantic surroundings, it was then and there that I first felt the urge to express myself in music.'

In 1885 Delius set up as a teacher of piano and violin first at Jacksonville and then at Danville, Virginia. After losing touch with him for some time, his parents eventually managed to re-establish contact and finally agreed to support his musical career. In August 1886 Delius went to the Leipzig Conservatorium where he met the Norwegian composer Edvard Grieg who, like Ward before him, recognised Delius's talent. In the spring of 1888, an orchestra was hired and the first performance was given of the *Florida suite*. It received an enthusiastic ovation from an audience that numbered precisely three people, Grieg and Delius being two. Grieg remained a lifelong friend and when he died in 1907, Delius felt that he had lost his best friend. After the performance of *Florida suite*, Delius left Leipzig and moved to Paris where he lived for the next ten years befriending artists, writers, and musicians in the fin-de-siecle culture of the city and becoming a full-time composer. His orchestral work *Paris* (1899) captured his fascination with that city.

In 1897 he married an artist Jelka Helen von Rosen from a German diplomatic family and moved to Grez-sur-Loing near Fontainbleau, where he spent the rest of his life. 'From then until 1921 all the great works were composed in the quiet home at Grez with the garden running down to the river. Here the couple mostly remained except when the war came too dangerously near for comfort. Then, having buried the wine, they sought the temporary shelter of these shores [and Norway]. Otherwise there would merely be trips to Germany and England in order to hear Delius' works performed, and to the Norwegian mountains for the summer holidays.'[3]

After the war he continued to compose until about 1924, when the symptoms of his previously contracted syphilis forced his retirement from composition until 1928. In pain, blind and paralysed, Delius remained in Grez with his wife and a stream of visitors and admirers. By this time he had composed numerous tone poems, songs, incidental music, concerti for violin, cello and piano, violin and cello sonatas, and two string quartets, among other works. His six operas including *Koanga* (1895–97), *A village Romeo and Juliet* (1900–01) and *Fennimore and Gerda* (1908–10). Major choral works included *A mass of life* (1904–05) and *Requiem* (1914–16). In 1928 his young amanuensis Eric Fenby arrived at Grez and helped in the composition and completion of several works. From this period come some of Delius' most poignant and profound works.

Delius' renown was first established in Germany, and not until about 1910, when a young conductor named Thomas Beecham took up his works, did he begin to achieve substantial recognition in the United Kingdom. There followed a steady increase in the performances of his works, and when Beecham returned from his period of self-imposed retirement in 1924 Delius rapidly became a popular success. A six-day Delius Festival was held at the Queen's Hall in the autumn of 1929 in the presence and to the pride and satisfaction of the composer, who was now confined to a wheelchair. He told Fenby, 'I have only one wish as far as my best music is concerned – I want Thomas to record it all.' In his biography of Delius, Thomas Beecham painted a picture of his favourite composer. 'His features had that mingled cast of asceticism and shrewdness one mentally associates with high-ranking ecclesiastics. I was also struck by a general air of fastidiousness and sober elegance rarely to be observed in artists of any kind. Unexpectedly contrasting, but not unpleasing, was his style of speech, of which the underlying basis was recognisably provincial. Not for him was the blameless diction so laboriously inculcated and standardised in our leading public schools and ancient universities. He loyally preserved his preference for the Doric dialect of that great northern county of broad acres . . . Upon this had been grafted a polyglot mish-mash, acquired during his twenty-four years self-imposed exile from England. Both French and German words interlarded his sentences, and he always spoke of the "orchester".'[4]

Like many creative and artistic individuals, Delius could be difficult. '"But it's not music," expostulated Delius one day, humming a misquotation from Beethoven. His bitterly caustic tongue, at strange variance with his music, in a harsh almost rasping accent, half Bradford, half foreign, would thus give pungent expression to his distaste for the classics. Another violent antipathy was towards the verbal discussion of composition technique . . . Both these traits explain to some extent his curious isolation in musical realms, for apart from a superficial affinity with Grieg's his music derives from nothing and leads nowhere.

Professional critics have decried his lack of "form" and amateur listeners have complained of monotony of texture. Both strictures are half just. He disdained the use of mechanical expedient to secure semblance of "form", so that the innocent listener, deprived of such adventitious aids to sustained attention, cannot always follow the composer's thought and tends to become drowsy with the sheer sensuous beauty of sound from moment to moment . . . Intensely susceptible to the beauties of nature and to the emotions, joys and sorrows of life, Delius made these the inspiration of all his most lovely works.'[5] By their titles, many of his works indicate an affinity with natural beauty: *Over the mountains high* (1885), *Florida suite* (1886–87), *Norwegian sleigh ride* (1887), *Summer evening* (1890), *Spring morning* (1890), *Over the hills and far away* (1893–97), *Appalachia* (1896), *Summer landscape* (1902), *Sea-Drift* (1903–04), *Songs of sunset* (1906–07), *Song of the high hills* (1911–12), *North country sketches* (1913–14), *On hearing the first cuckoo in spring* (1912), *Summer night on the river* (1911), *In a summer garden* (1908), *To be sung of a summer night on the water* (1917), *Song before sunrise* (1918), *A song of summer* (1929). One author advised of the risk in hearing Delius's music too often: 'Its sensuous autumnal beauty induces a profound nostalgia, a passionate and fruitless desire to stop the clocks, to recapture the past. I was once told of a man who on hearing Delius's more sensuous music was seized by an almost uncontrollable urge to remove all his clothing and engage in Pan-like diversions quite unsuited to his profession – which was that of a solicitor's clerk. He was, fortunately, sufficiently controlled to limit his response to the urge to the privacy of his chamber.'[6]

Although Bradford was by now a distant memory for Delius, the city conferred its freedom on him in 1932, and in 1933 he received an honorary doctorate of music from the University of Leeds. Oxford had intended to confer a DMus degree on him in 1929, but at the last moment he was unable to attend.

The CH was conferred on Delius in March 1929 for his services as a 'Composer', after Ralph Vaughan Williams, Sir Thomas Beecham, Lady Cunard, and Geoffrey Tancred, editor of the *Yorkshire Evening Post* had made representations. By this time Delius was unable to attend an investiture. 'I beg to acknowledge the receipt of the royal command. Unfortunately I am blind and paralysed and confined to my chair, so that the state of my health prevents me from attending the investiture on March 26th, to my great regret. I therefore beg His Royal Highness the Prince of Wales graciously to excuse me from being present. I remain faithfully yours, Frederick Delius.'[7] The badge was accordingly presented to Delius at his own home, by Sir Nevile Henderson, British ambassador in Paris, 'in an official and ceremonial manner in the presence of his family.'[8] In his biography of Delius, Beecham recalled the composer receiving the news with 'calm and dignity. . . I think he was on the whole gratified by this token of official recognition. He was sufficiently man of the world to know that any distinction of this kind raises the recipient in the estimation of the general public'.[9] He died in 1934 and after a temporary burial at Grez, his remains were interred at Limpsfield in Surrey in 1935.

The Reverend Edmund Horace Fellowes 1 January 1944
Edmund Fellowes was an Anglican priest and musicologist who spent his adult life in pioneering studies of English renaissance music.

Born in 1870 in Paddington, he was the second son of Horace Decimus Fellowes, assistant director of the Royal Army clothing depot. Both his parents were of landed gentry stock, his father from the Fellowes family of Shotesham Park, and his mother from the Packe family of Prestwold Hall, Leicestershire. With such a pedigree, it was inevitable that Edmund Fellowes should eventually find his way into a comfortable position within the church. He was educated at Winchester and at Oriel College, Oxford, from where he graduated in 1892 with a fourth class degree in theology. He found time to develop his musical interests and remained for a fourth year working towards a music degree. He was ordained in 1894, and after a short curacy in Wandsworth (1894–97) during which he took the Oxford BMus degree (1896), he was appointed precentor of Bristol Cathedral in 1897. In 1900 he was appointed to a minor canonry at St George's Chapel, Windsor, and there he remained until his death fifty-one years later.

From an early age, he demonstrated marked musical ability, and it was in this field that he achieved scholarship and renown. He was in charge of the choir of St George's Chapel between the death of Sir Walter Parratt in 1924 and the appointment of Sir Walford Davies in 1927, and he contributed five volumes to a series of historical monographs relating to the chapel. But his fame rested on his extensive work on sixteenth and seventeenth century English music. He became interested in the work of English madrigal composers in 1911, and it developed into a fascination that shaped the rest of his life. From that point he spent much of his spare time in studying and editing English music of the period 1545–1645, on which he became the leading authority. Single-handedly he edited thirty-six volumes of madrigals, thirty-two volumes of lute songs and twenty-nine volumes of Byrd's music. Among his significant published works were *The English madrigal composers* (1921) and *William Byrd* (1936). As honorary librarian of St Michael's College, Tenbury Wells, Worcestershire (1918–48), he arranged and catalogued the extensive music library left by Sir Frederick Ouseley. He was president of the Church Musical Society (1946–51) and president of the Royal Musical Association (1942–7). 'Scholar though he was, he was a performing musician even more, and his aim was to be not only accurate and informative but comprehensive and practical. His editions were intended to get the music performed, not to rest on a scholar's desk; but they were not to be mere selections. This conception was then a novelty; it has been amply justified by the natural familiarity of later generations with the field he tilled almost as a pioneer. When estimating his technical achievement as editor, as distinct from his range, discoveries and fruitful impact, it must be remembered that in Fellowes' day there was no organised training for musical research in England. He had to find his own way, and thereby contributed largely to the standards by which he will be judged. On his critical writings, whose contributions to knowledge are plain for all to see, it is a just comment that he viewed his subject in too insular a light.'[10] Fellowes had followed his own path with great proficiency, but he was still disappointed by his failure to obtain a canonry.

Honorary doctorates in music from Oxford (1939), Cambridge (1950) and Dublin (1917), and an honorary fellowship of Oriel College (1937), must have provided a measure of compensation, as did his CH in 1944, 'For services to the history of English music.' He had helped to make accessible in a scholarly way, a large amount of the finest music from the Tudor and Stuart periods, and Adrian Boult and Ralph Vaughan Williams and many others welcomed his candidature for an honour. He died in 1951.

Sir Henry Wood 8 June 1944
Henry Wood is remembered as the founder of the annual BBC Promenade Concerts at the Royal Albert Hall.

He was born in 1869, the only child of Henry Wood, an optician and model engineer who was a keen amateur cellist and for twenty-five years tenor soloist at St Sepulchre's Church, Holborn. His mother, the daughter of a Welsh farmer, had a natural soprano voice and developed her son's interest in music by providing him with tuition in his early years. 'Otherwise the child was self-taught and it is remarkable evidence of his gifts that at the age of ten he often acted as deputy organist at St Mary Aldermanbury.'[11] In childhood painting was as much an interest as music and for some years Wood studied in his spare time at the Slade School of Fine Art and the St John's Wood School of Fine Art. In 1911 he gave an exhibition of fifty sketches in oil at the Piccadilly Arcade in aid of the Queen's Hall Orchestra Endowment Fund. He studied composition and singing for two years at the Royal Academy of Music, and after leaving he composed a mass, a number of songs and arrangements of works by Purcell, Handel and J. S. Bach. But he never developed as a composer; his ability as an accompanist and his knowledge of singing led him inevitably to the musical stage and to conducting.

His first professional attempt at conducting was in 1889, and in the following year he was invited by Richard D'Oyly Carte to superintend the rehearsals of *Ivanhoe* for Sir Arthur Sullivan. A series of conducting engagements continued through the 1890s, though he continued his work as an accompanist and a teacher of singing. In 1894 Robert Newman, the manager of the Queen's Hall decided to run a series of promenade concerts and chose Wood to be the conductor. Beginning in 1895 the 'proms' became 'the most remarkable and influential series of concerts in the history of British music.'[12] The concerts were a popular success, and Wood conducted a command performance at Windsor Castle in 1898 before Queen Victoria. Despite the heavy schedule of London concerts, he found time to train and conduct an increasing number of provincial choral societies and orchestras. In 1898 he accepted the post of director of the Nottingham Sacred Harmonic Society and later founded the Nottingham City Orchestra. In 1900 he was appointed conductor of the Wolverhampton Festival Choral Society, in 1902 of the Sheffield, in 1904 of the Westmoreland, and in 1908 of the Norwich festivals. 'Such activity could only have been undertaken by a man of phenomenal energy who possessed also the most detailed knowledge of his work, a man who prepared everything minutely in advance, not only for himself but for all those with whom he was associated. A mere clockwork precision, however, was far from his ideal. Wood was one of the earliest British conductors to insist on the importance of interpretation, and his scores were invariably marked with a wealth of expressive detail. It was characteristic that when he was about to conduct Bach's B minor Mass at the Sheffield Festival of 1911, he sent each member of the choir 168 pages of notes on details of interpretation.'[13] Tempting offers came from America, and in 1918 he declined the offer of an appointment for six months each year with the Boston Symphony Orchestra.

As a result of Wood's negotiations, the promenade concerts came under the patronage of the BBC in 1927 and were broadcast for the first time. The earlier years of financial uncertainties were at an end, commercial considerations were excluded, and at a press interview, Wood declared that he was on the threshold of realising his lifelong ambition 'of truly democratising the message of music and making its beneficial effect universal.'[14] The 1939–45 war threatened the concerts when the BBC had to withdraw financial support and the Queen's Hall was destroyed by bombing in May 1941. The series was saved when the Royal Philharmonic Society agreed to fund the concerts in 1941, until the BBC resumed funding in 1942.

Wood was knighted in 1911 and his autobiography, *My life of music*, was published in 1938. Efforts were made to gain further recognition for him, and his supporters included such distinguished figures as Sir Hugh Allen, Sir Adrian Boult, Stanley Marchant, Lord Horder, Ralph Vaughan Williams, Sir James Jeans, Sir Walford Davies, George Dyson, W. Chetwynd Gardiner and Viscount Runciman of Doxford. Finally, he was appointed a CH in June 1944 at the age of seventy-five 'For services to music'. He conducted the opening night of the fiftieth promenade season a short while later, but his health had been failing and he died on 19 August 1944. His ashes were interred at the musician's church, St Sepulchre's, Holborn. 'By his thoroughness, integrity, enthusiasm and human understanding Wood did more than any other man to spread the love of orchestral music and raise its level of performance ... As a teacher of orchestras, choirs, and singers he influenced and developed almost every sphere of British music, while his constant encouragement of British composers was one of the greatest contributory factors in this country's musical renaissance.'[15]

Lord Britten 1 June 1953

Benjamin Britten was one of the foremost British composers of the twentieth century.

He was born in Lowestoft in 1913 – on St Cecilia's Day – the youngest child of a dental surgeon. His maternal grandfather was an active amateur singer and pianist, and secretary of the Lowestoft Choral Society. His mother, an amateur singer, gave him his first music lessons. He began composing his first works at the age of five, and produced prolifically throughout his childhood, despite his lack of musical guidance. He would compose before breakfast, to have time to go to school. He was educated at South Lodge Preparatory School, Lowestoft, where he caused a fuss in his last year by writing an essay that argued against hunting, and Gresham's School, Holt, then at the height of its 'progressive' reputation, selected by his parents as an environment that would encourage his talents and gifts.

Britten was 'discovered' by the composer Frank Bridge in 1927. Bridge gave him a technical foundation on which to base his creativity and introduced him to a wide range of composers from many different countries. Bridge was himself a pacifist, and their shared principle enabled the two men to empathise with each other, and Britten regarded Bridge as a 'musical conscience' throughout his life. In 1930, Britten went to the Royal College of Music to study piano and composition. According to Britten it was an unhelpful period and in his later years he remarked that he 'did not learn much'. Britten's antipathy to the college was partly due to a prevailing dislike in the musical establishment for the work of Bridge.

An invitation from the General Post Office film unit made Britten in effect the unit's resident composer and musical editor and in 1935 he collaborated with W. H. Auden on making two of the most memorable documentaries: *Coal Face* (1935) and *Night Mail* (1936). In the latter film, in order to recreate the effect of a train approaching through a tunnel, Britten recorded a cymbal crash, and reversed it. 'Auden's influence was profound: the apostle incarnate of Bohemianism blew away any vestiges of provinciality still clinging to Britten and it was probably about this time that he began to acknowledge and accept his homosexual nature.'[16]

He seemed set for a career of high promise but with his partner, the singer Peter Pears, he left England for the USA in May 1939. Various factors influenced the move: the worsening international situation, the examples of Auden and Isherwood who had already emigrated, the deaths of his father (in 1934) and his mother (in 1937), discouraging reviews of his music in the press, and the growth of his friendship with Pears (the two men had made their life together from 1937). 'An exemplary personal relationship that developed into one of the most distinguished and celebrated voice and piano duos of the twentieth century.'[17] They remained in Canada and the USA until March 1942 when they returned to England – the result of war time anxiety about family and friends, and a feeling of homesickness on the part of Britten. On their return they registered as conscientious objectors. The principal work of his war years was the bleak and pessimistic opera *Peter Grimes*, ironically performed on 7 June 1945 at the peak of the triumph of the allies. The success of the opera established Britten's international reputation, and he composed nine further operas including *The rape of Lucretia* (1946), *Albert Herring* (1947), *Little sweep or let's make an opera* (1949), *Billy Budd* (1951), *Gloriana* (1953), *The turn of the screw* (1954), *A midsummer night's dream* (1960) and *Death in Venice* (1973), each confirming the originality and range of his contribution to opera. From 1947 he and Pears lived at Aldeburgh in Suffolk and established the annual Aldeburgh Festival in 1948.

Britten was a prodigious composer in almost every genre: songs and song cycles, chamber music, orchestral music and choral music. His *War requiem* (1961), which used Auden's poetry, gave the fullest expression to his long-standing pacifist and anti-militarist beliefs and caught the imagination of a whole generation. It was held as the most impressive British choral work since Walton's *Belshazzar's feast* (1931). Another anti-war work, *Owen Wingrave* (1971) with words by Myfanwy Piper, was composed as a response to the Vietnam war. He wrote music for children, including *Noye's fludde* (1957) and *Young person's guide to the orchestra* (1945). An agnostic, Britten nevertheless composed some church music including *A boy was born* (1933), *Hymn to St Cecilia* (1942), *Rejoice in the lamb* (1943), *St Nicholas* (1948). A tribute to his mentor, *Variations on a theme of Frank Bridge*, appeared in 1937.

'Despite the assurance of public acclaim of a scale and global spread that had been enjoyed by no other British composer, Britten remained inwardly uncertain of his achievements. This insecurity was undoubtedly responsible for the unquestioning support he exacted of his friends and collaborators, and led in later years to an intellectual climate which did not much favour debate or dissonance . . . He was a truly modest, gentle, courteous, and generous man; but he could be ruthless when it came to professional standards or the achieving of a creative ambition, when he would absolutely not be thwarted. He was ready to sacrifice himself and others if the musical task demanded it.'[18] But he was not arrogant. 'People sometimes seem to think that, with a number of works now lying behind, one must be bursting with confidence. It is not so at all. I haven't achieved the simplicity I should like in my music, and I am enormously aware that I haven't yet come up to the technical standards Bridge set me.' Despite his own insecurities, his public reputation was assured.

He was plagued by ill-health in his last years. An attack of endocarditis in 1968 was followed by the discovery of a valvular heart-lesion, probably caused by rheumatic fever as a child. In 1971–72, symptoms of heart disease recurred, but he desperately wanted to finish his last opera, *Death in Venice*, and refused surgery until he had completed it. In 1973, he had an operation to replace a heart valve.

He was appointed a CH in 1953 for his services as 'Composer'. He was made an OM in 1965 and created a life peer in 1976. It was the first example of a peerage being conferred on a composer. He died in December of the same year, with no fear of dying and no conviction of what followed death.

John Christie 1 January 1954

The name of John Christie is commemorated by Glyndebourne, the opera house that he founded on his country estate near the town of Lewes in the Sussex countryside. Part country house and part opera house, it has for nearly seventy years, rightly or wrongly, evoked images of a gracious, elitist and plutocratic world of manicured lawns, dinner jackets, champagne picnics and operatic cognoscenti.

He was born in 1882 and educated at Eton and Trinity College, Cambridge. After service in the Boer War, he taught for a while at Eton and served again in the 1914–18 war. On the death of his father in 1931, Christie inherited substantial wealth and found himself able to give free rein to his love of music in a unique way – the construction of an opera house on his Sussex estate at Glyndebourne. He loved music and regularly visited the Bayreuth, Munich and Salzburg festivals. In 1931 he married Audrey Mildmay, an opera singer who was eighteen years his junior. Here lay the origins of what was to come. As the husband of an attractive and accomplished young soprano, John Christie grew more ambitious. In the grounds of his estate he proposed to build a small theatre with a proper stage and an orchestra pit big enough for a small string orchestra and an electric organ. His aim was to present opera in an 'undisturbed atmosphere', with 'unlimited' opportunity for rehearsal and with the purpose, as its founder said, of doing 'not the best we can do but the best that can be done anywhere.'

Intent on spending the substantial money required, Christie followed the advice of his wife to 'do the thing properly!' The theatre was redesigned to hold 300 people, with room for an orchestra of reasonable size and a stage with the most up-to-date lighting and technical equipment. He secured the services of Fritz Busch (1890–1951) as conductor and Carl Ebert (1887–1980) as producer and opera manager. Both men had left Germany after Hitler came to power and accepted Christie's offer on condition that in all artistic matters they were to have sole responsibility. (Many years later, Busch admitted that he had only agreed to conduct the first season as he didn't believe there could possibly be a second.) Christie's only condition was that they should leave all matters regarding the cost of running the opera festival to him.

Glyndebourne Festival Opera opened in May 1934 with a fortnight's season of Mozart operas. The first performance of *The marriage of Figaro* was unlike anything the audience had experienced before. The critics who journeyed from London to distant Sussex were sceptical about the worth of this rich man's private dream and a little resentful at having to put on evening dress and travel fifty miles in a special train from London just to listen to an opera. The rest of the audience, who also wore evening dress in response to Christie's recommendation that they should 'take trouble' as a compliment to the artists, came either out of curiosity, a sense of adventure or as a gesture of loyalty or friendship to Christie.

Had standards been lower than they were, the first night at Glyndebourne could have been dismissed as the amateurish result of a rich man's folly. In fact the combination of a good dinner during the long interval, a walk in the beautiful grounds, and a very high standard of performance achieved by endless rehearsal and concentration on detail, had given them a thoroughly pleasurable experience, and inaugurated the Glyndebourne festival as an international institution.

The subsequent years were not easy. The outbreak of war in 1939 ended performances, and it was not until a decade later that the festival began again. Between 1945 and 1950 there was relative inactivity at Glyndebourne for the simple reason that there was no money to fund the operas. John Christie had spent a large portion of his personal fortune on his enterprise and could no longer afford to fund his dream personally. From 1950–53 the work of Glyndebourne was continued by external sponsorship and Christie himself was relieved of the personal financial burden of maintaining the Festival Opera. In 1951 the Glyndebourne Festival Society was formed to secure annual financial support by way of a subscription scheme for each festival. In 1954 the Glyndebourne Arts Trust was formed to ensure the future of the Opera by the establishment of an endowment 'sufficient to maintain and improve Glyndebourne's amenities and to make good any annual deficit not covered by the Festival Society subscriptions.' Vita Sackville-West visited Glyndebourne in 1953 and was charmed by what she found. 'The graciousness of civilisation here surely touches a peak where the arts of music, architecture and gardening combine for the delight of man.'

John Christie's dream was secure, and he was appointed a CH in 1954 'For services to Opera'. In 1956 he handed over management of the festival to his son George, and died in 1962 at the age of eighty.

Sir Thomas Beecham 13 June 1957
Thomas Beecham was an eccentric conductor with a sharp wit who ran the Royal Philharmonic Orchestra as a private fiefdom.

He was born in 1879, the elder son of Sir Joseph Beecham, first baronet, a chemist and inheritor of a prosperous family business in digestive pills begun by his grandfather Joseph Beecham. At an early age Thomas Beecham showed a good memory for words and a passion for music. He was also taught to play the piano from the age of six. In 1899 he was given the opportunity to conduct the Hallé orchestra. He was educated at Rossall and Wadham College, Oxford, but left the university without taking a degree and went to live in London in 1900 where he studied musical composition. He married in 1903 the daughter of an American diplomat and there were two children of the marriage. It was short-lived, the separation was sad and bitter and Beecham rarely spoke about it in later life. They were divorced in 1943 and she died in 1977. He married for the second time in the year of his divorce.

An injury to his wrist ended his plans to become a concert pianist and he turned to the world of conducting. From 1902 to 1904 he led a small operatic ensemble and in 1906 he founded the New Symphony Orchestra (later renamed London Symphony Orchestra) and met Frederick Delius, whose music was to be an important part of Beecham's work. In 1910 he began a series of opera seasons at Covent Garden specialising in the performance of works unknown in Britain. He was the first in England to perform *The mastersingers of Nuremberg* by Wagner, *Elektra* and *Salome* by Strauss and invited Fyodor Shalyapin, Diaghilev's Ballets Russes, Wilhelm Furtwängler and Erich Kleiber to give guest performances in London. The series was ended by the outbreak of the 1914–18 war but Beecham remained indefatigable in his attempts to keep music going, and he sustained the Hallé Society and the London Symphony Orchestra with financial help. During the war he set up the Beecham Opera Company and supported it at his own expense until 1920 when the financial burden had become too great. His greatest achievement at this time was the touring of his opera company in theatres across the country, performing thirty different operas, including *The boatswain's mate* by Dame Ethel Smythe, at prices so low that they were within the reach of everyone. He was knighted in 1916 and succeeded to his father's baronetcy in the same year.

A final financially disastrous Covent Garden season in 1920 left him fighting to stave off bankruptcy and he was absent from the musical scene until 1923. He began the climb back from 1924 when he presented the first Delius festival in London (attended by the blind and paralysed composer, who for the first time began to receive the public appreciation he deserved). In 1932 he returned to Covent Garden and founded a permanent London orchestra, named the London Philharmonic. In 1936 he took the orchestra to Germany and caused a stir by refusing to precede Adolf Hitler into the concert hall, thereby avoiding having to salute the arrival of the Fuhrer. His comment on the age that saw the two world wars revealed his feelings. 'When the history of the first half of this century comes to be written – properly written – it will be acknowledged the most stupid and brutal in the history of civilisation.'[19]

From 1939 to 1944 he travelled constantly abroad in the USA and Australia, and his reputation as a wit and a raconteur grew as rapidly as his stature as a conductor. On his return to London in 1944 and after trials and arguments with the London Philharmonic Orchestra (which chose self-management and rejected his desire to be sole manager), he formed in 1946 the Royal Philharmonic Orchestra, his last and the one with which he had the longest association, though in the eyes of some observers that was not necessarily to the benefit of the orchestra. In the words of Arnold Goodman: 'The continued survival of the Royal Philharmonic Orchestra was a matter which had plagued everyone for years. The Arts Council took the view that the orchestra should not survive. This was based in part on a belief that it was redundant and in part on a belief that it was not very good and was musically low-class . . . The poor old RPO had a rather tatty record, having been the private orchestra of the capricious Sir Thomas Beecham. Needless to say, under his auspices they had attained splendours of performance and frequent threats of bankruptcy. Beecham was in my view this country's best conductor during his lifetime, but his treatment of musicians and his total want of concern for contractual obligations and the payment of debts were legends.'[20] Others were less complimentary than Goodman of Beecham's style of conducting. Toscanini dismissed him as a buffoon,[21] and Barbirolli likened his behaviour on the rostrum to that of 'a dancing dervish'.[22] Even Beecham himself admitted that he was not the greatest conductor in Britain, though he qualified it by adding that he was 'better than any damned foreigner.'[23]

His humour and wit were legendary and his style of conducting, which tended to be based rather on instinct than on intellect, was characteristic of a generation of musicians, to whom enthusiasm was more important than unrelenting strictness. He could be extremely caustic and some of his statements, whether authentic or not, have found their way into many dictionaries of quotations: 'the sound of a harpsichord resembles that of a bird-cage played with toasting forks'; 'brass bands are all very well in their place – out doors and several miles away'; 'I have recently been all round the world and have formed a very poor opinion of it'; 'a musicologist is a man who can read music but can't hear it.' 'Beecham was often a hard taskmaster and could sometimes be inconsiderate to those working for him. Punctuality was not among his most notable virtues. Nevertheless, such peccadilloes were easily overlooked in view of his effervescent enthusiasm which communicated itself to musicians and public alike. Orchestral players will long remember him as not only a great conductor, but a witty and stimulating person who could inspire them to produce their best and showed obvious pleasure in what he heard.'[24] He published a volume of autobiography, *A mingled chine* (1944) and a biography, *Frederick Delius* (1959).

Beecham had been knighted in 1916, but a further honour was a long time in coming. The CH was finally conferred on him in 1957 'For services to music'. It was overshadowed by the death of his second wife in 1958. He married for the third time in 1959 and died in 1961.

Sir Adrian Boult 1 January 1969
Adrian Boult was a prominent conductor who was a close friend of the most distinguished British composers of the first half of the twentieth century, and who championed their work throughout his long career.

He was born in 1889 in Chester into a Unitarian family, the only son of an oil merchant. He was educated at Westminster School and Christ Church, Oxford, where he was president of the university musical club in 1910. He studied Arthur Nikisch's methods of conducting at the Leipzig Conservatorium 1912–13. Returning to Oxford he took a BMus in 1914 and a DMus in 1921. At the beginning of 1914 he joined the staff of the Royal Opera House where he participated in the first British performance of Wagner's *Parsifal*, playing the off-stage bells. He suffered from a heart condition, which removed him from the need for military service in the 1914–18 war, but he helped to drill recruits from Cheshire for two years, worked in the war office in 1916–18 and found time to organize concerts in Liverpool with a small orchestra drawn from the ranks of the Liverpool Philharmonic Society. This led to an invitation to conduct the full orchestra in January 1916.

Boult came into prominence in 1918–19 with outstanding performances of works by Elgar, Vaughan Williams and Holst, all of whom became his close friends, and the championship of English composers was dominant in his career. He conducted the first performance of *The planets* (1918) at the Queen's Hall, London, at the invitation of the composer, and the London season of Diaghilev ballet and operas at the Empire Theatre in 1919.

He was a member of the teaching staff at the Royal College of Music (1919–30), and in 1926 he rejoined Covent Garden as a staff conductor. In 1928–31 he was conductor of the BBC Bach Choir, London and in 1924–30 he was musical director of the City of Birmingham Symphony Orchestra. In 1930–42 he was musical director of the BBC with responsibility for recruiting players for the BBC Symphony Orchestra, and becoming its chief conductor (1931–50). He took the orchestra on tour in Europe in 1935 and 1936, giving concerts in Brussels, Paris, Zurich, Vienna and Budapest. By this time Boult had become well known abroad having been invited to conduct the Vienna Philharmonic in Vienna in 1933, and later conducting in Boston and Salzburg in 1935, and in New York in 1938 and 1939. He was conductor of the orchestra at the coronation of King George VI in 1937 and at that of Queen Elizabeth II in 1953. In 1942 he became associate conductor of the promenade concerts and continued as conductor of the BBC Symphony Orchestra until 1950 when, having reached the age of sixty, he was retired by the BBC, and immediately became musical director of the London Philharmonic Orchestra, with whom he toured West Germany in 1951 and the Soviet Union in 1956. He retired from the LPO in 1957. In 1959 he was offered and accepted the presidency of the Royal Scottish Academy of Music in succession to Vaughan Williams, and was again musical director of the City of Birmingham Symphony Orchestra (1959–60), serving as its vice-president from 1960 until his death, and on the staff of the Royal College of Music (1962–66). His many other commitments included the presidency of the Incorporated Society of Musicians (1928–29), the National Youth Orchestra (1947–57), the Schools' Music Association (from 1947 until his death), and the Leith Hill Musical Festival (1955–78).

Apart from *The planets* in 1918, he had other 'firsts' to his credit: the first British performance of Mahler's third symphony; Vaughan Williams' *A pastoral symphony* (1922), fourth symphony (1935) and sixth symphony (1948), Bliss's *Music for strings* (1935), Tippett's second symphony (1958). the first English performance of Berg's *Wozzeck* (1934) and a concert performance of Busoni's *Doktor Faust* (1937). He wrote a handbook on conducting and a volume of autobiography *My own trumpet* (1973). 'He was in almost every sense a great man, even if no one would describe him as a great conductor. He was a conductor of high competence. He had the special value of being prepared to conduct any work undeterred by its difficulty – a quality which is not to be found in every conductor.'[25]

Boult was a prominent figure in English musical life and an advocate of English music at home and abroad. Vaughan Williams' *Job, a masque of dancing*, Herbert Howell's *Concert for strings* and Malcolm Williamson's *Concert for organ and orchestra* were dedicated to him. 'Boult was the least demonstrative of conductors on the concert platform, obtaining his effects by meticulous rehearsal, impeccable musicianship, and a natural authority. A tall man of erect, almost military bearing, Boult was taciturn by nature. However, his courteous manner could occasionally, at rehearsals, give way to storms of violent temper. He was always concerned to present the music as the composer conceived it, and was reluctant to impose his own personality upon a work in the name of interpretation.'[26]

Boult was knighted in 1937 and appointed a CH in 1969 'For services to Music'. Invested on 26 February 1969, he showed an unusual and refreshing interest in the honour. 'I had the honour of a presentation by Her Majesty the Queen yesterday of the Jewel of the Companionship of Honour, and I should be most grateful if you could kindly provide me with a history of the Honour, which I believe was instituted by King George V, and in particular the motto on the Jewel was new to me and I should be very interested to know where the quotation comes from.'[27] The reply from the Central Chancery was charmingly informal: 'Thanks to a brother-in-law who is an expert on crossword puzzles I have been able to answer your question on the origin of the motto . . .'[28]

Adrian Boult retired from conducting in 1979 at the age of ninety and died four years later.

Sir John Barbirolli 14 June 1969
John Barbirolli was a conductor whose name became firmly linked with the Hallé Orchestra.

He was born in 1899, the elder son of an émigré Italian violinist, Lorenzo Barbirolli and his French wife. Lorenzo and his father, Antonio, were distinguished Italian violinists and both were members of the La Scala Orchestra in Milan where, in February 1887, they played in the first performance of Verdi's *Otello*. John Barbirolli was educated at Trinity College of Music and made his debut in a cello concerto at the Queen's Hall in 1911. In 1912 he won a scholarship to the Royal Academy of Music (1912–16). In 1916 he became the youngest member of Henry Wood's Queen's Hall Orchestra and in 1917 gave his first solo cello recital in London.

He joined the army before the end of the 1914–18 war, serving in the Suffolk Regiment in 1918–19, and during this time, had his first opportunity to conduct an orchestra. He returned to civilian life in 1919, playing in the London Symphony Orchestra and in Beecham's Covent Garden Orchestra but he also played the cello in bands in dance halls, cinemas and circuses. He was gifted enough to be soloist in a performance of Elgar's Cello Concerto at Bournemouth in 1921. In 1926 he was invited by Frederic Austin, then artistic director of the British National Opera Company, to conduct on one of its provincial tours and made his operatic début in Newcastle upon Tyne in September that year, conducting Gounod's *Romeo et Juliette*. He conducted the London Symphony Orchestra in December 1926 when he deputised at short notice for Beecham, who was indisposed. He subsequently conducted a number of concerts in London with the LSO and the Royal Philharmonic Society but in 1936, though by now well established as permanent conductor of the Scottish Orchestra (from 1933), he was still considered by the English music establishment to be 'promising'.

When the BNOC foundered in 1929, Barbirolli was appointed conductor of the Covent Garden Opera touring company and also became a regular conductor at the Royal Opera House, Covent Garden. In 1931 the company staged thirteen operas including the revival of Dame Ethel Smythe's opera *The wreckers*. In 1936 he was invited to conduct the Philharmonic-Symphony Orchestra of New York for the first ten weeks of the 1936–37 season. He conducted at Carnegie Hall for the first time on 5 November 1936 and a month later he was offered a three-year contract. It was a rewarding and difficult time for him. He succeeded Toscanini who was idolised in New York, and the powerful and influential New York critics were savage in their attacks on his interpretations. But when his contract expired in 1940 it was renewed for a further two years and Barbirolli spent seven seasons in New York.

By 1942, home sick and worried about his family, he made a hazardous return sea crossing to Britain and conducted concerts throughout Britain with several of the country's leading orchestras. He had refused to take American citizenship in order to join the American Musicians' Union and the 1941–42 season was his last one as permanent conductor, though he did conduct concerts in New York in the 1942–3 season. In February 1943, he received a telegram from Manchester, enquiring if he was interested in becoming permanent conductor of the Hallé Orchestra. He accepted and found that he had to create a virtually new orchestra from a small residual nucleus of players who had refused to go over to a full-time contract with the BBC Northern Orchestra which was soon acclaimed as the best in the country. The task was so enervating that it bound him to his new orchestra for the rest of his life, despite lucrative offers from elsewhere and despite his own exasperation with its post-war financial problems. In 1959 he accepted engagements in the USA and returned to a rapturous welcome from public and critics in New York. From 1961 he was a regular guest-conductor with the Berlin Philharmonic and in 1961–67 he was conductor-in-chief of the Houston Symphony Orchestra; but the Hallé remained his principal concern. 'Barbirolli was a warm and interesting character, but he was not well liked by the orchestra. He was a severe disciplinarian, concerned above everything else to attain the highest musical standards, and he did in fact contrive to make it one of the best symphony orchestras in the country.'[29]

Barbirolli had a significant flaw: a intense dislike of distinguished soloists. He regarded them as potential and inveterate rivals to his own pre-eminence as conductor. Arnold Goodman remembered one preposterous tactic used by Barbirolli to ensure that he alone occupied the limelight. 'I particularly remember telephoning him one day to suggest that a concert should be held in which Yehudi Menuhin would perform. "No!" he said, "I will not appear with that man – he was a supporter of the Nazis!" This was as fanciful a piece of imagination as it was possible to devise. Yehudi was a firmly self-declared Jew and a man of great humanity and the idea that he had supported the Nazis was the most appalling scandal; but I formed the conclusion that to keep his concerts sanitised against any individual performer other than himself, Barbirolli would have invested almost any disparagement.'[30] 'No one who saw him – dynamic, with a touch of arrogance in his demeanour on the rostrum, small of stature, but big in every other way – would have guessed that after a concert he would often lapse into deep depression. He was prey to an insecurity which partly stemmed from his experiences during his rise to fame, was partly the result of his years in New York, and was also due to his own genuine humility in the face of great music.'[31]

Barbirolli once expressed the passion that he felt for his profession by using the metaphor of dealing with a cold. 'If you want a cure for a cold, put on two pullovers, take up a baton, poker or pencil, tune the radio to a symphony concert, stand on a chair, and conduct like mad for an hour and the cold will have vanished. It never fails. You know why conductors live so long? Because we perspire so much.'[32] In the case of Barbirolli himself, the comment proved inaccurate and he died at the comparatively early age of seventy. His last public concert was with the Hallé Orchestra at the King's Lynn Festival on 25th July 1970. A few days later, he died of a heart attack, in London, on 29 July. Only a few hours before, he had been busily rehearsing the Philharmonia Orchestra in preparation for his tour with them to Japan.

He was knighted in 1949, and made a CH in 1969 'For services to music.'

Sir Arthur Bliss 12 June 1971
Arthur Bliss was not a composer of the first rank, but he was a very effective and highly regarded court composer as master of the queen's music for more than twenty years

He was born in Barnes in 1891, the eldest of the three sons of an American businessman resident in England. He was educated at Rugby and Pembroke College, Cambridge and then the Royal College of Music for a single term before the 1914–18 war broke out and interrupted his studies for the duration. There he came to know Ralph Vaughan Williams and Gustav Holst. He spent the war in the Royal Fusiliers, being twice wounded, gassed and mentioned in despatches. He was discharged from the army in 1919 and began to produce a stream of compositions and established a reputation as an advanced and cosmopolitan composer. In *Madame Noy* (1918), *Rhapsody* (1919), and *Rout* (1920), he experimented with instrumental uses of the voice, in wordless vocalisation and nonsense syllables. 'He delighted in working in new mediums and was adept at providing fanfares, of which he wrote over thirty, each singularly apposite to the occasion celebrated . . . He possessed an abiding interest in painting, and one of his earliest large orchestral pieces, the balletic *Melée Fantasque* (1921) . . . evokes something of his fascination with colour, movement, and changing patterns.'[33] It was followed by the aptly named *A colour symphony* (1922).

In 1921 he became conductor of the Portsmouth Philharmonic Society, two years later moving to California where he continued to conduct. The *Introduction and allegro for orchestra* (1926), dedicated to the Philadelphia Orchestra and Stokowski, was the first of many works written for virtuoso ensembles or soloists. In 1930 the Norwich Festival produced one of the most deeply personal of his works, the choral symphony *Morning heroes*, written as a tribute to those who died in the 1914–18 war. In 1934–35 he began work in a new field, composing music for ballet and film. His works included music for six films, including Alexander Korda's *Things to come* (1936), based on a prophetic tract by H. G. Wells, and *Men of two worlds* (1945). His four ballets included *Checkmate* (1937), perhaps the most widely known, *Miracle in the Gorbals* (1944), *Adam Zero* (1946) and *Lady of Shallott* (1958). His *Piano concerto* was first performed at the New York World Fair in 1939 and he remained in the USA as visiting professor (from 1940) at the University of California, Berkeley until 1941 when he returned to England to join the BBC Overseas Music Service. There he framed a far-reaching memorandum that became a motivating factor in the creation of the Third Programme (later Radio 3) for BBC Radio. He was director of music at the BBC (1942–44). In 1953 he was appointed master of the queen's music. His later works include cantatas, several orchestral works, among which the *Meditations on a theme of John Blow* (1955) stands out as one of his finest scores, and two operas, *The Olympians* (1949), with a libretto by J. B. Priestley, and *Tobias and the angel* (1960), neither of great note. By the time of his death in 1975 he had written more than one hundred and fifty compositions, of which at least fifty are major works. His last cantata, entitled *Shield of faith* that he did not live to hear performed, was composed for the quincentenary of St George's Chapel, Windsor Castle in 1975. 'Through his exceptional ability to turn from the needful isolation of the creative artist to the pressures imposed upon the committee man and administrator, to both of which roles he brought an appraising and incisive mind, he became one of the outstanding musical personalities of the twentieth century.'[34]

He published a volume of memoirs, *As I remember* in 1970. He was knighted in 1950 and made a CH in 1971 in the year of his eightieth birthday 'For services to Music'.

Herbert Howells 3 June 1972
Herbert Howells was a self-effacing composer, teacher and writer on music, now known for little apart from his extensive repertoire of church music.

He was born at Lydney in Gloucestershire in 1892, the son of a painter and decorator of Gloucestershire stock. He was educated at Lydney Grammar School, where he came to the notice of Sir Herbert Brewer, organist of Gloucester Cathedral, who taught him until 1905 when he was ready to be formally articled. 'Howells was therefore one of the last English musicians to be brought up in the old apprentice system under which the aspirant was bound to a master, generally the nearest cathedral organist, who accepted full responsibility for his training and entry into the profession.'[35] Years of the daily routine of cathedral worship left an impression which lasted until the end of his life, and he later admitted that the main lines of his development had been moulded before he went to the Royal College of Music in 1912. He became the pupil of Sir Charles Stanford and Sir Hubert Parry and wrote a great deal of music. 'Even more significant than Stanford's discipline and Parry's generous friendship were the social and literary influences that flooded over him in the new world that welcomed his romantic good looks, charm and lively intelligence.'[36] In 1916, while assistant organist at Salisbury Cathedral, he suffered a complete breakdown of health and was not able to return to work and to London until 1918, where he lived for the rest of his life, except for a sojourn in Cambridge during the 1939–45 war. He earned his living by teaching theory and composition at the Royal College of Music for over fifty years and by lecturing and writing. If he had not been a musician he could have excelled as a poet, like his friend Walter de la Mare. In 1936–62 he was director of music at St Paul's Girls' School, Brook Green in succession to Gustav Holst, and in 1955–62 he was additionally King Edward VII professor of music at the University of London, an anomalous position since the university, at that date, had no music faculty.

Howells once stated that one of the two revelatory musical experiences of his youth was hearing the premiere of the *Fantasia on a theme by Thomas Tallis* in Gloucester Cathedral in 1910, the excitement of the performance being magnified by the coincidence that, after leaving the rostrum, Vaughan Williams happened to sit next to Howells and the two of them followed the same score through the subsequent performance of *The dream of Gerontius*. He was never a pupil of Vaughan Williams, and in fact both were colleagues at the Royal College of Music; Vaughan Williams taught composition there from 1919 and Howells joined him the following year. Howells seems to have lacked the self-promotional skills necessary for success as a composer, and few of his works were widely performed. But a handful of his works have become classics, and for those familiar with the extensive repertoire of church music, he is one of the major English composers of the twentieth century. The marvellously flowing *A spotless rose* is sung in many a carol service.

Powers of withdrawal and concentration enabled him to produce a great corpus of music, including besides early orchestral works, three concertos, six quartets, five instrumental sonatas, a large number of choral works, forty songs and much church and organ music. One of his outstanding songs is *King David*, with words by his favourite poet, Walter de la Mare. He also wrote the only substantial and successful body of music in the twentieth century for the clavichord. 'He had an unfailing insight into what is possible with a small choir and organ. Howells also wrote many short choral pieces for school and festival use, some of which are among his most distinguished works, imaginative, beautifully composed, and fastidious in choice and treatment of poetry . . . It is significant that he chose to write for the clavichord, most intimate of instruments, for his music often conveys a sense of privacy, of direct address to one friend, or of solitary meditation . . . One finds in Howells' music depth of feeling, tenderness, humour, and love of the English landscape, but seldom great exuberance. Especially after the death of his son in 1935 [from poliomyelitis], there is often a persistent note of nostalgia and regret that has led critics to compare him with Frederick Delius. But in Howell's music there are gleams of visionary hope that are not to be found in Delius and it is noticeable that in the last years of his life he wrote little or nothing except church music, as if, for the finale, he was returning home to Gloucester.'[37]

Howells was appointed a CBE in 1953 and a CH in 1972, in his eightieth year, for his services as a 'Composer'. He died in 1983 in his ninety-first year.

Sir Robert Mayer 1 January 1973

Robert Mayer is best remembered for his work in helping children to appreciate the beauty of music. His early musical gifts were never brought to fruition and he was essentially a businessman who could have had a career as a musician but instead used his wealth as a patron of that art to develop the nation's musical taste.

He was born in 1879 at Mannheim in Germany, the third son of a hop merchant and brewer with musical tendencies. He was a gifted pianist from his earliest years and his father entered him at the Mannheim Gymnasium and Conservatoire at the age of six. He was encouraged by a meeting with Johannes Brahms at the age of eleven and later recalled how the composer had patted him on the head and encouraged him to continue his studies. For whatever reason he never pursued a musical career. The rise of Prussian militarism led his father to send him to England in 1896 to work with a firm of stockbrokers. He later went into the non-ferrous metals business and remained in it until he had made his fortune in the USA and in London, and was able to retire in 1929 and concentrate on his musical work.

He was naturalised a British subject in 1902 and served in the army in 1917–19. His first wife, Dorothy Moulton, was a soprano singer and she encouraged him to support music and in particular to promote the musical development of children. His wife's recollection of a concert for children they had heard in New York decided the form their patronage would take, and Mayer was later to describe himself as 'a musical bricklayer with architectural aspirations.'

He and his wife instituted the Robert Mayer Concerts for Children, the first of which was held on 29 March 1923 at the Central Hall, London. It coincided with a transport strike in London, but the audience (300 for the first concert) grew to 1,360 by the third concert. Sir Malcolm Sargent succeeded Boult as conductor in the second season and continued as conductor until the outbreak of the 1939–45 war caused their suspension. 'The combination of Sargent's musicianship and skill with the young audience, Dorothy's enthusiasm and Robert's generosity and determination, ensured that the Robert Mayer Concerts became and remained an important institution in the musical life of London. They spread to a large number of provincial centres in the 1930s and made a significant contribution to the renaissance of music in England, as well as later in Ireland where Mayer supported his wife's foundation for the promotion of music.'[38]

The concerts began again after the 1939–45 war, which Mayer spent in the USA. 'In later years, Mayer's philanthropy was not confined to musical causes.

There were three threads that ran through it – music, young people, and the improvement of relations with citizens of other countries – and they were related in his mind: he saw music as a civilizing force in society and international relations.'[39] After the war he founded the Robert Mayer Trust for Youth and Music, in imitation of the Jeunesses Musicales (founded in wartime Brussels by Marcel Cuvelier). It was to cater for an older age group than the audience of the children's concerts, and in 1954 Mayer succeeded in rallying various musical interests to start it.

He was also interested in the problems of juvenile delinquency and in 1945 published a book *Young people in trouble*. He supported the Elizabeth Fry fund, the International Student Service, the Children's Theatre, the Transatlantic Foundation, and the Anglo-Israel foundation. In his nineties he was a strong supporter of the movement for British membership of the European community.

He was knighted in 1939 for his services to music and appointed a CH in 1973 also 'For services to Music', marking the fiftieth anniversary of the foundation of Youth and Music. His one hundredth birthday was celebrated by the publication of an autobiography *My first hundred years* (1979) and by a concert at the Festival Hall in the presence of Queen Elizabeth II who after the performance presented him with the insignia of a KCVO. He died in 1985 at the age of one hundred and five.

Sir Michael Tippett 16 June 1979

Michael Tippett ranks with Benjamin Britten as one of the principal British composers of the second half of the twentieth century.

He was born in 1905, the son of a Cornish lawyer, and his Celtic origins endowed him in old age with the looks of a hardy and weather-beaten Breton sailor. He spent the first fifteen years of his life in Suffolk and was educated at Stamford Grammar School. While at the school, near Peterborough, he took piano lessons from a local teacher, sang in the local church choir and took part in amateur stage-productions. It was the experience of hearing an orchestral concert in Leicester, conducted by Malcolm Sargent, that led him to decide to become a composer – even though he had little idea what it involved. His musical ambitions were not encouraged at school, so he pressed his parents into supporting him as a student at the Royal College of Music in London, where he enrolled in 1923. In his five years at the college, he studied composition with Charles Wood, and conducting with Adrian Boult and Malcolm Sargent. After leaving the RCM Tippett lived in Oxted, Surrey, taught French in a preparatory school (1929–34) and conducted a concert and operatic society. In April 1930 an Oxted concert featured his main works to date; but these he afterwards withdrew. He then went for further lessons with R. O. Morris on counterpoint and fugue, and from these he developed skills which produced the first works of his creative maturity, the *String Quartet No. 1* (1935; revised 1944) and *Piano Sonata No. 1* (1936–7).

During and after his student days, Tippett was deeply affected by the depression and mass unemployment of the 1930s, and he became involved in political radicalism, organised and conducted the South London Orchestra (of unemployed musicians) (1933–40), based at Morley College, and directed two choirs sponsored by the Royal Arsenal Co-operative Society. He was music director at the college from 1940 but resigned in 1951 to devote more time to composition, earning a small secondary income from radio talks.

Having seen the horrors of the 1914–18 war Tippett became an ardent pacifist, joined the Peace Pledge Union and declared himself a conscientious objector at the start of the 1939–45 war. He was allowed to register on condition that he entered full-time employment in civil defence, the NFS or on the land. In June 1943, he was sentenced to three months' imprisonment, not for *being* a conscientious objector, but for refusing to comply with these conditions of exemption from active war service. Ralph Vaughan Williams appeared as witness in his defence and said that he thought Tippett's compositions were a distinct musical asset.

Tippett was a known left wing radical. In the period 1935–45 he was a supporter of communism and of the Trotskyist movement in the United Kingdom, and belonged to a communist section of the musicians' union. In 1945 he was sponsor of the London committee of the freedom defence committee (an organisation associated with the union of anarchists' group), formed to assist in the defence of anarchists charged under the defence regulations. He later became a member of the national council of the Peace Pledge Union and spoke at meetings of the union in 1949 and 1950. In 1953 he was author of the foreword to the annual report of the central board for conscientious objectors.

Musically, he did not achieve any recognition until 1935 with his first string quartet, but the work which made his name familiar was the *Concerto for double string orchestra* (1938–39). His music often reflected his political and philosophical positions, which were reinforced by a friendship with T. S. Eliot who became a father figure to him, and with whom he enjoyed playing games of Monopoly. The outcome of his political standpoint was the oratorio *A child of our time* (1939–41), an impassioned protest against persecution and tyranny and now his most widely performed composition. It reflected the political and spiritual problems of the 1930s and 1940s and was inspired by the 1938 assassination of a German diplomat in Paris by a young Polish Jew. Tippett asked Eliot to write the libretto, but when the latter read the rough draft, he urged Tippett to write his own words.

His first symphony was finished in 1945 and he then embarked on his first opera, *The midsummer marriage*, which was completed in 1952 and performed at the Royal Opera House. It was not successful until its revival over twenty years later. *Fantasia concertante on a theme of Corelli* (1953) was composed for the Edinburgh Festival to mark the tercentenary of Corelli's birthday. A second opera *King Priam* was composed in 1962 and an elaborate choral work *The vision of St Augustine* (1966), the least accessible of his works. 'With the opera *The knot garden* (1970) Tippett entered a third period in which he fused his two earlier periods, the "lyrical" and the "disjunct" as they have been called, and also extended his bounds by reference to popular and serious music, past and present . . . But perhaps the most comprehensive synthesis of his work is the huge oratorio *The mask of time* [a commission from the USA]. . . Some of his determinedly popular passages in recent years, as in the opera *The ice break* (1973–76) [an allusion to Soviet dissidents], may come to sound increasingly self-conscious, but this is part of the price to be paid for Tippett's open-eyed, even naive outlook on the world expressed in music of exceptional technical sophistication.'[40]

Throughout his eighties, Tippett continued to compose, conduct and travel worldwide. His fifth and last opera, *New year*, commissioned jointly by Houston Grand Opera, Glyndebourne and the BBC, received its premiere in 1989, and the BBC screened a television production. Immediately after the opera came *Byzantium*, for soprano and orchestra (premiered in Chicago in 1991 and repeated the same year at the Proms) and a Fifth String Quartet (1992). Celebrations of his ninetieth birthday in 1995 opened with the BBC Music Magazine issuing a CD of his second and fourth symphonies, played by the BBC Symphony Orchestra conducted by the composer. A month-long Tippett festival at the Barbican reached a climax with the world premiere of his last major composition, *The rose lake*. It was subsequently performed eleven times during a two-month tour of the USA and Canada. In 1996, he moved from the isolated Wiltshire house in which he had lived for over twenty-five years to south London. In November 1997 the Stockholm Concert Hall mounted a retrospective of Tippett's concert music. But his advanced age was against him and he fell ill with pneumonia just after arriving in Stockholm. He recovered sufficiently to be brought home, where he died in January 1998, shortly after his ninety-third birthday.

A volume of autobiography *Those twentieth century blues* was published in 1991. He was appointed a CBE in 1959, although some took offence at his homosexuality and left wing politics. But Tippett went on to further honours. He was knighted in 1966 and appointed a CH in 1979 'For services to Music'. By the time he was appointed a CH, Benjamin Britten had been dead for three years and Tippett was regarded as the foremost British composer. Some thought that while his reputation was not as universal as that of Britten, his creative genius was in some ways higher. With the death of Sir William Walton in 1983, there was a vacancy for a musician in the ranks of the Order of Merit. Tippett was chosen, an irony considering that it had been a constant source of irritation to Walton that he and Tippett were mentioned in the same breath!

After Britten, Tippett was the second composer to have been honoured with both the CH and the OM. It was the ultimate accolade of state recognition for one who had arrived at Wormwood Scrubs prison forty years earlier, handcuffed to a prisoner convicted of manslaughter. 'The only truth I shall ever say,' he once said, 'was expressed in *A child of our time*: "I would know my shadow and my light. So shall I at least be whole." Anybody who can go down that very difficult road, and learn to know his darker side – his shadow – as his light, is approaching the truth.'[41]

Dame Janet Baker 31 December 1993
The mezzo-soprano Janet Baker broke new ground by becoming the first singer to be appointed a CH.

She was born at Hatfield, Doncaster in 1933. She was educated at the College for Girls at York, which she left at the age of seventeen to work as a clerk at a bank in Leeds to earn money for singing lessons. The manager heard her sing in a small part in which she was substituting for an indisposed singer and arranged for her to be transferred to the bank's headquarters in London where she would have better opportunities for musical study. In the back room of a London bank, she sang for hours while working on a coin-sorting machine. During that time she took singing lessons with Helene Isepp and Meriel St Clair. She joined the Ambrosian Singers in 1955; and won second prize in the Daily Mail Kathleen Ferrier Competition 1956. It brought her welcome publicity and enabled her to study at the Mozarteum at Salzburg.

She made her opera début in 1956 as Rosa in Smetana's *The secret*, at Oxford University's Opera Club. She also boosted her career by joining the

Glyndebourne Festival Chorus in 1956, and won the Queen's Prize from the Royal College of Music 1959, and an Arts Council grant in 1960 for further study. She performed at Wexford Festival 1959 and sang a leading role with the Handel Opera Society 1959. During 1960 she gave a recital at the Edinburgh International Festival and sang Sosotrice's aria from Michael Tippett's *A midsummer marriage* at the BBC Promenade Concerts. She joined Benjamin Britten's English Opera Group in 1961, giving performances of *Phaedra*, the work that Britten wrote for her, and continued to sing with the group until 1976.

From 1960 onwards Janet Baker sang in a succession of prominent roles which secured her reputation. She sang Dido in *Dido and Aeneas* (1961), followed by roles in *Tamerlano* (1962), *Ariodante* (1964), *Orlando* (1966), *Admeto* (1968), also Hippolyte in *Aricie* (1965). She sang at the Aldeburgh Festival from 1962 and recorded the Angel in Elgar's *Dream of Gerontius* with Barbirolli (1964). In 1966 she made her debut in New York (concert performance) and at Covent Garden as *Hermia* in *A midsummer night's dream*. She sang Dorabella (*Cosi fan tutte*) with Scottish Opera in 1967, followed by Dido (*Les Troyens*, 1969), Oktavien (*Der Rosenkavalier*, 1971), Composer (*Ariadne auf Naxos*, 1975), Orpheus in Gluck's opera (1979), Diana in *La Calisto* at Glyndebourne (1970), followed by Penelope in *Il ritorno d'Ulisse in patria* (1972), Poppea for English National Opera in *L'incoronazione di Poppea* (1971), *Mary Stuart* Donizetti, (1975), Charlotte in *Werther* (1977). She created the role of Kate in *Owen Wingrave*, on television in 1971 and at the Royal Opera House in 1973. She retired from the operatic stage in 1982, her last appearance being at Glyndebourne as Orpheus in Gluck's opera. Her voice was not remarkable for its volume or its weight and she never attempted Wagnerian roles, but she was, 'one of the most intense and intelligent of contemporary singers, as impressive in operatic parts as in the realm of lieder, English and French song, oratorio, and Mahler.'[42] Her autobiography *Full circle* was published in 1982. 'In singing a song,' she once said, 'one must be willing to stand aside all the time and not use the song as a vehicle for the personality, which is a dangerous temptation. It *is* a vehicle, but it must be for the right reason. The fundamental idea I have about my own singing is that it is a God-given gift to me and that the only way that it can work is if I give it back unstintingly.'[43]

Janet Baker was often known to be generous with the fees that she charged, so helping smaller and less well-endowed organisations to engage her. She was a leading figure in public life, including being a trustee of the Foundation for Sport and the Arts. In 1991 she accepted an invitation from the University of York to be its chancellor, in succession to Lord Swann. 'Her highly individual and beautiful voice, her warmth of personality, and her intelligent feeling for words, and a dramatic range which encompasses both tragic and comic roles, make her one of the outstanding artists of the day.'[44]

She was made a CBE in 1970, DBE in 1976 and a CH in 1993 'For services to the Arts'.

Sir Harrison Birtwistle 30 December 2000
The compositions of Harrison Birtwistle brought him to fame as a pioneering and challenging composer of pieces that sometimes required concentrated effort on the part of the listener.

He was born on a small farm near Accrington in 1934. 'He was gripped as a boy by an idea of Greek drama and the wail of a reedy pipe. He played clarinet in a town orchestra whose instruments were donated by a mill owner.'[45] He studied clarinet and composition at the Royal Manchester College of Music (1952–60). There he was one of the Manchester New Music Group, performing avant-garde works with a talented group of contemporaries including Peter Maxwell Davies, Alexander Goehr, John Ogdon and Elgar Howarth. After the RMCM in 1960 he spent a year at the Royal Academy of Music. From 1962–65 he was director of music at Cranborne Chase School. In 1965 he sold his clarinets to become a full-time composer and spent two years at Princeton University as a Harkness Fellow where he completed his first opera *Punch and Judy* (1966–67), a study of violence that included a costumed orchestra by the stage. It was followed by *The mask of Orpheus* (1973–84) for English National Opera, and *Gawain* (1987–90) for the Royal Opera House. His other operas include *Down by the greenwood side* (1968–69), a piece of cabaret-style music theatre, *Bow down* (1977), *Yan yan tethera* (1983–84) and *The second Mrs Kong* (1993–4). Other large-scale works included *Verses for ensembles* (1969), *The triumph of time* (1972), which established Birtwistle as a leading voice in British music; the concertos *Endless parade* (1987) for trumpet and *Antiphonies* (1992) for piano, the orchestral score *Earth dances* (1986), and a series of ensemble scores: *Silbury air* (1977), *Carmen arcadiae mechanicae perpetuum* (1978) and *Secret theatre* (1984). His most recent works include *Exody*, premiered by the Chicago Symphony Orchestra and *Panic* (1995), for saxophone, drummer and orchestra, first performed at the last night of the 1995 BBC Promenade. Recent chamber compositions include *Pulse shadows* (1996), an hour-long meditation for soprano, string quartet and chamber ensemble on poetry by Paul Celan, and the cycle of piano works *Harrison's clocks* (1998). His most recent stage-work, *The last supper*, received its first performances at the Deutsche Staatsoper in Berlin and at Glyndebourne in 2000. Though vague about any religious belief, 'he sought an echo of his Methodist upbringing, a hint of childhood hymnody, structured within a lifelong fascination for ecclesiastical architecture.'[46] His latest works include *The shadow of night* for the Cleveland Orchestra and a new stage work for the Royal Opera House.

He was an associate director of the National Theatre (1975–88) and with Maxwell Davies formed Pierrot Players in London for performance of new chamber music, initially Schoenberg's *Pierrot Lunaire*, involving theatrical elements. He is currently director of composition at the Royal College of Music in London, Henry Purcell professor of composition at King's College, London (from 1994), and composer in residence with the London Philharmonic Orchestra at the South Bank Centre (from 1993). He has received commissions for works from many organisations and is regarded as one of the most gifted and original of contemporary English composers, although his music seems – impishly and intentionally – designed to antagonise and to shock.

He accepted a knighthood in 1988, later claiming that he was tempted to refuse it,[47] and was made a CH in 2000 'For services to Music'.

Sir Colin Davis 16 June 2001
Colin Davis conducted some of the most prominent orchestras in the United Kingdom and was fifteen years music director of the Royal Opera House in London.

He was born in 1927 and educated at Christ's Hospital and the Royal College of Music. He began his career in Sweden in 1949 before becoming assistant conductor of the BBC Scottish Orchestra (1957–59). He first attracted widespread attention as an opera conductor with his *Die Entführung aus dem Serail* at Sadler's Wells in 1958. Further signs of his talent appeared when he substituted for Otto Klemperer with the Philharmonia Orchestra in *Don Giovanni* in 1959, and for Sir Thomas Beecham in *The magic flute* in Glyndebourne in 1960. He made his debut in the United States with the Minneapolis Symphony in 1961. His career took off in the early 1960s when he was appointed principal conductor of Sadler's Wells (1961–65) and later chief conductor of the BBC Symphony Orchestra (1967–71). He became the principal guest conductor of such prestigious ensembles as the London Symphony (1975–95), the Boston Symphony (1972–84) and the Concertgebouw Orchestra. He was music director of the Bavarian Radio Symphony Orchestra (1983–92) and has been honorary conductor of the Dresden Staatskapelle since 1990. He was named principal conductor of the London Symphony Orchestra in 1995 and became principal guest conductor of the New York Philharmonic in 1998.

His long tenure as music director of the Royal Opera House, Covent Garden (1971–86) was not without its storms at the beginning, especially as he had succeeded the revered George Solti. 'In straight terms,' he said, 'I was just not accepted. There were singers who did not like me and there were members of the orchestra who did not like me. I was criticised for not doing things the Solti way, but who is to say that he was wrong or that I was wrong.'[48] Davis was not a man to be defeated, and despite the early belligerent period, he survived at Covent Garden for fifteen years and became trusted and admired by its conservative audiences. The Royal Opera House was never able to provide him with all that he wished for, and at the end of his time he speculated that had he stayed at Sadler's Wells and gone on to the Coliseum he might have had more of the experiences for which he was looking.[49]

He championed contemporary composers including Hans Werner Henze, Peter Maxwell Davies and Michael Tippett, some of whose works he premiered. He is also known for his performances of Mozart, Sibelius, Britten and, above all, Berlioz. In addition to conducting the first full performance of Berlioz's monumental opera *Les Troyens* at Covent Garden in 1969 (which clinched his succession to Solti), he has also recorded all the works of Berlioz. In *The Times* profile of him which appeared in 1990, Richard Morrison wrote that Davis 'made his name by conducting Mozart like an angel. Then came his famous championing of Berlioz, his bold forays into Wagner, his oddly paced but deeply considered Beethoven, his pioneering of Tippett, his revival of Sibelius . . . the list goes on.'

Davis himself summed up the secret of being an effective conductor: 'Conducting is like holding the bird of life in your hand: hold it too tight and it dies, hold it too lightly and it flies away.' There is evidence of his modesty in his personal dislike of the personality cult adopted by many musicians. 'I detest all that charisma stuff. It leads to unmusical things like the pursuit of power. The older I get, the more wary I am of power. It is a beastly ingredient in our society.' Unlike many of his contemporary musicians Davis is not flamboyant and rarely temperamental. He never sought publicity and gave interviews infrequently and reluctantly. Yet he became one of the world's greatest conductors.

He was appointed a CBE in 1965, knighted in 1980, and made a CH in 2001. The citation read: 'Principal Conductor, London Symphony Orchestra. For services to Music.'

Sir George Christie 31 December 2001
Noted for his modesty, George Christie is not a nationally known figure outside the world of opera. He succeeded his father as the chairman of Glyndebourne – the literally homegrown East Sussex opera house.

He was born in 1934, the eldest son of John Christie, the man who conceived the Glyndebourne experience. He was educated at Eton and worked for five years as assistant to the secretary of the Calouste Gulbenkian Foundation (1957–62). Given the realised dreams of his father, a dream which the younger Christie shared, it was inevitable that he should inherit responsibility for its maintenance and future. With the retirement of his father he became chairman of Glyndebourne Productions Ltd in 1956 and was responsible for the development, administration and artistic direction of the Glyndebourne Festival until 1999, ensuring that this unique operatic experience continued to enjoy success and worldwide acclaim. Coupled with this, the touring company provided opportunities for regional audiences to share in the productions of a high quality, as well as helping launch the careers of many young British artists. Without public funding he oversaw the building of the new opera house, held concerts for charitable causes and extended the educational reach of Glyndebourne by providing operas with and for children. He handed over the chairmanship to his son on 31 December 1999, but remained involved in day to day matters behind the scenes. He was also a member of the Arts Council of Great Britain and chairman of the its advisory panel on music (1988–92), and was the founder chairman of the London Sinfonietta (1968–88). He continued on the board of trustees for Glyndebourne Productions Ltd.

He was knighted in 1984 and made a CH in 2001 'For services to Opera and to Glyndebourne'.

Bernard Haitink 12 June 2002
Dutch by birth and nationality, Bernard Haitink, one of the great conductors of the twentieth century has spent more than thirty years of his working life in the United Kingdom and was for fifteen years music director of the Royal Opera House, London.

He was born in Amsterdam in 1929 and studied music at the Amsterdam Conservatory. After beginning his career as an orchestral violinist, he was appointed second conductor with the Netherlands Radio Union in 1955 and principal conductor of the Netherlands Radio Philharmonic Orchestra in 1957. He was artistic director of the Concertgebouw Orchestra, Amsterdam (1964-88), and then principal conductor and artistic director of the London Philharmonic Orchestra (1967-79). During his time the LPO attracted larger audiences to the Royal Festival Hall than any other orchestra and a large part of the credit was due to his reputation.

Despite his Dutch origins and numerous foreign tours with the LPO, he always made a point of including works by British composers, including not only well-established works but also newer works which he considered merited special encouragement. He devoted part of his time to recording work, and during his time with the LPO he conducted recordings of works by Holst and Elgar, a Liszt tone poem cycle and all the Beethoven symphonies and concertos – the last project resulting from the great success of his Beethoven concert cycle at the Royal Festival Hall in 1974. His Concertgebouw recordings of the symphonies of Mahler, Bruckner and Beethoven, along with his Vienna Philharmonic recordings of Brahms and Bruckner rank among the best ever and he was recognised as an outstanding interpreter of Bruckner, Mahler, Liszt and Strauss.

He was a guest conductor at Glyndebourne Opera from 1972 and succeeded John Pritchard as musical director (1978–88). He was music director, the European Union Youth Orchestra (1994–99) and principal guest conductor, Boston Symphony Orchestra (1995–). He has also worked with the Berlin and Vienna Philharmonic Orchestras and with the New York Philharmonic and Chicago Symphony Orchestras. He made his first appearance as a guest conductor at the Royal Opera House, Covent Garden in 1977, and he succeeded Sir Colin Davis as music director, holding the office for fifteen distinguished years (1987-2002) during a succession of perilous financial crises which seemed to be endemic to that troubled institution. He did not take up his post at the Royal Opera House full time until 1988, insisting that he was duty bound to complete his contract at Glyndebourne. The news was greeted with delight. 'In Haitink [the Royal Opera House] has got a meticulous musician, a great believer in rehearsals, and in the quality of the music. He places these virtues above star names.'[50] He arrived there at a time of difficulty and change, but did his utmost within his own field to ensure that it remained a centre of excellence. Renowned for a retiring nature and modesty (exceptionally rare qualities in the musical world) he was popular with the orchestras that he conducted, for his commitment to the players under him as much as to the score on the rostrum before him. He was respected for his seriousness and a streak of stubborn toughness, both of which were essential qualifications for life at the Opera House.

In 1977 he was made an honorary KBE in recognition of his substantial contribution to the artistic life of the United Kingdom and to coincide with his tenth anniversary with the London Philharmonic Orchestra. He was made an honorary CH in 2002.

CHAPTER EIGHT

Portals of discovery

SCIENTISTS AND PHYSICIANS

Her eye fell upon a little bottle that stood near the looking-glass. There was no label this time with the words DRINK ME, but nevertheless she uncorked it and put it to her lips. 'I know something interesting is sure to happen . . . so I'll just see what this bottle does.

'The rabbit sends in a little bill', *Alice's adventures in wonderland*, Lewis Carroll

To someone whose life has been spent in the arts, the world of the experimental laboratory is a mysterious and awe-inspiring place where principles, theories and even basic conversation are well beyond the comprehension of the untrained and the uninitiated. Someone without a scientific background is well-advised to approach these disciplines in reverent silence.

The group of names in this chapter cannot easily be subdivided either by their subject field or by the reason for which the CH was conferred upon them. The category comprises a distinguished group of biologists, chemists, physicists and physicians, but the more closely one examines their life's work, the more difficult it becomes to create definite partitions between these fields and to place an individual scientist in one of them. It becomes a pointless piece of labelling which denies their broad-ranging knowledge and work. Few if any of them can be subjected to such restrictive and simple labelling.

Mixing the four disciplines produces the following list in chronological order: John Scott Haldane (1928), Lady Barrett (1929), Jane Walker (1931), Charles Wilson (1937), Archibald Hill (1946), Viscount Cherwell (1953), Lord Blackett (1965), Sir Lawrence Bragg (1967), Sir Harold Hartley (1967), Lord Boyd-Orr (1968), Sir James Chadwick (1970), Charles Herbert Best (1971), Sir Peter Medawar (1972), Lord Cohen (1974), Max Perutz (1975), Frederick Sanger (1981), Rodney Porter (1985), Sydney Brenner (1986), Stephen Hawking (1989), Elsie Widdowson (1993), Reginald Jones (1994), Cesar Milstein (1994), Sir Nevill Mott (1995) and Sir Richard Doll (1995). If they cannot be assigned to a subject field, they can be grouped according to the level and nature of their achievement, and here five separate groupings begin to emerge.

The first group consists of the first three appointments, and they fall in a category that is probably now closed and unlikely to be seen in the CH ranks of the future. John Scott Haldane (1928) was an occupational health physician whose work concentrated on the health of miners and those working in other dangerous industries. Florence Barrett (1929) was a gynaecologist and whose prime concern was the health care of women. Jane Walker (1931) was a pioneer in the fresh air treatment of tuberculosis. The service of these three individuals was impressive in its day, but viewed with hindsight, their work can be seen as less scientific than humanitarian and domestic, though certainly pioneering. They set out to alleviate the human condition in an age where industrial work was more dangerous and living conditions were less sanitary.

The second group moves from the domestic to the international stage. After the appointment of Jane Walker in 1931, no further 'scientist' was appointed a CH until Charles Wilson in 1937. Because of his eminence, Wilson set a standard that has continued to be one of a number of a measuring devices in assessing qualifications for membership of the Companions of Honour. He was the recipient of one significant tribute to his work – a Nobel prize. Founded by the will of Alfred Nobel, the Swedish inventor of dynamite, the status of the Nobel prizes (first awarded in 1901), in literature, physics, chemistry, physiology or medicine, peace and economics, has risen steadily through the years to the point where the work of its laureates is identified as the summit of human achievement. Nevertheless the prizes have not been free from controversy. Embarrassing mistakes have been made, the reputation of some prize winners has evaporated, and many have disappeared into total obscurity. Twelve British recipients of the Nobel science prizes have been made Companions of Honour: Charles Wilson (1937), a quantum physicist and inventor of the Wilson cloud chamber; Archibald Hill (1946), a physiologist; Patrick Blackett (1965), an expert on nuclear physics and cosmic radiation; Lawrence Bragg (1967), who founded X-ray crystallography with his father; James Chadwick (1970), discoverer of the neutron; Peter Medawar (1972), an immunologist whose research made organ transplants possible; Max Perutz (1975), a biochemist who studied the structures of globular proteins; Frederick Sanger (1981), a biochemist who was awarded two Nobel prizes for his work on insulin and nucleic acids; Rodney Porter (1985), an immunologist who discovered the chemical structure of antibodies; Sydney Brenner (1986), a molecular biologist who discovered messenger RNA; Cesar Milstein (1994), an immunologist who worked on the development and control of the immune system and discovered the principle for production of monoclonal antibodies; and Nevill Mott (1995), a physicist who worked on the electronic structure of magnetic and disordered systems. The agricultural scientist John Boyd Orr (1968) was awarded the 1949 peace prize for his work in the development of international food policies.

Although a Nobel prize might be one way of measuring eligibility for the CH, it is not the only way, nor does it guarantee that the CH will be conferred in due course. Any expectation that a CH will follow a Nobel prize, goes against one of the fundamental principles of the 1993 reform of the honours system – the abolition of automatic honours. Some Nobel prize winners have received the CH, some have received both the CH and the OM, some have received only the OM, some have received neither. A prize is not a clear route to a CH, and in an Order as numerically restricted as the CH, there is also a question of whether and when a vacancy should be allotted to a scientist; some prize winners have waited for many years before being made a CH. Charles Wilson waited ten years (Nobel laureate 1927, CH 1937), Archibald Hill, twenty-four years (Nobel laureate 1922, CH 1946); Patrick Blackett, seventeen years (Nobel laureate 1948, CH 1965); James Chadwick, thirty-five years (Nobel laureate 1935, CH 1970); John Boyd-Orr, nineteen years (Nobel laureate 1949, CH 1968); Peter Medawar, twelve years (Nobel laureate 1960, CH 1972); Max Perutz, thirteen years (Nobel laureate 1962, CH 1975); Frederick Sanger waited until he had accumulated two Nobel prizes, (1958 and 1980, CH 1981); Rodney Porter, thirteen years (Nobel laureate

1972, CH 1985), Cesar Milstein ten years (Nobel laureate 1984, CH 1994); and Nevill Mott, eighteen years (Nobel laureate 1977, CH 1995). Lawrence Bragg had the longest wait of all, fifty-two years (Nobel laureate 1915, CH 1967). Sydney Brenner was a reversal of the usual trend in being made a CH in 1986, sixteen years before receiving a nobel prize (in 2002).

The third group consists of those who were probably competent enough to win a Nobel prize but never did so, or have not yet done so. Charles Herbert Best (1971), was co-discoverer of insulin and probably should have jointly won the 1922 Nobel prize for physiology or medicine, instead of J. R. R. Macleod. The activities of the theoretical physicist Stephen Hawking (1989) have been restricted after the onset of motor neurone disease. Richard Doll (1995) was the first scientist to prove incontrovertibly the danger of tobacco to health.

The fourth group includes two people whose scientific work was probably never at Nobel level, but was nonetheless influential and represented a lifetime of service. The chemist Harold Hartley (1967) was honoured more for his application of chemistry to warfare and industry than for major pioneering research. The physician Henry Cohen (1974), had a voracious appetite for committee work, and his CH was more a recognition of his extensive public service than for scientific achievement. The chemist Elsie Widdowson (1993) spent more than sixty years of her life on research into the composition of food and had considerable influence on the British diet.

The fifth group includes two people who could be described as 'backroom boffins'. Viscount Cherwell (1953) and Reginald Jones (1994) were part of a group of scientists whose talents were dedicated to achieving victory in the 1939–45 war. Although their work was never at Nobel level, their ingenuity and support, especially in the case of Jones, provided the country with a level of scientific intelligence that helped to win the war.

John Scott Haldane 4 June 1928

John Haldane spent his working life concentrating on issues of occupational health, especially the working conditions of the mining industry.

He was born in Edinburgh in 1860 into the distinguished Scottish family of that name, and followed his sister Elizabeth into the ranks of the CH. He was educated at Edinburgh Academy and the universities of Edinburgh and Jena. Throughout his life, his researches, begun in 1885, centred on occupational health, in particular problems connected with the health of miners. As a member of the Safety in Mines Research Board since its inception in 1921, he was engaged with questions concerned with hot and deep mines, mine ventilation, mine-rescue apparatus, underground fires due to spontaneous oxidation of coal, illumination at the coal face, and pulmonary disease caused by the inhalation of dust – all problems directly bearing on the health and safety of the miner. Destined for a life of active research in natural science, Haldane was greatly attracted by philosophy, which guided and inspired his scientific work in a search for a consistent theory which would explain the phenomena of life.

His official appointments were numerous: demonstrator and reader in physiology at Oxford, Sillman lecturer at Yale in 1916, Gifford lecturer at Glasgow (1927–28), president of the Institution of Mining Engineers (1924–28), Donellan lecturer at Trinity College, Dublin in 1930, fellow of New College, Oxford, honorary professor and director, the Mining Research Laboratory at Birmingham, and gas referee at the board of trade. He also served on several royal commissions and carried out various special inquiries for government departments.

His publications included *Essays in philosophical criticism* (1885), *Blue-books on the causes of death in colliery explosions* (1896), *Mechanism, life and personality* (1913), *Organism and environment* (1917), *The new physiology* (1919), *Respiration* (1922 and 1935), *Gases and liquids* (1928), *The sciences and philosophy* (1929), *The theory of heat engines* (1930), *The philosophical basis of biology* (1931), *Materialism* (1932), *The philosophy of a biologist* (1935),

Haldane's capacity for work was astonishing and he rarely took a holiday. His outstanding personality, the simplicity and directness of his experimental methods, the clear reasoning which made the solution of the complex problems that he handled appear easy, his kindness and regard for others made an ineffaceable impression on those who worked with him. Perhaps not as narrowly focused as later scientific Companions of Honour, he was a product of the polymath family in which he was born and raised, and his life and career was an attractive amalgam of the physiologist, the philosopher and the humanitarian, and he received the CH in 1928 as 'Director of the Mining Research Laboratory of Birmingham University. For Scientific work in connection with industrial disease'. It was a rare combination and today, without an accompanying Nobel prize, it would probably not be found among the ranks of the Companions of Honour.

Haldane continued working until the end of his life. Shortly after returning from a visit to Persia to investigate cases of heatstroke in the oil refineries he died at Oxford from pneumonia at midnight on 14–15 March 1936.

Lady [Florence] Barrett 1 March 1929
In the age of women's suffrage, Florence Barrett was a pioneer in the world of women in medicine. She had a long career of social service and as a distinguished gynaecologist.

Florence Perry was born in Gloucestershire in 1867 at a time when a governess was considered sufficient for the education of a daughter. In her early teenage years she decided on a medical career and studied medicine at University College, Bristol (then one of the outposts of the University of London) and graduated with a conjoint MB and BS degree, qualifying and registering as a medical practitioner in 1900. She was appointed to the staff of the Royal Free Hospital, and there she remained for the rest of her working life, being successively assistant anaesthetist, ophthalmic assistant, house surgeon, clinical pathologist, surgical and gynaecological registrar, with charge of the X-ray department, and clinical gynaecological assistant and anaesthetist. In 1908 she was appointed to the honorary staff of the hospital as assistant physician for diseases of women and she took a leading role in the development of the Medical School for Women. She was lecturer in midwifery (1913–21). The final roll call of her appointments listed her as consulting obstetric and gynaecological surgeon at the Royal Free Hospital; consulting obstetric surgeon, Mother's Hospital, Clapton; honorary surgeon at the Marie Curie Hospital; dean of the London (Royal Free Hospital) School of Medicine for Women; and president of the Medical Women's International Association.

Throughout her career she did much to improve the standard and status of nursing. She served on a large number of committees concerned with social problems and women's roles in them. Not surprisingly she was a supporter of the women's suffrage movement, although she condemned militant suffragettes. In 1916 she married the physicist Sir William Barrett, FRS and they had nine years of happy marriage until his death in 1925. Spiritualism was a fashionable cult at the time and Sir William Barrett was founder and president of the Society for Psychical Research. Florence Barrett shared her husband's fascination with the 'beyond' and they regularly took part in 'sittings'. Her own interest in the subject found expression in her book *Personality survives death* (1937). Her other publications reflected her principal concerns: *A plea for the feeding of nursing mothers as a means of preventing the waste and maiming of child life*; *Diseases of women: A handbook for nurses* (1912); and *Conception control* (1922).

Before the 1914–18 war she was prominent in initiating voluntary centres in London for the feeding of expectant mothers and children, and for that work she was made a CBE in 1917 in the first honours list of that new Order. In 1929 she was made a CH for services as 'Dean of the London School of Medicine for Women, President of the Medical Women's International Association'. She died in 1945.

Jane Walker 1 January 1931

Jane Walker was a pioneer of the open-air treatment of tuberculosis at a time when the disease was both rife and feared in the United Kingdom.

She was born in 1859 at Dewsbury in Yorkshire, the daughter of a blanket manufacturer who, unusually for his time, encouraged his daughter to pursue a career in medicine. She was educated at Southport and the London School of Medicine for Women. She took an MD degree at Brussels in 1880 at a time when she could not have obtained such a degree from a British university. In 1884 she became a licentiate of the Royal College of Physicians and Licentiate in Midwifery. In 1889 she was admitted a licentiate of the Royal College of Surgeons of Edinburgh. At first she specialised in the illnesses of women and children, working at the East London Hospital and the Wirral Children's Hospital. But her life work was as a specialist in phthisis and she had a practice in London's Harley Street.

Early in her career she became convinced that the most effective method of combating tuberculosis was by systematic fresh-air treatment. In 1892 she was the first to introduce the open-air treatment of the disease into England. She opened her sanatorium firstly at Downham Market, Norfolk, subsequently transferring it to Nayland, Suffolk.

She recognised that prevention and health education were as important as treatment and cure, and throughout her life she preached the importance of improving social conditions and eradicating insanitary and overcrowded slum dwelling. 'Right up to the last days she was ready to help or even initiate any new scheme. Her activity was like the activity of a young person, in spite of the pain she suffered. She kept abreast of every new movement in thought, reading omnivorously. She was full of humour, and to the end of her days enjoyed anything that brightened her thoughts of men and women.'[1]

Her publications included *A handbook for mothers* (1893), *A book for every woman* (1895) and *Modern nursing of consumption* (1904).

The CH was conferred on her in 1931, for services as 'Founder and Medical Superintendent of the East Anglian Sanatorium, Nayland, Suffolk. Founder and first president of the Medical Women's Federation'. Although her work was prominent enough, she had the added advantage of gender at a time when more women were being sought for high honours. She died of a heart attack at her practice in Harley Street in 1938.

Charles Wilson 11 May 1937
Charles Wilson was a quantum physicist and the first of a series of Nobel laureates to be appointed a Companion of Honour. He received the physics prize in 1927 (shared with Arthur H. Compton, a U.S. physicist) for his method of making the paths of electrically charged particles visible by condensation of vapour.

He was born in 1869 in a farmhouse in the Pentland Hills near Edinburgh. The premature death of his father caused his mother to take him to Manchester where he was educated at Owens College on a biological course in preparation for medical training. From there he won a scholarship to Sidney Sussex College, Cambridge where his tutor encouraged him to study physics. He graduated in 1892 and taught for a short time at a grammar school in the Midlands. It was not a career at which he excelled and he quickly returned to Cambridge to the Cavendish laboratory, becoming Clerk Maxwell Scholar in 1895. In 1901 he became university lecturer in experimental physics and was Jacksonian professor of natural philosophy (1925–34).

Wilson never lost his love for the land of his birth, and it was there that he first conceived the instrument that won him a Nobel prize. At a meteorological observatory on the summit of Ben Nevis in 1894 he received the first impressions that led him to design the famous Wilson cloud chamber, the instrument described by Ernest Rutherford as 'the most original apparatus in the whole history of physics.'[2] He looked down from the summit of the mountain to the sea of cloud below. 'The shadow of the Ben on the surface of the sea of cloud at first reached to the western horizon; its upper edge came racing eastwards as the sun rose. On the cloud surface beyond the shadow would then appear a glory, the coloured rings incomplete and rather faint and diffuse. The most striking of all were to be seen from the edge of the precipice overlooking the great corrie when the observer's shadow was formed on a thin sheet of wisp of cloud only a few feet below . . . This greatly excited my interest and made me wish to imitate them in the laboratory.'[3] Many years of experimental work followed until in 1911 he perfected the cloud chamber detector for studying the activity of ionized particles. It worked on the principle that ions speeding through a vaporous medium leave thread-like trails of tiny water drops that can be photographed. For decades the cloud chamber was the mainstay of important experiments. P. M. S. Blackett (himself later a Nobel prize winner and CH) improved it in 1932. High energies finally made it obsolete, and it was superseded by the bubble chamber in 1952.

He was also noted for his studies of atmospheric electricity, and his entry in *Who's Who* recorded that he was 'engaged in research since 1895 on condensation nuclei, ions and atmospheric electricity.' His interest was stimulated again by standing on the summit of a Scottish mountain, this time during a thunderstorm. Feeling his hair standing on end, he promptly scrambled off the summit just before the occurrence of a vivid flash of lightning. 'This experience drew my attention very forcibly to the magnitude of the electric field of a thundercloud and to its sudden changes.'[4] He designed various forms of electrometer for measuring the surface density of the earth's changes during a thunderstorm, and he devised a method for the protection of barrage balloons from lightning during the 1939–45 war.

Wilson was a perfectionist but a modest and unassuming one, with an endearing absence of the personal arrogance and the desire to self-publicise his genius. He published little because of a belief that none of his work should be committed to print until it had been thoroughly tested and was proved to be sound.

He was elected a fellow of the Royal Society, and was made a CH in 1937, after his retirement from Edinburgh, 'For services to experimental physics'. He died in 1959 at the age of ninety.

Archibald Hill 1 January 1946
Archibald Hill won the 1922 Nobel prize for physiology or medicine for his discovery relating to the production of heat in the muscle.

He was born in Bristol in 1886, and educated at Blundells School, Tiverton and Trinity College, Cambridge. He took the natural sciences tripos and graduated in 1909. After graduation he began research on the nature of muscular contraction, studying the dependence of heat production on the length of muscle fibre. He was elected to a fellowship at Trinity in 1910, and then spent the winter of 1910–1911 in Germany, working with a number of prominent German scientists. From 1911 until 1914, he continued his work on the physiology of muscular contraction at Cambridge, developing interests in the nervous impulse, haemoglobin and the calorimetry of animals. After 1914 he tended to move away from physiology and was appointed university lecturer in physical chemistry. During the war he served as a captain and brevet-major, and as director of the anti-aircraft experimental section of the munitions inventions department.

In 1919 he resumed his study of the physiology of muscle. In 1920 he was appointed Brackenbury professor of physiology at Manchester, where he continued work on muscular activity and began to apply the results obtained on isolated muscles to the case of muscular exercise. In 1923 he became Jodrell professor of physiology at University College, London. In 1926 he was appointed the Royal Society's Fullerton research professor (an office he held until 1951) and was in charge of the Biophysics Laboratory at University College until 1952.

His work on muscle function, especially the observation and measurement of thermal changes associated with muscle function, was later extended to similar studies on the mechanism of the passage of nerve impulses. Techniques had to be developed and he was eventually able to measure temperature changes of the order of 0.003°C over periods of only hundredths of a second. He was the discoverer of the phenomenon that heat was produced as a result of the passage of nerve impulses. His researches gave rise to an enthusiastic following in the field of biophysics, a subject whose growth owes much to him.

He was the author of many scientific papers, lectures, and books, his best-known books being *Muscular activity* (1926), *Muscular movement in man* (1927), *Living machinery* (1927), *The ethical dilemma of science and other writings* (1960), and *Traits and trials in physiology* (1965).

He was a member of parliament (1940–45), when he represented Cambridge University in the house of commons as an Independent Conservative. During the 1939–45 war, he served on many commissions concerned with defence and scientific policy. He was a member of the war cabinet scientific advisory committee (1940–46), chairman of the Research Defence Society (1940–51), and chairman of the executive committee of the National Physical Laboratory (1939–45). He was a member of the University Grants Committee (1937–1944) and served on the science committee of the Society for the Protection of Science and Learning, (1946–1956). He was also a trustee of the British Museum (1947–63), and was president (in 1952) of the British Society for the Advancement of Science.

He was elected a fellow of the Royal Society in 1918, serving as secretary (1935–1945), and foreign secretary (1945–46). For his war service he was made a military OBE in 1918 and was appointed a CH in 1946 as 'a Secretary of the Royal Society. For scientific services'. He died in 1977.

Viscount Cherwell 10 November 1953

Frederick Alexander Lindemann, first and last Viscount Cherwell, was essentially a scientist, but his application was such that he was never likely to be ranked among the Nobel laureates. He was a trusted confidant of Winston Churchill, and his CH owed more to political service than to scientific eminence. He was a physics professor at Oxford for thirty-seven years, and science rather than politics was his first love.

He was born at Baden-Baden in 1886, the son of an Alsatian father and an English mother. His father eventually took British nationality and settled in Devon. 'It was largely his father's love of astronomy and skill as an instrument maker that inclined the son to mathematics and physics.' Lindemann was educated at Blairlodge School, a gymnasium at Darmstadt and the University of Berlin where he was awarded a PhD in 1910 on the atomic heat of metals at low temperatures. He studied with W. H. Nernst and developed with him the Nernst-Lindemann theory of specific heat. He continued his work in Paris and by 1914 his reputation was so high that he was given the directorship of the royal flying corps experimental physics station at Farnborough. His best known exploit at Farnborough was his courageous demonstration, as an experimental pilot, of how an aircraft could be pulled out of a spin.

In 1919 he was offered the university professorship of experimental philosophy at the then moribund Clarendon Laboratory, which carried with it a fellowship at Wadham College. It was a challenge; there was no research at all in physics in the university, and less than ten undergraduates were reading the subject. 'Oxford was glad to welcome this tall fine-looking, well-dressed, rich, athletic, Continentally educated stranger with a low voice and an informing and critical tongue, who in his fastidious way was a "card" . . . In the midst of luxury he preserved an attractive simplicity. He was an abstainer, a non-smoker, and a life-long vegetarian.'[5] At Oxford he met Lord Birkenhead, and through him Winston Churchill, a friendship which was to become important in the days after 1940. Although he certainly transformed the Clarendon Laboratory into a major research facility, his success as a professor was partial; there was a lack of personal determination and something of the dilettante about him. 'He never went hard and continuously at one important thing. He preferred to busy himself and his young men with a succession of smaller researches in various branches of physics . . . He was temperamentally averse from the hard drudgery of experimental work and more content to be a director, adviser and stimulator of young research men than their co-worker and leader.'[6]

In 1937, sensing the deteriorating political climate and feeling the need for increased British air power, he unsuccessfully stood for parliament as an Independent Conservative candidate. In this respect he was in tune with Winston Churchill who had remained a friend, and in 1940, the latter appointed him as his personal assistant. He was not required to deal with difficult scientific problems but to render advice generally, 'as a man of completely independent judgement, with a wide experience of French and German mentality, whose views on problems involving numbers and quantities of any kind were found to be unbiased and useful.'[7] His appointment was criticised in certain quarters, including ministers and civil servants, who thought it wrong that someone with the status of a private secretary should have the powers of a cabinet minister. That concern was addressed in 1941 when Lindemann was created a baron, and in 1942 when he entered the cabinet as paymaster-general. He served in the office until 1945 and again from 1951 to 1953, when he retired to resume his academic duties. In 1954 he was appointed a member of the United Kingdom Atomic Energy Authority, but his views would not find favour today. Speaking in a debate in the house of lords in May 1957 he said that he could see no argument against the testing of thermonuclear weapons. He dismissed the argument that the tests constituted a danger to the health of humanity as 'unmitigated nonsense.'

His publications included *The physical significance of the quantum theory* (1932) and a number of papers on physical, chemical and astrological subjects in the *Proceedings of the Royal Society* and other journals.

He was elected a fellow of the Royal Society in 1920, created a baron in 1941 and a viscount in 1956, taking the title of Cherwell in both cases. He was made a CH on his resignation from the government in November 1953. Unusually, no citation was included in the announcement in the *London Gazette*. Lindemann owed his honours and position to his patron Winston Churchill, and the latter paid tribute: 'There were no doubt greater scientists than Frederick Lindemann, though his credentials and genius command respect. But he had two qualifications of vital consequence to me. First . . . he was my trusted friend and confidant of twenty years . . . [Secondly] Lindemann could decipher the signals from the experts on the far horizon and explain to me in lucid, homely terms what the issues were.'[8]

Lindemann never married and the barony and viscountcy became extinct on his death in 1957.

Lord Blackett 12 June 1965

Patrick Blackett was one of the most eminent experimental physicists of his generation. He was awarded the 1948 Nobel prize for physics for his development of Charles Wilson's cloud chamber method and his discoveries in the fields of nuclear physics and cosmic radiation.

His early life had briefly pointed to a different career. He was born in 1897, the son of a stockbroker and seemed destined for a career in the royal navy. He was educated at the Royal Naval College at Osborne and Dartmouth and served with the navy in the 1914–18 war. He was present at the battle of the Falkland Islands before he was seventeen and at the battle of Jutland before he was nineteen. 'As a sub-lieutenant in a destroyer, his thoughts went to the design of a gun-sight. He knew he had a scientific talent, but it was boredom, not dislike of the service, that led him to speculate vaguely about changing his career.'[9] He went to Magdalene College, Cambridge from the royal navy in 1919, and was elected to a fellowship immediately after taking his degree in the natural sciences tripos. He became a member of Ernest Rutherford's Cavendish Laboratory and his reputation was established by the end of the 1920s, by which time he was a fellow of King's College.

In 1933 he discovered the positron, which was cited in the award of his Nobel prize fifteen years later. In the same year he left Cambridge, already a fellow of the Royal Society at the age of thirty-five, to be professor of physics at Birkbeck College, London (1933–37), Langworthy professor of physics at Manchester (1937–53), and finally professor of physics at Imperial College, London. He was additionally pro-vice-chancellor of Manchester (1950–52), dean of the Royal College of Science at Imperial College (1955–60) and pro-rector of Imperial College (1955–60). Parallel with his post at Birkbeck was an involvement with defence science. He was brought into the air defence committee in 1937 and was director of operational research at the admiralty (1942–45).

His public appointments were numerous: member of the board of the National Research Development Corporation (1949–64), member of the scientific policy committee of the European Research Development Corporation (1954–58), member of the governing body of National Institute for Research in Nuclear Science (1957–60), member of the council of the DSIR (1955–60), member of the council of the Overseas Development Institute, member of the Council for Scientific Policy (1955–60), president of the British Association for the Advancement of Science (1957–58), and a trustee of the British Museum (1963–65).

Blackett specialised in atomic theory, cosmic radiation, geophysics and wartime operational research. His left-wing views deprived him of the political influence that other leading scientists acquired during and after the 1939–45 war (he was too far to the left for the liking of the post-war Labour government), but he became scientific advisor to the Labour government of 1964 and to the government of India. His publications included scientific papers on nuclear and atomic physics, cosmic rays and rock magnetism, also *Rayons cosmiques* (1934), *Military and political consequences of atomic energy* (1948), *Lectures on rock magnetism* (1956), *Atomic weapons and east-west relations* (1956) and *Studies of war* (1962). Most of what he said in his 1948 and 1956 books on the military and political consequences of atomic energy now seems platitudinous, 'at the time it seemed to many to be inhumanly cold, perverse, and probably pro-communist.'[10]

Blackett was among the most eminent scientists of his generation, but not until the advent of the 1964–70 Labour government, and at the age of sixty-eight, did he very belatedly begin to receive honours that some felt he should have received many years earlier. The CH, long overdue, was conferred in 1965, the citation blandly describing him as 'lately Professor of Physics, Imperial College of Science and Technology, University of London'. In the same year his fellow scientists elected him to the most prestigious office in the British scientific world, president of the Royal Society (1965–70). The OM, a traditional accompaniment to the presidency of that body, followed in 1967, and a life peerage in 1969. He died in 1974.

Sir Lawrence Bragg 1 January 1967
William Lawrence Bragg holds a series of unsurpassed records. He shared a Nobel prize with his father, he was the youngest ever Nobel laureate in any field (he was twenty-five) and, because of his youth, he was a Nobel laureate for an unequalled fifty-six years. Bragg and his father (Sir William Henry Bragg) were awarded the 1915 Nobel prize in physics for their services in the analysis of crystal structure by means of X-rays. In 1912 Max von Laue was the first to prove that X-rays had an

extremely short wavelength, and he won the 1914 Nobel prize for physics. In the following year, the Braggs turned Laue's method around and showed how crystalline structures could be accurately measured using X rays. X-ray crystallography has been indispensable since that date and it played a key role in the discovery of the DNA structure in 1953.

He was born in Adelaide, South Australia in 1890, where his father was professor of physics and mathematics at Adelaide University. He was educated at St Peter's College Adelaide, Adelaide University and Trinity College, Cambridge where he was Allen Scholar. He was elected a fellow of Trinity College and was appointed college lecturer in natural sciences in 1914. During the 1914–18 war he was technical adviser on sound ranging to the map section at GHQ France (1915–19). He was appointed Langworthy professor of physics at Manchester (1919–37), director of the National Physical Laboratory (1937–38), and then Cavendish professor of experimental physics at Cambridge (1938–53). There he succeeded Ernest Rutherford who had died the previous year, and directed the Cavendish Laboratories. Under his directorship, the laboratory lost its world leadership in high-energy physics by 1946, a process actively encouraged by Bragg who instead developed the fields of radio astronomy and molecular biology. Neither field enjoyed any status in 1938, but Bragg employed Max Perutz (CH 1975, OM 1988) and Francis Crick (OM 1991) among others, and at the time of his departure in 1953, the laboratories had won a first class international reputation in both fields.

Bragg's remaining appointments included Fullerian professor of chemistry at the Royal Institution (1953–66), director of the Royal Institution (1954–66), and chairman of the Frequency Advisory Committee (1958–60).

His publications included various scientific papers on crystal structure, and (with his father) *X rays and crystal structure* (1915), *The structure of silicates* (1930), *The crystalline state* (1934), *Electricity* (1936), *Atomic structure of minerals* (1937), (with W. F. Claringbull) *Crystal structures of minerals* (1965), and *Ideas and discoveries in physics* (1970).

Bragg's honours began with an OBE in 1918 for his war work. He was elected a fellow of the Royal Society in 1921, knighted in 1941, and finally admitted to the ranks of the CH in 1967 'For services to Science', at the surprisingly late age of seventy-six. The truth of the matter was that Bragg never again did work in any way as good as that which had earned him the Nobel prize fifty years earlier, and the CH can be seen almost as a retrospective conferral. He died in 1971.

Brigadier General Sir Harold Hartley 10 June 1967
Harold Hartley was physical chemist whose work was essentially to apply chemistry to the fields of warfare and industry, and who received the CH long after the peak of his activity.

He was born in 1878 the only son of a mineral water manufacturer. After three years at Dulwich College he went to Balliol College, Oxford in 1897 and graduated with a first class honours degree in natural science (chemistry and mineralogy). In 1901 he was appointed a tutorial fellow at Balliol in the place of his tutor Sir John Conroy who had just died. He was given the additional responsibility of teaching in the Balliol-Trinity laboratory, which the two colleges had set up twenty years previously. In 1904 it was arranged that the laboratory should develop for the university course in the then novel subject of physical chemistry.

At the outbreak of the 1914–18 war Hartley joined the 7th Leicestershire Regiment, but early in 1915 when German gas attacks began, he was sent to France as chemical adviser to the Third Army (1915–17). He was promoted to lieutenant colonel and became assistant director of gas services at GHQ France (1917–18), was three times mentioned in despatches, and was awarded the MC (1916). He was promoted to brigadier-general in 1918 and given charge of the chemical warfare department of the ministry of munitions (1918–19).

He was released from the army in the summer of 1919 and was sent as the leader of a team to investigate the chemical side of German war time activities. There he met Fritz Haber, who had organised the use of gas by the German army, and was amused to discover that his opposite number had never risen above the rank of captain. What he saw made a lasting impression; it was a large industry led by high quality scientists with strong government support. The team's report recommending positive action for British industry had its effect and Hartley became a member of the chemical warfare board in which he played a prominent part until 1950. He never lost his interest in chemical defence and later in life he exchanged notes with Fritz Haber's son on the 1914–18 operations of gas warfare.

He returned to Oxford to start up work in physical chemistry and had a succession of able young Balliol scholars as his pupils, including Sir Cyril Hinshelwood, later to become a Nobel prize winner. He continued as natural science tutor and Bedford lecturer in physical chemistry until 1931, when he became a research fellow (1931–41). In research he returned to an earlier interest in the electrical conductivity of solutions. The subject then appeared to many as one already supplied with enough useful data but the situation was transformed in 1923 by the publication of the Debye-Huckel theory. Realising that a study of non-aqueous solutions afforded the best test Hartley began a systematic series of conductivity measurements of salts dissolved in alcohols and other organic solvents. His research made a substantial contribution towards the understanding of ionic solutions and in recognition he was elected a fellow of the Royal Society in 1926.

In 1922 he joined the Society of Chemical Engineers and the board of the Gas Light and Coke Company, on which he served until 1945, being a deputy governor (1942–45). In 1929 he joined the fuel research board of the department of scientific and industrial research, acting as its chairman (1932–47). His interest in the uses of fuel widened when he was appointed a vice-president and director of research for the London, Midland and Scottish Railway Company (1930–47). That led to his appointment as chairman of the newly formed Railway Air Services (1934–45), which in turn led to chairmanship of British European Airways (1946–47) and of the British Overseas Airways Corporation (1947–49), which led to a lifelong interest in air travel. He became first chairman of the Electricity Supply Council (1949–52), where he collected distinguished scientists to sit as members of the council, and he was later a consultant to the Central Electricity Generating Board.

He was president of the Institution of Chemical Engineering (1951–52 and 1954–55), and president of the Society of Instrument Technology (1957–61). The construction firm of John Brown appointed him its adviser (1954–61) enabling him to develop his views of the importance of replacing batch chemical and biochemical processes by continuous plant, and of the need for high-level studies of methods of precise control. He was chairman of the British national committee and international executive council of the world power conference (1935–50) and president of the conference (1950–56).

He was appointed an OBE in 1918, CBE in 1919, knighted in 1928, appointed KCVO in 1944, GCVO in 1957 and CH in 1967 'For services in Scientific and public affairs'. For the last thirty years of his life he suffered from arthritis and towards the end of his life he was confined to a London nursing home where he died in 1972 at the age of ninety-four.

Lord Boyd-Orr 1 January 1968

John Boyd-Orr was a Scottish nutritionist who became first director-general of the Food and Agriculture Organisation of the United Nations and was awarded the 1949 Nobel peace prize for his work in developing international food policies.

He was born in 1880 in Kilmaurs (East Ayrshire), the son of a quarry-owner, and educated at West Kilbride School, Kilmarnock Academy and the university of Glasgow, from where he graduated in 1901. He taught in a school for four years and then returned to the University of Glasgow to study medicine. He was awarded an MD degree in 1914 and was a locum tenens for one month before returning to the university to study metabolic disease, for which he was awarded a DSc in 1919. During the 1914–18 war he served in the Royal Army Medical Corps as regimental medical officer with the Sherwood Foresters, later transferring to the royal navy and serving in the Q ships. He was appointed a DSO in 1917 and was twice awarded an MC.

Moving to the University of Aberdeen, he established the Rowett Institute, named after John Quiller Rowett, a local Aberdeen businessman and a major benefactor. He established a programme of research on human and animal nutrition and his research had a significant impact on British health policy, including the introduction of free milk in schools. He was a member of the reorganisation commission for the fat stock industry (1932); the reorganisation commission for milk (1935–36); the cattle committee (ministry of agriculture); the colonial advisory council of agriculture and animal health; the advisory commission on nutrition (ministry of health); and the technical commission on nutrition (league of nations).

He was appointed professor of agriculture at Aberdeen in 1942 but retired in 1945 on being elected rector of the University of Glasgow (1945–47) (he was chancellor of the university 1947–71) and independent member of parliament for the Scottish universities (1945–47) and director-general of the newly established Food and Agriculture Organisation of the United Nations (1945–48). He made his lasting contribution in this latter position, becoming the architect of food policies aimed at helping starving nations, but he became frustrated at the lack of progress and exasperated by political procrastination. He resigned from the FAO, taking up the idealist cause of world government as the only means of preventing poverty and hunger. In recognition of this work he was awarded the Nobel peace prize in 1949 for advocating a world food policy based on human needs rather than trade interests.

His writings included *Minerals in pastures and their relation to animal nutrition* (1928), *The national food supply and its influence on public health* (1934), *Food, health and income* (1936), *Fighting for what* (1943), *Food and the people* (1944), *Food – the foundation of world unity* (1948), *The white man's dilemma* (1953), *Feast and famine* (1960), and *As I recall* (1966).

He was elected a fellow of the Royal Society in 1932, knighted in 1935, created baron in 1949, and rather belatedly made a CH in 1968 (he was then eighty-seven) 'For services to Human and Animal Nutrition.' His only son was killed in action in 1941 while serving with the RAF and the barony became extinct on his death in 1971.

Sir James Chadwick 1 January 1970

In 1932, after a search lasting eight years, James Chadwick discovered the existence of neutrons – elementary particles devoid of any electrical charge – and three years later he was awarded the Nobel prize for physics for one of the fundamental discoveries in the history of nuclear science. His discovery prepared the way towards the fission of uranium 235 and towards the creation of the atomic bomb.

Like many scientific discoveries, it was based on a degree of luck and chance. In the same year Irene and Frederic Joliot-Curie (Irene was the daughter of Marie Curie) explored what happened when a nucleus was bombarded with alpha rays. They concluded that gamma rays were ejecting protons from the nucleus, though they could not explain how the gamma rays could shoot out a sizeable entity like a proton, almost two thousand times heavier than an electron. They published their results quickly, since many others were working on the same problem, but it proved to be a mistake. Chadwick read their report and saw that they had the right data but the wrong answer. There must be another particle in the nucleus with a mass approximately that of a proton, and so he discovered the neutron. The Joliot-Curies were compensated by being awarded the chemistry prize in 1935, in the same year that Chadwick took the physics prize.

He was born in Cheshire in 1891 and educated at Manchester High School and Manchester University in 1908. He spent the next two years as a postgraduate in the physical laboratory in Manchester, where he worked on various radioactivity problems. In 1913 he was awarded the 1851 Exhibition Scholarship and proceeded to Berlin to work in the Physikalisch Technische Reichsanstalt at Charlottenburg with Professor Geiger of Geiger counter fame. As a British national he was interned during the 1914–18 war, though the Germans allowed him to continue his research, and he examined, among other things, German radioactive toothpaste.

In 1919 he returned to England to work with Ernest Rutherford, who in the meantime had moved to the Cavendish Laboratory, Cambridge. Chadwick joined Rutherford in accomplishing the transmutation of light elements by bombardment with alpha particles, and in making studies of the properties and structure of atomic nuclei. He received his PhD in 1921, was elected a fellow of Gonville and Caius College (1921–35) and was appointed the first ever assistant director of Research in the Cavendish Laboratory (1923), becoming the de facto director as Rutherford aged.

In 1927 he was elected a fellow of the Royal Society. He remained at Cambridge until 1935 when he was elected to the Lyon Jones chair of physics in the University of Liverpool. He used his Nobel prize money to buy a cyclotron, and, after the start of the 1939–45 war, he explored the possibility of building an atomic bomb. He was well aware of the progress to that end being made by German scientists and his motivation was a concern that the Allies would easily be defeated if the Germans won the race and Hitler was equipped with such a devastatingly powerful weapon. After the outbreak of the war he was chief advisor to the group of

British officials weighing the option of investing much of Britain's limited resources in the development of an atomic bomb. His reputation in the USA was such that his report persuaded administration officials of the feasibility of a fission device even before Pearl Harbour. In response to repeated requests by the American government from 1941 onwards, the British government allowed Chadwick to go to the USA where he worked as head of the British mission attached to the Manhattan Project for the development of the atomic bomb (1943–46). Chadwick was given authority over all non-American scientists in the project and used all his diplomatic skills in handling relations between them and General Leslie Groves the dictatorial US army officer in charge of the project. By virtue of his reputation, Chadwick was able to persuade the Danish physicist, Niels Böhr, to escape from Nazi-occupied Denmark in 1943, to work with him in the USA.

Chadwick returned to England and retired from active physics and his chair at Liverpool in 1948 on his election as master of Gonville and Caius College, Cambridge. He soon wearied of the factious nature of academic politics, retired in 1958, and is said never to have set foot in the college again. His successor Sir Nevill Mott had an equally difficult time. From 1957 to 1962 he was a part-time member of the United Kingdom Atomic Energy Authority, but he preferred obscurity to glory, and refrained from public statements on the politics of the atomic bomb; he held that such debates were for the public, not scientists, to dominate. He published several papers on radioactivity and connected problems and on the neutron and its properties, including *Radioactivity and radioactive substances* (1921), and with Rutherford and C. D. Ellis, he was co-author of *Radiations from radioactive substances* (1930).

For his critical efforts in the work leading to the creation of the first atomic bomb, Chadwick was knighted in 1945. In 1970, at the age of seventy-eight he was made a CH 'For services to Science'. Throughout his internment during the 1914–18 war he suffered from malnutrition, leaving him in poor health for the rest of his life. He died in 1974.

Charles Herbert Best *12 June 1971*

Charles Best was an unassuming Canadian scientist who ranks with Sir Frederick Banting as the co-discoverer of insulin and its use in the treatment of diabetes, although there was much controversy at the time and subsequently as to who had actually discovered the hormone.

He was born in Maine (of Canadian parents) in 1899 and inherited a predisposition to medicine from his father who was a physician. After war service in the 2nd Canadian Tank Corps (1918–19), he studied at Toronto University, and at the time of the discovery of insulin, he was a senior undergraduate physiology student.

Frederick Banting was a Canadian surgeon with little training in research. His medical education had been completed hastily in 1917 because of the war. His practice in London, Ontario, was not very exciting and certainly not remunerative. After he had become fascinated with the possibility of curing diabetes, Banting moved to Toronto to work with J. R. R. Macleod, the British-born professor of physiology at Toronto University. At first Macleod allowed Banting to use his laboratories for part of the summer with a supply of dogs for experiments, and with Best as an assistant. Macleod had his own assistant, J. B. Collip.

Relations between the two teams quickly deteriorated, and Banting and Macleod came to hate each other. Yet from their joint laboratory emerged the discovery of insulin in 1921. The Nobel committee had trouble deciding who had discovered insulin, and awarded the 1923 medicine prize jointly to Banting and Macleod. Banting was so incensed at Macleod being honoured that he decided to refuse the prize. When prevailed upon to accept (it would be the first time that any Nobel prize had gone to Canada), Banting announced that he would give half the prize money to Best, his real 'partner'. The next day Macleod announced that he would give half his share of the prize money to Collip. The controversy lingered on until 1962 when the Nobel Foundation declared that Macleod (who had died in 1935) had wrongly been given a share in the prize.

In 1928 Macleod went back to his native Scotland and Best succeeded him as professor of physiology at the University of Toronto in 1929. He served as associate director of the Connaught laboratories, in charge of the production of insulin, from 1932 to 1941, and became director of the Banting and Best department of medical research in 1941 (Banting having died in that year), holding the post until 1965, and becoming director emeritus in 1967. After the deaths of Banting and Macleod, Best was revered as the surviving discoverer of insulin and lived into honoured old age. He was made president of the International Diabetes Federation in 1949 and wrote numerous articles on insulin, carbohydrate and fat metabolism, and muscular exercise among others. Arguably Best was among the roll of distinguished scientists who perhaps should have had the Nobel prize but never did.

He was made a CBE in 1944 and a CC (Companion of the Order of Canada) in 1967. The CH 'For services to Medical Research' was conferred in 1971. The honour aroused Best's interest and he enquired whether he was the first Canadian to receive the award.[11] Regretfully not, was the reply; he was the fourth – after General Henry Crerar, Vincent Massey and General Andrew McNaughton. He died in 1978.

Sir Peter Medawar 1 January 1972

Peter Medawar was a medical scientist who was awarded the 1960 Nobel prize for physiology or medicine (shared with Sir Macfarlane Burnet) for his discovery of acquired immunological tolerance. His work centred on tissue transplantation which eventually helped make organ transplants possible.

He was born in 1915, in Rio de Janeiro, to a Lebanese businessman who was a naturalized British subject. Medawar was educated at Marlborough College and at Magdalen College, Oxford where he studied zoology. After graduation a period of work at the school of pathology at Oxford aroused his interest in research in areas of biology related to medicine. In 1935 he was appointed Christopher Welch scholar and senior demonstrator at Magdalen College, Oxford, and in 1938 he became a fellow of Magdalen College. In 1942 he was Rolleston Prizeman and in 1944 he became senior research fellow of St John's College, Oxford, and university demonstrator in zoology and comparative anatomy. He returned to Magdalen College as a fellow in 1946–47, leaving to become Mason professor of zoology at Birmingham University (1947–51). In 1951 he moved to London as Jodrell professor of zoology and comparative anatomy at University College, London, where he remained until 1962, when he was appointed director of the National Institute of Medical Research at Mill Hill, London. He was also a member of the Royal Commission on Medical Education (1965–68). He retired in 1975 at the age of sixty.

His earlier research at Oxford, concentrated on tissue culture, the regeneration of peripheral nerves and the mathematical analysis of the changes of shape of organisms that occur during this development. During the 1939–45 war he explored the problem of the failure of skin taken from one human being to form a permanent graft on the skin of another person and discovered a method for joining ends of severed nerves This research enabled him to establish theorems of transplantation immunity which formed the basis of his future research. At Birmingham he studied the problems of pigmentation and skin grafting in cattle and concluded that the phenomenon that they called 'actively acquired tolerance' of homografts could be artificially reproduced. When he moved to London he continued to work on this phenomenon of tolerance, and his detailed analysis of it occupied him for several years. Working on a theory proposed by an Australian virologist, Sir Macfarlane Burnet, he proved it was possible under certain circumstances for an organism to overcome its normal tendency to reject foreign tissue or organs, and the two men shared the 1960 Nobel prize for physiology or medicine.

He was a prolific writer, and his publications include works on philosophy as well as medical science: *The uniqueness of the individual* (1957), *The future of man* (1960), *The art of the soluble* (1967), *Induction and intuition* (1969), *The hope of progress* (1972), (with J. S. Medawar) *Life science* (1977), *Advice to a young scientist* (1979), *Pluto's republic* (1982), (with J. S. Medawar) *Aristotle to zoos* (1983), *The limits of science* (1984), and an autobiography *Memoir of a thinking radish* (1986). In that volume he complained that references to him being 'of Arab extraction' made him sound like a gum.

Medawar was knighted in 1965, and made a CBE in 1958 and a CH in 1972 'For services to Medical Research'. He was elected a fellow of the Royal Society in 1949, and it was no secret that but for the onset of ill-health, he would have been president in due course. Although the state of his health denied him the presidency, he was given the customary OM in 1981, and died in 1987.

Lord Cohen of Birkenhead 1 January 1974
Henry Cohen was a physician, who spent most of his life in the area of north-west England in which he was born, and who was renowned for his grasp of administration.

He was born in 1900, the youngest son of a Jewish draper from Liverpool. Throughout his life he was proud of his Jewish ancestry, but principally on ethical, cultural and historical grounds, and he was essentially a secular Jew who showed little interest in the religious side of his heritage. He was educated at St John's School, Birkenhead and at the University of Liverpool where he graduated with a first class MB BS degree in medicine in 1922. Further work led to an MD in 1924. He was appointed assistant physician at the Liverpool Royal Infirmary in 1924, and there he remained until his retirement in 1965. In 1934 he was appointed professor of medicine at Liverpool University. It was a part-time appointment, but not without its problems. Liverpool possessed four general teaching hospitals, each viewing itself as an autonomous unit, even when nominally incorporated into the United Liverpool Hospitals in 1936. 'Welding a teaching and research unit together under such circumstances presented insuperable difficulties to a young man of whom many people were jealous,'[12] and Cohen was not a notable success.

His lengthy entry in *Who's Who* records that he held a large number of fellowships, honorary or substantive, membership or chairmanship of countless committees, councils and boards, and the numerous lectures that he gave. Even Cohen himself seems to have found the enumeration wearisome and took refuge in the words: 'several committees and joint committees (Ministry of Health) including General Practice, Prescribing, Mental Nursing, Epilepsy, Welfare Foods, Poliomyelitis, Health and Education, Operation Research in Pharmaceutical Service, Safety on Drugs; Flour Panel, Ministry of Food, 1955.'

Among his committee work was the chairmanship of the committee dealing with the organisation of poliomyelitis vaccination in the United Kingdom, and the medical advisory committee of the ministry of health (1948–63). In 1949 he became first vice-chairman of the newly-formed Central Health Services Council, and then chairman (1957–63). He was president of the British Medical Association in 1951 and president of the Royal Society of Medicine in 1964. He was also editor-in-chief of the *British encyclopaedia for medical practice* (1955–70) and became well-known among general practitioners. Not all his activities were medical. He seemed to find time to be a deputy lieutenant for Lancashire, a justice of the peace, and chancellor of the University of Hull (1970–77). He loved the theatre and was president of the Liverpool Repertory Theatre, and its chairman (1948–61), and president of the Liverpool Playhouse (1961–77).

His publications include *New pathways in medicine* (1935), *Nature, method and purpose in diagnosis* (1943), *Sherrington: physiologist, philosopher and poet* (1958), and *The evolution of modern medicine* (1958).

He was knighted in 1949, created a baron (as Lord Cohen of Birkenhead) in 1956, and the CH was conferred on him in 1974 'For services to medicine.' Cohen seems to have been an inveterate gatherer of committees (which presumably he enjoyed and on which he was probably effective) and the extensive list included in his detailed entry in *Who's Who* inclines one to the believe that, physician though he was, his honours were for a career of public service that was primarily administrative. He never married and the peerage became extinct on his death in 1977.

Max Perutz 1 January 1975
Max Perutz was the joint recipient, with John Kendrew, of the 1962 Nobel prize for chemistry for their studies of the structures of globular proteins, in particular haemoglobin and myoglobin.

He was born in Vienna in 1914, his parents being Austrian Jews from families of textile manufacturers who had made their fortune in the nineteenth century by the introduction of mechanical spinning and weaving into the Habsburg empire. He was educated at the Theresianum, a grammar school derived from an officers academy of the days of the Empress Maria Theresa, and his parents suggested that he should study law in preparation for entering the family business. But a chemistry teacher awakened an interest in that subject, and he had no difficulty in persuading his parents to let him study the subject of his choice.

In 1932, he went to the University of Vienna where his curiosity was aroused by organic biochemistry. Hearing of the work of Sir Gowland Hopkins, the Cambridge scientist who discovered vitamins, he decided to go to Cambridge to work for a doctorate. With financial help from his father he became a research student at the Cavendish Laboratory at Cambridge under J. D. Bernal in September 1936, and stayed at Cambridge thereafter with a brief interregnum in the war.

With the German invasion of Austria in 1938, the family business was expropriated and Perutz survived because of a grant by the Rockefeller Foundation in 1939, engineered by Sir Lawrence Bragg who had become interested in Perutz's work. The grant continued until 1945, when he was given an Imperial Chemical Industries research fellowship. After the anschluss, Austria was no longer safe for Jews and he brought his parents to Britain. He and his parents were interned in 1940 in a number of locations throughout Britain until, in July that year, they were sent to Quebec. After a time his Cambridge friends and colleagues managed to secure his release and he returned to his research.

In 1937 Perutz began the analysis of haemoglobin, and ten years later, Kendrew set to work on the related protein myoglobin. Besides an analysis, they wanted to achieve a three-dimensional model of their molecules. The work was lengthy and painstaking. In Kendrew's case, the measurement of myoglobin required measuring the intensities of a quarter of a million X-ray reflections from 110 crystals. G. S. Adair made Perutz the first crystals of horse haemoglobin, and he was then shown how to take X-ray pictures and how to interpret them. Early in 1938 he published a joint paper on X-ray diffraction from crystals of haemoglobin and chymotrypsin. The chymotrypsin crystals were twinned and therefore difficult to work with, and so Perutz continued with haemoglobin. D. Keilin, then professor of biology and parasitology at Cambridge, became interested in the work and provided Perutz and his colleagues with the biochemical laboratory facilities that they lacked at the Cavendish. Perutz made many notable contributions particularly in connection with the allosteric changes associated with the oxygenation of haemoglobin; this led to an understanding of the functional characteristics of abnormal human haemoglobins. He also studied the crystal texture and mechanism of flow of glaciers, but as a keen mountaineer it was principally an excuse for working in mountains.

In 1947, he was made head of the newly constituted Medical Research Council's molecular biology unit; his entire staff consisting of J. C. Kendrew. It was a modest beginning for what was to become the world-famous Laboratory of Molecular Biology, and Perutz was effectively the founder. In 1962, the number of staff had grown to ninety and in that year four of the researchers who had worked there were give Nobel prizes. Perutz was the architect of the phenomenal success of the laboratory of which he became chairman in that year. 'His principles were to choose outstanding people and to give them intellectual freedom; to take a genuine interest in everyone's work and to give younger colleagues public credit; to enlist skilled support staff who could design and build sophisticated and advanced new apparatus and instruments; to facilitate the interchange of ideas, in the canteen as much as in seminars; to have no secrecy; to be in the laboratory most of the time and to be accessible as far as possible to everyone; and to engender a happy environment where there is high morale.'[13]

His publications include *Proteins and nucleic acids, structure and function* (1962), *Atlas of haemoglobin and myoglobin* (1981), *Is science necessary* (1988), *Mechanisms of co-operativity and allosteric control in proteins* (1990), *Protein structures: new approaches to disease and therapy* (1992), *Science is no quiet life* (1997), and *I wish I'd made you angry earlier: essays on science, scientists and humanity* (1998).

Perutz was naturalised a British subject in 1943. He was elected a fellow of the Royal Society in 1954, appointed CBE in 1963, the year following the Nobel prize, a CH in 1975 'For services to Molecular Biology' and an OM in 1988. He was generous and magnanimous to friend and stranger alike and was implaccably opposed to any unfairness. This innate egalitarianism perhaps explains the absence of a knighthood, which might reasonably have followed the CBE. He died in 2002.

Frederick Sanger 13 June 1981
The biochemist Frederick Sanger is a rare example of an individual who has twice won a Nobel prize, and he was the first person to win the chemistry prize twice. Although the work of Banting and Best had proved the beneficial effect of insulin on the treatment of diabetes, the structure of insulin remained a mystery until Sanger demonstrated its exact composition after eight years of hard work and was awarded a Nobel prize for chemistry in 1958. His scientific research continued unabated and in 1980 he won a second Nobel prize, also for chemistry, for determining the base sequence of the nucleic acids.

He was born in 1918 at Rendcomb in Gloucestershire, the second son of a medical practitioner. He was educated at Bryanston School and St John's College, Cambridge where he graduated with a degree in natural sciences in 1939. He then began research on the metabolism of the amino acid lysine, being awarded a PhD in 1943, and remained in Cambridge from that date. From 1944 to 1951 he held a Beit memorial fellowship for medical research and from 1951 he was a member of the external staff of the Medical Research Council, and worked at the council's Laboratory of Molecular Biology at Cambridge (1961–83).

From 1943 his work was concerned largely with problems related to the determination of the structure of proteins. He was a pioneer in the development of chemical methods to show how amino acids – the building blocks of proteins – are arranged in sequence in these very large molecules, and he won the 1958 Nobel chemistry prize for his studies on insulin, accomplishing the first determination of the amino acid sequence (primary structure) of a protein of the insulin molecule. After that, he turned his skills to other large molecules – the nucleic acids – and devised methods for sequencing both ribonucleic acids (RNA) and deoxyribonucleic acids (DNA). In 1980, he shared the Nobel prize (with Paul Berg and Walter Gilbert) for developing a method, important in recombinant DNA research, for rapidly determining the chemical structure of pieces of DNA.

Sanger was elected a fellow of the Royal Society in 1954. He was made a CBE in 1963, a CH in 1981 'For services to biochemistry', and an OM in 1986.

Rodney Porter 15 June 1985
Rodney Porter was an immunologist who made outstanding contributions to immunochemistry and was largely responsible for elucidating the chemical structure of antibodies. He was awarded the 1972 Nobel prize in physiology or medicine, shared with Gerald Edelman, for their discoveries concerning the chemical structure of antibodies.

He was born in 1917 at Newton-le-Willows, Lancashire. He was educated at the Ashton-in-Makerfield Grammar School, and at the University of Liverpool graduating in 1939 with a degree in biochemistry. In 1940–46 he served in the army with the Royal Artillery, the Royal Engineers, and the Royal Army Service Corps. He was with the First Army in 1942 in the invasion of Algeria and with the Eighth Army during the invasion of Sicily and then Italy. He served with the army in Italy, Austria, Greece and Crete until January 1946.

After demobilisation, he went to Pembroke College, Cambridge, joined the university department of biochemistry and became associated with Frederick Sanger who was developing methods for elucidating the detailed chemical structure of proteins. Porter worked on investigating protein chemistry for the PhD that he was awarded in 1948. While working in Cambridge his interest in immunochemistry, like many of his contemporaries, was aroused through reading Landsteiner's newly published book on the specificity of serological reactions. After a year's postdoctoral work on the structure of antibodies, he joined the scientific staff of the National Institute for Medical Research in 1949 where he worked with A. J. P. Martin, who during that time received a Nobel prize for his development of chromatographic methods of analysis. Porter himself worked on methods of protein fractionation, with a particular interest in chromatographic methods of fractionation. In 1958 he developed a method of using enzymes for splitting antibodies into two functionally distinct halves – one retaining the individual combining specificity of the molecules, and the other half associated with several other distinctive biological activities. This technique was extensively used to study the parts of the molecule responsible for many complex properties of antibodies. In 1960 he joined St Mary's Hospital Medical School, University of London, as Pfizer professor of immunology, the first chair of its kind created in the United Kingdom. There he continued the research he had developed at the NIMR. In 1960 'he made another fundamental contribution when he isolated the constituent peptide chains of antibody molecules in relatively unchanged form. On the basis of his work he proposed in 1962 a 4-chain structure for antibody which has proved applicable to all vertebrate species. This work led to a precise understanding of the chemical relationships which exist between different classes of antibodies, as well as those produced by normal and cancerous lymphoid tissues.'[14]

In 1967, he succeeded Sir Hans Krebs as Whitley professor of biochemistry in the University of Oxford and became honorary director of the Medical Research Council's immunology unit. 'His work at Oxford focused on a new theme, studying the complex mixture of proteins in the blood, called the complement system, which constitutes a major defence mechanism against invading foreign organisms. With the Medical Research Council team, created for this project in Oxford, he helped to clarify this complex system by providing detailed structural and functional analyses of many of the proteins in the system; and he was outstandingly successful in opening up a second major area of scientific research . . . Altogether his work contributed significantly to the understanding of immunological phenomena in molecular terms, and as a result immunology assumed an increasingly pervasive role in general biology and clinical medicine . . . Here he widened his research interests to include the nature of the molecular interactions of complement with antibodies, and he stimulated much research on the cells surface components of lymphocytes.'[15] When he reached the normal retiring age of sixty-five in 1982, he was invited to continue for a further five years. He was generally regarded as the most distinguished unit director of the Medical Research Council, and served as a member of the council (1970–74).

Porter was responsible for major advances in the understanding of immunological mechanisms. His demonstration that the immuno-globulin molecule consists of two pairs of polypeptide chains, with the antigen-combining associated part of these chain structures, was the basis for his prize. He continued to be a leading figure in the field until his untimely death.

He was elected a fellow of the Royal Society in 1964, and made a CH in 1985 'For services to Biochemistry', on his retirement from Oxford. Released from his teaching duties and departmental responsibilities, he was looking forward to devoting his whole attention to research. The hope was shattered by his death in a road accident three months after his retirement.

Sydney Brenner 31 December 1986

The molecular biologist Sydney Brenner is widely recognised as one of the founders of modern molecular genetics. He proved the existence of messenger RNA and demonstrated the genetic code, both important discoveries leading to the establishment of modern gene technology. He was awarded the 2002 Nobel prize for physiology or medicine (shared with Sir John Sulston and Robert Horvitz) for his work on genetic regulation of organ development and programmed cell death.

He was born in 1927 in Germiston, South Africa and educated at Germiston High School. His parents had no formal education and he had to teach himself and relied on what he could find in the local public library. He had his own laboratory in the garage by the age of ten. There he boiled flowers and wondered what made their pigment. He took degrees in science and medicine at the University of Witwatersrand and then moved to Exeter College, Oxford in 1951 to work for a DPhil degree in the physical chemistry laboratory.

After a brief return to South Africa he joined the Medical Research Council Unit in the Cavendish Laboratory in Cambridge in 1956. In 1959 he was elected a fellow of King's College. In 1964 he became joint head of the cell biology division of the Laboratory of Molecular Biology and was director of the laboratory (1979-86) and then director of the MRC Molecular Genetics Unit (1986-92). He was a member of the Medical Research Council (1978-82 and 1986-90), and honorary professor of genetic medicine at Cambridge (1989-92). In 1996 he started the new Institute of Molecular Sciences, a private research institute at Berkeley, California, retiring in 2001 at the age of seventy-four. The institute's endowment ended in July that year, and Brenner had no wish to spend much of his time raising more money to keep it going, nor did he want to be the head of a large organisation and push paper and people every day. But nor did he wish to retire and play golf. Scientific research was his hobby, his work and his pleasure and he accepted an offer to become a distinguished research professor at the Salk Institute for Biological Studies in La Jolla, California focussing on writing a book about the next step in research on the human genome.

Brenner is best known for his work in the 1960s, which established the existence of messenger RNA, which transmits information from DNA to proteins. He discovered messenger RNA (with Jacob and Meselson) and, with Francis Crick, showed that the code was composed of triplets. That discovery won him the prestigious Lasker Award in 1971 for basic medical research. In collaboration with colleagues, he made major theoretical or experimental contributions to the solving of the genetic code, the translation of genetic information into protein structure and mechanisms by which genes control the actions of other genes. He also contributed to the method of negative staining for electron microscopy.

In *Who's Who* he lists rumination as his only recreation, and when once asked what he was chewing over at the moment, he replied 'Everything!'

He was elected a fellow of the Royal Society in 1965 and was made a CH in 1986 'For services to Molecular Biology.'

Stephen Hawking 17 June 1989
Stephen Hawking achieved the status of a populist theoretical physicist, chiefly through his widely and successfully self-publicised interest in the origin and future of cosmic black holes and his best-selling book *A brief history of time*. Published in 1988, it acquired the not altogether enviable reputation of being a fashionable accoutrement – the book that everybody had but few ever read.

He was born in 1942 in Oxford. He was educated at St Albans School, and then at University College, Oxford. He graduated with a degree in natural science and then moved to Trinity Hall, Cambridge to do research in general relativity and cosmology, for which he was awarded a PhD. He stayed at Cambridge as first a research fellow, then a professorial fellow at Gonville and Caius College (1965–69). He was a member (1968–72) and then a research assistant (1972–73) at the Institute of Theoretical Astronomy. After leaving the institute he was appointed a research assistant at the department of applied mathematics and theoretical physics (1973–75), reader in gravitational physics (1975–77) and professor (1977–79). Since 1979 he has held the Lucasian chair of mathematics.

Hawking's research centred on the basic laws that govern the universe. He made a major contribution to the field of general relativity and its application to the study of astrophysics. His knowledge of mathematics and physics enabled him to demonstrate the basic theorems for the laws governing black holes. He showed that Einstein's general theory of relativity implied space and time would have a beginning in the big bang and an end in black holes. He conjectured that black holes should not be completely black, but should emit radiation and eventually evaporate and disappear. Another of his conjectures is that the universe has no edge or boundary in imaginary time.

His publications include (with G. F. R. Ellis) *The large scale structure of space-time* (1973), (edited by W. W. Israel) *General relativity: an Einstein centenary survey* (1979), (edited with M. Rocek) *Superspace and supergravity* (1981), (edited jointly) *The very early universe* (1983), (with W. Israel) *300 Years of Gravity* (1987), *A brief history of time* (1988), and *Black holes and baby universes* (1993). Despite its widespread popularity, *A brief history of time* was controversial and criticised by some academics, including two leading astronomers, for the errors that it contained. Some of his unproven and untested theories, although brilliant and plausible, were labelled 'exotic', and some of his later work was less securely based.

He was elected a fellow of the Royal Society in 1974. He was made a CBE in 1982, and a CH in 1989 'For services to Astronomical Research'. Hawking's comparative youth (he was forty-seven) and the absence of a Nobel prize, made the conferment of a CH a surprising and surprisingly early honour. The state of his health was almost certainly a contributory factor. While a postgraduate at Cambridge, he developed the progressive and incurable neurological disease amyotrophic lateral sclerosis, better known as motor neurone disease. Eventually he was confined to a wheelchair. In 1985 he developed pneumonia and had to have a tracheostomy operation which removed his ability to speak. Thereafter he needed twenty-four hour nursing care. The disease progressively paralyses and is fatal, but in Hawking's case the advance has been relatively slow, and by means of an electric wheelchair, a voice synthesiser and other technological devices he has been able to continue his research and writing though at a more restricted level. If the CH was given to him earlier than might have been expected, because his achievements were accomplished in the face of adversity, no one begrudged it.

Elsie Widdowson 12 June 1993
Elsie Widdowson was a pioneering British nutritionist who used wartime rationing to promote a healthy, lean diet of bread, cabbage, and potatoes. She was also known for her work analysing the chemical composition of food.

She was born at Dulwich in 1906. In the mid-1920s she became one of three female students in a class of about one hundred reading chemistry at Imperial College, London. She completed the course work in two years, but was obliged to stay a third year to be eligible for the degree. She used the time to study amino acid separations, breaking down proteins at a time when the number of constituent amino acids was still not known. She worked on the separation of carbohydrates from apples, and her first publication in 1931 described these studies which became the basis for the award of a PhD by the University of London.

Her research career began in 1933 when she enrolled at King's College of Household and Social Science to study for a one-year diploma in dietetics. There she met Dr Robert A. McCance, who was studying the loss of nutrients during cooking, and formed a partnership which lasted until his death in 1993. She moved with him to Cambridge in 1938 where she remained. In the 1930s McCance and Widdowson together put food under the microscope and for the first time prepared tables listing the energy values of all foods. The result was a book which no nutrition or dietetics department in a hospital or university can be without, and which has become something of a nutritionists' bible. *The composition of foods* by Robert McCance and Elsie Widdowson was first published in 1940, and a sixth edition was in preparation in 2000, the year of Elsie Widdowson's death. Her work was crucial in inaugurating scientific studies of human diets and nutrient intakes, and her reliable food composition tables made it possible for the first time to relate nutrient intakes to disease risks. Before the 1939–45 war her research centred on mineral metabolism and food composition. During the war she conducted studies on the effects of brown bread on the absorption of minerals, particularly calcium. As a result of her experiments a law was passed requiring that calcium carbonate be added to all flour used in breadmaking, and calcium carbonate is still in flour today.

The outbreak of the 1939–45 war caused the two dieticians to realise that the nation would have to tighten its belt because rationing was inevitable. Widdowson and McCance studied their own nutrient balance during a three months period of arduous climbing in the Lake District at the beginning of the war. 'They set out to make a virtue of a necessity. They began a scientific study of rationing that left Britain, ultimately, a healthier nation in spite of the privations of war.'[16]

After the war she spent three years in Germany studying the effect of undernutrition on the local population. This was followed by local studies on the effects of different kinds of bread on the health and growth of undernourished children. Gradually she became interested in the newborn, and a great deal of her later work was concerned with studies of newborn human infants and newborn animals. She worked at the department of experimental medicine at Cambridge, which was financed by the Medical Research Council, becoming assistant director of that department until 1966. During those years, using rats and pigs, she demonstrated that the earlier in life animals suffer from insufficient nutrition, the greater and longer lasting are the effects. In 1966 the infant nutrition research division was created, and she became head of that division at the Dunn Nutrition Laboratory until 1973 when she moved to the university's department of investigative medicine at Addenbrooke's

Hospital. 'She studied the early development of seals and black bears in collaboration with an American colleague. On one occasion she cheerfully transported the carcass of a seal . . . in her car boot for tissue analysis in Cambridge.'[17]

She was president of the Nutrition Society (1977–80), the Neonatal Society (1978–81) and the British Nutrition Foundation (1986–96). Although she had long been recognised as a good worker in her special field, the value of her work was not recognised until the last phase of her long life. She was elected a fellow of the Royal Society in 1976 at the age of seventy, made a CBE in 1979, and finally a CH in 1993 as 'President, British Nutrition Foundation. For services to Science.' She was a leading figure in nutritional research through her studies on food composition, chemical composition of the human body, iron balance, trace metal absorption and malnutrition, but most of her work had been done decades previously and was well in the past. By the early 1990s her intellectual influence had waned and it could have been argued that she had done nothing since being made a CBE in 1979 to justify a further honour. But on balance her career, influential even if it was not spectacular, merited a 'lifetime of service' award in the shape of the CH. 'Any comment from Elsie Widdowson had to be taken seriously, for it had been distilled from decades of incisive thought and extensive practical research.'[18]

For those who knew her work and her field, it raised the question of whether her co-worker Professor Robert McCance would have been similarly honoured had he survived; he died in March 1993 at the age of ninety-four, three months before her CH was announced. She was always noted for her humility. Shy, retiring and modest to the end, Elsie Widdowson said 'He was the one with the bright ideas, I followed.'[19] She died in 2000, at the age of ninety-three.

Reginald Jones 11 June 1994

Reginald Jones was a wartime intelligence scientist who was best known for his contribution to the air defence of the United Kingdom during the 1939–45 war and for his work on scientific intelligence. Like Lord Cherwell, Jones was highly regarded by Winston Churchill who did what he could to protect him. Jones could sometimes be his own worst enemy.

He was born in London in 1911 and educated at Alleyn's School, Dulwich. He graduated with a first class degree in physics from Wadham College, Oxford, where his teacher was Frederick Lindemann (later Viscount Cherwell CH). He carried out research on infrared radiation and was awarded a DPhil in 1934. In 1936 he began work as a scientific officer in the air ministry. By 1939 it had become clear that British intelligence knew very little about the scientific side of the German war machine, and Jones concentrated on Germany's innovative aerial weaponry, making his great breakthrough in 1940. He had been puzzling over radio beams transmitted from Germany during bombing raids in Britain. He became convinced that these beams were a navigation device for steering aircraft to their targets. Some were sceptical, refusing to believe that beams could be bent round the earth. Jones thought that they could and that they could be bent again by counter measures in order to redirect the aerial raiders away from urban areas to drop their bombs over open country. In June 1940 he was told to report to the cabinet room. To an astonished group he explained why it was that German bombers could bomb their targets with precision while the RAF could miss its targets by miles. Churchill ever afterwards described him as the man who 'broke the bloody beams.' Afterwards he discovered the technical and tactical details of the German radar-controlled night fighter defences and their airborne radar

He was appointed an assistant director of intelligence at the air ministry in 1941 and promoted to director in 1946. He left the secret intelligence service and the air ministry in the same year after a battle with the joint intelligence committee over the way post-war scientific intelligence should be organised. Jones never really made his peace with intelligence after his abrupt resignation. He argued that all the best work was done in huts and he hated bureaucracy, and he circumvented it as much as he could, sometimes to the annoyance of his superiors.

In 1946 he was appointed professor of natural philosophy at the University of Aberdeen (1946–81), where he stayed until retirement. He was additionally director of scientific intelligence at the ministry of defence (1952–53), chairman of the air defence working party (1963–64), chairman of the scientific advisory council at the war office (1963–66), chairman of the Safety in Mines Research Society (1956–60), and chairman of the Electronics Research Council (1964–70).

At Aberdeen his main research was to carry measurement to its fundamental limits. He devised many delicate instruments, including an optical lever to measure very small angles. He also initiated the growth of large crystals for optical and laser purposes. 'He was a devoted experimental physicist, never happier than when working on apparatus or in the workshop that he had developed.'[20] He vigorously opposed the rapid expansion of student numbers in the 1960s, voicing the traditional argument that this would reduce academic standards. After his retirement, the *Daily Express* included a report on 13 September 1982 that the university wanted to evict Jones and family from his house, which was university property.

In 1977 he was given leave to publish a book entitled *Most secret war*, which described British counter-measures against German beam-bombing, air defence, U-boat radar, and V1 and V2 rocket attacks. When Jones submitted the first draft, some intelligence officials, who argued that no member of the Secret Intelligence Service should ever disclose anything about the nature of his work, past or present, expressed residual doubts. Eyebrows were further raised when Jones revealed that he had taken away, in breach of regulations, war cabinet minutes, material from Bletchley Park, and about sixty of his personal war time reports, when he took up the chair of experimental philosophy at Aberdeen. He justified his action on the ground that air ministry officials, weeding files to save shelf space, would destroy the papers. He also wanted them for the lectures he gave at staff colleges. The documents were kept in his security safe at Aberdeen, and duplicates of them began to appear in the Public Record Office from 1972. With minor changes, including the deletion of names, publication was allowed.

For his war work, Jones was made a CBE in 1942 and a CB in 1946. It was said that Sir Horace Wilson, head of the home civil service, threatened to resign if Jones, a mere scientific officer, was a made a CBE at the age of twenty-eight.[21] In 1993 he was awarded a special medal named after him, by the CIA in their belief that the precision bombing at the start of the Gulf War was the direct result of Jones's technology.

The years went by, and some held the view that Jones' work deserved recognition beyond the 'slender' and 'minimal' CBE and CB that he had received several decades earlier. He was elected a fellow of the Royal Society in 1965 and there was a feeling in some scientific circles that his work had been under-acknowledged. In certain quarters he was esteemed and seen as a father figure. Others held that although he had done outstanding work during the war, he was not a first-rate scientist. He had demonstrated his ability as an effective broadcaster in the television documentary *The secret war* series. Whatever the merits of his case, a knighthood would have been a popular and eye-catching award. No knighthood was forthcoming; it was in any case not to his credit that he had removed many secret papers and sixty war time reports at the end of the war in breach of regulations. But Jones was not forgotten, and he was made a CH 'For services to Science' in 1994, three years before his death.

Cesar Milstein 31 December 1994

The British-Argentinian immunologist Cesar Milstein was awarded the 1984 Nobel prize for physiology or medicine (shared with Niels Jerne and Georges Köhler) for his theories concerning the specificity in development and control of the immune system and the discovery of the principle for production of monoclonal antibodies.

He was born at Bahia Blanca, Argentina in 1927, the son of Jewish immigrants and held both British and Argentine citizenship. He was educated at the Colegio Nacional de Bahia Blanca and read chemistry at the National University of Buenos Aires. A year-long honeymoon hitchhiking in Europe was followed by a return to Argentine to study for a doctorate (awarded in 1957) in kinetic analysis of the enzyme aldehyde dehydrogenase. After finishing it he won a British Council scholarship to Fitzwilliam College, Cambridge where he met Frederick Sanger and was awarded a second doctorate in 1960. From 1961–63 he studied enzymes in the molecular biology division at Argentina's National Institute of Microbiology in Buenos Aires. It was a difficult period for Milstein as for other intellectual liberals and scientists. Post-Peronist Argentina was still politically unstable and a vendetta against the director of the institute persuaded Milstein that there was no future for him in his home country. In 1963 he returned to Cambridge and spent the rest of his scientific career there. He visited Argentina from time to time but never stayed long and refused all temptations to return to lucrative appointments.

At Cambridge he worked with Sanger at the Medical Research Council's newly-founded Laboratory of Molecular Biology, and headed the laboratory's division of protein and nucleic acid chemistry (1983–94). At Sanger's suggestion Milstein changed his area of research from enzymes to immunology and it was in this field that he produced his greatest work. From 1974–76 he worked with Georges Köhler, a German research student biochemist, to produce monoclonal antibodies that could fight specific cells. Monoclonal antibodies are laboratory versions of the antibodies produced naturally by the immune system when foreign substances, such as bacteria and viruses, invade the body. Their technique enabled scientists to design antibodies to attack specific infectious agents and to produce identical copies of those antibodies in large quantities. Monoclonal antibodies can be used to study immunity or to diagnose and treat disease. Their technique for antibody production has since been adopted universally and the antibodies are used in diagnostics and in treating leukaemia. In later life Milstein followed the development of his discovery 'with huge interest and excitement, and lived long enough to see them beginning to transform the lives of many patients.'[22]

Milstein's contribution to immunology was seminal and had far-reaching consequences for biology and medicine as a whole, particularly in the treatment of cancer, arthritis and transplant rejection, and tests for the diagnosis of AIDS and pregnancy. 'His greatest joy came from understanding biological mechanisms,

The Insignia of the Order (obverse)
Badge as worn by a man, with St Edward's Crown (left above)
Badge as worn by a woman, with a Tudor Crown (left below)
Original prototype badge
[photograph by A.C. Cooper]

The Insignia of the Order (reverse)
Badge as worn by a man, bearing the cypher of Queen Elizabeth II (left above)
Badge as worn by a woman, bearing the cypher of Queen Elizabeth II (left below)
Original prototype badge bearing the cypher of King George V
[photograph by A.C. Cooper]

The Right Honourable the Lord Owen

Professor Amartya Sen
[photograph by Jon Chase]

Doris Lessing
[copyright Jill Furmanovsky]

The Right Honourable Douglas Anthony

The Right Honourable the Lord Brooke of Sutton Mandeville

Dame Janet Baker
[*photograph by Simon Francis*]

The Right Honourable the Lord Baker of Dorking

The Right Honourable the Lord Heseltine

Jack Jones

The Right Honourable the Lord Howe of Aberavon

The Right Honourable David Lange
[photograph by Woolf, Wellington, New Zealand]

The Right Honourable the Lord Hurd of Westwell

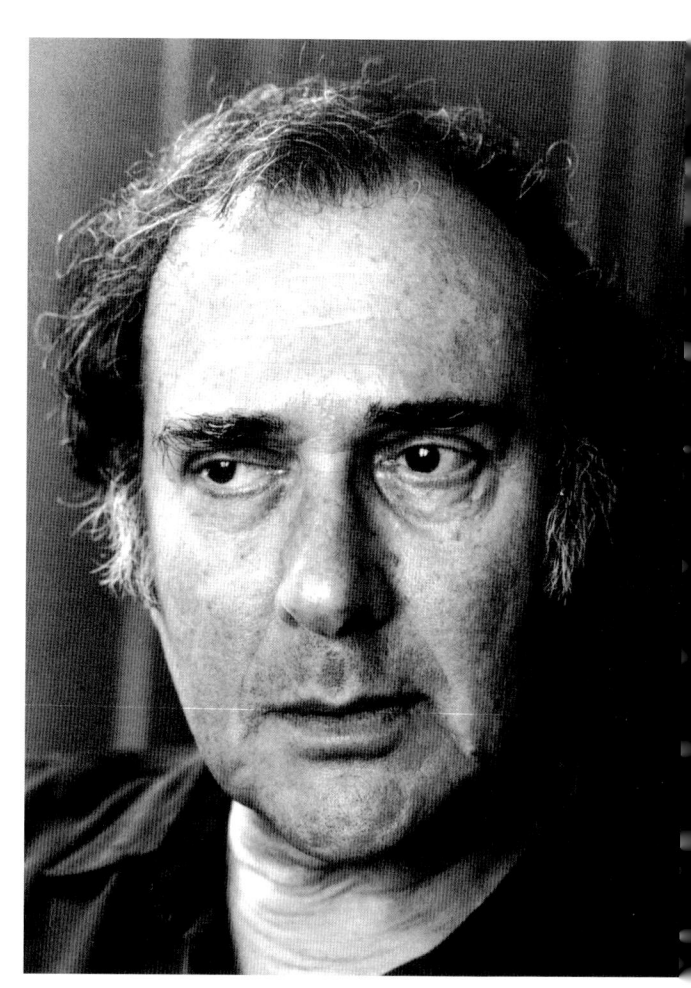

Harold Pinter

Sir Michael Howard
[photograph by Michael Marsland, Yale University, Office of Public Affairs]

The Right Honourable the Lord Glenamara

General John de Chastelain

Richard Hamilton
[photograph by Rita Donagh]

Dr Frederick Sanger

The Right Honourable Sir John Gorton

Lee Kuan Yew

David Hockney

The Right Honourable John Major

The Right Honourable the Lord Tebbit

The Right Honourable the Lord Carrington

Sir George Christie
[photograph by Mike Hoban]

The Right Honourable Malcolm Fraser

The Right Honourable the Lord King of Bridgwater

Sir Richard Doll
[copyright Robert Harris]

The Right Honourable the Lord Ashley of Stoke

C.H. Sisson and his wife Nora

The Right Honourable Christopher Patten

Sir Philip Powell

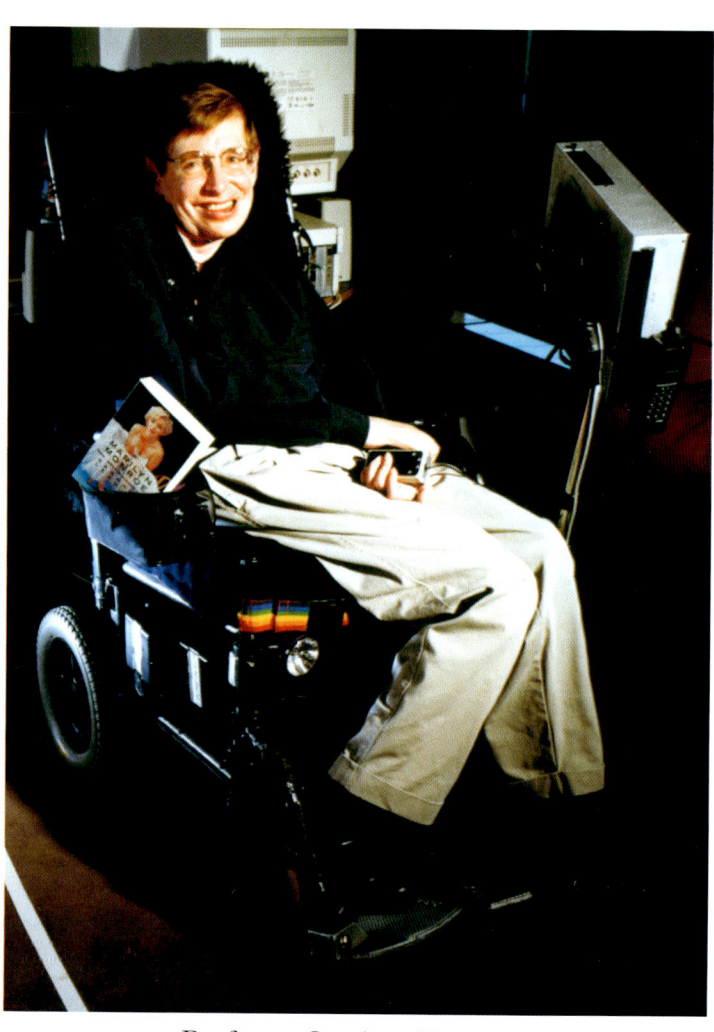

Professor Stephen Hawking
[photograph by Stewart Cohen Pictures, Dallas, Texas]

The Right Honourable the Lord Healey

Professor Eric Hobsbawm

Bernard Haitink
[photograph by Clive Barda]

Dr Sydney Brenner

Sir David Attenborough

Sir Harrison Birtwistle
[photograph by Richard Kalina]

Peter Brook
[photograph by Gilles Abegg]

Paul Scofield

Sir Colin Davis
[photograph by Keith Saunders]

The Reverend Prebendary Chad Varah
[photograph by Jonathan Manhire]

Sir John Smith
[photograph by Rex Coleman]

Bridget Riley

The Right Honourable Sir Brian Talboys

and he was never far from the laboratory bench. His style of science involved pacing around a problem in his mind, seeing it from every angle. He was not the kind of scientist who is certain of the outcome from the beginning and sweeps others along by force of conviction. Being decisive was not his greatest quality . . . He never ran a very large research group, but those lucky enough to work with him to some extent took the place of the children he never had.'[23] He had suffered from heart problems for many years and died in 2002.

He was elected a fellow of the Royal Society in 1975 and in 2000 he was awarded the Medical Research Council's first millennium gold medal with the comment that no other MRC scientist had made such an outstanding contribution to Britain's science, health and wealth creation. He was made a CH in 1995 'For services to Molecular Biology'.

Sir Nevill Mott 17 June 1995
Nevill Mott was one of the most distinguished theoretical physicists of the twentieth century. He was Cavendish professor of experimental physics at Cambridge (1954–71) and was awarded the 1977 Nobel prize for physics jointly with the US scientists Philip Anderson and John H. Van Fleck for their fundamental theoretical investigations of the electronic structure of magnetic and disordered systems. Mott's accomplishments include explaining theoretically the effect of light on a photographic emulsion and outlining the transition of substances from metallic to non-metallic states.

He was born in 1905, the child of parents who had met when students under J. J. Thomson at the Cavendish laboratory at Cambridge. He was educated at Clifton College and from there won a scholarship to St John's College, Cambridge in mathematics and physics in 1923, and read the mathematics tripos in 1924. At Cambridge he was introduced to a research problem that occupied him for much of his professional career, that of the metal-insulator transition. During this time he spent long enough in the practical physics classes run by G. F. C. Searle (who had taught Mott's parents) to establish that he found experiments dull, and he determined to be a theoretical physicist.

After graduation he spent three years' research in applied mathematics, including a year in Copenhagen working with Niels Böhr. He was appointed to a lecturership at Manchester in 1929 and worked with Lawrence Bragg. But he was invited back to Cambridge in 1930 to a university lectureship and college fellowship at Gonville and Caius College. He spent three years in Cambridge, working on problems in nuclear physics. In 1933, at the age of twenty-eight, he was appointed Melvill-Wills professor of theoretical physics at Bristol. There he switched from nuclear to solid-state physics, and built up Bristol as one of the leading groups in this rapidly emerging field. His ability to explain mathematics in physical terms was responsible for the immediate success of his book *An outline of wave mechanics* (1930) and its successor *Elements of wave mechanics* (1952), both of which exercised a profound influence on the teaching of wave mechanics in English universities. His other publications included *The theory of atomic collisions* (with H. S. W. Massey, 1933) and *The theory of the properties of metals and alloys* (with Harry Jones, 1936), *Metal-insulator transitions* (1970, 2nd ed, 1990) and *Electronic processes in ionic crystals* (with Ronald Gurney).

During the 1939–45 war he first worked on problems concerned with the propagation of radio waves. He was eventually brought in to head a theoretical physics group at Fort Halstead in 1943, working on problems related to munitions such as deformation in metals due to projectiles. As superintendent of theoretical research in armaments, he made outstanding contributions to the theory of the explosive fragmentation of shell and bomb cases. He was much concerned by the arrival of atomic energy, with which he was not directly involved, and was one of the founders, in 1946, of the Atomic Scientists' Association, set up to inform the public about the true facts of atomic energy. His own publications for the association were critical of British policy. He was also much involved in international scientific co-operation, and was active for many years with Pugwash, an international group set up to discuss ways of avoiding nuclear war and to use knowledge for peaceful ends. In 1948 he became Henry Overton Wills professor of physics and director of the Henry Herbert Wills physical laboratory at Bristol.

He returned to Cambridge in 1954 when he was elected to the Cavendish chair of expermiental physics at Cambridge, succeeding Lawrence Bragg who had succeeded Ernest Rutherford. Solid state physics and radio-astronomy were the two areas which particularly flourished during this period. By this stage his absent-mindedness had become legendary. It was said that when colleagues returned him to Didcot station from Harwell after a meeting there in 1954, he mistakenly took the train to Bristol, forgetting that he had just taken up the chair at Cambridge. At the time of his appointment to Cambridge there was a strong tradition of nuclear physics. He found a large and costly 'linear accelerator' under construction. He lost little time in closing the project down. 'This action determined, to a considerable extent, the future trend of the work at the Cavendish. It meant that nuclear physics could not much longer remain the central interest, and that the "Rutherford tradition" must soon cease.'[24] Research in solid state physics became a major activity of the laboratory and included the development of electron-microscopy and its use in the investigation of the properties of metals. He also encouraged the expansion of work in radio astronomy.

He was elected master of Gonville and Caius College in 1959, and had a generally uncomfortable time as did his predecessor, Sir James Chadwick. His research was at the centre of his life and the general administration of the college was not his forte. Following a very acrimonious battle within the fellowship over the appointment of a new professionally-trained bursar (which he had proposed) he resigned the mastership in 1966.

After his resignation he continued to work, not only with the research groups in the Cavendish laboratory but with workers in industrial research laboratories in the UK and in France, and, as a senior research fellow (1971–73) with the solid state physicists at Imperial College, London. He took up interest in the new field of non-crystalline semiconductors and 1971 when he retired as Cavendish professor, he was immersed in this field. He again produced the text that defined the field, co-authored with Ted Davis, *Electronic processes in non-crystalline materials*, which ran to two editions (1971 and 1979).

He won the Nobel prize in 1977, not for that one startling discovery for which the prize is often associated in the public mind, but for decades of excellent research in solid state physics, a subject at the heart of the contemporary electronics revolution. 'His work, and that of Anderson and van Beck, showed that certain cheap, glassy semiconductor materials had special electrical characteristics. He demonstrated that these could be used to improve the performance of circuits in computers, to increase enormously the memory of such systems, and to produce more efficient photovoltaic cells to convert solar energy into electricity. Such discoveries paved the way for a variety of now indispensable tools for the individual, ranging from the wafer-thin, battery-less pocket calculator to the PC and the desk-top publisher . . . Although unspectacular when described in purely scientific terms, these discoveries quite simply ended the notion of the computer as the preserve of aerospace and defence agencies, big industries and scientific research institutes, and added it to the list of household utensils.'[25]

His final research interest was the field of high temperature superconductors, which were discovered in 1986 and provided a 'gold rush' for many scientists. His publications included a volume of autobiography *A life in science* (1995).

Mott played a major role in the development of solid-state physics, from its infancy in the 1920s when the techniques of quantum mechanics first became available, through to his Nobel-prize winning work on non-crystalline semiconductors in the 1970s, and his final work on high temperature superconductors in the 1990s. He was the leading figure in solid state physics in the United Kingdom and led a long active life well beyond retirement. He made a central contribution to an amazingly wide range of problems in physics, especially the electronic properties of ionic crystals, the magnetism of the transition metals, the strength of solids and the field of metal-insulator transitions.

He was elected a fellow of the Royal Society in 1936 at the young age of thirty-one, knighted in 1962 and made a CH in 1995 'For services to Science', 'somewhat belated, but richly merited'[26] at the age of ninety. He died in 1996.

Sir Richard Doll 30 December 1995
Although Richard Doll never received a Nobel prize for physiology or medicine, he was probably the most distinguished British epidemiologist of the twentieth century. Beginning his research in the late 1940s, he was recognised as the first medical scientist to prove the link between smoking and lung cancer, and published the first work to demonstrate conclusively the carcinogenic nature of asbestos.

He was born in 1912 and educated at Westminster School. He qualified in medicine at St Thomas's Hospital Medical School, University of London in 1937. He served in the Royal Army Medical Corps during the 1939–45 war, and on demobilisation turned his interests towards research. From 1946 to 1969 he held various appointments with the Medical Research Council, becoming deputy director of the statistical research unit in 1959 and then director in 1961. In 1969 he became regius professor of medicine in Oxford and in 1979 the first warden of Green College, Oxford. After his retirement in 1983 he continued work as an honorary member of the clinical trials service unit and the epidemiological studies unit. He was additionally honorary associate physician at the Central Middlesex Hospital (1949–69), member of the Medical Research Council (1970–74), member of the Royal Commission on Environmental Pollution (1973–79), member of the Standing Commission on Energy and the Environment (1978–81), member of the scientific council of the World Health Organisation's international cancer research agency (1966–70 and 1975–78), and a member of the United Kingdom co-ordinating committee on cancer research (1972–77).

Richard Doll did more than any other epidemiologist to transform the general understanding of the avoidability of cancer and many other diseases linked to behaviour and environmental exposures. In 1950 his studies showed that smoking was a cause of most lung cancer deaths. A few smaller and earlier studies had already pointed to the hazards of tobacco, but Doll consolidated and extended the finding and inaugurated the modern era of cancer epidemiology. He also initiated the first relatively large cohort study, asking British doctors in 1951 what they smoked and then following them indefinitely to see what those doctors died of. The early results showed that smoking was a major cause of death from heart disease (and showed that many other diseases could also be caused by tobacco). The forty-year follow-up showed the absolute hazards of really prolonged smoking, demonstrating that about half of all persistent smokers would eventually be killed by their habit.

Having established the link between smoking and lung cancer, Doll explored further cancer-related areas including establishing a link between the dose of radiation and leukaemia. This was done at the request of the Medical Research Council's committee on hazards to men of nuclear and allied radiations. It was largely on the basis of this work that the committee was able to define safe limits for workers who in their occupations were exposed to chronic radiations.

Although a Nobel prize has eluded Richard Doll, many thought that he should have received the award. But his work led to a fundamental change of direction in personal and corporate life. Since his initial research in 1950, knowledge of the hazards of tobacco has already avoided many millions of deaths in the twentieth century, and no medical scientist contributed more to this prevention. Without his work and influence much less would be known about the industrial and social causes of ill-health, and there is much about Doll's career which places him with John Scott Haldane in his humanitarian concern for the health of men and women in the workplace.

Doll was elected a fellow of the Royal Society in 1966. Despite being a former member of the Communist Party, like many idealists of his generation, he was willing to be appointed an OBE in 1956, to be knighted in 1971 and made a CH 'For services to Epidemiology' in 1995 at the age of eighty-three.

CHAPTER NINE

To the well-trod stage

ACTORS, CHOREOGRAPHERS, PRODUCERS

'When I use a word,' Humpty Dumpty said, in a rather scornful tone, 'it means just what I choose it to mean – neither more nor less.' 'The question is,' said Alice, 'whether you <u>can</u> make words mean so many different things.'
'Humpty Dumpty', Through the looking-glass, Lewis Carroll

The category of 'the stage' is not unlike the category of 'science' in the previous chapter, in that the place in history of these recipients is mostly assured for all time and not subject to changing tastes. Whereas the work of an author can be subject to sometimes merciless reassessment by succeeding generations, the significance of those Companions of Honour whose life has revolved on or around the stage, has mostly been consistent and constant.

The Companions of Honour gathered in this chapter include actors, choreographers and producers. The word producer is used loosely to bring together the Companions whose work has effectively been 'back stage' – for want of a better description. Though none of them have 'trod the boards', except comparatively briefly or peripherally in some cases, their influence on the development of the theatre has been profound, and the list begins with two remarkable women. Lilian Baylis (1929), whose name is ever associated with the Old Vic and Sadler's Wells theatres, produced 'popular' productions of classics. Her stature has grown down the years as her work took root and flourished, and more than half a century after her death she was hailed as the grandmother of the National Theatre, the English National Opera and the Royal Ballet. Annie Horniman (1933), a northern contemporary of Lilian Baylis, was a determined, formidable and wealthy feminist who pioneered the modern theatre repertory movement. As a stage and scenery designer and a theoretician of the history of theatre, Gordon Craig (1956) was an unusual addition to the list. As the son of Ellen Terry, the blood of the stage coursed through his veins, but he was overlooked until he was well past eighty and had been forgotten. The name of the Cambridge academic Dadie Rylands (1987) was a questionable addition to the list, in that the extent of his influence is difficult to calculate. Not an actor (except as an amateur), not a director or producer (except on the rare occasions and essentially as a part-time hobby), not an academic (he did very little research), not a writer (to judge from the slender list of his publications), he was primarily a teacher who inspired and enthused his pupils, who responded with devotion. Though long resident in France, Peter Brook (1998), one of the United Kingdom's foremost directors, has stretched the bounds of theatrical production into the most unusual international arenas, and far beyond the pioneering work of Lilian Baylis and Annie Horniman. With the exception of Rylands, the other Companions – Baylis, Horniman, Craig and Brook – were pioneers who extended the previously accepted boundaries of the theatre, and such a quality would probably be looked for in any future theatrical 'back stagers'.

The acting profession only entered the ranks of the Companions of Honour in 1970 with the appointment of Dame Sybil Thorndike, to date the only actress CH, and the required standards have been very high indeed. Thorndike received the honour at the age of eighty-eight, in the year following the naming of a theatre in her honour, and after sixty-six years on the stage. Sir John Gielgud (1977), received the honour at the comparatively youthful age of seventy-three, though still with fifty-six years as professional actor behind him. With a voice like 'some gorgeous oboe miraculously playing itself', Gielgud was another long-lived actor who had a theatre named after him, and whose career spanned much of the twentieth century. With a retiring disposition, a tendency to self-effacement, and a desire to avoid publicity, Sir Alec Guinness (1994) received the CH at the age of eighty after a career of sixty years that encompassed a diversity of roles, from Shakespeare to *Star wars*. It was perhaps a mark of the competence and judgement of Lilian Baylis that Sybil Thorndike, John Gielgud and Alec Guinness had all performed at the Old Vic in her day. A desire to maintain his personal privacy placed Paul Scofield (2000) in the mould of Alec Guinness, and like Guinness he had completed a career of sixty years on the stage.

Any future members of the acting profession who are to become members of the Order of the Companions of Honour will probably be expected – like Thorndike, Gielgud, Guinness and Scofield – to have established consistently high and prominent professional reputations over a period of several decades.

The stage work of Sir Frederick Ashton (1970) and Dame Ninette de Valois (1981) revolved entirely around the performances of the ballet company founded by de Valois under the aegis of Lilian Baylis, which was to come to full flower as the Royal Ballet. De Valois was honoured with the CH fifty-five years after she founded her London Academy of Choreographic Art, and Ashton on his retirement after forty-six years as principal choreographer of the Royal Ballet and its predecessors. As the founder and the first principal choreographer, it seems unlikely but not impossible, that any future individual from the world of ballet will be able to equal the pioneering work of Frederick Ashton and Ninette de Valois.

One potential CH deserves a brief mention. *Harley Granville-Barker* (1877–1946) was an actor, producer, director, dramatist and Shakespearean scholar, and reckoned to be the first modern British director. He made his stage debut in 1891, and worked with the Ben Greet Company from 1895. In 1900, he joined the experimental Stage Society, and by 1904, he was manager of the Court Theatre where he introduced the public to the plays of Henrik Ibsen, Maurice Maeterlinck, and George Bernard Shaw. He was especially well known for his productions of Shakespeare which revolutionized the way the bard's plays would be performed in the theatre with their naturally spoken dialogue. He also produced several of his own plays including *The Voysey inheritance* (1905), *Prunella* (1906), *Waste* (1907), and *The Madras house* (1910). He managed a number of theatres, including the Savoy and the Duke of York's. During the 1914–18 war he served in the Red Cross. He was chairman of the British Drama League (1919–32), and director of the British Institute in Paris (1937–39). In 1923 he began writing his *Prefaces to Shakespeare* (1927–48). Previously, most Shakespearean analysis had been from the viewpoint of the critic. Granville-Barker looked at the plays from the practical perspective of the producer, and his writings became a cornerstone of Shakespearean criticism. During this period, he also collaborated with his second wife on translations of a number of works by French and Spanish playwrights. In

1940 he fled with his family from Paris to Spain. From there, they travelled to the United States where he worked for British Information Services and lectured at Harvard University. He returned to Paris in 1946 and died there later that same year. Although often overlooked during his lifetime, Granville-Barker's plays have come to be recognized as masterpieces of early twentieth century drama. He was a close friend of George Bernard Shaw (who had refused the Order of Merit), and his rumoured refusal of the CH in 1938 was almost certainly on ideological grounds. He saw society largely through Shaw's eyes.

Lilian Baylis 1 March 1929
Lilian Baylis was a formidable matriarch who developed and ran London's Old Vic and Sadler's Wells theatres and became known as the grandmother of the National Theatre, English National Opera and Royal Ballet.

She was born in Marylebone, London in 1874, the eldest of the nine children, five of whom died in infancy. Her father was the clerk of an Oxford Street store and her mother was a contralto who sang in concert parties. She was educated at home and trained as a violinist, first appearing in public at the age of seven, and her entry in *Who's Who* described her as a 'concert entertainer in England and South Africa in early youth.' In 1891 she emigrated to South Africa with her parents and two of her siblings as a singing troupe. It was not enough to make a living and they also worked in a drapery business in Johannesburg. Lilian worked hard as a music teacher in her spare time, but overwork and ill-health forced her return to London in 1897. There she joined her aunt and godmother, Emma Cons, in managing the Royal Victoria Hall in Lambeth, and became sole manager in 1912 on the death of her aunt. Emma and Lilian were two very tough ladies and ran the theatre by way of a matriarchal fiefdom for more than forty years.

Whereas her aunt's interests had been social and religious (she ran the theatre as a philanthropic temperance institution), Lilian Baylis raised the profile of the hall, which she advertised as the People's Opera House, and broadened the activities held there. Each of Shakespeare's plays was performed there, from *The taming of the shrew* in 1914 to *Troilus and Cressida* in 1923. By the end of the 1914–18 war, the 'Old Vic', as it was now known, had become one of London's leading theatres, and she ran it until her death in 1937. Though standards were high, it was a 'peoples' establishment and the emphasis was on the presentation of drama and opera in a way accessible to ordinary people. Her beliefs and her sheer determination in seeing them through to reality produced a remarkable legacy as much through what she enabled others to achieve as what she achieved herself. In her day she had the reputation of being a hard woman (some unkindly called her a skinflint), but she was not personally wealthy and continually struggled with inadequate resources and tight budgets. In South Africa she was able to earn eighty pounds a month as a teacher. In London her aunt was able to pay her only one pound each week, which explains her sometimes excessive thriftiness. For all that the Old Vic was run domestically on a tight budget, she made it a success because of her instinctively accurate choice of collaborators and she employed and encouraged many of the talented young actors of her day who found fame in the years after her death. Sybil Thorndike (CH 1970) appeared regularly at the Old Vic during the 1914–18 war, and John Gielgud (CH 1977) performed there throughout the 1920s and was one of a number of distinguished actors who began their careers under her tutelage. Alec Guinness (CH 1994) performed at the Old Vic in the last year of Baylis's life.

The Old Vic was her life and she all but lived within its portals. She also had her meals there as Russell Thorndike remembered. 'On the floor by the prompt corner of the Old Vic stage was a gas ring. It was not the sole means of boiling water for the stage or dressing rooms but it had a far more important function. It kept Miss Baylis alive. She was mortal enough to require a little food during the day besides her cups of tea and it was the gas ring that prepared it. Towards the end of a long matinee the salubrious fumes of sausage, bacon or kippers would float from the prompt corner over the footlights and fill the stalls accompanied by the sound of fizzling and spitting.'[1]

Her work in south London gained a counterpart in north London when she acquired Sadler's Wells Theatre in 1921 and ran it as a north London extension of the Old Vic. As they gradually developed, the Old Vic remained the showcase for drama, while Sadler's Wells became the opera house. In 1928 she engaged Ninette de Valois (CH 1981), under whose direction classical ballet was developed and, by doing so, Baylis had enabled the creation at Sadler's Wells of three significant national institutions: the Royal Ballet, the English National Opera and the Birmingham Royal Ballet, as well as the Royal Ballet School.

She was a devout high church Anglican and went to mass every day on her way to the theatre. Like many unmarried women she was believed to have harboured romantic feelings for an Anglican friar, Fr Andrew SDC, who regularly visited her, but she had the warmth of an east end Londoner and kept her theatre going mainly by the intense personal affection and idealism which she inspired in all who worked for her. Her working class origins (she was called 'Lil' by her friends) remained delightfully evident in her cockney accent and her homely, straightforward and fearless attitude towards even royal personages. Queen Mary visited the Old Vic on the occasion of the theatre's centenary matinee and was unavoidably late. Even the regal presence of the statuesque queen could not overawe the proprietress of the Old Vic. 'I'm glad you've turned up at last dear,' she said, 'and I know it's not your fault being late, as I hear that your dear husband going to the Union Jack Club has held up the road. But we've got a long programme to get through and had made a start. So let's get on with things.'[2] Baylis then pointed to the portrait of her aunt and to a smaller portrait of King George V both of which hung in the foyer. Indicating to the king's portrait she explained, 'It's not quite so large as Aunt Emma's because your dear husband has not done so much for the Old Vic.'[3]

Her standards were always high, as she said in 1931. 'I know . . . that those who have been nourished on great music and drama, or have discovered the true recreation that they will provide, will never again accept jejune and trashy entertainments whose claim on the mind is absolutely transitory.' Perhaps the greatest compliment that could be paid to Lilian Baylis is to regard her as the progenitor of popular theatre and opera, and as the ancestress of the National Theatre, the English National Opera and the Royal Ballet.

She made no pretence to education and admitted that she was ill-educated, but if that was a failing it did not affect her mission, and in 1924 the University of Oxford honoured her with an MA *honoris causa*. She was recommended for a state honour on more than one occasion, one of her supporters being Lord Stamfordham, private secretary to King George V. She herself was known to say that she had been formally offered a DBE – and swiftly rejected it. 'None of your dames for me! I don't want to go about the country labelled and be charged double for everything.'⁴ She was appointed a CH in 1929, one of an imaginative group of four appointed that year that included the composer Frederick Delius. Such was the reputation that she created for herself and her theatre, that the citation accurately, if prosaically, described her as 'Lessee and Manager, Old Vic Theatre.' She was pleased and proud of the recognition given to her efforts and at the end of each season she would make a speech from the stage, attired after 1924 in the gown and hood of an Oxford MA. After 1929 she added the badge and ribbon of a CH to her end of season stage costume.

Her work was her life and Lilian Baylis never married although she hinted that she had had many little romances. Before her death in 1937 she requested that instead of flowers at her funeral, donations should be sent either to the Vic-Wells Completion Fund, or to the St Giles Homes for British Lepers near Chelmsford.

Annie Horniman 3 June 1933
Annie Horniman was a fearless and formidable feminist who is remembered as a pioneer of the modern theatre repertory movement.

She was born in 1860, the daughter of Frederick John Horniman, a tea merchant, founder of the Horniman Museum and Liberal MP for Falmouth. She was educated privately by tutors and then studied at the Slade School of Art and in Antwerp. For five years she was secretary to W. B. Yeats. As her entry in *Who's Who* declaims, she interested herself originally in the theatre merely because her relatives strongly disapproved of it, though her association with Yeats probably influenced her to an extent. Her involvement with the theatre began in 1894–95 (badly as she frankly recorded) when she secretly sponsored a season of plays at the Avenue Theatre, London, which saw the first public production of plays by W. B. Yeats and George Bernard Shaw, including the latters' *Arms and the man.*

She had determined views and considerable wealth (she dressed with the utmost elegance and was always called 'Miss Horniman'), and minded not what people thought of her, and her entry in *Who's Who* is worth repeating more for what it reveals about her character than as a record of what she did. 'Observed her elders in early youth and by their disapproval became interested in theatres and the suffrage; learned and travelled as much as she could; studied astrology; had a fruitful failure at the Avenue Theatre in 1894, her first attempt with dramatic affairs; later on made the Abbey Theatre, Dublin, for the Irish National Theatre Society; bought the Gaiety Theatre, Manchester, and started the first theatre with a catholic repertoire in England.'

In 1904, as a result of her friendship with Yeats, she decided to subsidise the Irish National Theatre movement. She took over the old theatre of the Mechanics Institute in Abbey Street, Dublin and lent it rent free for six years to the Irish National Theatre Society. Regularly subsidised by her, the Abbey quickly established a wide reputation for its performance of new Irish plays and for the high standard of its acting.

Following disagreements with the Abbey she transferred her activities to Manchester in 1907. She established a theatre initially at the Midland Hotel, and in 1908 purchased the Gaiety Theatre and practically rebuilt it as the first full-scale modern repertory theatre in the country. Her policy was to produce plays by authors of all ages, with especial emphasis on new writers; they were to be performed by a permanent company of picked front-rank artists, and (echoing the work of Lilian Baylis in London) at prices within the reach of all. Sybil Thorndike

(CH 1970), a member of Annie Horniman's company in 1911–1913, was one of a number of distinguished actors and actresses who worked with her. The Gaiety's stock of plays was enormously varied, from Euripides to Shaw, but the theatre was most closely associated with writers of the so-called 'Manchester School', such as Harold Brighouse and Stanley Houghton. Unfortunately the enterprise collapsed after the 1914–18 war and in 1921 the theatre was sold to a cinema company.

She corresponded widely with journalists, playwrights, critics, actors, managers and other well-known figures of the day. The list includes J. M. Barrie, Arnold Bennett, James Bridie, Harold Brighouse, Millicent Garrett Fawcett, John Galsworthy, St John Hankin, C. H. Herford, Emmeline Pankhurst, George Bernard Shaw, Marie Stopes, Sybil Thorndike, Sir Herbert Beerbohm Tree, W. B. Yeats and Israel Zangwill.

The whole of the modern repertory theatre movement in the United Kingdom and the United States derives from the work of Annie Horniman in founding the Abbey and the Gaiety theatres. For her pioneering work she was made a CH in 1933 'For services to drama', and died in 1937 at the age of seventy-six.

Edward Gordon Craig 31 May 1956

Gordon Craig was a distinguished theatre scene designer and producer who flourished in the first forty years of the twentieth century.

He was born in 1872, the illegitimate son of the actress Dame Ellen Terry (1847–1928) and E. W. Godwin. His mother was Sir John Gielgud's great aunt and Gielgud referred to Craig as 'Uncle Ted'. As the son of such an eminent mother, it was inevitable that Craig himself should begin his working life with acting, and he spent twelve years with Henry Irving's Lyceum company (1885–97). In 1897 he abandoned acting for a new career as a producer and scene designer. Feeling that the realism then in vogue was too limiting, he developed new theories, strove for the poetic and the suggestive in his designs in order to capture the essential spirit of the play. His ideas gave new freedom to scene design, although many were impractical in execution. 'His theories on acting were criticised as reducing the actor to nothing more than a puppet working under the direction of a "master-mind". His theories on stage settings had an immense influence on the theatre in Europe and the USA more because of their originality and proliferation than because of Craig's actual achievements.'[5] His main influence was on lighting design where he used light to establish atmosphere and replace heavy scenic effects, not just to show the actors' faces. In his book *Changing stages*, Richard Eyre praised the pioneering work of both Craig and also Harley Granville-Barker: 'Craig was the first designer to use light as an element in design . . . He abolished overhead lighting battens and footlights, used concealed lighting bars, movable spots, colour changes and double gauzes: in effect he provided the twentieth-century lighting designer with his syntax . . . All the best theatre productions of today bear the marks of Harley Granville-Barker and Edward Gordon Craig: the determination to maximise the power of the text through the actor, allied to the desire to make staging as expressive as possible through the use of space, scenery, lighting and costume: in short, to exploit the the theatreness of the theatre.'[6]

Among his productions were *Dido and Aeneas* (1900), *The masque of love* (1901), Handel's *Acis and Galatea* (1902), Housman's *Bethlehem* (1902), Ibsen's *The Vikings*, and *Much ado about nothing* (both in 1903 for Ellen Terry), Ibsen's

Rosmerholm (in Florence for Eleanora Duse, 1906), and *Hamlet* (with the Moscow Art Theatre in 1912). In 1913 he founded the Gordon Craig School for the Art of the Theatre at Arena Goldoni, Florence.

He also founded and edited *The mask* (1908–29), a journal devoted to the art of the theatre and published in Florence, and his publications included *A book of penny toys* (1899), *On the art of the theatre* (1911, rev. ed. 1957), *A living theatre* (1913), *Towards a new theatre* (1913), *The marionette* (1918), *The theatre advancing* (1921), *Scene* (1923), *Woodcuts and some words* (1924) (he was a member of the English Woodgraving Society), *Books and theatres* (1925), *Henry Irving* (1930), *Fourteen notes* (1931) and *Ellen Terry and her secret self* (1931). A volume of autobiography, *Index to the story of my days*, appeared in 1957.

Craig was honoured with the Danish Order of Dannebrog in 1930, and elected a Royal Designer for Industry by the Royal Society of Arts in 1938, but a United Kingdom state honour eluded him until the last years of his life. Although he had been responsible for many stage productions in England and on the continent and had written widely on the art of the theatre, he was virtually completely retired after the 1939–45 war and some viewed him as an intellectual and theoretical 'back number'. By 1956 he was eighty-four years old, and while he had been a great innovator in his day, that day was more than thirty years previously. But his work was still revered by some and there was no doubting his considerable influence on theatre design.

He was made a CH in 1956 'For services to the Theatre'. He was living in retirement at Vence in the Alpes Maritimes département of France, and because of age and distance, it was not practicable for him to make the journey to Buckingham Palace. So the badge was dispatched to Sir Gladwyn Jebb, British ambassador in Paris to forward to Craig, whose slightly eccentric reply contained evident pleasure. 'Thank you for the safe sending of the Badge of the C of H. And especially for your words of congratulation. Shall I be able before long to call on you and thank you? Shall I be able to get to London, there to thank Her Majesty on behalf of the British Theatre? I hope to be able to do all this.'[7]

Even in extreme old age, Craig was still revered in theatrical circles, and in 1964, at the age of ninety-two, he was made president of the Mermaid Theatre, by its founder Bernard Miles. Craig died in 1966.

Dame Sybil Thorndike 13 June 1970
A distinguished and remarkably versatile actress, Agnes Sybil Thorndike was born in 1882 in Gainsborough, Lincolnshire, the daughter of an honorary canon of Rochester Cathedral, in which town she spent most of her childhood. She lived in Minor Canon Row behind Rochester Cathedral, where her house is marked with a plaque, and she was educated at Rochester High School. She initially trained as a pianist at the Guildhall School of Music but made her acting debut in 1904 with the Ben Greet Players as Palmis in *Palace of truth*, in the grounds of Downing College, Cambridge. She toured the United States with the company in 1904–07, taking more than one hundred parts in twenty-five Shakespearean plays.

Back in England, two ladies who were later to become Companions of Honour – Annie Horniman and Lilian Baylis – encouraged her talents. Thorndike performed with Annie Horniman's repertory company in Manchester (1908–09), Charles Frohman's Repertory at the Duke of York's Theatre in 1910, an American tour with John Drew in (1910–11) and again with Annie Horniman's company (1911–13). In 1914–18 she played Shakespearean leads at Lilian Baylis's Old Vic repertory theatre, and thereafter played hundreds of classic roles. She took every kind of role from the saint to the she-demon. During the 1914–18 war, when the Old Vic was short of men she even played male parts, including the fool in King Lear. She was acclaimed for her performances in Euripides' *Medea and the Trojan women* and created the title roles in George Bernard Shaw's *Candida* (1920) and *Saint Joan* (1924). Her success in the latter role was due to her ability to develop the character of Joan, using the gritty good sense of comedy to portray Joan as the peasant girl of Lorraine, before endowing the character with emotional tragedy, becoming a conquering heroine and national martyr.

She toured in South Africa (1928–29), and in Egypt, Palestine, Australia and New Zealand (1932–33), and regularly appeared in West End theatres throughout the 1930s. During the 1939–45 war she toured the mining areas playing Lady Macbeth, Medea and Candida. From the mid-1940s she broke new ground by acting the roles of a series of elderly women (she was then in her mid-60s): Mrs Wilson in *In time to come* at the King's Theatre, Hammersmith (1946), Mrs Fraser in *Call home the heart* at the St James's Theatre (1946–47), Mrs Linden in *The linden tree* at the Duchess Theatre (1947–48), Mrs Jackson in *The return of the prodigal* at the Globe Theatre (1948), Isobel Brocken in *The foolish gentlewoman* at the Duchess Theatre (1949), Aunt Anna Rose in *Treasure hunt* at the Apollo Theatre (1949), Lady Douglas in *Douglas* at the Edinburgh Festival (1950), Mrs Whyte in *Waters of the moon* at the Haymarket Theatre (1951), and Laura Anson in *A day by the sea* at the Haymarket (1953). In 1954–56 she travelled abroad giving recitals for the British Council in Australia, New Zealand, the Far East, Africa, Turkey and Israel, and she went to Australia again on tour (1957–58). She was back in the West End (1959–60), in Dublin in 1961, and in 1962 at the age of eighty she undertook another arduous tour of Australia, and was usually seen in West End theatres throughout the remainder of the 1960s. In 1969 the Thorndike Theatre at Leatherhead was named after her, and she performed at the opening in a play appositely entitled *There was an old woman* (she was then eighty-seven). Sadly, because of the withdrawal of its grant, the theatre closed in 1997.

Although she was primarily a stage actress, Sybil Thorndike had a number of films to her credit, including *Moths and rust* (1921), *Dawn* (1929), *To what red hell* (1930), *Hindle wakes* (1931), *Tudor rose* (1936), *Major Barbara* (1940), *Nicholas Nickleby* (1947), *Stage fright* (1950), *The magic box* (1951), *Melba* (1953), *The prince and the showgirl* (1956), *Shake hands with the devil* (1959), *Big gamble* (1960), and *Hand in hand* (1961)

She met her future husband, the actor and theatrical producer Sir Lewis Casson, in the lion house at Dublin Zoo. Dame Sybil recalled that 'Lewis was there trying to mesmerise the animals and ended by mesmerising me.' With wedding clothes said to have been borrowed from the theatre wardrobe, they found time to marry in 1906. Casson was a distinguished actor in his own right and appeared in several productions with his wife. He died in 1969 bringing their sixty-three years marriage to an end.

She was given the freedom of Rochester in 1929 and appointed a DBE in 1931. Her final honour, the CH, was conferred many years later, in the Birthday Honours List 1970 'For services to the Theatre'. She died of a heart attack in London in 1976.

Sir Frederick Ashton 13 June 1970
The founding choreographer of English ballet, Frederick Ashton worked for more than fifty years with the most famous dancers of his day. He was born in Guayaquil, Ecuador in 1904, the son of a minor diplomat who was working for a cable company. The family later moved to Peru where he was educated at the Dominican School at Lima. In 1917 he saw a performance by Anna Pavlova and resolved to make dancing his life. In 1919 he was sent to England to be educated at Dover College. Vacations were spent in London where he watched performances by Isadora Duncan and Anna Pavlova, and the last seasons of Serge Diaghilev's Ballets Russes. In 1922 he began to study dance with Léonide Massine and Marie Rambert. His talent for dance was not especially remarkable, and Rambert noted his 'passionate laziness'. But she sensed and encouraged his talent for choreography. He staged his first work, *A tragedy of fashion* in 1926, followed by *Façade* (1931).

In 1933 he joined forces with Ninette de Valois in what was later to become the Sadler's Wells Ballet (now the Royal Ballet) as chief choreographer, and later became associate director and then (1963) director of the company, holding both positions until retirement in 1970. Thereafter his ballets included *Les rendezvous* (1933), *Four saints in three acts* (1934), *Le baiser de la fée* (1935) which began his long partnership with Margot Fonteyn, *Apparitions* and *Nocturnes* (1936), *Les patineurs* and *A wedding bouquet* (1937), *Horoscope* (1938), *Dante sonata* and *The wise virgins* (1940–41) During the 1939–45 war he served with Royal Air Force Intelligence but was given leave of absence in 1943 to choreograph *The quest*, with a score by Sir William Walton.

His works were noted for their lyricism, quiet charm, and precision, and he was considered to be without equal in his field. His work included abstract ballets, such as *Symphonic variations* by César Franck (1946), which was considered to be his best; short dramatic works, such as *Daphnis and Chloë* and *Tiresias* (both 1951); and full-length traditional ballets, such as Prokofiev's *Cinderella* (1948), Délibe's *Sylvia* (a one-act ballet) (1952), *Ondine* (1958), and *The dream* (1964). Other works included *Homage to the queen* (he was a firm royalist) (1953), *Romeo and Juliet*, for the Royal Danish Ballet (1955), *La fille mal gardée* (1960), *Marguerite and Armand* (1963), *Enigma variations* (1968), and *A month in the country* (1976). His last major works as a choreographer were *La chatte metamorphosée en femmo* (1985) and *Fanfare for Elizabeth* (1986). He also appeared as a dancer in comedy and character roles, and perhaps his most popular and enduring work was the Royal Ballet's film of *The tales of Beatrix Potter* (1970), in which Ashton featured as Mrs Tiggy-Winkle. His international fame as a choreographer was undisputed, but his approach to choreography could be idiosyncratic. 'He seemed to plan little in advance, to arrive for the first rehearsals without any original ideas, and to use music suggested, even occasionally chosen by his friends. He would ask dancers to invent steps to musical phrases, sometimes selecting ones he liked and discarding others, sometimes discarding everything and commanding new inventions. In this unorthodox manner many of his best-known ballets were built.'[8]

After Ashton's death few of his ballets remained in the active repertoire of the Royal Ballet. *La fille mal gardée*, *The dream*, *A month in the country* became classics and *Cinderella* is a Christmas favourite. *Scènes de ballet*, in the opinion of many, including Ashton himself, his best ballet, is performed from time to time. He used to say that after his death most of his works would be considered passé and would fall into neglect, and so it quickly proved be. Ashton was replaced as choreographer by Kenneth MacMillan in 1970, who disparaged aspects of his predecessor's works as silly and irrelevant, and the number of performed Ashton ballets declined.

His honours, including the usual sprinkling of honorary doctorates were many, beginning with a CBE in 1950, a knighthood in 1962, a CH in 1970 'For services to the Ballet' and finally the OM in 1977.

Ashton was homosexual and had several enduring relationships throughout his life, though some did not bring the love and friendship that he so much wanted. 'He was a supreme socialite, loving gossip and good living, which caused a certain florid portliness in later years. His sense of humour was delightful and he was an amusing, often witty companion.'[9] A fay and whimsical old man in the last years of his life, he came to shun public transport because he didn't want to cause trouble by dying on a bus. As it was, he died peacefully at his country house at Eye in Suffolk in 1988.

Sir John Gielgud 11 June 1977

John Gielgud was born in London in 1904, the son of a prosperous stockbroker of Polish origin. Of more significance for his future career, was the fact that his great-aunt was the celebrated actress Ellen Terry, whom he saw every Christmas when the whole Terry clan descended on his parents home in Kensington. He was educated at Hillside and Westminster Schools, and trained as an actor at Lady Benson's School and the Royal Academy of Dramatic Art. His professional debut in 1921, playing a French herald in Shakespeare's *Henry V* at the Old Vic, began an acting life that was to last for more than seventy years. As the herald, his one line was 'here is the number of the slaughter'd French' and he claimed to have delivered it rather badly. His first major London role was as Trofimov in Chekhov's *The cherry orchard*. He went on to play Romeo and then two seasons at the Old Vic in 1929, in *Richard II* and *Hamlet*, marked him as a leading Shakespearean actor. By 1931, Gielgud was the toast of the town and he would remain in a position of eminence for 60 years. His first appearance on Broadway was in Alfred Neumann's *The patriot* in 1928, and he returned to the New York stage on many occasions. Reflecting on his early years in an interview in 1991 he said, 'I spoke rather well, but rather too well, and fell in love with my own voice.'[10] His diction was immaculate, and Laurence Olivier called his voice, 'the voice that wooed the world'. Alec McCowen called it 'the best voice of the century'. Alec Guinness called it 'a superb tenor voice'. Richard Briers described it as 'an intensely poetic voice that will be forever memorable.' Lee Strasberg, the American acting teacher likened it to 'some gorgeous oboe miraculously playing itself.' Gielgud once said of himself, 'I could never play a peasant or workman, or anything in dialect . . . I feel that it is a dreadful fault in me as an actor.'

His fully designed productions of *The merchant of Venice* at the Old Vic in 1932, *Hamlet* (1934), *Romeo and Juliet* (1935) and *Three sisters* (1938) marked his competence as a director and set new standards in the theatrical productions, and his sense of glamour and high comedy reached a peak when he appeared with Edith Evans in a legendary production of *The importance of being earnest* in 1939. Though his friends, colleagues and admirers might have wished him to do it, Gielgud was too anti-institutional ever to set up a permanent troupe of his own. 'It was his nature to move about within a large professional circle, forming and dissolving partnerships as he changed countries, switching between acting and directing, and rebounding – as he put it – "between the advance guard and the rear guard".'[11]

The new tendencies in drama that emerged after the 1939–45 war were not much to his liking. Always fastidious and elegant in speech and dress, he was disdainful of the scruffy and uncouth productions of Brecht and Beckett that captivated postwar audiences at the Royal Court Theatre, and he did not secure a foothold in the world of contemporary repertory for some time, nor easily adapt to changing times. When he was ninety he said 'I thought I was elderly, past my peak in 1944.' During the early postwar years he repeated his past successes, directed operas, made solo tours in his Shakespearean anthology *The ages of man*, devised by Dadie Rylands (CH 1987), and generally coasted along on his past reputation.

In 1968 he played the role of a bumbling traditionalist headmaster in Alan Bennett's *Forty years on*. It displayed his talent for self-mockery and marked an entry into the world of modern theatre and was followed by a series of parts in plays by David Storey, Peter Shaffer, Edward Bond and Harold Pinter. His last stage performance was in 1988 at the age of eighty-four when he played a museum curator, reminiscing on the disappointments of his life, in Hugh Whitemore's *The best of friends*.

His film career was not substantial, though later in his life he emerged as an effective character player. His first film, *Who is man*, was produced in 1924. Others included *The good companions* (1933), *The secret agent* (1936), *The prime minister* (starring as Disraeli) (1940), *A diary for Timothy* (1945), *Julius Caesar* (1953), *Richard III* (1955), *The Barretts of Wimpole Street* (1957), *St Joan* (1957), *Becket* (1964), *The loved one* (1965), *Chimes at midnight* (1966), *Mister Sebastian* (1967), *The charge of the light brigade* (1968), *Shoes of the fisherman* (1967), *Oh what a lovely war!* (1969), *Julius Caesar* (1970), *Eagle in a cage* (1973), *Lost horizon* (1973), *Murder on the Orient Express* (1974), *11 Harrowhouse* (1974), *Gold* (1974), *Aces high* (1976), a misanthropic dying novelist in *Providence* (1977), *Joseph Andrews* (1977), *Portrait of a young man* (1977), *Caligula* (1977), *The human factor* (1979), *The conductor* (1980), *Murder by decree* (1980), *The formula* (1980), a smutty-mouthed butler in *Arthur* (1980) (which made him a Hollywood star and brought him an Oscar, for best supporting actor), *The elephant man* (1980), *Lion of the desert* (1981), *Chariots of fire* (1981), *Priest of love* (1982), *Wagner* (1983), *Invitation to the wedding* (1983), *Scandalous* (1983), *The wicked lady* (1983), *Camille* (1984), *The shooting party* (1985), *Plenty* (1985), *Leave all fair* (1987), *The whistle blower* (1987), *Arthur on the rocks* (1988), *Getting things right* (1988), *Loser takes all* (1988), *Prospero's books* (1991), in a role which required him to perform naked, *Shining through* (1991), *Power of one* (1991), and an inspiring music professor in *Shine* (1996).

His television work included *The mayfly and the frog* (1966), *Dorian Grey* (1967), *In good King Charles's golden days* (1970), *Parson's pleasure* (1980), *Brideshead revisited* (1981), *The scarlet and the black* (1983), *Time after time* (1986), *Marco Polo* (1986), *Oedipus the king* (1986), *War and remembrance* (1987), *The Canterville ghost* (1987) *The Tichbourne claimant* (1998), a production of *Merlin* for Channel 4 television, and a month before his death he was filming the Samuel Beckett play *Catastrophe*.

He wrote a number of mostly autobiographical works. The first, *Early stages*, in 1939 (and revised in 1976) and the last, *Backward glances*, in 1989. His final publication, *Notes from the gods* (1994) was a collection of comments he had scribbled in programmes from his early years. He became legendary for a series of amusing, well-timed and quite deliberate gaffes. Sitting next to the then prime minister, Clement Attlee, he said 'Tell me, where are you living now?' Concluding a conversation with Christopher Reeve, at the time wearing his full *Superman* costume, he asked 'Christopher, I quite forgot to ask. What are you doing now?' Rehearsing for Benjamin Britten's *A midsummer night's dream*, Gielgud, anxious to interrupt the musicians, said 'Oh, for goodness sake, do stop that awful racket.' When Googie Withers asked him why he had never given her a job, he said, 'Because you have such a stupid name.' One morning Gielgud telephoned his biographer, Sheridan Morley to complain, 'You'll never believe this, in America they are actually about to name a theatre after a drama critic . . . Oh my God, you are one. Goodbye.'

In 1994 the Globe Theatre in London's Shaftesbury Avenue was renamed the Gielgud Theatre in his honour. He was knighted in 1953, appointed a CH in 1977 'For services to the Theatre' and an OM in 1996, although he said that public honours never really interested him. When his agent telephoned him after hearing that he had been appointed to the Order of Merit, Gielgud brushed aside the congratulations and asked impatiently, 'Any news about that part.'[12]

His final home was South Place, a seventeenth century house in Buckinghamshire, and described by Alec Guinness as 'a stately pleasure dome'. Gielgud had never made any secret of his homosexuality and in 1953 he pleaded guilty to a charge of importuning in Dudmaston Mews, Chelsea. For the last forty years of his life his companion was the Hungarian-born Martin Hensler who died in 1999. Gielgud aged visibly after Hensler's death, and died peacefully after lunch one Sunday at South Place in 2000.

Dame Ninette de Valois 31 December 1981

Ninette de Valois was one of the most influential figures in the world of dance in the twentieth century. She was revered by those who respected her outstanding achievements and disliked by those who had the misfortune to incur her wrath by crossing her or failing to rise to her expectations. Like a minor but all-powerful deity, 'Madam' as she was known throughout the world of ballet, was a small, formidable woman who worked as a choreographer, teacher, and director, and established ballet in a Britain that had no ballet tradition, and she watched and protectively interfered in the world of British ballet that she had created almost until the end of her long life.

'Ninette de Valois' was the stage name (created by her mother) of Edris Stannus, born in County Wicklow in 1898, the second daughter of an army colonel and a glass worker. The family moved to England when she was seven. She was sent to a London theatrical school also attended by Noel Coward, and at thirteen she was performing in Lila Field's *Wonder children* in commercial theatre. 'If they didn't like you, they threw things,' she once said. She went on to ballet, performed at seaside resorts when she was a teenager, and she danced Anna Pavlova's Dying Swan, as she recalled, 'dying twice nightly on all the coastal piers for my "death" was always ferociously encored.' At that date, ballet in Britain was little more than a novelty turn in the variety theatres.

Dame Ninette took lessons from Italian dance master Enrico Cecchetti, was premiere danseuse with the British National Opera Company in 1918 and prima ballerina at the Royal Opera Season at Covent Garden in 1919. She joined Diaghilev's Ballets Russes company in Monte Carlo (1923–26), but gave up dancing when she learned she had been struggling with the effects of undiagnosed childhood polio.

She came back to England and in 1926 opened her London Academy of Choreographic Art and formed a small group of dancers. She began a collaboration with Lilian Baylis at the Old Vic, teaching movement to the actors and giving ballet performances. In 1931, she moved to Baylis's second theatre, Sadler's Wells, persuaded Frederick Ashton from the Marie Rambert ballet company to join her company as choreographer, and signed Constant Lambert as musical director. Young dancers who later achieved international fame – Alicia Markova, Margot Fonteyn, Robert Helpmann, Rudolf Nureyev, Michael Soames, and Moira Shearer – performed with the company. It grew steadily and became the Sadler's Wells Ballet, which moved to the Opera House in Covent Garden in 1946. The company was renamed the Royal Ballet in 1956. Her Royal Ballet School became the cradle of an English ballet style, and she continued working with the school until 1971, having stepped down as director of the Royal Ballet in 1963.

She was strict, imperious, and did not accept laziness or incompetence in her dancers, and she could be ferocious towards fools, time wasters, and anyone less demanding of perfection in her companies, as her former students remembered. Meredith Daneman said, 'If she walked into classroom, our backs would stiffen and our knees would start to shake. A word from her could make or break you.' Peter Morris, a trustee of the Royal Ballet Benevolent Fund, remembered his hand shaking with nerves as he signed a birthday card to be sent to 'Madam' on her one hundredth birthday. Moira Shearer described her as 'a choreographer of immense talent and perception, and also a ruthless dictator. Rehearsals with her were hell. But performing these ballets was a delight.' David Bintley, who met her when he was eighteen and she was seventy-nine, said 'She could be absolutely terrifying and I count it as one of the blessings of my life that I never saw that side of her. She took an early shine to me which never wore off. The dragon manner was business. Outside of that she was the most witty, delightful, intelligent and informed of companions.'

She wrote three books, *Invitation to the ballet* (1937), *Come dance with me* (1957), and *Step by step* (1977). She was made a CBE in 1947 and, unusually rapidly, a DBE, in 1951 after two successive tours in the USA. Another thirty-one years passed before she was made a CH. She had become the grand old lady of ballet, she was past eighty, and she had devoted fifty years of her working life to promoting the cause of classical ballet in Britain. Without her, ballet of the standards and class by then customary would simply not exist. Her chief lieutenant, the choreographer Sir Frederick Ashton, had himself been made both a CH in 1970 and an OM in 1977. De Valois's contribution was equal if not greater than Ashton's and deserved further recognition. So she was made a CH in 1981 'For services to the ballet' and an OM in 1992.

In 1935, she married Arthur Connell, an Irish surgeon who died in 1986, but they had no children. When she was in her nineties, and living alone in an apartment in south-west London, Dame Ninette took to writing poetry. 'I'd rather have been a writer than a dancer. And I get more fun out of my poetry than I did out of choreography,' she said. To mark her one hundredth birthday, Dame Antoinette Sibley said of her mentor: 'She gave you enormous courage in life to take risks. Great people take risks, and she did so all the time.'

Ninette de Valois was frail for the last few years of her life, and it was feared she would not reach her centenary. But she lived to be 102, dying in her sleep at her home in 2001. On the evening of her death the audience at the Royal Opera House in Covent Garden stood for a minute's silence.

George Rylands 13 June 1987
Beyond the world of the University of Cambridge, the name of 'Dadie' Rylands, as his friends knew him, was not widely recognised. But within Cambridge he was an institution for more than seventy years.

He was born in 1902 at Tockington near Bristol, the son of a Gloucestershire estate agent, and educated at Eton and at King's College, Cambridge (from 1921), where he remained for the rest of his life in variety of roles. He was elected a fellow in 1927 on the strength of a dissertation published in 1928 as *Words and poetry*. He served the college as dean (appointed in 1930), bursar (1939), college lecturer and director of studies, and university lecturer in English literature. He was influenced by members of the Bloomsbury Group, and while writing his dissertation, he worked for Leonard and Virginia Woolf at the Hogarth Press. His rooms in the Old Lodge were decorated by Dora Carrington, and Lytton Strachey often visited him. In Virginia Woolf's *A room of one's own*, Rylands was the host at the luncheon described at the beginning of the book.

With Maynard Keynes he was one of the founders of the Cambridge Arts Theatre and the Marlowe Society. He himself acted in many plays at the ADC and Arts theatres. 'He was constantly devising and appearing in plays, masques, oratorios and other divertissements. A characteristic entertainment was the programme of ballet and poetry readings at the London Arts Theatre with Lydia Lopokova and Frederick Ashton. T. S. Eliot was pleased to hear the audience laughing delightedly at Ryland's production of *The family reunion*.'[13]

His greatest contribution was to drama and the theatre in Cambridge. In his first term at King's he played Electra in Aeschylus' *Oresteia*, and thereafter he was the centre of the dramatic life of Cambridge for several decades. Maynard Keynes presented the Arts Theatre to a theatre-less Cambridge in 1936 and on his death Rylands (who had been a director and trustee since the foundation of the project) succeeded him as chairman of the Arts Theatre Trust (1946–1982). The purpose of the theatre was to enable selected amateur groups from the town and the university to put on productions in the theatre and not risk a loss. The opportunity this provided resulted in the early entry to the professional stage of a steady stream of talented artists. Among well known personalities whose debut was in the Arts Theatre were Douglas Adams, Tim Brooke-Taylor, Margaret Drabble, Bamber Gascoigne, Germaine Greer, Clive James and Eric Idle. According to Jonathan Miller 'The Arts Theatre is probably the main reason that Cambridge has always taken the lead in producing England's most distinguished actors and directors.'

In the 1950s attendances slowly started to fall with the advent of television, and despite major fundraising, finances remained a major problem throughout the 70s and 80s. In April 1993, the theatre closed for the first time in its history, to prepare for a new development. The newly refurbished and enlarged theatre was opened in 1996, in the presence of Rylands then in his ninety-fourth year.

Rylands held a number of other public appointments – governor of the Old Vic (1945–78), chairman of the Apollo Society (1946–72), a member of the council of

Cheltenham College (1946–76), and a member of the council of RADA – but his first love remained the Cambridge Arts Theatre. He acted and directed as well – including John Gielgud and Peggy Ashcroft in *Hamlet* at the Haymarket in 1944, and *The duchess of Malfi* in 1945 – and he devised *The ages of man* for John Gielgud when the latter was 'out of fashion' in the later 1950s and early 1960s. The Marlowe Society recordings of the whole Shakespeare canon for the British Council, was one of his greatest achievements. Rylands' most notable productions were for the society. 'More than anyone he raised the standard of verse-speaking in the theatre so that critics used ruefully to compare Shakespearean performances in the West End with his amateur productions at Cambridge.'[14]

In an address as chairman of the Arts Theatre Trust at the launch of the Cambridge Theatre Club in 1953, he said: 'Look to the future. That is the theatre's motto. The drama is of itself ephemeral, fleeting, precarious; reputations wax and wane overnight; a West End triumph is a flop on Broadway – and vice versa. Every night in a thousand theatres and halls and social clubs and Women's Institutes the curtain rises and falls; and every performance is a new creation.'

For an academic, his output of publications was quite slender and relatively shallow. The Hogarth Press published his poem *Russet and Taffata* in 1925. His other publications included *Words and poetry* (1928) and a book of his *Poems* (1931) *A Shakespeare anthology* (1939), *Shakespeare's poetic energy* (British Academy lecture) (1951), and *A distraction of wits*, an anthology from the university's Elizabethan writers (1958). *Quoth the raven 'nevermore'. An anthology* (1984) and *Croaked the raven: One no more* (1988), both 'anthologies of negation' from favoured private presses. *College verse* appeared in 1989. His most valuable publication was thought to be *The ages of man*, an anthology of Shakespeare, which concentrated on the poet rather than the dramatist, and was made famous by the recitals of John Gielgud. Academic research was not Rylands' forte, and the stream of seminal or critical publications that emerged from the pens of his colleagues were not to his taste. 'He wanted to spread sweetness and light, and to encourage the public to love and be moved by literature . . . It was as a teacher that he excelled. He was always pleased if he could rouse a third-class man from laziness and see him get a good second . . . He could be sharp and cutting; if he detected in a friend a failure of sympathy, or incipient pomposity, he would deliver a devastating rebuke, but generations of undergraduates knew him as a wise confidant with a great understanding of human follies and frailties.'[15]

He was appointed a CBE in 1961 for services to Shakespearean studies and, slightly surprisingly, a CH in 1987 'For services to the Arts'. He was said to have influenced a generation of undergraduates who became prominent actors or directors in London or Cambridge, but it is difficult to calculate the extent or significance of this indirect influence, and outside the Cambridge world of his friends and devotees he was an obscure and peripheral figure. He did not welcome the onset of the restrictions of old age, complaining that he had lived too long and could no longer properly see, read, hear or walk. Probably to his relief, he died in 1999 in his ninety-seventh year.

Sir Alec Guinness 11 June 1994
Alec Guinness was an actor famous for the variety and excellence of his stage and screen characterizations, but throughout his life and distinguished career he craved privacy and shrank from all but the most unavoidable publicity.

His origins were mysterious in that he never knew the name of his father. His birth certificate registered him as Alec Guinness de Cuffe, born in London in April 1914, the son of a Miss Agnes Cuffe; the space for his father's name was left blank. Only at the age of fourteen was he told that his real name was Guinness. His early life was difficult as he recorded in his autobiography. 'I . . . was born to confusion and totally immersed in it for several years, owning three different names until the age of fourteen and living in about thirty different hotels, lodgings and flats, each of which was hailed as "home" until such time as my mother and I flitted, leaving behind, like a paper-chase, a wake of unpaid bills.'[16]

A tendency to act was demonstrated during his school days when he amused his classmates by acting out stories he had invented at the age of seven while ill. After school he worked for eighteen months as a copywriter for an advertising agency, then, after studying acting at the Fay Compton Studio of Dramatic Art, he made his stage debut in 1934 as an extra in *Libel* at the King's Theatre, Hammersmith. He was a member of the Old Vic company in 1936–37, John Gielgud's company 1937–38, and then the Old Vic again 1938–41. He appeared in such classics as *Richard II* (1937), *The school for scandal* (1937), *The three sisters* (1937), and *The merchant of Venice* (1938). In 1938 he starred in a popular modern-dress version of *Hamlet* at the Old Vic and produced *Twelfth night* for the Old Vic company in 1948. While on leave from the royal navy during the 1939–45 war (he had joined as a rating in 1941 and was commissioned in 1942), he made his New York stage debut in *Flare path* (1942–43) and later appeared there in *The cocktail party* (1964) and *Dylan* (1964).

Guinness's initial screen role was as Pip's friend Herbert Pocket in *Great expectations* (1946). He had written and produced the play (as well as playing the role of Pocket) in a small-scale stage production in London, and he repeated the role on screen. *Great expectations* launched his film career, and after its success, the producer David Lean decided to do another Dickens film, *Oliver Twist* (1948), and Alec Guinness asked to play Fagin. At thirty-two he was deemed to be far too young, and simply did not look right for the part. But he was persistent, arranged for himself to be made up, won the role and created the definitive Fagin.

Oliver Twist was followed by a series of Ealing studio comedies that included the internationally popular *Kind hearts and coronets* (1949), in which he played the eight heirs to the dukedom of Chalfont, each murdered in succession by Dennis Price; *The Lavender Hill mob* (1951), with himself as the mousy clerk turned bank robber; *The man in the white suit* (1951), with himself as the chemist who invents a fabric that will never wear out; and *The captain's paradise* (1953), in which he played a lovable bigamist. Other films included *The bridge on the River Kwai* (1957), in which he played an obsessed army officer, and for which he won the Academy Award for best actor; *Lawrence of Arabia* (1962), in which he played Prince Feisal; *Star wars* (1977), in which he played Obi-wan Kenobi; and *Little Dorrit* (1987), in which he played William Dorrit. His role in *Star wars* brought him international recognition among a younger generation who had never known his Dickens characters and the Ealing comedies. As Obi-wan Kenobi, he essentially played himself, speaking in his own voice and without character makeup. It was his favourite film, although he would often say that he hated the attention he received from that part. But through the generosity of George Lucas, who gave him a percentage of the gross, he became a millionaire many times over. 'Privately, he was very self-effacing and introverted, and although he had his little vanities he always liked to be anonymous, unnoticed and unobtrusive, unrecognised on the street. Yet he happily took on the part of a brash, gregarious charmer who swept his way up the social ladder on the strength of his hypnotic appeal. Between takes he would revert to being himself. In those days stars did not have the expensive trailers to rest in that they have today, and the back of a car was considered quite adequate. We were on location in the Potteries, and some kids came to see what was going on. They peered through the windows where Alec was resting. "Who's that?" said one. "Oh, it isn't anybody," said the other.'[17]

In 1980 he won a special Academy Award for memorable film performances. Guinness also wrote dramatizations (*The brothers Karamazov* and *Great expectations*) and a film script of *The horse's mouth* and co-authored the play *Yahoo* (1976), in which he played the role of Jonathan Swift. His television appearances included *Tinker, tailor, soldier, spy* (1979), *Smiley's people* (1981–82), *Tales from Hollywood* (1991), *A foreign field* (1993), and *Eskimo day* (1995). He published three volumes of autobiography: *Blessings in disguise* (1985), *My name escapes me. The diary of a retiring actor* (1996) and *A positively final appearance. A journal 1996–1998* (1999).

Alec Guinness was made a CBE in 1955, knighted in 1960 and appointed a CH in 1994 as 'Actor. For services to Drama'. After a long illness, he died in 2000, leaving his wife of sixty-two years, the playwright Merula Salaman, and a son Matthew. When his son had been stricken with polio years previously, Alec Guinness had made a private vow that if he recovered he would become a Roman Catholic, which he did. In death, the personal privacy that he had sought in life was continued. His funeral took place at St Lawrence's Roman Catholic Church, Petersfield, Hampshire. It was a private occasion for family and very close friends only, and at his request there was no memorial service. He was buried at an undisclosed destination.

Peter Brook 13 June 1998
Peter Brook was born in 1925, the son of Russian scientist, and educated at Westminster, Gresham's School and Magdalen College, Oxford. His career as one of the most prominent British theatre producers of the twentieth century began at the age of eighteen when he directed *Dr Faustus* at the Torch Theatre in 1943, followed by *The infernal machine* at the Chanticleer Theatre in 1945.

Brook is probably the most visionary and influential director Britain has ever produced. Many of his productions have become legendary, and his book *The empty space* (1968) has become a set text for numerous theatre workers, influencing directors worldwide as an acute analysis of the problems facing contemporary theatre. Often regarded as a theatrical guru, he has been a key figure in exploring and developing the possibilities of drama in his long career, taking productions from the West End to New York, disused quarries in Australia and African villages which have never seen a theatre company. His long association with the Royal Shakespeare Company resulted in a number of critically acclaimed productions, perhaps most famously with the seminal *A midsummer night's dream* (1970). It remains one of the most celebrated and discussed of Shakespeare productions and highlighted a new emphasis on visual style. In the same year he left the British theatre and founded an International Centre of Theatre Research in Paris, gathering an international company of actors dedicated to his way of working. The company's first play *Orghast* (1972) by Ted Hughes, established a policy of international touring, including to Africa where spontaneous improvisations to village audiences were performed. In 1980 the company took *The conference of birds* to aboriginal audiences in Australia, then to Paris and finally across the Sahara desert. Other productions include *The ilk* (1975), *The cherry orchard* (1981), and the much-acclaimed dramatisation of *The mahabharata* in a cycle of plays lasting nearly ten hours and with a multinational cast (Paris 1985, Glasgow 1988). It was televised in 1989 and won an International Emmy in 1990. 'Some actors talk about him as if he were an invisible magician always in control . . . Others talk about him as a great liberator of actor's instincts. He himself says that he usually starts with a pre-image of the play but that all rehearsal is a process of joint exploration. And he recalls with some amusement that when he directed *Timon of Athens* at the Theatre Bouffres du Nord in Paris . . . he began by telling the company that he didn't know much more about the play than they did.'[18]

Some have criticised his work as a form of self-indulgent escape, but Brook himself viewed it as a crucial period of questioning, of discovery, of experiment. He talked of a threefold responsibility: to the theatre-going audience; to people who would never set foot inside a theatre; and to the group itself. 'We also break into the monotonous regularity of playing every night whenever we can: we do everything we can to make a performance a total event.'[19] His concept was to free theatre from the tyranny of deadly repetition. He says he has seen this happen in Russia where an actor's house vibrates with excitement on the day he's due to perform in a *Three sisters* for the Moscow Arts: or in an opera where he remembers Carl Reinkel as musical director at Covent Garden thrilling to the prospect of a *Rosenkavalier* that night. 'It was like a boxing match, like a bout and I believe this is what it's essential to bring back into drama. Obviously we can't change the whole theatrical system overnight but we have to try and restore the magic of the event.'[20] Allied to this theory was a vision of freedom from the tyranny of crushingly expensive buildings with overheads that necessitate a factory-like output. 'Nothing will change because of what you and I say in this room. But the virtue of pioneer experiments, like the work in Paris is that it can make a chink somewhere and by going against the current it is possible that an embryonic scheme to spend a fortune on a building could be halted and transformed into that money being spent on the human element. Theatres don't benefit from vast technology, complex amenities, lavish comfort. Airports do. But theatres don't. One just hopes that some day the penny will drop.'[21] In his almost missionary endeavours, Brook has taken his productions not only to the civilised comforts of London, Glasgow, Paris and New York, but to the remoter areas of Australia, Iran, the Sahara, Niger and Nigeria.

He has directed a number of films, including *The beggar's opera* (1952), *Moderato cantabile* (1960), *Lord of the flies* (1962), *The Marat/Sade* (1967), *Tell me lies* (1968), *King Lear* (1969), *Meetings with remarkable men* (1979), and *The tragedy of Carmen* (1983). Apart from *The empty space*, his other publications include *The shifting point* (1988), a volume of autobiography, *Le diable c'est l'ennui* (1991), *There are no secrets* (1993), *Threads of time: a memoir* (1998), and *Evoking Shakespeare* (1999).

He has been twice decorated by the French government, being made a commandeur de l'Ordre des Arts and an officier de la Légion d'Honneur. On being admitted to the Légion d'Honneur, President Mitterand of France paid tribute to Brook. 'I have much joy in being able to meet a man who has assembled all talents. You create, you exhibit, you transmit.'[22]

Brook was destined for a state honour from an early age. His work was acknowledged as excellent and highly original, and by 1961 he was ranked as one of the top four or five British producers. He was appointed a CBE in 1965 at the age of forty, and then nothing further for more than thirty years. Towards the end of the twentieth century he was beginning to look like a prophet honoured more in his county of residence than in his country of origin. There was no doubting the genius displayed during more than fifty years as a theatre director and producer. The problem was that Brook had taken up residence in France and was unlikely ever to return to the United Kingdom, and permanent residence overseas tended to count against an individual on the ground that the conferment of a state honour required an element of service to the nation, not simply a 'reputation'. There was no doubt that he deserved further recognition above the CBE, but how could it be done? In Brook's case, a rare procedure was adopted. As he was resident in France, and had been for more than two decades, his CH appeared on the diplomatic and overseas service list (not the prime minister's list) of the birthday honours list 1998 'For services to the theatre'. His honour therefore came, appropriately, as a recommendation from the foreign and commonwealth office.

Paul Scofield 30 December 2000
Paul Scofield was born in Hurstpierpoint in Sussex in 1922, the son of a headmaster of a small church school. His mother was a Roman Catholic, and in later life he mused on the possibility of the then colourful and dramatic liturgies of the Roman Catholic Church having ignited his interest in the theatre. 'You know they just might have; certainly there was no theatre in our blood ... certainly they have something within the Mass: a marvellous atmosphere.'[23]

He was educated at Varndean Grammar School where he had his first stage appearance as Juliet (the school was a single sex) in a production of *Romeo and Juliet*. The experience was formative, and he came to believe emphatically that children should be encouraged to act in Shakespeare, and he himself made his name in Shakespearean roles. He left Varndean in 1939 at the age of seventeen to join Croydon Repertory Theatre School and train as a professional actor. His first role was a walk on in *Desire under the elms* at the Westminster Theatre in 1940. His first real break came when he joined Basil Langton's touring company in Birmingham in 1942. He played Horatio in *Hamlet*. There he met his future wife, Joy Parker, who played Ophelia. He left in 1944 to return to Birmingham and the permanent repertory company. In 1945 he went to Stratford for three years, one of the young stars in the Royal Shakespeare Company assembled by Sir Brian Jackson.

In the autumn of 1945 he met Peter Brook (who was to be made a CH in 1998). Brook directed him in Shaw's *Man and superman* and *The lady from the sea*, and their friendship lasted. It is arguable that both he and Scofield have done their best work together: the legendary production of Anouilh's *Ring round the moon* (1950), in which Scofield played the twins Hugo and Frederick; Otway's *Venice preserv'd* in 1953, in which he played Pierre; Scofield's *Hamlet* which was performed in 1955 at the Moscow Arts Theatre; and his *King Lear*, at Stratford in 1964 – all were described as touchstones of theatrical excellence, and all hinged on the collaboration between Scofield and Brook. 'We seemed to work together a lot then, Peter and I. I think his direction for me goes deepest. He strikes a bell.'[24]

Appointed a director of the Royal Shakespeare Company in 1966 (being one of three with Peter Brook and Peter Hall), he resigned two years later, discounting rumours of a personality clash. 'It is a personal decision, not a sudden one. In fact I resigned two weeks ago, and there are no dramatic reasons for it. At the time of my resignation I had no more theatre plans, but there is now a modern part being discussed with another management.'[25] The decision, he claimed, had nothing to do with the appointment of Trevor Nunn as the new artistic director of the company. He had been thinking of resigning before then. Nor, he said, had there been a disagreement with Peter Hall. But the projected film of the Royal Shakespeare Company's *Macbeth*, due to be directed by Hall was abandoned after Scofield said he preferred not to appear in it.[26]

Scofield was an avid filmgoer from an early age, with a particular affection for Laurel and Hardy. But although he appeared in several films, he showed no inclination to pursue a film career. His few films include *That lady* (1955), *Carve her name with pride* (1958), with Virginia McKenna, a film biography of Violette Szabo, *The train* (1964), another 1939–45 war drama, with Burt Lancaster, *A man for all seasons* (1966) a portrayal of Sir Thomas More in his dealings with King Henry VIII, *Bartleby* (1970), *King Lear* (1971), *Scorpio* (1973), in which he again starred with Burt Lancaster, *A delicate balance* (1973), with Katherine Hepburn, *Nineteen nineteen* (1985), *When the whales came* (1989), *Henry V* (1989), *Hamlet* (1991), *Utz* (1992), *Quiz Show* (1995), *The little riders* (1995) and *The crucible* (1997). His television work included *Anna Karenina* (1985), *The Attic* (1988), and *Martin Chuzzlewit* (1994). His performance as Sir Thomas More in *A man for all seasons*, which he had played on stage at the Globe Theatre in 1959, won him an Oscar, a BAFTA award, and won the prize for best actor at the Moscow Film Festival in 1967, and was hailed as one of the most definitive screen performances of all time.

Although he could probably have enjoyed a successful film career, he chose to forsake that glamorous route to stardom in favour of a hard-working life on the stage, which always remained his first love. 'Glamour is a trap if you go after success just for the fame and your face in the papers and all that. You are either an actor of ego or a worker. I am a worker. . . . I believe the theatre is more potent. I enjoy building up a rapport with the audience and developing a character as the play progresses. In films you are usually under-rehearsed, but your performance is committed for all time. If it's bad, well that's hard luck. If you aren't ready there is a danger you will fall back on your own personality rather than the author's creation. But I suppose that's film star acting.'[27]

Throughout his career, and much like Alec Guinness, Scofield acquired the honourable reputation as a man who preferred privacy and behaved with humility. 'I am not a star, 'he once said, 'I am a working actor, and I would hate that to change . . . to be recognised . . . to be followed by the press . . . It would interfere with my work. I like, you see, to avoid publicity. It always feels so false, somehow, talking about oneself.'[28] Interviews with him were rare and he went on record to say that he hadn't given many interviews in the past because he was afraid of boring people with that kind of self-exposure.[29]

Scofield emerged as a distinguished and highly professional actor and a natural candidate for state honours. His first, a CBE, came at the early age of thirty-four in 1956, but then a surprising gap of forty-four years, until the crowning honour of a CH in 2000. He would have been a natural candidate for a knighthood at a much earlier stage, and the absence of such an honour caused periodic speculation. Because he had accepted a CBE, he clearly had no ideological objections to honours. In a 1973 interview, he was asked how he felt about the possibility of becoming a knight. 'I don't have strong feelings about that. I could answer it to the extent of avoiding it by saying "I'm happy to be plain mister".'[30] Finally, after the award of a CH in 2000, he revealed that he had been offered, and declined, a knighthood on more than one occasion. On the first occasion he was playing in Moscow. 'I had to go and see the ambassador and explain that I didn't want it. He was surprised, but he was very nice about it.'[31] On each occasion he was fully supported by his wife. 'My wife backed me all the way. She didn't want to be known as Lady, just as I didn't wish to be a Sir.'[32]

Some individuals decline honours in the hope or the expectation that they will be offered something better, but apparently such was not the case with Scofield, and his genuine diffidence was counted to his credit. The CH that he was offered in 2000 came as a genuine and welcome surprise. 'I couldn't believe that they were considering me for such a high honour. I thought that by turning down a knighthood not once, but twice, I had ruled myself out of the reckoning . . . I decided that the Companion of Honour was something I couldn't turn down and I wrote off accepting it . . Although I'm not at all sure what a Companion of Honour actually is, I know it is a very high honour and that it is unusual for an actor to receive it. Sir John Gielgud and Sir Alec Guinness were I believe the only others. So now I have to find out just what it is about.'[33]

CHAPTER TEN

Interpreters of life and living

PHILOSOPHERS, HISTORIANS, ARCHAEOLOGISTS, ECONOMISTS

'Contrariwise,' continued Tweedledee, 'if it was so, it might be; and if it were so, it would be; but as it isn't, it ain't. That's logic.'
'Tweedledum and Tweedledee', Through the looking-glass, Lewis Carroll

Historians, philosophers, economists and archaeologists have been grouped together in this category entitled 'interpreters of life and living'. As interpreters of the course of human existence, historians, with their cousins the archaeologists, have predominated. The philosophers and the economists are accorded associate status, partly because they do not obviously fit into any other category, but mostly because their disciplines, although less factual and more theoretical, also concern themselves with the interpretation of life and living, and arguably make them more distant cousins of the historian.

Sir Henry Jones (1922) inaugurated the category of 'interpreters', but despite his undoubted eminence as a philosopher, he was appointed more because he was Welsh and highly regarded by the great Welsh prime minister David Lloyd George. Sixty years passed before the appointment of the only other philosopher, the Austrian-born Karl Popper (1982), whose lifelong obsession with human freedom was in accordance with a principal tenet of the philosophy of the Conservative government of Margaret Thatcher. Any further appointments from the discipline of these lovers of wisdom (*philos sophos*) will probably be motivated and justified by a very substantial international reputation.

The discipline of economics has so far had only three representatives among the ranks of the Companions of Honour: Lionel Robbins (1968), Friedrich von Hayek (1984), and Amartya Sen (2000). Robbins and von Hayek were colleagues at the London School of Economics from 1931 until 1950 when von Hayek went to Chicago. The reasoning behind their appointments as Companions of Honour is quite clear. Brilliant economist though he was, Lionel Robbins also undertook several public appointments in the world of arts administration and received the CH following his retirement as president of the British Academy and a trustee of the Tate Gallery. He is best remembered for producing the report which began the substantial expansion of higher education in the 1960s. Hayek was a prominent, outspoken and provocative conservative economist and critic of socialism and the welfare state, who was appointed a CH during a Conservative government. The Indian economist Amartya Sen, who himself taught at the London School of Economics in the 1970s, was in some ways the opposite of Hayek, a welfare economist passionately concerned with the economics of famine, drought and hunger, whose Nobel prize was attacked as an exercise in left-wing establishment economics, and whose CH came while a Labour government was in power. As with philosophers, any future economist CH will need to possess a very substantial international reputation, and probably one which is in accord with the prevailing ideology of the government in power.

The line of historians begins with the appointment of George Peabody Gooch (1939), a specialist in international and diplomatic relations, who never taught in a university, and who was honoured for his thirteen-volume *British documents on the origins of the war*. Arnold Toynbee (1956) worked on an even broader canvas as an historian of civilisations rather than events, and like Gooch he produced a multi-volume opus, *A study of history*. Sir Arthur Bryant (1967) was in the line of Gooch, a safe 'establishment' historian, if not a very well researched one. Son of a long-serving member of the royal household, he was the author of numerous 'popular' works that burnished the glories of English history. The Honourable Sir Steven Runciman (1983) was a linguistic child prodigy who developed an early fascination with the medieval history of Greece and the near east and wrote an unsurpassed three-volume history of the crusades. Sir Michael Howard (2002) became well known as a philosopher of the history of war. Joseph Needham, Leslie Rowse and Eric Hobsbawm were far from being 'safe establishment' figures; in each case the sub classification of 'controversial' or 'radical' describes their position in the ranks of historians. Yet each was unique and each made valuable contributions to the advancement of knowledge. After early training in biochemistry, Joseph Needham (1992) developed a greater interest in the history of science, and like Gooch and Toynbee, his fame rested on a remarkable multi-volume opus, *Science and civilisation in China*. Needham eventually managed to live down his early naive comments about Chinese communism to join the CH ranks late in his life. Leslie Rowse (1996), another entrant in old age, was a proud, passionate, angry and complex personality who ranged widely over the history and literature of Tudor England, and who had to wait for an honour until most of his opponents were dead. By that time, he himself was very nearly dead. The Marxist beliefs of Eric Hobsbawm (1997) made a CH, at the age of eighty, the most likely honour for this unrepentant communist, who studied history of the nineteenth and twentieth centuries from the view of the working classes in the age of revolution.

Two archaeologists have been made members of the Order. Sir John Beazley (1959) was part art historian and part academic archaeologist. He pioneered the study of the painting of Greek vases, effectively all that survived of Greek art, and knew everything there was to be known about the subject. Sir Mortimer Wheeler (1967) was much more a 'practical' archaeologist. He was a dashing, flamboyant and gallant hero of the 1914–18 war who popularised the work of 'the dig' and, through the medium of television, himself – to an extent that no subsequent archaeologist has managed.

There have been a number of other individuals eminent enough to be included in the ranks of the Order, and who, it is thought, refused the CH. *James Hammond* (1872–1949) and his wife Barbara were among the most innovative and influential social historians of modern England, especially the industrial revolution. Among their books were *The village labourer* (1911), *The town labourer* (1917) and *The skilled labourer* (1919). According to one writer he twice refused a knighthood (in 1931 and in 1946) on the ground that it would 'compromise his editorial independence.'[1] This seems unlikely, because having once refused a knighthood, a second offer would have been a very remote possibility, and as he was highly regarded by the postwar Labour government and that there was an offer of a second honour in 1946, it is much more likely to have been a CH. The socialist economic historian *R. H. Tawney* (1880–1962) was similarly highly regarded by Attlee's Labour government. Among his publications were *The agrarian problem in the sixteenth century* (1912), *The acquisitive society* (1920), *Religion and the rise of capitalism* (1926), *Land and labour in China* (1932) and *Business and politics under James I* (1958). It is certain that he refused a peerage from Ramsay MacDonald in 1933 and another honour, this time from Clement Attlee, and, as Tawney disapproved of titles, it was almost certainly a CH that was refused. 'He realized sadly that socialist politicians had still not renounced the toys of their opponents.'[2]

Michael Oakeshott (1901–1990) was the leading Conservative philosopher of the twentieth century. As an eloquent defender of conservative politics, he was a surprise choice to succeed Harold Laski as professor of political science at the London School of Economics (1951–69). There he influenced generations of students and readers who later became supporters of Margaret Thatcher. A political philosopher who established modesty as a philosophical principle, it was well known that he refused honours.[3] With the advent of a Conservative government in 1979, it is almost certain that he would have been offered recognition, and as he is known to have refused more than one honour, it is likely that this modest and retiring man declined both a knighthood and a CH.

Sir Henry Jones 2 January 1922

Henry Jones, whose liberal intellect led him to abandon early thoughts of entering the Welsh Presbyterian ministry, spent forty years teaching philosophy.

He was born at Llangernyw in north Wales in 1852, the son of a shoemaker, and rose from those humble beginnings to become the most eminent philosopher of his day. After a long struggle as a student in Wales, he was educated at the University of Glasgow where he graduated in 1878. He spent the next four years as an assistant lecturer at the university, while attending classes in the faculty of divinity with the intention of entering the Presbyterian ministry. The thought was abandoned, and in 1882 he accepted the post of lecturer in philosophy at University College, Aberystwyth, and two years later he became the first professor of logic and philosophy at the opening of the new University College of North Wales at Bangor. One of the selection panel challenged his theological soundness. 'We hear, Mr Jones that you deny the Divinity of our Lord.' Jones rose to the occasion. 'It is not true, Mr Thomas, I never yet denied the divinity of any man.'[4]

In 1891 he left Bangor to become professor of logic, rhetoric and metaphysics at the University of St Andrews, and in 1894, to his delight and pride, he returned to Glasgow as professor of moral philosophy. There he remained until his death nearly thirty years later, faithfully propagating the school of philosophy that he had learned from Edward Caird, his old tutor and immediate predecessor in the chair. 'He never swerved from the form of Hegelian idealism which he accepted as a student. He had accepted it as a man accepts religious truth which becomes the illuminating centre of his life; and his own conviction was so entire that he had comparatively little interest in other modes of approaching philosophical questions . . . His attitude had something of the impatience and intolerance which characterise the defender of the true faith, and in general his philosophy presented itself to him as a gospel which he preached with all the fervour of his Welsh temperament.'[5] His publications included *Browning as a religious and philosophical teacher* (1891), *The philosophy of Lotze* (1895), *Social responsibilities* (1905), *The philosophy of Martineau* (1905), *The immortality of the souls in the poems of Tennyson and Browning* (1905) *Idealism as a practical creed* (1909), *The working faith of the social reformer* (1910), *The immanence of God and the individuality of man*

(1912), *Social powers* (1913), *The idealism of Jesus* (1919), *The principles of citizenship* (1919) and *A faith that enquires* (1922).

In 1904 he was elected a fellow of the British Academy. He was knighted in 1912 and made a CH in 1922 within five weeks of his death. The appointment was made in the New Year Honours List for his services as 'Professor of Philosophy, Glasgow'. Jones was already seriously ill and there was no question of him attending an investiture. He was summoned to an investiture on 9 February but asked to be excused on the ground of illness and asked that the badge should be sent directly to him. 'As the matter appears to be very urgent,' recorded Sir Douglas Dawson, 'I sent the CH to Mr J. T. Davies [private secretary to Lloyd George] with a request that it should reach Sir Henry Jones as rapidly as possible.'[6] Lloyd George himself went to Scotland and presented the CH badge to his 'dear old friend' whose 'career and work will remain an encouragement and inspiration to Young Wales for many generations.'[7]

George Peabody Gooch 8 June 1939

George Peabody Gooch was an historian and politician who was honoured for his work in editing British government documents on the origins of the 1914–18 war.

He was born in 1873 in London into a comfortable middle class family, his father being a merchant. He was educated at Eton, King's College, London and Trinity College, Cambridge, graduating with a first class degree in the historical tripos in 1894, and then spent three years studying in Berlin. He failed to gain a fellowship at Trinity College in 1897, but being financially independent and having no great desire to become engrossed in a purely teaching career, he rejected advice to consider academic posts elsewhere.

The decisive factor in his formation was the South African War 1899–1902. 'Henceforward, it was not so much the social question but rather the problems of the empire, diplomacy, and war which stood in the forefront of his mind; and, apart from the tragedy of the conflict itself, he was troubled by the bitterness of the resulting controversy and the split in the ranks of the Liberals.'[8] He was elected Liberal MP in 1906 for Bath, but failed to secure re-election in 1910, and failed again at Reading in 1913. In 1911 he became joint editor of *Contemporary review* with J. Scott Lidgett, setting out to make it the leading monthly journal in foreign affairs. He held the post for an astonishing forty-nine years, until 1960 when he was eighty-seven.

Gooch developed a fundamental bias towards diplomatic history and international relations. His first book, *English democratic ideas in the seventeenth century* (1898), was assisted by Lord Acton. *Annals of politics and culture* (1910) itemised political events on the left hand pages and the contemporaneous cultural events on the right. *History and historians in the nineteenth century* (1913) was his finest production and was re-issued in 1952 to a wider audience. The outbreak of war in 1914 was painful, partly because Gooch had studied in Berlin and was attached to Germany and German historians, and partly because his wife was German, and after the 1914–18 war he tried hard to make Englishmen understand Germany. Seeing the clouds of war beginning to develop again, he was president of the national peace council (1933–36). *Germany and the French revolution* (1920) was his fourth book.

With Sir Adolphus Ward he edited the three-volume *Cambridge history of British foreign policy* (1922–23), and in 1924 he was invited by Ramsay MacDonald to edit the thirteen volumes of *British documents on the origins of the war* (1926–38). A by-product two volume work, *Before the war: studies in diplomacy*, appeared in 1936 and 1938. After the outbreak of the 1939–45 war he moved out of London but continued to write, publishing reminiscences of famous people he had known, and a series of essays on eighteenth and nineteenth century history including: *Courts and cabinets* (1944), *Frederick the great* (1947), *Studies in German history* (1948), *Maria Theresa and other studies* (1951), *Catherine the great and other studies* (1954), *Louis XV* (1956), *The second empire* (1960), and *French profiles* (1961). A volume of autobiography, *Under six reigns*, appeared in 1958.

Gooch was made an honorary fellow of Trinity College, Cambridge. The CH was conferred on him in 1939 'For services to historical research' in recognition of his work in editing *British documents on the origins of the war*. He was appointed in June 1939 but his investiture was delayed until February 1940 because of his ill-health. Shortly after the appointment was announced, his wife wrote to Buckingham Palace to say that her husband was too ill to attend an investiture. On 10 June *The Times* announced that he had undergone a 'serious operation' in a nursing home, and a week later, his condition was said to be critical after a heart attack. He was beginning to recover by the end of June, and lived for another twenty-eight years. In 1955 he was awarded the German Order of Pour le Mérite, a forerunner of the British Order of Merit that he received in 1963, two months before his ninetieth birthday. Sitting next to the Queen he recalled the visit to her father in 1940 to receive the CH. 'I told her I have never looked into kinder eyes . . . and she replied: "Yes, he was a very kind man".'[9] Gooch died in 1968 at the age of ninety-four, having been blind for the last few years of his life.

Arnold Toynbee 31 May 1956
Arnold Toynbee was an historian who specialised in studying the past by way of sweeping surveys of civilisations rather than political entities.

He was born in 1889, the only son of a worker for the Charity Organization Society. He was educated at Winchester and Balliol College, Oxford, where he acquired a remarkable knowledge of Latin and Greek, gaining first classes in both classical and honours moderations (1909) and literae humaniores (1911). In 1911 and 1912 he explored Greece and Italy alone and on foot, and for a year he became a student at the British School of Archaeology at Athens. He then became a tutor in ancient Greek and Roman history at Balliol (1912–15), and during the 1914–18 war he was employed in the political intelligence department of the foreign office, and was a member of the middle eastern section of the British delegation to the Paris peace conference in 1919.

In 1919 he was appointed to the Koraes chair of Byzantine and Modern Greek language, literature, and history in the University of London. He resigned in 1924. In 1925 he went to Chatham House (the Royal Institute of International Affairs) as director of studies and worked on the annual *Survey of international affairs*. Simultaneously he was research professor of international history in the University of London, retiring from both positions in 1955. During the 1939–45 war he was director of the foreign office research department.

His numerous publications include: *Nationality and the war* (1915), *The new Europe* (1915), *The western question in Greece and Turkey* (1922), *Greek historical thought* (1924), *Turkey* (1926), *A journey to China* (1931), *Civilisation on trial* (1948), *War and civilisation* (1951), *The world and the west* (1953), *Christianity among the religions of the world* (1958), *East to west; a journey round the world* (1958), *Hellenism* (1959), *Oxus and Jumna* (1961), *Comparing notes: a dialogue across a generation* (1963) *Between Niger and Nile* (1965), *Hannibal's legacy* (1965), *Change and habitat* (1966), *Acquaintances* (1967), *Between Maule and Mazon* (1967), *The crucible of Christianity* (1968), *Cities of destiny* (1969), *Cities on the move* (1970), *Surviving the future* (1971), and *Constantine Porphyrogenitus and his world* (1972). But his fame rests on his twelve-volume work, *A study of history*, published between 1934 and 1961. It was a massive comparative study of twenty-six civilizations in world history, analysing their genesis, growth, and disintegration. According to Toynbee's hypothesis, the failure of a civilization to survive was the result of its inability to respond to moral and religious challenges, rather than to physical or environmental challenges. Like many of his other publications it attracted controversy, but it has had considerable influence on modern attitudes toward history, religion, and international affairs, and Toynbee was secure and confident enough of his own work not to be bothered by criticism. Some of his contemporaries disagreed profoundly with his opinions and his methods, but they generously acknowledged his learning and his international fame.

He was an honorary fellow of Balliol College, Oxford. He was appointed a CH in 1956 on his retirement as director of the Royal Institute of International Affairs. The citation honoured him as 'lately Director of Studies, Royal Institute of International Affairs. Lately Research Professor of International History, University of London.' He was told of the offer while on board a ship between Panama and Auckland on an extended international tour. As he would be away from the country for some months, the Queen suggested that the badge should be sent to him, although she would like to receive him at some point in the future to talk about his tour.[10] Toynbee was delighted to accept the suggestion. 'He feels it is most kind of Her Majesty to think of having the Companion of Honour badge sent to him while he is on his journey. He would of course be much pleased to have it to wear on occasions when it should be worn before he gets back.'[11] As Toynbee was en route to Australia, the badge was posted to the governor general of Australia to allow him to be properly invested.

In 1974 a severe stroke deprived Arnold Toynbee of the power to communicate and the will to live and work. He died in a nursing home fourteen months later.

Sir John Beazley 1 January 1959
The reputation of archaeologist John Beazley rests entirely on his meticulous study of the painting of Greek vases.

He was born in Glasgow in 1885 the elder son of an interior decorator. He was educated at King Edward VI School, Southampton, Christ's Hospital and Balliol College, Oxford, where he took firsts in classical moderations (1905) and literae humaniores (1907), and held a number of scholarships. In 1908 he was made student of Christ Church and tutor in classics, and in 1925 he became Lincoln professor of classical archaeology, occupying the chair for thirty-one years. 'Long before this, however, although a fine classical scholar and an able and conscientious tutor, he has established his life's work as devoted to Greek art and in particular to Attic vase-painting. Greek vase painting, by virtue of its quality and in the all but total loss of other paintings from Greece, is of peculiar importance in the history of art. Its study is now on an entirely different footing from what it was seventy years ago; and that is Beazley's work.'[12]

The first phase of his work is summed up in *Attic red-figure vases in American museums* (1918), and the titles of succeeding publications express the consistency of his scholarship. *Greek vases in Poland* (1928), *Attic black-figure: a sketch* (1929), *Attic white lekythoi* (1938), *Attic vase-paintings in Boston* (1931–63), *Attic red-figure vase painters* (1942), *Potter and painter in ancient Athens* (1945), *Etruscan vase painting* (1947), *The development of Attic black-figure* (1951), *Attic black-figure vase painters* (1956), *Paralipomena: additions to Attic black-figured vase painters and to red-figured vase painters* (1969). His work on Attic vase-painters in the historiography of Greek art was pioneering and prodigious and at the highest level of originality, accuracy, insight and style. He not only created a new area of study, but himself studied it so comprehensively and exhaustively that he left very little for others to do in it.

He was an honorary fellow of Balliol and Lincoln colleges and an honorary student of Christ Church and the British School at Athens. He was elected a fellow of the British Academy in 1927. He was knighted in 1949 and the CH was conferred on him in 1959 as 'Emeritus Professor of Classical Archaeology, University of Oxford. For services to scholarship'.

He retired from his chair in 1956, and in old age he was afflicted by total deafness and increasing absorption in his work which led to a degree of isolation from other people. He never recovered from the death of his wife in 1967 and died in 1970.

Sir Mortimer Wheeler 1 January 1967
Mortimer Wheeler was an archaeologist who popularised his subject to the extent that no other archaeologist had done before him.

He was born in 1890, the eldest child of a Bradford journalist who inspired his son with a love of the arts and the open air. He was educated at Bradford Grammar School and University College, London where he read classics. He joined the Royal Commission on Historical Monuments in 1913 before enlisting in the Royal Field Artillery. He was posted to France in 1917 and was awarded the Military Cross in 1918 for conspicuous gallantry and initiative. 'While making a reconnaisance he saw two enemy field guns limbered up without horses within 300 yards of the outpost line. He returned for two six-horse teams, and under heavy fire, in full view of the enemy, successfully brought back both guns to his battery position and turned them on the enemy. He did fine work'.[13] The war had discovered his powers of leadership and dashing style.

After the war he returned briefly to the royal commission, but in 1920 was appointed keeper of archaeology in the National Museum of Wales and was promoted to director in 1924. Simultaneously, he and his wife and his students excavated Roman military sites, and his first book *Prehistoric and Roman Wales*, was published in 1925. He left Wales in 1926 to take on the directorship of the London Museum (1926–44), then housed at Lancaster House, and while there he launched campaigns to raise funds for the University of London's new Institute of Archaeology, which was opened in 1937. He and his wife continued to excavate, at Lydney in Gloucestershire (1928–29), at St Albans (1930–33) and at Maiden Castle in Dorset (1934–37). A happy marriage and partnership was broken by his wife's death in 1936 after a minor operation, and two subsequent marriages ended in failure.

In 1938–39 he explored the little known hill forts of Brittany and Normandy. At the outbreak of the 1939–45 war he raised an anti-aircraft battery that was subsequently incorporated into the Eighth Army and Wheeler saw service in north Africa. While there, his previous life surfaced and he took action to secure official protection of ancient monuments threatened by the war. In 1943 he accepted the post of director general of archaeology in India (1944–48). He returned to London in 1948 but served as architectural adviser to the government of Pakistan (1948–50). He held a part-time professorship at the University of London ('of the Archaeology of the Roman Provinces') (1948–55) and became honorary secretary to the British Academy 1949–68 (he had become a fellow in 1941), raising it to become the principal source of state aid to the humanities. He held many other offices, including director of the Society of Antiquaries (1940–44 and 1949–54) and president of the Society (1954–59); trustee of the British Museum (1963–73); president of the Royal Archaeological Institute (1951–53); chairman of the Ancient Monuments Board for England (1964–66); and professor of ancient history at the Royal Academy.

His many publications included: *The Roman fort near Brecon* (1926), *Prehistoric and Roman site at Lydney* (1932), *The Belgic and Roman cities at Verulamium* (1936), *Maiden Castle* (1943), *5,000 years of Pakistan* (1950), *The Indus civilization* (1953), *Archaeology from the earth* (1954), *The Stanwick fortifications* (1954), *Rome beyond the imperial frontiers* (1954), *Hill forts of northern France* (1957), *Early India and Pakistan* (1959), *Charsada* (1962), *Roman art and architecture* (1964), *Splendours of the east* (1965), *Alms for oblivion* (1966), *Roman Africa* (1966), *Flames over Persepolis* (1968) and *The British Academy 1949–68* (1968). He wrote a volume of autobiography, *Still digging* (1955).

As well as being a distinguished archaeologist, Wheeler also had a tendency to flamboyance, which not everyone appreciated. Lord Goodman in particular acknowledged Wheeler's competence but had little time for his style. 'Mortimer Wheeler struck me as a grotesque figure . . . My feeling towards him . . . was nothing but critical, and I realise that since he did me no harm, my judgement was anything but fair. But he seemed to me to be a posturing, preening, burlesque of a soldier, attired in the smartest of riding breeches although there was not a horse within miles, wearing shining riding boots which he forced his unfortunate batman – why he had a batman I never discovered – to polish. On the whole he was not a figure I admired, but he was certainly a brilliant archaeologist.' But he was generous enough to acknowledge Wheeler's gifts. 'As people who remember *Animal, mineral or vegetable* [a BBC television series] will know, he also had an extraordinary knowledge that distinguished him from every other poor wretch who was unwise enough to feature with him on the programme and which enabled him to identify any object that appeared. Where others would say that some unidentifiable lump was a primitive Indian weapon, he would immediately discern that it was a Hittite hot-water bottle. The programme became a public favourite as indeed he did.'[14]

Wheeler was elected a fellow of the Royal Society in 1968. He had been knighted in 1952 and received the CH in 1967 'For services to Archaeology.' When he heard of the offer, he was staying in the Lake Palace Hotel at Udaipur, and was reported to have been shaken by 'this wholly unexpected recognition'. He immediately cabled his grateful acceptance to the prime minister [then Harold Wilson], sent confirmation to the private office and then wrote two letters to Molly Myers, his assistant from his days at the British Academy and had them delivered by hand to Delhi airport. He gave the appearance of an elderly man alone in a strange place getting uncharacteristically fussed. His own response to the award was initially to describe it as 'the what-not' but then he went on, 'You know, the CH isn't bad – next to the OM which I can't imagine their giving to a mere me . . . On thinking it over I really am pleased about that CH – it's the first time it's happened to an archaeologist.'[15] Wheeler was either unaware that Sir John Beazeley had the CH, or he did not consider him an archaeologist.

In the last years of his life, Wheeler was cared for by Molly Myers and died in 1976.

Sir Arthur Bryant 10 June 1967
Arthur Bryant was the very antithesis of social, industrial and Marxist historians. With his father in royal service, Bryant was brought up in a house adjoining the gardens of Buckingham Palace. His childhood was saturated with the protocol, pomp and pageantry of the monarchy and it formed within him an attitude towards England and its history that infused his politics, his cultural attitudes and his writings until his death.

He was born in 1899 and educated at Pelham House, Sandgate and Harrow. He was the eldest son of Sir Francis Bryant, then chief clerk to the Prince of Wales. In 1916 he won an exhibition to Pembroke College, Cambridge, but declined it and instead joined the royal flying corps in 1917. Destined for the army, it was something of a surprise that Bryant, whose instincts were conservative and traditional, chose to join the newest of the three fighting forces, and one that was still in its infancy. In 1919 he went to Queen's College, Oxford to study modern history. After graduation he taught for a short while at a London County Council school and regularly attended debutante dances, where he persuaded his dancing partners to teach children of poverty-stricken families at the Dickens Library in Somers Town. For all the privilege of his education and his lifestyle, 'Bryant developed a strong social conscience and a deep belief in the importance of education as a bridge between the "two nations". It was this that later led him to become a popular historian.'[16]

He was called to the bar by the Inner Temple in 1923 but never practised law. In the same year he was appointed principal of the Cambridge School of Arts, Crafts and Technology, and in 1925 a lecturer in history for the Oxford University delegacy for extra-mural studies, where he remained until 1936. This teaching career, at the margins of academic life, also contributed to the style and level of his writings. His first book, *The spirit of conservatism*, was published in 1929, and in the same year, a publishing friend asked him to write a life of King Charles II. Because of its dramatic opening and its racy and readable style, the book was an immediate success, and the Book Society made it their 'choice' in October 1931. 'His success rightly convinced him that he could live by his pen. He did so for the rest of his life and lived very well.'[17]

Though he wrote over forty books, his most important contributions to English history were a three-volume life of Samuel Pepys (1933–38) and a two-volume edition of the diaries of Field Marshal Viscount Alanbrooke: *The turn of the tide* (1957) and *Triumph in the west* (1959). None of Bryant's other publications achieved the same level of scholarship. The manic speed of his prolific output inevitably caused scholarship and research to be sacrificed on the altar of readability. Professional academic historians were critical of his lack of research, and he never received high academic honours. But his broad outline histories of

England were solid and useful introductory works for those at the earliest stage of exploring the periods that they covered. His publications included biographies of King George V (1936), Stanley Baldwin (1937), Nelson (1970), and the Duke of Wellington (1971), and the titles of his books said as much about the predilections of the author as they did about the content: *The national character* (1934), *The England of Charles II* (1934), *English saga* (1940), *The years of endurance* (1942), *Years of victory* (1944), *The age of elegance* (1950), *The story of England: makers of the realm* (1953), *The age of chivalry* (1963), *The fire and the rose* (1965), *The lion and the unicorn* (1965), *The medieval foundation* (1966), *Protestant island* (1967), *Thousand years of British monarchy* (1975), *The Elizabethan deliverance* (1980), *Spirit of England* (1982) and *Set in a silver sea* (1984) 'He was a passionate believer in "communication" and has some claim to be the Lord Macaulay and G. M. Trevelyan of his day.'[18] Bryant wrote as an English patriot who recorded, and partly romanticised, all that was glorious and good in English history and communicated it very effectively. Not surprisingly, he opposed the entry of the United Kingdom into the European Economic Community in 1973.

He was made a CBE in 1949, knighted in 1954 and made a CH in 1967 for his services as 'Historian'. He died in 1985.

Lord Robbins 1 January 1968
Lionel Robbins had a varied career in public life, but made his reputation as an outstanding economist.

He was born in 1898, and educated at Southall County School, University College, London and the London School of Economics. He served in the Royal Field Artillery (1916–19), and in the mid-1920s began an academic career in the world of economics. He was a lecturer at New College, Oxford in 1924 and at the London School of Economics (1925–27), a fellow and lecturer at New College (1927–29), and finally held a long and distinguished occupancy of the chair of economics at the LSE. He was appointed to the chair in 1929 at the age of thirty and held it until his retirement in 1961 to become chairman of the *Financial Times* (1961–70). He later returned to the LSE as a member of its court of governors, serving as chairman (1968–74). He was also director of the economic section of the offices of the war cabinet (1941–45), president of the Royal Economic Society (1954–55), and president of the British Academy (1962–67).

Apart from many articles in economic journals, his publications included *Essay on the nature and significance of economic science* (1932), *The great depression* (1934), *Economic planning and international order* (1937), *The economic basis of class conflict and other essays in political economy* (1939), *The economic causes of war* (1939), *The economic problem in peace and war* (1947), *The theory of economic policy in English classical political economy* (1952), *The economist in the twentieth century and other lectures in political economy* (1954), *Robert Torrens and the evolution of classical economics* (1958), *Politics and economics* (1963), *The university in the modern world* (1966), *The theory of economic development in the history of economic thought* (1968), *The evolution of modern economic theory* (1970), *Autobiography of an economist* (1971), *Money, trade and international relations* (1971), *Political economy, past and present; a review of leading theories of economic policy* (1976) *Against inflation: speeches in the second chamber 1965–77* (1979), and *Higher education revisited* (1980).

There were other facets to the life of Robbins: arts administration and university expansion. He served as a trustee of the National Gallery (1952–59, 1960–67 and 1967–74), a trustee of the Tate Gallery (1953–59 and 1962–67), and a director of the Royal Opera House (1955–81). In the latter capacity, he was observed by Lord Goodman as 'The redoubtable Lord Robbins, the doyen of the world of artistic administration. Chairman then of the *Financial Times* of which Garrett Drogheda was managing director, chairman of the National Gallery and former chairman of the Tate, he was the most revered and powerful figure in the world of artistic boyars. But he was a man of strong preconceptions and of immense loyalty to his friends. Garrett was his friend and in anything to do with Covent Garden the two men stood shoulder to shoulder, a couple of very formidable musketeers.'[19]

Robbins was also the principal architect of the modern British university system – having advocated its massive expansion in the 1960s as chairman of the committee on higher education (1961–63). In the words of one observer, the report was 'one of the great state papers of this century, and possibly the last of its line.'[20] At the time there were some 113,000 students in British universities. Robbins proposed that the number should rise to 153,000 in 1967–68 and to 346,000 by 1980–81. Total numbers in higher education were to be increased from 216,000 in 1962–63 to 560,000 by 1980–81. The government accepted the report immediately. The colleges of advanced technology became technological universities, the size of all universities increased substantially, and a new degree-awarding body – the Council of National Academic Awards – was established to replace the external degree system of the University of London. 'Along with a gentle manner,' wrote a former secretary of the University Grants Committee, 'one sensed a giant paw from which a claw or two would sometimes make a carefully modulated appearance.'[21]

Robbins was honoured with a civil CB in 1944 for his civilian war work, and a life peerage in 1959. The CH was conferred on him in 1968 'For services to the Arts and to Learning'. In 1931, Robbins had secured the appointment of the distinguished Austrian economist, Friedrich von Hayek, as Tooke professor of economic science and statistics, and the two men formed an eminent duo at the LSE until von Hayek left in 1950. Dying in May 1984, Robbins did not live to see the conferment of a CH on his former colleague in the following month.

Karl Popper 12 June 1982
Karl Popper was a distinguished Austrian-born philosopher who taught at the London School of Economics.

He was born in Vienna in 1902 to parents of Jewish origin. He was raised in an atmosphere that he was later to describe as 'decidedly bookish'. His father, a lawyer by profession, also took an interest in the classics and in philosophy, and communicated to his son an interest in social and political issues which he was never to lose. From his mother he acquired a passion for music to the point where for a time he seriously contemplated taking it up as a career, and he initially chose the history of music as a second subject for his PhD examination. Subsequently, his love for music became one of the inspirational forces in the development of his thought.

He was educated at the local Realgymnasium, leaving at the age of fifteen because he felt the need to identify with the under-privileged, and became a cabinetmaker for a time. He went to the University of Vienna in 1918, but did not formally enrol at the university, by taking the matriculation examination, for another four years. In the chaos that followed the dissolution of the Austro-Hungarian empire in 1919 he took to left-wing politics, joined the Association of Socialist School Students, and became for a time a marxist. Disillusioned with its doctrinaire character, he soon abandoned it. He also discovered the psychoanalytic theories of Freud and Adler (under whose aegis he engaged briefly in social work with deprived children), and listened entranced to a lecture that Einstein gave in Vienna on relativity theory.

Popper obtained a primary school teaching diploma in 1925, took a PhD in philosophy in 1928, and qualified to teach mathematics and physics at secondary school level in 1929. The dominant philosophical group in Vienna from its inception in 1928 was the Wiener Kreis, a circle of 'scientifically-minded' intellectuals. Their principal objective was to unify the sciences, which carried with it, in their view, the need to eliminate metaphysics once and for all by showing that metaphysical propositions were meaningless. Although he was friendly with some of the circle's members and shared their esteem for science, Popper was heavily critical of the main tenets of logical positivism, especially of what he considered to be its misplaced focus on the theory of meaning in philosophy and upon verification in scientific methodology. In his view the real task was not to decide what was meaningful and what was nonsense, but to distinguish true science from pseudo-sciences such as astrology and metaphysics, while recognising that pseudo-science might serve a valuable purpose in inspiring true science. His own view of science was distinctive. It was not 'a plodding, logical investigation of the universe. It proceeds by flashes of intuition, exactly like poetry, and these are then subjected to the test of reason; it is essentially a process of learning by mistakes. But the intuition is, so to speak, the flash of lightning that starts the whole process.'[22] He had no radio, no television and never read any newspapers, but he was a man of enormous breadth of culture, a lover of music, poetry, art and literature, as well as having an abiding fascination with science and logic.

He articulated his own view of science, in his first work, published under the title *Logik der Forschung* in 1934. The book – which he was later to claim rang the death knell for logical positivism – attracted more attention than Popper had anticipated, and he was invited to lecture in England in 1935. The storm clouds were beginning to gather in the late 1930s and the growth of Nazism in Germany and Austria compelled him, like many other intellectuals of Jewish origin, to leave his native country. The experience contributed to his lifelong obsession with human freedom.

In 1937 he moved to New Zealand to teach philosophy at the University of Canterbury and remained there for the duration of the 1939–45 war. In 1946 he moved to London to teach at the London School of Economics, becoming professor of logic and scientific method in 1949, and stayed until his retirement in 1969. His reputation and stature as a philosopher of science and social thinker grew enormously, and he continued to write prolifically. His publications included *The logic of scientific discovery* (1935) – which made him famous and remains a classic, *The open society and its enemies* (1945) – an attack on Plato, Hegel and Marx for using metaphysics to buttress totalitarian ideas and threaten human freedom, and *Conjectures and refutations* (1963) – dedicated to the economist Friedrich von Hayek, himself to become a CH in 1984.

Popper was a gifted and original thinker, and one of the most important and influential thinkers of the twentieth century. He was knighted in 1965, and made a CH in 1982 'For services to philosophy'. In retirement he remained active as a writer, broadcaster and lecturer, living at his home in Buckinghamshire until his death in 1994.

The Honourable Sir Steven Runciman 31 December 1983
Steven Runciman was the pre-eminent British historian of the Byzantine empire and the crusades.

He was born in 1903, the younger son of the first Viscount Runciman of Doxford. His father was a member of Asquith's cabinet and his mother was MP for St Ives. He was a shy and clever child who developed the extraordinary ability to read French at three, Latin at six, Greek at seven and Russian at eleven. He won a scholarship to Eton, where a combination of an early interest in Greece and medievalism led to an interest in Byzantium.

In 1921, a further scholarship took him to Trinity College, Cambridge, where he demonstrated an elegant and fashionable aestheticism by papering his rooms with a French grisaille wallpaper depicting Cupid and Psyche, and being photographed by Cecil Beaton, with a parrot poised on his ringed finger. His undergraduate flamboyance was partnered by his homosexuality and he never married. Through his school friend George Rylands (himself to become a CH in 1987), he was introduced to John Maynard Keynes, Lytton Strachey and Virginia and Leonard Woolf.

After taking a first class degree in history, he became a research student for a while of J. B. Bury, the first British historian to take Byzantium seriously. Following an attack of pleurisy – and his doctor's prescription that his best chance of recovery would come from a long sea voyage – he visited China where he befriended and played piano duets with Pu Y'i, the last Chinese emperor. In 1924, he made his first trip to Greece, was enchanted by the Byzantine town of Monemvasia and, later, by the old city of Istanbul. On his return to Cambridge, he concentrated on his fellowship thesis, with pioneering investigations into Armenian and Syriac sources, which, in 1929, resulted in his first book, *The Emperor Romanus Lecapenus*. After that, in quick succession, came *The first Bulgarian empire* (1930) and *Byzantine civilisation* (1933).

He went back to Trinity College in 1927 to teach and hold a fellowship until 1938, becoming a university lecturer in 1932. The death of his grandfather in 1938, brought financial independence, and he gave up his fellowship, left Cambridge and concentrated on his writing. The outbreak of war took him back to the countries of his choice, first as press attaché in Sofia in 1940, then to Cairo in 1941 and to Jerusalem for the ministry of information, and finally to Istanbul for three years as professor of Byzantine art and history (1942–45). This gave him the opportunity to follow the tracks of the crusaders and plan his *History of the crusades* – as well as visiting Syria and becoming an honorary whirling dervish. After the war, he accepted an offer to direct the work of the British Council in Greece. While in Greece he wrote *The medieval Manichee* (1947) a study of the Christian dualist heresy. Some criticised it because it showed a defective grasp of theology. But Runciman himself had always found theology both fascinating and entertaining, particularly in its eastern forms. Although he did not belong to the Orthodox church, he had a profound commitment to orthodoxy and believed that it enshrined the future of Christianity.

He returned to Britain in 1947 dividing his time between his house in London, and the isle of Eigg, off the Scottish coast, which his father had bought in 1926, and working on the substantial three-volume work that established his reputation, *A history of the crusades*. Published between 1951 and 1954, it exemplified his belief that the main duty of the historian was 'to attempt to record, in one sweeping sequence, the greater events and movements that have swayed the destinies of man.' Having seen the damage done by those quasi-religious military escapades, he was no supporter. They were in his opinion, the last of the barbarian invasions and their disaster was their failure to understand Byzantium and see it as a vital Christian bulwark on the borders of Christian Europe. 'There was so much courage and so little honour, so much devotion and so little understanding. High ideals were besmirched by cruelty and greed, enterprise and endurance by a blind and narrow self-righteousness; and the holy war itself was nothing more than a long act of intolerance in the name of God, which is a sin against the Holy Ghost.'[23] His other publications included *The eastern schism* (1955), *The Sicilian vespers* (1958), *The white rajahs* (1960), *The fall of Constantinople 1453* (1965), *The great church in captivity* (1968), *The last Byzantine renaissance* (1970), *The Orthodox churches and the secular state* (1972), *Byzantine style and civilization* (1975), *The Byzantine theocracy* (1977), *Mistra* (1980) and *A traveller's alphabet: partial memoirs* (1991). *Mistra* was his expression of gratitude towards the Byzantine capital of the Peloponnese, when the town named a street after him. *A traveller's alphabet* colourfully recorded in alphabetical form – A for Athos, Z for Zion etc. – a lifetime of travels that had taken him round the world. In 1992, he rediscovered a short story or novella, written in 1935 and entitled *Paradise regained*. This fictional account of an expedition to Iraqi Kurdistan, dedicated to George Rylands and revealing both his wit and sharp sense of humour, was privately printed and distributed to his friends in place of a Christmas card.

When Eigg was sold in 1966, he moved to Elshieshields, a border tower in Dumfrieshire, where he happily entertained both old and new friends, introducing them to his collection of eighteenth and nineteenth century musical boxes, worry beads, a hubble bubble, the Alexander Runcimans and Edward Lears, the limericks as well as the watercolours. He could also display his knowledge of the genealogical ramifications of European royalty, often flavoured by well-informed gossip. Settled in Scotland, he made occasional visits to London where he could be seen dining at the Athenaeum, but he still travelled to lecture and discover new Coptic churches.

He held a number of public appointments: member of the advisory council of the Victoria and Albert Museum (1957–71), president of the British Institute of Archaeology, Ankara (1960–75), chairman of the Anglo-Hellenic League (1951–67) (which he nicknamed 'the Anglo-Hell'), president of the National Trust for Greece (1977–84), counsellor emeritus of the National Trust for Scotland (1985–2000), trustee of the British Museum (1960–67), and trustee of the Scottish National Museum of Antiquities (1972–77).

In September 1994, he took part in the ceremony on the island of Lemnos inaugurating the Aegean declaration, an agreement between UNESCO and the Greek ministry of culture to turn the Greek archipelago into a European cultural park. In 1995, in his capacity as president of the Friends of Mount Athos, he published a learned article in *The Times* deploring the fact that, on the Athonite peninsula, the tradition of faith transcending ethnic difference, which had been the practice for more than a millennium, was under threat. In extreme old age he still made regular visits to Bahrain and Greece, and went to Athens to receive the international prize for culture (arts and humanities) of the Onassis Foundation. In addition to its silver trophy, he received a substantial financial prize that he generously offered to Mount Athos.

He was knighted in 1958 and made a CH in 1984 'For services to Byzantine Art and History'. He was also made a knight commander of the Greek Order of the Phoenix in 1961 and received the first class of the Bulgarian Order of Madara Horseman in 1993. This generous, cultured, scholarly Christian aesthete died in 2000 in his ninety-eighth year.

Friedrich von Hayek 16 June 1984
Friedrich von Hayek was an Austrian-born economist noted for his conservative views and criticisms of the Keynesian welfare state.

He was born in Vienna in 1899, his father a municipal physician to the poor and his mother from a family of public servants and landowners. While still at school he was called up as an officer cadet in the field artillery and served in the Austro-Hungarian army on the Italian front in 1917–18. At the end of the war he enrolled in the University of Vienna and graduated with a law degree in 1921. He then started work as a lawyer in the government department carrying out the peace treaty provisions. Although previously a Fabian socialist, its implementation by the postwar social democratic governments of Austria and Germany was sufficient to convince Hayek that socialism would lead to a loss of freedom, or inflation, or both. While studying for his second doctoral degree in political science he began to work for Ludwig von Mises, the Austrian economist. Mises, soon became Hayek's mentor and in 1927 they founded the Österreichisches Institut für Konjunkturforschung (Austrian Institute for Trade Cycle Research).

Hayek's first book *Monetary theory and the trade cycle* (1929) set a standard in modern business cycle theory. One of the most striking characteristics of it is Hayek's insight that any shortage of capital immediately causes a crisis. Impressed by Hayek's new theory, Lionel Robbins invited him to lecture at the London School of Economics in 1931. These lectures were so successful that he was offered the position of Tooke professor of economic science almost immediately and he accepted gladly. At this time, when John Maynard Keynes' new theories began to dominate academic and political life it was unavoidable for Hayek not to be drawn into a fundamental debate with Keynes. Hayek opposed his theories and became the leading intellectual force against Keynes and his followers. While being involved in these heated debates, at the same time Hayek opened another intellectual front and published three essays designed to demolish the theoretical foundations of socialism. The essays are collected in his *Individualism and economic order* (1948).

His interest in technical economics culminated in his book *The pure theory of capital* (1942). But his intensive work on the insoluble economic and moral problems of socialism, the terror of fascism, and the outbreak of the 1939–45 war made him write *The road to serfdom* (1944). The book sold 100,000 copies in English. His conservative thesis was that governmental control of or intervention in a free market only forestalls such economic ailments as inflation, unemployment, recession, or depression, and he suggested that mild piecemeal reforms and governmental manipulations inevitably lead to the kind of ultimate domestic disaster that paves the way for totalitarian takeover by a Hitler. Churchill was said to have been influenced by *The road to serfdom* in his preparation for the general election in 1945.

In 1947 Hayek organized an international conference of economists, philosophers, and historians to discuss and exchange ideas about the nature of a free society and the means to strengthen its principles and intellectual support. This meeting in Switzerland resulted in the foundation of the exclusive 'Mont Pelerin Society', an international association of classical liberal scholars.

He became a naturalized British citizen in 1938, and left the London School of Economics, and went to the University of Chicago in 1950 as professor of moral and social science. At that time the university was the most celebrated centre in the United States of scholars championing the free market economy and the free society. His publications from these years include *The sensory order* (1952), probably his most difficult and least known work but containing some of his most original and important ideas. In *The constitution of liberty* (1960) he developed his idea of 'spontaneous order', and laid down the ethical, legal and economic principles of freedom and free markets.

In 1962 Hayek returned to Germany and joined the University of Freiburg im Breisgau. In his seven years there, he published, among others, *Studies in philosophy, politics and economics* (1967). This book covers his works dating from the early 1950s to the mid–1960s. After becoming professor emeritus at Freiburg in 1969, he accepted a visiting professorship at the University of Salzburg in Austria which he kept until 1977. In spite of poor health and intellectual isolation during these years he produced a number of significant works, including in 1973 the first volume of his trilogy, *Law, legislation, and liberty*.

In 1974 he was awarded the Nobel prize for economics. Probably for political reasons he had to share the prize with a complete adversary, Gunnar Myrdal, the intellectual force behind the socialist Swedish welfare state. It was said that both men were in danger of suffering a stroke on hearing that they had received the prize. Hayek at discovering that he had got the award at all. Myrdal at discovering that he had to share it with someone else. Both men later called for the economics prize to be abolished.

In 1977 he moved back to Freiburg where he completed the third volume of *Law, legislation, and liberty* in which he refined his critique of democracy and developed the principles of a political order for free people. As a side product he published *Denationalization of money* in 1977, in which he argued that inflation can be avoided only if the monopolistic power of issuing money is taken away from government and/or state authorities, and private industry be given the task of promoting competition in currencies. He continued to lecture, write and travel extensively until the late 1980s when he became ill and never fully recovered. He was unable to complete his last book *The fatal conceit* (1989) due to his inability to manage the huge manuscript, and it was heavily edited.

Because of his free market philosophy, Hayek became something of an intellectual guru to the Conservative Party under Margaret Thatcher from the mid–1970s. Although he was never the party theoretician, his views fitted perfectly with those of the developing party, and the Labour politician Michael Foot, excitably but inaccurately, described Margaret Thatcher as being 'in the clutches of a mad professor'.[24] In fact Hayek was a courteous and polite scholarly gentleman who gained little money from his career and who never allied himself with any political party.

After the award of the Nobel prize in 1974, the thought of a state honour began to emerge. Any question of an honour would have to surmount the perceived difficulty that he had lived outside the United Kingdom for more than thirty years – so long that he was hardly recognized as a British citizen. In 1977, a petition signed by Lords Grimond, Houghton, Joseph and Robbins and others urged an honour but his long absence from Britain remained a problem. A knighthood might have been appropriate had he lived in the United Kingdom, but it would be a bizarre honour for a resident in Germany where 'Sir Friedrich von Hayek' would mean little or nothing. So the CH was put to a new use – as an appropriate honour for a distinguished British subject long resident abroad. It was suggested by a peer who accompanied his recommendation with a lamentable display of ignorance: 'I believe his name would bring fresh lustre to the faded Order of Companion of Honour.' The citation read: 'For services to the study of Economics.' Hayek died at Freiburg im Breisgau in 1992.

Noel Joseph Terence Needham 13 June 1992

Joseph Needham was a historian of science who produced a monumental sixteen-volume history of science in China.

He was born in London in 1900. His father was a London doctor specialising in anaesthetics and his mother a pianist and composer of songs. He was educated at Oundle School and Gonville and Caius College, Cambridge where he studied for the natural sciences tripos, specialising in physiology with biochemistry as a subsidiary subject. He then went on to postgraduate research in the Cambridge biochemistry department under Frederick Gowland Hopkins (later an OM). He held a Benn Levy Studentship (1922–24), studying the biochemistry of inositol. He was elected a fellow of Gonville and Caius College in 1924 and appointed university demonstrator in biochemistry in 1928. In 1933 he succeeded J. B. S. Haldane as Sir William Dunn reader in biochemistry. He held the post until 1966 when he became master of Gonville and Caius College. He retired from the mastership in 1976.

Needham's early biochemical research focused on embryology. In his three-volume book *Chemical embryology* (1931) he explained embryological development as a chemical process, rejecting the view that such development was caused by an undefined vital spark. He then extended this work with research into various aspects of morphology, culminating in *Biochemistry and morphogenesis* (1942). As well as these two books, Needham produced three other major books on biochemistry and numerous scientific papers. He combined this high rate of productivity in biochemistry with a prolific output of articles on religious, political and philosophical subjects. Many of these were subsequently republished in four collections of articles and essays: *The sceptical biologist* (1929), *The great amphibium* (1931), *Time the refreshing river* (1943) and *History is on our side* (1946).

As well as his contributions to the development of biochemistry, he was also an important figure in the establishment of the history of science as an academic discipline at Cambridge. He was a founder member of the history of science lectures committee in 1936 which set up a programme of lectures in the history of science, featuring some of the greatest scientists of the time lecturing on the history of their disciplines. After the 1939–45 war he served on the history of science committee and the history and philosophy of science committee until 1971. He was also a leading figure in the International Union of the History and Philosophy of

Science. He served on the council of the division of the history of science (1969–77, president 1972–74) and was president of the Union (1972–75).

Needham is probably best known for his substantial history of the development of science in China. Chinese students at Cambridge awakened his interest in China from the mid-1930s. He began to learn Mandarin Chinese and study Chinese history, particularly the Chinese contribution to science and became an enthusiastic supporter of British academic assistance to Chinese universities. In 1942 he went to China as head of the British Scientific Mission and later Scientific Counsellor to the British Embassy at Chungking (then the 'acting capital' of China). Under the auspices of the British Council he established and became director of the Sino-British science cooperation office (SBSCO). The SBSCO was responsible for assessing the needs of Chinese scientific, technological and medical institutions and researchers, and facilitating the supply of equipment and medicines, books and journals to China. The success of the SBSCO was the immediate inspiration for his vision of postwar international science co-operation. With the form of the future United Nations organisation under intense discussion Needham sent three memoranda to a wide range of political and scientific leaders pressing for the inclusion of scientific co-operation under its auspices. He argued that the proposed United Nations Educational and Cultural Organisation should include science within its remit and he may have been the first to use the abbreviation 'UNESCO'. In 1946 when he left the SBSCO he was appointed the first director of the natural sciences section of UNESCO.

On his return to Cambridge in 1948 he began work on his masterpiece – a history of the contribution of China to science and civilisation. This monumental work occupied him for most of the rest of his life; the first volume of *Science and civilisation in China* appeared in 1954 and by his death it had run to sixteen volumes. This immense work of scholarship found a permanent home with the later establishment in Cambridge of the Needham Research Institute as a centre for research on Chinese science.

Needham's political sympathies lay very much with the left. He was a member of the Labour Party and in the 1930s served on the executive committee of the university branch. He was an early advocate of Keynsian economics, and introduced Keynes to the Labour Party. He was on the left of the party and from 1933 was chairman of the Cambridge branch of the Socialist League. This was dissolved in 1937 following its expulsion from the Labour Party for launching a 'Unity Manifesto' with the Independent Labour and Communist parties. In the 1930s Needham was also an active member of the Cambridge scientists' anti-war group, which campaigned against militarism and played an important part in securing better air raid precautions by illustrating the inadequacies of government preparations. From 1937 to 1939 he served as treasurer of the Cornford-Maclaurin memorial committee. This was established in memory of two Cambridge men, killed fighting with the International Brigade, to raise funds for the republican cause in Spain. On the outbreak of the 1939–45 war, Needham participated in discussions among Communist Party members and others on the left as to whether they should support the British war effort. After the German attack on the USSR in 1941 he was active in promoting Anglo-Soviet friendship until his departure for China.

After the war Needham supported peace and disarmament campaigns. His strong sympathies for China led to his being a founder of the Britain-China

Friendship Association, of which he was president, and its successor the Society for Anglo-Chinese Understanding, of which he was chairman. In 1952 he served on an international scientific commission investigating alleged American use of germ warfare in North Korea and China. The commission's report concluded that the USA had indeed been using such weapons and this led to intense criticism of Needham in the UK. He opposed the Vietnam war and this led him to refuse invitations to conferences or to lecture in the USA during the 1960s and early 1970s.

From his student days Needham was a high church Anglican, combining this with a commitment to social justice. In the 1930s he was active in propagating a highly political Christianity emphasising its closeness to Marxism and had a long association with the parish church of Thaxted, Essex, identified very closely with the Christian Socialist tradition under its famous socialist incumbent, Conrad Noel. Needham was a member of the editorial board behind the controversial book *Christianity and the social revolution* (1935), to which he contributed a chapter entitled 'Laud, the levellers and the virtuosi'. This and writings such as *The levellers and the English revolution* (1939), published under the name 'Henry Holorenshaw', linked radical Christianity of the seventeenth century with the politics of the twentieth century. In later years he was drawn away from Christianity and more to Daoism, which he believed offered hope of reconciliation between science and religion. This concern also led to his presidency of the Teilhard de Chardin centre for the future of mankind. His religious outlook notwithstanding, Needham was also an honorary associate of the Rationalist Press Association.

He was elected a fellow of the Royal Society in 1941 and in 1971 a fellow of the British Academy, becoming one of a very few to attain this double distinction. But a state honour was a long time coming, not in fact until he was ninety-one. His controversial views did not endear him to the foreign office. His monumental study of Chinese technology is a great work of scholarship – of that there was no doubt. But he was hopelessly naive about politics and about Chinese politics in particular. His 1952 visit to China during the Korean War, followed by his statements to the effect that he was firmly convinced that the USA had directed bacteriological attacks against North Korea and China, would have antagonised the foreign office. Others praised him as the inventor of a new field of study and the author of a unique masterpiece. Should his naive leftism and sinophilia constitute an impassable barrier to recognition? He was after all no more extreme than Lord Blackett or Dorothy Hodgkin, both of whom had received the OM.

By 1992 he was very old man and if he was to receive recognition it could not be delayed for much longer. His national and international eminence and his work which had laid the foundation for biochemical science development was evident. He was the world authority on the development of science in China and, despite the fact that he had effectively acted as an apologist for the communist regime in China, it was accepted that his massive work on Chinese science and culture was untainted by political sympathies. And in a sense he had 'redeemed' himself by speaking out against the suppression of the Tienanmen Square demonstration in 1989. The CH was conferred in 1992 for his services as 'Emeritus Director, Needham Research Institute (East Asian History of Science Library).'

He died in 1995, outliving his first wife Dorothy, who had died in 1987, and his second wife Lu Gwei-Djen, whom he had married in 1989 and who died in 1991.

Alfred Leslie Rowse 31 December 1996
Leslie Rowse, prolific historian, political commentator, man of letters and poet, was a controversial figure who attracted a combination of respect and hostility throughout his long life. He was a 'politically incorrect' Oxford don who said what he thought and acquired fame and popularity through his lively writing. His early life was marked by severe poverty and poor health, but he developed into a distinguished historian, an expert in Tudor and Elizabethan England, a poet, a biographer, and author of more than ninety books.

He was born in St Austell, Cornwall in 1903 and retained a love for that county, where he died, for the rest of his life. His background was humble and lay at the root of the insecurities that fuelled his egotism, a state which he ascribed to the lack of parental concern that he experienced as a child, as well as the coldness, egotism, and selfishness of his mother. He was the youngest of three siblings born to a china-clay worker turned shopkeeper in a village where illiteracy was rife. He was raised in a small, two-up, two-down house where books were non-existent.

His affection for Cornwall partly filled the gap left by the absence of loyalty to his home, and the county featured widely in his prodigious output. As a boy he fell in love with a local mansion overlooking the sea, and in 1953 he leased it. He attended a village school followed by a scholarship to a secondary school in St Austell, where his talents, interests and aspirations were recognised and encouraged. From secondary school, and with the assistance of Sir Arthur Quiller-Couch, he achieved the extraordinary success of winning one of only two county scholarships to Oxford. There, despite severe ill-health caused by duodenal ulcers he graduated with a first in history. In 1925, at the age of twenty-one, he was elected to a fellowship of All Souls College, becoming the first fellow to be recruited from the working class.

Memories of his poor childhood in Cornwall never left him 'It was the kind of circumstance, and there were many others, which made me bitterly resent my family background, which made me unyielding, obstinate, proud, determined never to make concessions or yield any respect to these grown-ups I had come to despise . . . I built myself a tower of unsmiling resentment.'[25] The result was a lifelong chip on his shoulder, a self-centredness, a resentment at being born into a poor uncultivated home, a vulnerability to criticism, a defensiveness, an unfortunate capacity to nurture a grudge, a refusal to admit to his own mistakes, and an intense and prickly pride. Although his published works rarely reveal this abrasive side to his character, he could be prone to overstatement, dismissal of his opponents, and lack of generosity to others. Given such a personality, knives were inevitably sharpened by his bitterest enemies, and the criticisms of his work only served to confirm his personal belief in his own superiority and worth. Rowse's homosexuality was another factor at work in his complex and creative personality.

He made two unsuccessful forays into the political arena, standing as Labour candidate for parliament at Penryn and Falmouth in 1931 and 1935. In 1952 he was defeated in the election for the wardenship of All Souls College, a position which he ardently desired, and which would have crowned his academic career. He perceived it as a massive snub and for more than twenty years, he spent much of his time in the universities and colleges of the USA, where he received the generous hospitality, remuneration, and acclaim that he felt he had been denied in his home country. He was appointed a senior fellow at the Huntington Library; as a result, for twenty years he usually wintered in California. In 1964 he was considered for the regius chair of modern history at Oxford, but the post went to Hugh Trevor-Roper.

Rowse is remembered primarily as an historian of Elizabethan England, but although his books were both lively and readable and his mastery of the sources undisputed, his interpretations and conclusions could be unsound and perverse, especially when he elevated personal conjecture to the level of dogmatic truth. He was especially proud of one piece of conjecture: his 'discovery' of the identity of the 'dark lady' in Shakespeare's sonnets, and he treasured a note from Agatha Christie signed: 'From a low brow detective to a high brow detective.' He wrote a number of books about his native Cornwall, including *A Cornish childhood* (1942), *A Cornishman at Oxford* (1965), *Tudor Cornwall* (1941), *A Cornish anthology* (1968) and *The Cornish in America* (1969). His many works of history and biography include *The England of Elizabeth* (1950), *The expansion of Elizabethan England* (1955), *The early Churchills* (1956), *The later Churchills* (1958), *William Shakespeare: a biography* (1963), *The Elizabethan renaissance* (1971–72), and an edition of *Shakespeare's sonnets* (1964). *The uses of history* (1946) was a product of his concern to cultivate a wide readership, far beyond the confines of the university common room which he inhabited on a strictly love-hate basis. *Glimpses of the great* (1985) was a collection of personal impressions of major figures of the twentieth century, from Bertrand Russell to C. S. Lewis. Even in old age, Rowse was still productive, and his last books included *All Souls in my time* (1993), *The regicides* (1994) and *Historians I have known* (1995).

If he was for so long denied an honour it was probably the result of the perceived flaws in his scholarship. Some academics accepted him as a famous and competent historian who had produced a succession of lively and readable books. Others considered him to be too much of a populariser and ranked him with Arthur Bryant. Others dismissed him as 'jokey' and pathetic and his own worst enemy, an historian who was not only disliked but also laughed at. His work on Shakespeare's sonnets in 1975, including his famous assertion of the identity of the 'dark lady', displayed skill and learning, but his arrogant nature would have made it difficult to defend his claims to an honour against those who took a different view of his merits. The affair of the sonnets almost certainly delayed an honour for Rowse. The dust had to be allowed to settle if undue controversy and criticism was to be avoided. Even in the 1980s he still enjoyed a general reputation for having said and done many silly things over a long period of time. Crueller comments dismissed him as a literary 'quack' with too high an opinion of his own worth. In the early 1990s he was still remembered by a few as a difficult and quirky historian who had too often strayed into the territory of others, whose overall output was uneven and who was known for pursuing minor theories and taking them beyond sensible bounds.

Throughout his life, Rowse had his friends and supporters who were scandalised by the lack of recognition of his talents, and they took to the newspapers to complain. In January 1993, eleven months before his ninetieth birthday, the *News of the World* took up arms with its usual passionate inaccuracies. Rowse, it claimed, was the son of 'a poor farm worker' who 'valiantly strove his way by work and brains to the top of the scholastic world'. 'Who,' it thundered, 'is spitefully blocking a proper honour for A. L. Rowse in Major's classless Britain?'[26] In April 1993 he was nominated for an honour by virtue of the newly introduced system of nominations for honours, and letters of support were sent by the Poet Laureate and Sir William Golding and a number of cabinet ministers including Kenneth Baker, Douglas Jay and William Waldegrave. In November of the same year, the *Evening Standard* urged the ridiculous course of making him a Knight of the Garter.[27] In November 1994 *The Times* reported that a government minister, William Waldegrave, was pressing for Rowse to be admitted to the Order of Merit. Publicly Rowse disclaimed any interest. 'You have to remember that I am rather politically incorrect. I have sometimes found myself out of step with the times. I was against appeasing Hitler, you know.'[28] In fact, Rowse had let it be known that his literary attainments justified him receiving the Order of Merit, and that he wished for nothing else. Waldegrave was not the only Rowse lobbyist. Others of high rank, some with Cornish interests, pressed the case for an honour for the aging scholar. On 23 July 1996, Rowse suffered a stroke and, at ninety-two years of age, the end could not be far off. Pressure was renewed in October of the same year to secure recognition for the sick old man before he died.

It was fortunate for Rowse that he did live into old age, because in doing so he probably outlived most of his sternest critics. By the late 1990s the controversies of the past were forgotten and his total contribution was distinguished enough to merit the CH in 1996 'For services to History and Literature'. By this stage, Rowse himself was unable to write or walk and had limited power of speech, and a letter of acceptance was written on his behalf by his executor, David Treffry. During a party, held to celebrate the long overdue honour, Rowse, who felt that his true destination should have been the Order of Merit, was heard to say 'I would have preferred something more academic'.[29] He died eight months later.

Eric Hobsbawm 31 December 1997
A lifelong communist, the historian Eric Hobsbawm has consistently written of developments in economic and social history through the prism of Marxist philosophy.

He was born in the symbolically revolutionary year of 1917, in Alexandria to Jewish parents, his father English and his mother Viennese. At the age of two he was taken to Vienna, capital of the recently disintegrated Habsburg empire and to Berlin in 1931. A tendency to the political left led to a reading of the works of Marx and Engels and confirmation as a lifelong communist. By 1933 both his parents were dead and his uncle took him to live in England. He arrived in England hardly able to speak English and went to St Marylebone Grammar School. He made huge strides and in 1936 he won a scholarship to King's College, Cambridge, where he acquired a reputation as an active communist. He graduated in 1939 and was offered a research studentship to study agrarian problems in French North Africa.

Research was cut short by the outbreak of war, and he served in the army until demobilisation. In 1946 he was appointed to a post at Birkbeck College, London, where he remained until retirement in 1982. He was promoted to reader in 1959, and professor of economic and social history in 1970. Although he produced a series of essays and pamphlets, the series of major publications which made his reputation did not begin to appear until the end of the 1950s: *Primitive rebels* (1959), *The age of revolution* (1962), *Labouring men* (1964). Hobsbawm's magnum opus is a four-volume history of the world over the two centuries since the French revolution: *The age of revolution* (1789–1848), *The age of capital* (1848–75), *The age of empire* (1875–1914) and *Age of extremes: the short twentieth century* (1914–91). Other publications include *Bandits* (1969), *Revolutionaries* (1973), *Worlds of labour* (1984),

Politics for a rational left (1989), *Nations and nationalism since 1780* (1990), *Echoes of the Marseillaise* (1990), *Uncommon people: resistance, rebellion and jazz* (1999).

As an unrepentant communist, revolution and economic concerns feature extensively in Hobsbawm's writings, especially the defining episodes of the French and industrial revolutions, the revolutions of 1848 and the two world wars of the twentieth century. There was a matching tendency to restrict the significance of the great and the good. Kings, emperors, presidents and prime ministers do not occupy a paramount place in the writings of an historian concerned with the role of the working classes, but he used an impressive breadth of source material. 'Whether writing about the Industrial or the French Revolution, bandits or the bourgeoisie, Count Basie or Count Bismarck, Wellington or Ellington, Vienna, Venice or Venezuela, Hobsbawm's erudition was dazzling and his breadth of allusion encyclopaedic. It is a rare historian who can draw upon so wide a variety of sources – in at least five languages – while yet remaining in total intellectual control of his material.'[30] Despite an element of embarrassment at the Soviet invasions of Hungary in 1956 and Czechoslovakia in 1968, and the evaporation of Soviet-style communism, Hobsbawm defiantly, some would say blindly, continued to take his stand on Marxist philosophy as 'the essential base of any adequate study of history'.

He was elected a fellow of the British Academy in 1976. Whereas he would have disparaged and declined a knighthood, he was prepared to accept the CH in 1997 at the age of eighty because of its non-titular and academic slant. He was appointed as 'Emeritus Professor of Economic and Social History, University of London. For services to History'.

Amartya Sen 11 May 2000

Amartya Sen is an academic economist who has specialized in the problems of third world economics. He was awarded the 1998 Nobel prize in economics.

He was born into the intellectual elite of Bengal in 1933. His father was a lecturer in chemistry at Dhaka University (now in Bangladesh) and his mother a writer and performer in many of the dance-dramas written by the writer, philosopher and poet, Rabindranath Tagore, the only Nobel laureate from India before Sen. Tagore was a close friend of Sen's maternal grandfather, and helped choose the name 'Amartya' which means 'immortal' and Sen himself was born on the campus of a school founded by Tagore.

From the first, he decided on an academic career and seriously considered Sanskrit, mathematics and physics in turn, before settling on economics. He studied at Presidency College, Calcutta and at Trinity College, Cambridge. He was professor of economics at Jadavpur University, Calcutta (1956–58), fellow of Trinity College, Cambridge (1957–63), professor of economics, Delhi University (1963–71), the London School of Economics (1971–77), and Oxford University (1977–80), fellow of Nuffield College, Oxford (1977–80), Drummond professor of political economy and fellow of All Souls College, Oxford (1980–88), professor of economics and philosophy, Harvard University (1987–97). In 1998 he was elected master of Trinity College, Cambridge, becoming the first Asian to head an Oxford or Cambridge college.

A childhood observation of poverty and victims of famine in India deeply affected him and led to a lifelong preoccupation with the causes of famine and poverty, and acceptance of the post of honorary president of Oxfam. 'I was upset by what I saw. My grandfather gave me a small cigarette tin, and said I could fill it with rice and give it to the starving, but only one tinful per family.'[31] He realised that the famine was class-dependent; only the people on the lowest rung of the economic ladder, such as landless labourers, were hungry, and the memory stayed with him, prompting him to develop a career as an welfare economist and to research the causes of famine. 'His work on the causes of famine changed public perceptions by showing why thousands might starve even when a country's food production has not diminished, and his analysis of poverty has been enormously influential. Arguing that simple measures of GNP were not enough to assess the standard of living, he helped to create the United Nations' Human Development Index, which has become the most authoritative international source of welfare comparisons between countries.'[32]

He articulated the view that no famine had ever occurred in a country with a free press and regular elections. Alternative political parties and a free press, he argued, would give early warning of economic disaster and lead to change and prevention. But he was careful not to enthuse about democracy. In his 1984 book *Resources, values and democracy*, he pointed out that in democratic India, free from the British raj, there was no famine, but still a third of the population went to bed hungry every night. 'The quiet presence of non-acute, endemic hunger leads to no newspaper turmoil, no political agitation, no riots in the Indian parliament. The system takes it in its stride.'[33]

In his teenage years, the days of British rule in India were drawing to a close, and the Indian subcontinent began to divide sharply along the sectarian lines of Hindu, Moslem and Sikh, and the horrors of communal massacres began to occur. The bloodbaths of the partition period turned him against the concept of prioritising communal identity, and taught him that economic poverty would only lead to the violation of human rights. In that spirit he criticised a report on multi-ethnicity in Britain for saying that Britain should be seen as a loose federation of cultures held together by common bonds of interest. Though it was meant to be a modern liberal vision, he felt that it devalued individual identity by lumping people together into 'communities' that they may not want to be part of, and interfered with a person's freedom to make his own choices.

His publications include *Choice of techniques* (1960), *Growth economics* (1970), *Collective choice and social welfare* (1971), *On economic inequality* (1973), *Employment technology and development* (1975), *Poverty and famines* (1981), *Utilitarianism and beyond* (1982), *Choice, welfare and measurement* (1982), *Resources, values and development* (1984), *Commodities and capabilities* (1985), *On ethics and economics* (1987), *The standard of living* (1987), *Hunger and public action* (1989), *The political economy of hunger* (1990–91), *Inequality re-examined* (1992), *India: economic development and social opportunity* (1995), and *Development as freedom* (1999).

He was elected a fellow of the British Academy in 1977 and awarded the Nobel prize for economics in 1998. Following the path of Hayek and others, Sen later told a reporter that he had always been sceptical of the worth of the economics prize but had not wished to say so before being awarded it because people would think it 'sour grapes'. Although long resident in the United Kingdom, he remained an Indian citizen, and so he was made an honorary CH in 2000.

Sir Michael Howard 15 June 2002
Michael Howard gained a reputation as one of the country's leading historians, by specialising in the history and philosophy of war.

He was born in 1922 and educated at Wellington and Christ Church, Oxford. During the 1939–45 war he served in the Coldstream Guards (1942–45), being awarded the Military Cross in 1943. After the war he embarked on an academic career serving as an assistant lecturer (1947–50) and lecturer (1950–53) at King's College, London. From 1953 he began to specialise in the history of war. He was lecturer then reader in war studies (1953–63), and professor of war studies (1963–68). In 1968 he moved to the University of Oxford as a fellow of All Souls College (1963–80) and became Chichele professor of the history of war (1977–80) and then regius professor of modern history (1980–89).

His other interests included the presidency of the international institute for strategic studies (of which he was the co-founder). He was also vice-president of the council on Christian approaches to defence and disarmament and vice-president of the army records society. His writing of military history was underpinned by a firm grasp of more general history and a gift for vivid narrative, and he transformed largely amateur accounts of battles and warfare into a serious scholarly subject with well-founded professional standards.

His publications include *The Coldstream Guards 1920–1946* (1951), *Disengagement in Europe* (1958), *Wellingtonian studies* (1959), *The Franco-Prussian war* (1961), *The theory and practice of war* (1965), *The Mediterranean strategy in the second world war* (1967), *Studies in war and peace* (1970), *Grand strategy (1971)*, *The continental commitment* (1972), *War in European history* (1976), *Clausewitz on war* (1977), *War and the liberal conscience* (1978), *Restraints on war* (1979), *The causes of wars* (1983), *Clausewitz* (1983), *Strategic deception in world war II* (1990) (a history of the British intelligence movement in the 1939–45 war), *The lessons of history* (1991), *The Oxford history of the twentieth century* (1998), and *The invention of peace* (2000).

He was made a CBE in 1977, knighted in 1986 and made a CH in 2002 as 'Emeritus Professor of Modern History, University of Oxford. For services to military studies.'

CHAPTER ELEVEN

Campaigning spirits

SOCIAL AND HUMANITARIAN PIONEERS

I took a kettle large and new:
Fit for the deed I had to do.
My heart went hop, my heart went thump:
I filled the kettle at the pump.

'Humpty Dumpty', *Through the looking-glass*, Lewis Carroll

The words 'miscellaneous service' are the first to come to mind in assessing this mixed group of social and humanitarian minded pioneers, whose work was broadly intended for the public good.

Margaret McMillan (1930) was a pioneer of elementary education for children and founded a teacher training college in the name of her sister Rachel. Albert Mansbridge (1931) pioneered adult education for the working class by founding the Worker's Educational Association. Helena Swanwick (1931) was a visionary internationalist and pacifist whose views increasingly isolated her from her contemporaries, and whose life and career ended sadly. By the nature of his lifelong interests and pursuits, Seebohm Rowntree (1931) chairman of the Rowntree chocolate and cocoa firm, could have been included among the industrialists. One of the most enlightened employers of his day, he worked over many years to improve the working conditions of his employees, partly from a genuine compassion for the poor and partly because he made the obvious connection between a contented work force and efficient productivity. His sociological surveys of poverty in York were pioneering and he remains the only Companion of Honour to have received the decoration 'for social service.' William Bruce (1935) was a modest and self-effacing civil servant who was a significant influence on the development of secondary education in England. Janet Trevelyan (1936) could have been completely overshadowed by her famous historian husband, but for her determined five-year fight which left central London with one of its largest and safest play areas for children. For nearly thirty years William Adams (1936) was chairman of the National Council of Social Service, a new body charged with promoting and developing social services and coordinating work between the statutory and voluntary services. The substantial benefactions of Gwendoline Davies (1937) did much to raise the profile of three Welsh national institutions and although she does not easily fit into this chapter her 'social' work embellished the culture of Wales. James Joseph Mallon (1939) laboured long and lovingly at Toynbee Hall in the east end of London, playing a role that was part teacher and part social worker. Lionel Curtis (1949) was another visionary internationalist who as he grew older argued with passionate conviction that the peace of the world could only be secured by a world government. Although a backbench Conservative member of parliament, and therefore ostensibly a politician, the name of Ian Fraser (1953) is always identified with his work at St Dunstan's with blinded ex-servicemen. Angela, Countess of Limerick (1974) devoted more than sixty years of her life to the work of the international Red Cross. Jack Ashley (1975), another backbench member of parliament lost his hearing in 1967 and thereafter became a vigorous campaigner on behalf of deaf people and the disabled generally. Barbara Wootton (1977) was a social philosopher whose concerns lay with remedying the problems of human society. Sir John Smith (1993) was a banker by profession and a director of Coutts and Co. for more than forty years. Although briefly a member of parliament in the 1960s, he devoted much of his life and his wealth to the cause of architectural conservation. The name of Chad Varah (1999) is indelibly associated with the organisation that he founded in 1953 to offer a listening service to the depressed and the suicidal – The Samaritans.

There is little to link the people in this chapter beyond their very different general public service, although it is interesting to observe that one third of them were women. The four women appointed between 1930 and 1937 can be seen as part of a broader design to 'find' suitable women candidates for the Order, probably in the aftermath of the 1928 legislation which finally gave women the right to vote at the same age as men. Women figured prominently among the new admissions to the Order in the following few years. Seven women were appointed between March 1929 and January 1931, and a further four were admitted between 1933 and 1937.

Margaret McMillan 3 June 1930

Margaret McMillan was an educational pioneer who tirelessly promoted the cause of improving the health and education of elementary schoolchildren

She was born in Westchester County, New York in 1860, the second of three daughters of James McMillan, who had emigrated to the USA in 1840 from Invernesshire. After the death of her father and her sister Elizabeth from scarlet fever in 1865, she returned with her mother to Inverness. Scarlet fever also left her deaf, though she recovered her hearing at the age of fourteen. Margaret and her surviving sister Rachel both attended the Inverness High School. Even for well-to-do children whose parents paid high fees, Margaret remembered that the school had a low standard of hygiene: dusty walls, greasy slates, no hot water and no health care.

When her mother died in 1877 it was decided that Rachel would remain in Inverness to nurse her sick grandmother, while Margaret was sent away to be trained as a governess. She went first to Frankfurt and then studied languages at Geneva and Lausanne. Later she thought of training for the stage, but developed an interest in social reform under the influence of her sister Rachel.

In 1887 Rachel visited a church in Edinburgh where she met John Glasse, a Christian Socialist. She was also introduced to John Gilray, another recent convert to this religious group. Gilray gave Rachel copies of *Justice*, a socialist newspaper and Peter Kropotkin's *Advice to the young*. She went with Gilray to several socialist meetings in Edinburgh and returned home to Inverness a convinced socialist. The death of her grandmother in 1888 freed her from nursing responsibilities and the two sisters remained inseparable until Rachel's death. Margaret, who was employed as a junior superintendent in a home for young girls in London, found Rachel a similar job. Rachel converted Margaret to socialism and together they attended political meetings and began contributing to the magazine *Christian Socialist* and gave free evening lessons to working class factory girls in Whitechapel. It was not an easy experience and Margaret remembered doing her best in a dim room with a sawdust floor, reached by climbing up some rickety steps from a muddy court, teaching girls brutalised by the poverty of their background who arrived at the end of a long working day and treated the classes as a source of fun.

In October 1889, the sisters helped the workers during the London dock strike. They continued to be involved in spreading the word of Christian Socialism to industrial workers and in 1892 it was suggested that their efforts would be appreciated in Bradford. Although for the next few years they were based in Bradford, Rachel and Margaret toured the industrial regions speaking at meetings and visiting the homes of the poor and experiencing the industrial pollution caused by factory chimneys from which black smoke fell in choking clouds on the city. As well as attending Christian Socialist meetings, they joined the Fabian Society, the Labour Church, the Social Democratic Federation, and in 1893 the newly formed Independent Labour Party.

Their work in Bradford convinced them that they should concentrate on trying to improve the physical and intellectual welfare of the slum child. In 1892 Margaret joined Dr James Kerr, Bradford's school medical officer, to carry out the first medical inspection of elementary school children in Britain. Kerr and McMillan published a report on the medical problems that they found and began a campaign to improve the health of children by arguing that local authorities should install bathrooms, improve ventilation and supply free school meals. Margaret became the Independent Labour Party candidate for the Bradford School Board. She was elected in 1894 and working closely with the leader of the ILP on the local council, she began to influence what went on in Bradford schools. Among other things, school baths and medical treatment were introduced, a physical care unknown in schools at that time, and for which no legal provision existed. About 1899 she compiled the first recorded medical inspection of schoolchildren at the Usher Street Schools. She also wrote several books and pamphlets on the subject including *Child labour and the half time system* (1896) and *Early childhood* (1900). In 1902 Margaret joined Rachel in London and the two became members of the recently formed Labour Party. She continued to write books on health and education including *Education through the imagination* (1904) and *The economic aspects of child labour and education* (1905).

The two sisters led a campaign for school meals that resulted in the Provision of School Meals Act 1906. The act accepted the argument put forward by the McMillan sisters that if the state insisted on compulsory education it must take responsibility for the proper nourishment of school children.

In 1908 the sisters opened the country's first school clinic in Bow. The Deptford Clinic followed in 1910 to serve a number of schools in that area. The clinic provided dental help, surgical aid and lessons in breathing and posture. They also established a night camp where slum children could wash and wear clean nightclothes. In 1911 Margaret published *The child and the state* in which she criticised the tendency of schools in working class areas to concentrate on preparing children for unskilled and monotonous jobs, and argued that instead schools should be offering a broad and humane education.

Inevitably the two sisters supported the campaign for universal suffrage, although they were against the use of violence. They disagreed with the force feeding of imprisoned suffragettes in prison and at a 1913 protest meeting against the Cat and Mouse Act, they were physically assaulted by a group of policemen.

In 1914 they decided to start an open-air nursery school and training centre in Peckham. Within a few weeks there were thirty children at the school ranging in age from eighteen months to seven years. Rachel, who was mainly responsible for the kindergarten, proudly pointed out that in the first six months there was only one case of illness and, because of precautions that she took, this case of measles did not spread to the other children.

Rachel McMillan died on 25 March 1917. Margaret was devastated by the loss of her sister, but she continued to run the Peckham nursery. She also served on London County Council and wrote a series of influential books that included *The nursery school* (1919) and *Nursery schools: a practical handbook* (1920). With financial help she established a new college to train nurses and teachers. Named after her beloved sister, Rachel McMillan College was opened in Deptford on 8 May 1930 by Queen Mary. It survived until 1977 when, after a government review of teacher training colleges, it was amalgamated with the nearby Goldsmiths College.

Margaret McMillan was made a CH in 1930 'For services to the Nursery School Movement.' She died less than a year later in March 1931. Her friend Walter Cresswell wrote a memoir of the McMillan sisters: 'Such persons, single-minded, pure in heart, blazing with selfless love, are the jewels of our species. There is more essential Christianity in them than in a multitude of bishops.' Her action and influence made Margaret McMillan the founder of medical inspection in English elementary schools and she improved the health and education of elementary schoolchildren more than any other person.

Helena Swanwick 1 January 1931
Helena Swanwick was a speaker and writer in the cause of internationalism, pacifism and feminism.

She was born at Munich, Bavaria in 1864, only daughter of Oswald Sickert, a commercial artist of Danish origin who became a German by virtue of the Prussian annexation of Schleswig-Holstein. One of her five brothers was the painter and etcher Walter Sickert; but as the only girl, she resented the greater freedom given to her brothers. She came to England with her family in 1868 and her father was naturalised a British subject. They lived first at Bedford before moving to Notting Hill where the family were part of artistic and literary circles that included William Morris, Edward Burne-Jones and Oscar Wilde. She was educated at Notting Hill High School and at Girton College, Cambridge from where she graduated in 1885 with a second class in the moral sciences tripos. In the same year she was appointed a lecturer in psychology at Westfield College, but in 1886 she married Frederick Swanwick, a lecturer in mathematics at Owen's College, Manchester. For the next eighteen years she wrote and reviewed regularly for the *Manchester Guardian* on domestic and feminist subjects and gardening. She also did voluntary work in a local girls' club, which brought her into contact with the local women's trade union council, the Women's Cooperative Guild and eventually the Labour Party.

Although she met the Pankhursts and was an early suffragette herself, there was too much of the pacifist in her and she was repelled by their militancy and rejected their use of physical force. In 1905 she joined the North of England Suffrage Society and was the first editor of its journal *Common Cause* (1909–14) She resigned from the National Union of Women's Suffrage Societies over the issue of pacifism and became a member of the executive committee of the Union of Democratic Control to campaign against secret diplomacy. She became the first president of the Women's International League for Peace (1915–22), an organisation that aimed to harness feminism to the peace movement and through which she tried hard to arouse women's interest in international affairs. Although she was passionately in favour of the concept of such an international organisation, she was critical of the League of Nations because it was permitted to use force and committed to supporting the clauses of the Versailles treaty – which she regarded as unjust and an unstable basis for peace. As editor of *Foreign Affairs* (1925–28), the journal of the Union of Democratic Control, she continually attacked the 'war guilt' clause in the treaty. She was British substitute-delegate to the fifth assembly of the League of Nations in 1924, and to the tenth assembly in 1929.

Her publications included numerous volumes on social questions: *The small town garden* (1907); *The future of the women's movement* (1913), an expression of her own views after her resignation as editor of *Common Cause*; *Women and war* (1915); *Women in the socialist state* (1921); *Builders of peace* (1924), a history of the Union of Democratic Control; and a volume of autobiography, *I have been young* (1935).

She was an independent-minded and spirited woman which made it difficult for her to work with others. In the late 1920s she and her husband, a tolerant and unselfish man, were in poor health and his death in 1931 ended her public life. She became an increasingly isolated figure, and her last two books – *Collective insecurity* (1937) and *The roots of peace* (1938) – were regrettable notes on which to end her career. She defended Adolf Hitler's foreign policies on the ground that they were no different from those of other imperialists, and naively argued for the development of a federal Europe with communal control of all vital strategic areas. The books confirmed her separation from all sections of British politics, and her career and her life ended rather sadly in November 1939 when she took an overdose of sleeping tablets at her home in Maidenhead.

She was made a CH in 1931 for her services as 'First President, Women's International League (British Section). Formerly delegate to the Assembly of the League of Nations.'

Albert Mansbridge *3 June 1931*

Albert Mansbridge was the founder of an organisation for which many working class people had reason to be grateful – the Workers' Educational Association – and seen by his contemporaries as the architect of modern adult education.

He was born in 1876 at Gloucester, the son of a carpenter. He was educated at board schools and at Battersea Grammar School. Home circumstances forced him to leave at the age of fourteen to go out to work. He began as a boy copyist in the department of inland revenue, and then in the same capacity in the privy council committee on education (later the ministry of education). Then he became a clerk in the Goldsmiths and Silversmiths Company. At the age of twenty he took a post as a desk clerk with the Co-operative Wholesale Society. From 1901 to 1905 he was a cashier with the Co-operative Building Society.

Mansbridge never ceased to regret that circumstances had denied him a university education, and while working at his various jobs he began to take an interest in further education and attended university extension lectures and classes at King's College, London. From 1899–1902 he taught industrial history, typewriting and economics at evening schools as well as working full time for the CWS during the day. The university extension movement had begun in 1873, but by 1900 it was still mainly a middle class movement. In January 1903 the *University Extension Journal* published an article by Mansbridge entitled 'Democracy and Education'. With two succeeding articles it outlined a scheme for a working alliance between the co-operative movement, trade unionism and university extension, and was the original blueprint of the Workers' Educational Association.

After the articles had appeared in print, Mansbridge decided to start 'An association to promote the higher education of working men,' with he and his wife as the first members. The first branch was formed at Reading in October 1904 and in 1905 the title Workers' Educational Association was adopted. Mansbridge resigned from his job with the CWS to become the general secretary of the WEA. He was a devout member of the Church of England (he had been licensed as a reader at the age of eighteen) and Charles Gore (later bishop of Oxford) was among his close friends, and William Temple (later archbishop of Canterbury) became first president of the WEA in 1908. Much was demanded of those who studied with the WEA; those who joined had to pledge themselves to attend for three years, write essays and read as widely as possible under the direction of highly qualified university tutors.

The movement rapidly spread throughout England and by 1914 there were 145 classes in England and Wales with 3,234 people attending them. In 1913 he visited Australia and organised a branch of the WEA in each state. He remained general secretary until he was forced to retire after an attack of cerebro-spinal meningitis in 1915, but his reputation was established and his work was flourishing.

He remained active in educational affairs until the end of his life. He was a member of the prime minister's committee on the teaching of foreign languages (1915–18), the royal commission on the universities of Oxford and Cambridge (1919–22), and the statutory commission on Oxford (1923) He worked for the foundation of the WEA's national central library. He established the central joint advisory committee on university tutorial classes (1908), and founded the Seafarers' Education Service (1919) which organised ships' libraries, the World Association of Adult Education (1918, president from 1929), and the British Institute of Adult Education (1921). He was also a director of the Co-operative Permanent Building Society (from 1910) where he had once worked as a cashier; that, together with a civil list pension and assistance from an educational trust fund formed by some of his friends, provided him with an adequate income.

His books included studies of Margaret McMillan and the Co-operative Building Society, and *An adventure in working class education* (1920), a history of the WEA. In 1944 he published his collected essays and addresses of 1903–37 under the title *The kingdom of God*. He died in 1952.

He was made a CH in 1931 'For services in connection with modern Adult Education.'

Benjamin Seebohm Rowntree 3 June 1931

Seebohm Rowntree was chairman of the York-based cocoa and chocolate firm that bore his family name, but he was far from being a typical industrialist. He had a strong conscience, born of his Quaker faith, that provoked concern for the downtrodden, and led him to spend much of his working life assessing and improving the working conditions of his employees.

He was born in 1871, the second son of Joseph Rowntree, and educated at Bootham School, York and Owen's College, Manchester. He joined the family firm of H. I. Rowntree in 1889, became a director when it was converted into a limited liability company in 1897, and was chairman 1923–41. But his claim to public recognition was his sociological and religious concern for the well being of the employees of his company. The management of his work force was his principal interest until his retirement from executive control in 1936 and Beatrice Webb described him as more philanthropist than capitalist. He endeavoured to develop the business as a trust, increasing its charitable and social service role, and in the twentieth century the firm became a leader in the field of scientific management and industrial welfare. As labour director, he introduced an eight-hour day in 1896, a pension scheme in 1906 and profit sharing in 1923. 'Social helpers' were recruited in 1891 to deal with the large numbers of women employees, a works doctor was appointed in 1904 and a psychology department set up in 1922. Works councils were established in 1919 and a 44-hour 5-day week was introduced in the same year. He believed that the promotion of comfortable working conditions would produce an efficient work force and his views were formulated in his books *Human needs of labour* and *Human factor in business* (1921). During the 1914–18 war he was employed as director of the welfare department of the ministry of munitions (1915–18) and a member of the reconstruction committee in (1917). He helped to found the Industrial Welfare Society (1908) and the National Institute of Industrial Psychology (1921), and was chairman of the latter organisation (1940–47). Lloyd George paid tribute to him, describing him as 'one of the foremost and most successful pioneers in the development of improved conditions in his works. I should like to pay tribute to the skill, energy, sympathy, and address with which he organised this new department. The work he did helped to transform the conditions for munition labour during the war, and has left a permanent mark upon conditions in our industries.'[1]

His concerns extended beyond the walls of his own factory towards the urban poor of his native city of York and were sharpened by a visit he made to the slums of Newcastle-upon-Tyne in 1895. He was also influenced by Charles Booth's investigation of poverty in London, and in 1897–98 he spent much of his time away from the factory investigating the state of the poor in York. The result was published in 1901 as *Poverty, a study of town life*. It was the first of his three great surveys of poverty in York during the next fifty years, and it became one of the classic texts of the social sciences. The second York survey was conducted in 1936 and published in 1941 with the title *Poverty and progress*, and in 1951 he collaborated with G. R. Lavers to produce the third survey, *Poverty and the welfare state*. Some sociologists criticised his surveys on the ground of their narrow definitions and criteria, but his work was always precisely researched and he accurately observed what he saw.

His interests also turned to working conditions on the land. *Land and labour, lessons from Belgium* was published in 1910 and led to his appointment by Lloyd George to the land inquiry committee (1912–14). A further book, *How the labourer lives* (1913) was written in collaboration with Mary Kendall, and dealt with the living and working conditions of the agricultural labourer. He later worked with Lord Astor on a series of studies of British agriculture in the hope that farming could be made to contribute to the relief of unemployment and the development of the economy. He was close to Lloyd George from 1926 to 1935 when he advised him on questions of unemployment, housing and agriculture. But the publication in 1935 of his first report *The agricultural dilemma* challenged Lloyd George's optimistic estimate of the number of people who could be settled on the land. Lloyd George did not care to have his views challenged and the friendship was at an end, though Rowntree continued his work with Astor until 1946.

Given Seebohm Rowntree's profound social conscience, he perhaps might have been expected to have close relations with the Labour Party, but an independent spirit and the self-effacing modesty of the Quaker made him shun limelight, whether political or of any kind. 'He had neither the necessary temperament nor the desire to play a leading role; he was not the kind of man to lead movements or to exercise power.'[2] He accepted the CH in 1931 'For social services', but 'rejected those distinctions which, he thought, might put a barrier between him and his fellow men.'[3]

He died in 1954 at his home in a wing of Hughenden Manor in Buckinghamshire, once the home of Benjamin Disraeli.

The Honourable William Bruce 3 June 1935
William Bruce was a civil servant who devoted his career to the establishment and improvement of secondary education in England and Wales.

He was born in 1858, son of the first Lord Aberdare who had played a leading role in the establishment of the University of Wales, and educated at Harrow and Balliol College, Oxford. He read classics, took a second class degree in greats in 1880 and was called to the bar at Lincoln's Inn in 1883. He began his official career in 1886 as an assistant commissioner in the Charities Commission under the Endowed Schools Act and spent several years travelling around every district of Wales. In 1894–95 he was secretary to the commission on secondary education and became very familiar with the needs of the country in regard to secondary education and with the problems of the curriculum and administration. He later played a significant role in the establishment of intermediate education in Wales as the result of his knowledge and experience of education in the principality.

In 1900 the education side of the Charities Commission was transferred to the new board of education. Bruce became an assistant secretary to the new board and in 1903 he was appointed a principal assistant secretary, responsible for the new branch concerned with secondary schools. From then until he retired as second secretary in 1921 he exercised a profound influence on the development of secondary education in England. 'It was largely due to his tact and conciliatory administration that the public schools came into contact, to their advantage, with the inspectors of the board, and his guidance did much to keep the secondary schools established under the Education Act of 1902 on sound and humane lines . . . He was an excellent chairman in a conference with people of conflicting views, and his character and personality did much at a critical time to make the schools and schoolmasters of England recognise the Board of Education as a friend anxious to serve them and make the most of them for the benefit of the country.'[4] From his father he inherited an active involvement in the work of the University of Wales (founded in 1893). His influence helped to secure its future through a number of difficult periods and he was its pro-chancellor from 1928 to 1934. After his retirement he also served for four years on the senate of the University of London.

Professionally, Bruce was the best type of civil servant: calm, quiet, conscientious, diligent and possessed of a statesmanlike frame of mind. Personally he was a modest and discreet individual, in part shown by his skeletal entry in *Who's Who*, who had 'neither the time nor the taste for general society.'[5] He wrote little (his friends regretted the paucity of his publications) including a short life of Sir William Napier (1885), an edition of the letters of Sir Henry Lavard (1903), and for a book on drawing by his friend W. A. S. Benson, published after Benson's death, a short sketch of the life of the author. He preferred to give his time to reading, and had a thorough knowledge of English poetry and English political history in the eighteenth and nineteenth centuries.

He was made a CB in 1905, and a CH in 1935 for his services as 'lately Pro-Chancellor of the University of Wales.' Bruce was too ill to attend an investiture and the insignia was sent by registered post to his home in Bath in December 1935. He died in March 1936.

Janet Trevelyan 23 June 1936
Janet Penrose Trevelyan lived her married life in the shadow of her eminent husband, G. M. Trevelyan OM (1876–1962), regius professor of modern history at the University of Cambridge and master of Trinity College (1940–51). But she carved a niche for herself by her passionate commitment for more than twenty years to the cause of providing play centres for the children of London and especially in preserving Coram's Fields as an open space.

She was born in 1879, the daughter of an art critic father and a novelist mother. The poet and critic Matthew Arnold (1822–88) was her great uncle and Thomas Arnold (1795–1842), the famous headmaster of Rugby School (1828–42) was her great-grandfather. She married the historian George Macaulay Trevelyan in 1904. Neither had any religious beliefs and the marriage took place in a registry office. 'By birth and marriage she was thus associated with a great tradition in literature and social beneficence,'[6] and she could more than hold her own with the formidably intellectual Trevelyans. 'She was always known as "the clever child" of the family, and from an early age was renowned for the force of her intellect and the independence of her spirit.'[7] At the age of sixteen she was already reading the works of Carlyle, and between the ages of seventeen and twenty-one she translated Julicher's *Commentary on the new testament* from German into English. She was devoted to Italian culture and was a member of the British-Italian League, a founding impulse behind the creation of the British Institute of Florence, and the author of *A short history of the Italian people* (1920), 'in which her keen intellectual appreciation of the glories of the Italian culture, and affection for Italians skilfully woven into the complex web of their history, open a welcoming door to newcomers.'[8]

Her other works included a biography of her mother (1923), Mary Augusta Ward (1851–1920), a pioneer in the movement for the provision of play centres for London children, and from whom her daughter inherited many of her own social concerns. In *Robert Elsmere*, her best known novel, Mrs Humphrey Ward, as she was known, envisaged a vigorous Christianity divested of its miraculous element and fulfilling the social gospel, and in 1890 she founded the Passmore Edwards Settlement. In 1909 she founded the Evening Play Centre Movement; it sought to provide children of school age, particularly in the poorer parts of the large cities, with facilities for recreation and a healthy social environment in the evenings. Janet Trevelyan continued her mother's work and became chairman and honorary treasurer of the Children's Play Centres Committee in 1920.

But her greatest triumph was the saving of Coram's Fields in London from the developer and the builder. Coram's Fields, now in the London Borough of Camden, was the site of the Foundling Hospital, founded in 1742 by Thomas Coram for deserted children. The hospital moved to the healthier climes of Berkhamstead in 1926 and the London buildings were demolished apart from the entrance arcades. From 1929 to 1936 Janet Trevelyan fought a spirited, determined and ultimately successful fight to keep the site as a children's playground, by raising funds for the purchase of the site.

In 1954 she published *Two stories*. The first was a tender reminiscence of the son that she lost when he was five years old. The second was a record of the fight to preserve Coram's Fields. 'In her fragile frame there was a large heart quick to understand, without intrusion, and resourceful to help the troubles of others. Her mind was penetrating, particularly in its insight into the complexities of character, but wholly simple in its own integrity. So friends found in her a good pilot through the straits of life, devoted to friendship, truth, kindness, and mirth.'[9] She died in 1956 after a long and debilitating illness, through which she was nursed by her husband.

She refused an OBE in 1928 but accepted a CH in 1936 for services as 'Honorary Secretary of the Foundling Site Appeal Council. Chairman and Honorary Treasurer of the Children's Play Centres Committees.' In 1945 her husband refused a knighthood, citing his wife's wish not to become 'Lady Trevelyan.'[10]

William Adams 23 June 1936
William Adams was an academic who reached the height of warden of All Souls College, Oxford (1933–45), yet who was equally at home as a farmer and sensitive to the needs of rural life, and was for nearly thirty years, chairman of the National Council of Social Service.

He was born in 1874, the son of a teacher. His father was the headteacher of a school in Lanarkshire, and one of his pupils was the future Conservative prime minister, Andrew Bonar Law (1922–23). He was educated at his father's school, St John's Grammar School, Hamilton, and then at the University of Glasgow and Balliol College, Oxford. Thereafter he developed as a lecturer on economic and social questions. His first appointment was as a lecturer at Borough Road Training College, London (1901–02). He spent a year at the University of Chicago as a lecturer in economics (1902) before returning to become a lecturer in economics at the University of Manchester (1903–04). The world of academia was abandoned for five years as the result of a meeting with Sir Horace Plunkett in the spring of 1904. Adams became superintendent of statistics and intelligence in the department of agriculture and technical instruction in Ireland. 'Plunkett helped to make a farmer of Adams and until he died in 1932 was a major influence in a life much of which was devoted to the improvement of the nation's agriculture by means of innumerable commissions and committees.'[11] Adams gave his spare time to running his own farm and he served as chairman of the Federation of Young Farmers' Clubs (1928–46).

In 1910 he was elected to a fellowship at All Souls College, Oxford, becoming a reader (1910–12) and then Gladstone professor of political theory and institutions (1912–33). As holder of the Gladstone chair, Adams was the only person at Oxford exclusively charged with the teaching of politics, but by his eminence and influence he succeeded in spreading the teaching of the subject throughout the university and helped to launch the degree course in philosophy, politics and economics. The subsequently large and flourishing sub-faculty of politics at Oxford was a tribute to Adams's faith in his subject 'at times when it was somewhat despised and when weaker men might have allowed it to fall into a subordinate position.'[12] He published very little and on that ground alone he would never have been appointed to a university chair by the more demanding standards of recent years.

Although an academic, his subject brought him into contact with politicians, especially during the 1914–18 war. Liberal in politics, Adams worked for the ministry of munitions (1915) and then joined the group of private secretaries to David Lloyd George (1916–19), where one of his colleagues was Philip Kerr CH. At first responsible for Labour questions, he transferred to dealing with Irish matters in July 1917, when Plunkett became chairman of the Irish convention, and edited the war cabinet reports for 1917 and 1918.

He returned to Oxford in 1919 and remained there until his retirement from the wardenship of All Souls in 1945. He was a member of the Development Commission (1923–49) and chairman of the National Council of Social Service (1920–49). The latter body was founded in 1919 with the aim of developing cooperation between statutory and voluntary social services, to provide a clearing house of information on the social services, and to promote and undertake experiments in social service. Services undertaken by the council included the development of social and cultural organisations, including the provision of village halls, community centres, and citizens' advice bureaux and the publication of citizens' advice notes. 'To all these manifold public services Adams contributed a character of great strength, loyalty and sincerity, wise and persuasive counsel, a vision of a better life and an incurable optimism in the possibility of its attainment.'[13]

After retirement he spent the rest of his life at his house in County Donegal where he died in 1966.

He was appointed a CH in 1936 for his services as 'Warden of All Souls College, Oxford. Chairman of the National Council of Social Service. Chairman of the National Federation of Young Farmers' Clubs.'

Gwendoline Davies 11 May 1937
Gwendoline Davies was prominent for many years in the cultural life of Wales, but virtually unknown outside the principality. She gave generously of her inherited and substantial wealth to support a number of Welsh national institutions.

She was born in 1882, the granddaughter of David Davies (1818–90) who had made his fortune as a contractor in coal and railways. Her mother had died when she was three and her father Edward Davies (1852–98) died when she was sixteen. Thereafter Gwendoline lived with her sister Margaret (1884–1963) and their stepmother at Plas Dinam, Llandinam. They were educated at Heathfield and at home and brought up as Calvinistic Methodists. Neither sister ever married. Margaret Davies briefly attended the Slade School as an external pupil, and later had a private tutor for her painting. From about 1908 they began jointly to form a collection of pictures, and by 1913 it was important enough to be exhibited at the national gallery of Wales. Their collection included works by Turner, Millet, Raeburn, Whistler, Monet, Boudin, Renoir, Cézanne, Van Gogh, Daumier and Carrière. They travelled widely in France and in 1916 Gwendoline organised a

Red Cross centre at Troyes. Both sisters helped to run it, but Margaret left in 1917 to work in Rouen.

In 1920 they bought Gregynog Hall, Newtown, Montgomeryshire, about ten miles from Llandinam where they had been raised. Their intention was to convert it into a centre for the arts in Wales, to be equipped with a printing press, artists' studios, pottery and music rooms. In August 1923 the first of what was intended to be a series of courses for Welsh art students took place there, but the schemes were curtailed in 1924 when the sisters themselves moved into Gregynog. Although the house did not develop along the lines initially envisaged, it did become a hub of cultural activity during their residence. Gregynog became famous in Wales for its concerts; Adrian Boult, Walford Davies and Gustav Holst were regular performers. Gwendoline also founded the Gregynog Press, which achieved a considerable reputation for fine binding and printing and ran until 1939.

By 1924 the sisters' collection of pictures was essentially complete and it was the largest collection of French impressionist and post-impressionist paintings in Britain at the time. Gwendoline stopped collecting in 1923. The conversion and modernisation of the hall was a substantial expense and, as mine owners and philanthropists, the 1926 general strike affected the Davies family. The strike was followed by the depression which further restricted their expenditure.

The two sisters were generous benefactors of educational and social movements in Wales (nearly always anonymously), including the University of Wales, the National Library of Wales and in particular the National Museum of Wales. By 1937, Gwendoline and her sister had given between them more than £756,600 to various objects in Wales, and they had regularly lent Gregynog and entertained the delegates to innumerable conferences connected with education, music and unemployment. They made frequent loans from their works of art to strengthen the young national collection and in 1940 they presented a small group of works by Rodin, Brangwyn and Augustus John. Gregynog Hall was given to the University of Wales in 1960 and their collection of paintings, drawings and sculptures to the National Museum of Wales in 1952 and 1963.

Gwendoline Davies, the elder and more active of the two sisters, was a founder of the Welsh national memorial association for the prevention and treatment of tuberculosis, and later president of the organisation until 1948, and received opinion had it that her CH in 1937 was 'for the many public services that she had performed, especially in the promotion of medical studies'.[14] She had been for many years a member of the council of the National Library of Wales, the court of governors of the University of Wales, and of the court of governors of the National Museum of Wales.

She was made a CH in the Coronation Honours List 1937 'For educational, social and philanthropic services in Wales. A Member of the Court of the University of Wales.' She died in 1951. Margaret Davies, who was two years younger than her sister, died in 1963.

James Joseph Mallon 8 June 1939

For thirty-five years, James Mallon was warden of Toynbee Hall in London's east end, and his social work was ranked with Lord Beveridge and R. H. Tawney; he was called 'the most popular man east of Aldgate Pump.'

He was born of Irish parents in Manchester in 1875, and was educated at Owen's College, Manchester from which he graduated with an MA. He was attracted by social work and joined the staff of the Ancoats Settlement devoted to the poor of Manchester. He soon became convinced of the social evil of sweated labour, and in 1906 was appointed secretary to the national league to establish a minimum wage. The agitation by this body led to the passing of the Trade Boards Act which fixed minimum wages in several industries. Mallon was a member of the first thirteen trade boards to be set up. He served on the Whitley Committee and was honorary secretary to the Trades Board Advisory Council.

In 1906 he moved from Manchester to Toynbee Hall. During the 1914–18 war he was a member of various committees under the Profiteering Act and in October 1919 he began his thirty-five years of being a teacher and social worker, as warden of Toynbee Hall. During his time, it became known as 'the poor man's university' and Mallon was responsible for the foundation of the Toynbee Hall theatre, the Workers' Travel Association and the John Benn Club for working boys. His efforts on behalf of the poor were not confined to material things. He believed in the need for the extension of opportunities for education to the working classes. He was a warm supporter of the work of Albert Mansbridge and became a member of the executive of the Workers' Educational Association. He was a strong advocate of raising the school leaving age to fifteen and of continued part-time education to the age of eighteen.

He took part in numerous national organisations and investigations. He served on the royal commission on licensing (1929–31), the executive of the League of Nations, departmental committees on the Cinematographic Films Act, and on the Adoption Societies and Agencies, the executive committee of the British Empire exhibition (1924), and the boards of governors of the Whitechapel Art Gallery and the London Museum. He was a member of the government's economic advisory council, the aliens deportation advisory committee, and was chairman of the London council for voluntary occupation in the 1930s. He was a governor of the BBC (1937–39 and 1941–46); the two-year break was due to a reduction in the number of governors. In October 1940 he was appointed by Lord Woolton to be adviser on the provision of food and refreshment in London air raid shelters.

He hoped on a number of occasions to become a Labour member of parliament, 'but his effervescence – and complete lack of gravitas – did not help him with selection committees or with the electorate.' Successive defeats were treated with good humour. In 1944 he addressed a meeting at Burslem: 'In this and many other constituencies I have been rejected by large and enthusiastic majorities.'[15] His only book, *Poverty yesterday and today*, was written with E. C. T. Lascelles and published in 1930.

He retired from Toynbee Hall in April 1954, but retained his honorary secretaryship of the Wages Council and his membership of the several trade boards connected with the clothing industry. Lord Salter, who had known him for half a century, recalled the charisma of Mallon: 'His friends will remember above all the depth of his rich humanity, expressed alike in his humour, his ardent feeling for the suffering of others (whether known personally to him or unknown), which gave the dynamic force to his social work, and the love of poetry which suffused his whole personality. I recall an evening in the first war when a small group of friends had met to discuss the practical problems of the time. He happened to quote from W. B. Yeats – with such felicity and feeling that we asked for more, and yet more and more; and in the end we listened entranced for the whole evening while he poured out the rich treasure of remembered passages of poetry from our own and earlier ages. Few indeed have inspired affection at once so deep and so wide.'[16] Another obituarist described him as 'a very eminent social organizer, a man of shining ideals, and the personal friend of many of London's working people.'[17]

He was made a CH in 1939 for his services as 'Warden of Toynbee Hall.' He died in 1961.

Lionel George Curtis 9 June 1949

Lionel Curtis was an internationalist who became a strong protagonist for the benefits of imperial federation. It eventually led him to a belief – romantic, naive, unrealistic and slightly eccentric, yet still passionate – that the problems of the world would be eradicated by a world government; and to those views he remained unshakably committed until the end of his life.

He was born in 1872 and educated at Haileybury and then at New College, Oxford from where he graduated with a degree in literae humaniores. He was later called to the bar at Inner Temple but never practised. His began his working life as a private secretary to Leonard Courtney MP, chairman of London County Council. Under the influence of Octavia Hill, the housing reformer, he spent a time disguised as a tramp, begging on the streets and sleeping in workhouses, to understand the working of the Poor Law.

He joined the City Imperial Volunteers in 1899 and served with them in the South African War until the occupation of Pretoria in 1900. He became one of Lord Milner's group of young men who were employed in reorganising South African government after the war. His first task was to organise municipal self-government in Johannesburg and in March 1901 he was appointed acting town clerk. Promotion brought him the office of assistant colonial secretary of the Transvaal in charge of local government. He held the office until 1907 when he became a member of the nominated upper house of the Transvaal legislature and devoted himself to the movement for creating a South African union.

The union accomplished in 1910 he left the country and spent the rest of his life applying the lesson of federation to the rest of the empire. 'For the next 30 years, in season and out of season, Curtis preached the doctrine of imperial federation, urging the need for a constitution which would unite Britain and the self-governing Dominions in a new Commonwealth entity; and then, for the rest of his life, he advocated a still wider federal unity in the approach to a world State.'[18]

In 1912 he was appointed Beit lecturer in colonial history at Oxford and the outbreak of the 1914–18 war gave fresh impetus to his dreams. He called for the establishment of an imperial parliament and in 1916 he published *The commonwealth of nations* in which he argued his case. Decades later it was recalled as the first recorded use of a term that came to identify the loose confederation that replaced the British empire. After the war he was instrumental in promoting and raising funds for the establishment of the Royal Institute of International Affairs. He made a substantial contribution to the work of the 1918 Montagu-Chelmsford report on changes to the governance of India, and published his opinions in *Dyarchy* (1920). From India he moved to Ireland and was secretary of the British delegation that negotiated the Anglo-Irish treaty of 1922. He remained at the colonial office as an adviser on Irish affairs until 1924. He then turned his interests to the problems of the far east and produced *The capital question of China* (1932).

Between 1934 and 1937 he produced his three volume opus magnus *Civitas dei*. The work was partly a product of his deeply religious upbringing and sought to show that the course of human history was ultimately guided by human beliefs. 'In a closely packed study he envisaged the growth of the commonwealth ideal into a society transcending the limits of nationality. The book was open to criticism by both historians and theologians, but there was no mistaking the author's fire and sincerity.'[19] He continued to argue for the immediate creation of a supranational state in the west and the outbreak of the 1939–45 war only strengthened his beliefs. Throughout the war he published pamphlets exhorting the creation of a United States of the World, to the point where he seemed to become a prophet of the apocalypse; he warned of impending global disaster as the result of failure to embrace what to him was now an article of faith. He could not or would not admit that his noble and beneficent visions of world peace through federal union were impractical dreams.

Towards the end of his life, by now a handsome old man with shaggy grey hair, his mind returned to his place in Lord Milner's South African kindergarten, the origin of his global federal dreams and in 1951 he published *With Milner in South Africa*, consisting largely of transcripts of the letters that he wrote to his mother in England. He died in 1955.

The CH was conferred on him in 1949 and the accompanying citation was 'President, Royal Institute of International Affairs.' The CH pleased him because it had been conferred on his old friend Philip Kerr in 1920; together they had served with Milner in South Africa.

Lord Fraser of Lonsdale 1 June 1953
Although a long-serving Conservative member of parliament, Ian Fraser never held ministerial office and remained firmly on the backbenches. For more than half a century he devoted his life to the well-being of disabled ex-servicemen and especially to those who, like himself, had lost their sight.

He was born in 1897 and educated at Marlborough and Sandhurst. In the 1914–18 war he served with the 1st Battalion, The King's (Shropshire) Light Infantry and was attached to the 1/4th Glosters. He had been in France for only a few weeks when he was blinded in the battle of the Somme in 1916. While recovering in hospital, he met his future wife who put him in touch with Sir Arthur Pearson, the blind newspaper proprietor who had founded St Dunstan's Lodge, Regents Park, London, for training blinded officers and men. His vision was that, given training, blind servicemen should be restored from being simply the recipients of charity, to people who could lead independent, useful and satisfying lives. The idea was revolutionary for its day. During the 1914–18 war, some 1,500 blinded ex-servicemen passed through St Dunstan's. Many were in poor health because of mustard gas poisoning. They were trained in a wide variety of trades and skills, and went on to pursue such diverse occupations as massage, boot repairing, poultry farming, telephone switchboard operating and joinery.

In 1917 Fraser started work as Pearson's assistant at St Dunstan's and in 1921 became his second in command. When Pearson died at the end of that year, Fraser, only twenty-four years old, was appointed to succeed him as chairman, and remained in office until his own death in 1974. He became the moving spirit behind the extension of Pearson's work. St Dunstan's was incorporated in 1923. New headquarters were acquired in Marylebone Road, offices in South Audley

Street, and a convalescent home was purpose built at Ovingdean, near Brighton in 1938.

Fraser was a passionate advocate of the needs of the disabled and sought a wider sphere of influence. He represented North St Pancras on London County Council (1922–25) and represented the same constituency in the house of commons (1924–29). He was defeated in 1929, used his time out of the commons to study law, and was called to the bar at Inner Temple in 1932. He was reelected for North St Pancras in 1931 and held it until 1936 when he was made a governor of the BBC. He had been a member of the broadcasting committee of enquiry (1925–26), and as representative of blind listeners, he made valuable contributions on their behalf. The outbreak of the 1939–45 war caused a reduction in the number of governors and Fraser resigned, and returned to the commons as member for Lonsdale, Lancashire (1940–50) and, as the result of a reorganisation of constituency boundaries, Morecambe and Lonsdale (1950–58). When the number of BBC governors was increased in 1941 he was reappointed and remained a governor until 1946.

He was a popular member of the commons and fought for increased pensions for disabled former servicemen and women. He was national president of the British Legion (1947–58) and represented its interests and concerns in parliament. That in itself brought a note of controversy at the legion's annual conference in 1952 when a group of members attempted to censure him for his attitude in the commons to the legion's demand for a weekly pension of £4 10s. Fraser was immensely popular and there was no doubting the result of the vote, in which only five of the 650 delegates voted against him.

He retired from the legion and from parliament in 1958 and died in 1974. Beneath his memorial is a tablet in braille. He published an autobiography *Whereas I was blind* (1942) and *My story of St Dunstan's* (1961).

He was appointed a CBE in 1922, knighted in 1934, appointed a CH in 1953 and created a life peer in 1958 but he always regarded his honours as a tribute to the blind community rather than to himself. The citation for the CH read: 'Unionist Member of Parliament for Morecambe and Lonsdale since 1950; for Lonsdale, 1940–1950; and for North St Pancras, 1924–1929 and 1931–36; Chairman, Executive Council of St Dunstan's since 1921. National President of the British Legion since 1947. For political and public services.'

Angela, Countess of Limerick 1 January 1974
Angela Limerick was a highly-regarded figure in the world of the many voluntary organisations to which she gave freely and conscientiously of her time for sixty-six years. Above all, she was devoted to the work of the Red Cross and in its service she travelled widely across the world.

She was born in 1897, the younger daughter of Lieutenant Colonel Sir Henry Trotter, a diplomat, and was educated at North Foreland School, Broadstairs and at the London School of Economics. She began more than sixty years of service to the Red Cross in 1915 when she trained as a VAD. Being officially too young for overseas service, she lied about her age to get to France, and until 1919 she nursed the sick and wounded at home and overseas. In 1926 she married the fifth Earl of Limerick. In the years after the 1914–18 war she became a pioneer campaigner for family planning and was active in local government, as a Poor Law Guardian (1928–30), a member of Kensington Borough Council (1929–35), and then a member of London County Council (1936–46). While on Kensington Council she served as chairman of the maternity and child welfare and public health committees. She also served as the privy council representative on the General Nursing Council for England and Wales (1933–50) and a member of the royal commission on equal pay.

Her local government work was matched by a developing interest in the work of the Red Cross, and this became a lifelong passion. She began as director and then president of the London branch of the British Red Cross Society; chairman of the joint war organisation of the British Red Cross Society and the Order of St John (1941–47), in which capacity she visited several battle fronts and fourteen countries; vice-chairman of the League of Red Cross Societies (1957–73); and chairman of the standing committee of the International Red Cross (1965–73). The standing committee was effectively the 'inner cabinet' of the worldwide Red Cross and convened the international conferences. She chaired the international conference in Istanbul in 1969 and retired after the conference in Tehran in 1973. She was then elected chairman of the council of the British Red Cross Society (1974–76) in succession to the Duke of Edinburgh, and on her retirement in 1976 she was appointed a life vice-president. 'She was an active and articulate leader of the British delegation at all international Red Cross meetings from 1948 onwards and her uncompromising support of the fundamental principles and integrity of the Red Cross movement was heard with growing respect.'[20]

The Red Cross and local government were not the only parts of her voluntary service. Among other organisations she was president of the Multiple Sclerosis Society (1968–76), president of the Hospital and Homes of St Giles, vice-president of the International Council of Social Service, vice-president of the Family Welfare Association, vice-president of the Star and Garter Home, and vice-president of the Queen Alexandra Home, Worthing. She was a hard-working volunteer who had no desire, and was not content, to be a 'name' on the notepaper, and she actively contributed to each of the organisations in which she held any official position. 'She had a great breadth of vision, an astonishing memory and grasp of detail, and an ability to establish close and lasting personal relationships after brief acquaintance. Above all, she had the gift of inspiring and encouraging others, and bringing out the best in them.'[21]

She was appointed a CBE in 1942, a DBE in 1946, a DStJ in 1952, a GBE in 1954 and a CH in 1974 'For services to the International Red Cross.' She died in 1981.

Lord Ashley of Stoke 1 January 1975

Jack Ashley was a backbench Labour member of parliament who made his reputation for his campaigning work on behalf of the deaf.

He was born in 1922 and educated at St Patrick's Elementary School, Widnes, Lancashire. After leaving school at the age of fourteen he worked as a factory labourer, furnace man, and crane operator (1936–46). In 1945 he was elected to Widnes borough council and in 1946 he was shop steward convenor and national executive member of the Chemical Workers' Union. In 1946 he won a scholarship to Ruskin College, Oxford (1946–48) and went from there to Gonville and Caius College, Cambridge (1948–51). He worked as a producer with BBC Radio (1951–57) and BBC Television (1957–66).

In 1966 he was elected Labour member of parliament for Stoke-on-Trent South, holding the seat until he retired from the house of commons in 1992. His government roles were limited to two short periods as a parliamentary private secretary; firstly to Peter Shore (1967–68) when he was secretary of state for economic affairs and secondly to Barbara Castle (1974–76) when she was secretary of state for the social services. Ashley was never a prominent parliamentarian or politician, but he made a name for himself as an outstanding backbencher, because of a personal disability. In 1967 he suffered a total and profound loss of hearing through a surgical procedure that went wrong. Suddenly he was unable to hear his own voice and he became familiar with the empty smiles and averted gaze that tends to greet the deaf, and he noticed that people hastened to a destination that had become more urgent than it would have been if he had not lost his hearing. He began to discover who his friends were as he found that invitations to dinner and to parties fell off very dramatically when he lost his hearing. The telephone fell silent, not only because he could no longer hear it but also because many people stopped telephoning him.

Some of his colleagues wondered how a totally deaf person could sustain a job as member of parliament and win elections by fighting vigorous campaigns. He himself wondered whether he could stay on and how he could function as a member of parliament. He seriously considered giving up politics but was encouraged to stay on by his constituents and parliamentary colleagues. He was able to continue through lip reading and other measures, including the support of his wife. He stayed and won six more elections over twenty-four years.

In the house of commons he found parliamentary colleagues who were willing to make notes for him and they helped him to follow proceedings. After eight years of lip reading he was given a stenographer and a visual display unit. He didn't court publicity as a deaf member of parliament, nor did he focus entirely on deafness and disability issues. He took up the rights of victims of the drug thalidomide, children damaged by vaccines, abuse in the army and battered women. There was however great public interest in the fact that someone who could hear nothing at all raised these issues, and the fact that he was doing these things naturally attracted far more attention than they would otherwise have done. By his campaigning spirit he persuaded the public to see deaf people in a very different light. He became a vigorous campaigner for the rights of deaf people in both houses of parliament. As a mostly invisible disability (a hearing aid usually indicates a difficulty), deafness is not as emotive or any where near as well supported and funded as blindness and other disabilities. Jack Ashley became a national public champion of a comparatively neglected disabled group and substantially raised its profile. He introduced bills and amendments to legislation on cochlear implants, subtitles on television and improvements to hearing aids. He took depositions to government ministers and pressed issues in parliament by questions, speeches and any other way that he could use to exert pressure.

He established the All Party Disablement Group (APDG, as it was initially called) during the parliamentary session of 1968–69 to provide a parliamentary forum to work for the interests of disabled people. Since then, the role of the APDG has grown and its remit and policies now cover the whole range of Government activity. It wields influence within and outside parliament and is respected by government as the parliamentary forum for the disabled. It was retitled the All Party Parliamentary Disablement Group in December 1998 and the All Party Parliamentary Disability Group early in 2001. The post–1998 name was a requirement of the Parliamentary Commissioner for Standards to indicate that the membership consisted exclusively of members and peers. Ashley also took on the presidencies of Defeating Deafness (the Hearing Research Trust) (1985–), the Royal National Institute for the Deaf (1987–), the Royal College of Speech and Language Therapists (1995–), the British Tinnitus Association, and the National Cochlear Implant Users' Association (2001–). He was also made chancellor of the University of Staffordshire (1993–). The National Deaf Children's Society established the Jack Ashley Millennium Awards, supported by a £1.7 million lottery grant from the Millennium Commission, designed to give young deaf people opportunities which their hearing peers can take for granted.

Later in his life, Ashley had a cochlear implant which restored a little of his hearing, but it never diminished his campaigning spirit of behalf of deaf people.

The question of honouring Ashley for his work was not slow in coming, although the precise nature and level of the honour needed thought. In the first instance a CBE or a knighthood might have been appropriate. But such was Ashley's national reputation for his work in bringing this invisible disability to greater prominence that he was made a CH in 1975. The citation read: 'Member of Parliament for Stoke on Trent South. For services to handicapped people.' He was appointed a member of the privy council in 1979; it was a rare honour for a backbencher without ministerial office. He was created a life peer on leaving the house of commons in 1992 and took the title of Lord Ashley of Stoke.

Baroness Wootton of Abinger 11 June 1977
Dismissed as forceful by some and opinionated by others, Barbara Wootton was a mixture of social philosopher, public servant, politician and pioneer of adult education, and a woman of intellectual distinction.

She was born in Cambridge in 1897 to a family of intellectuals. Both her parents were classical scholars; her father was a tutor at Emmanuel and her mother a fellow of Girton. She was educated at Perse High School for Girls and at Girton College, where she studied first classics and then economics. In 1917 she married her first husband, John Wesley Wootton (a research student at Trinity College, Cambridge), but their honeymoon had to be cancelled because he was recalled to his regiment. She had one and half days with the husband whose name she bore for the rest of her life; he was killed in action five weeks later. Although she married again many years later, her childlessness remained an underlying grief throughout her life.

After graduation with a first class honours degree she was elected to a fellowship at Girton and became director of studies in economics (1920–22). She left to become a research officer with the TUC and Labour Party joint research department (1922–26). She lost interest but remained 'absolutely wholehearted in my devotion to the Labour Movement and my adherence to socialism.'[22] For a short period (1926–27) she was principal of Morley College for Working Men and Women, and then the first director of studies for tutorial classes in the extramural department of the University of London (1927–44). In 1935 she married her second husband who had given up cab-driving to take a full-time scholarship at the London School of Economics. The marriage was not entirely successful because of his inability to be faithful to her, but he always made it clear to 'the others' that his wife came first, and she nursed him through cancer until his death in 1964.

In 1944 she became head of the department of sociology and social studies at Bedford College and then professor of social studies in 1948. Although she was a competent academic, she intensely disliked theoretical sociology and academic politics, and was never really content in that environment. 'She belonged to no school, she never sought or attracted disciples and her writing and research owed little to the influence or practices of conventional scholarship. She thought of herself as a social scientist, but claimed no more than a determination to apply scientific method to the problems of human society.'[23] She resigned her chair to take up a Nuffield research fellowship (1952–57), tenable at Bedford College and her research was published in 1959 as *Social science and social pathology*.

She had already begun a long career in public service as a member of the departmental committee on the national debt and taxation (1924–27). Many more appointments followed: member of the royal commission on workmen's compensation (1938), the interdepartmental committee on shop hours (1946–49), the royal commission on the press (1947), the university grants committee (1948–50), the royal commission on the civil service (1954), the interdepartmental committee on the business of the criminal courts (1958–61), the council on tribunals (1961–64), the interdepartmental committee on the criminal statistics (1963–67), the royal commission on the penal system (1964–66), the penal advisory council (1966–79), and the advisory council on the misuse of drugs (1971–74). She was also a governor of the BBC (1950–56), chairman of the national parks commission (1966–68) and its successor, the countryside commission (1968–70), a justice of the peace for Greater London (1926–70) and a member of the panel of chairmen for the metropolitan juvenile courts (1946–62). In the area of the law, her lasting claim to fame was her invention of the community service order (later renamed the community punishment order).

Her numerous publications reflected her experiences and concerns for society in the world around her: *Twos and threes* (1933), *Plan or no plan* (1934), *London's burning* (1936), *Lament for economics* (1938), *End social inequality* (1941), *Freedom under planning* (1945), *Testament for social science* (1950), *The social foundations of wage policy* (1955), *Crime and the criminal law* (1964), *Contemporary Britain* (1971), *Incomes policy: an inquest and a proposal* (1974), and *Crime and penal policy* (1978). A volume of autobiography, *In a world I never made*, appeared in 1967. 'She felt a passion to eliminate or reduce artificial and dehumanising inequalities. Throughout her life she rejected revolution as a way forward because she thought the price of the inevitable suffering was too heavy to be paid. A revolutionary in ideas, she always remained a democrat in politics, carrying in her bones an instinct for the future.'[24]

She was a woman of strong will and intellect and not everyone warmed to her, but there were many factors in her life that caused her to be the way she was, and A. H. Halsey delivered a good analysis. 'Her circumstances and her temperament formed her into a rationalist, an agnostic and a socialist . . . Her rationalism evolved, no doubt, in part from sheer intellectual power but also from the experience of bereavement and the illogicality of a gifted woman's place in society. Her agnosticism was nurtured by deep scepticism about the benevolence of any conceivable deity or principle of cosmic order in World War I. Her socialism was rooted in the same experiences which convinced her that, given sympathy for others, critical reason was the only road to salvation on this earth.'[25]

Her extensive record of public service made her once joke that the main committee room in the home office was the cell in which she served a life sentence. It was no surprise that in 1958 she became one of the first batch of life peers to be created under the Life Peerages Act, and in 1967 she became the first woman to sit as a deputy speaker in the house of lords. She was made a CH in 1977 'For public services', and died in 1988.

Sir John Smith 31 December 1993
John Smith was a banker by profession, and for a few years member of parliament. But his career was remarkable for the outstanding contribution he made over more than forty years to the conservation of historic buildings.

He was born in 1923, educated at Eton and New College, Oxford and served in the fleet air arm during the 1939–45 war. After the war he became a banker and was a director of Coutts & Co. (1950–93). He held a number of other business appointments including being a director of Financial Times Ltd (1958–65) and of Rolls Royce Ltd (1955–75). In November 1965 he won a by-election to serve as Conservative member of parliament for the cities of London and Westminster. During his time in parliament he was a member of the public accounts committee (1968–69) and the executive of the 1922 committee (1968–70). He did not stand again at the 1970 general election.

His interest in conservation began at an early age and he was associated with the National Trust from the age of twenty-nine in a variety of roles. He was a member of its historic buildings committee (1952–61), executive committee (1959–85), and council (1961–95); and he was deputy chairman (1980–85). He also held appointments with the Historic Buildings Council (predecessor to English Heritage) (1971–78), the National Heritage Memorial Fund (1980–82) and the Redundant Churches Fund (1972–74). He was also a member of the Standing Commission on Museums and Galleries (1958–66).

What made his contribution exceptional was his creation, from his own resources, of the Landmark and Manifold Trusts. The Landmark Trust, founded in 1965, specialises in acquiring vernacular buildings of outstanding quality, but with no viable use, restoring them and adapting them for use as high quality holiday accommodation. 'By sleeping under its roof they profit far more from each place than by looking at it only; they can study it at leisure, be there early and late, in all lights and weathers.'[26] Sir John's personal role in the enterprise was central. Although he had disagreements with English Heritage – he was notoriously impatient of bureaucracy – English Heritage officials had the highest admiration for his work and his success in securing the future of many small historic buildings which might otherwise have been lost. 'Few other organisations have done as much to demonstrate by practical example that our smaller historic buildings, of all kind, both deserved to be saved and can, in this way, have a viable future.'[27] The work of the Landmark and Manifold Trusts continued to grow. In the period 1988–93 the Landmark Trust acquired more than forty historic buildings, and by 1998 their total portfolio stood at 200 properties (including Lundy Island). In 1988–93 the Manifold Trust made grants of more than £7 million, some 80% of which assisted conservation work. He was also active in the field of maritime heritage, being almost single-handedly responsible for securing the restoration of *HMS Warrior*, Britain's first ironclad warship, and was a member of the inland waterways redevelopment committee (1958–62).

For his endeavours John Smith was held in high respect, and a national newspaper survey described him as 'the conservationist's conservationist'. He was made a CBE in 1975, knighted in 1988 and made a CH in 1993 'For services to Conservation and the Heritage.'

The Reverend Chad Varah 31 December 1999
Chad Varah has a reputation for a passionate involvement in a variety of groups concerned with human welfare, but he will be remembered as the founder (in 1953) of an organisation dedicated to providing a listening service for the depressed and the suicidal – the Samaritans.

He was born in 1911, son of the vicar of Barton-on-Humber, and educated at Worksop College, Keble College, Oxford (where he read philosophy, politics and economics) and Lincoln Theological College. He was ordained in 1935 and served curacies at St Giles, Lincoln (1935–38), St Mary, Putney (1938–40) and St John, Barrow-in-Furness (1940–42). He was vicar of Holy Trinity, Blackburn (1942–49) and St Paul, Clapham Junction (1949–53) before moving to the city of London parish of St Stephen, Wallbrook in 1953. Within weeks of his arrival in a city that still showed the extensive scars of bombing during the 1939–45 war, Varah established an organisation that was to become one of the principal passions and preoccupations of his life. With the aid of one telephone line that he found in the basement of the church, and a group of volunteers, he established a telephone service the prime purpose of which was to listen and befriend the depressed and the suicidal. He called it 'the Samaritans' and served as its director (1954–74) and president of the London branch (1974–86). He was also chairman of Befrienders International (Samaritans Worldwide) (1974–83) and president (1983–86). The test of any organisation is whether it can grow and develop to the point where it acquires its momentum and no longer needs to rely on the force and vigour of its founder. The Samaritans have passed the test.

He had other interests, including the Russian Orthodox Church. While at Oxford he was secretary of the Russian Club (1931) and the Slavonic Club (1932), and he was president of a committee for publishing the liturgical music of that church (1960–76). He would lend his name and support to organisations that embraced initially unfashionable causes. He was patron of the Terrence Higgins Trust (1987–99), the country's foremost AIDs charity, and founder (in 1992) of the bluntly titled Men Against the Genital Mutilation of Girls. But his prime interest remained the Samaritans, and his publications included: *The Samaritans* (1965), *Nobody understands Miranda* (1972), *The Samaritans in the 70s* (1973, revised 1977), *Telephone masturbators* (1976) and *The Samaritans in the 1980s* (1980, revised 1984 and 1988). A volume of autobiography, *Before I die*, was published in 1993. The title and the date seemed slightly premature; he was still alive nearly ten years later.

One of the few people to be honoured three times for doing the same thing, Varah was appointed an OBE in 1969 and a CBE in 1995. The CH was conferred on him in the New Year list 2000 'For services to The Samaritans.'

Addendum
As this book was about to go to press, the author's attention was drawn to an individual who is known to have refused the CH and the nature of whose work would have placed him in this chapter. *Group Captain the Lord Cheshire, VC, OM DSO, DFC (1917–1992)* was a distinguished pilot during the 1939–45 war, for which he was awarded the Victoria Cross, uniquely for four years of sustained courage rather than any specific deed. In 1946 he founded the first of what were to become known as the Cheshire Homes for the Disabled, and from that date, the rest of his life was dedicated to the relief of suffering. He was offered a CH in 1976 but politely refused[28] on a principle of co-equality, believing that he had not done any more than anyone else. It is believed that he refused a second offer some three years later. An ardent royalist, he accepted the Order of Merit in 1981 with deep appreciation. He was created a life peer in 1991, having been persuaded that it would provide him with a public platform to press his causes.

CHAPTER TWELVE

Sharp quillets

LAWYERS

'What do you know about this business?' the King said to Alice. 'Nothing,' said Alice. 'Nothing whatever?' persisted the King. 'Nothing whatever,' said Alice. 'That's very important,' the King said, turning to the jury.

'Alice's evidence', *Alice's adventures in wonderland*, Lewis Carroll

Six lawyers – five barristers and one solicitor – constitute the smallest category among the Companions of Honour, and none of them, with the possible exception of Lord Reid, have been appointed solely for their legal expertise; there has always been a 'value-added' factor.

A Scotsman by birth, James Reid (1967) was a rare example of a lawyer who was equally at home and equally expert in the differing laws and legal systems of both Scotland and England. Arnold Goodman (1972) was the solitary solicitor among the six, and his CH was conferred for a wide range of public service in the arts, a field in which, to judge from the content of his memoirs, he seemed to know everyone who was anyone. The flamboyant character of Quintin Hailsham (1974) found a more natural field of expression in the world of politics than in the courts of law, and he delighted in occupying the office of lord chancellor, once held by his father. His CH came immediately after the inconclusive first general election in 1974. Reserved and austere, Gerald Gardiner (1975) was the great reforming lord chancellor of the twentieth century who inaugurated a radical overhaul of the criminal justice system, yet who was honoured not for being lord chancellor, but for his libertarian work with the campaigning group Justice, of which he was chairman. John Morris (1975) was not an outstanding law lord, but he was an ardent Welshman and the CH was conferred on him for his public services in the principality. Another Welsh lawyer Elwyn Jones (1976), received the CH in Harold Wilson's controversial resignation honours list while still serving as lord chancellor, presumably as a token of the departing prime minister's affectionate regard.

With the exception of Arnold Goodman, whose national significance lay more as an *eminence grise* than as a lawyer, the other five were at least lords of appeal in ordinary, and three held the office of lord high chancellor. By virtue of their high rank, law lords and lord chancellors will usually though not always have collected knighthoods and peerages on or before reaching the summit of their profession. That raises the question of what then is the 'value-added' part of their work that would justify the additional honour of a CH? On the basis of this small and chronologically narrow legal group (Lord Goodman excepted), those holding the highest offices in their profession are the obvious candidates from which to pluck a legal CH. But there will almost certainly have to be a prominent additional factor; something 'more' than the high level of excellence to be found, for example, in a lord of appeal in ordinary.

Do the examples of the three lord chancellors – Gardiner, Hailsham and Elwyn-Jones – set a precedent? Is the office of lord chancellor threshold enough to presume a claim on the CH? Not, it would seem, in the category of law. Hailsham and Elwyn-Jones had both been members of the house of commons, were respected as politicians, and received the CH as a token of the esteem in which they were held by prime ministers Edward Heath and Harold Wilson. They were cabinet ministers, and during their long political careers, they would have seen a number of their fellow cabinet ministers given the CH, and not always for the best of reasons. Hailsham in particular would have been intimately aware of the use of the Order made by Harold Macmillan following the 'night of the long knives' in 1962. Although a cabinet minister, Gardiner was not a natural politician; his espousal of legal reform, civil liberties and human rights appears to have been the determining factor in his CH.

At the time of writing Hailsham was the last lord chancellor to receive the CH. Conferred on him at the conclusion of his first term (1970–74), he was made a Knight of the Garter after his second term (1979–87). His successor, Lord Mackay of Clashfern, was made a Knight of the Thistle at the end of his unprecedented (in the twentieth century) ten years in office (1987–97). The appointments of Hailsham, Gardiner and Elwyn-Jones do not amount to a trend, nor do they establish a precedent for conferring the CH on a lord chancellor by virtue of his office. Even if that were to be argued, Gardiner's CH cannot be cited in support. Such a practice could not in any case really be adopted without raising an undesirable reminder of the now discredited and abandoned days of 'automatic' honours, and a return to the 'badge of office' phase that the CH became for the prime ministers of Australia and New Zealand from the 1939–45 war until the end of the 1980s.

There seems to be no reason why lawyers could not be appointed to the Order in the future, but even the highest proficiency in the law is probably not enough. Despite – in the case of the law lords – the remote and almost unapproachable heights of their office, and their formidably forensic intellects, evidence will be sought of 'something more'; an adjunct to their work that will take them across the threshold of a CH.

Lord Reid 10 June 1967
Possessing an abundance of wisdom, shrewdness and common sense, James Reid was a Scottish lawyer and Conservative politician who reached the heights of a lord of appeal in ordinary by way of the patronage of an English Labour prime minister.

He was born in 1890 at Drem in the county of Haddington, the eldest son of a writer to the signet, who was also a farmer. He was educated at Edinburgh Academy and at Jesus College, Cambridge where he graduated with a first class honours in part one of both the natural sciences (1910) and law (1911) triposes. After Cambridge he attended Scots law classes to qualify himself for admission to the Faculty of Advocates. Qualification followed enlistment in the eighth battalion of the Royal Scots in November 1914, and Reid was the first advocate to be admitted to the faculty wearing uniform. He later transferred to the Machine Gun Corps.

After demobilisation, with the rank of major, he began a law practice in Edinburgh in 1919. He began writing and produced a book on the Agricultural

Holdings (Scotland) Act of 1923, which established his reputation as an authority on agricultural law. 'In time he came to be recognised as an exceptionally competent counsel in handling complex cases which gave scope for his quick analytical mind – his arguments in court being somewhat didactic in manner.'[1] His law practice was never extensive, partly because of his commitment to politics and partly because of prolonged service as a law officer. In 1932 he took silk and in 1945 the Faculty of Advocates elected him dean, holding the office until 1948. 'He did all he could to be helpful, friendly and hospitable, but his commitments in London prevented him from giving the guidance and support normally expected of the elected leader of the Scottish bar. Reid's professional career illustrates in striking fashion that eminence at the Scottish bar and a political career cannot be satisfactorily combined.'[2]

Reid was as much the politician as he was the lawyer. In 1931 he was elected Unionist member of parliament for Stirling and Falkirk Burghs. He lost the seat narrowly in 1935 but in 1937 he was elected for the Hillhead division of Glasgow which he represented until he was appointed a lord of appeal in 1948. In 1936 he joined Stanley Baldwin's government as solicitor general for Scotland and in 1941 Churchill promoted him to be lord advocate. He held office until the Labour victory at the 1945 general election. During the next three years on the opposition benches his acute and perceptive legal mind was put to political use in scrutinising the mass of emergency legislation, authorised by the continuance of wartime powers brought forward by the Labour government, arousing the hostility of sections of the Labour Party in the process. 'No one who sat in that House will ever forget his long frame leaning over the dispatch box while a long finger seemed to stab some transfixed and visibly shrinking minister while some unanswerable point was driven home with courteous but unanswerable logic.'[3]

Surprisingly, it was a Labour prime minister, Clement Attlee, who appointed Reid a lord of appeal in ordinary with a law life peerage in 1948. Some thought that Attlee was cleverly removing a powerful critic from the commons, others recognised that, discounting his political side, Reid was eminently qualified to be a law lord. Naturally desiring to know whether he had a political future, Reid consulted the Conservative Party hierarchy; the response did not encourage him to believe that he had much of a future, so he accepted Attlee's offer. He became the senior law lord in 1962 and held office until his retirement in January 1975 at the age of eighty-four. The quite different forms of law in England and Scotland made his appointment unusual. Although functioning as the supreme court of the United Kingdom, the law lords were almost invariably drawn from the ranks of the English judiciary and the intrusion of a Scottish advocate might have been a matter for resentment. Reid's evident ability confounded any concerns. One of his colleagues, Lord Morris of Borth-y-Gest, paid tribute to his remarkable mastery of law on both sides of the border: 'It was to all of us a constant source of wonder that one whose familiarity with the law and the history of the law of Scotland remained so profound and undimmed should possess an equal familiarity with the law and the history of the law of England.'[4]

Reid was shy, reserved and difficult to know, but his kindness and courtesy were apparent to all and he was held in high respect. After his death, Lord Wilberforce praised him as 'one of the greatest judges who ever sat in this house,' and noted his 'accuracy of thought and precision of reasoning, broad common sense, generous humanity, simple and elegant use of language . . . He was resistant to fashionable trends, but he always saw the law as a moving stream and he kept it moving at a pace unhurried and controlled.'[5]

Reid was made a privy councillor in 1941, a life peer in 1948 on his appointment as a law lord, and a CH in 1967, being cited as 'A Lord of Appeal in Ordinary'. He died in March 1975, two months after his retirement.

Lord Goodman 3 June 1972

Arnold Goodman was a solicitor who was coy about his private life, but turned his analytical mind to almost anything in the field of public life. He was a deeply ambitious man who established an extensive network of contacts and became a trusted confidant of Labour governments in the 1960s and 70s. He numbered a wide range of friends in the world of the arts through his chairmanship of the Arts Council.

He was born in 1913, and he revealed the names of his parents in his entry in *Who's Who*, but that was the extent of his revelation about his early life. He was reticent about the schools that he attended, but later went to University College, London and Downing College, Cambridge, taking first class honours degrees at both. He qualified as a solicitor and began work with a small firm in Grays Inn. At the outbreak of the 1939–45 war he enlisted as a gunner in the Royal Artillery. He joined an anti-aircraft battery then recently formed in Enfield under the command of Major Mortimer Wheeler (later Sir Mortimer Wheeler CH). Although never an orthodox Jew, his pride in his Jewish culture was deep enough for him to feel the call to fight against the anti-Semitic nature of German national socialism and he remained a Zionist to the end of his days.

He remained in Wheeler's unit for two years, and then went to a commission with the RAOC where he established a friendship with Colonel George Wigg (later Lord Wigg) who introduced him to rising figures in the Labour movement, such as Hugh Gaitskell and Harold Wilson. His credibility with the Labour movement rose to new heights in 1957 when he successfully acted on behalf of Aneurin Bevan in a controversial libel action against *The Spectator*. He built up a law practice orientated towards literature, the theatre and the arts generally. 'In the early 1960s the expanding world of commercial television beckoned him and the complex and remunerative law of copyright and libel sang its siren song to good effect.'[6] By now much in demand, he became chairman of the newly constituted board of British Lion Films (1965–72). Goodman was at the peak of his influence during Harold Wilson's premiership (1964–70) and in 1964 Wilson (on the advice of Wigg) used Goodman's negotiating skills to mediate in a strike in the television industry. Goodman was happy to help, but shrank from publicity, refusing to allow himself to be named or photographed, and Wilson thereafter referred to him as 'Mr X'. In recognition Goodman was created a life peer in 1965 but he kept clear of political commitments and sat on the crossbenches in the House of Lords.

After a period (1964–65) as chairman of a committee (on behalf of the Arts Council) looking at the future of London's orchestras, Bevan's widow, Jennie Lee, offered him the chairmanship of the Arts Council (1965–72). During this time he oversaw the planning of the National Theatre, the completion of the Hayward Gallery and the long-term future of London's symphony orchestras, and developed friendships with actors, artists and musicians including Laurence Olivier, Peter Hall, Sybil Thorndike, Francis Bacon, Bridget Riley and Yehudi Menuhin.

His public appointments were numerous and ranged widely through the arts field. He was chairman of Charter Film Productions (1973–84), The Observer Editorial Trust (1967–76), the Newspaper Publishers Association (1970–76), the Committee of Enquiry into Charity Law (1974–76), the Housing Corporation (1973–77), the National Building Agency (1973–78), Motability (1977–94), the Council for Charitable Support (1986–89), as well as deputy chairman of the British Council (1976–91), a director of the Royal Opera House (1972–83), a governor of the Royal Shakespeare Theatre (1972–94) and the College of Law (1975–84), and a member of the South Bank Theatre Board (1968–82). He was also president of the National Book League (1972–85), the Institute of Jewish Affairs (1975–90), the Theatres Advisory Council (1972–95), the Theatre Investment Fund (1985–95, chairman 1976–85), the English National Opera (1986–95), the Theatres Trust (1987–95, chairman 1976–87) and the Association for Business Sponsorship of the Arts (1989–95, chairman 1976–89). His Jewishness found expression in his chairmanship of the Jewish Chronicle Trust (1970–94), and his presidency of the Union of Liberal Progressive Synagogues (1988–95).

To the end of his life he was at his best when presiding over committees. 'He was reliably late in arriving [His volume of memoirs was appropriately entitled *Tell them I'm on my way*] and the more important items on the agenda were tactfully rearranged to coincide with his surprisingly inconspicuous entrances into the committee room. His lack of punctuality never gave offence because its cause was known to be an overloaded programme, not discourtesy . . . He continued at the same time to maintain a thriving practice as a solicitor and to serve the firm that bore his name. For this was the springboard from which he daily plunged into all his non-legal activities. And, by a natural reciprocity, the firm became the beneficiary of these activities, attracting an ever-increasing clientele.'[7]

Goodman was not always successful in his undertakings. Both Harold Wilson and Edward Heath used him in the fruitless negotiations to find a settlement to the problem of unilateral declaration of independence by Rhodesia, but both were doomed, and Goodman only undertook them because of his incurable optimism; and he willingly trekked to and from Rhodesia on several occasions in 1972. He opposed the divided professional legal system and largely on his advice, a royal commission was appointed in 1976 to examine the issue. The outcome was a deep disappointment, the commission deciding to leave the system unchanged and intact.

In 1976 David Astor decided that his resources could no longer maintain *The Observer* and it became necessary to find new owners. As chairman of the Newspaper Publishers Association, Goodman's London flat became the nerve centre of operations. 'Each morning at breakfast time his sitting room became the scene of an almost operatic tableau: the trustees and other notables connected with the paper in a semi-circle around Goodman himself clad in a glittering dressing gown and almost recumbent on a raised medical chair, while in adjoining rooms mandarins of the industrial, commercial and entertainments worlds patiently awaited their chance to consult the oracle if only for a few minutes.'[8]

In 1976 he accepted the appointment as master of University College, Oxford but retired in 1986. He could not give it full-time attention, but he was diligent and entertained every junior member of the college in his lodgings each year.

In 1987 he was honoured with a gala performance at the London Colosseum, and in 1993 his eightieth birthday was marked by a banquet for 400 of his friends at the hall of Lincoln's Inn. But at heart he was a lonely person. He never married and the person he felt closest to was his long-dead elder brother about whom, as about so much else in his private life, he was tantalisingly reticent in his memoirs. He died in 1995.

He was appointed a CH in 1972 on his retirement from the Arts Council and at the conclusion of a series of visits to Rhodesia, 'For public services'. 'I received a letter from Ted Heath,' he recalled, 'who asked whether it would be acceptable to me to receive a CH. The letter was couched in terms which contrived to suggest that if it was not acceptable then he would think of something better. But, if I may say so, it was totally acceptable, and I could not think of anything better, so I agreed with alacrity . . . The conferment of the CH stands out as something of special quality and considerable pleasure.'[9]

Lord Hailsham of St Marylebone 5 April 1974
Quintin Hogg was a flamboyant and ebullient lawyer and politician whose tendency to employ polemic and histrionics was always underpinned by an undisputed and generally admired integrity and courage. He was lord chancellor in three Conservative governments (1970–74, 1979–83 and 1983–87), and the longest serving holder of that office in the twentieth century.

He was born in 1907, the elder son of Douglas Hogg, first Viscount Hailsham, who was himself lord chancellor (1928–29 and 1935–38). He was educated at Eton and Christ Church, Oxford, where he gained firsts in both moderations and literae humaniores. He was elected a fellow of All Souls College in 1931 and was called to the bar by Lincoln's Inn in 1932. In 1938 he was elected to parliament as Conservative MP for the city of Oxford as a defender of Chamberlain's policy of appeasement, and resigned his fellowship (he was reelected in 1961). At the outbreak of the 1939–45 war he joined the Tower Hamlets Rifles in the Rifle Brigade, serving with the Middle Eastern land forces, and being wounded in the Western desert in 1941.

He returned to politics in 1942, becoming a founder member of the Tory reform committee, a pressure group of Conservative backbench members to commit the country to social reform and the creation of a welfare state. In the brief Conservative caretaker government of 1945 he was made joint parliamentary under-secretary of state for air, before spending five years relishing passionate assaults on the Labour government from the opposition benches. He used the time to explore the great themes of Conservative philosophy in a book, *The case for conservatism*, published in 1947. The need for continuity in social and political life, the importance of a proper balance between social cohesion and personal liberty, the connection between religious belief (he was a devout Anglican) and social stability, and the need to subordinate the nation's domestic ambitions to the demands of defence and foreign policy remained paramount until the 1960s, when they no longer appealed to a new generation of Conservative politicians.

On the death of his father in 1950 he became the second Viscount Hailsham, and resigned his seat in the house of commons. He took silk in 1953 and became a bencher of Lincoln's Inn in 1956. Competent lawyer though he was, the call of politics was still strong, and in September of the same year he was appointed first lord of the admiralty. He found it easy vigorously to defend the decisions first to enter and shortly afterwards to withdraw from the Suez debacle. His tenure of office lasted only until January 1957 when Harold Macmillan made him minister of education. 'He surprised teachers and education administrators by his freedom from doctrinaire prejudices over such matters as comprehensive education. He was admired by his civil servants as a doughty fighter for his department in and out of Cabinet.'[10] Trusted and well-liked, he was made lord president of the council, deputy leader of the house of lords, and chairman of the Conservative Party in September 1957. He gave a barnstorming performance at the Conservative Party's annual conference which contributed towards the party's victory at the 1959 election.

His reward was to be made lord privy seal (1959–60) in the new government and then again lord president of the council (1960–64). He was additionally minister for science and technology (1959–64), minister with special responsibility for sport (1962–64), minister dealing with unemployment in the north-east (1963–64), with higher education (1963–64), and secretary of state for education and science (April-October 1964). But his eyes had been set on higher things. At the party conference in 1963, Harold Macmillan intimated his intention to retire from the premiership, and Hailsham left no doubt in the minds of anyone that he intended to seek the post. He had many supporters, especially among the constituency representatives, but the decision rested with the party hierarchy, and his flamboyance, pugnaciousness and volatility made them wary of entrusting the future of the party to someone with a tendency to provoke rows. Much to his disappointment, he was defeated by the Earl of Home, another hereditary peer with a more ancient lineage. Like Home he renounced his peerage and was reelected to the Commons as member for St Marylebone in December 1963.

Six years on the opposition benches followed the government's defeat in the 1964 election, and by the time the Conservative Party was returned to power in 1970 under Edward Heath, Hogg was sixty-three and had made the transition to elder statesman. He was made lord chancellor, given a life peerage with the title of Lord Hailsham of St Marylebone, and held the office for a total of thirteen years. Conscientiously, but with a lack of enthusiasm (born of an innate sense of tradition) he implemented the radical overhaul of the criminal courts system – the basic principles of which had been initiated by his Labour predecessor Gerald Gardiner – under the terms of the Courts Act 1971.

As lord chancellor, his best work was probably done during Edward Heath's administration. Five more years in opposition followed (1974–79) and when the Conservatives returned to power under Margaret Thatcher he was then seventy-three, a widower (his second wife had died tragically in a riding accident in Australia in 1978), and wore an old-fashioned Edwardian air. That he was appointed lord chancellor in 1979 and reappointed in 1983 was a demonstration of Thatcher's regard and affection for him. But it was more a consolation after the death of his wife. His best work was in the past and in 1987 it was made clear to him that there would be no further extension. He was eighty years old and unable to deal swiftly and efficiently with the pressures of high office.

Among his extra-parliamentary activities he was rector of the University of Glasgow (1959–62) and chancellor of the University of Buckingham (1983–92). His publications included *The law of arbitration* (1935), *One year's work* (1944), *The law and employers' liability* (1944), *The times we live in* (1944), *Making peace* (1945), *The left was never right* (1945), *The purpose of parliament* (1946), *The case for conservatism* (1947), *The law of monopolies, restrictive practices and resale price maintenance* (1956), *The conservative case* (1959), *Interdependence* (1961), *Science and politics* (1963), *The devil's own song* (1968), *The door wherein I went* (1975), *Elective dictatorship* (1976), *The dilemma of democracy* (1978), *Hamlyn revisited: the British legal system* (1983), *A sparrow's flight* (1990), *On the constitution* (1992), and *Values: collapse and cure* (1994).

Unusually for a non-scientist, he was proud to be elected a fellow of the Royal Society in 1973. He was appointed a CH in 1974 shortly after Edward Heath relinquished office following an uncertain general election result. He was gazetted as 'Lord High Chancellor of Great Britain 1970–1974', leaving the reader to draw the inference that he was not expected to resume the office. After his second retirement he was created a Knight of the Garter in 1988. He lived to be ninety-four and died in 2001.

Lord Gardiner 1 January 1975

Gerald Gardiner, lord chancellor in the Labour governments of 1964–70, was a libertarian reformer who instituted far-reaching reforms of the criminal justice system, including the establishment of the Family Division of the High Court and the abolition of capital punishment.

He was born in 1900 at Cadogan Square, London, the son of Sir Robert Gardiner, an English businessman with interests in the theatre and shipping, and a Prussian mother. He was educated at Harrow and was just old enough to see service in the 1914–18 war, serving briefly in 1918 as a second lieutenant in the Coldstream Guards. At the end of the war he joined the Peace Pledge Union and went to Magdalen College, Cambridge from where he graduated with a fourth class degree in jurisprudence in 1923. His time at Cambridge was not easy, due at least in part to his libertarian and egalitarian spirit which led to a rebelliousness. He was rusticated for two terms in 1921 and threatened with rustication in November 1922 for publishing a pamphlet attacking the restrictions on women undergraduates.

He was called to the bar in 1925 and, initially supported by his father, he had a busy practice by the end of the 1930s, 'His success lay in meticulous preparation of cases and in the clarity and courteous, unrhetorical style with which he addressed judge, jury or witnesses, although with the last he could, if necessary, be icy.'[11] He was not called up during the 1939–45 war, but joined the Friends' Ambulance Unit (1943–45) and eventually commanded its sections on the western front. On leaving for war service he wrote to the lord chancellor, Viscount Simon, about the legal aid crisis arising from the departure for war service of the volunteers who provided the minimal aid then available. His initiative ultimately led to the Legal Aid and Advice Act of 1949. He joined the Haldane Society which supported law reform. In 1945 when it was threatened by a take-over of communist sympathisers he led a secession to form the Society of Labour Lawyers, of which he became chairman. His passion for reform brought him membership of the committee on supreme court practice and procedure (1947–53) and the lord chancellor's law reform committee (1952–63).

At the end of the war he returned to the bar, took silk in 1948, and served as chairman of the Bar Council in 1958 and 1959. He became known as fearless, tenacious and imperturbable and a master of lucid exposition. His notable cases included the prosecution in 1960 under the Obscene Publications Act (1959) of Penguin Books for publishing *Lady Chatterley's Lover* by D. H. Lawrence in which the acquittal Gardiner won for the defendants led to a significant widening of the permissible boundaries in literature; and in 1961 the proceedings against the Electrical Trades Union, in which he exposed the ballot-rigging of its communist officials.

Since Cambridge his sympathies had been with the political left and he joined the Labour Party in the 1930s. In 1951 he stood for West Croydon and although only narrowly defeated by the Conservative candidate, it was his only attempt to stand for election to the house of commons. He served as an alderman on London county council (1961–63) and in 1963 Harold Wilson nominated him for a life peerage. With the Labour victory in 1964 Gardiner became lord chancellor, the first person in modern times to fill the office without having previously sat either in the house of commons or on the bench of judges.

He gave expression to his desire for reform outlined in *Law reform now* (1963), which he edited. He had argued against capital punishment in his book *Capital punishment as a deterrent* (1956) He was joint chairman (with Victor Gollancz) of the national campaign for abolition of capital punishment, and during his time in office he had the pleasure of seeing it first temporarily (1965) and then permanently (1969) abolished. The laws on abortion and homosexuality were humanised and in 1966 he set up a commission to overhaul the machinery of the criminal courts, breaking with precedent and appointing a businessman (Lord Beeching) as its chairman. The commission's far-reaching recommendations, including the destruction of the ancient assize and the ending of the presence since medieval times of high court judges at many ancient towns, were embodied in the Courts Act 1971. He appointed the first woman high court judge (Dame Elizabeth Lane in 1965). He instituted compulsory and systematic training for lay magistrates ('who thus gradually ceased to be the great unlearned while remaining the great unpaid'[12]) and sought to ensure that they were drawn from as wide as possible a cross section of the community. Unlike other occupants of the office of lord chancellor, 'he was not really a politician, and he was ideologically perhaps less a socialist than an advanced and very independent radical . . . He made little impact on the political scene, and he remained to the end almost unknown to the general public.'[13]

He retired from the opposition front benches in 1971 but was kept active. In 1971–72 he was one of three privy councillors appointed by the Conservative government to investigate the alleged abuse of interrogation procedures in Northern Ireland. The majority were prepared to condone the procedures complained of, but it was Gardiner's minority report 'which in remarkable tribute to his legal and moral authority, was accepted by Edward Heath's government. Nevertheless he could make practical compromises, as when as chairman of another committee on Northern Ireland in 1975 he approved the continuation for the time being of detention without trial.'[14] Gardiner was also president of the Howard League for Penal Reform, and one of the people most instrumental in bringing about the formation of 'Justice', and as chairman of the executive committee he played a major part in successful campaigns for the appointment of a parliamentary commissioner and the scheme for compensating victims of crimes of violence, and he initiated and successfully carried through the campaign for the Rehabilitation of Offenders Act 1974.

A fellow lawyer, Arnold Goodman, did not warm to Gardiner's distant manner: 'There was a Puritan austerity about him that made one doubt whether he ever enjoyed anything at all. I never took a meal with him, but I should be surprised to find that he ate with a good appetite . . . I do not know if he was teetotal, but my guess would be that he was. He was a lord chancellor with a limited range. His practice was an entirely common-law one: he advised and appeared for parties on libel actions; he advised on contracts and similar matters dealt with in common-law courts. On chancery matters he was not well-known, nor indeed on matrimonial matters, although he appeared several times in leading divorce cases.'[15] Goodman's comment, while factually accurate was a shallow assessment. Although he could appear cold, Gardiner was essentially a shy man whose reserve and formality covered a painful inability to engage in small talk.

His lifelong egalitarianism found expression again when he accepted the chancellorship of the Open University (1973–78). As chancellor, he wanted to understand the life of the students of this innovative university, so he enrolled for and successfully completed a three year degree course in social sciences. He was proud of the achievement and included 'BA Open Univ., 1977' in his entry in *Who's Who*.

He was made a CH in 1975 as 'Chairman of the Council of Justice'. He died in 1990.

Lord Morris of Borth-y-Gest 14 June 1975

John William Morris, known as 'John Willie' was a lawyer who rose to be a lord of appeal in ordinary, and also – something that would have gladdened the heart of David Lloyd George – an ardent Welshman.

He was born in Liverpool in 1896, the younger son of a bank manager, and educated at the Liverpool Institute that he left in 1916 to join the Royal Welch Fusiliers. He served in France, rose to the rank of captain and was awarded the Military Cross. On demobilisation, he went to Trinity Hall, Cambridge from where he graduated in law in 1920. In 1921 he was called to the bar at Inner Temple and began practising on the northern circuit. He stood for parliament in 1923 and 1924, unsuccessfully contesting Ilford for the Liberal Party.

In 1935 he took silk and was judge of appeal in the Isle of Man (1935–45). In 1945 he was appointed a high court judge in the King's Bench division and from there he went to the highest ranks of his profession, becoming a lord justice of appeal in 1951 and a lord of appeal in ordinary in 1960. As a law lord he was made a peer and added the territorial designation 'of Borth-y-Gest' in affection for a seaside village near Porthmadog which he loved from his many childhood holidays there.

Morris was a hard working if not an outstanding law lord. He was remembered as a shy and hesitant man of strong opinions who was too hesitant to express them. 'Morris was the soul of consideration to those who appeared before him. Some would say that at times he was over-patient and could with advantage have speeded the hearing of a case. But in his determination to ensure that a just conclusion was arrived at, he saw to it that every point raised was carefully and, indeed, exhaustively examined. Above all he was vigilant in protecting the freedom of the individual when threatened by the Executive, and he exhibited judicial valour consistently and in full measure.'[16] In 1963–64 he chaired the Home Office committee on jury service.

Born in England and not fluent in Welsh, he was nevertheless devoted to Wales and proud of his Welsh ancestry. He was honorary standing counsel to the University of Wales (1938–45) and pro-chancellor (1956–74). In that capacity he lent his influence on the side of moderation during the difficult debates over the future of the university as a national institution. A member of the gorsedd of bards he regularly robed and processed at the annual Royal National Eisteddfod. He was a vice-president and life member of the Honourable Society of Cymmrodorion and chairman of the London Welsh Association (1951–53). For over a quarter of a century he sat as chairman of the Caernarfonshire quarter sessions. When in London he worshipped at the Welsh Congregational Chapel in King's Cross Road where Elvet Lewis CH had been minister before the 1939–45 war. He retired as a law lord in 1975, and during the 1977 debates he spoke eloquently in favour of devolution for Wales.

His professional eminence together with his personal qualities, marked by charm, modesty, affability and a gentle manner – both in court and out – made him possibly the most distinguished Welsh public figure outside Wales. He was one of the very few Welshmen – and probably the first – maintaining close connections with Wales to serve as a law lord.

He was appointed a CBE in 1945, knighted in 1945, made a privy councillor in 1951, and a CH in 1975 'For public services in Wales'. He never married and died in 1979 at Porthmadog.

Lord Elwyn-Jones 27 May 1976
Elwyn Jones was lord chancellor during the Labour government 1974–79. He was a warm-hearted man with an intense concern for human freedom and justice, born of poverty in the Welsh valleys and his experiences as a travelling lawyer in the cause of democracy in prewar Europe.

He was born in Llanelli in 1909, the youngest son of a tin plate rollerman. His father was an elder of the Tabernacle Congregational chapel and a lifelong socialist. Jones was educated at Llanelli Grammar School, University College, Aberystwyth and Gonville and Caius College, Cambridge from where he graduated with a degree in history in 1931. He went to Grays Inn and was called to the bar in 1935. Inheriting his father's concerns and political principles, he joined the Fabian Society. Through this connection he later responded to an urgent request from Hugh Gaitskell, then in Vienna, to go there and give legal help to the beleaguered Austrian Social Democrats during the time of the chancellorship of Engelbert Dolfuss (1932–34). What he saw led him to become involved in the deepening European problem and he accepted invitations from the International Association of Democratic Lawyers to attend political trials in Germany, Greece, Hungary and Romania. He was dismayed by the systematic persecution of the left, and organised help for those accused. He wrote three books for the Left Book Club: *Hitler's drive to the east* (1937), *The battle for peace* (1938) and *The attack from within* (1939).

Early in the 1930s he rejected his earlier pacifism and became a territorial army volunteer. During the 1939–45 war he served with the Royal Artillery in North Africa and Italy, but ended the war as a deputy judge advocate (1943–45) attending many courts martial and inquiries into alleged Nazi brutalities. He was elected to the House of Commons in 1945 as Labour member for Plaistow (West Ham). He became parliamentary private secretary (1946–51) to Sir Hartley Shawcross, the attorney general, and joined the team of counsel for the prosecution at the Nuremberg war trials. He was member for West Ham South (1950–74) and finally Newham South (1974).

A seat in the house of commons was no barrier to his legal career at first on the Wales and Chester circuit and then in London. He cherished his Welsh background and nothing pleased him more than his Welsh judicial appointments. He was recorder of Merthyr Tydfil (1949–53) and took silk in 1953. He was recorder of Swansea (1953–60), Cardiff (1960–64) and Kingston upon Thames (1964–74). With Labour victory at the 1964 election Harold Wilson appointed him attorney general. He was counsel for the tribunal in the enquiry into the 1965 Aberfan disaster, in which over 100 children had been killed in a Welsh village school by the movement of a coal slurry tip. He was the prosecutor in the moors murder case against Ian Brady and Myra Hindley.

With the defeat of the Labour government in the 1970 election, he returned to his legal practice. In the February 1974 election he was elected for the new constituency of Newham South, but when the Labour Party formed a government after a short hiatus, Harold Wilson appointed him lord chancellor and he resigned his seat. Urged to take a territorial title he decided instead (there were a few precedents) to hyphenate his first name and surname to produce the composite title of 'Lord Elwyn-Jones'.

His period as lord chancellor was not especially notable, though he encouraged the growth of law centres, whose numbers had quadrupled by the time he left office with the defeat of the Labour government in 1979. He was made a lord of appeal in ordinary in 1979 and continued in that office until his death. 'He was not a profound lawyer. Law as such was not his prime interest; politics were. He was very much a political lawyer of swift intelligence, good judgement and rare sensibility; more concerned that the legal system should provide the means of achieving true justice than with handing down great judgements himself.'[17] Outside the worlds of politics and the law, he was president of University College, Cardiff (1971–88) and of the Mental Heath Foundation (1980–89).

He was made a privy councillor in 1964, knighted in 1964 and uniquely made a CH in 1976 while still in office. He received the honour in Harold Wilson's controversial resignation honours list, as 'The Lord Chancellor'. He died in 1989.

CHAPTER THIRTEEN

National voices

JOURNALISTS AND BROADCASTERS

'Now I declare that's too bad!' Humpty Dumpty cried, breaking into a sudden passion. 'You've been listening at doors – and behind trees – and down chimneys – or you couldn't have known it!'

'Humpty Dumpty', *Through the looking-glass*, Lewis Carroll

A comparatively small group of ten journalists and two broadcasters have been appointed Companions of Honour, and the category will probably never be numerous. As with every other group, national prominence or national influence have been the broad criteria. The long-serving broadsheet editors of the twentieth century are no longer to be found, and newspapers themselves are no longer the foremost means of disseminating information and influencing public opinion. Their role has been at least complemented and probably overtaken by television in the second half of the twentieth century and by the worldwide web in the twenty-first century. With the exception of David Astor (1993), whose CH was more in recognition of a lifetime of service of which journalism was only a part, the other nine journalists were prominent in the years before 1950; the two broadcasters came to the public eye in the decades after 1950.

The first two appointments in the category were typical of the interests of David Lloyd George and do not reflect the standards of later appointments. Robertson Nicoll (1921) was the editor of the *British Weekly*, a journal that was the mouthpiece of the British nonconformist churches. Vincent Evans (1922), was given the CH for a mixture of public service in and to Wales, including services to Welsh literature, but his writing was never of the standard that would qualify him for a place among the 'literary' Companions of Honour. Looking at the totality of his public service, as much as the citation in the *London Gazette*, he was clearly honoured more for being 'Welsh' than for any specific aspect. His early journalistic work just about qualifies him for inclusion in this chapter.

Nicoll the nonconformist and Evans the Welshman were loyal supporters of the policies of David Lloyd George, the Welsh nonconformist prime minister, and their patriotic drum beating during the 1914–18 war was almost certainly a 'value added' factor leading to the CH.

After Evans' CH, ten years passed before the appointment of the dilettante Edward Verrall Lucas (1932), the lightweight nature, readable style and diverse content of whose books and articles gave him a popular appeal in the years between the two world wars. His populist writings were well known in his lifetime, but he is now completely forgotten.

Lucas was followed five years later by Alfred Spender (1937), the first of a small group of editors of national repute. Editor of the *Westminster Gazette* (1896–1922), Spender was highly influential with successive Liberal governments for a quarter of a century and was still sufficiently esteemed to be given a CH by a Conservative government in 1937 at the age of seventy-five. Howell Gwynne (1938) edited the *Morning Post* (1911–37) and was respected enough to enjoy a personal influence out of proportion to the small and declining circulation of his newspaper. James Garvin (1941) was a wilful maverick who edited the *Observer* for more than thirty years (1908–42) until forced to retire by an irritated proprietor whose views he had disregarded once too often. Arthur Mann (1941) was another independent-minded journalist, who edited the *Yorkshire Post* for twenty years (1919–39) and was remembered for his opposition to appeasement and for a strong leading article that broke the conspiracy of silence surrounding the crisis that led to the abdication of King Edward VIII. Robertson Scott (1947) was an unusual addition to the list. He was the founder, proprietor and one-man editor of *Countryman*, a quarterly journal in which he sought to convey his own love of the reality as well as the beauty of English rural life. James Bone (1947) loved London and for thirty-three years (1912–45) was London editor of the *Manchester Guardian*, daily revealing to the world anything of any importance that was happening in the capital city. At the time of writing, David Astor (1993) is the last of the long-serving and distinguished journalists to receive the CH. Editor of the *Observer* for twenty-seven years, he gave it a liberal and independent stance, and his retirement in 1975 marked the end of more than sixty years of the Astor family's proprietorship of the newspaper. The conferment of his CH, eighteen years after his retirement as editor, was more a recognition of his extensive humanitarian public service than his long editorship of a declining newspaper.

At the height of their careers, Spender, Gwynne, Garvin, Mann, Bone, Scott and Astor were influential and long-serving journalists with national reputations and with not less than twenty years in an editorial chair of some kind, and, with the exception of Astor, they operated in a pre-television age. In the generally changing world of the media, not least the development of cyberspace and electronic publication, it seems unlikely that journalists of their kind will again be accorded such a high level of national recognition.

The two broadcasters who feature in this chapter became national figures through the newer medium of television. Sir Peter Scott (1987) and Sir David Attenborough (1995) – the latter continuing and extending the work of the former – brought the fascinating and entrancing world of wildlife into the homes of the nation, and turned the British public into students without them realising it. Their work was fundamentally educational, and constituted a significant movement in the general extension of knowledge in the second half of the twentieth century, and was set against a growing interest in conservation and other 'green' issues.

Sir Robertson Nicoll 4 June 1921
Robertson Nicoll was a Scottish nonconformist minister turned journalist whose dated religious writings have not passed the test of time, but he was editor of *The British Weekly*, probably the most powerful voice in British nonconformity at the time, and a close political supporter of the policies of David Lloyd George.

He was born at Lumsden in Aberdeenshire in 1851, the elder son of a minister of the Free Church of Scotland. His father amassed some 17,000 volumes on a variety of subjects and his children, who were allowed free access to this large private library, developed a love of books.

Nicoll was educated at the parish school at Auchindoir, Aberdeenshire and then at the University of Aberdeen, from where he graduated in 1870. He seemed destined to follow his father into the ministry of the Free Church of Scotland, and after graduation, he spent four years in theological training, contributing regularly to the *Aberdeen Journal*, writing reviews and literary notes. He was ordained in 1874 and served as an assistant at Dufftown, Banffshire. In 1877 he was inducted as minister of the Free Church of Kelso and stayed there for seven and a half years until ill-health compelled his resignation in 1884. His mother, a sister and an only brother had died of consumption and he was ordered for the sake of his health to move to the south. He went to live at Norwood in southeast London. At Kelso he had established a connection with the publishers Hodder and Stoughton that lasted to the end of his life. They appointed him editor of their monthly theological magazine *The Expositor*, and he directed it from January 1885 until his death. In 1886 the company appointed him editor of a new magazine, *The British Weekly: A Journal of Social and Christian Progress*, which provided him with a nationwide voice until his death thirty-seven years later. His aim was to establish a penny religious journal in which 'everything should be treated in a Christian spirit.'[1] It became the most powerful nonconformist newspaper of its day, and with few interruptions, Nicoll contributed a weekly series of letters, signed 'Claudius Clear', for thirty years. Two volumes of selected letters were later published: *The daybook of Claudius Clear* (1905) and *A bookman's letters* (1913). Other literary efforts followed. In 1891 he founded *The Bookman*, a literary monthly, and in 1893, *The Woman at Home*, an illustrated magazine. In 1892 he moved from Norwood to an old Georgian house in Hampstead, which he extended by constructing a library to house his 24,000 volumes.

From about 1900, Nicoll threw himself into political controversies for the next twenty years and ended a passionate supporter of Lloyd George. He championed the movement of 'passive resistance' to Balfour's Education Bill of 1902. He became an ardent supporter of the social legislation identified with Lloyd George, and during the 1914–18 war he made *The British Weekly* a focus of nonconformist support of the government, adopting the violently bellicose language of many of his contemporaries. His nonconformism, his enthusiasm for radical Liberalism and his powerful journalistic platform made him a natural friend of Lloyd George and his cabinet, and he was a regular attender at the prime minister's political breakfasts at Downing Street. There he would find himself in the company of other distinguished voices of the Free Church such as J. H. Shakespeare, John Clifford and Scott Lidgett.

Nicoll was knighted in 1909 and made a CH by Lloyd George in 1921, as 'Editor of the "British Weekly" since 1886'. His health began to fail after 1920, but he continued to write until a few weeks before his death in 1923.

Sir Vincent Evans 19 October 1922
Vincent Evans was a London-based Welshman who was widely involved in Welsh institutions, and was made a CH for his services to Wales in the resignation list of the only Welsh prime minister. His appointment as a CH was undeniably due to his Welshness more than anything else.

He was the elder son a Welsh farmer and was born in the parish of Llangelynin, Merionethshire. He was said to have been born on 18 November 1851 according to the *Dictionary of national biography*, or 25 November 1852 according to the *Dictionary of Welsh biography*. At the time of his death, some sources stated that he was eighty-seven, which would place his year of birth around 1847. Given this uncertainty and that there is no official record of the date of his birth, two facts are undisputed: firstly, his birth was never registered, and secondly he himself never knew his date of birth.

After early years as a pupil teacher and then as an assistant in the village store, he moved to London in 1872, where he remained until his death. Clerical employment led to him becoming first secretary and then managing director of the Chancery Lane Safe Deposit and Offices Company Ltd. He was attracted to journalism and became a member of the parliamentary press gallery. He was responsible for the London letter in the *South Wales Daily News* for many years and became well acquainted with the younger Welsh members of parliament, especially with David Lloyd George, who was elected member for Caernarfon in 1880. 'The strong national feeling which manifested itself in Wales during the last two decades of the nineteenth century looked to the "London Welsh" for guidance, and Evan's interests and associations connected him with many bodies.'[2] In 1881 he became secretary and editor of the publications of the National Eisteddfod Association and in 1884 a member of the Honourable Society of Cymmrodorion, the council of which he joined in 1886. He became secretary of the society in 1887 and later undertook editorship of the society's publications and may be said to have re-established the society. He retained his offices in both these institutions until his death. He was a governor of the Welsh National Museum, the National Library of Wales, and the university colleges at Aberystwyth and Bangor; vice-president and member of the executive committee of the Cambrian Archaeological Society (he was president in 1918); chairman of the Royal Commission on Ancient Monuments in Wales and Monmouthshire, the Advisory Board on Ancient Monuments (Wales), the executive committee of the Welsh Bibliographical Society, and the London Welsh Aid Charitable Society; and a member of the executive committee and treasurer of the Welsh Folk Song Society. Although he made no claim to scholarship he published many articles in the *Cymmrodor* and the *Transactions* of the Cymmrodorion Society. He also took a large part in recruiting and organising the London Welsh battalions during the 1914–18 war and was chairman of the executive committee of the London Welsh Battalions (1914–18), honorary treasurer of the National Fund for Welsh Troops (1915–19), and trustee of the Welsh Troops' Children's Fund (1918–20).

He was knighted in 1909 for his services to Wales and appointed a CH in 1922 'For services to Welsh Literature and to Welsh National Institutions.' Against his name on a list of those submitted for honours to King George V was a terse note in the king's own handwriting: 'Too many Welshmen.'[3] Evans died in 1934.

Edward Verrall Lucas 3 June 1932

Edward Lucas was a well-known and popular journalist, essayist and critic between the two world wars who wrote prolifically, though never deeply, on any subject which happened to interest him.

He was born at Eltham in Kent in 1868, the son of Quaker parents, his father being an agent for insurance companies and building societies. He revolted against his father's piety without works and developed a strong streak of cynicism. His parents moved to Brighton shortly after his birth and he went to eleven schools in succession before being apprenticed at the age of sixteen to a Brighton bookseller. His first taste of journalism came when he joined the staff of the *Sussex Daily News* at eighteen. In 1892 he went to London to attend lectures at University College, read voraciously and in 1893 joined the staff of the *Globe* a London evening paper (absorbed by the *Pall Mall Gazette* in 1921). 'The manner that he cultivated for this purpose was, in appearance so effortless, that only by its readableness could its craft be ascertained. As a young journalist he spent many of his evenings translating Maupassant, not for publication, but as a practice in style.'[4]

His publications included *Listener's lure* (1905), *One day and another* (1909), *Old lamps for new* (1911), *Loiterer's harvest* (1913), *Cloud and silver* (1916), *A rover I would be* (1928). A series of travelogues included *Highways and byways in Sussex* (1904), *A wanderer in Holland* (1905), *A wanderer in Paris* (1909), *A wanderer in Florence* (1912), *Zigzags in France* (1925). Short books on painters included *Vermeer of Delft* (1922), *John Constable the painter* (1924) and *Vermeer the magical* (1929), 'I know very little about pictures,' he honestly admitted, 'but I like to write about them for the benefit of those who know less.'[5] He tried a few romances, including *Over Bemerton's* (1908), *Rose over Rose* (1921) and *Genevra's money* (1922). 'He was accustomed to say that he could not write a novel, because no novel made out human beings as bad as they really were.'[6] He produced an edition of *The works of Charles and Mary Lamb* (seven volumes, 1903–05) and a *Life of Charles Lamb* (two volumes 1905). He was a prolific contributor to *Punch* and a member of its staff and in 1924 he became chairman of Methuen's Publishing Company. 'He . . . emerged more and more as an apostle of the humanities, and if no optimist himself, a cause of optimism in others. He made it more and more his aim to communicate the delight which he found in art, travel and letters to a rapidly growing circle of readers. His publications include many anthologies and about thirty collections of light essays on almost any subject that took his fancy. To estimate the permanent value of his work is difficult, but he undoubtedly broadened the horizon of culture for a great number of readers by the easy introduction which he gave them to books that they would not otherwise have read, and pictures which they would not have seen; at the same time he helped to liberate the language of the critic and essayist from undue pedantry and affectation. Often preferring the quaint to the profound, and claiming neither deep study nor creative imagination, he established himself by dint of good taste, observation and wit as a man of letters, gaining friendship and admiration alike from the learned and the less critical.'[7]

He was made a CH in 1932 for his services as 'Author, Journalist and Publisher.' He died in 1938.

John Alfred Spender 11 May 1937
Alfred Spender was an influential political journalist, whose Liberal politics were declaimed for twenty-six years on the front page of the *Westminster Gazette*, and who enjoyed unrivalled access to government ministers during the last great years of the Liberal Party in the early twentieth century.

Spender was born in 1862 the son of a physician father and a novelist mother whose income enabled her to pay for the education of her children. He was educated at Bath College and at Balliol College, Oxford where he took a first class in classical moderations (1882) and narrowly missed a first class in literae humaniores (1885), largely owing to illness during the examination.

He left Oxford with vague thoughts of either teaching or studying for the bar. In the event he did neither. An uncle, who was both owner of the *Eastern Morning News* of Hull and also a Liberal parliamentary candidate, engaged him as his private secretary. Working in the newspaper office, he was soon deputising for the editor, and after a brief and chequered career on the London *Echo* he became editor of the *Eastern Morning News* in 1886 at the age of twenty-three. He left in 1891, after differences with his uncle, and went to live at Toynbee Hall, London where he wrote his first book: *The state and pensions in old age* (1892).

He had occasionally written for the *Pall Mall Gazette* and in 1892 he became its assistant editor. Within a month the journal had been sold to Waldorf Astor who objected to its Liberal politics. The entire staff resigned, and with financial support from Sir George Newnes, the founder of *Tit-Bits* and the *Strand Magazine*, they launched the *Westminster Gazette* in 1893 to keep alive the Liberal views of the *Pall Mall Gazette*. Spender became editor in 1896. 'So began one of the most remarkable editorships in British journalism, consisting as it did of the direction of a paper which never had a circulation greater than 27,000 and during most of its existence failed to touch 20,000; which regularly sustained a financial loss . . . and which undoubtedly exerted a greater influence per copy than any other paper in the kingdom . . . It was the front page leader – nearly always from Spender's pen – which sold the *Westminster*; of no other papers, certainly of no other evening paper, could as much be said . . . Day by day on that pea-green front page Spender preached a robust and reasoned Liberalism which sometimes left impetuous Radicals impatient but won high and constant commendation from such leaders as Rosebery, Campbell-Bannerman, Asquith, Haldane and Morley. With all of them Spender stood on terms of confidential friendship . . . It is not too much to say that but for his efforts at a critical moment in December 1905 Campbell-Bannerman's cabinet might never have been formed. Once it was formed, and the sweeping Liberal victory of 1906 achieved, Spender found himself the most influential political journalist of his day. On terms of intimacy with half the cabinet, described on occasions as an unofficial cabinet minister, he enjoyed regularly confidences which he was too scrupulous to use as news, but which enabled him to write of the political problems of the moment with a background of knowledge unique in the journalism of the period.'[8]

Spender's influence declined after 1916, as did the Liberal Party. The split between Herbert Asquith and Lloyd George dealt Liberalism a blow from which it never really recovered. Spender loyally supported Asquith, but there were now two factions within Liberalism and the *Westminster* could no longer appeal to the whole party. The proprietor decided to transform it into a morning paper in November 1921 and Spender's editorship ended in October 1922. He regularly contributed articles to the new *Westminster Gazette*, but the paper's decline paralleled that of the Liberal Party and it was incorporated with the *Daily News* in 1928.

Spender wrote biographies of Henry Campbell-Bannerman (1923), Viscount Cowdray (1930), Sir Robert Hudson (1930) and Herbert Asquith (1932) and a number of other works including *The public life* (1925), *The changing east* (1926), *Life, journalism and politics* (1927), *Fifty years of Europe* (1933), *These times* (1934), *A short history of our times* (1934), *Great Britain, empire and commonwealth 1886–1935* (1936), *Men and things* (1937), *The government of mankind* (1938), and *New lamps and ancient lights* (1940). He was a member of two royal commissions, on divorce and matrimonial causes (1909–12), and on the private manufacture of armaments (1935–36). He was a member of Lord Milner's mission to Egypt (1919–20). In 1926 he was president of the National Liberal Federation.

Spender had declined to be 'decorated' – probably with a knighthood – in Asquith's resignation honours list in 1916.[9] He was made a CH 'For services to literature and journalism' in the Coronation Honours List 1937, long after his greatest days of influence, and died in 1942.

Howell Gwynne 1 January 1938
Howell Gwynne's long career as a journalist was marked by editorships of two newspapers – the *Standard* and the *Morning Post* – both of which were relatively unsuccessful when measured by circulation, but the high respect in which he was held gave him considerable influence.

He was born in the district of Kilvey near Swansea in 1866, the son of a schoolmaster, and educated at Swansea Grammar School and 'abroad' according to his entry in *Who's Who*. In 1893 after a short spell as Balkans correspondent of *The Times*, he was appointed Reuter's correspondent in Romania, and remained with the agency until 1904. Reuter's used him as a war and special correspondent, and he covered a succession of wars. He went to Ashanti in 1895, and in 1896 he accompanied Kitchener to Dongola. In 1897 he followed the Greco-Turkish war, and in 1898–99 he was in Peking. He covered the South African War 1899–1902, organising Reuter's South African war service and becoming a lifelong friend of Lord Roberts, the supreme commander in South Africa. He returned to England in November 1902 but went back to South Africa later in the same month, accompanying Joseph Chamberlain, the colonial secretary. He went to Belgrade in 1903 to report on the grisly murders of King Alexander and Queen Draga of Serbia, and then to cover the rebellion in Macedonia against the Ottoman authorities. In 1904 he was appointed foreign director of Reuter's, but left in the same year to accept appointment as editor of the conservative *Morning Standard*, which he held until 1911. His wholehearted support of tariff reform as an economic link to bind together the empire made him a natural candidate for editorship of the paper when it was bought to support that policy.

Gwynne faced the formidable task of converting a readership dominated by moderate and old-fashioned Conservatives to a policy to which they were largely unsympathetic; the attempt failed. The circulation of the *Morning Standard* rapidly dwindled and in 1911 Gwynne left the paper (it closed in 1917) to become editor of the *Morning Post*, where the pattern was repeated. 'The readers of the *Morning Post* were of sterner stuff than those of the *Standard* and had long been nourished on protectionist dogma, but politics were changing, and it used to be said that each day the paper's circulation decreased by the number of deaths announced in its columns. Possibly a very great editor might have found new readers, but Gwynne lacked imagination and the breadth of view and elasticity of mind which might have enabled him to reconcile the policy he believed in with the spirit of the times . . . Yet there were few important political events of his time which he did not influence. He had a remarkable gift for making and keeping friends. People who mattered consulted "Taffy", knowing that he never betrayed a confidence, and they often followed the advice of one whose strength it was to be very much shrewder than he looked. Intimacy with Kitchener, Carson, Haig, Kipling, and indeed every person of note who shared his convictions gave to the paper he edited an influence out of proportion to its circulation, all the more because he never swerved in his respect for the highest principles and dignity of journalism.'[10]

Gwynne remained editor of the *Morning Post* until 1937 when it was merged with the *Daily Telegraph*. He was appointed CH in 1938 as 'lately Editor of the Morning Post.' He died in 1950.

James Garvin 1 January 1941

Of Liverpool Irish stock, James Garvin began his life in poverty and rose to be editor of the *Observer* for more than thirty years.

He was born at Birkenhead in 1868, the younger son of an Irish immigrant who was lost at sea when Garvin was two. He attended a Roman Catholic church school until he was twelve and a half, but had no formal education thereafter. In his spare time he helped his mother by delivering newspapers and medicines. They moved to Hull in 1884 and to Newcastle in 1889, where he worked as a clerk in corn, starch, electrical and coal businesses. He taught himself French, German and Spanish, and began writing regularly at Hull and sending letters to the *Eastern Morning News*, defending the cause of Irish Home Rule. In 1891 he wrote regularly to *United Ireland* and in the same year became a proof reader on the *Newcastle Chronicle*. After six weeks he began to write full time. In 1895 he began sending contributions on Irish politics to the *Fortnightly Review*. In 1899 he went to London to work as a leader and special writer for the *Daily Telegraph* on world issues. In 1905–06 he edited *Outlook*, in opposition to the unionist but free-trading *Spectator*, but left after a change of ownership.

In 1908 Lord Northcliffe who had bought the old but languishing Sunday paper, the *Observer*, appointed Garvin as the editor. He turned it around in two years and remained its editor until he retired thirty-four years later. In 1911 a dispute with Northcliffe led to the latter selling his share to Viscount Astor, who became sole owner of the *Observer*. Garvin was also employed by Astor as editor of the *Pall Mall Gazette* from 1912 until Astor sold it in 1915. Garvin, who was always a maverick, contrived to edit the paper almost exclusively via a special telephone line installed between the newspaper office and his luxurious house in Beaconsfield. His editorship ended in 1942 after a dispute with Astor. Garvin was an old-fashioned editor who ran the paper as his personal property with little concern for the wishes of the proprietor. His age and the length of his tenure only reinforced his intolerance of outside 'interference' and a clash became inevitable. Garvin had given his life to the paper and rescued it from decay and looming extinction. But Astor was the owner and desired to make changes. In 1942 they reached a compromise by which Garvin was to have remained as editor until the end of the war with an associate in London. But Garvin was too old to change, and contrary to Astor's known views, he used the paper to defend Winston Churchill's retention of the post of minister of defence and said that Lord Beaverbrook should soon return to the war cabinet. The two men were also in dispute over the terms of Garvin's contract that was due for renewal in February 1942. Astor, at the end of his patience, dismissed Garvin. It was an ignominious end to a distinguished career, but Garvin had brought it upon himself. Thereafter he wrote for the *Sunday Express* and then in March 1945 returned to the *Daily Telegraph* in which his last article appeared a week before he died in January 1947.

'As an editor Garvin said that he set out "to give the public what they don't want" by which he meant giving them something better than they knew. He communicated his vitality to the paper as a whole and his contributors found his encouragement bracing. Not only did he make the *Observer* a political force through his own comment, with which it was particularly identified, but helped by a change in social habits, he pioneered a new pattern of Sunday journal which was to be both a first class newspaper and a companion for the week-end with especially full treatment of the arts. As a writer he established a remarkable personal influence . . . The source of his authority, which made him appear at times inconsistent, was an intense capacity to enter into the life of events and yet to be outside them . . . His writing could be ponderous and too repetitive, but at its best . . . and in his quieter literary appreciations, there was a flow of feeling, imaginative and moral insight, wit and range of reference which found expression in bold and compelling phrases.'[11]

He also edited the supplementary volumes which made up the thirteenth edition of the *Encyclopaedia Britannica*. He then undertook the herculean task of editing the fourteenth edition (1926–29). He wrote three volumes of the *Life of Joseph Chamberlain* (1932–34) [The remaining two volumes were written by Julian Amery more than twenty years later]. He declined a knighthood from Lloyd George but accepted a CH in 1941 for his services as 'Editor of The Observer.'

Arthur Henry Mann 1 January 1941

Arthur Mann was for twenty years the proudly independent editor of the *Yorkshire Post*. He used its columns to fight against the appeasement prevalent at the time of the Munich crisis in 1938, and perhaps precipitated the abdication of King Edward VIII in December 1936.

He was born at Warwick in 1876, the eldest of the thirteen children of a merchant who was twice mayor of Warwick. He was educated at Warwick School, and at seventeen he was apprenticed as a reporter on the *Western Mail* in Cardiff. After three years as a reporter he was appointed to the company's evening paper which he sub-edited singled-handed. In 1900 he moved to Birmingham where he spent five years as sub-editor of the *Birmingham Daily Mail* and seven as editor of the *Birmingham Evening Dispatch*. He left in 1912 when the ownership of the paper changed hands, to work in London as London editor of the *Manchester Daily Dispatch* (1912–1915) and as editor of the *Evening Standard* (1915–19).

In 1919 he was offered the post of editor of the *Yorkshire Post*, which office he held for twenty years. In 1928 he was made managing editor with broad authority also over the editorial policy and staffing of the two other papers in the group. 'His tall figure and seeming air of quiet detachment were apt to create in others an impression of austerity, but behind his manner was penetrating observation combined with shrewd judgement. He wrote little, although his briefs to his leader-writers were sometimes nearly as long as the leading articles themselves, and he was exacting in his high standard of work from his staff.'[12] His editorship was associated with a steady growth in the prestige, if not in the circulation, of the *Post* and will be chiefly remembered for the paper's resolute opposition to Neville Chamberlain's policy of appeasement in 1938–39, as well as for the part it played in precipitating the abdication crisis when Mann on his own initiative published a strong leader on 2 December 1936 on the bishop of Bradford's address admonishing King Edward VIII.

Despite his own Conservative politics which mirrored those of the *Yorkshire Post* and its readers, Mann believed that a serious newspaper had a responsibility to inform and educate rather than entertain, and that it should above all be independent. He insisted on his right to decide what line the paper should take on important issues and on appeasement he made it clear that he would resign if overruled by the shareholders and the board of directors. The chairman, Rupert Beckett, privately urged Mann to moderate his views, but publicly supported him when an attempt was made at a shareholders' meeting to have the paper's policy changed. 'Mann's effectiveness as an editor rested on a flair for news, shrewd judgement of people, great strength and simplicity of character, and deep concern for the national interest as he saw it.'[13]

Declining circulation and deteriorating finances in 1936 brought Mann into conflict with the business managers of the paper who wanted to cut editorial costs and seek increased readership by reducing the price of the paper. The quality of the paper was high but its sales were low. Proposals for a merger had been made on a number of occasions, but it was implemented shortly after the outbreak of the 1939–45 war. The steep rise in the cost of newspaper production led to a proposal, vehemently opposed by Mann, to drop the price to one penny, to increase sales. The board then decided that the *Yorkshire Post* should be merged with its companion morning paper the *Leeds Mercury* in November 1939. Mann accordingly resigned and was succeeded by the editor of the *Mercury*. He served as governor of the BBC (1941–46) and a trustee of the *Observer* (1945–56) resigning because he disagreed with the paper's criticism of government policy over Suez. He rarely travelled and spent only a few weeks of his long life outside the United Kingdom. He died in 1972 at the age of ninety-six, eight weeks after the death of the Duke of Windsor, whose abdication as king he had unwittingly helped to bring about.

He was a staunch Conservative but, typical of his independent spirit, he twice declined a knighthood in the 1920s, writing that 'a journalist who receives a title, particularly if that title be regarded as a recognition of political services, may lessen his power to aid causes he has at heart.'[14] He accepted a CH in 1941 as 'lately Editor of The Yorkshire Post.'

John William Robertson Scott 12 June 1947
Robertson Scott was a journalist, who turned his back on a life of London-based politics to embrace and enjoy the English countryside, and to convey its beauties and its realities to the world of the towns.

He was born in 1866 at Wigton in Cumberland, the second child of a commercial traveller and temperance orator of broad and liberal views and he was educated at Quaker and grammar schools. In 1876 the family moved to Carlisle and three or four years later to Birmingham where his father was summoned to take charge of a quasi-masonic organisation: The Independent Order of Good Templars. One of his son's first jobs was to be secretary to the head of the Grand Lodge of the Good Templars of England.

His father died when Robertson Scott was still in his teens. He had settled on a career as a journalist and accepted responsibility for supporting his mother and siblings on his low earnings. He was contributing to several national journals when offered a staff appointment on the *Birmingham Gazette*. True to his upbringing and principles he had to leave when he stipulated that, as a Liberal, he should write nothing in support of the Conservative cause. After a period of freelance work he was invited to join the *Pall Mall Gazette* in 1887. With the rest of the staff, he left in 1893 when the new proprietor, Waldorf Astor, ordered the paper to change its Liberal politics. In 1952 he published his memories – *The life and death of a newspaper* – of its fate. With Alfred Spender, he worked on the new *Westminster Gazette*, for which he wrote a daily feature entitled 'Round the World'. In 1899 he transferred to the *Daily Chronicle* but his Quaker principles caused his resignation in November of the same year on the issue of the Boer War, with which the proprietors were in sympathy.

At that point he decided on a move that was to influence the rest of his life – to live and write in the country. He acquired a cottage in Essex and in 1902 he was invited to contribute farming articles to the *Country Gentleman*, and invented a pseudonym which passed into popular usage – "Home Counties". In the next few years, using the same pseudonym, he wrote for *World's Work*, *Field*, *Daily Chronicle*, *Country Gentleman*, *Quarterly Review*, *Nineteenth Century*, *Spectator*, *Nation*, and *The Times*.

Having discovered and grown to love the country, his articles (and several books and pamphlets) on all aspects of rural life, sought to reveal that world to town dwellers. He wrote about farmers and smallholders, farm workers and landowners, about how they lived and made a living. He and his wife contributed to the life of rural Essex, forming a Progressive Club 'for men and women of markedly different upbringings and associations, politics, denominations and incomes, and producing in Lady Warwick's big barn works by Synge, Barrie and Bensusan.'[15]

He was too old to serve in the 1914–18 war and adventurously decided to sell his cottage in Essex and go to Japan to study Japanese small farms. There he started and edited a monthly journal called the *New East*. In 1922 he returned to the United Kingdom via the United States and published *The foundations of Japan*, which became the standard work in English on the rural life and people of that country. The subtitle revealed the extent and the aim of the book: *Notes made during journeys of 6,000 miles in the rural districts as a basis for a sounder knowledge of the Japanese people*.

On his return he settled at the manor house in the Cotswold village of Idbury, near Kingham in Oxfordshire in 1923. He resumed his journalistic writing and became an enthusiastic adviser to the National Federation of Women's Institutes. He contributed a series of twenty-four articles to *Nation* which were collected and published in 1925 as *England's green and pleasant land*. It described frankly and penetratingly, through the people and their talk about neighbours and themselves, the life of the contemporary village. *The dying peasant and the future of his sons* followed in 1926, and both books were of considerable value to social historians.

In 1927 he founded the quarterly review, the *Countryman*. He and his wife were business and advertisement manager, editor, sub-editor, and principal contributors. Ignoring the advice of friends, and with never more than £500 capital, they made it the most successful venture in periodical publishing between the two world wars. 'Non-party, though firm enough in opinion, it was to be packed with rural life and character, to place before town, city and country dwellers vividly and convincingly the facts, and to strengthen the forces of rural progress.'[16] He sold the magazine in 1943 but continued to edit it with full independence until 1947.

He was also active in local government housing. For ten years he was chairman of his district council housing committee and served under four ministers on the Central Housing Advisory Committee.

After his retirement as editor of the *Countryman* in 1947 he was made a CH in 1947 as 'Author. Founder and lately Editor of the "The Countryman".' In 1956 he published a collection of reminiscences – *'We' and me. Memories of four eminent editors I worked with, a discussion by editors of the future of editing, and a candid account of the founding and the editing, for twenty-one years, of my own magazine* – in which he included a report of the experience of his CH. With permission, he included transcripts of the official letters that he had received. Generally no objections were made, although eyebrows were raised at his reference to the CH as 'my modest honour'. 'I trust,' wrote one official, 'that this is a clear example of a transferred epithet and that he is aware of the standing of the CH in relation to other honours. It might be better if he could convey the sense of his own modesty in some other way.'[17] He died in 1962 at the age of ninety-six.

James Bone 12 June 1947

For thirty-three years James Bone was the London editor of the *Manchester Guardian* and his 'London Letter' in that newspaper became renowned as the best of its kind.

He was born in Glasgow in 1872 the second of the six sons of a journalist. His brothers included Sir Muirhead Bone, the artist, Sir David Bone of Anchor Line and Alex Bone, the writer of seafaring reminiscences. 'We were born with a pencil in our mouths,' he was to say in later life.[18]

He left school at the age of fourteen and went to work in the waterfront office of the Laird Line until he could join the *North British Daily Mail*, the paper on which his father worked. The paper closed in 1901 and after a period of freelancing, he joined the London office of the *Manchester Guardian* in 1902. In 1912 he was made London editor although the parliamentary lobby work was excluded from his brief by decision of the retiring editor who recognised that Bone had no great political knowledge or interest. 'Bone, although fanatically loyal to the paper and its Liberal policies, was conservative by temperament and not radical; nor was he an intellectual, but rather an artist with a painter's vision and a poetic pen.'[19]

His life work was the 'London Letter' of the *Manchester Guardian*. Most provincial papers carried a London letter and that in the *Guardian* was reckoned to be the best. 'The feature was supposed to be a letter to the editor . . . Most of the paragraphs were written by Bone, two general reporters and their colleagues on the political staff. A miscellany of paragraphs told of sales and exhibitions of paintings and sculptures, the arrival of interesting visitors from abroad, what was happening at Court, buildings going up and coming down, the fashions, new Christmas party games, and even the weather.' 'Bone's "London Letter", never sour or malicious, was invested with his own blithe spirit and unquenchable Victorian optimism. He filled the London office with his own zest for the event of the hour, be it a test match, an abdication or a fog.'[20] On 31 December each year he published his 'Londoner's Retrospect', a social history of the year. In 1925 he published *The London Perambulator*, a description and an obituary of the London of the first twenty-five years of the twentieth century. 'Yet what Bone did was in his day perhaps less important than what Bone was. He moved in a group which might be described as "the higher Bohemia" – a circle of writers with style, wit and a fondness of one another's society.'[21] He had rooms in the Temple where he lived with his wife and his cat. Every evening he would visit three or four taverns in Fleet Street spending fifteen minutes in each and having only one small drink. When his home was bombed, he settled into the Strand Palace Hotel.

He retired in 1945 and was made a CH in 1947 as 'lately London Editor of the Manchester Guardian. For services to journalism.' He died in 1962 a few months after his ninetieth birthday.

Sir Peter Scott 13 June 1987
Joint founder of the World Wildlife Fund, Peter Scott was a multi-faceted character whose artistic and sporting interests were paralleled by a drive and determination to further the work of conservation, and which in turn led to a long broadcasting career that brought the world of wildlife to the British public.

He was born in London in 1909, the only child of the ill-fated Antarctic explorer, Captain Robert Falcon Scott. Being the son of national hero who died in tragic circumstances in 1912 profoundly influenced, but never blighted or overshadowed his career. He was educated at West Downs and Oundle schools and then went to Trinity College, Cambridge where he took a degree in zoology, botany and the history of art in 1930. Years later he was to say that it was his father's wish that he should become interested in natural history. He did and it gave him immense enjoyment during his life. He wanted as many people as possible to share that enjoyment at a time when the natural landscape was suffering constant encroachment and destruction.

While at Cambridge he took up wildfowling and in 1929 *Country Life* published two articles on the sport, written by him. Wildfowling led to the painting of wildfowl, and after two years at the Royal Academy Schools in London he held the first one-man exhibition of his work in 1933. Two books followed – *Morning flight* (1935) and *Wild chorus* (1938) – both illustrated by his evocative paintings of ducks, geese and swans (his speciality) flying across skies. To describe him as an artist would be too strong; he made no pretension to be more than an illustrator and painter of bird portraits and neither he nor other painters regarded his painting achievements as much more than a popular success.

Wildfowling was followed by the sport of sailing and he won a bronze medal at the Olympic Games in 1936 for single-handed yachting. He led the British dinghy team to Canada in 1936, and won the sailing speed record at Cowes in 1954. He was chairman of the Olympic Yachting Committee (1948) and the International Jury for Yachting at the Olympic Games (1956). Competence on the sea was followed by competence in the air. In the late 1950s he developed an interest in gliding, and in 1963 he won the British national gliding championships.

During the 1939–45 war he served in the royal naval volunteer reserve. He was commissioned and rose to the rank of lieutenant commander, serving in destroyers, gunboats in the English Channel (for which he was awarded a DSC) and finally commanding a new frigate. At the end of the war he briefly flirted with politics, standing as the Conservative candidate for Wembley North in the 1945 election. He was narrowly beaten (by 435 votes) by the Labour party candidate (a local alderman) and made no further attempt to seek election to parliament. Given the route along which he subsequently travelled, it was just as well.

In 1945 he visited the River Severn at a place in Gloucestershire with which he was to become synonymous – Slimbridge. The object was to search for a rare goose, but there he decided to establish a research organisation to study the swans, geese and ducks of the world. Known as the Severn Wildfowl Trust (later renamed the Wildfowl and Wetlands Trust), it was established in 1946. The trust was a success; in 1956 more than 1,200 organised parties visited Slimbridge, the trust had a membership of 5,000, and employed more than forty people. Scott had given up day to day management by 1960, but he remained its honorary director until his death, and was always remembered as warm, friendly, approachable and constantly full of ideas that enthused and inspired his staff.

He became famous for his work in studying and conserving endangered species, travelling to distant uncharted regions in search of the breeding grounds of rare varieties. He was a natural consultant in the creation of the BBC's natural history unit, and for them he presented for seventeen years a programme on natural history entitled *Look*, which did much to introduce natural history to the British public, and began a long series of radio and television broadcasts. In those more primitive days, many of the earlier episodes contained his own film which he shot on his travels.

The 1950s were marked by a deepening commitment to conservation. He became involved in the International Union for the Conservation of Nature and Natural Resources and became chairman of its Species Survival Commission (1962–81). In 1961, with two friends, he founded the World Wildlife Fund (later the World Wide Fund for Nature) to raise money for the conservation of nature around the world, and he travelled extensively in that cause. He designed the Fund's famous panda logo. He wrote and illustrated many books, including a volume of autobiography, *The eye of the wind* (1961).

He was rector of Aberdeen University (1960–63) and chancellor of Birmingham University (1974–83). He was appointed a military MBE in 1942, and a CBE in 1953. He was knighted in 1973 and appointed a CH in 1987 'For services to conservation.' He died in 1989 two weeks before his eightieth birthday.

The Honourable David Astor 31 December 1993
David Astor was editor and proprietor of the *Observer* newspaper for twenty-seven years until his retirement in 1975. The late arrival of the CH in 1993 (he was then eighty) was partly due to an independent spirit which balked at adherence to any one political party, and partly due to the self-effacing nature of his work which meant that few people knew the wide extent of his public and charitable services.

He was born in 1912, second son of the second Viscount Astor, owner of the *Observer*, and of the legendary Nancy, Viscountess Astor, who became the first woman to take her seat in the House of Commons and was herself a CH. He had the advantage of growing up in the shadow of the 'Cliveden Set', a group of right-wing politicians and journalists who gathered for weekend parties in the late 1930s at the Astor country home in Buckinghamshire. The set were intent on avoiding war to the point of appeasement, and the connection embarrassed David Astor in his later years.

He was educated at Eton and Balliol College, Oxford where he read politics, philosophy and economics. As the result of a breakdown he left in 1934 without taking a degree. After leaving Oxford he was involved in various activities including a period with the *Yorkshire Post* in 1936. At the outbreak of the 1939–45 war he was commissioned in the royal marines and received the Croix de Guerre in 1944. Astor had long been aware of the menace of German national socialism. While staying with a German family in Heidelberg in 1931 he had witnessed a day long Nazi rally and the event left an indelible impression.

He joined the *Observer* as its foreign editor in 1946, but his influence had begun earlier. The Astor family had owned the paper since 1911 and the dismissal of the obdurate James Garvin in 1942 had created a vacuum which Astor was destined to fill. A perfectly competent locum tenens editor – Ivor Brown – was appointed, but he was removed in 1948 to make way for Astor who became proprietor and editor.

He abandoned any specific political allegiance and turned the paper into a trust-owned non-party publication and helped to establish its reputation as the voice of post-war liberal Britain. During this period many famous writers were on the staff, including George Orwell, Anthony Sampson, Conor Cruise O'Brien, Barbara Ward, Sebastian Hoffman, Fritz Schumacher, Philip Toynbee, Kenneth Harris, Kenneth Tynan and more infamously Kim Philby. With such a group, Astor functioned as 'the inspired and creative conductor of an unusually talented journalistic orchestra.'[22]

Like James Garvin before him, Astor stayed too long at the helm of the paper. For a few years the paper prospered and in November 1956 it overtook the *Sunday Times* in circulation. But the achievement coincided with the Suez expedition, which the *Observer* denounced in an editorial (not by Astor). The article outraged Conservative opinion, and from that point the circulation of the *Observer* steadily declined. The launch of the *Sunday Telegraph* in 1961 and the *Sunday Times* colour magazine in 1962 made even more inroads into the paper's circulation. By 1975, the *Observer*'s circulation had decreased to the point where the paper was close to bankruptcy. It was a decline that had taken place over many years and was, in the opinion of Arnold Goodman, a consequence of the paper's hostility to Suez.[23] The paper had no significant capital reserves and was funded by its sales and by Astor family money.

Astor was persuaded to retire as editor in 1975. A reorganisation achieved a twenty-five percent reduction of staff, leading to hopes of solvency, but within a year it was again clear that resources were close to exhaustion and that the paper would be lucky to survive financially for twelve months. At that point Astor agreed that it should be sold to someone who was financially able to keep it going and would maintain its liberal traditions. The paper was sold to Atlantic Richfield in 1976 for £1 and Astor remained on the board of directors until, to his dismay, the paper was sold to Lonrho in 1981. He tried and failed to persuade the Monopolies Commission not to agree to the sale, and then resigned as a director. Astor was relieved when the Guardian Media Group bought the paper from Lonrho in 1993.

In his memoirs, Arnold Goodman, chairman of the *Observer* trustees, paid tribute to Astor: 'The *Observer* in those days proceeded under Astor's talented, if not wholly businesslike administration. David Astor is as big-hearted and liberal a man as can be found on this earth. He is a controversial figure: those who love him, love him without qualification, and I must admit that I am among the number. It would be uncandid indeed not to reveal that there are others who express a contrary view, often with vehemence. I will spare his blushes simply by recording that in my view he is overall a force for good . . . I took an active part in his campaign to establish hostels for beaten wives, and found myself dragged to the support of a lady named Erin Pizzey whose views I frequently found alarming but who had the force of persuasion of a steamroller . . . He was, in the view of many, and despite major idiosyncrasies, one of the great editors of the day. His triumph was to establish a newspaper which was widely respected everywhere that English was spoken and on which he induced a remarkable quality of journalists to serve.'[24]

Astor had many admirers and proposals for an honour were made on a number of occasions, some suggesting that his independent mind would be a valued addition to the cross benches in the house of lords. He had owned and edited one of the most respected weekly newspapers in the world and had never been afraid to champion unpopular causes. It was rightly said that the owners and editors of newspapers of vastly inferior quality (though with more clearly defined political sympathies) had been honoured with knighthoods and peerages, while Astor had nothing. He filled his retirement with continuous work in the institution and maintenance of humanitarian causes which became in part the justification for his CH. By the early 1990s it was far too late to honour him for his editorship of the *Observer*, but the brevity of his entry in *Who's Who* and his engaging modesty ensured that his other work in the field of international and domestic social problems remained unknown. The many organisations that he founded or funded were mostly low profile, but they were high-powered and Astor consistently avoided taking credit for them. His range of activity was impressive in its breadth: he convened the Anglo-German Konigswinter Conferences and the Anglo-Polish conferences in 1959 and 1961 for journalists and academics. He founded the British-Irish Association (with Garrett Fitzgerald and others) to bring together decision-makers and others in both countries; the Minority Rights Group; Index on Censorship; the World Security Council (set up in the late 1950s with the object of establishing a world peacekeeping role for the USA and the USSR); the Africa Bureau (in 1952), which became the principal body for disseminating information on black Africa to the western world in the 1950s and 1960s; the South African Advanced Education Project (for training black South Africans for senior positions); the Intermediate Technology group (to devise technology suitable for Third World countries – a practical application of Schumacher's *Small is beautiful*); the Home for Namibian Refugees, originally set up in Sutton Courtenay to provide housing and support, and later established in Oxford as the Namibian Social Centre; and groups making contacts between Israelis and Palestinians. He funded the Koestler Awards (founded by Arthur Koestler) to reward prisoners for art and craft work completed in prison, and the Butler Trust to improve the status and incentives of members of the prison service. He endowed a chair at the University of Sussex for the study of genocide, and was a firm supporter of Chiswick Women's Aid, the first ever refuge for women and children. Most famously he used the pages of the *Observer* to found Amnesty International in 1960.

Long after his retirement from the editorship of the *Observer* – when he would almost certainly have been considered for an honour for services to journalism – Astor was made a CH in 1993 'For public and charitable services'. Reserved and shy, he was not interested in conventional recognition and never used his birthright title of 'Honourable' if he could avoid it. Like his mother, he showed a compulsive desire for the betterment of humankind, and Nancy and David Astor remain the only known example of mother and son being made CH. David Astor died in 2001.

Sir David Attenborough 30 December 1995
In some ways David Attenborough was a successor to Peter Scott. By the beginning of the twenty-first century he had become Britain's best-known natural history filmmaker. His career had spanned four decades and he had travelled to some of the world's remotest regions.

He was born in 1926 and educated at Wyggeston Grammar School and Clare College, Cambridge. After the 1939–45 war he served in the royal navy (1947–49), hoping to travel. He later recalled being assigned to an aircraft carrier moored to a buoy in the middle of the Firth of Forth – not the kind of travel he had in mind. The navy was followed by a short stint as a junior editorial assistant in a publishing house (1949–52).

In 1952 he joined the BBC as a trainee producer and thereafter the corporation was the medium of his work as he travelled around the world. At first, the television service had no money and it was regarded as a rather raffish arm of the BBC. He found the studio format unimaginative and longed to take a camera outside to film. He eventually succeeded and his first expedition was to Freetown, Sierra Leone in 1954 with a team from the London Zoo. In those days of less developed aviation, the journey took three days, and trips to the Far East took a week. Thereafter he undertook zoological and ethnographic filming expeditions to British Guiana (1955), Indonesia (1956), New Guinea (1957), Paraguay and Argentina (1958), the south west Pacific (1959), Madagascar (1960), the Northern Territory of Australia (1962), the Zambesi (1964), Bali (1969), Central New Guinea (1971), Celebes, Borneo, Peru and Colombia (1973), Mali, British Columbia, Iran and the Solomon Islands (1974), and Nigeria (1975).

His mission to collect exotic animals for London Zoo occasionally caused problems The journey to Paraguay in 1958 involved collecting armadillos and anacondas which were due to arrive in Britain on Christmas Eve. On arrival at Puerto Rico, the airline had cancelled all the outbound flights and he asked the airline staff for help with the animals as he was running out of food for them. An American airline agreed to carry him and his cargo. It was a first class-only plane and the air stewardess told him that she only had caviar and Californian peaches. The armadillos dined on them all the way to New York. There was occasionally trouble with hotel management when animals were smuggled into hotel rooms. Pythons and anacondas were in sacks under the beds, armadillos in the bath and bats were hanging up on the curtains. And many escaped in the middle of the night. In Madagascar he collected a group of one hundred pill millipedes, creatures about the size of a golf ball, and put them in a sack. In the middle of the night they found a hole in the sack and the next morning, they were found wandering around in the hotel corridor.

Although he occupied two managerial posts: Controller, BBC Television Service (1965–68), and director of programmes, television, and member of the BBC board of management (1969–72), it was as a writer and presenter of a succession of television series that he excelled and which established his fame: *Tribal Eye* (1976), *Wildlife on one* (from 1977), *Life on earth* (1979), *The living planet* (1984), *The first Eden* (1987), *Lost worlds* (1989), *Vanished lives* (1989), *The trials of life* (1990), *Life in the freezer* (1993), *The private life of plants* (1995), *The life of birds* (1998), *State of the planet* (2000), and *The blue planet* (2001). His television series have attracted television audiences of 500 million and more, and the books accompanying the series have been international bestsellers.

Concerned generally with conservation, the disappearance of species, and industrial pollution, he was a member of the Nature Conservancy Council (1973–82), and joined Sir Peter Scott as a trustee of the World Wildlife Fund, UK (1965–69, 1972–82 and 1984–90), and the World Wildlife Fund International (1979–86). He has also been a trustee of the British Museum (1980–2001), the Science Museum (1984–87), and the Royal Botanic Gardens, Kew (1986–92). He was also president of the British Association for the Advancement of Science (1990–91) and of the

Royal Society for Nature Conservation (1991–96). In interview, he once summed up his work philosophy: 'The public won't care tuppence about wildlife,' he has said, 'unless they think that butterflies, birds and badgers are wonderful things that lift the heart and the spirit when you see them. Unless they believe that, they won't help WWF or anyone else work towards the preservation of species and ecosystems. That's why the BBC Natural History Unit makes the kind of programmes it does. The basis of conservation is the comprehension of the natural world, and that's my game.'

He was made a CBE in 1974 and knighted in 1985. He was made a CVO in 1991 for producing the Queen's Christmas broadcast for a few years, and a CH in 1995 as 'Broadcaster and Naturalist. For services to nature broadcasting.'

CHAPTER FOURTEEN

Forth to his work

BUSINESSMEN AND TRADES UNIONISTS

A great many voices all said together ('like the chorus of a song,' thought Alice) 'Don't keep him waiting child! Why, his time is worth a thousand pounds a minute!'
'Looking-glass insects', Through the looking-glass, Lewis Carroll

Businessmen and trades unionists fell naturally together in chapter two by virtue of their common effort towards achieving victory in the 1914–18 war. In the years since 1921, eleven individuals have been appointed to the Order under the broad heading of businessmen and trade unionists. The latter group is a more easily identifiable and coherent than the former. Trade unionists are quite sharply defined by their services towards their unions or to employees in general. Businessmen are less well defined, and more diverse in their public services and for the most part their honours, including the CH were conferred not for being businessmen, but for what they chose to do with their time and their wealth. Each of them had what might be called a bolt-on module and none of them were honoured purely for their services to industry.

The ship owner Sir John Ellerman (1921) was a secretive figure who protected his privacy and about whose personal life and personal fortune little was known or revealed. As no citation or description of appointment was included in his entry in the *London Gazette*, what public service earned him his CH in 1921 cannot be definitely established, though it included elements of war service and mostly unrecorded philanthropy.

The work of Lord Hives (1943) at Rolls-Royce in developing the 'Merlin' aero engine, and Essington Lewis (1943) in masterminding the manufacture of munitions in Australia, put them firmly in the category of 'war service'.

Viscount Nuffield (1958) developed the legendary Morris Minor car and made a substantial fortune in the process. But his philanthropy was equally legendary and he had disbursed a substantial fortune by the time of his death, for the advancement of health and social well-being and the care of the elderly.

The Earl of Limerick (1960) was a city businessman whose public service was less visible and concerned mostly with the Territorial Army, though his CH was earned for his eight successful years as chairman of the Medical Research Council. He and his wife, Angela, remain the only husband and wife to have been made Companions of Honour.

Sir Allen Lane (1969) was a publisher who developed the phenomenally successful Penguin paperback books from the 1930s. Being unsuccessfully prosecuted for publishing a complete version of *Lady Chatterley's lover* in 1960 only raised his reputation and the profits of his company.

From one perspective, the five trade unionists are as diverse a group as the businessmen, although their common aim was to improve the pay and working conditions of their members. Joseph Havelock Wilson (1922) of the National Sailors' and

Firemen's Union and the Merchant Seaman's League was highly regarded by many for his work in organising the nation's sailors. Others despised him as a traitor to his class by opposing the nationalisation of the mines, and helping to break the general strike of 1926. By later standards, his other 'public service' was minimal, but he was a 'moderate' trade union leader and favoured Lloyd George, who was duly grateful.

Gertrude Tuckwell (1930), a founding member of the Women's Trade Union League, eschewed a comfortable upper middle class background to campaign vigorously against the contemporary supine acceptance of the often poisonous and dangerous working conditions of women. In the workplace, her pioneering and persistent efforts on behalf of working women paralleled the more militant political work of the Pankhursts.

George Gibson (1946) was instrumental in founding the Mental Hospital and Institutional Workers' Union in 1910. It merged with others to become the Confederation of Health Service Employees – of which he became the first general secretary. Well regarded by prime minister Clement Attlee, and appointed a governor of the Bank of England, his career in public service was terminated abruptly when he was implicated in a financial scandal.

Arthur Deakin (1949) was general secretary of the Transport and General Workers' Union for fifteen years in the 1940s and 50s. Autocratic, interfering and intolerant of opposition, he was a close ally of Labour prime minister Clement Attlee.

Jack Jones (1977) was another general secretary of the Transport and General Workers' Union. During his tenure of office in the 1970s, the union was at the height of its numerical strength and power, and he was in demand for membership of numerous committees and commissions. On retirement he began work again, this time becoming the voice of the elderly.

Of the five trade unionists appointed after 1921, Havelock Wilson can be counted as one of Lloyd George's allies and his mixed efforts would not have raised him to the higher standards of the CH in later years. Gertrude Tuckwell was a pioneer on behalf of the rights of women and she received her CH as one of a group of seven prominent and equally pioneering women similarly honoured between March 1929 and January 1931. George Gibson and Arthur Deakin reached the peak of their prominence during the first substantial Labour government (1945–51). Deakin especially saw his union membership grow from 650,000 (1940) to 1,230,000 (1946). During Jack Jones' seven years as general secretary of the TGWU, its membership rose from 1,530,000 (1969) to 2,073,000 (1978). When he retired, the trade union movement had reached its high water mark and the election of the Conservative government in 1979 began its decline. Among other factors, the curtailment of union privileges by statute and the privatisation of the monolithic nationalised industries led to a steep downward trend in membership figures, and by 1998 the TGWU membership had shrunk to 882,000. By the beginning of the twenty-first century, trade union leaders were no longer the prominent, recognisable and familiar figures in the life of the nation that they had been in the 1970s.

Sir John Ellerman 1 January 1921
John Ellerman was a financier and ship owner, who was reputed at his death to be possibly the richest man and certainly one of the greatest forces behind shipping that Britain had ever known.[1]

He was born in 1862, the son of a Hamburg corn merchant who had settled in Hull in 1854. Ellerman was a private individual who revealed little about his early life, but it was known that shipping had fascinated him for many years before he joined the board of the Leyland line in 1892, and it was not long before he became chairman of the company. He founded the Ellerman line in 1901 by acquiring a series of historic shipping lines: Westcott and Lawrence (founded in 1857), the Papayanni group (founded in 1854), the City line (founded in 1839) and the Hall line (founded about 1863). He subsequently acquired Bucknall's Steamship Company, the Shaw, Albion and a number of others. In 1915 he absorbed Wilson's of Hull. During the 1914–18 war he placed his ships at the disposal of the war effort, a gesture which would have contributed towards his CH in 1921.

After the 1914–18 war he took an interest in newspapers and purchased the bulk of the shares in the *Illustrated London News*, the *Sphere*, the *Tatler*, the *Sketch*, *Eve*, and the *Illustrated Sporting and Dramatic News*. He began to suggest books for review, drafting new features and even on one occasion interviewing an individual contributor who had attracted his attention. He delighted in his private collection housed in his large Mayfair mansion at 1 South Audley Street. The house was packed with mosaics, tapestries, carvings, furniture and objets d'art (not all of them valuable) which had caught his attention on his many trips to the bazaars of Europe and Africa. His artistic instincts ran deep but they were overpowered by his financial acumen which enabled him to amass his vast fortune.

Ellerman could be extraordinarily secretive about his personal life. His 'dominant characteristic was his unmitigated determination to keep his private life and that of his family from public knowledge. The more astonishing his financial achievements became the deeper he burrowed into anonymity . . . As a result of his almost morbid passion for secrecy, much material about his business career will never be known, because he obscured his vast transactions in shipping, newspapers, and periodicals, London real estate, breweries, and other interests, under the guise of trust companies, the shares of which he held.'[2] He could have been a great public benefactor, but the theme of secrecy extended to a desire for anonymity. Few knew the amounts that he gave to good causes and struggling individuals. 'The things he shrank from doing are illuminating; rarely if ever did he dine at a restaurant, or have his photograph taken, or go to a race-meeting or public banquet, make a speech, or accept invitations from any but his few intimate friends, attend a club, public conference, concert or even a church. His great delight was to bring business friends home to a lunch which he had planned down to the minutest detail in conference with his chef. It remained only for his wife to preside at the table and arrange the flowers. Afterwards he would show his guests his fine library and large collection of paintings of the conventional Royal Academy type . . . He moved in a routine so rigid as to approach the ritualistic. His weakness was that he made no attempt to understand the new forces working beneath the surface of his time. Generous and sympathetic in his own small circle, he was lacking in a broad humanitarian outlook and had little social imagination.'[3]

He was created a baronet in 1905 and a CH in 1921, but even with the latter high honour the secrecy that he would have wanted prevailed. In 1919 Sir Thomas Royden, Bt, vice-chairman of the Cunard line, was given a CH for his shipping work during the war and received an effusive citation in the London Gazette. Two years later, his fellow shipowner was listed simply as 'Sir John Reeves Ellerman,

Bart.' with not a hint of the services rendered. He died after a short illness at the Hotel Royal, Dieppe in 1933, leaving a vast fortune of £36 million.

Joseph Havelock Wilson 2 January 1922

Joseph Wilson was a trade unionist and member of parliament. There was no doubting his imagination and energy as a union organiser, but he was incompetent in financial matters and his increasingly autocratic personality brought him many enemies and made him something of a pariah within the trade union movement by the time of his death.

He was born in 1858, the son of a foreman draper who died when his son was three. His mother opened a greengrocer's shop and later became the proprietor of a small boarding house. At the age of six Wilson began selling newspapers out of school hours and at the age of nine he left the Boy's British School at Sunderland to work as an errand boy on a newspaper. A thirteen he was apprenticed to a local lithographic printer but ran away to sea after a few months. After several short voyages, his family accepted his determination to become a seaman, and he was apprenticed to a Sunderland ship owner where he stayed for the next eleven years, serving as boy steward, cook, able seaman to boatswain and second mate. Having married in 1879, his wife persuaded him to abandon his sea fever in 1882. He opened a small cook-shop in Monkwearmouth, moving to larger premises in the same town two years later, known as 'Wilson's Temperance Hotel and Dining Rooms.'

Wilson never lost his love of the sea and before long the contact was renewed by proxy. The North of England Sailors' and Seagoing Fireman's Friendly Society was founded in 1879, and by 1885 it was meeting in Wilson's hotel and he had become the president. In that capacity he gave evidence before the royal commission on loss of life at sea in 1886. In 1887 he resigned from the society because of disputes with his colleagues over the direction the union was to take. He established his own union in August 1887 under the title 'the National Amalgamated Sailors' and Firemen's Union of Great Britain and Ireland, becoming its general secretary, and the union affiliated to the Trades Union Congress in 1888.

It was an era of rapid expansion in foreign trade, and a new mood of militancy about the working conditions and low wages of seafarers brought a rash of strikes. Both factors led to a dramatic increase in the membership of Wilson's union, and by 1889 it had 65,000 members. The union disintegrated in 1894 because of a determined and ruthless onslaught by the Shipping Federation against unions of dockers and seamen. In 1891 Wilson was convicted of unlawful assembly and riot and sentenced to six weeks imprisonment. He resigned as general secretary in 1893 to become president, and in 1894 the union went into voluntary liquidation. A new union with the same name was formed, with Wilson as its president, but it remained weak until the period of industrial unrest of 1910–11. Though this was immediately followed by the breakaway of dissident branches in 1911 and 1912.

Wilson had political ambition and after several unsuccessful attempts, he was elected Liberal member of parliament for Middlesbrough in 1892. He retained the seat in 1895, lost it in 1900 and regained it in 1905. Inside the commons, most often his work was concerned with extending the work for the improvement of seafaring conditions. 'He always regarded politics as an adjunct to industrial action and for this, as well as for many other reasons, he never became a parliamentarian of any stature.'[4] He had a mania for litigation and was involved in legal cases almost continuously. On more than one occasion he had to be declared bankrupt as a result of damages and costs which he was unable to meet.

He decided that his union would fully cooperate with the war effort. He had served in the royal naval reserve and had been a patriotic supporter of the Boer War. He did not stand in the elections of 1910 but made attempts at by-elections in 1913 and 1914.

He was surprisingly moderate at the beginning of the 1914–18 war until submarine warfare in particular helped to push him into the pathological anti-German attitudes typical of the day. He remained primarily a Liberal and was virulently hostile towards the Labour Party and its antiwar stance. Beatrice Webb remembered him making 'patriotic speeches of the savage and uncompromising type, accusing the anti-war party of being "cowards and traitors".'[5]

At a by-election at South Shields in 1918 he was returned unopposed and likewise at the general election in the same year. Between 1918 and 1922 his union voted to affiliate with the Labour Party though he obstinately continued to represent himself to the people of South Shields as a National Liberal. He was opposed in 1922 by the official Labour Party candidate, came third in the poll, and his parliamentary career was finished. He remained prominent in the increasingly turbulent affairs of shipping unions throughout the 1920s, though his increasingly conservative views put him at odds with the British labour movement. In 1919 he gave evidence to the Sankey commission into the future of the coal industry. The report urged the nationalisation of the coal mines, but in his evidence to the commission, Wilson argued that the mines should be left in private ownership. The mining unions never forgave him for that and for his later opposition to their cause. In 1921 changes of government policy removed subsidies on housing, and controls on food, the mines and agriculture. A miners' strike began on 1 April, and within a week a general strike was threatened. The threat never materialised because of disunity within the trade union movement, and Wilson among others was applauded (and honoured) in government circles for refusing to bring in his union and thereby helping to break the strike. In 1926 he characterised the general strike as a vast communist plot and refused to obey the instructions of the TUC general council that all transport workers should withdraw their labour, and he took to court a number of his own officials who supported the strike, and supplied cars, officials and financial assistance to breakaway unions opposed to the strike. His union was expelled from the TUC in 1928, an event that allowed the powerful TGWU to begin recruiting seamen.

By this date Wilson was a sick man. He had suffered from progressive rheumatoid arthritis since 1910 and suffered from heart trouble in his last years. He died in office in 1929, leaving only £428. An obituary in the *Miner* summed up this complex man. 'In his early years he performed magnificent work in organising the much ill-used seamen of this country. The war had a most disturbing affect on his outlook, and in postwar years he has been, in plain language, a faithful ally of the employing class. His union organisation has been the faithful servant of the ship owners and he himself used the whole of his own and his union's influence to disrupt and demoralise other sections of workers. We miners were honoured by the major share of his attentions. It cannot be said that his efforts met with a considerable degree of success; but they must necessarily have the effect of causing him to be remembered less as the organiser of the seamen 30 years ago than as the stepfather of Spencerism of the coal industry. Havelock Wilson will go down in history as one of the tragedies of the twentieth century working-class movement in Britain. We would very much rather it had been otherwise.'[6]

Wilson published an accurately titled volume of autobiography in 1925 – *My stormy voyage through life*. He was made a CBE in 1917 and a CH in 1922 for his services as 'General President, National Sailors' and Firemen's Union. Secretary, Merchant Seaman's League.' Whatever the strengths and failings of Joseph Havelock Wilson, he was a loyal trade union supporter of the government of Lloyd George at a crucial time.

Gertrude Tuckwell 1 January 1930

Gertrude Tuckwell was an early trade unionist and campaigner for women's rights who inherited a radical streak from her father and her aunt. One of a group of middle class energetic and enthusiastic women to whom the Labour movement owed much in its earliest days, she worked with May Tennant CH, dedicating her life to the cause of working women. Like Tennant, her life could have been one of luxury and ease, but instead it was a long record of selfless service.

She was born in Oxford in 1861 where her father was the chaplain of New College. He was a Christian socialist at a time when being called a socialist brought opprobrium and social ostracism. His autobiography, *Reminiscences of a radical parson* (1905), was dedicated to Gertrude. She was strongly influenced by her maternal aunt, born Emilia Strong, then married to Mark Pattison, rector of Lincoln College, Oxford, and later to Sir Charles Dilke, the radical politician. While staying with her aunt in 1878 she met two members of the Women's Trade Union League, who urged her to become a teacher. She went to a teacher training college at Liverpool where she met poverty and slums for the first time in her life. She left Liverpool in 1882 and went to Bishop Otter's College, Chichester, leaving in 1884. From 1884 until 1890 or 1892 she taught in an elementary school in Chelsea (dealing incredibly with classes of up to seventy children) and lived modestly in Oakley Street and then Tite Street. Her resignation was precipitated by ill-health and her first book *The state and its children* (1894) was a personal statement of her experiences.

After leaving the school she developed an interest in the condition of women workers, campaigning for protective labour legislation and trade union organisation. Inevitably she favoured women's suffrage, though she eschewed the more militant suffragettes, preferring to work through the Women's Trade Union League, the Women's Industrial Council and the Labour Party. She had been a member of the committee of the Women's Trade Union League since 1891. She succeeded May Abraham (later May Tennant CH) as secretary to Lady Dilke in 1892 and became honorary secretary of the league and editor of its journal the *Women's Trade Union Review*, a post she held until 1905. She was especially active in the league's campaign for the protection of women workers from injuries sustained at work, particularly from lead poisoning and sulphuric necrosis. From 1892 to 1895 she personally investigated the pottery industry areas and the white lead mills of Newcastle under Lyme.

In 1908 she was appointed to the departmental committee on dangers attendant on the use of lead. The committee refused to recommend the outright prohibition of the use of lead in pottery glazes and Tuckwell registered a protest by issuing a dissenting minority report. She called on the Home Office to compile a list of goods in which the use of lead would be prohibited and to ban the importation of goods containing lead glaze as had been done in the case of yellow phosphorus. From 1905 to 1923 she was a member of the advisory committee to the ministry of health.

She joined the International Association for Labour Legislation in 1897 and went on to its executive committee in 1906. She founded the British section in 1904 with Sidney Webb as the chairman and Arthur Henderson as honorary treasurer. In 1910 she attended the international meeting at Lugano at which she presented a paper on lead poisoning. She took part in the formation of the National Anti-Sweating League in 1907 and arranged the Guildhall conference on the minimum wage in the same year.

She believed in women's trade unionism not only as a means of improving working conditions but also because it assisted in raising women's consciousness and she travelled across the country to address meetings and organise union branches. She became president of the Women's Trade Union League in 1905 in succession to Lady Dilke (who had died in 1904), and in 1908 she became president of the National Federation of Women Workers (founded in 1906) with the object of organising women workers who were not being admitted to other trade unions. She remained active in both organisations until 1918 when she announced her retirement. In 1918 she was appointed to the labour advisory panel of the ministry of reconstruction and in 1920–22 she was a member of the central committee on women's training and employment.

She enjoyed a parallel career in the promotion of women in the lower ranks of the law. In 1920 was appointed a justice of the peace for St Pancras and became one of the first women justices in the country, and at the same time was chosen, with Beatrice Webb, to be a member of the lord chancellor's advisory committee for the selection of women justices. She was active in the Magistrates' Association (founded in 1920) and was elected to its council in 1921. She retired from the bench in 1931 but remained on the Magistrates' Association Council until 1940. She was also a member of the association's treatment of offenders committee and the poor persons defence committee, through which she campaigned for the extension of legal aid. The lessons that she had learned in the elementary school in Chelsea remained with her for the rest of her life and she channelled her concern for children into probation work, and became deeply committed to extending its reforming functions. She saw crime as taking its origin from poverty and deprivation and became interested in the possible correlation between the physiology of delinquents and their crimes, and in the biological basis of the delinquent personality. In 1927 she became president of the National Association of Probation Officers, vice-president in 1930 and was chairman from 1933–41.

She was president of the Women Sanitary Inspector's and Health Visitors' Association (1922–29) and in 1928 she launched the maternal mortality conference and remained active in her efforts to reduce maternal mortality. Her concern for women's health was reinforced by her participation in the 1926 royal commission on national health insurance. In a minority report she recommended the provision of medical care for children and the extension of benefit to women of childbearing age, and she campaigned for better maternity services and for higher sickness benefit.

She was designated literary executor to her uncle Sir Charles Dilke and after his death in 1911 she undertook the task of writing his biography. In a blinkered spirit of dedication to his memory, she tried to clear his name of the scandal (he was cited as co-respondent in a divorce case) that had damaged his career, and she ill-served history by destroying many of his papers on the ground that they might have contained incriminating material. Given her social background, she was able to establish easy relations with politicians of all parties and was described by one of her associates as having a 'distinguished appearance, being rather imperious in manner, and having about her an air of plumes, lace and elegant clothes.'[7]

She was made a CH in 1930 with the long citation: 'Member of the Advisory Committee to the Lord Chancellor for Women Justices of the Peace; Member of the Women's Central Committee on Women's Training and Employment; Member of the Executive of the Magistrates' Association.' It was an understandably brief conflation of a fascinating life that ended in 1951 with her death at the age of ninety.

Lord Hives 2 June 1943

Ernest Walter Hives was employed in a succession of posts in a company that achieved worldwide admiration through its meticulous engineering in the production of beautiful and opulent cars: Rolls Royce. He joined the company in 1908, and lived for it (outside his domestic life) until his retirement in 1957.

He was born in 1886, the son of a Reading schoolmaster and educated at Redlands School, Reading. After working in a Reading garage in 1903 he got a job at the garage of C. S. Rolls' car sales company. After a brief period with another firm he joined the Napier company where he spent three years and in 1908 he joined Rolls Royce, the company with which he was to be identified for the rest of his working life

He was originally engaged at Derby to supervise experimental road testing and he became one of the firm's outstanding drivers in the major automobile trials which were a feature of the European scene before the 1914–18 war. He was one of the first men to achieve a speed of 100mph on a race track. C. S. Rolls had died in 1910, but his name was perpetuated in the company made famous by the talents of Sir Henry Royce who designed his first aero-engine in 1915. Hives began its development in the same year and in 1919 it powered the twin-engined Vickers-Vimy bomber on the first direct flight across the Atlantic. Other notable engines followed, all of which were developed under Hives' direction. In 1936 he succeeded to the general works management of the factory and in 1937 he was elected to the board.

In 1941 the first British jet-propelled aeroplane, powered by the Whittle W1 gas turbine engine, flew. Sir Frank Whittle's company, Power Jets Ltd., was collaborating with other companies and by 1942 particularly with the Rover Company. In that year Hives made the most important policy decision in the company's history until that point. His decision to go all out for the gas turbine engine had a significant effect on the future of his company, and he arranged with the ministry of aircraft production to take over the Rover gas turbine engine while Rover took over from Rolls Royce the production tank, in which a variant of the 'Merlin' engine was installed. It was a shrewd decision. The evolution of the Rolls-Royce 'Merlin' was probably the most remarkable feat that had ever been achieved in the history of the internal combustion engine and Hives was regarded as the most outstanding internal combustion engineer in the country. Under his direction the company achieved a commanding world lead in the design, development and manufacture of gas turbine engine aircrafts

In the years before the 1939–45 war, Hives had developed intimate contacts with the air force and the government departments which supplied it. Due to Hives' relations with ministers, service chiefs and civil servants and his perception of what the service required, as well as the reputation of the technological abilities of Rolls Royce, the company enjoyed unparalleled official confidence. After the war, Hives became managing director (1946–50) and finally chairman of the board (1950–57).

He was made an MBE in 1920, and a CH in 1943, 'For services in the design of aero-engines'. He was created a baron in 1950 and the supporters for his coat of arms were a mechanic in overalls holding a micrometer and a draughtsman holding a set-square and T-square. He died in 1965.

A footnote to Hives' CH adds a note of irony, and evidence of how far the CH had moved on. Nineteen years earlier, in May 1924, the Labour government of Ramsay MacDonald proposed a CH for Henry Royce, the engine designer whose name was enshrined in the name of the company that he jointly founded. Twenty years later his pioneering work would have certainly qualified him for the honour, but six years after the foundation of the Order was just too soon for King George V. 'The King desires me to ask if there is any special reason why Mr Frederick Henry Royce is selected for a Companion of Honour? It strikes His Majesty as rather an unusual distinction to confer and the King would have thought that, if Mr Royce's public service for aircraft are of such value, a Knighthood would have been a more suitable recognition. His Majesty knows that the CH has in the past been given somewhat promiscuously: but he feels sure that the Prime Minister will agree that it is of the utmost importance, especially in a young Order, to preserve the highest possible standard of membership.'[8] Royce received a baronetcy in 1930 and died in 1933.

Essington Lewis 24 September 1943 [Australia]
Essington Lewis was the first Australian to be appointed to the Order, who had not previously been prime minister of the federation. The story of how he came to be recommended for a CH, and the consequential introduction of empire and commonwealth quotas, is covered in chapter fifteen. The purpose of this section is to look at his life and work and to review his place in Australian history.

He was born in Burra, South Australia, in 1881, the son of John Lewis CMG, partner in a firm of stock and station agents and a member of the South Australian Legislative Council, and the grandson of a Welsh immigrant who had gone to Australia in 1836 to help survey the new city of Adelaide. He was educated at St Peter's College, Adelaide, leaving at the age of thirteen and working for a while on one of his father's cattle stations, before returning to school. He left again at seventeen and after another period with cattle, he went to Adelaide University and graduated in law. He never practised, deciding that mining offered more opportunity than the law. The work was not unfamiliar; during his school holidays, he had worked underground at Broken Hill and Mount Lyell, and having become the foreman of a sulphuric acid and zinc plant, he was awarded a diploma by the South Australian School of Mines in 1905. His career thereafter was exclusively concerned with the business of mining, metallurgy and finally munitions in one of Australia's greatest industrial concerns, the Broken Hill Proprietary Company Ltd. He began as assistant manager of the smelting plant at Port Pirie, and then production engineer at the new steel works at Port Waratah. In 1920 he was made assistant general manager of the whole company, and in 1921 general manager at the age of forty. He was managing director (1926–38), chief general manager (1938–50), chairman (1950–52) and deputy chairman (1952–61). BHP as it was known was the largest steel producer in the British Commonwealth, 'and it inspired and provided the firmest base for Australia's general industrial development. Essington Lewis from the very early days, foresaw this role for BHP and fashioned it deliberately. He was a remarkable managing technician, with a splendid vision of what ought to be and what could be.'[9]

His early publications included *The iron and steel industry of Australia* (1929) and *The economics of the Australian iron and steel industry* (1938), and his breadth of experience and knowledge and his outstanding business and administrative abilities marked him for government service. In 1938 the government made him chairman of its advisory panel on industrial organisation and business consultant to the department of defence, and in 1939 chairman of the defence board of business administration. But it was during the 1939–45 war that he reached the summit of government service. At the request of Sir Robert Menzies, he became director general of munitions (1940–45) and director general of aircraft production and chairman of the aircraft advisory committee (1942–45).

His role was crucial to Australia's effective contribution to the war. By 1943 he had increased the number of government munitions factories from four to forty-eight, and the number of private industries with specially created munitions annexes was two hundred and thirteen. It was due largely to his efforts that Australia was self-sufficient in munitions. The iron, steel and allied industries of Australia were extended, made highly efficient, and organised as far as possible for conversion to war purposes. During his period as director general of munitions he co-ordinated the organisation of the production of munitions of war and equipment in the federally-owned and controlled industrial factories. 'Vast powers have been vested in him, and these powers have been so wisely and capably used as to have a highly stimulating effect on a great number of workmen, and also on the executives of these workmen. It is doubtful whether Australia would have reached anything like its present state of effectiveness for prosecuting the war but for the outstanding services Mr Essington Lewis has rendered.'[10]

Such was his success that in 1942 the government asked him to take over the administration and control of aircraft manufacture, in addition to his munitions work. His work in co-ordinating and improving the work of an industry which was causing the government anxiety, was also an unqualified success. John Curtin, the Australian prime minister warmly commended Lewis for the CH. 'No Australian has placed his talents and energies more unreservedly at the disposal of his country, or rendered greater service in production of the means for defending, not only the Commonwealth and its territories, but the Empire. As head of the government for the past twelve months and as Leader of the Opposition for 6 years previously, I have had a close knowledge of the value of the work rendered to the Commonwealth by citizens generally, and I am certain that my predecessor, as well as myself, would find it extraordinarily difficult to name any other Australian whose services industrially have been so valuable to the nation . . . The present satisfactory output of munitions, equipment and aircraft is due more to the ability and energy of Mr Essington Lewis than of any other man in Australia, and without his invaluable services these satisfactory results could not have been achieved.'[11]

Despite the irritable exchanges between London and Australia over the relative merits of Forgan Smith and Essington Lewis, the tendency is to accept Curtin's view that Lewis did have the better claim. Whereas Smith's work was limited to Queensland, Lewis's was nationwide and at a time of international crisis. The regret of the affair is that, good candidate though Lewis was, his candidature for the CH could have waited until the end of the war, and seems to have been brought forward with the sole purpose of foiling the recommendation of Forgan Smith.

After the war Lewis resigned from government service and returned to his work with BHP. He was additionally the first chairman of the Australian Administrative Staff College (1954–59), and the first chairman of the Industrial Design Council of Australia from 1957.

He was made a CH in 1943 for his services as 'Director-General of Munitions and of Aircraft Production in the Commonwealth of Australia.' He died in 1961.

George Gibson 13 June 1946
The life of George Gibson was the story of one who rose from working class obscurity to become general secretary of the foremost health service trade union and a member of the board of directors of the Bank of England, only through financial impropriety to end his life once again in obscurity.

He was born in Glasgow in 1885, one of the nine children of a drysalter. He left school at the age of twelve to become a tailor's messenger boy and went through a succession of other jobs before an economic depression forced him to leave his native land and move to Manchester, where he found work as an attendant in an asylum. Working conditions in asylums, as in many other trades, were grim and Gibson set about improving them by organising labour to secure improvements. His efforts led to the creation of the Mental Hospital and Institutional Workers' Union in 1910, which eventually merged with a number of small hospital unions to become the Confederation of Health Service Employees. His energy, ability and shrewdness were recognised in 1913 when he was elected general secretary of the union (holding the office for more than thirty years), and in that capacity he was called in 1925 to give evidence on staff conditions and the treatment of patients to the royal commission on Lunacy. He spoke and wrote frequently on institutional problems and became a considerable influence in the trade union world. He was elected to the general council of the Trades Union Congress (1928–48) and represented it at the annual conference of the American Federation of Labour in 1936.

He had no scruples about participation in the 1939–45 war (he had served as a gunner with the Royal Garrison Artillery in the 1914–18 war, and was commissioned and mentioned in despatches), though on his election as chairman of the TUC (1940–41) he declared: 'The main job facing the trade union movement is to prosecute the war to a successful conclusion and to prepare for meeting the legitimate aspirations of the working classes in all lands.'[12] He had many other activities including membership of the Overseas Settlement Board (1936–39) and the Lancashire Industrial Development Council, vice chairman of the National Savings Committee (1943–49) 'for which he worked strenuously and with marked success;'[13] and chairman of the Children's Overseas Committee (1944–53), the North West Regional Board for Industry (1945–48), and the North West Area Electricity Board (1948–49).

In the aftermath of the 1939–45 war Gibson was at the height of his influence. A Labour government was in power, and in 1946 he was appointed by that government to the board of directors of the Bank of England. His public life collapsed in the autumn of 1948 when a government tribunal criticised his involvement in a corruption scandal centred on the bank. The tribunal was set up to investigate a flurry of accusations and rumours that ministers and civil servants had been taking bribes. Given the general economic austerity of the time, even suggestions that the powerful were feathering their nests led to widespread public indignation. The chief subject of investigation was the relationship between John Belcher (parliamentary secretary to the president of the board of trade), George Gibson and Sidney Stanley, a Polish-born confidence trickster who made money by representing himself as a friend of the powerful. The tribunal met from October to December 1948, and Stanley, Belcher and Gibson were called upon to give evidence to the tribunal, while Hugh Dalton, president of the board of trade, gave evidence at his own request. Gibson denied that he had received any money, gift or loan or that he had exercised an influence on the bank's capital issues committee over a possible company flotation. Belcher admitted receipt of certain gifts, but not corruptly or to influence him.

The tribunal finished its work on 21 December 1948. Without waiting for its report, Gibson resigned as a director of the Bank of England on 23 December. The report was published on 25 January 1949. It rejected as baseless rumours of the payment of large sums of money to ministers or public servants, but found that there was justification for some of the allegations against Belcher and Gibson but none for any other ministers or public servants. Belcher (who was Labour member for the Sowerby division of the West Riding) had resigned his seat after giving evidence. On 26 January Gibson resigned his chairmanship of the north-western electricity board, though refusing to accept the tribunal's decision as just, and on the following day he resigned his other honorary appointments. In a statement to the house of commons, the prime minister declared that it would be 'conducive to the public good' that Sidney Stanley should leave the country. Gibson retired into obscurity at his home in Manchester where he died in 1953.

Gibson had refused a knighthood in 1941 at the conclusion of his chairmanship of the TUC, and twice refused a CBE in 1946 – offered for his services as general secretary of his union. His sole honour was the CH, conferred in 1946 for his services as 'Vice-Chairman of the National Savings Committee. A Past Chairman of the Trades Union Congress.' By repute he worked hard for the savings committee, but the citing of his chairmanship of the TUC (a ceremonial twelve-months appointment) was an odd addition – a pointless and unnecessary piece of gloss. After the report of the Lynsky tribunal, it was suggested that Gibson be removed from the CH Order, but no action was taken.

Arthur Deakin 1 January 1949
Arthur Deakin was the autocratic general secretary of the Transport and General Workers Union. Intolerant of communists, militants and any form of opposition, he ruled the union from 1940 until his death fifteen years later.

He was born in 1890 in Sutton Coldfield, Warwickshire, where his mother was a domestic servant. When he was ten, he moved with his mother and stepfather to Dowlais in south Wales, starting work at the steel firm of Guest, Keen and Nettlefolds at the age of thirteen. He joined the National Union of Gas Workers and was strongly influenced by the charismatic figure of Keir Hardie, member of parliament for Merthyr Tydfil, of which Dowlais was a part. In 1910 he moved to north Wales and took a job with another firm as a roll turner. He was briefly a member of the Amalgamated Society of Engineers, before joining the Dock, Wharf, Riverside and General Workers Union. He also belonged to the small British Roll Turners Society, of which he was general secretary for a short period. In 1919 he became a full-time official of the dock union and in 1922, when it joined others to form the Transport and General Workers Union, he became assistant general secretary for the north Wales area. A career as a union official was paralleled by a career in local government. In 1919 he was elected an alderman of Flintshire county council and became chairman of the council in 1932.

In 1932 he moved to London as national secretary of the General Workers' Trade Group where he came to the attention of Ernest Bevin, who had been general secretary of the TGWU since its formation. Bevin recognised Deakin's talents and appointed him assistant general secretary in 1935. In 1940 Bevin became minister of labour in the coalition government during the 1939–45 war. Deakin replaced him as acting general secretary, until Bevin's formal retirement in 1946 when he was elected to the substantive office.

A protégé of Bevin, Deakin lived for many years in the shadow of his mentor. He was 'essentially a Bevin creation and perhaps the most loyal supporter of a man upon whom he modelled himself to the extent of copying some of his public mannerisms'.[14] He was a member of the general council of the Trades Union Congress, a body dominated by Bevin and Walter Citrine, and was unable to make any influential contribution. He committed an embarrassing faux pas in 1943 when he visited neutral Sweden as a fraternal delegate to the congress of the Swedish Transport Workers' Union. While there he conferred with a Finnish trade union leader on the possibilities of a peace treaty. It was a well-intentioned but naive move which received wide publicity – and for which he was widely criticised. A peace treaty between the allied and axis powers at the height of the war was not on anyone's agenda.

The retirement of Bevin and Citrine in 1946 brought Deakin a much greater prominence in the trade union world and revealed him as a firm ally of the Attlee Labour government. His accession to the general secretaryship took place against the background of severe postwar economic restraint, and Deakin loyally supported government policy by urging unions to increase productivity and to restrain demands for wage increases – much to the displeasure of militants within his own union who expected him to fight the government on their behalf. He was increasingly hostile to communism especially within his own union, and in 1949 he persuaded it to bar communists from holding office. 'The attitude . . . was in part a reflection of his attitude towards opposition. He believed in the sanctity of majority decisions and was intolerant of those who opposed them. He attacked minorities in his own union and in the Labour Party with invective and organisational measures. He would defy conventions and precedents to get his own way and was often accused by his antagonists as being a dictator. By his public manner, outspoken, brusque and intolerant, and by his manner of handling internal union affairs he lent support to the accusation . . . He possessed a vital reluctance to delegate authority and maintained a strict control over even the smallest administrative detail in the union's head office. He would sometimes speak on behalf of his union without consulting the general executive council which constitutionally controlled him.'[15]

Deakin was also chairman of the TUC general council (1951–52), and a member of the advisory committees of the ministries of reconstruction and materials, the national advisory council of the ministry of labour, the British Transport advisory council, and the executive committee to provide a national memorial to King George VI. He was also a director of the *Daily Herald*, a national daily newspaper of which 49% of the shares were held by the TUC.

Deakin twice refused a knighthood, but he accepted a CBE in 1943, and a CH in 1949 for his services as 'General Secretary, Transport and General Workers' Union', and was made a privy councillor in 1954. He died, still in harness, in 1955.

Viscount Nuffield 1 January 1958
William Richard Morris, first Viscount Nuffield, was a single-minded and far-sighted pioneering automobile manufacturer and kind-hearted philanthropist, who during his working life donated staggering amounts of money to various causes.

He was born in Worcester in 1877. At the time his father was working in a draper's shop in the city, but returned to farming in Oxfordshire when Morris was three years old. He grew up in Cowley and went to the village school. He worked for a short period in a local cycle firm, then started on his own at the age of sixteen with a capital of £4. In 1901 he advertised himself as 'sole maker of the celebrated Morris cycles.' Beginning his career as the proprietor of a bicycle shop, he later became a manufacturer of motorcycles and then cars, and by 1910, he was described as a 'motor car engineer and agent and garage proprietor.' His plans for a car of his own were well advanced and when the 'Morris-Oxford' was announced at the 1912 motor show he received an order for four hundred cars. The first was produced in April 1913; it could reach a speed of 50mph in top gear and was priced at £165.

The Morris cars quickly became one of the biggest mass-production industries in the United Kingdom, and Morris became known as the 'British Ford.' During the 1914–18 war his factory at Cowley continued to make a small number of cars but like many other factories at the time, its principal work was the output of munitions. (In the 1939–45 war it concentrated on the production of tanks and aircraft.) The company produced 20,000 cars in 1923 and 50,000 in 1926, at that time one third of the national output. The 1930s depression saw a change of focus to smaller models, and it was claimed that the Morris Minor of 1931, which sold at £100, was able to do more than one hundred miles to the gallon.

Nuffield was now an extremely wealthy man. In 1935 the ordinary share capital of the company, all owned by Nuffield, consisted of £2,650,000. In 1936 the issue of one quarter of the shares raised his personal fortune to £20 million. He had no miserly tendencies and delighted in giving his money away to good causes. His donations had begun in 1926, and by the time of his death, it is thought that he had given away something like £30 million, the largest part of which was directed to research in medicine and social services with the principal aim of reducing human suffering. In 1936 he endowed a medical school at Oxford for £2 million, and added a further £1 million in 1937. In the same year he founded Nuffield College, Oxford, for the study of social, economic and political problems. In 1939 he gave £1½ million to form the Nuffield Provincial Hospitals Trust. In 1948 he established the Nuffield Foundation with an endowment of £10 million, its purposes being the advancement of health and the prevention and relief of sickness, the advancement of social well-being and the care and comfort of the aged poor. He was conservative in politics and made comparatively small donations to the Conservative Party: £20,000 in 1938; £25,000 in 1941; a seven year covenant in 1943 totalling £25,000, a post-election gift of £100,000 in 1945; £50,000 in 1947; and £10,000 in 1951.

Nuffield was neither scholar nor academic. He read very little and despite the large sums that he gave for academic activity, he was not interested in the process of research, only in the extent to which its results led to progress in dealing with medical problems.

His immense generosity led to a succession of honours. He was made an OBE in 1917 for his contributions to munitions in the 1914–18 war. He was created a baronet in 1929, a baron in 1934 and a viscount in 1938. His contribution to the manufacture of tanks and aircraft in the 1939–45 war brought him a GBE in 1941. It is thought that he was considered for an earldom in 1944 and in 1954 but the last of his honours was the CH, conferred in 1958 'For public and philanthropic services.' He retired in 1952 and died in 1963. He and his wife had no children, and the baronetcy, barony and viscountcy became extinct at his death.

Earl of Limerick 31 December 1960
Edmund Colquhoun Pery, fifth Earl of Limerick, was a wealthy and successful businessman. As such he represented the type of hereditary peer whose sense of noblesse oblige led him to give freely of his time for a mixture of public service.

He was born in 1888 and educated at Eton and New College, Oxford, and served in Egypt, Gallipoli and France during the 1914–18 war, being appointed to the DSO in 1918. He succeeded his half-brother, the fourth earl, in 1929.

His business life can be mentioned briefly because it bears no relation to the honours that he received. He was a director of the Industrial and Commercial Finance Corporation Ltd, the London Life Association Ltd, and the National Discount Company Ltd. He was also chairman of Mutual Finance Ltd and Parnall (Yate) Ltd and a number of subsidiary companies.

From the end of the 1914–18 war until the 1950s his principal area of service was the territorial army. He commanded the 11th brigade, Royal Horse Artillery (TA), from which he retired in 1931, and was honorary colonel of the City of London Yeomanry, Royal Armoured Corps (TA) (1932–52). He was chairman of the City of London Territorial and Auxiliary Forces Association (1941–50) (vice-chairman 1937–41), and national chairman of the council of Territorial and Auxiliary Forces Associations (1949–54) (vice-chairman (1942–49), and president (1954–56).

The public service which led to the conferment of the CH was his work as chairman of the Medical Research Council (1952–60), in which post he was outstandingly successful and well-liked. His complete fairness, shrewd sense of perspective, and obvious integrity won him both the full trust of the council members and the high respect of those with whom the council had to deal. That enabled him to guide the council smoothly, and through a number of difficult situations, during nearly nine years. His chairmanship saw a great expansion of the medical research council's activities, including in particular the shouldering of major responsibilities for clinical research within the national health service and for research in tropical medicine in collaboration with the colonial and commonwealth relations offices. His foresight and understanding of the significance of those developments were an important factor in ensuring their acceptance and successful progress. Because of his public spirit and his sense of the importance of the period of expansion, he was persuaded, despite personal inconvenience, to remain as chairman for so long a period.

For his work with the territorial army he was made a KCB in 1945 and a GBE in 1953. The CH came in 1960 for his services as 'Chairman, Medical Research Council'. It was perhaps too high an honour for someone who had only been chairman of a research council for less than eight years, but as he was an earl and already a GBE, the choice was between a CH or nothing. He died in 1967.

Sir Allen Lane 14 June 1969
Allen Lane was the founder of Penguin books and major contributor to the so-called paperback revolution in the 1920s and 30s. He also achieved an undeserved notoriety in 1961 when he and his company were prosecuted under the Obscene Publications Act for publishing an unexpurgated version of D. H. Lawrence's novel *Lady Chatterley's lover*.

He was born in 1902 in Bristol and educated at Bristol Grammar School. With his brothers he began his career in the book trade in 1919 by working in the bookshop and publishing house in London of their uncle John Lane, The Bodley Head. He remained with the company until 1936 when he resigned to establish his own publishing house – Penguin Books.

The birth of the company can be traced to a train trip on which Allen Lane was returning from a visit to his friend Agatha Christie. He found himself facing a return trip with nothing to read. Browsing the bookseller's stall in the station, he could find only magazines and expensive new hardbacks and nothing to interest him. On the train back to London, he began to consider seriously an idea that he had been thinking about for some time – to publish new fiction, quality reprints, and nonfiction in an inexpensive format. The books would have attractive paper covers and would sell for sixpence – at the time, the price of a packet of cigarettes. Furthermore, Lane envisaged the books being offered for sale at convenient venues apart from bookshops – such as train stations. Acquiring the capital he needed he settled on the name 'Penguin' – rejecting 'Dolphin' and 'Porpoise'. The first ten titles from the new press appeared in July 1935 and included works by Agatha Christie, Ernest Hemingway, and Dorothy Sayers. By publishing quality titles in well-designed formats at a low price, the venture was an instant success. He could not claim to be the first to publish paperbacks, but he was the first to be successful on a major scale. In 1967 Penguin launched its first line of hardback titles, under the name 'The Allen Lane Press.'

In 1936 the company broke from the Bodley Head, and Penguin Books Ltd. was established. In 1936, Penguin published its first nonfiction work – *A short history of the world*, by H. G. Wells. In its first year of business, Penguin sold over three million books and made approximately £75,000. In the next few years, other ornithologically titled series including 'Pelican' and 'Puffin' added to the success of Penguin.

One of the most infamous events in Lane's career was the Penguin publication of D. H. Lawrence's *Lady Chatterley's lover* in 1960. Lawrence's last novel, it was notable for the controversy surrounding its publication and it underwent various printings due to its sexual content. It was published privately in Florence in 1928, in a censored version in London in 1932 and finally unexpurgated by Grove Press in the USA in 1959. The appearance of the American edition persuaded Lane that there was no longer any reason for not publishing the full version in the United Kingdom. The main reason for the censorship of the book in the United Kingdom was the unprecedented, unrestrained and explicit language used to describe Lady Chatterley's affair with Oliver Mellors. But Lawrence had died in 1930 and his powerful works had long been accepted into the literary canon, and the full text was in print in the USA. The authorities took a different view. Lane and Penguin were charged under the Obscene Publications Act for publishing the unexpurgated version. The case went to trial and a jury eventually acquitted Lane and his company in November 1960. The case was a major event in the history of censorship in the United Kingdom and it turned *Lady Chatterley's lover* into one of Penguin's all time bestsellers, selling over three million copies in the two years following publication.

The company grew larger and larger and in 1967 Penguin Publishing was awarded The Queen's Award to Industry, for export achievement by Penguin Books Ltd. As Lane grew older his direct involvement in publishing diminished and he acquired the aura of being the elder statesman among publishers. By his vision, literary taste, marketing flair, and perseverance, he became and remains a significant figure in the history of publishing.

He was knighted in 1952 and made a CH in 1969 for his services as 'Chairman, Penguin Publishing Company'. He died in 1970.

James (Jack) Jones 31 December 1977

Jack Jones was general secretary of the TGWU – the vast and then powerful Transport and General Workers' Union – from 1969 to 1978, and in old age he found a new career championing the needs and rights of pensioners.

He was born in 1913 and educated at an elementary school in Liverpool. Leaving school at the age of fourteen, he worked for twelve years in the engineering and docks industries (1927–39) For the last three years of that period he was a councillor on Liverpool city council (1936–39). During that time he fought with the international brigade in the Spanish civil war on the side of the republican government and was wounded at the battle of Ebro in August 1938.

In 1939 he began what was to be a lifetime career as a trade union official. He started at a local level as district secretary for the TGWU and district secretary of the Confederation of Shipbuilding and Engineering Unions (1939–55), both in Coventry. Promotion followed in the TGWU in subsequent years: Midlands regional secretary (1955–63); executive officer (1963–69) and finally national general secretary (1969–78). The TGWU was one of the largest and most powerful trade unions, and Jones was its general secretary in what proved to be the last period of great trade union power. With Hugh Scanlon of the Amalgamated Union of Engineering Workers, Jones was one of the two most prominent trade union leaders of his day and was often seen on television and heard on radio, speaking on behalf of his members and disputing not only with employers but also with government ministers.

An able organiser and speaker, he was much in demand for committee work, and the roll call of his voluntary appointments was considerable: chairman, Midlands TUC advisory committee (1948–63); member, Midlands regional board for industry (1942–46 and 1954–63); justice of the peace for the city of Coventry (1950–63); executive chairman, Birmingham productivity committee

(1957–63); member, Labour Party national executive committee (1964–67); member, national committee for commonwealth immigrants (1965–69); member, national economic development committee (1969–78); member, advisory conciliation and arbitration service council (1974–78); member, British overseas trade board (1974–79); member, committee of enquiry into industrial democracy (1976–77); member, Crown Agents board (1978–80); member, royal commission on criminal procedure (1978–80); chairman, TUC international, transport and nationalised industries committees (1972–78); executive board member, international confederation of free trade unions; member, TUC general council (1968–78); deputy chairman, national ports council (1967–79); and joint chairman (with Lord Aldington), special committee on the ports (1972).

His public service lasted into his old age, and in retirement he took up a new career acting as the foremost spokesperson of a hitherto voiceless section of society – the elderly. As he was now a pensioner himself, it was typical of Jones that he should willingly campaign for others on the basis of his personal experience. A new collection of appointments appeared on his curriculum vitae: vice-president, Age Concern (1978-); vice-president, European Federation of Elderly and Retired Persons (1991-); president, Retired Members Association (1979-); and chairman, National Pensioners' Convention (1992-). In old age he had lost none of his spirited desire to remedy injustice and to right wrongs, and long after his contemporaries had retired and been forgotten, the voice of Jack Jones is still regularly heard on the media, passionately campaigning for his fellow pensioners.

His public service was recognised by appointment as an MBE in 1950, and a CH in 1977 for his services as 'General Secretary, Transport and General Workers' Union.' The then prime minister, Jim Callaghan, suggested to Jones that he should take a peerage. The latter had no time for the house of lords and had no desire to join a chamber that he wished to see abolished. Callaghan then raised the offer of the CH: 'It was set up to take the point of view of people like you into account. It carries no title and no privileges . . . I agreed to accept it, perhaps somewhat against my better judgement.'[16]

Aged eighty-nine at the time of writing, and more than sixty years after he was first appointed a trade union official, he is still as active as ever on behalf of his adopted cause.

CHAPTER FIFTEEN

A grant of honours

THE 1943 ENLARGEMENT AND THE COMMONWEALTH QUOTAS

> *Four other Oysters followed them,*
> *And yet another four;*
> *And thick and fast they came at last,*
> *And more, and more, and more –*
> *All hopping through the frothy waves,*
> *And scrambling to the shore.*
>
> 'Tweedledum and Tweedledee', *Through the looking-glass*, Lewis Carroll

The establishment of a Dominions quota 1942–43
The statutory size of the Order of the Companions of Honour, set at fifty in 1917, remained at that level until 1943 when it was enlarged to sixty-five. The expansion inaugurated a separate section of the Order, by providing official and agreed quotas for Australia, New Zealand and South Africa, and a fourth quota for the rest of the empire. Between 1917 and 1943 only five individuals from the empire had been appointed Companions of Honour. Four were from Australia: Stanley Bruce (1927), Joseph Lyons (1936), William Hughes (1941) and Earle Page (1942); and one from India: Valingaman Sankarana-Rayana Srinivasa Sastri (1930). Although occasional appointments from the empire might have continued from time to time, Australia seemed to have established a pre-eminent use of the CH Order by the early years of the 1939–45 war, and it was from Australia that there came in 1943 an initiative to create a ring-fenced 'imperial' section. Technically the decision was a formal recommendation by the Committee on the Grant of Honours, Decorations and Medals, but the work of the committee tended to be reactive rather than proactive, and in this case the decision was made in response to an outflanking manoeuvre by John Joseph Curtin, the prime minister of Australia.

Curtin was of Irish-Catholic descent and born into a family that knew poverty when he was a child, because of the ill-health of his father. Battling alcoholism, loneliness and uncertainty, his natural persona was austere and he could be shy and reserved in 'society' company. But he had a passionate concern for the underprivileged. He had no choice but to go out to work at thirteen, and he was successively a printer's helper, hotel pageboy, labourer in a pottery works, copyboy on the *Melbourne Age* and clerk in a factory. This first-hand experience of working-class conditions and a wide reading of socialist literature, turned him into a radical activist. By 1906, as a founder-member of the Victorian Socialist Party, he was a regular speaker at political meetings. In 1916, as secretary of the Victorian Anti-Conscription League, he was sentenced to three months imprisonment for failing to enlist under the Military Service Proclamation. It was an attempt to force conscription on Australians, but was withdrawn when Curtin had served only three days in prison. Soon afterwards he accepted the editorial chair of the *Perth*

Westralian Worker and took his wife and children to Western Australia. During a second attempt at conscription he escaped a second spell in prison even though he was charged with sedition. He was elected to the federal parliament in 1928, leader of the Australian Labour Party in 1934, and prime minister of Australia in 1941. Curtin's stand against conscription in the 1914–18 war was early evidence of a man who was devoted to peace, but he became such a notable wartime leader in the Second World War that even Churchill described him as 'commanding and successful'. He clashed with Churchill on a number of issues, for example his refusal to divert Australian troops to Burma to assist British forces, when they were needed to defend Australia against the real threat of an imminent Japanese attack.

The stress of leading Australia through the 1939–45 war contributed to his sudden death on 5 July 1945. Had he lived, he would have been an ideal Companion of Honour. As it was, he clashed with Churchill on the conferment of the CH Order on Australians – and won.

The story began in September 1942 with the resignation of Forgan Smith, after a long (1934–42) and successful tenure as premier of Queensland. By tradition established towards the end of the nineteenth century, the premiers of Australian states were traditionally given a KCMG at some point during their tenure, or on retirement. Forgan Smith, like John Curtin, belonged to the Australian Labour Party and had an aversion to titles. Sir Leslie Wilson, governor of Queensland, wrote to Lord Gowrie, governor general of Australia, recommending that in view of Smith's ideological objections, he should be offered not a KCMG but a CH. Gowrie was concerned that the conferral of the CH on a state premier would establish an undesirable precedent. The CH had previously been conferred only on four prime ministers of the Australian federal government. There were six Australian states, of which Queensland was one, and were the CH to be given to one state premier, it would be difficult to withhold it from others of identical rank and with a similar aversion to titles, and raise the prospect that the small Order might eventually be swamped by Australian state premiers. Gowrie agreed that Smith deserved an honour, but the KCMG not the CH was his preferred option and he sought the advice of the dominions office.[1]

Before the office had time to respond, Gowrie quickly followed his telegram with another. 'Have just received telegram from Governor of Queensland in which he states Forgan Smith desires him to withdraw recommendation for KCMG for himself. Governor desires that his recommendation for CH for Forgan Smith should stand. I am unable to vary the opinion expressed in my telegram.'[2]

The next few weeks saw an exchange of telegrams between the dominions office and the governor general. Gowrie's opinion was not immediately shared by Clement Attlee, deputy prime minister and dominions secretary in Churchill's wartime coalition government. Although Attlee had no personal dislike of honours that carried titles, he headed Britain's Labour Party, and must have felt an instinctive sympathy with the Australian Labour premier. 'I feel myself that in view of Forgan Smith's long and successful tenure of the Premiership of Queensland, his case is an exceptional one and I should like to see his services rewarded by a suitable mark of distinction. It would, I think, be a pity if this were found to be impracticable on account of the technical difficulties which undoubtedly exist. The difficulty as regards a KCMG, which would be the ordinary reward for a state premier on retirement is no doubt that Forgan Smith himself and his Labour successor would feel unable to support a recommendation carrying a title. If this is insuperable, it becomes a question of a CH or nothing. I realise that hitherto in Australia no-one less than an ex-Prime Minister of the Commonwealth has received this award. In this country however, the CH has been awarded on a somewhat broader basis and in particular it has from the beginning been used to distinguish prominent persons in the Labour Party who presumably would have felt difficulty in accepting awards carrying titles. If CH were awarded to Forgan Smith, it would, I agree, afford a precedent for future claims by other State ex-Premiers, but it should . . . be possible to limit awards to cases of outstanding service like that of Forgan Smith.' Attlee's point about the broader basis of conferment of the CH in the United Kingdom was valid and one that Curtin later used to clinch his argument.

Gowrie stood firm on his advice to the dominions office. He was still of the opinion that to confer the CH on someone who, however eminent, stood outside the federal sphere, would create an awkward precedent for the future. It was all very well to say that Forgan Smith had performed outstanding service. But the qualification of outstanding service and where the line of period of service should be drawn would be difficult to define. Although it carried no title, the CH ranked above the KCMG and the Knight Bachelor, and those prominent in the federal political sphere would consider that their federal service had been assessed below the service of one particular state; such action would create surprise and comment. 'The question of the Labour Government being averse to the bestowal of the title has caused injustice to many prominent men outside political circles who have well earned recognition . . . If the principle is accepted that Labour politicians themselves can be awarded even higher honours than they would otherwise have received it would give rise to grave dissatisfaction. Unless therefore you are prepared to enlarge the distribution of the CH and thereby lower its status in Australia by including not only State Premiers but other deserving citizens as well, I would suggest that the bestowal of a CH on Mr Forgan Smith would create an embarrassing precedent and should not be proceeded with.'[4]

The argument was faultless, and the award of a CH to a state premier would certainly have formed the basis for further claims. On occasions state premiers had been candidates for the federal parliament and there was no reason to suppose this trend would not continue in the future. Because of their experience in state government, they would be prime candidates to become federal ministers, and the situation would then arise where a federal minister would enjoy a high honour not yet conferred on a federal prime minister. 'I still feel,' wrote Gowrie to the dominions office, 'that to go beyond the Federal sphere would lead to embarrassment in the future; but if you are prepared to accept this possibility and are still of the opinion that the bestowal of this honour on Forgan Smith would not lead to an increase beyond the numbers allowed, then I will agree to your proposal.'[5]

The matter was thrashed around Whitehall for a while. Robert Knox of the ceremonial office was inclined to agree with Attlee and be generous. Smith had held a state premiership with great success for nine consecutive years, a record unequalled in the history of the Australian state premierships, and as the dominions office pressed for his appointment as a CH, 'I think that in spite of the various difficulties, the recommendation might be favourably considered.'[6] Although there was a certain risk involved, the Order had been designed from the beginning to accommodate those who were disinclined from principle or other reason to accept an honour that conferred a title, for example a number of Labour MPs and trades union general secretaries. But there was a danger that the award of the CH could become a convenient way of rewarding those who, for principle or other reason, could not or would not accept a knighthood, and the result might be the inclusion in the Order of too large a proportion of such groups as the clergy or Labour politicians. 'Two Australian Federal Ministers or ex-Ministers, Mr Hughes and Sir Earle Page, already have it, and it would certainly be undesirable that any Labour Federal Minister in Australia should think that he was entitled to be considered for it. Nevertheless Mr Forgan Smith's record is so exceptional that I think the Prime Minister would be justified in recommending him.'[7]

In November, Curtin entered the debate – firmly against a CH for Forgan Smith. As a ceremonial governor general, Gowrie did his constitutional duty and discussed the issue with his prime minister. Curtin agreed with Gowrie that a CH for Forgan Smith was out of the question. Such an award would cause members of the federal parliament who were ex-prime ministers or even a present minister to expect similar recognition, and would place him in difficult position. 'He expressed strong views against the principles involved . . . He has asked me to do my best to prevent that situation arising.'[8]

The battle lines had been drawn. On one side was the Australian prime minister, supported by the governor general, adamant that the CH should not go to an Australian state premier. On the other side, the dominions office in London, impressed by Forgan Smith's record, who could see no serious objection to giving him the CH. The line taken by Curtin was not so surprising since it was based on an issue which had bedevilled Australia since the formation of the federation in 1901 – the interests of the federation versus the interests of the states. Throughout the discussion, the dominions office took a view that was as reasonable as it was detached from the ferment of Australian politics. There was no question of setting up a new standard for the CH in Australia in respect of political services, and the comparative merits of federal or state services respectively should not be allowed to enter into the matter. The proposal of a CH for Forgan Smith was a case of recognising outstanding merit by an individual, and what was wrong with that.[9] Clement Attlee delivered what he thought was the final word on the subject. 'Mr Attlee does not regard Mr Curtin's intervention as conclusive against the suggested award to Mr Forgan Smith. The matter is not one which, in his view, ought to be dealt with from the aspect of jealousies between the Commonwealth and the States.'[10]

Attlee had not reckoned with the determination of Curtin not to be overruled by politicians or civil servants in London. Doubtless in alliance with his governor general, he moved swiftly to adopt a tactic that effectively outflanked the Queensland nomination. In late November telegrams were sent by Gowrie to the Dominions Office and by Curtin to Churchill, recommending the name of Essington Lewis, the Commonwealth director general of munitions and director general of aircraft production, for the CH. The Australian strategy was obvious to London. 'There seems no doubt that Mr Curtin has put forward this recommendation mainly with a view to preventing effect being given to the recommendation in the case of Mr Forgan Smith . . . since it would clearly be impossible to award two CH's to Australians in the same Honours list. The Commonwealth Government have not been making any recommendations for *Civil* honours since

Mr Curtin assumed office in the autumn of 1941, and this supports the view as to the purpose of the present recommendation . . . In any event, this does not seem to be a case in which the CH would be the appropriate award and the most suitable Honour would be a KBE, or perhaps a GBE.'[11]

Churchill consulted his advisers, decided to oppose the recommendation and telegraphed directly to Curtin. 'I fully appreciate the great services which Mr Essington Lewis has rendered towards the war effort . . . I am afraid, however, that having regard to the standards of appointment generally adopted, the CH would not be appropriate. The right honour would, I think, be a KBE or even perhaps a GBE, and if you care to put him forward for one of these I should be most glad to consider the possibility of submitting his name accordingly.'[12]

From December 1942 until March 1943 there then followed a game of table tennis, in which Churchill and Curtin courteously but firmly batted the ball back and forth across the net, each with the expectation that the other side must and would give way. Having offered an honour as high as the GBE (in fact it ranked above a CH) Churchill could not conceive that Curtin would do anything other than acquiesce. Not so Curtin; despite Churchill's formidable personality, he was not prepared to be bullied by the British prime minister. 'Glad your interest in, and appreciation of, services of Essington Lewis which, as set out in Governor-General's telegram, has had a profound effect on war effort of the Empire. My recommendation was made with due regard to standard of appointments made in the past. Although GBE would be a suitable form of recognition in ordinary circumstances, there are several reasons why, in this case, it would not be suitable. Mr Lewis has rendered services of such national importance to Australia that any recognition of his work involves a distinction not generally accorded. I would not ask him to accept a distinction now shared by Australians whose services are not comparable. Difficulties which might be visualised by Officers of the Order should not be allowed to stand in the way, particularly in view of Section five of the Statutes of the Order referring to eligibility. I would greatly value your concurrence in my views, and help in having recommendation accepted.'[13] The problem was undoubtedly partly ideological, Curtin not desiring to recommend any Australian for any honour that carried a title, but it was partly practical – to circumvent the appointment of Forgan Smith – and Curtin did have a point. He *was* ideologically opposed to titles and he was more sensitive to the tensions of Australian politics than either Churchill or Attlee.

Churchill, in true Churchillian form, did not take kindly to what he saw as irrational opposition to a perfectly reasonable solution. On some matters he could be quite oblivious and insensitive to matters of political delicacy. In the question of the CH and Australia, he really couldn't see what all the fuss was about – at least until it was explained to him – and his contemporary attitude towards Irish politics and the fate of the Order of St Patrick bears this out.[14] He had no intention of yielding to Curtin. If the latter would not agree to a KBE or a GBE for Lewis, then it would be nothing. 'I recognize the high value to be placed on Essington Lewis's services, but I am sorry that you still feel that the CH is the only appropriate award. The CH in fact ranks lower than the GBE. I do not understand what you mean by 'the Officers of the Order' being concerned in the matter. I am the only one who knows about it, and I am totally indifferent. There is of course nothing in the Statutes of the Order to preclude the appointment, but I am advised that the regular practice in the case of Australia has hitherto been to limit the conferment of the CH to Prime Ministers and ex-Prime Ministers. However that may be, I am afraid there is no prospect of a CH being available in the New Year's List. I am so sorry.'[15]

Curtin could be as obstreperous as Churchill and he was not about to give way. Had he been less obsessed with the exclusion of titles from Australia, he would have accepted Churchill's correct statement that a member of the Order of the Companions of Honour ranked below a knight grand cross of the Order of the British Empire, and been delighted to recommend Lewis for a GBE. But his position was unshakeable, and on 11 December, he supplied a coda which implied that he had selected Lewis because he *knew* that the latter would not accept a knighthood. 'I consulted Essington Lewis on the question of a knighthood. Naturally he asked the reason for my enquiry, as I had known his objections to that class of distinction which knowledge led to the recommendation I had made. In reply to Mr Lewis' query, I said there were difficulties. Thereupon he informed me that he would wish to be relieved of any obligation to accept any honour.'[16] Deserving though his qualities might have been, it is not difficult to see that Lewis was in part being used as a pawn by Curtin in a game with Churchill, and Curtin did not intend to lose the game.

Although Curtin had been told that there was no prospect of a CH being made available in the New Year List 1943, there were other future lists in which Lewis might appear. Having recommended Lewis, who clearly had federal responsibilities, Curtin continued to press his candidate in January, after the publication of the New Year List – which contained a name that supported his arguments. 'Now that I know the New Year Honours I do desire you to reconsider my request that Mr Essington Lewis be put forward for membership of the Order of the Companions of Honour. There is no other Order which will be appropriate as marking his great services to the Empire, and I am confident that in my place you would assess the matter as I do.'[17] Curtin had announced his final stand – 'there was no other Order' that was acceptable for Lewis.

The dominions office meanwhile continued to view the Smith-Lewis affair with a faultless logic that seemed to be not quite capable of grasping that they were dealing with a very determined Australian prime minister. Forgan Smith's case had been disposed of by the decision that a CH could not be made available in the New Year List, but in their view it was still necessary to keep him in mind when considering the recommendation of Essington Lewis. There was also formal recognition that the regular practice in the case of Australia was to limit the conferment of the CH to prime ministers and former prime ministers. Forgan Smith's distinguished record as premier of Queensland would have justified an exception to existing practice. But was it possible to take the line that Essington Lewis' merits were sufficiently outstanding to justify a similar exception, or would his appointment as a CH create another embarrassing precedent? There was further strength for Curtin's candidate, as he himself had implied, in that the New Year List had included (for a CH) the name of Lord Leathers, minister of war transport. When the name of Leathers was combined with those of Lord Woolton, minister of food, who had received the CH in the Birthday List 1942, and A. V. Alexander, first lord of the admiralty, who had received the CH in the Birthday List 1941, it produced a trio of ministers who played a significant role in the war effort. Curtin portrayed Lewis as occupying a position at least as important as that of Lord Leathers. It was true that he was not a government minister, but his status had to be properly assessed. Sir Eric Machtig, permanent under secretary at the dominions office asked for the opinion of Robert Knox, the treasury ceremonial officer, who for more than thirty years guarded the United Kingdom honours system. 'In the circumstances,' wrote Machtig, 'we seem to need, in the first instance, your views as to the effect upon standards if a CH were conferred upon Mr Essington Lewis.'[18]

Because of his breadth of experience, Knox was able to rise above Australian politics and to take a broader view of the conferment of honours. He was also wise enough to see that nothing would be achieved by needlessly antagonising a dominions prime minister at a time of international crisis, especially not one as wedded to his convictions as Curtin. Armed with the benefit of his reply, Machtig presented the arguments to Churchill. The conferment of a CH on Essington Lewis in the Birthday Honours List might present less difficulty in relation to the refusal of a CH to Forgan Smith, but he personally still felt that of the two, Forgan Smith was the better candidate. Machtig pointed to the recent conferments of the CH on Alexander, Woolton and Leathers as a possible precedent for the appointment of Lewis. True, he was not a government minister but, because of the method of government war organization adopted in Australia, his position could be regarded as approximating to that of a cabinet minister. For ideological reasons, Curtin was not making any recommendations for the award of *civil* honours to Australians, and therefore the selection of Lewis as the one Australian on whom such an honour was being conferred would look curious, but that was a matter for the Australian prime minister. Furthermore, if a CH was to be conferred on anyone in a dominion of a status comparable to that of Essington Lewis, 'there is a strong candidate in Canada who had been performing similar functions and whose services are, in the opinion of the United Kingdom departments concerned, in every way as deserving of recognition than those of Mr Essington Lewis. If, in the circumstance, you should feel that the case was not one for the conferment of a CH, you might like to sound Mr Curtin as to whether the conferment of a GCMG would meet the case, though in view of your earlier correspondence with Mr Curtin in which he indicated that a GBE would not be acceptable, it is by no means certain that he would accept this. I still think, however, that a GBE is the right award.'[19]

So back went the ball to Curtin – with the unusually high offer of a GCMG – although any further argument with him was now quite futile. Forgan Smith had by now disappeared into the wings and Curtin had secured the upper hand by presenting Essington Lewis and challenging London to say why he was not an acceptable candidate for the CH. At this stage, early in March 1943, the size of the Order was cited as an additional obstacle. The number of candidates was limited to fifty and vacancies were in consequence few in number. By inference, Curtin had suggested an enlargement, but such an extension in the case of the dominions 'as is implied in your prime minister's proposal', wrote Attlee to Gowrie, would require a very considerable increase in the number of vacancies and also of Companions and this in turn would result in lessening the value of the Order and so defeat its own purpose. 'He is sorry therefore that at present he sees no prospect of submitting person named for CH. He cannot but feel that a GBE is the appropriate award in this instance though special difficulties as to this in the present case are fully recognized.'[20]

Curtin now began to display his irritation. On 17 March 1943 he drafted a full reply and sent it to Gowrie for onward transmission to London. He dealt with all the difficulties raised by Churchill, raised the complaint that this was an unwarranted interference in Australian affairs, and made it clear that he would not tolerate further delay. Firstly there was the question of precedent. True all previous Australians appointed to the Order had been prime ministers of the commonwealth, but that did not mean that they needed to be so in the future. 'I am not aware of any reason or provision in the statutes for confining the award of this honour in Australia to men who have filled the office of Prime Minister. The fact that up to the present four Australian men have been admitted to this Order upon the grounds of one and the same qualification has not in my opinion established a practice which would exclude all other Australian men and all Australian women whatever their service to the Crown may have been.'

Curtin observed that the same rule did not apply in the United Kingdom. 'I note that men and women who have been admitted to the Order in the United Kingdom appear to have been selected for a very wide range of services.' If the nomination of Essington Lewis was rejected because he had not filled the office of prime minister, 'it must be assumed that there is a distinction between the eligibility of persons in the United Kingdom and Australia respectively.' Curtin then proceeded to offer a solution to this discrepancy of standard. If this distinction did not exist in fact, there appeared to be no reason for not extending membership of the Order to enable the dominion governments to recommend directly to the sovereign that appointments be made to the Order. 'An increase of the membership provided for in the Statutes, namely fifty, in order to provide an allocation for Australia on a population basis, would amount to an increase of say five. This number would meet present and immediate future requirements . . . provided without increase of the statutory number, namely by making five available from the fifty provided for in the Statutes.'

The United Kingdom need not fear the provision of an Australian quota, because Curtin had read the statutes and knew what was required. 'Whether an allocation is made from the number provided under the Statutes, or by extension, there is no reason to suppose that the admission of Australians would cause a "lessening of purpose" of the Order which, according to the provision in the Statutes, is for bestowal on "subjects of our Crown as may have rendered conspicuous service of national importance." Then he returned to Essington Lewis, proposing an unusual course. 'In regard to vacancies it is obvious that whether the person recommended is domiciled in the United Kingdom or elsewhere his immediate appointment would depend on the existence of a vacancy. I suggest that His Majesty in these circumstances would be pleased to approve admission to the Order pending a vacancy and I have no doubt such a course could be taken in the case of Mr Essington Lewis.'

Curtin concluded his letter by warning that the interference of United Kingdom ministers in Australian recommendations was not acceptable, and reiterating his nomination of Lewis. 'I am not satisfied that it is fitting that my proposal should have been rejected by a United Kingdom minister or that it has been refused on reasonable grounds. I must again request that my original recommendation together with my advice forwarded since, be submitted to His Majesty with a request that, if necessary, the Order be extended to provide an allocation for Australian purposes or that my recommendation be approved pending the next vacancy.'

Lord Gowrie added his own entreaty that Curtin's request should be complied with. 'In your Secret Honours telegram dated 23rd October 1942, the following statement appears – "The CH is as you know strictly limited in numbers and it was definitely designed to meet the case of a man who has rendered outstanding services in any particular sphere of public life but I understand does not for adequate personal reasons feel disposed to accept an honour involving knighthood." "It should in my view be our endeavour to award men in accordance with their services and not on account of their status." Such statements would clearly embrace the case of Essington Lewis. I most strongly urge that the above submission from my Prime Minister be laid before His Majesty.'[21]

The question of Lewis aside, Curtin had raised two issues which deserved consideration. Firstly, should the Order be reconstituted so as to allot a quota to Australia (and presumably to the other dominions) either by population basis or some similar proportionate basis? Secondly, Curtin argued that his recommendation of Essington Lewis should have been submitted directly to the sovereign, irrespective of the view taken by the British government or any individual British minister.

The second point raised a delicate constitutional issue which needed careful consideration. In theory there was no doubt that the prime minister of Australia had the right to make whatever submission that he pleased to the sovereign, on a matter affecting Australia. But what of the question of honours, which did not relate to Australia alone? This demonstrated the weakness if not of the imperial honours system then certainly of the CH Order. It was a small British Order to which a few exceptional dominions appointments had been allowed. 'In its inception, and to some extent in its application, the Companionship of Honour is primarily a United Kingdom matter, and it is clear that, having regard more especially to the fixed number of Companions, any recommendation of a particular individual for appointment to the Order must affect other appointments to the Order and particularly concerns the United Kingdom government which has hitherto been responsible for making recommendations for appointment to the Order. It is not possible to admit, therefore, that we committed any error in not submitting Mr Curtin's recommendation of Mr Essington Lewis for a CH to the King, irrespective of our own views, or that we are now bound to lay the matter before the King without further consideration. I might also mention that the line which Mr Curtin is at present taking is quite different from that which he previously took when we were desirous of seeing a CH conferred upon Mr Forgan Smith, the ex-Premier of Queensland.'[22]

Such was Attlee's opinion. Churchill himself could see no difficulty. 'I presume that he is entitled to advise the King in one sense, and I am entitled to advise him in the other. The King could then be advised to reply that such an Order was primarily a United Kingdom Order, and as a difference of view had been expressed by two of his Prime Ministers, he hoped the matter might be the subject of further discussion between them in order that, if possible, he might receive similar advice from both quarters.' But he did see the force of the argument of disparity between the two nations. 'I must say however that I think there is something in Curtin's point that only Australian Prime Ministers should be eligible while any old Britisher can be given it, and that therefore the Australians are placed in a definitely lower category.'[23]

The question of honours was a comparatively minor issue on the imperial stage in the mid–1940s, but it could have been unnecessarily divisive, and provoked ill-feeling between allies if it was not carefully handled. The crown was the focus of unity of the world-wide empire and commonwealth, and it must not be brought into a dispute. It had always been the endeavour to avoid a situation where conflicting advice was given to the King by his separate governments and to compose any differences at government level before a submission was made to the sovereign, and that was the best way to proceed. Attlee, however, still objected to Curtin's nomination of Lewis as a ploy to suppress the nomination of Smith. 'Curtin has some justification for his view that the standard of CH awards in this country is on a lower level than it has been hitherto in Australia. But I think myself that he has put himself altogether out of court by his opposition to the award of a CH to Forgan Smith who was clearly the most distinguished man in Australia in State, as opposed to Federal, politics.'[24] Nevertheless he agreed that the best way forward was to adopt Curtin's suggestion that the Order should be reconstituted in some way so as to allot a quota to Australia and the other dominions. That would also provide a means for delaying the appointment of Essington Lewis, although it could not be delayed for ever.[25]

Curtin was duly informed that the matter would be resolved in this way, but for the time being it must be allowed to rest. The United Kingdom had a prime interest in the Order, and therefore the prime minister of the United Kingdom had an equal right with the prime minister of Australia to advise the sovereign. 'But the King must not be embarrassed by receiving on the same matter divergent advice from his several Prime Ministers. Mr Curtin will surely therefore agree that best course is for the matter to be fully discussed and prior agreement reached between the two Governments as to the submission which should be made to the King.'[26]

There was no reason why the CH should not have a discrete dominions quota, and there was also precedent for dominions to make their submission directly to the sovereign. For many years it had been the regular practice to allocate to Australia, as well as New Zealand definite quotas in the Order of St Michael and St George, the civil and military divisions of the Order of the British Empire and the military division of the Order of the Bath, for each New Year and Birthday Honours List. When Canada resumed recommendations for honours in the 1930s, quotas were also allocated for Canada in the three Orders. Previously, recommendations from Australia within the agreed quotas had been submitted to the sovereign by United Kingdom ministers. It had, however, been agreed that dominions ministers had the right to submit such recommendations direct to the King if they so desired, and the statutes of the Order of the British Empire had recently been amended so as to provide in terms for this. When making recommendations for military honours during the 1939–45 war, the Canadian government submitted its recommendations to the sovereign through the governor general of Canada and without any intervention by United Kingdom ministers. When Richard Bedford Bennett was prime minister of Canada, he followed the same procedure when he submitted a batch of recommendations in 1933–35. Whether such an arrangement could be extended to the Companions of Honour was a matter for consideration but the principle of a dominion quota and of direct submission by a dominion within the quota was a well established one. The CH was established to meet the case of those who had rendered outstanding services in any particular sphere of public life but who could not or would not accept an honour involving a title. This consideration had been present in Canada since the Canadian parliament's 1918 resolution petitioning the sovereign to refrain from conferring titular honours on Canadian citizens, and with a Labour government in power, it was becoming a controversial issue in Australia. 'It is largely this which has inspired Mr Curtin's insistence on a CH for Essington

Lewis, whom he is unwilling to recommend for a GBE,' wrote Attlee to Churchill, and he advised that the time had come to bring the CH into line with the other United Kingdom Orders. 'You have yourself made the point that in existing conditions the Australians are placed in a definitely lower category than people belonging to this country as regards eligibility for the CH. In the circumstances it seems to me that there is much to be said for letting the Australian government have a small quota (say 5) of their own which they would themselves have the responsibility of filling within the requirements of the Statutes of the Order. It would avoid the kind of controversy which has arisen between the Australian Prime Minister and ourselves over the last two cases – Forgan Smith and Essington Lewis – which does not help matters and usually ends, anyhow, in the Dominion getting its own way. The position in Canada is much the same. As you probably know, the Canadian government have considered the possibility of instituting a special Canadian Order of Merit to cover cases which merit high distinction but cannot be recognized by appointment to knighthoods. This has been found to present considerable difficulties and the proposal has, I understand, been abandoned, at any rate for the time being. It seems possible that the allocation to Canada of a small quota in the Order of Companions of Honour (say seven) would go some way towards solving the problem there. I am sure that you will agree that it would be far preferable that the Dominion Governments should be encouraged to make recommendations for appointments to existing Orders which are open to British subjects in any part of the Empire, rather than that they should institute new Orders of their own, limited to citizens of the particular Dominion. In the circumstances, I hope that you will be willing that the question should at any rate be examined by the Committee on the Grant of Honours, Decorations and Medals in Time of War. This would not, of course, commit anyone, and the views of the Committee would, as a next step, be submitted to you for consideration.'[27]

The proposal was referred to Robert Knox, who agreed that a dominions quota would have to be instituted, if only to keep the dominions within the structure of an imperial honours system. 'The system proposed would rob the Prime Minister of the ability to recommend Dominion candidates for the CH. This would be unfortunate. Postponement of such a new system could probably be managed by giving way at once in the case of Essington Lewis. No very great harm would be done by that but I do not consider that it would enable us to postpone a change in the system for more than a year or two. Most of the arguments in the Dominions Office memorandum are sound, and sooner or later I think it will be necessary to provide Dominion allocations. This is especially desirable if it is likely to prevent applications for new Orders in the Dominions.'[28]

On 27 April 1943, the Committee on the Grant of Honours, Decorations and Medals in Time of War proposed that the statutory size of the Order be increased from fifty to seventy, the distribution being as follows:

The Commonwealth of Australia	5
The Dominion of New Zealand	2
The Union of South Africa	2
The Dominion of Canada	7
The United Kingdom	45
India, Burma and the Colonies	9
TOTAL	70

The figures were approved by Attlee on 3 May, by Churchill on 5 May,[29] and the King's approval was reported on 14 May.[30] On 18 May telegrams were sent to the governments of Canada and South Africa and to the governor generals of Australia and New Zealand. 'We are . . . impressed by the considerations in favour of such a step and we are accordingly prepared to recommend to the King that the Statutes of the Order should be amended . . . it would be made clear that these figures would cover existing members of the Order belonging to a Dominion.'[31]

Although the figures were somewhat arbitrary, the principle was sound and well-intentioned – but it was not enough to satisfy Curtin – who now saw victory within sight and pressed home his advantage – as Gowrie reported to the dominions office. 'My Prime Minister would be glad to be informed of the method employed in arriving at the proposed apportionment of 70 . . . between the United Kingdom and the four Dominions. My Prime Minister has nothing to add to what has already been forwarded to London in regard to Essington Lewis and desires that his original recommendation with subsequent advice and communication be submitted to His Majesty when the next vacancy occurs without waiting for the amendment of the Statute.'[32]

It was difficult to give a satisfactory reply to Curtin's enquiry as to the method employed in arriving at the proposed apportionment of seventy Companions of Honour. On the basis of a strict comparison between populations, Australia could claim more than five. In fact the Australian figure would then be seven and the Canadian figure would be eleven. But that would mean increasing the total establishment still further to seventy-six, a fifty percent increase in the size of the Order. But if Australia was limited to five, the corresponding figure for the United Kingdom on a population basis would be only about thirty. In fact, the figure of five was taken for Australia because it appeared from the governor-general's telegram of 17 March that Curtin would be satisfied with that figure.

Curtin could also have made use of the argument (from a situation of his own making) that as Australians in existing circumstances were to a great extent debarred from accepting high honours (i.e. knighthoods in the various Orders) normally awarded to United Kingdom citizens, Australia was entitled to a certain measure of liberality in the matter of an honour not carrying a title, and could claim many more places in the CH than the five on offer. But it was doubtful how far he could seriously argue that, because of differences in the attitudes of Australia and the United Kingdom on titular honours, the United Kingdom ought to go out of its way to assist by giving Australia a special allocation in what was primarily a United Kingdom Order.

In the circumstances, it was decided not to send an answer to Curtin until a reply had been received from the Canadian government (to whom a reminder had been sent) on the general question. If the Canadian government was also to argue that its allocation should be increased above the proposed figure of seven, the whole matter would have to be further considered. On the other hand, if Canada accepted the figure of seven without question, it would strengthen the decision to decline to consider a higher figure for Australia. As regards Curtin's yet again reiterated request that his recommendation of Essington Lewis should be submitted to the sovereign when the next vacancy occurred without waiting for the amendment of the statutes, the reply was simply that it would be open to Mr Curtin to submit Lewis's name to the King as soon as the new proposals had been approved and without awaiting the completion of the amending statutes. But again it would be better to defer a reply on this point as well until the Canadian government's answer had been received.[33]

The Canadian government's reply was received by telegram dated 6 July; it was a firm and not altogether unexpected refusal to participate in the Order of the Companions of Honour. Documents in the National Archives of Canada show that proposals were discussed in the Canadian Privy Council Office in May 1943 for the creation of two honours to be styled 'The Canadian Award of Honour' and 'The Canadian Decoration of Honour'.[34] Although neither honour was instituted, the question of an indigenous honours system was sufficiently high on the agenda of the Canadian government for them swiftly to reject a CH quota.

The Canadian refusal presented an additional difficulty. Should the United Kingdom go ahead with Australia, New Zealand and South Africa who were willing to participate, notwithstanding Canada's withdrawal? If so, could the revised statutes be drafted in such a way as to avoid making an express reference to the figures allocated to the other dominions, which would obviously disclose the fact that Canada was not taking part? The general view was that it was best to go ahead with the remaining three dominions, and that if it was necessary, a new statute could be drafted to allocate shares to Australia, New Zealand and the Union of South Africa. The alternative would be to dispense with any numerical allocation in the statutes, leaving the actual figures to be agreed separately between the several governments. In many ways this was thought to be preferable, on the understanding that the statutes should provide that dominion nominations should be made by dominion prime ministers; this would avoid a public revelation of the Canadian snub.

In the meantime Curtin had requested that the Australian allocation should be increased from five to seven, for reasons which were not difficult to see. An allocation of five would leave him with just one vacancy. Former Australian prime ministers Stanley Bruce, William Hughes and Earle Page occupied three places, and Lewis was about to take a fourth. Given the Canadian refusal to participate, the suggestion was made that Curtin's request should be allowed. Australia should have seven places, leaving New Zealand and South Africa with two each, giving a total establishment of sixty-five instead of the seventy originally proposed. 'This leaves Canada out of account, but we can deal with their case later if they change their minds.'[35] In fact eight Canadians were appointed to the CH Order from 1945 onwards, but often for service outside Canada, and never enough to establish a trend and warrant a separate Canadian quota.

Given that the Canadian government had refused to join the proposed scheme, the new quotas were formally established by the Committee on the Grant of Honours, Decorations and Medals in Time of War.[36] A Canadian quota was abandoned and Curtin was given two extra places, leading to a total increase from fifty to sixty-five.

The Commonwealth of Australia	7
The Dominion of New Zealand	2
The Union of South Africa	2
The United Kingdom	45
India, Burma and the Colonies	9
TOTAL	65

On the issue whether an amendment should be made in the statutes so as to provide for recommendations to be made by dominions prime ministers, the position of the South African government was that such a change must be made. In those circumstances the dominions office favoured the responsibility for dominions recommendations being the formal responsibility of the dominion concerned.[37] The issue was technical and tedious and of no consequence to anyone who was not closely involved in the internal running of Whitehall departments, but it had been established that dominions prime ministers could submit their recommendations directly to the sovereign, and in the eyes of those concerned, this was such a change of practice that it really should be incorporated in the statutes for the further avoidance of doubt. 'All that seems necessary is the inclusion, at some appropriate place, of a provision that "the names of persons to be appointed to be members of the Order may, in the case of any Dominion the Government whereof shall so desire, be laid before the King by the Prime Minister of the said Dominion." We quite see that a provision of this kind might appear somewhat curious in a Statute which contains no provision at all as to Ministerial recommendation. To meet this difficulty, would it be possible to include an express provision that the name of every person to be appointed to be a member of the Order "shall be laid before the King by the Prime Minister of the United Kingdom or, in the case of any Dominion, the Government whereof shall so desire, by the Prime Minister of the said Dominion?" We do not think that the inclusion of a provision of this kind need prejudice the position in the case of the Statutes of other Orders, such as the Bath, which at present contain no provision as to Ministerial recommendation. In the case of the Bath (and equally the SMG), recommendations are made to the King by a number of different Ministers according to the circumstances of the case, and it can reasonably be argued that there would be no special advantages (and indeed definite disadvantages) in attempting to define in precise terms in the Statutes the channel by which recommendations may be made. On the other hand, in the case of such an Order as the CH, where it is clearly desirable that the authority for recommendations should be centralised in the Prime Ministers of the United Kingdom and the respective Dominions, there seems much to be said for laying down expressly in the Statutes the channel by which recommendations are to be made. There is the further consideration that the Statutes of the CH will in any case have to be amended and it is convenient to take this opportunity of amending them comprehensively. This does not apply in the case of the other Orders.'[38]

The provision for dominions recommendations to be submitted by dominions prime ministers was incorporated by additional statute dated 18 August 1943, and remained in force until it was amended by a further additional statute dated 7 November 1969. The phrase 'the Prime Minister of the said Dominion' was replaced with 'the appropriate Minister of any other Member of the Commonwealth of which We are Queen.' The change was designed to avoid the embarrassment which might arise from the fact that, however much he might like to receive the CH, the prime minister of a dominion would not feel it proper to put forward his own name.[39]

Amendments to statutes might fascinate and excite Whitehall civil servants, but it was more important that the dominions office should be able to inform Curtin as soon as possible that approval had been given for the increase of the total establishment to sixty-five, of which seven would be allocated to Australia to be awarded on the recommendation of the prime minister of Australia. 'The Secretary of State is anxious to be in a position to telegraph to the Governor General as to this as soon as possible, in view of the tenor of the previous correspondence with Mr Curtin and what we know of Mr Curtin's strong views on this matter. Surely it will not be necessary to defer submission of this question to the King until the precise form of the amendment of the Statutes has been settled? Equally we hope that when His Majesty has approved the total establishment and the Dominions allocations, there will be no question but that Mr Curtin will be in a position to submit the name of Mr Essington Lewis for appointment and that this will not have to wait until the Statutes have been amended. As to this our telegram to the Governor General of the 19th May, in which you concurred, said: "As regards Essington Lewis, as soon as new proposals have been approved by His Majesty, it will, of course, be open to your Prime Minister to submit his name to His Majesty for the proposed award." Mr Curtin will certainly, therefore, be assuming that he is at liberty to go ahead as soon as His Majesty's approval of the Australian allocation has been signified. In any case, having regard to the protracted correspondence which there has been on the matter, we are afraid that it will be out of the question to suggest to him that there must be further delay before he can act. There have been a number of private indirect representations (apart from telegraphic correspondence on record) as to the importance which Mr Curtin attaches to getting Mr Essington Lewis a CH as quickly as possible, and for political reasons, the Secretary of State feels that we ought now to facilitate this as much as we possibly can.'[40]

By telegram on 24 August, South Africa, Australia and New Zealand were officially informed of the revised increased establishment of the Order, and that each dominion quota was to include existing members.[41] In response to his question of 14 June, Curtin was informed separately that the quotas were based on the relative populations of the United Kingdom and the dominions. The allowance of nine for India, Burma and the Colonial Empire together was entirely notional. The vast population of the Indian subcontinent made a population basis clearly inapplicable,[42] although in the years since 1943 the quota for 'the rest' has been very little used.

Twelve months after the proposal to nominate Forgan Smith for the CH, Essington Lewis was formally appointed a Companion of Honour on 24 September 1943. Whether Smith was offered any other honour is unknown, but given his reported aversion to titles and the strong request for a CH, the suspicion is that he was not. He died in 1953 without an honour.

Quota changes in 1970
The quota figures established in 1943 remained in force until 1970, when they were reconsidered in the light of political and constitutional changes in the empire and commonwealth.

By February 1970, the United Kingdom quota of forty-five was full. The Birthday Honours List was four months away, and the prime minister might wish to appoint some new Companions of Honour. There was no obvious explanation for the full quota. Harold Wilson, the then prime minister, did not seem to have made particularly heavy use of the CH; an average of two names per list was standard throughout his premiership (1964–70), and there was no evidence of bias towards appointing more politicians than usual. Whether recipients were living longer or being appointed at younger ages, the quota was full. So the choice lay between telling the prime minister that there were no vacancies and that he could not appoint any new CHs, enlarging the size of the Order, or revisiting the 1943 Commonwealth quotas to see whether some additional vacancies could be 'created' for the UK. The first option was not considered at all – although there would have been no harm in a pause, and the second option was considered undesirable unless it was unavoidable. 'I am very reluctant to recommend an increase in the complement unless it proves inescapable. The value of the CH lies in its rarity, and to make public an increase in the complement might suggest that it was being cheapened.'[43] There remained the third option. 'I would like, therefore, to ask you whether you would see any objection to the UK using some of the spares out of the other allocations.'[44] Borrowing from the other allocations was not a simple matter because of the official nature of the 1943 decision and the desire not offend the sensitivities of the Commonwealth nations. But what could be done was to review the 1943 quotas to see how far they were still operable or needed. As of the 16 February 1970, the position was as follows:

	Quota	Appointments	Vacancies
The Commonwealth of Australia	7	3*	4
The Dominion of New Zealand	2	1**	1
The Union of South Africa	2	0	2
The United Kingdom	45	45	0
India, Burma and the Colonies	9	4***	5

*   Lord Casey, Sir Robert Menzies, Sir John McEwen
**   Sir Keith Holyoake
*** Viscount Malvern (Rhodesia), Sir John Kotelawala (Ceylon), Tunku Abdul Rahman (Malaysia), and Eric Williams (Trinidad and Tobago)

There could be no question of borrowing from the Australian or New Zealand quotas – which would have to be explained to them and might have political repercussions – but the two South African vacancies could be regarded as genuinely free. The South African quota had technically never been put into operation because no citizens of that country were appointed to the Order between the establishment of the quota in 1943 and South Africa leaving the Commonwealth in 1961. The formation of a government by the Nationalist Party after the general election in June 1948 marked the end of recommendations from South Africa, and in the history of the Order only one South African – Jan Christian Smuts – received the CH. By 1970 the South African quota had been redundant for years and could well be used without any fear of repercussion. That would add an additional two places to the United Kingdom quota, and another three were added from the 'India, Burma and the Colonies' quota. The 1943 name for the quota was itself redundant. There was no longer any need for provisions for India and Burma, nor for that matter for Ceylon and Pakistan. Malaysia had been an independent monarchy since 1957, and although the appointment of Tunku Abdul Rahman, the Malaysian prime minister, as a CH in 1960, was assigned to the 'India' quota, it would have been better as an honorary appointment like that of Lee Kuan Yew of Singapore in 1970. Since the unilateral declaration of independence by Southern Rhodesia in 1965, there was unlikely to be any further appointment from that country. Stuart Milner-Barry, successor to Robert Knox as the treasury ceremonial officer adopted a pragmatic view of the now historic quotas. 'I cannot imagine that more will be required in the ordinary course of nature, but how would you view the possibility that we might, if necessary, borrow two or three more from the quota for 'the rest', on the understanding in the unlikely event that it became necessary? I would suppose that the prospect of 'the rest' requiring five fresh appointments in the foreseeable future is fairly remote . . . All that I need . . . is your sanction to our using up the 2 South African vacancies; but perhaps you might give thought to the proposition that we might consider the effective limit on the UK allocation as being 50 for the future rather than 45, the tally of 'the rest' being reduced from 9 to 6 – subject, as I say, to these being restored by means of the Statutes if that should become necessary. If you thought that was a reasonable proposition, would you think it necessary to say anything to the Commonwealth countries?'[45]

Some fluttering was caused in official circles when it was discovered that the South African quota had already been quietly abandoned, and that it had been absorbed into the category known as 'the rest' at some date in or before 1957. No one seemed to know quite when or by whom it had been done. 'Neither the Foreign and Commonwealth Office nor ourselves seem to have any papers to indicate exactly how and why the South African quota disappeared . . . and I do not know whether this particular matter was ever submitted to the Queen.'[46] This was confirmed by the Queen's Assistant Private Secretary, Sir Martin Charteris, who also could find no record of the fate of the South African quota.[47] All that could be certain was that the *List of Members* produced by the Central Chancery of the Orders of Knighthood had, from 1957, listed the quotas as forty-five for the United Kingdom, seven for Australia, two for New Zealand and eleven for the rest.[48] In the absence of documentation, the only explanation is that the decision to revoke the South African quota was made informally at some date in the years after 1948, when the advent of the Nationalist government ended South Africa's involvement in the system of imperial honours.

By 1970 the dismantling of the British empire was well under way. Australia and New Zealand had their own quotas, and with the United Kingdom hungry for additional places among the Companions of Honour, was a figure of eleven places not too generous a provision for what remained of the empire and those independent countries that still made use of United Kingdom honours? 'Whether 'the rest' need as many as eleven depended on the transition of countries from colonial status to independent monarchical status and from that to republican status. With the departmental mergers of 1967–68, responsibility for the Commonwealth quotas now belonged to the new foreign and commonwealth office, and Lees Mayall, vice marshal of the diplomatic corps, accepted that the figure of eleven could be reduced. 'Even if the drain to republican status were to stop now, and the 'viable' monarchies were all to be added to the existing number of independent monarchies . . . I doubt if, given their size and degree of importance, they would together need as big an allocation as eleven. I think this view is justified by the fact that, over the past ten years, there has been a constant figure of about six vacancies in the allocation for 'the rest'. I would therefore see no objection on this account to the United Kingdom appropriating and keeping two from the eleven now available to 'the rest.'[49]

Since among 'the rest' no individual country had any particular entitlement, no consultation would be necessary, and no publicity need be given to the change since the distribution had never been publicly announced and the figures had never been detailed in the statutes. 'It is clear that there has never been any announcement in Parliament about the United Kingdom quota, and we have no record here of any kind referring to the distribution of the complement . . . This has never been considered and I think, therefore, that we can safely proceed on the assumption that the change will not come to light unless we ourselves wish it. There is no reference in any of the books of reference to the distribution of the quotas. The only place where they appear (so far as we know) is on page 3 of the *List of Members* of the CH which is prepared and published by the Central Chancery of the Orders of Knighthood. Moreover, since this list is issued to a Member only on his first appointment, there is no means of his comparing the list of members for 1969 with that for 1970 or 1971. Thus, relevant inferences could only be drawn by those in the central honours machine like ourselves, who are already aware that the quotas have been changed.'[50]

It was possible that the United Kingdom would need more than the two places that were being appropriated to its quota, but it was at least sufficient for the Birthday Honours List 1970. The two additional places would be enough for the time being, but Stuart Miner-Barry thought that it could have been more. 'Whether we should need more than two I do not know, but at any rate it would keep us going for the time being . . . I myself think it would be not unreasonable to put the United Kingdom quota up to fifty (rather than forty-seven) reducing the quota for 'the rest' from eleven to six.'[51] The Foreign and Commonwealth Office was reluctant to reduce their patronage further by surrendering more than the agreed two vacancies in favour of the United Kingdom list. In any case a general election was imminent, and Milner-Barry felt that the fewer vacancies there were, the better. 'They would probably not resist strongly if pressed, but I am not myself particularly anxious to press them at present. Indeed, in an election year there is much to be said for having the complement of the Companionship of Honour pretty well up against the ceiling.'[52] So from 1970 the new quotas were as follows:

Australia	7
New Zealand	2
The United Kingdom	47
The rest of the Commonwealth	9

Though they were never aware of it at the time, the recipients of the redundant former South African quota were the choreographer, Sir Frederick Ashton, and the actress, Dame Sybil Thorndike.

Quota changes in 1975
Further changes to the quotas were made in 1975 at the request of the New Zealand government. The New Zealand quota of two was full up (the places being held by Sir Keith Holyoake and Sir John Marshall) and the government of Robert Muldoon requested that the New Zealand allocation should be enlarged to four places. (Muldoon was the first to benefit from the enlarged allocation, being appointed a CH in 1977). The foreign and commonwealth office accepted the

increase and were willing for the general Commonwealth quota to be further reduced to seven, so avoiding any overall increase in the complement of the Order. Following precedent, no publicity was given to the change, because the distribution was not detailed in the Statutes and the existing quotas had never been publicly announced.[53] The new quota arrangement provided the following places:

Australia	7
New Zealand	4
The United Kingdom	47
Other Commonwealth countries	7

The future

At the time of writing, the changes of 1975 were the last made to the Commonwealth quotas established in 1943, and it seems likely that the inauguration of indigenous and complete honours systems in Australia and New Zealand will eventually lead to their CH quotas being formally abolished. The delay in that occurrence is due to the fact that the quotas are still in use even if they are now obsolescent. Australia has made no recommendations for the CH since 1981 and New Zealand has made no recommendations since 1989. The use of the quota for the rest of the Commonwealth has similarly declined, and the situation at 1 January 2002 makes that clear.

	Quota	Appointments	Vacancies
Australia	7	2*	5
New Zealand	4	2**	2
Other Commonwealth countries	7	2***	5

*	Malcolm Fraser and Douglas Anthony
**	Sir Brian Talboys and David Lange
***	Sir Michael Somare (Papua New Guinea) and General John de Chastelain (Canada)

A case could be made for retaining a quota for the entire Commonwealth, but the separate quotas for Australia and New Zealand are likely to become redundant in due course and allocated elsewhere.

CHAPTER SIXTEEN

Over the bright blue sea

OVERSEAS APPOINTMENTS

'I declare its marked out just like a large chess-board!' Alice said at last. 'There ought to be some men moving about somewhere – and so there are!' she added in a tone of delight, and her heart began to beat quick with excitement as she went on. 'It's a great huge game of chess that's being played – all over the world . . . Oh, what fun it is! How I wish I was one of them!'

'The garden of live flowers', *Through the looking-glass*, Lewis Carroll

Those members of the Order assembled in this chapter fall under the general heading of 'overseas', though closer analysis reveals a more complicated picture. The statutes of the Order provide for a distinction between 'substantive' and 'honorary' members, but to have limited this chapter only to 'honorary' appointments would have reduced it to nine individuals: René Massigli (1954), Nuri es-Said (1956), Paul-Henri Spaak (1963), Lee Kuan Yew (1970), Joseph Luns (1971), Jean Monnet (1972) Amartya Sen (2000) and Bernard Haitink (2002); and two of them – Lee Kuan Yew and Amartya Sen – are citizens of Commonwealth countries. The picture would be further confused if the name of Kenneth Quinan (1917) was added. As a United States citizen resident in South Africa he should have been made an honorary member, but at the time there was no provision for such in the Statutes and consequently his CH was substantive – as it would probably have become when he took South African nationality in 1939.

With the exceptions of Lee and Sen, all other Commonwealth citizens have been appointed substantive members of the Order, and it seemed unnecessary to subdivide the 'Commonwealth' category on grounds that are purely technical and of no great significance. Broadly speaking, 'substantive' members are counted against the statutory maximum of sixty-five members; 'honorary' members are additional to that number and in theory unlimited though in practice very few in number.

This chapter has divided the 'overseas' members into citizens of Commonwealth countries and citizens of foreign countries (although Kenneth Quinan later moved from the latter to the former) and lists thirty-seven politicians or diplomats, three soldiers (all of them Canadian generals, one of whom briefly attempted a political career), two industrialists, one medical scientist, one economist and one musician. As founder members, honoured for their war service, Jan Smuts (1917) and Kenneth Quinan (1917) are included in chapter two. Because of the specialist nature of their work, Essington Lewis (1943), Charles Herbert Best (1971), Amartya Sen (2000), and Bernard Haitink (2002) are included in the chapters appropriate to their work. For the sake of completeness, their names and dates of appointment are noted in chronological order in this chapter, which otherwise consists entirely of politicians.

Part 1 Commonwealth appointments

A clear pattern emerges from an analysis of the Commonwealth Companions of Honour: it was primarily a decoration for Commonwealth prime ministers. In Australia and New Zealand, the CH came to be used mostly as an automatic honour, conferred almost as a badge of office on successive prime ministers (at least on those who were prepared to accept it), during or after their tenure of power. Because of the 1918 Canadian resolution, the CH was used more diversely in that country, principally because the honour was of high rank and conveniently did not carry the encumbrance of a title. With the exception of Srinivasa Sastri and Amartya Sen of India, the remaining Commonwealth Companions of Honour were mainly prime ministers of their respective nations, four of them being the first holders of the office after independence. Because of the tendency of Commonwealth nations to introduce their own honours systems in the last quarter of the twentieth century, this practice has ceased and future appointments to the Order from the Commonwealth will be rare.

Australia (13)

Viscount Bruce of Melbourne (1927), Joseph Lyons (1936), William Hughes (1941), Sir Earle Page (1942), Essington Lewis (1943), Lord Casey (1944), Sir Robert Menzies (1951), Harold Holt (1967), Sir John McEwen (1969), Sir John Gorton (1971), Sir William McMahon, (1972), Malcolm Fraser (1977) and Douglas Anthony (1981).

Ten of the thirteen Australians were prime ministers of the Australian commonwealth. Lord Casey became governor-general, Douglas Anthony was deputy prime minister, and Essington Lewis was an industrialist, whose work is covered in chapter fourteen.

Canada (8)

General Henry Crerar (1945), Vincent Massey (1946), General Andrew McNaughton (1946), Charles Herbert Best (1971), Arnold Smith (1975), John Diefenbaker (1976), Pierre Trudeau (1984) and General John de Chastelain (1998).

By resolution of the Canadian House of Commons in 1918, Canada had eschewed British honours in general and titular honours in particular, so on a number of occasions, the CH has been a usefully high honour to confer on Canadians without offending Canadian sensitivities. History has seen the CH used almost entirely as a civil honour, and only in the case of Generals Crerar and McNaughton, has it been conferred for distinguished military service. Vincent Massey was governor general, John Diefenbaker and Pierre Trudeau were prime ministers, Arnold Smith was a diplomat, Charles Herbert Best was a medical scientist whose work is covered in chapter eight, and General de Chastelain received the honour for his delicate diplomacy in Northern Ireland.

New Zealand (8)

Peter Fraser (1946), Sir Sidney Holland (1951), Sir Walter Nash (1959), Sir Keith Holyoake, (1963), Sir John Marshall (1973), Sir Robert Muldoon (1977), Sir Brian Talboys (1981), and David Lange (1989).

Seven of the New Zealand Companions of Honour were prime ministers of the country. The exception was Sir Brian Talboys, who was deputy prime minister and received the CH in anticipation of his retirement from parliament.

India (2)
Valingaman Sankarana-Rayana Srinivasa Sastri (1930) and Amartya Sen (2000). Sastri was a voice of moderation in the rise of Indian nationalism and demands for home rule. He was highly regarded in his day and declined a KCSI but accepted a CH. Sen is an economist resident in the United Kingdom, and his work is covered in chapter ten.

South Africa (1)
Jan Smuts (1917), soldier and prime minister of South Africa, was one of the founding members of the Order, and his life and work are covered in chapter two.

Sri Lanka (1)
Sir John Kotelawala (1956) was the pro-western and anti-communist prime minister of Ceylon (as it was then named) in the mid-1950s.

Malaya (1)
Tunku Abdul Rahman (1960) was a prince of the royal house of Kedah who became the first prime minister of Malaya at independence in 1957.

Papua New Guinea (1)
Sir Michael Somare (1978) became the first prime minister of Papua New Guinea at independence in 1975.

Singapore (1)
Lee Kuan Yew (1970) was the first prime minister of Singapore after secession from Malaysia in 1965.

Southern Rhodesia (1)
Viscount Malvern (1944), better known as Sir Godfrey Huggins, was prime minister of Southern Rhodesia for twenty years before he became the first prime minister of the ill fated Federation of Rhodesia and Nyasaland.

Trinidad and Tobago (1)
Eric Williams (1969) became the first prime minister of Trinidad and Tobago at independence in 1961 and died in office in 1981.

Part 2 Foreign appointments
The work of the American explosives expert, Kenneth Quinan (1917) *[United States of America]*, is covered in chapter two. René Massigli (1954) *[France]* was an anglophile French diplomat who served for ten years as French ambassador in London. Nuri es Said (1956) *[Iraq]* was a key figure in the history of his country for more than thirty years, serving as prime minister on numerous occasions, and remains the only CH to have been assassinated. Paul Henri Spaak (1963) *[Belgium]* was a long-serving Belgian foreign minister who was perhaps more devoted to the cause of European unity than he was to his own country. Joseph Luns (1971) *[Netherlands]* was a long-serving foreign minister of the Netherlands and subsequently secretary general of the North Atlantic Treaty Organisation. Jean Monnet (1972) *[France]* was the architect of a number of schemes to bring about a greater European unity and came to be revered almost as the 'father of Europe.' Bernard

Haitink (2002) was a distinguished Dutch-born conductor who spent most of his working life in the United Kingdom, and his work is covered in chapter seven.

Commonwealth appointments

Field Marshal Jan Smuts 4 June 1917 [South Africa] (see Chapter 2)

Viscount Bruce of Melbourne 9 May 1927 [Australia]
Stanley Bruce was prime minister of Australia 1923–29. Tall, stately, formal, detached, and always impeccably dressed, he was the most British of Australian prime ministers. Becoming prime minister at the age of thirty-nine, he had already spent fifteen years living overseas, and about half his long life was spent in the United Kingdom.

Bruce was born in Melbourne in 1883. His father was an Irishman of Scottish origin who arrived in Melbourne and swept floors. He prospered and became a founder of Laing, Patterson and Bruce, one of the largest of soft goods houses in Australia. His son was educated at Melbourne Grammar School. On the death of his father in 1901 he went into the family business for a year before going to Trinity Hall, Cambridge where he read law. After graduation he settled in London and was called to the bar at Middle Temple in 1906 and practiced for several years. At the outbreak of the 1914–18 war he was commissioned as an officer in the Royal Fusiliers and fought in Gallipoli and France. In 1917, decorated with the Military Cross and Croix de Guerre and having been twice wounded, he was invalided out of the army and returned to Melbourne to take charge of the family business after the death of his elder brother.

Australian patriots soon persuaded this war hero to make recruiting speeches, which he did so effectively that he attracted the attention of the National Party. The party offered him the federal seat of Flinders for the 1918 elections and he won comfortably, holding the seat until 1929 and then again from 1931–33. In 1921 he was overseas on a business trip when the then prime minister William Hughes asked him to represent Australia at the League of Nations. Bruce performed so effectively that, when he returned home, Hughes appointed him treasurer. He retained his seat in the 1922 general election, but the National Party won only twenty-eight seats against thirty for the Labour Party. The Nationals could govern only with the support of the new Country Party's fourteen seats. Earle Page, leader of the Country Party, agreed to a coalition but objected to Hughes. Bruce proved the only man acceptable to both sides of the coalition and, after only five years in politics, he became prime minister of Australia and the youngest member of his own cabinet. It was a meteoric rise to the highest office, but he was untarnished by the political squabbling of previous years, it was a period of Anglo-Australian euphoria, and he was an Anglicised Australian war hero.

Australia was by then well into the postwar boom and Bruce saw the time as ripe for a businessmen's government, under the slogan 'Men, Money and Markets'. He wanted British immigration to build up the workforce, British loan capital to fuel the economy and British markets for Australian primary produce. At the same time, he kept the Country Party on side with export subsidies and price support for primary produce. Possibly his most significant achievement was the establishment of what is now the Commonwealth Scientific and

Industrial Research Organization. His policies called for a strong, unified Australia which would attract overseas investors, and for closer ties with Britain on foreign affairs, and he organised the 1927 transfer of the federal parliament to Canberra.

He was typical of the businessmen of his time in regarding socialists as disruptive and dangerous. The 1917 Russian revolution was still recent history and there was a fear in the minds of many that the Australian Labour Party would be the spearhead of a similar revolution. Bruce brought in anti-union legislation and proposals to abandon the arbitration system. When the 1920s boom began to fade, Australia quickly felt the results. Wheat and wool prices collapsed, unemployment rose and British loan funds dried up. The October 1929 elections were held only seventeen days before the collapse of the Wall Street stockmarket and the onset of the Great Depression. The government itself was defeated and Bruce lost his own seat. At forty-six, he was embarrassingly young to be an ex-prime minister, and for the rest of his life he spent very little time in Australia.

He regained his seat in parliament in 1931 and held it until his appointment as high commissioner in London (1933–45). He had left high level Australian politics as abruptly as he had entered it and made no spectacular comeback. According to Bruce himself, he was sounded out about succeeding Lyons as prime minister in 1939, but it came to nothing. For most of the rest of his long life he held a 'roving commission' which enabled him to serve both Australia and his adopted country, Britain, in a number of official positions in both peace and war. In 1942 John Curtin, the Labour prime minister, appointed him Australian representative in the British war cabinet and on the Pacific war council but Bruce soon found that these positions carried little participation in the conduct of the war and was resentful of the scant respect shown for Australian attitudes. 'Bruce clashed more than once with Churchill, a conflict of two unbending, sometimes overbearing men, but inevitably an unequal one.'[1]

The Labour government ended his role as high commissioner in 1945 and he had no further official connection with Australian government and politics. In 1947 he was made chairman of the Finance Corporation for Industry and contributed during the next decade to the recovery of British industry. He was also chairman of the World Food Council (1947–51). His last appointment in Australia was to become the first chancellor of the National University of Canberra in 1951, retiring in 1961.

In 1927 he was the first Australian to be appointed a CH, and in 1947, ennobled as Viscount Bruce of Melbourne, becoming the first Australian to sit in the house of lords. He remained resident in London for the rest of his life, and then returned to the land of his birth. When he died in 1967, his will provided for his ashes to be sprinkled over Lake Burley Griffin in Canberra. He had no children and the viscountcy became extinct.

The wording of the CH citation – that Bruce was receiving it as 'Prime Minister of the Commonwealth of Australia' – established a policy that lasted for more than sixty years. When given to a prime minister of one of the commonwealth realms, it came to have the appearance of being more a badge of office than recognition of merit.

Valingaman Sankarana-Rayana Srinivasa Sastri 1 January 1930 [India]
Born into an orthodox high caste Hindu family, V. S. Srinivasa Sastri was a shy softly spoken agnostic teacher, who developed into a liberal nationalist with decid-

edly pro-British sympathies, and a strong humanitarian concern for the well-being of Indians in other parts of the British empire.

He was born at Valangaiman, a village in Madras province, in 1869, the eldest of the four sons of a Brahmin priest and Sanskrit scholar. He was educated at the Native High School and the Government College at Kumbakonam, where he trained as a teacher and eventually rose to be headmaster of the Hindu High School, Triplicane, Madras. He resigned in 1907 to become a member of the Servants of India Society, an organisation of Indian political liberals, and assisted in its campaign for free and compulsory primary education for Indian children. An interest in the right to education paralleled a growing involvement with the movement for Indian self-government. In 1908 he became secretary of the Madras session of the Indian National Congress, and helped to formulate the Lucknow Pact between the Congress and the Muslim League, which demanded self-government. In 1913 he was nominated to the Madras Legislative Council and elected by it to the Imperial Legislative Council in 1915.

He broke with the Congress in 1918 over its opposition to the declared British aim of responsible government for India along the lines of the British parliamentary system. Sastri founded the National Liberal Federation in 1918 to support the British plan and travelled to London to give evidence to a parliamentary joint select committee. Having found an ally among Indian nationalists, the government made him a member of the Southborough Committee on franchise, and he unofficially cooperated with E. S. Montague, the secretary of state for India, in finalising the Government of India Act 1919. The Montague constitution was opposed by the Congress, under the leadership of Mahatma Gandhi, who formulated a non-violent and non-cooperation policy of boycott. Sastri opposed Gandhi's policy as harmful to India.

As a moderate nationalist, Sastri was well regarded by successive British governments, if not always by individual ministers, and he became something of a roving international ambassador for India. In 1921 he went to Geneva as a member of the Indian delegation to the League of Nations and in 1922 he attended the limitation of naval armaments conference in Washington, as head of the Indian delegation. But his best work was probably done in his concern for the welfare of Indians living outside India. In 1921 he was elected to the council of state and chosen as the delegate of India to the imperial conference in London. With the support of Montague, and against the opposition of J. C. Smuts, prime minister of South Africa, the conference agreed to a resolution stating that British subjects of Indian origin, lawfully settled anywhere in the British dominions, should be entitled to vote. The resolution was not binding, and the prime ministers of Australia, Canada and New Zealand, requested that Sastri should visit their dominions to canvass support for its implementation. He made the tour in 1922, though South Africa was excluded from his itinerary. The welfare of Indians in South Africa did concern him and he was a member of the Indian delegation to the conference between South Africa and India in 1926. The conference led to the Cape Town Agreement, which committed the South Africa government to abandon its Class Areas Bill, an early piece of segregation legislation. At the request of the governments of India and South African, and also Gandhi, Sastri agreed to stay in South Africa to ensure the implementation of the resolution. In 1932 he was a member of a further conference on the same subject which, with minor changes, renewed the agreement. His concern for Indians abroad extended to east Africa, and in

1923 he campaigned in England for increased rights for Indians living in Kenya. He went to Kenya in 1929 to help local Indians present their case to the under-secretary of state for the colonies. In 1936 he was sent by the government of India to look into the conditions of Indian workers in Malaya.

Sastri's nationalism was as gentle, broad and liberal as his education and his interests, and he was influenced by the works of Shakespeare, Edmund Burke, Walter Scott, George Eliot, T. H. Huxley, Herbert Spencer, John Stuart Mill, Marcus Aurelius, Tolstoy, Thomas Hardy and Victor Hugo. His educated and tolerant mind could see and understand the arguments of all sides, and he was often accused of presenting his opponent's case better than his own. Though he had parted company with the Congress Party, he advocated in 1943 that Gandhi should be invited to attend the peace conference at the end of the 1939–45 war, where he could make an effective contribution to world peace. He was alarmed by the increasing vociferousness and polarisation that marked demands for independence, and in 1945 he strongly opposed Jinnah's demand for the partition of India and the creation of a separate Moslem state. He had long suffered from heart problems and died in 1946, sixteen months before the independence which he would have welcomed, and the partition and its bloody aftermath, which would have distressed him.

Sastri was made a privy councillor in 1921 and received the freedom of the city of London in 1921 and the city of Edinburgh in 1931. He was offered a KCSI (Knight Commander of the Order of the Star of India) which he declined, and then a CH, which he accepted, in the New Year Honours List 1930. He was honoured 'for his eminent services in Indian affairs and as first incumbent of the post of Agent of the Government of India in South Africa.'

Joseph Lyons 23 June 1936 [Australia]

Joseph Aloysius Lyons was prime minister of Australia 1932–39. He was a kindly, genial, unostentatious extrovert who believed in making friends with everyone, including members of opposition parties and, rarely for a politician, he was generally well liked and died poor.

He was born at Stanley, Tasmania, in 1879 into an Irish Catholic family. His parents ran a small farm but, when he was nine, his father's illness forced him to leave school and seek odd jobs to help support the family. After three years, a spinster aunt intervened to pay for his education. At the age of seventeen he qualified as a teacher and taught for a number of years in country schools. The domination of northern Tasmania by Protestant landowners, raised his Irish resentments and political aspirations and he joined the Workers' Political League. He responded to a sharp reproof from the department of education by resigning and standing for election to the Tasmanian house of assembly.

He canvassed his electorate by bicycle, speaking so vigorously for the Labour cause that an outraged landowner horsewhipped him. He won the election and in 1909 at the age of thirty, he began nineteen years in the Tasmanian legislature. His talents brought him into the Tasmanian cabinet and he was premier of the state (1923–28). His ministry was the first to have a clear Labour majority in Tasmania and to show a surplus in the state's shaky finances.

He resigned in 1928 to pursue a career in federal politics and was given a place in the 1929 Labour government of his fellow Irish Catholic James Scullin. He was postmaster-general and minister of public works (1929–31) and acting treasurer

(1930–31). He was dismayed by the Australian Labour Party's in-fighting over depression finances and he was deeply offended by Scullin's re-appointment of 'Red Ted' Theodore as treasurer. He began discussions with four other dissatisfied Labour members and with a body of supporters known as 'The Group' – which comprised Melbourne businessmen, the National Union and some civic leaders and Opposition politicians. With this backing, Lyons and his four followers first broke away from the Labour Party and then supported the vote of no confidence in Scullin's government. During the last few months of Scullin's administration, 'The Group' allied with the National Party to form the United Australia Party which won a clear majority in December 1931. A 1934 coalition with the Country Party helped Lyons to win two more elections.

As an Irish Catholic, Lyons had been an anti-conscription activist during the 1914–18 war and hated the waste and horror of war. But it fell to him, as prime minister, to prepare Australia for another war at a time when the armed forces had been allowed to run down to a skeleton level. His government began to re-equip the army, double voluntary recruitment and strengthen the air force and the navy. It also broadened the industrial base essential for the war effort by opening the first Commonwealth aircraft factory and planning munitions works and shipyards. Lyons had to hold the balance between a collection of powerful personalities in the two coalition parties; it forced him into consensus politics and inevitably he could not please everyone. As the shadows of impending war darkened, he became more decisive and determined, but letters to his wife during his final year in government reveal the unhappiness of a man under many conflicting pressures. He died of a heart attack in 1939.

The CH, his only honour, was conferred in 1936, and as with Lord Bruce the citation was only a record that Lyons was 'Prime Minister of the Commonwealth of Australia.'

In 1915 he married Enid Muriel Burnell, a Protestant who joined the Roman Catholic Church on her marriage. They had five sons and six daughters. Dame Enid Lyons (she was made a GBE in 1937) followed her husband into politics. She had gained a reputation in Tasmania as a civic leader and social worker and, in 1943, she won the seat of Darwin, Tasmania. She was the first woman member of the house of representatives in the Commonwealth parliament, where she served for eight years until ill health compelled her retirement. She survived her husband by more than forty years, dying in 1981, the year following her appointment as one of only two dames of the Order of Australia.

William Hughes 1 January 1941 [Australia]
'Billy' Hughes was prime minister of Australia 1915–23. Voluble, volatile, stubborn, shrewd and artful, and with a substantial ego, he became the target of both hatred and admiration. But he was also a vigorous and inspiring leader during the 1914–18 war who forced British recognition of Australia as an independent military power. He insisted on an Australian seat at the Versailles peace conference, secured the Australian mandate over German New Guinea, and effectively pulled Australia on to the world stage.

He was born in London in 1864 of Welsh-English parentage and educated at Llandudno Grammar School and St Stephen's School, Westminster. He began his working life as a teenage pupil teacher until he emigrated to Australia in 1884. His first years in Australia are known only through his own colourful and probably embellished reminiscences. The story depicts him as ship's cook, seaman, drover, swagman, boundary rider, factory hand, umbrella mender and railway fettler. By 1890 he was working in Sydney, where he married his landlady's daughter and opened a small mixed business. His background and working life gave him natural Labour sympathies and a first-hand knowledge of Australian workers. He joined the Socialist League, held meetings in the back room of his shop, and became a full-time union organiser. In 1894 his Labour friends nominated him for a seat in the state parliament of New South Wales – and bought him a new suit when he won. He founded the Waterside Workers' Federation in 1900 and became its first president. In 1901 he was elected to the first Commonwealth parliament. Part-time law studies brought his admission to the New South Wales bar and secured his promotion to attorney-general in Andrew Fisher's three governments (1908–09, 1910–13 and 1914–15). When Fisher retired as prime minister in 1915, the Labour Party chose Hughes as his natural successor.

During the 1914–18 war, Hughes was among many Australians who advocated conscription for overseas service, but a Labour majority would accept conscription only for home defence. In 1916 he brought the issue to a head with a referendum on conscription. When it was defeated, he split Labour by leading twenty-three defectors to form the National Labour Party, and was thereafter known among his erstwhile colleagues as a 'rat'. He survived as prime minister with the support of the Liberal Party and then merged the NLP and Liberals as the National Party. In May 1917, he led this new alliance to a general election victory. But when he put another conscription referendum to the public, his opponents campaigned against it even more bitterly than before. The 'no' vote won again and Australia's 226,073 war casualties were all volunteers. With Labour in disarray because of his defection, he called a general election in 1919 but discovered he could govern only with the help of the new Country Party. Another election, in late 1922, made the new party even stronger. It refused to accept Hughes as prime minister and he resigned in favour of Stanley Bruce.

For the next twenty-nine years his political life was one of frequent manoeuvring, but much as he wanted it, he never succeeded in regaining the office of prime minister. In 1929 he sided with Labour to dismiss Bruce, failed to form a new party and joined the right-wing United Australia Party. He held several ministerial portfolios in the 1930s: health and repatriation (1934–35 and 1936–37); minister in charge of territories (1937–38); minister of external affairs (1937–39); minister for industry; attorney-general (1939–41); and minister of the navy (1940–41). He was also vice-president of the executive council (1934–35 and 1937–38). He made a bid to become prime minister in 1939 (losing to Robert Menzies), worked with Labour on the 1941–45 advisory war council, was expelled by the UAP and finally joined Menzies in the revival of the Liberal Party. The CH came in the New Year List 1941 as his political career was drawing to an end. The citation followed the precedent set by Bruce and Lyons, of naming the office – 'Minister for the Navy and Attorney-General, Commonwealth of Australia.' – rather than acknowledging the services.

Despite a meagre physique and nagging disabilities, including deafness, he lived to be eighty-eight, dying in 1952.

Sir Earle Page 23 June 1942 [Australia]
Earle Page holds the record for the second-shortest period as prime minister of

Australia, holding the office in a caretaker capacity for just fourteen days in 1939. Blunt, shrewd and earthy, he had no delusions that he would ever achieve the substantive office and was content to act as a powerful second in command. His claim to fame rests more on the fact that he was the instigator of Australia's national health service.

Born in Grafton, New South Wales in 1880, into a prosperous country family, Page was educated at Sydney High School and the University of Sydney. He studied medicine because his mother had suffered an accident when he was a child and there was no medical help available locally. He was a popular student at the university especially for his ability to pick winners in the Melbourne Cup, but his basic attitude to medicine is perhaps reflected in the title of his autobiography, *Truant doctor*.

He qualified in 1904, and his devotion to the Clarence River region drew him back to open a practice in his home town. He established one of the first hospitals in the area. During the next twelve years he began to take an interest in state politics, especially in the move to create a separate state in northern New South Wales, and to invest in farming and grazing properties. Eighteen months as a surgeon in the Army Medical Corps, dealing with the debris of war in Egypt and on the western front, made him feel he would enjoy politics better than medicine, and when he returned to Australia he found the time was ripe for an entry into that arena.

Australia was steadily evolving into an urban-industrial nation in which labour and capitalism battled with each other, with scant regard for farmers. Billy Hughes' alliance with the National Party caused a feeling in the country that he would 'socialise' the Nationalists. In a nationwide movement, men of influence in the bush and outback founded the Country Party. Having served as mayor of South Grafton in 1918, Page presented himself to an electorate closely acquainted with him and his family and in 1919 he was elected as independent member for Cowper in the federal parliament. He was co-founder of the new Country Party, and in 1920 he became its leader.

After the 1923 elections, the new Country Party held the balance of power between Labour and Nationalists. Page disliked Hughes and did not hesitate to say so. His price for supporting the Nationalists was the dismissal of Hughes as prime minister in favour of Stanley Bruce and his own appointment as treasurer and deputy prime minister. He also demanded certain ministerial posts for members of his own party. Page rose from obscurity to power faster than Stanley Bruce, and Hughes never forgave him for this ruthless strategy.

During his years as treasurer (1923–29), Page negotiated the financial agreement between the federal government and the state governments, and established the Loan Council, the National Debt Sinking Fund and the Federal Aid Roads Fund, and placed the Commonwealth Bank under an independent board of directors. Page supported Bruce's anti-union legislation and fought for the rights of his Country Party supporters. The 1929 elections swept the Bruce-Page coalition out of office and the depression eroded the Country Party's power base among farmers. Page retained his seat, but had only minimal influence until he allied his party with the United Australia Party in 1934 and became deputy prime minister under Joseph Lyons.

As minister for commerce in the new government, he established the Australian agricultural council, which gave Australia a common voice in overseas markets, and arranged for the sale of export surpluses to Britain. Lyons died in April 1939, some two years before a general election needed to be called. Page advised the governor-general to appoint him as 'caretaker' prime minister while the United Australia Party chose a new leader. He announced that he himself supported Stanley Bruce, while other members of both the Country Party and the UAP canvassed Robert Menzies as prime minister. Page was determined that Menzies should not win the contest and attacked Menzies' credibility in a savage speech, claiming he would be a frail reed during the war which now seemed inevitable. His attack was so personally offensive that it swung support to Menzies and offended Page's own supporters so much that he was removed as leader of the Country Party. Menzies, a pragmatic politician, later gave Page office in his governments. He was minister of commerce (1940–41) and minister of health (1949–56), when he introduced Australia's first comprehensive and workable national health care scheme.

In 1941–42 John Curtin appointed Page special Australian envoy to the British war cabinet, and it was in that period that he was made a CH. Page had already received the higher honour of GCMG in 1938. During his time in London he impressed Winston Churchill, who wrote to Curtin suggesting an honour. 'Sir Earle Page is leaving here shortly having largely recovered from his dangerous illness. Would you like me to submit his name to The King for the Companionship of Honour. Everybody here feels very warmly towards him and we are grateful to Australia for sending him as your first representative to the council.'[2] Curtin, was delighted to accede. 'I am delighted to request you to do this. As our first representative on the council he will have a notable position in Australian annals to add to his already distinguished role in Australian internal government.'[3] Unlike Bruce, Lyons and Page before him, the *London Gazette* only recorded the date of his appointment and no details were given of the office he held.

Page died in December 1961 at the age of eighty-one, a few hours before the news that he had been defeated in the constituency that he had represented in the federal parliament since 1919.

Essington Lewis 24 September 1943 [Australia] (see Chapter 14)

Lord Casey 1 January 1944 [Australia]
Richard Gardiner Casey was an Australian politician and diplomat who could have become prime minister in 1939, but was defeated by a lack of political judgement and instead rose to be governor-general of Australia and the first Australian knight of the Garter.

He was born at Brisbane, Queensland in 1890, the son of a farmer with mining interests who had once been a member of the Queensland legislature. He was educated at Melbourne Church of England Grammar School, Melbourne University, and Trinity College, Cambridge, from where he graduated with a degree in mechanical sciences in 1913. A brief engineering career in Australia was terminated by the outbreak of the 1914–18 war. He joined the Australian Imperial Force in October 1914 and served in Egypt, Gallipoli and France. He was appointed to the DSO in 1918 and awarded the MC in 1917. At the end of the war he began a career in the mining industry and took over several of his father's directorships, but he abandoned the work in 1924 for a career in politics and public service that lasted until his retirement in 1969.

In 1924 Stanley Bruce, the Australian prime minister, appointed Casey liaison officer with the cabinet secretariat in London. In effect he was the Australian diplomat and trade representative in London from 1924 until 1931, apart from a short break in 1927. In 1931 he was elected to the federal parliament for the United Australia Party as member for Corio, Victoria, and held the seat until 1940. He served as assistant treasurer (1933–35) and treasurer (1935–39) of the federal government under Joseph Lyons. Casey was Lyons' favoured successor, but on Lyons' death in 1939, he stood aside in favour of Stanley Bruce. When Bruce then decided not to stand, Casey's rival, Robert Menzies, was elected, and Casey was removed from the treasurership and given the compensatory post of minister for supply and development, charged with preparing the Australian economy for the impending war. Further marginalisation by Menzies caused Casey to resign his seat in parliament and become Australian minister to the United States. In harness with the British ambassador, Casey worked to bring the United States into the war against Germany and to secure its aid against potential Japanese attacks on British possessions in the Pacific.

Impressed by his ability, Winston Churchill made Casey British minister resident in the Middle East (1942–43) with a seat in the war cabinet. Among his difficult tasks was negotiating the replacement of Sir Claude Auchinleck by Generals Montgomery and Alexander, persuading the British cabinet to deal with inflation in the Middle East, engineering procurement campaigns to deal with wheat shortages, and persuading the French to release the Lebanese cabinet from prison. He was now recognised as an effective troubleshooter and was made governor of Bengal (1944–46) to secure the base for a drive against the Japanese in Burma. He reorganised the administration of the state, inoculated most of the population against smallpox, and implemented a food procurement programme to offset the likelihood of a famine.

He returned to Australia in 1946 and was president of the federal Liberal Party (1947–49). In 1949 he was reelected to the federal parliament, for the constituency of Latrobe and brought into the cabinet by Robert Menzies, as minister of works and housing (1949–51), of supply and development (1949–50), of national development (1950–51), in charge of the commonwealth scientific and industrial research organisation (1950–60), and of external affairs (1951–60). During his time at external affairs he encouraged closer relations with Asia and the United States through the Colombo Plan and the ANZUS and SEATO (of which he was the principal architect) alliances. His private opposition to the British invasion of Suez caused his defeat in the ballot for deputy leader of the Liberal Party. In 1960 he retired from parliament, largely because he could not tolerate Menzies' domination of the cabinet and interference in the external affairs ministry.

There remained only the ceremonial office of governor general which he held from 1964 to 1969. Sounded by Menzies, Casey was astonished that his old rival should have considered him for the office. More cynical observers believed that Menzies was simply preparing the way for his own appointment as Casey's successor. He filled the viceregal office with conscientious dignity for five years. 'Tall, handsome and dignified, he was respected by political friends and foes alike for his integrity. He lacked, perhaps, the driving ambition and capacity for intrigue which might have made him prime minister. When Menzies had been manoeuvring for the leadership in 1938 and 1939, Lyons knew that some ministers were plotting his downfall but rightly dismissed the possibility of Casey being involved with the remark that he was a gentleman'.[4]

Casey was made a privy councillor in 1939, appointed a CH in 1944, a GCMG in 1965 (a standard honour for a governor-general) and a KG in 1969. The CH was almost certainly conferred at the instigation of Winston Churchill who admired Casey's able work in the Middle East. Casey was an Australian citizen and in theory his CH should have been recommended by the Australian prime minister and set against the Australian quota. But as the honour was for his work as 'Minister of State Resident in the Middle East', John Curtin, the Australian prime minister, agreed that Casey's appointment should be set against the United Kingdom quota. He died in 1976.

Viscount Malvern 4 August 1944 [Southern Rhodesia]
Sir Godfrey Huggins, first Viscount Malvern, was prime minister of Southern Rhodesia (1933–1953) and then the first prime minister of the ill-fated Federation of Rhodesia and Nyasaland (1953–56), of which he was the chief architect.

He was born in 1883 at Bexley in Kent, the eldest son of a member of the London Stock Exchange. He was educated at Malvern College, where mastoid problems left him permanently deaf. At the age of eighteen he went to St Thomas's Hospital in London and qualified as a doctor in 1906. After postgraduate appointments at St Thomas', he went to the Hospital for Sick Children at Great Ormond Street. In 1911 he went to Southern Rhodesia for a rest and acted as locum for a doctor in Salisbury. Developing a liking for the country, he decided to remain as a general practitioner and surgeon. During the 1914–18 war he served with the Royal Army Medical Corps as a surgical specialist in England, France and Malta. In 1921 he gave up general practice to concentrate on surgery. As a surgeon, Huggins acquired a substantial following who were reluctant to see him abandon them for a career in politics. In 1923 he was elected to represent Salisbury North in the legislative assembly of Northern Rhodesia, but he continued his medical career, operating early in the morning before going on to his ministerial duties, and he did not finally retire from surgery until 1950.

He was an independent-minded figure who did not always agree with the policy of the Rhodesia Party to which he belonged. During the depression years he resigned on an economic matter and sat as an independent. In 1933 he was persuaded to accept the leadership of the Reform Party, shortly before the election that year, and, to his surprise, the party was returned to power with an absolute majority and Huggins found himself prime minister. Within a year, a series of splits and mergers found Huggins as the leader of the new United Party and with another absolute majority at the election in November 1934. His government survived with greater or lesser majorities until 1953, when he resigned to become the first prime minister of the new Federation of Rhodesia and Nyasaland. On 17 February 1955 he achieved the record as the longest-serving prime minister in the Commonwealth, having continuously held office for 7,829 days since 1933. He retired as prime minister of the federation on 1 November 1956.

Huggins was an old-fashioned liberal who repeatedly argued that no civilised society should be built up at the expense of any class or any race. For many years in Southern Rhodesia, he simultaneously held the office of minister of native affairs (1933–49), and he oversaw substantial improvements in native education, housing and clinics. But he regarded the economic and social advancement of native Africans as being more important than political advancement; the former would gradually justify and bring about the latter. The victory of the Rhodesian Front Party at the 1962 election in Southern Rhodesia caused him great concern, a concern which deepened as that government became increasingly intolerant and sought to entrench rule by the white minority of Rhodesians. To the end of his life Huggins was an imperial loyalist, and he condemned the unilateral declaration of independence in 1965 and the declaration of a republic in 1970. His attack on the Rhodesian government for abandoning the Union flag and adopting a new flag for the illegal republic was one of his last public appearances before his death in 1971.

In 1941 Huggins received a KCMG, the traditional honour for colonial premiers, putting him on a par with the premiers of the Australian states. But the high regard in which he was held in Britain was proved by the two further honours – a CH and a viscountcy – that he received in 1944 and 1955 respectively. There was no precedent for conferring a CH on a Commonwealth prime minister, whose country did not have dominion status, but the honour was given on the recommendation of Lord Cranborne, secretary of state for dominions affairs. 'He showed himself to be a considerable personality while he was here for the Dominion Prime Ministers' meeting, and I have been considering whether there is anything that could be done by the conferment upon him of an honour to signalize his visit here and to strengthen his position in Southern Rhodesia. His long tenure (11 years) of the appointment of Prime Minister in Southern Rhodesia and the striking war effort which Southern Rhodesia has achieved under his leadership are additional reasons why a signal honour would be appropriate . . . If this is to be done, the most appropriate honour would be the CH . . . If so, it should, I think, be announced specially at some suitable date – say, about August – and not kept for the next general Honours List at the New Year, 1945.[5]

General Henry Crerar 5 July 1945 [Canada]
Harry Crerar was the first Canadian to be appointed a CH. On the formation of the First Canadian Army in 1944, he became its first general officer commanding-in-chief and directed its successful progress through France, Belgium and the Netherlands into Germany. 'No other single officer had such impact on the raising, fighting, and eventual disbanding of the greatest army Canada has ever known. Crerar was unquestionably the most important Canadian soldier of the war.'[6]

He was born in 1888 in Hamilton, Ontario, the son of a lawyer born and educated in Scotland, who emigrated to Canada in his twenties. He was educated at a local school in Hamilton, at Upper Canada College, then a year at a school at Lausanne in Switzerland. He went to the Royal Military College (at Kingston, Ontario) in 1906, graduated in 1909 and was commissioned as an officer in the Fourth Field Battery, Canadian Field Artillery. He had hoped to join either the British or the Indian armies, but decided against a military career because it would have meant relying on financial support from his father. Instead he entered the world of industry, joining the Canadian Tungsten Lamp Company in 1910 and learning a great deal about the manufacture of light bulbs. In 1912 he joined the Hydro-Electric Power Commission of Ontario as an illuminating engineer.

At the outbreak of war he joined the Eleventh Battery of the Third Brigade, Canadian Field Artillery and served in the first actions of the Canadian Division at Ypres. He took command of a battery in 1915 and by 1917 he was an acting lieutenant colonel. He was mentioned in despatches and appointed a DSO in 1917; no citation was recorded in the *London Gazette*. He remained in the permanent force after the war. He joined the artillery as a major and was soon promoted to temporary lieutenant colonel. He attended a course at the British staff college at Camberley in 1923 and afterwards remained on secondment to the war office in London. He returned to Canada in 1927 and had a period as professor of tactics at the Royal Military College (1928–29). When General Andrew McNaughton was made chief of the General Staff in 1929, he summoned Crerar to work with him in Ottawa as a planning officer. Over the next decade he produced a series of planning papers on various aspects of Canadian defence and, like McNaughton, his imperialism lessened after the 1931 Statute of Westminster had recognised the effective independence of the dominions. There was no longer any such thing as the Canadian section of the Imperial General Staff. In 1934 he was selected to attend the Imperial Defence College in London for a year's advanced military schooling, and the reports on his progress commented on his outstanding ability 'with all the attributes for high command.'[7] In 1935–38 he was director of military operations and intelligence in the department of National Defence, and commandant of the Royal Military College 1938–39.

Crerar was nothing if not ambitious; humility and selflessness were not fundamental to his character. On more than one occasion he lobbied for promotion 'for the sake of my personal security and my future career.'[8] 'His ambition was unbounded, his self-seeking unlimited. What was worse was the piety with which his demands were couched.'[9]

In 1939–40 he organised the Canadian military headquarters in London, but after the fall of France he was recalled to Ottawa in 1940 as vice-chief of the general staff with the rank of major general. Two days after his arrival in Canada, he was promoted to chief of the general staff. He found a sleepy and inefficient organisation, unprepared for the impending task of fighting a war, and used his considerable administrative and planning skills to bring order out of chaos. Political subtlety was not one of his strengths and he gave voice, indiscreetly, to his serious reservations about Colonel J. R. Ralston, the Canadian minister of national defence, who in turn began to make it clear that he hated Crerar. 'He has very grave weaknesses of character. He is intensely ambitious and is constantly seeking to arrogate to himself the whole business of the department. He even demands copies of letters coming to [the minister] personally.'[10] Crerar confirmed Ralston's suspicions by starting a year-long campaign to get the minister to promote him to lieutenant general. When the commander of the Canadian navy was promoted to vice-admiral (naval equivalent of a lieutenant general) in March 1941, Crerar was almost beside himself. 'Quite apart from my personal feelings, it seems to me not only illogical but highly undesirable that the Chief of the Army Staff should remain inferior in rank to the Chief of another Canadian Service, the operational responsibilities of which are measurably less in scale.'[11]

Crerar yearned not only for promotion but for a command in the field and both were satisfied in November 1941. He was promoted by way of Cabinet decision that the heads of the three services should be of the same rank, and the illness of General Andrew McNaughton brought him to the front line of battle in Europe. He was given command of the Canadian Corps two days before Christmas 1941 and began to deal with the areas of weakness left by his predecessor. Politically and militarily, Crerar was a far better army commander, and his judgement that McNaughton was incompetent was harsh but true. Of his methods in securing the removal of McNaughton, perhaps the less said the better. 'It was one thing to gossip maliciously about one's superior, but it was quite different for Crerar to undercut so consistently and with such force, the man who had fostered his career – and in such high places. Unfortunately, and despite his protestations, it *had* become Crerar's habit to knife his superior in the back.'[12]

Crerar took command and served in Britain and Italy 1942–44. He became commander of the First Canadian Corps, which patrolled in Sicily (July 1943) and in mainland Italy (from September 1943). He was recalled to England in early 1944 to take command of the First Canadian Army, units of which landed on Juno Beach on D-Day during the Normandy invasion. Operating temporarily under the British Second Army, Canadian units took part in bitter fighting for the city of Caen and then helped to close the northern arm of the Falaise-Argentan gap, in which large numbers of Germans were encircled. By that time Crerar's army was directly under Field Marshal Bernard Montgomery as part of the 21st Army Group. Operating on the extreme left flank of the allied drive across France, the First Canadian Army took the French Channel ports of Le Havre and Dieppe and then cleared the Scheldt River estuary and captured Antwerp in Belgium. From there, they drove into The Netherlands and then breached the northern end of the Siegfried Line. Crerar had to work with the egotistical Field Marshal Montgomery who ordered dominions troops about as though the devolution of the British empire had never happened, and held to the view that Crerar had no operational responsibilities for Canadian troops temporarily serving with another army! Of Crerar himself, Montgomery was particularly damning. 'He is a most awfully nice chap, but he is very prosy and stodgy, and he is very definitely not a commander.'[13] Throughout his period of command, Crerar continuously stood firm for Canadian interests in the face of Montgomery's bullying behaviour. Crerar was promoted to general in November 1944 by McNaughton who was now defence minister, and even then Montgomery tried to intervene and insist that it was a normal promotion and not for distinguished service in the field.

Crerar retired from the army in 1946. He was offered the post of lieutenant governor of Ontario but declined, feeling that it was not really his type of job. A few minor diplomatic appointments were undertaken. In 1947 he headed a Canadian mission to Japan in connection with the Japanese peace settlement. In 1948 he was appointed the first Canadian ADC to King George VI, and received the same appointment with Queen Elizabeth II in 1952. He represented Canada at the installation of Queen Juliana of the Netherlands in 1948. He was grand president of the Canadian Legion, president of the Canadian Citizenship Council (1948–50), and a member of the Canadian Institute of International Affairs.

Crerar was appointed a CB in 1943, and in 1945 Montgomery recommended him for a KBE, saying 'no commander ever has had a more loyal subordinate than I have had in you.'[14] Because of the 1918 resolution, he could not accept a KBE because of its knighthood, and a CBE was felt to be poor recognition. The only realistic choice was the CH which carried neither precedence nor title. As Canadians were allowed to accept gallantry awards, he was given the CH on the submission of the Canadian minister of national defence to King George VI 'in recognition of his gallant and distinguished service in north west

Europe.' It was the only example of the flexible CH being overtly used as a gallantry decoration. Crerar died at Ottawa in 1965 at the age of seventy-seven, largely forgotten.

Peter Fraser 4 January 1946 [New Zealand]
Peter Fraser rose from a humble beginning in Scotland, to work as a carpenter in the house of commons, to adopt passionately-held socialist beliefs, to spend twelve months in prison for sedition, and at the last to reach the pinnacle of being prime minister of New Zealand (1940–49).

He was born in the highland village of Fearn, Ross-shire in 1884 where his father was a bootmaker. His attended the village school for a while, but left to go out to work, first as a postman and then as a carpenter, to bring needed additional income into his home. His father was an active member of the local branch of the Liberal Party and his son was imbued with political knowledge from an early age. In 1907 he went to London where he was employed as a construction worker on the White City at Shepherd's Bush and also with the board of works on repair carpentering at the house of commons. Initially a Liberal, he became an ardent socialist and a convert to the Independent Labour Party.

He was unemployed in 1910, decided to emigrate to New Zealand, and arrived in Auckland in January 1911. He quickly joined the New Zealand Socialist Party and worked as a labourer. His political activity and open-air speaking in the socialist cause brought him to prominence in the Auckland General Labourers Union. He was elected its president in 1911, but his involvement in a series of damaging and inconclusive strikes cost him his reputation, and in 1913 he went to Wellington to work as a docker. In the same year he was elected secretary-treasurer of the new Social Democratic Party. During another strike he was arrested and bound over to keep the peace. He was typical of many socialists in opposing the 1914–18 war, denouncing it as an 'imperialist' war and opposing conscription. In 1916 he was arrested on a charge of sedition for inciting opposition to conscription, and was sentenced to twelve months imprisonment. He served the full term.

Before his imprisonment, he had taken a prominent role in the formation of the New Zealand Labour Party in 1916, and in 1918 he was elected to parliament as Labour member for Wellington Central. He was renowned as an effective and devastatingly incisive debater with a flair for sarcasm. For some years his politics were militant but they gradually mellowed under a growing pragmatism. In 1919 he had supported land nationalisation. In 1927 he was one of those who persuaded the party to abandon it as unrealistic. In 1933 he was elected deputy leader of the party, and when the party was elected to government in 1935 he was given the education, health, marine and police portfolios. When the prime minister, M. J. Savage, fell ill in 1939, Fraser became acting prime minister, and was effective head of the government until Savage's death in March 1940, when he was elected leader by a majority vote.

The 1939–45 war years were not easy for Fraser. His desire was to see the formation of a national government for the duration, and a joint war cabinet was created. It collapsed in the summer of 1942 when the National Party withdrew. Thereafter Fraser had to run the country on a war footing and contend with the continuation of party politics at peacetime level – and fight and win a general election in 1943 at the height of the war. He showed an authoritarian streak in his introduction of conscription, comprehensive censorship and emergency regulation. Like his neighbouring prime minister, John Curtin of Australia, Fraser faced difficulties with the allies in the use and location of New Zealand troops, but unlike Curtin, he was more inclined to follow the wishes of the allied command.

He was an ardent supporter of the League of Nations and he was equally fervent in his support for its successor, the United Nations Organisation, though he was disappointed (a) that the UN was not given supranational authority and the means to enforce its decisions, (b) that the veto rights of the great powers were unlimited, and (c) that there were no guarantees binding member states to come the aid of a victim of aggression. He was more successful in achieving the establishment of the Trusteeship Council (of which he became the first chairman) and the elevation of the Economic and Social Council to the status of a principal body of the UN, and he emerged from the early UN debates as a respected figure of importance on the international stage.

The postwar years were difficult and less happy. He narrowly won the 1946 election with support from the right wing majority of the trades unions. But he came under increasing pressure from rising militancy on the left and the National Party on the right. Although he won a 1949 referendum on peacetime compulsory military training, in the face of considerable hostility, he was heavily defeated at the ensuing general election. Either in name or in effect he had been prime minister for ten years and the strain had begun to show. He suffered a stroke in October 1949 and died fourteen months later. It was typical of the man that as he lay ill he worried because the chauffeurs who drove his car while he was prime minister had been given no opportunity to visit him.[15]

He was certainly among the greatest of New Zealand prime ministers, though also among the most complex and most underestimated. 'He had much of the Scottish Calvinist in his moral make-up – a certain dourness of nature, personal asceticism, great industry and firm strength of conviction. He possessed a sharp and capacious intellect and his thinking extended over a tremendous range of interests . . . He combined a pride in intellectual dispute with a thorough-going distrust of intellectuals. He was a shrewd judge of a situation but, influenced too greatly at times by personal likes and dislikes, was not always the best judge of men. Steeped in the standing orders of the House, he was a skilled parliamentarian able, when he "took notice" of a developing situation, by breadth of knowledge and sheer force of personality, to command it.'[16]

Fraser was honoured by his native land when the University of Aberdeen conferred the degree of LLD on him in 1941. On his appointment as prime minister in 1940 he was made a member of the privy council, and the CH was conferred on him in 1946. The proposal came from New Zealand's first native-born governor general, Lord Freyberg, who had taken office in February that year. 'Suggest for your consideration that on his arrival in England my Prime Minister might be offered a Companion of Honour. He does not know of this suggestion, and I do not of course know whether he would accept, but in any event it would be a good gesture.'[17] Clement Attlee accepted Freyberg's recommendation. There was every reason why Fraser should have the honour. Using a comparative ranking among Commonwealth prime ministers, based on tenure, in judging their readiness for the CH, Fraser was next in line. Mackenzie King of Canada was senior to Fraser but his attitude towards honours was that he would not accept them. Fraser was second on the list as Smuts of South Africa had been made a CH in 1917 and was promoted field marshal in 1941. Chifley of Australia was comparatively new and had only recently been made a privy councillor. 'Prime Minister would very much like to submit to the King Mr Peter Fraser's name for a CH in recognition of his outstanding services to the empire during the war.'[18]

Fraser accepted the CH after the personal hesitation natural in a Labour politician, and his acceptance set a trend for four decades. He was the first of seven New Zealand prime ministers to receive the honour, and the Australian precedent was followed, citing Fraser as 'Prime Minister of New Zealand'. There was no better form of wording, but it seemed to imply that the honour was more official than meritorious, and so it proved to be with his successors. As with the Australian prime ministers, it became more a badge of office than an honour.

Vincent Massey 22 May 1946 [Canada]
Vincent Massey was high commissioner for Canada in the United Kingdom for an unequalled period of eleven years, of which six encompassed the 1939–45 war. An ardent royalist anglophile who delighted in English aristocratic society, he was equally a persistent and firm defender of Canadian rights and a vigorous exponent of Canadian cultural achievements. He came from a prominent Canadian family, his father being president of the Massey-Harris Company, known for manufacturing agricultural equipment and his brother being the actor Raymond Massey.

He was born in Toronto in 1887 into one of Canada's wealthiest and most prominent families. He was educated at St Andrew's College, Toronto, the University of Toronto, and Balliol College, Oxford. This early experience of England gave him a lasting appreciation of its traditions and institutions, and led in later years to him being lampooned as 'a precious colonial version of an English gentleman who made up in aristocratic manners what he lacked in aristocratic ancestry.'[19] He began his working life as a lecturer in modern history at the University of Toronto (1913–15). His academic career was cut short by the 1914–18 war and he was a staff officer of Military District No. 2 (Canada) (1915–18), associate secretary of the war cabinet committee (January-December 1918), secretary and later director of the government repatriation committee (1918–19). In the early 1920s, he was active as an actor and director in Hart House Theatre at the University of Toronto. He served as president of the family business (1921–25).

His career in public life began in September 1925 when he joined the Liberal cabinet as minister without portfolio at the invitation of the prime minister. In the federal election of October 1925 he ran in the riding of Durham but was defeated. He served as Canada's first diplomatic representative in the USA (1926–30) and was Canadian high commissioner in the United Kingdom (1935–46). While in Britain, Massey served as a trustee of the National Gallery (1941–46) and was chairman (1943–46). It was not a polite diplomatic gesture, but an affirmation of Massey's knowledge and influence in the art world. On his return to Canada, he was chairman of the National Gallery of Canada (1948–52). From 1949 to 1951, he was chairman of the royal commission on national development in the arts, letters and sciences. The historic report of the Massey Commission, as it became known, included recommendations on broadcasting, the creation of the Canada Council, the establishment of a national library and financial aid to universities, and ultimately a Canadian honours system. All of the major recommendations of the report were implemented by 1957. 'More than any other Canadian, he was responsible for the first major movement of the arts and letters from the periphery of national concern towards the centre.'[20]

The culmination of his career in public life was as Canada's first post-confederation native-born governor general (1952–59), in succession to Field Marshal Earl Alexander of Tunis. It was an innovation and there was some muted criticism of the appointment as repugnant to the tradition of Canadian loyalism. But Louis St Laurent, the prime minister, was insistent. 'I would not like to think that a Canadian, alone of the Queen's subjects, would not be considered fit to represent her in Canada'.[21] Massey confounded his detractors by his impeccable behaviour, performing the role with a dignity appropriate to the crown representative. He was personally loyal to the monarchy and held that it was his duty to strengthen the bond between Canada and the crown. He combined a respect for the crown and its ceremonies with a commitment to using his office to promote Canadian unity and identity. He revived the use of the state landau in 1953 when it was used in Ottawa for the coronation celebrations of Queen Elizabeth II. Amid much pageantry, the landau conveyed the governor general and his staff to Parliament Hill under escort by members of the Royal Canadian Mounted Police, and the landau that he used that day is still used for the opening of parliament and during state visits. Though his position was ceremonial, he was assiduous and conscientious in his duties, travelling widely throughout Canada and using canoe or dog team to visit places beyond the reach of train and airplane.

He continued the work that he had begun with the Massey Commission and promoted the concept of a national festival of the arts which began a movement that eventually led to the founding of the National Arts Centre. At Rideau Hall, the governor general's residence, he established writers' weekends to help create a Canadian literary identity. The then fledgling Stratford Shakespearean Festival received his enthusiastic support and he lent the prestige of his position to the opening of numerous art exhibitions. His term as governor general was extended twice, first by prime minister Louis St. Laurent, and then by prime minister John Diefenbaker who regarded Massey as 'sound, learned, wise and thoughtful' and wanted him to continue in office.[22]

After leaving office in 1959, he retired to Batterwood, his home near Port Hope, Ontario, and continued as chairman of the Massey Foundation, as he had done since 1926. The foundation, incorporated in 1918, was the first trust of its kind to be established in Canada. He devoted his time to two of the foundation's endowments on the University of Toronto campus – Massey College and Hart House, a student centre – and he was chancellor of the university (1947–53).

Massey had a good understanding of the need for honours of various kinds. He had proposed the establishment of a system of Canadian honours to Lord Tweedsmuir as early as 1935, and regretted the disinclination of successive Canadian governments to establish indigenous honours. In 1953 he established the Governor General's Awards for Architecture; in 1954 the Governor General's Gold Medal for the Institute of Chartered Accountants; and in 1959 the Massey Medal to recognise national exploration, development, and description of geography for the Royal Canadian Geographical Society. Though he did not see his dream of Canadian honours established during his tenure as governor general, he was appointed one of the first thirty-five Companions of the new Order of Canada at its foundation in 1967. Had the attitude of the Canadian government been more favourable to the use of imperial honours, Massey could have been showered with them. As it was he had two United Kingdom honours: the CH in 1946 and the Royal Victorian Chain in 1960.

The CH came in 1946 at the conclusion of his eleven years as Canadian high commissioner in London, though no citation or description of appointment was included in the entry in the *London Gazette*. Evidence shows that the honour for Massey originated with the personal initiative of King George VI.[23] On 8 May he was informed by King George VI's private secretary that the King desired Massey to have the CH. Given long-standing Canadian antipathy towards the use of United Kingdom honours in Canada, Massey could not accept without the approval of his government, and the Canadian prime minister would not agree before consulting his colleagues. Mackenzie King, a strange individual, was at first opposed, as he was generally opposed to all honours (though he accepted a CMG in 1906 and the Order of Merit in 1947), but he later changed his mind and recommended that his colleagues might wish to see Massey as highly deserving of this gesture of royal appreciation. 'They, I think, would feel that Massey had really rendered great service over the ten years that he had been here, and that now that he is leaving, recognition of the kind would be appropriate; also it would appropriately come within the honours that would be related specially to services rendered by civilians during the war.'[24] Another account presents King as almost contemptuous of Massey's desperation. 'The Order of the Companion of Honour was on the arm of a chair and Vincent had been looking at it, if not worshipping it. This was, of course, the apex of Vincent's ambitions and career.'[25] King was in London at the time and went to convey the news to Massey, who was staying at the Dorchester Hotel. According to King's account, Massey was overjoyed. 'This means so much. There is nothing I would rather have than this. I cannot tell you how deeply I feel or how grateful I am to you.'[26]

Massey was personally invested by King George VI on the night before he and his wife sailed for Canada. 'We appeared in our travelling clothes, as everything else had been packed and sent to the ship, and were received by the King and Queen, who were accompanied by Princess Elizabeth. The King rather shyly gave me the little case with the decoration inside it. The Queen suggested that they should drink our health, the champagne was ready and the toast was drunk – by the King, in tea. The intimacy and charm and warmth of this private investiture moved us both deeply.'[27]

In 1954 the Duke of Edinburgh, when on a private visit to Canada, asked Massey whether he would be prepared to accept the Order of the Garter. 'I was completely overwhelmed by the thought and told him that I hoped he would tell the Queen how touched I was . . . What a wonderful idea it is! And how I would love to be able to accept this fabulous honour.'[28] Like the CH eight years earlier, he knew it would need government approval and hoped that this would be forthcoming. Prime minister Louis St Laurent told Massey quite definitely that, in the light of past decisions, it would, in his view, be politically embarrassing to the government if Massey accepted the honour while in office.[29] For six years Massey clung to the hope, and in 1959 prime minister John Diefenbaker gave him every reason to think that there would be no objection. But the prime minister subsequently withdrew his approval leaving Massey with a lingering feeling of bitterness and betrayal, although the letter that he received from London was charm itself. 'The Queen has instructed me to let you know in confidence that as much as she would like to make you a Knight of the Garter — the first in the Commonwealth overseas — it is not possible for her to do so because her government in Canada . . . advised her that this would be inappropriate . . . Her Majesty does not wish to bring it to a close without assuring you once again of her great appreciation of your service as her representative in Canada and of her deep regard for you and gratitude for what you have done.'[30]

Instead of the Order of the Garter, Massey was given the Royal Victorian Chain – a non-titular honour – on 22 July 1960, one month later. 'At the appointed hour I arrived at the Palace, and was received by the Queen in a small drawing-room. She gave me the Chain, with a very charming reference to my time at Government House as her representative. I was deeply moved and told her how much this honour meant to me.'[31]

Massey died in 1967 while on a visit to England and was given a state funeral in Canada.

General Andrew McNaughton 13 June 1946 [Canada]
Andrew McNaughton was general officer commanding in chief, First Canadian Army in 1942–43, and second of three Canadian generals to be made CH.

McNaughton was born in 1887, in Moosomin in the North-West Territories, where his father ran a trading post. He grew up on the prairies and went to Bishop's College School in Lennoxville, Quebec. He studied electrical engineering at McGill University, graduating with a BSc in 1910 and an MSc in 1912, and joined the teaching staff of the university. In 1914 he went into a private engineering practice. Like many of his contemporaries he sampled soldiering on the side and was commissioned into the Canadian militia in 1909. After the outbreak of the 1914–18 war he served in the Second Brigade, Canadian Field Artillery, being twice wounded and three times mentioned in despatches. By 1916 he was a lieutenant colonel and in 1917 he became counter-battery staff officer of the Canadian Corps, charged with locating and neutralising enemy guns. It was designed for a scientifically minded officer, and McNaughton rose to the challenge. He was awarded the DSO in 1918 'for conspicuous gallantry and devotion to duty as counter-battery staff officer. He carried out daring reconnaissances, and observed the enemy's batteries from an exposed position under heavy fire. On one occasion he crossed the enemy's lines in a low-flying airplane, obtaining valuable information as to the enemy's batteries. He rendered most valuable service during a long period.' He was credited with developing techniques for locating enemy artillery so that it could be disabled and was co-inventor of a cathode-ray direction finder used in aircraft. He was promoted to brigadier general and given command of the Canadian Corps Heavy Artillery during the final weeks of the war.

After the war he was encouraged to remain in the army, and held a succession of staff and command appointments in the permanent active militia. In 1921 he attended the British Army Staff College at Camberley where the commandant described him as 'an officer of exceptional attainments, with immense powers of concentration, and great strength of character . . . He has good tactical ability, and as a scientific gunner, he is quite outstanding . . . He expresses himself with conviction . . . He is tactful, and has a good manner, in which the intenseness of the man is evident.'[32] Praise of that level was rarely lavished on dominions officers, and McNaughton decided to remain with the permanent force. By 1923 he was deputy chief of the general staff, and in 1927 he went to London to attend the Imperial Defence College, where again he received glowing praise for his 'ability, knowledge, experience and enthusiasm . . . He has shown himself to be a man of great determination and thoroughness, and an admirable debater. He has certainly left no stone unturned to add to his knowledge of the military problems of the Empire.'[33]

In 1929 he was promoted to major general and appointed chief of the Canadian general staff at the young age of forty-two. 'His rise had been simply phenomenal in a military force bound up in seniority and red tape, and he had made it to the top on ability alone.'[34] He appealed to politicians because he combined military genius with an understanding of the budgetary problems that dictated a small professional army. But he had his opponents, even within the army. There were those who saw his application of science to warfare as a downgrading of the significance of the infantry and the cavalry. In 1930 he was described by one of his officers as 'a vindictive and conceited man. He doesn't like advice and does not ask it and is much annoyed if anyone has diff[erent] views to himself . . . He is uncouth and slovenly in his makeup . . . and forgets that he is dealing with men, the most of them on a lower mental capacity than himself but general[ly] with more balance and more business sense.'[35] It was not far short of the mark. McNaughton was brighter and more able than many of his colleagues and could forget to make allowances when dealing with men not as intellectually able as himself.

He resigned as chief of the general staff in 1935 to become president of the National Research Council, and the resignation was not voluntary. R. B. Bennett, the Canadian prime minister, was facing a general election, and McNaughton was one of a number of people attracting criticism to his government. Bennett offered him the post in terms which made it clear that it was not a request. McNaughton, hesitant at first, accepted it on the understanding that he was being seconded and would not therefore sever his links with the army.

McNaughton's reputation as a scientist ensured his recall to the army at the outbreak of war. Because he preferred the use of machines to manpower, there would be less loss of life, therefore less demand for conscription, and less risk of a damaging split between the English and French-speaking sections of the government. In fact McNaughton insisted on Canada being represented by a fighting unit in the field of battle. He was given command of the First Canadian Division and led it overseas in December 1939. He was promoted lieutenant general and commanded the Canadian Corps from its inception in December 1940. In April 1942 an army headquarters with two corps was formed and he became commander of the First Canadian Army, although his troops remained mostly in Britain. He firmly supported the policy of keeping the Canadian army as a complete and separate force, but he also tended to run the Canadian army in Europe with scant regard to the wishes of the Canadian cabinet in Ottawa. In fact he simply ran his section of the war, in full cooperation with his military allies, but without seeing the need to consult the government at home, unless there was a question of the principle of Canadian independence. Vincent Massey, the Canadian high commissioner in London, viewed McNaughton with irritation. 'Generally he has his mind made up on the matters he wishes to discuss, and cooperation with him is a bit like cooperation with an Act of Parliament . . . I'm afraid he's rather a spoiled darling with a prima donna complex – despite his great ability.'[36]

Although he cooperated with the allies, he would not always take orders from them without reference to Ottawa. As a result he was severely criticised by the British general, Alan Brooke for being unwilling to agree to greater integration on the grounds of tactical necessity. Brooke also complained that McNaughton had neglected the training of the Canadian troops and highlighted the inefficiency of their commanders. McNaughton showed signs of nervous strain, fell ill and went on sick leave, not returning to his post until March 1942, but thereafter he was often ill and hypertense. The death in action of his son, a squadron leader, in June 1942 added an extra strain. He badly mishandled a joint military exercise with the British in the spring of 1943 and Brooke wrote that he was 'quite incompetent to command an Army! He does not know how to begin to cope with the job and he was tying his force up into the most awful muddle.'[37]

After the exercise the writing was on the wall. McNaughton was relieved of his command in December 1943 on the grounds of ill-health. He returned to Canada early in 1944, retiring in September that year with the rank of general. King liked the wayward general if only because of his opposition to conscription and offered him the chance to become the first Canadian governor general of Canada. McNaughton was attracted by the idea and accepted. Within a few weeks King changed his mind and decided that McNaughton could be more use in the political arena. At the end of October 1944 King summoned this 'gaunt, grizzled yet still wonderfully magnetic figure'[38] and unwisely made him minister of national defence. The appointment was controversial – with the army, with the opposition Conservative Party and within King's own party. He was too much of a loose cannon to give time to the more subtle and more deadly world of politics, and he never became a member of the Canadian parliament. He was defeated in a by-election at Grey North in February 1945 and at Qu'Appelle in the general election in August. Because he was now tainted by political partisanship the offer of the governor generalship evaporated.

After the war he served as president of the Canadian Atomic Energy Control Board (1946–48), as Canada's representative on the United Nations Security Council (1948–49), and represented Canada on the United Nations Atomic Energy Commission (1946–66). He was also Canadian chairman of the International Joint Commission with the United States (1950–62). He never changed his nature, and in the late 1950s, John Diefenbaker remembered that he 'sometimes acted so imperiously that one might have assumed that he was the Canadian government.'[39]

McNaughton was made a CMG in 1919, a CB in 1935 and a CH in 1946 for his services as 'General Officer Commanding in Chief, First Canadian Army, 1942–43'. It was an irony in the extreme. 'He was a great man, highly intelligent, a compelling personality and one who did well in every single endeavour that he took on – except as commander of the First Canadian Army.'[40] The only explanation is that the Canadian prime minister decided that he 'owed' something to McNaughton, and certainly King himself pressed for McNaughton to be given a CH.

In the case of Crerar, the initiative for an honour (eventually the CH) had come from Montgomery, and King had acquiesced and signed the submission. In the case of McNaughton, the initiative came from the Canadian prime minister himself. 'I feel that he is entitled to the same recognition as Crerar having regard to what he did in organising Canada's armies and in training them for war. He is now out of Parliament. This may be the last list that will relate particularly to the war and it seems to me that his services might well be given recognition at this time.'[41]

King himself was quite willing again to sign a submission to the King.[42] Unfortunately it was not that easy. Had not the Canadian prime minister declined the proposal to establish a Canadian CH quota in 1943? Although there was no objection to McNaughton on the ground of merit, he would have to be included either in the United Kingdom quota or in the quota for 'the rest', and in either case the British prime minister would be the appropriate authorised signatory. The question had not arisen in the case of Crerar where, probably on the assumption that it was a 'one-off', King had been accepted without demur as the signatory. But the appointment of three Canadians, two of them generals, within a period of twelve months was beginning to look like the start of a trend, and there was much muttering in Whitehall about the irregularity of it all. 'It is of course the case that Mr Mackenzie King signed a submission in General Crerar's case and Sir Robert Knox's view is that under the statute it would have been possible for him to sign in this case also. Nevertheless it seems difficult to go on borrowing in this way from other people's quotas and it looked as if insistence on the strictest method in this case might provoke a change in the Canadian attitude. After all they cannot have the best of both worlds.'[43] So what was to be said to the Canadian prime minister? The same note revealed that the refusal of a CH quota on doctrinal grounds was now regretted at least in certain Canadian quarters. 'I had earlier discussed with Sir Alan Lascelles and Sir Eric Machtig the question of what was to be said to Mr Mackenzie King when he wrote and it was agreed that the general line should be to point out that under the statute it was not possible to deal with this except by taking one of our quota but without rubbing it in too much and Sir Alan Lascelles told me that he thought Mr Mackenzie King realised that he had made a mistake in refusing a quota and certainly that his staff took that view.'[44] McNaughton's submission was duly signed by Clement Attlee. McNaughton died at Montebello, Quebec, in 1966.

Sir Robert Menzies 1 January 1951 [Australia]

A powerful intellect and ambition led Robert Menzies to become the longest serving prime minister of Australia, holding the office for a total of eighteen years (1939–41 and 1949–66).

He was born at Jeparit in 1894, the son of a first-generation Scottish Australian who ran a general store. He was proud of his Scottish ancestry and remained unswervingly pro-British throughout his life. Education at Jeparit State School was followed by a periods at a series of Melbourne colleges and finally to the University of Melbourne, from where he graduated with a first class degree in law. A family conference had decided that he should continue his studies while his two brothers enlisted during the 1914–18 war, and he was admitted as a barrister in 1918.

By 1923 he was Australia's youngest-ever King's Counsel and one of the nation's best-known and best-paid barristers. He could have had a long and successful career at the bar, but he was raised in an atmosphere of politics (both his father and his uncle had held seats in the Victoria legislature) and the world of politics soon began to attract him. He entered the Victoria legislature as a member of the legislative council in 1928 and as a member of the legislative assembly in 1929. In 1932, he could have become premier of Victoria but preferred to be deputy premier and attorney-general. In 1934 he was elected to the federal parliament and immediately made attorney-general of Australia and minister for industry by Joseph Lyons. By 1935 he was deputy leader of the United Australia Party. During the late 1930s he acquired the unaffectionate nicknames of 'Ming the Merciless' and 'Pig-iron Bob'. The first derived from a character in the contemporary *Flash Gordon* serials, and referred to his attempt to deport an anti-fascist, anti-war Czech author as an illegal immigrant. The second came from his battle with dockers who refused to load ships with scrap iron for Japan, claiming that it would be used for armaments.

In 1939 he was one of the two candidates to succeed Lyons, and his election was brought about in part by the foolishness of Earle Page, the caretaker prime minister, who attempted to sabotage Menzies' chances. Within a few months he was leader of a country that was at war. He failed in an attempt to persuade the Labour Party to join an all-party wartime coalition, and in the 1941 elections his own party disintegrated, Labour won power and his career seemed to be finished. But he created a new party, the Liberals, from anti-Labour elements and after the war, when Labour launched a nationalisation programme, he played on national fears that Australia was on the road to communism. He was helped by postwar industrial turbulence and won the 1949 general election.

His victory coincided with the start of a postwar boom, which gave the Liberal-Country coalition more than twenty years in government. Menzies implemented policies of massive immigration, medical and hospital benefits, advances in education and the development of Canberra. In foreign affairs, he linked Australia more closely to south-east Asia and the USA to counter what was seen as the spread of communism and the possible isolation of Australia. In support of offensives against communism, he sent Australian troops to fight in the Korean War, and with the Americans in Vietnam.

During his premiership Australians enjoyed unprecedented prosperity and development, and in later years, many looked back to his time as a golden era. He could be aloof and authoritarian, almost revelling in his role as the dominant father-figure and protector of the traditional values of the nation. He inspired awe and respect rather than affection and was well known for his razor tongue and rapier wit. Given the prosperous and healthy economy, he was seen as the architect of Australian postwar progress and there were no serious challenges to his leadership. He retired in January 1966.

He was made a CH in 1951, and the citation followed the practice of Bruce, Lyons and Hughes, recording that he was 'Prime Minister of the Commonwealth of Australia.' He was made a Knight of the Thistle (an extremely rare honour for a non-British national) in 1963, in recognition of his Scottish ancestry, and in 1976 one of the handful to be made knights of the Order of Australia. He died in 1978.

Sir Sidney Holland 7 June 1951 [New Zealand]
Sidney Holland was a frank, friendly and pragmatic politician who was prime minister of New Zealand 1949–57.

He was born at Greendale, Canterbury in 1893, the son of a Yorkshire father and a Lancashire mother. His father was the proprietor of a haulage business in Christchurch, and later mayor of Christchurch and a member of parliament. He was educated at West Christchurch School, but left at the age of fifteen to work for a hardware company. When his father was elected mayor of Christchurch, he joined the family company as an accountant. After the outbreak of the 1914–18 war, he joined the army in 1915, was commissioned in the New Zealand Field Artillery and served on the western front. He fell seriously ill during the battle of Messines in June 1917, was sent home and discharged from the army in November. A long period of convalescence was followed by renewed involvement in business. He became a director in several companies, including founding the Midland Engineering Company with his brother, and taking part in provincial politics. In 1925 his father was elected to parliament as the representative for Christchurch North, and his son served as his campaign manager. When an accident compelled Henry Holland's retirement, shortly before the 1935 general election, the younger Holland was nominated by the National Party to succeed his father. The party was left with only nineteen members after the election, and a further defeat in the 1938 election increased party discontent with the then leader. In November 1940 Holland, popular with younger members of the party, was elected leader. He joined the war cabinet in 1942 as minister in charge of war expenditure, but a comparatively minor dispute caused him to withdraw and the joint war cabinet collapsed. He was sometimes blamed for causing the breakdown, but substantial numbers in both the Labour and National parties opposed the wartime coalition.

A narrow victory for the Labour Party in 1946 was followed by a substantial victory for Holland and the Liberal Party in 1949. The first two years of his administration were marked by two controversial acts. In 1950 he secured the abolition of the legislative council, the upper chamber of the New Zealand parliament, and was criticised for not replacing it with a more powerful body. In 1951, a strike by the Waterside Workers' Union caused Holland to declare a state of national emergency and use all the government's powers to break the strike. 'He broke it by a well-judged blend of resolution and restraint, and though the losers accused him of dictation, his measures in fact reflected determination to eschew class policies or the excitement of class feeling.'[45] Holland, like other prime ministers in a similar situation, saw the issue as one of who ruled the country, and in the subsequent general election he won with a substantial majority. He was additionally minister of finance, but dropped the portfolio after the 1954 election when the Liberal Party was returned with a reduced majority.

The strain of office began to show and by 1957 there were evident signs of deterioration in his health. At the National Party conference that year he nominated Keith Holyoake as his successor, resigned as prime minister, and remained in the cabinet under Holyoake as a minister without portfolio until the 1957 election. He lived quietly in Wellington for much of his retirement, and for a while his health showed signs of improvement. His retirement gave him the leisure he coveted to enjoy his farm at North Canterbury, where he bred Romney sheep and Polled Angus cattle. He never fully recovered from a stroke in 1960 and died in the following year.

Holland was more a shrewd pragmatist than a doctrinaire conservative, respected for his sincerity and liked for his frank and friendly manner. Before taking office he had shown little interest in international affairs and his grasp of the subject was tenuous. He often spoke of 'the dear old Empire,' and referred to hoisting the flag 'for Britain, the British Empire and Imperial Preference', and he had an obvious pride in New Zealand's association with the Crown.[46] 'Despite his belief in the principles of private enterprise, he was not a deep political thinker . . . Rather he was a practical New Zealander who looked at a problem and found what he thought was the most satisfactory solution regardless of politics.'[47]

He was made a privy councillor in 1950 and a CH in 1951. Following the practice established with Australian appointments, and followed in the case of Peter Fraser in 1946, Holland was cited only as 'Prime Minister of New Zealand' in the *London Gazette*. On his retirement as prime minister he was made a GCB.

Sir John Kotelawala 2 January 1956 [Sri Lanka]
The third prime minister of independent Ceylon (now Sri Lanka), John Kotelawala was unusual among the Asian leaders of his day in being decidedly pro-western and having an almost pathological hatred of communism. He was a colourful ebullient personality who aroused controversy in almost everything he did.

He was born in 1897, the son of a police inspector who committed suicide, and from whom he inherited an impulsive forthright temperament. He was educated at the Royal College, Colombo until 1915 when he went to Europe. His five-year sojourn included a year studying agriculture at Christ's College, Cambridge. He returned to his native land and joined the Ceylon Light Infantry in 1922, reaching the rank of colonel. He retired from the army in 1930 and entered politics in 1931, representing his home district in the state council.

He was briefly acting minister of agriculture and lands in 1934, and became minister of communications and works in 1935, holding the office until he became prime minister in 1953. During the 1939–45 war he served on the war council and afterwards became chairman of the post-war problems committee.

He was a co-founder of the United National Party in 1946 and was elected a vice-president of the party. By 1947 the pressure for independence was growing within Ceylon. Persistent efforts by high Ceylonese officials had forced the British government to reform the Ceylon constitution in 1943, and one of the officials was D. S. Senanayake, a relative of Kotelawala. Senanayake's push for independence led to his election as independent Ceylon's first prime minister in 1948, with Kotelawala continuing as minister of transport and works, and also serving as leader of the house of representatives (1950–53).

The newly-independent state faced several problems, not least of which was the strained relationship with India over the question of the Indian Tamil population, who constituted more than 20% of Ceylon's population and were resident in the north of the island. The economy was weak, caused by the high price of rice – the staple food of the people – and the falling price of rubber – the country's main export. Senanayake was killed in a riding accident in April 1952, and Kotelawala expected to be named prime minister. But Senanayake had left instructions that his son Dudley was to succeed him. Kotelawala was told privately and was mortified, believing for a time that he was the victim of a conspiracy to keep him from the premiership. He didn't have long to wait. Dudley Senanayake's tenure was brief. He was forced to resign as prime minister in October 1953, ostensibly on the grounds of ill health, but following a series of nationwide strikes which had led to a state of emergency. Kotelawala was the natural successor, and took office with a nation on the verge of revolution because of the government's decision to increase the price of rationed rice. Kotelawala declared that he would have no truck with those who supported revolutionary methods in politics and would do his utmost to stamp out communism in the country. He had an intense hatred of communism, calling it the 'new colonialism' and 'nakedly totalitarian'. A series of quiet measures and a visit by Queen Elizabeth II in 1954 assuaged immediate unrest, but there remained the unresolved difficulty of the Tamil population. Despite agreement between the government and the opposition, prime minister Nehru of India steadfastly refused to recognise them as Indian citizens.

In 1954 Kotelawala called a conference of south-east Asian prime ministers, attended by the prime ministers of India, Pakistan, Burma and Indonesia, which led to the creation of an association of Asian states. It was the precursor of the Bandung Conference, held in Indonesia in 1955, at which twenty-nine African and Asian nations met to plan economic and cultural cooperation and oppose colonialism. While speaker after speaker attacked western colonialism, Kotelawala swam strongly against the tide and made a courageous and memorable speech condemning Soviet domination of its satellites as another form of colonialism, and his declaration that communism was a form of imperialism shocked the Communist Chinese delegation led by Zhou Enlai and embarrassed Jawahalal Nehru of India. It won him support from Iraq, Lebanon, Turkey and Pakistan and gained him international headlines. He urged the conference to declare its opposition to Russian colonialism in eastern Europe, but the final resolution simply condemned colonialism in all its forms as an evil to be brought to an end. 'If the devil had wanted to fight communism,' he once said, 'I would be on his side.'[48] He was never afraid of criticising even the giant of Communist China: 'We sell you rubber, you sell us rice. Ceylon has no other friendship or dealing with Communist China. Nor does she want it.'[49] As prime minister he created a special public security department to maintain surveillance on communists and all those suspected of communist sympathies.

Despite his prominent place on the international stage, he faced increasing opposition at home. The high price of rice was still a cause of unrest, and his speech at the Bandung Conference fuelled opposition charges that his pro-western stance was isolating Ceylon from its neighbours. He was defeated at the 1956 elections which swept the left-wing United Peoples' Front into power. In the same year he published his forthright memoirs, *An Asian prime minister's story*, in which he referred to reactions at the time of his assumption of the premiership. 'I was described as being as rugged as the graphite that gave me my enormous wealth; a man of action with a supreme belief in myself; notable for my courage, my ruthless tongue, and my lively sense of humour. One writer peered into the future and asked a pertinent question: "Will Asia's playboy politician ever become tame, mature, important, and dull enough to be a Premier true to type? Who knows? The spoilt child might at last become the leader of a great nation." I hope I am fulfilling this prophecy. But never let it be said of me that I am dull.'[50]

He never held office again. He was wealthy and bought an estate called Brogues Wood, at Biddenden in Kent where he lived and lavishly entertained. With the onset of old age he returned to Ceylon and in September 1980, a month before his death, he gave his residence on the outskirts of Colombo to house a national defence academy, and was promoted to the rank of general in gratitude.

Kotelawala was not destitute of honours. Despite the comparative brevity of his premiership, his membership of the cabinet lasted more than twenty years. He was made a KBE in 1948 and a privy councillor in 1954. He also received the Grand Cross of the Legion of Honour (France) in 1954, the Grand Cross of the Order of Merit (Italy) in 1954 and the Grand Cross of the Order of the White Elephant (Thailand) in 1955. In 1954 Sir Oliver Goonetilleke was appointed the first Ceylonese governor general of Ceylon, and from him there came a request that the prime minister should be made a GCMG. The commonwealth relations office resisted the request, arguing that the honour was not held by any existing Commonwealth prime minister (i.e. the United Kingdom, Canada, Australia, New Zealand, South Africa, India and Pakistan) and to confer the honour on the prime minister of Ceylon would look incongruous. Although Sir Earle Page (Australia) had received the GCMG in 1938, the honour was still viewed in the mid-1950s as an honour appropriate for a governor general not for a prime minister. There was also a perception that Kotelawala had acquired a taste for such things. 'The Prime Minister of Ceylon has an insatiable appetite for honours and has now collected large numbers, very much against the wish of the Palace. I do not really think that there is a case for a GCMG for him at this stage. Try to get away with a CH . . . . it is eminently a Prime Minister's honour.'[51] The CH was conferred on Kotelawala in the New Year Honours List 1956 to mark his twenty-five years in the Ceylonese parliament. Following the now well-established tradition, the citation was only a description of his appointment: 'Prime Minister of Ceylon.'

Sir Walter Nash 13 June 1959 [New Zealand]
Idealist and visionary, Walter Nash was prime minister of New Zealand 1957–60 and received the CH in that capacity, but his greatest work was done as a cabinet minister in the 1930s and 1940s.

He was born in a two-storey brick cottage at Kidderminster, Worcestershire in 1882. His father was a clerk who spent much of his adult life in a cycle of alcohol and poverty, and his mother was a weaver at a local mill. He was educated at St John's, the local church primary school. At the age of eleven he won a scholarship to the local grammar school, but could not take up the place because his mother could not afford the three suits of clothes which were required. So he left school and had a variety of jobs: first a messenger for a local solicitor, then a metal worker for a bicycle manufacturing firm in Selly Oak where he stayed for ten years, eventually becoming a kind of unqualified accountant as head of the cost analysis department. In about 1906 he acquired his own shop and set up a small business as a wholesale and retail tobacconist and confectioner.

Although his business did relatively well, he and his wife decided to emigrate to New Zealand in 1909 during a period of recession for British industry. His first job was as secretary to a tailoring company in Wellington and a zeal for reforming social and economic injustice led him to join the New Zealand Labour Party in 1912, of which he was later secretary 1922–32 and president 1935–36. Although he learned his views from the writings of Victorian and Edwardian radicals, his views were strengthened by Christian socialism and he was a devout Anglican throughout his adult life. 'Many people who knew Nash later believed that he was a lay reader, licensed by the bishop to take part in divine service. No evidence for this can be found. But he was often asked to preach. And all his life there was something a little parsonical about his personality and voice, which contributed to the strong impression of sincerity which he gave.'[52] The cathartic experience of strikes in 1912–13 shifted his views to the left and he was quoted as saying that there was more Christianity in the strike leaders than in the church leaders.[53] He was a pacifist in the 1914–18 war and courageously allowed a German to stay in his house.

He was elected member of parliament for Hutt in 1929 and retained the seat until his death in 1968. He became minister of finance, customs and stamp duties in the first Labour government (1935–49). He was additionally minister of marketing (1936–41), social security (1938), and deputy prime minister (1940–49). In 1942 he was appointed New Zealand minister in the United States and a member of the Pacific war council. During his years as a cabinet minister, Nash was responsible for initiating far-reaching financial and social reforms, including the bitterly contested social welfare legislation of 1939 which made New Zealand a welfare state. He was also responsible for bringing the Reserve Bank under state ownership and control, for the acquisition of the privately owned shares in the Bank of New Zealand, and for the nationalisation of the major domestic airline. His opponents came to mark him as a stern tax-gatherer, but he was highly successful in his handling of New Zealand's finances during the heavy demands of the 1939–45 war.

He became leader of the New Zealand Labour Party in 1950 after the death of Peter Fraser in 1950, and following a narrow election victory he became prime minister (1957–60), and additionally minister for external affairs and Maori affairs, at the now inconceivable age of seventy-five. He was criticised on frequent occasions for his inability to delegate, but he had the difficult task of heading a government with a working majority of only two seats. In fact his greatest work was done in his days as a cabinet minister 1935–49, and his comparatively short premiership can be seen almost as a coda or an epilogue to a distinguished career. In his later years, feeling that he had achieved all the social reforms that he had desired to see in New Zealand, his interests turned more towards the welfare of the world's starving and underprivileged, and he considered that New Zealand should make greater efforts to contribute towards the well-being of the Asian peoples. He loved the power and influence of the premiership and the wide range of social engagements that it brought him, and he never declined an invitation to any function if he could possibly attend, 'and he loved still more the wider personal contacts, the visiting politicians, the politicians overseas – he was an unwearied and inveterate traveller – and his own countrymen, of every party and profession up and down New Zealand. He missed nothing. The annual dinner of the local rugby team was to him as interesting and exciting as a state banquet for the Queen Mother, and he gave himself equally and tirelessly to both, talking on, reminiscing, holding the floor, while men of half his age prayed in silence for their beds.'[54] 'Well-dressed and courteous, he was at home in any company and was capable of making an appropriate and thought-provoking speech. He gave the impression of possessing in good measure the reliable common sense that most people wish to recognise in their politicians. He was unwavering in his belief in the value of the Commonwealth and of its influence for peace.'[55]

During a period of prosperity, the Labour Party was defeated at the general election in November 1960, but Nash took his loss of office philosophically. He was seventy-eight and had achieved his ambition to be prime minister. In May 1960, he had returned to Kidderminster to be entertained by the town council at a civic dinner In 1963 he resigned the leadership of the Labour Party but remained a member of parliament until his death in 1968. He was made a privy councillor in 1946 and a CH in 1959 as 'Prime Minister of New Zealand'. He was appointed a GCMG in 1965 and received over a thousand messages of congratulation, including one from the distinguished historian J. C. Beaglehole – who said that he would not congratulate Nash but Saint George, on acquiring a great dragon slayer for his Order.[56]

Tunku Abdul Rahman 31 December 1960 [Malaya]
Tunku Abdul Rahman was a Malay prince and politician who led his country to independence in 1957, and became the first and longest-serving prime minister of independent Malaysia until his retirement in 1970.

He was born in Alor Setah, Kedah in 1903, the fifth son and twentieth child of Abdul Hamid Halim Shah, twenty-fourth Sultan of Kedah, one of the nine principalities within the Malay federation. He was educated at local schools until 1913, when his mother sent him to Bangkok to stay with his eldest brother, Tunku Yusuf, who was working there. He returned to Kedah in 1915 on the death of his brother. When he was seventeen he went to England, to St Catherine's College, Cambridge. His application to stay in the college was rejected because of his colour, but when his royal status was recognised, he was offered a place, but refused on principle and stayed in rented rooms throughout his university course.

He graduated with a degree in law in 1925, though with the lowest possible number of marks to secure a pass, and returned to Kedah in the following year. After four months he was sent back to England by his family to study for the bar at Inner Temple. He abandoned his studies in 1931 (horse-racing, dog-racing and dancing were more to his taste than the law) and returned to Kedah and joined the Kedah civil service as a cadet in the legal advisor's office, and then district officer in several districts of Kedah. In 1940, Tunku was appointed deputy director of civil defence, southern Kedah. When the Japanese handed Kedah over to Thailand in 1941, he was made supervisor of education, a post he held until British rule was restored in 1945.

He returned to London in 1947 to complete his training as a barrister, qualified in 1949 and returned to Kedah. He had long been a nationalist and helped to found the United Malay National Organisation in 1945, becoming its president in 1951. Having the reputation of being a playboy, an uninspiring speaker and a poor administrator, he was an unlikely candidate to lead a Malayan nationalist organisation, and at first the British were disinclined to take him seriously. Although he was co-opted by the British governor to the executive council, he often arrived at meetings without reading the papers in advance and consequently either had nothing to say or spoke irrelevantly. Even after he became chief minister in 1955 he was not diligent in reading briefs presented to him by civil servants. Embarrassed civil servants often had to correct the blunders he made when announcing government policies.

But there was more to the prince than there first seemed. The details might have escaped him, but he could grasp important essentials. He constantly travelled throughout Malaya and kept in touch with Malay opinion, but he saw that Malaya's future would be as a multiracial state, and he publicly opposed Malay xenophobia and promoted alliances or at least tacit agreements with the Malayan Chinese Association and the Malayan Indian Congress. Through the 1950s he gradually shed his old playboy image and emerged as the one leader who could carry the Malays into alliances with the other two racial groups. The push towards independence was gathering momentum and the first general election was held in July 1955, his three-party alliance won 51 out of the 52 seats contested, and Rahman was appointed chief minister and minister of home affairs.

Abdul Rahman had to face five years of communist insurgency, at first trying to end it by declaring an amnesty for communist terrorists who surrendered and holding talks with leaders of the Malayan Communist Party. But his innate anti-communism was too strong, and the Malay communists themselves never received Russian or Chinese support.

Independence was achieved on 31 August 1957. In the following years multiracial alliance governments governed the country and in 1963 it was enlarged by the inclusion of Singapore, British North Borneo (Sabah), and Sarawak. Brunei decided not to join the enlarged federation and Singapore left in 1965. The addition of 1.5 million Singaporean Chinese was acceptable when balanced by the populations of Sabah and Sarawak, but as the influence of the intelligent and dynamic Lee Kuan Yew of Singapore began to spread into mainland Malaya, the Tunku sensed a Chinese takeover and a threat to his conservative alliance government. Singapore, Malaysia's biggest city, was duly expelled from the federation when Lee refused to implement a federal edict granting a privileged economic position to the Malays.

Although once dismissed as a British lackey by President Sukarno of Indonesia, Rahman matured into a powerful and influential politician who set Malaysia securely on a course of peace and prosperity. He remained prime minister until his retirement in 1970 and despite his failings, he retained the affection of the Malays until the end of his life. 'No one could confuse an issue more verbosely than the Tunku: soft-spoken and unemotional, he could keep talking until persistent questioners were lost. Few politicians shared his ability, when asked a difficult or embarrassing question, to appear genuinely not to understand. He did not like being compared unfavourably to Lee Kuan Yew, but, that apart, he did not mind if Chinese and western intellectuals dismissed him as dim. He knew he could outlast them and that he could maintain something they all respected: a tolerant, multiracial government . . . With his princely ways, his instinct for compromise and his robust modesty, he was one of the most acceptable to the British of all the leaders who assumed power from them. Perhaps it was the fact that many of them looked down on him intellectually – he always consulted the racing calendar before agreeing to an official engagement – that made them so fond of him.'[57]

The end of his long premiership was overshadowed by vicious Malay-Chinese riots in May 1969. An emergency was declared, parliament suspended, and the country governed by the national operations council chaired by the deputy prime minister, Tun Abdul Razak. Saddened by events, Tunku Abdul Rahman resigned as prime minister in September 1970. He lived for another twenty years, writing newspaper columns and books and making occasional speeches, mostly commentaries on matters of contemporary concern. He continued to emphasise the importance of national unity, religious tolerance and the values of truth, justice, freedom and compassion.

He received many honours in his home nation in addition to the CH that he received in 1960. He remains the only Malay to have been appointed to the Order. As the citizen of a Commonwealth country of which Queen Elizabeth II was not head of state, he should perhaps have been made an honorary CH, as was Lee

Kuan Yew of Singapore ten years later. Instead he was made substantive and included in the under used 'rest of the Commonwealth' quota.

Sir Keith Holyoake 1 January 1963 [New Zealand]
Keith Holyoake was twice prime minister of New Zealand, briefly in 1957 and again from 1960 to 1972, and finally governor general of the country in 1977–80. He was one of New Zealand's longest serving prime ministers and led the National Party to four election victories. His public life spanned nearly half a century, entering parliament in 1932 and retiring as governor general in 1980.

He was born in 1904, the son of a storekeeper, at Mangamutu near Pahiatua. He left school at the age of twelve and had a variety of experience in farming, including dairying, fruit, hops, and tobacco growing, and in later years of sheep and cattle grazing. He was actively involved in agricultural organisations, including being Nelson provincial president of the Farmers' Union (1930–41), New Zealand vice-president of the Farmers' Union (1940–50), and president of the New Zealand hop marketing committee (1938–41). Such involvements led to an interest in politics and in 1932 he was elected Reform Party member of parliament for Motueka. He held the seat in 1935, but lost it as a National Party member in 1938. He re-entered parliament as member for Pahiatua in 1943 (holding the seat until his retirement in 1977) and became deputy leader of the party in 1947. After the National Party's victory at the 1949 election he was named deputy prime minister and minister of agriculture, marketing and scientific research. When Sidney Holland retired as leader of the party, shortly before the 1957 election, Holyoake succeeded him as prime minister. It was unfair to Holyoake to make him prime minister three months before the election, and his first taste of the premiership lasted for seventy-three days. The National Party was defeated in the election, and Holyoake spent three years as leader of the opposition before resuming the office after the 1960 election.

Like Sidney Holland, he was more a pragmatist than a doctrinaire conservative. He opposed state control, supported private enterprise and controversially backed United States involvement in Vietnam, but mindful of his responsibility for New Zealand, he opposed and protested against French nuclear testing in the Pacific, and worked to protect New Zealand's economic stability in the event of Britain joining the European Community. His long premiership coincided with an era of prosperity for New Zealand. Full employment, economic growth, and a desire for consensus politics helped him to win four successive elections – 1960, 1963, 1966 and 1969 – and he came to be seen as the embodiment of the National Party. He could appear pompous and vain, but he lived and worked modestly and had a quirky sense of humour.

Following the precedent of Sidney Holland in 1957, Holyoake retired in February 1972, nine months before a general election was due, in order to give his successor time to prepare. The ploy hadn't worked for Holyoake in 1957 and it failed again for his deputy John Marshall in 1972. The Labour Party won the election.

With the re-election of the National Party three years later in 1975, the new prime minister, Robert Muldoon, appointed Holyoake to his cabinet in the non-portfolio role as minister of state (1975–77). In 1977 he became the first New Zealand politician to be appointed governor general (1977–80). The appointment was controversial, the ceremonial office being above the world of politics, but Holyoake behaved with dignity and with impeccable impartiality. He died in 1983.

He was made a privy councillor in 1954, a CH in 1963 as 'Prime Minister and Minister of External Affairs, New Zealand', a GCMG in 1970, and finally a KG in 1980, the only New Zealand prime minister to be made a Knight of the Garter.

Harold Holt 14 June 1967 [Australia]

Heir and successor of Sir Robert Menzies who had groomed him for the office, Harold Holt was prime minister of Australia from January 1966 to December 1967. The comparative brevity of his premiership, in the shadow of the long and towering rule of his predecessor, ensured that Holt would be one of the lesser-known Australian prime ministers – but for the exception of his fate. He disappeared into the sea on 17 December 1967 and was never seen again.

Holt was born in Sydney in 1908, the son of a schoolteacher who became the London director of J. C. Williamson Theatres. He was educated at Wesley College, Melbourne and Queen's College, University of Melbourne. He graduated with a degree in law and practiced as a solicitor for a time, but while a law student, he had developed an interest in politics. In 1935 he was elected to the federal parliament at a by-election for the seat of Fawkner as a candidate of the United Australia Party. A supporter of Robert Menzies, he joined the army in 1940 but served only five months when Menzies lost three of his leading ministers in an air crash and recalled Holt to Canberra. He was appointed minister of labour and national service at the age of thirty-two, but the defeat of the Menzies government in the 1941 election led to eight years on the back benches.

With the 1949 Liberal victory, Holt was again made minister of labour and national service (1949–58) and additionally minister for immigration (1949–56). He was deputy leader of the party and leader of the house of representatives (1956–66) and treasurer (1958–66). Holt succeeded Menzies as prime minister in January 1966 at a time of change in Australia. At first he seemed quite different from his patriarchal predecessor. He was an able spear-fisherman and the first photographs of Australia's new prime minister showed him wearing goggles and a wet suit.

He faced increasing opposition from Australians opposed to involvement in the Vietnam war. Menzies had reintroduced conscription in 1965, compelling Australians to fight in Vietnam even though Australia was not formally at war. In March 1966 he announced that Australia's military force in Vietnam would be tripled, and in April he visited Australian troops in Vietnam. His welcome of President Lyndon Johnson to Australia with Johnson's election slogan 'All the way with LBJ', caused an uproar of protest from a section of Australian opinion. But he won a record majority in the November 1966 general election, and he seemed to be at his zenith.

He recognised that Australia could not exist in isolation from its neighbours and began the process of changing direction. He was the first Australian prime minister to visit south-east Asian leaders in their own countries and worked to strengthen trade and political links with Asia. Noted for his debonair charm and taste for socialising, he was not unlike Sir Anthony Eden, Britain's prime minister a decade earlier. Critics said that he was a better lieutenant than commander, and an indecisive prime minister, fortunate to have the support of capable ministers. 'He was a likeable, decent man who wanted to be helpful to everyone. Perhaps he dissipated too much the limited strength he had.'[58]

His premiership ended early on the morning of 17 December 1967 when he went for a swim at Cheviot Beach, Victoria. At the time, rumours said the strain of office had been too much for him, that he had committed suicide or even contrived his own disappearance. But it seems more likely that the surf crashed him against a rock, drowned him while he was unconscious and dragged his body out to sea.

Six months before his death, Holt was appointed a CH in an unprecedented and relatively swift promotion. The request came from Lord Casey, governor general of Australia, to Harold Wilson, the United Kingdom prime minister. Wilson had not been properly briefed. He seems to have known nothing about the Australian 'quota' and at first parried by saying that the request would be considered, although there would be difficulty about finding a vacancy. Menzies had not received a CH until twelve years after first becoming prime minister and two years after he became prime minister for the second time. Casey replied that Australia was not well off in respect of CHs and said that Holt had of course endured a very long apprenticeship as second string to Menzies.[59] The point about Australia not being well-off for honours was valid. Although he must have known of the Australia quota of seven places, Menzies had made no effort to recommend an Australian since his own appointment in 1951. In 1967 there were only three Australian CHs – Viscount Bruce (who lived in London), Sir Robert Menzies and Lord Casey. Conjecturally, Menzies made no recommendations for the CH because he wanted to revert to previous practice and retain it, in Australia, as a decoration for prime ministers. Holt's citation followed the practice of Bruce, Lyons, Hughes and Menzies by only naming his office: 'Prime Minister of the Commonwealth of Australia.'

Holt's name could clearly be set against the Australian quota and there was no question of the British government intervening in any recommendations made by the Australian government, provided they were within their allocation. But although an Australian prime minister could recommend others, it would be embarrassing for him to recommend himself. To circumvent the additional statute of 18 August 1943, which provided that dominions citizens should be recommended by dominions prime ministers, Holt's name was formally recommended by Harold Wilson. An additional statute dated 7 November 1969 substituted the phrase 'the Prime Minister of the said Dominion' with 'the appropriate Minister of any other Member of the Commonwealth of which We are Queen.'

Sir John McEwen 1 January 1969 [Australia]
John McEwen was, like Sir Earle Page in 1939, a caretaker prime minister of Australia (1967–68) who never had any hope of attaining the substantive office.

Known as 'Black Jack', John McEwen was born in Chiltern, Victoria in 1900, orphaned at the age of seven and brought up by his widowed grandmother. He was educated at the local school and at the age of thirteen he began work as a messenger boy. Chiltern offered little in the way of opportunity and he went to Melbourne where, at the age of fifteen he became a junior clerk in the crown solicitor's office. In 1918 he volunteered for the army but the war ended before he could be shipped overseas. Army service entitled him to put his name down for one of the soldier settlers' blocks which rewarded many ex-servicemen. The belief was that the ex-servicemen could make a good living by opening up undeveloped country. McEwen and his new wife cleared a block in the Goulburn Valley and produced milk, wool and lambs. He led local farmers in forming a cooperative dairy factory, became secretary of the Water Users' League and a member of the Victorian Farmers' Union. He was a natural member of the Country Party and stood (and was defeated) for the state legislature in 1932. In 1934, the retirement of a sitting Country Party member gave McEwen an opening for a federal constituency. He was elected and remained in the federal parliament for thirty-seven years until his retirement in 1971.

He served in the governments of Joseph Lyons and Robert Menzies as minister for the interior (1937–39), external affairs (1940), and air and civil aviation (1940–41). When Menzies regained power in 1949, McEwen was made minister for commerce and agriculture (1949–56), trade (1956–63), and trade and industry (1963–71). He was deputy leader (1943–58) and leader (1958–71) of the Country Party, and deputy prime minister (1958–71). Some saw McEwen as the right man to succeed Menzies as prime minister in 1966, but he was too narrowly intent on pursuing Country Party objectives to win a sufficiently broad enough cross-section of support. He proved himself a loyal lieutenant to Holt and whenever the latter was absent overseas, he always appointed McEwen acting prime minister.

The shock of Holt's disappearance on 17 December 1967 led to a two-day interregnum before the coalition could accept the probability of his death. McEwen was installed as a caretaker prime minister, to allow time for the Liberal Party to compose itself and elect a new leader. McEwen was the principal powerbroker and effectively vetoed the Liberal Party's first choice of William McMahon, when he declared that he would not serve in a cabinet headed by McMahon. The Liberals were virtually compelled to elect their second choice, John Gorton, and McEwen returned to his post of minister for trade. He retired from parliament in 1971 and enjoyed nine peaceful years before his death in 1980.

McEwen was made a CH in 1969. The citation followed the practice of previous Australian appointments and recorded his office: 'Deputy Prime Minister and Minister for Trade and Industry.' He was made a GCMG in 1971 on his retirement from parliament.

Eric Williams 14 June 1969 [Trinidad and Tobago]
Eric Williams was an academic sociologist with a meticulously chiselled intellect who led Trinidad and Tobago to independence from Britain in 1962, and served as its prime minister until his death in 1981.

He was born in Trinidad in 1911, the son of a postal clerk, and in his autobiography, *Inward hunger*, he recalled the straitened circumstances of his early life. He blamed a serious fall in his youth and the inability of his family to afford a doctor's fees, to his progressive loss of hearing in his adult life. There was no evidence for this, but Williams was convinced that it was the origin of his hearing difficulties, leading to the need for a hearing aid many years later.[60] He was educated at Tranquillity Boy's School and Queen's Royal College, Trinidad. He won a scholarship to St Catherine's College, Oxford where he was subjected to a degree of racism that affected him to the end of his life. He took a first class degree in history and remained to study for a doctorate. His thesis was published in 1944 under the title *Capitalism and slavery*. It was the product of a modified Marxist approach to history, but it was innovative in its choice of subject and in the polemic that underlay its scholarship. 'Here for the first time, was a top West Indian scholar taking as his theme the history of the West Indies. Here was a black man concealing the dagger of his raw rage beneath a cloak of selective research directed against the white man's outrageous version of history.'[61]

Armed with an Oxford doctorate, he took a teaching position at Howard University, Washington DC in 1939 as an assistant professor of social and political science. He was promoted to associate professor in 1944 and full professor in 1947 and published a number of books including: *The Negro in the Caribbean* (1942); *The economic future of the Caribbean* (1943); *History of the people of Trinidad and Tobago* (1964); *British historians and the West Indies* (1964); and *From Columbus to Castro: the history of the Caribbean 1492–1969* (1970).

In 1948 he left the university to work for the Caribbean Commission and Research Council at its headquarters in Trinidad. The commission (later the Anglo-American Commission) was an international organisation dedicated to the study of Caribbean problems, and while it might have suited Williams at first, he became increasingly frustrated, uncomfortable and bitter in his role. Embroiled in a battle with the commission about his future he was dismissed in 1955.

Williams had latent political ambitions that were realised by his dismissal from the commission. In January 1955 he launched the country's first political party, the Peoples' National Movement. Ominously it attracted the support of the oilfield workers, who were predominantly African, but not of the sugar workers who were mostly Indian. Williams' strength was his intellectualism, which raised his competency far above other aspiring Trinidadian politicians, and a gift for oracular pronouncements. His audiences were left spellbound by his ability to quote Aristotle and to translate complex philosophy into comprehensible realities. 'He . . . understood the mentality of the society. He gave them what they wanted, thereby facilitating his control over the political apparatus. The crowds probably never understood much of his public addresses, yet he mesmerized them over the years, and they loved him for it.'[62]

With the grant of internal self-government, Williams became chief minister of Trinidad and Tobago in 1956, premier in 1959 and, with independence, prime minister in 1961. Successive elections reaffirmed his position and, as he would probably have wished, he died in office in 1981. His method of rule was unashamedly populist and deviously autocratic with his ministerial colleagues, and towards the end of his life began to show signs of the inevitable tendency towards megalomania. 'One tactic at which he was a consummate artist was to shift consultation from the Cabinet to the Party and vice versa as the situation demanded. He used another method to diminish ministers and amplify his image. It was the Meet-the-People tours which, when analysed, seemed to show conclusively that, in Williams' opinion, many ministers were not doing their job, and he had to fill the breach personally. During these tours Cabinet meetings were suspended. Williams visited every constituency – a commendable feat. He gave on-the-spot orders to build post offices, pave roads, dig drains, erect standpipes, bring electricity, remove police stations, acquire land, reclaim land. The Opposition and the Press raised the usual alarms about dictatorship in the guise of democracy. As Cabinet members we did not agree with many of Williams' moves but when he developed a notion to pursue something there was no one to stop him . . . Williams also had a disturbing habit of appearing not to listen to what certain ministers thought were sound propositions. Subsequent experience showed that these propositions often surfaced from his ministry with him as their advertised progenitor.'[63] He was a brilliant political strategist who was able to stay two steps ahead of his opponents and three steps ahead of his cabinet colleagues. It was said of him that he arrived at Cabinet meetings never knowing what he wanted to achieve, and he would pragmatically change his mind from year to year as he determined it to be necessary.

In 1964 he was made a privy councillor and in 1969 he was made a CH, as 'Prime Minister and Minister of Finance, Planning and Development, Trinidad and Tobago.' Four years later a rising and vocal tide of black nationalism in Trinidad caused him to realise that changes were needed. He moved Trinidad towards republican status, asked to resign as a privy councillor, and returned his CH badge. But whatever he might have thought at the time, his appointment as a CH was never cancelled, and his action was treated only as a request that his badge be kept 'in custody' until he should require it again.

Lee Kuan Yew 1 January 1970 [Singapore]
Lee Kuan Yew was a dynamic socialist lawyer who led the crowded and prosperous island city of Singapore from British colony to independence, and served as its prime minister from 1959 to 1990.

He was born in Singapore in 1923 and was educated at Raffles Institution, Raffles College and Fitzwilliam College, Cambridge where he read law. After graduating in 1949 with a double first class honours and a star for 'special distinction', he was called to the bar at Middle Temple in 1950. He returned to Singapore to practice law with his wife, the first Malayan woman to achieve a first class honours degree at Cambridge. Attracted by politics, he founded the People's Action Party (PAP) in 1954 and served as its secretary general from 1954 to 1992. He was elected to the legislative assembly for the constituency of Tanjong Pagar in 1955. In 1959, at the age of thirty-five, he led the PAP to victory in the legislative assembly elections and became Singapore's first prime minister. The manner in which he won the election was politically clever. At a private meeting with Alan Lennox-Boyd, the British colonial secretary, the two men agreed that the British would arrest several leading communists in Singapore, who were Lee's allies in the election campaign. Lee would make speeches denouncing this illiberal act of imperialism, but when he won the election and released his former allies, he would find grounds to imprison them again. He was one of the few political leaders to ally himself with communists and then successfully dump them.

The country remained independent apart from a two year period in 1963–65 when it was included, with Sabah and Sarawak, in the enlarged federation of Malaysia. The federation could have worked but for historic Malay jealousy of the industrious Chinese and because Lee's political ambitions extended to mainland Malaya. Within a year of Singapore joining the federation, Lee had begun to extend the influence of his political party into Malaya. The conservative Alliance government of Tunku Abdul Rahman in Kuala Lumpur became fearful of being displaced by a Chinese dominated party, and Singapore was ejected from the federation in August 1965. The catalyst occurred when Lee Kuan Yew refused to implement a federal edict granting Malays a privileged economic position. He could hardly do otherwise in a city of 1.5 million Chinese, but the demerger left him angry and bruised. The island had not sought independence, and seventy per cent of the electorate had voted in favour of merger with Malaya, persuaded that an independent Singapore was simply not viable. Now the city state was on its own and had to be made to work.

The economic prospects were not good, since Singapore was small and had no natural resources apart from a harbour. However, during Lee's rule a strong, export-led manufacturing and service economy was developed, and Singapore became a financial and industrial powerhouse. Lee governed as a benevolent if intrusive autocrat, and his zeal for law and order was legendary. He fashioned a government intent on the suppression of political opposition and on anything deemed even slightly socially undesirable. Among others, regulations were introduced banning the chewing of gum and smoking in public. Elections were held at regular intervals – 1963, 1968, 1972, 1976, 1980, 1984 and 1988, and his charisma and popularity, as much his power, gradually ensured that his party had an absolute monopoly on power by winning every seat at every election from 1972. When at last, in the 1988 elections, a solitary seat was won by the Singapore Democratic Party, Lee was shocked and angry and did not trouble to conceal it – though with eighty government seats to the opposition's one, he had a comfortable working majority. He announced that he would not complete his eighth term of office, nor seek subsequent office. He retired as prime minister in 1990, though his unparalleled thirty-one years as head of government had ensured abiding respect for the father of the nation. After his resignation he remained in the cabinet with the newly-created title of 'Senior Minister, Prime Minister's Office'.

Lee was twice honoured by the United Kingdom, with a CH in 1970 and a GCMG in 1972. As the citizen of a Commonwealth republic, he was appointed an honorary CH (he was not gazetted), highlighting the paradox that his former political rival, Tunku Abdul Rahman of Malaysia was a substantive CH.

Sir John Gorton 12 June 1971 [Australia]
A man of wilful and independent spirit, John Gorton was prime minister of Australia (1968–71). He was the penultimate of the four Liberal-Country coalition prime ministers who presided over the decline of the Menzies heritage.

He was born illegitimate in 1911 and made no mention of his parentage in *Who's Who*. His mother was a young Irish woman who died when he was nine. He was raised by his father and stepmother in the affluent North Shore area of Sydney. He was educated at Geelong Grammar School and then worked for a while on his father's property, an orange grove at Mystic Park near Kerang in northern Victoria, before going to Brasenose College, Oxford. He returned to Australia in 1936 and was offered a trainee journalist post on the *Melbourne Herald*. He refused and preferred managing the property he had inherited on the death of his father.

In 1940 he joined the Australian air force and was almost immediately seconded to the royal air force and spent four years as a fighter pilot in Britain, Malaysia and New Guinea. In 1942 his squadron was posted to Singapore. On 25 January that year his Hurricane aircraft crashed into the sea and inflicted severe facial injuries. Prolonged plastic surgery repaired the damage but the marks remained with him for the rest of his life and gave him something of a cherubic countenance even in old age. He was discharged in 1944 with the rank of flight lieutenant and returned to run his orange grove in Victoria. 'It was hard and back-breaking work in arid country. Water was brought by petrol-engined pumps from Lake Kangaroo to the trees planted in circles on a low hill. Gorton devised a primitive irrigational trickle system that was effective so long as the pumps worked. The fruit markets were fickle and the banks capricious when capital was required to finance plant-and-pay labour,'[64] and Gorton did most of the physical work himself.

He had become interested in country politics and by 1939 he was secretary of the local branch of the Country Party. After the war he ventured into local government, becoming a member of the Kerang shire council (1947–52) and eventually shire president for two years. In 1947 he stood unsuccessfully for the Victorian legislative council (the upper house of the Victorian parliament). Admiration for Robert Menzies made him abandon the Country Party to join the new Liberal Party. In 1949 he was elected as a Liberal senator for the state of Victoria in the federal parliament. 'It was a late start in politics and – despite his qualities of intellect and character – did not result in rapid promotion.'[65] Menzies appointed him minister for the navy (1958–63). From 1960 he was also minister assisting the minister for external affairs and in 1962 he was made minister in charge of the Commonwealth Scientific Industrial Research Organisation. A succession of cabinet posts ensued, including minister for works (1963–1967), the interior (1963–1964) education and science (1966–68), and government leader in the senate (1967–68). Gorton was a competent minister known for his charm, humour, decisiveness and his ability to foster good public relations. He invariably received a good press and was widely known as 'Jolly John'. He inspired loyalty and was a popular figure. Denis Healey likened Gorton to Pierre Trudeau of Canada in his charismatic nature.[66] Tall, lean and athletic he usually dressed casually and had the informality which appealed to Australians at a time when attachment to the formal ways of the 'mother country' was beginning to weaken and an Australian republican movement was beginning to emerge. Declaring that he was 'Australian to his boot straps' and that his appreciation of culture extended little beyond 'rootin', shootin', son-of-a-gun cowboy flicks,'[67] he had in fact the best of both worlds. He had also been educated in exclusive Australian schools and at Oxford. He had a good war record, a country property, and a strong anti-communist bias, all of which appealed to the Liberal Party.

After the premature and mysterious death of Harold Holt in December 1967, Gorton was a natural contender for the Liberal leadership. In the final round he won by 43 votes to the 38 cast for Paul Hasluck. As the first senator ever to be elected prime minister, constitutional law obliged him to win a seat in the house of representatives, and he won the seat left vacant by Holt's death. As prime minister Gorton protested vigorously against British plans to withdraw its troops from Malaysia and Singapore, while withdrawing Australian troops in 1970 from the Vietnam war. Legislation was passed to protect the Great Barrier Reef, to increase social security for the disadvantaged, and to improve relations with the aboriginal people.

He might have continued in office for much longer but for emerging traits in his personality that began to cause alarm within the Liberal Party, and he proved to be a far more complex character than his public image had indicated. He was given to making extempore speeches that included mixtures of fact and fantasy. He began to show a reluctance to consult the cabinet, an obstinate determination to get his own way and a worrying tendency to rely less on his colleagues than on a 'cocktail cabinet' of young cronies. He could be intolerant and belligerent, and offended state premiers and members of his own party. Scandalous rumours were circulated by his enemies including one that his attractive young female secretary, Ainslie Gotto, exerted undue influence over him. His cabinet colleagues resented her influence and were said to dread her forceful telephone calls.

The climax came on 10 March 1971 when Malcolm Fraser resigned as minister of defence and indicted Gorton for frittering away the inheritance of the Menzies years. Divisions over the Vietnam war and major reductions in the government's support at elections in 1969 and 1970, led to a party vote of confidence in him as leader. The vote was equally divided for and against him. Gorton's situation was impossible, and he honourably used his own casting vote as chairman to vote himself out of office.

His successor, William McMahon, appointed him minister for defence and deputy leader of the party, but Gorton continued to defy the proprieties by publishing a series of newspaper articles entitled *I did it my way* and McMahon finally lost patience and dismissed him in August. After the Liberal defeat in 1972 he was Liberal Party spokesman on the environment, conservation and regional development (1973–75) but he stood down from parliament and resigned from the party in 1975. His political career ended when he stood unsuccessfully as an independent candidate for the Australian Capital Territory in the senate elections in December 1975. He died in 2002.

He was appointed a CH in 1971, after his departure from the office. Like the citations for all previous Australians, he was noted by his office, though he was the first and the last to be recorded as 'Minister for Defence, lately Prime Minister of the Commonwealth of Australia.' He was also made a GCMG in 1977 and an AC (Companion of the Order of Australia) in 1988.

Charles Herbert Best 12 June 1971 [Canada] (see Chapter 8)

Sir William McMahon 1 January 1972 [Australia]
William McMahon was prime minister of Australia (1971–72) and the fourth and final inheritor of the strong Liberal-Country coalition legacy of Sir Robert Menzies. Severely weakened by internal strife, the coalition needed stronger leadership and it was McMahon's misfortune to be the wrong person at the wrong time. Conscientious and efficient though he was, his almost total lack of flair and charisma contributed to the Labour landslide at the general election of December 1972.

He was born in Sydney in 1908, the son of a successful lawyer. His mother died when he was four, and his father twelve years later. He was educated at Sydney Grammar School, and St Paul's College, University of Sydney, from where he graduated in law and economics. He qualified as a solicitor and worked for a firm in Sydney. At the outbreak of the 1939–45 war he joined the army, but a hearing problem – later corrected – kept him from overseas service. He felt the call of politics during the postwar years of the Labour government of Ben Chifley, and he won the Sydney constituency of Lowe in the 1949 election.

McMahon had a talent for hard work and organisation. It came to the notice of Robert Menzies who gave him a succession of cabinet posts: minister for the navy and air (1951–54), social services (1954–56), primary industry (1956–58), and labour and national service (1958–66). He served under Menzies' successors, Holt, McEwen and Gorton, as treasurer (1966–69), minister for external (later foreign) affairs (1969–71), and was deputy leader of the Liberal Party (1966–71), in succession to Harold Holt. His wide range of portfolios gave him immense administrative experience, which occasionally irritated other ministers because it caused McMahon to pontificate on matters which were not his responsibility.

When Holt died, McMahon could have expected to succeed him as prime minister, but suffered the humiliation of an effective veto when John McEwen, leader of the Country Party, refused to serve under him. He was moved by Gorton to the treasury and further humiliations followed. Gorton interfered with his 1968–69 budgets and then moved him to the ministry of foreign affairs. McMahon remained deputy leader and when Gorton was obliged to resign in 1971, he was the obvious successor. It was too late for him to have an appreciable effect on the inexorable decline of the coalition. The Liberal Party had lost the impetus accumulated during the Menzies era. The premature death of Holt, the internal strife of the Gorton years, rising opposition to Australian participation in the Vietnam war, the growing popularity of the Labour Party, and an impending economic recession were among the factors that brought twenty-three years of continuous Liberal-Country rule to an end.

McMahon himself was earnest and well meaning, but his persona looked decidedly dull against the charismatic Labour Party leader, Gough Whitlam. He eroded support within his own party by moving or demoting ministers appointed by Gorton, regardless of their ability, apparently to prove that his administration would be different from his predecessor. He was no match for the Labour Party which swept to power in the general election of December 1972. Although he continued as a member of the federal parliament until 1982, McMahon disappeared into political obscurity.

He was made a CH in 1972 as 'Prime Minister of Australia' (for some reason the words 'Commonwealth of' were omitted from the *London Gazette* entry), and he was made a GCMG in 1977. His final years were blighted by cancer, which led to his death in 1988.

Sir John Marshall 1 January 1973 [New Zealand]
John Marshall (better known as 'Jack') served briefly as New Zealand's prime minister from February to November 1972, but achieved his greatest success in 1971 when, as minister of overseas trade, he stalled Britain's admission to the European Economic Community until the EEC agreed to continue the importation of New Zealand dairy products for at least five years.

He was born in 1912, the son of a Scottish immigrant, and educated at Whangerei High School and Otago Boy's High School, and studied law at the Victoria University of Wellington, qualifying as a barrister and a solicitor in 1936. He served in the Second New Zealand Expeditionary Force in the Pacific islands and in Europe (1941–46) and developed an outward looking approach that served him well as leader of the New Zealand team in the EEC negotiations.

He was first elected to parliament in 1946, representing Mount Victoria (1946–54) and Karori (1954–75) for the National Party. He was a part time lecturer in law at Victoria University (1948–51), but in 1949 Sidney Holland took him into his cabinet as minister assisting the prime minister with the portfolios of state advances, public trust, and statistics. He was then given a series of major portfolios including health (1951–54), justice (1954–57), industry and commerce (1960–69), customs (1960–61), and labour and immigration (1969–72). He gained a reputation for his liberal and imaginative policies and for his thorough and methodical preparation of the legislation which enacted them. As deputy leader of the National Party from 1957 (and deputy prime minister from 1960) he was chosen to succeed Sir Keith Holyoake in 1972, but the party was defeated in the November election that year. Holyoake might have known from his own experience in 1957 that a few months was no time to allow his successor to prepare for a general election.

Shortly before the 1975 election, which saw the National Party return to power, Marshall was ousted as leader of the opposition by his rival Robert Muldoon and retired from politics. 'He represented essentially the enlightened conservative wing of his party . . . His strength both as an administrator and in debates was that he managed always to be persuasive without ever being aggressive.[68] It was perhaps Marshall's misfortune that he was not aggressive enough to hold on to the leadership in the face of an opponent who was determined to have it. He took no further role in politics, though he served as chairman of the board of directors of the National Bank of New Zealand (1975–83) and was appointed to the boards of a number of companies. He also wrote four books for children, featuring a character called Dr Duffer. They originated with some fifty stories, written for New Zealand radio and broadcast by Marshall himself between 1934 and 1936. They recounted the adventures of Dr Duffer and his friends: Hiccup, the Polynesian boy, Peter the Parrot, and Patches the Fox Terrier. They made voyages of exploration in a machine called *Aeronaut* which took them on land and sea, through the air and under the sea.

Shortly before his death, he looked back to the EEC negotiations of 1971 as his proudest achievement, commenting with satisfaction that the arrangements outlined in the protocol with Brussels in 1972 had proved its validity, with New Zealand butter still available to Britain's housewives in the shops and supermarkets to show it.[69]

Marshall received the CH, by now almost automatic for a New Zealand prime minister, in the New Year List 1973 which described him as 'lately Prime Minister of New Zealand'. He was also appointed a GBE, an unusual honour for a Commonwealth prime minister, in 1974. He died in 1988 while on a private visit to the United Kingdom.

Arnold Smith 29 April 1975 [Canada]
Arnold Smith was an experienced Canadian diplomat who became first secretary general of the Commonwealth (1965–75). Despite that organisation's tendency to fractiousness in the face of a number of serious crises, his belief in the worth of the Commonwealth never wavered.

He was born in 1915 at Toronto and educated at Upper Canada College, Toronto; Lycée Champoleon, Grenoble University, the University of Toronto and Christ Church, Oxford where he was a Rhodes scholar. Anxious to see more of Europe before returning to Canada, he answered a newspaper advertisement and in 1939 became editor of the *Baltic Times*, a bi-monthly journal published in Tallin, Estonia. His salary was slender, so he supplemented it by working as a part time associate professor of political economy at the University of Tartu (1939–40), and an attaché at the British legation in Tallin (1940). After the Russian invasion and annexation of the Baltic states, he and his family were allowed to make their way through Russia to Egypt where he spent two years as an attaché in the political warfare section of the British embassy in Cairo and a part time lecturer in political science and economics, Egyptian State University, Cairo (1940–42).

He transferred to the Canadian diplomatic service in 1942, returned to Russia and served as secretary at the Canadian legation at Kuibyshev (1943) and the Canadian embassy at Moscow (1943–45). A period at the department of external affairs in Ottawa (1946–47) and as associate director of the National Defence College of Canada (1947–49) was followed by appointments as a counsellor, Canadian embassy in Brussels (1950–53), special assistant to the secretary of state for external affairs (1953–55), international truce commissioner in Indo-China (1955–56), Canadian minister to the United Kingdom (1956–58), and then ambassador to the United Arab Republic (1958–61). In the latter post, he showed considerable diplomatic skill in repairing the almost non-existent relations between Britain and Egypt in the aftermath of Suez. 'He succeeded in winning Nasser's personal regard and made a prime contribution to overcoming the differences and injured pride and arrogance between the two countries.'[70] He was then Canadian ambassador in Moscow (1961–63) before his appointment as secretary general of the Commonwealth in 1965.

During his ten years in office, he tactfully handled a number of serious crises that might otherwise have threatened to destroy the Commonwealth. When the white minority government in Southern Rhodesia proclaimed the country independent in 1965, the Organisation of African Unity threatened that all its members would break diplomatic ties with Britain. During the Nigerian civil war (1967–70), caused by the attempted secession of Biafra, Smith visited leaders on both sides attempting to bring an end to the violence, each recognising him to be fair and impartial. In 1971, when the United Kingdom proposed selling arms to South Africa, he forcefully transmitted to British leaders the profound concern felt in many Commonwealth countries. In 1972 Pakistan left the Commonwealth after a war with India which led to the creation of Bangladesh, and it was to his great satisfaction that it rejoined seventeen years later. In 1973 the United Kingdom became a member of the European Economic Community, and Smith cautioned worried members of the Commonwealth not to be hostile to the idea, arguing that it could build a better relationship between developed and developing nations. He seemed to enjoy the biennial Commonwealth heads of government meetings, but he was not alone in expressing strong disapproval of the formality and rigidity which appeared at the 1971 meeting in Singapore, arguing that the Commonwealth should not become institutionalised.

Smith served for two five-year terms and retired in 1975 to become Lester B. Pearson professor of international affairs at Carleton University, Ottawa (1975–81). Among his publications was *Stitches in time: The Commonwealth in world politics* (1981), which by its title indicated his faith in the usefulness of the Commonwealth. In 1976 he was co-founder of the North-South Institute in Ottawa and served as its chairman until 1991. In retirement he divided his time between his homes in Canada and France and proudly included in his entry in *Who's Who*, the fact that during the 'summer' he could be reached at Monflanquin in France. He died in 1994.

The possibility of an honour for Smith was considered towards the end of his time at the Commonwealth secretariat. The approaching Commonwealth heads of government conference in Jamaica would be his last conference as secretary-general and there was something to be said for making it possible for the Queen to invest Smith with an honour at some point during the conference. As Smith was a Canadian citizen, any honour would have to be agreed with the Canadian government. Canada had long since ceased to recommend British honours, and the 1918 resolution of the Canadian parliament had ruled out the possibility of any honour which conveyed a title. With its 'Commonwealth' category, the CH appeared to be the right honour. Informal soundings were taken of the Canadian government, which agreed to the honour 'with considerable pleasure'. A tradition had developed whereby recipients of the CH were received in private audience by the Queen, and Smith was invested before dinner on board HM Yacht Britannia off Kingston Harbour, Jamaica on 29 April 1975. He was honoured by his own nation with the insignia of an Officer of the Order of Canada in 1984.

John Diefenbaker 1 January 1976 [Canada]
John George Diefenbaker was prime minister of Canada 1957–63, and despite heading the first Conservative government in Canada for twenty-two years, his policies were radical and reformist and often in contradiction to 'traditional' Conservative values. While previous prime ministers had concerned themselves with the reconciliation of French and English culture in Canada, Diefenbaker aspired to include those of other ethnic extractions in the national identity. He also drew attention to the rights of Canada's indigenous population, who had also been left out of the 'two founding nations' equation. During his period in office they were allowed to vote in federal elections for the first time, and a member of the Blood tribe was the first native person appointed to the Senate.

He was born in Neustadt, Ontario in 1895 to parents of German and Scottish descent. His family moved to Fort Carlton, north of Saskatoon in 1903 where his father taught in a local school and encouraged his sons to read. Diefenbaker attended the University of Saskatchewan, graduating with a BA in 1915 and an MA in political science and economics in 1916. He was commissioned in the 196th Battalion in 1916, and served briefly in the United Kingdom before being invalided home in 1917. Returning to the university to study law, he graduated in 1919, and set up a law practice in Wakaw, near Prince Albert, specialising in criminal law.

Parallel with his law practice was a rising political ambition that took some years to bear fruit. He unsuccessfully contested a seat in the house of commons in 1925 and 1926, and stood, also unsuccessfully, for the provincial legislature in 1929 and 1938. An attempt to run for mayor of Prince Albert in 1933 also ended in failure. Diefenbaker was elected leader of the Conservative Party of Saskatchewan in 1936, but the party won no seats in the 1938 election. Success came at last in the 1940 general election, when he won Lake Place for the Conservative Party. The party remained in opposition until 1957, and during this long period of waiting, Diefenbaker began a campaign for the better treatment of ethnic minorities. In 1942, at the height of the 1939–45 war, he bravely criticised the government's treatment of Japanese-Canadians. He was sufficiently convinced of the rightness of his principles to oppose his own party when he blocked a 1948 Conservative campaign to outlaw the Communist Party.

He stood as a candidate for the leadership of the party in 1942 and in 1948, but lost both times. He succeeded in 1956 at the third attempt, and won the 1957 election with a barnstorming, theatrical and egocentric campaign that appealed to farmers, store-owners and factory-workers. He acquired the nickname of 'Dief the Chief.' The Conservatives formed a minority government in 1957 but in the following year they were returned with a large majority.

During his years in power Diefenbaker pursued radical policies that demonstrated his social concerns. The Agricultural Rehabilitation and Development Act helped farmers across Canada and he found a new market in China for their wheat. He initiated projects to revive the maritime provinces. He appointed the first woman federal cabinet minister, Ellen Fairclough. He championed human rights outside Canada by supporting the independence of many non-white Commonwealth countries and his anti-apartheid statement in 1961 contributed to the withdrawal of South Africa from the Commonwealth. He also antagonised the Americans by refusing to support their blockade of Cuba. However he had been in opposition for too long. 'For all his patient homework and ceaseless study, he had learned no philosophy of government. He lacked any experience of management in politics or business, any real comprehension of the social process or indeed, of himself. Beyond mere craftsmanship and political ingenuity he had only hunches, sometimes benign, sometimes malignant, always inchoate and disjointed.'[71] High unemployment, the devaluation of the Canadian dollar and other issues eroded the popularity of the Conservatives. The 1962 election reduced them to a minority government and they were defeated by the Liberal Party in the 1963 election. The Conservative Party viewed Diefenbaker as a liability and he lost the leadership in 1967. He stayed in the house of commons, winning his last election in 1979, three months before his death.

Diefenbaker refused a CH in 1962, but accepted it when the offer was renewed in 1976 three years before his death. He received it on the recommendation of Harold Wilson, following a written request to that effect from the Canadian prime minister Pierre Trudeau after prior consultations between the two governments. By 1976 the new Order of Canada was in full working condition, and a Companionship in that Order would have been appropriate; but by tradition it was not possible. Although there was no formal provision in the constitution of the Order of Canada, convention dictated that a Canadian politician was not given a Canadian honour while still active in political life. Diefenbaker's successor, Lester Pearson, retired from the house of commons when he left office and was eligible for the Order of Canada, which he received, and was never made a CH. Diefenbaker never retired from parliament, was not given a Canadian honour, and received the CH instead. It was the appropriate option. Diefenbaker never approved of the Order of Canada. When he visited London to receive the badge of the CH from Queen Elizabeth II, he described the Companion of the Order of Canada as the 'cuckoo' award when compared to his own CH.[72]

Malcolm Fraser 26 January 1977 [Australia]

After Robert Menzies sixteen-year record, Malcolm Fraser was the second longest serving prime minister of Australia, in office from 1975–83. The circumstances surrounding his coming to power were unique but, despite his somewhat formal and aloof manner, he was popular enough with the electorate to win three successive general elections.

He was born in 1930, into a prosperous landowning family with an estate at Nareen in Victoria, and was educated at Melbourne Grammar School and

Magdalen College, Oxford, where he read philosophy, politics and economics. An early interest in politics led him to win the federal seat of Wannon for the Liberal Party in the 1955 general election. He attracted the interest of Robert Menzies, who appreciated and admired his qualities of resolution, resourcefulness and refusal to be swayed by unpopularity. In 1966 Harold Holt made Fraser minister for the army (1966–68), and he served under Gorton and McMahon. His ministerial appointments included education and science (1968–69) and defence (1969–71). Fraser's first moment as a kingmaker came on 10 March 1971, when he resigned as a minister and delivered a passionate condemnation of John Gorton which led to the latter's resignation. The new prime minister, William McMahon, appointed him minister for education and science (1971–72).

In three years of opposition that followed the Labour landslide victory of 1972, Fraser served successively as Liberal Party spokesman on primary industry, labour and immigration, and on labour relations. He made two challenges for the leadership of the Liberal Party, but Billy Snedden defeated him on both occasions. Speculation over the leadership continued until Fraser won the position in March 1975. He mounted a fierce and sustained attack on the Labour government of Gough Whitlam, whose early popularity had dwindled. Controversially, he instructed the Liberal Party senators to block the 1975 budget in the senate. It was an unprecedented political manoeuvre and denied the government the money it needed to govern. The move was intended at forcing Whitlam to dissolve the parliament. Whitlam obstinately refused, leaving Sir John Kerr, the governor general with no choice but to dismiss the government in November 1975 and appoint Fraser as prime minister of a caretaker government pending the outcome of a general election.

On 13 December 1975, the electorate gave the Fraser government an overwhelming majority and started him on the longest period in office of any prime minister apart from Menzies. His administration was marked by firm leadership, spending restraint, control of trade unions, encouragement of private enterprise and anti-communism in foreign affairs. But he introduced other reforms that might not have appeared in previous Liberal manifestos, such as direct payment of family allowances to mothers, an increased federal role in aboriginal affairs and a number of initiatives in the areas of human rights, civil liberties and the environment.

In 1975 his tall physique and strong image seemed like a reassuring reincarnation of the confident years of Robert Menzies. The economy improved during the first years of his regime and his government was reelected in 1977 and 1980. By early 1983, increasing unemployment, decreasing business activity and a severe recession caused him to call an early election. He was defeated by the resurgent Labour Party under Robert Hawke. Fraser, like McMahon before him, quickly resigned from the party leadership and then from parliament later in 1983. His successor said of him: 'he won the votes of the Australian electorate, but not their hearts.'

After 1983 he developed a surprising interest in a number of humanitarian issues. He became a spokesperson against apartheid and other systems of racial discrimination. He was chairman of the United Nations Panel of Eminent Persons on the Role of Transnational Corporations in South Africa in 1985, and co-chairman of the Commonwealth Group of Eminent Persons on South Africa (1985–86). He was also chairman of the United Nations Secretary-General's

Expert Group on African Commodity Issues (1989–90). From 1991 he was president of CARE International, a foreign aid organisation dedicated to providing humanitarian assistance across the globe.

Malcolm Fraser was made a CH in 1976, the last of eight Companions of Honour to receive the honour for being 'Prime Minister of the Commonwealth of Australia'. He was made a Companion of the Order of Australia in 1988.

Sir Robert Muldoon 11 June 1977 [New Zealand]
A pugnacious appearance and personality made Robert Muldoon one of New Zealand's most dynamic and controversial politicians. He was elected prime minister in 1975 and maintained an extraordinary hold over the country until his defeat in 1984.

He was born in Auckland in 1921 and educated at Mount Albert Grammar School. Leaving school he worked for the local power board while studying for accountancy examinations. He joined the Third Battalion, the Auckland Regiment in November 1940, continuing to study accountancy, and was admitted to the New Zealand Society of Accountants in 1942. He studied cost accounting in England after the war ended in 1945. In 1947 he started work for an Auckland accountancy firm.

In 1949, he became the chairman of the Young Nationals. After two unsuccessful attempts to enter parliament – in 1954 and 1957 – he was elected in 1960 for the seat of Tamaki and held it until his retirement from politics in 1991. His experience with accountancy soon marked out his career. In 1964 he became parliamentary under-secretary (finance) with responsibility for changing the nation to a decimal currency. He became minister of finance, holding the portfolio until the defeat of the government in 1972, and again, simultaneously with the office of prime minister, 1975–84.

With the retirement of Sir Keith Holyoake in February 1972, Jack Marshall was elected to succeed him, and Muldoon became deputy leader of the party and deputy prime minister. In December 1972 the National Party was defeated at the general election and Muldoon became deputy leader of the opposition. In 1974, he succeeded Marshall as the leader of the National Party, and in the 1975 election he reversed the Labour landslide of 1972 and became prime minister.

During his premiership, he introduced a scheme giving universal superannuation at the age of sixty without a means test, which gained him enormous popularity. After the oil crisis in the seventies, he introduced the short-lived 'carless days', where every car had a day of the week on which it could not be used. He also introduced a 'wage and price freeze' to reduce inflation. He paid generous subsidies to farmers in the form of supplementary minimum prices, arousing allegations that he was favouring the areas where his vote was strongest.

Muldoon had messianic qualities and was either loved or hated. His short stature belied the fact that he was a powerful, charismatic and intelligent person whose absolute convictions and decisiveness appealed to the electorate. He had an enormous following, known as 'Rob's Mob', predictably including the elderly and the farmers, but also a substantial following among the young. He was known for his honesty and integrity and would state his opinions in a way that was as provocative as it was fearless. He was aggressive, abrasive and confrontational and disliked losing an argument, but he had always mastered his brief and his memory was said to be phenomenal. He worked hard, and had no time for people who had not 'done their homework'. In 1981 South Africa's Springbok Rugby team was scheduled to tour New Zealand. The anti-tour movement asked Muldoon to deny them entry visas, arguing that South Africa was a country whose politics condoned racism, and therefore should be boycotted. Muldoon refused and countered that it was wrong for a government to interfere with anyone's right of free movement.

Towards the end of his premiership, some accused him of dictatorial practices, and certainly those around him preferred to do what he said because it was easier than engaging with him in a forceful argument that they would probably lose. He called a snap election in 1984 and was defeated. Replaced as leader of the National Party, he remained a member of parliament until his retirement in 1991.

Despite his widespread appeal across New Zealand and his incessant travels throughout the country, he was a loner and his interests were solitary. He enjoyed reading, preferred to drive himself to work rather than use the chauffeur service, shunned the cocktail party circuit, had few friends, and protected his private life. Despite his ostensible toughness, he had a gentle side; he loved his garden and was at his happiest tending it wearing a pair of old shorts and a ragged shirt, and was particularly knowledgeable about lilies.

The CH was conferred on him in 1977 as 'Prime Minister of New Zealand', and a GCMG followed in 1984. He died in 1992.

Sir Michael Somare 3 June 1978 [Papua New Guinea]
An account of the career of Michael Somare is still incomplete. First prime minister of the independent state of Papua New Guinea, and respected as the constitutional architect and the 'father' of his nation, he is still actively involved in politics at the time of writing.

Born in 1936 his education led initially to a career in teaching (1956–64), culminating in appointment as an area education officer at Madang (1962–63). He then moved to a career in broadcasting and journalism, becoming a broadcasts officer in the department of information and extension services at Weewack (1963–66) and a full-time journalist (1966–68). Journalism led to politics, and in 1968 he was elected member for East Sepik region in the house of assembly and became leader of the Pangu Party, and a member of the select committee on constitutional development (1968–72). With the introduction of self-government in 1972, elections resulted in the formation of a ministry by Somare who became the first chief minister of Papua New Guinea in a national coalition government (1972–75). Somare pledged to lead the country to independence from Australian trusteeship.

Papua New Guinea achieved independence in September 1975 with Somare as the first prime minister, and the 1977 national elections confirmed him in office at the head of a coalition led by his Pangu Party. He remained as prime minister, despite widespread allegations of inefficiency in government ministries and of discrimination against highland provinces, until in 1980 he lost a vote of confidence, the fourth in fifteen months. Since independence Papua New Guinea politics has been characterised by a plethora of political parties, quixotic coalitions, shifting party loyalties, claims of corruption, and motions of no confidence, all of which have lent an air of instability to political proceedings.

Somare's task was made more difficult by Papua New Guinea being given independence despite Indonesia's feverish efforts to absorb it. Indonesia's expansionist tendencies were rejected by the United Nations, but tension between the two countries has been a mark of the years since independence. Papuans in particular had a tendency to suspect Indonesia of harbouring territorial ambitions, at least on New Guinea. Somare endeavoured to reduce tensions between the two countries, agreeing to repatriate 10,000 Melanesian refugees from Indonesian New Guinea (Irian Jaya) and dismissed his defence minister for verbally abusing the Indonesian government. In 1984 the two countries signed a five-year agreement setting up a joint border security committee to mediate disputes between the two governments.

After being voted out of office in 1980 his government was replaced by a new cabinet headed by Sir Julius Chan as prime minister, and Somare became leader of the opposition. After the 1982 elections parliament again chose Somare as prime minister. In 1983 he effected a constitutional change to provide central authorities with greater control of the provincial governments as a means of preventing abuse of their powers. He was defeated in a motion of no confidence in 1985 that criticised the government's handling of the economy, and parliament elected Paias Wingti, at the head of a five-party coalition, as prime minister. Although victorious in the 1987 elections, a no-confidence vote in 1988 toppled Wingti and brought to power Rabbie Namaliu, who a few weeks earlier had replaced Somare as leader of the Pangu Party. Namaliu appointed Somare as minister of foreign affairs (1988–92).

With the election of Sir Mekere Morauta as prime minister in 1999, Somare, now head of the National Alliance Party, was brought back into the cabinet, first as minister of foreign affairs, and then as minister of mining and Bougainville affairs. For nearly ten years (1989–98), a secessionist movement had fought for the independence of the island of the Bougainville and Somare was seen by some as the best hope for maintaining peace on the war-ravaged island. The hope was shortlived. Somare was abruptly dismissed from office in May 2001 by Morauta who accused him of trying to destabilise the government, and expelled the National Alliance Party from the ruling coalition.

He was made a CH in 1978. Following established precedent, he was cited as 'Prime Minister of Papua New Guinea.' He remains the first and probably the last prime minister of the nation to be made a CH. None of his numerous successors have received the honour, and in May 2000 Somare himself began to encourage thoughts of Papua New Guinea moving to republican status. He was made a GCMG in 1990.

Sir Brian Talboys 30 April 1981 [New Zealand]
Of the eight New Zealand politicians appointed Companions of Honour, Brian Talboys was the only one not to have held the office of prime minister.

He was born in 1921 at Wanganui and educated at Wanganui Collegiate School, the University of Manitoba, and Victoria University (1947–50). He worked for Dalgety and Company, Wanganui (1937–41), served in the New Zealand air force (1941–47), and worked for the New Zealand *Dairy Exporter* (1950–54). He was a farmer at Heddon Bush, Southland (1954–57), before being elected as National Party member of parliament for Wallace in 1957. He held that seat until he retired in 1981. He held a number of ministerial appointments in the government of Keith Holyoake: parliamentary under secretary to the minister of customs (1961), minister of agriculture (1962–69), science (1964–71), education (1970–71), and trade and industry (1972).

On the return of a National government under Robert Muldoon in 1975, he was minister of national development (1975–77), deputy prime minister (1976–80), and minister of foreign affairs and overseas trade (1976–81).

He retired from parliament in 1981 and took up a number of business and public appointments: chairman of Ericsson Communications (NZ) Ltd (1983–89), chairman of the Australia-New Zealand Federation, chairman of the Banque Indosuez (NZ) (1982-), chairman of the Technical Aids Trust (1983–88), chairman of the New Zealand committee for Pacific economic co-operation (1983–90), and chairman of the standing committee of the Pacific economic cooperation Conference (1988–89).

He was made a CH in 1981 in anticipation of his impending retirement from parliament. Following tradition, the citation only recorded his appointment: 'Minister of Foreign Affairs and Minister of Trade, lately Deputy Prime Minister of New Zealand.' He was also made a Companion of the Order of Australia in 1982 and a KCB in 1991.

Douglas Anthony 31 December 1981 [Australia]

Douglas Anthony, last of the thirteen Australian Companions of Honour, was leader of the Country Party, the traditional ally of the Liberal Party, and therefore destined, like Sir Earle Page and Sir John McEwen before him, to be deputy prime minister. Although both Page and McEwen became prime ministers of Australia on an interim basis at a time of crisis, no such chance came to Anthony and he remained deputy to prime ministers William McMahon and Malcolm Fraser.

He was born in 1929 and educated at The King's School, Parramatta, and Queensland Agricultural College. He was elected to the federal parliament in 1957, representing Richmond, New South Wales for the Country (later National) Party, and held the seat until his retirement in 1984. He was deputy leader of the Country Party (1966–71) and leader (1971–84). He held ministerial office under five prime ministers: Robert Menzies, Harold Holt, John Gorton, William McMahon and Malcolm Fraser, and was given various ministerial appointments: the interior (1964–67), primary industry (1967–71), trade and industry (1971–72), overseas trade, minerals and energy (November-December 1975), natural resources (1975–77), trade and resources (1977–83). As leader of the Country Party, he was also deputy prime minister (1971–2 and 1975–83). After leaving parliament in 1984 he returned to farming and took on a number of business interests.

He was made a privy councillor in 1971 and a CH in 1981 as 'Deputy Prime Minister'. Of where was not specified in the *London Gazette* entry, but as he was appointed by the Queen 'on the advice of her Australian Ministers', the inference was clear.

Pierre Trudeau 4 July 1984 [Canada]

A charismatic, handsome, youthful, glamorous intellectual, Pierre Elliott Trudeau became prime minister of Canada in 1968 on a wave of national euphoria and, with a six months interlude in 1979–80, he remained in office for the next sixteen years.

He was born in 1919 at Montréal, Québec to a millionaire French Canadian businessman who had developed a chain of petrol stations on Montreal Island, and a mother of Scottish descent. Part of his success was this useful racial blending of English and French Canada. He was educated at Jean-de-Brebeuf College where he was known for his brilliance and intractability, and the University of Montreal, where he graduated with a degree in law. He was called to the bar at Quebec in 1943. Further postgraduate studies took him to Harvard University where he was awarded an MA in political economy in 1945, the École des Sciences Politiques, Paris (1946–47) and the London School of Economics (1947–48). During his time at the University of Montreal, Trudeau was required to join the Canadian Officers Training Corps, but like most other Québècois, he opposed the conscription. After his year at the LSE, he travelled for a year to see Europe and Asia before returning to Canada.

Many stories circulated about his year abroad. He once swept into an underground train in Paris bestowing kisses on pretty girls. He wandered through Germany, using papers he had faked himself, and flew to Belgrade, in an attempt to get into Yugoslavia without a visa. He was jailed, then deported to Bulgaria, where he joined a group of Spanish-speaking Jewish refugees, with whom he rambled through Greece and Turkey. He wandered into Palestine and was arrested as an Israeli spy; he was released and began wandering again, only to be picked up by desert bandits, whom he frightened off by feigning madness. He wandered to India, where he was attacked by pirates whilst travelling in a sampan, and escaped in a providential fog. He visited the Khyber Pass during the India-Pakistan conflict, crossed Burma and Vietnam and then got into China during the final throes of the civil war. He was also arrested by Moscow police for throwing snowballs at a statue of Karl Marx. 'I liked to make experiments, to push things to the limit, run risks, court adventure,' he recalled in later years.[73] 'What he brought back ... was self-sufficiency, highly-developed physical courage, and a profound distrust of the nationalist movements that seemed to be at the heart of the violence he had seen.'[74]

On his return to Canada, Trudeau was given a job with the Canadian privy council in Ottawa (1949–51), specialising in employment law, and he became well known for supporting the trades unions in the asbestos strike of Québec. He was a co-founder and co-director of the paper *Cité Libre* (1950), a radical monthly review which combined criticism of the reactionary and oppressive Maurice Duplessis regime in Québec with original views on the balance of authority between Canada's federal and provincial governments. He was once branded a dangerous radical by the Americans, and placed on a US immigration blacklist for a period in the 1950s. He practiced law for a while and then returned to academe as associate professor of law at the University of Montreal and researcher at the Institut de Récherches en Droit Publique (1961–1965). He was called to the Ontario bar in 1967.

Because of his anti-separatist stand, he was invited by Lester Pearson to enter federal politics. He won Mount Royal, Québec in the 1965 general election, retaining the seat until 1984. Pearson appointed him as his parliamentary secretary in 1966, and minister of justice (1967–1968). Within a year, he had reformed the divorce laws and had liberalised the laws on abortion and homosexuality, declaring that the government had no business in the bedrooms of the nation.

After Pearson's resignation, Trudeau stood as a candidate in the leadership election in 1968. His openness, honesty, youth and vigour, like those of John Kennedy in the United States seven years earlier, aroused the fascination of the Canadians and inspired the media term 'Trudeaumania'. He was elected leader of the Liberal Party on 6 April, and became Canada's fifteenth prime minister. Less than three weeks later he called a general election, which resulted in the first majority government since 1958. Many thought that Trudeau would soon tire of the responsibilities of high office, but Canadians never entirely lost their affection for their wealthy playboy prime minister and he was continually reelected. The 1972 election reduced the Liberals to a minority government and, beaten in a non-confidence motion in May 1974, a further election in July returned the Liberals to power with a comfortable majority. A sense of alienation in western Canada led to his defeat by the Progressive Conservatives in the 1979 general election and, deciding not to serve as leader of the opposition, he announced his retirement as leader of the Liberal Party. Within six months the Progressive Conservative Party was defeated in a non-confidence vote, his party encouraged him back to office and he won the ensuing election, forming a majority government. He resigned on 29 February 1984. The president of the Liberal Party commented: 'I should have known he would pick that day.'

Trudeau was a strong advocate of a single Canada, with all nationalities, cultures and languages living in harmony, and spent his political career in strengthening Canadian unity and federalism. His government introduced the Official Languages Act, 1969, guaranteeing a bilingual civil service. In 1970 he faced the 'October Crisis', during which he implemented the War Measures Act at the request of Robert Bourassa, the premier of Québec. The Front de Libération de Québec, a terrorist group, kidnapped a British diplomat and Pierre Laporte, a Québec cabinet minister. The British diplomat was rescued and the terrorists were captured, but Laporte was murdered. The War Measures Act gave the police wide powers of arrest and detention, and more than 400 people were arrested – though later released without being charged. He devoted his efforts during his final term as prime minister to opposing the separatist goals of the Parti Québècois in power in Québec. He campaigned vigorously against the separatists and played a significant role in the victory of the 'No' vote in the Québec referendum on sovereignty association in 1980.

The most public achievement of his 1980–84 government was the introduction of the Canadian charter of rights and freedoms and the patriation of the Canadian constitution in 1982. The Canadian constitution was enshrined in the wording of the British North America Act of 1867. Efforts to replace it had always foundered on disagreement between the provinces and the federal government. Trudeau needed the cooperation of all the provinces and negotiations continued for eighteen months, during which dissenting ministers, along with rulings from the supreme court and various provincial courts, threatened to derail the effort. Despite the lack of cooperation from René Lévèsque, the premier of Québec, consent was finally given. On 5 November 1981, the provinces and the federal government reached an historic agreement over the patriation and substance of the Canadian constitution. On 17 April 1982 the constitution, with its endorsement of the Canadian charter of rights and freedoms, was brought home and the Constitution Act was signed by Queen Elizabeth II in a special ceremony on Parliament Hill in Ottawa.

Trudeau was responsible for other 'firsts', including the promotion of women. He appointed Muriel McQueen Fergusson as the first woman speaker of the senate in 1972, and Jeanne Sauvé as Canada's first woman speaker of the house of the commons in 1980. One of his last acts was to appoint Sauvé as first woman governor general in 1984. He also campaigned for world peace and worked to improve the relationships between the industrialised nations and the third world countries. The establishment of diplomatic relations between Canada and the Peoples' Republic of China in 1971 helped to pave the way for China's admission to the United Nations, and a rapprochement between Beijing and Washington. He also drastically reduced Canada's contribution to NATO, and tried to establish a special relationship with the Soviet Union. He was initially cool towards the Commonwealth, but later became a warm supporter.

On his retirement from politics in 1984 he became a senior consultant with the law firm of Heenan Blaikie in Montreal. He married in 1971 and had three children by his wife; they were separated in 1977 and divorced in 1984. He had another child, a daughter, in 1992. His youngest son died in 1998 in an avalanche while skiing. Stricken with Parkinson's Disease and prostate cancer, Trudeau died in his sleep surrounded by his family in 2000, three weeks before his eighty-first birthday.

Trudeau received the CH after his retirement from parliament in 1984. He had been a controversial figure in Canada throughout most of his time in office, but after his departure he was acclaimed as a remarkable leader and an historic figure. A CH was seen as appropriate in view of his exceptionally long incumbency, his considerable experience of international affairs, his position as a major figure in the Commonwealth, and on the grounds of his service to Canada. The suggestion emerged from the United Kingdom government, but the Canadian government was consulted and Trudeau himself informally sounded. Although he had on several occasions refused offers to become a member of the United Kingdom privy council, he responded graciously to the offer of a CH. Carrying the implication of British interference, 'for services to Canada' would not have been an appropriate citation, and Trudeau was listed in the *London Gazette* as 'lately Prime Minister of Canada.'

David Lange 30 December 1989 [New Zealand]
David Lange was prime minister of New Zealand (1984–89) and the seventh and last of the New Zealand prime ministers to become a Companion of Honour.

Of German ancestry, David Lange was born in 1942 at Otahuhu, the son of a general practitioner. His grandfather, John Lange, had been drawn into the New Zealand Labour movement in 1917, and Walter Nash, then a young cloth salesman and later prime minister of New Zealand, was a frequent visitor.

Lange was educated at Otara College and Auckland University, from where he graduated with a degree in law. He was called to the bar and admitted a solicitor in 1966. He spent a year in the United Kingdom (1967–68), meeting the woman who was to become his wife, and being fascinated by the radical socialist preaching of the Methodist theologian Donald Soper. On returning to New Zealand he practiced law in Kaikohe (1968–70) and Auckland (1970–77), during which time he was known to take the cases of people who could not afford to pay. He also studied for an LLM degree in criminal law, criminal behaviour and medico-legal ethics at Auckland University.

He entered parliament in 1977, winning the seat of Mangere at a by-election, and holding it until 1990. He was deputy leader of the Labour Party (1979–83) and leader (1983–84). The popularity of Robert Muldoon's government was beginning to wane and Lange was not afraid to challenge the formidable economic expertise of the prime minister. He once famously described him as 'an economic ignoramus unfit to oversee a fifty cent raffle,'[75] He became prime minister when the Labour Party won the 1984 general election. Lange had portrayed Muldoon as an uncaring man who had no understanding of the problems of ordinary people; the latter said that he would never forgive Lange for the 'vicious and personal' way in which he had conducted the election campaign, although the statement was probably more an emotional concession of electoral defeat.[76] During his tenure, he held a number of additional portfolios: minister of foreign affairs (1984–87), minister in charge of the New Zealand Security Intelligence Service (1984–89), and minister of education (1987–89).

A moderate socialist, Lange favoured a mixture of state and private ownership of industries, encouraged free market reforms and cut the federal budget. Under his government, New Zealand moved to the monetary right. Many of the government's inefficient bureaucracies, including the railways and the post office, were sold, and all subsidies and tariffs were gradually eliminated. In foreign policy, he supported greater independence from the United Kingdom and the United States, and his government established a policy that excluded from New Zealand ports and territorial waters all ships powered by nuclear fuel or armed with nuclear weapons. In 1985 a US destroyer was denied access to a New Zealand port after US officials refused to reveal whether or not the ship carried nuclear weapons.

The Labour Party won the 1987 election, and Lange remained prime minister and would have carried on until the election due in 1990, but for a personality clash. In 1988 Roger Douglas, the minister of finance, resigned from the cabinet, claiming that he could no longer work with Lange. On 3 August 1989 the parliamentary Labour Party reelected Douglas to the cabinet. Four days later, Lange abruptly resigned, saying that the party had effectively 'stabbed him in the back'.

After his resignation, his successor, Geoffrey Palmer, made him attorney general and minister in charge of the serious fraud office (1989–90), both portfolios being outside the cabinet. He was made a CH in 1989 as 'Attorney General and Minister of State, lately Prime Minister of New Zealand.' He retired from parliament in 1996.

General John de Chastelain 31 December 1998 [Canada]

John de Chastelain was an unusual appointment to the Order, in that this distinguished Canadian soldier and diplomat earned a CH entirely for his services in Northern Ireland.

His family and background had a slightly cosmopolitan air. His unusual name revealed his French Huguenot ancestry and he was born in Bucharest in 1937, the son of a Scottish petroleum engineer and an American-born mother. Both his parents were spies. His father was attached to the Special Operations Executive during the 1939–45 war, was awarded the DSO and was captured behind enemy lines after parachuting into Romania. His mother spent much of the war working at the London headquarters of the Secret Intelligence Service (MI6). He was educated at Fettes College, Edinburgh, emigrated to Canada in 1955 to join his parents, and went to Mount Royal College, Calgary, Alberta. At the age of eighteen he enlisted as a private in the Calgary Highlanders, then enrolled as an officer cadet at the Royal Military College, Kingston, Ontario, graduating in 1960 with a degree in history, and went to the British staff college at Camberley. When he was invited to work in the religious and political cauldron of Northern Ireland, he remarked: 'It's not the sort of background many in Ulster would find acceptable. I'm British-born, attended the British army's staff college, have parents who were with British espionage and, to top it all off, I'm a Presbyterian.'[77]

He was commander of Canadian Forces Base, Montreal (1974–76) and the Canadian Contingent, UN Forces, Cyprus (1976–77); commandant of the Royal Military College (1977–80); commander of the 4th Canadian Mechanized Brigade Group, Germany (1980–82); deputy commander, Mobile Command, Québec (1983–86); assistant deputy minister (personnel), National Defence Headquarters (1986–88); vice-chief of the defence staff (1988–89); chief of the defence staff (1989–92); Canadian ambassador to the USA (1993); and again chief of the defence staff (1994–95).

He was made a Commander of the [Canadian] Order of Military Merit in 1984 and an Officer of the Order of Canada in 1993. The citation for his OC read: 'As a professional soldier, he has served with distinction for more than thirty-five years. In the role of Chief of the Defence Staff, he led the Canadian Forces through extremely challenging times, marked by a war in the Persian Gulf, a major domestic crisis and an unprecedented growth in the number of peacekeeping operations, in parallel with a significant down sizing of the Forces. He also devoted a great deal of time and energy to Scouts Canada's National Council and to the organisation's Substance Abuse Task Force. He is now Canadian ambassador to the United States.'

It was only after his retirement from the Canadian army that he began his most difficult assignment. He was asked to take an active role in the tentative peace process in Northern Ireland and to oversee the process of decommissioning of paramilitary weapons in the province, as chairman of the Independent International Commission on Decommissioning. It has been a long and delicate task that began in 1995 and is still unfinished at the time of writing. The CH came in 1998 for his services as 'Co-Chairman, Northern Ireland Talks'. Although it was certainly well deserved, the course of developments in Northern Ireland may prove it to be an interim honour.

Amartya Sen 11 May 2000 [India] (see Chapter 10)

Foreign appointments

Kenneth Quinan 4 June 1917 [United States of America] (see Chapter 2)

René Massigli 21 December 1954 [France]
René Massigli was an anglophile French diplomat who for ten years was the French ambassador in London.

He was born in 1888 and educated at the Ecole Normale. He left with a degree in history and taught at the Ecole Francaise de Rome (1910–13), then became a lecturer in literature at Lille University (1913–14). After serving in the 1914–18 war he was attached to the secretariat at the Paris peace conference in 1919. He was appointed secretary to the conference of ambassadors in 1920, assistant general secretary at the Washington conference in 1921, and in 1922 headed the secretariat of the Geneva conference and was French delegate at The Hague. He was a member of the Conseil d'État (1924–28) then head of the League of Nations section at the Quai d'Orsay until 1933. In 1933 he was promoted to assistant director of the political section and in 1937 he became director.

In 1938 he became ambassador at Ankara. After the outbreak of war he proved that his sympathies lay firmly with the allies and not with the Vichy government.

'In close and sympathetic accord with his British colleague [he] served the allied cause to signal advantage while Turkey sought anxiously to safeguard her neutrality.'[78] Well known for his anti-Nazi sentiments, he was recalled and dismissed by the Vichy authorities on the instructions of the German government.

Returning to France he lived in the south in close contact with the resistance, until November 1942 when German troops occupied the Vichy zone. The order for his arrest went out in twenty-four hours, but he evaded capture and escaped to London by courtesy of the royal air force in January 1943. General Charles de Gaulle made him commissioner for foreign affairs in the provisional government set up in Algiers, and he helped to preserve Anglo-French understanding when it was clouded by storms between Winston Churchill and de Gaulle. 'His overall success was due in large measure to the fact that he liked the British, felt at home with them, and believed strongly in the need for Franco-British friendship . . . Churchill said of him that he was "half-English and wholly French." He was French in his logical and precise cast of mind, which was reflected in his clipped and economical speech; he often expressing himself far more dogmatically and impatiently than is the English habit.'[79]

After the liberation of France in 1944 he was a natural candidate to be French ambassador to London, and was welcomed in London as a friend by government ministers 'who knew that their views would be interpreted as expertly in Paris as he explained French views in London.'[80] He stayed for ten years and left in 1954 to become head of the Quai d'Orsay. He retired in 1956 at the age of sixty-eight. On his retirement he was given the gold medal of the French foreign ministry, the first to be struck for some decades. From 1958–69 he was French president of the channel tunnel study group. He died in 1988, a few weeks before his one hundredth birthday.

He was made an honorary KBE in 1938, a GCVO after the state visit by President Vincent Auriol of France in 1950 and, unusually, a CH in 1954. The CH was a signal and unique honour for an ambassador, not all to the liking of Sir Robert Knox of the treasury ceremonial branch, and arose from an initiative within the foreign office. 'The Foreign Office have written informally to the Palace asking whether the French Ambassador, Massigli, could be given a CH (honorary) on his departure and they give a list of precedents given to important ambassadors on leaving (contrary, I think, to the customary rule). The Prime Minister is annoyed that this informal submission should have gone to the Palace and he proposes to send a note to the Foreign Office reminding them that recommendations for the CH should go through him. Major Ford thinks that the CH is the wrong honour for an ambassador. Why should he not have, for instance, the GBE?'[81] The foreign office won the argument.

Nuri es Said 16 July 1956 [Iraq]

Vigorous, intelligent and charming, General Nuri es-Said was prime minister of the kingdom of Iraq, and reckoned, in western opinion, to be the most distinguished Iraqi since the foundation of that state in 1921. He was certainly a continuing presence in the government of his particularly unstable homeland, but his friendship towards the west, particularly Britain, and his devotion to the Iraqi monarchy, alienated radical Arab nationalists, and he was shot while trying to escape from a mob during a savage and bloodthirsty revolution in 1958.

He was born in Baghdad in 1888, the son of an Ottoman empire official. In 1903 he went to the military academy in Istanbul and returned to Iraq in 1908 as a commissioned officer. He returned to Turkey in 1910 to study at the Army Staff College. Between 1910 and 1914 he became an active supporter of Arab nationalism. He was captured by the British at the start of the 1914–18 war and taken to India. Thereafter he joined the Arab revolt and fought with Emir Faisal and T. E. Lawrence against Ottoman rule. He remained loyal to the emir and his family to the end of his life. He acted as the emir's personal escort or envoy during Faisal's brief reign as king of Syria from April to June 1920. In the following year Faisal was established as king of Iraq and from that point onwards Nuri es-Said became a pivotal and enduring figure in Iraqi politics. He was appointed to his first cabinet post – minister of defence – in November 1922 and remained in office under three prime ministers until 1928. In 1930 he became prime minister himself, resigning in 1932 in the face of growing opposition. He was too important to be entirely excluded from the political scene, and in 1932–36 he was minister for foreign affairs in a series of short-lived governments. He escaped with his life during a coup d'etat in 1936 by leaving the country in an RAF airplane. He returned some months later when the coup leader was assassinated and then occupied diplomatic appointments abroad until he was recalled to the premiership in 1938. Opposition again caused his resignation in 1940, though he continued as a cabinet minister. A coup by four generals intent on allying Iraq with Germany led to a brief period of exile, before he was again prime minister 1941–44. He ensured that Iraq declared war on the Axis powers and made the allied powers regard him as a firm friend. He began moves towards an organisation for Arab unity that culminated in the foundation of the Arab League in 1945. He was prime minister again in 1946–47, from January to December 1949, 1950–52, 1954–57, and finally from March to May 1958.

Gerald de Gaury knew Nuri es-Said from 1925 and regarded him highly. 'He was an example of extreme intelligence, wedded to unusual adaptability and good political sense. He . . . never wavered in loyalty to the dynasty or . . . in faith in Britain as the supporter of the Arab movement . . . At work he was full of nervous energy and high inquisitiveness, usually concealed by a statesmanlike reticence while in official European circles . . . It was said of Nuri that he "never read a file", and, broadly speaking it was true. He came to know what he wanted about any subject by asking those who understood the question best. I never heard him make an original remark, but I never heard him make an unwise one.'[82]

After the coup that overthrew King Farouk of Egypt in 1952, Nuri gradually became unpopular with those who looked towards Gamal Nasser of Egypt as the focus of Arab nationalism. The British invasion of the Suez Canal was a blow to his pro-western policies, though he deftly expressed support for Egypt while refusing to break off relations with Britain. Nasser in turn was irrationally jealous of Nuri and regarded him as his principal opponent in the contest for leadership of the Arab world. Nuri was nearly seventy, and younger dissatisfied nationalist officers of the Iraqi army looked towards Nasser and Egypt, but when the coup came, it was unpleasantly brutal and more reminiscent of the murder of the Russian royal family in 1917 than the exile of the Egyptian royal family in 1952.

The coup took place on 14–15 July 1958. It was led by a group of army officers and met no armed opposition. King Faisal II and most of the royal family were shot at the palace, and Nuri survived them for only a few hours. Alarmed by the cutting of his telephone wires and new reports, he left his house in his pyjamas and went by river – rowed by two fishermen at the point of his two pistols – to the east

bank where a general commotion made it unsafe for him to land. He returned to
the west bank to the house of a friend, where he learned that there was a price of
ten thousand dinars on his head. From there he was smuggled back to Baghdad
to seek refuge in the house of a friend. As he wandered through the streets trying
to find the house he was spotted and a chased by a group. He ran and then turned
and fired with his pistols on the group. They, with some men of the volunteer
police, fired in return and he was killed. His body was buried, but not for long. A
group of revolutionaries disinterred his body and dragged it through the streets. A
passing car was order to stop and the driver ordered to run over the body, reverse
and then run over it again. 'Still not satisfied, they went on into the city and strung
it up, then lugged it down again and pulled it to bits, souvenir hunters having their
way with it, until it was unrecognisable as the corpse of the man who had been the
best-known patriot in the Arab world. At last the trunk was set afire. Not much
petrol was needed to consume in flame the little that remained.'[83]

Nuri es-Said was made a CH in 1956 while accompanying King Faisal II on a state
visit to London. It was a high recognition of his long-standing pro-British stance, and
Nuri became the first and so far the only Arab to have been made a Companion of
Honour. The conferral on 16 July was made at almost the last possible moment. Ten
days later, the Egyptians nationalised the Suez Canal, and the following sequence of
events effected a profound change in Britain's relations with the Arab world. Nuri es-
Said remains the only member of the Order to have died by violence.

Paul-Henri Spaak 14 May 1963 [Belgium]
The first socialist prime minister of Belgium, Paul-Henri Spaak was better known
after the 1939–45 war as the pioneer of the Western European Union who made
his country the home of NATO and the European Economic Community, aspects
of the new Europe that developed from the wreckage of the war hostilities. He was
prime minister for three short periods in coalition government (1938–39, 1946,
1947–49), but was better known as Belgium's foreign minister (1935–39, 1939–49,
1954–57 and 1961–66).

He was born in Brussels in 1899, the grandson of a barrister and left-wing parliamentarian. His father was a translator of Shakespeare and co-director of the
Brussels Monnaie Theatre, while his mother was a socialist member of the Belgian
senate (from 1921). He spent two years in a German prisoner of war camp during the 1914–18 war, and afterwards rapidly qualified as a barrister. His brief
career in the law was marked by his defence of a young Italian who attempted to
assassinate the crown prince of Italy at Brussels in 1929.

Recognised as a powerful socialist orator and writer, he was elected as a far left
republican socialist deputy for Brussels in 1932. His calls for revolutionary action
quickly ended in 1935 when he was appointed minister of transport, and from
then on he became decidedly more right wing in his views and statements. He also
became an ardent royalist and trusted friend of King Leopold III. After a few
months he became foreign minister and in May 1938 he became Belgium's first
socialist prime minister at the age of thirty-nine. He resigned both offices early in
1939, but resumed the foreign ministry one day after the British declaration of war
on Germany, with the sole aim of keeping Belgium out of the war. The German
invasion of Belgium in May 1940 ended his hopes, and the Belgian government
moved southwards through France, Spain and Portugal to London where it
remained until the liberation of Brussels in 1944.

King Leopold III's order to the Belgian army to surrender after two weeks of fighting in 1940, and his decision to stay in Belgium with his people, divided the country in the postwar years, and Spaak in particular became intensely hostile to the king. In 1935 Spaak had sat alone with the king after the death of Queen Astrid, and contrived to say exactly the right thing to the bereaved monarch, and the two became friends. In 1940 Spaak denounced the king for ordering the Belgian army to surrender. In 1941–44 he again praised the king to the world, but in 1945 he realised that he would have to condemn the king in line with his socialist colleagues. When the king returned from exile to Belgium in 1950, Spaak led a hostile demonstration to the royal palace to force the king's withdrawal from power, and his eventual abdication. He recanted his behaviour during a television interview in 1968. The king's attitude was more consistent and more generous. 'If I were to meet him somewhere, I would still hold out my hand to him, for we have been such friends in the past and have been through so much together. He is fat and jolly and likes all the good things of life. He can always see the funny side of things. We would sit down together, and in no time he would be making me laugh – probably with some outrageous story about one of his colleagues. I can forgive him anything for that.'[84]

In 1944 Spaak and the Dutch foreign minister conceived the idea of 'Benelux', an economic union of Belgium, the Netherlands, and Luxembourg which they hoped would become the nucleus of an even larger union. He was elected first president of the United Nations general assembly in 1946, chairman of the newly founded Organisation for European Economic Cooperation in 1948, and in 1949 president of the consultative assembly of the Council of Europe. The last appointment came in the immediate aftermath of the electoral defeat of the socialist government in Belgium. Hearing that Spaak was free, the delegates to the consultative assembly delayed the election until he could reach Strasbourg where he was given the office spontaneously and unanimously. He resigned in 1951, disappointed in the council's ineffectiveness and dismayed by Britain's refusal to take a more prominent role in the European movement. Two later projects – for a European Political Community and a European Defence Community – also failed, although in 1952 he was elected president of the European Coal and Steel Community.

In 1954 he was again appointed foreign minister of Belgium and enthusiastically entered the negotiations, leading to the establishment of the European Economic Community and the European Atomic Energy Community. He was chairman of the six-nation team which drafted the 1957 Treaty of Rome, 'after months of relentless and powerful effort, during which time he amazed everyone by his persistence and resourcefulness in complex bargaining. Never losing sight of basic principles, he wheedled, bullied, and cajoled the delegates of the six countries until the Rome Treaty was at last signed.'[85]

He was secretary-general of NATO (1957–61) before returning for a final period as Belgium's foreign minister (1961–66). With difficulty he had to address the problems arising from the grant of independence to the Congo in 1960. In 1963 he was appalled by General de Gaulle's veto of British membership of the European Economic Community and the following year at French intransigence towards political unity. In the mid-1960s when quarrels developed between Belgium's two linguistic groups, Spaak was criticised for his evident devotion to European unity while showing little concern for developing the unity that was needed in his own country. The criticisms were thought to have precipitated his resignation as Belgium's foreign minister in July 1966. Although he was a master of his native tongue of French, he could not speak Flemish, his country's second language, and although he learned English, he found great difficulty in speaking any foreign language. In appearance he looked like Winston Churchill and even affected the same bow ties. During the war he said: 'I am often told that I look like Winston Churchill and speak English like Charles Boyer, but I wish it were the other way round.'[86]

His many honours included decorations from Belgium, Finland, Yugoslavia, Sweden and Lithuania. He was probably the only Belgian foreign minister to accompany two Belgian monarchs on state visits to the United Kingdom. In November 1937 he received the customary GCMG while accompanying King Leopold III. In May 1963 he accompanied King Baudoin and Queen Fabiola and was made a CH in recognition of his broadly pro-British attitudes as much as his role in endeavouring to bind Europe together. He died in 1972.

Joseph Luns 14 June 1971 [The Netherlands]

Joseph Luns was a Roman Catholic Dutch politician and diplomat of conservative beliefs, elegant appearance, gracious style and humorous wit, who for nearly twenty years was the seemingly permanent foreign minister of the Netherlands, and for thirteen years secretary general of NATO. Six feet seven inches in height, he was one of the few European statesmen who was tall enough to look General Charles de Gaulle in the eyes.

He was born at Rotterdam in 1911, the son of a French father and a Belgian mother. His father was a member of the Netherlands Academy of Fine Art and a professor of art history. When he was seven, his family moved to Amsterdam where he attended St Ignatius College, a Roman Catholic classical high school. He completed his high school education at the Institute Saint Louis in Brussels. He was drafted into the Royal Netherlands Navy in 1931 and served a year as a signalman. He then studied law at the universities of Leiden and Amsterdam and received a doctorate in jurisprudence at the latter in 1937. The following year he took courses in political economy at the London School of Economics and at the German Institute for Foreigners of the University of Berlin.

He joined the Netherlands diplomatic corps in September 1938 as a junior attaché at the ministry of foreign affairs in The Hague. In January 1940 he was transferred to a similar position at the Dutch legation in Berne and was serving there when the German forces invaded the Netherlands that year. The Dutch government in exile sent Luns to the legation at Lisbon in March 1941 and there he was promoted to the rank of second secretary. Called to London in 1943 he served on the staff of the ministry of foreign affairs for several months then returned briefly to Lisbon as chargé d'affaires. Back in London in 1944 he was promoted to the rank of first secretary at the embassy, which he held until 1949. His last diplomatic posting was as a member of the Netherlands permanent delegation to the UN in New York (1949-52).

In the general election of 1952, Luns, who belonged to the moderate Catholic Peoples' Party, was appointed minister without portfolio in the government of Willem Drees. The Labour Party and the moderate Catholic Peoples' Party took an equal number of seats in both chambers of the States General, but with support from several minor parties, Drees succeeded in forming a government.

'Minister without portfolio' was technical rank. In an unusual but amicable arrangement Luns was effectively joint foreign minister with J. W. Beyen, and was given specific responsibility for international affairs outside Europe, including the United Nations, various aspects of international commerce, and for the Benelux trade union. When asked why two foreign ministers were needed, he replied, 'As a small country we have such a tremendous amount of outside world to cope with.'[87]

He was elected to the lower chamber of the States General in 1956, but following the requirement of Dutch law, he surrendered his seat when Drees named him minister for foreign affairs in October that year. He was reelected to the States General in 1959, 1963, 1967 and 1971 and was appointed foreign minister by each of the governments formed after the first three of those elections, and managed to serve under seven prime ministers. During his nineteen years as foreign minister, he was a staunch supporter of the United States on such controversial issues as Vietnam, and as secretary general of NATO (1971-84) he continued to back the Americans on most policy matters. 'His almost uncritical support of American foreign policy, as many of his countrymen saw it, would have rapidly become untenable in The Netherlands in the 1970s. As Secretary-General he was almost continually at loggerheads with successive Dutch cabinets.'[88] During his time at NATO he had to deal with internal dissension as much as with international crises. The feud between Greece and Turkey over the festering sore of Cyprus caused Greek withdrawal from the military wing of NATO in 1974 and the clash between Britain and Iceland over fishing rights in 1976 caused a breach in diplomatic relations. Luns was a continuous supporter of British membership of the European Community and no one worked harder than him to bring Britain into membership.

He was fundamentally conservative, and had little time for liberals of any kind, and as Dutch politics moved steadily to the left, Luns moved steadily to the right. 'I get up and leave when some leftist starts saving the whole world', he was reported as saying.[89] He was also often at odds with the reform-minded hierarchy of the Dutch Roman Catholic Church. 'The Lord protects the Head of the Church against grave errors, and in that context I prefer to accept the Pope, not the 300 or 400 mini-Popes in Holland.'[90] He was well-liked and respected in the Netherlands. In 1979 it was revealed that his name had been found on the rolls of the Dutch Nazi party in the mid-1930s. But the States General accepted without question, Luns' statement that his brother had submitted his name without his knowledge or permission, and no inquiry was held.

Luns received numerous foreign honours, including a GCMG in 1958 and a CH in 1971. He suffered a stroke in 1997 and died in 2002.

Jean Monnet 22 January 1972 [France]

A French economist and public official, Jean Monnet was a long time proponent of European unity for which he strove unceasingly, and which earned him the informal title of 'Father of Europe'.

He was born in Cognac, Charente in 1888 and educated at Cognac College. He spent his youth helping his father in the family business. During the 1914–18 war, he was the French representative on the inter-allied maritime commission, an international committee designed to secure war materials, foodstuffs, and shipping facilities for the allies. The problem of organising supplies could have com promised the outcome of the conflict. Having worked out the solution, namely joint planning by France and England he persuaded the president of the council, René Viviani, to adopt his proposal. Monnet was sent to London, where he set up an Anglo-French organisation that coordinated the acquisition and transport of supplies. At the end of the war, his considerable achievements were recognised by his appointment as deputy secretary-general of the League of Nations (1919–23).

Like many others, he was enthusiastic and had high hopes that this new international organisation would be able to deal with the problems of the world by its moral force and appeal to public opinion, and like many others, he was soon forced to recognise that the league was simply unable to achieve the goals of peace and harmony which it had set itself. Decisions had to be unanimous and Monnet was later to say that the power of veto was the prime cause and the symbol of the impossibility of overcoming national egotism. Neither a common will nor a common good could be achieved on such a basis. In 1923 he resigned his office and returned to his family's cognac business for the next fifteen years. He was also active in banking, acting as a financial adviser to several eastern European countries (1923–39), and helping to reorganise the Chinese railway system in 1932.

His talents were not forgotten, and at the outbreak of the 1939–45 war they were brought into use once again, and he was sent to London as chairman of the Franco-British committee for co-ordinating economic and financial requirements, armaments and transport (1939–40). In London in June 1940, while the French army was being overwhelmed by the German army, Monnet conceived an impractical dream. He proposed a project for immediate federal union between France and the United Kingdom to Churchill and de Gaulle, who accepted it. The two governments should declare that in future France and Great Britain would no longer be two nations but a single Anglo-French Union. The constitution of the union would entail common organisations for defence, foreign policy and economic affairs and the two parliaments would be officially united. It was effectively a naive desperate attempt to prevent the defeat of France, but it failed. The French government was already resigned to surrender, and the union never became a reality.

From London he went to the USA to be a member of the Washington-based British Supply Council (1940–43) where he was instrumental in coordinating the allied war effort. The economist John Maynard Keynes was to say at the end of the war that through his coordinating work Monnet had probably shortened the war by one year. He moved to Algiers in 1943, to join Charles de Gaulle's National Liberation Committee of 'Free France', as commissioner for armament, supplies and reconstruction (1943–44). He was convinced, and tried to convince the committee, that there would be no peace in Europe if, at the end of the war, European states were to be reconstituted on the basis of national sovereignty. He held that the countries of Europe were too small to guarantee their peoples the necessary prosperity and social development, and that a federation was best solution.

In 1946 he was appointed general commissioner of the plan for the modernisation and equipment of France, and was charged with rebuilding the French economy. Ever after known as the Monnet Plan, and published in 1947, it called for the modernisation of French industry and agriculture with government help and supervision, and provided for a 48-hour working week to achieve economic goals.

The resultant redevelopment encouraged French participation in the Marshall Plan and also in the Schuman Plan, drafted by Monnet himself. In 1949 friction between Germany and France for control of the Ruhr, an important coal and steel region, was rising to dangerous levels, presaging a possible return to hostilities as had happened after the 1914–18 war. There was no question of federation being the solution. The memories of the war were still too vivid and France, having recovered its sovereignty after the German occupation, was not enthusiastic to see it limited by federation with Germany. Monnet saw Franco-German pacification as vital to the peace of Europe, and believed that European peace and stability would be built on practical achievements, and that common institutions were the key to a durable European Community. With others he drafted a new proposal – to merge Franco-German coal and steel resources, under the control of a European government – and submitted 'the Monnet Memorandum' to foreign minister Robert Schuman. By pooling basic production and the establishment of a new high authority, whose decisions would be binding on France, Germany and the countries that join them, the proposal would lay the first concrete foundations of a European federation that was, in his view, indispensable to the maintenance of peace. Schuman accepted the proposal and, in agreement with Konrad Adenauer, the German chancellor, published 'the Schuman Plan' (so titled, although Monnet was the author) in 1950. In 1951 the Treaty of Paris, signed by France, Germany, Italy, Belgium, Holland and Luxembourg, established the European Coal and Steel Community (ECSC).

Monnet became the first president of the ECSC when it came into being in 1952 and there is no doubt that his international mind conceived it as the initial step toward European economic and political integration. Another of his dreams was the European Defence Community, but it came to nothing. NATO was already in active existence and in 1955 France refused to ratify the plans for the EDC and Monnet resigned as president of the ECSC. In the same year he founded the Action Committee for the United States of Europe, becoming its first chairman a year later, and until his death, he continued to call on the European political class not to abandon the path of European unity. The group supported the establishment of the Common Market (the European Economic Community), which developed from many of Monnet's ideas. With European economic union well under way, the committee was disbanded in 1975.

In 1976 at a meeting of heads of state in Luxembourg, it was decided to confer the title 'Honorary Citizen of Europe' on Monnet for his work as a founder of the European Community. He died in 1979.

For his services to British interests, Monnet was recognised on several occasions by the British government, by way of a series of honorary appointments in the Order of the British Empire. He was made a CBE in 1919, a KBE in 1920, and a GBE in 1946. He was made a CH in 1972 at the age of eighty-three. Not surprisingly the honour came on the initiative of Edward Heath, that most pro-European of prime ministers, in recognition of the outstanding contribution Monnet had made to Anglo-French relations and the civilisation of Europe and for consistently supporting full British participation in the movement towards unity in western Europe.

Bernard Haitink 12 June 2002 [The Netherlands] (see Chapter 7)

CHAPTER SEVENTEEN

Emblem of honour

THE RIBBON AND BADGE OF THE ORDER

> *Years afterwards she could bring the whole scene back again, as if it had been only yesterday – the mild blue eyes and kindly smile of the Knight – the setting sun gleaming through his hair, and shining on his armour in a blaze of light that quite dazzled her – the horse quietly moving about, with the reins hanging loose on his neck . . . and the black shadows of the forest behind.*
>
> 'It's my own invention', *Through the looking-glass*, Lewis Carroll

Although the first members of the Order were named on 24 August 1917, it was not until November 1918 that they were given the riband and badge of their new honour. That the statutes were published as late as 15 October 1919, more than two years after the institution of the Order, was at least in part caused by the long delay in agreeing the appearance of the insignia. As with the Order of the British Empire, the Order of the Companions of Honour was part of the war effort; it was needed quickly, and it was important to publicise the foundation of the Order and the names of its members. Of course the insignia was important, but design and manufacture could be allowed to proceed at a less urgent pace. In fact a cavalier eagerness to produce the insignia as quickly as possible only served to delay its appearance by many months.

The statutes describe the badge as follows: 'the oval shaped badge of the Order which shall consist of a gold medallion with a representation of an oak tree and pendant from a branch a shield of the Royal Arms on the dexter a representation of a Knight and in armour mounted on a horse, the whole within a circle azure inscribed with the motto, "In action faithful and in honour clear".' As with the insignia of the Order of the British Empire, the essence of the design came from the mind of one individual, while several others, not least the King, periodically intervened with comparatively minor suggestions to produce the design that is still in use.

Four individuals figure prominently in the correspondence dealing with the design and manufacture of the insignia of the Order between April 1917 and November 1918: Prince Louis of Battenberg (Marquess of Milford Haven from June 1917), Sir Frederick Ponsonby, keeper of the privy purse, Sir Douglas Dawson, state chamberlain and secretary of the central chancery of the orders of knighthood, and principally the artist Elinor Hallé. All the surviving documentation shows that the tablet that forms the centrepiece of the present badge, was essentially the work of Elinor Hallé, under the supervision of Prince Louis of Battenberg.[1]

Prince Louis of Battenberg (1854–1921) was married to a granddaughter of Queen Victoria, and despite his Germanic title, had been a naturalised British subject since 1868. His father, Prince Alexander of Hesse, an experienced numismatist, had been an ardent collector of the coins and medals of the grand duchy of

Hesse and Prince Louis in his turn developed a similar taste. A deep interest in naval history combined with an early gift of a few naval commemorative medals, themselves mementoes of sea fights and sea captains, began a life-long fascination with the subject of medals and inaugurated his large personal collection, and his three-volume work on the history and design of naval medals is the definitive study on the subject. It was natural that the King should turn to his cousin to guide the design of the badge of the new Order. Prince Louis enjoyed a distinguished career in the royal navy until a wave of anti-German hysteria swept the country at the outbreak of the 1914–18 war and forced him to resign as first sea lord in 1914. Anti-German feeling claimed him a second time in June 1917 when, with other German-titled members of the royal family, he was obliged to relinquish his name and princely rank, and thoroughly Anglicise himself by accepting a peerage and taking the title of Marquess of Milford Haven. Throughout most of the war he lived in virtual retirement at his house at East Cowes on the Isle of Wight.

On 23 April 1917 a letter was despatched to Prince Louis from Sir Frederick Ponsonby entrusting him with responsibility for the design of the insignia. 'His Majesty hopes that you will undertake to have suitable designs prepared for this new decoration. It is to be an equivalent of the DSO and ISO and will therefore be worn on the coat, and not round the neck . . . As you are down in the Isle of Wight, if you wish anything done, perhaps you will let me know, and I will carry out any instructions you choose to send me, but the King wishes the design of this new decoration placed entirely in your hands.'[2] Despite the King's desire for the insignia to be a breast decoration Ponsonby was in principle against the badge being worn on the coat. Not only would the place of wearing determine the design, it would also determine the status of the Order. A member of the Order of the Companions of Honour ranked high in the table of precedence; he or she would be the equivalent of a knight grand cross of the Order of the British Empire, and Ponsonby wondered whether it was appropriate to have it worn on the breast. Did its high rank not require that it *should* be worn as a neck decoration?[3] 'Certainly', was Prince Louis's succinct reply.[4]

The first reference to a design occurs on 12 May when, apparently without his being asked, Henry Farnham Burke, Garter King of Arms, submitted his own suggestion. Sir Douglas Dawson forwarded it to Prince Louis, but without any enthusiasm. 'It looks expensive', wrote Dawson to Ponsonby, 'but of course there would be very few given.'[5] Ponsonby later described it as 'vulgar and banal'.[6] The influence of Prince Louis was paramount and it was consigned to oblivion.

The design finally approved was the work of Elinor Hallé (1856–1926), designer of the insignia of the Order of the British Empire in 1916 and the collar of the Royal Victorian Order in 1911, both at the instigation of Ponsonby. Prince Louis had worked with her on the design of the insignia of the Order of the British Empire, and he had no hesitation in inviting her to design a badge for the Companions of Honour. Daughter of Sir Charles Hallé, founder of the Hallé Orchestra, Elinor Hallé was a noted sculptress, enamellist and medallist in her day, exhibiting at the Royal Academy on a number of occasions between 1892 and 1914. Among her works were a bronze medal of Cardinal Newman in 1887, and one of Countess Feodora Gleichen in 1914. Forrer's *Biographical Dictionary of Medallists*, published in 1904 records that 'she first made her mark at the Grosvenor Gallery in 1884 with a low-relief of "Music". She later abandoned the field of sculpture for medal-designing and enamelling. She became a member of the Society of Medallists, at the exhibitions of which 'she has exhibited some nice works'.

On 29 June, Elinor Hallé wrote to Ponsonby, enclosing what proved in substance to be the final design of the badge of the Order of the Companions of Honour. 'I have been asked to design the new 'Honour' Order. I sent in a few designs to Prince Louis the other day, but since then I have worked a little badge in relief which I would very much like the King to see. I heard from Lord Milford Haven last night that he had sent the designs in to the King and that he himself was just off to France, so I am sending the new one to you in the hope that perhaps you might be able to insert it among the others in case the King has not chosen yet. I should be very glad if this could be done. I was asked to do an emblem of Honour and this, as you will see, is a knight guarding the British shield, hung on an oak. The inscription, which is a little difficult to read in the plaster, is a nice quotation from Pope "In action faithful and in honour clear". Of course it is all much rougher in plaster than it would be in metal and enamel, but it gives an idea of what it means.'[7]

On 2 July, Ponsonby reported that Milford Haven had suggested that the badge should be the same height as the badge of knight grand cross of the Order of the Bath (three and a half inches for a military GCB and two and a half inches for a civil GCB). 'Until this is settled it is rather difficult for the artist to produce any design. Milford Haven has now gone to France and therefore it will not be possible to consult him any more for the present. But he asks me to get this information so that he might have it when he returned.'[8]

On 11 July Lord Milford Haven proposed an oval crowned badge, the size of a civil KCB (two and a quarter inches).[9] By 14 July he had seen and generally approved Miss Hallé's design, though with a few suggestions of his own. 'Pope's words FAITHFUL IN ACTION AND IN HONOUR CLEAR are to be used as a legend – not in the order you placed them. Personally I would suggest you showing the sea horizon behind the tree, with one or two old sailing vessels on it. Will you please now prepare the model for the die-sinker, presumably Pinches. Will you undertake to see to the manufacture of the finished badge (we want to cut out Garrards.) It should be the exact size of your cast in the box. The back to be quite smooth except for the GRI and crown, engraved or stamped. The metal for everything to be silver gilt. The legend in gold letters on dark blue enamel . . . The crown should be enamelled as regards the jewels on circlet, the pearls on the arches, and the red cap, and ermine lining, showing below the gold circlet. The ermine should form a continuous curve with top of medallion. A flat ring for the ribbon should pass through the orb on top of crown.' His last words must have given Miss Hallé much encouragement. 'I rejoice that we shall have at least one Order, entirely the work of an artist.'[10]

Milford Haven's rendering of the motto, 'FAITHFUL IN ACTION AND IN HONOUR CLEAR', was in fact a misquotation, almost certainly derived from Ponsonby, who in turn got it from J. W. Mackail, assistant secretary in the secondary school branch of the board for education. Ponsonby had written to Mackail on 2 July, sounding him about the appropriateness of the proposed motto: 'I am also engaged in finding a suitable inscription for "The Order of the Companions of Honour." This must be English, and the one suggested is "In action faithful and in honour clear".'[11] Mackail's reply was as brief as it was inaccurate: 'I don't know why the well-known line of Pope's has been altered: he wrote "Faithful in action, and in honour clear" . . . ; and I think his order of words is better in itself, apart from the undesirability of altering a celebrated quotation. Subject to this criticism, I don't think I can better the inscription.'[12] That John William Mackail should make such a blunder was surprising considering his knowledge of the subject field. In addition to his work as examiner and assistant secretary at the board of education (1885–1919), he was also professor of literature at the Royal Academy and had been professor of poetry at Oxford (1906–11). But his misquotation of Pope had long been forgotten and was not held against him when he was appointed a member of the Order of Merit in 1935.

IN ACTION FAITHFUL AND IN HONOUR CLEAR certainly derives from an elegy by the eighteenth century English poet Alexander Pope (1688–1744), but the lines have a complicated history. The full text of the passage is:

> *Statesman, yet friend to truth! of soul sincere,*
> *In action faithful, and in honour clear;*
> *Who broke no promise, serv'd no private end,*
> *Who gain'd no title, and who lost no friend.*

According to the Twickenham edition of Pope's poems, these lines, in quotation marks, first appeared as an imaginary inscription at the end of *Verses occasion'd by Mr. Addison's treatise of medals*, now known to have been published in 1720. The lines refer not to Pope's contemporary, the poet and essayist Joseph Addison (1672–1719), but to the politician James Craggs (1657–1721), and were subsequently published as an epitaph on Craggs after his death in 1721. It is now thought that these concluding lines, in celebration of Craggs, were written shortly after Addison's death (in 1719), when Pope learned that Addison had bequeathed to Craggs the edition of his works then in preparation, and when he assumed that it was in this book that his epistle would first appear. The lines were undoubtedly written before Craggs's death on 16 February 1721 since they were printed with the rest of the epistle in some copies of a (possibly) pirated edition of Pope's *Works* in 1720. Whether Craggs himself was worthy of the ascription 'in action faithful and in honour clear, who broke no promise, serv'd no private end', is another matter. He accepted at least £30,000 in stock of the South Sea Company from its directors. He was implicated in the speculation and ultimate bursting of the 'South Sea Bubble' and died soon after examination by a parliamentary committee. It is impossible to say whether Elinor Hallé knew of any of this, but the words 'gain'd no title' were certainly apposite for Craggs and have remained so for many of those appointed to the Order of the Companions of Honour.

On 19 July, Ponsonby reported that Milford Haven was 'getting on with the badge'.[13] On 25 July Milford Haven himself told Dawson that he had seen 'a beautiful badge modelled by Miss Hallé and for £5 a piece she will make them herself: cast and chased by hand – real works of art.'[14] With an eye to expense Dawson suspected that '£5 a piece' would not include the cost of the riband and the case, but considering the small number of pieces that would be required, he hoped that the treasury would allow him to spend beyond budget to cover the cost of those items.[15] 'We will raise no objection to this arrangement', replied the treasury, 'in view of the small number that will be wanted; and we will agree to the cost falling on the Miscellaneous Expenses Vote in due course.'[16] As Dawson suspected, '£5 a piece' did not include case and ribbon, and the final cost was much higher due to wasted work. 'I suppose we must get Garrard, or some other jeweller, to mount Miss Hallé's badges on the ribbons and put them in cases? This will necessitate a further expenditure for which I shall have to make a second appeal to the Treasury.'[17] Ponsonby replied that as the treasury had agreed the sum of £5 a piece, it would have to stand – for badge, riband, case and mounting – and wrote to Miss Hallé to break the news.[18]

The badge was ready to go into production. Ponsonby had seen the design by 9 August 1917 and described the result as 'really beautiful'.[19] Milford Haven himself was very pleased with Miss Hallé's work: 'This Order will really be a thing of beauty.'[20] But who was to manufacture the pieces? Garrard, the crown jewellers, was foremost in the market place, but there was a degree of antipathy towards the company because of their perceived monopoly. 'As you may remember when the OBE was discussed I found a great deal of opposition to the employment of Garrard. The Treasury seems to think that Garrard has the monopoly of decorations and that they were making large profits. It was said that questions would be asked in the House as to why it was not put out to open tender. If you remember we went carefully into all this and we found that Garrards was the only firm capable of producing the OBE in large numbers, and that there was really no alternative. The Treasury accepted this explanation but now if we again employ Garrards we shall be up against this opposition with no satisfactory explanation as almost any firm can turn out the small quantities required. I therefore told Prince Louis to let Miss Hallé employ what firm she liked. There should be no difficulty and I have told her to get a regular estimate from Pinches or whatever firm she likes but the whole thing is not to cost more than £5.'[21]

Elinor Hallé herself was almost ready to start work on manufacture. She had received the approved pattern of riband and only needed to know the width and length for each badge. 'Then I will be able to deliver the whole thing complete, cases included. I think it would be more expeditious and satisfactory. The diesinker is to begin his work tomorrow, so I hope the badge will be ready in a few weeks.'[22] The commission went not to Garrard but to the London firm of Pinches, and that company had notified Miss Hallé, on or before 22 September, that the completed badges would be ready in 'six weeks or two months from now.'[23] So far, everything was going well, but at this stage, disastrously as it proved in terms of timing, King George V decided to intervene on almost every front, not least on the question of the colour of the riband.

According to Ponsonby, the design of the riband had been settled (presumably by Elinor Hallé or by himself, or by both of them) by 19 July, but Milford Haven cautioned that further advice should be taken. 'He suggested that as the bow which women would wear was so much more important than the small piece of riband which would show in the case of men, it would be wise to take the Queen's advice in this matter.'[24] Ponsonby obediently sent the Queen 'a mass of coloured ribands and also a book of different coloured distempers', but considering the intense interest shown by the Queen in the riband of the Order of the British Empire, she at first showed little interest in the Companions of Honour. 'Lady Mary Trefusis wrote to me and said that the Queen had no time to go into the whole thing but thought a light colour would be best such as jade green.'[25] Milford Haven then suggested that a gold line would make the riband very distinctive. 'Apparently the Russian Order of St Catherine has a red riband with a gold edge.

I have therefore had the enclosed bows made up in accordance with these suggestions. On one I have had a gold line put on one side so as to judge the effect with and without the gold edge. Now can you see the Queen and ascertain Her Majesty's wishes and then finally submit something definite for the King's approval. There may be some difficulty in getting the riband made and so no time should be lost . . . The only objection I see to jade green is that green more or less denotes Ireland.'[26]

Presented with the made-up bows, Queen Mary then began to take as serious an interest as she had done with the Order of the British Empire ribbon. She was not greatly taken with jade green and suggested alternatives of either cerise (a light clear red) or the colour of a malmaison carnation (pink), a petal of which she sent to Dawson.[27] The latter duly had ribands of cerise and malmaison made up and sent them on to Milford Haven on 23 July.[28] Four days later, Dawson was worried; the atmosphere was taking its toll of the malmaison petal, which was changing colour from day to day, 'and in the absence of the box of pattern ribbons which is following you about, it is very difficult to fix on the colour The Queen selected. The last I heard of the pattern ribands was that they were sent to you in the Isle of Wight. Can you return them to me, indicating as near as you can the colour The Queen selected.'[29] Milford Haven obliged, and Dawson then took his life in his hands by writing to Queen Mary on 30 July cautioning against the colour she had chosen. 'If I might humbly suggest', he wrote to the Queen, 'the lighter tints resembling malmaison, seem to me hardly suitable for men to wear. If Your Majesty will return to me the colour selected I will take the necessary steps.'[30] Dawson's advice appears to have been taken, and his letter of 30 July was duly returned by Sir Derek Keppel, with a piece of red ribbon pinned to it, and a brief annotation by Keppel, dated 31 July, to the effect that 'This colour has been approved by Their Majesties.'

Subsequent correspondence raises a doubt about Keppel's statement that the colour had been approved by *Their* Majesties, and suggests at least the possibility that the King had not been shown the ribbon. Queen Mary's intervention in the debate surrounding the ribbon of the Order of the British Empire indicates that, having been defeated in that contest,[31] she might have tried once again to press the cause of her favourite dusky pink as the colour for the ribbon of the Order of the Companions of Honour, before accepting a darker shade. Certainly by mid-September the King was still waiting to be consulted on the colour of the ribbon, as Ponsonby wrote to Dawson. 'The King tells me he has never seen any ribbon for the Order . . . I was under the impression that you had fixed all this up with the King, but His Majesty apparently has not yet had any proposals submitted to him.'[32] The reply that Dawson sent to Ponsonby's challenge was a bare-faced lie. 'I have never been consulted or even shown what is under consideration. The matter has been conducted entirely by Lord Milford Haven and Miss Hallé. I believe the latter was to send me the riband when approved.'[33] Dawson's untruthfulness was revealed when Ponsonby was shown the letter marked with Keppel's annotation.

Ignoring Dawson's desire to extricate himself, there remains a degree of uncertainty about who saw what and when, and more importantly, who had approved what? Did the Queen select the colour of the riband and approve it herself without reference to the King? Did she in passing mention a possible colour to the King and assume his approval? Did she tell Keppel that the King had seen and approved the ribbon? Did Keppel assume that the King had approved the Queen's selection? The questions are impossible to answer, but one thing is certain, and that is that Queen Mary had very firm views in matters of artistic taste.

The King had a right to be consulted and to be the final authority, but his involvement in the preparatory work for the Order led to a delay of more than a year before the insignia finally appeared. The first members of the Order had been named on 24 August 1917, but it was now late September 1917, and they still had no insignia, not even so much as a ribbon. If the King had been kept informed of progress from the beginning, the process of design and manufacture might have moved more swiftly than it did, but now that he had become formally involved, it was impossible to by-pass his ultimate authority; and now his attention was turned not only to the riband but to other aspects of the new Order. On 22 September Ponsonby reported that the King had reiterated his decision that the badge should not be worn from a riband around the neck, but from a riband on the breast. 'His Majesty says that this decoration is now being given to Labour leaders and others who have not hitherto been decorated. Such invariably wear a neck decoration with a long ribbon, somewhat in the manner of the wine butler at the Ritz Hotel. It is for this reason that the King thinks it would be far simpler if the decoration were worn on the breast. In the case of women it makes no difference as they wear it in any case on the shoulder.'[34] In April Ponsonby and Prince Louis had agreed that this was utterly illogical, but neither it seems had thought to tell the King what they had agreed between themselves; now it would have to be done. The CH was the non-titled equivalent of the GBE, and it was difficult to conceive of a decoration worn on the breast as being equivalent to a knight or dame grand cross of the Order of the British Empire. Then there was the attitude of the new members themselves to consider. 'Take for instance the case of General Smuts: he accepted this decoration under the impression that it was equivalent to the Order of Merit, but if he finds it is worn in a place usually associated with the lower classes of other decorations, he may resent having been offered such an apparently low decoration.'[35]

In April 1917 Prince Louis had agreed with Ponsonby that the CH should be a neck decoration, and now in September 1917 Dawson supported Ponsonby. The CH ranked above the KBE and CBE, the badges of which grades were worn from the neck. 'The CBE has been given to labour men and the objection that they would not know how to wear insignia around the neck would apply equally in these cases.'[36] The King's attitude towards 'labour men' and their knowledge of protocol in the wearing of decorations was slightly patronising, and confronted with Ponsonby's logic, he had reversed his decision by 23 October 1917.[37]

Where the riband and badge were to be worn was a comparatively minor issue when compared with the colour of the riband and the design of the badge. The King did not object in principle to the reddish colour, that he was said already to have approved, but he regarded the proposed shade of plain red as too like the ribbon of the French Legion of Honour. When worn with other Order and medal ribbons, the Companion of Honour ribbon would be virtually indistinguishable from the Legion ribbon, and he followed Ponsonby's suggestion that it should be given a gold edge.[38] On 23 October Elinor Hallé was informed, only just in time, of the King's decision.[39] 'I had fortunately only sent the order for the ribbon yesterday' she wrote 'so I will cancel it at once and tell them to wait. I suppose you know that the ribbon will have to be woven specially? I wrote to the firm which serves Garrard, Spinks, and they tell me it will take from three to four weeks to make the hundred yards that will be wanted, and so if the badges are wanted before the end of the year, there is not very much time. The die of the medallion is finished and the enamelling is being done. Will you let me know, when you write about the ribbon, how many will be wanted for men and how many for ladies in the first batch of fifteen or twenty? And are the initials on the case to be OH or CH. I have not ordered the cases yet, as I must wait for a proof of the badge, but I don't think they will take long to make.'[40] Elinor Hallé contacted the ribbon manufacturer, H. V. Caldicott of 8 Wood Street, London, EC2, who came up with a further suggestion. Rather than a red ribbon with gold edges, why not a red ribbon with a central gold stripe which would be much more distinctive. Furthermore, a red ribbon with gold edges would look almost identical to the ribbons of the Russian Order of Saint Anne and the China War Medal. 'Do you know if there is already one with a stripe in the middle?' she wrote to F. S. Osgood at the Lord Chamberlain's Office, 'I expect Caldicott would not have suggested it, if there is, as he seems to make most of the ribbons. Do you think the watered silk or the plain would be best? The watered one is more brilliant at night.'[41]

The problem of the ribbon lingered on. No decision had been reached by 29 October, when she wrote again with worrying news about an ambitious draper. 'Caldicott's manager came to see me today and said he had been asked by Peter Robinson to supply him with 100 yards of the red ribbon, as he supposed, for the Order of Honour. I am afraid this will be a complication. My agreement with Sir Frederick Ponsonby was to supply the badges with their cases and ribbons complete for the sum of £5 each badge. I shall not be able to do this, including it all in one account, if the ribbons are ordered separately through any other firm. And also it might be difficult to keep within the price, as Peter Robinson or any other draper would require his profit and would always have to go to Caldicott, who seem to be the only firm who make this particular sort of ribbon. Will you kindly let me know what I am to do about this, and if, when the design has been decided on, I am to tell Caldicott to proceed with the work. He told me this morning that it will take at least one month to weave the ribbon, but I think he has the plain colour in stock.'[42] She was assured that no decision had been taken, nor would anyone else be asked to furnish the ribbon apart from herself. As soon as the King and Queen had decided on the design, she would be notified, and she would then be free to go to whichever firm she wished.[43]

Some combination of red with gold or yellow now looked likely, but still the details continued to provoke correspondence and debate into November. Dawson was not opposed to the either edging or a central stripe, but he did not care at all for the use of gold on red. 'The addition of gold gives the ribbon such a tawdry appearance that it would not be worth while to proceed further with the idea. I would suggest that any combination of red and *gold* is out of the question. Red and *yellow* might be made to look well.'[44]

On 14 November Ponsonby reported to Dawson that the King had decided to use the style of the silver edging of the ribbon of the Russian Order of St Catherine, although half the width of that used in the Russian Order.[45] The Order of St Catherine was instituted by Tsar Peter I of Russia soon after the conclusion of the campaign he had begun in 1711 against the Ottoman Sultan Ahmed III. The Order was awarded exclusively to women and, despite adopting the name of the obscure female saint, the title was a definite allusion to the tsar's wife, also

Catherine. The ribbon was originally white moiré edged with gold but it was later changed to red moiré with edges of interlaced woven silver thread. An example of the ribbon of that Order had been borrowed from Princess Beatrice, the King's aunt, to illustrate the King's wishes.[46] The unusual style of the edging of the CH ribbon, not found in any other British Order, is clearly modelled on that of the Order of St Catherine. With the other imperial Russian Orders, the Order of St Catherine was swept away in the revolution of 1917, and the ribbon of the Companions of Honour is the only memory of a long forgotten honour.

Elinor Hallé was duly given her instructions to proceed with the ribbon on 16 November,[47] but Mr Caldicott was pessimistic about timing when he was shown the design. 'I am afraid that it will be some time before we can submit samples as the fancy edges are very slow weaving and it is possible that the gold wire is not obtainable just now, but I will write to you again as soon as I get the factory's report.'[48] To speed the process Elinor Hallé herself recommended gold silk instead of gilt wire, which would be 'quicker and much less expensive', and ordered a sample while waiting for the wire.[49] Caldicott was quicker than expected, and Hallé was able to send samples of both on 29 November. To the factor of expense she added the problem of durability, cautioning against the use of gold wire, 'as it is certain to turn black very soon'. The gold border was not as narrow as she had asked, and she preferred the ribbon to be plain rather than watered, which she dismissed as 'gaudy', and expressed her worry about the shortage of time. 'He [Caldicott] says that "the factory will do their best to deliver the first length of 36 yards in about one month from confirmation of the order, the remainder to follow at intervals". The "about" is rather ominous, but I think they really will do their best.'[50]

Dawson, who supported every point that Hallé had made, sent the specimen pieces to the King. The King had decided views on badges and ribands, but he agreed with some of the objections. He approved a plain rather than a watered ribbon, but did not think that the ribands had been made in the correct shade of red. Although early specimen samples of red ribbon with interlaced gold wire were made, the King rejected the use of gold wire, but insisted on gold thread rather than yellow thread. 'The King does not agree with you and Miss Hallé that the yellow silk is preferable to the gold, which may tarnish in London. His Majesty considers that the yellow is too staring, and that the gold would blend better with the correct colour. The King asks whether it would be possible to have a bow made of the correct colour with the gold thread interwoven for him to see, before he finally decides'.[51]

Back to Miss Hallé went the desired specimen and instructions for the work to proceed on yet another specimen. There was however one last insurmountable problem, as she reported: 'I have written to Caldicott to make the ribbon as quickly as possible. I expect he could not get the exact red, as dyes are so difficult now, but I am glad this shade will do.'[52] Mr Caldicott produced yet another and final specimen which Hallé forwarded on 8 January 1918. She again reiterated the concerns that Caldicott had voiced about the use of gold thread. 'He says the one with gold thread is certain to turn black after a time, but I don't suppose they will be much exposed to the air.'[53] The ribbon appears to have been made of a slightly different shade of red, though it is now difficult to determine how much the colour had altered. In any case the King now signified his approval. 'The King approves of the colour of the ribbon as shown in this pattern. This is not the colour first decided upon, of which I gave you a piece of ribbon when I saw you, but His Majesty prefers it to the original selection.'[54] The colour eventually settled on is described in the Statutes as 'carmine', a crimson pigment of cochineal, and is virtually the same shade of red as the ribbon of the Legion of Honour. The word is derived from the French or Spanish *carmin*, itself derived from the medieval Latin cremesinus, variations of which, in *kermesimus* and *carmeminus*, gave rise to 'crimson' and 'carmine'.

The insignia had still not appeared by the early days of February 1918. Eight months had now passed since the creation of the Order, and occasional apologies had to be made. Viscount Chetwynd CH, was to be given a presentation portrait of himself by his munitions workers at Chilwell. The portrait would depict Chetwynd in his peer's robes, and they wanted the CH insignia to be included. 'Would you be so kind', wrote the King's assistant private secretary to Dawson, 'as to let me know if you could help what seems to be a reasonable request by lending the artist the insignia of a Companion of Honour.'[55] Dawson could only admit that the insignia was not yet in existence, but he hoped that it would be ready by the end of the month, when he would be delighted to help. If there was any immediate necessity, he had a rough coloured plaster cast of the badge, which the artist, Mr George Hall Neale, could see if he cared to call at the Central Chancery.[56] The reply satisfied Wigram, but such excuses could not continue indefinitely.

On 28 February, the King himself expressed a wish to know when the insignia would be ready, and asked to see a specimen.[57] Dawson then tried to distance himself from the affair. 'The insignia . . . is in the hands of Lord Milford Haven and Miss Hallé, who he instructed to make it. I hear *privately* from Mr Pinches, who is manufacturing the insignia for Miss Hallé, that he is sending her ten of the badges on Saturday next . . . Shall I ask her to send you a badge for His Majesty's inspection as soon as she receives them, or, as I did not order the insignia, perhaps you would like to write to her yourself?'[58] Elinor Hallé despatched a badge for the King to see on 5 March. She had hoped that the first twenty would all have been finished before this, but Pinches reported that they had had 'unexpected difficulties' with the gilding.[59]

If there had been any hope on any side that the King would simply approve the specimen, it was swiftly disappointed. King George V took a deep interest in the appearance of honours, and had an obsessive preference for small insignia. A completed badge was shown to him and, no doubt to the dismay of all concerned, he immediately rejected it. The specimen badge measured $3\frac{3}{8}$ inches by $1\frac{3}{4}$ inches. 'The King thinks that the badge of the Companions of Honour is much too big, and is of the opinion that even if it takes several months to produce a new badge, it is worth while having it reduced. I have shown His Majesty specimens of other Orders, but he still thinks it must be altered. If this badge was worn only by men, it might perhaps do, but the King is convinced that women will dislike wearing such an unwieldy decoration, as it is far larger than anything at present worn by a woman. In fact the King thinks that with well developed ladies it will stick out at right angles. I have explained to His Majesty that this may necessitate 6 or 8 months more work, but he thinks that even so it is worth while getting a better sized badge made. The King does not like the wreath at the bottom of the badge. This may have looked well in a drawing, but does not come out well in enamel and gold.'[60] The badge of the Secretary of the Order of the Garter would do well as a guide to size, but if anything the badge of the Order of the Companions of

Honour should be even smaller. 'The King is sure that she will see that the wreath at the base of the present badge is out of place. Of course it must not be anything in the nature of a Garter, but perhaps some sort of device could be added at the base of the outside scroll.'[61] So Miss Hallé and Mr Pinches were called in for a meeting at the central chancery[62] and the design effectively went back to the drawing board and the factory for another five months.

A specimen reduced size badge, measuring 2¾ inches by 1½ inches, was submitted to the King in August 1918, but by this time Elinor Hallé had developed further thoughts of her own. The badge was now an oblong silver gilt tablet within an oval azure frame bearing the motto, but although the wreath at the bottom was now omitted, she now proposed to fill in the spaces between the tablet and the frame with decorative scroll work. 'Time is of importance', wrote Dawson, 'and there may be other alterations to make, which Pinches could do at the same time he adds the scroll work, if the addition is required.'[63] There was an element of irony in the remark about time because of the increasing number of Companions of Honour. Seventeen founder members had been named in August 1917, to which had been added a further three in January 1918, one in February 1918 and two more in June 1918. There were now twenty-three Companions of Honour with postnominal letters but still with no badge or ribbon.

Dawson argued against the suggestion of scroll work around the central tablet, thinking it would detract from the lightness of the design, nor had it been found possible 'to pierce the design of the horse and the tree.'[64] The King however approved of the scroll work, saying that the basic design of an oblong tablet in an oval frame was 'not pretty', and in another note of irony, 'His Majesty hopes you will tell Miss Hallé to get on with this as soon as possible',[65] as though the continued delays were her fault. She did her best, and the amended design was sent to Ponsonby on 7 September 1918. One last fault did unfortunately appear. 'By an error in workmanship the bottom right hand end of the Motto has been brought too far round, but this would be rectified.'[66] The design was approved by the King with the added hope that manufacture would now begin, 'so that the Companion of Honour badges may be available for bestowal at as early a date as possible.'[67]

An order was placed on 11 September 1918, and Elinor Hallé reported to Dawson that Pinches had promised them by 15 November. 'It would be best to give a margin of a day or two, but I really think we begin to see day-light at last.'[68] The margin proved to be a little too hopeful, but twenty-three completed badges, nineteen for men and four for ladies, were delivered to the central chancery on 25 November 1918,[69] and the sixteen months' story of design was concluded at last. A postscript to the question of size can be mentioned here. In March 1918, King George V had criticised the dimensions of Hallé's design and ordered a reduction to a smaller size, but these things are matters of personal taste. Receiving her CH in 1948, the novelist Vita Sackville-West complained: 'It seems so enormous.'[70]

Running parallel to the matter of design was the question of cost. In July 1917, Miss Hallé had estimated the cost of the badges at £5 each, but the long delay, caused by the number of alterations required by the King, inevitably caused the figure to rise by November 1918. In May 1918 she tentatively asked whether she could have £150 or £200 on account. 'I have had to pay for the cases and the ribbon and now Pinches is asking for £150 for work done up to the present.'[71] Her request for '£150 or £200' and the absence of any supporting invoices or other documentation, was sufficiently vague for the lord chamberlain's office to give careful consideration to what exactly she was due. There could be no question of parting with any money without precise accounting. 'I don't know how many badges of the discarded design Miss Hallé produced, but I believe not more than 20, therefore she has only £100 due to her. As her design was passed, of course she must be paid, but doubtless it has cost far more than she anticipated. The initial arrangements were wrong, as she could not possibly turn out a respectable looking badge at £5.'[72] Ponsonby was inclined to be generous. 'I presume . . . that Miss Hallé was to receive no remuneration for her design, but that she was to arrange with Pinches to have a certain percentage on the profits of each badge. I think that clearly she should be paid for the badges that were made and as no doubt she is a poor woman, there would be no objection to advancing her another £100, making £200 in all, for the badges Pinches are now making.'[73] She was asked to provide a detailed account, and returned a bill from Pinches for £150 showing that work on the old design was well advanced by the time of the intervention of King George V. One hundred badges had been ordered: twenty had been enamelled and finished and eighty had been partly finished; all had to be scrapped.[74] The eighty partly finished badges were probably melted down for the metal to be reused, but at least some of the twenty completed prototype badges have survived; there is one in official custody and others have appeared for sale from time to time.

Dawson wrote to Sir Thomas Heath, permanent secretary of the treasury, asking for approval of the sum of £150, on the ground that Elinor Hallé was not a rich woman and that it was not her fault that the badges she had made did not meet with the King's approval.[75] Given that they were at least in part at fault, Ponsonby and Dawson were instinctively inclined to be kind to her and to help her out of any financial difficulties, but kindness and spontaneous generosity were not the principal hallmarks of the treasury, and Heath returned a very searching letter that must have caused Dawson some embarrassment. 'Could you say how much of the £200 represents *wasted* expenditure (e.g. on material which can't be used again) and how much is for work which has been done on the new badges or can be utilised for them? What will be the total cost which we shall be asked to pay altogether for the badges old and new, and how many of the new ones will there be. In your original letter of 27th July 1917 you said that "a very small number will be required, the statutory limit being 50". But you seem to have ordered 100. Is not this rather a large extra provision for casualties?'[76] Dawson's reply was beyond belief. 'I did not order 100 of the Order badges . . . but I will see that no more than 50 of the new style are ordered, when the order is given . . . I am not responsible for the muddle which I must confess has been made . . . All this arises because the matter was referred to and dealt with by irresponsible people, and I was only called in when the details were all settled.'[77] At the stroke of a pen, the Marquess of Milford Haven, Sir Frederick Ponsonby and Elinor Hallé were labelled 'irresponsible'.

If anyone was irresponsible it was Dawson, for his very refusal to take responsibility, and a continuous juvenile desire to exonerate himself. Elinor Hallé was beyond reproach. She produced evidence, in the shape of letters from Milford Haven and Ponsonby to prove the fact, and the content of those letters only confirmed her innocent role. If Milford Haven and Ponsonby were guilty of anything, their offence was enthusiasm not irresponsibility. They delighted in her design and they wanted to proceed to manufacture as quickly as possible. Milford

Haven's letter was dated 14 July 1917. 'I am at last able to tell you', he wrote to Miss Hallé, 'that the King has approved of the beautiful design I return herewith.'[78] There is no reason to doubt the implication that the King was shown at least a drawing of the design for the new badge, but having given it his approval, no one then seems to have thought that he should also see a made-up specimen badge before production started.

The treasury eventually agreed to pay the sum of £192 4s 9d. The sum of £150 was written off in payment to Pinches for materials used in the discarded badges; £12 4s 9d went to Caldicott for 75 yards of ribbon, which would be reusable; £30 to the firm of Wootton for 100 cases which could be used with only slight alteration.[79] Dawson requested the accounts of the three firms from Miss Hallé, and in return received another bill for £339 4s 9d for making the new approved insignia: £231 5s 0d for Pinches, for cutting dies and tools for the new design (£50) and for supplying the new badges in silver gilt and enamel at £3 12s 6d each. £12 4s 9d went to Caldicott for the ribbon, and £18 5s to Wootton to make 50 cases. She also submitted her own bill for £75 'for designs and superintending and carrying out of work'. Heath's eagle eye immediately vetoed the expenditure for ribbon and cases. 'I am afraid we are in danger of getting into some muddle or overlap with the former account.'[80] There was nothing that Dawson could do except to exonerate himself once again. 'I must admit that the financial arrangements with regard to this Order are distinctly unbusinesslike, but we are dealing with a lady who, whatever her artistic merits may be, has the proverbial vagueness of her sex with regard to accounts.'[81]

Dawson's comment, admittedly the product of an age that knew nothing of political correctness, was nevertheless unworthy. Whatever her lack of financial acumen, Elinor Hallé produced a design, to her enduring credit, that is still delightfully charming. Her armoured and mounted knight with uplifted lance and fluttering pennant, 'in action faithful and in honour clear', guarding a shield, ablaze with the Royal Arms, set safely in the branches of an English oak tree, evokes the more romantic aspects of a departed age of chivalry and honour that has gone for ever.

Changes since 1918

Since the drafting of the statutes in 1918, there has been very little change to the insignia of the Order. As with the insignia of its companion honour – The Order of Merit – the badge of the Order of the Companions of Honour may not be worn in miniature. No provision for a miniature was ever made in the statutes, and as they were mostly copied from the statutes of the Order of Merit where there is no mention of a miniature, the Companions were obliged to follow the practice of their senior brethren. In 1927, Stanley Bruce, prime minister of Australia, enquired in a four-word telegram: 'Has Companion Honor Miniature.'[82] The reply was a firm 'no'.

With the death of King George V in January 1936 came the traditional debate to consider what changes should be made to the insignia of the Orders and Medals of the nation. Although names and substantial design tend to remain unchanged, attention is focused on whether royal cyphers and the royal effigies should be changed to represent the new reign. The practice was well established. The insignia of the Order of the Bath and the Order of St Michael and St George do not contain a royal cypher or the royal effigy and no alteration was required on a change of reign. The insignia of the now dormant Orders of the Star of India and the Indian Empire had always incorporated the effigy of Queen Victoria and no alteration was made on the commencement of a new reign. The Royal Victorian Order had always been specially identified with Queen Victoria, and the insignia of all classes incorporate the monogram 'V. R. I.' whatever the reign. Among the medals, the now defunct Albert Medal incorporated the monogram composed of the letters 'V' and 'A', and that remained unaltered from one reign to the next. The similarly defunct Edward Medal bore the cypher of the reigning sovereign as did the Royal Victorian Medal, and these were both changed. The medal of the Imperial Service Order bore the effigy of King George V and that was also changed. By 1936 it had become the custom to alter the effigy of practically all medals both civil and military on a change of reign.

Of particular interest in 1936 were the two new honours that had been instituted since the last change of reign in 1910 – The Order of the British Empire and the Order of the Companions of Honour – and the most radical of the 1936 changes was in the appearance of the insignia of the Order of the British Empire, which was altered almost beyond recognition.[83] The Order of the Companions of Honour followed the practice of the Order of Merit and the Imperial Service Order, and the cypher on the reverse of the badge was changed;[84] it changed again with the accession of Queen Elizabeth II in 1953.

At the time of her accession, the Queen indicated, on the advice of Garter King of Arms, that she wished the traditional 'imperial' or 'Tudor' crown that surmounted the royal cypher, effigy and insignia, to be changed to the St Edward Crown, representing that item of the regalia with which she would be crowned. The 'imperial' or 'Tudor' crown, depicted on medals, coins, royal cyphers, regimental colours, representations of the royal arms etc., was not a reproduction of any actual crown, but a standardized representation of the symbol of sovereignty. At his accession in 1901 King Edward VII, finding various representations of this symbol in use, standardized the representation for all purposes in the style of the 'imperial' or 'Tudor' crown, and directed that no other form should be used, whether in the United Kingdom, India or the colonies. Those directions remained in force throughout succeeding reigns until the accession of Queen Elizabeth II.[85]

The change of design after 1953 involved a considerable number of changes, from insignia to buttons, and to avoid unnecessary expense, it was done over many years as old stock was used up, and inevitably some items slipped through the net. CH insignia, bearing a representation of the Tudor crown, was still being used in 1988. It had not been amended although the Central Chancery had ordered several batches of insignia since 1952 when the Queen made her wishes known. A degree of embarrassment was averted by the Queen's decision that the existing stocks should be used up and the St Edward Crown then be substituted for the Tudor crown, providing the cost was not large. The photograph of the badge used in the statutes, continued to show a badge with the Tudor crown.[86]

Very few changes were made to the statutes of the Order after 1919. An additional statute of 7 March 1935 provided for the appointment of additional members at the time of the silver jubilee of King George V. A similar additional statute was made on 17 April 1937 to provide for additional appointments to commemorate the coronation of King George VI. The statute of 18 August 1943 increased the statutory complement from 50 to 65. Another statute of 30 May 1953 provided for additional appointments to commemorate the coronation of Queen

Elizabeth II. Another statute, of 7 November 1969, provided for varying sources of submission of names to the sovereign from Commonwealth countries. The last additional statute provided for appointments to be made at the time of the silver jubilee of Queen Elizabeth II in 1977.

By 1988, the statutes of the Order were substantially more than seventy years old, and new members of the Order continued to be given reprints of the 1919 version with the six additional statutes inserted at the end. It was time to consolidate the statutes, and also to revisit the 1918 drafting of Farnham Burke. As a one-class Order, Burke seems to have based his draft statutes for the Order of the Companions of Honour on the statutes of the Order of Merit, with only the most essential changes. Seventy years later, did his work still hold good, or had the passing of time introduced an element of redundancy?

The statutes were examined in detail between August and October 1988 and although Burke's work was basically sound, there were areas of obsolescence and inaccuracy. The 1919 statutes had provided for a sovereign's badge, 'of the same material and fashion as are hereinafter appointed for the members of the Order, save only with those alterations which distinguish our royal dignity'. Had a sovereign's badge ever been made? A search of the strong rooms of the central chancery failed to unearth a sovereign's badge, so the answer was 'no'. Not at any time in its history had the members of the Order gathered as a corporate entity in the presence of the sovereign; the only occasion on which a sovereign's badge might have been appropriately worn. Should a sovereign's badge be manufactured? Although there was none in existence, there was nothing to stop the sovereign having one designed in accordance with the wording of the 1919 statutes, and the matter was referred to the Queen. The answer was again 'no'. The Queen decided to follow the pattern of the Order of Merit and if, as sovereign of the Order, she ever needed to wear its insignia, she would wear the badge as worn by ladies of the Order,[87] and appropriate wording was devised for the new statute.

The vague wording describing the nonexistent sovereign's badge was surpassed by the precise description of the nonexistent badge of the secretary and registrar, and here Burke's lack of care was revealed for all to see. The 1919 statutes had prescribed 'a like badge to that appointed for members of the Order, with the addition of two silver pens saltirewise between the angles of the cross.' The description was clear; but nowhere on the badge of members was there a cross of any description. The only explanation for the text is that Burke had hastily and thoughtlessly copied the wording of the relevant statute of the Order of Merit, describing the badge of the secretary and registrar of that Order: 'a like badge to that appointed for members of the Order, with the addition of two silver pens, saltirewise between the cross.' The cross forms the principal element in the design of the badge of the Order of Merit.

As with 'the sovereign's badge', a search failed to disclose the existence of a badge for the secretary and registrar of the Order of the Companions of Honour, and almost certainly none was made at the foundation of the Order. Badges for fifty members were more important than a badge for one officer, and as it was of so little consequence, it never became an issue that needed to be addressed. Now that it had been raised, what was to be done? It would be wrong for the secretary and registrar to wear the badge as worn by members of the Order. If he was to have a badge it would have to be specially made. Perhaps the shape would be the same, but in place of *In action faithful and in honour clear* the words *The Order of*

Companions of Honour might be appropriate? The central cameo could be replaced by a book with two silver pens saltirewise across the book, reflecting the dual role of secretary and registrar? The question was referred to the Queen for decision,[88] but the answer was a predictable 'not necessary.'[89] After seventy years, was there need or any other justification to provide such a badge? The Order was a dispersed community with no focal point or periodic gatherings, at which an identifiably labelled secretary and registrar would be required to attend his members.

The solitary officer of the Order of the Companions of Honour has had very little more than administrative duties in connection with servicing of the members. The 1919 statutes provided that 'on the day of investiture the person to be invested shall be introduced into the presence of the Sovereign by the Officer of the Order in attendance bearing the proper Insignia of the Order, when the Sovereign shall proceed to invest him with the Ensigns of the said Order with the Riband and Badge.' This statute was again a copy by Farnham Burke of the relevant statute of the Order of Merit, and has been honoured more in the breach than in the observance. Twenty Companions of Honour were summoned to an investiture by King George V at Buckingham Palace on 17 December 1918. For the first and last time, the court circular recorded the occasion as 'An investiture of the Order of the Companions of Honour and of the Most Excellent Order of the British Empire.' From 1918 until 1941 recipients resident in the United Kingdom were usually invested with their badge at general investitures. Exceptions were made in the case of those who lived abroad or who were too frail or too ill to attend an investiture. Private investitures were allowed on two occasions: for Dick Sheppard in 1927 and Nancy Astor in 1937.

In 1941 King George VI privately invested A. V. Alexander, first lord of the admiralty, setting a practice (residence and health permitting) which continued without interruption until 1992. Members of the Order of the Companions of Honour were given the same status and privilege as members of the Order of Merit, by being accorded the privilege of a private investiture by the sovereign. Private investitures were abandoned from June 1992 to March 1994 when eight CHs were summoned to general investitures. From July 1994 to October 1997 private investitures were resumed for the thirteen CHs invested in those years. Christopher Patten and Peter Brook attended public investitures in 1998, as did Chad Varah in 2000 and Sir Colin Davis in 2002.

Although a rare privilege, a private investiture does have the disadvantage of being 'private'. The recipient is invested with the badge and then spends a short time in conversation with the sovereign, no others being present. Some recipients have understandably opted for public investitures, allowing them to bring guests.

By the statutes, the Secretary and Registrar is charged with the custody of the seal of the Order, 'which he shall affix, or cause to be affixed, to all Statutes and other documents or instruments connected therewith.' The design of the seal had been approved by February 1918.[90] The statutes describe it: 'Upon a white field, a representation of the Badge of the Order, as hereinafter described, impaled with Our Royal Arms, with this circumscription *The Seal of the Order of the Companions of Honour.*'

CHAPTER EIGHTEEN

Gallery of conspicuous service

A RETROSPECT OF EIGHTY-FIVE YEARS

> *Alice glanced nervously along the table, as she walked up the large hall, and noticed that there were about fifty guests, of all kinds: some were animals, some birds, and there were even a few flowers among them. 'I'm glad they've come without waiting to be asked,' she thought: I should never have known who were the right people to invite.'*
>
> 'Queen Alice', *Through the looking-glass*, Lewis Carroll

Every honour has 'evolved' since its foundation and the Order of the Companions of Honour is no exception, although its evolutionary process has been more subtle than most. In outward appearance it remains much as it was at its foundation in 1917: a single class honour for 'conspicuous service of national importance'. What has changed is the use to which the Order has been put. The hurried assembly of war service names in 1917 was succeeded in later years by a more measured and thoughtful selection that reflected the interests and concerns of the passing ages. 'Conspicuous service of national importance' had a very definite meaning in 1917. It provided a broad measurement and a high threshold to recognise an eminent level of effort and endeavour in the task of winning a long and protracted war against the central powers, a war that had lasted for nearly three years and was far from being won. Elinor Hallé's design for the badge of the Order is a romantically medievalised exemplification of national service – an armed and armoured knight 'in action faithful and in honour clear', seated on horseback beneath an English oak, ready to ride to the defence of the realm.

Eighty-five years have passed since the rapid gathering of the names of the original members, and in that time the CH has stabilised, developed, matured and increased in stature. From the beginning it was understood (although unwritten) that the Order was partly intended to satisfy a perceived contemporary need for a high honour that carried no title. In that respect, it bore a passing resemblance to the Order of Merit, though the similarity was superficial. Although they were both one-class honours, the CH and the OM were really very different from each other in 1917 and for some twenty years afterwards. The Order of Merit honoured high thought in theory and strategy; the CH honoured the practical application of those thoughts and strategies. The early Companions of Honour included Labour backbench members of parliament and general secretaries of trades unions; none of whom were traditional candidates for the OM. The absence of an accompanying title for members of the CH was a deliberate policy to make the Order acceptable to the new and increasingly powerful socialist and labour movement; the OM was an honour well above and beyond a title. The sovereign conferred the OM; the disposal of the CH rested with the prime minister. From 1917 to 1920 membership of the CH was exclusive to those civilians who played a significant role in the war effort. (Although they held high military rank neither Jan Smuts nor Alfred

Keogh received the CH for their fighting abilities.) Military and naval figures at one time accounted for half the membership of the Order of Merit, and a military division of the Order of the British Empire was created in 1918. The CH has never had a military division, nor has it possessed a distinctive badge for military members, as with the OM. The CH has remained a civil honour, conceived for those who 'kept the home fires burning' and not for those engaged in defending the nation by force of arms. The only proven examples of conferment specifically for military service were those of the Canadian generals Henry Crerar (1945) and Andrew McNaughton (1946). They were incongruous appointments in what was a fully civil and civilian Order, but in each case the CH usefully accommodated the scruples of a Canadian government, instinctively hostile to the conferral of titular honours on its citizens. No artists, writers, musicians or scientists appeared in the Order until 1921, and not for another generation or so did the CH begin to resemble the OM, by including within its ranks the high levels of learning previously recognised principally by the OM.

Recognition of war services had finished by 1921, and a series of peacetime categories then began to emerge slowly. Before the inauguration of the welfare state, voluntary social and humanitarian work ranked highly in public esteem and the exponents of peace and social work dominated the Order in the 1920s and 1930s. A line of clergy began with John Clifford in 1921, and thereafter the churches received a generous allocation of places in the 1920s and 1930s. Thirteen clergy of one kind or another were appointed in the sixteen years from 1921 to 1937. They were a mixed group, predominantly from the free churches and usually with a strong bias toward ecumenism and social work, both of which went down well in the inter-war years. The frequency of clergy appointments slowed down and tailed off after the 1939–45 war. The names of Derek Worlock (1995) and Chad Varah (1999) were fleeting and atypical postscripts to a category long thought to have become extinct.

Women featured very prominently in the 1930s. Four had been included among the first appointments to the Order: the Marchioness of Lansdowne (1917), Elizabeth Haldane (1917), May Tennant (1917) and Violet Markham (1917), all for their war services. The work of women in the 1914–18 war had enhanced their role in society and added impetus to their campaign for the right to vote. Women were given the right to vote in 1918 (above the age of thirty) and in 1928 (above the age of twenty-one). Lilian Baylis (1929) was the first of a new influx of prominent women. She was followed by Florence Barrett (1929), Maude Royden (1930), Gertrude Tuckwell (1930), Margaret McMillan (1930), Helena Swanwick (1931), Jane Walker (1931), Annie Horniman (1933), Janet Trevelyan (1936), Nancy Astor (1937), Gwendoline Davies (1937), Margaret Bondfield (1948), Vita Sackville-West (1948), Edith Summerskill (1966), Megan Lloyd George (1966), Sybil Thorndike (1970), Irene Ward (1973), Angela Limerick (1974), Barbara Wootton (1977), Ninette de Valois (1981), Elisabeth Frink (1992), Elsie Widdowson (1993), Janet Baker (1993), Bridget Riley (1998) and Doris Lessing (1999). The greatest concentration occurred in the years before the 1939–45 war with eleven women made CH between 1929 and 1937. Only fourteen were added to the Order in the half century between 1948 and 1999. No emphasis should be placed on these facts, nor on this compiled list of women members of the Order. In each case the honour was for personal achievement irrespective of gender, and not because the candidate was a woman, although exceptions could be made in the cases of Nancy Astor, Edith Summerskill, Megan Lloyd George and Irene Ward, each of whom was a feminine force in the then masculine stronghold of the house of commons.

The increasing sense of equal rights for women after 1929 prompted a debate in 1932–33 on the institution of a new and wider honour for women, that would provide a title to rank alongside knight bachelor for men.[1] The plan was abortive, but it progressed far enough for prime minister Ramsay MacDonald to direct that three prominent women should be consulted.[2] Among them was Violet Markham CH who was dismissive of this proposal to create the title of 'Lady of Grace'. 'The more I think, the more doubtful I become. Some further recognition of women's work would I am sure be appreciated, but this effort to put the women's honours on an equality with those of the men won't I fear be satisfactory. You *can't* force men & *women* into the same mould, & the abstract feminism that aspires to do so, only ends in absurdity. The overwhelming majority of women will continue in the future as in the past to be supported by their husbands & take their status from their husbands. And it seems to me more & more on reflection that Mr Josiah and Lady Buggins fit nowhere into our social framework. For if Josiah can turn Mary Buggins into a Lady why shouldn't Mary turn Josiah into a Sir? I am afraid an equivalent knighthood for ladies will involve some rather ludicrous situations & nothing kills like ridicule. But if, without getting mixed up with the knighthood difficulties, you could devise something on the lines of a Legion of Honour for women, then you would have the advantages without the drawbacks of the present suggestion. I take it that you want to recognise good *work* without pandering to the social snobbery involved in Lady Buggins walking into the room ahead of Mrs Smith. I have racked my brains for a suggestion as to names. Why not call them "Ladies of the Rose" (the rose has the only possible symbolism on which I can hit – it is the emblem of England & has *many* beautiful suggestions in literature from Dante onwards), and give them a little rose to wear? They would have the prestige of the title without any of the *social* anomalies bound up with the present proposal.'[3] Markham's criticism was probably one factor among several that contributed to the abandonment of the concept before the end of 1933. Considered in isolation, the 'Lady of Grace' plan is only one of numerous proposals for new honours that have surfaced down the years, although it seems to have got further than some. However, set in the context of its time, it can be seen as an aspect of the movement for women's rights and a tangential development to the number of women appointed to the CH in the early 1930s.

In 1952 Winston Churchill, who was devoted to the royal family, suggested that the CH should be given to Princess Marina, Duchess of Kent at the conclusion of her successful tour of the far east in that year. The proposal was unprecedented and was rejected. Members of the royal family were not specially decorated by the sovereign for individual tours, which were regarded as part of the job and all in a day's work, and no member of the royal family has ever been given the CH.

The first representatives of the world of writing emerged with popular novelists: Henry Newbolt (1922), whose works were probably known by every public schoolboy in the country; Hall Caine (1922), whose stories were consistently set against Manx scenery, yet who was phenomenally popular in his time; and John Buchan (1932), forever remembered for *The thirty-nine steps*. Their successors, Laurence Binyon (1932), Thomas Page (1934) and John Dover Wilson (1936) were more scholars than writers, and in the 1930s and 1940s long-serving newspaper editors were preferred to serious writers. The line of writers resumed with Elfed Lewis (1948) and Vita Sackville-West (1948), but by the end of the twentieth century, the popular adventures of Newbolt, Caine and Buchan had given way to the austere gloom of the poems of C. H. Sisson (1993) and the grimmer social realities of the novels of Doris Lessing (1999) and the plays of Harold Pinter (2002)

A gap of fifteen years followed the composer Frederick Delius (1929) before the appointment of Henry Wood (1944) but the world of music did not begin to be routinely represented in the Order until Benjamin Britten (1953). By the end of the twentieth century, music had moved from the lyrical romanticism of Delius to the atonal compositions of Harrison Birtwistle (2000).

In the world of the arts, Viscount Dillon (1921) was hardly typical and the line properly begins with the sculptor Henry Moore (1955). The artist Companions of Honour have generally been those who have pioneered and stretched the boundaries of art beyond the photographic confectionery portraiture much loved by earlier generations. Bridget Riley (1998) of 'Op Art' and David Hockney (1997) and Richard Hamilton (1999) of 'Pop Art' are the latest examples.

From the world of the stage came the redoubtable and determined Lilian Baylis (1929), grandmother of the National Theatre, the English National Opera and the Royal Ballet, and the equally redoubtable and determined Annie Horniman (1933) who pioneered the modern theatre repertory movement. As a stage and scenery designer and historian of theatre, Gordon Craig (1956) and Peter Brook (1998) were backstage theoreticians who extended the art of the theatre into new concepts and fields. From the world of ballet came other 'founding' figures – Frederick Ashton (1970) and Ninette de Valois (1981). Each of the select group of distinguished actors – Sybil Thorndike (1970), John Gielgud (1977), Alec Guinness (1994) and Paul Scofield (2000) – had accumulated several decades of service to their profession.

The Welsh philosopher Henry Jones (1922) was given the CH on his deathbed, and received it as much for being Welsh as for his love of wisdom. It was the historian George Peabody Gooch (1939) who inaugurated a line of historians, philosophers, archaeologists and economists who examined and analysed human life and living in the past and the present. Most of them have been pioneeringly radical theorists, very well known in their own disciplines but rarely beyond. Arthur Bryant (1967) and Mortimer Wheeler (1967) were well known and popular practitioners.

Science and medicine – a mysterious world enveloped by a protective and secretive jargon not easily understood by those outside – began with John Scott Haldane (1928), Florence Barrett (1929) and Jane Walker (1931). Their work was largely domestic and humanitarian. The line of scientists with international reputations begins properly with the cloud chamber of Charles Wilson (1937), first of a series of Nobel prize winners to receive the CH.

Trades unionists and philanthropic businessmen have been few and scattered thinly throughout the history of the Order. Sir John Ellerman (1921) was the first postwar businessman (though there could well have been a war service element in considering him for the CH), and the controversial Joseph Havelock Wilson (1922) was the first postwar trade unionist. Although trades unionists featured prominently in the early war service lists, the trade union movement has declined in recent decades and they have long since ceased to be natural candidates for the

CH. Lawyers flourished for a short while in the 1960s and 1970s, but the legal profession has not featured in the Order for many years.

From overseas, the Commonwealth was once widely represented by numerous prime ministers from Australia and New Zealand, but the regular Commonwealth use of the Order has ceased. In the last three decades of the twentieth century the Commonwealth realms began to establish their own systems of honours and the CH ceased to be a traditional adornment for Commonwealth prime ministers.

Politicians – the most numerous category – started to gather speed in the 1940s. There were earlier isolated examples: Winston Churchill (1922), John Davidson (1923), Hugh Pollock (1936) and Nancy Astor (1937), and the category rapidly developed from Churchill's use of the CH (beginning in 1941) to recognise the services of the sometimes shadowy figures who were ministers in the wartime coalition government. The Order had acquired high prestige by 1939, and although Churchill used it to recognise 'war service', the numbers were few compared with 1917–21 and there is no record of any proposal to enlarge the Order (other than the provision of an empire quota in 1943) to allow 'additional' appointments for war service. By the beginning of the 1939–45 war the status of the CH had reached too high a level for it to be enlarged on the grounds of expediency. It was unfortunate that Churchill should have chosen A. V. Alexander – the weakest of his cabinet ministers – to be the first of them to receive the CH. But the world of politics is unlike the worlds of literature or science or art or music or humanitarian endeavour, where more exacting standards have been applied. A meteoric rise in the world of politics is no guarantee of lifelong eminence, and an abrupt ending to a political career is a routine occurrence, whether through personal scandal, government rating in opinion polls (e.g. the 'night of the long knives') or simply prime ministerial whim. The ignominious ending of a ministerial career through personal scandal would hardly lead to the conferral of the CH, but different prime ministers have used the CH for different 'political' reasons at different times: sometimes as a public expression of confidence; sometimes as a sincere 'thank you' for old friends and for work well done; sometimes as consolation for a terminated career; sometimes as a way to assuage or expunge feelings of personal guilt. Politicians should best be seen as a subgroup within the Order, where different rules apply because their profession works differently. But whatever view might be taken about the number of politicians who have received the CH, the status of the Order remains undiminished. If anything its reputation has steadily risen with the passing years.

As the CH gradually broadened its scope to include a wider range of disciplines, and as its status rose, another new role for the Order emerged in the late 1940s; that of a nursery school or breeding ground for the Order of Merit. It was only one of a number of pools from which to select recruits for the smaller Order, but the CH had been tried and tested and the increasingly high standard of its recipients made them potential recruits for the OM after the elapse of a suitable period of time. The first of the dual members was Winston Churchill who was made a CH in 1922 and appointed to the OM in 1946. With the 1939–45 war successfully concluded, King George VI rightly believed that Churchill, although out of power, deserved recognition for the exhausting efforts he had made in leading the nation to victory in the face of overwhelming odds. Churchill already had the CH and had also given it to eight of his ministerial colleagues during his premiership: A. V. Alexander (1941), Lord Woolton (1942), Lord Leathers (1943), Lord Snell

(1943), Lord Swinton (1943), Robert Hudson (1944), Lord Selborne (1945) and Clement Attlee (1945). Set in that context Churchill was relegated to the status of just one political CH among several, and he was due for some further mark of distinction. He refused the Order of the Garter in 1944 and had no desire to go to the house of lords, and no other honour was appropriate for one who had done so much for his country. His appointment to the Order of Merit in 1946 began a trend, and nineteen Companions of Honour have been made members of the Order of Merit since that date.

	CH	*OM*
Jan Christian Smuts	1917	1947
Winston Churchill	1922	1946
George Peabody Gooch	1939	1963
Clement Attlee	1945	1951
Walter de la Mare	1948	1953
E. M. Forster	1953	1969
Benjamin Britten	1953	1965
Henry Moore	1955	1963
Kenneth Clark	1959	1976
Patrick Blackett	1965	1967
Graham Greene	1966	1986
Frederick Ashton	1970	1977
Peter Medawar	1972	1981
Max Perutz	1975	1988
John Gielgud	1977	1996
Michael Tippett	1979	1983
Frederick Sanger	1981	1986
Ninette de Valois	1981	1992
Lucien Freud	1983	1993

The CH is a high and rare honour and – on the basis that a knighthood has already been conferred or declined – the OM remains the only possibility for promotion.

One aspect of the CH has not been satisfactorily addressed, and that is the way and the extent to which it is used as an honour for those who do not desire a title. In its first application the CH was designed to bring into the honours system at a high level those whose ideology was uncomfortable with titular honours. However, the CH has not been given exclusively to those who refuse titles, and of the more than three hundred appointments to the Order since 1917, roughly half have also been given an honour conferring a title, whether a knighthood or peerage. This gives the CH a composite appearance and membership. The first group consists of those for whom the CH is a high and crowning honour that follows a knighthood for a man (or the equivalent title of dame for a woman). In the second group are those (mostly but not entirely politicians) for whom the CH has been an interim honour until a higher honour, usually a peerage is in prospect. (It remains to be seen whether the reforms to the house of lords will end that practice.) In the third group are those for whom the CH is the high and sometimes the only honour for those who would not accept any title.

In the first and second cases the CH is additional to a title. The third case raises the question of the level of titular honour at which the CH is an alternative. There are many honours that confer titles – from knight bachelor to peer. In the ranking of honours the CH comes immediately after the GBE (knights and dames grand cross of the Order of the British Empire) and immediately before knights and dames commander of the Order of the Bath (KCB and DCB). The Order of the British Empire gave birth to the Order of the Companions of Honour and originally the CH was the untitled equivalent of a GBE and historically its status is therefore high. The conferral of the CH on those who have refused the grade of knight bachelor arguably lowers the high status of the CH. It rightly includes those to whom titles are objectionable, but there is always a risk that it can be too freely given to people who refuse any titular honour from the lowest to the highest. Whether or not that is a valid concern depends on which of two arguments is adopted. The first would emphasise the continuing relevance of the founding principles of the Order. On that basis should not eminent candidates be offered either the GBE or the CH depending on their personal predilections? The second and opposing argument would say that the composite nature of the CH is a principal strength and that it provides a place in which ranks and grades are irrelevant. On that ground is not the CH a good example of 'a classless society'?

An honour is not everybody's heart's desire and refusals of the CH have occurred in the past. However, they are rare occurrences. Scattered throughout this book, according to their subject field, are the names of the sixteen or so individuals who are known (or reputed) to have refused the CH: Frederick Treves, Virginia Woolf, Edward Garnett, Harley Granville-Barker, Hilaire Belloc, James Hammond, R. H. Tawney, Robert Graves, Ben Nicholson, Leonard Woolf, Malcolm Macdonald, J. B. Priestley, L. S. Lowry, Leonard Cheshire, Francis Bacon and Michael Oakeshott. The grounds for refusal of an honour are few, sometimes laudable and sometimes eccentric. Sometimes the motive is ideological, the individual concerned disagreeing with the principle of an honours system; this was the belief of Virginia and Leonard Woolf and R. H. Tawney. Others believe, wrongly, that the acceptance of an honour will compromise their independence and inhibit their freedom of speech. Edward Garnett laboured under this curious misapprehension. Some, like Ben Nicholson and J. B. Priestley, refuse in the hope or the expectation that something higher will be offered at a later date. Then there are those, such as L. S. Lowry and Michael Oakeshott, who shrink from publicity, and refuse from a sincere wish to let their work speak for itself.

The CH is an honour almost of the last resort. When the Order of the British Empire, a knighthood or even a peerage are rejected, the 'classless' CH remains the highest and the most select honour in the gift of the prime minister and tends to be offered when all else has failed. Those who refuse it are therefore, mostly, inclined to refuse everything. A very few, including Nicholson and Priestley, were captivated by the Order of Merit and, by banking on their reputations, they played a high risk strategy to get it. Such a tactic is reprehensible, but when set beside the humility of Lowry, it appears grubby.

The CH is an unusual honour that simply does not fit easily into the structure of the honours system, and this has caused some uncertainty about the qualifications for membership. It is not easy to devise and apply a standard beyond the historically high level enshrined in the Order's statutes – 'conspicuous service of national importance'. Although the phrase is a child of its time, redolent of emergency and duty, it has remained unchanged in succeeding ages and offers little guidance in the selection process. Consequently, the definition has changed from decade to decade and from war to peace to war again and then back to peace. The Order has been pressed into recognising different forms of service at different times to meet different national concerns and the preoccupations of different prime ministers. What can be confidently asserted on the basis of evidence is the fact that the overall standard of the CH has risen continuously throughout its history. Many of the Companions of Honour appointed in the 1920s and 1930s were well known within the United Kingdom. By the beginning of the twenty-first century, the majority of members had international reputations.

Age alone is not a totally reliable yardstick, but aggregates can indicate a trend. The average age of the twenty-seven Companions of Honour appointed in 1917–20 was fifty-seven on appointment. The similar average of the thirty Companions appointed in 1930–39 was sixty-four. The average of the thirty-six appointed in 1992–99 was seventy-two. If the eight politicians (usually appointed at a younger age than the non-politicians) are removed from the last group, the average age for that group rises to seventy-six. These statistics do not warrant too detailed an analysis, but they could be interpreted to suggest that as the century progressed longer periods of service were expected of those considered for the CH. Age mattered less in the 1917–20 period when the intensity of commitment in the four years of war was more important than length of service. In 1917 the CH was also a brand new Order with fifty vacancies and there were no established criteria for filling them. Violet Markham was made a CH in June 1917 at the age of forty-four and died in February 1959 at the age of eighty-six, having been a member of the Order for forty-one years. Walter Layton was only thirty-five when he was made a CH in April 1919. He died in February 1966 at the age of eighty-one, having been a member for more than forty-six years. Age is not a factor in the selection of names, and the appointment of younger men and women is not precluded, but it is now unlikely that a man or woman would have established a national reputation for consistently long and eminent service or achievement when still only in the comparatively youthful periods of their fourth and fifth decades of life. Of course fate occasionally intervenes to render age completely irrelevant. Dame Elisabeth Frink was made a CH in June 1992 and died ten months later. Longevity can also seriously distort any neat statistical table. Dame Ninette de Valois was made a CH in December 1981 at the age of eighty-three. She lived for nearly twenty more years, dying in March 2001 at the age of one hundred and two.

The CH is not a well-known honour; few honours are. This one however suffers more than most. As with each of the small one-class United Kingdom honours, it is simply too small to have a registered importance in the national consciousness. The MBE and the OBE, for example, have basked in the spotlight of popular recognition for generations, as have the VC and the GC at the pinnacle of the gallantry decorations. At best references to 'the CH' might arouse mild curiosity; but more probably a blank stare. It is too small to be well known, and perhaps not small enough to be thought exclusive. Although it is an 'Order' with a badge and a registered membership (not a medal with a list of recipients), it has hardly any of the hallmarks of the other Orders; little more in fact than the title of 'Order'. It is diminished by a complete absence of the level of corporate activity and organisation that would give it greater identity and profile, and it could benefit from a little more ceremonial and superstructure. It has no grand master, no chapel, no stalls, no stall plates or banners displaying the armorial bearings of its members, no regular gatherings and only one administrative officer. It is a notional 'paper' society with a minimalist structure and no sense of cohesion or corporate life. On one view it could be described as the very model of a modern secular Order; laudably classless and democratic, and totally devoid of religious symbol or occasion. Another view would say that this has worked to the disadvantage of an honour that is largely unknown and slightly colourless. The CH is an Order, not a medal. It has a select and registered membership, and its members wear not a 'medal' but a badge to indicate that they belong to this 'society'. In eighty-five years they have never been called together because there is neither provision nor precedent for convening them. Yet a gathering of the members of the Order of the Companions of Honour would produce an assembly of men and women as distinguished as members of the Order of Merit.

Despite the historic phrase 'conspicuous service of national importance', it is not easy to define precisely what the CH is for. It has enveloped a number of different constituencies, which have variously risen and waned in line with changing national tastes and perceptions. However, it would be broadly true to say that it has become the appropriate honour for people of eminence who so epitomise achievement in their chosen field that their stature is recognised not only by those among their own kind, but by the public at large. Whereas the Order itself is generally unrecognised, its members have been mostly well known and well regarded in their own time and among their own peers. Reading through the chapters of this book will provide a roll call of the renowned. But what were the common threads that individually and collectively hallmarked them as CH material?

An analysis of the life and work of the Companions of Honour produces four principle qualifications of membership: popular, prominent, pioneering and political. Of course the boundary line between each is well blurred, there is much overlapping, and many recipients can claim more than one of these benchmarks. However, they do provide a good base for working up to an assessment of each of the Companions of Honour, although they are of course subject to personal interpretation. Popularity is a dangerous delusion and a fickle measurement of the worth of a human being when it is born from a mindless adulation of mediocre talent, and it should never be used as a starting point. It comes later, when an individual is widely known, liked, admired and respected for his or her rare and indisputable gifts – even when those gifts are accompanied by a difficult temperament. F. R. Leavis (1977) and A. L. Rowse (1996), for example, were two irascible if inspirational individuals whose theories, comments and behaviour bordered on the eccentric. Prominence can arise from infamy and notoriety and a self-enhancing and self-seeking desire for fame, to the point of cultivating publicity and seeking recognition. Yet many of the most prominent Companions of Honour have been self-effacing individuals whose lives were marked by modesty and humility; unwanted fame was thrust upon them by virtue of their good works and achievements. Pioneers can be egotistical and self-indulgent, desirous of adventure and new experiences, but they can also demonstrate a genuine and altruistic desire to push further the boundaries of knowledge and taste (sometimes in the face of initial disdain or hostility) for the benefit or for the enlightenment of humankind. Politics is an often despised profession, characterised (in the minds of many external observers) by an avid desire for power, authority and acclaim, and a disregard for ethics. Yet at their best, politicians can show a commitment to public service, marked by the highest standards of integrity, sagacity, duty and prudence. The value of the CH as an honour has risen to its present high level because these qualities have been looked for in potential members, and also because the establishment has not been continually increased for the purposes of need and convenience. Set at fifty in 1917 and increased to sixty-five in 1943, the Order has continued a select group. There is no annual allocation and there are no promotions, and vacancies become available only through the death of a member. As the Commonwealth quota has fallen into disuse in recent decades, the size of the Order has gradually returned to its original figure of fifty, and there it should desirably remain. A restriction on numbers always adds to the prestige of an honour, and concentrates the minds of those responsible for selecting names to adorn its ranks.

The conferral of a CH represents the recognition of high achievement, public eminence and conspicuous service across several decades – despite the fact that the work of many Companions of Honour has long been forgotten, and their former fame has been erased by the passage of time. Presented with an unfamiliar name the observer asks the obvious question: 'who was he or she?' or 'what did he or she do to get it?' These questions are not unique to the CH; many honoured individuals, including those with high honours, were famous for a while and then faded into obscurity. Among the ranks of the Companions of Honour who now remembers William Davies, general secretary of the Amalgamated Society of Brassworkers; John Henry Jowett, minister of Westminster Chapel; Hugh Pollock, deputy prime minister of Northern Ireland; Sir Hall Caine and his Isle of Man novels; Viscount Dillon, curator of the Tower of London armouries; the cloud chamber of Charles Wilson; the theatre scenery and theories of Gordon Craig; the philosophy of Henry Jones; Helena Swanwick the pacifist; James Reid the lawyer; Edward Lucas the journalist; or John Ellerman the shipowner? Yet they were all thought worthy of the CH in their time. The answer is that specialist historians of those fields will of course know their names and their work; but very few others. All these people were renowned in their day but disappeared into the shadows many years ago, and memories of their work have died with the passing of the generations. They shone brightly in their own times and were honoured by their contemporaries – the better judges of their services.

Another argument can be adduced in urging caution and refraining from judgement in the question of suitability for honours, and that is to look backwards in time and to ponder whether individuals who have been given the CH in recent years would have been seen as natural candidates in earlier times. Sir John Smith was made a CH in 1993 'For services to Conservation and the Heritage'. His work in founding and endowing the Landmark Trust in 1965 has saved and preserved a broad range of historic, scenic, attractive and sometimes downright quirky architectural gems as important parts of the national heritage. Yet the period from 1920 to 1960 saw the rampaging destruction of numerous country houses. It was a shattering loss, but the voice of conservation was still in its infancy, and few seriously challenged the wholesale demolition. Would an architectural conservationist have been thanked and honoured for his work in the 1920s or 1930s? Conservation of a different kind can be seen in the wildlife broadcasting work of Sir Peter Scott (1987) and Sir David Attenborough (1995). Admittedly the reputations of both were diffused by the medium of television, but it is difficult to imagine either of them as natural CH material in the first twenty years of the Order's history. Conservation and preservation began to flower in the late twentieth century, but is this contemporary concern here to stay, or will it have been surpassed by more pressing concerns, as yet unpredictable, in fifty or sixty years time?

The appropriateness of conferring the CH should be mostly beyond question – although the temptation to put question marks against certain names is admittedly overwhelming and irresistible. These people were honoured for what they did at the time at which they did it – when their reputations had reached a peak. They were vivid and prominent names in their own times. In some cases, and with the benefit of hindsight, history may reconsider their work and pass a different judgement, but it would be wrong to assess earlier Companions of Honour by the standards or interests of succeeding generations. Human memories are short, heavily edited and often quite unreliable. Fame is usually transitory, occasionally long lasting, but never eternal. Let each generation judge its own.

APPENDIX 1

Members of the Order of the Companions of Honour

1   Field Marshal Jan Christian Smuts, OM, CH   4 June 1917
       born   24 May 1870
       invested   17 December 1918 (at an investiture of the Order of the Companions of Honour and of the Most Excellent Order of the British Empire by King George V at Buckingham Palace)
       died   11 September 1950

2   Henry Gosling, CH   4 June 1917
       born   9 June 1861
       invested   17 December 1918 (at an investiture of the Order of the Companions of Honour and of the Most Excellent Order of the British Empire by King George V at Buckingham Palace)
       died   24 October 1930

3   Lady Maud Evelyn Hamilton
       The Marchioness of Lansdowne, CI, GBE, CH, VA   4 June 1917
       born   17 December 1850
       invested   17 December 1918 (at an investiture of the Order of the Companions of Honour and of the Most Excellent Order of the British Empire by King George V at Buckingham Palace)
       died   21 October 1932

4   Elizabeth Sanderson Haldane, CH   4 June 1917
       born   27 May 1862
       invested   17 December 1918 (at an investiture of the Order of the Companions of Honour and of the Most Excellent Order of the British Empire by King George V at Buckingham Palace)
       died   24 December 1937

5   Kenneth Bingham Quinan, CH   4 June 1917
       born   3 July 1878
       invested   23 May 1922 (by the Governor General of South Africa)
       died   26 January 1948

6   Sir Henry Babington Smith, GBE, CH, KCB, CSI   4 June 1917
       born   29 January 1863
       invested   3 April 1919 (at a general investiture by King George V at Buckingham Palace)
       died   29 September 1923

7   Harry Lawson Webster Levy-Lawson
       The Right Honourable the Viscount Burnham, Bt, GCMG, CH   4 June 1917
       born   18 December 1862
       invested   17 December 1918 (at an investiture of the Order of the Companions of Honour and of the Most Excellent Order of the British Empire by King George V at Buckingham Palace)
       died   20 July 1933

8   Sir Frank Athelstane Swettenham, GCMG, CH   4 June 1917
       born   28 March 1850
       invested   17 December 1918 (at an investiture of the Order of the Companions of Honour and of the Most Excellent Order of the British Empire by King George V at Buckingham Palace)
       died   11 June 1946

APPENDIX I

9   The Honourable Edward Gerald Strutt, CH   4 June 1917
    born   10 April 1854
    invested 17 December 1918 (at an investiture of the Order of the Companions of Honour and of the Most Excellent Order of the British Empire by King George V at Buckingham Palace)
    died   8 March 1930

10 Alexander Henderson
    The Right Honourable the Lord Faringdon, Bt, CH   4 June 1917
    born   28 September 1850
    invested 17 December 1918 (at an investiture of the Order of the Companions of Honour and of the Most Excellent Order of the British Empire by King George V at Buckingham Palace)
    died   17 March 1934

11 Godfrey John Boyle Chetwynd
    The Right Honourable the Viscount Chetwynd, CH   4 June 1917
    born   3 October 1863
    invested 17 December 1918 (at an investiture of the Order of the Companions of Honour and of the Most Excellent Order of the British Empire by King George V at Buckingham Palace)
    died   22 March 1936

12 William Ripper, CH   4 June 1917
    born   10 February 1853
    invested 17 December 1918 (at an investiture of the Order of the Companions of Honour and of the Most Excellent Order of the British Empire by King George V at Buckingham Palace)
    died   13 August 1937

13 Margaret Edith Tennant, CH   4 June 1917
    born   5 April 1869
    invested 18 February 1919 (at a general investiture by King George V at Buckingham Palace)
    died   11 July 1946

14 Violet Rosa Markham
    Mrs James Carruthers, CH   4 June 1917
    born   3 October 1872
    invested 17 December 1918 (at an investiture of the Order of the Companions of Honour and of the Most Excellent Order of the British Empire by King George V at Buckingham Palace)
    died   2 February 1959

15 William John Davies, CH   4 June 1917
    born   6 August 1848
    invested 17 December 1918 (at an investiture of the Order of the Companions of Honour and of the Most Excellent Order of the British Empire by King George V at Buckingham Palace)
    died   12 October 1934

16 George James Wardle, CH   4 June 1917
    born   15 May 1865
    invested 17 December 1918 (at an investiture of the Order of the Companions of Honour and of the Most Excellent Order of the British Empire by King George V at Buckingham Palace)
    died   18 June 1947

17 Alexander Wilkie, CH   4 June 1917
       born   30 September 1850
       invested 17 December 1918 (at an investiture of the Order of the Companions of
                 Honour and of the Most Excellent Order of the British Empire by King
                 George V at Buckingham Palace)
       died   2 September 1928

18 Sir John Furley, CH, CB   1 January 1918
       born   19 March 1836
       invested 17 December 1918 (at an investiture of the Order of the Companions of
                 Honour and of the Most Excellent Order of the British Empire by King
                 George V at Buckingham Palace)
       died   27 September 1919

19 James Andrew Seddon, CH   1 January 1918
       born   7 May 1868
       invested 17 December 1918 (at an investiture of the Order of the Companions of
                 Honour and of the Most Excellent Order of the British Empire by King
                 George V at Buckingham Palace)
       died   31 May 1939

20 James Parker, CH   1 January 1918
       born   9 December 1863
       invested 21 December 1918 (at a general investiture by King George V at
                 Buckingham Palace)
       died   11 February 1948

21 Lieutenant General Sir Alfred Keogh, GCB, GCVO, CH   25 February 1918
       born   3 July 1857
       invested 17 December 1918 (at an investiture of the Order of the Companions of
                 Honour and of the Most Excellent Order of the British Empire by King
                 George V at Buckingham Palace)
       died   30 July 1936

22 Colonel Sir Herbert Charles Perrott Bt, CH, CB   3 June 1918
       born   26 October 1849
       invested 17 December 1918 (at an investiture of the Order of the Companions of
                 Honour and of the Most Excellent Order of the British Empire by King
                 George V at Buckingham Palace)
       died   15 February 1922

23 Sir Samuel Butler Provis, CH, KCB   3 June 1918
       born   9 February 1845
       invested 17 December 1918 (at an investiture of the Order of the Companions of
                 Honour and of the Most Excellent Order of the British Empire by King
                 George V at Buckingham Palace)
       died   11 July 1926

24 Walter Thomas Layton
    The Right Honourable the Lord Layton, CH, CBE   29 April 1919
       born   15 March 1884
       invested 17 July 1919 (at a general investiture by King George V at Buckingham
                 Palace)
       died   14 February 1966

25 Thomas Royden
    The Right Honourable the Lord Royden, CH   29 April 1919
       born   22 May 1871
       invested 17 July 1919 (at a general investiture by King George V at Buckingham
                 Palace)
       died   6 May 1950

APPENDIX I 519

26 **The Right Honourable George Nicoll Barnes, CH**   1 January 1920
    born   2 January 1859
    invested   12 May 1920 (at a general investiture by King George V at Buckingham Palace)
    died   21 April 1940

27 **Philip Henry Kerr**
The Most Honourable the Marquess of Lothian, KT, CH   1 January 1920
    born   18 April 1882
    invested   12 May 1920 (at a general investiture by King George V at Buckingham Palace)
    died   12 December 1940

28 **The Reverend John Clifford, CH**   1 January 1921
    born   16 October 1836
    invested   18 November 1921 (at a general investiture by King George V at Buckingham Palace)
    died   20 November 1923

29 **Sir John Reeves Ellerman, Bt, CH**   1 January 1921
    born   15 May 1862
    invested   8 March 1921 (at a general investiture by King George V at Buckingham Palace)
    died   16 July 1933

30 **Harold Arthur Dillon**
The Right Honourable the Viscount Dillon, CH   4 June 1921
    born   24 January 1844
    invested   19 July 1921 (at a general investiture by King George V at Buckingham Palace)
    died   18 December 1932

31 **The Right Reverend Arthur Cayley Headlam, CH**   4 June 1921
    born   2 August 1862
    invested   19 July 1921 (at a general investiture by King George V at Buckingham Palace)
    died   17 January 1947

32 **Sir William Robertson Nicoll, CH**   4 June 1921
    born   10 October 1851
    invested   19 July 1921 (at a general investiture by King George V at Buckingham Palace)
    died   4 May 1923

33 **Sir Henry Jones, CH, FBA**   2 January 1922
    born   30 November 1852
    invested   [not invested; the insignia was forwarded by the State Chamberlain to the Private Secretary to the Prime Minister for presentation, 20 January 1922]
    died   4 February 1922

34 **Sir Henry Newbolt, CH**   2 January 1922
    born   6 June 1862
    invested   9 February 1922 (at a general investiture by King George V at Buckingham Palace)
    died   19 April 1938

35 **Joseph Havelock Wilson, CH, CBE**   2 January 1922
    born   16 August 1858
    invested   9 February 1922 (at a general investiture by King George V at Buckingham Palace)
    died   16 April 1929

36   Sir Thomas Hall Caine, CH, KBE   19 October 1922
        born   14 May 1853
        invested 16 June 1923 (at a general investiture by King George V at Buckingham
                  Palace)
        died   31 August 1931

37   The Right Honourable Sir Winston Leonard Spencer Churchill, KG, OM, CH`
                                                                              19 October 1922
        born   30 November 1874
        invested 16 June 1923 (at a general investiture by King George V at Buckingham
                  Palace)
        died   24 January 1965

38   Sir Evan Vincent Evans, CH   19 October 1922
        born   [There is no record of the registration of his birth. He was reputedly born on
                  18 November 1851, (Dictionary of National Biography) or 25 November
                  1852 (Dictionary of Welsh Biography). Other sources state that he was
                  eighty-seven at the time of his death, giving a date of about 1847]
        invested 22 February 1923 (at a general investiture by King George V at Buckingham
                  Palace)
        died   13 November 1934

39   The Reverend John Henry Jowett, CH   19 October 1922
        born   25 August 1863
        invested 25 July 1923 (at a general investiture by King George V at Buckingham
                  Palace)
        died   19 December 1923

40   John Colin Campbell Davidson
     The Right Honourable the Viscount Davidson, GCVO, CH, CB   25 May 1923
        born   23 February 1889
        invested 16 June 1923 (at a general investiture by King George V at Buckingham
                  Palace)
        died   11 December 1970

41   The Reverend Prebendary Wilson Carlile, CH   1 January 1926
        born   17 January 1847
        invested 4 February 1926 (at a general investiture by King George V at Buckingham
                  Palace)
        died   26 September 1942

42   The Reverend Herbert Armitage James, CH   5 June 1926
        born   3 August 1844
        invested 12 July 1926 (at a general investiture by King George V at Buckingham
                  Palace)
        died   15 November 1931

43   The Reverend Hugh Richard Lawrie Sheppard, CH   1 January 1927
        born   2 September 1880
        invested 21 March 1927 (privately by King George V at Buckingham Palace)
        died   31 October 1937

44   Stanley Melbourne Bruce
     The Right Honourable the Viscount Bruce of Melbourne, CH, MC, FRS   9 May 1927
        born   15 April 1883
        invested 9 May 1927 (by the Duke of York at Parliament House, Canberra)
        died   25 August 1967

45 The Reverend John Daniel Jones, CH   3 June 1927
    born   *13 April 1865*
    invested   *21 June 1927 (at a general investiture by King George V at Buckingham Palace)*
    died   *19 April 1942*

46 John Scott Haldane, CH, FRS   4 June 1928
    born   *3 May 1860*
    invested   *27 June 1928 (at a general investiture by King George V at Buckingham Palace)*
    died   *15 March 1936*

47 Lady Florence Elizabeth Barrett, CH, CBE   1 March 1929
    born   *18 February 1867*
    invested   *28 March 1929 (at a general investiture by the Prince of Wales at St James's Palace)*
    died   *7 August 1945*

48 Lilian Mary Baylis, CH   1 March 1929
    born   *9 May 1874*
    invested   *28 March 1929 (at a general investiture by the Prince of Wales at St James's Palace)*
    died   *25 November 1937*

49 The Reverend John Charles Carlile, CH, CBE   1 March 1929
    born   *22 March 1862*
    invested   *28 March 1929 (at a general investiture by the Prince of Wales at St James's Palace)*
    died   *16 August 1941*

50 Fritz Theodor Albert (Frederick) Delius, CH   1 March 1929
    born   *29 January 1862*
    invested   *[insignia presented by the chargé d'affaires (Paris) at Grez-sur-Loing, 21 April 1929]*
    died   *10 June 1934*

51 William Bramwell Booth, CH   30 April 1929
    born   *8 March 1856*
    invested   *[insignia was handed to Mrs Bramwell Booth by Sir George Crichton at The Homestead, Hadley Wood, Barnet, Hertfordshire, 1 July 1929]*
    died   *16 June 1929*

52 Thomas Jones, CH   3 June 1929
    born   *27 September 1870*
    invested   *9 July 1929 (at a general investiture by the Prince of Wales at St James's Palace)*
    died   *15 October 1955*

53 Agnes Maude Royden
    Mrs George William Hudson Shaw, CH   1 January 1930
    born   *23 November 1876*
    invested   *26 February 1931 (at a general investiture by King George V at Buckingham Palace)*
    died   *30 July 1956*

54 The Right Honourable Valingaman Sankarana-Rayana Srinivasa Sastri, CH
                                                                      1 January 1930
    born   *22 September 1869*
    invested   *28 March 1930 (by Lord Irwin, the Viceroy of India, at New Delhi)*
    died   *17 April 1946*

55 Gertrude Mary Tuckwell, CH 1 January 1930
    born 25 April 1861
    invested 5 July 1930 (at a general investiture by King George V at Buckingham Palace)
    died 5 August 1951

56 Margaret McMillan, CH, CBE 3 June 1930
    born 20 July 1860
    invested 5 July 1930 (at a general investiture by King George V at Buckingham Palace)
    died 29 March 1931

57 Helena Maria Lucy Swanwick, CH 1 January 1931
    born 1864 (at Munich)
    invested [presented with the insignia by Sir George Crichton at 26 Lawn Crescent, Kew]
    died 16 November 1939

58 Jane Harriet Walker, CH 1 January 1931
    born 24 October 1859
    invested 26 February 1931 (at a general investiture by King George V at Buckingham Palace)
    died 17 November 1938

59 Albert Mansbridge, CH 3 June 1931
    born 10 January 1876
    invested 25 June 1931 (at a general investiture by King George V at Buckingham Palace)
    died 22 August 1952

60 Benjamin Seebohm Rowntree, CH 3 June 1931
    born 7 July 1871
    invested 25 June 1931 (at a general investiture by King George V at Buckingham Palace)
    died 7 October 1954

61 John Buchan
    The Right Honourable the Lord Tweedsmuir, GCMG, GCVO, CH 1 January 1932
    born 26 August 1875
    invested 23 February 1932 (at a general investiture by King George V at Buckingham Palace)
    died 11 February 1940

62 Robert Laurence Binyon, CH 3 June 1932
    born 10 August 1869
    invested 21 June 1932 (at a general investiture by King George V at Buckingham Palace)
    died 10 March 1943

63 Edward Verrall Lucas, CH 3 June 1932
    born 11 June 1868
    invested 21 June 1932 (at a general investiture by King George V at Buckingham Palace)
    died 26 June 1938

64 The Revd Philip Thomas Byard Clayton, CH 2 January 1933
    born 12 December 1885
    invested 11 June 1933 (at a general investiture by King George V at Buckingham Palace)
    died 15 December 1972

APPENDIX I 523

65 The Reverend John Scott Lidgett, CH   2 January 1933
    born   *10 August 1854*
    invested *22 February 1933 (at a general investiture by King George V at Buckingham*
               Palace)
    died   *16 June 1953*

66 Annie Elizabeth Fredericka Horniman, CH   3 June 1933
    born   *3 October 1860*
    invested *11 July 1933 (at a general investiture by King George V at Buckingham*
               Palace)
    died   *6 August 1937*

67 Thomas Ethelbert Page, CH   1 January 1934
    born   *27 March 1850*
    invested *27 February 1934 (at a general investiture by King George V at Buckingham*
               Palace)
    died   *1 April 1936*

68 The Honourable William Napier Bruce, CH, CB   3 June 1935
    born   *15 January 1858*
    invested *[insignia sent by registered post to Westfield House, Western Road, Bath,*
               2 December 1935]
    died   *20 March 1936*

69 The Right Reverend John White, CH   3 June 1935
    born   *16 December 1867*
    invested *9 July 1935 (at a general investiture by King George V at Buckingham*
               Palace)
    died   *20 August 1951*

70 John Dover Wilson, CH   1 January 1936
    born   *13 July 1881*
    invested *18 February 1936 (at a general investiture by King George V at Buckingham*
               Palace)
    died   *15 January 1969*

71 William George Stewart Adams, CH   23 June 1936
    born   *8 November 1874*
    invested *14 July 1936 (at a general investiture by King Edward VIII at Buckingham*
               Palace)
    died   *30 January 1966*

72 The Right Honourable Joseph Aloysius Lyons, CH   23 June 1936
    born   *15 September 1879*
    invested *6 November 1936 (by the Governor General of Australia in Queen's Hall,*
               Parliament House, Melbourne)
    died   *7 April 1939*

73 The Right Honourable Hugh McDowell Pollock, CH   23 June 1936
    born   *16 November 1852*
    invested *[insignia posted to Arlington, 18 Windsor Avenue, Belfast]*
    died   *15 April 1937*

74 Janet Penrose Trevelyan   23 June 1936
    Mrs George Macaulay Trevelyan, CH
    born   *6 November 1879*
    invested *14 July 1936 (at a general investiture by King Edward VIII at Buckingham*
               Palace)
    died   *7 September 1956*

75 Nancy Witcher
    Viscountess Astor, CH   11 May 1937
        born   *19 May 1879*
        invested *23 July 1937 (privately by King George VI at Buckingham Palace)*
        died   *2 May 1964*

76 The Reverend Melbourn Evans Aubrey, CH   11 May 1937
        born   *21 April 1885*
        invested *10 June 1937 (at a general investiture by King George VI at Buckingham Palace)*
        died   *18 October 1957*

77 Gwendoline Elizabeth Davies, CH   11 May 1937
        born   *11 February 1882*
        invested *10 June 1937 (at a general investiture by King George VI at Buckingham Palace)*
        died   *3 July 1951*

78 John Alfred Spender, CH   11 May 1937
        born   *23 December 1862*
        invested *10 June 1937 (at a general investiture by King George VI at Buckingham Palace)*
        died   *21 June 1942*

79 Charles Thomson Rees Wilson, CH, FRS   11 May 1937
        born   *14 February 1869*
        invested *10 June 1937 (at a general investiture by King George VI at Buckingham Palace)*
        died   *15 November 1959*

80 Howell Arthur Gwynne, CH   1 January 1938
        born   *3 September 1866*
        invested *15 February 1938 (at a general investiture by King George VI at Buckingham Palace)*
        died   *26 June 1950*

81 George Peabody Gooch, OM, CH   8 June 1939
        born   *21 October 1873*
        invested *6 February 1940 (at a general investiture by King George VI at Buckingham Palace)*
        died   *31 August 1968*

82 James Joseph Mallon, CH   8 June 1939
        born   *9 May 1875*
        invested *11 July 1939 (at a general investiture by King George VI at Buckingham Palace)*
        died   *12 April 1961*

83 James Louis Garvin, CH   1 January 1941
        born   *12 April 1868*
        invested *15 February 1941 (at a general investiture by King George VI at Buckingham Palace)*
        died   *23 January 1947*

84 The Right Honourable William Morris Hughes, CH   1 January 1941
        born   *25 September 1864*
        invested *27 September 1941 (by the Governor General of Australia at Admiralty House, Sydney)*
        died   *28 October 1952*

85 Arthur Henry Mann, CH   1 January 1941
        born   7 *July 1876*
        invested   *15 February 1941 (at a general investiture by King George VI at*
                      Buckingham Palace)
        died   *23 July 1972*

86 Albert Victor Alexander
   The Right Honourable the Earl Alexander of Hillsborough, KG, CH   12 June 1941
        born   *1 May 1885*
        invested   *26 June 1941 (privately by King George VI at Buckingham Palace)*
        died   *11 January 1965*

87 Frederick James Marquis
   The Right Honourable the Earl of Woolton, CH   11 June 1942
        born   *24 August 1883*
        invested   *2 July 1942 (privately by King George VI at Buckingham Palace)*
        died   *14 December 1964*

88 The Right Honourable Sir Earle Christmas Grafton Page, GCMG, CH   23 June 1942
        born   *8 August 1880*
        invested   *23 June 1942 (privately by King George VI at Buckingham Palace)*
        died   *20 December 1961*

89 The Very Reverend Joseph Herman Hertz, CH   1 January 1943
        born   *25 September 1872*
        invested   *5 February 1943 (privately by King George VI at Buckingham Palace)*
        died   *14 January 1946*

90 Frederick James Leathers
   The Right Honourable the Viscount Leathers, CH   1 January 1943
        born   *21 November 1883*
        invested   *3 February 1943 (privately by King George VI at Buckingham Palace)*
        died   *19 March 1965*

91 The Right Honourable John Miller Andrews, CH   21 May 1943
        born   *17 July 1871*
        invested   *22 July 1943 (privately by King George VI at Buckingham Palace)*
        died   *5 August 1956*

92 Ernest Walter Hives
   The Right Honourable the Lord Hives, CH, MBE   2 June 1943
        born   *21 April 1886*
        invested   *8 July 1943 (privately by King George VI at Buckingham Palace)*
        died   *24 April 1965*

93 Henry Snell
   The Right Honourable the Lord Snell, CH, CBE   2 June 1943
        born   *1 April 1865*
        invested   *30 June 1943 (privately by King George VI at Buckingham Palace)*
        died   *21 April 1944*

94 Philip Cunliffe-Lister
   The Right Honourable the Earl of Swinton, GBE, CH   9 August 1943
        born   *1 May 1884*
        invested   *11 August 1943 (privately by King George VI at Buckingham Palace)*
        died   *27 July 1972*

95 Essington Lewis, CH   24 September 1943
        born   *13 January 1881*
        invested   *22 March 1944 (by the Governor General of Australia at Canberra)*
        died   *2 October 1961*

96 Richard Gardiner Casey
   The Right Honourable the Lord Casey, KG, GCMG, CH, DSO, MC   1 January 1944
      born   29 August 1890
      invested   3 June 1944 *(privately by King George VI at Sandringham House)*
      died   17 June 1976

97 The Reverend Edmund Horace Fellowes, CH, MVO   1 January 1944
      born   11 November 1870
      invested   6 February 1944 *(privately by King George VI at Windsor Castle)*
      died   20 December 1951

98 Robert Spear Hudson
   The Right Honourable the Viscount Hudson, CH   1 January 1944
      born   15 August 1886
      invested   3 February 1944 *(privately by King George VI at Buckingham Palace)*
      died   2 February 1957

99 Sir Henry Joseph Wood, CH   8 June 1944
      born   3 March 1869
      invested   21 June 1944 *(privately by King George VI at Bukingham Palace)*
      died   19 August 1944

100 Godfrey Martin Huggins
   The Right Honourable the Viscount Malvern, CH, KCMG   4 August 1944
      born   6 July 1883
      invested   [grant and warrant sent to the Colonial Office, 13 October 1944]
      died   8 May 1971

101 Roundell Cecil Palmer
   The Right Honourable the Earl of Selborne, CH   1 January 1945
      born   15 April 1887
      invested   22 February 1945 *(privately by King George VI at Buckingham Palace)*
      died   3 September 1971

102 Clement Richard Attlee
   The Right Honourable the Earl Attlee, KG, OM, CH, FRS   8 June 1945
      born   3 January 1883
      invested   15 June 1945 *(privately by King George VI at Buckingham Palace)*
      died   8 October 1967

103 The Right Honourable Arthur Greenwood, CH   8 June 1945
      born   8 February 1880
      invested   15 June 1945 *(privately by King George VI at Buckingham Palace)*
      died   9 June 1954

104 The Right Reverend Henry Herbert Williams, CH   14 June 1945
      born   19 December 1872
      invested   9 July 1946 *(privately by King George VI at Buckingham Palace)*
      died   29 September 1961

105 General Henry Duncan Graham Crerar, CH, CB, DSO, CD   5 July 1945
      born   28 April 1888
      invested   24 July 1945 *(privately by King George VI at Buckingham Palace)*
      died   1 April 1965

106 The Right Honourable Leopold Charles Moritz Stennett Amery, CH   17 August 1945
      born   22 November 1873
      invested   20 August 1945 *(privately by King George VI at Buckingham Palace)*
      died   16 September 1955

107 The Right Honourable Alfred Ernest Brown, CH 17 August 1945
 born *27 August 1881*
 invested *14 August 1945 (privately by King George VI at Buckingham Palace)*
 died *16 February 1962*

108 Hastings Lionel Ismay
 General the Right Honourable the Lord Ismay, KG, GCB, CH, DSO 17 August 1945
 born *21 June 1887*
 invested *20 August 1945 (privately by King George VI at Buckingham Palace)*
 died *17 December 1965*

109 Archibald Vivian Hill, CH, OBE, FRS 1 January 1946
 born *26 September 1886*
 invested *21 February 1946 (privately by King George VI at Buckingham Palace)*
 died *3 June 1977*

110 The Right Honourable Peter Fraser, CH 4 January 1946
 born *28 August 1884*
 invested *9 January 1946 (privately by King George VI at Buckingham Palace)*
 died *12 December 1950*

111 The Right Honourable Charles Vincent Massey, CC, CH 22 May 1946
 born *20 February 1887*
 invested *22 May 1946 (privately by King George VI at Buckingham Palace)*
 died *30 December 1967*

112 George Gibson, CH 13 June 1946
 born *3 April 1885*
 invested *26 June 1946 (privately by King George VI at Buckingham Palace)*
 died *4 February 1953*

113 General the Honourable Andrew George Latta McNaughton, CH, CB, CMG, DSO, CD
 13 June 1946
 born *25 February 1887*
 invested *18 April 1947 (by the Governor General of Canada at Government House, Ottawa)*
 died *11 July 1966*

114 James Bone, CH 12 June 1947
 born *16 May 1872*
 invested *25 July 1947 (privately by King George VI at Buckingham Palace)*
 died *23 November 1962*

115 John William Robertson Scott, CH 12 June 1947
 born *20 April 1866*
 invested *25 July 1947 (privately by King George VI at Buckingham Palace)*
 died *21 December 1962*

116 The Right Honourable Margaret Grace Bondfield, CH 1 January 1948
 born *17 March 1873*
 invested *12 February 1948 (privately by King George VI at Buckingham Palace)*
 died *16 June 1953*

117 Victoria Mary Sackville-West
 The Honourable Lady Nicolson, CH 1 January 1948
 born *3 March 1892*
 invested *12 February 1948 (privately by King George VI at Buckingham Palace)*
 died *2 June 1962*

118 Walter John de la Mare, OM, CH   10 June 1948
     born   25 April 1873
     invested 16 July 1948 *(privately by King George VI at Buckingham Palace)*
     died   22 June 1956

119 The Reverend Howell Elvet Lewis, CH   10 June 1948
     born   14 April 1860
     invested 16 July 1948 *(privately by King George VI at Buckingham Palace)*
     died   10 December 1953

120 The Right Honourable William Whiteley, CH   10 June 1948
     born   3 October 1882
     invested 16 July 1948 *(privately by King George VI at Buckingham Palace)*
     died   3 November 1955

121 The Lord Edward Christian David Gascoyne-Cecil, CH   1 January 1949
     born   9 April 1902
     invested 9 March 1949 *(privately by King George VI at Buckingham Palace)*
     died   1 January 1986

122 The Right Honourable Arthur Deakin, CH   1 January 1949
     born   11 November 1890
     invested 9 March 1949 *(privately by King George VI at Buckingham Palace)*
     died   1 May 1955

123 Lionel George Curtis, CH   9 June 1949
     born   7 March 1872
     invested 6 July 1949 *(privately by King George VI at Buckingham Palace)*
     died   24 November 1955

124 The Right Honourable Sir Richard Stafford Cripps, CH, FRS, QC   1 January 1951
     born   24 April 1889
     invested *[insignia sent to Lady Cripps 29 April 1952]*
     died   21 April 1952

125 The Right Honourable Sir Robert Gordon Menzies, KT, AK, CH, QC, FRS
                                                                               1 January 1951
     born   20 December 1894
     invested 3 January 1951 *(privately by King George VI at Buckingham Palace)*
     died   15 May 1978

126 The Right Honourable Sir Sidney George Holland, GCB, CH   7 June 1951
     born   18 October 1893
     invested 29 January 1952 *(privately by King George VI at Buckingham Palace)*
     died   4 August 1961

127 Herbert Stanley Morrison
     The Right Honourable the Lord Morrison of Lambeth, CH   30 November 1951
     born   3 January 1888
     invested 13 December 1951 *(privately by King George VI at Buckingham Palace)*
     died   6 March 1965

128 The Right Honourable Walter Elliot Elliot, CH, MC, FRS   5 June 1952
     born   19 September 1888
     invested 12 June 1952 *(privately by Queen Elizabeth II at Buckingham Palace)*
     died   8 January 1958

129 Edward Morgan Forster, OM, CH   1 January 1953
     born   1 January 1879
     invested 13 February 1952 *(privately by Queen Elizabeth II at Buckingham Palace)*
     died   7 June 1970

APPENDIX I

130 Edward Benjamin Britten
   The Right Honourable the Lord Britten, OM, CH   1 June 1953
       born   22 November 1913
       invested 1 July 1953 (privately by Queen Elizabeth II at Buckingham Palace)
       died   4 December 1976

131 James Chuter-Ede
   The Right Honourable the Lord Chuter-Ede, CH   1 June 1953
       born   11 September 1882
       invested 1 July 1953 (privately by Queen Elizabeth II at Buckingham Palace)
       died   11 November 1965

132 William Jocelyn Ian Fraser
   The Right Honourable the Lord Fraser of Lonsdale, CH, CBE   1 June 1953
       born   30 August 1897
       invested 1 July 1953 (privately by Queen Elizabeth II at Buckingham Palace)
       died   19 December 1974

133 The Right Honourable Thomas Johnston, CH   1 June 1953
       born   2 November 1881
       invested 24 June 1953 (privately by Queen Elizabeth II at the Palace of Holyrood
                House)
       died   5 September 1965

134 Frederick Alexander Lindemann
   The Right Honourable the Viscount Cherwell, CH, FRS   10 November 1953
       born   5 April 1886
       invested 10 December 1953 (privately by Queen Elizabeth II at Buckingham Palace)
       died   3 July 1957

135 John Christie, CH, MC   1 January 1954
       born   14 December 1882
       invested 18 February 1954 (privately by Queen Elizabeth the Queen Mother at
                Clarence House)
       died   4 July 1962

136 Richard Austen Butler
   The Right Honourable the Lord Butler of Saffron Walden, KG, CH   8 January 1954
       born   9 December 1902
       invested 25 February 1954 (privately by Queen Elizabeth the Queen Mother at
                Clarence House)
       died   8 March 1982

137 William Somerset Maugham, CH   10 June 1954
       born   25 January 1874
       invested 14 July 1954 (privately by Queen Elizabeth II at Buckingham Palace)
       died   16 December 1965

138 René Lucien Daniel Massigli, GCVO, CH, KBE, (Honorary) 21 December 1954
       born   22 March 1888
       invested (presented with the badge by Queen Elizabeth II at Buckingham Palace, 21
                December 1954)
       died   3 February 1988

139 Harry Frederick Comfort Crookshank
   The Right Honourable the Viscount Crookshank, CH   1 January 1955
       born   27 May 1893
       invested 1 February 1955 (privately by Queen Elizabeth II at Buckingham Palace)
       died   17 October 1961

140 The Reverend Hugh Martin, CH   1 January 1955
    born   7 *April 1890*
    invested   *16 February 1955 (privately by Queen Elizabeth II at Buckingham Palace)*
    died   *1 July 1964*

141 Henry Spencer Moore, OM, CH   9 June 1955
    born   *30 July 1898*
    invested   *14 July 1955 (privately by Queen Elizabeth II at Buckingham Palace)*
    died   *13 August 1986*

142 Edgar Algernon Robert Cecil
    The Right Honourable the Viscount Cecil of Chelwood, CH, QC   2 January 1956
    born   *18 September 1864*
    invested   *[badge sent by registered post, 24 February 1956]*
    died   *24 November 1958*

143 The Right Honourable Sir John Lionel Kotelawala, CH, KBE   2 January 1956
    born   *4 April 1897*
    invested   *13 July 1956 (privately by Queen Elizabeth II at Buckingham Palace)*
    died   *2 October 1980*

144 Arthur David Waley, CH, CBE   2 January 1956
    born   *19 August 1889*
    invested   *24 February 1956 (privately by Queen Elizabeth II at Buckingham Palace)*
    died   *27 June 1966*

145 Edward Henry Gordon Craig, CH   31 May 1956
    born   *16 January 1872*
    invested   *[badge sent to HM ambassador at Paris, 30 June 1956]*
    died   *29 July 1966*

146 Arnold Joseph Toynbee, CH   31 May 1956
    born   *14 April 1889*
    invested   *[badge sent to Governor General of Australia for delivery, 23 July 1956]*
    died   *22 October 1975*

147 General Nuri-es-Said, CH (Honorary)   16 July 1956
    born   *December 1888*
    invested   *[received badge at Buckingham Palace 16 July 1956 during state visit of*
               King Faisal II]
    died   *14 July 1958*

148 The Very Reverend John Baillie, CH   1 January 1957
    born   *26 March 1886*
    invested   *18 July 1957 (privately by Queen Elizabeth II at Buckingham Palace)*
    died   *29 September 1960*

149 James Gray Stuart
    The Right Honourable the Viscount Stuart of Findhorn, CH, MVO   14 January 1957
    born   *9 February 1897*
    invested   *14 January 1957 (privately by Queen Elizabeth II at Buckingham*
               Palace)
    died   *20 February 1971*

150 Sir Thomas Beecham, Bt, CH   13 June 1957
    born   *29 April 1879*
    invested   *12 July 1957 (privately by Queen Elizabeth II at Buckingham Palace)*
    died   *8 March 1961*

APPENDIX I 531

151 The Most Reverend John Allen Fitzgerald Gregg, CH   13 June 1957
 born   *4 July 1873*
 invested   *24 July 1957 (privately by Queen Elizabeth II at Buckingham Palace)*
 died   *2 May 1961*

152 William Richard Morris
 The Right Honourable the Viscount Nuffield, GBE, CH, FRS   1 January 1958
 born   *10 October 1877*
 invested   *18 March 1958 (privately by Queen Elizabeth II at Buckingham Palace)*
 died   *22 August 1963*

153 Sir Francis Osbert Sacheverell Sitwell, Bt, CH, CBE   12 June 1958
 born   *6 December 1892*
 invested   *6 August 1958 (privately by Queen Elizabeth II at Buckingham Palace)*
 died   *4 May 1969*

154 Sir John Davidson Beazley, CH   1 January 1959
 born   *13 September 1885*
 invested   *4 February 1959 (privately by Queen Elizabeth II at Buckingham Palace)*
 died   *6 May 1970*

155 Kenneth Mackenzie Clark
 The Right Honourable the Lord Clark, OM, CH, KCB, FBA   1 January 1959
 born   *13 July 1903*
 invested   *11 February 1959 (privately by Queen Elizabeth II at Buckingham Palace)*
 died   *21 May 1983*

156 The Right Honourable Sir Walter Nash, GCMG, CH   13 June 1959
 born   *12 February 1882*
 invested   *6 November 1959 (privately by Queen Elizabeth II at Buckingham Palace)*
 died   *4 June 1968*

157 Alan Tindal Lennox-Boyd
 The Right Honourable the Viscount Boyd of Merton, CH   1 January 1960
 born   *18 November 1904*
 invested   *28 March 1960 (privately by Queen Elizabeth II at Buckingham Palace)*
 died   *8 March 1983*

158 Edmund Colquhoun Pery
 The Right Honourable the Earl of Limerick, GBE, CH, KCB, DSO, TD
     31 December 1960
 born   *16 October 1888*
 invested   *13 January 1961 (privately by Queen Elizabeth II at Buckingham Palace)*
 died   *4 August 1967*

159 Tunku Abdul Rahman Putra, CH, AC   31 December 1960
 born   *8 February 1903*
 invested   *14 March 1961 (privately by Queen Elizabeth II at Buckingham Palace)*
 died   *6 December 1990*

160 The Reverend Charles Harold Dodd, CH   10 June 1961
 born   *7 April 1884*
 invested   *22 June 1961 (privately by Queen Elizabeth II at Buckingham Palace)*
 died   *21 September 1973*

161 The Very Reverend Walter Robert Matthews, KCVO, CH   1 January 1962
 born   *22 September 1881*
 invested   *9 February 1962 (privately by Queen Elizabeth II at Buckingham Palace)*
 died   *5 December 1973*

162 Patrick George Thomas Buchan-Hepburn
    The Right Honourable the Lord Hailes, GBE, CH   2 June 1962
        born   2 April 1901
        invested 17 July 1962 (privately by Queen Elizabeth II at Buckingham Palace)
        died   5 November 1974

163 John Selwyn Brooke Selwyn-Lloyd
    The Right Honourable the Lord Selwyn-Lloyd, CH   20 July 1962
        born   28 July 1904
        invested 24 July 1962 (privately by Queen Elizabeth II at Buckingham Palace)
        died   17 May 1978

164 John Scott Maclay
    The Right Honourable the Viscount Muirshiel, KT, CH, CMG   20 July 1962
        born   26 October 1905
        invested 24 July 1962 (privately by Queen Elizabeth II at Buckingham Palace)
        died   17 August 1992

165 Harold Arthur Watkinson
    The Right Honourable the Viscount Watkinson, CH   20 July 1962
        born   25 January 1910
        invested 24 July 1962 (privately by Queen Elizabeth II at Buckingham Palace)
        died   19 December 1995

166 Sir Keith Jacka Holyoake, KG, GCMG, CH   1 January 1963
        born   11 February 1904
        invested [received the badge during the Queen's visit to New Zealand,
                    February/March 1963]
        died   8 December 1983

167 Paul-Henri Spaak, CH (Honorary)   14 May 1963
        born   25 January 1899
        invested [received the badge at Buckingham Palace during the state visit of King
                    Baudoin of the Belgians, 14 May 1963]
        died   31 July 1972

168 Ivor Armstrong Richards, CH   1 January 1964
        born   26 February 1893
        invested 12 June 1964 (privately by Queen Elizabeth II at Buckingham Palace)
        died   7 September 1979

169 Henry Brooke
    The Right Honourable the Lord Brooke of Cumnor, CH   1 December 1964
        born   9 April 1903
        invested 22 December 1964 (privately by Queen Elizabeth II at Buckingham
                    Palace)
        died   29 March 1984

170 Lewis Silkin
    The Right Honourable the Lord Silkin, CH   1 January 1965
        born   14 November 1889
        invested 29 January 1965 (privately by Queen Elizabeth II at Buckingham Palace)
        died   11 May 1972

171 Patrick Maynard Stuart Blackett
    The Right Honourable the Lord Blackett, OM, CH, FRS   12 June 1965
        born   18 November 1897
        invested 14 July 1965 (privately by Queen Elizabeth II at Buckingham Palace)
        died   13 July 1974

APPENDIX I

172 Emanuel Shinwell
    The Right Honourable the Lord Shinwell, CH   12 June 1965
        born   18 October 1884
        invested 14 July 1965 (privately by Queen Elizabeth II at Buckingham Palace)
        died   8 May 1986

173 Henry Graham Greene, OM, CH   1 January 1966
        born   2 October 1904
        invested 11 March 1966 (privately by Queen Elizabeth II at Buckingham Palace)
        died   3 April 1991

174 Edith Clara Summerskill
    The Right Honourable the Baroness Summerskill, CH   1 January 1966
        born   19 April 1901
        invested 18 March 1966 (privately by Queen Elizabeth II at Buckingham Palace)
        died   4 February 1980

175 The Right Honourable James Griffiths, CH   19 May 1966
        born   19 September 1890
        invested 20 July 1966 (privately by Queen Elizabeth II at Buckingham Palace)
        died   7 August 1975

176 The Lady Megan Arfon Lloyd George, CH   19 May 1966
        born   22 April 1902
        invested [badge delivered to her sister, Lady Olwen Carey Evans, c/o 137 Sloane Street, SW1]
        died   14 May 1966

177 Sir William Lawrence Bragg, CH, OBE, MC, FRS   1 January 1967
        born   31 March 1890
        invested 8 March 1967 (privately by Queen Elizabeth II at Buckingham Palace)
        died   1 July 1971

178 Sir Robert Eric Mortimer Wheeler, CH, CIE, MC, TD   1 January 1967
        born   10 September 1890
        invested 1 March 1967 (privately by Queen Elizabeth II at Buckingham Palace)
        died   22 July 1976

179 Arthur Leslie Noel Douglas Houghton
    The Right Honourable the Lord Houghton of Sowerby, CH   5 January 1967
        born   11 August 1898
        invested 8 February 1967 (privately by Queen Elizabeth II at Buckingham Palace)
        died   2 May 1996

180 Sir Arthur Wynne Morgan Bryant, CH, CBE   10 June 1967
        born   18 February 1899
        invested 20 July 1967 (privately by Queen Elizabeth II at Buckingham Palace)
        died   22 January 1985

181 Brigadier General Sir Harold Brewer Hartley, GCVO, CH, CBE, MC, FRS   10 June 1967
        born   3 September 1878
        invested 21 July 1967 (privately by Queen Elizabeth II at Buckingham Palace)
        died   9 September 1972

182 James Scott Cumberland Reid
    The Right Honourable the Lord Reid, CH, QC   10 June 1967
        born   30 July 1890
        invested 18 July 1967 (privately by Queen Elizabeth II at Buckingham Palace)
        died   29 March 1975

183 The Right Honourable Harold Edward Holt, CH   14 June 1967
    born   5 August 1908
    invested   14 June 1967 (privately by Queen Elizabeth II at Buckingham Palace)
    died   17 December 1967

184 John Boyd Orr
    The Right Honourable the Lord Boyd Orr, CH, DSO, MC, FRS   1 January 1968
    born   23 September 1880
    invested   22 February 1968 (privately by Queen Elizabeth II at Buckingham Palace)
    died   25 June 1971

185 The Reverend Ernest Alexander Payne, CH   1 January 1968
    born   19 February 1902
    invested   29 February 1968 (privately by Queen Elizabeth II at Buckingham Palace)
    died   14 January 1980

186 Lionel Charles Robbins
    The Right Honourable the Lord Robbins, CH, CB, FBA   1 January 1968
    born   22 November 1898
    invested   29 February 1968 (privately by Queen Elizabeth II at Buckingham Palace)
    died   15 May 1984

187 Patrick Chrestien Gordon Walker
    The Right Honourable the Lord Gordon-Walker, CH   8 June 1968
    born   7 April 1907
    invested   26 June 1968 (privately by Queen Elizabeth II at Buckingham Palace)
    died   2 December 1980

188 Sir Adrian Cedric Boult, CH   1 January 1969
    born   8 April 1889
    invested   26 February 1969 (privately by Queen Elizabeth II at Buckingham Palace)
    died   22 February 1983

189 The Right Honourable Sir John McEwen, GCMG, CH   1 January 1969
    born   29 March 1900
    invested   26 March 1969 (by the Governor General of Australia at Government House, Canberra)
    died   21 November 1980

190 Robert Michael Maitland Stewart
    The Right Honourable the Lord Stewart of Fulham, CH   1 January 1969
    born   6 November 1906
    invested   13 February 1969 (privately by Queen Elizabeth II at Buckingham Palace)
    died   10 March 1990

191 Sir John Giovanni Battista Barbirolli, CH   14 June 1969
    born   2 December 1899
    invested   31 October 1969 (privately by Queen Elizabeth II at Buckingham Palace)
    died   29 July 1970

192 Sir Allen Lane Williams Lane, CH   14 June 1969
    born   21 September 1902
    invested   [badge sent by post, 2 February 1970]
    died   7 July 1970

193 The Right Honourable Eric Eustace Williams, CH   14 June 1969
    born   25 September 1911
    invested   17 July 1969 (privately by Queen Elizabeth II at Buckingham Palace)
    died   29 March 1981

APPENDIX I

194 Sir James Chadwick, CH, FRS 1 January 1970
  born 20 October 1891
  invested 5 February 1970 (privately by Queen Elizabeth II at Buckingham Palace)
  died 24 July 1974

195 Sir Alan Patrick Herbert, CH 1 January 1970
  born 24 September 1890
  invested 6 February 1970 (privately by Queen Elizabeth II at Buckingham Palace)
  died 11 November 1971

196 The Right Honourable Lee Kuan Yew, GCMG, CH (Honorary) 1 January 1970
  born 16 September 1923
  invested [badge presented by the United Kingdom High Commissioner to Singapore, 18 July 1970]

197 Sir Frederick William Mallandine Ashton, OM, CH, CBE 13 June 1970
  born 17 September 1904
  invested 3 July 1970 (privately by Queen Elizabeth II at Buckingham Palace)
  died 18 August 1988

198 Dame Agnes Sybil Thorndike, CH, DBE 13 June 1970
  born 24 October 1882
  invested 3 July 1970 (privately by Queen Elizabeth II at Buckingham Palace)
  died 9 June 1976

199 Sir Cecil Maurice Bowra 1 January 1971
  born 8 April 1898
  invested 10 February 1971 (privately by Queen Elizabeth II at Buckingham Palace)
  died 4 July 1971

200 Charles Herbert Best, CC, CH, CBE 12 June 1971
  born 27 February 1899
  invested 16 December 1971 (privately by Queen Elizabeth II at Buckingham Palace)
  died 31 March 1978

201 Sir Arthur Edward Drummond Bliss, CH, KCVO 12 June 1971
  born 2 August 1891
  invested 15 July 1971 (privately by Queen Elizabeth II at Buckingham Palace)
  died 27 March 1975

202 The Right Honourable Sir John Grey Gorton, GCMG, AC, CH 12 June 1971
  born 9 September 1911
  invested ?
  died 19 May 2002

203 Joseph Marie Antoine Hubert Luns, GCMG, CH (Honorary) 14 June 1971
  born 28 August 1911
  invested [presented with the badge by Queen Elizabeth II at the Palace of Holyrood House, 1 July 1971]
  died 17 July 2002

204 The Right Honourable Sir William McMahon, GCMG, CH 1 January 1972
  born 23 February 1908
  invested ?
  died 31 March 1988

205 Sir Peter Brian Medawar, OM, CH, CBE, FRS 1 January 1972
  born 28 February 1915
  invested 4 February 1972 (privately by Queen Elizabeth II at Buckingham Palace)
  died 2 October 1987

206   Jean Monnet, CH (Honorary)   22 January 1972
- *born*   9 November 1888
- *invested*   *[presented with the badge by the Prime Minister, Brussels, 22 January 1972]*
- *died*   16 March 1979

207   Arnold Abraham Goodman
The Right Honourable the Lord Goodman, CH   3 June 1972
- *born*   21 August 1913
- *invested*   *14 June 1972 (privately by Queen Elizabeth II at Buckingham Palace)*
- *died*   12 May 1995

208   Herbert Norman Howells, CH, CBE   3 June 1972
- *born*   17 October 1892
- *invested*   *14 June 1972 (privately by Queen Elizabeth II at Buckingham Palace)*
- *died*   23 February 1983

209   John Egerton Christmas Piper, CH   3 June 1972
- *born*   13 December 1903
- *invested*   *14 June 1972 (privately by Queen Elizabeth II at Buckingham Palace)*
- *died*   28 June 1992

210   The Right Honourable Sir John Ross Marshall, GBE, CH   1 January 1973
- *born*   5 March 1912
- *invested*   *11 February 1973 (by the Governor General of New Zealand at Government House, Wellington)*
- *died*   30 August 1988

211   Sir Robert Mayer, CH, KCVO   1 January 1973
- *born*   5 June 1879
- *invested*   *29 March 1973 (privately by Queen Elizabeth II at Buckingham Palace)*
- *died*   9 January 1985

212   Duncan Edwin Duncan-Sandys
The Right Honourable the Lord Duncan-Sandys, CH   1 January 1973
- *born*   24 January 1908
- *invested*   *9 February 1973 (privately by Queen Elizabeth II at Buckingham Palace)*
- *died*   26 November 1987

213   Bernard Howell Leach, CH, CBE   2 June 1973
- *born*   5 January 1887
- *invested*   *8 August 1973 (privately by Queen Elizabeth II at Buckingham Palace)*
- *died*   6 May 1979

214   Irene Mary Bewick Ward
The Right Honourable the Baroness Ward of North Tyneside, CH, DBE   2 June 1973
- *born*   1 January 1895
- *invested*   *8 August 1973 (privately by Queen Elizabeth II at Buckingham Palace)*
- *died*   26 April 1980

215   Henry Cohen
The Right Honourable the Lord Cohen of Birkenhead, CH   1 January 1974
- *born*   21 February 1900
- *invested*   *25 January 1974 (privately by Queen Elizabeth II at Buckingham Palace)*
- *died*   7 August 1977

216   Angela Olivia Pery
The Dowager Countess of Limerick, GBE, CH   1 January 1974
- *born*   27 August 1897
- *invested*   *25 January 1974 (privately by Queen Elizabeth II at Buckingham Palace)*
- *died*   25 April 1981

217	William Stephen Ian Whitelaw The Right Honourable the Viscount Whitelaw, KT, CH, MC	1 January 1974

    born   28 June 1918
    invested   25 January 1974 *(privately by Queen Elizabeth II at Buckingham Palace)*
    died   1 July 1999

218	Quintin McGarel Hogg The Right Honourable the Lord Hailsham of St Marylebone, KG, CH, FRS	5 April 1974

    born   9 October 1907
    invested   4 June 1974 *(privately by Queen Elizabeth II at Buckingham Palace)*
    died   12 October 2001

219	David Jones, CH, CBE	15 June 1974

    born   1 November 1895
    invested   [badge sent by post to Calvary Nursing Home, Sudbury Hill, Harrow on the Hill, 2 July 1974]
    died   28 October 1974

220	The Reverend Nathaniel Micklem, CH	15 June 1974

    born   10 April 1888
    invested   27 June 1974 *(privately by Queen Elizabeth II at Buckingham Palace)*
    died   26 December 1976

221	Jack Ashley The Right Honourable the Lord Ashley of Stoke, CH	1 January 1975

    born   6 December 1922
    invested   13 February 1975 *(privately by Queen Elizabeth II at Buckingham Palace)*

222	Gerald Austin Gardiner The Right Honourable the Lord Gardiner, CH	1 January 1975

    born   30 May 1900
    invested   14 February 1975 *(privately by Queen Elizabeth II at Buckingham Palace)*
    died   7 January 1990

223	Max Ferdinand Perutz, OM, CH, CBE, FRS	1 January 1975

    born   19 May 1914
    invested   11 February 1975 *(privately by Queen Elizabeth II at Buckingham Palace)*
    died   6 February 2002

224	Arnold Cantwell Smith, OC, CH	29 April 1975

    born   18 January 1915
    invested   29 April 1975 *(privately by Queen Elizabeth II on board HM Yacht Britannia off Kingston Harbour, Jamaica)*
    died   7 February 1994

225	Herbert William Bowden The Right Honourable the Lord Aylestone, CH, CBE	14 June 1975

    born   20 January 1905
    invested   11 July 1975 *(privately by Queen Elizabeth II at Buckingham Palace)*
    died   30 April 1994

226	John William Morris The Right Honourable the Lord Morris of Borth-y-Gest, CH, CBE, MC	14 June 1975

    born   11 September 1896
    invested   11 July 1975 *(privately by Queen Elizabeth II at Buckingham Palace)*
    died   9 June 1979

227   The Right Honourable John George Diefenbaker, CH, QC   1 January 1976
        born   18 September 1895
        invested 1 April 1976 (privately by Queen Elizabeth II at Windsor Castle)
        died   16 August 1979

228   Frederick Elywn Elwyn-Jones
      The Right Honourable the Lord Elwyn-Jones, CH   27 May 1976
        born   24 October 1909
        invested 2 July 1976 (privately by Queen Elizabeth II at Buckingham Palace)
        died   4 December 1989

229   Edward Watson Short
      The Right Honourable the Lord Glenamara, CH   27 May 1976
        born   17 December 1912
        invested 1 July 1976 (privately by Queen Elizabeth II at Buckingham Palace)

230   Cledwyn Hughes
      The Right Honourable the Lord Cledwyn of Penrhos, CH   31 December 1976
        born   14 September 1916
        invested 22 February 1977 (privately by Queen Elizabeth the Queen Mother)
        died   22 February 2001

231   The Right Honourable John Malcolm Fraser, AC, CH   26 January 1977
        born   21 May 1930
        invested ? (by Queen Elizabeth II in Australia)

232   Sir Arthur John Gielgud, OM, CH   11 June 1977
        born   14 April 1904
        invested 8 July 1977 (privately by Queen Elizabeth II at Buckingham Palace)
        died   21 May 2000

233   The Right Honourable Sir Robert David Muldoon, GCMG, CH   11 June 1977
        born   21 September 1921 (or 25 September 1921)
        invested 10 June 1977 (privately by Queen Elizabeth II at Buckingham Palace)
        died   4 August 1992

234   Barbara Frances Wootton
      The Right Honourable the Baroness Wootton of Abinger, CH   11 June 1977
        born   14 April 1897
        invested 8 July 1977 (privately by Queen Elizabeth II at Buckingham Palace)
        died   11 July 1988

235   James Larkin Jones, CH, MBE   31 December 1977
        born   29 March 1913
        invested 16 March 1978 (privately by Queen Elizabeth II at Buckingham Palace)

236   Frank Raymond Leavis, CH   31 December 1977
        born   14 July 1895
        invested [badge sent by the Private Secretary to 12 Bulstrode Gardens, Cambridge,
                  11 January 1978]
        died   14 April 1978

237   The Right Honourable Sir Michael Thomas Somare, GCMG, CH   3 June 1978
        born   9 April 1936
        invested 12 October 1978 (by the Governor General of Papua New Guinea)

238   Denis Winston Healey
      The Right Honourable the Lord Healey, CH, MBE   12 June 1979
        born   30 August 1917
        invested 10 July 1979 (privately by Queen Elizabeth II at Buckingham Palace)

APPENDIX I

239   Sir Michael Kemp Tippett, OM, CH, CBE   16 June 1979
      born   2 *January 1905*
      invested   *12 July 1979 (privately by Queen Elizabeth II at Buckingham Palace)*
      died   8 *January 1998*

240   George Edward Peter Thorneycroft
       The Right Honourable the Lord Thorneycroft, CH   31 December 1979
      born   *26 July 1909*
      invested   *20 February 1980 (privately by Queen Elizabeth II at Buckingham Palace)*
      died   *4 June 1994*

241   Arthur Christopher Soames
       The Right Honourable the Lord Soames, GCMG, GCVO, CH, CBE   14 June 1980
      born   *12 October 1920*
      invested   *8 July 1980 (privately by Queen Elizabeth II at Buckingham Palace)*
      died   *16 September 1987*

242   Edwin John Victor Pasmore, CH, CBE, RA   31 December 1980
      born   *3 December 1908*
      invested   *11 February 1981 (privately by Queen Elizabeth II at Buckingham Palace)*
      died   *23 January 1998*

243   The Right Honourable Sir Brian Edward Talboys, AC, CH, KCB   30 April 1981
      born   *7 June 1921*
      invested   *15 October 1981 (by Queen Elizabeth II at Government House, Wellington)*

244   Edward Charles Gurney Boyle
       The Right Honourable the Lord Boyle of Handsworth, Bt, CH   13 June 1981
      born   *31 August 1923*
      invested   *30 June 1981 (privately by Queen Elizabeth II at Buckingham Palace)*
      died   *28 September 1981*

245   Frederick Sanger, OM, CH, CBE, FRS   13 June 1981
      born   *13 August 1918*
      invested   *1 July 1981 (privately by Queen Elizabeth II at Buckingham Palace)*

246   The Right Honourable John Douglas Anthony, CH   31 December 1981
      born   *31 December 1929*
      invested   *8 June 1982 (privately by Queen Elizabeth II at Windsor Castle)*

247   Dame Edris Ninette de Valois, OM, CH, CBE   31 December 1981
      born   *6 June 1898*
      invested   *10 February 1982 (privately by Queen Elizabeth II at Buckingham Palace)*
      died   *8 March 2001*

248   Sir Karl Raimund Popper, CH, FBA   12 June 1982
      born   *28 July 1902*
      invested   *9 July 1982 (privately by Queen Elizabeth II at Buckingham Palace)*
      died   *17 September 1994*

249   Peter Alexander Rupert Carrington
       The Right Honourable the Lord Carrington, KG, GCMG, CH   11 June 1983
      born   *6 June 1919*
      invested   *24 June 1983 (privately by Queen Elizabeth II at Buckingham Palace)*

250   Lucian Freud, OM, CH   11 June 1983
      born   *8 December 1922*
      invested   *24 June 1983 (privately by Queen Elizabeth II at Buckingham Palace)*

251   The Honourable Sir James Cochrane Stevenson Runciman, CH, FBA   31 December 1983
       born   7 July 1903
       invested   10 February 1984 *(privately by Queen Elizabeth II at Buckingham Palace)*
       died   1 November 2000

252   Sir Sacheverell Sitwell, Bt, CH   31 December 1983
       born   15 November 1897
       invested   10 February 1984 *(privately by Queen Elizabeth II at Buckingham Palace)*
       died   1 October 1988

253   David McAdam Eccles
       The Right Honourable the Viscount Eccles, CH, KCVO   16 June 1984
       born   18 September 1904
       invested   28 June 1984 *(privately by Queen Elizabeth II at Buckingham Palace)*
       died   24 February 1999

254   Friedrich August von Hayek, CH   16 June 1984
       born   8 May 1899
       invested   25 October 1984 *(privately by Queen Elizabeth II at Buckingham Palace)*
       died   23 March 1992

255   Sir Arnold Joseph Philip Powell, CH, OBE, RA   16 June 1984
       born   15 March 1921
       invested   28 June 1984 *(privately by Queen Elizabeth II at Buckingham Palace)*

256   The Right Honourable Joseph Pierre Yves Elliote Trudeau, CC, CH, QC   4 July 1984
       born   18 October 1919
       invested   29 September 1984 *(by Queen Elizabeth II on board HM Yacht Britannia)*
       died   28 September 2000

257   Sir Hugh Maxwell Casson, CH, KCVO, RA   31 December 1984
       born   23 May 1910
       invested   27 February 1985 *(privately by Queen Elizabeth II at Buckingham Palace)*
       died   15 August 1999

258   Philip Arthur Larkin, CH, CBE   15 June 1985
       born   9 August 1922
       invested   *[not invested; badge sent by post to Miss Margaret Jones, 19 February 1986]*
       died   2 December 1985

259   Rodney Robert Porter, CH, FRS   15 June 1985
       born   8 October 1917
       invested   10 July 1985 *(privately by Queen Elizabeth II at Buckingham Palace)*
       died   6 September 1985

260   Keith Sinjohn Joseph
       The Right Honourable the Lord Joseph, CH   21 May 1986
       born   17 January 1918
       invested   28 July 1987 *(privately by Queen Elizabeth II at Buckingham Palace)*
       died   10 December 1994

261   Sydney Brenner, CH, FRS   31 December 1986
       born   13 January 1927
       invested   19 February 1987 *(privately by Queen Elizabeth II at Buckingham Palace)*

262   Sir John Newenham Summerson, CH, CBE, FBA   31 December 1986
       born   25 November 1904
       invested   19 February 1987 *(privately by Queen Elizabeth II at Buckingham Palace)*
       died   10 November 1992

APPENDIX I 541

263 George Humphrey Wolferstan Rylands, CH, CBE 13 June 1987
born 23 October 1902
invested 29 July 1987 (privately by Queen Elizabeth II at Buckingham Palace)
died 16 January 1999

264 Sir Peter Markham Scott, CH, CBE, DSC, FRS 13 June 1987
born 14 September 1909
invested 16 July 1987 (privately by Queen Elizabeth II at Buckingham Palace)
died 29 August 1989

265 Norman Beresford Tebbit
The Right Honourable the Lord Tebbit, CH 31 July 1987
born 29 March 1931
invested 5 November 1987 (privately by Queen Elizabeth II at Buckingham Palace)

266 Anthony Dymoke Powell, CH, CBE 31 December 1987
born 21 December 1905
invested 17 February 1988 (privately by Queen Elizabeth II at Buckingham Palace)
died 28 March 2000

267 Stephen William Hawking, CH, CBE, FRS 17 June 1989
born 8 January 1942
invested 19 July 1989 (privately by Queen Elizabeth II at Buckingham Palace)

268 The Right Honourable David Russell Lange, CH 30 December 1989
born 4 August 1942
invested ...... February 1990 (by Queen Elizabeth II at Government House, Wellington)

269 Kenneth Wilfred Baker
The Right Honourable the Lord Baker of Dorking, CH 13 April 1992
born 3 November 1934
invested 13 April 1992 (privately by Queen Elizabeth II at Buckingham Palace)

270 Peter Leonard Brooke
The Right Honourable the Lord Brooke of Sutton Mandeville, CH 13 April 1992
born 3 March 1934
invested 13 April 1992 (privately by Queen Elizabeth II at Buckingham Palace)

271 Thomas Jeremy King
The Right Honourable the Lord King of Bridgwater, CH 13 April 1992
born 13 June 1933
invested 14 April 1992 (privately by Queen Elizabeth II at Windsor Castle)

272 Dame Elisabeth Jean Frink, CH, DBE 13 June 1992
born 14 November 1930
invested 29 October 1992 (at a general investiture by Queen Elizabeth II at Buckingham Palace)
died 18 April 1993

273 Noel Joseph Terence Montgomery Needham, CH, FRS, FBA 13 June 1992
born 9 December 1900
invested 27 October 1992 (at a general investiture by Queen Elizabeth II at Buckingham Palace)
died 24 March 1995

274 Sir Victor Sawdon Pritchett, CH, CBE 31 December 1992
born 16 December 1900
invested 10 February 1993 (at a general investiture by Queen Elizabeth II at Buckingham Palace)
died 20 March 1997

275	Charles Hubert Sisson, CH		12 June 1993
	born	22 April 1914	
	invested	2 November 1993 (at a general investiture by Queen Elizabeth II at Buckingham Palace)	
276	Elsie May Widdowson, CH, CBE, FRS		12 June 1993
	born	21 October 1906	
	invested	23 November 1993 (at a general investiture by Queen Elizabeth II at Buckingham Palace)	
	died	14 June 2000	
277	The Honourable Francis David Langhorne Astor, CH		31 December 1993
	born	5 March 1912	
	invested	29 March 1994 (at a general investiture by Queen Elizabeth II at Buckingham Palace)	
	died	6 December 2001	
278	Dame Janet Abbott Baker, CH, DBE		31 December 1993
	born	21 August 1933	
	invested	31 March 1994 (at a general investiture by the Prince of Wales at Buckingham Palace)	
279	Sir John Lindsay Eric Smith, CH, CBE		31 December 1993
	born	3 April 1923	
	invested	8 March 1994 (at a general investiture by the Prince of Wales at Buckingham Palace)	
280	Sir Alec Guinness, CH, CBE		11 June 1994
	born	2 April 1914	
	invested	28 July 1994 (privately by Queen Elizabeth II at Buckingham Palace)	
	died	5 August 2000	
281	Reginald Victor Jones, CH, CB, CBE, FRS		11 June 1994
	born	29 September 1911	
	invested	2 October 1994 (privately by Queen Elizabeth II at Balmoral Castle)	
	died	17 December 1997	
282	David Anthony Llewellyn Owen The Right Honourable the Lord Owen, CH		11 June 1994
	born	2 July 1938	
	invested	12 July 1994 (privately by Queen Elizabeth II at Buckingham Palace)	
283	Cesar Milstein, CH, FRS		31 December 1994
	born	8 October 1927	
	invested	1 March 1995 (privately by Queen Elizabeth II at Buckingham Palace)	
	died	24 March 2002	
284	Carel Victor Morlais Weight, CH, CBE, RA		31 December 1994
	born	10 September 1908	
	invested	1 March 1995 (privately by Queen Elizabeth II at Buckingham Palace)	
	died	13 August 1997	
285	Sir Denys Louis Lasdun, CH, CBE, RA		17 June 1995
	born	8 September 1914	
	invested	13 July 1995 (privately by Queen Elizabeth II at Buckingham Palace)	
	died	11 January 2001	
286	Sir Nevill Francis Mott, CH, FRS		17 June 1995
	born	30 September 1905	
	invested	14 July 1995 (privately by Queen Elizabeth II at Buckingham Palace)	
	died	8 August 1996	

APPENDIX I

287   Sir David Frederick Attenborough, CH, CVO, CBE, FRS   30 December 1995
- *born*   8 May 1926
- *invested*   29 February 1996 (privately by Queen Elizabeth II at Buckingham Palace)

288   Sir Richard William Shaboe Doll, CH, OBE, FRS   30 December 1995
- *born*   28 October 1912
- *invested*   29 February 1996 (privately by Queen Elizabeth II at Buckingham Palace)

289   Douglas Richard Hurd
The Right Honourable the Lord Hurd of Westwell, CH, CBE   30 December 1995
- *born*   8 March 1930
- *invested*   29 February 1996 (privately by Queen Elizabeth II at Buckingham Palace)

290   The Most Reverend Derek John Hartford Worlock, CH   30 December 1995
- *born*   4 February 1920
- *invested*   [badge sent by registered post to the Lord Lieutenant of Merseyside, 7 February 1996]
- *died*   8 February 1996

291   Richard Edward Geoffrey Howe
The Right Honourable the Lord Howe of Aberavon, CH, QC   15 June 1996
- *born*   20 December 1926
- *invested*   15 October 1996 (privately by Queen Elizabeth II at Buckingham Palace)

292   Alfred Leslie Rowse, CH, FBA   31 December 1996
- *born*   4 December 1903
- *invested*   [badge sent by registered post to the Lord Lieutenant of Cornwall, 21 February 1997]
- *died*   3 October 1997

293   David Hockney, CH, RA   14 June 1997
- *born*   9 July 1937
- *invested*   30 July 1997 (privately by Queen Elizabeth II at Buckingham Palace)

294   Michael Ray Dibdin Heseltine
The Right Honourable the Lord Heseltine, CH   2 August 1997
- *born*   21 March 1933
- *invested*   30 October 1997 (privately by Queen Elizabeth II at Buckingham Palace)

295   Eric John Ernest Hobsbawm, CH, FBA   31 December 1997
- *born*   9 June 1917
- *invested*   3 March 1998 (at a general investiture by Queen Elizabeth II at Buckingham Palace)

296   The Right Honourable Christopher Francis Patten, CH, CBE   31 December 1997
- *born*   12 May 1944
- *invested*   8 May 1998 (at a general investiture by the Prince of Wales at Buckingham Palace)

297   Peter Stephen Paul Brook, CH, CBE   13 June 1998
- *born*   21 March 1925
- *invested*   4 November 1998 (at a general investiture by Queen Elizabeth II at Buckingham Palace)

298   The Right Honourable John [Roy*] Major, CH   31 December 1998
- *born*   29 March 1943
- *invested*   9 June 1999 (privately by Queen Elizabeth II at Buckingham Palace)
- * a baptismal name which does not appear on his birth certificate

544 COMPANIONS OF HONOUR

299 Bridget Louise Riley, CH, CBE 31 December 1998
born 24 April 1931
invested 18 February 1999 *(privately by Queen Elizabeth II at Buckingham Palace)*

300 General Alfred John Gardyne Drummond De Chastelain, CMM, OC, CH
 31 December 1998
born 30 July 1937
invested 15 July 1999 *(privately by Queen Elizabeth II at Buckingham Palace)*

301 Richard Hamilton, CH 31 December 1999
born 24 February 1922
invested 10 February 2000 *(privately by Queen Elizabeth II at Buckingham Palace)*

302 Doris May Lessing, CH 31 December 1999
born 22 October 1919
invested 2 March 2000 *(privately by Queen Elizabeth II at Buckingham Palace)*

303 The Reverend Prebendary Edward Chad Varah, CH, CBE 31 December 1999
born 12 November 1911
invested 7 March 2000 *(at a general investiture by Queen Elizabeth II at Buckingham Palace)*

304 Amartya Kumar Sen, CH, FBA (Honorary) 11 May 2000
born 3 November 1933
invested 30 November 2000 *(privately by Queen Elizabeth II at Buckingham Palace)*

305 Sir Harrison Birtwistle, CH 30 December 2000
born 15 July 1934
invested 7 March 2001 *(privately by Queen Elizabeth II at Buckingham Palace)*

306 David Paul Scofield, CH, CBE 30 December 2000
born 21 January 1922
invested 13 February 2001 *(privately by Queen Elizabeth II at Buckingham Palace)*

307 Sir Colin Rex Davis, CH, CBE 16 June 2001
born 25 September 1927
invested 13 February 2002 *(at a general investiture by Queen Elizabeth II at Buckingham Palace)*

308 Sir George William Langham Christie, CH 31 December 2001
born 31 December 1934
invested 16 July 2002 *(privately by Queen Elizabeth II at Buckingham Palace)*

309 Bernard Haitink, CH, KBE (Honorary) 12 June 2002
born 4 March 1929
invested 5 December 2002 *(presented with the badge by Queen Elizabeth II at Buckingham Palace)*

310 Harold Pinter, CH, CBE 15 June 2002
born 10 October 1930
invested 6 November 2002 *(privately by Queen Elizabeth II at Buckingham Palace)*

311 Sir Michael Eliot Howard, CH, CBE, FBA 15 June 2002
born 29 November 1922
invested 30 October 2002 *(privately by Queen Elizabeth II at Buckingham Palace)*

APPENDIX 2

Officer of the Order of the Companions of Honour
The Secretary and Registrar

The first statutes of the Order, dated 15 October 1919, formally established the office of Secretary and Registrar and provided that appointments to the office should be made by warrant. In practice the office has always been held by the Secretary of the Central Chancery of the Orders of Knighthood, and the revised statutes of 11 November 1988 formally provide that it should be held ex officio.

Brigadier General Sir Douglas Frederick Rawdon Dawson   1919–1921
       born   25 April 1854
       died   20 January 1933

Colonel the Honourable Sir George Arthur Charles Crichton   1921–1936
       born   6 September 1874
       died   5 March 1952

Major Sir Henry Hudson Fraser Stockley   1936–1946
       born   30 October 1878
       died   30 July 1951

Brigadier Sir Ivan De la Bere   1946–1960
       born   25 April 1893
       died   27 December 1970

Major General Sir Cyril Harry Colquhoun   1960–1968
       born   16 August 1903
       died   5 June 1996

Major General Sir Peter Bernard Gillett   1968–1979
       born   8 December 1913
       died   4 July 1989

Major General Sir Desmond Hind Garrett Rice   1980–1989
       born   1 December 1924

Lieutenant Colonel Walter Hugh Malcolm Ross   1989–1991
       born   27 October 1943

Lieutenant Colonel Anthony Charles McClure Mather   1991–1999
       born   21 April 1942

Lieutenant Colonel Robert Guy Cartwright   1999–
       born   6 August 1950

BIBLIOGRAPHY

Adams, Jad, *Tony Benn. A biography*, (London, 1992).
Attlee, Clement, *As it happened*, (London, 1954).
Ayre, Leslie, *The wit of music*, (London, 1971).
Balsan, Consuelo Vanderbilt, *Glitter and gold*, (London, 1952).
Banks, Olive, *The biographical dictionary of British feminists*, 2 volumes, (Brighton, 1985–90).
Bardon, Jonathan, *A history of Ulster*, (Belfast, 2001).
Battiscombe, Georgina, *Queen Alexandra*, (London, 1969).
Beecham, Thomas, *Frederick Delius*, (London, 1959).
Bellamy, Joyce and John Saville, *Dictionary of labour biography*, 9 volumes to date, (London, 1972–).
Berthoud, Roger, *The life of Henry Moore*, (London, 1987).
Beyers, C. J., (ed), *Dictionary of South African biography*, 5 volumes, (Durban, 1968–87).
Bissell, Claude, *The imperial Canadian. Vincent Massey in office*, (Toronto, 1986).
Boodhoo, Ken I. (ed), *Eric Williams. The man and the leader*, (Lanham, Maryland, 1986).
Bradford, Sarah, *George VI*, (London, 1989).
Bramwell-Booth, Catherine, *Bramwell Booth*, (London, 1933).
Brome, Vincent, *J. B. Priestley*, (London, 1988).
Buckland, Patrick, *A history of Northern Ireland*, (Dublin, 1981).
Bullock, Alan and R. B. Woodings, *The Fontana biographical companion to modern thought*, (London, 1983).
Bunting, Sir John, *R. G. Menzies. A portrait*, (Australia, 1988).
Butler, J. R. M., *Lord Lothian (Philip Kerr) 1882–1940*, (London, 1960).
Byrt, G. W., *John Clifford. A fighting free churchman*, (London, 1947).
Cannadine, David, *G. M. Trevelyan. A life in history*, (London, 1992).
Carlile, John Charles, *My life's little day*, (London, 1935).
Carrington, Lord, *Reflect on things past*, (London, 1988).
Carswell, John, *Government and the universities in Britain: programme and performance 1960–1980*, (Cambridge, 1985).
Chadwick, Owen,
 – *Michael Ramsey. A life*, (London, 1990).
 – *The Victorian church*, third edition, 2 volumes, (London, 1971).
Checkland, Sarah Jane, *Ben Nicholson. The vicious circles of his life and art*, (London, 2000).
Chilvers, Ian, *A dictionary of twentieth-century art*, (Oxford, 1999).
Churchill, Randolph S., *Lord Derby 'King of Lancashire'*, (London, 1959).
Churchill, Winston, *The second world war*, 6 volumes, (London, 1948–1954).
Clynes, J. R., *Memoirs*, 2 volumes, (London, 1937).
Cole-Mackintosh, Ronnie, *A century of service towards mankind. The story of the St John Ambulance Brigade*, second edition, (London, 1994).
Cooke, Colin, *The life of Richard Stafford Cripps*, (London, 1957).
Craig, Edward Anthony, *Gordon Craig: the story of his life*, (London, 1968).
Cresswell, Walter, *Margaret McMillan. A memoir*, (London, 1948).
Cross, J. A., *Lord Swinton*, (Oxford, 1982).
Current biography yearbook, (New York, 1940–).
Daniell, A. E., *London city churches*, (London, 1895).
Dark, Sidney, *Wilson Carlile. The laughing cavalier of Christ*, (London, 1944).
Darlow, T. H., *William Robertson Nicoll: Life and letters*, (London, 1925).
Davies, Rupert, *John Scott Lidgett: a symposium*, (London, 1957).
de Gaury, Gerald, *Three kings in Baghdad 1921–1958*, (London, 1961).
De la Bere, Sir Ivan, *The queen's orders of chivalry*, (London, 1964).
De-la-Noy, Michael, *The honours system*, (London, 1985).
Dictionary of national biography.
Diefenbaker, John G.,
 – *One Canada. The crusading years 1895–1956*, (Toronto, 1975).
 – *One Canada. The tumultuous years 1962–1967*, (Toronto, 1977)
 – *One Canada. The years of achievement 1957–1962*, (Toronto, 1976).

Dimbleby, Jonathan, *The last governor. Chris Patten and the handover of Hong Kong*, (London, 1997).
Dimond, Frances and Roger Taylor, *Crown and camera. The royal family and photography 1842–1910*, (London, 1987).
Dorey, Peter, *The Major premiership. Politics and policies under John Major 1990–1997*, (London, 1999).
Drabble, Margaret, *The Oxford companion to English literature*, fifth edition, (Oxford, 1985).
Duchene, Francois, *Jean Monnet. The first statesmen of interdependence*,
(New York, 1994).
Eden, Anthony, *Full circle*, (London, 1960).
Encyclopedia Canadiana. The encyclopedia of Canada, 10 volumes (Toronto, 1975).
Ervine, St John, *God's soldier. General William Booth*, (London, 1934).
Eyck, Frank, *G. P. Gooch. A study in history and politics*, (London, 1982).
Eynat-Confino, Irene, *Beyond the mask: Edward Gordon Craig, movement, and the actor* (Carbondale, Illinois, USA, 1987).
Eyre, Richard, *Changing stages. A view of British theatre in the twentieth century*, (London, 2000).
Feldman, Burton, *The Nobel prize. A history of genius, controversy and prestige*, (New York, 2000).
Forbes, Grania, *My darling Buffy. The early life of the queen mother*, (London, 1997).
Fransen, Frederic, *The supranational politics of Jean Monnet. Ideas and origins of the European Community*, (Westport, USA, 2000).
Galloway, Peter,
 – *The Most Illustrious Order*, (London, 1999).
 – *The Order of the British Empire*, (London, 1996).
 – *The Order of St Michael and St George*, (London, 2000).
Gilbert, Martin, *Winston Churchill*, (London, 1979).
Gladwyn, Cynthia, *The Paris embassy*, (London, 1976).
Glendinning, Victoria, *Vita. The life of V. Sackville West*, (London, 1983).
Gooch, George Peabody, *Under six reigns*, (London, 1958).
Goodman, Arnold, *Tell them I'm on my way*, (London, 1993).
Goring, Rosemary,
 – *Chambers Scottish biographical dictionary*, (Edinburgh, 1992).
 – *Larousse dictionary of writers*, (Edinburgh, 1994).
Granatstein, J. L., *The generals. The Canadian army's senior commanders in the Second World War*, (Toronto, c.1993).
Greig, Geordie, *Louis and the prince. A story of politics, intrigue and royal friendship*, (London, 1999).
Guinness, Alec, *Blessings in disguise*, (London, 1985).
Hailsham, Lord, *A sparrow's flight. The memoirs of Lord Hailsham*, (London, 1990).
Haldane, Elizabeth Sanderson, *From one century to another*, (London, 1937).
Hamilton, Ian, *The Oxford companion to twentieth-century poetry in English*, (Oxford, 1994).
Harcourt, Melville, *Tubby Clayton, a personal saga*, (London, 1953).
Harte, Negley, *The university of London 1836–1986*, (London, 1986).
Hartnoll, Phyllis, *The Oxford companion to the theatre*, fourth edition, (London, 1995).
Haste, Kate, *Keep the home fires burning. Propaganda in the first world war*, (London, 1977).
Hastings, Adrian, *A history of English Christianity 1920–1985*, (London, 1986).
Hawkes, Jacquetta, *Mortimer Wheeler. Adventurer in archaeology*, (London, 1982).
Headley, Gwyn *and* Wim Meulenkamp, *Follies, grottoes and garden buildings*, (London, 1999).
Healey, Denis, *The time of my life*, (London, 1989).
Hearnshaw, F. J. C., *The centenary history of King's College London 1828–1928*, (London, 1929).
Hillman, Judy, and Peter Clarke, *Geoffrey Howe. A quiet revolutionary*, (London, 1988).
Howe, Geoffrey, *Conflict of loyalty*, (London, 1994).
Hubback, David, *No ordinary press baron. A life of Walter Layton*, (London, 1985).
Huelin, Gordon, *King's College London 1828–1978*, (London, 1978).
Hutchison, Bruce, *Mr prime minister 1867–1964*, (Ontario, 1964).
Ingamells, John, *The Davies collection of French art*, (Cardiff, 1967).
Ingham, Kenneth, *Jan Christian Smuts. The conscience of a South African*, (London, 1986).
Innes, Christopher, *Edward Gordon Craig*, (Cambridge, 1983).
Jasper, R. C. D., *Life and letters of Arthur Cayley Headlam*, (London, 1960).
Jefferson, George, *Edward Garnett. A life in literature*, (London, 1982).
Jenkins, Emlyn G., *Cofiant Elfed 1860–1953*, (Aberystwyth, 1957).

Jenkins, Roy, *Portraits and miniatures*, (London, 1993).
Jones, Anthony Mark, *Eric Eustace Williams. 'A very private person' and his publics* (sic), (Trinidad and Tobago, c.1983).
Jones, Jack, *Union man. The autobiography of Jack Jones*, (London, 1986).
Jones, John Daniel, *Three score years and ten*, (London, 1940).
Kemp, Sandra, and Charlotte Mitchell and David Trotter, *Edwardian fiction. An Oxford companion*, (Oxford, 1997).
Kennedy, Michael, *The Oxford dictionary of music*, (London, 1994).
Kerr, Mark, *The life of Prince Louis of Battenberg. Admiral of the Fleet*, (London, 1934).
Keyes, Roger, *Outrageous fortune. The tragedy of Leopold III of the Belgians 1901–1941*, (London, 1984).
King, Sir Edwin and Luke, Sir Harry, *The knights of St John in the British realm*, (London, 1967).
Kirk, John Foster, *A supplement to Allibone's critical dictionary of English literature and British American authors*, 2 volumes, (Philadelphia, 1891).
Koss, Stephen, *Fleet Street radical. A. G. Gardiner and the Daily News*, (London, 1973).
Kotelawala, Sir John, *An Asian prime minister's story*, (London, 1956).
Landmark Trust, *The landmark trust handbook*, (Maidenhead, 1998).
Lapping, Brian, *End of empire*, (London, 1985).
Laybourn, Keith, *Philip Snowden: a biography 1864–1937*, (Aldershot, 1988).
Lever, Tresham, *Clayton of Toc H*, (London, 1971).
Lidgett, John Scott,
 – *Reminiscences*, (London, 1928).
 – *My guided life*, (London, 1936).
Lloyd, Selwyn,
 – *Mr Speaker, Sir*, (London, 1976).
 – *Suez 1956: a personal account*, (London, 1978).
Lloyd George, David, *War memoirs of David Lloyd George*, 6 volumes, (London, 1933–36).
Lockhart, J. G., *Cosmo Gordon Lang*, (London, 1949).
McLintock, A. H. (ed), *An encyclopaedia of New Zealand*, 3 volumes, (Wellington, 1966).
McRedmond, Louis, *Modern Irish lives. Dictionary of 20th-century Irish biography*, (Dublin, 1996).
Madol, Hans Roger, *The private life of Queen Alexandra*, (London, 1940).
Mahabir, Winston, *In and out of politics. Tales of the government of Dr Eric Williams from the notebooks of a former minister*, (Trinidad and Tobago, 1978).
Manser, Jose, *Hugh Casson. The biography*, (London, 2000).
Marchant, Sir James, *Dr John Clifford. Life, letters and reminiscences*, (London, 1924).
Markham, Violet, *May Tennant. A portrait*, (London, 1949).
Marshall, John, *Memoirs, volume 1: 1912–1960*, (Auckland, 1983).
Martin, Paul, *A very public life*, (Toronto, 1983).
Martindale, Hilda, *From one generation to another 1839–1944. A book of memoirs*, (London, 1944).
Massey, Vincent, *What's past is prologue*, (London, 1963).
Matthews, W. R., *Memories and meanings*, (London, 1969).
Maugham, W. Somerset,
 – *A writer's notebook*, (London, 1967).
 – *The summing up*, (London, 1963).
Micklem, Nathaniel, *The box and the puppets 1888–1953*, (London, 1957).
Morris, Richard, *Cheshire. The biography of Leonard Cheshire, VC, OM*, (London, 2000).
Muldoon, R. D., *Muldoon*, (Wellington, 1977).
Murphy, Brian, *Dictionary of Australian history*, (Sydney, 1982).
Murphy, Edward F., *The Macmillan treasury of relevant quotations*, (London, 1979).
Murphy, Philip, *Alan Lennox-Boyd. A biography*, (London, 1999).
National Museum of Wales, *Catalogue of the Gwendoline E. Davies bequest of paintings, drawings and sculpture*, (Cardiff, 1952).
Newbolt, Sir Henry, *My world as in my time. Memoirs of Sir Henry Newbolt 1862–1932*, (London, 1932).
Newman, Peter C., *Renegade in power. The Diefenbaker years*, (Toronto, 1963).
Nicolson, Harold, *Diaries and letters 1930–1964*, (London, 1980).
Norman, Jesse, *The achievement of Michael Oakeshott*, (London, 1993).
O'Connor, Garry, *Paul Scofield – the biography*, (London, 2002).
Ousby, Ian, *The Cambridge guide to literature in English*, (Cambridge, 1993).
Owen, David, *Time to declare*, (London, 1991).

Owen, H. P., *W. R. Matthews: philosopher and theologian*, (London, 1976).
Patten, Christopher, *East and west*, (London, 1998).
Payne, Ernest A., *The Baptist Union. A short history*, (London, 1959).
Pimlott, Ben, *Hugh Dalton*, (London, 1985).
Plarr, Victor G., *Men and women of the time. A dictionary of contemporaries*, fifteenth edition, (London 1889).
Pogson, Rex, *Miss Horniman and the Gaiety Theatre, Manchester*, (London, 1952).
Ponsonby, Frederick, *Recollections of three reigns*, (London, 1951).
Porritt, Arthur, *J. D. Jones of Bournemouth*, (London, 1942).
Powell, Anthony, *Journals 1987–1989*, (London, 1996).
Proctor-Gregg, Humphrey, *Beecham remembered*, (London, 1976).
Purdom, C. B., *Harley Granville Barker. Man of the theatre, dramatist and scholar*, (London, 1955).
Reeve, James, *Cocktails, crises and cockroaches. A diplomatic trail*, (London, 1999).
Reid, Charles, *John Barbirolli*, (London, 1971).
Ripper, William, *Ripper's steam engine theory and practice*, eighth edition rewritten and enlarged by William J Goudie, (London, 1932).
Roberts, Peter, *The Old Vic story. A nation's theatre 1818–1976*, (London, 1976).
Robertson, Alec, *More than music*, (London. 1961).
Rohde, Shelley, *L. S. Lowry. A biography*, third edition, (London, 1999).
Romanov, Prince Dimitri, *The orders, medals and history of imperial Russia*, (Denmark, 2000).
Rose, Kenneth,
  - *King George V*, (London, 1983).
  - *Kings, queens and courtiers*, (London, 1985).
Rose, M., *Artist potters in England*, (London, 1970).
Rosenthal, Harold and John Warrack, *The concise Oxford dictionary of opera*, (Oxford, 1987).
Rothenstein, Sir John, *Modern English painters*, 3 volumes, (London, 1976).
Rowan, Edgar, *Wilson Carlile and the Church Army*, fifth edition, (London, 1956).
Rowse, A. L., *A Cornish childhood*, (London, 1942).
Salter, Lord, *Memoirs of a public servant*, (London, 1961).
Sanger, Clyde, *Malcolm Macdonald. Bringing an end to empire*, (Liverpool, 1995).
Sen, S. P. (ed), *Dictionary of national biography*, 4 volumes, (Calcutta, 1972–74).
Shuckburgh, Evelyn, *Descent to Suez. Diaries 1951–56*, (London, 1986).
Sinclair, Andrew, *Francis Bacon. His life and violent times*, (London, 1993).
Sinclair, Keith, *Walter Nash*, (Oxford and Auckland, 1976).
Snowden, Philip, Viscount, *An autobiography*, 2 volumes, (London, 1934).
Somerset Fry, Peter and Fiona, *A history of Ireland*, (London, 1988).
Spater, George and Ian Parsons, *A marriage of true minds. An intimate portrait of Leonard and Virginia Woolf*, (London, 1977).
Spender, Stephen, *World within world*, (London, 1977).
Spuler, Bertold, *Rulers and governments of the world*, volume 3, 1930–1975, (London, 1977).
Stenton, Michael and Stephen Lees, *Who's Who of British members of parliament*, volume 3 1919–1945 (Sussex, 1979) and volume 4 1945–1979 (Sussex, 1981).
Stephens, Meic,
  - *The Oxford companion to the literature of Wales*, (Oxford, 1986).
  - *The new companion to the literature of Wales*, (Cardiff, 1998).
Stewart, Walter, *Shrug. Trudeau in power*, (Toronto, 1971).
Stuart, James, *Within the fringe. An autobiography*, (London, 1967).
Stuart, Mark, *Douglas Hurd. The public servant. An authorised biography*, (Edinburgh, 1998).
Sutherland, John, *The Longman companion to Victorian fiction*, (London, 1988).
Tebbit, Norman, *Upwardly mobile*, (London, 1989).
Terrill, Ross, *R. H. Tawney and his times*, (London, 1974).
Thorn, James, *Peter Fraser. New Zealand's wartime prime minister*, (London, 1952).
Thorpe, D. R., *Selwyn Lloyd*, (London, 1989).
Trombley, Stephen, *Sir Frederick Treves*, (London, 1989).
Trotter, Ann, *New Zealand and Japan 1945–1952: the occupation and the peace treaty*, (London, 1990).
Vansittart, Lord, *The mist procession – the autobiography of Lord Vansittart*, (London, 1958).
Vinson, James (ed), *Twentieth-century fiction*, (London, 1983).
Walker, Patrick Gordon, *Restatement of liberty*, (London, 1951).
Ward, A. C., *Longman's companion to twentieth century literature*, second edition, (London, 1975).

Ward, Russel, *The history of Australia. The twentieth century 1901–1975*, (London, 1978).
Watkinson, Harold, *Turning points. A record of our times*, (London, 1986).
Webb, Beatrice, *The diary of Beatrice Webb*, 4 volumes, edited by Norman MacKenzie and Jean Mackenzie, (London, 1983–85).
Weaver, Stewart, *The Hammonds. A marriage in history*, (Stanford, USA, 1997).
Westell, Anthony, *Paradox. Trudeau as prime minister*, (Scarborough, Ontario, 1972).
Who's who in New Zealand, twelfth edition, (Wellington, 1991).
Williams, Eric, *Inward hunger. The education of a prime minister*, (London, 1969).
Wilson, Duncan, *Leonard Woolf. A political biography*, (London, 1978).
Wingate, Sir Ronald, *Lord Ismay. A biography*, (London, 1970).
Winnifrith, Alfred, *Men of Kent and Kentishmen, Biographical notices of 680 worthies of Kent, written by a man of Kent*, (Folkestone, 1913).
Winterton, Earl, *Orders of the day*, (London, 1953).
Woolf, Virginia, *The diary of Virginia Woolf, volume IV 1931–1935*, (London, 1983).
Wright, Vernon, *David Lange. Prime minister*, (Wellington, 1984).
Zavos, Spiro, *The real Muldoon*, (Wellington, 1978).

Thorn, James, *Peter Fraser. New Zealand's wartime prime minister*, London, 1952).
Thorpe, D. R., *Selwyn Lloyd*, (London, 1989).
Trombley, Stephen, *Sir Frederick Treves*, (London, 1989).
Trotter, Ann, *New Zealand and Japan 1945–1952: the occupation and the peace treaty*, (London, 1990).
Vansittart, Lord, *The mist procession – the autobiography of Lord Vansittart*, (London, 1958).
Vinson, James (ed), *Twentieth-century fiction*, (London, 1983).
Walker, Patrick Gordon, *Restatement of liberty*, (London, 1951).
Ward, A. C., *Longman's companion to twentieth century literature*, second edition, (London, 1975).
Ward, Russel, *The history of Australia. The twentieth century 1901–1975*, (London, 1978).
Watkinson, Harold, *Turning points. A record of our times*, (London, 1986).
Webb, Beatrice, *The diary of Beatrice Webb*, 4 volumes, edited by Norman MacKenzie and Jean Mackenzie, (London, 1983–85).
Westell, Anthony, *Paradox. Trudeau as prime minister*, (Scarborough, Ontario, 1972).
Who's who in New Zealand, twelfth edition, (Wellington, 1991).
Williams, Eric, *Inward hunger. The education of a prime minister*, (London, 1969).
Wilson, Duncan, *Leonard Woolf. A political biography*, (London, 1978).
Wingate, Sir Ronald, *Lord Ismay. A biography*, (London, 1970).
Winnifrith, Alfred, *Men of Kent and Kentishmen, Biographical notices of 680 worthies of Kent, written by a man of Kent*, (Folkestone, 1913).
Winterton, Earl, *Orders of the day*, (London, 1953).
Woolf, Virginia, *The diary of Virginia Woolf, volume IV 1931–1935*, (London, 1983).
Wright, Vernon, *David Lange. Prime minister*, (Wellington, 1984).
Zavos, Spiro, *The real Muldoon*, (Wellington, 1978).

REFERENCES

Archive Sources

CCOK   Central Chancery of the Orders of Knighthood, St James's Palace
COCS   Cabinet Office, Ceremonial Secretariat
RA   Royal Archives

Chapter 1   In the beginning

1. Sir Ivan De la Bere, *The queen's orders of chivalry*, p. 170.
2. CCOK, OBE Letters, Box Misc., Report of the committee appointed to enquire into the advisability of instituting a new decoration for services in connection with the war. Printed for the use of the cabinet, 8 July 1916, p. 2.
3. CCOK, OBE Institution Letters Box, Sir Frederick Ponsonby to the Comptroller, the Lord Chamberlain's Office, 23 June 1916.
4. ibid., an unsigned and undated memorandum headed, 'New Order. Note on Committee's Report'.
5. CCOK, OBE Letters, Box 1, Sir Frederick Ponsonby to Sir Edward Troup, 13 October, 1916.
6. ibid., Memorandum by Sir Douglas Dawson, 11 December 1916.
7. CCOK, OBE Letters, Box 2, Memorandum by Lord Curzon submitted to the war cabinet, 1 April 1917.
8. ibid., Sir Frederick Ponsonby to Sir Douglas Dawson, 5 April 1917.
9. ibid., paraphrase of a circular telegram by the secretary of state for the colonies, sent 8pm, 25 April 1917.
10. ibid., Sir Amherst Selby-Bigge to Sir Frederick Ponsonby, 26 April 1917.
11. ibid., Sir Frederick Ponsonby to Sir Amherst Selby-Bigge, 27 April 1917.
12. ibid., George Cunningham to Sir Frederick Ponsonby, 1 May 1917.
13. CCOK, 37/18, Memorandum by F. S. Osgood on a meeting held on 15 May 1917.
14. COCS, BE1A, Minutes of a meeting, 1 May 1917.
15. ibid.
16. CCOK, OBE Letters, Box 2, Sir Frederick Ponsonby to J. T. Davies, 2 May 1917.
17. ibid., Prince Louis of Battenberg to Sir Frederick Ponsonby, 8 May 1917.
18. ibid., Sir Frederick Ponsonby to Earl Curzon of Kedleston, 23 May 1917.
19. CCOK, OBE Letters, Box 1, Sir Frederick Ponsonby to Prince Louis of Battenberg, 10 February 1917.
20. ibid., Sir Frederick Ponsonby to Prince Louis of Battenberg, 10 February 1917.
21. CCOK, OBE Letters, Box 2, Earl Curzon of Kedleston to Sir Frederick Ponsonby, 26 May 1917.
22. ibid., Sir Frederick Ponsonby to Prince Louis of Battenberg, 8 June 1917.
23. ibid., Sir Frederick Ponsonby to Earl Curzon of Kedleston, 8 June 1917.
24. ibid., 9 June 1917.
25. ibid., draft press release by Earl Curzon of Kedleston, no date, but June 1917.
26. CCOK, 37/18, H. Farnham Burke to Sir Douglas Dawson, 30 January 1918.
27. CCOK, 37/19, Sir Douglas Dawson to Earl of Crawford and Balcarres, 23 April 1918.
28. ibid., Earl of Crawford and Balcarres to Sir Douglas Dawson, 24 April 1918.
29. ibid., Sir Douglas Dawson to Earl of Crawford and Balcarres, 25 April 1918.
30. ibid., Earl of Crawford and Balcarres to David Lloyd George, 26 April 1918.
31. ibid., C. A. Kemball to Sir Douglas Dawson, 11 January 1919.
32. ibid., Sir Thomas Holdernesse to Sir Douglas Dawson, 12 May 1919.
33. ibid., R. Graham to Sir Douglas Dawson, 30 May 1919.
34. ibid., H. Farnham Burke to H. H. Stockley, 26 June 1919.

Chapter 2   The dogs of war

1. CCOK, OBE Letters, Box 2, Sir Frederick Ponsonby to Prince Louis of Battenberg, 8 June 1917.
2. ibid., Sir Frederick Ponsonby to Prince Louis of Battenberg, 8 June 1917.
3. ibid., Sir Frederick Ponsonby to S. W. Harris, 15 June 1917.

4 ibid., Sir Frederick Ponsonby to Earl Curzon of Kedleston, 8 June 1917.
5 RA, PS/GV/P284, Lord Stamfordham to the Governor General of Australia, 11 September 1917.
6 CCOK, OBE Letters Box 2, Lord Curzon to Sir Frederick Ponsonby, 7 June 1917.
7 ibid., Sir Frederick Ponsonby to J. T. Davies, 27 June 1917.
8 Sir Frederick Ponsonby to Earl Curzon of Kedleston, 28 June 1917.
9 RA, PS/GV/P284, Lord Stamfordham to the Governor General of Australia, 11 September 1917.
10 Kenneth Ingham, *The conscience of a South African*, pp. 101–02.
11 Joyce Bellamy and John Saville, *Dictionary of labour biography*, volume 2, p. 375.
12 ibid.
13 *The Times*, 3 September 1928.
14 CCOK, 37/21, H. Stockley to W. Scott, 13 June 1921 and 29 June 1921.
15 Lloyd George, *War memoirs*, volume 2, pp. 596–98.
16 ibid., p. 598.
17 William Ripper, *Ripper's steam engine theory and practice*, eighth edition rewritten and enlarged by William J Goudie.
18 CCOK, OBE Letters, Box 2, Lord Stamfordham to Sir Frederick Ponsonby, 20 August 1917.
19 *Dictionary of national biography 1931–40*, p. 368.
20 ibid., p. 389
21 Violet Markham, *May Tennant. A portrait*, p. 34.
22 Lloyd George, *War memoirs*, volume 3, p. 1367.
23 Violet Markham, *May Tennant. A portrait*, pp. 49–50.
24 Claude Bisell, *The imperial Canadian. Vincent Massey in office*, p.17.
25 Vincent Massey, *What's past is prologue*, p. 441.
26 Lloyd George, *War memoirs*, volume 6, p. 3339.
27 *Dictionary of national biography 1931–40*, p. 534.
28 ibid., *1922–1930*, pp. 819–20.
29 *The Times*, 19 March 1934.
30 Victor G. Plarr, *Men and women of the time. A dictionary of contemporaries*, p. 396.
31 *The Times*, 29 September 1919.
32 John Foster Kirk, *A supplement to Allibone's critical dictionary of English literature and British American authors*, volume 1, p. 639.
33 Joyce Bellamy and John Saville, *Dictionary of labour biography*, volume 2, p. 290.
34 *The Times*, 16 February 1922.
35 ibid., 13 July 1926.
36 Sir Frederick Ponsonby, *Recollections of three reigns*, p. 142.
37 Stephen Trombley, *Sir Frederick Treves*, p. 171.
38 ibid., p. 186.
39 ibid., p. 148.
40 CCOK, 37/18, note by Sir Frederick Ponsonby on a memorandum from Sir Douglas Dawson, 21 June 1918.
41 *Dictionary of national biography 1961–1970*, p. 637.
42 David Hubback, *No ordinary press baron*, p. 38.
43 Lloyd George, *War memoirs*, volume 1, p. 251.
44 ibid., volume 3, p. 1587.
45 *Dictionary of national biography 1961–1970*, p. 638.
46 CCOK, OBE Letters Box 2, W. Graham Greene to Sir Frederick Ponsonby, 25 August 1917.
47 Lloyd George, *War memoirs*, volume 3, p. 1220.
48 ibid., p. 1079.
49 CCOK, 37/18, Sir Douglas Dawson to Sir Frederick Ponsonby, 9 December 1918.
50 COCS, H59, Sir Arthur Stanley to Sir Frederick Ponsonby, 19 August 1919.
51 ibid., Sir Frederick Ponsonby to Sir Arthur Stanley, 24 August 1919.
52 ibid., Sir Arthur Stanley to Sir Frederick Ponsonby, 27 August 1919.
53 ibid., 28 April 1920.
54 ibid., Sir Frederick Ponsonby to Sir Arthur Stanley, 29 April 1920.
55 ibid., 30 November 1920.
56 ibid., Sir Frederick Ponsonby to J. T. Davies, 7 December 1920.
57 RA, PS/GV/J1866/10, Sir Frederick Ponsonby to Lieutenant Colonel Ronald Waterhouse, 27 April 1923.
58 RA, PS/GV/J1964/4, Lord Stamfordham to Ramsay Macdonald, 6 November 1924.
59 RA, PS/GV/J1964/9, Stanley Baldwin to Lord Stamfordham, 20 November 1924.
60 RA, PS/GV/J1964/10, Lord Stamfordham to the Prime Minister, 28 November 1924.
61 RA, PS/GV/J1964/11, Stanley Baldwin to Lord Stamfordham, 28 November 1924.

Chapter 3 In God's name

1 RA, PS/GV/J1707/25, J. T. Davies to Lord Stamfordham, 25 May 1921.
2 ibid.

3 RA, PS/GV/J1707/30, Randall Davidson to Lord Stamfordham, 25 May 1921.
4 RA, PS/GV/J1707/31, note by Lord Stamfordham, 26 May 1921.
5 RA, PS/GV/J1813/25, List of suggested honours. Mr Lloyd George and Mr Austen Chamberlain, no date. Annotated in the handwriting of King George V.
6 RA, PS/GV/J1707/29, unsigned memorandum, no date, but after 26 May 1921.
7 RA, PS/GV/J1813/25, List of suggested honours. Mr Lloyd George and Mr Austen Chamberlain, no date. Annotated in the handwriting of King George V.
8 Adrian Hastings, *A history of English Christianity 1920–1985*, p. 97.
9 Sir James Marchant, *Dr John Clifford*, p. 79.
10 *Dictionary of national biography 1941–50*, pp. 369–71.
11 ibid.
12 *Annual Register*, 1923, p. 164.
13 ibid.
14 A. E. Daniell, *London city churches*, p. 241.
15 *The Times*, 16 November 1931, p. 17.
16 ibid.
17 J. G. Lockhart, *Cosmo Gordon Lang*, p. 332.
18 ibid., p. 375.
19 *Dictionary of national biography 1941–50*, p. 438.
20 COCS, H59, Robert Fitzarcher to the Prime Minister, 13 April 1929.
21 ibid., Sir James Marchant to the Prime Minister, 16 April 1929.
22 ibid., 18 April 1929.
23 *The Times*, 2 August 1956.
24 *Dictionary of national biography 1971–80*, p. 157.
25 ibid.
26 Adrian Hastings, *A history of English Christianity 1920–1985*, p. 120.
27 ibid.
28 *Dictionary of national biography 1951–60*, p. 635.
29 *Dictionary of national biography 1941–50*, p. 380
30 ibid.
31 *The Times*, 30 September 1961.
32 ibid.
33 Adrian Hastings, *A history of English Christianity 1920–1985*, p. 179.
34 *Dictionary of national biography 1971–80*, p. 243.
35 ibid.
36 *The Times*, 24 September 1973.
37 *Dictionary of national biography 1971–80*, p. 244.
38 ibid., p. 556.
39 Adrian Hastings, *A history of English Christianity 1920–1985*, p. 470.
40 *Dictionary of national biography 1971–80*, p. 569.
41 Adrian Hastings, *A history of English Christianity 1920–1985*, p. 271.
42 *Dictionary of national biography 1971–80*, p. 570.
43 *The Times*, 9 February 1996, p. 19.

Chapter 4 All the pride of power

1 Selwyn Lloyd, *Mr speaker, sir*, p. 160.
2 Clyde Sanger, *Malcolm Macdonald. Bringing an end to empire*, p. 257.
3 ibid., p. 283.
4 *Dictionary of national biography 1981–1985*, p. 256.
5 Beatrice Webb, *Diary of Beatrice Webb*, volume 2, p. 287, 8 July 1903.
6 J. R. Clynes, *Memoirs*, volume 1, p. 97.
7 Philip Snowden, *An autobiography*, volume 2, p. 723.
8 *The Times*, 12 November 1965.
9 ibid.
10 ibid.
11 Martin Gilbert, *Winston S. Churchill*, volume VIII 1945–1965, p. 1124.
12 *The Times*, 14 December 1970.
13 ibid., 17 October 1955.
14 *Dictionary of national biography 1931–1940*, p. 713.
15 Consuelo Vanderbilt Balsan, *Glitter and gold*, p. 161.
16 ibid., p. 162.
17 *Dictionary of national biography 1961–1970*, p. 44.
18 *The Times*, 12 January 1965.
19 ibid.
20 ibid., 15 December 1964.
21 ibid., 20 March 1965.
22 ibid., 6 August 1956.
23 Peter and Fiona Somerset Fry, *A history of Ireland*, p. 330.
24 Jonathan Bardon, *A history of Ulster*, p. 564.
25 ibid., p. 573.
26 Patrick Buckland, *A history of Northern Ireland*, p. 91.
27 *Dictionary of national biography 1941–1950*, p. 807.
28 ibid.
29 *The Times*, 29 July 1972.
30 ibid.
31 ibid., 4 February 1957.
32 ibid., 6 September 1971.
33 Clement Attlee, *As it happened*, pp. 28–29.
34 *The Times*, 9 October 1967.

35 ibid.
36 ibid.
37 Denis Healey, *The time of my life*, p. 153.
38 *The Times*, 10 June 1954.
39 ibid.
40 *The Times*, 18 December 1965.
41 ibid.
42 ibid.
43 ibid.
44 Sir Ronald Wingate, *Lord Ismay*, pp. 128–29.
45 Roy Jenkins, *Portraits and miniatures*, p. 242.
46 *The Times*, 17 September 1955.
47 Roy Jenkins, *Portraits and miniatures*, p. 243.
48 *The Times*, 16 February 1962.
49 Hilda Martindale, *From one generation to another*, pp. 34–35
50 *The Times*, 4 November 1955.
51 COCS, H59, 'Extract from Mr Rowan's minute to the Prime Minister', 4 May 1947.
52 *British Weekly*, 5 October 1933.
53 Denis Healey, *The time of my life*, p. 471.
54 Colin Cooke, *The life of Richard Stafford Cripps*, p. 405.
55 *The Times*, 8 March 1965.
56 ibid.
57 ibid., 9 January 1958.
58 ibid., 12 November 1965.
59 ibid., 6 September 1965.
60 *Dictionary of national biography 1981–1985*, p. 64.
61 ibid., p. 55.
62 Anthony Eden, *Full circle*, p. 318.
63 *The Times*, 18 October 1961.
64 Lord Winterton, *Orders of the day*, p. 64.
65 Geordie Greig, *Louis and the prince*, p. 184.
66 Sarah Bradford, *George VI*, p. 101.
67 Kenneth Rose, *Kings, queens and courtiers*, p. 269.
68 Grania Forbes, *My darling Buffy*, p. 156.
69 *The Times*, 22 February 1971.
70 James Stuart, *Within the fringe*, p. 48.
71 Kenneth Rose, *Kings, queens and courtiers*, p. 270.
72 *Dictionary of national biography 1981–1985*, p. 238.
73 Philip Murphy, *Alan Lennox-Boyd*, p. 259.
74 *The Times*, 6 November 1974.
75 ibid.
76 *The Times*, 21 August 1992.
77 ibid.
78 ibid., 19 December 1995.
79 D. R. Thorpe, *Selwyn Lloyd*, p. 346.
80 Harold Watkinson, *Turning points*, p. 162.
81 D. R. Thorpe, *Selwyn Lloyd*, p. 273.
82 James Reeve, *Cocktails, crises and cockroaches*, p. 78.
83 D. R. Thorpe, *Selwyn Lloyd*, p. 340.
84 ibid., p. 278.
85 ibid., p. 274.
86 Roy Jenkins, *Portraits and miniatures*, pp. 272–73.
87 D. R. Thorpe, *Selwyn Lloyd*, p. 441.
88 ibid., p. 349.
89 *Dictionary of national biography 1981–1985*, p. 92.
90 ibid.
91 *The Times*, 12 May 1972.
92 ibid., 8 August 1975.
93 ibid.
94 ibid., 16 May 1966.
95 *Dictionary of national biography 1961–1970*, p. 488.
96 *The Times*, 16 May 1966.
97 ibid., 3 May 1996.
98 ibid.
99 ibid.
100 *Dictionary of national biography 1971–1980*, p. 354.
101 *The Times*, 19 March 1990.
102 Denis Healey, *The time of my life*, p. 297.
103 *The Times*, 19 March 1990.
104 ibid.
105 ibid., 27 November 1987.
106 ibid.
107 ibid., 24 April 1980.
108 ibid., 2 July 1999.
109 ibid.
110 ibid.
111 ibid.
112 ibid., 6 June 1994.
113 ibid.
114 ibid.
115 ibid.
116 ibid.
117 ibid., 17 September 1987.
118 ibid.
119 ibid.
120 *Dictionary of national biography 1981–1985*, p. 50.
121 Lord Carrington, *Reflect on things past*, p. 372.
122 *The Times*, 12 December 1994.
123 Denis Healey, *The time of my life*, p. 488.
124 *The Times*, 16 September 1994.
125 ibid.
126 ibid.
127 Norman Tebbit, *Upwardly mobile*, p. 12.
128 ibid., p. 47.
129 ibid., pp. 54–55.
130 Geoffrey Howe, *Conflict of loyalty*, p. 425.
131 Denis Healey, *The time of my life*, p. 458.
132 David Owen, *Time to declare*, p. 624.
133 ibid.

134 ibid., p. 20.
135 Mark Stuart, *Douglas Hurd*, p. 93.
136 Judy Hillman and Peter Clarke, *Geoffrey Howe*, p. 122.
137 ibid., p. 147.
138 Geoffrey Howe, *Conflict of loyalty*, p. 567.
139 ibid. Full text is in appendix 2.
140 ibid., p. 677.
141 ibid., p. 672.
142 Christopher Patten, *East and west*, p. 14.
143 Jonathan Dimbleby, *The last governor*, p. 11.
144 *The Times*, 30 June 1997.
145 Jonathan Dimbleby, *The last governor*, p. 3.
146 Peter Dorey, *The Major premiership*, p. 217.

Chapter 5   Bright is the ring of words

1 Virginia Woolf, *The diary of Virginia Woolf*, volume IV 1931–1935, p. 314.
2 George Jefferson, *Edward Garnett. A life in literature*, p. 282. Letter to Barker Fairley, 30 January 1936.
3 *Dictionary of national biography 1951–1960*, p. 88.
4 George Spater and Ian Parsons, *A marriage of true minds. An intimate portrait of Leonard and Virginia Woolf*, p. 187.
5 Vincent Brome, *J. B. Priestley*, p. 454.
6 *Dictionary of national biography 1931–40*, p. 650.
7 ibid.
8 ibid., p. 651.
9 Margaret Drabble, *The Oxford companion to English literature*, p. 380.
10 Sandra Kemp, *Edwardian fiction*, p. 52.
11 Hans Roger Madol, *The private life of Queen Alexandra*, pp. 194–95.
12 Georgina Battiscombe, *Queen Alexandra*, p. 251
13 *Dictionary of national biography 1931–40*, p. 137.
14 ibid., p. 111.
15 ibid.
16 Claude Bissell, *The imperial Canadian. Vincent Massey in office*, p. 65.
17 Peter Galloway, *The Order of St Michael and St George*, p. 223.
18 *Dictionary of national biography 1941–50*, p. 80.
19 ibid.
20 ibid.
21 ibid., p. 81.
22 *Dictionary of national biography 1931–40*, p. 666.
23 *The Times*, 17 January 1969.
24 ibid.
25 *Dictionary of national biography 1961–70*, p. 913.
26 ibid., p. 914.
27 ibid.
28 Harold Nicolson, *Diaries and letters 1930–1964*, 24 December 1933.
29 Stephen Spender, *World within world*, p. 145.
30 Victoria Glendinning, *Vita. The life of V. Sackville-West*, pp. 350–51.
31 CCOK, 64/1/48, Vita Nicolson to Ivan De la Bere, 5 May 1948.
32 Emlyn Jenkins, *Cofiant Elfed 1860–1953*, p. 215.
33 ibid.
34 ibid.
35 ibid., p. 216.
36 *Dictionary of national biography 1951–60*, p. 293.
37 ibid., p. 294.
38 Ian Hamilton, *The Oxford companion to twentieth-century poetry in English*, p. 123.
39 *Dictionary of national biography 1981–86*, p. 64.
40 ibid.
41 ibid., p. 65.
42 *Dictionary of national biography 1961–70*, p. 381.
43 T. E. Lawrence in *The Spectator*, 6 August 1927.
44 *Dictionary of national biography 1961–70*, p. 383.
45 W. S. Maugham, *A writer's notebook*, p. 237.
46 *Dictionary of national biography 1961–70*, p. 742.
47 ibid., p. 743.
48 W. S. Maugham, *The summing up*, p. 23.
49 *Dictionary of national biography 1961–70*, p. 1044.
50 *The Times*, 12 May 2001.
51 ibid.
52 Ian Hamilton, *The Oxford companion to twentieth-century poetry in English*, p. 495.
53 *Dictionary of national biography 1961–70*, p. 952.
54 ibid.
55 ibid., pp. 952–53.
56 ibid., p. 953.
57 Michael De-la-Noy, *The honours system*, p. 152.
58 *Daily Telegraph*, 8 September 1979.
59 *Dictionary of national biography 1971–1980*, p. 721.
60 ibid.
61 Rosemary Goring, *Larousse dictionary of writers*, p. 394.
62 A. C. Ward, *Longman's companion to twentieth century literature*, p. 234.

63 *Dictionary of national biography 1971–80*, p. 400.
64 ibid.
65 *The Guardian*, 18 April 1978.
66 *Dictionary of national biography 1986–90*, p. 416.
67 ibid.
68 *The Times*, 15 November 1982.
69 *Dictionary of national biography 1986–90*, p. 416.
70 *The Times*, 10 November 1980.
71 Ian Hamilton, *The Oxford companion to twentieth-century poetry in English*, p. 495.
72 *The Times*, 15 November 1982.
73 A. R. Bullock and R. B. Woodings, *The Fontana biographical companion to modern thought*, p. 426.
74 *The Times*, February 2001.
75 Ian Hamilton, *The Oxford companion to twentieth-century poetry in English*, p. 288.
76 CCOK, 64/1/86, Sir William Heseline to Philip Larkin, 21 June 1985.
77 *The Independent*, 29 March 2000.
78 ibid.
79 Margaret Drabble, *The Oxford companion to English literature*, p. 782.
80 ibid., p. 783.
81 Anthony Powell, *Journals 1987–1989*, pp. 53–54, 13 November 1987.
82 ibid.
83 *The Times*, 22 March 1997.
84 Margaret Drabble, *The Oxford companion to English literature*, p. 791.
85 *The Times*, 22 March 1997.
86 ibid.
87 ibid.
88 Ian Hamilton, *The Oxford companion to twentieth-century poetry in English*, p. 494.
89 *The Times*, 19 April 1984.
90 ibid.
91 Ian Ousby, *The Cambridge guide to literature in English*, p. 878.
92 *Larousse dictionary of writers*, p. 576.
93 *The Times*, 1 February 2002.
94 *The Guardian*, 29 November 1990.
95 ibid.
96 ibid.

Chapter 6 Famed in all great arts

1 Sarah Jane Checkland, *Ben Nicholson, The vicious circles of his life and and art*, p. 345.
2 Andrew Sinclair, *Francis Bacon. His life and violent times*, p. 145.
3 Shelley Rohde, *L. S. Lowry. A biography*, p. 353.
4 ibid., p. 356.

5 *Dictionary of national biography 1931–40*, p. 229.
6 A. R. Bullock and R. B. Woodings, *The Fontana biographical companion to modern thought*, p. 528.
7 *Dictionary of national biography 1986–90*, p. 315.
8 ibid., p. 314.
9 ibid., p. 315.
10 Arnold Goodman, *Tell them I'm on my way*, p. 333.
11 Roger Berthoud, *The life of Henry Moore*, p. 259.
12 *Dictionary of national biography 1981–85*, p. 85.
13 ibid., pp. 85–86.
14 ibid., pp. 86–87.
15 *The Times*, 30 June 1992.
16 ibid.
17 ibid.
18 ibid.
19 *Dictionary of national biography 1971–80*, p. 488.
20 ibid., p. 489.
21 ibid.
22 ibid., p. 455.
23 ibid.
24 *The Guardian*, 11 February 1972.
25 Ian Chilvers, *Oxford dictionary of twentieth century art*, p. 464.
26 *Sunday Times magazine*, 2 June 1963.
27 *Manchester Guardian*, 30 September 1958.
28 *The Times*, 13 May 1980.
29 *Heritage today*, Spring 1996, p. 37.
30 Gwyn Headley and Wim Meulenkamp, *Follies, grottoes and garden buildings*, pp. 217–18.
31 *Sunday Times magazine*, 2 June 1963.
32 *Financial Times*, 5 February 1980.
33 Charles Moritz, *Current biography yearbook* 1988, p. 174.
34 ibid., p. 172.
35 *The Times*, T2, 17 June 2002.
36 *Evening Standard*, 28 October 1982.
37 Arnold Goodman, *Tell them I'm on my way*, p. 332.
38 Ian Chilvers, *Oxford dictionary of twentieth century art*, p. 221.
39 *The Guardian*, 12 November 1974.
40 *The Times*, 17 August 1999.
41 ibid.
42 *The Times*, 12 November 1992.
43 ibid.
44 *The Times*, 20 April 1993.
45 Ian Chilvers, *Oxford dictionary of twentieth century art*, p. 222.
46 *The Times*, 20 April 1993.
47 ibid., 14 August 1997.
48 ibid.

49 ibid.
50 Ian Chilvers, *Oxford dictionary of twentieth century art*, p. 651.
51 ibid.
52 ibid., 12 January 2001.
53 Arnold Goodman, *Tell them I'm on my way*, p. 342.
54 *The Times*, 12 January 2001.
55 A. R. Bullock and R. B. Woodings, *The Fontana biographical companion to modern thought*, p. 333.
56 *The Times*, 23 May 2000.
57 Arnold Goodman, *Tell them I'm on my way*, pp. 332–33.
58 *Daily Telegraph*, 1 January 1999.
59 Ian Chilvers, *Oxford dictionary of twentieth century art*, p. 518.

Chapter 7   Music of the spheres

1 Arnold Goodman, *Tell them I'm on my way*, p. 315.
2 *Dictionary of national biography 1931–40*, p. 218.
3 ibid., pp. 218–19.
4 Thomas Beecham, *Frederick Delius*, p. 146.
5 *Dictionary of national biography 1931–40*, p. 220.
6 Alec Robertson, *More than music*, p. 132.
7 CCOK, 64/29, Frederick Delius to the Registrar of the Central Chancery of the Orders of Knighthood, 10 March 1929.
8 ibid., Sir Nevile Henderson to Sir Austen Chamberlain, 23 April 1929.
9 Thomas Beecham, *Frederick Delius*, p. 200.
10 *Dictionary of national biography 1951–60*, pp. 350–51.
11 *Dictionary of national biography 1941–50*, p. 967.
12 ibid., p. 968.
13 ibid., pp. 968–69.
14 ibid., p. 970.
15 ibid.
16 *Dictionary of national biography 1971–80*, p. 84.
17 ibid., p. 85.
18 ibid., p. 86.
19 H. Proctor-Gregg, *Beecham remembered*, p.153.
20 Arnold Goodman, *Tell them I'm on my way*, p. 298.
21 Gerald Jackson in *Reader's digest*, July 1972.
22 Charles Reid, *John Barbirolli*, p. 79.
23 *Daily Express*, 9 March 1961.
24 *Dictionary of national biography 1961–70*, p. 89.
25 Arnold Goodman, *Tell them I'm on my way*, p. 315.
26 ibid., *1981–85*, p. 46.
27 CCOK, 64/1/69, Sir Adrian Boult to the Central Chancery of the Orders of Knighthood, 27 February 1969.
28 ibid., Major General P. B. Gillett to Sir Adrian Boult, 3 March 1969.
29 Arnold Goodman, *Tell them I'm on my way*, p. 104.
30 ibid., p. 103.
31 *Dictionary of national biography 1961–70*, p. 69.
32 Leslie Ayre, *The wit of music*, p. 12.
33 ibid., *1971–80*, p. 65.
34 ibid., p. 66.
35 ibid., *1981–90*, p. 201.
36 ibid.
37 ibid., p. 202.
38 *Dictionary of national biography 1981–85*, p. 275.
39 ibid., p. 276.
40 Michael Kennedy, *Oxford dictionary of music*, p. 891.
41 Charles Moritz (ed), *Current biography yearbook 1974*, p. 416.
42 *Oxford dictionary of music*, p. 49.
43 Charles Moritz (ed), *Current biography yearbook 1971*, p. 22.
44 Harold Rosenthal and John Warrack, *The concise Oxford dictionary of opera*, p. 28.
45 *Daily Telegraph*, Arts and Books section, 14 October 2000.
46 ibid.
47 ibid.
48 *The Times*, 16 July 1986.
49 *The Guardian*, 19 July 1986.
50 *The Financial Times*, 4 November 1983.

Chapter 8   Portals of discovery

1 *The Times*, 18 November 1938.
2 ibid., 16 November 1959.
3 ibid.
4 ibid.
5 ibid., 4 July 1957.
6 ibid.
7 ibid.
8 Winston Churchill, *The second world war*, volume 2, pp. 337–39.
9 *The Times*, 15 July 1974.
10 ibid.
11 CCOK, 64/2/71, A G Morgan to G A Harris, 22 June 1971.
12 *Dictionary of national biography 1971–1980*, p. 161.
13 *The Times*, 7 February 2002.
14 ibid., 9 September 1985.
15 ibid.

16 ibid., 11 June 1993.
17 ibid., 27 June 2000.
18 ibid.
19 ibid., 11 June 1993.
20 ibid., 19 December 1997.
21 ibid., 13 March 1978.
22 ibid., 26 March 2002.
23 ibid.
24 ibid., 12 August 1996.
25 ibid.
26 ibid.

Chapter 9 To the well trod stage

1   Peter Roberts, *The Old Vic story*, p. 69.
2   ibid., p. 70.
3   ibid., p. 68.
4   ibid., p. 71.
5   Phyllis Hartnoll (ed), *The Oxford companion to the theatre*, p. 191.
6   Richard Eyre, *Changing stages. A view of British theatre in the twentieth century*, p. 34.
7   CCOK, 64/4/56, Gordon Craig to Sir Gladwyn Jebb, 12 July 1956.
8   *Dictionary of national biography 1986–1990*, p. 16.
9   ibid.
10 *The Times*, 23 May 2000.
11 ibid.
12 ibid.
13 *The Times*, 18 January 1999.
14 ibid.
15 ibid.
16 Alec Guinness, *Blessings in disguise*, p. 1.
17 *The Times*, 13 August 2000.
18 *The Guardian*, 11 October 1978.
19 ibid.
20 ibid.
21 ibid.
22 *The Times*, 15 May 1987.
23 Garry O'Connor, *Paul Scofield*, p. 14.
24 *The Guardian*, 4 August 1971.
25 *Daily Telegraph*, 23 February 1968.
26 *The Guardian*, 23 February 1968.
27 *Daily Mail*, 3 September 1973.
28 *Daily Telegraph magazine*, 6 March 1970.
29 *The Guardian*, 4 August 1971.
30 *Daily Mail*, 3 September 1973.
31 ibid., 30 December 2000.
32 ibid.
33 ibid.

Chapter 10 Interpreters of life and living

1   Stewart Weaver, *The Hammonds. A marriage in history*, p. 254.

2   Ross Terrill, *R. H. Tawney and his times. Socialism as fellowship*, p. 97.
3   Jesse Norman, *The achievement of Michael Oakeshott*, p. 63.
4   *Proceedings of the British Academy 1921–23*, p. 552.
5   *The Times*, 6 February 1922.
6   CCOK, 64/22, Sir Douglas Dawson to The Honourable George Crichton, 23 January 1922.
7   *The Times*, 6 February 1922.
8   *Dictionary of national biography 1961–70*, p. 439.
9   Frank Eyck, *G. P. Gooch*, p. 441.
10 CCOK, 64/3/56, Edward Ford to Ivan De la Bere, 25 June 1956.
11 ibid., Norah Williams to Brigadier Ivan De la Bere, 19 July 1956.
12 *Dictionary of national biography 1961–70*, pp. 84–85.
13 *London Gazette*, 2 December 1918.
14 Arnold Goodman, *Tell them I'm on my way*, p. 49.
15 Jacquetta Hawkes, *Mortimer Wheeler. Adventurer in archaeology*, p. 312.
16 *Dictionary of national biography 1981–85*, p. 56.
17 ibid.
18 ibid., p. 57.
19 Arnold Goodman, *Tell them I'm on my way*, p. 304.
20 John Carswell, *Government and the universities in Britain: programme and performance 1960–1980*, p. 38.
21 Negley Harte, *The university of London 1836–1986*, p. 261.
22 *Week-end Telegraph*, 1 November 1968.
23 Steven Runciman, *A history of the crusades. Volume 3. The kingdom of Acre and the later crusades*, p. 401.
24 *Daily Mail*, 15 September 1978.
25 A. L. Rowse, *A Cornish childhood*, p. 203.
26 *News of the World*, 31 January 1993.
27 *Evening Standard*, 19 November 1993.
28 *The Times*, 29 November 1994.
29 Information supplied to the author by Dr Donald Adamson.
30 *History Today*, January 1999.
31 *The Times Saturday Review*, 31 March 2001.
32 ibid.
33 ibid.

Chapter 11 Campaigning spirits

1   David Lloyd George, *War memoirs*, volume 1, p. 347.
2   *Dictionary of national biography 1951–1960*, p. 854.

3 ibid.
4 *The Times*, 21 March 1936.
5 ibid.
6 ibid., 10 September 1956.
7 David Cannandine, *G. M. Trevelyan*, p. 9.
8 *The Times*, 10 September 1956.
9 ibid.
10 David Cannandine, *G. M. Trevelyan*, p. 18.
11 *The Times*, 1 February 1966.
12 ibid.
13 ibid.
14 John Ingamells, *The Davies collection of French art*, p. 4.
15 *Dictionary of national biography 1961–1970*, p. 718.
16 *The Times*, 14 April 1961.
17 ibid., 13 April 1961.
18 ibid., 25 November 1955.
19 ibid.
20 ibid., 27 April 1981.
21 ibid.
22 ibid., 18 July 1988.
23 ibid.
24 ibid.
25 *Dictionary of national biography 1986–1990*, p. 492.
26 *The landmark trust handbook*, p. 6.
27 ibid., p. 5
28 COCS, H59, Air Chief Marshal Sir Christopher Foxley-Norris to the Prime Minister, 11 July 1978

Chapter 12 Sharp quillets

1 *Dictionary of national biography 1971–1980*, p. 712.
2 ibid.
3 *The Times* 3 April 1975.
4 ibid., 5 April 1975.
5 ibid., 9 April 1975.
6 ibid., 15 May 1995.
7 ibid.
8 ibid.
9 Arnold Goodman, *Tell them, I'm on my way*, p. 229.
10 *The Times*, 15 October 2001.
11 *Dictionary of national biography 1986–1990*, p. 152.
12 *The Times*, 9 January 1990.
13 ibid.
14 *Dictionary of national biography 1986–1990*, p. 153.
15 Arnold Goodman, *Tell them I'm on my way*, p. 188.
16 *Dictionary of national biography 1971–1980*, pp. 591–92.
17 ibid., *1986–1990*, p. 236.

Chapter 13 National voices

1 *Dictionary of national biography 1922–1930*, p. 637.
2 ibid., *1931–1940*, pp. 261–62.
3 RA, PS/GV/J1813/25, List of suggested honours. Mr Lloyd George and Mr Austen Chamberlain, no date. Annotated in the handwriting of King George V.
4 *Dictionary of national biography 1931–1940*, p. 549.
5 ibid.
6 ibid.
7 ibid., pp. 549–50.
8 ibid., *1941–1950*, p. 813.
9 Stephen Koss, *Fleet Street radical*, p. 205.
10 *Dictionary of national biography 1941–1950*, pp. 336–37.
11 ibid., p. 292.
12 *The Times*, 28 July 1972.
13 *Dictionary of national biography 1971–1980*, p. 542.
14 ibid.
15 ibid., *1961–1970*, pp. 889–90.
16 ibid., p. 890.
17 CCOK, 64/54, D. B. Pitblado to Sir Alan Lascelles, 8 March 1954.
18 *Dictionary of national biography 1961–1970*, p. 118.
19 ibid.
20 ibid., p. 119.
21 ibid.
22 *The Times*, 8 December 2001.
23 Arnold Goodman, *Tell them I'm on my way*, p. 394.
24 ibid., pp. 378–79.

Chapter 14 Forth to his work

1 *Dictionary of national biography 1931–40*, p. 255.
2 ibid., p. 256.
3 ibid., p. 257.
4 *Dictionary of labour biography*, volume 4, p. 202.
5 Beatrice Webb, *The diary of Beatrice Webb*, volume 3, p. 237.
6 ibid., p. 207.
7 ibid., volume 6, p. 257.
8 RA, PS/GV/J1936/36, Lord Stamfordham to Lieutenant Colonel Ronald Waterhouse, 24 May 1924.
9 *The Times*, 3 October 1961.
10 COCS, H59, Governor General of Australia to Dominions Office, 20 November 1942.
11 ibid.
12 *The Times*, 5 February 1953.
13 ibid.

14 *Dictionary of national biography 1951–60*, p. 289.
15 ibid., p. 290.
16 Jack Jones, *Union man*, p. 333.

Chapter 15 A grant of honours

1 COCS, H59, Telegram from Governor General of Australia to Dominions Office, 23 September 1942.
2 ibid., 25 September 1942.
3 ibid., Dominions Office to Governor General of Australia, 2 October 1942.
4 ibid., Governor General of Australia to Dominions Office, 7 October 1942.
5 ibid., 26 October 1942.
6 ibid., Robert Knox to Sir Richard Hopkins and J. M. Martin, 7 November 1942.
7 ibid., Sir Richard. Hopkins to J. M. Martin, 7 November 1942.
8 ibid., Governor General of Australia to Dominions Office, 18 November 1942.
9 ibid., Dominions Office to Governor General of Australia, 20 November 1942.
10 ibid., J. J. S. Garner to J. M. Martin, 21 November 1942.
11 ibid., Clement Attlee to Winston Churchill, 24 November 1942.
12 ibid., Winston Churchill to John Curtin, 29 November 1942.
13 ibid., John Curtin to Winston Churchill, 1 December 1942.
14 Peter Galloway, *The Most Illustrious Order. The Order of St Patrick and its knights*, p. 152.
15 COCS, H59, Winston Churchill to John Curtin, 9 December 1942.
16 ibid., John Curtin to Winston Churchill, 11 December 1942.
17 ibid., John Curtin to Dominions Office, 12 January 1943.
18 ibid., Sir Eric Machtig to Robert Knox, 15 January 1943.
19 ibid., Sir Eric Machtig to Prime Minister, 25 January 1943.
20 ibid., Clement Attlee to Lord Gowrie, 3 March 1943.
21 ibid., Lord Gowrie to Dominions Office, 17 March 1943, quoting reply by John Curtin dated 15 March 1943.
22 ibid., Clement Attlee to Winston Churchill, 19 March 1943.
23 ibid., Winston Churchill to Clement Attlee, 22 March 1943.
24 ibid., Clement Attlee to Winston Churchill, 23 March 1943.
25 ibid., 25 March 1943.
26 ibid., Dominions Office to Governor General of Australia, 26 March 1943.
27 ibid., Clement Attlee to Winston Churchill, 29 March 1943.
28 ibid., Robert Knox to Sir R Hopkins and J. Martin, 30 March 1943.
29 ibid., Clement Attlee to Winston Churchill, 3 May 1945, initialled by Churchill 5 May 1943.
30 ibid., Alan Lascelles to Sir Richard Hopkins, 14 May 1943.
31 ibid., Dominions Office telegram to governments of Canada and South Africa and to the governor generals of Australia and New Zealand, 18 May 1943.
32 ibid., Governor General of Australia to Dominions Office, 14 June 1943.
33 ibid., C. W. Dixon to Robert Knox, 18 June 1943.
34 National Archives of Canada, Record Group 2, The Privy Council Office, Volume 9, Page 10, File H–5 (1943 January to May).
35 COCS, H59, J. A. Stephenson to Robert Knox, 13 July 1943.
36 ibid., HW951, Committee on the Grant of Honours, Decorations and Medals in Time of War, One hundred and sixty-ninth report, The Order of the Companions of Honour.
37 ibid., Eric Machtig to Robert Knox, 9 August 1943.
38 ibid., Eric Machtig to Robert Knox, 13 August 1943.
39 ibid., HD7089, Committee on the Grant of Honours, Decorations and Medals, One thousand and thirty-second report, 3 November 1969.
40 ibid., Eric Machtig to Robert Knox, 13 August 1943.
41 ibid., Dominions Office telegram to the governments of Canada and South Africa and to the governor generals of Australia and New Zealand, 24 August 1943.
42 ibid., Dominions Office telegram to Governor General of Australia, 18 September 1943.
43 ibid., P. S. Milner-Barry to A. Lees Mayall, 16 February 1970.
44 ibid.
45 ibid.
46 ibid.
47 ibid., Martin Charteris to P. S. Milner-Barry, 18 March 1970.
48 ibid., A. Lees Mayall to P. S. Milner-Barry, 2 March 1970.
49 ibid.
50 ibid., P. S. Milner-Barry to D. H. Andrews, 16 April 1970.
51 ibid., P. S. Milner-Barry to Sir Michael Adeane, 9 March 1970.

52 ibid., P. S. Milner-Barry to Sir William Armstrong, 9 April 1970.
53 ibid., HD7237, Committee on the Grant of Honours, Decorations and Medals. Allocation of the Companionship of Honour. One thousand and seventy-first report, 27 February 1975.

Chapter 16 Over the bright blue sea

1 *The Times*, 26 August 1967.
2 COCS, H59, prime minister's personal telegram to Australian government, 13 June 1942.
3 ibid., John Curtin to Dominions Office, 16 June 1942.
4 Russel Ward, *The history of Australia. The twentieth century 1901–1975*, p. 321.
5 COCS, H59, Lord Cranborne to the prime minister, 20 June 1944.
6 J. L. Granatstein, *The generals*, p. 83.
7 ibid., p. 89.
8 ibid., p. 92.
9 ibid., p. 93.
10 ibid., p. 96.
11 ibid., p. 97.
12 ibid., p. 105.
13 ibid., p. 109.
14 ibid., p. 115
15 James Thorn, *Peter Fraser. New Zealand's wartime prime minister*, p. 279.
16 *An encyclopaedia of New Zealand*, volume 1, p. 751.
17 COCS, H59, Governor General of New Zealand to Dominions Office, 19 December 1945.
18 ibid., Lord Addison to Lord Halifax, 21 December 1945.
19 Claude Bissell, *The imperial Canadian*, p. 4.
20 ibid., p. x.
21 Bruce Hutchison, *Mr prime minister*, p. 298.
22 John Diefenbaker, *The years of achievement*, p. 58.
23 National Archives of Canada, W. L. M. King papers, MG–26–J1, Note for the record by J. A. Gibson, 22 May 1946.
24 ibid., William Mackenzie King to Louis St Laurent, 22 May 1946.
25 Claude Bissell, *The imperial Canadian*, p. 175.
26 ibid.
27 Vincent Massey, *What's past is prologue*, p. 441.
28 Claude Bissell, *The imperial Canadian*, p. 264.
29 University of Toronto Archives, Massey Papers, Vincent Massey to Sir Michael Adeane, 26 January 1955.
30 ibid., Sir Michael Adeane to Vincent Massey, 13 June 1960.
31 ibid., p. 525.
32 J. L. Granatstein, *The generals*, p. 57.
33 ibid.
34 ibid.
35 ibid., p. 58.
36 Claude Bissell, *The imperial Canadian*, p. 143.
37 J. L. Granatstein, *The generals*, p. 72.
38 Bruce Hutchinson, *Mr prime minister*, p. 275.
39 John Diefenbaker, *The years of achievement*, p. 156.
40 J. L. Granatstein, *The generals*, p. 82.
41 National Archives of Canada, W. L. M. King Papers, MG–26–J1, volume 413, William Lyon Mackenzie King to Louis St Laurent, 22 May 1946.
42 COCS, H59, note for the record by A. Bevir, 9 June 1946.
43 ibid.
44 ibid.
45 *The Times*, 5 August 1961.
46 Ann Trotter, *New Zealand and Japan 1945–52*, chapter 6, p.1.
47 *An encyclopaedia of New Zealand*, volume 2, p. 108.
48 *The Times*, 3 October 1980
49 Roland Turner, *The annual obituary 1980*, p. 584.
50 Sir John Kotelawala, *An Asian prime minister's story*, p. 92.
51 COCS, H59, Commonwealth Relations Office to prime minister, 15 August 1955.
52 Keith Sinclair, *Walter Nash*, p. 17.
53 ibid., p. 37.
54 ibid., p. 338.
55 *The Times*, 5 June 1968.
56 Keith Sinclair, *Walter Nash*, p. 357.
57 Brian Lapping, *End of empire*, p. 190.
58 *The Times*, 19 December 1967.
59 COCS, H59, note on a discussion on honours between the prime minister and Lord Casey, Governor General of Australia, 1 May 1967.
60 Eric Williams, *Inward hunger*, pp. 28–29.
61 Winston Mahabir, *In and out of politics*, p. 13.
62 Ken Boodhoo, *Eric Williams*, Conclusion, p. 5.
63 Winston Mahabir, *In and out of politics*, p. 53.
64 *The Times*, 21 May 2002.
65 ibid.
66 Denis Healey, *The time of my life*, p. 296.
67 *The Times*, 21 May 2002.
68 *The Times*, 31 October 1988.

69 ibid.
70 ibid., 9 February 1994.
71 Bruce Hutchison, *Mr prime minister*, p. 316.
72 Paul Martin, *A very public life*, p. 436.
73 *The Times*, 30 September 2000.
74 Walter Stewart, *Shrug. Trudeau in power*, p. 10.
75 Vernon Wright, *David Lange*, p. 128.
76 ibid., pp. 142–43.
77 *Maclean's Magazine*, 6 December 1999.
78 *The Times*, 4 October 1988.
79 ibid.
80 ibid.
81 COCS, H59, note by Robert Knox, 7 December 1954.
82 Gerald de Gaury, *Three kings in Baghdad*, pp. 49–50.
83 ibid., p. 197.
84 Roger Keyes, *Outrageous fortune*, p. 39.
85 *The Times*, 1 August 1972.
86 ibid.
87 *The Times*, 18 July 2002.
88 ibid.
89 *Time*, 14 June 1971.
90 *The Observer*, 6 June 1971.

Chapter 17 Emblem of honour

1 CCOK, 39/18, Sir Frederick Ponsonby to Elinor Hallé, 5 August 1917.
2 CCOK, OBE Letters, Box 2, Sir Frederick Ponsonby to Prince Louis of Battenberg, 23 April 1917.
3 ibid., Sir Frederick Ponsonby to Prince Louis of Battenberg, 7 May 1917.
4 CCOK, OBE Letters, Box 2, Prince Louis of Battenberg to Sir Frederick Ponsonby, 8 May 1917.
5 CCOK, 37/18, Sir Douglas Dawson to Sir Frederick Ponsonby, 12 May 1917.
6 CCOK, 39/18, Sir Frederick Ponsonby to Elinor Hallé, 5 August 1917.
7 CCOK, OBE Letters, Box 2, Elinor Hallé to Sir Frederick Ponsonby, 29 June 1917.
8 CCOK, 37/18, Sir Frederick Ponsonby to Sir Douglas Dawson, 2 July 1917.
9 ibid., Marquess of Milford Haven to Sir Douglas Dawson, 11 July 1917.
10 CCOK, 39/18, Marquess of Milford Haven to Elinor Hallé, 14 July 1917.
11 COCS, H59, Sir Frederick Ponsonby to J. W. Mackail, 2 July 1917.
12 ibid., J. W. Mackail to Sir Frederick Ponsonby, 10 July 1917.
13 CCOK, 37/18, Sir Frederick Ponsonby to Sir Douglas Dawson, 19 July 1917.
14 ibid., Marquess of Milford Haven to Sir Douglas Dawson, 25 July 1917.
15 ibid., Sir Douglas Dawson to Sir Thomas Heath, 27 July 1917.
16 ibid., Sir Thomas Heath to Sir Douglas Dawson, 31 July 1917.
17 ibid., Sir Douglas Dawson to Sir Frederick Ponsonby, no date, but between 2 and 7 August 1917.
18 ibid., Sir Frederick Ponsonby to Sir Douglas Dawson, 9 August 1917.
19 ibid.
20 ibid., Marquess of Milford Haven to Sir Douglas Dawson, 17 August 1917.
21 ibid., Sir Frederick Ponsonby to Sir Douglas Dawson, 9 August 1917.
22 ibid., Elinor Hallé to F. S. Osgood, 15 August 1917.
23 ibid., 22 September 1917.
24 ibid., Sir Frederick Ponsonby to Sir Douglas Dawson, 19 July 1917.
25 ibid.
26 ibid.
27 ibid., Sir Douglas Dawson to Marquess of Milford Haven, 21 July 1917.
28 ibid.
29 ibid., Sir Douglas Dawson to Marquess of Milford Haven, 27 July 1917.
30 ibid., Sir Douglas Dawson to Queen Mary, 30 July 1917.
31 Peter Galloway, *The Order of the British Empire*, pp. 85–86.
32 CCOK, 37/18, Sir Frederick Ponsonby to Sir Douglas Dawson, 15 September 1917.
33 ibid., Sir Douglas Dawson to Sir Frederick Ponsonby, 18 September 1917.
34 ibid., Sir Frederick Ponsonby to Sir Douglas Dawson, 22 September 1917.
35 ibid.
36 ibid., Sir Douglas Dawson to Sir Frederick Ponsonby, 3 October 1917.
37 ibid., note dated 23 October 1917 on a letter from Sir Douglas Dawson to Sir Frederick Ponsonby, 3 October 1917.
38 ibid., Sir Frederick Ponsonby to Sir Douglas Dawson, 22 September 1917.
39 ibid., F. S. Osgood to Elinor Hallé, 24 October 1917.
40 ibid., Elinor Hallé to F. S. Osgood, 24 October 1917.
41 ibid.
42 ibid., Elinor Hallé to F. S. Osgood, 29 October 1917.
43 ibid., F. S. Osgood to Elinor Hallé, 2 November 1917.
44 ibid., Sir Douglas Dawson to Sir Frederick Ponsonby, 6 November 1917.
45 ibid., Sir Frederick Ponsonby to Sir Douglas Dawson, 14 November 1917.
46 ibid.
47 ibid., F. S. Osgood to Elinor Hallé, 16 November 1917.

48 ibid., H. V. Caldicott to Elinor Hallé, 19 November 1917.
49 ibid., Elinor Hallé to F. S. Osgood, 25 November 1917.
50 ibid., 29 November 1917.
51 ibid., Sir Frederick Ponsonby to Sir Douglas Dawson, 5 December 1917.
52 ibid., Elinor Hallé to F. S. Osgood, 15 December 1917.
53 ibid., 8 January 1918.
54 ibid., F. S. Osgood to Elinor Hallé, 9 January 1918.
55 ibid., Clive Wigram to Sir Douglas Dawson, 4 February 1918.
56 ibid., Sir Douglas Dawson to Clive Wigram, 5 February 1918.
57 ibid., Sir Frederick Ponsonby to Sir Douglas Dawson, 28 February 1918.
58 ibid., Sir Douglas Dawson to Sir Frederick Ponsonby, 28 February 1918.
59 ibid., Elinor Hallé to F. S. Osgood, 5 March 1918.
60 ibid., Sir Frederick Ponsonby to Sir Douglas Dawson, 8 March 1918.
61 ibid.
62 ibid., F. S. Osgood to Elinor Hallé, 11 March 1918.
63 ibid., Sir Douglas Dawson to Elinor Hallé, 20 August 1918.
64 ibid., Sir Douglas Dawson to Sir Frederick Ponsonby, 20 August 1918.
65 ibid., Sir Frederick Ponsonby to Sir Douglas Dawson, 21 August 1918.
66 ibid., Sir Douglas Dawson to Sir Frederick Ponsonby, 7 September 1918.
67 ibid., Earl of Cromer to Sir Douglas Dawson, 10 September 1918.
68 ibid., Elinor Hallé to F. S. Osgood, 3 November 1918.
69 ibid., 25 November 1918.
70 CCOK, 39/18, Elinor Hallé to F. S. Osgood, 30 May 1918.
71 CCOK, 64/1/48, Vita Nicolson to Ivan De la Bere, 5 May 1948.
72 CCOK, 39/18, F. S. Osgood to Sir Douglas Dawson, 30 May 1918.
73 ibid., Sir Frederick Ponsonby to Sir Douglas Dawson, 1 June 1918.
74 ibid., Elinor Hallé to F. S. Osgood, 5 June 1918.
75 ibid., Sir Douglas Dawson to Sir Thomas Heath, 2 July 1918.
76 ibid., Sir Thomas Heath to Sir Douglas Dawson, 5 July 1918.
77 ibid., Sir Douglas Dawson to Sir Thomas Heath, 9 July 1918.
78 ibid., Marquess of Milford Haven to Elinor Hallé, 14 July 1917.
79 ibid., Sir Thomas Heath to Sir Douglas Dawson, 10 September 1918.
80 ibid., 21 September 1918.
81 ibid., Sir Douglas Dawson to Sir Thomas Heath, 24 September 1918.
82 CCOK, 64/27, telegram from S. M. Bruce to Sir Harry Batterbee, Dominions Office, 14 September 1927.
83 Peter Galloway, *The Order of the British Empire*, chapter 9.
84 RA, PS/GVI/PS00077/02, memorandum from the Treasury, 17 February 1936.
85 COCS, H77F, extract from ODM 19.
86 CCOK, 64/1/88, Desmond Rice to Ruth Gardner, 8 August 1988.
87 ibid., 31 October 1988.
88 ibid., 20 October 1988.
89 ibid., 31 October 1988.
90 CCOK, 37/18, F. S. Osgood to Mr Pinches, 7 February 1918.

Chapter 18 Gallery of conspicuous service

1 Peter Galloway, *The Order of the British Empire*, pp. 54–55.
2 COCS, H13, J. A. Barlow to R. U. E. Knox, 24 March 1933.
3 ibid., Violet Markham to J. A. Barlow, 30 June 1933.

INDEX

Abercorn, 1st Duke of, 20
Abraham, May (see Tennant, May)
Aberdare, 1st Lord, 342
Adams, William George Stewart, (CH 1936), 335, **344–345**
Addison, Sir Christopher, 11
Addison, Joseph, 492
Adler, Hermann, 57
Alexander, Albert Victor, (see Alexander of Hillsborough, Earl)
Alexander, King of Serbia, 375
Alexander of Hillsborough, Earl, (CH 1941), 68, **78–80**, 410, 411, 504, 509
Alexander of Tunis, Field Marshal Earl, 435, 443
Alexandra, Queen, 20, 172
Allen, Sir Hugh, 238
Amery, Julian, 377
Amery, Leopold Charles Moritz Stennett, (CH 1945), **94–96**
Amis, Kingsley, 195
Anderson, Philip, 285
Andrew, Fr, 292
Andrews, John Miller, (CH 1943), 68, **82–83**
Anthony, John Douglas, (CH 1981), 425, **475**
Armagh, Archbishop of (see Gregg, John Allen Fitzgerald)
Arnold, Matthew, 343
Arnold, Thomas, 343
Ashcroft, Dame Peggy, 303
Ashley, Jack (see Ashley of Stoke, Lord)
Ashley of Stoke, Lord, (CH 1975), 71, 336, **351–353**
Ashton, Sir Frederick William Mallandine, (CH 1970), 290, **297–298**, 301, 302, 508, 510
Astor, The Honourable Francis David Langhorne, (CH 1993), 361, 369, 370, **382–384**
Astor, Lord, 341
Astor, Nancy Witcher, Viscountess, (CH 1937), 68, **77–78**, 384, 504, 506, 507, 509
Astor, Waldorf, Viscount, 374, 376, 378
Astrid, Queen, 484
Athlone, Princess Alice, Countess of, 35
Attenborough, Sir David Frederick, (CH 1995), 370, **384–386**, 514
Attlee, Clement Richard, Earl, (CH 1945), chapter 4 passim, **88–91**, 178, 300, 359, 408, 413, 441, 448, 510
Aubrey, Melbourn Evans, (CH 1937), 41, **56–57**
Auchinleck, Field Marshal Sir Claude, 435
Auden, W. H., 193, 238–239
Auriol, Vincent, 481
Austin, Frederic, 245

Avon, Anthony, Earl of, 69, 106, 108, 115, 117, 141, 143, 145, 458
Aylestone, Lord, (CH 1975), 69, **136–137**
Bacon, Francis, 206, 360, 511
Baillie, John, (CH 1957), 41, **60–61**
Baker, Dame Janet Abbott, (CH 1993), 232, **252–253**, 506
Baker, Kenneth Wilfrid (see Baker of Dorking, Lord), 70
Baker of Dorking, Lord, (CH 1992), **151–152**, 331
Baldwin, Stanley (see Baldwin of Bewdley, Earl)
Baldwin of Bewdley, Earl, 37, 68, 72, 74, 75, 359
Balfour, Arthur (later the Earl of Balfour), 2, 12
Banting, Sir Frederick, 272, 273, 277
Barbirolli, Sir John Giovanni Battista, (CH 1969), 232, 242, **245–246**
Barnes, George Nicoll, (CH 1920), 11, 13, 17, **33–34**
Barrett, Lady Florence Elizabeth, (CH 1929), 258, **261–262**, 506, 508
Barrett, Sir William, 262
Barrie, J. M., 294
Barry, F. R., 53
Battenberg, Prince Louis of (see Milford Haven, 1st Marquess of)
Baylis, Lilian Mary, (CH 1929), 289 290, **291–293**, 295, 296, 301, 506, 508
Beaglehole, J. C., 455
Beaton, Cecil, 322
Beatrice, Princess, 497
Beaufort, Louise, Duchess of, 36–37
Beazley, Sir John Davidson, (CH 1959), 311, **315–316**
Beckett, Rupert, 377
Beecham, Sir Thomas, (CH 1957), 231, 232, 234, 235, **241–243**, 255
Belcher, John, 126, 398
Belloc, Hilaire, 166, 511
Benn, Tony, 140
Bennett, Arnold, 294
Bennett, Richard Redford, Viscount, 414, 446
Bennett, Sir William, 36–37
Benson, W. A. S., 343
Berenson, Bernhard, 210
Berg, Paul, 277
Bernal, J. D., 275
Best, Charles Herbert, (CH 1971), 258, 260, **272–273**, 277, 424, 425, 465
Betjeman, Sir John, 212, 213
Bevan, Aneurin, 102, 360
Beveridge, Lord, 346
Bevin, Ernest, 90, 399

Beyen, J. W., 486
Bigge, Sir Arthur (See Stamfordham, Lord)
Bintley, David, 301
Binyon, Robert Laurence, (CH 1932), 165, **174–175**, 507
Birch, Nigel, 141–142
Birkenhead, Earl of, 265
Birtwistle, Sir Harrison, (CH 2000), 232, **253–254**, 508
Blackett, Patrick Maynard Stuart, Lord, (CH 1965), 258, 259, 263, **266–267**, 328, 510
Blair, Tony, 70
Bliss, Sir Arthur Edward Drummond, (CH 1971), 232, **246–247**
Bohr, Niels, 272, 285
Bonar Law, Andrew, 3, 37, 74, 75
Bondfield, Margaret Grace, (CH 1948), 69, **97–98**, 133, 506
Bone, Sir David, 380
Bone, James, (CH 1947), 370, **380**
Bone, Sir Muirhead, 380
Booth, Charles, 341
Booth, William Bramwell, (CH 1929), 41, **50–52**
Boothroyd, Betty, Baroness, 153
Boult, Sir Adrian Cedric, (CH 1969), 232, 238, **243–244**, 250, 346
Bourassa, Robert, 477
Bowden, Herbert William 'Bert' (see Aylestone, Lord)
Bower, Commander Robert, 121
Bowes-Lyon, Lady Elizabeth (see Elizabeth, Queen, the Queen Mother)
Bowra, Sir Cecil Maurice, (CH 1971), 166, **191–192**
Boyd of Merton, Viscount, (CH 1960), 69, **111–113**
Boyd-Orr, John Boyd Orr, Lord, (CH 1968), 258, 259, **270–271**
Boyer, Charles, 485
Boyle, Edward Charles Gurney (see Boyle of Handsworth, Lord)
Boyle of Handsworth, Lord, (CH 1981), 70, **144–145**
Braddock, Bessie, 133
Bragg, Sir William Henry, 267
Bragg, Sir William Lawrence, (CH 1967), 258, 259, 260, **267–268**, 276, 285
Brenner, Sydney, (CH 1986), 258, 259, 260, **279**
Brewer, Sir Herbert, 248
Bridge, Frank, 238, 239
Bridges, Robert, 170
Bridie, James, 294
Briers, Richard, 298
Brighouse, Harold, 294
Britten, Edward Benjamin, Lord, (CH 1953), 212, 231, **238–240**, 253, 508 510
Brook, Peter Stephen Paul, (CH 1998), 289, **305–307**, 307, 308, 504
Brooke, General Sir Alan, 447

Brooke, Henry (see Brooke of Cumnor, Lord)
Brooke, Peter Leonard (see Brooke of Sutton Mandeville, Lord), 70
Brooke of Cumnor, Lord, (CH 1964), 69, **119**, 153
Brooke of Sutton Mandeville, Lord, (CH 1992), **152–153**
Brooke of Ystradfellte, Baroness, 119, 153
Brown, Alfred Ernest, (CH 1945), 68, **96–97**
Brown, George, (see George-Brown, Lord)
Brown, Ivor, 382
Bruce, Stanley Melbourne (see Bruce of Melbourne, Viscount)
Bruce, The Honourable William Napier, (CH 1935), 335, **342–343**
Bruce of Melbourne, Viscount, (CH 1927), 405, 417, 425, **427–428**, 431, 432, 435, 459, 501
Bryant, Sir Arthur Wynne Morgan, (CH 1967), 311, **318–319**, 330, 508
Bryant, Sir Francis, 318
Buchan, John (see Tweedsmuir, Lord)
Buchan-Hepburn, Patrick George Thomas (see Hailes, Lord)
Buchanan, Sir George, 35
Burke, Sir Henry Farnham Burke, 3, 5, 10, 490, 503, 504
Burkitt, F. C., 62
Burnet, Sir Macfarlane, 273
Burnham, Viscount, (CH 1917), 13, **23–24**
Bury, J. B., 322
Busch, Fritz, 240
Butler, Sir Montague, 105
Butler, Richard Austen (see Butler of Saffron Walden, Lord)
Butler of Saffron Walden, Lord, (CH 1954), 69, **105–107**, 112, 119
Caine, Sir Thomas Hall, (CH 1922), 165, **171–172**, 507, 508, 514
Caird, Edward, 312
Caldicott, H. V., 496, 497, 501
Callaghan, James (see Callaghan of Cardiff, Lord)
Callaghan of Cardiff, Lord, 70, 126, 136, 139, 140, 141
Carlile, John Charles, (CH 1929), 42, **50**, 56
Carlile, Wilson, (CH 1926), 41, **46–47**, 51
Carlisle, Bishop of (see Williams, Henry Herbert)
Carrington, Dora, 302
Carrington, Peter Alexander Rupert, Lord, (CH 1983), 70, 145, **145–147**, 162
Carruthers, Lieutenant Colonel James, 23
Carruthers, Violet (see Markham, Violet Rosa, Mrs James Carruthers) Carson, Lord, 375
Casey, Richard Gardiner, Lord, (CH 1944), 425, **434–436**, 459
Cassels, Sir Ernest, 25

Casson, Sir Hugh Maxwell, (CH 1984), 206, **220–221**
Casson, Sir Lewis, 221, 296
Castle, Barbara (see Castle of Blackburn, Baroness)
Castle of Blackburn, Baroness, 127, 352
Cave, Sir George, 3
Cave, Viscount, 48
Cavendish, Lady Rachel, 110
Cecchetti, Enrico, 300
Cecil, Lord David (see Gascoyne-Cecil, Lord Edward David Christian)
Cecil, Henry Algernon (see Cecil of Chelwood, Viscount)
Cecil, Lord Robert, 174
Cecil of Chelwood, Edgar Algernon Robert, Viscount, (CH 1956), 69, **108–110**
Ceylon (see Sri Lanka)
Chadwick, Sir James, (CH 1970), 258, 259, **271–272**, 286
Chamberlain, Sir Austen, 48
Chamberlain, Joseph, 112
Chamberlain, Neville, 6–7, 72, 79, 86, 95, 377
Chan, Sir Julius, 474
Charteris, Sir Martin, 421
Cherwell, Frederick Alexander Lindemann, Viscount, (CH 1953), 258, 260, **265–266**, 282
Cheshire, Group Captain Lord, 356, 511
Chetwynd, Godfrey John Boyle (see Chetwynd, Viscount)
Chetwynd, Viscount, (CH 1917), 13, **18–19**, 498
Chifley, Joseph, 442
Christie, Agatha, 330, 402
Christie, Sir George William Langham, (CH 2001), 153, 232, **256**
Christie, John, (CH 1954), 153, 232, **240–241**, 256
Churchill, Randolph, 147
Churchill, Sir Winston Leonard Spencer, (CH 1922), 49, **71–73**, chapter 4 *passim*, 174, 190, 265, 282, 325, 359, chapter 15 *passim*, 434, 481, 485, 487, 507, 509, 510
Chuter-Ede, James, Lord, (CH 1953), 69, **103–104**
Citrine, Walter, 399
Clark, Kenneth Mackenzie, Lord, (CH 1959), 206, 207, 208, **209–11**, 212, 510
Clayton, Philip Thomas Byard 'Tubby', (CH 1933), 41, **53–54**
Cledwyn of Penrhos, Lord, (CH 1976), 70, **138–139**
Clifford, John, (CH 1921), 39, 40, 41, **42–44**, 371, 506
Clynes, J. L., 71
Cohen, Henry (see Cohen of Birkenhead, Lord)

Cohen of Birkenhead, Lord, (CH 1974), 258, 260, **274–275**
Collip, J. B., 272
Colmore, T. M., 15
Compton, Arthur H., 263
Connaught, Princess Arthur of, 35
Connaught, Princess Patricia of, 35
Connell, Arthur, 301
Connolly, Cyril, 193, 197
Conroy, Sir John, 268
Cons, Emma, 291, 292
Cooper, Duff, 143
Coram, Thomas, 344
Corbett, Sir James, 171
Coward, Noel, 300
Craggs, James, 492
Craig, Edward Henry Gordon, (CH 1956), 289, **294–295**, 514
Craigavon, Lord, 82
Cranborne, Lord, 437
Crawford and Balcarres, Earl of, 9, 10
Crerar, General Henry Duncan Graham, (CH 1945), 273, 425, **437–440**, 447, 448, 506
Cresswell, Walter, 338
Crick, Francis, 268, 279
Cripps, Sir Richard Stafford, (CH 1951), 69, 90, **99–100**, 102, 117
Cromer, Earl of, 173
Crookshank, Harry Frederick Comfort, Viscount, (CH 1955), 69, **107–108**
Crosland, Anthony, 154
Crossman, Richard, 137
Cuffe, Agnes, 304
Cullen, Gordon, 213
Cunard, Lady, 235
Cunliffe-Lister, Philip (see Swinton, Earl of)
Curtin, John, chapter 15 *passim*, 428, 434, 441
Curtis, Lionel George, (CH 1949), 335, **348–349**
Curzon of Kedleston, Earl (later Marquess), 3, 4, 5, 7, 8, 11, 12, 13, 32, 36
Dalton, Hugh, 92, 100, 102, 398
Danemann, Meredith, 301
Darwin, Charles, 43
Davidson, Sir James, 74
Davidson, John Colin Campbell, Viscount, (CH 1923), 68, 73, **74–75**, 509
Davidson, Randall (Archbishop of Canterbury), 39, 40, 53, 55
Davies, Gwendoline Elizabeth, (CH 1937), 76, 335, **345–346**, 506
Davies, Sir Henry Walford, 236, 238, 346
Davies, Jennie, 125
Davies, J. T., 11, 36, 39, 313
Davies, Margaret, 345–346
Davies, Peter Maxwell, 254, 255
Davies, William John, (CH 1917), 13, **15–16**, 514

Davis, Sir Colin Rex, (CH 2001), 232, **254–56**, 257, 504
Dawson, Sir Douglas, 3, 5, 9, 10, 35, 313, chapter 17 *passim*
Dawson of Penn, Lord, 147
De Chastelain, General Alfred John Gardyne Drummond, (CH 1998), 425, **479–480**
de Gaulle, General Charles, 143, 481, 487
de Gaury, Gerald, 482
De la Bere, Sir Ivan, 1
de la Mare, Walter John, (CH 1948), 166, **180–181**, 190, 248, 510
de Valera, Eamonn, 61
de Valois, Dame Ninette, (CH 1981), 290, **300–302**, 506, 508, 510, 512
de Zoete, Beryl, 186
Deakin, Arthur, (CH 1949), 388, **398–400**,
Delius, Fritz Theodor Albert (Frederick), (CH 1929), 231, **233–235**, 241, 248, 293, 508
Devonshire, Duchess of, 110
Devonshire, Duke of, 110
Diamond, Lord, 137
Diefenbaker, John George, (CH 1976), 425, 443, **469–470**
Dilke, Sir Charles and Lady, 22, 392, 393
Dillon, Harold Arthur, Viscount, (CH 1921), 206, **207–08**, 508, 514
Dodd, Charles Harold, (CH 1961), 41, **62–63**, 64
Dolfuss, Engelbert, 367
Doll, Sir Richard William Shaboe, (CH 1995), 258, 260, **287–288**
Douglas, Roger, 479
Douglas-Home, Sir Alec (see Home of the Hirsel, Lord)
Dover Wilson, John (see Wilson, John Dover)
D'Oyly Carte, Richard, 237
Draga, Queen of Serbia, 375
Drees, Willem, 485, 486
Drogheda, Garrett, Earl of, 320
Driver, Sir Godfrey, 62
Dudley, Dowager Countess of, 35
Duncan, Isadora, 297
Duncan-Sandys, Duncan Edwin **Duncan-Sandys, Lord**, (CH 1973), 69, **130–133**,
Duplessis, Maurice, 476
Duveen, Lord, 210
Dyson, George, 238
Ebert, Carl, 240
Eccles, David McAdam, Viscount, (CH 1984), 70, **147–148**
Ede, Chuter (see Chuter-Ede, Lord)
Edelman, Gerald
Eden, Sir Anthony, (see Avon, Anthony, Earl of)
Edinburgh, Prince Philip, Duke of, 351, 444
Edward VII, King, 5, 39, 172, 502
Edward VIII, King (Duke of Windsor), 370, 377, 378

Elgar, Sir Edward, 231, 232, 243
Elgin, Earl of, 25
Eliot, T. S., 251, 302
Elizabeth, Queen, the Queen Mother, 110, 111, 212, 454
Elizabeth II, Queen, 65, 73, 111, 132, 198, 221, 231, 244, 314, 315, 439, 444–445, 452, 456, 469, 470, 477, 502, 502–503
Ellerman, Sir John Reeves, (CH 1921), 387, **388–390**, 508, 514
Elliott, Walter Elliot, (CH 1952), 69, **102–103**
Elliott of Harwood, Baroness, 103
Ellis, G. F. R., 280
Elwyn-Jones, Frederick Elwyn, Lord, (CH 1976), 357, 358, **367–368**
Emerson, Ralph Waldo, 42
Evans, Sir Evan Vincent, (CH 1922), 369, **371–372**
Eyre, Richard, 294
Fairclough, Ellen, 470
Faisal I, King, 482
Faisal II, King, 483
Faringdon, Alexander Henderson, Lord, (CH 1917), 13, **26**
Farouk, King, 482
Fawcett, Millicent Garrett, 294
Fellowes, Edmund Horace, (CH 1944), 42, 58, 233, **235–236**
Fenby, Eric, 234
Fergusson, Muriel McQueen, 477
Fiddes, Sir George, 3, 6
Finlay, Lord, 35
Fisher, Geoffrey Francis, 64
Fonteyn, Margot, 301
Foot, Michael, 137, 140, 325
Forster, Edward Morgan, (CH 1953), 166, **182–183**, 190, 510
Fraser, John Malcolm, (CH 1977), 425, 465, **470–472**, 475
Fraser, Peter, (CH 1946), 425, **440–442**, 451
Fraser, Sir Robert, 137
Fraser, William Jocelyn Ian (see Fraser of Lonsdale, Lord)
Fraser of Lonsdale, Lord, (CH 1953), 71, 335, **349–350**
Freud, Lucian, (CH 1983), 205, 207, **217–219**, 510
Freyberg, Lord, 441
Frink, Dame Elisabeth Jean, (CH 1992), 205, **223–224**, 506, 512
Furley, Sir John, (CH 1918), 13, **26–27**
Furtwangler, Wilhelm, 242
Gaitskell, Hugh, 102, 128, 129, 136, 360, 367
Galsworthy, John, 294
Gandhi, Mahatma, 429
Garbett, Cyril, 53
Gardiner, Gerald Austin, Lord, (CH 1975), 357, 358, **364–366**
Gardiner, W. Chetwynd, 238
Garnett, Edward, 166, 511

Garrard, 493, 496
Garvin, James Louis, (CH 1941), 370, **376–377**, 382, 383
Gascoyne-Cecil, Lord Edward Christian David, (CH 1949), 166, **181–182**
George V, King, 3, 6, 31, 37, 39–40, 47, 74, 75, 244, 292, 395, 490, 493, 494–495, 496, 497–498, 498–499, 500, 501, 502, 504
George VI, King, 14, 147, 180, 244, 400, 416, 439, 444, 502, 504, 509
George-Brown, Lord, 129, 136, 143
Gibson, George, (CH 1946), 388, **397–398**
Gielgud, Sir Arthur John, (CH 1977), 290, 294, **298–300**, 303, 309, 508, 510
Gilbert, Walter, 277
Gill, Eric, 214
Gilmour, J., 13
Glasse, John, 336
Glenamara, Edward Watson Short, Lord, (CH 1976), 69, **137–138**
Godwin, E. W., 294
Goehr, Alexander, 254
Golding, Sir William, 331
Gollancz, Victor, 365
Gooch, George Peabody, (CH 1939), 311, **313–314**, 508, 510
Goodman, Arnold Abraham, Lord, (CH 1972), 219, 226, 232, 242, 317, 320, 357, **360–362**, 365–366, 383
Goonetilleke, Sir Oliver, 453
Gordon-Walker, Patrick Chrestien, Lord, (CH 1968), 69, **127–129**
Gore, Charles, 340
Gorton, Sir John Grey, (CH 1971), 425, 460, **463–465**, 466, 471, 475
Gosling, Henry, (CH 1917), 13, **14–15**
Gower, Sir Patrick, 37
Gowrie, Lord, 406, 407, 408, 412
Granville-Barker, Harley, 290–291, 294, 511
Graves, Robert, 166, 511
Green, Henry, 197
Greene, Henry Graham, (CH 1966), 166, **189–190**, 197, 510
Greenwood, Anthony (Lord Greenwood of Rossendale), 92
Greenwood, Arthur, (CH 1945), **91–92**
Greenwood, Thomas, 26
Gregg, John Allen Fitzgerald, (CH 1957), 41, **61–62**
Gregg, Robert Gregg, 61
Grey, Sir Edward, 158
Grieg, Edvard, 233
Griffiths, James, (CH 1966), 69, **123–124**, 139
Grimond, Lord, 326
Groves, General Leslie, 272
Guinness, Sir Alec, (CH 1994), 290, 298, **303–305**, 308, 309, 508
Gurney, Sir Ronald, 285

Gwynne, Howell Arthur, (CH 1938), 370, **375–376**
Haber, Fritz, 270
Haig, Field Marshal Earl, 375
Hailes, Lord, (CH 1962), 69, **113–114**
Hailsham of St Marylebone, Lord, (CH 1974), 145, 357, 358, **362–364**
Haitink, Bernard, (CH 2002), 232, **256–257**, 424, 426–427, 488
Haldane, Elizabeth Sanderson, (CH 1917), 13, **21–22**, 260, 506
Haldane, John Burdon Sanderson, 326
Haldane, John Scott, (CH 1928), 21, 258, **260–261**, 508
Haldane, Richard B., 21, 29
Hall, Peter, 308, 360
Hallé, Sir Charles, 490
Hallé, Elinor, chapter 17 *passim*
Halifax, Earl of, 35
Halsey, A. H., 354
Hamilton, Lady Maud Evelyn, (see Lansdowne, Marchioness of)
Hamilton, Richard, (CH 1999), 205, 207, **229–230**, 508
Hammond, James and Barbara, 311, 511
Hankin, St John, 294
Harcourt, Lord, 74
Hardie, Keir, 399
Hardy, Thomas, 183
Hare, David, 204
Hartley, Brigadier General Sir Harold Brewer, (CH 1967), 258, 260, **268–270**
Hasluck, Sir Paul, 464
Havelock Wilson, Joseph (see Wilson, Joseph Havelock)
Hawke, Robert, 471
Hawking, Stephen William, (CH 1989), 258, 260, **280**
Haxton, Gerald, 184
Headlam, Arthur Cayley, (CH 1921), 39, 41, **44–45**
Healey, Denis Winston, Lord, (CH 1979), 70, 90, 100, **139–141**, 149, 157–158, 464
Heath, Edward, 69, 143, 145, 148, 149, 152, 157, 161, 206, 361, 363, 364, 365
Heath, Sir Thomas, 3, 500, 501
Helpmann, Robert, 301
Henderson, Alexander (see Faringdon, Lord)
Henderson, Arthur, 3, 8, 12, 393
Hensler, Martin, 300
Henze, Hans Werner, 255
Hepworth, Dame Barbara, 206, 214, 222
Herbert, Sir Alan Patrick, (CH 1970), 166, **190–191**
Herford, C. H., 294
Hertz, Joseph Herman, (CH 1943), 41, **57–58**
Heseltine, Michael Ray Dibdin, Lord, (CH 1997), 70, 157, **159–161**, 164
Hesse, Prince Alexander of, 489

Hill, Archibald Vivian, (CH 1946), 258, 259, 264–265
Hill, J., 13
Hill, Octavia, 21
Hinshelwood, Sir Cyril, 270
Hitchcock, Alfred, 166, 184
Hives, Ernest Walter, Lord, (CH 1943), 387, **394–395**
Hobsbawm, Eric John Ernest, (CH 1997), 311, **331–332**
Hockney, David, (CH 1997), 205, 207, **226–228**, 508
Hodgkin, Dorothy, 328
Hogg, Quintin McGarel (see Hailsham of St Marylebone, Lord)
Holland, Sir Sidney George, (CH 1951), 425, **449–451**, 457
Holst, Gustav, 247, 248, 346
Holt, Harold Edward, (CH 1967), 425, **458–459**, 464, 465, 471, 475
Holyoake, Sir Keith Jacka, (CH 1963), 422, 425, 450, **457–458**, 467, 472
Home of the Hirsel, Alec, Lord, 69, 107, 118, 148, 363
Hopkins, Sir Gowland, 275
Horder, Lord, 238
Horner, David, 187
Horniman, Annie Elizabeth Frederica, (CH 1933), 289, **293–294**, 295–296, 506, 508
Houghton, Arthur Leslie Noel Douglas (see Houghton of Sowerby, Lord)
Houghton of Sowerby, Lord, (CH 1967), 69, **125–127**, 326
Howard, Sir Michael Eliot, (CH 2002), 311, **333–334**
Howarth, Elgar, 254
Howe, Richard Edward Geoffrey (see Howe of Aberavon, Lord)
Howe of Aberavon, Lord, (CH 1996), 70, 140, 154, **157–159**, 160
Howells, Herbert Norman, (CH 1972), 232, **247–249**
Hudson, Robert Spear, Viscount, (CH 1944), 68, **86–87**, 132, 510
Huggins, Godfrey Martin (see Malvern, Viscount)
Hughes Cledwyn, (see Cledwyn of Penrhos, Lord)
Hughes, William Morris, (CH 1941), 405, 408, 417, 425, 427, **431–432**, 433, 459
Hurd, Anthony (see Hurd, Lord)
Hurd, Douglas (see Hurd of Westwell, Lord)
Hurd, Sir Percy, 155
Hurd, Lord, 155
Hurd of Westwell, Douglas Richard, Lord, (CH 1995), 70, 152, **155–157**, 164
Irving, Sir Henry, 294
Isepp, Helene, 252
Ismay, Hastings Lionel, General Lord, (CH 1945), 68, **92–94**

Israel, W., 280
James, Herbert Armitage, (CH 1926), 41, **47–48**
Jay, Douglas, 331
Jeans, Sir James, 238
Jebb, Sir Gladwyn, 295
Jenkins, Emlyn, 180
Jenkins, Roy (see Jenkins of Hillhead, Lord)
Jenkins of Hillhead, Lord, 155
Jinnah, Mohammed Ali, 430
Johnson, Lyndon Baines, 458
Johnston, Thomas, (CH 1953), 69, **104–105**
Joliot-Curie, Frederic and Irene, 271
Jones, David, (CH 1974), 205, 207, **214–215**
Jones, Frederick Elwyn (see Elwyn-Jones, Lord)
Jones, Harry, 285
Jones, Sir Henry, (CH 1922), 310, **312–313**, 508, 514
Jones, James Larkin (Jack), (CH 1977), 388, **403–404**
Jones, John Daniel, (CH 1927), 41, **49–50**
Jones, Monica, 196–197
Jones, Reginald Victor, (CH 1994), 258, 260, **282–284**
Jones, Thomas, (CH 1929), 68, **75–76**
Joseph, Keith Sinjohn, Lord, (CH 1986), 70, **148–150**, 157, 326
Jowett, John Henry, (CH 1922), 40, 42, **45**, 514
Jowitt, Lord, 79
Keilin, D., 276
Kendall, Mary, 341
Kendrew, John C., 275, 276
Kent, Princess Marina, Duchess of, 507
Keogh, Sir Alfred, (CH 1918), 13, **29**, 505–506
Keppel, Sir Derek, 494, 495
Kerr, James, 337
Kerr, Sir John, 471
Kerr, Philip Henry (see Lothian, Philip Henry Kerr, Marquess of)
Keynes, John Maynard, 302, 322, 324, 327
King, Horace, 133
King, Thomas Jeremy (see King of Bridgwater, Lord)
King, William Lyon Mackenzie, 174, 441, 444, 447, 448
King of Bridgwater, Lord, (CH 1992), 70, **153–154**
Kipling, Rudyard, 375
Kitchener of Khartoum, Field Marshal Earl, 29, 375
Kleiber, Erich, 242
Klemperer, Otto, 255
Knox, Sir Robert, 407, 411, 415, 448
Kohler, Georges, 284
Kotelawala, Sir John Lionel, (CH 1956), 426, **451–453**
Krebs, Sir Hans, 278

Kruger, Paul, 57
Lambert, Constance, 301
Lancaster, Osbert, 212
Lane, Sir Allen Lane Williams, (CH 1969), 387, **402–403**
Lane, Dame Elizabeth, 365
Lang, Cosmo Gordon (Archbishop of Canterbury), 41, 49
Lange, David Russell, (CH 1989), 425, **478–479**
Lansbury, George, 89, 90
Lansdowne, Marchioness of, (CH 1917), 13, **20–21**, 24, 506
Lansdowne, Marquess of, 20
Laporte, Pierre, 477
Larkin, Philip Arthur, (CH 1985), 166, **195–197**
Lascelles, Sir Alan, 178
Lasdun, Sir Denys Louis, (CH 1995), 206, **225–226**
Laski, Harold, 102, 312
Lavers, G. R., 341
Law, Andrew Bonar (see Bonar Law, Andrew)
Lawrence, D. H., 183, 364, 402–403
Lawrence, T. E., 183, 482
Lawson, Nigel (see Lawson of Blaby, Lord)
Lawson of Blaby, Lord, 164
Layton, Walter Thomas, Lord, (CH 1919), 13, **31–32**, 512
Leach, Bernard Howell, (CH 1973), 206, **213–214**
Lean, Sir David, 304
Leathers, Frederick James, Viscount, (CH 1943), 68, **81–82**, 410, 411, 509
Leavis, Frank Raymond, (CH 1977), 166, **192–194**, 513
Leavis, Queenie Dorothy, 193
Lechmere, Sir Edmund, 27
Lee, Jennie, 360
Lee Kuan Yew, (CH 1970), 113, 424 426, 456–457, **462–463**
Lennox-Boyd, Alan Tindal, (see Boyd of Merton, Viscount)
Leopold III, King, 483, 484
Lessing, Doris May, (CH 1999), 166, **201–202**, 506, 508
Lévèsque, René, 477
Levy-Lawson, Harry Lawson Webster (see Burnham, Viscount)
Lewis, Essington, (CH 1943), **395–397**, 409, 410, 411, 412, 413, 414–415, 416, 419, 424, 425, 434
Lewis, Howell Elvet, (CH 1948), 42, 59, 165, **179–180**, 367, 508
Lidgett, John Scott, (CH 1933), 41, **54–56**, 313, 371
Limerick, Angela Olivia Pery, Countess of, (CH 1974), 336, **350–351**, 506

Limerick, Edmund Colquhoun Pery, Earl of, (CH 1960), 350, 387, **401–402**
Lindemann, Frederick Alexander, (see Cherwell, Viscount)
Lloyd, John Selwyn Brooke (see Selwyn-Lloyd, Lord)
Lloyd George, David, 3, 6–7, 8, 9, 18, 19, 28, 33, 34, 36, 40, 41, 72, 125, 310, 313, 341, 342, 345, 369, 370, 371, 372, 374, 377, 388
Lloyd George. Gwilym, 125
Lloyd George, Lady Megan Arfon, (CH 1966), 69, **124–125**, 138, 506, 507
Long, Walter, 2
Lopokova, Lydia, 302
Lothian, Philip Henry Kerr, Marquess of, (CH 1920), 13, **34–35**, 37, 174, 345, 349
Lowry, L. S., 206, 511
Lucas, Edward Verrall, (CH 1932), 369, **372–373**, 514
Lucas, George, 304
Luns, Joseph Marie Antoine Hubert, (CH 1971), 424, 426, **485–486**
Lyons, Dame Enid, 431
Lyons, Joseph Aloysius, (CH 1936), 405, 425, 428, **430–431**, 432, 435, 449, 459
McCance, Robert A., 281–282
McCowen, Alec, 298
MacDonald, Malcolm, 70, 511
MacDonald, Ramsay, 35, 37, 89, 92, 98, 101, 395, 507
McEwen, Sir John, (CH 1969), 425, **459–460**, 465, 475
Machtig, Sir Eric, 410, 411
Mackail, J. W., 491, 492
Mackay of Clashfern, 358
McKenna, Reginald, 71
Maclay, John Scott (see Muirshiel, Viscount)
Maclay, 1st Lord, 114
Macleod, Iain, 107
Macleod, J. R. R., 260, 272, 273
McMahon, Sir William, (CH 1972), 425, 460, **465–466**, 471, 475
Macmillan, Harold, chapter 4 *passim*, 358, 362, 363
Macmillan, Kenneth, 298
McMillan, Margaret, (CH 1930), 335, **336–338**, 340, 506
McMillan, Rachel, 336–338
McNaughton, General the Honourable Andrew George Latta, (CH 1946), 273, 425, 438, 439, **445–448**, 506
Magro, Frank, 187
Major, John Roy, (CH 1998), 70, 153, 157, 159, 161, 162, **163–164**
Mallon, James Joseph, (CH 1939) 335, **346–348**
Malvern, Godfrey Martin, Viscount, (CH 1944), 426, **436–437**

Mann, Arthur Henry, (CH 1941), 370, 377–378
Manning, Cardinal Henry, 50
Mansbridge, Albert, (CH 1931), 335, **339–340**
Marchant, Stanley, 238
Markham, Violet Rosa (Mrs James Carruthers) (CH 1917), 13, **23**, 506, 507, 512
Markova, Alicia, 301
Marquis, Frederick James, (see Woolton, Earl of)
Marshall, Sir John Ross, (CH 1973), 422, 425, 457, **466–467**, 472
Martin, A. J. P., 278
Martin, Hugh, (CH 1955), 41, **59–60**
Martindale, Louisa, 97
Mary, Queen, 31, 292, 493, 494, 496
Maryon-Wilson, Canon Sir Percy, 53,
Massey, Charles Vincent, (CH 1946), 273, 425, **442–445**, 446
Massey, H. S. W., 285
Massigli, René Lucien Daniel, (CH 1954), 424, 426, **480–481**
Massine, Leonide, 297
Matthews, Walter Robert, (CH 1962), 41, **63**
Maugham, William Somerset, (CH 1954), 165, 166, **183–185**, 199
Mayall, Lees, 421
Mayer, Sir Robert, (CH 1973), 232, **249–250**
Medawar, Sir Peter Brian, (CH 1972), 258, 259, **273–274**, 510
Mellor, David, 153,
Menuhin, Yehudi, Lord, 246, 360
Menzies, Sir Robert Gordon, (CH 1951), 396, 425, 432, 434, 435, **448–449**, 458, 459, 460, 465, 466, 470, 471, 475
Merrick, Joseph, 30
Micklem, Nathaniel, (CH 1974), 41, **64–65**
Mikardo, Ian, 138
Mildmay, Audrey, 240
Milford Haven, 1st Marquess of (formerly Prince Louis of Battenberg), 3, 5, 7, chapter 17 *passim*
Miller, Jonathan, 302
Milner, Lord, 348, 349
Milner-Barry, Sir Stuart, 421, 422,
Milstein, Cesar, (CH 1994), 258, 260, **284–285**
Mitterrand, Francois, 306
Monnet, Jean, (CH 1972), 424, 426, **486–488**
Montague, E. S., 429
Montgomery of Alamein, Field Marshal Viscount, 79, 435, 439
Moore, Henry Spencer, (CH 1955), 205–206, 207, **208–209**, 214, 508, 510
Morauta, Sir Mekere, 474
Morley, Sheridan, 300
Morris, Cedric, 218
Morris, John William (see Morris of Borth-y Gest, Lord)

Morris, Peter, 301
Morris of Borth-y-Gest, Lord, (CH 1975), 357, 359, **366–367**
Morris, William Richard (see Nuffield, Viscount)
Morrison, Herbert Stanley (see Morrison of Lambeth, Lord)
Morrison of Lambeth, Lord, (CH 1951), 69, 90, 92, **100–102**, 127
Moseley, Sir Oswald, 89
Mott, Sir Nevill Francis, (CH 1995), 258, 260, 272, **285–287**
Moulton, Dorothy (Lady Mayer), 249
Moulton, W. F., 55
Mountbatten of Burma, Earl
Muirshiel, John Scott Maclay, Viscount, (CH 1962), 67, 69, **114–115**
Muggeridge, Malcolm, 197
Muldoon, Sir Robert David, (CH 1977) 422, 425, 457, 467, **472–473**, 475, 478–479
Myers, Molly, 317, 318
Myrdal, Gunnar, 325
Namaliu, Rabbie, 474
Nash, Sir Walter, (CH 1959), 425, **453–455**, 478
Nasser, Gamal, 482
Neale, George Hall, 498
Needham, Noel Joseph Terence Montgomery, (CH 1992), 311, **326–328**
Nehru, Jawaharlal, 452
Newbolt, Sir Henry, (CH 1922), 165, **170–171**, 507, 508
Nicholson, Ben, 206, 214, 511
Nicholson, Christopher, 220
Nicoll, Sir William Robertson, (CH 1921), 39–40, 369, **370–371**
Nicolson, Sir Harold, 178
Nicolson, The Honourable Lady (see Sackville-West, Vita)
Nobel, Alfred, 259
Northcliffe, Viscount, 35, 376
Nuffield, William Richard Morris, Viscount, (CH 1958), 387, **400–401**
Nunn, Trevor, 308
Nureyev, Rudolf, 301
Oakeshott, Michael, 312, 511
Ogden, D. K., 187, 188
Ogdon, John, 254
O'Grady, J., 13
Olivier, Laurence, 298, 360
Orr, John Boyd (see Boyd Orr, Lord)
Orwell, George, 197
Osgood, F. S., 496
Ouseley, Sir Frederick, 236
Owen, David Anthony Llewellyn, Lord, (CH 1994), 70, **154–155**
Page, Sir Earle Christmas Grafton, (CH 1942), 405, 408, 417, 425, 427, **432–434**, 449, 475

Page, Thomas Ethelbert, (CH 1934), 166, **175–176**, 507
Pakenham, Lady Violet (see Powell, Lady Violet)
Pakenham, Vice Admiral Sir William, 35
Palmer, Geoffrey, 479
Palmer, Roundell Cecil (see Selborne, Earl of),
Pankhurst, Emmeline, 294
Parker, James, (CH 1918), 13, 17, **28–29**
Parmoor, Lord, 99
Parratt, Sir Walter, 236
Parry, Sir Hubert, 248
Pasmore, Edwin John Victor, (CH 1980), 205, 207, **215–217**
Patten, Christopher Francis, (CH 1997), 70, **161–163**, 504
Pattison, Mark, 392
Pavlova, Anna, 297
Payne, Ernest Alexander, (CH 1968), 41, **63–64**
Peake, A. S., 62
Pears, Sir Peter, 239
Pearson, Sir Arthur, 349
Pearson, Lester, 470, 476
Peart, Lord, 139
Perrott, Colonel Sir Herbert Charles, (CH 1918), 13, **29–30**
Perutz, Max Ferdinand, (CH 1975), 258, 259, 268, **275–277**, 510
Pery, Angela Olivia (see Limerick, Angela, Countess of)
Pery, Edmund Colquhoun (see Limerick, Earl of)
Pevsner, Niklaus, 213
Phipps, E. H., 11
Pinches, 491, 493, 499, 501
Pinter, Harold, (CH 2002), 166, **202–204**, 508
Piper, John Egerton Christmas, (CH 1972), 205, 207, **211–213**, 214
Pollock, Hugh McDowell, (CH 1936), 68, **76–77**, 82, 509, 514
Ponsonby, Sir Frederick, 2–3, 5, 6, 7, 11, 13–14, 30, 35–36, chapter 17 *passim*
Pope, Alexander, 492
Popper, Karl Raimund, (CH 1982), 310, **320–322**
Porter, Rodney Robert, (CH 1985), 258, 259, **277–279**
Powell, Anthony Dymoke, (CH 1987), 166, **197–198**
Powell, Sir Arnold Joseph Philip, (CH 1984), 206, **219–220**
Powell, J. Enoch, 141–142
Powell, Lady Violet, 198
Priestley, John Boyton, 166, 247, 511
Pritchard, John, 257
Pritchett, Sir Victor Sawdon, (CH 1992), 166, **198–200**

Provis, Sir Samuel Butler, (CH 1918), 13, **30–31**
Pu Y'i, 322
Quiller Couch, Sir Arthur, 329
Quinan, Kenneth Bingham, (CH 1917), 13, **17–18**, 424, 426, 480
Rahman Putra, Tunku Abdul, (CH 1960), 420, 426, **455–457**, 462
Ralston, Colonel J. R., 438
Rambert, Marie, 297, 301
Ramsey, Arthur Michael, 79
Rayleigh, Lord, 26
Razak, Tun Abdul, 456
Reeve, Christopher, 300
Reid, James Scott Cumberland, Lord, (CH 1967), 357, **358–359**, 514
Reinkel, Carl, 306
Reyntiens, Patrick, 212
Richards, Ivor Armstrong, (CH 1964), 166, **187–188**
Richards, J. M., 213
Riley, Bridget Louise, (CH 1998), 205, **228–229**, 360, 506, 508
Ripper, William, (CH 1917), 13, 18, **19–20**
Robbins, Lionel Charles, Lord, (CH 1968), 310, **319–320**, 324, 326
Roberts, Field Marshal Earl, 375
Roberts, G. H., 17
Robinson, Alison (see Waley, Alison)
Robinson, Peter, 496
Rolls, C. S., 394
Roosevelt, Franklin, 174
Rossetti, Gabriel Dante, 171
Rowntree, Benjamin Seebohm, (CH 1931), 335, **340–342**
Rowse, Alfred Leslie, (CH 1996), 311, **329–331**, 513
Royce, Sir Henry, 394, 395
Royden, Agnes Maude, (CH 1930), 42, **52–53**, 506
Royden, Thomas, Lord, (CH 1919), 13, **32–33**, 389
Runciman, The Honourable Sir James Cochrane Stevenson, (CH 1983), 311, **322–324**
Runciman of Doxford, Viscount, 238, 322
Russell, Theo, 6
Rutherford, Ernest, 263, 271
Rylands, George Humphrey Wolferstan, (CH 1987), 289, 299, **302–303**, 322
Sackville-West, Victoria Mary (Vita), (CH 1948), 166, **177–179**, 499, 506, 508
es-Said, Nuri, (CH 1956), 424, 426, **481–483**
St Clair, Meriel, 252
St Laurent, Louis, 443, 444
Salaman, Merula, 305
Salter, Arthur, Lord, 347–348
Sandys, Duncan Edwin (see Duncan-Sandys, Lord)

Sanger, Frederick, (CH 1981), 258, 259, **277**, 278, 284, 510
Sankey, Ira, 46
Sargent, Sir Malcolm, 250
Sassoon, Siegfried, 183
Sastri, Valingaman Sankarana-Rayana Srinivasa, (CH 1930), 9, 405, 425, 426, **428–430**
Sauvé, Jeanne, 477
Savage, M. J., 440
Schuman, Robert, 488
Scofield, David Paul, (CH 2000), 290, **307–309**, 508
Scott, John William Robertson, (CH 1947), 370, **378–380**
Scott, Sir Peter Markham, (CH 1987), 370, **381–382**, 384, 385, 514
Scott, Robert Falcon, 382
Scullin, James, 430, 431
Searle, Alan, 184
Searle, G. F. C., 285
Seddon, James Andrew, (CH 1918), 13, **28**
Selborne, Earl of, (CH 1945), **87–88**, 510
Selwyn-Lloyd, Lord, (CH 1962), 67, 69, **117–118**
Sen, Amartya Kumar, (CH 2000), 310, **332–333**, 424, 425, 426, 480
Senanayake, D. S., 451
Senanayake, Dudley, 451
Shakespeare, John H., 40, 56, 371
Shalyapin, Fyodor, 242
Shaw, George Bernard, 290, 291, 293, 294
Shaw, Mrs George William Hudson (see Royden, Agnes Maud)
Shaw, George William Hudson, 52, 53
Shawcross, Hartley, Lord, 367
Shearer, Moira, 301
Sheppard, David, 65, 66
Sheppard, Hugh Richard Lawrie, (CH 1927), 41, **48–49**, 504
Shinwell, Emanuel, Lord, (CH 1965), 69, **121–122**
Shore, Peter (see Shore of Stepney, Lord)
Shore of Stepney, Lord, 352
Short, Edward Watson (see Glenamara, Lord)
Sibley, Dame Antoinette, 301–302
Sickert, Oswald, 338
Sickert, Walter, 339
Silkin, Lewis, Lord, (CH 1965), 69, **120**
Simon, Viscount, 364
Sisson, Charles Hubert, (CH 1993), 166, **200–201**, 508
Sitwell, Sir Francis Osbert Sacheverell, (CH 1958), 165, **186–187**
Sitwell, Sir Sacheverell, (CH 1983), 165, **194–195**
Smith, Arnold Cantwell, (CH 1975), 425, **467–469**
Smith, Forgan, 397, 406, 407, 409, 410, 411, 414, 419

Smith, Sir Henry Babington, (CH 1917), 13, **25**
Smith, Sir John Lindsay Eric, (CH 1993), 336, **355**, 514
Smuts, Field Marshal Jan Christian, (CH 1917), 9, 13, **14**, 420, 424, 426, 427, 429, 495, 505, 510
Snedden, Billy, 471
Snell, Henry, Lord, (CH 1943), 68, **83–85**, 509–510
Soames, Arthur Christopher, Lord, (CH 1980), 70, 73, **143–144**
Soames, Michael, 301
Solti, Sir Georg, 255
Somare, Sir Michael Thomas, (CH 1978), 426, **473–474**
Sorensen, Reginald, Lord, 128
Spaak, Paul-Henri, (CH 1963), 424, 426, **483–485**
Spender, John Alfred, (CH 1937), 369, **373–375**, 378
Spink's, 496
Spurgeon, Charles Haddon, 43
Stamfordham, Lord, 12, 37, 39, 292
Stanford, Sir Charles Villiers, 170, 248
Stanley, Sir Arthur, 35–36
Stanley, Sidney, 398
Stannus, Dame Edris (see de Valois, Dame Ninette)
Stead, William Thomas, 51
Stewart, Robert Michael Maitland (see Stewart of Fulham, Lord)
Stewart of Fulham, Lord, (CH 1969) 67, 69, 128, **129–130**
Stopes, Marie, 294
Stoppard, Sir Tom, 204
Strachey, Lytton, 302, 322
Strutt, The Honourable Edward Gerald, (CH 1917), 13, **25–26**
Strutt and Parker, 26
Stuart, James Gray (see Stuart of Findhorn, Viscount)
Stuart of Findhorn, Viscount, (CH 1957), 69, **110–111**
Sukarno, Ahmed, 456
Sullivan, Sir Arthur, 237
Summerskill, Edith Clara, Baroness, 69, 102, (CH 1966), **122–123**, 506, 507
Summerson, Sir John Newenham, (CH 1986), 206, **222–223**
Swanwick, Frederick, 338
Swanwick, Helena Maria Lucy, (CH 1931), 335, **338–339**, 506, 514
Swettenham, Sir Frank Athelstane, (CH 1917), 13, **25**
Swinton, Earl of, (CH 1943), 68, **85–86**, 510
Tagore, Rabindranath, 332
Talbot, Neville, 53
Talboys, Sir Brian Edward, (CH 1981), 425, **474–475**

Tancred, Geoffrey, 235
Tawney, R. H., 311–312, 346, 511
Tebbit, Norman Beresford, Lord, (CH 1987), 70, **150–151**
Temple, Sir Richard, 36
Temple, William, 48, 52, 59, 340
Tennant, Henry, 23
Tennant, John, 22
Tennant, Margaret Edith (May), (CH 1917), 13, **22–23**, 392, 506
Terry, Ellen, 289, 294, 298
Thatcher, Margaret, Baroness, 70, 139, 142, 143, 146, 147, 149, 150, 151, 152, 153, 156, 157, 158, 160–161, 162, 164, 198, 310, 312, 325, 363
Thompson, J. J., 285
Thorndike, Dame Agnes Sybil, (CH 1970), 290, 293–294, **295–296**, 360, 506, 508
Thorndike, Russell, 292
Thorneycroft, George Edward Peter, Lord, (CH 1979), 70, **141–143**
Tippett, Sir Michael Kemp, (CH 1979), 232, **250–252**, 253, 255, 510
Toynbee, Arnold Joseph, (CH 1956), 311, **314–315**
Toynbee, Philip, 193
Tree, Sir Herbert Beerbohm, 294
Treffry, David, 331
Trefusis, Lady Mary, 493
Trefusis, Violet, 178
Trevelyan, Janet Penrose, (CH 1936), 335, **343–344**, 506
Trevelyan, George Macaulay, 343
Trevelyan, Mrs George Macaulay (see Trevelyan, Janet Penrose)
Treves, Sir Frederick, 30–31, 511
Trevor-Roper, Hugh, 330
Trimmings, Lionel, 183
Trotter, Sir Henry, 350
Troup, Sir Edward, 3
Trudeau, Joseph Pierre Yves Elliote, (CH 1984), 425, 464, 470, **475–478**
Tuckwell, Gertrude Mary, (CH 1930), 22, 388, **392–394**, 506
Tweedsmuir, Lord, (CH 1932), 165, **173–174**, 507, 508
Van Deventer, Lieutenant General Sir Jacob, 35
Van Fleck, John H., 285
Varah, Edward Chad, (CH 1999), 42, 66, 336, **356**, 504, 506
Victoria, Queen, 237, 502
von Hayek, Friedrich August, (CH 1984), 310, 320, 321, **324–326**, 333
Von Laue, Max, 267–268
Von Mises, Ludwig, 324
Von Rosen, Jelka Helen, 234
Waldegrave, William, 331
Wales, Charles, Prince of, 139, 221
Waley, Alison, 186

Waley, Arthur David, (CH 1956), 166, **185–186**
Walker, Jane Harriet, (CH 1931), 258, 259, **262–263**, 506, 508
Walker, Patrick Chrestien Gordon (see Gordon-Walker, Lord)
Wallis, Helen, 148
Walton, Sir William, 252, 297
Ward, Sir Adolphus, 313
Ward, Mrs Humphrey (see Ward, Mary Augusta)
Ward, Irene Mary Bewick (see Ward of North Tyneside, Baroness)
Ward, Mary Augusta, 343
Ward, Thomas F., 233
Ward of North Tyneside, Baroness, (CH 1973), 69, **133–134**, 506, 507
Wardle, George James, (CH 1917), 13, **16–17**
Waterhouse, Sir Ronald, 37, 74
Watkinson, Harold Arthur, Viscount, (CH 1962), 67, 69, **115–117**
Waugh, Evelyn, 197
Webb, Beatrice, 71, 72, 393
Weight, Carel Victor Morlais, (CH 1994), 205, 207, **224–225**
Wheeler, Sir Robert Eric Mortimer, (CH 1967), 311, **316–318**, 360, 508
White, Eirene, Baroness, 76
White, John, (CH 1935), 41, **56–57**
Whitelaw, William Stephen Ian, Viscount, (CH 1974), 67, 69, **134–136**, 157
Whitlam, Gough, 466, 471
Whiteley, William, (CH 1948), 69, **98–99**, 136
Whittle, Sir Frank, 394
Widdowson, Elsie May, (CH 1993), 258, 260, **281–282**, 506
Wigg, Lord, 360
Wigram, Clive, Lord, 498
Wilberforce, Lord, 359
Wilkie, Alexander, (CH 1917), 13, **17**
Williams, Eric Eustace, (CH 1969), 426, **460–462**
Williams, Henry Herbert, (CH 1945), 41, **58–59**
Williams, Ralph Vaughan, 235, 238, 247, 248, 251
Williams, Shirley (see Williams of Crosby, Baroness)
Williams of Crosby, Baroness, 155
Wilson, Charles Thomson Rees, (CH 1937), 258, 259, **263–264**, 508, 514
Wilson, David (see Wilson of Tillyorn, Lord)
Wilson, Harold (see Wilson of Rievaulx, Lord)
Wilson, Sir Horace, 283
Wilson, John Dover, (CH 1936), 166, **176–177**, 507
Wilson, Joseph Havelock, (CH 1922), 13, 387, **390–392**, 508
Wilson, Sir Leslie, 406

Wilson, Woodrow, 109
Wilson of Rievaulx, Lord, 65, 69, 126, 127, 128, 129, 136, 137, 138, 139, 140, 206, 360, 361, 365, 368, 419, 459, 470
Wilson of Tillyorn, Lord, 162
Windsor, Duke of (see Edward VIII, King)
Wingate, Sir Ronald, 94
Wingti, Paias, 474
Withers, Googie, 300
Wood, Charles, 250
Wood, Sir Henry Joseph, (CH 1944), 232, **237–238**, 508
Wood, James, 188
Woolf, Leonard, 166, 302, 322, 511
Woolf, Virginia, 166, 178, 302, 322, 511
Woolton, Frederick James Marquis, Earl of, (CH 1942), 68, **80–81**, 142, 410, 411, 509
Wootton, 501
Wootton, Barbara Frances (see Wootton of Abinger, Baroness)
Wootton of Abinger, Baroness, (CH 1977), 336, **353–355**, 506
Worlock, Derek John Hartford, (CH 1995), 42, **65–66**, 506
Yeats, W. B., 293, 294
York, Duke of (see George VI, King)
York, Duchess of (see Queen Elizabeth the Queen Mother)
Zangwill, Israel, 294
Zhou Enlai, 452